AI in Medical Imaging and Image Processing—Volume I

AI in Medical Imaging and Image Processing—Volume I

Topic Editors

Karolina Nurzynska
Michał Strzelecki
Adam Piórkowski
Rafał Obuchowicz

MDPI Basel • Beijing • Wuhan • Barcelona • Belgrade • Novi Sad • Cluj • Manchester

Topic Editors
Karolina Nurzynska
Department of Algorithmics and Software
Silesian University of Technology
Gliwice
Poland

Michał Strzelecki
Institute of Electronics
Lodz University of Technology
Lodz
Poland

Adam Piórkowski
Department of Biocybernetics and Biomedical Engineering
AGH University of Krakow
Krakow
Poland

Rafał Obuchowicz
Department of Diagnostic Imaging
Jagiellonian University Medical College
Krakow
Poland

Editorial Office
MDPI AG
Grosspeteranlage 5
4052 Basel, Switzerland

This is a reprint of the Topic, published open access by the journals *Cancers* (ISSN 2072-6694), *Diagnostics* (ISSN 2075-4418), *Journal of Clinical Medicine* (ISSN 2077-0383) and *Tomography* (ISSN 2379-139X), freely accessible at: https://www.mdpi.com/topics/P281D89UL6.

For citation purposes, cite each article independently as indicated on the article page online and as indicated below:

Lastname, A.A.; Lastname, B.B. Article Title. *Journal Name* **Year**, *Volume Number*, Page Range.

Volume I
ISBN 978-3-7258-4513-2 (Hbk)
ISBN 978-3-7258-4514-9 (PDF)
https://doi.org/10.3390/books978-3-7258-4514-9

Set
ISBN 978-3-7258-4517-0 (Hbk)
ISBN 978-3-7258-4518-7 (PDF)

Cover image courtesy of Karolina Nurzynska

Contents

About the Editors

Karolina Nurzynska

Karolina Nurzyńska obtained a PhD in computer science in 2009 and a post-doctoral degree in 2019. Since then, she has held the position of professor at the Silesian University of Technology. She collaborates with national and international teams, tackling research topics concerning the application of artificial intelligence methods in image understanding. Her main interest involves automating medical image analysis and determining techniques that could simplify and assure repeatability in medical data understanding. However, the design of chatbots dedicated to communication within closed topics has become one of her new interests. In her free time, she loves traveling and spending time in nature.

Michał Strzelecki

Prof. Michał Strzelecki has been employed at the Institute of Electronics, Lodz University of Technology (TUL), since 1988, and since 2007, he has been a Full Professor. In the years 2004–2019, he was the Deputy Director of the Institute for Teaching and Research. He also served as the Vice Dean for Research at the Faculty of Electrical, Electronic, Computer and Control Engineering, TUL, until 2020. His scientific interests include the processing and analysis of biomedical signals and images, data analysis methods, and artificial intelligence. In particular, he is interested in issues related to image texture analysis and the applications and hardware implementations of artificial neural networks. He also works on the development of software aimed at supporting medical imaging diagnostics. Within these interests, Prof. Strzelecki conducts extensive cooperation with domestic and foreign medical universities on the construction and development of systems supporting the diagnostic process. He has participated in numerous international research programs, including COST B21, BM1103, TD1007 (a member of the Management Committee), DGF, 7FP, and projects funded by the National Science Centre (Poland) and the National Centre for Research and Development (Poland). He is the author and co-author of more than 200 scientific publications. In 2006–2008, he was employed at the Jeonbuk National University, Jeonju, Republic of Korea, as a Visiting Professor.

Adam Piórkowski

Adam Piórkowski obtained a PhD in computer science in 2005. In 2015, he obtained a post-doctoral degree in biomedical engineering, and in 2019, he became a professor at AGH in Krakow. He has been involved in medical image processing since 2003, where his particular interests are the segmentation, normalization, and textural analysis of visual data. He conducts scientific projects generally related to medical informatics. He is also an active programmer.

Rafał Obuchowicz

Rafał Obuchowicz currently works in the Department of Radiology of the University Hospital, Krakow, and heads the Imaging Diagnostics department at Lux Med, Krakow. His professional interests are focused on the problems of focal change detection and shape detection in various radiological techniques using classical methods and deep learning machine algorithms. The result of the work undertaken in this direction is the NCBiR project "XR-AI A diagnostic browser for radiology with computer-aided use of artificial intelligence," of which he is the originator and head of the medical team. He also has a professional interest in analyzing image quality using MR and X-ray techniques, resulting in the completed habilitation procedure entitled "Analysis and parametrization of information in selected techniques of radiological diagnostics." His hobbies include environmental psychology, history, ecology, and urbanization, and he is the husband of Barbra and father of Isabella and Wiktor.

Journal of
Clinical Medicine

MDPI

Editorial

AI in Medical Imaging and Image Processing

Karolina Nurzynska [1,*], Michał Strzelecki [2], Adam Piórkowski [3] and Rafał Obuchowicz [4]

1 Algorithmics and Software Division, Silesian University of Technology, 44-100 Gliwice, Poland
2 Institute of Electronics, Lodz University of Technology, 90-924 Lodz, Poland; michal.strzelecki@p.lodz.pl
3 Department of Biocybernetics and Biomedical Engineering, AGH University of Krakow, 30-059 Krakow, Poland; pioro@agh.edu.pl
4 Department of Diagnostic Imaging, Jagiellonian University Medical College, 31-501 Krakow, Poland; r.obuchowicz@gmail.com
* Correspondence: karolina.nurzynska@polsl.pl

Artificial intelligence methods have evolved sufficiently to be widely applied in automatic data analysis, providing standardized and reproducible results comparable to those of highly skilled specialists, while assisting less experienced personnel. This allows for a reduction in repetitive work and draws attention to the choice of medical treatment and accurate patient cases. Convolutional neural networks, attention-based transformers, and traditional machine learning approaches using radiomics features are at the forefront of medical applications, where the automatic understanding of various imaging techniques is needed (such as computed tomography—CT, magnetic resonance imaging—MRI, X-ray, radiographs, and positron emission tomography—PET) to examine internal organs and tissues. Moreover, graph neural networks are also making strides in this field. Finally, rapid progress in large language models has led to the integration of speech recognition and text analysis technologies, further streamlining radiologists' workflows [1].

This collection of research highlights the influence of artificial intelligence (AI) and machine learning (ML) on healthcare, demonstrating their capacity to improve diagnostics, treatment strategies, and patient care. The presented studies address critical healthcare challenges, offering solutions that enhance precision, productivity, and healthcare accessibility. The compilation includes works on diagnostic improvement, featuring models such as convolutional neural networks (CNNs) and transformers for the early and accurate identification of various conditions, including different types of cancer, stroke, intracranial hemorrhage, and acute aortic syndrome (AAS). AI's integration into radiology is showcased, facilitating tasks like the automatic segmentation of anatomical structures, cancer prediction using radiomics, and image quality optimization, thereby enhancing workflow efficiency and consistency. The collection also presents AI applications in surgical planning and intraoperative guidance, as evidenced by studies evaluating preoperative imaging predictors and AI tools for detecting surgical wound infections. These advancements enable personalized medicine by customizing interventions based on individual patient characteristics. Innovative technologies such as microwave imaging for breast cancer detection and steady-state thermal imaging are featured, illustrating AI's role in developing non-invasive diagnostic methods that offer safer and more accessible alternatives to conventional techniques. The compilation also includes insights into AI-driven tools designed to track disease progression in chronic conditions and monitor postoperative recovery. Novel AI methodologies addressing rare and complex diagnoses, such as early-stage osteosarcoma detection, bone mineral density screening in cystic fibrosis, and biomarker identification in leukemia, are presented. The collection incorporates articles on AI-powered tools for emergency settings, capable of detecting rib fractures, coronary occlusion, or chest abnormalities, ensuring effective patient management in critical scenarios. Studies focusing on tuberculosis and COVID-19 detection from radiographs emphasize AI's potential in global health applications, reflecting the development of AI-powered tools aimed at democratizing healthcare. The compilation also addresses practical aspects of AI integration, such as interrater variability, reproducibility, and the need for standardized benchmarks. This comprehensive collection serves as a valuable resource for healthcare professionals, researchers, and technologists seeking to understand and leverage AI's potential in medicine. By combining in-depth technical insights with practical clinical applications, these studies contribute to improving patient outcomes, streamlining workflows, and promoting a more equitable healthcare system.

Deep learning models can be valuable when quick assessment of chest X-rays is needed to differentiate between acute aortic syndrome and thoracic aortic aneurysm without expert personnel available, as indicated in [2]. Employing a four-view network based on EfficientNet and incorporating an attention module could enhance breast cancer diagnosis from mammograms [3]. Implementing data augmentation techniques and developing novel network architectures may substantially improve the detection of tuberculosis and COVID-19 in CT scans [4]. Selecting the appropriate hyperparameters can optimize deep model performance, as shown in the case of brain tumor classification using MRI data [5].

Object localization within medical data can be accomplished through various methods. The most prevalent approach involves semantic segmentation using the U-Net network architecture, which assigns each pixel to a specific class. For example, when examining H&E (haematoxylin and eosin)-stained images, an accurate cell count across different classes is crucial for proper diagnosis, making precise segmentation, often achieved through U-Net architecture, essential [6]. The U-Net model facilitates the identification of heart and lung anatomy in chest X-rays, necessary for cardiothoracic ratio calculation, as shown in [7]. It can also be employed for the precise segmentation of the appendix with distinct boundaries, critical for diagnosing acute appendicitis from CT scans [8]. The determination of temporomandibular joint placement in ultrasonography images is explored in [9]. U-Net networks enhanced with pyramid attention modules and preprocessed with stick filter derivatives demonstrate 91–93% accuracy in lung fissure segmentation in CT images [10]. Despite its power, the U-Net architecture has limitations. In [11], researchers propose augmenting features derived from this model with a graph neural network to better capture the spatial relationships of features significant in COVID-19 diagnosis from CT scans. Moreover, repurposing existing datasets for different applications is challenging. In [12], researchers propose an algorithm to convert the original three-label annotation in the BraTS dataset to two-label annotations suitable for post-operative settings, which were then used to train the nnU-Net for brain segmentation in treatment response monitoring. The same network architecture proved to yield very good outcomes, with an F1-score of 94% for the automatic segmentation of the nasolacrimal canal in CBCT (cone beam computed tomography) imaging [13]. Ref. [14] introduces a novel semantic segmentation network for brain tumor annotation within the BraTS dataset, achieving 88–93% segmentation accuracy depending on the category. It is noteworthy that determining the training methodology can be complex, as the number of classes used may influence the outcomes, as demonstrated in research on osteosarcoma in X-rays and normal radiographs, where using more classes for model training yielded better quality results [15]. An alternative approach to object detection employs variations in Mask R-CNNs to determine approximate rectangular region boundaries. Enhancing mask detection with Mask R-CNN enables high-quality appendix segmentation in CT scans, as evidenced in [16]. Utilizing Faster R-CNN with the Feature Pyramid Network allows for rib fracture detection on chest radiographs with 89% accuracy [17].

Convolutional neural networks have numerous potential applications beyond those already mentioned. The detection of anomalies in optical coherence tomography (OCT) images using local region analysis has demonstrated 99% accuracy [18]. Denoising techniques are valuable for enhancing the quality of the medical data obtained from non-contrast chest and low-dose abdominal CT scans, as the image quality can vary depending on the equipment used [19]. Research presented in [20] indicates that employing denoising methods can particularly improve the output of older imaging devices. In the context of diffusion tensor imaging, while deep learning denoising techniques reduce femorotibial factorial anisotropy regardless of voxel size, these approaches may help to address the challenge of lower signal-to-noise ratios [21]. A broad review of various techniques concerning coronary artery calcium scoring on non-dedicated CT is described in [22]. An application of CNNs for pediatric neuroimaging presents the potential of this approach in [23].

Recent advancements have shown that attention mechanisms and transformer networks are not only effective in automated text analysis, but also yield impressive results in image processing. For example, [24] introduced the Vertebrae-aware Vision Transformer to ensure precise and efficient spine segmentation from CT scans. A transformer-based model was employed for bone age estimation from radiographs, achieving a mean absolute error of 4.1 months [25], which surpasses the traditional machine learning methods outlined in [26]. The tedious task of manually analyzing H&E-stained WSI (whole slide images) can now be replaced by an attention-based network, enhancing accuracy and subsequently reducing the number of required surgeries [27]. The Efficient Spatial Channel Attention Network for breast cancer detection in histopathological images has demonstrated superior performance compared to conventional convolutional neural networks, attaining 94% accuracy [28]. Transformers used in combination with the inverse Fourier transform enhance the performance of the convolution layer in rosette trajectory magnetic resonance imaging [29].

Numerous organizations opt to enhance their medical data acquisition equipment with artificial intelligence-based analysis software. The research outlined in [30] indicates that an AI-powered ECG (electrocardiogram) biomarker could identify coronary occlusion in resuscitated patients, performing comparably to an expert consensus. The application of AI systems for detecting dental caries enables the establishment of a gold standard and minimizes discrepancies among dentists' assessments [31]. The findings presented in [32] demonstrate that implementing an AI-based system for identifying limb fractures in radiographs decreased the overall disagreement between physicians. An AI-driven system for screening low bone mineral density in low-dose chest CT scans proves valuable [33], as does AI support in OCTA (optical coherence tomography angiography) analysis for diagnosing various medical conditions [34]. These AI models can also streamline effective dose calculations in PET/CT, eliminating variations between operators [35]. There are also approaches on how to create simple, mobile applications that could enhance physician work. In [36], a RedScar mobile application for post-operative scar healing condition determination is introduced. The newly suggested, highly sensitive imaging technique proved to better detect breast cancer compared to MRI and infrared imaging [37]. The conclusions in [38] indicate that collaborative analysis and discussion accelerate the achievement of more accurate results when humans are learning to use new equipment.

The effectiveness of radiomic features in describing image content has been demonstrated, enabling further data classification. Research in [39] indicates that when extracted from CT or MRI scans of lung or prostate tumors, these features are influenced by individual variations in contrast. This underscores the importance of normalizing data before applying such methods [40]. Conversely, radiomic information derived from the MRI T2W modality yields more standardized results, potentially enhancing PIRADS (prostate imaging reporting data system) scores in a broader context [41]. Texture analysis, specifically gray-level co-occurrence matrix parameters, has shown a strong correlation with the histopathological grades of head and neck squamous cell carcinoma, emerging as an age-independent marker according to the study presented in [42]. A comparison of several traditional classification methods based on radiomic features with convolutional neural networks, trained both with and without transfer learning, was conducted to reduce the false-positive rates in prostate cancer detection using MRI images. The findings reveal that the tumor location affects the performance of all approaches, though deep learning models appear to be less susceptible to this issue [43].

A system for categorizing patients with idiopathic macular holes into those with favorable or unfavorable vision six months post vitrectomy can be developed using logistic regression, based on carefully chosen features from OCT data and medical records [44]. In another study, logistic regression and XGBoost were employed on features extracted via casual forest from functional MRI time series data, achieving 97% accuracy in distinguishing between healthy individuals and Parkinson's disease patients [45]. A comparable approach demonstrated the effectiveness of the SAFE (scan and find early) microwave imaging device in detecting breast cancer in young women (83%) and those with dense breasts (91%) [46]. Various machine learning models were assessed to identify an accurate model for dose estimation in CT [47].

Statistical analyses reveal that the left atrial volume and function derived from four-chamber measurements are equivalent to biplane methods when appropriate bias correction factors are applied [48]. Preoperative CT findings correlate with the duration of laparoscopic appendectomy in pediatric cases, as demonstrated in [49]. Research has also shown that categorizing osteophytes into four distinct types based on CT scans impacts the planning of surgical interventions [50]. Statistical analysis of multi-color flow cytometry data using t-SNE (t-distributed stochastic neighbor embedding) enabled the identification of multiple clusters in leukemic cells, based on their antigen expression composition and intensity [51]. K-means analysis was applied to determine the separation of the total kidney volume in patients treated with tolvaptan and allowed it to be shown between others that high annual growth was associated with a responder phenotype [52].

Utilizing fully labeled data to train models enables the resolution of numerous challenges in automated medical data analysis. However, the process of creating annotations is time-consuming and costly, necessitating the exploration of alternative methods when labels are unavailable. In such cases, unsupervised algorithms prove valuable. For instance, research in [53] demonstrates that employing non-linear dimensionality reduction techniques, such as locally linear embedding and isometric feature maps, facilitates the identification of active lesions in MRI scans during the planning of multiple sclerosis diagnosis and treatment. A study in [54] introduces a k-means approach for detecting and quantifying immunohistochemical staining. This method, when applied to the tissue of interest with normalized color and a removed extraneous background, yields good outcomes.

Transformer networks emerged as a solution to various challenges in automated text processing and comprehension. When trained on extensive datasets, these models demonstrate good capabilities in swift knowledge acquisition and, through generative approaches, can operate across different modalities. Consequently, their application as a supportive tool in medicine is a logical choice. For example, in medical imaging analysis for diagnosis and treatment planning, findings must be documented textually, forming the basis of communication. To streamline this process, an automatic speech recognition system can be employed, as shown in [55]. Advanced language models such as GPT-4 can automatically describe the imaging data content, serving as an initial step towards assisting radiologists in image description. However, using these models without proper preparation leads to high error rates, while employing the current prompts can enhance results, as outlined in [56], along with appropriate tuning [57]. In [58], researchers compare

GPT-4o with Cloud 3.5 Sonnet models for the automatic detection of acute ischemic stroke in diffusion-weighted imaging, revealing superior diagnostic abilities in the latter model, albeit still noting a high error rate that necessitates further investigation.

Table 1 summarizes the application of various AI approaches to medical data. Within the publication cycle, three main areas related to the topic of artificial intelligence in medicine can be distinguished. The largest group of articles (24) is the implementation of systems in specific medical issues, mainly using deep learning, U-Net, or CNNs. Most of them are studies of the proposed architecture for one problem, but there are also four publications testing and comparing different architectures. Three of the publications concern histopathological images. A very frequently discussed issue in this group of publications is image segmentation applied to a wide class of organs and tissues. A summary of such papers is presented in Table 2.

Table 1. Summary of medical research using various AI techniques.

AI Technique	Medical Problem
Data classification (CNN)	Chest [2], mammograms [3], tuberculosis [4], brain tumor [5]
Data segmentation (CNN)	Cell counting in H&E-stained images [6], heart and lung anatomy [7], appendix segmentation [8], temporomandibular joints [9], lung fissure [10], COVID-19 diagnosis [11], brain [12], nasolacrimal canal [13], brain tumor [14], osteosarcoma [15], appendix [16], rib fracture [17]
Other applications of CNNs	Detection of anomalies in OCT [18], denoising in chest [19], working with older equipment [20], technical improvements [21], review [1,22,23]
Data analysis with transformers	Spine segmentation [24], bone age estimation [25], analysis of H&E WSI [27], breast [28], brain [29]
Gold standard definitions	Coronary occlusion identification [30], dental caries [31], limb fractures [32], chest [33], OCTA [34], PET [35], scar healing [36], breast cancer [37], discussion helps to apply new technology [38]
ML with radiomics	Lung/prostate tumors [39], PIRADS [41], cell carcinoma [42], prostate cancer [43]
Other applications	Idiopathic macular hole [44], Parkinson's disease [45], breast cancer [46], dose estimation in CT [47], left atrial volume is equivalent to biplane methods [48], laparoscopy duration [49], osteophytes impact planning of surgical interventions [50], leukemic cells [51], kidney [52]
Unsupervised ML	Active lesions [53], immunohistochemical staining [54]
LLM	Speech recognition [55], describing image content [56,57], detection of acute ischemic stroke [58]

The second largest group of publications (12) concerned the use of artificial intelligence systems for the classification of medical data. The most commonly used method was logistic regression, but other regressors were also used, e.g., random forest, and once the stochastic t-SNE method was used. A summary of topic papers focused on pathology detection and classification is shown in Table 3.

Table 2. Summary of topic papers focused on cell or organ segmentation (MAE—mean absolute error, IoU—intersection over union, F1—F1-score, DSC—Dice similarity coefficient, HD—Hausdorff distance, and JAFROC—free-response receiver operating characteristic).

DL Tools	Problem	Modality	Algorithm	Results
CNN [6]	The automatic cell counting on images of H&E-stained slides	H&E-stained images	U-Net	Good agreement between pathologists and AI: MAE(pat) = 13.3%, MAE(AI) = 10.9
CNN [7]	Lung and heart segmentation for cardiothoracic ratio calculation	Chest radiographs	U-Net	Segmentation accuracy: IoU = 0.83, F1 = 0.91
CNN [8]	The accurate segmentation of the appendix	CT	Modified U-Net, DenseNet, Resnet	Segmentation accuracy of modified U-Net: DSC = 0.87, HD = 3.95 mm
CNN [10]	Lung lobe segmentation and lung fissure segmentation	CT	U-Net, Derivative-of-Stick Filter	Segmentation accuracy: F1 = (0.894–0.899), for left and right lung fissures, average DSC = 0.989
CNN [14]	Brain tumor segmentation	MRI	Enhanced by Hierarchical Feature Fusion module	Accuracies of three tumor subregions (enhanced tumor, tumor core, entire tumor): DSC = 88.27%, 91.31%, and 92.96%, respectively
CNN [15]	A novel annotation method for preparing training data for osteosarcoma detection	X-ray	U-Net	Segmentation accuracy for three classes: DSC = 0.644
CNN [16]	Automatic and accurate segmentation of the appendix	CT	Mask R-CNN, Reset101, Grad-CAM	Segmentation accuracy: DSC = 0.87
CNN [17]	Segmentation of rib fractures	Chest radiography	Detectron2 with feature pyramid network	Radiograph with rib fracture classification: AUC = 0.89, rib fracture detection: JAFROC = 0.76
Transformers [24]	The accurate and efficient segmentation of the spine and vertebrae identification	CT	Vertebrae-aware Vision Transformer (a variant of Vision Transformer)	Segmentation accuracy: DSC = (0.95–0.94), IoU = (0.96–0.94) for VerSe2019 and VerSe2020 datasets

Table 3. Summary of topic papers focused on pathology detection and classification (AUC—area under the curve).

AI Tools	Problem	Modality	Algorithm	Results
DL [2]	Identifying acute aortic syndrome and thoracic aortic aneurysm in emergency departments	Chest radiographs	InceptionV3, ResNet101, VGG19, nception-ResNet-v2	InceptionV3 F1 = 0.76 for identification of patients with chest pain and suspected acute aortic syndrome/thoracic aortic aneurysm

Table 3. *Cont.*

AI Tools	Problem	Modality	Algorithm	Results
DL [5]	Brain tumor detection and classification	MRI	Optimized CNN	Accuracy of classification (three tumor types) = 0.97
DL [4]	Identification of pneumonia, COVID-19, and tuberculosis	Chest radiographs	ResNet50, VGG16	ResNet50's precision and recall rates are close to 0.99 in disease identification
DL with attention module [3]	Computer-aided systems for breast cancer diagnosis in mammograms	X-ray	EfficientNet-b0, cross-mammogram dual-pathway attention module	Classification accuracy = 98.02%, AUC = 0.9664
DL with attention module [5]	Breast cancer diagnosis from histopathology images	Microscope histopathology images	Efficient channel-spatial attention network, improved version of EfficientNetV2	Accuracies of 94.2% at 40×, 92.96% at 100×, 88.41% at 200×, 89.42% at 400× magnifications
DL with attention module [27]	Prediction of lymph node metastasis in colorectal cancer images	H&E-stained whole slide images	Customized deep convolutional neural network attention module, classification module	Accuracy = 0.92, AUC = 0.781–0.824
Radiomics, Statistical analysis [42]	Determination of the grade of cellular differentiation in head and neck squamous cell carcinoma	Multi-Slice Spiral CT	Texture analysis (TA), gray-level co-occurrence matrix	The correlations found between texture parameters and histopathological features suggest that TA is a useful tool in the prognosis and tailoring of treatment strategies for patients with different tumor types
ML/DL, Radiomics [5]	Segmentation and classification of prostate lesions using different ML models	MRI	Texture features, support vector machine, random forest, multiple perceptron, ConvNeXt, ConvNet, ResNet	CNN-based approaches obtained better results compared to the classical machine learning approaches

The third group of publications are analyses of the use of existing software based on artificial intelligence (e.g., The Quantitative ECG (QCG™) system, PixelShine, or A.I. DeNoise™). The cycle also contains three review papers.

Figure 1 illustrates the distribution of imaging modalities used in publications within this topic. CT and MRI are predominant, which is expected given their widespread use across medical specialties. This correlates with the number of commercially available AI solutions for CT and MRI [1], representing the modalities with the most developed image-based diagnostic algorithms. Radiography is the next most common modality, and similarly, numerous FDA-approved (Food and Drug Administration) machine learning models exist for the analysis of X-ray images. Optical imaging, primarily microscopy of histological specimens, follows in prevalence. Other modalities such as OCT, ultrasound (US), and thermography are utilized to a much lesser extent. Regarding medical specialties (shown in Figure 2), publications on image analysis methods for neurology, pulmonology, and oncology (excluding brain and lung cancers) are the most prevalent. This is due to the advanced development of these medical fields and the very large number of conditions where the use of diagnostic imaging is essential. The number of described methods for these specialties also correlates with the number of commercially available AI algorithms, which are the most abundant for neurology and pulmonology applications [1]. The number of AI algorithms presented for other specialties is relatively similar and small.

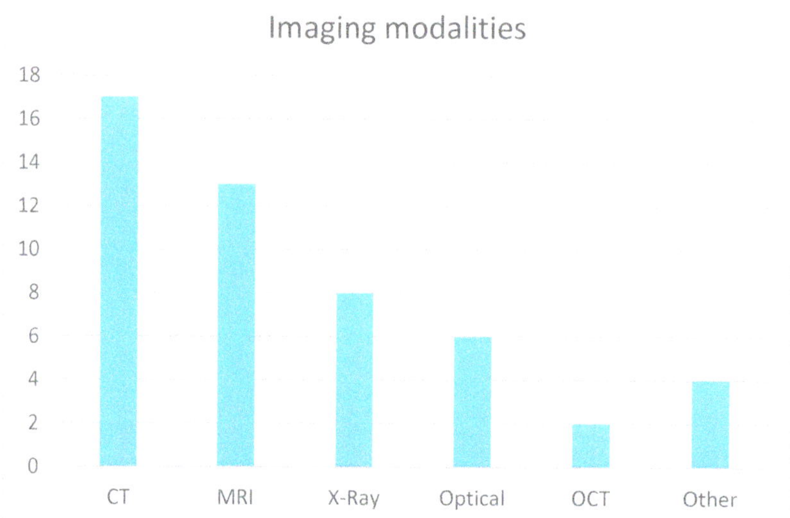

Figure 1. Modality distribution in topic publications.

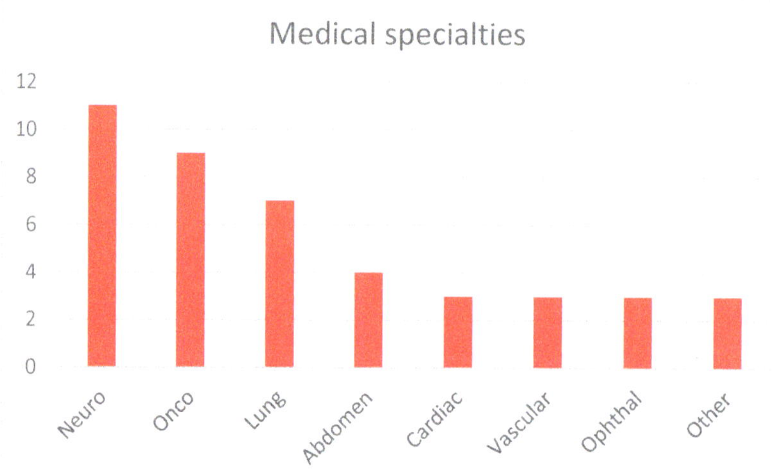

Figure 2. Medical specialties addressed by the described AI methods.

In image analysis tasks, where the primary research problem involves detecting and classifying pathologies or predicting their occurrence, algorithms based on deep learning dominate. It is noteworthy that deep learning methods increasingly incorporate attention mechanisms, which often lead to improved performance. The topic also includes studies employing radiomics, particularly texture analysis [59]. These methods, combined with classical machine learning algorithms or statistical analysis, remain effective tools for biomedical image analysis. However, their popularity is declining in favor of deep learning-based approaches.

For the segmentation tasks described in the topic papers, dedicated deep learning architectures dominate. In particular, the U-Net architecture and its variants are prevalent. Alternative approaches, such as oscillator neural networks, which have proven effective in biomedical image segmentation [60], are virtually absent. The transformer-based models, previously employed in large language models like ChatGPT, are emerging. However, due to the limited number of topic publications utilizing these methods, comparing their performance with classical convolutional neural networks is challenging. The growing popularity of transformer-based algorithms in biomedical image analysis is noteworthy, due to their often-superior performance compared to deep neural networks [24].

Conflicts of Interest: The authors declare no conflicts of interest.

References

1. Obuchowicz, R.; Lasek, J.; Wodziński, M.; Piórkowski, A.; Strzelecki, M.; Nurzynska, K. Artificial Intelligence-Empowered Radiology—Current Status and Critical Review. *Diagnostics* **2025**, *15*, 282. [CrossRef] [PubMed]
2. Lin, Y.-T.; Wang, B.-C.; Chung, J.-Y. Identifying Acute Aortic Syndrome and Thoracic Aortic Aneurysm from Chest Radiography in the Emergency Department Using Convolutional Neural Network Models. *Diagnostics* **2024**, *14*, 1646. [CrossRef] [PubMed]
3. Wen, X.; Li, J.; Yang, L. Breast Cancer Diagnosis Method Based on Cross-Mammogram Four-View Interactive Learning. *Tomography* **2024**, *10*, 848–868. [CrossRef]
4. Kolhar, M.; Al Rajeh, A.M.; Kazi, R.N.A. Augmenting Radiological Diagnostics with AI for Tuberculosis and COVID-19 Disease Detection: Deep Learning Detection of Chest Radiographs. *Diagnostics* **2024**, *14*, 1334. [CrossRef]
5. Aamir, M.; Namoun, A.; Munir, S.; Aljohani, N.; Alanazi, M.H.; Alsahafi, Y.; Alotibi, F. Brain Tumor Detection and Classification Using an Optimized Convolutional Neural Network. *Diagnostics* **2024**, *14*, 1714. [CrossRef]
6. Kiyuna, T.; Cosatto, E.; Hatanaka, K.C.; Yokose, T.; Tsuta, K.; Motoi, N.; Makita, K.; Shimizu, A.; Shinohara, T.; Suzuki, A.; et al. Evaluating Cellularity Estimation Methods: Comparing AI Counting with Pathologists' Visual Estimates. *Diagnostics* **2024**, *14*, 1115. [CrossRef] [PubMed]
7. Kufel, J.; Paszkiewicz, I.; Kocot, S.; Lis, A.; Dudek, P.; Czogalik, Ł.; Janik, M.; Bargieł-Łączek, K.; Bartnikowska, W.; Koźlik, M.; et al. Deep Learning in Cardiothoracic Ratio Calculation and Cardiomegaly Detection. *J. Clin. Med.* **2024**, *13*, 4180. [CrossRef]
8. Baştuğ, B.T.; Güneri, G.; Yıldırım, M.S.; Çorbacı, K.; Dandıl, E. Fully Automated Detection of the Appendix Using U-Net Deep Learning Architecture in CT Scans. *J. Clin. Med.* **2024**, *13*, 5893. [CrossRef]
9. Lasek, J.; Nurzynska, K.; Piórkowski, A.; Strzelecki, M.; Obuchowicz, R. Deep Learning for Ultrasonographic Assessment of Temporomandibular Joint Morphology. *Tomography* **2025**, *11*, 27. [CrossRef]
10. Fufin, M.; Makarov, V.; Alfimov, V.I.; Ananev, V.V.; Ananeva, A. Pulmonary Fissure Segmentation in CT Images Using Image Filtering and Machine Learning. *Tomography* **2024**, *10*, 1645–1664. [CrossRef]
11. Rashid, P.Q.; Türker, I. Lung Disease Detection Using U-Net Feature Extractor Cascaded by Graph Convolutional Network. *Diagnostics* **2024**, *14*, 1313. [CrossRef] [PubMed]
12. Sørensen, P.J.; Ladefoged, C.N.; Larsen, V.A.; Andersen, F.L.; Nielsen, M.B.; Poulsen, H.S.; Carlsen, J.F.; Hansen, A.E. Repurposing the Public BraTS Dataset for Postoperative Brain Tumour Treatment Response Monitoring. *Tomography* **2024**, *10*, 1397–1410. [CrossRef] [PubMed]
13. Haylaz, E.; Gumussoy, I.; Duman, S.B.; Kalabalik, F.; Eren, M.C.; Demirsoy, M.S.; Celik, O.; Bayrakdar, I.S. Automatic Segmentation of the Nasolacrimal Canal: Application of the nnU-Net v2 Model in CBCT Imaging. *J. Clin. Med.* **2025**, *14*, 778. [CrossRef]
14. Zhang, L.; Zhang, R.; Zhu, Z.; Li, P.; Bai, Y.; Wang, M. Lightweight MRI Brain Tumor Segmentation Enhanced by Hierarchical Feature Fusion. *Tomography* **2024**, *10*, 1577–1590. [CrossRef]
15. Hasei, J.; Nakahara, R.; Otsuka, Y.; Nakamura, Y.; Ikuta, K.; Osaki, S.; Hironari, T.; Miwa, S.; Ohshika, S.; Nishimura, S.; et al. The Three-Class Annotation Method Improves the AI Detection of Early-Stage Osteosarcoma on Plain Radiographs: A Novel Approach for Rare Cancer Diagnosis. *Cancers* **2025**, *17*, 29. [CrossRef]
16. Dandıl, E.; Baştuğ, B.T.; Yıldırım, M.S.; Çorbacı, K.; Güneri, G. MaskAppendix: Backbone-Enriched Mask R-CNN Based on Grad-CAM for Automatic Appendix Segmentation. *Diagnostics* **2024**, *14*, 2346. [CrossRef]
17. Lee, K.; Lee, S.; Kwak, J.S.; Park, H.; Oh, H.; Koh, J.C. Development and Validation of an Artificial Intelligence Model for Detecting Rib Fractures on Chest Radiographs. *J. Clin. Med.* **2024**, *13*, 3850. [CrossRef]
18. Tiosano, L.; Abutbul, R.; Lender, R.; Shwartz, Y.; Chowers, I.; Hoshen, Y.; Levy, J. Anomaly Detection and Biomarkers Localization in Retinal Images. *J. Clin. Med.* **2024**, *13*, 3093. [CrossRef] [PubMed]

19. Gohmann, R.F.; Schug, A.; Krieghoff, C.; Seitz, P.; Majunke, N.; Buske, M.; Kaiser, F.; Schaudt, S.; Renatus, K.; Desch, S.; et al. Interrater Variability of ML-Based CT-FFR in Patients without Obstructive CAD before TAVR: Influence of Image Quality, Coronary Artery Calcifications, and Location of Measurement. *J. Clin. Med.* **2024**, *13*, 5247. [CrossRef]
20. Drews, M.A.; Demircioğlu, A.; Neuhoff, J.; Haubold, J.; Zensen, S.; Opitz, M.K.; Forsting, M.; Nassenstein, K.; Bos, D. Impact of AI-Based Post-Processing on Image Quality o Non-Contrast Computed Tomography of the Chest and Abdomen. *Diagnostics* **2024**, *14*, 612. [CrossRef]
21. Santos, L.; Hsu, H.-Y.; Nelson, R.R.; Sullivan, B.; Shin, J.; Fung, M.; Lebel, M.R.; Jambawalikar, S.; Jaramillo, D. Impact of Deep Learning Denoising Algorithm on Diffusion Tensor Imaging of the Growth Plate on Different Spatial Resolutions. *Tomography* **2024**, *10*, 504–519. [CrossRef] [PubMed]
22. Aromiwura, A.A.; Kalra, D.K. Artificial Intelligence in Coronary Artery Calcium Scoring. *J. Clin. Med.* **2024**, *13*, 3453. [CrossRef]
23. da Rocha, J.L.D.; Lai, J.; Pandey, P.; Myat, P.S.M.; Loschinskey, Z.; Bag, A.K.; Sitaram, R. Artificial Intelligence for Neuroimaging in Pediatric Cancer. *Cancers* **2025**, *17*, 622. [CrossRef]
24. Li, X.; Hong, Y.; Xu, Y.; Hu, M. VerFormer: Vertebrae-Aware Transformer for Automatic Spine Segmentation from CT Images. *Diagnostics* **2024**, *14*, 1859. [CrossRef] [PubMed]
25. Zhang, J.; Chen, W.; Joshi, T.; Zhang, X.; Loh, P.-L.; Jog, V.; Bruce, R.J.; Garrett, J.W.; McMillan, A.B. BAE-ViT: An Efficient Multimodal Vision Transformer for Bone Age Estimation. *Tomography* **2024**, *10*, 2058–2072. [CrossRef] [PubMed]
26. Nurzyńska, K.; Piórkowski, A.; Strzelecki, M.; Kociołek, M.; Banyś, R.P.; Obuchowicz, R. Differentiating age and sex in vertebral body CT scans—Texture analysis versus deep learning approach. *Biocybern. Biomed. Eng.* **2024**, *44*, 20–30. [CrossRef]
27. Song, J.H.; Kim, E.R.; Hong, Y.; Sohn, I.; Ahn, S.; Kim, S.-H.; Jang, K.-T. Prediction of Lymph Node Metastasis in T1 Colorectal Cancer Using Artificial Intelligence with Hematoxylin and Eosin-Stained Whole-Slide-Images of Endoscopic and Surgical Resection Specimens. *Cancers* **2024**, *16*, 1900. [CrossRef]
28. Aldakhil, L.A.; Alhasson, H.F.; Alharbi, S.S. Attention-Based Deep Learning Approach for Breast Cancer Histopathological Image Multi-Classification. *Diagnostics* **2024**, *14*, 1402. [CrossRef]
29. Yalcinbas, M.F.; Ozturk, C.; Ozyurt, O.; Emir, U.E.; Bagci, U. Rosette Trajectory MRI Reconstruction with Vision Transformers. *Tomography* **2025**, *11*, 41. [CrossRef]
30. Park, M.J.; Choi, Y.J.; Shim, M.; Cho, Y.; Park, J.; Choi, J.; Kim, J.; Lee, E.; Kim, S.-Y. Performance of ECG-Derived Digital Biomarker for Screening Coronary Occlusion in Resuscitated Out-of-Hospital Cardiac Arrest Patients: A Comparative Study between Artificial Intelligence and a Group of Experts. *J. Clin. Med.* **2024**, *13*, 1354. [CrossRef]
31. Boldt, J.; Schuster, M.; Krastl, G.; Schmitter, M.; Pfundt, J.; Stellzig-Eisenhauer, A.; Kunz, F. Developing the Benchmark: Establishing a Gold Standard for the Evaluation of AI Caries Diagnostics. *J. Clin. Med.* **2024**, *13*, 3846. [CrossRef] [PubMed]
32. Herpe, G.; Nelken, H.; Vendeuvre, T.; Guenezan, J.; Giraud, C.; Mimoz, O.; Feydy, A.; Tasu, J.-P.; Guillevin, R. Effectiveness of an Artificial Intelligence Software for Limb Radiographic Fracture Recognition in an Emergency Department. *J. Clin. Med.* **2024**, *13*, 5575. [CrossRef] [PubMed]
33. Welsner, M.; Navel, H.; Hosch, R.; Rathsmann, P.; Stehling, F.; Mathew, A.; Sutharsan, S.; Strassburg, S.; Westhölter, D.; Taube, C.; et al. Opportunistic Screening for Low Bone Mineral Density in Adults with Cystic Fibrosis Using Low-Dose Computed Tomography of the Chest with Artificial Intelligence. *J. Clin. Med.* **2024**, *13*, 5961. [CrossRef]
34. Barca, I.C.; Potop, V.; Arama, S.S. Monitoring Progression in Hypertensive Patients with Dyslipidemia Using Optical Coherence Tomography Angiography: Can A.I. Be Improved? *J. Clin. Med.* **2024**, *13*, 7584. [CrossRef] [PubMed]
35. Eom, Y.; Park, Y.-J.; Lee, S.; Lee, S.-J.; An, Y.-S.; Park, B.-N.; Yoon, J.-K. Automated Measurement of Effective Radiation Dose by ^{18}F-Fluorodeoxyglucose Positron Emission Tomography/Computed Tomography. *Tomography* **2024**, *10*, 2144–2157. [CrossRef]
36. Craus-Miguel, A.; Munar, M.; Moyà-Alcover, G.; Contreras-Nogales, A.M.; González-Hidalgo, M.; Segura-Sampedro, J.J. Enhancing Surgical Wound Monitoring: A Paired Cohort Study Evaluating a New AI-Based Application for Automatic Detection of Potential Infections. *J. Clin. Med.* **2024**, *13*, 7863. [CrossRef]
37. Sritharan, N.; Gutierrez, C.; Perez-Raya, I.; Gonzalez-Hernandez, J.-L.; Owens, A.; Dabydeen, D.; Medeiros, L.; Kandlikar, S.; Phatak, P. Breast Cancer Screening Using Inverse Modeling of Surface Temperatures and Steady-State Thermal Imaging. *Cancers* **2024**, *16*, 2264. [CrossRef]
38. Nielsen, M.Ø.; Ljoki, A.; Zerahn, B.; Jensen, L.T.; Kristensen, B. Reproducibility and Repeatability in Focus: Evaluating LVEF Measurements with 3D Echocardiography by Medical Technologists. *Diagnostics* **2024**, *14*, 1729. [CrossRef]
39. Watzenboeck, M.L.; Beer, L.; Kifjak, D.; Röhrich, S.; Heidinger, B.H.; Prayer, F.; Milos, R.-I.; Apfaltrer, P.; Langs, G.; Baltzer, P.A.T.; et al. Contrast Agent Dynamics Determine Radiomics Profiles in Oncologic Imaging. *Cancers* **2024**, *16*, 1519. [CrossRef]
40. Gibała, S.; Obuchowicz, R.; Lasek, J.; Piórkowski, A.; Nurzynska, K. Textural Analysis Supports Prostate MR Diagnosis in PIRADS Protocol. *Appl. Sci.* **2023**, *13*, 9871. [CrossRef]
41. Liu, J.-C.; Ruan, X.-H.; Chun, T.-T.; Yao, C.; Huang, D.; Wong, H.-L.; Lai, C.-T.; Tsang, C.-F.; Ho, S.-H.; Ng, T.-L.; et al. MRI T2w Radiomics-Based Machine Learning Models in Imaging Simulated Biopsy Add Diagnostic Value to PI-RADS in Predicting Prostate Cancer: A Retrospective Diagnostic Study. *Cancers* **2024**, *16*, 2944. [CrossRef] [PubMed]

42. de Oliveira, L.A.P.; Lopes, D.L.G.; Gomes, J.P.P.; da Silveira, R.V.; Nozaki, D.V.A.; Santos, L.F.; Castellano, G.; Lopes, S.L.P.d.C.; Costa, A.L.F. Enhanced Diagnostic Precision: Assessing Tumor Differentiation in Head and Neck Squamous Cell Carcinoma Using Multi-Slice Spiral CT Texture Analysis. *J. Clin. Med.* **2024**, *13*, 4038. [CrossRef] [PubMed]
43. Rippa, M.; Schulze, R.; Kenyon, G.; Himstedt, M.; Kwiatkowski, M.; Grobholz, R.; Wyler, S.; Cornelius, A.; Schindera, S.; Burn, F. Evaluation of Machine Learning Classification Models for False-Positive Reduction in Prostate Cancer Detection Using MRI Data. *Diagnostics* **2024**, *14*, 1677. [CrossRef] [PubMed]
44. Mase, Y.; Matsui, Y.; Imai, K.; Imamura, K.; Irie-Ota, A.; Chujo, S.; Matsubara, H.; Kawanaka, H.; Kondo, M. Preoperative OCT Characteristics Contributing to Prediction of Postoperative Visual Acuity in Eyes with Macular Hole. *J. Clin. Med.* **2024**, *13*, 4826. [CrossRef]
45. Solana-Lavalle, G.; Cusimano, M.D.; Steeves, T.; Rosas-Romero, R.; Tyrrell, P.N. Causal Forest Machine Learning Analysis of Parkinson's Disease in Resting-State Functional Magnetic Resonance Imaging. *Tomography* **2024**, *10*, 894–911. [CrossRef]
46. Yurtseven, A.; Janjic, A.; Cayoren, M.; Bugdayci, O.; Aribal, M.E.; Akduman, I. XGBoost Enhances the Performance of SAFE: A Novel Microwave Imaging System for Early Detection of Malignant Breast Cancer. *Cancers* **2025**, *17*, 214. [CrossRef]
47. Ferrante, M.; De Marco, P.; Rampado, O.; Gianusso, L.; Origgi, D. Effective Dose Estimation in Computed Tomography by Machine Learning. *Tomography* **2025**, *11*, 2. [CrossRef]
48. Assadi, H.; Sawh, N.; Bailey, C.; Matthews, G.; Li, R.; Grafton-Clarke, C.; Mehmood, Z.; Kasmai, B.; Swoboda, P.P.; Swift, A.J.; et al. Validation of Left Atrial Volume Correction for Single Plane Method on Four-Chamber Cine Cardiac MRI. *Tomography* **2024**, *10*, 459–470. [CrossRef]
49. Taskent, I.; Ece, B.; Narsat, M.A. Are Preoperative CT Findings Useful in Predicting the Duration of Laparoscopic Appendectomy in Pediatric Patients? A Single Center Study. *J. Clin. Med.* **2024**, *13*, 5504. [CrossRef]
50. Taçyıldız, A.E.; İnceoğlu, F. Classification of Osteophytes Occurring in the Lumbar Intervertebral Foramen. *Tomography* **2024**, *10*, 618–631. [CrossRef]
51. Nollmann, C.; Moskorz, W.; Wimmenauer, C.; Jäger, P.S.; Cadeddu, R.P.; Timm, J.; Heinzel, T.; Haas, R. Characterization of $CD34^+$ Cells from Patients with Acute Myeloid Leukemia (AML) and Myelodysplastic Syndromes (MDS) Using a t-Distributed Stochastic Neighbor Embedding (t-SNE) Protocol. *Cancers* **2024**, *16*, 1320. [CrossRef] [PubMed]
52. Dev, H.; Hu, Z.; Blumenfeld, J.D.; Sharbatdaran, A.; Kim, Y.; Zhu, C.; Shimonov, D.; Chevalier, J.M.; Donahue, S.; Wu, A.; et al. The Role of Baseline Total Kidney Volume Growth Rate in Predicting Tolvaptan Efficacy for ADPKD Patients: A Feasibility Study. *J. Clin. Med.* **2025**, *14*, 1449. [CrossRef]
53. Uwaeze, J.; Narayana, P.A.; Kamali, A.; Braverman, V.; Jacobs, M.A.; Akhbardeh, A. Automatic Active Lesion Tracking in Multiple Sclerosis Using Unsupervised Machine Learning. *Diagnostics* **2024**, *14*, 632. [CrossRef]
54. Zamojski, D.; Gogler, A.; Scieglinska, D.; Marczyk, M. EpidermaQuant: Unsupervised Detection and Quantification of Epidermal Differentiation Markers on H-DAB-Stained Images of Reconstructed Human Epidermis. *Diagnostics* **2024**, *14*, 1904. [CrossRef] [PubMed]
55. Jelassi, M.; Jemai, O.; Demongeot, J. Revolutionizing Radiological Analysis: The Future of French Language Automatic Speech Recognition in Healthcare. *Diagnostics* **2024**, *14*, 895. [CrossRef] [PubMed]
56. Wada, A.; Akashi, T.; Shih, G.; Hagiwara, A.; Nishizawa, M.; Hayakawa, Y.; Kikuta, J.; Shimoji, K.; Sano, K.; Kamagata, K.; et al. Optimizing GPT-4 Turbo Diagnostic Accuracy in Neuroradiology through Prompt Engineering and Confidence Thresholds. *Diagnostics* **2024**, *14*, 1541. [CrossRef]
57. Koyun, M.; Cevval, Z.K.; Reis, B.; Ece, B. Detection of Intracranial Hemorrhage from Computed Tomography Images: Diagnostic Role and Efficacy of ChatGPT-4o. *Diagnostics* **2025**, *15*, 143. [CrossRef]
58. Koyun, M.; Taskent, I. Evaluation of Advanced Artificial Intelligence Algorithms' Diagnostic Efficacy in Acute Ischemic Stroke: A Comparative Analysis of ChatGPT-4o and Claude 3.5 Sonnet Models. *J. Clin. Med.* **2025**, *14*, 571. [CrossRef]
59. Szczypiński, P.M.; Strzelecki, M.; Materka, A.; Klepaczko, A. Mazda—The Software Package for Textural Analysis of Biomedical Images. In *Computers in Medical Activity*; Kącki, E., Rudnicki, M., Stempczyńska, J., Eds.; Advances in Soft Computing; Springer: Berlin/Heidelberg, Germany, 2009; Volume 65, pp. 73–84. [CrossRef]
60. Strzelecki, M. Texture boundary detection using network of synchronised oscillators. *Electron. Lett.* **2004**, *40*, 466–467. [CrossRef]

Journal of
Clinical Medicine

MDPI

Article

Performance of ECG-Derived Digital Biomarker for Screening Coronary Occlusion in Resuscitated Out-of-Hospital Cardiac Arrest Patients: A Comparative Study between Artificial Intelligence and a Group of Experts

Min Ji Park [1], Yoo Jin Choi [1,*], Moonki Shim [1], Youngjin Cho [2], Jiesuck Park [2], Jina Choi [2], Joonghee Kim [3,4], Eunkyoung Lee [3,4] and Seo-Yoon Kim [1]

1 Department of Emergency Medicine, Ajou University School of Medicine, Suwon-si 16499, Republic of Korea; parkmjem@gmail.com (M.J.P.); moonki.shim@gmail.com (M.S.); seoyoon426@aumc.ac.kr (S.-Y.K.)
2 Department of Cardiology, Seoul National University Bundang Hospital, Seongnam-si 13620, Republic of Korea; cho_y@snubh.org (Y.C.); cardio.jspark@gmail.com (J.P.); mdmiki0552@gmail.com (J.C.)
3 Department of Emergency Medicine, Seoul National University Bundang Hospital, Seongnam-si 13620, Republic of Korea; joonghee79@gmail.com (J.K.); heayang0418@naver.com (E.L.)
4 Big Data Center, Seoul National University Bundang Hospital, Seongnam-si 13620, Republic of Korea
* Correspondence: choiyj0729@naver.com; Tel.: +82-31-219-7777

Abstract: Acute coronary syndrome is a significant part of cardiac etiology contributing to out-of-hospital cardiac arrest (OHCA), and immediate coronary angiography has been proposed to improve survival. This study evaluated the effectiveness of an AI algorithm in diagnosing near-total or total occlusion of coronary arteries in OHCA patients who regained spontaneous circulation. Conducted from 1 July 2019 to 30 June 2022 at a tertiary university hospital emergency department, it involved 82 OHCA patients, with 58 qualifying after exclusions. The AI used was the Quantitative ECG (QCG™) system, which provides a STEMI diagnostic score ranging from 0 to 100. The QCG score's diagnostic performance was compared to assessments by two emergency physicians and three cardiologists. Among the patients, coronary occlusion was identified in 24. The QCG score showed a significant difference between occlusion and non-occlusion groups, with the former scoring higher. The QCG biomarker had an area under the curve (AUC) of 0.770, outperforming the expert group's AUC of 0.676. It demonstrated 70.8% sensitivity and 79.4% specificity. These findings suggest that the AI-based ECG biomarker could predict coronary occlusion in resuscitated OHCA patients, and it was non-inferior to the consensus of the expert group.

Keywords: out-of-hospital cardiac arrest; ST elevation myocardial infarction; artificial intelligence; electrocardiography

1. Introduction

EMS-assisted out-of-hospital cardiac arrests (OHCAs) have an annual incidence of up to 35,000 cases in the United States, and the rate of survival-to-discharge is known to be approximately 9% [1]. Since cardiac causes are implicated as a major contributor to OHCA, representing around 60.8% [2], and as acute coronary syndrome (ACS) accounts for 16% of OHCA cases [3], previous studies have suggested that immediate coronary angiography (CAG) for the identification of individuals who require emergency coronary angioplasty could potentially improve patient survival by addressing reversible causes [4–7]. While the role of immediate CAG in patients with cardiac arrest without ST-segment elevation on electrocardiography (ECG) remains debatable [8–10], the importance of prompt revascularization for acute coronary occlusion in patients showing ST-segment elevation after return of spontaneous circulation (ROSC) remains unchanged [11,12].

An acute ST-elevation myocardial infarction (STEMI) is an event in which transmural myocardial ischemia results in myocardial injury or necrosis with typical changes in the ST segment on an ECG. This condition arises due to the occlusion of one or more coronary arteries, which are vital for supplying blood to the heart [13]. However, it is difficult to accurately identify such coronary occlusions from 12-lead ECGs in resuscitated OHCA patients. ECGs after ROSC can show various changes due to factors like electrolyte imbalances, post-arrest myocardial dysfunction, or intracranial bleeding, such as subarachnoid hemorrhages which can mimic or mask underlying coronary occlusion [14].

Recently, we have developed an artificial intelligence (AI) system (QCG™) that can extract various digital biomarkers from printed 12-lead ECGs. This biomarker demonstrated high accuracy in identifying acute total or near-total coronary occlusion in emergency department settings [15]. As the system has also been implemented on smartphones with camera functionality, it can be easily used in the resuscitation room. However, its accuracy for screening acute coronary occlusion in resuscitated OHCA patients has not been evaluated. Therefore, our aim was to assess the performance of the system's occlusive myocardial infarction (MI) biomarker, qSTEMI, in screening for acute coronary occlusion in post-ROSC patients.

2. Materials and Methods

2.1. The AI Algorithm

The Quantitative ECG (QCG™) system (ARPI Inc., Seongnam-si, Gyenggi-do, Republic of Korea) version 1.0.1. comprises a heterogeneous set of deep learning-based ECG encoders designed to evaluate various cardiac conditions using printed ECGs [15]. We utilized its STEMI digital biomarker, qSTEMI, which is designed to assess acute coronary occlusion. This biomarker outputs a score between 0 and 100, which is correlated with the risk of coronary occlusion. The algorithm has been externally validated and has shown superior performance compared to a group of emergency physicians and cardiologists in detecting coronary occlusion [15].

2.2. Study Setting, Participants, and Data Preparation

This retrospective observational study was conducted at a tertiary university hospital with an annual emergency department (ED) attendance of over 70,000 individuals. The study population included adult patients aged 18 years or older who presented to the ED with OHCA from 1 July 2019 to 30 June 2022. The inclusion criteria were patients who arrived at the emergency department with OHCA, underwent coronary angiography and underwent a 12-lead ECG within one hour post-ROSC. The exclusion criteria were as follows: (1) cases of ventricular tachycardia (VT), (2) pacemaker interference, and (3) cases where coronary angiography suggested vasospasm, where ST-elevations are indistinguishable from those of actual STEMI.

Medical records were reviewed to collect demographic details, pre-existing conditions, laboratory results, Utstein variables, initial post-ROSC ECGs, outcomes of CAG, and treatment outcomes, including the 30-day survival data. The laboratory results were obtained from the first blood test conducted immediately after ROSC and utilized to assess the patient's initial state following ROSC. ECG evaluations utilized the first ECG conducted within one hour after ROSC, with all of these ECGs being performed prior to coronary angiography. The Institutional Review Board (IRB) of the hospitals approved the use of data.

2.3. Definitions

Cardiac arrest is defined as the cessation of cardiac mechanical activity and is confirmed by the absence of signs of circulation [16]. OHCA refers to cardiac arrest that occurs outside of a hospital setting. The presence of coronary occlusion was determined based on the results of coronary angiography performed after resuscitation. Near-total or total occlusion was defined as a positive case of acute coronary occlusion, while cases without such findings were defined as negative. However, if the report described the occlusion as chronic, it was considered an existing lesion and defined as a negative case.

2.4. Measurements of Human and AI Performance

Both experts and the AI system used the same ECG images for interpretation. These images were derived from screen captures of the waveform area of the original 12-lead ECG reports generated by MAC® 5500 HD (General Electric, Boston, MA, USA) at a 25-mm paper speed and were accessed from the electronic medical records (EMR). To simulate a typical clinical scenario involving multiple experts in decision-making, a consensus score of a group of experts, including two board-certified emergency physicians and three board-certified cardiologists, was calculated. They were informed that the supplied ECGs were the initial ones obtained after ROSC in OHCA patients, without disclosure of any other details, such as age, gender, and underlying diseases. The participants reviewed the ECGs at their own pace and provided binary responses ("yes" or "no" for STEMI). The performance of the AI was assessed using the same ECGs (PNG format) as those used for human evaluation, obtaining qSTEMI. A QCG value of 50 or higher was considered a positive diagnosis for coronary occlusion.

2.5. Statistical Analysis

Categorical variables were reported as frequencies and proportions. Continuous variables were reported as mean and standard deviation (SD) or median and interquartile range (IQR) as appropriate. Sensitivity, specificity, positive predictive value (PPV), and negative predictive value (NPV) of the quantitative electrocardiography (QCG) score and the consensus scores of the expert groups were calculated based on the Youden Index. The 95% confidence interval (CI) of the difference between the area under the curve (AUC) of the QCG score and the consensus score was calculated using DeLong's method to confirm the non-inferiority of the biomarker over human experts' consensus decision. Non-inferiority was confirmed if the lower margin of the 95% CI was larger than our predetermined non-inferiority margin (−0.05 difference). p-values < 0.05 were considered statistically significant. Data handling and statistical analyses were performed using the R-package version 3.3.2 (R Foundation for Statistical Computing, Vienna, Austria).

3. Results

3.1. Baseline Characteristics

A total of 82 OHCA patients were admitted to the emergency department and underwent CAG. A total of 75 of these 82 patients underwent a 12-lead ECG(s) within one hour of resuscitation. After the exclusion of a patient with VT ECG and 16 patients with vasospasm, a total of 58 patients were included in the study. Coronary occlusion (either near-total or total) was identified in 24 patients (Table 1). There were no significant differences in demographics, underlying diseases, 30-day survival, or discharge neurological outcomes. Emergency angiography was performed more frequently in patients with obstruction: 19 (79.2%) vs. 15 (44.1%).

Table 1. Patient Characteristics.

	Occlusion (n = 24)	No Occlusion (n = 34)	p
Age, mean (SD)	55.1 (10.4)	51.8 (13.5)	0.318
Sex, frequency (%)			1.000
Male	21 (87.5)	29 (85.3)	
Female	3 (12.5)	5 (14.7)	
Height, median (IQR)	170.0 (166.5–175.0)	170.0 (165.0–176.0)	0.623
Weight, mean (SD)	68.6 (10.1)	70.0 (12.9)	0.664
HTN, frequency (%)			1.000
Yes	10 (41.7)	14 (41.2)	
No	14 (58.3)	20 (58.8)	

Table 1. *Cont.*

	Occlusion (*n* = 24)	No Occlusion (*n* = 34)	*p*
DM, frequency (%)			0.883
Yes	4 (16.7)	4 (11.8)	
No	20 (83.3)	30 (88.2)	
CVD, frequency (%)			0.706
Yes	5 (20.8)	8 (23.5)	
No	17 (70.8)	21 (61.8)	
Unknown	2 (8.3)	5 (14.7)	
Witnessed, frequency (%)			1.000
Yes	20 (83.3)	29 (85.3)	
No	4 (16.7)	5 (14.7)	
Bystander CPR, frequency (%)			0.474
Yes	17 (70.8)	28 (82.4)	
No	7 (29.2)	6 (17.6)	
30-day Survival, frequency (%)			0.755
Yes	20 (83.3)	26 (76.5)	
No	2 (8.3)	5 (14.7)	
Unknown	2 (8.3)	3 (8.8)	
Discharge CPC, frequency (%)			0.765
1	17 (70.8)	22 (64.7)	
2	3 (12.5)	3 (8.8)	
3	0 (0.0)	0 (0.0)	
4	2 (8.3)	3 (8.8)	
5	2 (8.3)	4 (11.8)	
Unknown	0 (0.0)	2 (5.9)	
Emergency Angiography (<24 h), frequency (%)			0.016
Emergency	19 (79.2)	15 (44.1)	
Delayed	5 (20.8)	19 (55.9)	
Initial Rhythm (Prehospital), frequency (%)			0.583
Shockable	21 (87.5)	29 (85.3)	
Asystole	1 (4.2)	3 (8.8)	
PEA	2 (8.3)	1 (2.9)	
Unknown	0 (0.0)	1 (2.9)	
Initial Rhythm (ED Arrival), frequency (%)			0.172
Shockable	5 (20.8)	1 (2.9)	
Asystole	1 (4.2)	2 (5.9)	
PEA	3 (12.5)	4 (11.8)	
Prehospital ROSC	15 (62.5)	27 (79.4)	
Rhythm (After ROSC), frequency (%)			0.329
Sinus Rhythm	8 (33.3)	15 (44.1)	
Sinus Tachycardia	5 (20.8)	10 (29.4)	
Atrial Fibrillation	7 (29.2)	4 (11.8)	
Accelerated Junctional Rhythm	3 (12.5)	1 (2.9)	
Atrial Flutter	0 (0.0)	1 (2.9)	
Escape Bradycardia	1 (4.2)	0 (0.0)	
Escape Capture Bigeminy	0 (0.0)	1 (2.9)	
Supraventricular Tachycardia	0 (0.0)	1 (2.9)	
Ventricular Bigeminy	0 (0.0)	1 (2.9)	
Troponin I *, ng/mL, median (IQR)	0.300 (0.100–1.350)	0.200 (0.100–0.700)	0.381
QCG, median (IQR)	0.625 (0.208–0.988)	0.145 (0.015–0.320)	0.001
Consensus Score, median (IQR)	0.9 (0.3–1.0)	0.4 (0.0–0.8)	0.2

* The reference value of troponin I: <0.028 ng/mL. SD: standard deviation, IQR: interquartile range, HTN: hypertension, DM: diabetes mellitus, CVD: cardiovascular disease, CPR: cardiopulmonary resuscitation, CPC: cerebral performance scale, PEA: pulseless electrical activity, ED: emergency department, ROSC: return of spontaneous circulation.

Figure 1 and Table 1 show the differences in the QCG score, consensus score, and Troponin I between the two groups. The QCG score showed a significant difference, with the occlusion group showing a score of 0.625 (0.208–0.988) and the non-occlusion group showing a score of 0.145 (0.015–0.320) (p = 0.001). The Consensus Score also showed a significant difference: the occlusive group showed a score of 0.9 (0.3–1.0) and the non-occlusion group showed a score of 0.4 (0.0–0.8) (p = 0.020). Troponin levels showed no significant differences: 0.300 ng/mL (0.100–1.350) vs. 0.200 ng/mL (0.100–0.700) (p = 0.381).

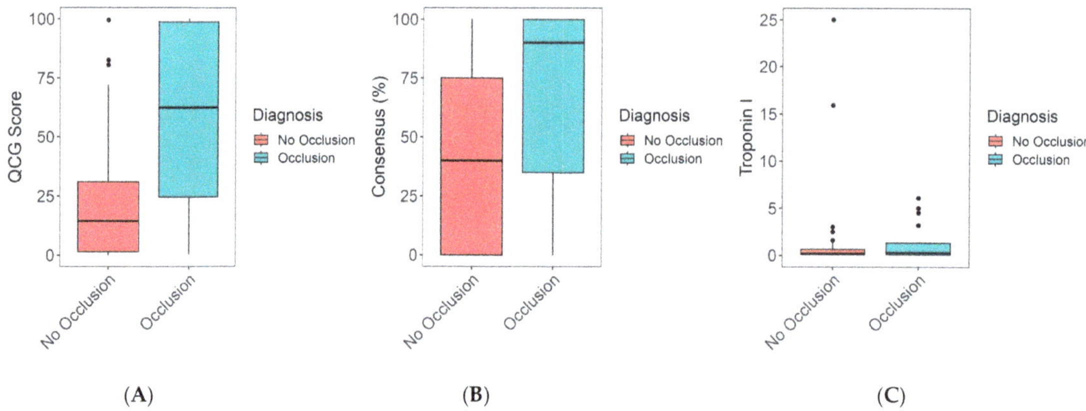

Figure 1. Boxplot of (**A**) QCG scores of the coronary occlusion group and the non-occlusion group. (**B**) Experts' consensus of the two groups. (**C**) Troponin I level in the two groups.

3.2. QCG Biomarker Versus Expert Group

The classification ability of the QCG biomarker had an AUC of 0.770 (0.641–0.900). On applying a threshold of 0.376, the sensitivity was 70.8 (48.9–87.4), the specificity was 79.4 (62.1–91.3), the positive predictive value (PPV) was 70.8 (54.5–83.1), and the negative predictive value (NPV) was 79.4 (66.9–88.0) (Table 2, Figure 2). The classification abilities of emergency physicians and cardiologists varied from an AUC of 0.592 to 0.648. When combined into a consensus score, the expert group's AUC was 0.676 (0.532–0.820), with a sensitivity of 70.8 (48.9–87.4), specificity of 64.7 (46.5–80.3), PPV of 58.6 (45.7–70.5), and NPV of 75.9 (61.6–86.0).

Table 2. Diagnostic accuracies of the QCG score and the experts.

	AUC (95% CI)	Threshold	Sensitivity (95% CI)	Specificity (95% CI)	PLR (95% CI)	NLR (95% CI)	PPV (95% CI)	NPV (95% CI)
QCG	0.770 (0.641–0.900)	0.376	70.8 (48.9–87.4)	79.4 (62.1–91.3)	3.44 (1.69–6.99	0.37 (0.19–0.70)	70.8 (54.5–83.1)	79.4 (66.9–88.0)
Consensus *	0.676 (0.532–0.820)	0.500	70.8 (48.9–87.4)	64.7 (46.5–80.3)	2.01 (1.19–3.38)	0.45 (0.23–0.88)	58.6 (45.7–70.5)	75.9 (61.6–86.0)
EP#1	0.619 (0.493–0.745)	-	70.8 (48.9–87.4)	52.9 (35.1–70.2)	1.51 (0.97–2.34)	0.55 (0.27–1.11)	51.5 (40.6–62.3)	72.0 (56.1–83.8)
EP#2	0.592 (0.462–0.722)	-	62.5 (40.6–81.2)	55.9 (37.9–72.8)	1.42 (0.87–2.31)	0.67 (0.37–1.22)	50.0 (38.0–62.0)	67.9 (53.8–79.3)
CA#1	0.645 (0.517–0.772)	-	58.3 (36.6–77.9)	70.6 (52.5–84.9)	1.98 (1.07–3.69)	0.59 (0.35–0.99)	58.3 (42.9–72.3)	70.6 (58.8–80.2)
CA#2	0.648 (0.523–0.773)	-	70.8 (48.9–87.4)	58.8 (40.7–75.4)	1.72 (1.07–2.77)	0.50 (0.25–0.98)	54.8 (43.0–66.2)	74.1 (59.1–85.0)
CA#3	0.627 (0.500–0.755)	-	66.7 (44.7–84.4)	58.8 (40.7–75.4)	1.62 (0.99–2.65)	0.57 (0.30–1.07)	53.3 (41.2–65.1)	71.4 (57.1–82.5)

* Consensus of experts. CI: confidence interval, PLR: positive likelihood ratio, NLR: negative likelihood ratio, PPV: positive predictive value, NPV: negative predictive value, EP: emergency physician, CA: cardiologist.

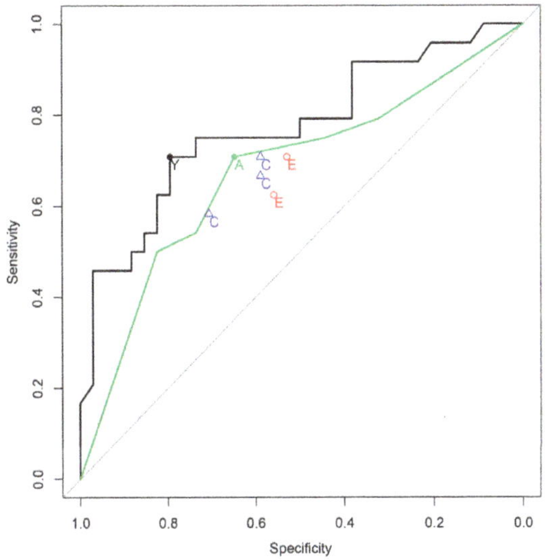

Figure 2. ROC curves for the prediction of coronary occlusion. Black solid line: ROC curve of QCG, Green solid line: ROC curve of experts' consensus, Y (black filled circle): Youden Index Point of QCG, E (red hollow circles): Emergency Physicians, C (blue hollow triangles): Cardiologists, A (green filled circle): Youden Index Point of the Consensus score.

The difference in classification ability between the QCG score and the consensus score was found to be 0.094 (−0.017–0.205). As the lower margin of this range was greater than −0.05, the QCG score was not inferior to the consensus of the five experts (Table 3).

Table 3. Non-inferiority test.

Non-Inferiority Margin	Difference	95% CI	Non-Inferiority
−0.05	0.094	−0.017 to 0.205	Confirmed

CI: confidence interval.

4. Discussion

In this study, we tested the performance of an AI-based digital biomarker in screening for occlusive MI in out-of-hospital cardiac arrest patients. The biomarker demonstrated its non-inferiority compared to the combined judgment of cardiologists and emergency medicine physicians. Data in Table 3, showing the AUC confidence interval ranging from −0.017 to 0.205, suggests no significant difference, underlining our goal to prove the AI's non-inferiority rather than its superiority. It is also worth considering that the AI was compared against the consensus score of five experts in cardiology and emergency medicine from a university hospital. Given that the sensitivity and specificity coordinates of the experts are all located below the ROC curve of the consensus score, we believe that our algorithm could be more useful in real clinical situations when evaluated by a single physician for making more accurate assessments. According to our previous study [15], in patients presenting with chest pain rather than cardiac arrest, the AUC for STEMI diagnosis was high in both AI and the consensus of experts, at 0.919 and 0.856, respectively. However, in the case of cardiac arrest in this study, the AUCs were relatively lower in both groups. This indicates that diagnosing coronary occlusion using the initial ECG of patients resuscitated after cardiac arrest is a challenging task. We believe this study is significant in demonstrating that the AI-based ECG biomarker achieved non-inferior results compared to a group of experts, even in cases of cardiac arrest. This research is the first of its kind globally, revealing the potential role of AI in decision-making regarding CAG in

OHCA patients, especially in scenarios where specialized experts like cardiologists are not available.

The COACT trial, a significant study in the field of cardiac arrest management, explored the efficacy of immediate versus delayed coronary angiography in patients who had been resuscitated from out-of-hospital cardiac arrest without ST-segment elevation on ECG. The study included 538 participants, with a follow-up duration of 90 days and 1 year. It revealed that immediate angiography with the intent to revascularize was not superior to delayed angiography among these patients. The primary outcome measured was survival at 90 days, and secondary outcomes included survival with good cerebral performance, survival to hospital discharge, and incidences of major bleeding and need for renal replacement therapy [17,18]. The downsides of performing early CAG on patients following OHCA include logistical challenges and increased risk exposure. Early CAG necessitates moving patients at a time when they may be hemodynamically unstable, which can lead to exposure to contrast agents and entail procedural risks such as bleeding, stroke, and other complications [19]. Furthermore, prioritizing CAG as the primary intervention may not only delay other crucial, potentially life-saving treatments but also slow down the process of identifying the underlying cause, especially when a coronary lesion is not the trigger for the event. This approach underscores the need for careful consideration of the timing and prioritization of CAG in the acute management of OHCA patients [20]. This suggests that the benefit of CAG can be limited to the patient with actual acute coronary occlusion and therefore it is important to accurately identify such patients.

Cardiac troponins are the biomarkers of choice for acute myocardial infarction [21]. Troponin is released into the bloodstream 4–6 h after acute MI, and peaks after approximately 18–24 h [22]. According to Wereski R. et al., at presentation in STEMI patients, the median troponin concentration was 0.196 ng/mL, and in 2.2% of patients, it was less than 0.005 ng/mL. When a threshold of 0.052 ng/mL was applied, only 73.2% were reported as positive [23]. Therefore, the initial troponin level immediately after ROSC may not be diagnostic in deciding to proceed with emergency coronary angiography, highlighting the need for a more accurate and rapid assessment of the ECG.

In this context, the need for an objective and quantifiable ECG biomarker for acute coronary occlusion has become increasingly vital. AI's ability to discern subtle patterns and variations in ECGs, which might be overlooked or misinterpreted in chaotic emergency settings, offers a significant advantage. By providing a more nuanced and detailed analysis of ECG data, AI can aid in more accurate identification of patients who may benefit from immediate CAG among resuscitated OHCA patients.

In this study, we used initial ECG only. However, ECG changes dynamically after ROSC, making it challenging to rely on a single ECG for clinical decision-making. This is corroborated by findings from the PEACE study, which indicate that early ECG acquisition post-ROSC is associated with a higher percentage of false-positive findings for STEMI [24]. In fact, ECGs obtained within 8 min post-ROSC showed a significantly higher false-positive rate compared to those obtained later. This suggests that delaying ECG acquisition by at least 8 min post-ROSC may improve its accuracy in diagnosing actual acute coronary occlusion, thus aiding in better patient selection for urgent CAG and minimizing false-positive diagnoses. Considering the dynamic nature of ECG changes post-ROSC, an approach that involves delayed or repeated ECGs could provide a more accurate and reliable assessment for guiding clinical interventions, such as CAG.

In this context, incorporating AI into serial ECG testing and harnessing its ability to provide a quantified digital biomarker for coronary occlusion may allow clinicians to objectively track the trend of coronary occlusion risk over time. As ECGs dynamically change post-ROSC, this approach may ensure that decisions regarding CAG are based on the trajectory of a measurable biomarker rather than a single snapshot in time. By observing changes in this biomarker, clinicians can make more accurate, objective, and reproducible decisions, potentially reducing unnecessary angiographies and focusing interventions on patients with a quantifiable high risk of occlusion.

Another promising aspect of the digital biomarker is its ability to utilize printed ECG images, enabling analysis through mobile phone cameras. This feature allows for the use of smartphone-based AI services even in chaotic environments of a resuscitation room. Traditional approaches, which rely on raw ECG data, often encounter practical challenges unless a data pipeline and AI integration are already in place. In contrast, our approach makes it exceptionally versatile and adaptable to various clinical settings, including those where traditional ECG data process infrastructures might be lacking.

This study has several limitations that warrant consideration. Firstly, its retrospective design may have introduced biases that could have affected the interpretation of results. Secondly, the study might have introduced selection bias by analyzing only patients who underwent CAG after ROSC. Thirdly, the number of patients analyzed in this study is less than 100, making it a relatively small-scale study. This was due to the low number of patients who underwent coronary angiography after cardiac arrest. Based on the results of this study, the authors plan to conduct further multi-institutional research based on the collection of data from multiple sources. Fourth, the study dataset was constrained in its ability to assess the diagnostic efficacy of the QCG for identifying new-onset left bundle branch block (LBBB), which is one of the diagnostic criteria for STEMI, because no cases of LBBB were found among those finally included in the study. Fifth, reliance on printed ECGs could raise concerns about image quality and interpretation. Finally, the AI algorithm's diagnostic accuracy and clinical utility require further validation in larger, prospective studies to establish efficacy across diverse clinical settings.

5. Conclusions

An ECG-based digital biomarker could predict total or near-total coronary occlusion in resuscitated OHCA patients, and it was non-inferior to the consensus of a group of clinical experts. Combined with serial ECG analysis and other clinical information, it could provide objective and reproducible decision-making criteria for immediate angiography in resuscitated OHCA patients.

Author Contributions: Conceptualization: M.J.P., Y.J.C. and J.K. Data curation: M.J.P., Y.J.C., S.-Y.K. and E.L. Formal analysis: M.J.P., Y.J.C. and J.K. Methodology: M.J.P., Y.J.C., M.S., Y.C., J.P. and J.C. Writing—original draft: M.J.P., Y.J.C. and J.K. Writing—review and editing: M.J.P., Y.J.C. and J.K. All authors have read and agreed to the published version of the manuscript.

Funding: This research did not receive any specific grant from funding agencies in the public, commercial, or not-for-profit sectors.

Institutional Review Board Statement: The Institutional Review Board of Ajou Medical Center approved the analysis and waived the informed consent requirement. (IRB Number: AJOUIRB-DB-2022-346, date of approval 16 August 2022).

Informed Consent Statement: Patient consent was waived due to the study being a retrospective observational study based on medical records and not including private personal information.

Data Availability Statement: The original contributions presented in the study are included in the article. Further inquiries can be directed to the corresponding author/s.

Acknowledgments: The authors thank the Big Data Center of Seoul National University Bundang Hospital for assistance with data analysis and the excellent work of all the staff who participated in the study.

Conflicts of Interest: Joonghee Kim developed the algorithm and founded a start-up company, ARPI Inc. He is the CEO of the company. Eunkyoung Lee works for the company as a part-time data scientist. Min Ji Park and Yoo Jin Choi hold stocks in ARPI Inc. Otherwise, there are no conflicts of interest for the other authors.

References

1. Tsao, C.W.; Aday, A.W.; Almarzooq, Z.I.; Anderson, C.A.; Arora, P.; Avery, C.L.; Baker-Smith, C.M.; Beaton, A.Z.; Boehme, A.K.; Buxton, A.E.; et al. Heart Disease and Stroke Statistics-2023 Update: A Report From the American Heart Association. *Circulation* **2023**, *147*, e93–e621, Correction in *Circulation* **2023**, *147*, e622. [CrossRef]
2. Hawkes, C.; Booth, S.; Ji, C.; Brace-McDonnell, S.J.; Whittington, A.; Mapstone, J.; Cooke, M.W.; Deakin, C.D.; Gale, C.P.; Fothergill, R.; et al. Epidemiology and outcomes from out-of-hospital cardiac arrests in England. *Resuscitation* **2016**, *110*, 133–140. [CrossRef]
3. Chen, N.; Callaway, C.W.; Guyette, F.X.; Rittenberger, J.C.; Doshi, A.A.; Dezfulian, C.; Elmer, J. Arrest etiology among patients resuscitated from cardiac arrest. *Resuscitation* **2018**, *130*, 33–40. [CrossRef] [PubMed]
4. Spaulding, C.M.; Joly, L.-M.; Rosenberg, A.; Monchi, M.; Weber, S.N.; Dhainaut, J.-F.A.; Carli, P. Immediate Coronary Angiography in Survivors of Out-of-Hospital Cardiac Arrest. *N. Engl. J. Med.* **1997**, *336*, 1629–1633. [CrossRef] [PubMed]
5. Noc, M.; Fajadet, J.; Lassen, J.F.; Kala, P.; MacCarthy, P.; Olivecrona, G.K.; Windecker, S.; Spaulding, C. Invasive coronary treatment strategies for out-of-hospital cardiac arrest: A consensus statement from the European Association for Percutaneous Cardiovascular Interventions (EAPCI)/Stent For Life (SFL) groups. *EuroIntervention* **2014**, *10*, 31–37. [CrossRef] [PubMed]
6. Batista, L.M.; Lima, F.O.; Januzzi, J.L.; Donahue, V.; Snydeman, C.; Greer, D.M. Feasibility and safety of combined percutaneous coronary intervention and therapeutic hypothermia following cardiac arrest. *Resuscitation* **2010**, *81*, 398–403. [CrossRef] [PubMed]
7. Welsford, M.; Bossard, M.; Shortt, C.; Pritchard, J.; Natarajan, M.K.; Belley-Côté, E.P. Does Early Coronary Angiography Improve Survival After out-of-Hospital Cardiac Arrest? A Systematic Review with Meta-Analysis. *Can. J. Cardiol.* **2018**, *34*, 180–194. [CrossRef]
8. Lemkes, J.S.; Janssens, G.N.; van der Hoeven, N.W.; Jewbali, L.S.; Dubois, E.A.; Meuwissen, M.; Rijpstra, T.A.; Bosker, H.A.; Blans, M.J.; Bleeker, G.B.; et al. Coronary Angiography after Cardiac Arrest without ST-Segment Elevation. *N. Engl. J. Med.* **2019**, *380*, 1397–1407. [CrossRef]
9. Staudacher, I.I.; den Uil, C.; Jewbali, L.; van Zandvoort, L.; Zijlstra, F.; Van Mieghem, N.; Boersma, E.; Daemen, J. Timing of coronary angiography in survivors of out-of-hospital cardiac arrest without obvious extracardiac causes. *Resuscitation* **2018**, *123*, 98–104. [CrossRef]
10. Hollenbeck, R.D.; McPherson, J.A.; Mooney, M.R.; Unger, B.T.; Patel, N.C.; McMullan, P.W.; Hsu, C.-H.; Seder, D.B.; Kern, K.B. Early cardiac catheterization is associated with improved survival in comatose survivors of cardiac arrest without STEMI. *Resuscitation* **2014**, *85*, 88–95. [CrossRef]
11. Ibanez, B.; James, S.; Agewall, S.; Antunes, M.J.; Bucciarelli-Ducci, C.; Bueno, H.; Caforio, A.L.; Crea, F.; Goudevenos, J.A.; Halvorsen, S.; et al. 2017 ESC Guidelines for the management of acute myocardial infarction in patients presenting with ST-segment elevation: The Task Force for the management of acute myocardial infarction in patients presenting with ST-segment elevation of the European Society of Cardiology (ESC). *Eur. Heart J.* **2018**, *39*, 119–177.
12. Peberdy, M.A.; Callaway, C.W.; Neumar, R.W.; Geocadin, R.G.; Zimmerman, J.L.; Donnino, M.; Gabrielli, A.; Silvers, S.M.; Zaritsky, A.L.; Merchant, R.; et al. Part 9: Post-cardiac arrest care: 2010 American Heart Association Guidelines for Cardiopulmonary Resuscitation and Emergency Cardiovascular Care. *Circulation* **2010**, *122* (18 Suppl. 3), S768–S786; Correction in *Circulation* **2011**, *123*, e237. [CrossRef]
13. Alpert, J.S.; Thygesen, K.; Antman, E.; Bassand, J.P. Myocardial infarction redefined—A consensus document of The Joint European Society of Cardiology/American College of Cardiology Committee for the redefinition of myocardial infarction. *J. Am. Coll. Cardiol.* **2000**, *36*, 959–969.
14. Kim, Y.-J.; Min, S.-Y.; Lee, D.H.; Lee, B.K.; Jeung, K.W.; Lee, H.J.; Shin, J.; Ko, B.S.; Ahn, S.; Nam, G.-B.; et al. The Role of Post-Resuscitation Electrocardiogram in Patients With ST-Segment Changes in the Immediate Post-Cardiac Arrest Period. *JACC Cardiovasc. Interv.* **2017**, *10*, 451–459. [CrossRef] [PubMed]
15. Choi, Y.J.; Park, M.J.; Ko, Y.; Soh, M.-S.; Kim, H.M.; Kim, C.H.; Lee, E.; Kim, J. Artificial intelligence versus physicians on interpretation of printed ECG images: Diagnostic performance of ST-elevation myocardial infarction on electrocardiography. *Int. J. Cardiol.* **2022**, *363*, 6–10. [CrossRef] [PubMed]
16. Roger, V.L.; Go, A.S.; Lloyd-Jones, D.M.; Adams, R.J.; Berry, J.D.; Brown, T.M.; Carnethon, M.R.; Dai, S.; De Simone, G.; Ford, E.S.; et al. Heart Disease and Stroke Statistics-2011 Update A Report From the American Heart Association. *Circulation* **2011**, *123*, e18–e209. [CrossRef] [PubMed]
17. Desch, S.; Freund, A.; Akin, I.; Behnes, M.; Preusch, M.R.; Zelniker, T.A.; Skurk, C.; Landmesser, U.; Graf, T.; Eitel, I.; et al. Angiography after Out-of-Hospital Cardiac Arrest without ST-Segment Elevation. *N. Engl. J. Med.* **2021**, *385*, 2544–2553. [CrossRef] [PubMed]
18. Lemkes, J.S.; Janssens, G.N.; van der Hoeven, N.W.; Jewbali, L.S.; Dubois, E.A.; Meuwissen, M.M.; Rijpstra, T.A.; Bosker, H.A.; Blans, M.J.; Bleeker, G.B.; et al. Coronary Angiography After Cardiac Arrest Without ST Segment Elevation: One-Year Outcomes of the COACT Randomized Clinical Trial. *JAMA Cardiol.* **2020**, *5*, 1358–1365. [CrossRef] [PubMed]
19. Joffre, J.; Varenne, O.; Bougouin, W.; Rosencher, J.; Mira, J.-P.; Cariou, A. Stent thrombosis: An increased adverse event after angioplasty following resuscitated cardiac arrest. *Resuscitation* **2014**, *85*, 769–773. [CrossRef] [PubMed]
20. Laver, S.; Farrow, C.; Turner, D.; Nolan, J. Mode of death after admission to an intensive care unit following cardiac arrest. *Intensiv. Care Med.* **2004**, *30*, 2126–2128. [CrossRef] [PubMed]

21. Roffi, M.; Patrono, C.; Collet, J.-P.; Mueller, C.; Valgimigli, M.; Andreotti, F.; Bax, J.J.; Borger, M.A.; Brotons, C.; Chew, D.P.; et al. 2015 ESC Guidelines for the management of acute coronary syndromes in patients presenting without persistent ST-segment elevation: Task Force for the Management of Acute Coronary Syndromes in Patients Presenting without Persistent ST-Segment Elevation of the European Society of Cardiology (ESC). *Eur. Heart J.* **2016**, *37*, 267–315. [CrossRef] [PubMed]
22. Madsen, L.H.; Christensen, G.; Lund, T.; Serebruany, V.L.; Granger, C.B.; Hoen, I.; Grieg, Z.; Alexander, J.H.; Jaffe, A.S.; Van Eyk, J.E.; et al. Time course of degradation of cardiac troponin I in patients with acute ST-elevation myocardial infarction: The ASSENT-2 troponin substudy. *Circ. Res.* **2006**, *99*, 1141–1147. [CrossRef] [PubMed]
23. Wereski, R.; Chapman, A.R.; Lee, K.K.; Smith, S.W.; Lowe, D.J.; Gray, A.; Mills, N.L. High-Sensitivity Cardiac Troponin Concentrations at Presentation in Patients With ST-Segment Elevation Myocardial Infarction. *JAMA Cardiol.* **2020**, *5*, 1302–1304. [CrossRef] [PubMed]
24. Baldi, E.; Schnaubelt, S.; Caputo, M.L.; Klersy, C.; Clodi, C.; Bruno, J.; Compagnoni, S.; Benvenuti, C.; Domanovits, H.; Burkart, R.; et al. Association of Timing of Electrocardiogram Acquisition After Return of Spontaneous Circulation With Coronary Angiography Findings in Patients With Out-of-Hospital Cardiac Arrest. *JAMA Netw. Open* **2021**, *4*, e2032875. [CrossRef]

diagnostics

MDPI

Article

Impact of AI-Based Post-Processing on Image Quality of Non-Contrast Computed Tomography of the Chest and Abdomen

Marcel A. Drews [1,*], Aydin Demircioğlu [1], Julia Neuhoff [2], Johannes Haubold [1], Sebastian Zensen [1], Marcel K. Opitz [1], Michael Forsting [1], Kai Nassenstein [1] and Denise Bos [1]

1 Institute of Diagnostic and Interventional Radiology and Neuroradiology, University Hospital Essen, Hufelandstraße 55, 45147 Essen, Germany; aydin.demircioglu@uk-essen.de (A.D.); johannes.haubold@uk-essen.de (J.H.); sebastian.zensen@uk-essen.de (S.Z.); marcel.opitz@uk-essen.de (M.K.O.); michael.forsting@uk-essen.de (M.F.); kai.nassenstein@uk-essen.de (K.N.); denise.bos@uk-essen.de (D.B.)

2 Faculty of Medicine, University Duisburg-Essen, Hufelandstraße 55, 45122 Essen, Germany

* Correspondence: marcelalexander.drews@uk-essen.de; Tel.: +49-201-723-84502

Abstract: Non-contrast computed tomography (CT) is commonly used for the evaluation of various pathologies including pulmonary infections or urolithiasis but, especially in low-dose protocols, image quality is reduced. To improve this, deep learning-based post-processing approaches are being developed. Therefore, we aimed to compare the objective and subjective image quality of different reconstruction techniques and a deep learning-based software on non-contrast chest and low-dose abdominal CTs. In this retrospective study, non-contrast chest CTs of patients suspected of COVID-19 pneumonia and low-dose abdominal CTs suspected of urolithiasis were analysed. All images were reconstructed using filtered back-projection (FBP) and were post-processed using an artificial intelligence (AI)-based commercial software (PixelShine (PS)). Additional iterative reconstruction (IR) was performed for abdominal CTs. Objective and subjective image quality were evaluated. AI-based post-processing led to an overall significant noise reduction independent of the protocol (chest or abdomen) while maintaining image information (max. difference in SNR 2.59 ± 2.9 and CNR 15.92 ± 8.9, $p < 0.001$). Post-processing of FBP-reconstructed abdominal images was even superior to IR alone (max. difference in SNR 0.76 ± 0.5, $p \leq 0.001$). Subjective assessments verified these results, partly suggesting benefits, especially in soft-tissue imaging ($p < 0.001$). All in all, the deep learning-based denoising—which was non-inferior to IR—offers an opportunity for image quality improvement especially in institutions using older scanners without IR availability. Further studies are necessary to evaluate potential effects on dose reduction benefits.

Keywords: computed tomography; image reconstruction; image quality; chest; abdomen; urolithiasis; COVID-19; deep learning

1. Introduction

Obtaining excellent image quality on the one hand and reducing radiation exposure to the patients on the other hand is an ongoing challenge in modern computed tomography (CT) [1,2]. In this context, low-dose computed tomography (LD-CT) is an important diagnostic tool in clinical routine for detecting various pathologies including pulmonary infections or urinary stones [3,4]. Here, a lower radiation dose reduces the carcinogenic risk by ionizing radiation based on the assumption of the linear no-threshold model [5,6]. On the other hand, this leads to a weaker signal received by the image detector, which generally results in a lower image resolution [1]. However, the final image quality depends on the reconstruction algorithm applied to the raw image data.

A traditional method for image reconstruction is filtered back-projection (FBP), which is based on the idea that a projection consisting of measurements at multiple angles can be back-projected into a model of the scanned object using an inverse radon transformation with a high-pass filter [7]. The advantages of FBP are a high computational efficacy, stability, and speed in image reconstruction; while on the other hand, a high noise level and significant artifacts in low-contrast structures occur, especially in LD-CT. However, its advantages make it a widespread reconstruction method for old-generation CT scanners. Another modern approach is iterative reconstruction (IR), which requires more computational power and time but reduces image noise by cyclic imaging processing [8,9]. This leads to an overall better image quality, particularly in LD-CT, but can result in a plastic-like smooth appearance of the images [10].

With further increasing computational power within the last years, modern approaches to image noise reduction have been developed that are based on imaging post-processing including machine learning techniques [2,7,11]. A promising commercially available software solution is PixelShine v. 1.3.004 (AlgoMedica, Inc., Sunnyvale, CA, USA), which is based on a deep learning approach, trained by a high amount of imaging data [12].

First, clinical data in low-dose abdominal, pediatric thoracal, or midfacial trauma CT imply a significant noise reduction following PixelShine image reconstruction compared to FBP, but additional studies are necessary to evaluate its impact in different settings [13–16]. In our study, we evaluated the impact of the novel deep learning-based reconstruction algorithm on image quality in abdominal LD-CT for the detection of urinary stones as well as in chest CT for COVID-19 pneumonia diagnostics and compared it to FBP and IR.

2. Materials and Methods

2.1. Patients and Image Acquisition

Patient data were collected at two different sites of one radiological institution (site I (primary care): St. Marien-Hospital, Mülheim an der Ruhr, Germany; site II (tertiary care): University Hospital Essen, Essen, Germany). The institutional database of site I was searched for patients who underwent non-contrast thoracal between September 2020 and October 2021 for evaluation of pulmonary status for suspected COVID-19 pneumonia. Only examinations with the lowest available dose protocol were included. Because of the old scanner model (SOMATOM Emotion 6, Siemens Healthineers, Erlangen, Germany), this was not a real low-dose protocol as available in modern scanners. Twenty-nine patients were identified, of which three were excluded due to a different protocol (n = 2) and missing dose sheet (n = 1), leading to a final study population of 26 patients (8 female, 18 male) (Figure 1A). At site II, most thoracal CTs for suspected SARS-CoV-2 pneumonia were pulmonary artery CTs or full-dose thoracal CTs, mainly because of more severe disease or additional suspected pulmonary embolism. Therefore, no comparison was made between the sites.

Furthermore, the PACS of site I and institutional databases of site II were evaluated for patients with suspected urolithiasis who received low-dose, non-contrast abdominal CT between June 2019 and July 2021. A total of 48 patients from site I (17 female, 31 male) and 48 patients (17 female, 31 male) from site II were included (Figure 1B).

All scans (chest and abdomen) at site I were performed using SOMATOM Emotion 6 (Siemens Healthineers, Erlangen, Germany), while scans at site II were obtained using SOMATOM Force (Siemens Healthineers, Erlangen, Germany), a dual-source scanner which was used in single-source mode. Technical CT parameters were extracted from the DICOM header, and dose sheets were stored in the PACS and are summed up in Table 1. Raw image data of lung scans were reconstructed using FBP, using lung kernel (B70) and soft-tissue kernel (B40). Abdominal imaging was reconstructed using FBP (site I and site II) and IR with strengths 3 of 5 (site II only), applying a soft-tissue kernel. To reduce image noise, all reconstructed images (FBP and IR) were post-processed using the commercially available deep learning software PixelShine v. 1.3.004 (AlgoMedica Inc., Sunnyvale, CA, USA), resulting in PixelShine-processed FBP (FBP + PS) and IR (IR + PS) images. Following software reconstruction, parameters were used according to the manufacturer's recommendations as follows: for the lung kernel, streak artifact reduction of R1, target noise level 12 (based on Hounsfield unit, HU), maximum strength of noise reduction A7, and lung kernel L6; for the soft-tissue kernel, streak artifact reduction of R2, sharpening P3, and target noise level 12 (based on Hounsfield unit, HU).

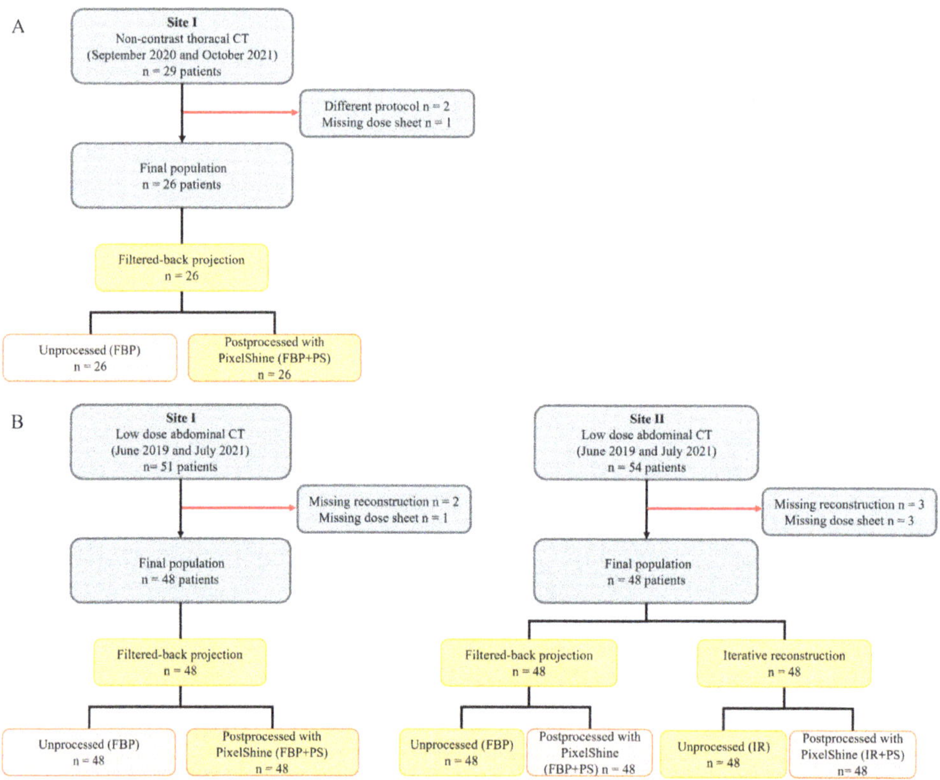

Figure 1. Patient flowchart and study design for assessment of thoracal (**A**) and abdominal LD-CT (**B**).

Table 1. Technical protocols for non-contrast thoracal and abdominal CT.

	Thorax	**Abdomen**	
	Site I	Site I	Site II
Scanner model	SOMATOM Emotion 6 (Siemens Healthineers)	SOMATOM Emotion 6 (Siemens Healthineers)	SOMATOM Force (Siemens Healthineers)
Scanner slices	6	6	192
Scanner mode	sequential	sequential	spiral
Tube potential (kVp)	130	130	150 or 100
Reference tube current time product (mAs)	70	40	40 or 244
Reconstructed slice thickness (mm)	2.5	5	5
Single collimation width (mm)	2	2	0.6
Total collimation width (mm)	12	12	57.6
Pitch factor	-	-	0.9

2.2. Objective Image Quality Analysis

For an objective analysis of thoracal and abdominal CTs, different regions-of-interest (ROIs) were evaluated (Figure 2). For thoracal CT, seven ROIs were defined as follows: ascending aorta (AAC), pulmonary trunk (TRP), descending aorta (ADE), lung (LUN), autochthonous back muscle (AUM), subcutaneous fat tissue (FAT), and air (AIR). Six ROIs were used for abdominal CT as follows: left liver lobule (LLL), spleen (SPL), descending aorta (AOD), autochthonous back muscle (AUM), subcutaneous fat tissue (FAT), and air (AIR). For each ROI, mean CT number and noise (SD of CT number as a surrogative parameter) were measured by evaluating a circular ROI (99.0 $mm^2 \pm 1.18$ [thorax] and 99.2 $mm^2 \pm 1.22$ [abdomen]). ROI annotation was performed on the FBP-reconstructed scan and was then automatically copied to each scan to ensure that all ROIs in each scan had the same annotation location. A custom tool written in Python was used for this.

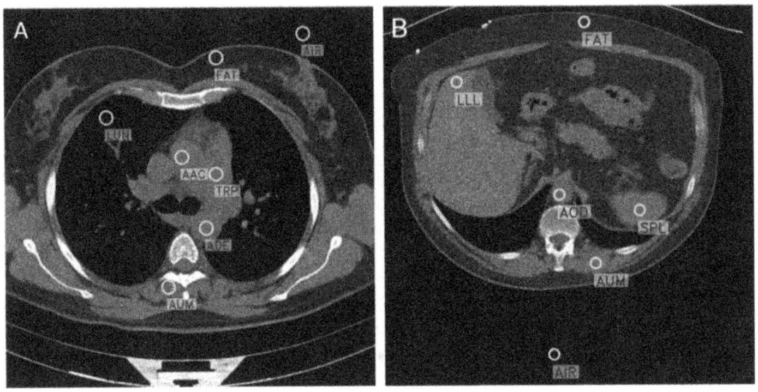

Figure 2. Axial CT slices reconstructed with FBP showing the positions of seven evaluated ROIs (green circle) for thoracal CT (**A**) and six ROIs for abdominal CT (**B**). AAC = ascending aorta, ADE = descending thoracal aorta, AOD = descending abdominal aorta, AIR = air, AUM = autochthonous muscle, FAT = subcutaneous fat, LLL = left liver lobule, LUN = lung tissue, TRP = pulmonary trunk, SPL = spleen.

Furthermore, the contrast-to-noise ratio (CNR) as well as the signal-to-noise ratio (SNR) were calculated using the following formulas [13]:

$$CNR_{ROI} = \frac{\left|CT_{ROI} - CT_{fat}\right|}{SD_{fat}} \quad (1)$$

$$SNR_{ROI} = \frac{\left|CT_{ROI}\right|}{SD_{ROI}} \quad (2)$$

2.3. *Subjective Image Quality Analysis*

Three radiologists with 5 years (D.B., M.O.) and over 10 years (K.N.) of experience in CT independently evaluated the image quality of different methods for the reconstruction of thoracal as well as abdominal CT using a self-developed web-based application. In a blinded fashion, two differently reconstructed images showing the same slice of the same study were presented to the rater simultaneously in a randomized order (Figures 3 and 4). Raters were able to vary the zoom level. Firstly, the rater had to rank the images using 1 for the better and 2 for the worse images. Equality could be expressed using 1 for both. Secondly, each image was rated with the help of a 5-point Likert scale ("excellent", "completely acceptable", "mostly acceptable", "suboptimal", and "unacceptable"). For thoracal CT, FBP and FBP + PS were compared for the lung as well as for the soft-tissue kernel. Comparisons of abdominal CTs were made between FBP and FBP + PS (site I + site II) as well as FBP + PS and IR (site II only) only for the soft-tissue kernel.

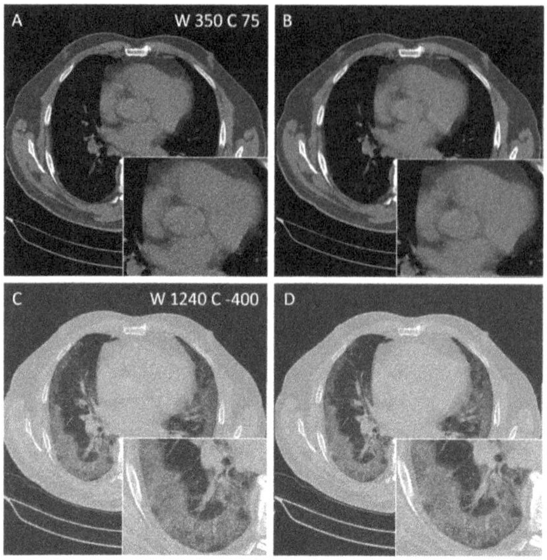

Figure 3. Axial CT of a 65-year-old patient with COVID-19 pneumonia comparing FBP reconstruction (**A**,**C**) and post-processing with PS (**B**,**D**) using soft-tissue (**A**,**B**) and lung kernel (**C**,**D**). Window width (W) and centre (C) are given.

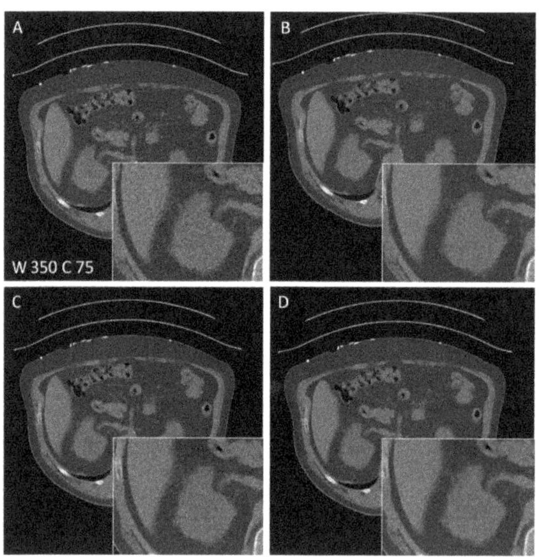

Figure 4. Axial CT of a 63-year-old patient suspected of urolithiasis comparing FBP reconstruction (**A**), FBP post-processed with PS (**B**), IR (**C**), and IR post-processed with PS (**D**). Window width (W) and centre (C) are given.

2.4. Statistical Analysis

The objective and subjective image quality of FBP + PS and FBP were compared for thoracal and abdominal CTs. An additional comparison of abdominal CTs between IR + PS and IR, as well as IR and FBP + PS, was performed for site II only, due to the unavailability of IR in site I. Mean and standard deviation (SD) or median and interquartile range (IQR)—in cases lacking a normal distribution—were used to report descriptive statistics. To compare demographics, Wilcoxon or $\chi2$ tests were used. Concordance between subjective ratings were evaluated using Kendall's coefficient of concordance W. A p-value < 0.05 was considered statistically significant. Statistical analysis was performed using R v4.2.0 and commercially available software (Microsoft Excel 2021, Redmond, WA, USA and SPSS 29.0, Inc., Chicago, IL, USA).

3. Results

3.1. Patient Cohort

Thoracal non-contrast CTs of 26 patients with suspected SARS-CoV-2 pneumonia (17 male, 9 females, median age 77.0 IQR: 16.5 years) and abdominal non-contrast LD-CTs of 48 patients (31 male, 17 female) at site I and site II, each suspected of urolithiasis, were evaluated (Table 2). For thoracal scans, median DLP was 301.4 mGy·cm (IQR: 188.6). For abdominal CT, median DLPs were 178.4 mGy·cm (IQR: 108.1) at site I and 60.0 mGy·cm (IQR: 40.2) at site II.

Table 2. Patient characteristics and radiation dose.

	Thorax	Abdomen	
	Site I	Site I	Site II
Patients	26 (9 female/17 male)	48 (17 female/31 male)	48 (17 female/31 male)
Median age (years)	77.0 (IQR 16.5)	55.5 (IQR 25)	39.0 (IQR 18)
Median tube Current time product (mAs) [Tube potential kVp]	86.5 (IQR 45) [130]	32.0 (IQR 18) [130]	220 (IQR 89.0) [100] 50 (IQR 25) [150]
Median scan length (cm)	32.1 (IQR 4.8)	47.6 (IQR 6.1)	49.6 (IQR 11.1)
Median $CTDI_{vol}$ (mGy)	9.5 (IQR 4.9)	3.5 (IQR 1.9)	1.21 (IQR 0.6)
Median DLP (mGy·cm)	301.4 (IQR 188.6)	178.4 (IQR 108.1)	60.0 (IQR 40.2)

3.2. Objective Image Quality of Thoracal CT

Objective image quality was assessed by evaluating mean CT values and their standard deviation (as surrogate parameters for image noise) as well as SNR and CNR. Regarding thoracal CT, the mean difference of CT numbers between FBP + PS and FBP measured within the soft-tissue kernel varied between 1.11 HU (FAT) and −0.09 HU (AUM) and 1.98 HU (FAT) and 0.08 HU (ADE) for the lung kernel (Table 3). Significantly different CT values were detected only for lung, fat, and air independently of the kernel (<±2 HU). Noise (SD) was significantly reduced following PS processing in all ROIs in both kernels, with differences between −9.68 (ADE) and −2.33 (LUN) [lung kernel] and −28.98 (ADE) and −14.69 (FAT) [soft-tissue kernel]. Furthermore, all evaluated ROIs revealed significantly higher SNRs as well as CNRs in PS-post-processed images compared to FBP alone for both lung and soft-tissue kernels (Tables 3 and S1).

Table 3. Mean differences of CT values, noise, CNR, and SNR between FBP and FBP + PS reconstructed thoracal CT with lung and soft-tissue kernels. Significant p-values (<0.05) are in bold.

	Ascending Aorta	Pulmonary Trunk	Descending Aorta	Lung	Autochthonous Muscle	Fat	Air
			B40 [soft-tissue kernel]				
CT FBP + PS vs. FBP	-0.08 ± 0.4 $p = 0.116$	-0.01 ± 0.4 $p = 0.708$	0.06 ± 0.5 $p = 0.423$	0.52 ± 0.5 $\mathbf{p \leq 0.001}$	-0.09 ± 0.6 $p = 0.94$	1.11 ± 0.4 $\mathbf{p \leq 0.001}$	0.79 ± 0.4 $\mathbf{p \leq 0.001}$
Noise FBP + PS vs. FBP	-8.72 ± 3.4 $\mathbf{p \leq 0.001}$	-9.28 ± 3.2 $\mathbf{p \leq 0.001}$	-9.68 ± 3.4 $\mathbf{p \leq 0.001}$	-2.33 ± 2.3 $\mathbf{p \leq 0.001}$	-6.49 ± 2.1 $\mathbf{p \leq 0.001}$	-4.10 ± 2.1 $\mathbf{p \leq 0.001}$	-6.53 ± 2.6 $\mathbf{p \leq 0.001}$
SNR FBP + PS vs. FBP	1.69 ± 0.6 $\mathbf{p \leq 0.001}$	1.61 ± 0.5 $\mathbf{p \leq 0.001}$	1.30 ± 0.5 $\mathbf{p \leq 0.001}$	2.59 ± 2.9 $\mathbf{p \leq 0.001}$	0.34 ± 0.3 $\mathbf{p \leq 0.001}$	-2.11 ± 1.2 $\mathbf{p \leq 0.001}$	-
CNR FBP + PS vs. FBP	2.99 ± 1.7 $\mathbf{p \leq 0.001}$	2.96 ± 1.7 $\mathbf{p \leq 0.001}$	2.92 ± 1.7 $\mathbf{p \leq 0.001}$	15.92 ± 8.9 $\mathbf{p \leq 0.001}$	2.60 ± 1.4 $\mathbf{p \leq 0.001}$	-	-

Table 3. *Cont.*

	Ascending Aorta	Pulmonary Trunk	Descending Aorta	Lung	Autochthonous Muscle	Fat	Air
			B70 [lung kernel]				
CT FBP + PS vs. FBP	0.17 ± 0.6 $p = 0.328$	0.19 ± 0.5 $p = 0.054$	0.08 ± 0.7 $p = 0.861$	1.63 ± 0.8 $\boldsymbol{p \leq 0.001}$	0.58 ± 0.9 $\boldsymbol{p = 0.002}$	1.98 ± 0.4 $\boldsymbol{p \leq 0.001}$	1.78 ± 0.6 $\boldsymbol{p \leq 0.001}$
Noise FBP + PS vs. FBP	−27.95 ± 12.7 $\boldsymbol{p \leq 0.001}$	−28.91 ± 12.0 $\boldsymbol{p \leq 0.001}$	−28.98 ± 10.6 $\boldsymbol{p \leq 0.001}$	−5.59 ± 8.3 $\boldsymbol{p = 0.001}$	−20.60 ± 8.3 $\boldsymbol{p \leq 0.001}$	−14.69 ± 8.9 $\boldsymbol{p \leq 0.001}$	−14.93 ± 6.8 $\boldsymbol{p \leq 0.001}$
SNR FBP + PS vs. FBP	0.46 ± 0.2 $\boldsymbol{p \leq 0.001}$	0.44 ± 0.2 $\boldsymbol{p \leq 0.001}$	0.38 ± 0.2 $\boldsymbol{p \leq 0.001}$	1.63 ± 2.4 $\boldsymbol{p = 0.001}$	0.14 ± 0.1 $\boldsymbol{p \leq 0.001}$	−0.66 ± 0.46 $\boldsymbol{p \leq 0.001}$	-
CNR FBP + PS vs. FBP	0.95 ± 0.6 $\boldsymbol{p \leq 0.001}$	0.94 ± 0.6 $\boldsymbol{p \leq 0.001}$	0.93 ± 0.6 $\boldsymbol{p \leq 0.001}$	5.22 ± 3.4 $\boldsymbol{p \leq 0.001}$	0.83 ± 0.5 $\boldsymbol{p \leq 0.001}$	-	-

3.3. *Objective Image Quality of Abdominal CT*

The analysis of abdominal CTs delivered similar results when comparing FBP and FBP + PS in site I and site II (Tables 4 and S2). PS led to small differences in CT values which were again only significant for fat (1.00 ± 0.5 [site I] and 1.08 ± 0.6 [site II]) and air (0.83 ± 0.4 [site I] and 0.65 ± 0.5 [site II]). Noise was significantly reduced in all ROIs while SNR and CNR increased overall. Comparing IR + PS and IR, PS post-processing also decreased image noise and elevated SNR and CNR significantly, independently of the analysed ROI. Additionally, differences in CT values were low but significant not only for fat (0.92 ± 0.2) and air (0.98 ± 0.3) but also for the descending aorta (0.31 ± 0.4) and autochthonous muscle (0.10 ± 0.2). Finally, a comparison of FBP + PS and unprocessed IR images revealed that noise was also lower in FBP + PS while SNR was higher. Differences were significant for all ROIs except fat. No significant differences were seen with regard to CNR. Again, CT values were significantly altered for fat (1.15 ± 0.5) and air (1.68 ± 0.7).

Table 4. Mean differences of CT values, noise, SNR, and CNR comparing FBP + PS vs. FBP at site I and II and, additionally, IR + PS vs. IR and FBP + PS vs. IR reconstructed abdominal LD-CT at site II only. Significant p-values (<0.05) are in bold.

		Left Liver Lobule	Spleen	Descending Aorta	Autochthonous Muscle	Fat	Air
				Site I			
FBP + PS vs. FBP	CT	0.05 ± 0.5 $p = 0.532$	−0.15 ± 0.7 $p = 0.189$	−0.05 ± 0.5 $p = 0.579$	−0.09 ± 0.5 $p = 0.367$	1.00 ± 0.5 $\boldsymbol{p \leq 0.001}$	0.83 ± 0.4 $\boldsymbol{p \leq 0.001}$
	Noise	−11.35 ± 5.3 $\boldsymbol{p \leq 0.001}$	−8.67 ± 4.5 $\boldsymbol{p \leq 0.001}$	−11.15 ± 4.6 $\boldsymbol{p \leq 0.001}$	−7.00 ± 4.1 $\boldsymbol{p \leq 0.001}$	−5.32 ± 3.5 $\boldsymbol{p \leq 0.001}$	−6.80 ± 3.4 $\boldsymbol{p \leq 0.001}$
	SNR	1.37 ± 0.5 $\boldsymbol{p \leq 0.001}$	1.41 ± 0.5 $\boldsymbol{p \leq 0.001}$	1.10 ± 0.4 $\boldsymbol{p \leq 0.001}$	1.00 ± 0.5 $\boldsymbol{p \leq 0.001}$	3.16 ± 2.32 $\boldsymbol{p \leq 0.001}$	-
	CNR	4.68 ± 3.3 $\boldsymbol{p \leq 0.001}$	4.51 ± 3.1 $\boldsymbol{p \leq 0.001}$	4.46 ± 3.2 $\boldsymbol{p \leq 0.001}$	4.31 ± 2.9 $\boldsymbol{p \leq 0.001}$	-	-
				Site II			
FBP + PS vs. FBP	CT	0.09 ± 0.7 $p = 0.772$	−0.11 ± 0.7 $p = 0.291$	0.26 ± 0.7 $\boldsymbol{p = 0.008}$	−0.13 ± 0.6 $p = 0.154$	1.08 ± 0.6 $\boldsymbol{p \leq 0.001}$	0.65 ± 0.5 $\boldsymbol{p \leq 0.001}$
	Noise	−11.92 ± 2.8 $\boldsymbol{p \leq 0.001}$	−9.98 ± 2.5 $\boldsymbol{p \leq 0.001}$	−10.44 ± 2.9 $\boldsymbol{p \leq 0.001}$	−8.25 ± 2.7 $\boldsymbol{p \leq 0.001}$	−6.93 ± 2.3 $\boldsymbol{p \leq 0.001}$	−6.55 ± 1.5 $\boldsymbol{p \leq 0.001}$
	SNR	1.87 ± 0.5 $\boldsymbol{p \leq 0.001}$	1.72 ± 0.6 $\boldsymbol{p \leq 0.001}$	1.41 ± 0.5 $\boldsymbol{p \leq 0.001}$	1.50 ± 0.6 $\boldsymbol{p \leq 0.001}$	1.89 ± 0.9 $\boldsymbol{p \leq 0.001}$	-
	CNR	3.12 ± 1.5 $\boldsymbol{p \leq 0.001}$	3.01 ± 1.4 $\boldsymbol{p \leq 0.001}$	2.80 ± 1.3 $\boldsymbol{p \leq 0.001}$	3.03 ± 1.5 $\boldsymbol{p \leq 0.001}$	-	-
IR + PS vs. IR	CT	0.10 ± 0.3 $p = 0.06$	0.01 ± 0.25 $p = 0.495$	0.31 ± 0.4 $\boldsymbol{p \leq 0.001}$	0.10 ± 0.2 $\boldsymbol{p = 0.001}$	0.92 ± 0.2 $\boldsymbol{p \leq 0.001}$	0.98 ± 0.3 $\boldsymbol{p \leq 0.001}$
	Noise	−4.03 ± 1.6 $\boldsymbol{p \leq 0.001}$	−2.69 ± 1.3 $\boldsymbol{p \leq 0.001}$	−3.32 ± 1.5 $\boldsymbol{p \leq 0.001}$	−1.69 ± 1.3 $\boldsymbol{p \leq 0.001}$	−1.13 ± 1.1 $\boldsymbol{p \leq 0.001}$	−1.94 ± 1.3 $\boldsymbol{p \leq 0.001}$
	SNR	1.00 ± 0.4 $\boldsymbol{p \leq 0.001}$	0.72 ± 0.4 $\boldsymbol{p \leq 0.001}$	0.73 ± 0.4 $\boldsymbol{p \leq 0.001}$	0.47 ± 0.3 $\boldsymbol{p \leq 0.001}$	−0.41 ± 0.5 $\boldsymbol{p \leq 0.001}$	-
	CNR	0.71 ± 0.7 $\boldsymbol{p \leq 0.001}$	0.69 ± 0.7 $\boldsymbol{p \leq 0.001}$	0.65 ± 0.7 $\boldsymbol{p \leq 0.001}$	0.70 ± 0.7 $\boldsymbol{p \leq 0.001}$	-	-

Table 4. *Cont.*

		Left Liver Lobule	Spleen	Descending Aorta	Autochthonous Muscle	Fat	Air
FBP + PS vs. IR	CT	0.09 ± 0.6 $p = 0.636$	0.05 ± 0.6 $p = 0.715$	−0.09 ± 0.8 $p = 0.367$	−0.07 ± 0.5 $p = 0.351$	1.15 ± 0.5 $\boldsymbol{p \leq 0.001}$	1.68 ± 0.7 $\boldsymbol{p \leq 0.001}$
	Noise	−3.21 ± 1.9 $\boldsymbol{p \leq 0.001}$	−1.96 ± 1.9 $\boldsymbol{p \leq 0.001}$	−2.36 ± 1.9 $\boldsymbol{p \leq 0.001}$	−0.90 ± 1.9 $\boldsymbol{p = 0.004}$	0.20 ± 1.9 $p = 0.373$	−3.54 ± 1.3 $\boldsymbol{p \leq 0.001}$
	SNR	0.76 ± 0.5 $\boldsymbol{p \leq 0.001}$	0.55 ± 0.5 $\boldsymbol{p \leq 0.001}$	0.48 ± 0.4 $\boldsymbol{p \leq 0.001}$	0.27 ± 0.5 $\boldsymbol{p = 0.001}$	0.05 ± 0.8 $p = 0.221$	-
	CNR	−0.01 ± 1.3 $p = 0.378$	−0.02 ± 1.3 $p = 0.322$	−0.03 ± 1.2 $p = 0.278$	−0.02 ± 1.3 $p = 0.362$	-	-

3.4. Subjective Image Quality of Thoracal CT

Subjective image quality, comparing FBP + PS and FBP, was evaluated in thoracal CTs using the soft-tissue and lung kernels (Figure 3). All three raters preferred the PS post-processed images over the unprocessed ones for both the lung as well as the soft-tissue kernels. The agreement between the raters was moderate for the lung kernel (Kendalls's W = 0.5, $p = 0.01$, Table 5) and perfect for the soft-tissue kernel (Kendalls's W = 1, $p < 0.001$). The rating of the image quality on a 5-point Likert-scale could not deliver such a strong tendency. Regarding the lung kernel, two raters did not find any difference in image quality (mean difference = 0) while the third rated the FBP + PS just slightly better than FBP (mean difference 0.08). For the lung kernel, again one rater did not detect any quality difference while the others rated FBP + PS higher than FBP (mean differences 0.04 and 0.89, respectively). Interrater reliability was moderate for both kernels (Kendall's W = 0.51 for soft tissue and 0.40 for lung) and was only significant for the soft-tissue kernel ($p = 0.006$).

Table 5. Evaluation of subjective image quality ranking. Mean differences in ranking are shown for each rater (Raters 1–3) individually. Positive values indicate that the images of the first method were ranked higher. Interrater reliability was evaluated using Kendall's W (W) and its *p*-value (*p*).

	Rater 1	Rater 2	Rater 3	W	*p*
		Thorax			
B40 (FBP + PS vs. FBP)	1	1	1	1	<0.001
B70 (FBP + PS vs. FBP)	0.04	0.35	0.65	0.50	0.01
		Abdomen (Site I)			
FBP + PS vs. FBP	0.96	1	1	0.98	<0.001
		Abdomen (Site II)			
FBP + PS vs. FBP	1	0.96	1	0.98	<0.001
FBP + PS vs. IR	−0.81	0.44	0.79	0.19	1

3.5. Subjective Image Quality of Abdominal CT

In abdominal CTs, subjective image quality was compared using the soft-tissue kernel only (Figure 4A,B) and delivered similar results (Table 5). All raters strongly preferred FBP + PS over FBP (mean difference between 0.96 and 1) with an almost perfect interrater reliability for both sites (Kendall's W = 0.98, $p < 0.001$).

In addition, a comparison betweem FBP + PS and IR was performed at site II (Figure 4C,D). Here, two raters ranked FBP + PS higher than IR (mean differences 0.44 and 0.79, respectively), while the third favoured IR over FBP + PS (mean difference −0.81), leading to a low interrater-reliability with a Kendall's W of 0.19 ($p = 1$). Regarding the subjective quality rating, all observers strongly preferred FBP + PS over FBP (mean difference 0.63 to 0.96), with a significant interrater agreement ($p < 0.001$) (Table 6). Moreover, two observers preferred FBP + PS over IR (mean difference in rating: 0.5 and 0.19, respectively), while the third one did not show any preference. This resulted in moderate agreement, with a Kendall's W of 0.44 ($p = 0.02$).

Table 6. Evaluation of subjective image quality rating on a 5-point Likert scale. Mean ratings ± SD and mean differences in rating are shown for each rater (Raters 1–3) individually. Positive difference values indicate that the images of the first method were rated higher. Interrater reliability was evaluated using Kendall's W (W) and its *p*-value (*p*).

	Rater 1	Rater 2	Rater 3	W	*p*
		Thorax			
B40 (FBP + PS vs. FBP)	4.0 ± 0 vs. 4.0 ± 0	4.0 ± 0 vs. 3.6 ± 0.5	4.0 ± 0.4 vs. 3.1 ± 0.3	1	<0.001
Mean difference	0	0.38	0.88		
B70 (FBP + PS vs. FBP)	4.0 ± 0 vs. 4.0 ± 0	4.1 ± 0.3 vs. 4.0 ± 0.2	3.4 ± 0.8 vs. 3.4 ± 0.8	0.50	0.01
Mean difference	0	0.08	0		
		Abdomen (Site I)			
FBP + PS vs. FBP	4.4 ± 0.5 vs. 3.6 ± 0.5	4.3 ± 0.4 vs. 3.7 ± 0.6	4.2 ± 0.6 vs. 3.3 ± 0.5	0.59	<0.001
Mean difference	0.80	0.63	0.92		
		Abdomen (Site II)			
FBP + PS vs. FBP	4.1 ± 0.4 vs. 3.2 ± 0.5	4.1 ± 0.3 vs. 3.3 ± 0.5	3.95 ± 0.3 vs. 3.0 ± 0.1	0.98	<0.001
Mean difference	0.96	0.85	0.94		
FBP + PS vs. IR	3.0 ± 0 vs. 3.0 ± 0	4.0 ± 0.2 vs. 3.8 ± 0.4	4.6 ± 0.6 vs. 4.1 ± 0.6	0.19	1
Mean difference	0	0.19	0.5		

4. Discussion

In this retrospective analysis, the impact of AI-based post-processing of non-contrast chest and low-dose abdominal CT images was evaluated by comparing the commercial software PixelShine with unprocessed FBP and IR images in thoracal and abdominal CTs, showing the non-inferiority of PS post-processing compared to IR alone and therefore offering an opportunity for image quality improvement in institutions using older scanners without IR availability.

4.1. Objective Image Quality

Different CT reconstruction methods have various effects on image quality and noise. FBP is an efficient and stable approach but results in a high noise level and significant artifacts in low-contrast structures [17]. On the other hand, IR shows a better noise reduction but can result in a plastic-like smooth appearance of the images [7]. These differences in reconstruction techniques are foremost observed in chest and abdominal protocols [18]. The post-processing of FBP or IR images with PixelShine is advertised as reducing image noise but maintaining image information. However, published data on the impact of PixelShine on image quality are scarce.

As expected, image information was maintained using PixelShine as determined by changes in the CT values as a surrogative parameter. Small but significant alterations were only seen regarding fat, air, and lung tissue. This could be explained by their overall lower density and higher contrast between containing structures, which is affected by smoothing as it is caused by PixelShine more easily. However, since the differences were small (<±2 HU) and did not alter the visual impression, these are not considered clinically relevant, as similarly stated by Steuwe et al. [15].

Our study revealed an overall significant reduction of image noise on the one hand and a significant increase of CNR and SNR while maintaining image information for thoracal as well as abdominal non-contrast CT scans by post-processing FBP reconstructed images using PixelShine.

These findings were mostly independent of the applied kernel and the examined tissues/organs. These results are in line with previous reports. Brendlin et al. also stated that PixelShine improves the image quality of FBP-reconstructed thoracal LD-CT in paediatric patients, while Wisselink et al. described noise reduction, especially in air and emphysema, evaluating a COPDGene phantom [14,19]. But to our knowledge, our study is the first evaluation of PixelShine in adult chest CT in vivo—especially in the context of COVID-19 pneumonia. Regarding abdominal LD-CT, a study comparable to ours but with a lower number of patients was performed by Steuwe et al. and concluded that PixelShine reduces image noise and shows improved SNR and CNR [13]. Also, for other CT protocols including pelvic arterial phase CT or midfacial trauma imaging, image quality improvement was described by comparing FBP + PS and FBP resp. IR [16,20,21].

Importantly, we were also able to show that the image quality of PixelShine-processed images was at least not inferior to that of iteratively reconstructed abdominal CTs, as we found that noise and SNR were improved, while no significant differences were observed regarding CNR. Similar observations had earlier been made by Brendlin and Steuwe [13–15]. Although PixelShine is recommended by the vendor for quality improvement of FBP-reconstructed images, our additional analysis of PS-post-processed IR images also showed an optimization of CNR and SNR. But further studies are necessary to evaluate its clinical relevance. Therefore, additional subjective analyses are recommended and an evaluation of the plastic-like smooth appearance of IR images following PS-post-processing would especially be of interest [7].

4.2. Subjective Image Quality

Our subjective imaging evaluation confirmed the results from the objective analysis to a large extent. Imaging ranking as well as ranking on a 5-point Likert scale revealed a strong preference of the raters towards FBP + PS in abdominal LD-CT and in the thoracal CT image regarding the soft-tissue kernel. However, with regard to the lung kernel, no superiority of FBP + PS was seen. As this is the clinically relevant kernel in patients suspected of pneumonia, FBP + PS does not deliver a subjective benefit for these indications, which contrasts with observations made in paediatric chest CTs by Brendlin et al. [14]. But this could be explained by the patient selection, because Brendlin et al. evaluated ultra-low-dose CTs in children while we examined non-contrast CTs in adults with higher doses. Furthermore, the raters confirmed the non-inferiority of FBP + PS compared to IR-processed abdominal CT. This is important because modern CT scanners usually offer IR algorithms but there are still institutions with older machines where FBP is the only available reconstruction method; for these institutions especially, PixelShine could also offer a suitable opportunity for CT image quality improvement.

Another possible benefit of PixelShine is a further reduction of radiation exposure. Brendlin et al. could show, in a retrospective analysis of whole-body LD-staging CTs in melanoma patients using simulation software, that a dose reduction of up to 30% could be achieved without image quality loss using DL-based post-processing with PixelShine [22]. Although prospective data are not available yet, these findings underline the opportunities for dose reduction offered by DL-based post-processing software, which is especially important for commonly used protocols including thoracal and LD-abdominal CTs.

4.3. Limitations

We evaluated the usage of PixelShine in very narrowly defined CT indications (examination of suspected COVID-19 and urolithiasis), leading especially to a quite small population size for the thoracal imaging. This makes a generalization of our results difficult, although they are mostly in line with previous studies as described above. Due to the commercial character of the software, we had no insight into the detailed underlying algorithm, so our information on that fully relies on the vendor. A comparison with other commercial or non-commercial DL approaches such as ClariCT.AI (ClariPi, Seoul, Republic of Korea) [23–25], AiCE (advanced intelligent Clear-IQ Engine, Canon, Tokyo, Japan) [26–28], or TrueFidelity™ (GE Healthcare, Chicago, IL, USA) would be favourable [29,30]. Moreover, we used the software's parameters as recommended by the vendor. A detailed analysis comparing different software parameters was not feasible. In terms of image analysis, we assessed subjective image quality based on the raters' overall impressions of the images and an additional ranking. No detailed analysis regarding the textural properties or visibility of artifacts was performed. Moreover, low-contrast features were not explicitly considered in our study as they were expected to play an overall minor role in low(er) dose CTs. Generally, a subjective assessment with a broader range of radiologists is recommended for future studies to evaluate its usability in clinical routines more specifically. With regard to future studies, a longitudinal follow-up of patients could be beneficial for investigating the impact of AI-based post-processing on clinical outcomes including diagnostic accuracy, changes in patient management, and potential dose reduction benefits.

In conclusion, we show that using PixelShine for deep learning-based post-processing of non-contrast thoracal and non-contrast, low-dose abdominal CT scans that were reconstructed using filtered back-projection leads to a significant increase in objective image quality and in subjective image quality, depending on the kernel in thoracal imaging and with the strongest effects in soft-tissue imaging. However, this post-processed image quality was not inferior to iterative reconstruction techniques, making it a promising approach for medical institutions where IR reconstruction methods are not available. Further studies are necessary to evaluate whether AI-based post-processing could allow for a further reduction of radiation dose while maintaining image quality.

Supplementary Materials: The following supporting information can be downloaded at: https://www.mdpi.com/article/10.3390/diagnostics14060612/s1, Table S1. Mean relative differences of CT values, noise, SNR and CNR comparing FBP + PS vs. FBP reconstructed thoracal CT. Table S2. Mean relative differences of CT values, noise, SNR and CNR comparing FBP + PS vs. FBP, IR + PS vs. IR and FBP + PS vs. IR reconstructed abdominal LD-CT in Site I and Site II.

Author Contributions: All authors contributed to the study's conception and design. Material preparation, data collection, and analysis were performed by J.N., D.B. and A.D. The first draft of the manuscript was written by M.A.D. and all authors commented on previous versions of the manuscript. All authors have read and agreed to the published version of the manuscript.

Funding: We acknowledge support by the Open Access Publication Fund of the University of Duisburg-Essen. D.B. and J.H. were supported as Clinician Scientists within the University Medicine Essen Academy (UMEA) program, funded by the German Research Foundation (DFG; grant FU356/12-2) and the Faculty of Medicine, University of Duisburg-Essen.

Institutional Review Board Statement: Ethical approval was given by the Ethics Committee of the Medical Faculty of the University of Duisburg-Essen on 19 April 2021 (21-9996-BO) and the requirement to obtain informed consent was waived. All procedures in the studies involving human participants were performed according to the ethical standards of the institutional and/or national research committee and the 1964 Helsinki Declaration and its later amendments or comparable ethical standards.

Informed Consent Statement: Patient consent was waived due to the retrospective design of the study. All CT examinations were performed as part of the clinical routine of the hospital.

Data Availability Statement: Dataset available on request from the authors.

Acknowledgments: The authors would like to thank AlgoMedica Inc. for the opportunity to test their product and for their help with technical questions.

Conflicts of Interest: The commercial software PixelShine (AlgoMedica Inc., Sunnyvale, CA, USA) was provided for testing purposes, but the company had no role in the design, conduct, or publication of the study. Further, the authors declare that they have no conflicts of interest.

References

1. Brenner, D.J.; Hall, E.J. Computed tomography—An increasing source of radiation exposure. *New Engl. J. Med.* **2007**, *357*, 2277–2284. [CrossRef]
2. Lell, M.M.; Kachelriess, M. Recent and Upcoming Technological Developments in Computed Tomography: High Speed, Low Dose, Deep Learning, Multienergy. *Investig. Radiol.* **2020**, *55*, 8–19. [CrossRef] [PubMed]
3. Andrabi, Y.; Patino, M.; Das, C.J.; Eisner, B.; Sahani, D.V.; Kambadakone, A. Advances in CT imaging for urolithiasis. *Indian J. Urol.* **2015**, *31*, 185–193. [CrossRef] [PubMed]
4. Suliman, I.I.; Khouqeer, G.A.; Ahmed, N.A.; Abuzaid, M.M.; Sulieman, A. Low-Dose Chest CT Protocols for Imaging COVID-19 Pneumonia: Technique Parameters and Radiation Dose. *Life* **2023**, *13*, 992. [CrossRef]

5. ICRP. *The 2007 Recommendations of the International Commission on Radiological Protection*; ICRP Publication 103; SAGE Publications: Thousand Oaks, CA, USA, 2007; Volume 37, pp. 1–332. [CrossRef]
6. Calabrese, E.J.; O'Connor, M.K. Estimating risk of low radiation doses—A critical review of the BEIR VII report and its use of the linear no-threshold (LNT) hypothesis. *Radiat. Res.* **2014**, *182*, 463–474. [CrossRef] [PubMed]
7. Arndt, C.; Guttler, F.; Heinrich, A.; Burckenmeyer, F.; Diamantis, I.; Teichgraber, U. Deep Learning CT Image Reconstruction in Clinical Practice. *Rofo* **2021**, *193*, 252–261. [CrossRef]
8. Lim, K.; Kwon, H.; Cho, J.; Oh, J.; Yoon, S.; Kang, M.; Ha, D.; Lee, J.; Kang, E. Initial phantom study comparing image quality in computed tomography using adaptive statistical iterative reconstruction and new adaptive statistical iterative reconstruction v. *J. Comput. Assist. Tomogr.* **2015**, *39*, 443–448. [CrossRef]
9. Geyer, L.L.; Schoepf, U.J.; Meinel, F.G.; Nance, J.W., Jr.; Bastarrika, G.; Leipsic, J.A.; Paul, N.S.; Rengo, M.; Laghi, A.; De Cecco, C.N. State of the Art: Iterative CT Reconstruction Techniques. *Radiology* **2015**, *276*, 339–357. [CrossRef]
10. Stiller, W. Basics of iterative reconstruction methods in computed tomography: A vendor-independent overview. *Eur. J. Radiol.* **2018**, *109*, 147–154. [CrossRef]
11. Oostveen, L.J.; Meijer, F.J.A.; de Lange, F.; Smit, E.J.; Pegge, S.A.; Steens, S.C.A.; van Amerongen, M.J.; Prokop, M.; Sechopoulos, I. Deep learning-based reconstruction may improve non-contrast cerebral CT imaging compared to other current reconstruction algorithms. *Eur. Radiol.* **2021**, *31*, 5498–5506. [CrossRef] [PubMed]
12. Pan, T.; Hasegawa, A.; Luo, D.; Wu, C.C.; Vikram, R. Technical Note: Impact on central frequency and noise magnitude ratios by advanced CT image reconstruction techniques. *Med. Phys.* **2020**, *47*, 480–487. [CrossRef]
13. Steuwe, A.; Valentin, B.; Bethge, O.T.; Ljimani, A.; Niegisch, G.; Antoch, G.; Aissa, J. Influence of a Deep Learning Noise Reduction on the CT Values, Image Noise and Characterization of Kidney and Ureter Stones. *Diagnostics* **2022**, *12*, 1627. [CrossRef]
14. Brendlin, A.S.; Schmid, U.; Plajer, D.; Chaika, M.; Mader, M.; Wrazidlo, R.; Mannlin, S.; Spogis, J.; Estler, A.; Esser, M.; et al. AI Denoising Improves Image Quality and Radiological Workflows in Pediatric Ultra-Low-Dose Thorax Computed Tomography Scans. *Tomography* **2022**, *8*, 1678–1689. [CrossRef]
15. Steuwe, A.; Weber, M.; Bethge, O.T.; Rademacher, C.; Boschheidgen, M.; Sawicki, L.M.; Antoch, G.; Aissa, J. Influence of a novel deep-learning based reconstruction software on the objective and subjective image quality in low-dose abdominal computed tomography. *Br. J. Radiol.* **2021**, *94*, 20200677. [CrossRef]
16. Rozema, R.; Kruitbosch, H.T.; van Minnen, B.; Dorgelo, B.; Kraeima, J.; van Ooijen, P.M.A. Iterative reconstruction and deep learning algorithms for enabling low-dose computed tomography in midfacial trauma. *Oral Surg. Oral Med. Oral Pathol. Oral Radiol.* **2021**, *132*, 247–254. [CrossRef]
17. May, M.S.; Wust, W.; Brand, M.; Stahl, C.; Allmendinger, T.; Schmidt, B.; Uder, M.; Lell, M.M. Dose reduction in abdominal computed tomography: Intraindividual comparison of image quality of full-dose standard and half-dose iterative reconstructions with dual-source computed tomography. *Investig. Radiol.* **2011**, *46*, 465–470. [CrossRef] [PubMed]
18. Fletcher, J.G.; Leng, S.; Yu, L.; McCollough, C.H. Dealing with Uncertainty in CT Images. *Radiology* **2016**, *279*, 5–10. [CrossRef] [PubMed]
19. Wisselink, H.J.; Pelgrim, G.J.; Rook, M.; van den Berge, M.; Slump, K.; Nagaraj, Y.; van Ooijen, P.; Oudkerk, M.; Vliegenthart, R. Potential for dose reduction in CT emphysema densitometry with post-scan noise reduction: A phantom study. *Br. J. Radiol.* **2020**, *93*, 20181019. [CrossRef] [PubMed]
20. Tian, S.F.; Liu, A.L.; Liu, J.H.; Liu, Y.J.; Pan, J.D. Potential value of the PixelShine deep learning algorithm for increasing quality of 70 kVp+ASiR-V reconstruction pelvic arterial phase CT images. *Jpn. J. Radiol.* **2019**, *37*, 186–190. [CrossRef]
21. Rozema, R.; Kruitbosch, H.T.; van Minnen, B.; Dorgelo, B.; Kraeima, J.; van Ooijen, P.M.A. Structural similarity analysis of midfacial fractures-a feasibility study. *Quant. Imaging Med. Surg.* **2022**, *12*, 1571–1578. [CrossRef]
22. Brendlin, A.S.; Plajer, D.; Chaika, M.; Wrazidlo, R.; Estler, A.; Tsiflikas, I.; Artzner, C.P.; Afat, S.; Bongers, M.N. AI Denoising Significantly Improves Image Quality in Whole-Body Low-Dose Computed Tomography Staging. *Diagnostics* **2022**, *12*, 225. [CrossRef]
23. Nam, J.G.; Ahn, C.; Choi, H.; Hong, W.; Park, J.; Kim, J.H.; Goo, J.M. Image quality of ultralow-dose chest CT using deep learning techniques: Potential superiority of vendor-agnostic post-processing over vendor-specific techniques. *Eur. Radiol.* **2021**, *31*, 5139–5147. [CrossRef] [PubMed]
24. Hong, J.H.; Park, E.-A.; Lee, W.; Ahn, C.; Kim, J.-H. Incremental image noise reduction in coronary CT angiography using a deep learning-based technique with iterative reconstruction. *Korean J. Radiol.* **2020**, *21*, 1165. [CrossRef] [PubMed]
25. Yeoh, H.; Hong, S.H.; Ahn, C.; Choi, J.-Y.; Chae, H.-D.; Yoo, H.J.; Kim, J.H. Deep learning algorithm for simultaneous noise reduction and edge sharpening in low-dose CT images: A pilot study using lumbar spine CT. *Korean J. Radiol.* **2021**, *22*, 1850. [CrossRef]
26. Noda, Y.; Iritani, Y.; Kawai, N.; Miyoshi, T.; Ishihara, T.; Hyodo, F.; Matsuo, M. Deep learning image reconstruction for pancreatic low-dose computed tomography: Comparison with hybrid iterative reconstruction. *Abdom. Radiol.* **2021**, *46*, 4238–4244. [CrossRef] [PubMed]
27. Singh, R.; Digumarthy, S.R.; Muse, V.V.; Kambadakone, A.R.; Blake, M.A.; Tabari, A.; Hoi, Y.; Akino, N.; Angel, E.; Madan, R. Image quality and lesion detection on deep learning reconstruction and iterative reconstruction of submillisievert chest and abdominal CT. *Am. J. Roentgenol.* **2020**, *214*, 566–573. [CrossRef]

28. Tanabe, N.; Sakamoto, R.; Kozawa, S.; Oguma, T.; Shima, H.; Shiraishi, Y.; Koizumi, K.; Sato, S.; Nakamoto, Y.; Hirai, T. Deep learning-based reconstruction of chest ultra-high-resolution computed tomography and quantitative evaluations of smaller airways. *Respir. Investig.* **2022**, *60*, 167–170. [CrossRef]
29. Kim, J.H.; Yoon, H.J.; Lee, E.; Kim, I.; Cha, Y.K.; Bak, S.H. Validation of Deep-Learning Image Reconstruction for Low-Dose Chest Computed Tomography Scan: Emphasis on Image Quality and Noise. *Korean J. Radiol.* **2021**, *22*, 131–138. [CrossRef]
30. Shin, Y.J.; Chang, W.; Ye, J.C.; Kang, E.; Oh, D.Y.; Lee, Y.J.; Park, J.H.; Kim, Y.H. Low-Dose Abdominal CT Using a Deep Learning-Based Denoising Algorithm: A Comparison with CT Reconstructed with Filtered Back Projection or Iterative Reconstruction Algorithm. *Korean J. Radiol.* **2020**, *21*, 356–364. [CrossRef]

diagnostics MDPI

Article

Automatic Active Lesion Tracking in Multiple Sclerosis Using Unsupervised Machine Learning

Jason Uwaeze [1], Ponnada A. Narayana [2], Arash Kamali [2], Vladimir Braverman [1], Michael A. Jacobs [1,2,3,4] and Alireza Akhbardeh [2,4,*]

1 Department of Computer Science, Rice University, Houston, TX 77005, USA
2 Department of Diagnostic and Interventional Imaging, The University of Texas Health Science Center at Houston, Houston, TX 77030, USA
3 Department of Radiology and Radiological Science and Sidney Kimmel Comprehensive Cancer, Johns Hopkins University School of Medicine, Baltimore, MD 21287, USA
4 The University of Texas MD Anderson Cancer Center UT Health Houston Graduate School of Biomedical Sciences, Houston, TX 77030, USA
* Correspondence: alireza.akhbardeh@uth.tmc.edu

Abstract: Background: Identifying active lesions in magnetic resonance imaging (MRI) is crucial for the diagnosis and treatment planning of multiple sclerosis (MS). Active lesions on MRI are identified following the administration of Gadolinium-based contrast agents (GBCAs). However, recent studies have reported that repeated administration of GBCA results in the accumulation of Gd in tissues. In addition, GBCA administration increases health care costs. Thus, reducing or eliminating GBCA administration for active lesion detection is important for improved patient safety and reduced healthcare costs. Current state-of-the-art methods for identifying active lesions in brain MRI without GBCA administration utilize data-intensive deep learning methods. Objective: To implement nonlinear dimensionality reduction (NLDR) methods, locally linear embedding (LLE) and isometric feature mapping (Isomap), which are less data-intensive, for automatically identifying active lesions on brain MRI in MS patients, without the administration of contrast agents. Materials and Methods: Fluid-attenuated inversion recovery (FLAIR), T2-weighted, proton density-weighted, and pre- and post-contrast T1-weighted images were included in the multiparametric MRI dataset used in this study. Subtracted pre- and post-contrast T1-weighted images were labeled by experts as active lesions (ground truth). Unsupervised methods, LLE and Isomap, were used to reconstruct multiparametric brain MR images into a single embedded image. Active lesions were identified on the embedded images and compared with ground truth lesions. The performance of NLDR methods was evaluated by calculating the Dice similarity (DS) index between the observed and identified active lesions in embedded images. Results: LLE and Isomap, were applied to 40 MS patients, achieving median DS scores of 0.74 ± 0.1 and 0.78 ± 0.09, respectively, outperforming current state-of-the-art methods. Conclusions: NLDR methods, Isomap and LLE, are viable options for the identification of active MS lesions on non-contrast images, and potentially could be used as a clinical decision tool.

Keywords: multiple sclerosis; dimensionality reduction; multiparametric MRI; lesion segmentation

1. Introduction

Multiple sclerosis (MS) is the most common demyelinating disease in humans and it affects both white matter and gray matter of the central nervous system (CNS; brain and spinal cord). The etiology of MS is not completely understood [1,2]. Magnetic resonance imaging (MRI) is the most common radiologic modality for noninvasive visualization of MS pathology in the CNS. MRI plays a crucial role in both diagnosis and patient management. A hallmark of MS is the presence of hyperintense lesions on T2-weighted (T2W), including T2-weighted Fluid Attenuation by Inversion Recovery (FLAIR), and proton-density-weighted (PDW) MRI. However, not all hyperintense lesions seen on T2W MRI are active. Identification of active lesions is essential for patient management [3–7]. Regionally compromised blood–brain barrier (BBB) is believed to be a pathologic feature of active lesions. The compromised BBB is the result of repeated venular inflammation [8]. The compromised BBB allows the leakage of gadolinium (Gd)-based contrast agents (GBCAs) from the vasculature into the brain parenchyma, which results in reduced T1 relaxation time because of the paramagnetic nature of GBCA. Consequently, on MRI, active lesions appear hyperintense on post-contrast T1-weighted (T1W) images (contrast enhancement). An association between Gd enhancement and clinical activity in MS patients has been reported [8,9]. Moreover, the number of volumes of enhancing lesions may be important in the evaluation of treatment efficacy [9,10].

Recent studies have reported that GBCA administration results in long-term accumulation of gadolinium (Gd) in various tissues [11]. While there is no definite evidence demonstrating any physiologic effect of accumulated Gd, the Food and Drug Administration issued a cautionary note that "clinicians should limit GBCA use to circumstances in which additional information provided by the contrast agent is necessary, and assess the necessity of repetitive MRIs with GBCAs" [12]. In response to these concerns, a number of techniques for identifying active lesions on unenhanced scans have been proposed [13]. Perhaps the most widely accepted method for detecting active lesions is through subtraction MRI. These methods are mainly based on the subtraction of MR images acquired at two different time points to detect expanding lesions that are considered to represent lesion activity [14]. However, all these techniques have been introduced to identify active lesions, but not quantitatively compare with the ground truth, post-contrast T1-weighted images. More recently deep learning (DL) has started making inroads in automatically identifying active lesions on unenhanced scans [15].

A number of automatic and semi-automatic techniques for identifying and segmenting enhancing lesions in MS have been reported [5,10,16–18]. As described by Coronado et al. [17], these methods have limitations that include the need for specialized MRI pulse sequence, extensive pre-processing, minimizing false lesion classification etc. Therefore, more recently, deep learning was used to delineate enhancing lesions in MS [16,17,19]. These DL methods are mainly based on convolutional neural networks (CNNs).

The majority of MS segmentation methods, including DL, are based on multiparametric MRI. While multiparametric-based segmentation is shown to provide excellent results, it also suffers from a few weaknesses. These include the following: (1) high dimensional feature space that increases the computational complexity, (2) ineffectiveness in explicitly capturing the spatial relationship between voxels, (3) inability to effectively capture nonlinear relationships between different voxels, since it linearly combines voxel intensities of images with different contrasts, (4) noise within MRI can compromise segmentation quality, and (5) requiring registration of multiparametric images. Many of these problems can be potentially alleviated using nonlinear dimensionality reduction (NLDR) techniques.

Machine learning is broadly divided into supervised and unsupervised learning methods [20]. Supervised learning requires labeled data created by experts to establish the ground truth. The labeling by experts could be expensive in time and cost. While CNNs are excellent at extracting global features and detecting large lesions, they may have limitations in extracting multi-scale local features, thus making it hard to detect active lesions, which may vary in size. Data-intensive tasks, like segmentation, often suffer from the curse of dimensionality, which suggests that the required sparsity and sample size needed to achieve optimal results increase with the dimensionality of the data [21]. To overcome these limitations, in this preliminary study, we have applied an unsupervised NLDR method for segmenting active lesions in MS.

Non-linear dimensionality reduction is an unsupervised machine learning technique [22–24]. Unlike linear dimensionality reduction (LDR), NLDR captures complex nonlinear data structures that are prominent in brain MR images. In a high-dimensional feature space, NLDR uses local features from nearest-neighbor graphs to create a lower-dimensional subspace. NLDR requires far fewer images to train than DL-based methods. This work investigates how NLDR techniques can be used to identify active MS lesions.

The objective of this study was to demonstrate that unsupervised NLDR methods outperform supervised machine learning methods in identifying active lesions. To accomplish this, we introduce key differences between LDR and NLDR. Subsequently, we establish the motivation behind applying NLDR to brain MRI data. Then, we provide details for the MR imaging dataset and performance evaluation metrics used in this work. Furthermore, we compare NLDR methods to current state-of-the-art methods for active MS lesion identification. Lastly, we discuss the potential limitations of this work.

2. Materials and Methods

2.1. Dimensionality Reduction

For combining multiparametric MRI data while maintaining inherent data structure, also called the manifold, we used dimensionality reduction (DR). A manifold is a subspace that allows the visualization of curves and surfaces through multiple coordinate systems, or charts [23]. Intuitively, a manifold is any object that can be "charted". DR is achieved by either keeping a small subset of the most relevant information and features or by finding a smaller subset of data points [24]. DR maps high dimensional dataset X, with D dimensions, to a lower dimensional dataset Y, with d dimensions, such that $d < D$ and X can be represented by d points.

Dimensionality reduction can be divided into two categories, LDR and NLDR, which make assumptions about X lying in a linear and nonlinear subspace, respectively, [25,26]. While both methods can find the lowest number of data points that are able to represent the structure of X, there are key differences between LDR and NLDR that are briefly described below.

2.2. Linear Dimensionality Reduction

LDR might reduce the complexity of high-dimensional data through a linear mapping of all data points. With LDR, we assume that the subspace that best fits X is linear. LDR has been used in several healthcare applications because it is highly adaptable and effective in extracting features from large high dimensional datasets [27–29]. An example of LDR is multidimensional scaling (MDS).

Multidimensional Scaling

MDS finds a linear subspace, Y, that best represents the high dimensional dataset, X, by minimizing the cost function below

$$\sum_{ij}(||x_i - x_{ij}|| - ||y_i - y_{ij}||)^2 \tag{1}$$

such that, given the i, j-th components of X and Y, $||x_i - x_{ij}||$ and $||y_i - y_{ij}||$ are the respective Euclidean distances. To minimize this cost function, MDS uses eigenvalue decomposition defined as

$$B = X^T * X, \tag{2}$$

$$M = [V_1, V_2, ...Vd], \tag{3}$$

$$Y = M * X, \tag{4}$$

where V are the eigenvectors, M is a feature matrix containing the first d largest eigenvalues, and B is the pairwise distances matrix of X.

Recently, Knezek et al. [27] used DR to assess various learning approaches to improve motivation amongst young learners. These authors applied MDS to add meaning and understanding to educational game play, and its effect on children's learning performance. This work goes beyond DR for conducting statistical analysis. Malone et al. [28] proposed a Clinical Sustainability Assessment Tool (CSAT) for grouping health concepts, collected from

64 healthcare and research professionals, into several domains (e.g., engaged staff, planning, and monitoring) to create a meaningful tool for improving sustainable healthcare service delivery. Both studies used MDS to remove redundant information from high-dimensional data and create helpful insights. Although MDS effectively reduces high dimensional data, it struggles to uncover the true manifold of non-linear data, thus motivating the use of NLDR.

2.3. Non-Linear Dimensionality Reduction

We used NLDR, to uncover the true manifold of multiparametric brain MR images by reconstructing a single embedded image. While LDR assumes that the data lie in a linear subspace, NLDR can perform more intricate embeddings of nonlinear data [22]. Brain MRI is one of the primary methods for diagnosing MS, often requiring multiple image sequences to identify and characterize pathology. Brain MRI sequences, such as T2-weighted (T2W) and T1W images, provide different contrast information that aids patient management in MS. Since brain MR images share a nonlinear subspace, we employed NLDR for segmentation of active lesions. This is accomplished by reducing the dimensionality of MRI sequences into lower dimensions while preserving contrast information. Specifically, we used two NLDR algorithms, isometric feature mapping (Isomap) [22,30] and locally linear embedding (LLE) [31] to segment MS lesions using multiparametric MRI. The following sections will briefly describe how Isomap and LLE create a low-dimensional representation of high-dimensional data.

2.3.1. Isometric Feature Mapping

Isomap maps a high-dimensional dataset, X, to a lower-dimension dataset, Y, while retaining maximum geometric information. To reconstruct Y, Isomap first uses a K nearest neighbor graph G [32] to calculate geodesic distances (GDs) [33,34] of all data points of X. This creates a distance matrix, such that every data point, x_i, is connected to its K nearest neighbors, x_{ij}. Isomap then utilizes MDS to map all data points in X to a lower dimension [22,35]. To preserve the distance of X, MDS employs eigenvalue decomposition of the pairwise distance matrix. Specifically, we used the K neighbors classifier for the implementation of G and MDS. We used both G and MDS to reconstruct multiparametric brain MRI into a single embedded image. To maintain the manifold of X, MDS minimizes the error between pair-wise distances defined below

$$\sum (||x_i - x_{ij}|| - ||y_i - y_{ij}||)^2 \tag{5}$$

where $||x_i - x_{ij}||$ and $||y_i - y_{ij}||$ are the geodesic distances between data points in higher and lower dimensions, respectively. Isomap finally uses MDS mappings to create Y, a single image embedding X. The steps to create Isomap embeddings are shown in Figure 1.

We used two shortest path algorithms to construct pairwise distance matrices, crucial for Isomap geodesic distance calculations. In Tenenbaum et al. [22], Isomap was introduced using shortest path algorithm, a recursive method which attempts to create M while holding the following recurrence relation [36,37], to create a geodesic distance matrix. Floyd Warshall is a recursive method which attempts to create M while holding the following recurrence relation

$$d_{ij}^{k} = \begin{cases} w_{ij} & \text{if,} \quad k = 0 \\ \min\left(d_{ij}^{k-1}, d_{ik}^{k-1}, d_{kj}^{k-1}\right), & \text{if,} \quad k > 0 \end{cases} \tag{6}$$

where w_{ij} and d_{ij}^{k} represent the initialized and shortest distance lengths between points i and j, respectively, for all of data points X. Dijkstra's is another popular shortest distance algorithm [37], which first selects a starting data point, labeled as the source, and finds the shortest path from the source to all other data points of X. According to Wang [37], Dijkstra is defined by the following relation

$$D_{ij} = \min\left(D_{ij}, D_{ij} + dist(x_j, x_k)\right) \tag{7}$$

where D_{ij} is the current distance from data point i to j, $dist(x_j, x_k)$ is the distance between two abutting data points, and matrix M is created by recursively finding the pairwise distances of all data points of X. Due to the simplicity of the Floyd Warshall algorithm, it is often preferred over Dijkstra's algorithm. Set to default in the scikit learning library, the best algorithm was automatically selected at run time, to assume optimal performance.

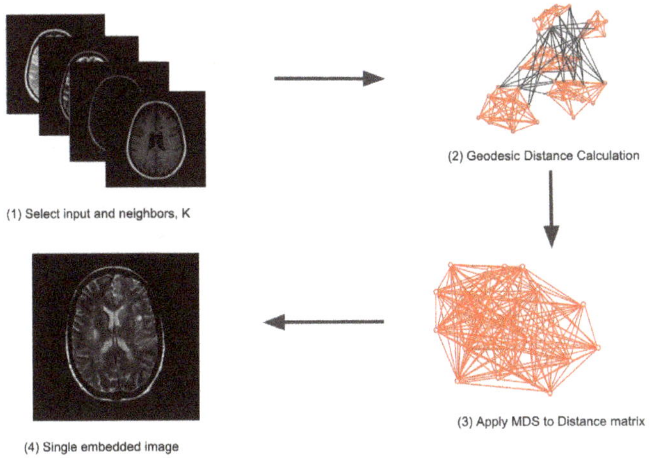

Figure 1. The Isomap algorithm can be summarized in four steps: (1) select a nearest neighbor algorithm, (2) calculate geodesic distances for all data points (3) apply multidimensional scaling to geodesic distance matrix, (4) output single embedded image.

2.3.2. Locally Linear Embedding (LLE)

Similar to Isomap, LLE creates a mapping from X to a lower dimension while preserving its local properties. LLE assumes that embeddings can be created through small regions of X, such that any data points, x_i, and its neighbors, x_{ij}, lie on or near a linear patch of X. By assuming that the manifold is approximately linear, LLE reconstructs the properties of the data by calculating the sum of K nearest neighbors for each data point. We used G in order to calculate the Euclidean distances for all data points in X. LLE identifies coordinates of Y or y_i that best align with the embedding of X [31].

To create an embedding of X, LLE characterizes the local geometry of all patches of X, as linear coefficients, and reconstructs each data point from its neighbors. The reconstruction error is defined as

$$\epsilon(W) = \sum_{n=1}^{n} ||x_i - \sum_{j=1}^{k} w_{ij}x_{ij}||^2, \tag{8}$$

which is constrained by $w_{ij} = 0$ when x_i has no neighbors (i.e., $x_{ij} = 0$) and $\sum_{j=1}^{k} w_{ij} = 1$. To perform embedding of X in Y, LLE chooses the best coordinates of Y to minimize the embedding error defined as

$$\phi(Y) = \sum_{n=1}^{n} ||y_i - \sum_{j=1}^{k} w_{ij}y_j||^2. \tag{9}$$

The mapping from X to Y in LLE is carried out by minimizing the reconstruction and embedding error in Equations (2) and (5).

2.3.3. Applications of Non-Linear Dimensionality Reduction

Recently in healthcare, NLDR techniques have been incorporated to extract important features from medical data. Sharma et al. [38] introduced a framework for thyroid abnormality detection, applying various dimensionality reduction techniques to ultrasound and histopathological datasets. Results based on NLDR methods outperformed current state-of-the-art computer-assisted diagnostic systems. In this work, LLE and Isomap exceeded other DR techniques, such as principal component analysis and singular value decomposition, in extracting features from ultrasound data, demonstrating that NLDR is able to reconstruct nonlinear ultrasound imaging data. We chose to use NLDR methods, LLE and Isomap, to segment active MS lesions. NLDR has been shown to outperform LDR methods in extracting features from imaging datasets [21,25,38].

In Figure 2, we show how NLDR compares to the LDR method, MDS. Dimensions of the Swiss roll were successfully reduced to a lower dimension by using LLE and Isomap, meaning both pairwise distances of all data points and the geometric shape of the Swiss roll were preserved in the embedded images. While successfully creating a lower dimensional representation, MDS failed to unfold the manifold while maintaining its underlying structure. This suggests that LLE and Isomap effectively understand complex manifolds and can be applied to real-world data. We further validated this hypothesis on multiparametric brain MRI data and showed how LLE and Isomap are able to segment active MS lesions.

Figure 2. Embedding of the 3-dimensional Swiss roll to 2 dimensions using MDS, LLE, and Isomap. Neighborhood size, k, was set to 12 for all methods. Both NLDR methods, LLE and Isomap, unfolded the Swiss roll in lower dimensions while the linear DR method, MDS, failed to unfold and preserve the manifold. Results that best retained the shape of the Swiss roll were derived by Isomap.

2.4. Patients

The MRI data were acquired as a part of CombiRx, a multi-center, phase 3, double-blinded, randomized clinical trial (Clinical Trial Identifier: NCT00211887) [39] that was supported by the National Institute of Health (NIH). Table 1 summarizes the demographics and clinical data of the clinical trial cohort at baseline. The main objective of the CombiRx clinical trial is to evaluate if treating MS patients with a combination interferon-β1a (IFNB) and glatiramer acetate (GA) results in a better patient outcome compared to treating them with these two drugs separately. Only patients with the relapsing–remitting (RRMS) phenotype are included in this trial. Our dataset included MRIs from 46 randomly selected patients. All patients provided signed written consent and this study was approved by the local IRB. All patients had MRI-detectable MS brain lesions and were administered GBCA during the MRI scan. In total, 6 subjects were excluded due to image misregistration issues, bringing the total number of subjects to 40.

Table 1. Demographic and clinical data acquired as part of CombiRx randomized clinical trial.

Demographics and Clinical Data on the CombiRx Cohort		
Age (yrs)		37.7 ± 9.7
Female/Male (ratio)		72/28
Race (%)	Caucasian	87.6
	African American	7.2
	Other	5.2
Ethnicity (%)	Hispanic	6.3
	Non-Hispanic	89.5
	Other	4.3
Symptom Duration (yrs)		4.8 ± 5.6

2.5. Image Dataset

Anonymized brain MR images from 46 subjects with relapsing–remitting MS were used in this work. MRIs were acquired on Philips (Best, The Netherlands) or General Electric (Milwaukee, USA), or Siemens (Erlangen, Germany) scanners operating at either 1.5T or 3T field strengths. The images included proton density (PDW), T2W, 2D FLAIR, and pre- and post-contrast T1W with voxel dimensions of (0.94 mm × 0.94 mm × 1.5 mm). All images were reviewed by two neuro MRI experts (more than 30+ years of experience) [40,41]. The MRI protocol and the acquisition details were provided elsewhere. Image preprocessing methods including co-registration, bias field correction and intensity normalization were applied [39].

The target lesions of this study are active white matter lesions. Grey matter lesions are not included because they rarely show enhancement. Also, grey matter lesion detection requires specialized MRI sequences such as double inversion recovery (DIR) sequence [42] and the CombiRx MRI did not include DIR imaging.

2.6. Multiparametric Brain MRI

We used LLE and Isomap to differentiate different tissue types and identify active lesions from multiparametric brain MRI. Specifically, we used PDW, FLAIR, T2W, and pre-contrast T1W as our high-dimensional dataset, and applied NLDR methods in identifying active MS lesions in brain MRI. Post-contrast T1W images were excluded from the input but were used for validation of the embedded image-based active lesion identification. The ground truth used was subtracted pre- and post-contrast T1-weighted image, referred to as the subimage. Lesions identified in subimages are labeled as active. To obtain lesion regions, we performed binary thresholding on all the ground truth and embedded images. Lower dimensional images, created by LLE and Isomap embeddings, were verified to include MS lesions by one of the authors (P.A.N).

As summarized in Figure 3, active lesion segmentation was accomplished by (1) embedding of brain MRI images through LLE and Isomap applications, (2) calculating of the subimage, and (3) generating binary images followed by thresholding to isolate lesions. The performance of LLE and Isomap was evaluated using thresholded binary images. To quantitatively evaluate the performance of LLE and Isomap, we used Dice similarity to measure the overlap between lesion boundaries in embedded and ground truth lesions. By converting LLE and Isomap embedding to binary images, we assigned "1" to pixels related to active MS lesions, and a zero to all other pixels.

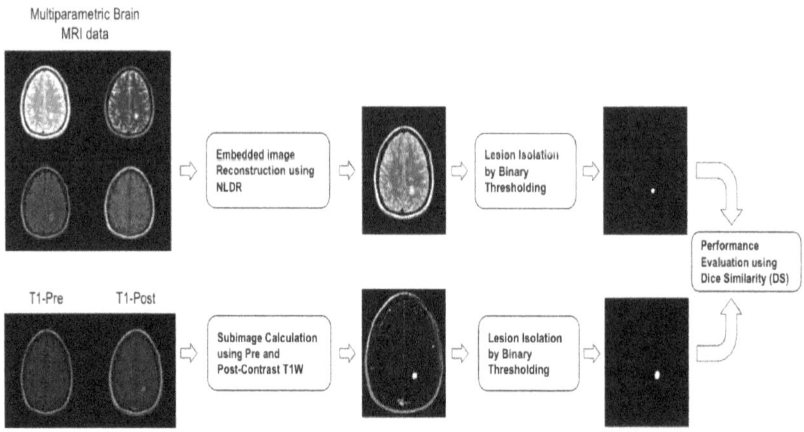

Figure 3. Multiparametric input brain MRI integration framework for embedding reconstruction. (**Top row**) Four brain MRIs are inputted and then integrated into a single embedded image using NLDR methods. The NLDR maps are thresholded for lesions. (**Bottom row**) T1-pre and post are subtracted. Next, active lesions are masked to obtain the ground truths binary masks. At the end, the two binary images are compared using dice similarity (DS) score, for the evaluation of proposed methods.

2.7. Performance Evaluation

To describe the overlap between the embedded and ground truth binary images, we use DS

$$DS = 2\frac{A \cap B}{A + B} \tag{10}$$

where A is the ground truth and B represents lesions identified on the binary thresholded images.

$$DS = \frac{2TP}{2TP + FN + FP} \tag{11}$$

Equation (11), as shown in Figure 4, TP, FP, FN, represent the true positive, false positive, and false negative sets of pixels [43], based on the overlap between A and B. Thus, if no overlap is found, DS = 0, or 1 if A and B perfectly overlap. Brain MR image resolution and the nearest neighbor value, K, were the input parameters to the model. We empirically evaluated the performance of LLE and Isomap for optimizing different input parameters.

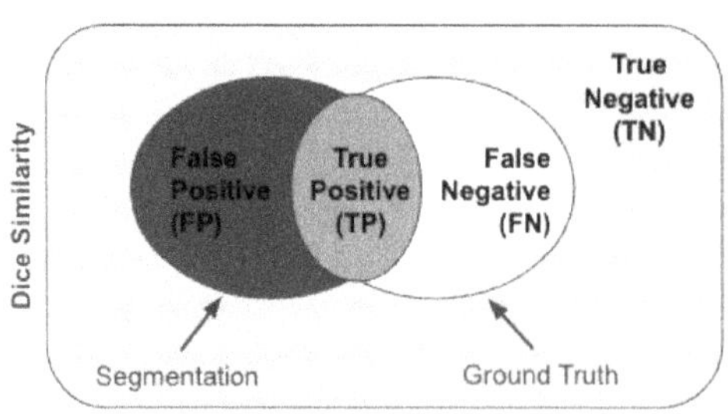

Figure 4. Dice Similarity is used to describe the overlap between embedded and ground truth active lesions.

3. Results

In order to choose the optimal input parameters for Isomap and LLE, we evaluated their sensitivity to various input resolutions and nearest neighbor values, K.

Due to high computational times in testing Isomap and LLE on original brain MR images, we initially reduced the input resolutions. However, Figure 5 shows that reducing the input resolution of LLE and Isomap degrades both methods' ability to provide accurate DS scores due to the blurring of active lesion boundaries. Our results suggest that Isomap and LLE are able to segment active lesions given 128^2 input images but achieve optimal performance on the original 256^2 input resolution. As a result, we chose 256^2 as the input resolution for LLE and Isomap to obtain accurate DS measurements.

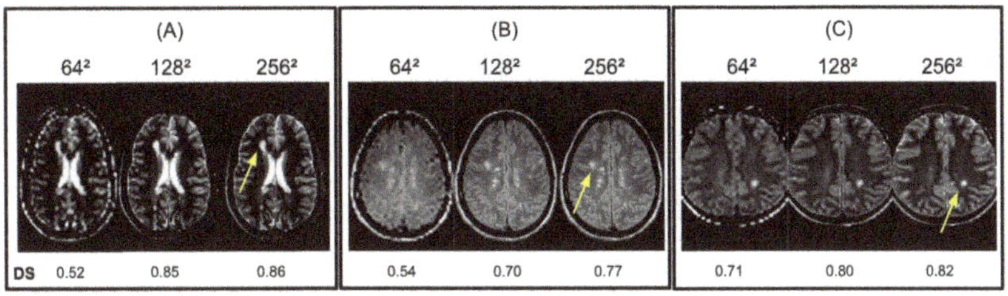

Figure 5. Examples of LLE algorithm sensitivity to different image matrix sizes and resolutions. We compared the active lesion (yellow arrow) in the embedded image to ground truth lesions using DS scores. (**A–C**) As shown in 64^2 images, (bottom row) DS was significantly lower. However, no significant differences were observed between 256^2 and 128^2.

As shown in Figure 6, both Isomap and LLE are insensitive to $K \geq 100$. However, LLE appears to have a minor fluctuation of dice scores across k-values, and thus is more sensitive to k-values compared to Isomap, which is more stable.

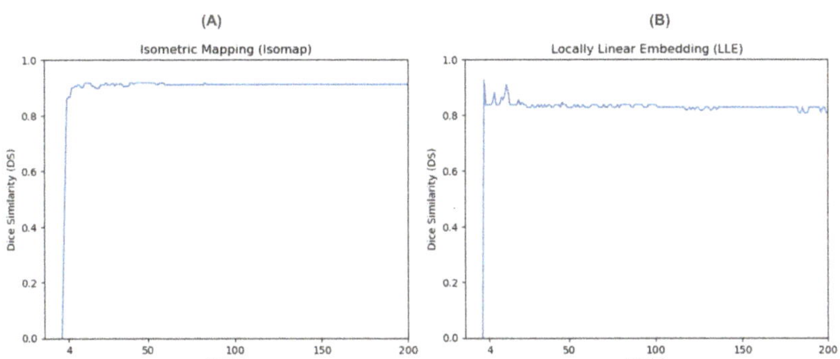

Figure 6. Evaluation of the sensitivity of NLDR methods to control parameters (K; neighborhood size): (**A**) Isomap (**B**) LLE.

To evaluate Isomap and LLE on all MS patients (n = 40), we chose K to be 100. With the chosen input resolution and K value, Isomap and LLE successfully segmented active lesions from brain MRI. Figure 7 shows single embedded images reconstructed by Isomap and LLE, while Figure 8 shows the segmentation performance of Isomap and LLE on all subjects. Isomap achieved a median DS of 0.78 ± 0.09, compared to LLE with a median DS of 0.74 ± 0.1. These results need to be further validated on a larger sample size.

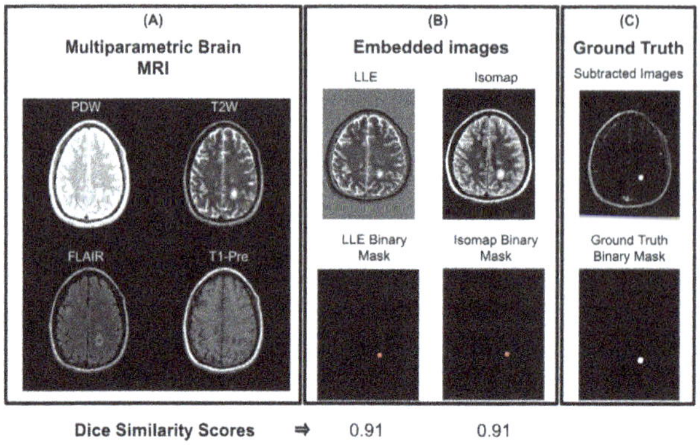

Figure 7. (**A**) Multiparametric brain MRI data as input to nonlinear dimensionality reduction (NLDR) methods. (**B-upper**) Output embedded images from locally linear embedding (LLE) and isometric feature mapping (Isomap). (**B-lower**) The resulting binary masks are shown. (**C-upper**) The ground truth (contrast subtraction image). (**C-lower**) Corresponding binary image for ground truth, used to evaluate methods using dice similarity scores.

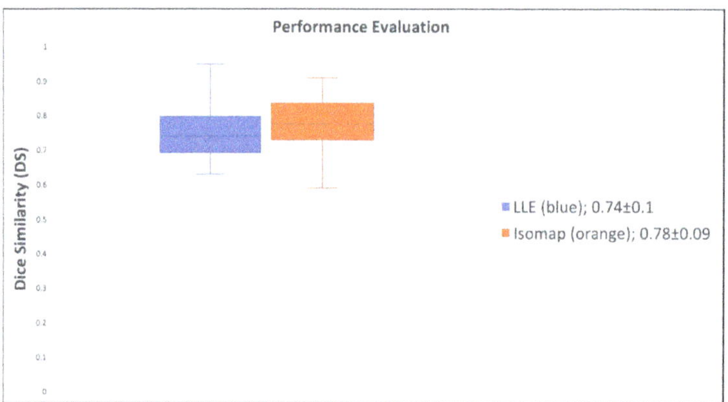

Figure 8. The performance of nonlinear dimensionality reduction methods, locally linear embedding (LLE) and isometric feature mapping (Isomap), are shown in the box plot. Isomap marginally outperformed LLE with a median and standard deviation for dice similarity (DS) score, respectively, as 0.78 ± 0.09 and 0.74 ± 0.09.

4. Discussion

To the best of our knowledge, this is one of the first implementations of Isomap and LLE for gadolinium (Gd) enhancing (active) lesion segmentation. We utilized NLDR techniques to combine brain MR images into an embedded image and identify lesions. Our results show, based on DS, that both Isomap and LLE were excellent at identifying active lesions, with Isomap providing slightly better results relative to LLE. Based on our results, LLE and Isomap could potentially reduce the need for the administration of contrast agents and outperform previous state-of-the-art active lesion segmentation DL methods.

Administration of GBCA [7,44,45] is still used for identifying active lesions in MS. With recent observations about GBCA retention in various tissues, different methods have been proposed to identify Gd-enhancing lesions, either by reducing the amount of GBCA administered or eliminating it. However, the majority of published methods, particularly those based on DL, utilized multiparametric MRI and supervised learning. These methods have their own disadvantages. In this preliminary study, we attempted to overcome these disadvantages by using unsupervised techniques, Isomap, and LLE. Our results suggest that NLDR methods if confirmed on a larger sample size, can be deployed in a clinical setting.

Multiple MRI studies are reported on the detection of active lesions on unenhanced scans. The results of subtraction images are compared with post-T1W images to assess the accuracy. However, they did not perform lesion segmentation [7,14,46–48]. Thus, it is very difficult to compare our results with these published ones. On the other hand, there are existing AI-based clinical applications for active lesion identification. In [7], Rudie et al. identified active MS lesions on non-contrast images using a computer-assisted-detection (CAD)-based system. This work demonstrated that it is possible to perform real-time assessments of non-contrast images to determine the necessity of contrast administration. However, this work requires manual annotations of MS lesions to achieve optimal performance. LLE and Isomap achieved excellent performance in identifying active MS lesions without need for manual annotated trained images as input. Identifying active lesions without contrast agents and less supervision could potentially improve patient safety and reduce the cost of clinical care.

Based on Coronado et al. [17], our work appears to outperform current state-of-the-art (SOTA) DL methods in segmenting active lesions in brain MRI. However, this work included GBCA imaging while we excluded post-contrast T1W images from testing. Current methods for active MS lesion segmentation use deep convolutional neural networks (CNNs) [17,19,40,41] to segment active lesions from brain MRI. Coronado et al. achieved a mean dice similarity score of 0.77 which is considered to be excellent. Our method offered a very comparable score of 0.78. Our method offers a number of advantages over the CNN method, which typically needs a large amount of annotated imaging data by experts, which could be very time-consuming and not feasible for large data. Although this work achieved dice similarity performance as shown in this preliminary study, our method is an unsupervised machine learning technique and does not require using a subset of data for training and the entire dataset could be used as a validation set.

Instead of using manual lesion annotations to guide reconstruction, LLE and Isomap use local image features from K nearest neighbor graphs to reconstruct high dimensional inputs in a lower dimensional space. This suggests NLDR performance is dependent on local topological features [22,32]. Other segmentation studies of breast [25], and ischemic lesions in brain MRI [49], used Isomap and LLE to reconstruct multiparametric MRI data with fewer than 30 subjects.

Akhbardeh et al. [25] used DR to embed multiple breast MR images and segment breast lesions. The performance of linear and nonlinear DR methods was compared to determine the best method for breast tissue segmentation. Both LLE and Isomap outperformed LDR methods, principal component analysis and MDS, and resulted in excellent similarity to post-contrast T1-weighted images that are consistent with our results. In this work, we exploited the robustness of NLDR methods for segmenting smaller embedded MS lesions compared to larger breast lesions.

To segment tissue at risk in stroke patients and quantify the amount of salvageable brain tissue, Parekh et al. [49] integrated multiparametric stroke MRI data using LLE and Isomap, demonstrating high similarity to radiological gold standards. However, this study was limited to animal MRI data, and thus needs to be further validated on human subjects. With the application of NLDR in early cerebral ischemia detection, this work shows NLDR methods as potential solutions for other diseases that require multiparametric MRI data to perform accurate diagnosis. Similarly, with brain MRI data, Park [50] used Isomap to quantify the shape of brain MRI and detection of Alzheimer's Disease. This work revealed that Isomap can delineate the true shape of brain MR images, distinguish between AD and normal manifolds, and potentially be used for brain MRI time-series analysis.

There are potential limitations in our study. For example, there is increased computational complexity, in both Isomap and LLE, when reconstructing embedded images. This is largely due to shortest path distance and eigenvalue calculations. This limitation could be overcome using a subset, "landmarks", of high dimensional data points to reduce the computations required for both Isomap and LLE [51–54].

Another limitation is that our sample size was 40 subjects. Further validation is needed on a larger and independent sample size that is drawn from a different distribution. Lastly, this work does not measure the sensitivity of LLE and Isomap to different lesion sizes. Investigating and addressing active MS lesion identification performance as a function of lesion sizes could further improve the performance of LLE and Isomap.

5. Conclusions

In conclusion, we demonstrated unsupervised learning techniques, LLE and Isomap, are able to capture the manifold of multiparametric MRI data and segment active MS lesions. Although both methods exhibited excellent performance, Isomap slightly outperformed LLE and showed more consistent results in the sensitivity analysis of input parameters. LLE and Isomap potentially could assist in the clinical management of MS patients, and reduce the usage of GBCAs for identifying active lesions in brain MRIs.

6. Patents

A.A. and M.A.J. have patent, "Multiparametric non-linear dimension reduction methods and systems related thereto", US Patent 9,256,966.

Author Contributions: Methodology, A.A. and M.A.J.; software and code, A.A. and J.U.; validation, A.A., M.A.J. and J.U.; formal analysis, J.U. and A.A.; resources, M.A.J., A.A., P.A.N. and V.B.; data curation, P.A.N. and A.A.; writing—original draft preparation, J.U. and A.A.; writing—review and editing, J.U., M.A.J., P.A.N., A.K., A.A. and V.B.; visualization, J.U.; supervision, A.A., M.A.J., P.A.N. and V.B.; project administration, A.A., M.A.J. and V.B.; funding acquisition, V.B., A.A. and M.A.J. served as the driving force and guidance in implementing the project, data analysis, and results throughout the execution of the project. All authors have read and agreed to the published version of the manuscript.

Funding: This work was supported by the Defense Advanced Research Projects Agency, Navy, the National GEM consortium and University of Texas Health Science Center Houston, UT-Health Endowed Chair in Biomedical Engineering for Michael A. Jacobs, PhD.

Institutional Review Board Statement: This research was approved by the Committee for the Protection of Human Subjects of the University of Texas Health Science Center Houston and started on January 2005 and completed in March 2013. It was a double-blind, multicenter phase III clinical trial (clinicaltrials.gov code is NCT00211887).

Informed Consent Statement: Patient consent was waived due to the fact that no patient personal information was retrieved or processed off-site.

Data Availability Statement: Data will be made available upon request, and availability is determined by the institutional guidelines.

Acknowledgments: We thank Jerry S. Wolinsky and Fred D. Lublin for providing access to the CombiRx MRI data.

Conflicts of Interest: The authors declare no conflicts of interest.

References

1. Dobson, R.; Giovannoni, G. Multiple sclerosis—A review. *Eur. J. Neurol.* **2019**, *26*, 27–40. [CrossRef] [PubMed]
2. Dilokthornsakul, P.; Valuck, R.J.; Nair, K.V.; Corboy, J.R.; Allen, R.R.; Campbell, J.D. Multiple sclerosis prevalence in the United States commercially insured population. *Neurology* **2016**, *86*, 1014–1021. [CrossRef] [PubMed]
3. Sadigh, G.; Saindane, A.; Waldman, A.; Lava, N.; Hu, R. Comparison of unenhanced and gadolinium-enhanced imaging in multiple sclerosis: Is contrast needed for routine follow-up MRI? *Am. J. Neuroradiol.* **2019**, *40*, 1476–1480. [CrossRef] [PubMed]
4. Saade, C.; Bou-Fakhredin, R.; Yousem, D.M.; Asmar, K.; Naffaa, L.; El-Merhi, F. Gadolinium and multiple sclerosis: Vessels, barriers of the brain, and glymphatics. *Am. J. Neuroradiol.* **2018**, *39*, 2168–2176. [CrossRef] [PubMed]
5. Datta, S.; Sajja, B.R.; He, R.; Gupta, R.K.; Wolinsky, J.S.; Narayana, P.A. Segmentation of gadolinium-enhanced lesions on MRI in multiple sclerosis. *J. Magn. Reson. Imaging Off. J. Int. Soc. Magn. Reson. Med.* **2007**, *25*, 932–937. [CrossRef]

6. Warntjes, J.; Tisell, A.; Landtblom, A.M.; Lundberg, P. Effects of gadolinium contrast agent administration on automatic brain tissue classification of patients with multiple sclerosis. *Am. J. Neuroradiol.* **2014**, *35*, 1330–1336. [CrossRef] [PubMed]
7. Rudie, J.D.; Mattay, R.R.; Schindler, M.; Steingall, S.; Cook, T.S.; Loevner, L.A.; Schnall, M.D.; Mamourian, A.C.; Bilello, M. An Initiative to Reduce Unnecessary Gadolinium-Based Contrast in Multiple Sclerosis Patients. *J. Am. Coll. Radiol.* **2019**, *16*, 1158–1164. [CrossRef]
8. Karimian-Jazi, K.; Wildemann, B.; Diem, R.; Schwarz, D.; Hielscher, T.; Wick, W.; Bendszus, M.; Breckwoldt, M.O. Gd contrast administration is dispensable in patients with MS without new T2 lesions on follow-up MRI. *Neurol.-Neuroimmunol. Neuroinflamm.* **2018**, *5*, e480. [CrossRef]
9. Rovira, À.; Doniselli, F.M.; Auger, C.; Haider, L.; Hodel, J.; Severino, M.; Wattjes, M.P.; van der Molen, A.J.; Jasperse, B.; Mallio, C.A.; et al. Use of gadolinium-based contrast agents in multiple sclerosis: A review by the ESMRMB-GREC and ESNR Multiple Sclerosis Working Group. *Eur. Radiol.* **2023**, *34*, 1726–1735.
10. Zeng, C.; Gu, L.; Liu, Z.; Zhao, S. Review of deep learning approaches for the segmentation of multiple sclerosis lesions on brain MRI. *Front. Neuroinform.* **2020**, *14*, 610967. [CrossRef]
11. Starekova, J.; Pirasteh, A.; Reeder, S.B. Update on Gadolinium Based Contrast Agent Safety, From the AJR Special Series on Contrast Media. *Am. J. Roentgenol.* **2023**. [CrossRef]
12. FDA Drug Safety Communication. FDA Warns That Gadolinium-Based Contrast Agents (GBCAs) Are Retained in the Body. 2018. Available online: https://www.fda.gov/drugs/drug-safety-and-availability/fda-drug-safety-communication-fda-warns-gadolinium-based-contrast-agents-gbcas-are-retained-body (accessed on 7 March 2024).
13. Eichinger, P.; Schön, S.; Pongratz, V.; Wiestler, H.; Zhang, H.; Bussas, M.; Hoshi, M.M.; Kirschke, J.; Berthele, A.; Zimmer, C.; et al. Accuracy of unenhanced MRI in the detection of new brain lesions in multiple sclerosis. *Radiology* **2019**, *291*, 429–435. [CrossRef]
14. Moraal, B.; Meier, D.S.; Poppe, P.A.; Geurts, J.J.; Vrenken, H.; Jonker, W.M.; Knol, D.L.; van Schijndel, R.A.; Pouwels, P.J.; Pohl, C.; et al. Subtraction MR images in a multiple sclerosis multicenter clinical trial setting. *Radiology* **2009**, *250*, 506–514. [CrossRef]
15. Narayana, P.A.; Coronado, I.; Sujit, S.J.; Wolinsky, J.S.; Lublin, F.D.; Gabr, R.E. Deep Learning for Predicting Enhancing Lesions in Multiple Sclerosis from Noncontrast MRI. *Radiology* **2020**, *294*, 398–404. [CrossRef]
16. Schlaeger, S.; Shit, S.; Eichinger, P.; Hamann, M.; Opfer, R.; Krüger, J.; Dieckmeyer, M.; Schön, S.; Mühlau, M.; Zimmer, C.; et al. AI-based detection of contrast-enhancing MRI lesions in patients with multiple sclerosis. *Insights Into Imaging* **2023**, *14*, 123. [CrossRef]
17. Coronado, I.; Gabr, R.E.; Narayana, P.A. Deep learning segmentation of gadolinium-enhancing lesions in multiple sclerosis. *Mult. Scler. J.* **2021**, *27*, 519–527. [CrossRef]
18. Karimaghaloo, Z.; Shah, M.; Francis, S.J.; Arnold, D.L.; Collins, D.L.; Arbel, T. Automatic detection of gadolinium-enhancing multiple sclerosis lesions in brain MRI using conditional random fields. *IEEE Trans. Med. Imaging* **2012**, *31*, 1181–1194. [CrossRef]
19. Gaj, S.; Ontaneda, D.; Nakamura, K. Automatic segmentation of gadolinium-enhancing lesions in multiple sclerosis using deep learning from clinical MRI. *PLoS ONE* **2021**, *16*, e0255939. [CrossRef]
20. Russell, S.J.; Norvig, P. *Artificial Intelligence: A Modern Approach*, 3rd ed.; Pearson: London, UK, 2010.
21. Liu, N.; Chee, M.L.; Koh, Z.X.; Leow, S.L.; Ho, A.F.W.; Guo, D.; Ong, M.E.H. Utilizing machine learning dimensionality reduction for risk stratification of chest pain patients in the emergency department. *BMC Med. Res. Methodol.* **2021**, *21*, 74. [CrossRef]
22. Tenenbaum, J.B.; Silva, V.d.; Langford, J.C. A global geometric framework for nonlinear dimensionality reduction. *Science* **2000**, *290*, 2319–2323. [CrossRef]
23. Sorzano, C.O.S.; Vargas, J.; Montano, A.P. A survey of dimensionality reduction techniques. *arXiv* **2014**, arXiv:1403.2877.
24. Meilă, M.; Zhang, H. Manifold learning: What, how, and why. *Annu. Rev. Stat. Its Appl.* **2023**, *11*. [CrossRef]
25. Akhbardeh, A.; Jacobs, M.A. Comparative analysis of nonlinear dimensionality reduction techniques for breast MRI segmentation. *Med. Phys.* **2012**, *39*, 2275–2289. [CrossRef]
26. Linting, M.; Meulman, J.J.; Groenen, P.J.; van der Koojj, A.J. Nonlinear principal components analysis: Introduction and application. *Psychol. Methods* **2007**, *12*, 336. [CrossRef]
27. Knezek, G.; Gibson, D.; Christensen, R.; Trevisan, O.; Carter, M. Assessing approaches to learning with nonparametric multidimensional scaling. *Br. J. Educ. Technol.* **2023**, *54*, 126–141. [CrossRef]
28. Malone, S.; Prewitt, K.; Hackett, R.; Lin, J.C.; McKay, V.; Walsh-Bailey, C.; Luke, D.A. The clinical sustainability assessment tool: Measuring organizational capacity to promote sustainability in healthcare. *Implement. Sci. Commun.* **2021**, *2*, 1–12. [CrossRef]
29. Patra, S.S.; Harshvardhan, G.; Gourisaria, M.K.; Mohanty, J.R.; Choudhury, S. Emerging healthcare problems in high-dimensional data and dimension reduction. In *Advanced Prognostic Predictive Modelling in Healthcare Data Analytics*; Springer: Singapore, 2021; pp. 25–49.
30. Law, M.H.; Jain, A.K. Incremental nonlinear dimensionality reduction by manifold learning. *IEEE Trans. Pattern Anal. Mach. Intell.* **2006**, *28*, 377–391. [CrossRef] [PubMed]
31. Roweis, S.T.; Saul, L.K. Nonlinear dimensionality reduction by locally linear embedding. *Science* **2000**, *290*, 2323–2326. [CrossRef]
32. Kim, J.; Kim, B.S.; Savarese, S. Comparing image classification methods: K-nearest-neighbor and support-vector-machines. In Proceedings of the 6th WSEAS international conference on Computer Engineering and Applications, and Proceedings of the 2012 American conference on Applied Mathematics, Stevens Point, WI, USA, 25–27 January 2012; pp. 133–138.
33. Shamai, G.; Kimmel, R. Geodesic distance descriptors. In Proceedings of the IEEE Conference on Computer Vision and Pattern Recognition, Honolulu, HI, USA, 21–26 July 2017; pp. 6410–6418.

34. Crane, K.; Livesu, M.; Puppo, E.; Qin, Y. A survey of algorithms for geodesic paths and distances. *arXiv* **2020**, arXiv:2007.10430.
35. Steyvers, M. Multidimensional scaling. In *Encyclopedia of Cognitive Science*; Nature Publishing Group: Berlin, Germany, 2002; Volume 1, pp. 160–165.
36. Toroslu, I.H. Improving the floyd-warshall all pairs shortest paths algorithm. *arXiv* **2021**, arXiv:2109.01872.
37. Wang, X.Z. The comparison of three algorithms in shortest path issue. *J. Phys. Conf. Ser.* **2018**, *1087*, 022011. [CrossRef]
38. Sharma, R.; Mahanti, G.K.; Panda, G.; Rath, A.; Dash, S.; Mallik, S.; Hu, R. A framework for detecting thyroid cancer from ultrasound and histopathological images using deep learning, meta-heuristics, and MCDM algorithms. *J. Imaging* **2023**, *9*, 173. [CrossRef] [PubMed]
39. Lublin, F.D.; Cofield, S.S.; Cutter, G.R.; Conwit, R.; Narayana, P.A.; Nelson, F.; Salter, A.R.; Gustafson, T.; Wolinsky, J.S.; Investigators, C. Randomized study combining interferon and glatiramer acetate in multiple sclerosis. *Ann. Neurol.* **2013**, *73*, 327–340. [CrossRef] [PubMed]
40. Sajja, B.R.; Datta, S.; He, R.; Mehta, M.; Gupta, R.K.; Wolinsky, J.S.; Narayana, P.A. Unified approach for multiple sclerosis lesion segmentation on brain MRI. *Ann. Biomed. Eng.* **2006**, *34*, 142–151. [CrossRef] [PubMed]
41. Datta, S.; Sajja, B.R.; He, R.; Wolinsky, J.S.; Gupta, R.K.; Narayana, P.A. Segmentation and quantification of black holes in multiple sclerosis. *Neuroimage* **2006**, *29*, 467–474. [CrossRef]
42. Bedell, B.J.; Narayana, P.A. Implementation and evaluation of a new pulse sequence for rapid acquisition of double inversion recovery images for simultaneous suppression of white matter and CSF. *J. Magn. Reson. Imaging* **1998**, *8*, 544–547. [CrossRef]
43. Bokhovkin, A.; Burnaev, E. Boundary loss for remote sensing imagery semantic segmentation. In Proceedings of the International Symposium on Neural Networks, Moscow, Russia, 10–12 July 2019; Springer: Berlin, Germany, 2019; pp. 388–401.
44. Falk Delgado, A.; Van Westen, D.; Nilsson, M.; Knutsson, L.; Sundgren, P.C.; Larsson, E.M.; Falk Delgado, A. Diagnostic value of alternative techniques to gadolinium-based contrast agents in MR neuroimaging—A comprehensive overview. *Insights Into Imaging* **2019**, *10*, 1–15. [CrossRef]
45. Rogosnitzky, M.; Branch, S. Gadolinium-based contrast agent toxicity: A review of known and proposed mechanisms. *Biometals* **2016**, *29*, 365–376. [CrossRef] [PubMed]
46. Donatelli, G.; Cecchi, P.; Migaleddu, G.; Cencini, M.; Frumento, P.; D'Amelio, C.; Peretti, L.; Buonincontri, G.; Pasquali, L.; Tosetti, M.; et al. Quantitative T1 mapping detects blood–brain barrier breakdown in apparently non-enhancing multiple sclerosis lesions. *NeuroImage Clin.* **2023**, *40*, 103509. [CrossRef]
47. Liguori, M.; Meier, D.S.; Hildenbrand, P.; Healy, B.C.; Chitnis, T.; Baruch, N.F.; Khoury, S.J.; Weiner, H.L.; Bakshi, R.; Barkhof, F.; et al. One year activity on subtraction MRI predicts subsequent 4 year activity and progression in multiple sclerosis. *J. Neurol. Neurosurg. Psychiatry* **2011**, *82*, 1125–1131. [CrossRef]
48. Schlaeger, S.; Li, H.B.; Baum, T.; Zimmer, C.; Moosbauer, J.; Byas, S.; Mühlau, M.; Wiestler, B.; Finck, T. Longitudinal Assessment of Multiple Sclerosis Lesion Load With Synthetic Magnetic Resonance Imaging—A Multicenter Validation Study. *Investig. Radiol.* **2023**, *58*, 320–326. [CrossRef] [PubMed]
49. Parekh, V.S.; Jacobs, J.R.; Jacobs, M.A. Unsupervised nonlinear dimensionality reduction machine learning methods applied to multiparametric MRI in cerebral ischemia: Preliminary results. In Proceedings of the Medical Imaging 2014: Image Processing, San Diego, CA, USA, 16–18 February 2014; Volume 9034, pp. 681–689.
50. Park, H.; The ADNI. ISOMAP induced manifold embedding and its application to Alzheimer's disease and mild cognitive impairment. *Neurosci. Lett.* **2012**, *513*, 141–145. [CrossRef] [PubMed]
51. Silva, V.; Tenenbaum, J. Global versus local methods in nonlinear dimensionality reduction. *Adv. Neural Inf. Process. Syst.* **2002**, *15*, 721–728.
52. Chen, Y.; Crawford, M.; Ghosh, J. Improved nonlinear manifold learning for land cover classification via intelligent landmark selection. In Proceedings of the 2006 IEEE International Symposium on Geoscience and Remote Sensing, Denver, CO, USA, 31 July–4 August 2006; pp. 545–548.
53. Shi, H.; Yin, B.; Bao, Y.; Lei, Y. A novel landmark point selection method for L-ISOMAP. In Proceedings of the 2016 12th IEEE International Conference on Control and Automation (ICCA), Kathmandu, Nepal, 1–3 June 2016; pp. 621–625.
54. Braverman, V.; Feldman, D.; Lang, H.; Statman, A.; Zhou, S. Efficient coreset constructions via sensitivity sampling. In Proceedings of the Asian Conference on Machine Learning, Virtual, 17–19 November 2021; pp. 948–963.

tomography

MDPI

Article

Validation of Left Atrial Volume Correction for Single Plane Method on Four-Chamber Cine Cardiac MRI

Hosamadin Assadi [1,2], Nicholas Sawh [3], Ciara Bailey [1,2], Gareth Matthews [1,2], Rui Li [1,2], Ciaran Grafton-Clarke [1,2], Zia Mehmood [1,2], Bahman Kasmai [1,2], Peter P. Swoboda [4], Andrew J. Swift [5], Rob J. van der Geest [6] and Pankaj Garg [1,2,*]

1 Department of Cardiovascular and Metabolic Health, Norwich Medical School, University of East Anglia, Norwich NR4 7TJ, UK
2 Department of Cardiology, Norfolk and Norwich University Hospitals NHS Foundation Trust, Norwich NR4 7UY, UK
3 Faculty of Medicine, Medical University of Sofia, Blvd Akademik Ivan Evstratiev Geshov 15, 1431 Sofia, Bulgaria
4 Division of Biomedical Imaging, Leeds Institute of Cardiovascular and Metabolic Medicine, University of Leeds, Leeds LS2 9JT, UK
5 Department of Infection, Immunity & Cardiovascular Disease, University of Sheffield, Sheffield S10 2RX, UK
6 Department of Radiology, Division of Image Processing, Leiden University Medical Center, 2333 ZA Leiden, The Netherlands
* Correspondence: p.garg@uea.ac.uk

Abstract: Background: Left atrial (LA) assessment is an important marker of adverse cardiovascular outcomes. Cardiovascular magnetic resonance (CMR) accurately quantifies LA volume and function based on biplane long-axis imaging. We aimed to validate single-plane-derived LA indices against the biplane method to simplify the post-processing of cine CMR. Methods: In this study, 100 patients from Leeds Teaching Hospitals were used as the derivation cohort. Bias correction for the single plane method was applied and subsequently validated in 79 subjects. Results: There were significant differences between the biplane and single plane mean LA maximum and minimum volumes and LA ejection fraction (EF) (all $p < 0.01$). After correcting for biases in the validation cohort, significant correlations in all LA indices were observed (0.89 to 0.98). The area under the curve (AUC) for the single plane to predict biplane cutoffs of LA maximum volume $\geq$ 112 mL was 0.97, LA minimum volume $\geq$ 44 mL was 0.99, LA stroke volume (SV) $\leq$ 21 mL was 1, and LA EF $\leq$ 46% was 1, (all $p < 0.001$). Conclusions: LA volumetric and functional assessment by the single plane method has a systematic bias compared to the biplane method. After bias correction, single plane LA volume and function are comparable to the biplane method.

Keywords: heart atria; magnetic resonance imaging; CMR; image processing; atrial function

1. Introduction

The importance of the left atrium (LA) structure and function in predicting cardiovascular health outcomes is well established. For instance, an enlarged LA size has been linked to a higher risk of cardiovascular events in the general population, as well as a poorer prognosis for patients with heart failure and myocardial infarction [1–4]. Furthermore, an enlarged LA size has been associated with the onset of atrial fibrillation (AF) and stroke [5–7]. Similarly, diminished LA function correlates with cardiovascular events in the general population and in patients with preserved left ventricular (LV) systolic function [8]. In clinical practice, cardiovascular magnetic resonance (CMR) offers precise and reproducible LA structure and function measurements with high spatial and temporal resolution without the risk of radiation exposure [9,10]. The American College of Cardiology Foundation and the American Heart Association recommend using noninvasive imaging modalities, including CMR, when transthoracic echocardiography is unable to evaluate cardiac structure and function accurately [11,12]. LA structure and functional assessment are mainly done using biplane long-axis views, including four-chamber and two-chamber views [13,14]. In addition, more recently, the CMR assessment of LA has been shown to be important in assessing left ventricular filling pressure (LVFP) and hemodynamics as it can measure acute and dynamic changes in preloading conditions on the left ventricle [15]. CMR can estimate LVFP in patients with suspected heart failure, and CMR-modelled LVFP has been shown to have prognostic power [15,16].

To streamline the workflow in daily clinical practice, quantifying LA function and structure from a single plane may be sufficient [17]. However, the accuracy of these measurements from a single plane method is yet to be determined. In addition, sometimes, due to temporal differences in four-chamber and two-chamber cines, errors can be introduced in quantifying LA volume and function [18]. Finally, occasionally, some patients do not complete their CMR examination due to claustrophobia, which can further limit the application of the biplane method. Hence, an alternative single plane four-chamber method would be desirable for LA quantification.

We hypothesize that four-chamber imaging alone can provide accurate and reliable measurements of LA volumes and function.

2. Materials and Methods

2.1. Study Cohort

This study consisted of a cohort of 179 patients with several cardiovascular diseases who have been previously prospectively recruited to other studies between 2014 to 2018 [19,20]. The group was divided into derivation (n = 100) and validation (n = 79) cohorts. The inclusion criteria specific to this study were individuals over the age of 18 who provided written informed consent. In addition, a four-chamber, well-planned cine and two-chamber cine were needed for the patients to be enrolled to this work. The exclusion criteria were estimated glomerular filtration rate (eGFR) < 30 mL/min/1.73 m^2, claustrophobia and any CMR contraindications.

2.2. Ethics Approval and Consent to Participate

The research adhered to the guidelines outlined in the 2013 version of the Declaration of Helsinki. Data acquisition and handling were authorised by the National Research Ethics Service in the UK, with approval number 21/NE/0149.

2.3. Cardiac Magnetic Resonance Protocol

The CMR images for this study were performed on a 1.5 T Ingenia system by Philips Healthcare (Best, The Netherlands) equipped with a Biometric body with 28-channel coils and digitisation of the CMR signal in the receiver coil. The CMR protocol included baseline survey images, cines (vertical long-axis, horizontal long-axis, 3-chamber and the LV volume contiguous short axis stack), early and late gadolinium enhancement imaging, two-dimensional phase contrast and four-dimensional flow acquisition methods previously described by our group [19,20]. Following planning sequences, four-chamber cine images were acquired, followed by a stack of short-axis cine images covering apex to base. For standard cines, we acquired 30 phases throughout the cardiac cycle. Other cine acquisition parameters include an 8-mm slice thickness, repetition time of 2.72 ms and echo time of 1.36 ms using a standard cardiac-gated balanced steady-state free precession (bSSFP) sequence.

2.4. CMR Analysis

All analyses used MASS research software (version 2023—EXP, Leiden University Medical Center, Leiden, The Netherlands). Endocardial contours for the left and right ventricle and atria structures were drawn in all cardiac phases using artificial intelligence models previously described [21] in the four-chamber cine. Epicardial contours were also drawn for the left ventricle. Endocardial contours for the left ventricle and left atria structures were drawn for the two-chamber cine. For quality control, the AI-generated segmentations and time-resolved volume curves throughout all cardiac phases for all four chambers were evaluated by one of the authors (HA) and double-checked by an experienced clinician (SCMR Level 3).

2.5. Statistical Analysis

Data were analysed using MedCalc® Statistical Software, version 22.014 (MedCalc Software Ltd., Ostend, Belgium). Continuous variables were expressed as the mean ± standard deviation (SD). Discrete data were presented as numbers (n) and percentages (%). All data were treated as parametric. Variables were compared between groups using an independent sample t-test. Correlations between the two methods were evaluated using Pearson's coefficient of rank correlation (r). We used Bland Altman plot analysis to check for agreement and bias between the methods. The discriminative capability was evaluated by calculating the area under the curve (AUC) using receiver operating characteristic (ROC) curves. The statistical significance was set at $p < 0.05$.

3. Results

3.1. Left Atrial Biplanar Volume Assessment in the Whole Cohort

In total, we enrolled 179 patients. Figure 1 demonstrates the broad cumulative distribution of LA volume and functional metrics across all normal and abnormal values ranges. In the total cohort, 40 patients (22%) had elevated LA maximum volume (≥112 mL). For LA minimum volume, 79 patients (44%) had high LA minimum volume (≥44 mL). Only four patients (2%) had reduced LA SV (≤21 mL). However, 56 patients (31%) had reduced LA EF (≤46%).

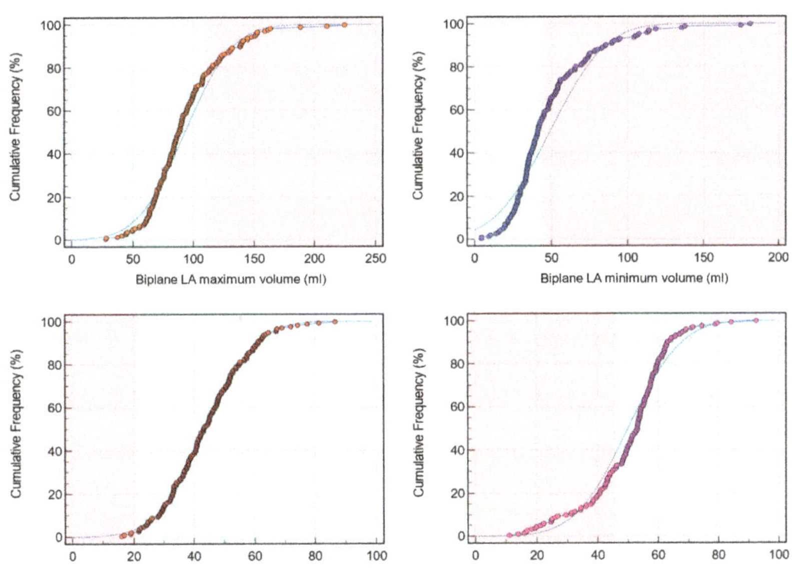

Figure 1. Cumulative frequency distribution of biplane left atrial (LA) parameters in the whole study cohort ($n = 179$). Each graph's two distinct background colors divide them at the halfway point of the y-axis, indicating different zones or reference ranges for easier visual interpretation. The figure effectively visualizes the distributions of the biplane LA parameters measured in the study.

For the LA maximum volume, the biplane method showed a range of 28–225 mL, with a mean of 93 mL (95% CI: 89–98 mL), median of 88 mL (95% CI: 84–91 mL), and standard deviation of 31 mL. The relative standard deviation was 34%, and the standard error was 2.3 mL. For the LA minimum volume, the range was 4.5–181 mL, with a mean of 49 mL (95% CI: 45–53 mL), median of 41 mL (95% CI: 38–45 mL), and standard deviation of 29 mL. The relative standard deviation was 58%, and the standard error was 2 mL. For the LA SV, the biplane method showed a range of 16–87 mL, with a mean of 44 mL (95% CI: 42–46 mL), median of 43 mL (95% CI: 41–46 mL), and standard deviation of 13 mL. The relative standard deviation was 30%, and the standard error was 1 mL. For the LA EF, the range was 11–93%, with a mean of 50% (95% CI: 48–52%), median of 53% (95% CI: 51–54%), and standard deviation of 14%. The relative standard deviation was 27%, and the standard error was 1%.

3.2. *Derivation Cohort (n = 100)*

3.2.1. Correlations between Biplanar and Single Planar Methods

The regression equations and scatter plots are presented in Figure 2. The regression analysis of the dependent variable biplane maximum LA volume (in mL) on the independent variable single plane maximum LA volume (in mL) yielded a highly significant model ($p < 0.001$) with a strong coefficient of determination (r = 0.96), indicating that approximately 96% of the variation in biplane maximum LA volume can be explained by single plane maximum LA volume. The regression equation is y = 16.193 + 0.917x. The intercept is 16.2 (95% CI: 11.0 to 21.3, t = 6.2, $p < 0.001$), and the slope is 0.9 (95% CI: 0.9 to 1.0, t = 32.4, $p < 0.001$), both of which are statistically significant.

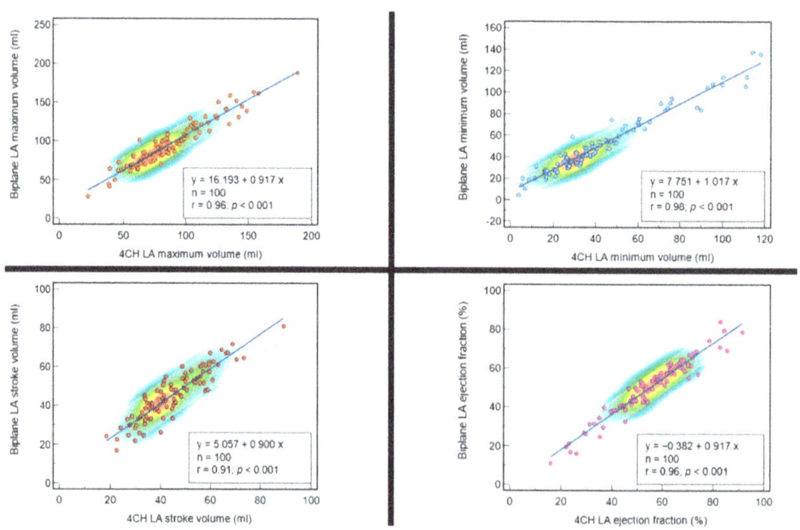

Figure 2. Scatter plots with heat maps demonstrating correlations between single plane four-chamber cine (4CH) left atrial (LA) parameters and biplane LA parameters. The color-coding of data points represents data density, with red indicating higher density and blue signifying lower density. Each plot includes a linear regression line with confidence intervals, demonstrating the strength and direction of the correlations. The figure effectively visualizes the strong positive correlations between the single plane and biplane LA parameters measured in the study.

The regression analysis of the dependent variable biplane minimum LA volume (in mL) on the independent variable single plane minimum LA volume (in mL) yielded a highly significant model ($p < 0.001$) with a strong coefficient of determination (r = 0.98), indicating that approximately 98% of the variation in biplane minimum LA volume can be explained by single plane minimum LA volume. The regression equation is y = 7.751 + 1.017x. The intercept is 7.8 (95% CI: 5.5 to 10.0, t = 6.9, $p < 0.001$), and the slope is 1.0 (95% CI: 0.97 to 1.06, t = 44.2, $p < 0.001$), both of which are statistically significant.

The regression analysis of the dependent variable biplane LA SV (in mL) on the independent variable single plane LA SV (in mL) yielded a significant model ($p < 0.001$) with a strong coefficient of determination (r = 0.91), indicating that approximately 91% of the variation in biplane LA SV can be explained by single plane LA SV. The regression equation is y = 5.057 + 0.900x. The intercept is 5.1 (95% CI: 1.2 to 8.9, t = 2.6, $p = 0.01$), and the slope is 0.9 (95% CI: 0.82 to 0.98, t = 21.4, $p < 0.001$), both of which are statistically significant.

The regression analysis of the dependent variable biplane LA EF (in %) on the independent variable single plane LA EF (in %) yielded a significant model ($p < 0.001$) with a strong coefficient of determination (r = 0.96), indicating that approximately 96% of the variation in biplane LA EF can be explained by single plane LA EF. The regression equation is y = −0.382 + 0.917x. The intercept is −0.4 (95% CI: −3.2 to 2.5, t = −0.3, $p = 0.79$), and the slope is 0.9 (95% CI: 0.87 to 0.97, t = 36.3, $p < 0.001$), both of which are statistically significant.

3.2.2. Bland–Altman Plots and Bias Investigation

In a derivation cohort of 100 subjects, the comparison between the biplane and single plane methods for measuring LA volume and function revealed significant differences (Table 1). The Bland–Altman plots are presented in Figure 3. The mean ± SD of maximum LA volume was found to be lower in the single plane method (86 ± 30 mL) compared to the biplane method (96 ± 29 mL), with a bias of −9 mL and a standard deviation of bias of 9 mL ($p < 0.01$). Similarly, the mean minimum LA volume was also lower in the single plane method (42 ± 26 mL) compared to the biplane method (50 ± 27 mL), with a bias of −8 mL and a standard deviation of bias of 6 mL ($p < 0.01$). However, there was no significant difference in the LA SV between the two methods (45 ± 13 mL for both), with a negligible bias of −1 mL and an SD of bias of 6 mL ($p = 0.27$). Interestingly, the mean LA EF was found to be higher in the single plane method (55 ± 15%) compared to the biplane method (50 ± 14%), with a bias of 5% and an SD of bias of 4% ($p < 0.01$). The SD of the bias was used to correct the systematic bias in these measurements.

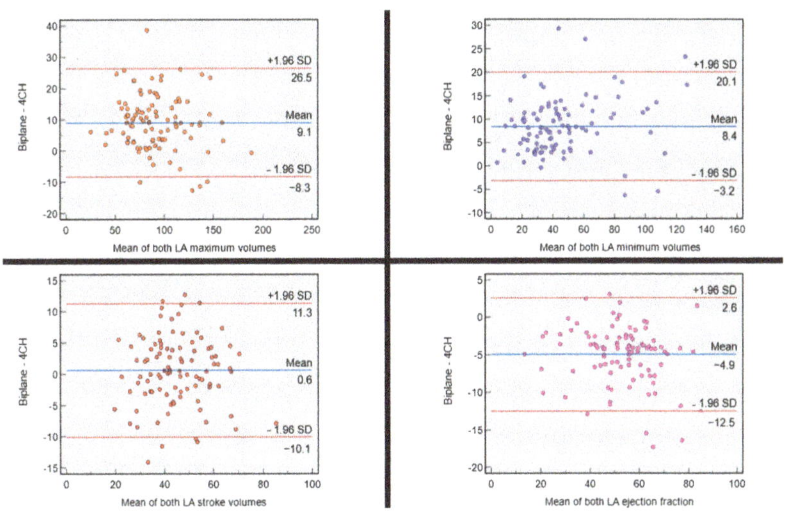

Figure 3. Bland–Altman plots for all left atrial (LA) variables demonstrate significant bias between biplane and single plane methods for LA maximum and minimum volumes. Both are systematically underestimated by the single plane method. Stroke volume (SV) is similar between both groups. Due to the relative difference in maximum and minimum volumes, the single plane method systematically overestimates the LA ejection fraction (EF). Other than for stroke volume, all *p*-values are significant for paired comparison.

Table 1. Left atrial volumetric measurements by biplane and single plane analysis methods of the derivation cohort (n = 100).

Derivation Cohort	Biplane Method	Single Plane Method	Bias	SD of Bias	p
LA maximum volume, mL	96 ± 29	86 ± 30	−9	9 *	<0.01
LA minimum volume, mL	50 ± 27	42 ± 26	−8	6 *	<0.01
LA stroke volume, mL	45 ± 13	45 ± 13	−1	6	0.27
LA ejection fraction, %	50 ± 14	55 ± 15	−5	4 *	<0.01

Mean ± standard deviation. * The standard deviation of the bias has been used to correct the systematic bias. Abbreviations: LA, left atrium; SD, standard deviation.

3.3. *Validation Cohort (n = 79)*

3.3.1. Left Atrial Volumetric Assessment

The arithmetic mean ± SD of the LA maximum volume derived using the biplane and single plane methods were (90 ± 34 mL, 95% CI: 82.8 to 97.9 mL) and (83 ± 34 mL, 95% CI: 75.8 to 90.8 mL), respectively, indicating that the true population mean is likely within this range. The median values for the biplane and single plane methods were (86 mL, 95% CI: 78.9 to 90.7 mL) and (76 mL, 95% CI: 71.4 to 86.3 mL), respectively. The variance, which is a measure of dispersion for biplane and single plane methods, was 1132 mL and 1127 mL, respectively. The relative standard deviation for the biplane method was 37%, and the single plane method was 34%, providing a measure of dispersion relative to the mean. The standard error of the mean, which estimates the precision of the sample mean as an estimate of the population mean, was 3.8 mL for both methods.

For LA minimum volume, the arithmetic mean ± SD using the biplane and single plane methods were (48 ± 30 mL, 95% CI: 40.9 to 54.6 mL) and (41 ± 30 mL, 95% CI: 34.6 to 47.9 mL), respectively, indicating that the true population mean is likely within this range. The median values for the biplane and single plane methods were (39 mL, 95% CI: 34.9 to 44.8 mL) and (32 mL, 95% CI: 28.5 to 38.5 mL), respectively. The variance, which is a measure of dispersion for the biplane and single plane methods, was 923 mL and 883 mL, respectively. The relative standard deviation for the biplane method was 64%, and the single plane method was 72%, providing a measure of dispersion relative to the mean. The standard error of the mean, which estimates the precision of the sample mean as an estimate of the population mean, was 3.4 mL and 3.3 mL for biplane and single plane methods, respectively.

The biplane and single plane LA SV's arithmetic mean ± SD were (43 ± 14 mL, 95% CI: 39.6 to 45.7 mL) and (42 ± 13 mL, 95% CI: 39.3 to 44.9 mL), respectively, indicating that the true population mean is likely within this range. The median values for the biplane and single plane methods were (41 mL, 95% CI: 37.6 to 45.9 mL) and (41 mL, 95% CI: 38.9 to 45.2 mL), respectively. The variance, which is a measure of dispersion for the biplane and single plane methods, was 184 mL and 158 mL, respectively. The relative standard deviation for the biplane method was 32%, and the single plane method was 30%, providing a measure of dispersion relative to the mean. The standard error of the mean, which estimates the precision of the sample mean as an estimate of the population mean, was 1.5 mL and 1.4 mL for biplane and single plane methods, respectively.

The biplane and single plane method derived LA EF's arithmetic mean ± SD were (50 ± 14%, 95% CI: 47 to 53.1%) and (54 ± 15%, 95% CI: 50.9 to 57.5%), respectively, indicating that the true population mean is likely within this range. The median values for the biplane and single plane methods were (54%, 95% CI: 50.5 to 55.8%) and (59%, 95% CI: 54.1 to 61%), respectively. The variance, which is a measure of dispersion for the biplane and single plane methods, was 187% and 213%, respectively. The relative standard deviation for both was 27%, providing a measure of dispersion relative to the mean. The standard error of the mean, which estimates the precision of the sample mean as an estimate of the population mean, was 1.5% for the biplane method and 1.6% for the single plane method.

3.3.2. Correlations between Biplanar and Single-Planar after Bias Correction

In a validation cohort of 79 subjects, the regression analysis of the dependent variable biplane LA maximum volume (in mL) on the independent variable single plane LA maximum volume (in mL) yielded a significant model ($p < 0.001$) with a strong coefficient of determination (r = 0.96). The regression equation was y = 1.429 + 0.963x. The intercept was 1.4 (95% CI: −4.8 to 7.6, t = 0.5, $p = 0.65$), and the slope was 1.0 (95% CI: 0.9 to 1.0, t = 30.4, $p < 0.0001$) (Figure 4). For biplane LA minimum volume (in mL) and single plane LA minimum volume (in mL), the regression equation was y = 0.343 + 1.003x with a strong coefficient of determination (r = 0.98, $p < 0.001$). For biplane LA EF (in %) and single plane LA EF (in %), the regression equation was y = 4.617 + 0.905x with a strong coefficient of determination (r = 0.97, $p < 0.001$). For biplane LA SV (in mL) and single plane LA SV (in mL), the regression equation was y = 2.397 + 0.955x with a strong coefficient of determination (r = 0.89, $p < 0.001$). These findings suggest a strong positive linear relationship between each pair's dependent and independent variables.

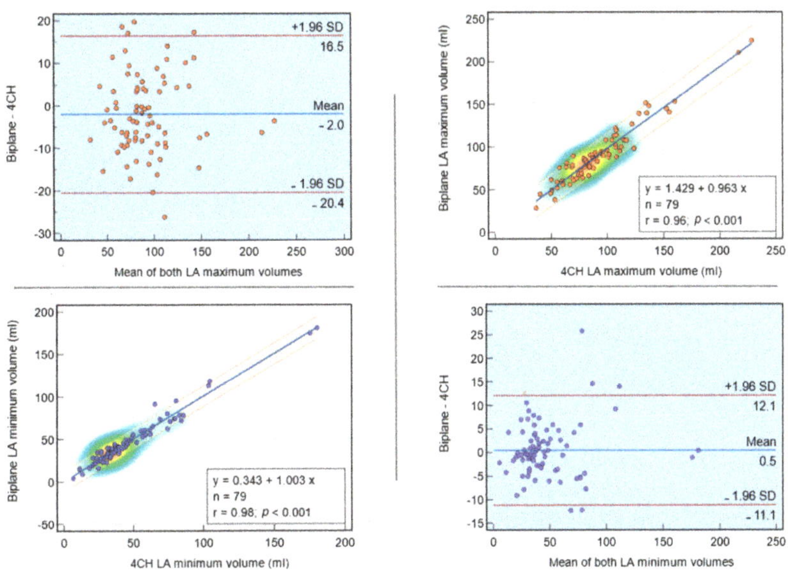

Figure 4. Post-bias correction agreement investigation in the validation cohort ($n = 79$): Bland–Altman plot agreement and correlation between biplane and single plane methods of left atrial (LA) maximum and minimum volumes assessment methods. Both Bland–Altman and regression analyses demonstrate the agreement of biplane versus single plane measurements for these two variables.

3.3.3. Bland–Altman Plots and Bias Investigation after Bias Correction

Comparison between the biplane and single plane post-bias correction methods for measuring LA volumes are demonstrated in Table 2. Bland–Altman plots illustrating the agreement between biplane and single plane methods are shown in Figures 4 and 5. In a comparative analysis of biplane and single plane analysis methods, for biplane LA maximum volume, the arithmetic mean difference was −2 mL (95% CI: −20.4 to 16.5 mL, $p = 0.05$), indicating a slight underestimation by single plane, but this difference was not statistically significant. Similarly, for biplane LA minimum volume, the mean difference was 0.5 mL (95% CI: −11.1 to 12.1 mL, $p = 0.47$), suggesting a slight underestimation by single plane, but again, this difference was not statistically significant. For biplane and single plane LA SV and LA EF, the mean differences were 0.5 mL (95% CI: −11.8 to 12.8, $p = 0.47$) and −0.2% (95% CI: −7.7 to 7.3, $p = 0.75$), respectively, indicating no significant differences between the two methods. These findings suggest that the two methods are comparable for measuring LA maximum volume, LA minimum volume, LA SV and LA EF.

Table 2. Left atrial volumetric measurements by biplane and single plane post-bias correction analysis methods of the validation cohort (n = 79).

Validation Cohort	Biplane Method	Single Plane	Bias	p
LA maximum volume, mL	90 ± 34	92 ± 34	−2	0.06
LA minimum volume, mL	48 ± 30	47 ± 30	0.5	0.47
LA stroke volume, mL	43 ± 14	42 ± 13	0.5	0.47
LA ejection fraction, %	50 ± 14	50 ± 15	−0.2	0.69

Mean ± standard deviation. Abbreviations: LA, left atrium; SD, standard deviation.

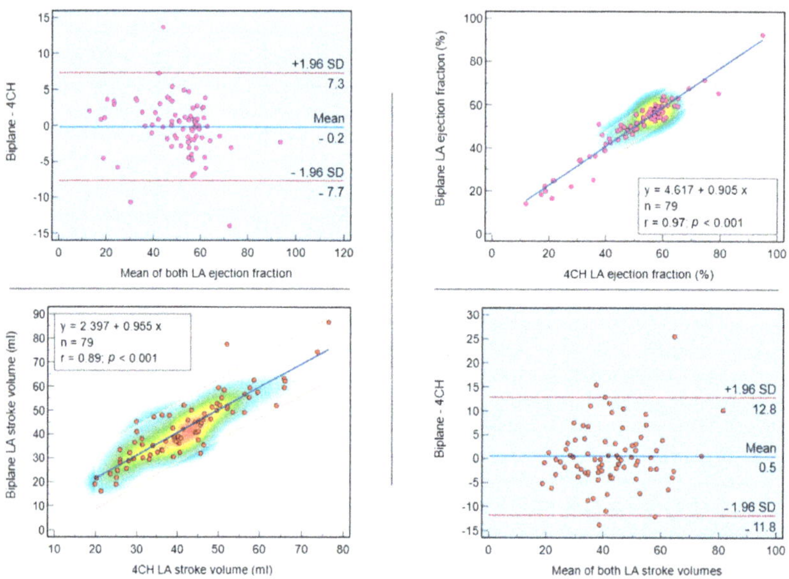

Figure 5. Post-bias correction agreement investigation in the validation cohort (n = 79): Bland–Altman plot agreement and correlation between biplane and single plane methods of left atrial (LA) ejection fraction (EF) and stroke volume (SV) assessment. Both Bland–Altman and regression analyses demonstrate the agreement of biplane versus single plane measurements for these two variables.

3.3.4. Receiver Operator Characteristics

The area under the curve (AUC) for the single plane method to predict biplane method cutoff of LA maximum volume of ≥112 mL was (AUC = 0.97, $p < 0.001$), indicating a high level of accuracy in distinguishing between normal and abnormal states. Moreover, the single plane method to predict the biplane method cutoff of LA minimum volume of ≥44 had an even higher AUC = 0.99 ($p < 0.001$), suggesting excellent accuracy. Additionally, single-plane-derived LA parameters to predict biplane LA SV of ≤21 mL had an AUC of 1 ($p < 0.001$). Finally, single-plane-derived LA parameters to predict biplane LA EF of ≤46% had an AUC of 1 ($p < 0.001$), indicating ideal accuracy (Figure 6).

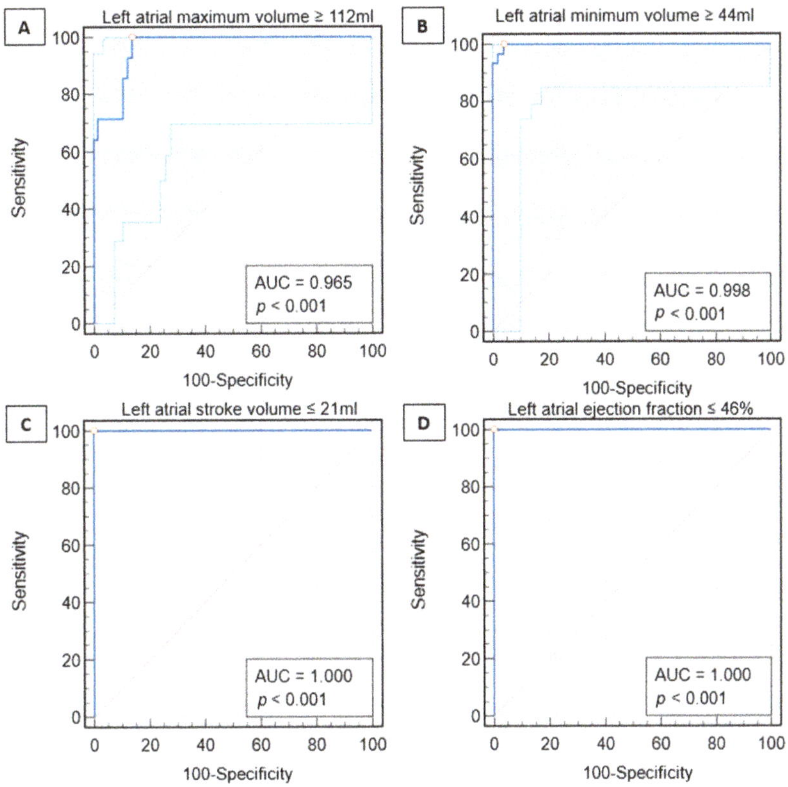

Figure 6. Receiver operating characteristic (ROC) Curves for left atrial (LA) parameters in predicting biplane cutoffs of abnormal values using the upper limit of normal values. [(**A**) maximum volume $\geq$ 112 mL, (**B**) minimum volume $\geq$ 44 mL, (**C**) stroke volume $\leq$ 21 mL, and (**D**) ejection fraction $\leq$ 46%]. Each panel displays the sensitivity (y-axis) against 100-specificity (x-axis). All p-values are less than 0.001, indicating significant predictive power for all metrics.

The results suggest that these variables are highly predictive and could be useful in disease diagnosis or prognosis. The standard errors were 0.02 mL for LA maximum volume, 0.002 mL for LA minimum volume, 0 mL for LA SV and 0% for LA EF. The 95% confidence intervals ranged from 0.89 to 0.99 mL for the LA maximum volume, 0.95 to 1.0 mL for the LA minimum volume, 0.95 to 1.0 mL for the LA SV and 0.95 to 1.0% for the LA EF. These findings provide robust evidence for the reliability of these variables in the study context.

4. Discussion

This study aimed to investigate if the single plane method for LA volume assessment on CMR is as good as the biplane method for clinical assessment. We observed that both methods had an excellent association with each other with some systematic biases. After correcting for biases, both methods are comparable and in strong agreement with each other. When we looked at clinically relevant cutoffs in the validation cohort, the single plane method demonstrated a high area under the curve for diagnosing a dilated left atrium, as per the biplane method.

Previous studies used CMR to compare LA indices derived from biplane and single plane methods [17]. Tao et al. [17] demonstrated that the single plane tissue tracking CMR underestimated LA volume and strain compared to the biplane method. To compensate for that, they used regression equations to further quantify LA indices from a single plane. They found no significant differences between single plane and biplane methods in all LA volume and strain parameters. They concluded that the single-plane-derived CMR method is reproducible and as accurate as the standard biplane method. The relevant findings in this study provided the foundation we used to evaluate our study's data further. However, despite demonstrating consistency and agreement between single plane and biplane methods, their method did not appear to account for any systematic bias. The single plane method underestimates volumes systematically; therefore, our study used a systematic correction factor to correct it to the biplane method. Given that their method does not routinely incorporate LA volumetric assessment, our approach offers broader applicability compared to tissue tracking or strain analysis. Moreover, our segmentation analysis method was completely automated, making it more feasible than tissue tracking CMR.

LA volume is considered more reproducible than left atrial strain [22,23] as it is less affected by the acoustic window and image quality, and it is based on geometric assumptions that are less complex than those required for strain analysis [24]. The reproducibility of left atrial strain can be affected by the load dependency of the parameter and the wide range of normal values, which can introduce variability in the assessment of left atrial function, particularly in patients with normal left ventricular EF [25]. It is also worth noting that several software vendors have different strain algorithms, which further prohibit its broader clinical adoption. Meanwhile, the area-length method for volumetric assessment is already largely used and is available in many cardiac-specific and generic applications. In summary, the more reproducible nature of LA volume measurements can be attributed to the established and standardised techniques for volume quantification, less sensitivity to image quality and operator dependency, and the geometric simplicity of the measurements compared to the complexity of strain analysis.

In routine clinical practice, the use of the biplane method for computing LA volume can be hindered by several challenges. These include temporal misalignment between the four-chamber and two-chamber cines, and improper planning of either cine. A well-executed four-chamber cine is of significant clinical value as it facilitates a comparative analysis of the LA and other chambers. Moreover, it enables the assessment of the pericardium, subcutaneous adipose tissue and descending aorta. Therefore, in situations where high-quality cines in other views are unavailable due to arrhythmias or other issues, a four-chamber analysis can prove to be invaluable. This study enhances the clinical applicability of four-chamber analysis by calibrating several methods for LA volume assessment. Consequently, this research significantly advances the field.

Limitations

The four-chamber CMR analysis depends on acquisition; if wrongly planned, it can lead to under or overestimating LA volumes. However, we had clear acquisition protocols, likely reducing this error. We used already developed artificial intelligence (AI) deep-learnt contours to derive both biplane and single plane volumes. There is room for error in the accuracy of the AI contours; however, in our in-house testing, this has been minimal. Even though both derivation and validation datasets include a broad range of left ventricular impairment patients, we did not include congenital studies, which may limit our methods' more general clinical applicability. Future studies are needed to test the prognostic relevance of our single plane method to measure LA volume.

5. Conclusions

LA volumetric and functional assessment by the single plane method has a systematic bias compared to the biplane method. After applying the bias correction factors, single plane four-chamber-derived LA volume and function are comparable to the biplane method.

Author Contributions: Conceptualization, P.P.S., A.J.S., R.J.v.d.G. and P.G.; Data curation, H.A., R.L. and P.G.; Formal analysis, H.A. and P.G.; Funding acquisition, P.G.; Investigation, H.A. and P.G.; Methodology, H.A., R.J.v.d.G. and P.G.; Project administration, P.G.; Resources, P.P.S., R.J.v.d.G. and P.G.; Software, B.K. and R.J.v.d.G.; Supervision, P.G.; Validation, R.J.v.d.G. and P.G.; Visualization, H.A. and P.G.; Writing—original draft, H.A., N.S., C.B. and P.G.; Writing—review and editing, H.A., N.S., C.B., G.M., R.L., C.G.-C., Z.M., B.K., P.P.S., A.J.S., R.J.v.d.G. and P.G. All authors have read and agreed to the published version of the manuscript.

Funding: P.G. is funded by Wellcome Trust Clinical Research Career Development Fellowships (220703/Z/20/Z). For the purpose of Open Access, these authors have applied a CC BY public copyright license to any Author Accepted Manuscript version arising from this submission. The funders had no role in study design, data collection and analysis, publishing decisions, or manuscript preparation.

Institutional Review Board Statement: The research adhered to the guidelines outlined in the 2013 version of the Declaration of Helsinki. Data acquisition and handling were authorized by the National Research Ethics Service in the United Kingdom in October 2017, with approval number 21/NE/0149.

Informed Consent Statement: Informed consent was obtained from all subjects involved in the study.

Data Availability Statement: The datasets generated and analyzed during the current study are not publicly available. Access to the raw images of patients is not permitted since specialized post-processing imaging-based solutions can identify the study patients in the future. Data are available from the corresponding author upon reasonable request.

Conflicts of Interest: PG is a clinical advisor for Neosoft, Pie Medical Imaging and Medis Medical Imaging. PG consults for Anteris and Edward Life Sciences. All other authors have no competing interests to declare.

Abbreviations

AF	atrial fibrillation
AUC	area under the curve
CMR	cardiovascular magnetic resonance
EF	ejection fraction
LA	left atrium
LVFP	left ventricular filling pressure
ROC	receiver operator curve
SD	standard deviation
SV	stroke volume

References

1. Hoit, B.D. Left atrial size and function: Role in prognosis. *J. Am. Coll. Cardiol.* **2014**, *63*, 493–505. [CrossRef]
2. Rossi, A.; Temporelli, P.L.; Quintana, M.; Dini, F.L.; Ghio, S.; Hillis, G.S.; Klein, A.L.; Marsan, N.A.; Prior, D.L.; Yu, C.M.; et al. Independent relationship of left atrial size and mortality in patients with heart failure: An individual patient meta-analysis of longitudinal data (MeRGE Heart Failure). *Eur. J. Heart Fail.* **2009**, *11*, 929–936. [CrossRef]
3. Raisi-Estabragh, Z.; McCracken, C.; Condurache, D.; Aung, N.; Vargas, J.D.; Naderi, H.; Munroe, P.B.; Neubauer, S.; Harvey, N.C.; Petersen, S.E. Left atrial structure and function are associated with cardiovascular outcomes independent of left ventricular measures: A UK Biobank CMR study. *Eur. Heart J. Cardiovasc. Imaging* **2022**, *23*, 1191–1200. [CrossRef]
4. Bombelli, M.; Facchetti, R.; Cuspidi, C.; Villa, P.; Dozio, D.; Brambilla, G.; Grassi, G.; Mancia, G. Prognostic Significance of Left Atrial Enlargement in a General Population. *Hypertension* **2014**, *64*, 1205–1211. [CrossRef]
5. Inciardi, R.M.; Giugliano, R.P.; Claggett, B.; Gupta, D.K.; Chandra, A.; Ruff, C.T.; Antman, E.M.; Mercuri, M.F.; Grosso, M.A.; Braunwald, E.; et al. Left atrial structure and function and the risk of death or heart failure in atrial fibrillation. *Eur. J. Heart Fail.* **2019**, *21*, 1571–1579. [CrossRef]
6. Di Tullio, M.R.; Sacco, R.L.; Sciacca, R.R.; Homma, S. Left atrial size and the risk of ischemic stroke in an ethnically mixed population. *Stroke* **1999**, *30*, 2019–2024. [CrossRef]
7. Hosseini Farahabadi, M.; Milani-Nejad, S.; Liu, S.; Yu, W.; Shafie, M. Left Atrial Dilatation and Reduced Left Ventricular Ejection Fraction Are Associated with Cardioembolic Stroke. *Front. Neurol.* **2021**, *12*, 680651. [CrossRef] [PubMed]
8. Welles, C.C.; Ku, I.A.; Kwan, D.M.; Whooley, M.A.; Schiller, N.B.; Turakhia, M.P. Left atrial function predicts heart failure hospitalization in subjects with preserved ejection fraction and coronary heart disease: Longitudinal data from the Heart and Soul Study. *J. Am. Coll. Cardiol.* **2012**, *59*, 673–680. [CrossRef] [PubMed]

9. Kawel-Boehm, N.; Hetzel, S.J.; Ambale-Venkatesh, B.; Captur, G.; Francois, C.J.; Jerosch-Herold, M.; Salerno, M.; Teague, S.D.; Valsangiacomo-Buechel, E.; van der Geest, R.J.; et al. Reference ranges ('normal values') for cardiovascular magnetic resonance (CMR) in adults and children: 2020 update. *J. Cardiovasc. Magn. Reson. Off. J. Soc. Cardiovasc. Magn. Reson.* **2020**, *22*, 87. [CrossRef] [PubMed]
10. Kowallick, J.T.; Kutty, S.; Edelmann, F.; Chiribiri, A.; Villa, A.; Steinmetz, M.; Sohns, J.M.; Staab, W.; Bettencourt, N.; Unterberg-Buchwald, C.; et al. Quantification of left atrial strain and strain rate using Cardiovascular Magnetic Resonance myocardial feature tracking: A feasibility study. *J. Cardiovasc. Magn. Reson.* **2014**, *16*, 60. [CrossRef] [PubMed]
11. Yancy, C.W.; Jessup, M.; Bozkurt, B.; Butler, J.; Casey, D.E.; Drazner, M.H.; Fonarow, G.C.; Geraci, S.A.; Horwich, T.; Januzzi, J.L.; et al. 2013 ACCF/AHA guideline for the management of heart failure: A report of the American College of Cardiology Foundation/American Heart Association Task Force on practice guidelines. *Circulation* **2013**, *128*, e240–e327. [CrossRef] [PubMed]
12. Heidenreich, P.A.; Bozkurt, B.; Aguilar, D.; Allen, L.A.; Byun, J.J.; Colvin, M.M.; Deswal, A.; Drazner, M.H.; Dunlay, S.M.; Evers, L.R.; et al. 2022 AHA/ACC/HFSA Guideline for the Management of Heart Failure: A Report of the American College of Cardiology/American Heart Association Joint Committee on Clinical Practice Guidelines. *Circulation* **2022**, *145*, e895–e1032. [CrossRef]
13. Kawel-Boehm, N.; Maceira, A.; Valsangiacomo-Buechel, E.R.; Vogel-Claussen, J.; Turkbey, E.B.; Williams, R.; Plein, S.; Tee, M.; Eng, J.; Bluemke, D.A. Normal values for cardiovascular magnetic resonance in adults and children. *J. Cardiovasc. Magn. Reson. Off. J. Soc. Cardiovasc. Magn. Reson.* **2015**, *17*, 29. [CrossRef] [PubMed]
14. Petersen, S.E.; Khanji, M.Y.; Plein, S.; Lancellotti, P.; Bucciarelli-Ducci, C. European Association of Cardiovascular Imaging expert consensus paper: A comprehensive review of cardiovascular magnetic resonance normal values of cardiac chamber size and aortic root in adults and recommendations for grading severity. *Eur. Heart J. Cardiovasc. Imaging* **2019**, *20*, 1321–1331. [CrossRef]
15. Garg, P.; Gosling, R.; Swoboda, P.; Jones, R.; Rothman, A.; Wild, J.M.; Kiely, D.G.; Condliffe, R.; Alabed, S.; Swift, A.J. Cardiac magnetic resonance identifies raised left ventricular filling pressure: Prognostic implications. *Eur. Heart J.* **2022**, *43*, 2511–2522. [CrossRef]
16. Assadi, H.; Matthews, G.; Chambers, B.; Grafton-Clarke, C.; Shabi, M.; Plein, S.; Swoboda, P.P.; Garg, P. Cardiac Magnetic Resonance Left Ventricular Filling Pressure Is Associated with NT-proBNP in Patients with New Onset Heart Failure. *Medicina* **2023**, *59*, 1924. [CrossRef]
17. Tao, S.; Ciuffo, L.A.; Lima, J.A.C.; Wu, K.C.; Ashikaga, H. Quantifying left atrial structure and function using single-plane tissue-tracking cardiac magnetic resonance. *Magn. Reson. Imaging* **2017**, *42*, 130–138. [CrossRef]
18. Mitchell, C.; Rahko, P.S.; Blauwet, L.A.; Canaday, B.; Finstuen, J.A.; Foster, M.C.; Horton, K.; Ogunyankin, K.O.; Palma, R.A.; Velazquez, E.J. Guidelines for Performing a Comprehensive Transthoracic Echocardiographic Examination in Adults: Recommendations from the American Society of Echocardiography. *J. Am. Soc. Echocardiogr. Off. Publ. Am. Soc. Echocardiogr.* **2019**, *32*, 1–64. [CrossRef] [PubMed]
19. Crandon, S.; Westenberg, J.J.M.; Swoboda, P.P.; Fent, G.J.; Foley, J.R.J.; Chew, P.G.; Brown, L.A.E.; Saunderson, C.; Al-Mohammad, A.; Greenwood, J.P.; et al. Impact of Age and Diastolic Function on Novel, 4D flow CMR Biomarkers of Left Ventricular Blood Flow Kinetic Energy. *Sci. Rep.* **2018**, *8*, 14436. [CrossRef] [PubMed]
20. Garg, P.; Crandon, S.; Swoboda, P.P.; Fent, G.J.; Foley, J.R.J.; Chew, P.G.; Brown, L.A.E.; Vijayan, S.; Hassell, M.E.C.J.; Nijveldt, R.; et al. Left ventricular blood flow kinetic energy after myocardial infarction—Insights from 4D flow cardiovascular magnetic resonance. *J. Cardiovasc. Magn. Reson. Off. J. Soc. Cardiovasc. Magn. Reson.* **2018**, *20*, 61. [CrossRef] [PubMed]
21. Alandejani, F.; Alabed, S.; Garg, P.; Goh, Z.M.; Karunasaagarar, K.; Sharkey, M.; Salehi, M.; Aldabbagh, Z.; Dwivedi, K.; Mamalakis, M.; et al. Training and clinical testing of artificial intelligence derived right atrial cardiovascular magnetic resonance measurements. *J. Cardiovasc. Magn. Reson. Off. J. Soc. Cardiovasc. Magn. Reson.* **2022**, *24*, 25. [CrossRef] [PubMed]
22. Alfuhied, A.; Marrow, B.A.; Elfawal, S.; Gulsin, G.S.; Graham-Brown, M.P.; Steadman, C.D.; Kanagala, P.; McCann, G.P.; Singh, A. Reproducibility of left atrial function using cardiac magnetic resonance imaging. *Eur. Radiol.* **2021**, *31*, 2788–2797. [CrossRef] [PubMed]
23. Zareian, M.; Ciuffo, L.; Habibi, M.; Opdahl, A.; Chamera, E.H.; Wu, C.O.; Bluemke, D.A.; Lima, J.A.C.; Venkatesh, B.A. Left atrial structure and functional quantitation using cardiovascular magnetic resonance and multimodality tissue tracking: Validation and reproducibility assessment. *J. Cardiovasc. Magn. Reson. Off. J. Soc. Cardiovasc. Magn. Reson.* **2015**, *17*, 52. [CrossRef] [PubMed]
24. Jenkins, C.; Bricknell, K.; Marwick, T.H. Use of real-time three-dimensional echocardiography to measure left atrial volume: Comparison with other echocardiographic techniques. *J. Am. Soc. Echocardiogr. Off. Publ. Am. Soc. Echocardiogr.* **2005**, *18*, 991–997. [CrossRef]
25. Nagueh, S.F.; Khan, S.U. Left Atrial Strain for Assessment of Left Ventricular Diastolic Function: Focus on Populations with Normal LVEF. *JACC Cardiovasc. Imaging* **2023**, *16*, 691–707. [CrossRef]

cancers

MDPI

Article

Characterization of CD34⁺ Cells from Patients with Acute Myeloid Leukemia (AML) and Myelodysplastic Syndromes (MDS) Using a t-Distributed Stochastic Neighbor Embedding (t-SNE) Protocol

Cathrin Nollmann [1], Wiebke Moskorz [2], Christian Wimmenauer [1], Paul S. Jäger [3], Ron P. Cadeddu [3], Jörg Timm [2], Thomas Heinzel [1,*] and Rainer Haas [3,*]

1 Condensed Matter Physics Laboratory, Heinrich-Heine-University, 40204 Düsseldorf, Germany; cathrin.nollmann@hhu.de (C.N.)
2 Institute of Virology, Heinrich-Heine-University, 40204 Düsseldorf, Germany; joerg.timm@med.uni-duesseldorf.de (J.T.)
3 Department of Hematology, Oncology and Clinical Immunology, Medical Faculty, Heinrich-Heine-University, 40225 Düsseldorf, Germany; paulsebastian.jaeger@med.uni-duesseldorf.de (P.S.J.)
* Correspondence: thomas.heinzel@hhu.de (T.H.); haas@med.uni-duesseldorf.de (R.H.)

Simple Summary: Hematopoietic stem and progenitor cells (HSPCs) play a pivotal role in maintaining the homeostasis of the blood and immune systems. Acute myeloid leukemia (AML) and myelodysplastic syndromes (MDS) represent heterogeneous hematologic malignancies resulting from genetic mutations within cells of the hematopoietic lineage, leading to the expansion of leukemic blasts including leukemic stem cells (LSCs). Using the t-distributed stochastic neighbor embedding (t-SNE) methodology, we examined the immunological phenotype of HSPCs based on the differential expression of CD34, CD38, CD45RA, CD123 and programmed death ligand 1 (PD-L1) antigens, and contrasted it with the immunophenotype of blasts and LSCs in AML and MDS.

Abstract: Using multi-color flow cytometry analysis, we studied the immunophenotypical differences between leukemic cells from patients with AML/MDS and hematopoietic stem and progenitor cells (HSPCs) from patients in complete remission (CR) following their successful treatment. The panel of markers included CD34, CD38, CD45RA, CD123 as representatives for a hierarchical hematopoietic stem and progenitor cell (HSPC) classification as well as programmed death ligand 1 (PD-L1). Rather than restricting the evaluation on a 2- or 3-dimensional analysis, we applied a t-distributed stochastic neighbor embedding (t-SNE) approach to obtain deeper insight and segregation between leukemic cells and normal HPSCs. For that purpose, we created a t-SNE map, which resulted in the visualization of 27 cell clusters based on their similarity concerning the composition and intensity of antigen expression. Two of these clusters were "leukemia-related" containing a great proportion of CD34⁺/CD38⁻ hematopoietic stem cells (HSCs) or CD34⁺ cells with a strong co-expression of CD45RA/CD123, respectively. CD34⁺ cells within the latter cluster were also highly positive for PD-L1 reflecting their immunosuppressive capacity. Beyond this proof of principle study, the inclusion of additional markers will be helpful to refine the differentiation between normal HSPCs and leukemic cells, particularly in the context of minimal disease detection and antigen-targeted therapeutic interventions. Furthermore, we suggest a protocol for the assignment of new cell ensembles in quantitative terms, via a numerical value, the Pearson coefficient, based on a similarity comparison of the t-SNE pattern with a reference.

Keywords: hematopoietic stem and progenitor cell (HSPC); acute myeloid leukemia (AML); myelodysplastic syndromes (MDS); leukemic stem cells (LSC); CD34; CD38; CD45RA; CD123; PD-L1; flow cytometry; t-SNE; high-dimensional space analyses; classification; dimensionality reduction; immunophenotyping

1. Introduction

Acute myeloid leukemia (AML) and myelodysplastic syndromes (MDS) are heterogeneous disorders originating from hematopoietic stem cells (HSCs) through the progressive and sequential acquisition of genetic and epigenetic alterations. As a result, there is a clonal expansion of myeloid progenitors/precursors in the bone marrow (BM) and peripheral blood (PB), associated with impaired cell differentiation leading to hematopoietic insufficiency [1–3]. Drug resistance and dormancy of the leukemic stem cells (LSC) with a reduced susceptibility to cytotoxic drugs are the main reasons for treatment failure [4,5]. To tackle the problem of resistance and dormancy, a subtle characterization of the leukemic blast population including the LSC is a prerequisite for a more efficacious targeting and eradication.

The search for a better characterization of the various subsets contained within the bulk mass of leukemic blasts from patients with acute leukemia has prompted a constant increase in the number of antigens in panels for single-cell cytometry, reaching numbers from 14 to 28 colors [6–8]. In order to visualize and interpret that kind of multidimensional marker expression function (MEF), the traditional representation via two-dimensional scatter plots increases correspondingly and reaches its limits.

Mathematically, these scatter plots represent two-dimensional projections of the multidimensional function, by which some information of the original distribution is inevitably lost. Consequently, rare or so far unknown leukemic subpopulations of pathophysiological relevance may be not detected [9,10] or multi-dimensional structural information may get lost. This prompted the search for two-dimensional, graphical representations of the MEF, which preserve the full representations [11]. Among such mapping algorithms, t-distributed stochastic neighbor embedding (t-SNE) [12] is a promising candidate [13–17]. We opted for the t-SNE algorithm as compared to equally valid alternatives like uniform manifold approximation and projection (UMAP) [18] since it has a long and successful track record over the past decade and is one of the most widely used for comparable tasks [19,20]. Using this methodology, we aimed at elucidating the $CD34^+$ cell population in more depth in samples from patients with AML and MDS in comparison to samples from patients in complete remission (CR) following antineoplastic therapy.

2. Materials and Methods

2.1. Patients

BM samples of 21 patients with MDS (6 patients) and AML (15 patients) were obtained at the Department of Hematology, Oncology and Clinical Immunology from the University Hospital Düsseldorf on their regular follow-up visits for routine diagnostics. Our control population consisted of 12 patients following allografting, cytotoxic chemotherapy or both who were in CR, with 2 patients (#8 and #21 marked with asterisks in Table 1) still not having achieved full hematological reconstitution. The characteristics of the entire group of patients are shown in Table 1.

Table 1. Patient characteristics. The samples are grouped according to whether the patients have active disease (AD) or are in complete remission (CR). All patients in CR are MRD negative (see Supplemental Table S2 for the MRD analysis).

Group	Pat. ID	Age	Sex	WHO Classification	Status of Disease	Initial Mutation	Cytogenetic	Time ** (Months)
AD	1	61	m	MDS-IB2	AD	-	46, XY	11
AD	4	58	f	AML	Mr	-	47, XX, +11	10
AD	10	58	m	MDS-IB2	Hr	-	46, XY	30
AD	11	67	m	AML, md-r	Mr/p	*FLT3-ITD, RUNX1, EZH2*	46, XY	5
AD	12	65	f	AML, md-r	Hr	*ASXL1*	46, XX, del(11)(q21,q24) [21]	26

Table 1. *Cont.*

Group	Pat. ID	Age	Sex	WHO Classification	Status of Disease	Initial Mutation	Cytogenetic	Time ** (Months)
AD	13	60	m	AML	Id	*IDH1*	47, XY, +8[22]/46, XY[2]	0
AD	14	69	f	AML, md-r	Hr	*JAK2*	45, XX, -7	39
AD	16	60	m	AML, md-r	Hr	*ASXL1, RUNX1*	not initial: 46, XY, del(3)(q21q25)[23]/47idem+8[5]	53
AD	17	60	f	AML with minimal differentiation	Hr	*IDH2*	47, XX, +mar[4]/46, XX [22], cytogenetic aberration: 7(4;12)	216
CR	2	76	m	MDS-IB2	CR	*ASXL1*	46, XY	13
CR	3	67	f	AML with CEBPA mutation	CR	*CEBPA*	46, XX	21
CR	5	56	f	AML with maturation	CR	*DNMT3A, IDH1*	46, XX	4
CR	6	41	m	AML, md-r	CR	*RUNX1*	complex karyotype	3
CR	7	54	f	AML with NPM1 mutation	CR	*NPM1, IDH2*	46, XX	8
CR	8	51	m	MDS with low blasts and SF3B1 mutation (MDS-SF3B1)	CR *	*JAK2, SF3B1*	complex karyotype	60
CR	9	67	f	AML with CBFB-MYH11 fusion	CR	*CBFB-MYH11*	46, XX, inv(16)(p13q22)[24]/ 46, XX [3]	29
CR	15	28	f	AML, md-r	CR	*RUNX1*	complex karyotype	47
CR	18	39	f	AML, md-r	CR	*FLT3-ITD*	del(7)(q22[22]/46, XX [3]	2
CR	19	40	m	AML, md-r	CR	*ASXL1, c-KIT, TET2*	+8, XXY, add(21p)	32
CR	20	61	f	AML, md-r	CR	*ASXL1, RUNX1*	46, XX	57
CR	21	70	m	AML, md-r	CR *	*ASXL1, RUNX1, TET2, EZH2*	46, XY	11

* Patients who still not having achieved full hematological reconstitution; ** time difference between initial diagnosis and sample collection; md-r: myelodysplasia-related; CR: complete remission; Hr: hematological recurrence; Mr: molecular recurrence; Mr/p: molecular recurrence/persistence; Id: initial diagnosis; AD: active disease; MDS: myelodysplastic syndrome.

2.2. Isolation and Phenotyping of White Blood Cells

White blood cells (WBCs) were isolated via red blood cell lysis. For that, BM was collected in EDTA coated syringes or blood collection tubes and bone fragments were removed by filtering the BM with a 70 µm cell strainer. The BM was then incubated 1:10 for 10 min with isotonic ammonium chloride solution (155 mM NH_4Cl, 10 mM $KHCO_3$ and 0.1 mM EDTA, pH 7.4, purchased from the University Hospital Düsseldorf Pharmacy, Düsseldorf, Germany). WBCs were pelleted for 5 min at 500 g, supernatant was discarded and the remaining WBCs were washed twice with DPBS prior to staining. For each sample, one to four million cells were transferred to a 96 well U-Bottom plate and dead cells were stained with fixable viability dye (#65-08666-14, Thermo Fisher Scientific, 1:1000 in DPBS), washed with DPBS and subsequently stained for cell surface molecules. Dead cells and surface molecules were each stained for 15 min at room temperature in the dark. Antibodies for cell surface molecules (see Table 2) were diluted in Brilliant Stain Buffer (#566349, BD Horizon, BD Bioscience, Franklin Lakes, NJ, USA) to prevent staining artifacts due to polymer dyes. Prior to data acquisition at a BD LSR Fortessa (V/B/YG/R), cells were washed with DPBS, fixed overnight (IC Fixation Buffer, #00-8222, Thermo Fisher Scientific, Waltham, MA, USA) and washed again. Cells were taken up in DPBS and acquired at up to 3000 events/s. All samples contain more than 10^5 cells.

Table 2. WBC staining panel.

Specificity	Clone	Fluorescence Dye	Vendor	Cat #	RRID	Concentration
Fixable viability dye	/	eFlour506	TFS *	65-0866-14	/	1:1000
PD-L1	MIH5	PerCP-eFlour710	TFS	46-5983-42	AB_11041815	1:50
CD123	6H6	PE	TFS	12-1239-42	AB_10609206	1:100
CD45	HI30	PE-Cy5	BioLegend	304010	AB_314398	1:200
CD45RA	HI100	PE-Cy7	TFS	25-0458-42	AB_1548774	1:200
CD34	4H11	APC	TFS	17-0349-41	AB_2016604	1:50
CD38	HIT2	APC-eFlour780	TFS	47-0389-41	AB_11217871	1:50

* TFS: Thermo Fisher Scientific.

2.3. Gating Strategy

In the study presented here, we were particularly interested in a detailed, multi-color flow cytometry-based characterization of the $CD34^+$ cells focusing on a subtle comparison between the $CD34^+$ cell subsets of patients with active disease (AD) and those of patients in CR. For that purpose, we used a panel of the following monoclonal antibodies: CD34, CD38, CD45, CD45RA and CD123, as it provides the basis for defining the various types of HSPCs (Table 3). In addition, the programmed death ligand 1 (PD-L1) was included, since it is also expressed on normal hematopoietic cells, exerting a suppressive effect on the immunological response. We consider this panel suitable and sufficient to demonstrate strengths and pitfalls of a t-SNE-based analysis.

Table 3. Antigen combinations for HSPC characterization.

Cell Type	Label	Antigen Combination
Hematopoietic stem cells	HSC	$CD34^+$ $CD38^-$ ($CD90^+$ not included)
Multipotent progenitor cells	MPP	$CD34^+$ $CD38^-$ ($CD90^-$ not included)
Common lymphoid progenitors	CLP	$CD34^+$ $CD38^-$ $CD45RA^+$
Common myeloid progenitors	CMP	$CD34^+$ $CD38^+$ $CD45RA^-$ $CD123^{low}$ *
Megakaryocyte/erythroid progenitors	MEP	$CD34^+$ $CD38^+$ $CD45RA^-$ $CD123^-$
Granulocyte-macrophage progenitors	GMP	$CD34^+$ $CD38^+$ $CD45RA^+$ $CD123^+$
Not identified by this set of antigens	Other	Various combinations

* By the term "low" we refer to weakly positive.

Our gating strategy for the cells of interest, i.e., the $CD34^+$ cells, encompassed six steps including: (1) an FSC vs. SSC gate, (2) a CD45 vs. SSC gate, (3) an exclusion step for the elimination of doublets, and (4) a viability check using eF506 dye for the exclusion of dead cells. As a result, the (5) final gate of interest (GOI) contained $CD34^+$ cells excluding the population of granulocytes. Afterwards (6), only the $CD34^+$ cells were selected, as shown in Figure 1A and B for patient 1. The gating was carried out in FlowJo® (FlowJo, Ashland, OR, USA). The number of $CD34^+$ positive cells of an individual patient varied between 129 and 207,994 (Figure 1C). To avoid domination of features in the t-SNE plots by individual patients, a maximum of 1000 cells was randomly selected in patients with high cell numbers.

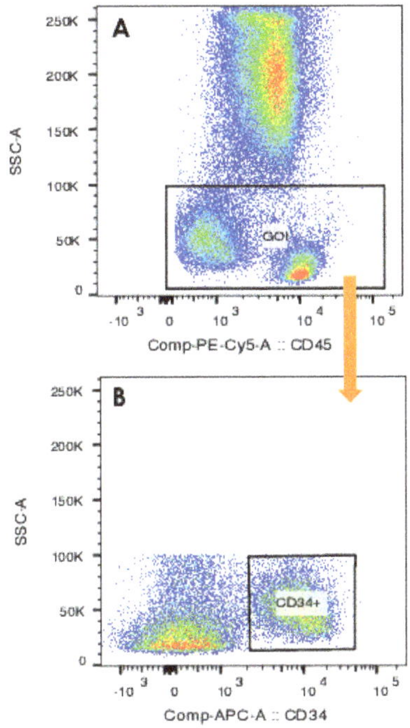

C Patient	cell no. CD34⁺	cell no. included
1	12171	1000
2	656	656
3	303	303
4	3006	1000
5	2044	1000
6	1046	1000
7	204	204
8	1104	1000
9	4384	1000
10	129	129
11	4030	1000
12	18247	1000
13	207994	1000
14	9694	1000
15	1304	1000
16	3280	1000
17	14248	1000
18	1310	1000
19	879	879
20	3202	1000
21	4379	1000

Figure 1. In (**A**) and (**B**), steps (5) and (6) of the gating strategy are shown. The orange arrow means that in B only the cells from the gate of interest (GOI, black frame) were analyzed. (**A**) The exclusion of the population of granulocytes with (5) a GOI; (**B**) The final step (6), selection of the $CD34^+$ cells; In (**C**), the numbers of $CD34^+$ cells after the gating are shown for each patient as well as the numbers thereof included in the t-SNE analysis.

2.4. *Visualization by t-SNE*

In a second step, we applied t-SNE for the visualization of different cell clusters based on their similarity with regards to the composition and intensity of antigen expression. The t-SNE algorithm is a nonlinear dimensionality reduction technique which visualizes high-dimensional data in a two-dimensional scatter plot in such a way that the clustering in high dimensions is preserved. Cells exhibiting comparable protein-expression patterns are positioned adjacently on the t-SNE map, facilitating the depiction of distinct cellular subgroups. The nature of this algorithm is to preserve the local relationships and not the global structure [21]. This is one of the well-known limitations of t-SNE [22–24]. Thus, global structures such as the arrangement of the clusters and their distances in the t-SNE plane provide no basis for interpretation. A principal component analysis (PCA) was therefore carried out for the initialization to improve the global structure of the plot, as established in the literature [21,25].

To enable comparability between the t-SNE plots, the gated $CD34^+$ cells from all patients were first merged into a common data set. The patient ID and the group assignment were appended to the expression matrix prior to data merger permitting the subsequent separation according to these characteristics after the t-SNE analysis. The fluorescence data were scaled biexponentially in a preliminary step [26]. The t-SNE analysis was carried out using the Barnes–Hut implementation of t-SNE by the Rtsne package (Version 0.16, Open Source). The code is available in the Supplement (Code S1). For the PCA the predefined value of 50 for the number of retained dimensions was used. The perplexity as well as the number of iterations were varied over wide intervals. These variations, shown in Supplement Figure S1, not only reassure us that the structures to be interpreted are robust, but also demonstrate that a perplexity of 70 and 3000 iterations is a reasonable choice providing visibility of the relevant morphology within an acceptable computation time [27]. The t-SNE coordinates (t-SNE1, t-SNE2) were also appended to the expression matrix as novel parameters. The entire data set as well as a data set of only patients in CR and a data set of the patients with AD were then exported as FSC files for further analysis in FlowJo ®. The t-SNE plot is created as a function of the two parameters (t-SNE1 and t-SNE2). Since distances within a t-SNE plot cannot be interpreted in a straightforward way for reasons mentioned above, axis labels are omitted for all t-SNE plots, in agreement with common practice.

2.5. Defining Gates in the t-SNE Plots

The expression matrix with the t-SNE coordinates of the three data sets (All patients, only CR, only AD) were imported into FlowJo®. A group was created therein containing all three data sets. Density-based polygon gates were manually drawn on the common t-SNE plot of all patients in CR. Afterward, the 27 gates were applied to the FlowJo® group in order to transfer them to the remaining two data sets.

2.6. Determination of the Immunological Phenotypes of HSPCs

The immunological phenotype of HSPCs was determined using the markers CD34, CD38, CD123 and CD45RA. For this purpose, the limits for the classification into positive (+) and negative (−) according to the marker expression were determined in FlowJo® on the common data set of all patients using scatter plots (Supplement Figure S2). The fluorescence values for the markers used were exported separately for the patients in CR and patients with AD for all gates and then displayed as boxplots (Supplement Figure S3). The commonly used limits for the classification were drawn into the boxplots with the antigen expression levels and the immunological phenotype of the HSPCs was then determined for the respective gate depending on whether the mean value of the respective marker was above or below the limit.

2.7. Quantitative Comparison of t-SNE Plots Using the Pearson Correlation Coefficient

For the quantitative comparison of the t-SNE plots, the density matrix for the respective t-SNE plot was first calculated in R, e.g., for a single patient or for the cumulative image of all patients with AD. The density matrices were exported and the Pearson coefficients between the t-SNE plots were determined using Python. The code is available in the Supplement (Code S2). The density plots of all patients are shown in Supplement Figure S4.

3. Results and Discussion

3.1. Design of a t-SNE-Based Protocol for Multicolor Flow Cytometry Analysis

For the t-SNE analysis, a common data set of all FSC files from all patients was created, so that the t-SNE plots are comparable between the patients. The t-SNE analysis was carried out based on the expressions of CD34, CD38, CD45RA, CD123 and PD-L1. In general, the CD34 antigen permits the identification of hematopoietic stem and progenitor cells, while CD38 is considered a marker associated with differentiation [28,29]. The combination of these two antigens with CD45RA and CD123 permits a characterization and quantification within a BM of the HSC/HPC within a BM sample [30,31].

After the t-SNE run on the combined data set (Figure 2A), the contributions of the CR and AD patients were visualized separately to recognize their contributions to the combined t-SNE picture (Figure 2B,C).

By t-SNE, the cells are arranged in five islands (I–V) of different sizes. It becomes immediately apparent that the CR (in 2B) and the AD (in 2C) samples contribute almost complementarily to the combined representation (A). While in the CR patients, most of the cells are in the east part of the main island (I) plus in three of the four separated islands (II, III, V), the cells from the AD patients accumulate more to the west of the main island as well as in island IV. However, the populations are not mutually exclusive, as all cell types are present in both groups, albeit in some regions with strikingly different prevalence. This phenomenon is most likely not related to "contaminating" leukemic cells within the CR samples as the CR patients are MDR negative. In the t-SNE representation, the cells are distributed according to marker-specific gradients, as shown in the bottom row of Figure 2 D–H for the combined data set, where the black horizontal bars in the color scale column define the corresponding intensity intervals. The overlay of the different markers is shown separately for AD and CR in Supplement Figure S5, as well as an example for two patients from each of the groups in Supplement Figure S6.

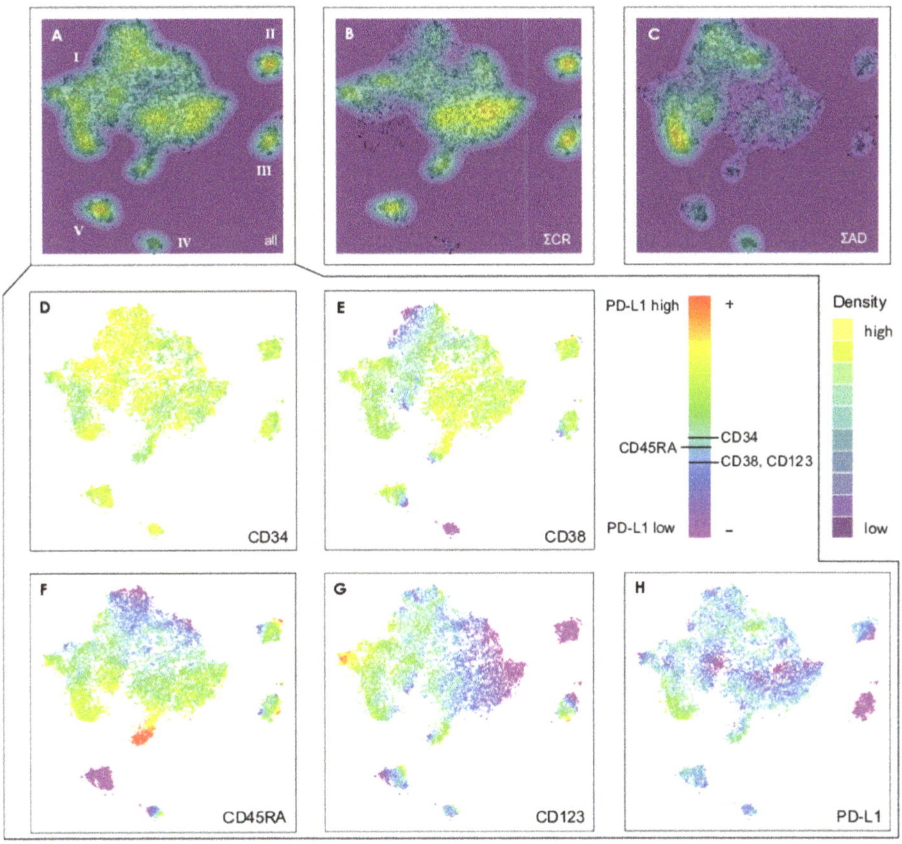

Figure 2. (**A**) t-SNE representation of the combined data set (cells of patients with active disease (AD) and in complete remission (CR)), and the contributions from patients in CR (**B**) as well as from the patients with AD (**C**). The color scale for (**A–C**) corresponds to the local density of cells in arbitrary units. In each t-SNE plot, the color scale starts at zero and is normalized to the maximum density in the respective plot. In (**D–H**), the prevalence of the various markers entering the t-SNE algorithm are reproduced, for CD34, CD38, CD45RA, CD123 and PD-L1. The color scale represents the expression level. The classification in terms of *positive* (+) and *negative* (−) expression is indicated by the black horizontal lines in the color bar.

As far as CD34 is concerned, the corresponding intensities in (Figure 2D) comprise only positive values since per definition only cells above the threshold of expression were included. Still, the islands in the t-SNE plot show quite varying CD34 expression levels. With respect to CD38, the cells are assorted from northwest to southeast of the main island with increasing expression level, while it is particularly low in island IV. A pronounced

CD38 gradient is visible in island III and V, indicating a sub-ensemble of cells undergoing some kind of development. The CD123 concentration, on the other hand, increases from east to west across island I, is almost zero in island II, and shows gradients within islands III and V. The CD45RA expression increases strongly from north to south. Finally, the PD-L1 expression, which is not considered in the assignment of the cells according to Table 3, is non-monotonously distributed across island I and takes characteristic low values in islands II and III.

We can therefore conclude that the gradients in the intensities of CD38, CD45RA and CD123 cause the main substructure in island I, while the expression levels of CD34 and PD-L1 refine this landscape.

3.2. Exemplifying Discussion of t-SNE Gates

For a more detailed study of the five islands, we have defined 27 gates in the t-SNE plot of the CR samples, each with a characteristic set of expression levels for the markers used (Figure 3A). This gate pattern was then transferred without modifications to the AD data as described in Section 2.5, shown in Figure 3B. The percentage distribution of the cells in the 27 gates for the three datasets (all patients, only CR, only AD) is shown in Supplement Table S1.

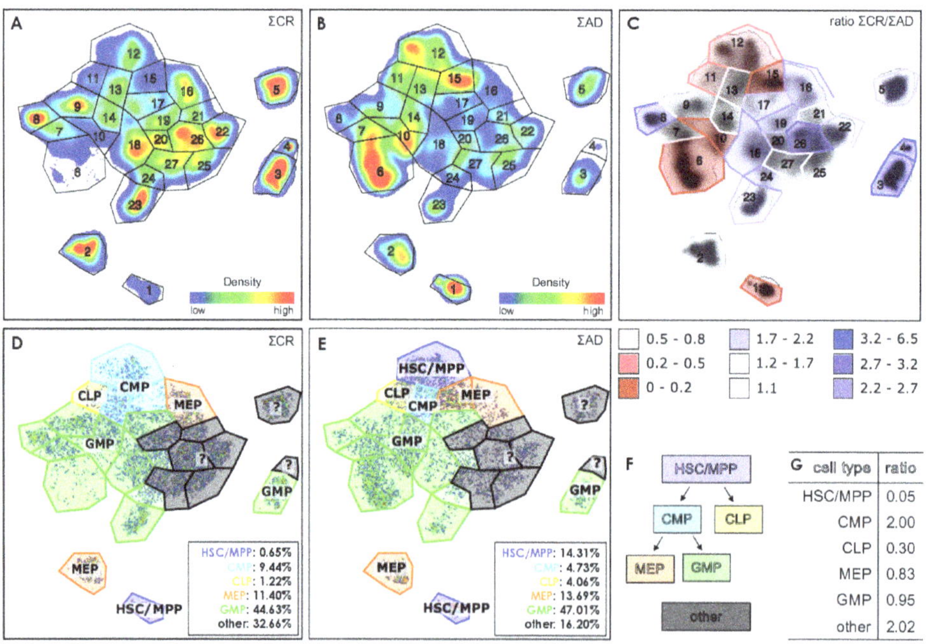

Figure 3. (**A**) Density-based gate definition on the t-SNE plot of the CR data set, performed by visual inspection; (**B**) Application of the gates on the AD data set; In (**C**), the ratio of the percentage distribution of the cells for the CR to the AD samples is given for each gate; The gates are inked in red if this ratio is smaller than 1, i.e., most of the cells in this gate come from AD samples, and blue for ratios larger than 1. The cell type identification for the gates is represented in (**D**,**E**) for the CR samples and for the AD samples, respectively; (**F**) Evolution scheme for the relevant cell types; The ratios of the percentage distribution of cells for the different types in CR samples vs. AD samples are listed in (**G**).

From that kind of visualization, eight gates emerge, namely gates 1, 6, 7, 10–13 and 15, in which the cells of patients with AD dominate. The remaining gates contain more cells from the CR patients, while within gate 14 the ratio is very close to 1.

The box plots of the 27 gates (Supplement Figure S3) were used to assign the cells within each gate according to the classification scheme as detailed in Table 3 and shown in Figure 3F. As can be extracted from Figure 3, the CR subsets are composed of 0.7% HSC/MPP, 9.4% CMP, 1.2% CLP, 11.4% MEP and 44.6% GMP. A proportion of cells (32.7%) could not be allocated according to the classification scheme. On the other hand, the samples of the patients with AD comprised 14.3% HSC/MPP, 4.7% CMP, 4.1% CLP, 13.7% MEP and 47.0% GMP with a proportion of 16.2% of the cells which could not be classified. Clearly, in comparison with the CR samples the AD samples show a significantly greater proportion of HSC/MPP as well as CLP cells, while there are smaller percentages of CMP cells as well as of those cells that cannot be allocated. The fractions of MEP cells are approximately equal for both groups.

Beyond this canonical classification, the t-SNE representation provides a rich substructure within the regions of particular cellular subtypes, reflecting subtle differences between the various populations. A complete delineation of all 27 gates would be certainly beyond the scope of our presentation. We therefore selected gates representing five characteristic cellular subsets, namely gates 1, 3, 6, 12 and 26, to illustrate the possibilities, but also the potential shortcomings associated with a t-SNE representation. The corresponding box plots are shown in Figure 4.

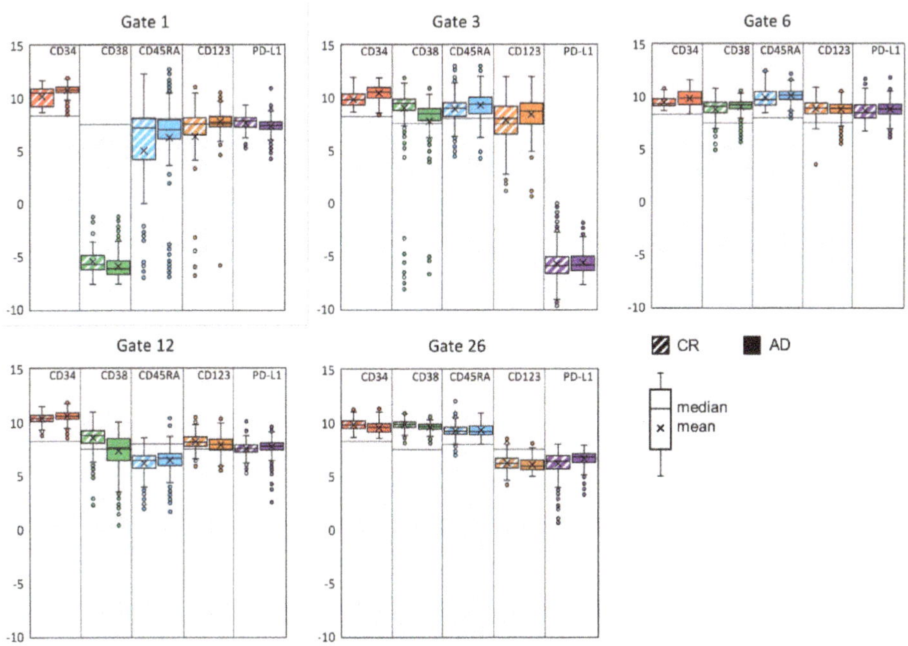

Figure 4. Box plots of the antigen expression levels (red: CD34, green: CD38, blue: CD45RA, orange: CD123, purple: PD-L1) within 5 selected gates from the 27 shown in Figure 3. The fluorescence data were scaled biexponentially in a preliminary step. The light blue and red background indicate the expression levels classified as *negative* (blue) and *positive* (red), respectively. The PD-L1 antigen was not used for the cell classification.

In general, a clear distinction of one gate from the others originates from a particularly low expression of one antigen within this gate.

We begin with gate 1, a well-separated island containing the great majority of HSC/MPP cells, as defined by the lack, or extremely low expression, of CD38. Since the differentiation between HSC and MPP is based on the CD90 marker (with CD38 negative in both cases) which was not included in our panel, we cannot distinguish these two cell types within our data set. As far as CD45RA and CD123 are concerned, their expression levels show a broad distribution spanning almost the full intensity range. Since AD cells contribute 88% to this population, this gate represents a predominantly leukemic-related gate and is compatible with the signature of leukemic stem cells. We note that the patients' ID and the group assignment were added to the expression matrix prior to the data merging, which allows us to determine the contribution of each patient group (CR and AD) to each gate. To relate these findings to the results of Kersten et al. [32], we looked at the expression level of CD45RA and CD123 on the CD34^{+} cells within this gate and found a greater expression of these antigens on the leukemic cells compared to those from the control samples. The aforementioned investigators examined the potency of CD45RA to specifically discriminate LSC and normal HSC for a better LSC quantification and found that in comparison to other markers such as CLEC12A, CD33 and CD123, CD45RA was the most reliable antigen. From a clinical point of view, it was interesting to note that CD45RA^{+} LSC tended to be associated with a more favorable cytogenetic/molecular marker constellation. However, it is important to recognize that the expression of CD45RA in AML is not as straightforward as in the immune system T cell subsets, and the functional implications can be quite diverse [33]. With regard to CD123, the study by Testa et al. based on the screening of CD123 expression in various hematopoietic malignancies shows that this antigen not only frequently expressed at high levels in AMLs but also on B-ALLs [34]. In an earlier report, they had explored a large set of AML patients and reported that 45% of these patients overexpress CD123 [35]. Similar to their results, Al-Mawali et al. [36] found that overall, this antigen was expressed in 37 (97%) out of 38 AML cases analyzed. The median expression of CD123 was 90% (range 21%–99%). Interestingly, the proportion of cells co-expressing CD123 on CD34^{+}/CD38^{-} leukemic stem cells was also 37 (97%) out of the 38 AML patients with a broad range from 0.0262% to 39.7% (median 0.8164, mean 4.45) at the time of diagnosis. These results are in line with our findings regarding the expression pattern of the CD34^{+}/CD38^{-} in our gate 1.

Gate 3, on the other hand, has been selected as an example for a cell cluster mainly encompassing CD34^{+} normal progenitor cells of GMP subtype, as the great majority of cells show a strong CD38 expression in the presence of CD45RA and CD123. Different from this normal signature, the few CD34^{+} cells falling onto this gate from patients with AD are lacking or only faintly expressing CD38 while the intensity for CD45RA and CD123 tends to be stronger in comparison to their normal counterparts.

Gate 6 resides at the edge of the main island with a proportion of 93% of cells from AD samples. Since the expression levels of all antigens are above the threshold of detection, they are formally classified as GMP. Still, a specific property of gate 6 in comparison to other gates containing GMP-like cells is that the PD-L1 expression level is relatively high—well above the levels in all other gates—and the levels of CD45RA and CD38 are also above the average observed for GMP cells. Furthermore, it is remarkable that these cells have a relatively low CD34 antigen expression and that all antigens display a relatively sharp intensity distribution with relatively low standard deviations. This suggests that there is no ongoing evolution among the cells in this gate. The CD34^{+} cells of this cluster were to some extent CD38^{+}, indicating a kind of "late" HSC on its way towards an abnormal stage of differentiation. As far as PD-L1 is concerned, our t-SNE-based data confirm the results obtained previously in a study focusing on the immunophenotype of T cells in patients with MDS and AML [37]. The mechanisms underlying T cell evasion to immune checkpoint inhibitors in acute myeloid leukemia have been recently elucidated by Gurska et al. [38].

We now take a closer look at the cells in gate 12, where two-thirds of the cells originate from AD samples. This gate represents a kind of borderline cell pool regarding the AD samples. In general, the expression level of CD45RA is very low, and the CD34 level is extraordinarily high with a relatively broad distribution of CD38 expression. While the cells in this gate from the CR patients are unequivocally classified as CMP, this is not possible for the AD samples, as they rather appear to be a mixture of CMP with HSC/MPP. This gate is, therefore, distinct from most other gates due to its internal shift of the t-SNE intensity between AD and CR samples. Accordingly, the AD cells with a lack or very low expression of CD38 reside more at the left side of this gate, whereas the cells of the CR samples preferentially group around its center. This indicates that the cells undergo an evolution from HSC/MPP when the disease is active, towards CMP during remission. The cluster contained within gate 12 is thus a nice example for the discriminative strength of t-SNE. In comparison to gate 1, the CR group shows a positive CD38 signal, while the AD group in this gate is CD38 negative, even though these values are significantly higher than in gate 1.

Gate 26 is dominated by a proportion of 68% of CR cells. It is a kind of enigmatic cluster, as this subpopulation of $CD34^{+}$ cells could not be allocated unequivocally according to the classification scheme as described in Figure 3F. Their characterization certainly requires an extended labelling for the lymphoid progenitor cells including antigen markers like CD10, CD7 or CD19. With regard to the leukemic cells contained within this cluster, aberrant marker constellations not related to the canonic scheme are also conceivable. Therefore, starting from our proof-of-principle marker panel, modifications including new monoclonal antibodies are necessary taking into account the steadily evolving knowledge and discovery of leukemic-related antigens and their co-expression patterns. Within this process, our efforts should be geared towards linking the phenotypical characterization to the molecular signature of the leukemic cells in the sense of a phenotype–genotype linkage. In the context of an antigen-targeted therapy, this could be helpful in defining the most relevant subset, i.e., leukemic stem cell, within the bulk mass of leukemic cells.

We proceed by drawing some general conclusions from these characteristic examples.

First, carefully selected additional markers can discriminate the cells to a deeper level. In that respect, we found a strong correlation between the expression level of the PD-L1 antigen and the percentage of predominantly leukemic cells in a particular gate. Considering that PD-L1 is an immunoprotective antigen, one may speculate that by increasing the PD-L1 expression during the evolution from healthy towards malignant, the cells protect themselves with respect to the immune system.

On the other hand, disregarding a relevant marker can leave the cell population within some of the gates unspecified, as has been seen from the example of gate 26. Moreover, since the markers used tend to show a continuous expression on this cell ensemble, only a few distinct islands became apparent in the t-SNE plot. This means that with manual density-based gating, the areas sometimes do not have a distinct border, which is reflected by the variability of the box plots for the respective gates. By using more markers that ideally exclude each other, better separation within the t-SNE plot [39] may improve subsequent gating or also enable the use of more automated density-based gating, such as DBSCAN [40] or HDBSCAN [41].

Furthermore, in our control samples of patients (CR), the composition of the cell ensemble was similar to our previous findings in normal donors showing a predominance of the GMP followed by the CMP, HSC and the MEP [42]. Subtle differences may be explained by the fact that in our study, BM samples of patients in CR served as normal controls, as BM from normal volunteers were not available. More specifically, normal hematopoietic cells that express high levels of CD34 lacking CD38 are considered stem cells, whereas those that express low levels of CD34 and high levels of CD38 represent more differentiated progenitor cells [43]. The lack of CD38 on leukemic blast cells is also characteristic for the leukemic stem cell [4].

3.3. Quantification of the t-SNE Representation

We proceed by asking to what extent a t-SNE-based assessment can be quantified. Based on quantitative evaluations already proposed [44,45], we suggest an analysis in terms of the Pearson correlation coefficient r (A, B), a well-established measure for the similarity of two pictures labelled A and B. The two pictures are composed of N pixels each, with pixel density A_j and B_j, respectively. The Pearson coefficient is defined as

$$r(A,B) = \frac{cov(A,B)}{\sigma_A \sigma_B} \quad (1)$$

with the covariance of the two pictures given by

$$cov(A,B) = \frac{\sum_{j=1}^{N} A_j B_j - \left(\sum_{j=1}^{N} A_j\right) \cdot \left(\sum_{j=1}^{N} B_j\right)}{N} \quad (2)$$

and the standard deviation of the pixel densities of picture X (X = A, B) given by

$$\sigma_X = \sqrt{\frac{\sum_{j=1}^{N} X_j^2 - \left(\sum_{j=1}^{N} X_j\right)^2}{N}} \quad (3)$$

For r (A, B) = 1, the two pictures are identical, and they are maximally different, i.e., their sum picture has a density of zero at all sites, for r (A, B) = −1.

The comparison of the two representations of the combined data sets, Figure 2B,C gives $r_{\sum CR, \sum AD} = 0.46$. Here, ∑AD and ∑CR denote the sum pictures of all AD and all CR samples, respectively.

Based on this value, we evaluate a classification protocol in which the t-SNE representation of a new sample is generated by first merging it with a reference plot composed of a sufficient number of samples, which is split up again into the two reference pictures ∑AD and ∑CR plus the contribution from the new sample labelled as N.

When we refer to the sample N including its classification, we label it by NCR or NAD, respectively. In the next step, the Pearson coefficients of N with the two reference pictures $r_{\sum AD,N}$ and $r_{\sum CR,N}$ are computed.

We have implemented this protocol with the present data set as follows. From our data set, we have removed each sample separately and considered the remaining combined pictures as reference pictures. We now treat the individual sample N as unknown and compute $r_{\sum AD,N}$ as well as $r_{\sum CR,N}$. This implementation is represented schematically in Figure 5.

The results are the values without parentheses listed in Table 4. For all but one of the twelve control samples, we measure $r_{\sum CR,NCR} > r_{\sum AD,NCR}$, with differences up to 0.47 for sample 20. Therefore, only in the case of $N = 18$, the sample would have been classified as AD in contrast to the correct classification. We will elucidate the reasons for the wrong classification below.

Regarding the identification of an AD sample, the situation is less clear. While samples 1, 12, 13, 14 and 16 show $r_{\sum AD,NAD} > r_{\sum CR,NAD}$ and are thus classified correctly, we observe that $r_{\sum AD,NAD}$ is just slightly smaller than $r_{\sum CR,NAD}$ in samples 10 and 17, but find dramatic deviations from the classification for samples 4 and 11, with r value differences of 0.68 and 0.42, respectively.

In order to investigate how stably the classification works with respect to multiple t-SNE runs, two further runs were performed, and the classification was carried out as described previously. The AD samples were assigned to the same group in all runs as described above. In two out of three runs, all CR samples except $N = 18$ were identified as CR samples and in the third run, all were classified as CR.

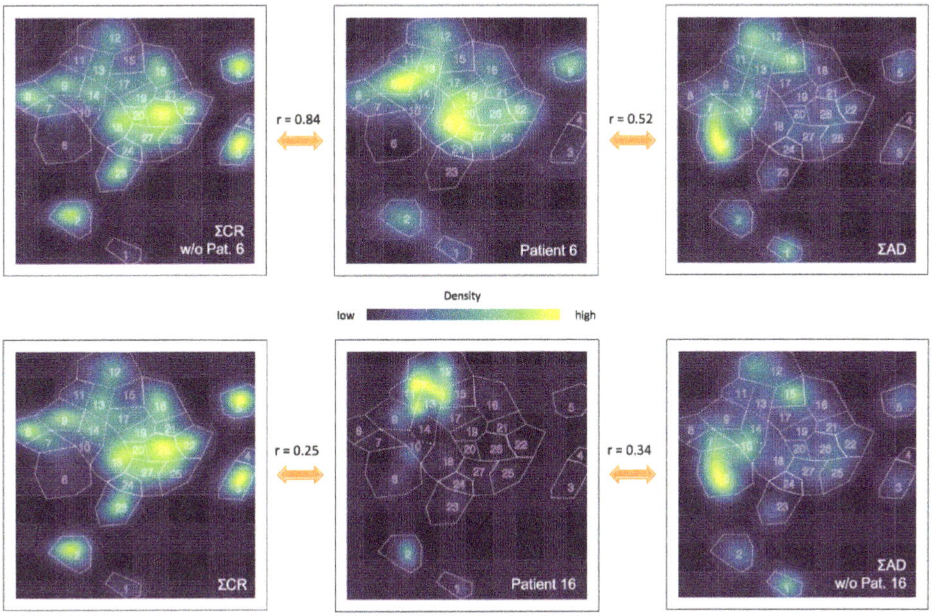

Figure 5. Graphic representation of the calculation of the r value as an example for two patients, 6 (CR group, top center) and 16 (AD group, bottom center). For patient 6, the density distribution is compared with those containing all patients with AD (top right) and for all patients of the CR group except patient 6 (top left). Likewise, we compare for patient 16 the density with the t-SNE plots containing all patients with AD except patient 16 (bottom right) and all patients of the CR group (bottom left). The orange arrows indicate which two plots were compared with each other. The r values are given in between the compared plots. The density is normalized to the respective maximum value of the plot. The gates are shown as an overlay for all plots.

The failure of allocating samples 4 and 11 asks for refined consideration. Despite their different subtype of AML, the leukemic cells show a monoblastic differentiation reflecting a more "mature" subtype not necessarily reflected by a particular CD34/CD38 subset. Since the cells of these misassigned patients represent a more mature type and the patients had only a molecular relapse, it is very likely that they could not be adequately assigned, since the leukemic cells were not contained within the $CD34^+$ cell population. For the detection of that kind of subtype, additional markers such as CD33 and CD14, for example, would still be necessary. Rather, the antigen markers used should show expression levels quite similar to those of the CR samples. Since it is of great interest to study how such a misallocation influences the t-SNE representation and the corresponding Pearson coefficients, we remove patients 4 and 11 from the ensemble and repeat the quantitative analysis. The modified t-SNE plot in comparison to the plots of these two patients, shown in Figure 6, illustrates the dissimilarity of the density distributions. The obtained r values are given in Table 4 in parentheses. First, we notice a striking decrease of $r_{\sum \mathrm{AD},\sum \mathrm{CR}}$ by 0.22. Apparently, these two samples have been responsible for a significant similarity between the two t-SNE representations, again indicating that samples 4 and 11 generate a pattern that resembles more CR samples than AD cases. Second, for all control samples, the values of $r_{\sum \mathrm{AD},\mathrm{NCR}}$ improve, some of them dramatically, e.g. for patient 9, r drops from 0.24 to −0.05. Third, however, we observe some effect on the $r_{\sum \mathrm{AD},\mathrm{NAD}}$ values, which change by no more than 0.19. It increases only for patients 1 and 13 but decreases for the remaining cases. This impressively shows how the lack of a relevant marker for clear characterization can lead to false similarities and thus impede the classification. It is therefore conceivable that with each additional diagnostically relevant marker the characterization becomes better, the t-SNE image becomes more differentiated and thus the classification becomes more reliable.

Table 4. The calculated r values are shown, in the second respective third column, the density of the t-SNE plot of the individual patient (first column) with AD is compared with the density of the t-SNE plot containing all patients with AD (∑AD) respective of the density of the t-SNE plot containing all patients of the CR group (∑CR). In columns 4 to 6, this is shown accordingly for the individual patients from the CR group (fourth column), in each case compared to the density of the t-SNE plot of the entire CR group (∑CR) or entire group of patients with AD (∑AD). In the seventh column, the r value for the comparison between the densities of the two t-SNE plots with all patients from the CR group (∑CR) and with all patients with AD (∑AD) is shown. The calculated r values from the analysis in which patients 4 and 11 were excluded from the AD group are given in parentheses in the respective column.

1	2	3	4	5	6	7
Pat.	**NAD vs. ∑AD**	**NAD vs. ∑CR**	**Pat.**	**NCR vs. ∑CR**	**NCR vs. ∑AD**	**∑CR vs. ∑AD**
1	0.23 (0.25)	0.17	2	0.46	0.17 (0.00)	0.46 (0.24)
4	0.12	0.80	3	0.53	0.41 (0.36)	
10	−0.01 (−0.2)	0.06	5	0.77	0.44 (0.23)	
11	0.29	0.71	6	0.84	0.52 (0.31)	
12	0.14 (0.13)	0.12	7	0.50	0.43 (0.41)	
13	0.05 (0.07)	−0.06	8	0.56	0.19 (0.02)	
14	0.22 (0.19)	0.14	9	0.61	0.24 (-0.05)	
16	0.34 (0.33)	0.25	15	0.70	0.55 (0.43)	
17	0.12 (0.11)	0.15	18	0.43	0.48 (0.42)	
			19	0.28	0.18 (0.16)	
			20	0.67	0.25 (0.01)	
			21	0.69	0.43 (0.28)	

As an evaluation of this proposed identification protocol, we note that the values of $r_{\sum CR,NCR}$ are large, a fact which quantifies the high similarity of the cell population in the CR stage. They are furthermore significantly larger than $r_{\sum AD,NCR}$ and we can thus conclude that the state of CR is safely identified and clearly distinguished from the AD state. Furthermore, it can be characterized by a single number with the t-SNE-based protocol, namely by $r_{\sum CR,N}$. The identification of an AD case, however, has remained ambiguous. All values for $r_{\sum AD,NAD}$ and $r_{\sum CR,NAD}$ are close to zero, with correspondingly small differences which in some cases would even indicate a remission. This situation reflects, in our opinion, the heterogeneity of the considered AD cases. Since these samples generate widely varying t-SNE patterns, they have relatively low r values and if such a reference pattern is compared with a new sample, a t-SNE-based identification is ambiguous if not impossible. On the other hand, we have seen in the example of patients 4 and 11 how the t-SNE-based identification can be improved considering blasts of a more "mature" type. We therefore expect that sufficiently differentiated t-SNE reference maps for AD subtypes will also allow the unique identification of an AD as well as its predominant blast population. To be on the safe side, we estimate that t-SNE subtype reference maps should be constructed from at least ten samples.

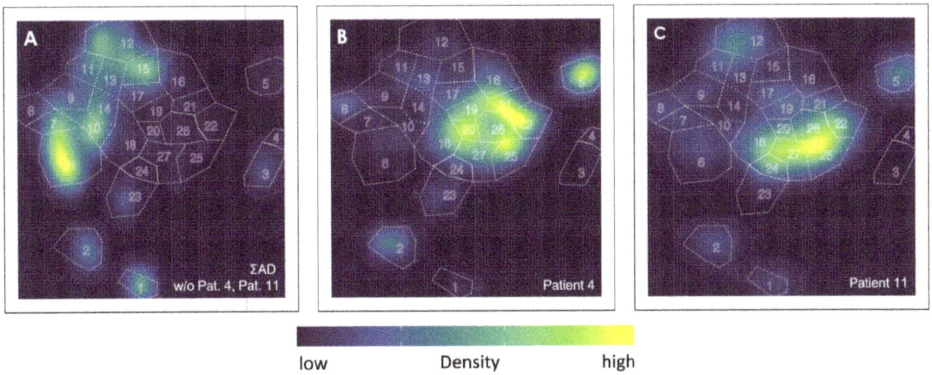

Figure 6. (**A**) Density plot of all patients with AD without patient 4 and patient 11; (**B**) density plot of patient 4, and (**C**) of patient 11. The gates are shown as an overlay in all plots.

4. Conclusions

Our study has evaluated the potential of t-SNE to represent multi-dimensional cell ensemble data from AML and MDS patients in a compact, two-dimensional form, thereby condensing the widely spread information of the scatter plots in a single picture. In order to develop this mapping into a diagnostically valuable tool, the mapping has to be capable of handling the specific challenges of such data sets, namely the large variance of the cell numbers per sample, the diverse manifestations of the diseases and their subtypes, as well as the unavoidable smearing of the map by the continuous cell evolution. Our protocol takes these initial conditions into account providing a meaningful clustering with gates containing diagnostically relevant cell populations. Additional markers may facilitate further dissection of otherwise homogeneous cell populations or hidden subtypes including rare cells not detectable in the two-dimensional scatter plots. We have also demonstrated how new samples may be diagnosed with the help of reference t-SNE patterns, based on similarities or dissimilarities, respectively. A quantified approach may comprise a statistical measure of the similarity of two pictures, like the Pearson coefficient. Our study shows that such an approach may work even for relatively poorly defined reference pictures. It is straightforward to adapt this concept to the evolution of the cell population of individual patients under therapy.

To facilitate the continued advancement of the t-SNE method, it is essential to establish a consistent and unchanging assignment of cells to a predefined t-SNE map representing "normality," as detailed earlier. This reference map should remain constant regardless of the introduction of new samples. Recent developments by Kobak, D. and Berens, P. [21] and Policar et al. [46] have introduced methods for embedding new samples into an existing t-SNE plot in single-cell transcriptomics data. The integration of corresponding tools in the mapping algorithm was, however, beyond the scope of the present work and will be the topic of future studies. Finally, it should be emphasized that these concepts are not limited to AML/MDS cells but can be applied to essentially all multidimensional diagnostic fluorescence flow cytometry data.

Supplementary Materials: The following supporting information can be downloaded at: https://www.mdpi.com/article/10.3390/cancers16071320/s1, Figure S1: Evaluation of the impact of varying the t-SNE parameters number of iterations and perplexity; Figure S2: Scatter plots to determine the classification limits; Figure S3: Box plots with antigen expression levels of all 27 gates; Figure S4: Density-plots of all patients; Figure S5: t-SNE plots of the common datasets of the CR and AD group; Figure S6: t-SNE plots as an example for four patients; Table S1: Percentage distribution of the calls in the 27 gates; Table S2: MRD analysis; Code S1: R script for the t-SNE analysis, calculation of the density matrices and some figures; Code S2: Python script for quantitative analysis of the t-SNE plots with the Pearson coefficient.

Author Contributions: Conceptualization: C.N., C.W., W.M., T.H. and R.H.; methodology: C.N., C.W., W.M., T.H. and R.H.; software: C.N. and C.W.; validation and formal analysis: C.N., C.W. and T.H.; investigation: C.N., C.W. and W.M.; resources: J.T., R.H. and T.H.; data curation: W.M., C.N., R.P.C. and P.S.J.; writing—original draft preparation, review and editing: C.N., T.H. and R.H.; visualization: C.N.; supervision: J.T., T.H. and R.H. All authors have read and agreed to the published version of the manuscript.

Funding: This research was funded by a grant of the Jürgen-Manchot-Stiftung, Düsseldorf.

Institutional Review Board Statement: The study was conducted in accordance with the Declaration of Helsinki and approved by the Institutional Ethics Committee of the University Hospital of the Heinrich-Heine-University (2020–1222) on 8 December 2020.

Informed Consent Statement: Informed consent was obtained from all subjects involved in the study. Written informed consent for publication was not explicitly asked for, as the participating patients agreed on the exploitation of the scientific findings for the public in general.

Data Availability Statement: Data can be provided by the authors upon reasonable request.

Acknowledgments: We thank Stefanie Geyh, Ramona Grothmann, Irmgard Hamann, Saskia Mayer and all participating physicians for their assistance in sample collection and preparation as well as all patients for participating in the study. C.N. gratefully acknowledges the support by the Jürgen-Manchot-Stiftung. W.M. gratefully acknowledges the support by the Düsseldorf School of Oncology (funded by the Comprehensive Cancer Center Düsseldorf/Deutsche Krebshilfe and the Medical Faculty HHU Düsseldorf).

Conflicts of Interest: The authors declare no conflicts of interest.

Abbreviations

AD	active disease
AML	acute myeloid leukemia
BM	bone marrow
CLP	common lymphoid progenitors
CMP	common myeloid progenitors
CR	complete remission
GMP	granulocyte-macrophage progenitors
GOI	gate of interest
HSCs	hematopoietic stem cells
HSPC	hematopoietic stem and progenitor cell
HSPCs	hematopoietic stem and progenitor cells
LSC	leukemic stem cell
LSCs	leukemic stem cells
MDS	myelodysplastic syndromes
MEF	marker expression function
MEP	megakaryocyte/erythroid progenitors
MPP	multipotent progenitor cells
PB	peripheral blood
PCA	principal component analysis
PD-L1	programmed death ligand 1
t-SNE	t-distributed stochastic neighbor embedding
UMAP	uniform manifold approximation and projection

References

1. Bonnet, D.; Dick, J.E. Human acute myeloid leukemia is organized as a hierarchy that originates from a primitive hematopoietic cell. *Nat. Med.* **1997**, *3*, 730–737. [CrossRef] [PubMed]
2. Döhner, H.; Wei, A.H.; Appelbaum, F.R.; Craddock, C.; DiNardo, C.D.; Dombret, H.; Ebert, B.L.; Fenaux, P.; Godley, L.A.; Hasserjian, R.P.; et al. Diagnosis and management of AML in adults: 2022 recommendations from an international expert panel on behalf of the ELN. *Blood* **2022**, *140*, 1345–1377. [CrossRef]
3. Tran, T.B.; Siddon, A.J. Molecular findings in myeloid neoplasms. *Int. J. Lab. Hematol.* **2023**, *45*, 442–448. [CrossRef] [PubMed]
4. Lapidot, T.; Sirard, C.; Vormoor, J.; Murdoch, B.; Hoang, T.; Cacerescortes, J.; Minden, M.; Paterson, B.; Caligiuri, M.A.; Dick, J.E. A cell initiating human acute myeloid-leukemia after transplantation into SCID mice. *Nature* **1994**, *367*, 645–648. [CrossRef]

5. Niu, J.L.; Peng, D.Y.; Liu, L.B. Drug Resistance Mechanisms of Acute Myeloid Leukemia Stem Cells. *Front. Oncol.* **2022**, *12*, 896426. [CrossRef] [PubMed]
6. Adan, A.; Alizada, G.; Kiraz, Y.; Baran, Y.; Nalbant, A. Flow cytometry: Basic principles and applications. *Crit. Rev. Biotechnol.* **2017**, *37*, 163–176. [CrossRef] [PubMed]
7. Liechti, T.; Roederer, M. OMIP-051-28-color flow cytometry panel to characterize B cells and myeloid cells. *Cytom. A* **2019**, *95*, 150–155. [CrossRef] [PubMed]
8. Fokken, H.; Waclawski, J.; Kattre, N.; Kloos, A.; Müller, S.; Ettinger, M.; Kacprowski, T.; Heuser, M.; Maetzig, T.; Schwarzer, A. A 19-color single-tube full spectrum flow cytometry assay for the detection of measurable residual disease in acute myeloid leukemia. *Cytom. A* **2023**, *105*, 181–195. [CrossRef] [PubMed]
9. Pyne, S.; Hu, X.L.; Wang, K.; Rossin, E.; Lin, T.I.; Maier, L.M.; Baecher-Allan, C.; McLachlan, G.J.; Tamayo, P.; Hafler, D.A.; et al. Automated high-dimensional flow cytometric data analysis. *Proc. Natl. Acad. Sci. USA* **2009**, *106*, 8519–8524. [CrossRef]
10. Verschoor, C.P.; Lelic, A.; Bramson, J.L.; Bowdish, D.M.E. An introduction to automated flow cytometry gating tools and their implementation. *Front. Immunol.* **2015**, *6*, 380. [CrossRef]
11. Moon, K.R.; van Dijk, D.; Wang, Z.; Gigante, S.; Burkhardt, D.B.; Chen, W.S.; Yim, K.; van den Elzen, A.; Hirn, M.J.; Coifman, R.R.; et al. Visualizing structure and transitions in high-dimensional biological data. *Nat. Biotechnol.* **2019**, *37*, 1482–1492. [CrossRef]
12. van der Maaten, L.; Hinton, G. Visualizing Data using t-SNE. *J. Mach. Learn. Res.* **2008**, *9*, 2579–2605.
13. Diggins, K.E.; Ferrell, P.B.; Irish, J.M. Methods for discovery and characterization of cell subsets in high dimensional mass cytometry data. *Methods* **2015**, *82*, 55–63. [CrossRef]
14. Saeys, Y.; Van Gassen, S.; Lambrecht, B.N. Computational flow cytometry: Helping to make sense of high-dimensional immunology data. *Nat. Rev. Immunol.* **2016**, *16*, 449–462. [CrossRef]
15. Mair, F.; Hartmann, F.J.; Mrdjen, D.; Tosevski, V.; Krieg, C.; Becher, B. The end of gating? An introduction to automated analysis of high dimensional cytometry data. *Eur. J. Immunol.* **2016**, *46*, 34–43. [CrossRef]
16. Hu, Z.C.; Bhattacharya, S.; Butte, A.J. Application of Machine Learning for Cytometry Data. *Front. Immunol.* **2022**, *12*, 787574. [CrossRef]
17. Amir, E.D.; Davis, K.L.; Tadmor, M.D.; Simonds, E.F.; Levine, J.H.; Bendall, S.C.; Shenfeld, D.K.; Krishnaswamy, S.; Nolan, G.P.; Pe'er, D. viSNE enables visualization of high dimensional single-cell data and reveals phenotypic heterogeneity of leukemia. *Nat. Biotechnol.* **2013**, *31*, 545–552. [CrossRef]
18. McInnes, L.; Healy, J.; and Melville, J. UMAP: Uniform manifold approximation and projection for dimension reduction. *arXiv* **2018**, arXiv:1802.03426.
19. Becht, E.; McInnes, L.; Healy, J.; Dutertre, C.A.; Kwok, I.W.H.; Ng, L.G.; Ginhoux, F.; Newell, E.W. Dimensionality reduction for visualizing single-cell data using UMAP. *Nat. Biotechnol.* **2019**, *37*, 38–44. [CrossRef]
20. Cheung, M.; Campbell, J.J.; Whitby, L.; Thomas, R.J.; Braybrook, J.; Petzing, J. Current trends in flow cytometry automated data analysis software. *Cytom. A* **2021**, *99*, 1007–1021. [CrossRef]
21. Kobak, D.; Berens, P. The art of using t-SNE for single-cell transcriptomics. *Nat. Commun.* **2019**, *10*, 5416. [CrossRef]
22. Wattenberg, M.; Viégas, F.; Johnson, I. How to use t-SNE effectively. *Distill* **2016**. Available online: https://distill.pub/2016/misread-tsne (accessed on 15 November 2023). [CrossRef]
23. Huang, H.Y.; Wang, Y.F.; Rudin, C.; Browne, E.P. Towards a comprehensive evaluation of dimension reduction methods for transcriptomic data visualization. *Commun. Biol.* **2022**, *5*, 719. [CrossRef]
24. Wang, Y.F.; Huang, H.Y.; Rudin, C.; Shaposhnik, Y. Understanding How Dimension Reduction Tools Work: An Empirical Approach to Deciphering t-SNE, UMAP, TriMap, and PaCMAP for Data Visualization. *J. Mach. Learn. Res.* **2021**, *22*, 1–73.
25. Kobak, D.; Linderman, G.C. Initialization is critical for preserving global data structure in both t-SNE and UMAP. *Nat. Biotechnol.* **2021**, *39*, 156–157. [CrossRef]
26. Finak, G.; Perez, J.M.; Weng, A.; Gottardo, R. Optimizing transformations for automated, high throughput analysis of flow cytometry data. *Bmc Bioinform.* **2010**, *11*, 546. [CrossRef]
27. Belkina, A.C.; Ciccolella, C.O.; Anno, R.; Halpert, R.; Spidlen, J.; Snyder-Cappione, J.E. Automated optimized parameters for T-distributed stochastic neighbor embedding improve visualization and analysis of large datasets. *Nat. Commun.* **2019**, *10*, 5415. [CrossRef]
28. Civin, C.I.; Loken, M.R. Cell-surface antigens on human marrow-cells—Dissection of hematopoietic development using monoclonal-antibodies and multiparameter flow-cytometry. *Int. J. Cell Cloning* **1987**, *5*, 267–288. [CrossRef]
29. Terstappen, L.; Huang, S.; Safford, M.; Lansdorp, P.M.; Loken, M.R. Sequential generations of hematopoietic colonies derived from single nonlineage-committed CD34+CD38- progenitor cells. *Blood* **1991**, *77*, 1218–1227. [CrossRef] [PubMed]
30. Lansdorp, P.M.; Sutherland, H.J.; Eaves, C.J. Selective expression of CD45 isoforms on functional subpopulations of CD34+ hematopoietic-cells from human bone-marrow. *J. Exp. Med.* **1990**, *172*, 363–366. [CrossRef] [PubMed]
31. Sato, N.; Caux, C.; Kitamura, T.; Watanabe, Y.; Arai, K.; Banchereau, J.; Miyajima, A. Expression and factor-dependent modulation of the interleukin-3 receptor subunits on human hematopoietic-cells. *Blood* **1993**, *82*, 752–761. [CrossRef]
32. Kersten, B.; Valkering, M.; Wouters, R.; van Amerongen, R.; Hanekamp, D.; Kwidama, Z.; Valk, P.; Ossenkoppele, G.; Zeijlemaker, W.; Kaspers, G.; et al. CD45RA, a specific marker for leukaemia stem cell sub-populations in acute myeloid leukaemia. *Br. J. Haematol.* **2016**, *173*, 219–235. [CrossRef] [PubMed]

33. Brod, S.A.; Rudd, C.E.; Purvee, M.; Hafler, D.A. Lymphokine regulation of CD45R expression on human t-cell clones. *J. Exp. Med.* **1989**, *170*, 2147–2152. [CrossRef]
34. Testa, U.; Pelosi, E.; Castelli, G. CD123 as a Therapeutic Target in the Treatment of Hematological Malignancies. *Cancers* **2019**, *11*, 1358. [CrossRef]
35. Testa, U.; Riccioni, R.; Militi, S.; Coccia, E.; Stellacci, E.; Samoggia, P.; Latagliata, R.; Mariani, G.; Rossini, A.; Battistini, A.; et al. Elevated expression of IL-3Rα in acute myelogenous leukemia is associated with enhanced blast proliferation, increased cellularity, and poor prognosis. *Blood* **2002**, *100*, 2980–2988. [CrossRef] [PubMed]
36. Al-Mawali, A.; Pinto, A.D.; Al-Zadijali, S. CD34+CD38–CD123+ Cells are present in virtually all Acute Myeloid Leukaemia Blasts: A promising single unique phenotype for minimal residual disease detection. *Acta Haematol.* **2017**, *138*, 75–181. [CrossRef]
37. Moskorz, W.; Cosmovici, C.; Jäger, P.S.; Cadeddu, R.P.; Timm, J.; Haas, R. Myelodysplastic syndrome patients display alterations in their immune status reflected by increased PD-L1-expressing stem cells and highly dynamic exhausted T-cell frequencies. *Br. J. Haematol.* **2021**, *193*, 941–945. [CrossRef]
38. Gurska, L.; Gritsman, K. Unveiling T cell evasion mechanisms to immune checkpoint inhibitors in acute myeloid leukemia. *CDR* **2023**, *6*, 674–687. [CrossRef] [PubMed]
39. Eshghi, S.T.; Au-Yeung, A.; Takahashi, C.; Bolen, C.R.; Nyachienga, M.N.; Lear, S.P.; Green, C.; Mathews, W.R.; O'Gorman, W.E. Quantitative Comparison of Conventional and t-SNE-guided Gating Analyses. *Front. Immunol.* **2019**, *10*, 1194. [CrossRef]
40. Ester, M.; Krigel, H.P.; Sander, J.; Xu, X. A density-based algorithm for discovering clusters in large spatial databases with noise. In Proceedings of the 2nd International Conference on Knowledge Discovery and Data Mining, Portland, OR, USA, 2 August 1996; pp. 226–231.
41. Campello, R.J.; Moulavi, D.; Sander, J. Density-Based Clustering Based on Hierarchical Density Estimates. In *Pacific-Asia Conference on Knowledge Discovery and Data Mining*; Springer: Berlin/Heidelberg, Germany, 2013; pp. 160–172.
42. Bruns, I.; Cadeddu, R.P.; Brueckmann, I.; Fröbel, J.; Geyh, S.; Büst, S.; Fischer, J.C.; Roels, F.; Wilk, C.M.; Schildberg, F.A.; et al. Multiple myeloma-related deregulation of bone marrow-derived CD34+ hematopoietic stem and progenitor cells. *Blood* **2012**, *120*, 2620–2630. [CrossRef]
43. Terstappen, L.; Huang, S. Analysis of bone-marrow stem-cell. *Blood Cells* **1994**, *20*, 45–63.
44. Ho, T.C.; LaMere, M.; Stevens, B.M.; Ashton, J.M.; Myers, J.R.; O'Dwyer, K.M.; Liesveld, J.L.; Mendler, J.H.; Guzman, M.; Morrissette, J.D.; et al. Evolution of acute myelogenous leukemia stem cell properties after treatment and progression. *Blood* **2016**, *128*, 1671–1678. [CrossRef]
45. Roca, C.P.; Burton, O.T.; Neumann, J.; Tareen, S.; Whyte, C.E.; Gergelits, V.; Veiga, R.V.; Humblet-Baron, S.; Liston, A. A cross entropy test allows quantitative statistical comparison of t-SNE and UMAP representations. *Cell Rep. Methods* **2023**, *3*, 100390. [CrossRef] [PubMed]
46. Policar, P.G.; Strazar, M.; Zupan, B. Embedding to reference t-SNE space addresses batch effects in single-cell classification. *Mach. Learn.* **2023**, *112*, 721–740. [CrossRef]

tomography

Article

Impact of Deep Learning Denoising Algorithm on Diffusion Tensor Imaging of the Growth Plate on Different Spatial Resolutions

Laura Santos [1,*], Hao-Yun Hsu [1], Ronald R. Nelson, Jr. [1], Brendan Sullivan [1], Jaemin Shin [2], Maggie Fung [2], Marc R. Lebel [2], Sachin Jambawalikar [1] and Diego Jaramillo [1]

1 Radiology Department, Columbia University Irving Medical Center, New York, NY 10032, USA
2 GE Healthcare, New York, NY 10032, USA
* Correspondence: ls3865@cumc.columbia.edu

Abstract: To assess the impact of a deep learning (DL) denoising reconstruction algorithm applied to identical patient scans acquired with two different voxel dimensions, representing distinct spatial resolutions, this IRB-approved prospective study was conducted at a tertiary pediatric center in compliance with the Health Insurance Portability and Accountability Act. A General Electric Signa Premier unit (GE Medical Systems, Milwaukee, WI) was employed to acquire two DTI (diffusion tensor imaging) sequences of the left knee on each child at 3T: an in-plane 2.0 × 2.0 mm^2 with section thickness of 3.0 mm and a 2 mm^3 isovolumetric voxel; neither had an intersection gap. For image acquisition, a multi-band DTI with a fat-suppressed single-shot spin-echo echo-planar sequence (20 non-collinear directions; b-values of 0 and 600 s/mm^2) was utilized. The MR vendor-provided a commercially available DL model which was applied with 75% noise reduction settings to the same subject DTI sequences at different spatial resolutions. We compared DTI tract metrics from both DL-reconstructed scans and non-denoised scans for the femur and tibia at each spatial resolution. Differences were evaluated using Wilcoxon-signed ranked test and Bland–Altman plots. When comparing DL versus non-denoised diffusion metrics in femur and tibia using the 2 mm × 2 mm × 3 mm voxel dimension, there were no significant differences between tract count (p = 0.1, p = 0.14) tract volume (p = 0.1, p = 0.29) or tibial tract length (p = 0.16); femur tract length exhibited a significant difference ($p < 0.01$). All diffusion metrics (tract count, volume, length, and fractional anisotropy (FA)) derived from the DL-reconstructed scans, were significantly different from the non-denoised scan DTI metrics in both the femur and tibial physes using the 2 mm^3 voxel size ($p < 0.001$). DL reconstruction resulted in a significant decrease in femorotibial FA for both voxel dimensions ($p < 0.01$). Leveraging denoising algorithms could address the drawbacks of lower signal-to-noise ratios (SNRs) associated with smaller voxel volumes and capitalize on their better spatial resolutions, allowing for more accurate quantification of diffusion metrics.

Keywords: diffusion tensor imaging; spatial resolution; denoising; pediatrics; growth; voxel size

1. Introduction

Diffusion tensor imaging (DTI) can characterize tissue microstructure and microarchitecture inside a voxel of interest [1], thus providing new information previously unavailable from conventional magnetic resonance imaging (MRI). DTI techniques have been rigorously studied and well described within the fields of brain, spine, and nerve imaging [2–6]. The use of DTI in the physeal–metaphyseal complex for prediction of pediatric growth has been studied for approximately 10 years [7]. Characterization of columns of cartilage and newly formed bone in the physis and adjacent metaphysis through tractography has proven useful for the determination of height gain and the evaluation of growth failure in pediatric subjects [7–13]. Tractography is the result of tensor estimation inside each voxel;

the tensor depicts the main direction of unrestricted water diffusion inside the columns running perpendicular to the growth plate [2,7].

Accurate quantitative DTI metrics rely on specific acquisition parameters and the achievement of satisfactory SNRs due to the intrinsic vulnerability of MR-DTI to artifacts caused by diffusion gradients and motion [1]. Ample studies have used DL to optimize DTI in the central nervous system, from basic denoising to using denoising algorithms to minimize the diffusion weighted data requirements, and even to asses sensitivity and specificity of the technique for classification of white matter disorders [14–18]. However, only a few studies have investigated the effects of varying acquisition parameters on DTI metrics in the orthopedic field, which were predominantly performed on adults or animal models, primarily focusing on adult muscle fibers or articular structures in rat knees [19–24]. These studies highlighted the sensitivity of knee connective tissues, specifically ligaments, to changes in spatial resolution [24]. Surprisingly, the rat knee physes demonstrated no significant variations in fractional anisotropy (FA) or mean diffusion across different spatial resolutions. Furthermore, the influence of these variations on physeal–metaphyseal tractographic diffusion metrics such as tract count, volume, and length remains unassessed [24].

Spatial resolution plays an essential role in ensuring the quality and reliability of DTI by influencing and modulating the occurrence of partial volume effects (PVEs) [25]. Larger voxel dimensions (associated with lower spatial resolution) offer higher SNRs but increase the probability of PVEs. In contrast, smaller voxel dimensions provide better spatial resolution and reduce the likelihood of PVEs at the cost of lower SNRs.

Our study aims to assess the impact of a deep learning (DL) denoising reconstruction algorithm applied to identical patient scans acquired with two different voxel dimensions, representing distinct spatial resolutions. We hypothesize that the denoising reconstruction algorithm will have a more pronounced effect on the smaller voxel dimensions, given their inherently lower SNR and consequent higher level of noise, which can be more effectively eliminated through the algorithm. Through this study, we hope to obtain valuable insights into the potential benefits of employing the denoising reconstruction technique in the context of varying spatial resolutions in DTI of the growth plate.

Our research presents a novel application of a deep learning (DL) denoising algorithm to DTI data of the knee growth plate. This application has not previously been explored or validated. The commercial software provided by the manufacturer was designed for denoising clinical structural images such as 2D T1 and T2 weighted scans. However, we will utilize a prototype denoising reconstruction algorithm applied to diffusion EPI scans, which is not yet commercially approved or tested for DTI scans. Our study will evaluate the effectiveness of this prototype denoising reconstruction in evaluating microstructural diffusion metrics, possibly demonstrating its potential to enhance the spatial resolution of DTI scans and offering novel insights into more reliable growth plate DTI metric changes over time.

2. Materials and Methods

2.1. Subjects

A prospective study was conducted at our tertiary pediatric center, in compliance with the Health Insurance Portability and Accountability Act and approved by the institutional review board, to evaluate growth using DTI of the knee. Healthy girls (8–15 years old) and boys (10–16 years old) (14 girls, 13 boys) during the pubertal and adolescent expected growth spurt, were recruited between August 2022 and November 2023. Informed consent and assent were provided by every parent/legal guardian and child, respectively before they participated in the study. The study was conducted in accordance with the Declaration of Helsinki, and the protocol was approved by the Ethics Committee of Columbia University Irving Medical Center (AAAS9882).

2.2. MRI

We performed two DTI sequences of the left knee on each child at our pediatric center at 3T. We used a multi-band DTI acquisition with a fat-suppressed single-shot spin-echo echo-planar sequence (20 non-collinear directions; b-values of 0 and 600 s/mm^2). Slice-selective gradient reversal was used for fat suppression. Two voxel dimensions were acquired on each subject, an in-plane 2.0 × 2.0 mm^2 with section thickness of 3.0 mm and a 2 mm^3 isovolumetric voxel, both without inter-section gap. We used a General Electric Signa Premier unit (GE HealthCare, Waukesha, WI, USA) with an 18-channel knee coil (Quality Electrodynamics, Mayfield Village, OH, USA). Parameters: repetition time (TR)/echo time (TE); 3000/51.7 ms; bandwidth 1953.12 Hz/pixel; parallel imaging factor, 2; signal averages, 5 for 600 b-value scans; matrix 128 × 128; field of view, 256 × 256 mm.

2.3. Intra-Voxel Tensor Visualization at Different Spatial Resolutions

To illustrate how acquisition at different spatial resolution (smaller versus larger 3D voxels) influences diffusion tensor direction, we employed MRtrix3 3.0.4 [26]. This software package is commonly used in diffusion imaging to visualize intravoxel tensors. The diffusion tensor is a mathematical model that characterizes the diffusion properties within a voxel, capturing the directionality and magnitude of water diffusion in three-dimensional space [27]. MRtrix3 uses the acquired MR-DTI data to estimate the diffusion orientation at each voxel [26], making it a useful tool to visualize and examine fiber tractography in the physes.

A diffusion-weighted image was selected as input for MRtrix3—2 mm × 2 mm × 3 mm volume. The volume was resampled into 2 mm^3 image using MRtrix3's regrid command. Confirmed successful resampling was achieved with the mrinfo command from MRtrix3 toolbox. Both the original and resampled images were saved into separate folders along with their corresponding .bval and .bvec files. For each corresponding image, the Dhollander algorithm was employed [28]. This method is instrumental in creating basis functions essential for estimating fiber orientation distributions (FODs) derived from the diffusion signal. Consequently, a model was established to project how the diffusion signal changes in different orientations and with varying diffusion gradients applied. The outputs from this algorithm provided the corresponding voxels used to build the basis function. Subsequently, the dwi2fod command from MRtrix3 toolbox was utilized to apply this basis function to each voxel in the input volume [29]. Finally, the mrcat command was used to concatenate these into a single volume, enabling the visualization of tensor ellipsoids that are representative of the fiber orientation directions.

2.4. AIRTM Recon DL Algorithm (GE Healthcare, Waukesha, WI)

The MR vendor provided a commercially available DL model with 75% noise reduction settings (Recon DL strength: High) applied. This model was applied on the same subject DTI sequences acquired at two different spatial resolutions (isovolumetric 2 mm^3 and 2 mm × 2 mm × 3 mm).

2.5. Segmentation

Using fiber tract reconstruction software, Diffusion Toolkit v. 0.6.4 (trackvis.org, Martinos Center for Biomedical Imaging, Massachusetts General Hospital, Boston, MA, USA) and Trackvis (FACT algorithm), the brightest voxel inside the physes was used as the reference point to locate the physes. A region of interest (ROI) was drawn intersecting the distal femoral and proximal tibial growth plates perpendicular to the long axis of the bone on every slice. ROIs were manually drawn in the AIRTM Recon DL reconstructed scans (n = 54 DL reconstructed scans) over the distal femur and proximal tibia physes. The same ROIs were applied to non-denoised scans (n = 54 non-denoised scans) for consistency. Diffusion metrics (tract count, tract volume, tract length, and fractional anisotropy (FA)) were obtained from the resultant tractography.

2.6. Signal-to-Noise Ratio Measurements

The signal-to-noise ratio (SNR) serves as an important metric when assessing the quality of DTI data. Enhanced SNR results in more dependable tensor estimation, consequently boosting the reliability and clarity of DTI-derived metrics, like FA, mean diffusivity, tract length etc. In MRI data, particularly DTI, noise can vary spatially due to elements like multi-channel coil sensitivity profiles, parallel imaging, and susceptibility artifacts. Traditional methodologies might not effectively capture this noise variance. To tackle this, SNR was calculated using the validated single-image set method applied by Wang et al. for the assessment of SNR in muscle diffusion tensor imaging [30]. Imaged volumes were paired with others that had proximally aligned diffusion encoding directions. We performed a subtraction of each DWI to yield initial noise image volumes. Each slice was transformed to k-space using 2D Fourier transformation, followed by Butterworth filtering and 2-D inverse transformation to image space, resulting in the final noise image volumes. Finally, the average noise variance was calculated from the same local ROI for both b0 and b600 images.

2.7. Statistical Analysis

We compared the tract count, volume, length and FA, derived from both reconstructed scans and non-denoised scans for femur and tibia, at each spatial resolution. Differences between spatial resolutions were evaluated using Wilcoxon-signed ranked test and Bland–Altman plots. All statistical analysis was performed on JMP®, Version <17>. SAS Institute Inc., Cary, NC, USA, 1989–2023.

3. Results

Twenty-seven subjects (14 girls, 13 boys) were included in the study; each subject had 2 DTI sequences to which a DL reconstruction algorithm was applied ($n = 27$ subjects, $n = 54$ non-denoised DTI scans, $n = 54$ DL reconstructed scans). In all subjects, isovolumetric 2 mm^3 DTI scans exhibited a visibly higher quantity of tensor ellipsoids compared to the 2 mm $\times$ 2 mm $\times$ 3 mm acquisition, a more defined diffusion direction was observed in the smaller voxel size, as shown in Figure 1. Fiber tract count, volume, and length were consistently larger in both the femur and tibia physes when using the isovolumetric 2 mm^3 voxel size in both the DL reconstructed scans and non-denoised scans, as shown in Tables 1 and 2.

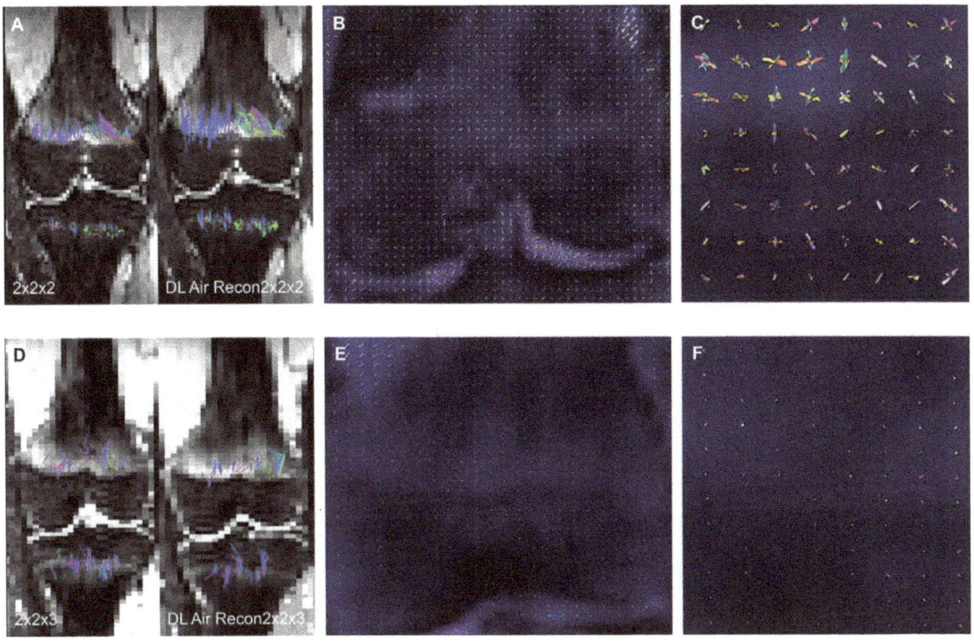

Figure 1. Same subject DTI acquisition using voxel sizes of (**A**) 2 mm^3 and (**D**) 2 mm × 2 mm × 3 mm. The image quality is visibly better when DL reconstruction is applied in the 2 mm^3 voxel size (**A**), with sharper bone contours and an increase in fiber tracts on both the femur and tibia. Conversely, in the 2 mm × 2 mm × 3 mm voxel size, both the non-denoised and DL denoise images (**D**) appear equally pixelated, and there are minimal changes in tractography. The tensor ellipsoid representation of intravoxel eigen vectors is substantially larger and more numerous in the 2 mm^3 voxel size (**B**,**C**) compared to the 2 mm × 2 mm × 3 mm voxel size (**E**,**F**).

Table 1. Denoised AIr Recon DL DTI metrics: 2 mm^3 versus 2 mm × 2 mm × 3 mm.

DTI METRIC	AIr Recon DL Isovolumetric 2 mm^3	AIr Recon DL 2 mm × 2 mm × 3 mm	*p*-Value
femur tract count	753.03 ± 409.17	410.37 ± 308.29	<0.0001 *
femur tract volume	12.47 ± 7.05	9.52 ± 7.17	<0.0006 *
femur tract length	8.83 ± 2.48	9.07 ± 3.93	0.9
femur FA	0.29 ± 0.04	0.25 ± 0.02	<0.0001 *
tibia tract count	341.62 ± 187.3	137.44 ± 177.31	<0.0001 *
tibia tract volume	5.34 ± 2.7	4.50 ± 8.36	0.0005 *
tibia tract length	5.36 ± 0.84	6.81 ± 2.42	0.002 *
tibia FA	0.34 ± 0.05	0.24 ± 0.03	<0.0001 *

Wilcoxon signed rank test; *p*-value < 0.05 was considered significant (*).

Table 2. Raw Data DTI metrics: 2 mm^3 versus 2 mm × 2 mm × 3 mm.

DTI METRIC	Raw Data Isovolumetric 2 mm^3	Raw Data 2 mm × 2 mm × 3 mm	*p*-Value
femur tract count	576.85 ± 257.21	388.62 ± 274.57	<0.0001 *
femur tract volume	9.3 ± 4.45	9.03 ± 6.4	0.13
femur tract length	6.11 ± 1.39	7.96 ± 3.25	0.001 *
femur FA	0.31 ± 0.04	0.26 ± 0.03	0.0001 *
tibia tract count	277.22 ± 133.89	123.44 ± 112.03	0.0001 *
tibia tract volume	4.33 ± 1.99	2.74 ± 2.2	0.0001 *
tibia tract length	4.26 ± 0.62	6.43 ± 1.75	0.0001 *
tibia FA	0.36 ± 0.06	0.26 ± 0.04	0.0001 *

Wilcoxon signed rank test; *p*-value < 0.05 was considered significant (*).

Applying the reconstruction algorithm led to an increase in femorotibial tract count, volume, and length in both DL reconstructed voxel dimensions compared to non-denoised scans (Tables 3 and 4). DTI metrics showed a greater increase in scans acquired using isovolumetric 2 mm^3 compared to the scans acquired with 2 mm × 2 mm × 3 mm voxel dimensions ($p = 0.04$). Diffusion metrics (tract count, volume, and length) derived from the DL reconstructed scans were significantly higher from the non-denoised scan DTI metrics in both the femur and tibial physes using the 2 mm^3 voxel dimension ($p < 0.001$ (Table 3, Figures 2 and 3).

Table 3. Raw data versus DL denoised DTI metrics: 2 mm^3.

DTI METRIC	Raw Data Isovolumetric 2 mm^3	AIr Recon DL Isovolumetric 2 mm^3	*p*-Value
femur tract count	576.85	753.03	<0.0001 *
femur tract volume	9.3	12.47	<0.0001 *
femur tract length	6.11	8.83	<0.0001 *
femur FA	0.31	0.29	<0.0001 *
tibia tract count	277.22	341.62	0.013 *
tibia tract volume	4.33	5.34	0.001 *
tibia tract length	4.26	5.36	<0.0001 *
tibia FA	0.36	0.34	0.005 *

Wilcoxon signed rank test; *p*-value < 0.05 was considered significant (*).

Table 4. Raw data versus DL denoised DTI metrics: 2 mm × 2 mm × 3 mm.

DTI METRIC	Raw Data 2 mm × 2 mm × 3 mm	AIr Recon DL 2 mm × 2 mm × 3 mm	*p*-Value
femur tract count	388.62	410.37	0.1
femur tract volume	9.03	9.52	0.14
femur tract length	7.96	9.07	0.001 *
femur FA	0.26	0.25	0.017 *
tibia tract count	123.44	137.44	0.14
tibia tract volume	2.74	4.5	0.29
tibia tract length	6.43	6.81	0.16
tibia FA	0.26	0.24	<0.0001 *

Wilcoxon signed rank test; *p*-value < 0.05 was considered significant (*).

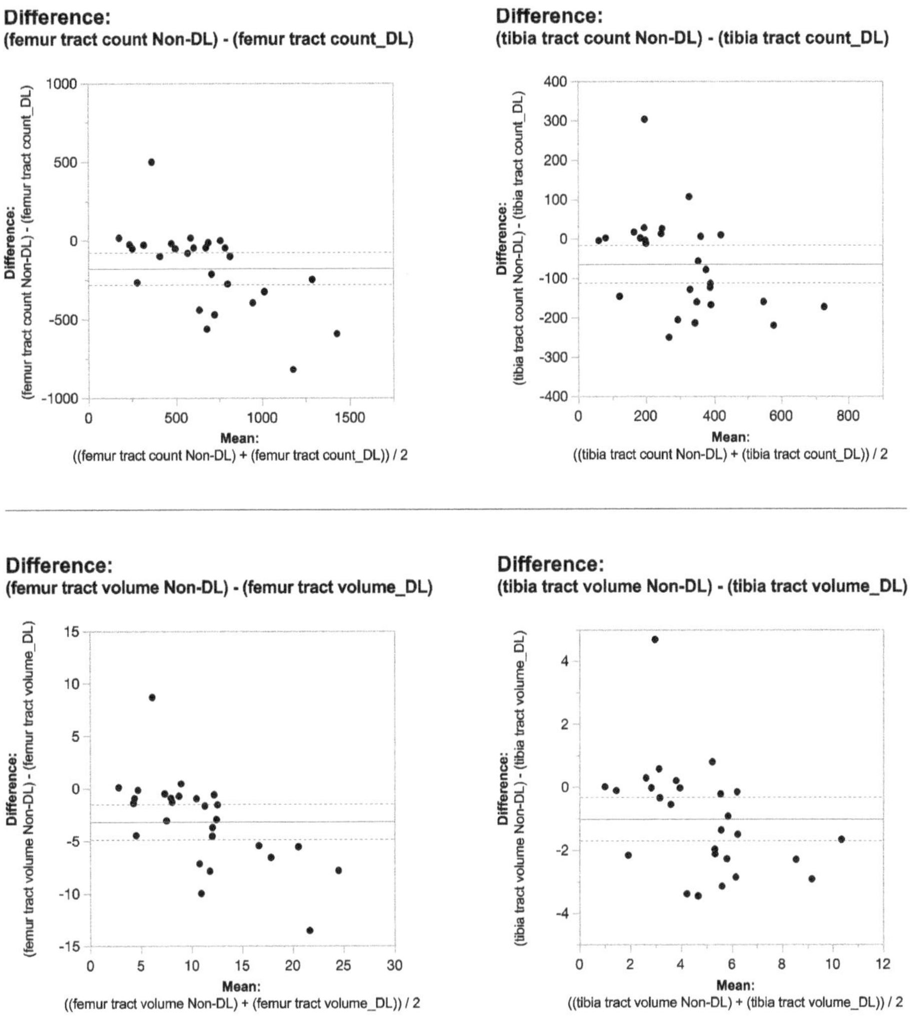

Figure 2. Bland–Altman plots regarding the difference in DTI metrics for same physeal ROIs between DL reconstructed-and non-denoised (Non-DL) image DTIs. The horizontal axis represents the mean of the two methods and the vertical axis, the difference between them. The solid line (red) shows the mean difference (close to zero) and the dashed lines show the 95% limits of agreement.

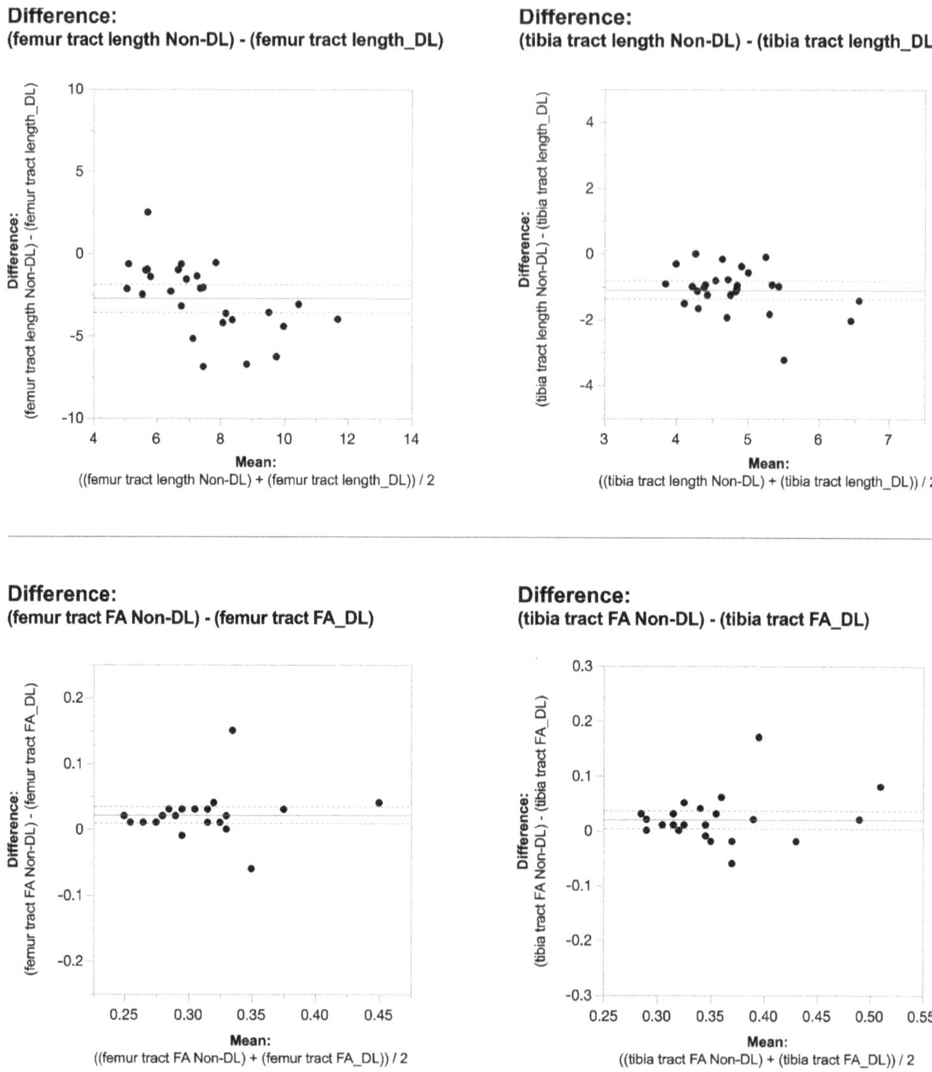

Figure 3. Bland–Altman plots regarding the difference in DTI metrics for same physeal ROIs between DL-reconstructed and non-denoised (non-DL) image DTIs. The horizontal axis represents the mean of the two methods and the vertical axis, the difference between them. The solid line (red) shows the mean difference (close to zero) and the dashed lines show the 95% limits of agreement.

When comparing DL versus non-denoised diffusion metrics in femur and tibia using the 2 mm × 2 mm × 3 mm voxel dimension there were no significant differences between tract count ($p = 0.1$, $p = 0.14$) tract volume ($p = 0.14$, $p = 0.29$), or tibial tract length ($p = 0.16$); femur tract length exhibited a significant difference ($p < 0.01$) (Table 4, Figures 4 and 5). DL reconstruction resulted in a significant decrease in femorotibial fractional anisotropy (FA) for both voxel dimensions ($p < 0.01$) (Figures 3 and 5). Figure 6A,B show DTI tractography changes in non-denoised and denoised 2 mm^3 versus non-denoised and denoised 2 mm × 2 mm × 3 mm in a 9-year-old girl and a 10-year-old boy.

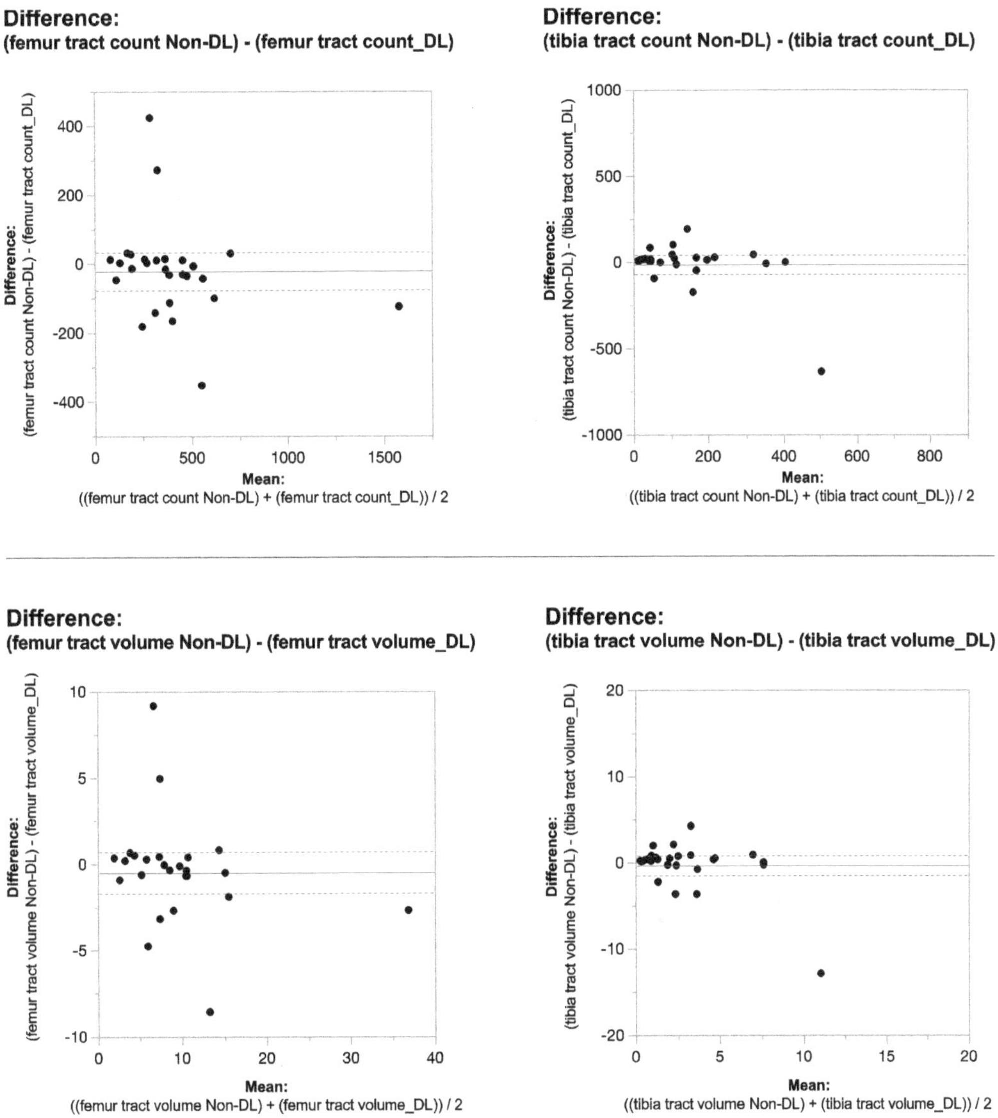

Figure 4. Bland–Altman plots regarding the difference in DTI metrics for same physeal ROIs between DL reconstructed and non-denoised (non-DL) DTIs. The zero value is indicated by the red line. The horizontal axis represents the mean of the two methods and the vertical axis, the difference between them. The solid line (red) shows the mean difference (close to zero) and the dashed lines show the 95% limits of agreement. The mean is very close to zero for most cases, indicating little difference between the methods, and the range of LoA is relatively small indicating a good numerical agreement in the methods among the majority of patients for the 2 mm × 2 mm × 3 mm voxel size.

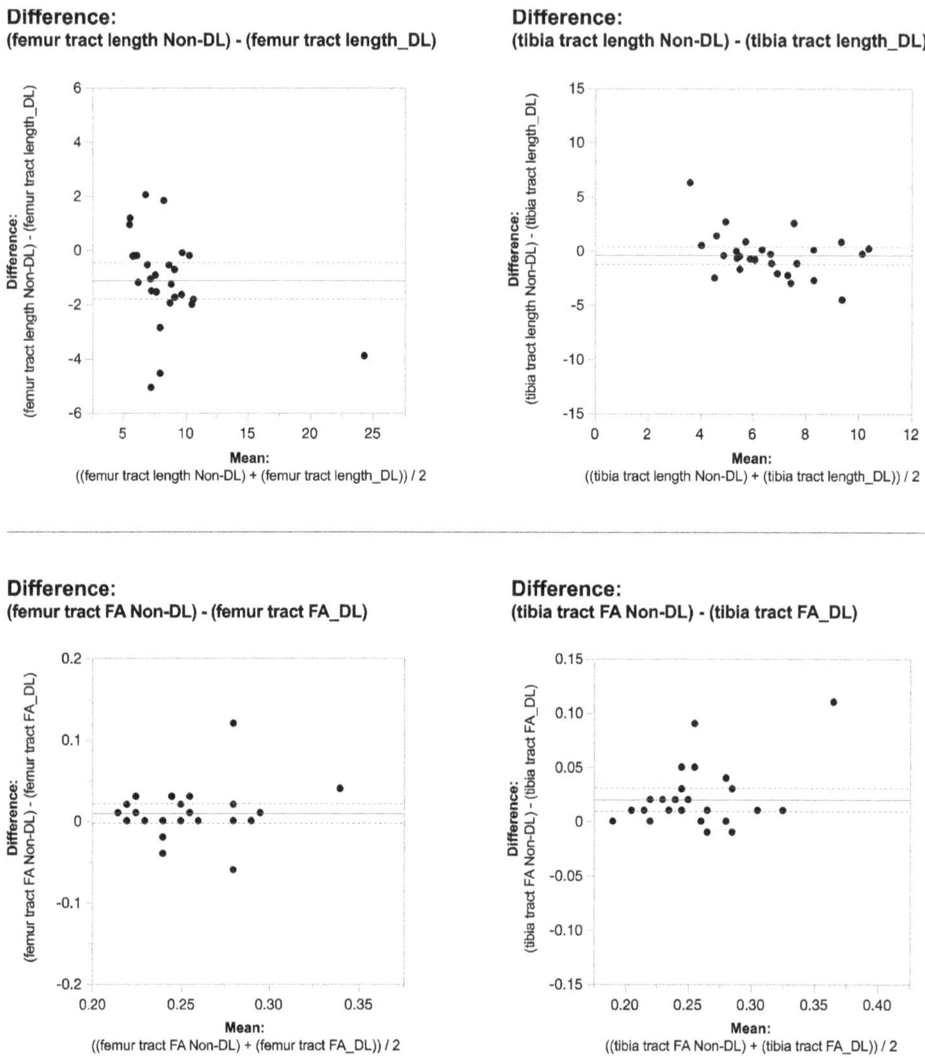

Figure 5. Bland–Altman plots regarding the difference in DTI metrics for same physeal ROIs between DL reconstructed and non-denoised (non-DL) DTIs. The zero value is indicated by the red line. The horizontal axis represents the mean of the two methods and the vertical axis, the difference between them. The solid line (red) shows the mean difference (close to zero) and the dashed lines show the 95% limits of agreement. The mean is very close to zero for most cases, indicating little difference between the methods, and the range of LoA is relatively small indicating a good numerical agreement in the methods among the majority of patients for the 2 mm × 2 mm × 3 mm voxel size.

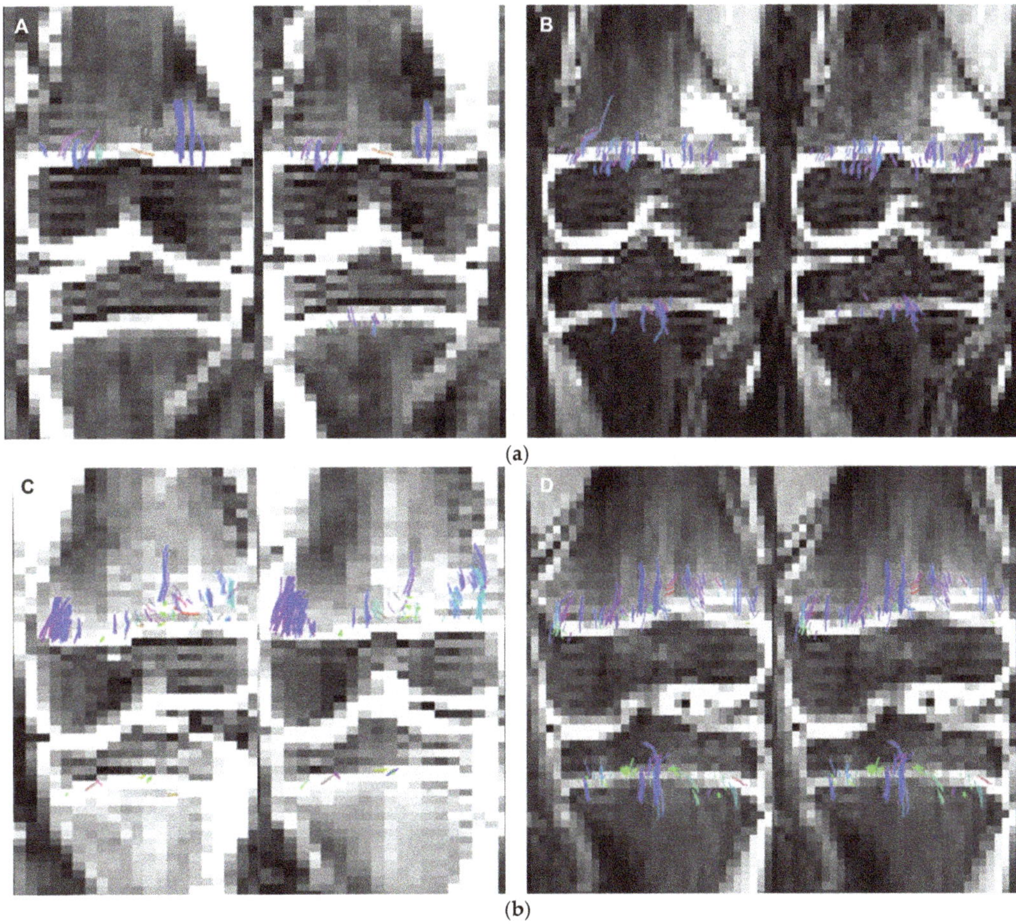

Figure 6. (**a**). 2 mm × 2 mm × 3 mm (**A**) non-denoised (**left**) and 2 mm × 2 mm × 3 mm denoised (**right**) versus 2 mm^3 (**B**) non-denoised (**left**) and denoised (**right**) in a 9-year-old girl. There is an evident increase in fiber tract on the denoised images acquired with a 2 mm^3, while denoised and non-denoised images are very similar using 2 mm × 2 mm × 3 mm voxel size. (**b**). 2 mm × 2 mm × 3 mm (**C**) non-denoised (**left**) and denoised (**right**), versus 2 mm^3 (**D**) non-denoised (**left**) and denoised (**right**) in a10 year-old boy. There is an evident increase in fiber tract on the denoised images acquired with a 2 mm^3, while denoised and non-denoised images are very similar using 2 mm × 2 mm × 3 mm voxel size.

SNR values were significantly higher in the non-denoised femur and tibia ROIs in the 2 mm × 2 mm × 3 mm voxel dimension compared to the 2 mm^3 voxel size ($p < 0.0001$), a pattern observed both before and after applying DL-denoising (Table 5). Following the application of DL-denoising, the femur and tibia ROI SNR on b0 exhibited a 39% and 41% increase in the 2 mm3 voxel dimension, respectively, in contrast to the 37% and 38% increase in the 2 mm × 2 mm × 3 mm (Table 5). Moreover, the SNR for the femur and tibia ROI on b600 experienced a 39% and 40% increase in the 2 mm^3 voxel size, whereas a more pronounced increment of 40% and 42% was observed in the 2 mm × 2 mm × 3 mm (Table 6).

Table 5. SNR values in the non-denoised femur and tibia ROIs: 2 mm × 2 mm × 3 mm voxel dimension compared to 2 mm^3 voxel size.

Voxel Size Comparison of ROI SNRs for b0 and b600 DTI with and without DL			
2 mm^3	**DL**	**Non-DL**	***p*-value**
femur_b0	44.2	31.7	<0.0001 *
femur_b600	18.9	13.7	<0.0001 *
tibia_b0	36.4	25.8	<0.0001 *
tibia_b600	16.6	11.9	<0.0001 *
2 mm × 2 mm × 3 mm	**DL**	**Non-DL**	***p*-value**
femur_b0	67.1	49.0	<0.0001 *
femur_b600	29.6	20.9	<0.0001 *
tibia_b0	54.1	39.3	<0.0001 *
tibia_b600	25.4	17.9	<0.0001 *

Wilcoxon signed rank test; p-value < 0.05 was considered significant (*).

Table 6. SNR Increase.

SNR Increase (Mean Difference SNR/Non-DL SNR)	2 mm^3	2 mm × 2 mm × 3 mm
femur_b0	0.39	0.37
tibia_b0	0.41	0.38
femur_b600	0.39	0.42
tibia_b600	0.4	0.42

4. Discussion

Voxel dimension is one of the factors that influences fiber tracking and the degree of PVEs [25]. Larger voxel sizes can contain more than one dominant diffusion orientation, thereby causing possible errors in estimating the primary tensor direction which ultimately impacts fiber tracking and the resultant diffusion metrics [1,25]. This may explain the markedly smaller tensor ellipsoid representations inside a voxel with a less defined direction observed in the larger voxel dimension (which results in lower microscopic resolution) compared to the smaller isotropic voxel size used (2 mm^3). The relationship between voxel resolution and image quality is evident in Figure 1, where the knee bones and physes are more sharply defined on the isotropic 2 mm^3 voxel size [31].

The use of larger voxels resulted in smaller fiber tract diffusion metrics. Larger 3D voxels can cover the entire field of view (FOV) and thickness with fewer voxels overall at a lower spatial resolution, the opposite is true when using smaller voxel sizes, hence fewer tensors overall are calculated on bigger voxels (as more area is covered by one 3D voxel and a single dominant tensor is calculated per voxel) accounting for lower tract count, length, and volume when using a larger voxel size.

We hypothesize the significant increase in both femur and tibia fiber tract count, volume, and length after denoising isovolumetric 2 mm^3 scans is due to the removal of intrinsically increased noise by the applied reconstruction algorithm. Diffusion metrics on the bigger voxel size in same subject scans, however, had better SNR and lower microscopic resolution, which was not improved with the reconstruction algorithm. This may possibly explain the small changes in tract count and volume in both physis after reconstruction algorithm application, which were not significant. The change in femoral tract length after denoising the 2 mm × 2 mm × 3 mm voxel size was small yet statistically significant, suggesting tract length is more sensitive to small SNR changes when compared to tract volume and tract count. In previous femur and tibia physeal DTI studies evaluating growth, tract length results have been variable: showing poor interobserver reliability compared to other fiber tract diffusion metrics (count, volume, length, and FA) evaluated in the same specimens [8], and it also did not show the expected change with age in animal models [8], which could suggest tract length is susceptible to small changes.

FA is the measurement of the degree of restricted water diffusion, calculated from the eigen value of the diffusion tensor [32]. In brain white matter, FA has been seen to decrease steadily after 20 years of age. Previous studies on the knee physes, have shown increasing FA with age as the closing physes, now ossified cartilage, show greater water diffusion restriction [7,9]. FA contrasts the principal eigenvalues of diffusivity and is considered to be limited by noise, making it susceptible to voxel size effects [33]. A previous study evaluating FA in brain white matter fiber tracts in different subjects using increasing voxel sizes found voxel size to significantly affect FA with smaller voxels giving higher FA values and reporting the impact was strongest at the highest spatial resolutions [33]. These mirrors our findings where same subject mean femur and the tibia FA values were 0.34 and 0.36 (2 mm^3) and 0.26 for both femur and tibia (2 mm × 2 mm × 3 mm).

High noise levels can bias DTI measurements, which can consequently produce errors in estimation of fiber tract parameters [34]. Low SNR can cause overestimation and underestimation of the largest and smallest eigenvalues, respectively [35]. A previous study evaluating DL noise reduction effects on FA in CNS structures in 20 patients, performed one image acquisition (NAQ1) versus five image acquisitions (NAQ5), and compared FA values after DL denoising was applied in NAQ1 [36]. They found FA to be overestimated when the number of image acquisitions was one (NAQ1), and after denoising NAQ1's FA decreased and came closer to that of NAQ5 [36]. In our study, a similar decrease in FA values on both spatial resolutions after application of the DL reconstruction occurred likely due to noise elimination and the resultant increased signal, with greater signal achieved in the intrinsically noisier 2 mm^3 spatial resolution explaining the greater drop in FA in the smaller voxel size (non-denoised versus denoised FA for the femur, 0.31 and 0.29, and the tibia, 0.36 to 0.34). This finding is also consistent with previous studies that low SNR leads to overestimation of FA on skeletal muscle [37], and the positive bias in FA values on peripheral nerve was removed after denoising [18].

We observed that the ROI SNR values for both the femur and tibia were higher when utilizing the larger voxel size (2 mm × 2 mm × 3 mm), irrespective of denoising. This aligns with the acknowledged trade-off between spatial resolution and SNR. Initially we anticipated a higher increase in SNR after denoising the smaller voxel dimensions (2 mm^3). The signal-to-noise ratio (SNR) quantitatively increased slightly more for the b600 images in the 2 mm × 2 mm × 3 mm voxel size than for the 2 mm^3. The 2 mm × 2 mm × 3 mm demonstrated higher SNR before denoising and the subsequent increase in SNR did not impact the metrics as observed in the smaller, noisier voxel dimensions.

The children imaged in this study are part of an ongoing longitudinal cohort, focusing on predicting growth in healthy children using DTI of the physeal–metaphyseal complex. As a standard practice, the left knee was chosen for imaging as it was more likely to be the non-dominant knee and less prone to injury, ensuring consistency and reducing potential confounding factors for analysis. No differences are predicted in the equally healthy right contralateral extremity in terms of SNR or imaging acquisition that would alter the findings on this study.

This study is limited by the small sample size used. To address this, the methods could be replicated in a bigger subject population to determine if the effects observed are consistent. The data can also be compared in groups of children in the clinical setting, with musculoskeletal disease for example and/or adult population. This study provides information to support the leveraging of denoising algorithms, such as AIRTM Recon DL, on DTI acquisition with smaller voxel volumes. The noise is reduced while preserving the higher spatial resolution, allowing for more accurate quantification of diffusion metrics.

This approach could address the drawbacks of lower SNR associated with smaller voxel volumes and capitalizes on their better spatial resolutions. This allows clinicians a clearer view of growth plate tissue microstructures without sacrificing signal. In addition, it may be possible to take advantage of better image resolution without a greater acquisition time which is essential when imaging pediatric subjects. In cases where there will be various same subject acquisitions, FA values are more reliable when they are denoised than when they are not.

Recognizing DTI's inherent sensitivity to noise, which significantly impacts the reliability of metrics such as fractional anisotropy (FA) and tract count, our discussion delves into the effectiveness of the DL denoising algorithm. This pretrained prototype is adept at generating noise-tolerant, reliable DTI metrics, a critical advancement for interpreting complex microstructures like the knee growth plate in the context of skeletal growth. This capability to reduce noise while preserving essential diffusion signals is pivotal, especially for the knee growth plate, where precise visualization and accurate tract counts and other diffusion metrics are crucial for assessing prediction of post-imaging growth and growth plate closure as well as positive and negative effect of treatments like growth hormone administration for potential growth disorders in pediatric patients. The significant improvements in DTI metrics following denoising underscore the impact of DL techniques in addressing DTI's traditional challenges. Given its fixed pretrained parameters, this inference network seamlessly translates across different body parts for DTI scans, negating the need for retraining. This characteristic is helpful in clinical and research settings, offering a stable, reliable tool to enhance DTI data quality.

5. Conclusions

A DL reconstruction algorithm may lead to significant increase in femorotibial DTI metrics (tract count, volume, and length) when applied on smaller voxel sizes, while causing a significant decrease in FA regardless of voxel dimension, larger cohorts should be used to asses validation.

Leveraging denoising algorithms could address the drawbacks of lower SNR associated with smaller voxel volumes and capitalizes on their better spatial resolutions, allowing for more accurate quantification of diffusion metrics.

Author Contributions: Author contributions included conceptualization by L.S., S.J., D.J. and J.S.; methodology by L.S., H.-Y.H., S.J., D.J., M.F. and M.R.L.; software development by R.R.N.J., J.S., M.F. and M.R.L.; validation by J.S., H.-Y.H. and B.S.; formal analysis by S.J., D.J., B.S. and H.-Y.H.; investigation conducted by L.S., H.-Y.H., R.R.N.J. and D.J.; resources provided by D.J., M.F. and J.S.; data curation managed by L.S., D.J. and B.S.; original draft preparation by L.S., B.S., M.F., J.S. and M.R.L.; review and editing performed by M.F., J.S. and M.R.L.; visualization by S.J. and R.R.N.J.; supervision overseen by D.J. and S.J.; project administration handled by D.J. and H.-Y.H.; and funding acquisition by D.J. All authors have read and agreed to the published version of the manuscript.

Funding: This research was funded by both the Society for Pediatric Radiology Research and Education Foundation and National Institutes of Health R01 grant number HD104720.

Institutional Review Board Statement: The study was conducted in accordance with the Declaration of Helsinki, and approved by the Institutional Review Board (or Ethics Committee) of Columbia University Irving Medical Center (AAS988 approved 27 March 2020).

Informed Consent Statement: Informed consent and assent was obtained from all subjects and legal guardians respectively, involved in the study. Written informed consent has been obtained from the patients to publish this paper.

Data Availability Statement: Data generated and analyzed during this study are not publicly available due to subject imaging containing protected health information but are available from the corresponding author on reasonable request.

Conflicts of Interest: Authors Jaemin Shin, Maggie Fung, and Marc Leber report a relationship with General Electric Company that includes employment. For the remaining authors, none are declared. The funders had no role in the design of the study; in the collection, analyses, or interpretation of data; in the writing of the manuscript; or in the decision to publish the results.

References

1. Soares, J.M.; Marques, P.; Alves, V.; Sousa, N. A Hitchhiker's Guide to Diffusion Tensor Imaging. *Front. Neurosci.* **2013**, *7*, 31. [CrossRef] [PubMed]
2. Ranzenberger, L.R.; Das, M.; Snyder, T. Diffusion Tensor Imaging. In *StatPearls 2023, November 12*; StatPearls Publishing: Treasure Island, FL, USA, 2024.
3. Chen, Q.; Abrigo, J.; Deng, M.; Shi, L.; Wang, Y.X.; Chu, W.C.W. Alzheimer's Disease Neuroimaging Initiative. Diffusion Changes in Hippocampal Cingulum in Early Biologically Defined Alzheimer's Disease. *J. Alzheimer's Dis.* **2023**, *91*, 1007–1017. [CrossRef] [PubMed]
4. Alexander, A.L.; Lee, J.E.; Lazar, M.; Field, A.S. Diffusion Tensor Imaging of the Brain. *Neurotherapeutics* **2007**, *4*, 316–329. [CrossRef] [PubMed]
5. Vedantam, A.; Jirjis, M.B.; Schmit, B.D.; Wang, M.C.; Ulmer, J.L.; Kurpad, S.N. Diffusion Tensor Imaging of the Spinal Cord: Insights from Animal and Human Studies. *Neurosurgery* **2014**, *74*, 1–8. [CrossRef] [PubMed]
6. Jambawalikar, S.; Baum, J.; Button, T.; Li, H.; Geronimo, V.; Gould, E.S. Diffusion Tensor Imaging of Peripheral Nerves. *Skelet. Radiol.* **2010**, *39*, 1073–1079. [CrossRef] [PubMed]
7. Jaimes, C.; Berman, J.I.; Delgado, J.; Ho-Fung, V.; Jaramillo, D. Diffusion-Tensor Imaging of the Growing Ends of Long Bones: Pilot Demonstration of Columnar Structure in the Physes and Metaphyses of the Knee. *Radiology* **2014**, *273*, 491–501. [CrossRef] [PubMed]
8. Kvist, O.; Damberg, P.; Dou, Z.; Berglund, J.S.; Flodmark, C.E.; Nilsson, O.; Diaz, S. Magnetic Resonance and Diffusion Tensor Imaging of the Adolescent Rabbit Growth Plate of the Knee. *Magn. Reson. Med.* **2023**, *89*, 331–342. [CrossRef] [PubMed]
9. Bedoya, M.A.; Delgado, J.; Berman, J.I.; Chauvin, N.A.; Zurakowski, D.; Ramirez-Grueso, R.; Ntoulia, A.; Jaramillo, D. Diffusion-Tensor Imaging of the Physes: A Possible Biomarker for Skeletal Growth-Experience with 151 Children. *Radiology* **2017**, *284*, 210–218. [CrossRef]
10. Delgado, J.; Jaramillo, D.; Chauvin, N.A.; Chauvin, N.A.; Zurakowski, D.; Ramirez-Grueso, R.; Ntoulia, A.; Jaramillo, D. Evaluating Growth Failure with Diffusion Tensor Imaging in Pediatric Survivors of High-Risk Neuroblastoma Treated with High-Dose cis-Retinoic Acid. *Pediatr. Radiol.* **2019**, *49*, 1056–1065. [CrossRef]
11. Duong, P.; Mostoufi-Moab, S.; Raya, J.G.; Jaimes, C.; Delgado, J.; Jaramillo, D. Imaging Biomarkers of the Physis: Cartilage Volume on MRI vs. Tract Volume and Length on Diffusion Tensor Imaging. *J. Magn. Reson. Imaging* **2020**, *52*, 544–551. [CrossRef]
12. Barrera, C.A.; Bedoya, M.A.; Delgado, J.; Berman, J.I.; Chauvin, N.A.; Edgar, J.C. Correlation between Diffusion Tensor Imaging Parameters of the Distal Femoral Physis and Adjacent Metaphysis, and Subsequent Adolescent Growth. *Pediatr. Radiol.* **2019**, *49*, 1192–1200. [CrossRef] [PubMed]
13. Jaramillo, D.; Duong, P.; Nguyen, J.C.; Mostoufi-Moab, S.; Nguyen, M.K.; Moreau, A.; Barrera, C.A.; Hong, S.; Raya, J.G. Diffusion Tensor Imaging of the Knee to Predict Childhood Growth. *Radiology* **2022**, *303*, 655–663. [CrossRef] [PubMed]
14. Tian, Q.; Li, Z.; Fan, Q.; Polimeni, J.R.; Bilgic, B.; Salat, D.H.; Huang, S.Y. SDnDTI: Self-supervised Deep Learning-based Denoising for Diffusion Tensor MRI. *Neuroimage* **2022**, *253*, 119033. [CrossRef] [PubMed]
15. Tian, C.; Fei, L.; Zheng, W.; Xu, Y.; Zuo, W.; Lin, C.W. Deep Learning on Image Denoising: An Overview. *Neural Netw.* **2020**, *131*, 251–275. [CrossRef] [PubMed]
16. Tian, Q.; Bilgic, B.; Fan, Q.; Liao, C.; Ngamsombat, C.; Hu, Y.; Witzel, T.; Setsompop, K.; Polimeni, J.R.; Huang, S.Y. DeepDTI: High-fidelity Six-direction Diffusion Tensor Imaging using Deep Learning. *Neuroimage* **2020**, *219*, 117017. [CrossRef] [PubMed]
17. Vidyadharan, S.; Prabhakar Rao, B.V.V.S.N.; Perumal, Y.; Chandrasekharan, K.; Rajagopalan, V. Deep Learning Classifies Low- and High-Grade Glioma Patients with High Accuracy, Sensitivity, and Specificity Based on Their Brain White Matter Networks Derived from Diffusion Tensor Imaging. *Diagnostics* **2022**, *12*, 3216. [CrossRef] [PubMed]
18. Sneag, D.B.; Zochowski, K.C.; Tan, E.T.; Queler, S.C.; Burge, A.; Endo, Y.; Lin, B.; Fung, M.; Shin, J. Denoising of Diffusion MRI Improves Peripheral Nerve Conspicuity and Reproducibility. *J. Magn. Reson. Imaging* **2020**, *51*, 1128–1137. [CrossRef] [PubMed]
19. Charles, J.P.; Grant, B.; D'Août, K.; Bates, K.T. Subject-specific Muscle Properties from Diffusion Tensor Imaging Significantly Improve the Accuracy of Musculoskeletal Models. *J. Anat.* **2020**, *237*, 941–959. [CrossRef] [PubMed]
20. Malis, V.; Sinha, U.; Csapo, R.; Narici, M.; Smitaman, E.; Sinha, S. Diffusion Tensor Imaging and Diffusion Modeling: Application to Monitoring Changes in the Medial Gastrocnemius in Disuse Atrophy Induced by Unilateral Limb Suspension. *J. Magn. Reson. Imaging* **2019**, *49*, 1655–1664. [CrossRef]
21. Mazzoli, V.; Moulin, K.; Kogan, F.; Hargreaves, B.A.; Gold, G.E. Diffusion Tensor Imaging of Skeletal Muscle Contraction Using Oscillating Gradient Spin Echo. *Front. Neurol.* **2021**, *12*, 608549. [CrossRef]
22. Zhao, Q.; Ridout, R.P.; Shen, J.; Wang, N. Effects of Angular Resolution and b Value on Diffusion Tensor Imaging in Knee Joint. *Cartilage* **2021**, *13* (Suppl. S2), 295S–303S. [CrossRef] [PubMed]
23. Wang, N.; Mirando, A.J.; Cofer, G.; Qi, Y.; Hilton, M.J.; Johnson, G.A. Characterization complex collagen fiber architecture in knee joint using high-resolution diffusion imaging. *Magn. Reson. Med.* **2020**, *84*, 908–919. [CrossRef] [PubMed]
24. Wang, N.; Mirando, A.J.; Cofer, G.; Qi, Y.; Hilton, M.J.; Johnson, G.A. Diffusion tractography of the rat knee at microscopic resolution. *Magn. Reson. Med.* **2019**, *81*, 3775–3786. [CrossRef] [PubMed]
25. Mukherjee, P.; Chung, S.W.; Berman, J.I.; Hess, C.P.; Henry, R.G. Diffusion Tensor MR Imaging and Fiber Tractography: Technical Considerations. *AJNR Am. J. Neuroradiol.* **2008**, *29*, 843–852. [CrossRef] [PubMed]

26. Tournier, J.D.; Smith, R.; Raffelt, D.; Tabbara, R.; Dhollander, T.; Pietsch, M.; Christiaens, D.; Jeurissen, B.; Yeh, C.-H.; Connelly, A. *MRtrix3*: A Fast, Flexible and Open Software Framework for Medical Image Processing and Visualisation. *Neuroimage* **2019**, *202*, 116137. [CrossRef] [PubMed]
27. O'Donnell, L.J.; Westin, C.F. An Introduction to Diffusion Tensor Image Analysis. *Neurosurg. Clin. N. Am.* **2011**, *22*, 185–196. [CrossRef] [PubMed]
28. Dhollander, T.; Raffelt, D.; Connelly, A. Unsupervised 3-tissue Response Function Estimation from Single-shell or Multi-shell Diffusion MR Data without a Co-registered T1 Image. In Proceedings of the ISMRM Workshop on Breaking the Barriers of Diffusion MRI, Lisbon, Portugal, 11–16 September 2016.
29. Tournier, J.D.; Calamante, F.; Connelly, A. Robust Determination of the Fibre Orientation Distribution in Diffusion MRI: Non-negativity Constrained Super-resolved Spherical Deconvolution. *Neuroimage* **2007**, *35*, 1459–1472. [CrossRef] [PubMed]
30. Wang, Z.J.; Yamamura, J.; Keller, S. Signal-to-noise Ratio Assessment of Muscle Diffusion Tensor Imaging using Single Image Set and Validation by the Difference Image Method. *Br. J. Radiol.* **2019**, *92*, 20190133. [CrossRef] [PubMed]
31. Mulder, M.J.; Keuken, M.C.; Bazin, P.L.; Alkemade, A.; Forstmann, B.U. Size and shape matter: The impact of voxel geometry on the identification of small nuclei. *PLoS ONE* **2019**, *14*, e0215382. [CrossRef]
32. Kaplan, P.E. Fractional Anisotropy. In *Encyclopedia of Clinical Neuropsychology*; Kreutzer, J.S., DeLuca, J., Caplan, B., Eds.; Springer: New York, NY, USA, 2011. [CrossRef]
33. Gattu, R.; Latif, Z.; Kou, Z.; Haacke, E.M.; Benson, R.R. Effect of Voxel Size on DTI Fractional Anisotropy. *Proc. Intl. Soc. Mag. Reson. Med.* **2009**, *17*, 3578. Available online: https://archive.ismrm.org/2009/3579.html (accessed on 21 June 2023).
34. St-Jean, S.; Coupé, P.; Descoteaux, M. Non Local Spatial and Angular Matching: Enabling higher spatial resolution diffusion MRI datasets through adaptive denoising. *Med. Image Anal.* **2016**, *32*, 115–130. [CrossRef] [PubMed]
35. Seo, Y.; Rollins, N.K.; Wang, Z.J. Reduction of Bias in the Evaluation of Fractional Anisotropy and Mean Diffusivity in Magnetic Resonance Diffusion Tensor Imaging Using Region-of-Interest Methodology. *Sci. Rep.* **2019**, *9*, 13095. [CrossRef] [PubMed]
36. Sagawa, H.; Fushimi, Y.; Nakajima, S.; Fujimoto, K.; Miyake, K.K.; Numamoto, H.; Koizumi, K.; Nambu, M.; Kataoka, H.; Nakamoto, Y.; et al. Deep Learning-based Noise Reduction for Fast Volume Diffusion Tensor Imaging: Assessing the Noise Reduction Effect and Reliability of Diffusion Metrics. *Magn. Reson. Med. Sci.* **2021**, *20*, 450–456. [CrossRef] [PubMed]
37. Froeling, M.; Nederveen, A.J.; Nicolay, K.; Strijkers, G.J. DTI of Human Skeletal Muscle: The Effects of Diffusion Encoding Parameters, Signal-to-noise Ratio and T2 on Tensor Indices and Fiber Tracts. *NMR Biomed.* **2013**, *26*, 1339–1352. [CrossRef] [PubMed]

cancers

MDPI

Article

Contrast Agent Dynamics Determine Radiomics Profiles in Oncologic Imaging

Martin L. Watzenboeck [1,2], Lucian Beer [1,2,*], Daria Kifjak [1,2], Sebastian Röhrich [1,2], Benedikt H. Heidinger [1,2], Florian Prayer [1,2], Ruxandra-Iulia Milos [1,2], Paul Apfaltrer [3], Georg Langs [1,2], Pascal A. T. Baltzer [1] and Helmut Prosch [1,2]

[1] Department of Biomedical Imaging and Image-Guided Therapy, Medical University of Vienna, 1090 Vienna, Austria; georg.langs@meduniwien.ac.at (G.L.); pascal.baltzer@meduniwien.ac.at (P.A.T.B.); helmut.prosch@meduniwien.ac.at (H.P.)

[2] Computational Imaging Research Lab, Christian Doppler Laboratory for Machine Learning Driven Precision Medicine, Department of Biomedical Imaging and Image-Guided Therapy, Medical University of Vienna, 1090 Vienna, Austria

[3] Zentralröntgeninstitut für Diagnostik, Interventionelle Radiologie und Nuklearmedizin, Landesklinikum Wiener Neustadt, 2700 Wiener Neustadt, Austria

* Correspondence: lucian.beer@meduniwien.ac.at; Tel.: +43-1-40400-48180

Simple Summary: Radiomics is the extraction of high-dimensional quantitative features from medical images. These features have shown potential to provide diagnostic and prognostic information in various oncological settings, but their reproducibility and stability can be affected by multiple physiological and technical factors. In this study, we assessed the effect of contrast agent timing on radiomics features using dynamic contrast-enhanced CT or MRI in prostate and lung cancers, whereby multiple images are acquired with a high temporal resolution after contrast agent application. We observed that a substantial number of radiomics features are contrast perfusion dependent and prone to bias. Therefore, when using contrast-enhanced scans for radiomics studies, patient-specific perfusion timing (e.g., test bolus protocol) should be applied.

Abstract: Background: The reproducibility of radiomics features extracted from CT and MRI examinations depends on several physiological and technical factors. The aim was to evaluate the impact of contrast agent timing on the stability of radiomics features using dynamic contrast-enhanced perfusion CT (dceCT) or MRI (dceMRI) in prostate and lung cancers. Methods: Radiomics features were extracted from dceCT or dceMRI images in patients with biopsy-proven peripheral prostate cancer (pzPC) or biopsy-proven non-small cell lung cancer (NSCLC), respectively. Features that showed significant differences between contrast phases were identified using linear mixed models. An L2-penalized logistic regression classifier was used to predict class labels for pzPC and unaffected prostate regions-of-interest (ROIs). Results: Nine pzPC and 28 NSCLC patients, who were imaged with dceCT and/or dceMRI, were included in this study. After normalizing for individual enhancement patterns by defining seven individual phases based on a reference vessel, 19, 467 and 128 out of 1204 CT features showed significant temporal dynamics in healthy prostate parenchyma, prostate tumors and lung tumors, respectively. CT radiomics-based classification accuracy of healthy and tumor ROIs was highly dependent on contrast agent phase. For dceMRI, 899 and 1027 out of 1118 features were significantly dependent on time after contrast agent injection for prostate and lung tumors. Conclusions: CT and MRI radiomics features in both prostate and lung tumors are significantly affected by interindividual differences in contrast agent dynamics.

Keywords: radiomics; machine-learning; contrast agent; lung cancer; prostate cancer

1. Introduction

Radiomics is the automated high-throughput extraction of a large number of quantitative features from radiologic/medical imaging data [1]. While radiomics features have successfully been applied in oncologic imaging to gain insights into tumor biology [2,3] and predict clinical responses and outcomes [4–7], the repeatability and reproducibility of such features is influenced by several patient-related and technical factors. For example, inspiration depth, examination protocol, slice thickness and the reconstruction kernel have all been shown to alter the extracted radiomics features [8]. Common practice is to exclude unstable features based on test–retest studies [9,10].

The administration of intravenous (i.v.) contrast agent may be another potential source of variation. In oncologic imaging, i.v. contrast agents are used in clinical practice to enhance the tissue contrast between the tumor and surrounding structures. However, the protocols for the timing between the start of i.v. contrast injection and scan acquisition are set individually at the respective institutions or between scanners within the same institution according to local preferences. In addition, even when standardized contrast injection protocols are used, the pharmacokinetics of the injected contrast material can vary substantially from patient to patient due to patient-specific factors, such as the cardiac output and blood volume [11,12]. While these factors might impair the stability of radiomics features extracted from contrast-enhanced computed tomography (CT) or magnetic resonance imaging (MRI) and can limit the use these data in quantitative research settings [13], at present, no comprehensive analyses of the magnitude of these effects exist. The lack of these studies may be the reason that, despite the potential effects of i.v. contrast agents on radiomics features, recently published guidelines on data acquisition and analysis do not address these effects and their consequences for the design of radiomics studies [13,14].

Therefore, the aim of this study was to evaluate the impact of contrast agents on the stability of radiomics features at different timepoints. For the purpose of this study, two tumor entities were examined: peripheral zone prostate cancer (pzPC) and non-small cell lung cancer (NSCLC); each of which are exemplified by distinct contrast agent uptake characteristics. pzPC is characterized by rapid intense contrast agent uptake compared to the surrounding non-tumoral peripheral zone tissue [15], while NSCLC shows a more heterogeneous and less intense uptake [16]. Dynamic contrast-enhanced computed tomography (dceCT) or MRI (dceMRI) images, which provided a high temporal resolution of radiomics profiles after contrast agent application (see graphical abstract), were included in this study. Seven distinct contrast agent phases were defined, and radiomics features which are dependent on contrast agent phase for NSCLC or pzPC tumors were identified. Furthermore, the dependency of contrast agent phases on machine-learning-based differentiation between healthy prostate parenchyma and pzPC lesions were evaluated. Finally, the influence of contrast agent phases on radiomics features could also be observed in dceMRI, where even stronger effects were observed.

2. Materials and Methods

2.1. Ethics

This retrospective study was approved by the Institutional Review Board of the Medical University of Vienna (Numbers 1764/2016 and 1789/2015) and performed in accordance with the Declaration of Helsinki. Written informed consent was obtained from all patients.

The cohort of pzPC patients has been described previously [10]. Briefly, patients without contraindications to MRI or CT of the prostate from December 2015 to May 2018, who presented with an MRI-proven suspicious lesion of the prostate (≥PI-RADS 3), and who were scheduled for MRI-guided transrectal biopsy, were eligible for this study. Exclusion criteria were a prior local therapy to the prostate (e.g., brachytherapy) or to other organs in the vicinity.

MRI protocols and target-MRI in-bore biopsy details were performed as described, and 14 patients with biopsy-proven peripheral zone prostate cancer, who received a multiparametric MRI within a 3-month time window of the dynamic contrast-enhanced CT and/or MRI were further included. For dceCT images, seven of these patients were excluded, since prostate tumors were too small to be reliably segmented on CT. For dceMRI images, five patients were excluded, since tumors could not be reliably segmented on dceMRI. Patient characteristics for the cohort of included prostate cancer patients are shown in Table 1.

Table 1. Prostate cancer patient cohort.

ID	Age (Years)	Tumor Location	PI-RADS	Gleason Score	Number of CT Scans	Number of MRI Scans
1	78	Left peripheral zone	5	3 + 4	26	70
2	75	Left peripheral zone	4	3 + 3	33	70
3	64	Left peripheral zone	4	3 + 4	26	21
4	57	Right peripheral zone	4	3 + 3	26	No MRI included
5	76	Left peripheral zone	4	3 + 4	33	70
6	71	Left peripheral zone	4	4 + 3	26	No MRI included
7	57	Left peripheral zone	4	3 + 3	26	No MRI included
8	76	Right peripheral zone	4	3 + 4	No CT included	70
9	63	Left peripheral zone	4	3 + 3	No CT included	70
10	84	Left peripheral zone	4	3 + 3	No CT included	70
11	58	Right peripheral zone	4	3 + 3	No CT included	70
12	63	Right peripheral zone	4	4 + 3	No CT included	70

The dceCT cohort of NSCLC patients consisted of nine patients with histologically verified adenocarcinoma or squamous cell carcinoma who were scheduled for adjuvant therapy.

Patient characteristics for the cohort of NSCLC patients imaged with dceCT can be found in Table 2.

Table 2. CT lung cancer patient cohort.

ID	Age (Years)	Sex	Histology	Target Lesion	Stage	Number of CT Scans
1	70	Male	Squamous cell carcinoma	Primary tumor	IV	20
2	77	Male	Squamous cell carcinoma	Primary tumor	IV	30
3	74	Female	Adenocarcinoma	Primary tumor	IV	20
4	61	Male	Squamous cell carcinoma	Lymph node metastasis	IV	30
5	60	Male	Adenocarcinoma	Lymph node metastasis	IV	20
6	67	Male	Squamous cell carcinoma	Primary tumor	III	30
7	81	Male	Squamous cell carcinoma	Lymph node metastasis	IV	30

An additional cohort of NSCLC patients, consisting of 21 patients, was imaged with dceMRI of the lung. If available, not only was the initial scan included, but so were follow-up investigations (between one and five investigations per patient), resulting in a total of 36 investigations being included in the final cohort (Table 3).

Table 3. MRI lung cancer patient cohort.

ID	Age (Years)	Sex	Histology	Target Lesion	Stage	Number of Visits	Number of Scans
1	55	Male	Squamous cell carcinoma	Primary tumor	IV	5	60–78 per visit
2	76	Male	Squamous cell carcinoma	Primary tumor	IV	2	76 per visit
3	43	Female	Adenocarcinoma	Primary tumor	IV	2	76 per visit
4	76	Male	Adenocarcinoma	Primary tumor	IV	2	76 per visit
5	66	Female	Squamous cell carcinoma	Primary tumor	IV	1	76
6	64	Male	Squamous cell carcinoma	Primary tumor	IV	2	74–76 per visit
7	70	Male	Adenocarcinoma	Primary tumor	IV	1	76
8	55	Female	Squamous cell carcinoma	Primary tumor	IV	2	76–78 per visit
9	67	Male	Squamous cell carcinoma	Primary tumor	IV	1	16
10	54	Male	Squamous cell carcinoma	Primary tumor	IV	1	76
11	74	Male	Adenocarcinoma	Primary tumor	IV	3	70–76 per visit
12	56	Male	Adenocarcinoma	Primary tumor	IV	2	76 per visit
13	69	Female	Adenocarcinoma	Primary tumor	IV	2	76 per visit
14	52	Female	Squamous cell carcinoma	Primary tumor	IV	3	76 per visit
15	81	Female	Adenocarcinoma	Primary tumor	IV	1	76
16	54	Male	Adenocarcinoma	Primary tumor	IV	1	76
17	64	Male	Squamous cell carcinoma	Primary tumor	IV	1	76
18	68	Female	Squamous cell carcinoma	Primary tumor	IV	1	76
19	50	Female	Adenocarcinoma	Primary tumor	IV	1	70
20	74	Male	Adenocarcinoma	Primary tumor	IV	1	76
21	60	Female	Squamous cell carcinoma	Primary tumor	IV	1	76

2.2. Inclusion and Exclusion Criteria

For NSCLC patients the inclusion criteria were as follows: an identifiable thoracic target lesion larger than 1 cm and the ability to undergo a CT examination. Exclusion criteria were radiotherapy within three months of inclusion or low image quality ($n = 2$).

For pzPC patients the inclusion criteria were as follows: an identifiable thoracic target lesion larger than 0.5 cm and the ability to undergo a CT examination. Exclusion criteria were previous therapy or low image quality.

2.3. Dynamic Contrast-Enhanced CT Imaging Protocol

A SOMATOM Definition Flash CT scanner (Siemens Healthineers, Erlangen, Germany) was utilized for all patients. An a priori performed non-contrast pelvis CT (for pzPC patients) or thoracic CT (for NSCLC patients) was used for planning, in which the prostate or index lesion (for NSCLC patients) was delineated. After i.v. injection of 40 mL of non-ionic iodinated contrast agent at an injection rate of 5 mL/second (Iomeron 400, Bracco Imaging, S.p.A., Rome, Italy), followed by a saline chaser of 40 mL, 26–33 scans of the prostate or 20–30 scans of the tumor in the thorax were acquired. The first 20 examinations were performed at 1.5 s intervals, and the following scans at 3 s intervals, to reduce the radiation dose after the initial arterial influx. A tube voltage of 80 or 90 kVp was used, depending on patient body weight. Slice width was 5 mm for prostate scans and 1.5 mm for lung scans, rotation time 0.25 s, slice collimation 48 × 1.2 mm; and scan length was 114 mm for prostate scans, and 110 or 174 mm for lung scans.

2.4. Dynamic Contrast-Enhanced MRI Imaging Protocol for pzPC Patients

Patients with pzCT were scanned on a Magnetom Trio (A Tim; Siemens Healthineers, Erlangen, Germany) scanner. Dynamic contrast-enhanced (DCE) MRI was acquired using a three-dimensional, T1-weighted gradient echo sequence (TWIST) with a temporal resolution of 4.22 s (FOV 260 mm; matrix 160). Before dynamic scanning, T1-mapping sequences using the variable flip-angle method were applied. Gadoterate meglumine (Gd-DOTA, Dotarem®, Guerbet, France) was injected after three baseline scans intravenously as a bolus (0.2 mL/kg body weight) using a power injector at a flow rate of 4 mL/s, followed by a flush of 20 mL of saline solution.

2.5. Dynamic Contrast-Enhanced MRI Imaging Protocol for NSCLC Patients

A SiemensBiograph mMR 3T system (Tim Trio, Siemens Healthineers, Erlangen, Germany) was used to scan NSCLC patients. Dynamic contrast-enhanced (DCE) MRI was acquired using a three-dimensional, T1-weighted gradient echo sequence (TWIST) with a temporal resolution of 11.025 s (FOV 280 mm; matrix 192). Before dynamic scanning, T1-mapping sequences using the variable flip-angle method were applied. Gadoterate meglumine (Gd-DOTA, Dotarem®, Guerbet, France) was injected after three baseline scans intravenously as a bolus (0.2 mL/kg body weight) using a power injector at a flow rate of 5 mL/s, followed by a flush of 40 mL of saline solution.

2.6. Region-of-Interest Segmentation

Region-of-interest (ROI) segmentation was performed using a Microsoft Advanced Imaging Labeler (Microsoft, 2022, Redmond, Washington, DC, USA) by a radiology resident (M.W., with three years' experience in oncologic imaging) under the supervision of a board certified radiologist (L.B., with nine years' experience in oncologic imaging). For pzPC patients, tumors were segmented on consecutive slices in venous phase scans. To investigate whether the dynamics of radiomics features after contrast agent injection differed between tumors and healthy tissue, for pzPC patients imaged with dceCT, an additional ROI was placed in the contralateral, tumor-free prostatic hemisphere. For both dceCT and dceMRI of pzPC patients, a cylindric ROI was placed in the common femoral artery lumen. For NSCLC patients, the best visible (index) lesion was segmented in a venous phase scan, which was the primary tumor in four patients, and a lymph node metastasis in three patients imaged with dceCT, and the primary tumor in all patients was imaged with dceMRI. Analogous to pzPC patients, an additional ROI was placed in the descending aortic lumen. For each patient, masks were propagated across different dynamic contrast CT or MRI series. Propagated masks were inspected visually to ensure that tumors, the healthy prostate parenchyma and the arterial lumen were accurately delineated in all series. Segmentation masks were exported as DICOM-RT files. Both images and segmentation masks were subsequently converted to an NRRD file format using the open source software plastimatch (version 1.9.0, The General Hospital Corporation, Inc., Boston, MA, USA).

2.7. Radiomics Feature Extraction

Pyradiomics [17] version 3.0.1 running under Python 3.7.1 was used to extract radiomics features from segmented ROIs. Example settings for CT images, included in the pyradiomics library (specified in the file exampleCT.yaml), were used for feature extractions, and shape features were a priori excluded from the study, since regions were propagated across different dynamic contrast series, and therefore shape features were not expected to change across series. The binWidth parameter (specifying the number of bins for image discretization) was set to 25, the voxelArrayShift parameter to 1000 (to prevent negative values from being squared), sitkBSpline was used for image resampling, resampledPixelSpacing was defined as [1, 1, 1], and padDistance as 10. A total of 13 different filtering transformations were applied to the original images: Laplacian of Gaussian (LoG) edge enhancement filters, with sigma values (defining the coarseness of the emphasized texture) set to 1, 2, 3, 4 and 5 mm; and wavelet filtering for all possible combinations of applying High or Low pass filters along the x, y and z axes, which resulted in eight (23) different combinations. Including the original unfiltered CT scans, this resulted in 14 different sets of images, from which 18 first-order, 22 gray-level co-occurrence matrix (GLCM), 14 gray-level dependence matrix (GLDM), 16 gray-level run length matrix (GLRLM) and 16 gray-level size zone matrix (GLSZM) features (a total of 14 × 86 = 1204 features) were extracted.

For MR images, example settings specified in the file exampleMR_3 mm.yaml were used for feature extractions. The binWidth parameter was set to 5, the voxelArrayShift parameter to 300, sitkBSpline was used for image resampling, resampledPixelSpacing was defined as [2, 2, 2], normalize was set to true, and normalizeScale to 100. A total of 12 filtering transformations (LoG edge enhancement filters, with sigma values set to 2, 3, 4, and 5 mm, and eight different combinations of wavelet filtering with High or Low pass filters) were applied to the original images (13 different sets of images, including the original MRI scans). From the resulting images, 18 first-order, 22 GLCM, 14 GLDM, 16 GLRLM and 16 gray-level size zone matrix (GLSZM) features (a total of 13 × 86 = 1118 features) were extracted.

2.8. Statistical Analysis

All statistical analyses were performed using R version 4.0.5 (R Foundation for Statistical Computing, Vienna, Austria) or Python 3.7.1. Custom R functions were used to define contrast agent phases according to arterial lumen median voxel intensity (see Results section). To assess the temporal dynamics after contrast agent injection, linear mixed models (R package lmerTest version 3.1.3) were applied, using the following formulas:

For pzPC and NSCLC dceCT and pzPC dceMRI data:

1. $Feature \sim Timepoint + (1|Patient)$

For NSCLC dceMRI data, where multiple visits per patient were included:

2. $Feature \sim Timepoint + (1|Patient) + (1|Visit)$

Therefore, timepoints (after contrast injection) were treated as a fixed covariate and patient identity and visit as random covariates, as applicable. p-values for the timepoint covariate were calculated using the Satterthwaite approximation and corrected for multiple testing with the false discovery rate (FDR) method of Benjamini and Hochberg [18]. Features with a p-value and FDR of <0.05 were considered to show significant temporal dynamics after contrast agent application. These approaches and thresholds were chosen to maintain a high statistical power, but keep the proportion of false-positives low. For the features wavelet.HHH_firstorder_TotalEnergy, wavelet.HHL_firstorder_TotalEnergy, wavelet.HHL_firstorder_Energy and wavelet.HHH_firstorder_Energy extracted from lung tumor sections, linear mixed models failed to converge. Thus, these features had to be excluded from the analysis. Heatmaps of features with significant temporal dynamics were generated using the R package ComplexHeatmap version 2.6.2, after calculating the mean value for each feature over all patients and applying a z-score transformation over all seven timepoints. Clustering of features with similar temporal dynamics was performed using the complete linkage method on Euclidean distance matrices. For visualization as heatmaps, median voxel intensities of the aortal lumen or radiomics features were standardized across timepoints the using a z-score transformation. This method involves subtracting the mean and dividing by the standard deviation, resulting in transformed data with a mean of zero and a standard deviation of one.

Classification of healthy prostate and tumor regions-of-interest (ROIs) based on CT radiomics features was performed using the Python package scikit-learn version 1.0.2. Logistic regression classifiers with default settings (which uses L2 regularization with regularization strength C = 1) was applied. Receiver operator characteristic (ROC) curves were generated using leave-one-out cross validation, whereby for each of the timepoints, each (healthy or tumor) ROI was iteratively left out; classifiers were trained on the remaining ROIs, and class probability was predicted for the left-out ROI.

3. Results

3.1. Contrast Agent Dynamics Vary between Patients and Require Standardization for Systematic Analysis

Arterial lumen voxel median intensity values showed a high variability between patients throughout the acquisition phase (Figure 1A), with peaks occurring between 15 and 26 s and peak values between 520 and 827 HU. Taking fixed timepoints for radiomics evaluation (and thus simulating a standard CT protocol with a limited number of scans) led to a high variability of radiomics features in both tumors and healthy tissue (Figures S1 and S2).

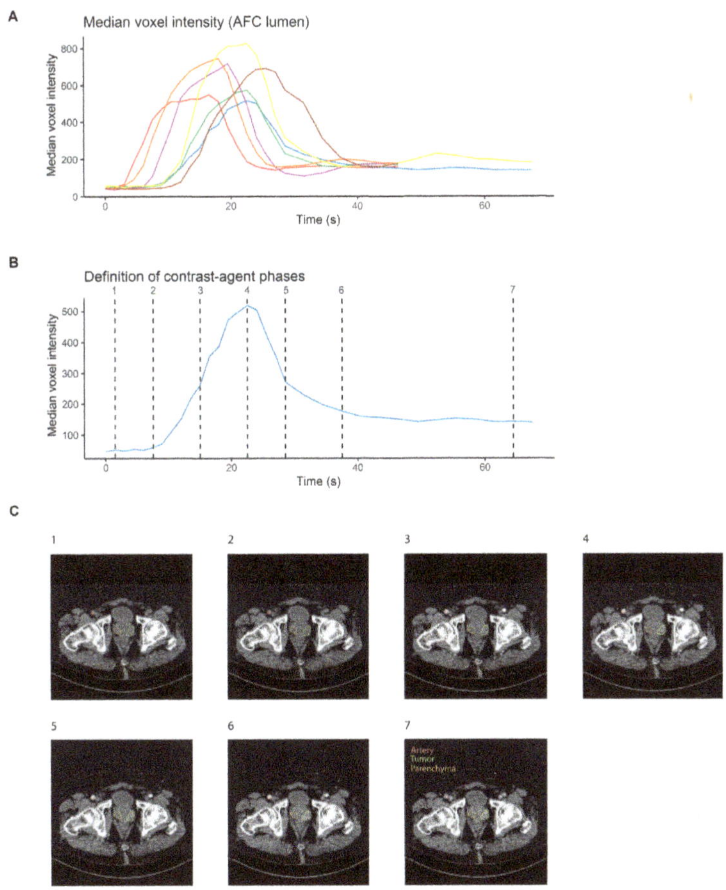

Figure 1. Synchronization of CT image series across prostate cancer patients. (**A**) Median voxel intensity as a function of time for each of the seven pzPC patients who were imaged with dceCT after intravenous injection of contrast medium. Lines are colored according to patients. (**B**) Definition of seven contrast agent phases on a single patient, to enable synchronization of image series across patients. (**C**) Representative slices for the seven defined contrast agent phases of a single prostate cancer patient.

To enable the identification of radiomics features that depended on the contrast agent phase across patients, arterial median intensity values were used to define seven distinct contrast agent phases. Timepoint (TP) 1 was defined as the second acquired scan, TP2 as the scan closest to an increase of at least 15% in median voxel intensity in the arterial lumen t compared to the mean of the first two scans. TP4 was the scan with peak voxel intensity,

TP3 was the scan closest to the center between TP2 and TP4. Similarly, TP6 was defined as the last scan with a median voxel intensity at least 15% higher than the mean of the last two acquired scans, TP5 was the scan closest to the center between TP4 and TP6, and TP7 was the second-to-last acquired scan. Contrast agent phase definition according to the arterial lumen median intensity values for a representative patient are shown in Figure 1B, and representative slices for a single patient and for all seven contrast agent phases are shown in Figure 1C.

3.2. *Contrast Agent Injection Induces Changes in CT Radiomics Features in Peripheral Zone Prostate Cancer and Healthy Prostate Parenchyma*

Having defined contrast agent phases across patients, the next aim was to identify radiomics features that depended on contrast agent phase; i.e., showed significant temporal changes after contrast agent application. Using linear mixed models to determine feature values according to timepoints after injection, 19 (1.6%) and 467 (38.8%) of the 1204 features that showed significant (FDR < 0.05) temporal dynamics in healthy prostate parenchyma and prostate tumors, respectively, were identified (Figure 2B,C). The z-score-transformed arterial lumen median voxel intensities for each timepoint are shown as a reference (Figure 2A). Using hierarchical clustering, two diverging clusters of radiomics features could be identified for both healthy prostate parenchyma and prostate tumors. Linear mixed model *p* values and cluster membership of all features for both healthy prostate parenchyma and prostate tumors can be found in Supplementary Tables S1 and S2, respectively.

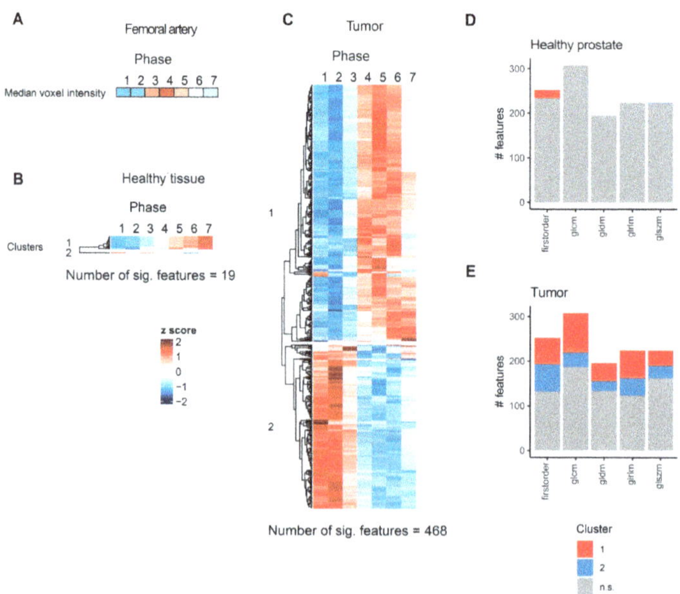

Figure 2. Significantly affected CT radiomics features in healthy prostate tissue and pzPC. (**A**) Heatmap of arterial lumen median voxel intensity. (**B**,**C**) Heatmaps of radiomics features with significant temporal dynamics after intravenous contrast agent injection for healthy prostate parenchyma (**B**) and pzPC (**C**) sections. For each feature, mean values for all seven patients were z-score transformed over the seven timepoints. Features are grouped according to hierarchical clustering, which is represented by dendrograms. (**D**,**E**) Number of radiomics features with and without significant temporal dynamics, grouped by feature class and colored according to clusters as defined in (**B**,**C**). glcm: gray level co-occurrence matrix, gldm: gray level dependence matrix, glrlm: gray level run length matrix, glszm: gray level size zone matrix.

For healthy prostate parenchyma, 18 of the 19 significant features belonged to the first cluster, which displayed low values initially and a monotonous increase after contrast agent injection. All these 18 features belonged to the first order class of radiomics features (Figure 2D, Supplementary Table S1). The only feature belonging to the second cluster, which showed high values initially and subsequently declined after contrast agent injection, was the feature wavelet.LLL_glszm_GrayLevelNonUniformityNormalized. On the other hand, in prostate tumors, more than one-third of all features showed significant temporal dynamics. Of note, while the strongest effect sizes and lowest *p* values were observed for first-order features, contrast media led to significant alterations in features that belonged to all radiomics feature classes (Figure 2E, Supplementary Table S2).

3.3. Machine-Learning-Based Classification of Healthy and Tumor ROIs Depends on Contrast Agent Phase

The next aim was to evaluate whether the ability of machine-learning classifiers to discriminate between healthy prostate tissue and prostate tumors is dependent on contrast agent phase. To this end, penalized logistic regression classifiers were trained on radiomics features to differentiate between healthy and tumor ROIs, and evaluated predictive accuracy using leave-one-out cross validation. Classification accuracy showed a high dependence on contrast agent phase (Figure 3A,B). As expected, classifiers could not differentiate well between healthy prostate tissue and tumors early after contrast agent application, with AUROC values ranging from 0.46 to 0.59 for the first three timepoints. In contrast, the highest predictive accuracies (AUROC 0.92) were found on TP4 (during peak arterial contrast enhancement) and TP5. Classification accuracy subsequently declined, but remained higher than during the initial phase after contrast agent injection (AUROC 0.86 and 0.72 for TP6 and TP7, respectively).

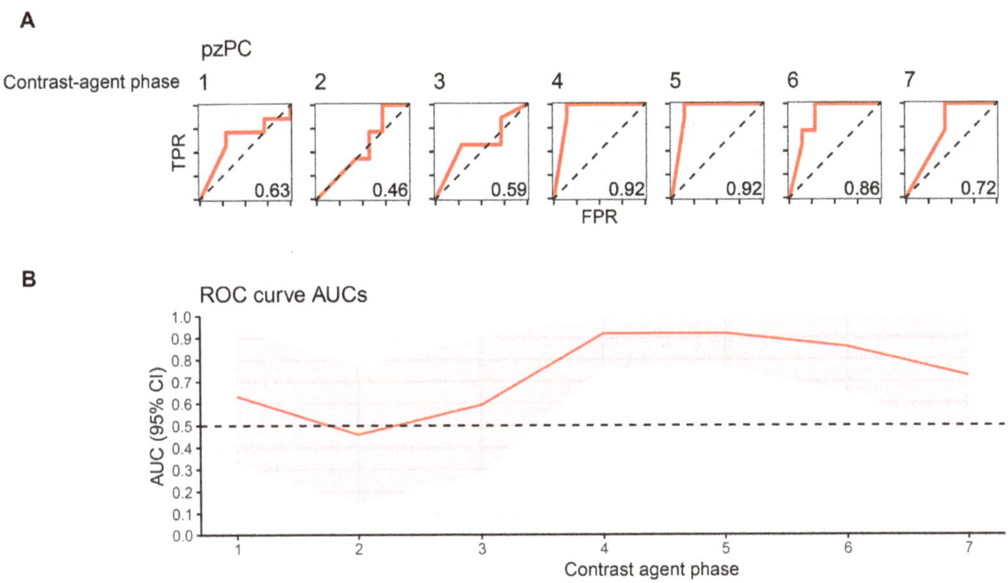

Figure 3. Machine-learning-based classification of healthy and pzPC ROIs depends on contrast agent phase. (**A**) ROC curves for logistic regression classifiers with an L2 penalty differentiating between healthy and tumor ROIs. Numbering above the curves denotes the timepoint after contrast agent injection. (**B**) AUC and 95% confidence intervals for each timepoint, which is represented on the *x*-axis. ROI, region-of-interest; pzPC, peripheral zone prostate cancer; TPR, true-positive rate; FPR, false-positive rate.

3.4. CT Radiomics Features Show Distinct Contrast Agent Dynamics in Lung Cancer

To determine how contrast agent application affected radiomics features in NSCLC, a similar methodology was applied, but the seven contrast agent phases were defined based on the descending aortal lumen median voxel intensity. Representative slices for a single patient are shown in Figure 4A. A total of 128 (10.6%) features with significant temporal dynamics after contrast agent application were identified, which, unlike in prostate tumors, could be grouped into three different clusters (Figure 4C, Supplementary Table S3). As in Figure 3, z-score transformed aortal lumen median voxel intensities for each timepoint are shown as a reference (Figure 4B). The first cluster consisted of features belonging to all radiomics feature classes, all of which were extracted from images after wavelet filter transformations (Supplementary Table S3). The second cluster, which gradually increased after contrast agent administration—and thus most likely reflected contrast agent influx into the tumor—was the smallest cluster in terms of the number of significant features. However, it included the features with the strongest effect sizes and lowest p values (Supplementary Table S3) and consisted exclusively of first-order features (Figure 4D). The third cluster, to which the highest number of features with significant temporal dynamics belonged, included radiomics features of all classes (Figure 4D), most of which were also extracted from images after wavelet filter transformations (Supplementary Table S3).

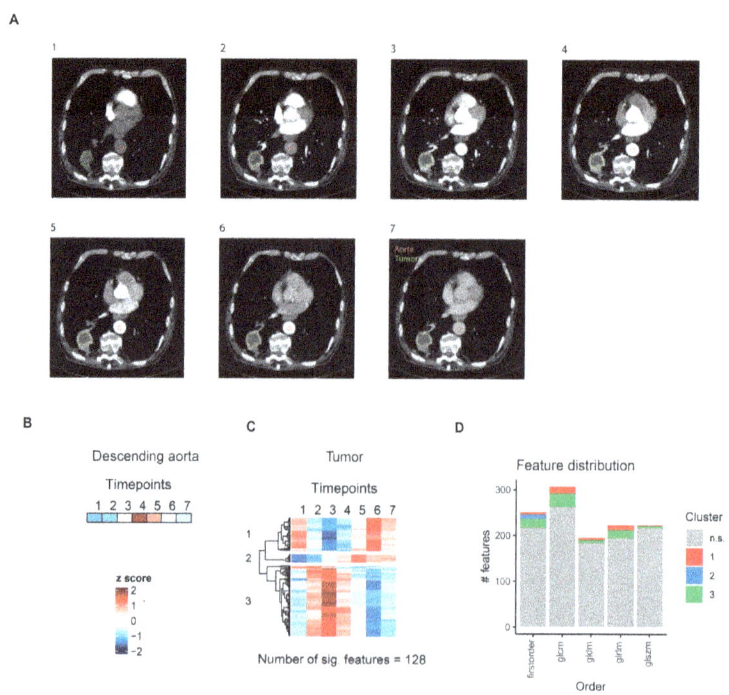

Figure 4. CT radiomics feature dynamics in lung cancer. (**A**) Representative slices for the seven defined contrast agent phases of a single lung cancer patient. (**B**) Heatmap of aortal lumen median voxel intensity. (**C**) Heatmap of radiomics features with significant temporal dynamics after intravenous contrast agent injection in solid lung tumors. For each feature, mean values for all seven patients are z-score transformed over the seven timepoints. Features are grouped by hierarchical clustering. (**D**) Distribution of radiomics features across different feature classes. Features are colored according to clusters defined in (**C**). glcm: gray level co-occurrence matrix, gldm: gray level dependence matrix, glrlm: gray level run length matrix, glszm: gray level size zone matrix.

3.5. Contrast Agent Application Induces Drastic Changes in MRI Radiomics Features in pzPC and NSCLC Tumors

Next, the effects of contrast agent administration on the MRI radiomics profiles of pzPC or NSCLC tumors were examined. Tumors were segmented on T1-weighted sequences (Figures 5A and 6A), and contrast agent phases were manually identified based on signal intensities in the femoral artery (for prostate MR images) or the aortal (for lung MR images) lumen. Z-score-transformed arterial or aortal lumen median voxel intensities for each timepoint are shown in Figures 5B and 6B.

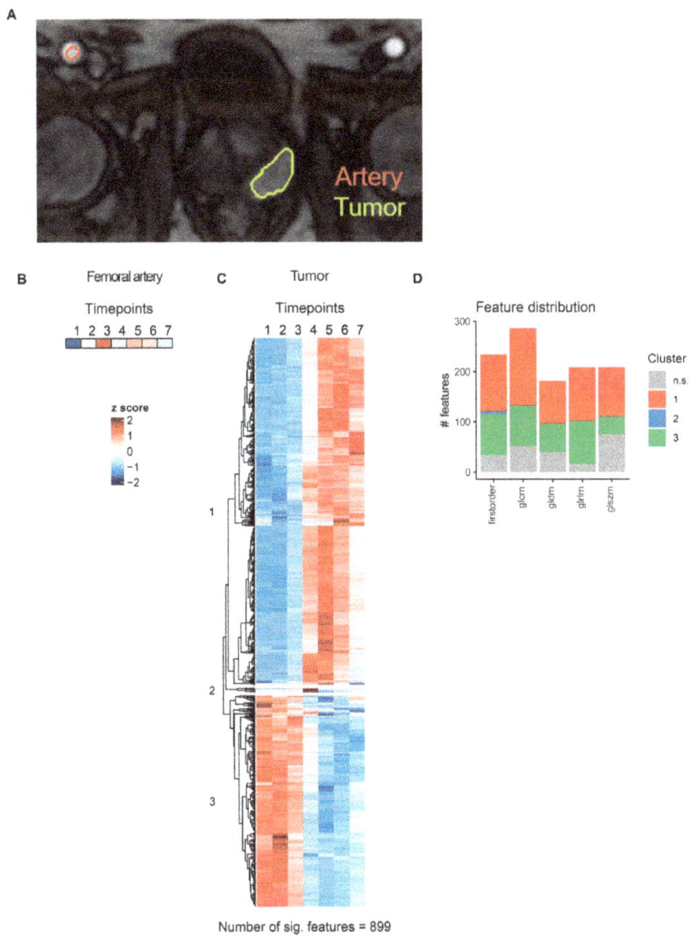

Figure 5. MRI radiomics feature dynamics in prostate cancer. (**A**) Representative slice illustrating segmentation of femoral artery and pzPC lesions in a single pzPC patient. (**B**) Heatmap of the femoral artery lumen median voxel intensity. (**C**) Heatmap of radiomics features with significant temporal dynamics after intravenous contrast agent injection in pzPC lesions. Features are grouped by hierarchical clustering. (**D**) Distribution of radiomics features across different feature classes. Features are colored according to clusters defined in (**C**). glcm: gray level co-occurrence matrix, gldm: gray level dependence matrix, glrlm: gray level run length matrix, glszm: gray level size zone matrix.

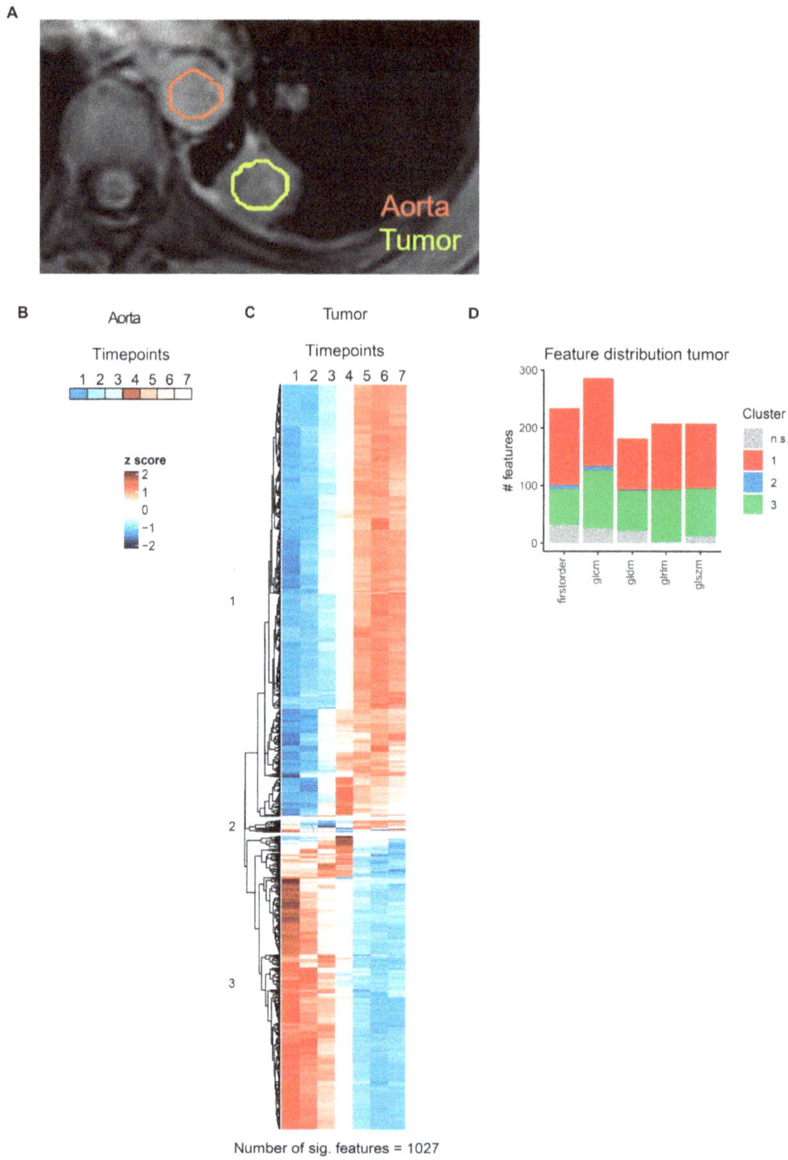

Figure 6. MRI radiomics feature dynamics in lung cancer. (**A**) Representative slice illustrating segmentation of thoracic aorta and NSCLC lesions in a single NSCLC patient. (**B**) Heatmap of aortal lumen median voxel intensity. (**C**) Heatmap of radiomics features with significant temporal dynamics after intravenous contrast agent injection in solid lung tumors. Features are grouped by hierarchical clustering. (**D**) Distribution of radiomics features across different feature classes. Features are colored according to clusters defined in (**C**). glcm: gray level co-occurrence matrix, gldm: gray level dependence matrix, glrlm: gray level run length matrix, glszm: gray level size zone matrix.

For pzPC tumors, 899 of 1118 (80.4%) MRI radiomics features showed significant temporal dynamics after multiple testing correction (Figure 5C, Supplementary Table S4). Hierarchical clustering grouped these features into three distinct clusters (Figure 5C,D).

Similarly, for NSCLC tumors, 1027 of 1118 (91.9%) MRI radiomics features were significantly associated with time after contrast agent injection (Figure 6C, Supplementary Table S5). As in pzPC tumors, these features could be grouped into three clusters via hierarchical clustering (Figure 6C,D).

4. Discussion

The data presented in this study show that radiomics profiles of pZC and NSCLC are highly dependent on the contrast agent phase. Data from patients with pzPC and NSCLC with dynamic contrast-enhanced computed tomography (dceCT) were analyzed. These two cancer types were selected due to their contrary contrast agent uptake characteristics: PzC is characterized by rapid, intense contrast agent uptake compared to the surrounding non-tumoral peripheral zone tissue. This enables the visualization of pzPC using dynamic imaging techniques such as dynamic contrast-enhanced magnetic resonance imaging (dceMRI) [19] or dceCT [15]. In contrast, NSCLC does show a more heterogonous and weaker contrast agent uptake compared to pzPC, and is characterized by a longer contrast agent plateau phase with a slower in- and out-flow of the contrast agent [16]. Based on this difference in vascularity, it was hypothesized that contrast agent timing would have a more pronounced effect on radiomics features in patients with pzPC compared to NSCLC.

The use of dynamic scanning protocols, in which multiple scans are acquired at short (1.5–3 s) pre-defined intervals after contrast agent injection, enabled us to examine the potential effects of contrast agents on radiomics features at an unprecedented temporal resolution. These data provide insights into the impact of contrast agent timing on the stability of radiomics features extracted from pzPC and NSCLC tumors.

Several other studies have analyzed the robustness of MRI- and CT-based radiomics features. These include phantom studies [9,20], test–retest studies [21,22], and reports on reproducibility and repeatability in oncological settings [23,24]. However, alterations in radiomics features in dceCT imaging have not been investigated systematically. In contrast to noise observed in test–retest variability, radiomics feature changes during dceCT time series may reflect the characteristics of the tumor. Hence, in this paper, important considerations for the analysis of radiomics features for contrast agent-enhanced CT and MRI data sets are described.

First, this study shows that CT and MRI radiomics profiles of tumor ROIs in pzPC and NSCLC are dependent on contrast perfusion timing. There were 468 (38.8%) CT radiomics features that showed contrast agent timing-dependent alterations in pzPC, highlighting the effect of contrast agent timing on radiomics feature profiles. In contrast to the highly perfused pzPC, CT radiomics changes in NSCLC were less pronounced with 128 (10.6%) of features showing time-dependent changes. On MRI, radiomics features were considerably contrast agent-dependent in both pzPC and NSCLC patients. These changes are important for the further analysis of the features, as well as for the correlation of radiomics features with clinical outcomes and need to be dealt with in any quantitative imaging study involving the use of contrast agents. While heterogeneity-inducing scanning parameters (such as kVp, slice thickness, reconstruction kernel) and post-processing parameters (such as the reconstruction bins) can be standardized, harmonization of contrast agent timing is more challenging. This is particularly important for large-scale, multi-center studies with heterogeneous contrast agent timing protocols. The use of bolus tracking systems that start the scan once a certain amount of contrast attenuation reaches a tracking vessel improves the comparability between patients compared to fixed delay protocols. However, these bolus tracking protocols face problems in patients who suffer from low cardiac output [12], or who are unable to perform the examination with the planned i.v. injection flow rate, or in elderly patients [11]. Awareness of this potential problem when dealing with contrast agent enhanced datasets is needed. Simple quantitative measurements in reference vessels visible on all study participants (i.e., aorta, femoral vessel) could provide an overview of the data heterogeneity in terms of contrast distribution, and could be used to adequately implement time-scanning protocols, enabling standardization of contrast agent phases across patients and exclusion of obvious outliers. Alternatively, post hoc temporal alignment of contrast agent phases based on voxel intensity in time series with high temporal resolution may establish sufficient temporal correspondence among radiomics profiles, if contrast perfusion data sets are available.

A possible solution to address the variability introduced by contrast agent dynamics is to utilize non-contrast scans whenever feasible and diagnostically meaningful. This approach would mitigate the bias introduced by contrast agent dynamics and could enhance the reproducibility of radiomics results.

Furthermore, this study underscores the importance of addressing contrast agent protocols. For multi-center studies, standardized contrast agent protocols are essential. These standardization efforts may involve recommendations for uniform timing, dosage and the specific types of contrast agents utilized. Nevertheless, even after controlling and harmonizing all these parameters, intra-patient differences in cardiac output will still significantly impact contrast dynamics

The data on machine-learning-based classification of healthy and tumorous prostate ROIs proves the relevance of contrast agent-induced changes in radiomics features for further analysis. Given that, even for a relatively simple classification task (i.e., differentiation between healthy and tumor ROIs), accuracy was greatly dependent on contrast agent phase, vast implications for more sophisticated approaches (e.g., prediction of survival or therapeutic response based on radiomics data) can be expected.

Further advantages of this study include the high temporal resolution at which dceCT or dceMRI scans were performed, which gives unprecedented insights into the dynamics of radiomics features after contrast agent application, the robust statistical analysis, which was performed using linear mixed models.

The main limitation of this study was the small size of the cohorts and that only two cancer types were investigated. However, this was sufficient to perform basic analysis due to the large number of effects observed for multiple radiomics features, but associations of even more radiomics features with contrast agent phases with a larger cohort size could be expected. A further limitation is the retrospective, single-center study design. Nevertheless, the presented data clearly show the influence of agent dynamics on radiomics features, and a prospective study design would likely yield similar results. Finally, the NSCLC included both adenocarcinomas and squamous cell carcinomas, and this heterogeneity may have influenced the results to a certain degree. This can, however, also be interpreted as a strength, since it suggests that the presented findings are generalizable across different NSCLC subtypes.

The presented data open up multiple avenues for further research. Future studies may explore the influence of contrast agent timing on radiomics features in other types of cancers, such as breast or ovarian cancer, in which radiomics have shown potential [25–27]. Additionally, radiomics feature dynamics after contrast agent application may harbor biological information, which might be useful to infer quantifiable data on tumor heterogeneity and predict outcome. Radiomics features are quantitative measurements extracted from CT or MRI scans, capturing various aspects of tumor morphology, texture and intensity. In lung or prostate cancer, certain features may reveal unique patterns in contrast agent dynamics, reflecting characteristics such as vascularity and perfusion within the tumor microenvironment. Identifying these features can provide insights into tumor biology, aiding in diagnosis, prognosis and treatment planning by differentiating between subtypes, assessing treatment response and predicting outcomes. Overall, these features might offer a non-invasive method to understand tumor behavior and personalize patient management.

5. Conclusions

This study shows that CT and MRI radiomics profiles of pZC and NSCLC are highly dependent on the contrast agent dynamics. This highlights the need for careful design of radiomics studies when contrast media are involved, as a substantial number of radiomics features are dependent on individual contrast perfusion dynamics and are therefore prone to bias. When using contrast-enhanced scans for radiomics studies, care should be taken to ensure a patient-specific perfusion timing for radiomics analysis, which could be achieved by a test bolus application.

Supplementary Materials: The following supporting information can be downloaded at: https://www.mdpi.com/article/10.3390/cancers16081519/s1, Figure S1: Perfusion dynamics of selected CT radiomics features in prostate tumors; Figure S2: Perfusion dynamics of selected CT radiomics features in in healthy prostate tissue; Table S1: Linear mixed model *p* values and cluster membership of all CT radiomics features for prostate parenchyma; Table S2: Linear mixed model *p* values and cluster membership of all CT radiomics features for prostate tumors; Table S3: Linear mixed model *p* values and cluster membership of all CT radiomics features for lung tumors; Table S4: Linear mixed model *p* values and cluster membership of all MRI radiomics features for pzPC tumors; Table S5: Linear mixed model *p* values and cluster membership of all MRI radiomics features for NSCLC tumors.

Author Contributions: M.L.W., L.B. and H.P. conceptualized the study. M.L.W. performed data analysis and visualization with assistance from G.L., L.B., F.P., D.K., P.A. and P.A.T.B. recruited patients and managed patient data. M.L.W., L.B. and H.P. wrote the original draft of the manuscript. S.R., B.H.H., R.-I.M., P.A.T.B. and G.L. edited the manuscript. All authors have read and agreed to the published version of the manuscript.

Funding: The financial support by the Austrian Federal Ministry for Labour and Economy, the National Foundation for Research, Technology and Development and the Christian Doppler Research Association, FWF (P 35189), WWTF (10.47379/LS20065, 10.47379/LS20030), EU Horizon Europe (101100633, 101080302 101136299) is gratefully acknowledged.

Institutional Review Board Statement: This retrospective study was approved by the Institutional Review Board of the Medical University of Vienna (Numbers 1764/2016 and 1789/2015) and performed in accordance with the Declaration of Helsinki.

Informed Consent Statement: Informed consent was obtained from all subjects involved in the study.

Data Availability Statement: Radiomics data and analysis scripts are available upon request.

Acknowledgments: We thank the patients and their families who participated in this study.

Conflicts of Interest: The authors declare no conflicts of interest.

Abbreviations

CT	Computed tomography
dceCT	Dynamic contrast-enhanced CT
dceMRI	Dynamic contrast-enhanced MRI
FDR	False discovery rate
GLCM	Gray level co-occurrence matrix
GLDM	Gray level dependence matrix
GLRLM	Gray level run length matrix
GLSZM	Gray level size zone matrix
i.v.	Intravenous
kVp	Kilovolt pascal
LoG	Laplacian of Gaussian
mL	Mililiter
MRI	Magnetic resonance imaging
NSCLC	Non-small cell lung cancer
PI-RADS	Prostate Imaging-Reporting and Data System
pzPC	Peripheral zone prostate cancer
ROC	Receiver-operator-characteristics
ROI	Region-of-interest

References

1. Lambin, P.; Rios-Velazquez, E.; Leijenaar, R.; Carvalho, S.; van Stiphout, R.G.; Granton, P.; Zegers, C.M.; Gillies, R.; Boellard, R.; Dekker, A.; et al. Radiomics: Extracting more information from medical images using advanced feature analysis. *Eur. J. Cancer* **2012**, *48*, 441–446. [CrossRef] [PubMed]
2. Dinis Fernandes, C.; Schaap, A.; Kant, J.; van Houdt, P.; Wijkstra, H.; Bekers, E.; Linder, S.; Bergman, A.M.; van der Heide, U.; Mischi, M.; et al. Radiogenomics Analysis Linking Multiparametric MRI and Transcriptomics in Prostate Cancer. *Cancers* **2023**, *15*, 3074. [CrossRef] [PubMed]
3. Nicoletti, G.; Mazzetti, S.; Maimone, G.; Cignini, V.; Cuocolo, R.; Faletti, R.; Gatti, M.; Imbriaco, M.; Longo, N.; Ponsiglione, A.; et al. Development and Validation of an Explainable Radiomics Model to Predict High-Aggressive Prostate Cancer: A Multicenter Radiomics Study Based on Biparametric MRI. *Cancers* **2024**, *16*, 203. [CrossRef] [PubMed]
4. Coroller, T.P.; Agrawal, V.; Huynh, E.; Narayan, V.; Lee, S.W.; Mak, R.H.; Aerts, H. Radiomic-Based Pathological Response Prediction from Primary Tumors and Lymph Nodes in NSCLC. *J. Thorac. Oncol.* **2017**, *12*, 467–476. [CrossRef] [PubMed]
5. Ligero, M.; Garcia-Ruiz, A.; Viaplana, C.; Villacampa, G.; Raciti, M.V.; Landa, J.; Matos, I.; Martin-Liberal, J.; Ochoa-de-Olza, M.; Hierro, C.; et al. A CT-based Radiomics Signature Is Associated with Response to Immune Checkpoint Inhibitors in Advanced Solid Tumors. *Radiology* **2021**, *299*, 109–119. [CrossRef] [PubMed]
6. Martin, A.; Marcelin, C.; Petitpierre, F.; Jambon, E.; Maaloum, R.; Grenier, N.; Le Bras, Y.; Crombe, A. Clinical, Technical, and MRI Features Associated with Patients' Outcome at 3 Months and 2 Years following Prostate Artery Embolization: Is There an Added Value of Radiomics? *J. Pers. Med.* **2024**, *14*, 67. [CrossRef] [PubMed]
7. Wang, T.W.; Chao, H.S.; Chiu, H.Y.; Lin, Y.H.; Chen, H.C.; Lu, C.F.; Liao, C.Y.; Lee, Y.; Shiao, T.H.; Chen, Y.M.; et al. Evaluating the Potential of Delta Radiomics for Assessing Tyrosine Kinase Inhibitor Treatment Response in Non-Small Cell Lung Cancer Patients. *Cancers* **2023**, *15*, 5125. [CrossRef] [PubMed]
8. Zhao, B. Understanding Sources of Variation to Improve the Reproducibility of Radiomics. *Front. Oncol.* **2021**, *11*, 633176. [CrossRef] [PubMed]
9. Jha, A.K.; Mithun, S.; Jaiswar, V.; Sherkhane, U.B.; Purandare, N.C.; Prabhash, K.; Rangarajan, V.; Dekker, A.; Wee, L.; Traverso, A. Repeatability and reproducibility study of radiomic features on a phantom and human cohort. *Sci. Rep.* **2021**, *11*, 2055. [CrossRef] [PubMed]
10. Zhang, X.; Lu, B.; Yang, X.; Lan, D.; Lin, S.; Zhou, Z.; Li, K.; Deng, D.; Peng, P.; Zeng, Z.; et al. Prognostic analysis and risk stratification of lung adenocarcinoma undergoing EGFR-TKI therapy with time-serial CT-based radiomics signature. *Eur. Radiol.* **2023**, *33*, 825–835. [CrossRef]
11. Johnson, D.Y.; Farjat, A.E.; Vernuccio, F.; Hurwitz, L.M.; Nelson, R.C.; Marin, D. Evaluation of Intraindividual Contrast Enhancement Variability for Determining the Maximum Achievable Consistency in CT. *AJR Am. J. Roentgenol.* **2020**, *214*, 18–23. [CrossRef] [PubMed]
12. Sakai, S.; Yabuuchi, H.; Chishaki, A.; Okafuji, T.; Matsuo, Y.; Kamitani, T.; Setoguchi, T.; Honda, H. Effect of cardiac function on aortic peak time and peak enhancement during coronary CT angiography. *Eur. J. Radiol.* **2010**, *75*, 173–177. [CrossRef] [PubMed]
13. van Timmeren, J.E.; Cester, D.; Tanadini-Lang, S.; Alkadhi, H.; Baessler, B. Radiomics in medical imaging-"how-to" guide and critical reflection. *Insights Into Imaging* **2020**, *11*, 91. [CrossRef] [PubMed]
14. Shur, J.D.; Doran, S.J.; Kumar, S.; Ap Dafydd, D.; Downey, K.; O'Connor, J.P.B.; Papanikolaou, N.; Messiou, C.; Koh, D.M.; Orton, M.R. Radiomics in Oncology: A Practical Guide. *Radiogr. A Rev. Publ. Radiol. Soc. N. Am. Inc.* **2021**, *41*, 1717–1732. [CrossRef] [PubMed]
15. Beer, L.; Polanec, S.H.; Baltzer, P.A.T.; Schatzl, G.; Georg, D.; Schestak, C.; Dutschke, A.; Herrmann, H.; Mazal, P.; Brendel, A.K.; et al. 4D perfusion CT of prostate cancer for image-guided radiotherapy planning: A proof of concept study. *PLoS ONE* **2019**, *14*, e0225673. [CrossRef] [PubMed]
16. Ohno, Y.; Koyama, H.; Matsumoto, K.; Onishi, Y.; Takenaka, D.; Fujisawa, Y.; Yoshikawa, T.; Konishi, M.; Maniwa, Y.; Nishimura, Y.; et al. Differentiation of malignant and benign pulmonary nodules with quantitative first-pass 320-detector row perfusion CT versus FDG PET/CT. *Radiology* **2011**, *258*, 599–609. [CrossRef] [PubMed]
17. van Griethuysen, J.J.M.; Fedorov, A.; Parmar, C.; Hosny, A.; Aucoin, N.; Narayan, V.; Beets-Tan, R.G.H.; Fillion-Robin, J.C.; Pieper, S.; Aerts, H. Computational Radiomics System to Decode the Radiographic Phenotype. *Cancer Res.* **2017**, *77*, e104–e107. [CrossRef] [PubMed]
18. Benjamini, Y.; Hochberg, Y. Controlling the False Discovery Rate: A Practical and Powerful Approach to Multiple Testing. *J. R. Stat. Soc. Ser. B Methodol.* **1995**, *57*, 289–300.
19. Polanec, S.H.; Bickel, H.; Wengert, G.J.; Arnoldner, M.; Clauser, P.; Susani, M.; Shariat, S.F.; Pinker, K.; Helbich, T.H.; Baltzer, P.A.T. Can the addition of clinical information improve the accuracy of PI-RADS version 2 for the diagnosis of clinically significant prostate cancer in positive MRI? *Clin. Radiol.* **2020**, *75*, 157.E1–157.E7. [CrossRef] [PubMed]
20. Lee, J.; Steinmann, A.; Ding, Y.; Lee, H.; Owens, C.; Wang, J.; Yang, J.; Followill, D.; Ger, R.; MacKin, D.; et al. Radiomics feature robustness as measured using an MRI phantom. *Sci. Rep.* **2021**, *11*, 3973. [CrossRef] [PubMed]
21. Prayer, F.; Hofmanninger, J.; Weber, M.; Kifjak, D.; Willenpart, A.; Pan, J.; Rohrich, S.; Langs, G.; Prosch, H. Variability of computed tomography radiomics features of fibrosing interstitial lung disease: A test-retest study. *Methods* **2021**, *188*, 98–104. [CrossRef] [PubMed]

22. van Timmeren, J.E.; Leijenaar, R.T.H.; van Elmpt, W.; Wang, J.; Zhang, Z.; Dekker, A.; Lambin, P. Test-Retest Data for Radiomics Feature Stability Analysis: Generalizable or Study-Specific? *Tomography* **2016**, *2*, 361–365. [CrossRef] [PubMed]
23. Escudero Sanchez, L.; Rundo, L.; Gill, A.B.; Hoare, M.; Mendes Serrao, E.; Sala, E. Robustness of radiomic features in CT images with different slice thickness, comparing liver tumour and muscle. *Sci. Rep.* **2021**, *11*, 8262. [CrossRef] [PubMed]
24. Zhao, B.; Tan, Y.; Tsai, W.Y.; Qi, J.; Xie, C.; Lu, L.; Schwartz, L.H. Reproducibility of radiomics for deciphering tumor phenotype with imaging. *Sci. Rep.* **2016**, *6*, 23428. [CrossRef] [PubMed]
25. Guo, L.; Du, S.; Gao, S.; Zhao, R.; Huang, G.; Jin, F.; Teng, Y.; Zhang, L. Delta-Radiomics Based on Dynamic Contrast-Enhanced MRI Predicts Pathologic Complete Response in Breast Cancer Patients Treated with Neoadjuvant Chemotherapy. *Cancers* **2022**, *14*, 3515. [CrossRef] [PubMed]
26. Pesapane, F.; Rotili, A.; Agazzi, G.M.; Botta, F.; Raimondi, S.; Penco, S.; Dominelli, V.; Cremonesi, M.; Jereczek-Fossa, B.A.; Carrafiello, G.; et al. Recent Radiomics Advancements in Breast Cancer: Lessons and Pitfalls for the Next Future. *Curr. Oncol.* **2021**, *28*, 2351–2372. [CrossRef] [PubMed]
27. Miceli, V.; Gennarini, M.; Tomao, F.; Cupertino, A.; Lombardo, D.; Palaia, I.; Curti, F.; Riccardi, S.; Ninkova, R.; Maccioni, F.; et al. Imaging of Peritoneal Carcinomatosis in Advanced Ovarian Cancer: CT, MRI, Radiomic Features and Resectability Criteria. *Cancers* **2023**, *15*, 5827. [CrossRef] [PubMed]

tomography

MDPI

Article

Classification of Osteophytes Occurring in the Lumbar Intervertebral Foramen

Abdullah Emre Taçyıldız [1,2,*] and Feyza İnceoğlu [3]

[1] Department of Neurosurgery, Faculty of Medicine, Turgut Özal University, Malatya 44090, Turkey
[2] Department of Neurosurgery, Faculty of Medicine, Karabuk University, Karabuk 78200, Turkey
[3] Department of Biostatistics, Faculty of Medicine, Turgut Özal University, Malatya 44090, Turkey; feyza.inceoglu@ozal.edu.tr
* Correspondence: abdullahtacyildiz@karabuk.edu.tr; Tel.: +90-370-415-80-00

Abstract: Background: Surgeons have limited knowledge of the lumbar intervertebral foramina. This study aimed to classify osteophytes in the lumbar intervertebral foramen and to determine their pathoanatomical characteristics, discuss their potential biomechanical effects, and contribute to developing surgical methods. Methods: We conducted a retrospective, non-randomized, single-center study involving 1224 patients. The gender, age, and anatomical location of the osteophytes in the lumbar intervertebral foramina of the patients were recorded. Results: Two hundred and forty-nine (20.34%) patients had one or more osteophytes in their lumbar 4 and 5 foramina. Of the 4896 foramina, 337 (6.88%) contained different types of osteophytes. Moreover, four anatomical types of osteophytes were found: mixed osteophytes in 181 (3.69%) foramina, osteophytes from the lower endplate of the superior vertebrae in 91 (1.85%) foramina, osteophytes from the junction of the pedicle and lamina of the upper vertebrae in 39 foramina (0.79%), and osteophytes from the upper endplate of the lower vertebrae in 26 (0.53%) foramina. The L4 foramen contained a significantly higher number of osteophytes than the L5 foramen. Osteophyte development increased significantly with age, with no difference between males and females. Conclusions: The findings show that osteophytic extrusions, which alter the natural anatomical structure of the lumbar intervertebral foramina, are common and can narrow the foramen.

Keywords: foraminal stenosis; lumbar intervertebral foramen; osteophyte

1. Introduction

The lumbar intervertebral foramen (IVF) comprises two movable joints and a complex three-dimensional (volumetric) structure that few surgeons understand [1,2]. The lumbar IVF contributes to the development of radiculopathy and its surgical treatment [2].

In general, osteophytes are a feature of osteoarthritis and are classified as extraspinal or vertebral [3]. The pathophysiology of osteoarthritis involves the proliferation of periosteal cells at the bone–cartilage border. Mechanical stimuli are the most likely cause of this proliferation [3]. TGF-β and morphogenetic protein 2 play critical roles in osteophyte formation [3].

Back pain is a personal and societal burden that significantly reduces the quality of life worldwide; it causes severe disability and requires substantial healthcare resources [4,5]. Significant evidence suggests a relationship between the severity of low back pain and the presence of spinal osteoarthritis and disk space narrowing [6]. Osteoarthritis in the lumbar spine causes low back pain and lowers the quality of life [7]. Low back pain is not observed in people without degenerative osteoarthritis, as confirmed through lumbar magnetic resonance images [7]. Obesity, lumbar disk degeneration, and spinal osteoarthritis contribute to spinal degeneration [8].

Foraminal stenosis is one of the most common findings (25–29%), and it is used to diagnose failed back surgery syndrome [9]. Previous studies have focused on the intervertebral foramen—a critical area for surgeons—and its morphology and anatomy [1,2]. However, a literature review revealed a lack of research on foraminal osteophytic pathologies in the sagittal plane [10]. The present study aims to visualize the location of osteophytes in the intervertebral foramen. The study also identifies the frequency, anatomical regions, and distribution of the osteophytes involved in lumbar IVF. Another aim is to statistically present the presence of osteophytes based on age and gender. This study aims to detect pathologies in this region, provide a clinical guideline, and contribute to biomechanics research. Foraminal space narrowing, osteoarthritic processes, and the distribution of osteophytes in the intervertebral foramina are important factors to consider when performing surgery and conducting biomechanical studies. Understanding lumbar IVF osteophytes could help us better understand one of the causes of low back pain.

2. Materials and Methods

2.1. Patient Population

Our study is a retrospective, non-randomized, single-center study involving 1224 patients who presented to the Faculty of Medicine, Malatya Turgut Özal University, between 1 January and 31 December 2021. The data from patients who were asked to undergo computed tomography (CT) of the lower abdomen after visiting the emergency department, urology clinic, or general surgery clinic were reviewed retrospectively. CT scans of the lower abdomen were reconstructed in the bone window using the PACS v4.1.2.40 software from our hospital's electronic database. Moreover, the L4 (L4–L5) and L5 (L5–S1) intervertebral foramina were evaluated bilaterally. The gender, age, and anatomical location of the osteophytes in the lumbar intervertebral foramina of the patients were recorded. This retrospective study was approved by the Ethics Committee of Clinical Research of the Faculty of Medicine, Malatya Turgut Özal University, with decision no. 2021/111, dated 16 December 2021.

2.2. Inclusion and Exclusion Criteria

Patients who had undergone a neurosurgical procedure and those for whom neurosurgeons requested lumbar CT scans were excluded from this study. Moreover, patients whose post-reconstruction images had visibility issues that interfered with interpretation were excluded from the study. Patients under 18 years old were not allowed to participate.

2.3. Image Analysis and Research Methods

The sagittal plane was used to examine the reconstructed lumbar vertebrae. Foramina L4 and L5 were evaluated bilaterally by a single observer. The sagittal section was evaluated until both foramina exited, allowing visualization of the right and left sides (until the sagittal sections were completed). The natural anatomical boundaries of the evaluated lumbar vertebrae were determined using standard atlases of human anatomy [11]. The osteophytes were defined as extrusions from the natural anatomical boundaries of the lumbar vertebrae and classified based on the anatomical region in which they originated from the lumbar vertebrae (i.e., the junctions of the pedicles and laminae, the upper endplate of the lower vertebrae, and the lower endplate of the upper vertebrae). If they extruded from multiple regions, they were classified as a mixed type.

The imaging equipment included Philips Ingenuity CT, 2014, 128 slices, serial no. 600021 (Philips Healthcare, Eindhoven, The Netherlands) and Philips MX, 2014, 16 slices, serial no. EP16E140004 (Philips Healthcare, Eindhoven, The Netherlands). The slice thickness (for both CT machines) was 2.5 mm. First, axial sections were created. The image was then reconstructed into sagittal sections using the PACS v4.1.2.40 software.

2.4. Statistical Analysis

The data from this study were analyzed using the statistical program in the Social Sciences 25 software. The Shapiro–Wilk test was used to determine whether the data from this study followed a normal distribution. For comparison tests, a significance level (p) of 0.05 was used. Because the variables did not follow the normal distribution ($p > 0.05$), the analysis was continued using nonparametric tests. The Mann–Whitney U test was used for independent paired group comparisons because the normality assumptions were not met. The Kruskal–Wallis test was used to compare multiple independent groups. As the number of comparisons between the variables showing differences increased, the Bonferroni corrected p-value was used and calculated as 0.05 (binary comparison). This study had four groups and two comparisons, resulting in the following calculation: =6, $\alpha_{BD} = 0.05/6 = 0.008$. After the Kruskal–Wallis test was conducted, the p-values obtained from the Mann–Whitney U test were compared with the value of 0.008, and the results were determined. To analyze the categorical data, we created cross tables and used chi-square (χ^2) analysis.

3. Results

In this study, 1224 cases and 4896 lumbar intervertebral foramina were examined. Of the cases, 527 (43.1%) were females and 697 (56.9%) were males. The mean age of the participants was 47.75 ± 19.03 years. Among the study participants, the highest age was 109 years, and the lowest age was 18 years (Table 1). The lowest ages at which osteophytes were discovered were 19 and 20 in 1 and 3 patients, respectively. One or more osteophytes were found in the lumbar 4 and 5 foramina in 249 (20.34%) patients.

Table 1. Descriptive values of variables.

Variable	Group	Frequency	Percentage
Gender	Male	697	56.9
	Female	527	43.1
L5–S1	None	1025	83.7
	Left	65	5.3
	Right	57	4.7
	Right and Left	77	6.3
L4–L5	None	1151	94.0
	Left	27	2.2
	Right	27	2.2
	Right and Left	19	1.6
	Total	1224	100.0
Variable	Mean ± SD	Min–Max	
Age	47.75 ± 19.03	18–109	

Mean ± SD, mean ± standard deviation; Min, minimum value; Max, maximum value.

Various types of osteophytes were found in 337 (6.88%) of the 4896 foramina. Moreover, mixed-type osteophytes were found in 181 foramina (3.69%, Figure 1), and osteophytes extruded from the lower endplate of the superior vertebrae in 91 foramina (1.85%, Figure 2), from the junction of the pedicle and lamina of the upper vertebrae in 39 foramina (0.79%, Figure 3A,B), and from the upper endplate of the lower vertebrae in 26 (0.53%) foramina (Figure 3C,D). Overall, 248 and 89 osteophytes were found in the L5 and L4 intervertebral foramina, respectively. Four different types of osteophytes were identified (Figure 4).

There was a significant difference between the measurements of the L5 and L4 foramina in the participants. The L5 foramen had a higher incidence of osteophytes than the L4 foramen ($p < 0.05$, Table 2). Among the participants included in the study, there was no statistically significant difference between the males and females in terms of the measurements of the right L5–S1, the left L5–S1, both the right and left L5–S1, the right L4–L5, the left L4–L5, and both the right and left L4–L5 ($p > 0.05$, Table 3). The osteophyte formations in the foramen increased significantly with age ($p < 0.05$, Table 4).

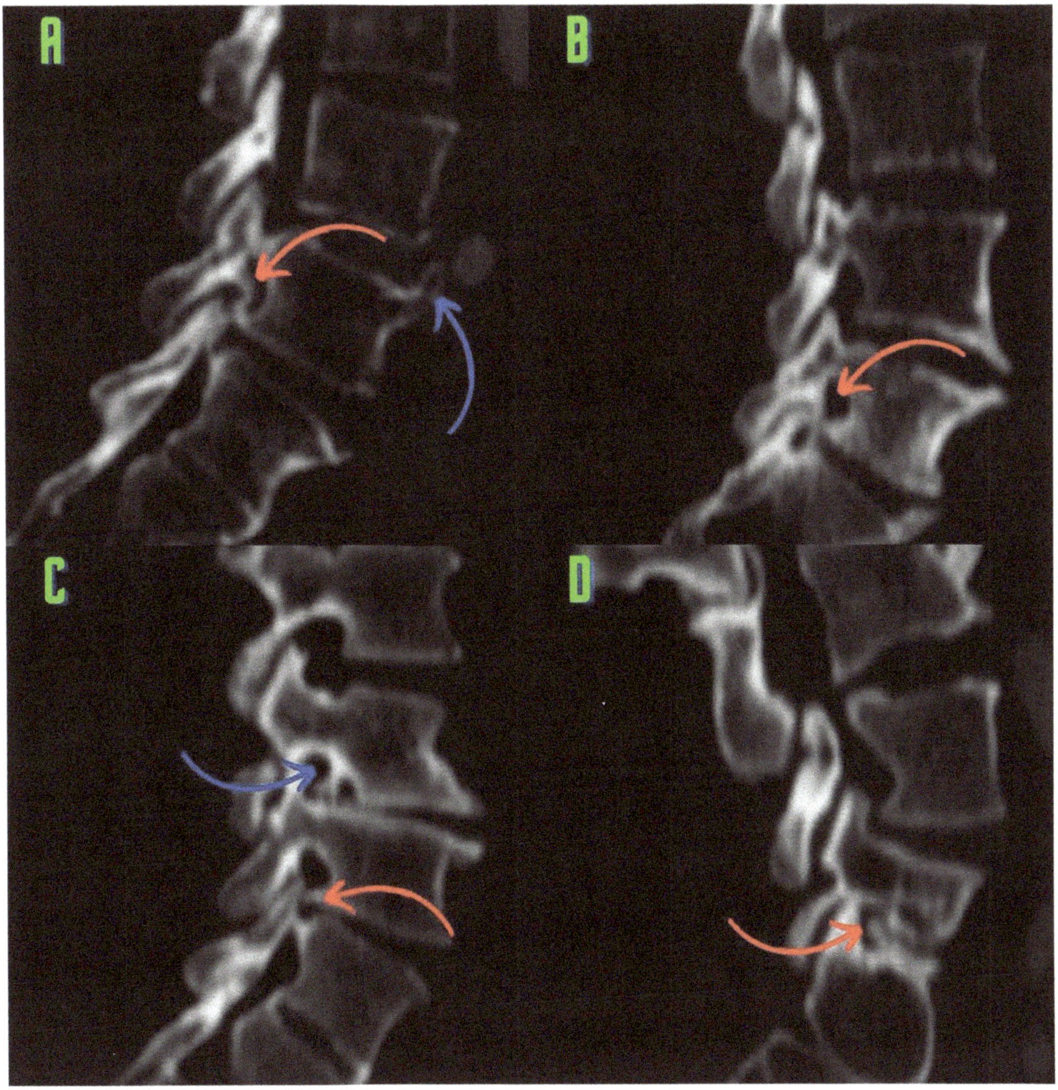

Figure 1. Mixed-type osteophytosis is observed. (**A**) An osteophyte (red arrow) arising from the pedicle–lamina junction and the inferior endplate of the superior vertebrae is observed in the L5–S1 foramen. Vertebral osteophytes (blue arrow) are also observed at a position anterior to the vertebrae. (**B**) Osteophytes (red arrow) arising from three different points united in the foramen. A mixed-type osteophyte arising from the pedicle–lamina junction, lower endplate of the superior vertebrae, and upper endplate of the inferior vertebrae formed an interesting pathoanatomical structure in the foramen. (**C**) A mixed-type osteophyte (blue arrow) arising from the pedicle–lamina junction in the L4–5 foramen and an osteophyte (red arrow) arising from the lower endplate of the superior vertebrae in the L5–S1 foramen are observed. (**D**) The L5–S1 disk space appears to have collapsed. A mixed-type osteophyte (red arrow) is seen to be arising from both the lower endplate of the superior vertebrae and the upper endplate of the inferior vertebrae. The fact that the spines are not in the same plane in sagittal images gives the impression of degenerative scoliosis.

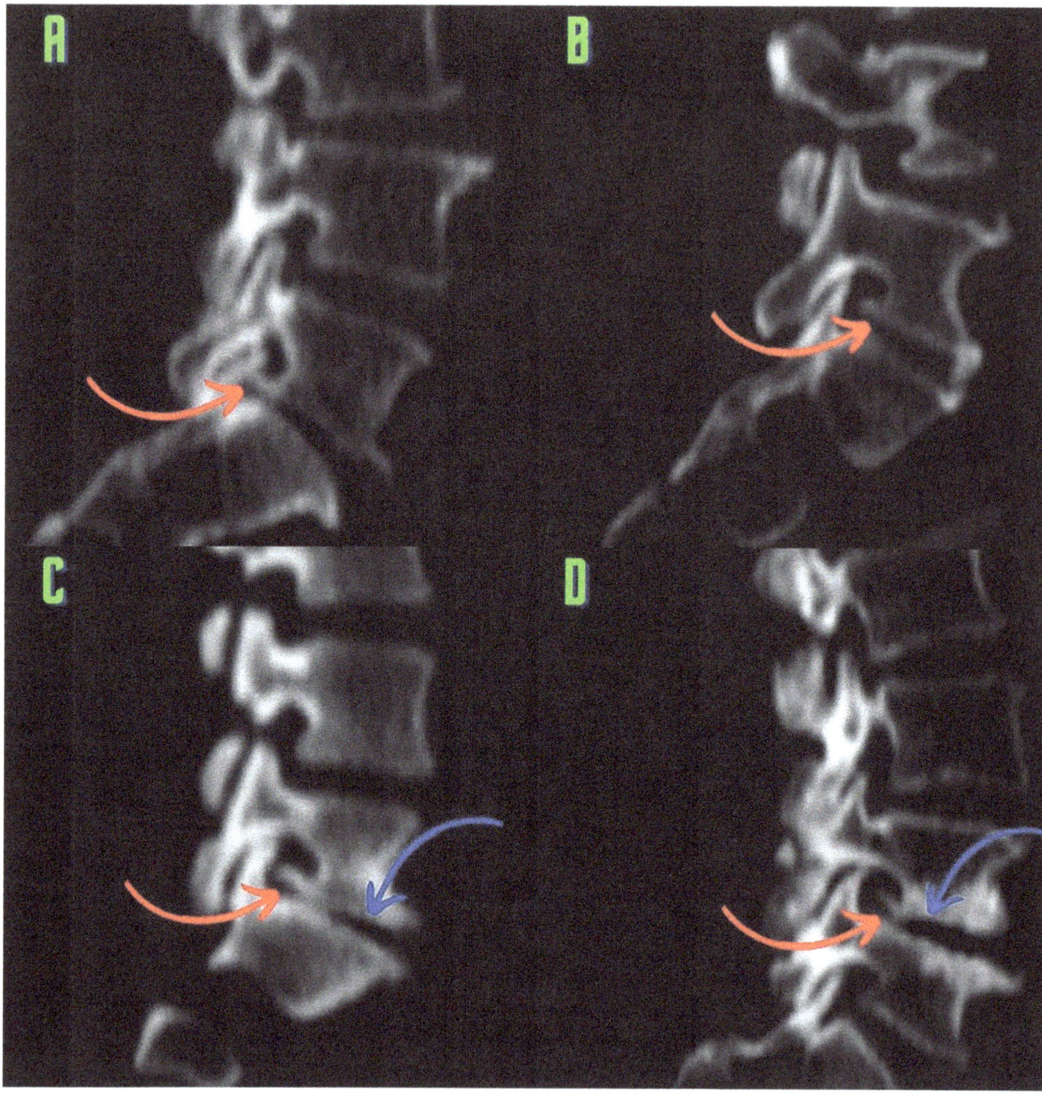

Figure 2. Osteophytes arising from the lower endplate of the superior vertebrae are observed. (**A**) An osteophyte arising from the lower endplate of the superior vertebrae (red arrow) in the L5–S1 foramen. It is observed that the intervertebral foramen is narrowed. (**B**) An osteophyte arising from the lower endplate of the superior vertebrae (red arrow) in the L5–S1 foramen. (**C**) In the L5–S1 foramen, the osteophyte arising from the inferior endplate of the superior vertebrae (red arrow) almost merges with the superior articular facet. The disk space is narrowed, and the vacuum phenomenon (blue arrow) is observed. (**D**) An osteophyte (red arrow) extending cranially from the inferior endplate of the superior vertebrae potentially narrows the foraminal space. Vacuum phenomenon (blue arrow) is observed.

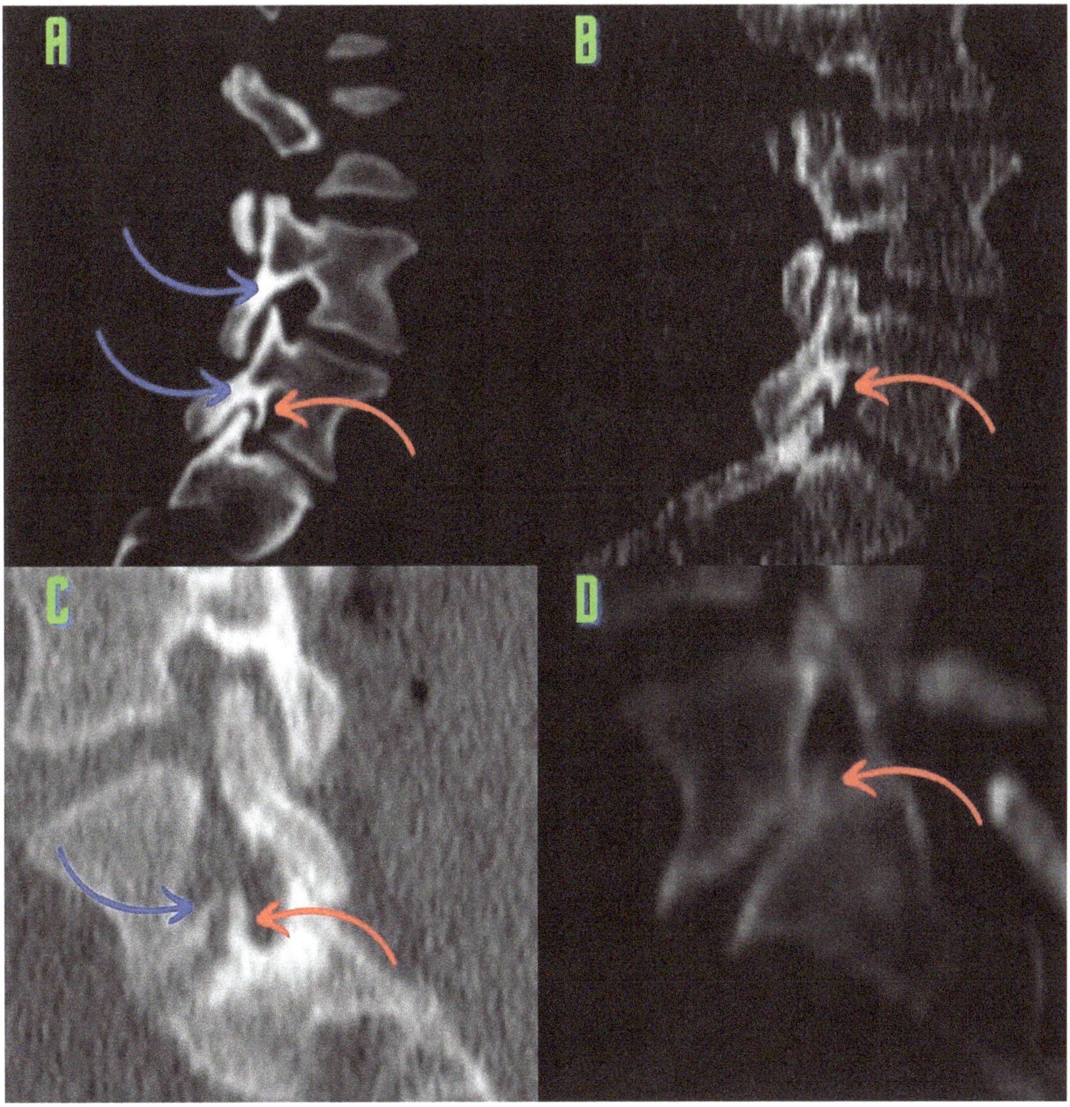

Figure 3. In the L5 (L5–S1) foramina, osteophytes arising from the pedicle–lamina junction and osteophytes arising from the superior endplate of the lower vertebrae are observed. (**A**) An osteophyte (red arrow) is observed in the L5–S1 foramen originating from the pedicle–lamina junction and extending to the anterior of the superior articular process. Hyperostosis (blue arrow) is observed in the pars region. (**B**) An osteophyte (red arrow) arising from the pedicle–lamina junction is observed in the L5–S1 foramen. (**C**) An osteophyte (red arrow) arising from the lower vertebral endplate of the intervertebral foramen is observed. Moreover, an osteophyte (blue arrow) arising from the lower endplate of the superior vertebrae is observed. (**D**) An osteophyte (red arrow) arising from the superior endplate of the lower vertebrae in the L5–S1 foramen exhibits oblique extension and occupies the foramen.

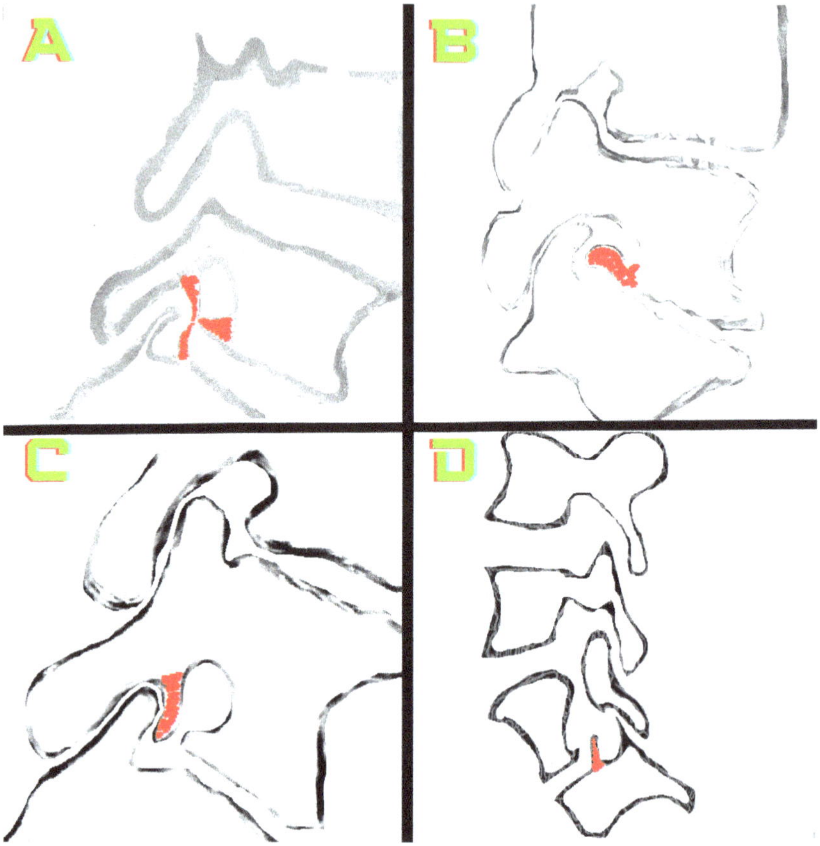

Figure 4. Intervertebral foramina and osteophytes are illustrated. (**A**) Osteophytes (red area) arising from three different points. (**B**) An osteophyte (red area) arising from the inferior endplate of the superior vertebrae. (**C**) An osteophyte (red area) arising from the pedicle–lamina junction. (**D**) A big osteophyte (red area) arising from the lower vertebral endplate of the intervertebral foramen is observed. Simultaneously, osteophytization is observed at two distinct points.

Table 2. Comparison between the measurements of osteophyte counts in L5 and L4 foramina.

Variable	Group	n/%	L5–S1		Total	Test Value [a]	*p*-Value
			Absent	Present			
L4–L5	**Absent**	n	957	176	1151	**12,094**	**<0.001 ***
		%	95.1%	88.4%	94.0%		
	Present	n	50	23	73		
		%	4.9%	11.6%	6.0%		
Total		n	**1025**	**199**	**1224**		
		%	**100.0%**	**100.0%**	**100.0%**		

n, number of samples; %, percentage; test value [a], chi-square test value (χ^2); *p*-value, statistical significance; * $p < 0.05$. There is a statistically significant difference between the groups. Bold numbers (for test value and *p*-value) indicate significant difference.

Table 3. Comparison of measurements by gender.

Variable	Group	n/%	Gender		Total	Test Value [a]	*p*-Value
			Male	Female			
		%	**10.1%**	**10.6%**	**10.3%**		
L5–S1	Absent	n	589	436	1025	3259	0.353
		%	84.5%	82.7%	83.7%		
	Left	n	33	32	65		
		%	4.7%	6.1%	5.3%		
	Right	n	36	21	57		
		%	5.2%	4.0%	4.7%		
	Right and Left (Bilateral)	n	39	38	77		
		%	5.6%	7.2%	6.3%		
L4–L5	Absent	n	654	497	1151	1837	0.607
		%	93.8%	94.3%	94.0%		
	Left	n	16	11	27		
		%	2.3%	2.1%	2.2%		
	Right	n	18	9	27		
		%	2.6%	1.7%	2.2%		
	Right and Left (Bilateral)	n	9	10	19		
		%	1.3%	1.9%	1.6%		
Total		n	**697**	**527**	**1224**		
		%	**100.0%**	**100.0%**	**100.0%**		

n, sample size; %, percentage; test value [a], chi-square test value (χ^2); *p*-value. There is a statistically significant difference between the groups. Bold letters and numbers (for test value and *p*-value) indicate significant difference.

Table 4. Comparison of measurements by age.

Variable	Group	Mean ± SD	M	Min–Max	Test Value	*p*-Value	Difference
Left L5–S1	Absent	46.01 ± 18.6	43.00	18–109	**42,068.000 [a]**	**<0.001 ***	Present
	Present	61.08 ± 16.91	61.00	19–101			
Right L5–S1	Absent	45.94 ± 18.37	43.00	18–109	**37,973.000 [a]**	**<0.001 ***	Present
	Present	62.52 ± 17.95	63.00	20–101			
L5–S1	Absent	45.17 ± 18.22	42.00	18–109	**112,789 [b]**	**<0.001 ***	1 and 2, 1 and 3, 1 and 4
	Left	58.08 ± 16.36	56.00	19–93			
	Right	61.05 ± 19.14	62.00	20–99			
	Right and Left	63.61 ± 17.06	64.00	20–101			
Left L4–L5	Absent	47.00 ± 18.77	44.00	18–109	**11,234.000 [a]**	**<0.001 ***	Present
	Present	67.07 ± 15.25	66.50	20–92			
Right L4–L5	Absent	47.09 ± 18.09	44.00	18–109	**12,662.500 [a]**	**<0.001 ***	Present
	Present	64.7 ± 14.00	62.00	33–92			
L4–L5	Absent	46.63 ± 18.71	44.00	18–109	**65,559 [b]**	**<0.001 ***	1 and 2, 1 and 3, 1 and 4
	Left	66.85 ± 16.28	69.00	20–87			
	Right	62.81 ± 13.9	63.00	33–87			
	Right and Left	67.37 ± 14.07	61.00	38–92			

SD, standard deviation; M, median; Min, the smallest value obtained; Max, the largest value obtained; test value [a], Mann–Whitney test; test value [b], Kruskal–Wallis test; *p*-value, statistical significance; * $p < 0.05$. There is a statistically significant difference between the groups. Bold letters and numbers (for test value and *p*-value) indicate significant difference.

4. Discussion

This study presented descriptive statistics and visual evidence for the morphology and distribution of lumbar foraminal osteophytes. The study also allowed a discussion of various points of view on the potential effects of lumbar foraminal osteophytes. To the best of our knowledge, there are no similar studies in the literature, which made making comparisons challenging at some points.

This study suggests that classifying the different types of osteophytes can play a critical role in the planning of surgical interventions. Treatment approaches that are tailored to the locations of the osteophytes can significantly improve patients' recovery processes. This information enables surgeons to select more accurate intervention methods and to reduce the risk of potential complications. Accurately identifying osteophytes (e.g., the lower endplates of the upper vertebrae) can improve the effectiveness of targeted surgical interventions and result in significant pain relief for the patient (Figures 3C,D and 4D). Our findings provide visual evidence of foraminal stenosis (Figures 1–4). Additionally, this classification system can be used as an effective teaching tool in spinal surgery training programs (Figures 1–4). Young surgeons can use this information to better understand the anatomical variations of osteophytes and their potential clinical implications. This classification provides a foundation for a more in-depth study of osteophytes and their clinical outcomes. Future research can contribute to the development of customized approaches in spinal surgery by evaluating the impact of this classification on surgical outcomes in greater detail.

The study results provide a detailed map of the foraminal osteophytes. Four osteophytes were identified based on their anatomical locations in the L4–L5 and L5–S1 foramina (Figures 1–4). Lumbar spinal osteophytes are more prevalent in the L5 (L5–S1 level) foramen (Table 2). The presence of these osteophytes does not vary by gender (Table 3), and age plays an important role in osteophyte formation (Table 4). This finding is consistent with those reported in the relevant literature. Previous research has found that osteophytes increase with age in other anatomical regions of the body (such as the knees) [3].

4.1. Osteophytes and Facet Osteoarthritis

Facet osteoarthritis is recognized as a cause of severe low back pain, affecting the economy through lost labor and, more importantly, health. Some studies have found that the facet joint and osteoarthritis can be the source of pain in these patients [12,13]. Facet osteoarthritis is a pathological condition characterized by degenerative and proliferative processes, such as subarticular bony erosions, joint space narrowing, articular process hypertrophy, osteophytosis, and an imbalance between destruction and repair [14]. Previous research has shown that facet osteoarthritis is more common at the L4–L5 level [15]. Our study revealed that osteophyte rates were higher in the L5 foramen (i.e., at the L5–S1 level; $p < 0.05$, Table 2). This finding is also consistent with the findings in the existing literature. Although osteophytes and osteoarthritis are correlated, they are different concepts [3]. Therefore, the presence of more osteophytes in the L5 (L5–S1 level) foramen than in the L4 (L4–L5 level) foramen can be explained by the increased interaction of weight-bearing and other forces in the spine from top to bottom [3,16]. This could be because osteophytes form in response to biomechanical stimuli, as reported in the literature [3].

An imbalance in load distribution is considered to be the primary cause of facet osteoarthritis [17]. The three joints in the motion segment are functionally related [10]. Biomechanical studies have shown that the lumbar disk and two facet joints work together to carry loads [18,19]. Moreover, facet osteoarthritis has a close pathological relationship with lumbar disk degeneration [14,15]. Autopsy studies revealed that facet joint degeneration is always associated with disk degeneration. The autopsy study of Vernon-Roberts and Pirie found that disk degeneration was almost always associated with osteophyte formation in the vertebral margins [20]. As a result, it is widely known that the three segments of motion (the lumbar disk and two facet joints) interact and can degenerate together [10,14,15,18,19]. In our study, disk degeneration accompanied foraminal osteophytes in many cases (Figure 1B–D, Figure 2A,C,D and Figure 3D). Notably, the visual findings of our study support and contribute to the existing literature. Moreover, vertebral osteophytes (Figures 1B and 2A,C,D) are another indicator of disk degeneration and commonly coexist with foraminal osteophytes [3]. At the foraminal region, the parts of the triple motion system are most closely related [1]. Therefore, osteophytes, for which visual evidence was provided in the present study, are candidates for strong radiographic markers of facet osteoarthritis because they represent a pathoanatomical structure that may affect the musculoskeletal system.

Facet osteoarthritis and motion segment failure are thought to contribute to degenerative spondylolisthesis and scoliosis [21]. The visual evidence of the present study supports the literature on the subject. In this study, we presented foraminal osteophytes with sagittal sections, and some cases had concomitant degenerative scoliosis (Figure 1D). According to previous studies, sagittal sections can reveal deformity in degenerative scoliosis [22].

Atul Goel linked the development of facet joint osteophytes to degeneration and instability in this region [23,24]. The visual findings of our study, particularly the signs of degeneration associated with osteophytes (decreased disk height, vertebral osteophytes, and the vacuum phenomenon), are consistent with those of previous studies (Figures 1A,C and 2A,C,D) [23]. The periosteal reaction is thought to be responsible for osteophyte-induced degeneration [24]. It is also noted that these degenerative osteophytes that form around the facet joint narrow the intervertebral neural foramen [24]. Our findings are consistent with those of Atul Goel, who found visual evidence that osteophytes cause foraminal stenosis (Figures 1–4) [24].

4.2. Potential Effect of Osteophytes on Biomechanics

The findings of the present study may have significant biomechanical and kinematic implications. Kozanek et al. [25] found that in asymptomatic participants, the movement of the facet joints during the flexion–extension movement of the L4–L5 segment was less than that of the upper lumbar segments. In general, they found that the flexion and extension movements were more limited at the lower lumbar levels, whereas the torsion and lateral bending movements were more limited at the upper lumbar levels [25]. These movements involve both the lower lumbar spine, which is coronal and horizontal, and the upper lumbar spine, which is sagittal and vertical [25]. The orientation of the facets directs and limits the movements of the spine. Thus, the orientation aims to reduce mechanical forces while protecting the annulus fibrosus cells from overstretching [16]. Kozanek et al. [25] found that the lower lumbar facet joints limit flexion and extension movements. Moreover, Wilke [26] and Nachemson et al. [27] found that intradiscal pressure is higher in the flexion positions of the spine (i.e., the flexion position while sitting, standing, and lifting weights in the standing position) than in other positions. Mechanical stress is thought to be the first event that causes the formation of osteophytes [3]. We believe that mixed-type osteophytes (Figure 1) and extrusions that develop into osteophytes behind the superior facet at the pedicle–lamina junction (Figures 1 and 3A,B) are modular (regionally independent) responses that aim to further restrict (even immobilize) lumbar flexion and extension movements. Atul Goel [28] suggests that the formation of osteophytes around the facet joint may provide protection by reducing instability. Our modular response view is consistent with Atul Goel's thoughts. There are three explanations for this viewpoint. First, the natural anatomical (coronal and horizontal) structures of the lower lumbar facet joints limit the flexion and extension movements of the spine to reduce the mechanical forces [16,25]. Second, it has been documented that spinal flexion and extension cause an increase in intradiscal pressure [26,27]. Third, during lumbar extension, particularly if the disk height is decreased, the ends of the inferior articular processes may come into contact with the pars interarticularis and lamina, which is thought to cause pain [29]. These stimuli could be biomechanical initiators of foraminal osteophytic processes [3].

According to Dunlop et al. [30], significant loads are transmitted to the facets more effectively than to the pars interarticularis. According to their findings, the pars interarticularis, one of the load-bearing regions, is the anatomical region where osteophytes originate from the pedicle–lamina junction described in our study (Figure 3A,B). According to Prasad et al. [31], hyperextension of the spine increases the load on the facet joints. Many studies have found that lumbar extension may cause pain [30,32]. Moreover, Yang and King [19] found that further overloading of the facet joints altered the anatomical orientation of the facets. As the disk height decreases, the tip of the inferior articular processes makes contact with the surrounding bone tissue during forward flexion [29]. Several authors have reported that the normal compressive loads carried by the facets increase with unrestricted (above physiological limits) lumbar flexion movement [33–35]. These concepts contribute to a better understanding of the process that causes mechanically induced lumbar foraminal osteophytes. The movement segment becoming more immobile supports our claim that it serves as a protective mechanism [29,30,32–35]. However, further studies with high levels of evidence are required to verify this. Atul Goel suggests that the formation of osteophytes around the facet joint may have a protective rather than a harmful or pathological effect [28].

4.3. Osteophytes and Foraminal Stenosis

Lumbar foraminal stenosis is one of the causes of pain associated with radiculopathy [36]. Foraminal stenosis can be caused by various factors, including disk protrusion, decreased disk height, facet hypertrophy, and osteophytes on the vertebral endplates [37]. Lee et al. [37] developed a grading system for foraminal stenosis. When evaluating foraminal stenosis, morphological parameters, such as foraminal height, superior foraminal width, middle foraminal width, minimum foraminal height, pedicle length, and posterior disk height, must be considered [38]. The osteophytes described in this study provide visual evidence of stenosis in the foraminal volume (Figures 1–4). Identifying these osteophytes before surgery has the potential to improve surgical outcomes. Foraminal pathologies are among the leading causes of failed back surgery syndrome. Furthermore, the osteophytes described in the present study (Figures 1–4) will improve preoperative assessment and awareness. This will help to explain some clinical findings observed after surgery. Our results provide surgeons with a therapeutic target within a novel framework.

In a recent and significant study, Murata et al. [39] linked insufficient decompression of the vertebral osteophyte and intervertebral disc complex (O/D complex) to poor surgical outcomes. Murata et al. specifically recommend removing osteophytes from the lower endplates of the upper vertebrae (Figure 2A–D) for foraminal decompression. Moreover, Murata et al. identified the osteophyte size (O/D complex) as a predictor of recovery. They emphasize the importance of osteophyte size in treating back and leg pain. However, Murata et al. have only focused on one type of osteophyte (originating from the lower endplate of the upper vertebrae). Despite the excision of a single osteophyte, the 2- and 5-year outcomes are quite successful [39]. In our study, we found four osteophytes that narrow the foramen (Figures 1–4). The osteophytes we described (Figures 1–4) could help surgeons perform foraminal decompression [39]. Murata et al. emphasize that the structure known as an osteophyte, which originates from the lower endplates of the upper vertebrae, is also an important factor in patient selection and surgical planning. Therefore, the four osteophytes we identified (Figures 1–4) may be important in patient selection and surgical decision making. Like Murata et al., Atul Goel [24] observes that osteophytes narrow the lumbar intervertebral foramen. Our visual findings show that osteophytes significantly narrow the lumbar intervertebral foramen; these findings are consistent with those of previous studies (Figures 1–4).

4.4. Limitations of this Study

The present study has several limitations. First, there is no precise definition of foraminal osteophytes in the literature. Second, millimetric osteophytes can cause observers to make different observations, which affects the calculation of their incidence. Third, we reconstructed the images that the other branches requested. We assumed this patient group was asymptomatic, but some patients likely experienced symptoms. Fourth, the images in this study were reconstructed, and they may not have met the requirements of the study. The L4–L5 and L5–S1 levels are very common for osteophyte formation but are not limited to these regions. The paper only reported on the L4–L5 and L5–S1 levels. The L1–L2, L2–L3, and L3–L4 foramen could also be investigated. The images were analyzed without the expertise of a radiologist, which may have had an impact on the results of the study.

This is because partial volume effects, motion artifacts, or foraminal variations may be misidentified as osteophyte formations. The images used in the study came from two multi-detector CT machines (one with 128 slices and the other with 16 slices). Despite attempts to control for confounding variables, the inherent observational nature of the study may have allowed residual confounding factors to persist. Future studies across multiple centers must confirm our findings in diverse patient populations.

5. Conclusions

This study presented the distribution and morphology of foraminal osteophytes in the sagittal plane in a large number of patients. We identified four types of osteophytes in the L4–L5 and L5–S1 foramina and discussed their potential effects on osteoarthritis, biomechanics, and foraminal stenosis. Awareness of foraminal osteophytes before, during, and after surgery will improve patient management. However, additional research is needed to collect data with high levels of evidence.

Author Contributions: A.E.T. and F.İ. contributed to the concept and design of the study; F.İ. and A.E.T. acquired the data; F.İ. and A.E.T. analyzed and interpreted the data; A.E.T. drafted the manuscript; F.İ. edited the statistical data; A.E.T. revised the manuscript critically; A.E.T. made the illustrations. All authors have read and agreed to the published version of the manuscript.

Funding: This research received no external funding.

Institutional Review Board Statement: This retrospective study was approved by the Ethics Committee of Clinical Research of the Faculty of Medicine, Malatya Turgut Özal University, with decision no. 2021/111, dated 16 December 2021.

Informed Consent Statement: Informed consent was waived due to the retrospective nature of our cohort.

Data Availability Statement: The raw data supporting the findings of this study are available from the corresponding authors upon reasonable request.

Acknowledgments: My deep gratitude goes to Cevat Akıncı and Şeyda Sevde Kaya for the provided training on ChatGPT 4 and Canva. We would like to express our gratitude to OpenAI for building ChatGPT4, which helped in the grammar-checking procedures during the manuscript writing process of some parts of the article. (Source: https://chat.openai.com/ accessed on 5 March 2024). The authors thank Canva "https://www.canva.com.tr/ (accessed on 24 March 2024)". Figure 4 was created using Canva-design. (Source: https://www.canva.com.tr/ accessed on 24 March 2024). The content, results, and methods seen in this manuscript are entirely the work of the authors, as listed in the author contributions section.

Conflicts of Interest: The authors declare no conflicts of interest.

Abbreviations

IVF: lumbar intervertebral foramen, SD: standard deviation, Min: minimum, Max: maximum.

References

1. Gkasdaris, G.; Kapetanakis, S. Clinical anatomy and significance of the lumbar intervertebral foramen: A review. *J. Anat. Soc. India* **2015**, *64*, 166–173. [CrossRef]
2. Yan, S.; Zhang, Y.; Wang, K.; Han, Y.; Zhu, K.; He, F.; Tan, J. Three-Dimensional Morphological Characteristics of Lower Lumbar Intervertebral Foramen with Age. *BioMed Res. Int.* **2018**, *2018*, 8157061. [CrossRef]
3. Wong, S.H.J.; Chiu, K.Y.; Yan, C.H. Osteophytes. *J. Orthop. Surg.* **2016**, *24*, 403–410. [CrossRef]
4. GBD 2017 Disease and Injury Incidence and Prevalence Collaborators. Global, regional, and national incidence, prevalence, and years lived with disability for 354 diseases and injuries for 195 countries and territories, 1990–2017: A systematic analysis for the Global Burden of Disease Study 2017. *Lancet* **2018**, *392*, 1789–1858. [CrossRef]
5. Lambeek, L.C.; van Tulder, M.W.; Swinkels, I.C.; Koppes, L.L.; Anema, J.R.; van Mechelen, W. The Trend in Total Cost of Back Pain in the Netherlands in the Period 2002 to 2007. *Spine* **2011**, *36*, 1050–1058. [CrossRef]

6. Chamoro, M.; de Luca, K.; Ozbulut, O.; Oei, E.H.G.; Vleggeert-Lankamp, C.L.A.; Koes, B.W.; Bierma-Zeinstra, S.M.A.; Chiarotto, A. Association between clinical findings and the presence of lumbar spine osteoarthritis imaging features: A systematic review. *Osteoarthr. Cartil.* **2023**, *31*, 1158–1175. [CrossRef] [PubMed]
7. Borenstein, D. Does osteoarthritis of the lumbar spine cause chronic low back pain? *Curr. Pain Headache Rep.* **2004**, *8*, 512–517. [CrossRef]
8. Goode, A.P.; Cleveland, R.J.; George, S.Z.; Schwartz, T.A.; Kraus, V.B.; Renner, J.B.; Gracely, R.H.; DeFrate, L.E.; Hu, D.; Jordan, J.M.; et al. Predictors of Lumbar Spine Degeneration and Low Back Pain in the Community: The Johnston County Osteoarthritis Project. *Arthritis Care Res.* **2021**, *74*, 1659–1666. [CrossRef] [PubMed]
9. Schofferman, J.; Reynolds, J.; Herzog, R.; Covington, E.; Dreyfuss, P.; O'Neill, C. Failed back surgery: Etiology and diagnostic evaluation. *Spine J.* **2003**, *3*, 400–403. [CrossRef] [PubMed]
10. Gellhorn, A.C.; Katz, J.N.; Suri, P. Osteoarthritis of the spine: The facet joints. *Nat. Rev. Rheumatol.* **2013**, *9*, 216–224. [CrossRef]
11. Rohen, J.W.; Yokochi, C.; Lütjen-Drecoll, E. *Color Atlas of Anatomy: A Photographic Study of the Human Body*; Schattauer: Stuttgart, Germany, 2006.
12. Kang, Y.-M.; Choi, W.-S.; Pickar, J.G. Electrophysiologic Evidence for an Intersegmental Reflex Pathway Between Lumbar Paraspinal Tissues. *Spine* **2002**, *27*, E56–E63. [CrossRef] [PubMed]
13. Schwarzer, A.C.; Aprill, C.N.; Derby, R.; Fortin, J.; Kine, G.; Bogduk, N. Clinical Features of Patients with Pain Stemming from the Lumbar Zygapophysial Joints. Is the lumbar facet syndrome a clinical entity? *Spine* **1994**, *19*, 1132–1137. [CrossRef] [PubMed]
14. Pathria, M.; Sartoris, D.J.; Resnick, D. Osteoarthritis of the facet joints: Accuracy of oblique radiographic assessment. *Radiology* **1987**, *164*, 227–230. [CrossRef] [PubMed]
15. Fujiwara, A.; Tamai, K.; Yamato, M.; An, H.S.; Yoshida, H.; Saotome, K.; Kurihashi, A. The relationship between facet joint osteoarthritis and disc degeneration of the lumbar spine: An MRI study. *Eur. Spine J.* **1999**, *8*, 396–401. [CrossRef]
16. Taylor, J.R.; Twomey, L.T. Structure and Function of Lumbar Zygapophyseal (facet) Joints: A Review. *J. Orthop. Med.* **1992**, *14*, 71–78. [CrossRef]
17. Kettler, A.; Wilke, H.-J. Review of existing grading systems for cervical or lumbar disc and facet joint degeneration. *Eur. Spine J.* **2005**, *15*, 705–718. [CrossRef] [PubMed]
18. Putz, R. The functional morphology of the superior articular processes of the lumbar vertebrae. *J. Anat.* **1985**, *143*, 181–187. [PubMed]
19. Yang, K.H.; King, A.I. Mechanism of Facet Load Transmission as a Hypothesis for Low-Back Pain. *Spine* **1984**, *9*, 557–565. [CrossRef] [PubMed]
20. Vernon-Roberts, B.; Pirie, C.J. Healing trabecular microfractures in the bodies of lumbar vertebrae. *Ann. Rheum. Dis.* **1973**, *32*, 406–412. [CrossRef]
21. Wang, J.; Yang, X. Age-Related Changes in the Orientation of Lumbar Facet Joints. *Spine* **2009**, *34*, E596–E598. [CrossRef]
22. Kim, W.; Porrino, J.A.; Hood, K.A.; Chadaz, T.S.; Klauser, A.S.; Taljanovic, M.S. Clinical Evaluation, Imaging, and Management of Adolescent Idiopathic and Adult Degenerative Scoliosis. *Curr. Probl. Diagn. Radiol.* **2019**, *48*, 402–414. [CrossRef] [PubMed]
23. Goel, A. 'Only fixation' as rationale treatment for spinal canal stenosis. *J. Craniovertebral Junction Spine* **2011**, *2*, 55–56. [CrossRef] [PubMed]
24. Goel, A. Facet distraction spacers for treatment of degenerative disease of the spine: Rationale and an alternative hypothesis of spinal degeneration. *J. Craniovertebral Junction Spine* **2010**, *1*, 65–66. [CrossRef] [PubMed]
25. Kozanek, M.; Wang, S.; Passias, P.G.; Xia, Q.; Li, G.; Bono, C.M.; Wood, K.B.; Li, G. Range of Motion and Orientation of the Lumbar Facet Joints In Vivo. *Spine* **2009**, *34*, E689–E696. [CrossRef]
26. Wilke, H.; Neef, P.; Caimi, M.; Hoogland, T.; Claes, L.E. New In Vivo Measurements of Pressures in the Intervertebral Disc in Daily Life. *Spine* **1999**, *24*, 755–762. [CrossRef] [PubMed]
27. Nachemson, A.L. Disc Pressure Measurements. *Spine* **1981**, *6*, 93–97. [CrossRef] [PubMed]
28. Goel, A. Vertical facetal instability: Is it the point of genesis of spinal spondylotic disease? *J. Craniovertebral Junction Spine* **2015**, *6*, 47–48. [CrossRef] [PubMed]
29. Inoue, N.; Orías, A.A.E.; Segami, K. Biomechanics of the lumbar facet joint, Spine surgery and related research. *Spine Surg. Relat. Res.* **2019**, *4*, 1–7. [CrossRef] [PubMed]
30. Dunlop, R.B.; Adams, M.A.; Hutton, W.C. Disc space narrowing and the lumbar facet joints. *J. Bone Jt. Surg.* **1984**, *66*, 706–710. [CrossRef]
31. Prasad, P.; King, A.I.; Ewing, C.L. The Role of Articular Facets During +Gz Acceleration. *J. Appl. Mech.* **1974**, *41*, 321–326. [CrossRef]
32. Gorniak, G.; Conrad, W. Lower lumbar facet joint complex anatomy. *Austin. J. Anat.* **2015**, *2*, 1–8.
33. Ivicsics, M.; Bishop, N.; Püschel, K.; Morlock, M.; Huber, G. Increase in facet joint loading after nucleotomy in the human lumbar spine. *J. Biomech.* **2014**, *47*, 1712–1717. [CrossRef] [PubMed]
34. Ianuzzi, A.; Little, J.S.; Chiu, J.B.; Baitner, A.; Kawchuk, G.; Khalsa, P.S. Human lumbar facet joint capsule strains: I. During physiological motions. *Spine J.* **2004**, *4*, 141–152. [CrossRef]
35. Claeson, A.A.; Barocas, V.H. Computer simulation of lumbar flexion shows shear of the facet capsular ligament. *Spine J.* **2016**, *17*, 109–119. [CrossRef] [PubMed]
36. Jenis, L.G.; An, H.S. Spine update: Lumbar foraminal stenosis. *Spine* **2000**, *25*, 389–394. [CrossRef] [PubMed]

37. Lee, S.; Lee, J.W.; Yeom, J.S.; Kim, K.-J.; Kim, H.-J.; Chung, S.K.; Kang, H.S. A Practical MRI Grading System for Lumbar Foraminal Stenosis. *Am. J. Roentgenol.* **2010**, *194*, 1095–1098. [CrossRef] [PubMed]
38. Attias, N.; Hayman, A.; Hipp, J.A.; Noble, P.; Esses, S.I. Assessment of magnetic resonance imaging in the diagnosis of lumbar spine foraminal stenosis—A surgeon's perspective. *Clin. Spine Surg.* **2006**, *19*, 249–256. [CrossRef]
39. Murata, S.; Takami, M.; Iwasaki, H.; Hashizume, H.; Yukawa, Y.; Minamide, A.; Nakagawa, Y.; Tsutsui, S.; Okada, M.; Nagata, K.; et al. Outcomes and Vertebral Osteophytes and Bulging Intervertebral Discs Occupancy as a Decision-Making Tool for Surgical Success in Patients Undergoing Microendoscopic Foraminotomy for Lumbar Foraminal Stenosis. *World Neurosurg.* **2024**, *182*, e570–e578. [CrossRef]

diagnostics

MDPI

Article

Revolutionizing Radiological Analysis: The Future of French Language Automatic Speech Recognition in Healthcare

Mariem Jelassi [1,2], Oumaima Jemai [2,3] and Jacques Demongeot [4,*]

1 RIADI Laboratory, Ecole Nationale des Sciences de l'Informatique (ENSI), Manouba University, La Manouba 2010, Tunisia; jlassi.mariem.esti@gmail.com
2 Health Tech Innovation Systems Inc., ENSI Innovation Hub, La Manouba 2010, Tunisia; jemaioumayma98@gmail.com
3 Ecole Supérieure des Communications de Tunis (SUP'COM), Carthage University, Ariana 2083, Tunisia
4 AGEIS Laboratory, Faculté de Médecine, Université Grenoble Alpes (UGA), 38700 La Tronche, France
* Correspondence: jacques.demongeot@univ-grenoble-alpes.fr

Abstract: This study introduces a specialized Automatic Speech Recognition (ASR) system, leveraging the Whisper Large-v2 model, specifically adapted for radiological applications in the French language. The methodology focused on adapting the model to accurately transcribe medical terminology and diverse accents within the French language context, achieving a notable Word Error Rate (WER) of 17.121%. This research involved extensive data collection and preprocessing, utilizing a wide range of French medical audio content. The results demonstrate the system's effectiveness in transcribing complex radiological data, underscoring its potential to enhance medical documentation efficiency in French-speaking clinical settings. The discussion extends to the broader implications of this technology in healthcare, including its potential integration with electronic health records (EHRs) and its utility in medical education. This study also explores future research directions, such as tailoring ASR systems to specific medical specialties and languages. Overall, this research contributes significantly to the field of medical ASR systems, presenting a robust tool for radiological transcription in the French language and paving the way for advanced technology-enhanced healthcare solutions.

Keywords: automatic speech recognition (ASR); medical transcription; radiology; whisper large-v2 model; language-specific ASR systems; French language processing; AI in healthcare

1. Introduction

The integration of Artificial Intelligence (AI) in healthcare, particularly through Automatic Speech Recognition (ASR) systems, has been a subject of increasing interest in recent years. These systems, demonstrating significant potential in various medical applications, have revolutionized the way patient–physician interactions are transcribed and clinical documentation is managed [1]. Recent explorations into online therapy platforms underscore ASR's expanding role in mental health, where nuanced language processing enhances therapeutic outcomes [2]. In the field of radiology, where accuracy and efficiency in reporting are paramount, the application of ASR technology can be particularly transformative, offering a new paradigm in the way radiologists work and interact with diagnostic data [3]. Similarly, advancements in ASR for cochlear implants illustrate the technology's potential to improve communication for individuals with hearing impairments, showcasing its adaptability to diverse healthcare needs [4].

Despite the global advancements in ASR technology, its application within the French medical context has been limited. This gap is further addressed by recent studies leveraging Large Language Models to refine the accuracy of ASR in medical transcription, promising more reliable patient records [5]. This gap is primarily due to the linguistic and terminological specificity required in medical ASR systems, which are often not met by general-purpose

ASR tools [6]. The development of a French-language medical ASR system is thus a technological and linguistic challenge, requiring a deep understanding of medical terminologies and the nuances of spoken French in a clinical setting [7]. The need for extensive and specialized datasets, encompassing a wide range of medical terminologies, accents, and speech patterns specific to the medical profession, poses a significant hurdle [7]. While the broader application of ASR technology shows immense promise, the French radiological sector presents unique challenges such as the need for highly specialized terminologies and the accommodation of diverse French dialects and accents, which our research specifically aims to address. However, this also presents an opportunity to develop tailored solutions that can significantly benefit the medical community, particularly in non-English-speaking regions. Recent studies have shown promising results in cross-lingual applications of ASR, adapting systems to work with low-resource languages [8]. Moreover, the development of specialized ASR systems for healthcare chatbots in schools demonstrates this technology's potential in pediatric care, contributing to early health assessments [9].

While ASR's impact spans across multiple medical disciplines, the field of radiology in French healthcare settings remains largely untapped, marked by a critical need for customized ASR solutions. Our research directly responds to this gap by offering an ASR system that is not only linguistically and terminologically precise but also attuned to the operational workflows of French radiologists, thereby promising a significant leap towards streamlined radiological reporting and enhanced diagnostic efficiencies.

The use of advanced neural network models and language processing techniques has been explored to enhance the accuracy and reliability of medical ASR systems [10,11]. These advancements are not only technical but also encompass a broader understanding of the medical field, ensuring that the developed systems are finely tuned to the specific needs of healthcare professionals. Amidst these advancements, our study carves out a distinct niche by developing an ASR system that not only caters to the French-speaking medical community but is also intricately tailored to the nuanced demands of radiological terminology and practices in Francophone countries. Such nuanced applications of ASR, from enhancing mental health support to improving medical equipment interaction, underscore the technology's evolving role in facilitating comprehensive and personalized care [12].

The primary objective of this research was to develop a specialized French-language ASR system, tailored for radiological applications. This system aims to facilitate radiologists in efficiently generating medical image reports, thereby enhancing the overall workflow in diagnostic procedures [13]. The novelty of this project lies in its focus on creating a dedicated ASR tool for radiology, addressing the scarcity of French-language audio datasets in the medical domain. By leveraging machine learning techniques, specifically tailored for medical jargon and radiological terms, this tool aims to provide accurate and efficient transcription services [14]. The potential of ASR in medicine is vast, ranging from automated transcriptions of medical reports to assisting in the drafting process, indexing medical data, and enabling voice-based queries in medical databases [15].

The implications of ASR technology extend beyond radiology to other medical fields. For instance, in emergency medical services, ASR has been assessed for its impact on stroke detection, showing potential for improving response times and diagnostic accuracy [16]. In long-term care for older adults, ASR models have been used to facilitate interview data transcription, saving time and resources [17]. Even in operating rooms, ASR techniques can be used to improve the dialogue between the surgeon and their human (e.g., surgical nurses) or digital (e.g., robotic arms) assistants [18,19]. Additionally, in pediatric care, ASR and voice interaction technologies have been explored for remote care management, demonstrating feasibility and effectiveness in tracking symptoms and health events [20].

Recent reviews in the field of healthcare have highlighted significant advancements in Automatic Speech Recognition (ASR) technology and its diverse applications. These advancements underscore the transformative potential of ASR in healthcare, paving the way for more efficient, accurate, and patient-centered medical practices.

A comprehensive review of state-of-the-art approaches in ASR, speech synthesis, and health detection using speech signals has shed light on the current capabilities and future directions of speech technology in healthcare [21]. This review emphasizes the growing importance of ASR in various healthcare settings, from clinical documentation to patient monitoring.

Another study explored the potential of real-time speech-to-text and text-to-speech converters, using Natural Language Grammar (NLG) and Abstract Meaning Representation (AMR) graphs, to enhance healthcare communication and documentation [22]. This technology could revolutionize how medical professionals interact with electronic health records, making the process more intuitive and efficient.

The robustness of ASR systems in noisy environments, a common challenge in medical settings, has also been a focus of recent research [23]. Enhancing the noise robustness of ASR systems is crucial for their effective deployment in diverse healthcare environments, from busy emergency rooms to outpatient clinics.

Furthermore, a systematic literature review on various techniques within the domain of speech recognition provides a comprehensive understanding of the advancements and challenges in this field [24]. This review highlights the rapid evolution of ASR technology and its increasing relevance in healthcare.

In addition to these technical advancements, the integration of ASR with patient-reported outcomes and value-based healthcare has been explored [25]. This integration signifies a shift towards more personalized and patient-centered healthcare models, where patient voices and experiences are directly captured and analyzed through advanced speech recognition technologies.

These reviews and studies collectively illustrate the significant strides made in ASR technology and its increasing applicability in healthcare. From enhancing clinical workflows to improving patient engagement, ASR technology is set to play a pivotal role in the future of healthcare delivery.

2. Methods

This study on developing an Automatic Speech Recognition (ASR) system tailored for radiological applications meticulously documents the methods and processes integral to this research. This section begins with a detailed description of the data preprocessing techniques and datasets foundational to the ASR system. It then describes the model selection criteria, training processes, and the deployment of the speech recognition application. The subsequent sections delve into the tasks and design of the system, followed by an outline of the evaluation metrics that quantify the performance of the system.

2.1. Data Preprocessing

2.1.1. Data Source Selection and Collection Methodology

This research utilized a diverse array of audio content, with a primary focus on YouTube, which constituted approximately 90% of the sourced data. This was supplemented by audiobooks and podcasts. The selection strategy was driven by the need to cover a broad spectrum of radiological topics. YouTube, as a rich repository, provided access to a wealth of relevant material including radiology conferences, online courses, and medical descriptions. The integration of audiobooks and podcasts, forming about 10% of the dataset, enriched it with detailed presentations on radiological themes, ensuring a rich variety of accents and tonalities crucial for the development of a robust ASR system.

In this comprehensive approach to data collection, a multi-tiered methodology was employed. This involved systematic categorization based on human body systems, a targeted keyword analysis for each organ and imaging type, and the inclusion of diverse pedagogical voices. A critical component of the methodology was the technical extraction of audio from YouTube videos and podcasts, using sophisticated software tools to isolate the audio track from visual elements and to extract high-quality audio. This process created an audio-centric dataset, focusing on the auditory dimensions of medical instruction.

The compiled dataset boasts over 240 h of audio content, representing a vast educational repository.

2.1.2. Data Collection Methodology

The methodology adopted for our exhaustive research and diverse data collection covering the entire human body was based on a methodical approach. This process revolved around a detailed exploration of various body systems, including the nervous system, circulatory system, digestive system, respiratory system, and skeletal system, among others. Each of these systems was meticulously investigated to identify the organs they comprise. This targeted and comprehensive approach facilitated the gathering of data specifically suited for radiology.

Simultaneously, each organ underwent an in-depth exploration aimed at classifying various pathologies and abnormalities diagnosable through radiographic images. This step was crucial to ensure precise and complete data collection.

To enrich the database, each consulted video was supplemented with relevant metadata. This includes vital information such as the type of imaging described in the video, whether MRI, X-ray, or another type. This step aimed to ensure sufficient diversity in imaging, considering that each imaging type is associated with specific terms. Furthermore, the metadata includes details such as the speaker's accent and gender, the total video duration, the organ described in the video, and the body system to which the presented organs belong. This information was methodically organized and stored in a .csv file for efficient management and future reference. Table 1 details the distribution of this material among the various body systems, highlighting the dataset's depth and scope:

Table 1. Distribution of audio content duration by body system.

Body System	Duration (Hours)
Nervous System	53 h 32 min
Musculoskeletal System	61 h 27 min
Endocrine System	23 h 42 min
Respiratory System	22 h 54 min
Cardiovascular System	26 h 11 min
Digestive System	19 h 43 min
Reproductive System	17 h
Urinary System	6 h 17 min
Auditory System	5 h 10 min
Lymphatic and Blood System	4 h 21 min

Additionally, the number of hours of data collected for each speaker accent was calculated, as demonstrated in Table 2, to ensure a diverse representation of accents in the dataset.

Table 2. Distribution of audio content duration by accent.

Accent	Duration (Hours)
African	16 h 33 min
Algerian	25 h 19 min
Canadian	2 h 38 min
Native French	155 h 22 min
Moroccan	29 h 17 min
Tunisian	11 h 13 min

2.1.3. Transcription Generation

The transcription generation phase was a pivotal component of this study, entailing a rigorous evaluation of various transcription tools and models. This evaluation was meticulously orchestrated to not only gauge the performance of these tools but also to ascertain their alignment with the intricate requirements characteristic of radiological audio content. An extensive exploration of transcription tools was undertaken, encompassing leading-edge models such as Whisper, Conformer-CTC Large, and Wav2Vec 2.0. These models were deliberately selected for their avant-garde capabilities in speech recognition, alongside their potential applicability in the domain of medical imaging. This exploration was further augmented through the integration of Python's SpeechRecognition library and specialized online transcription services like oTranscribe, thereby facilitating a holistic comparison between traditional transcription methodologies and contemporary machine learning-driven approaches.

To objectively evaluate the efficacy of each transcription tool, the Word Error Rate (WER) metric was employed as the principal evaluative criterion. A reference transcription was meticulously constructed for a specific 12 s audio sequence, serving as a benchmark for this assessment. The WER, recognized as a gold standard in speech recognition research, was computed utilizing Python's Jiwer library, thus providing a quantitative foundation for the comparative analysis of transcription accuracy across various tools. This evaluative process was intricately designed to surmount the challenges inherent in transcribing medical imaging content, which is frequently imbued with specialized terminology and encompasses a spectrum of accents. As a result, the efficacy of each tool was appraised not solely on the grounds of its overall accuracy but also in terms of its adeptness in navigating the linguistic and acoustic idiosyncrasies intrinsic to the dataset.

The culmination of this exhaustive evaluation is encapsulated in Table 3, presenting a nuanced comparison of the WER scores attributed to each transcription tool. This table furnishes invaluable insights into the comparative strengths and limitations of each tool within the context of this research. The insights derived from this analysis were instrumental in guiding our selection of the most apt transcription tool for the dataset.

Table 3. Comparative analysis of transcription tool performance based on word error rate.

Transcription Tools	WER
SpeechRecognition (Python library supporting various engines including Google Web Speech API, Sphinx, etc.)	0.228
oTranscribe (free online tool designed for audio transcription with features like playback speed control, bookmarking, etc.)	0.628
Conformer-CTC Large (voice recognition model based on the Conformer-CTC architecture, optimized for automatic speech transcription)	0.2
AssemblyAI (automatic speech transcription service using machine learning models)	0.100
Whisper Large-v2 (voice recognition model developed by OpenAI, designed for automatic speech transcription)	0.142
Wav2Vec 2.0 (model developed by Facebook AI that excels in Automatic Speech Recognition using a self-supervised learning approach)	0.257

In the pursuit of selecting an apt transcription tool for the ASR system, a comparative analysis was conducted, centering on both the accuracy and practical applicability relative to the extensive dataset at hand. The Whisper Large-v2 model, developed by OpenAI, was identified as the optimal tool for this research endeavor. Despite the Assembly AI tool manifesting the lowest WER, its utility was constrained by a usage limitation of three hours per month, rendering it incompatible with the expansive scale of the dataset. In contrast, Whisper Large-v2 showcased a competitive WER of 0.142 and afforded the requisite flexibility for processing extensive audio inputs, accommodating sessions extending up to two hours.

The selection of the Whisper model was underpinned by its proven adeptness in navigating diverse and challenging audio environments, a capability of paramount importance given that the dataset comprised YouTube videos and podcasts often interlaced with background noise and music. The efficacy of Whisper in such scenarios has been substantiated through rigorous comparative evaluations with leading commercial and open-source ASR systems [26]. These evaluations underscored Whisper's superiority over the premier open-source model, NVIDIA STT, across a multitude of datasets, and its competitive stance against commercial ASR systems, thereby underscoring its adaptability and reliability across varied transcription contexts. This comprehensive performance assessment, as evidenced in Figure 1, affirmed our decision to utilize Whisper Large-v2 for the dataset's transcription needs.

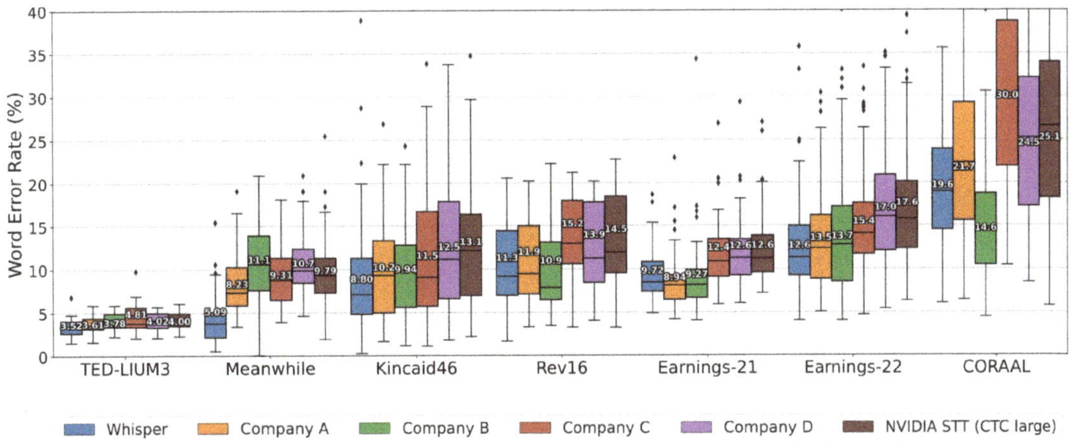

Figure 1. Comparative performance of the Whisper model in long-form transcription against leading ASR systems [26].

Figure 1 offers a visual summary of the Whisper Large-v2 model's Word Error Rates (WERs) juxtaposed with those of other prominent ASR systems. It depicts a boxplot distribution for each system, which includes the median WER and the interquartile ranges, thereby furnishing a statistical comparison of the performance metrics. The selection of the Whisper model was substantiated by this extensive assessment, affirming its capacity to outperform the well-established NVIDIA STT model across diverse datasets and to maintain competitive accuracy alongside proprietary ASR systems. The entire dataset was transcribed using the Whisper Large-v2 model, developed by OpenAI, due to its proficiency in handling diverse audio environments and its flexibility in processing extensive inputs. This model processes audio in segments of 2 to 30 s, generating detailed transcriptions for each, which are then combined to form the transcription for the entire audio file. Upon transcription, the Whisper model generates a TSV file for each audio recording. This file details the start and end times of each sound segment and its corresponding transcription, ensuring a precise match between audio and text. The "start" and "end" columns within the TSV file demarcate the commencement and conclusion of each sequence, offering a precise temporal framework for the segmentation of both audio files and their transcriptions, as illustrated in Figure 2.

This segmentation was essential for achieving an exact match between the audio content and its textual representation. It ensured the generation of detailed and precise transcriptions for each segment, which were subsequently amalgamated to formulate a comprehensive transcription for each audio file. This methodological choice was predicated on its efficacy in managing the voluminous audio dataset and its proficiency in capturing the nuanced variations prevalent in medical dialogue.

To ensure transcription accuracy, an automated correction process was employed using the Checkspeller library, supplemented by a custom script for specialized medical terminologies. This dual approach effectively addressed both common grammatical errors and the unique challenges posed by complex medical terms. To mitigate this limitation, an integration of a specialized lexicon encompassing technical terms was undertaken, significantly enhancing the transcription accuracy, as depicted in Figure 3.

```
start end text
0 4800  Chers maîtres, chers collègues, permettez-moi de vous présenter le cas radioclinique du jour.
9000  13880 Il s'agit d'un patient ayant 33 ans, sans antécédent pathologique particulier, victime
13880 16920 d'un accident de la voie publique, motocycliste heurté par une voiture,
16920 21800 occasionnant chez lui un traumatisme à point d'impact crânien. Ramené aux urgences inconscients,
21800 26640 l'examen clinique objectif a un Glasgow à 8 15ème et une anisocorie droite. Une
26640 33480 TDM cérébrale a été réalisée. Voici la TDM cérébrale du patient en coupe axiale,
33480 37080 fenêtres par enchimateuse, sans injection du produit de contraste.
52080 53320 En coupe coronale.
86640 89640 Puis en coupe sagittale.
116640  121640  Ensuite, la TDM cérébrale du patient en coupe axiale, fenêtres osseuses.
136640  141640  Le scanner objectif valora un hématome extradural frontoparietal droit, siège de bulles d'ai
141640  147640  mesurant 30 mm d'épaisseur maximale, étendu sur 80 mm de hauteur, exerçant un effet de masse
147640  151160  sur le système ventriculaire et la ligne médiane, responsable donc d'un engagement
151160  157640  souffle-alcooliel. Il s'y associe à un hématome extradural temporal droit, mesurant 17,5 mm
157640  163640  étendu sur 26 mm de hauteur, présence d'un trait de fracture parietal droit, d'une fracture
163640  168000  bifocale de la cloison nasale avec angulation, d'une fracture de l'arcade zygomastique droit
168000  169640  et des os propres du nez.
171640  176640  Le patient fut en urgence acheminé au bloc opératoire et a bénéficié d'un volet osseux
176640  181640  centré sur l'hématome extradural et évacuation de celui-ci, avec suspension de la durmère
181640  183640  afin d'éviter une éventuelle récidive.
185640  189640  Les engagements cérébraux résultent d'un processus expansif intracérébral au sein
189640  193640  d'une voûte crânienne inextensible. Les structures encéphaliques vont donc se déplacer
193640  198640  vers les orifices de communication des différents secteurs intracrâniens, c'est-à-dire les
199640  203640  foramen, notamment les foramen magnum, incisures tentorielles, voire en extracérébrale s'il
203640  208640  existe une perte de substance osseuse. Il n'existe pas de diagnostic différentiel et
208640  212640  le pronostic est lié à la rapidité de la prise en charge des lésions causables.
```

Figure 2. Audio file sample transcribed using Whisper Large-v2.

```
terms_hip.txt

Fichier   Modifier   Affichage
opothalmoplegie
craniopharyngiome
acromégalie
hyperprolactinémie
neuropathie
optique
compressive
insuffisance hypophysaire
prolactinome invasif
hormonothérapie
vacuolisation cytoplasmique
inhibiteurs de la dopamine
hyperplasie corticotrope
vasopressinergique
adénomectomie transsphénoidale
transsphénoidale
angiogenèse
adénylate cyclase
corticotropine
somatostatine
glycoprotéine alpha
diabète insipide
sécrétion pulsatile
corticotrophine corticotrope
tumeur chromophobe
syndrome de Sheehan
Ln 1, Col 1   100%   Unix (LF)   UTF-8
```

Figure 3. Exemplar list of technical terms.

The aforementioned enhancements and rigorous verification processes underscore the meticulous approach adopted in this study to ensure the generation of high-quality accurate transcriptions. This commitment to precision laid a robust foundation for the subsequent phases of the research, particularly in the development and fine-tuning of the Automatic Speech Recognition (ASR) system tailored for radiological applications.

To demystify the transcription process and the concomitant verification mechanism with greater granularity, the subsequent Table 4 delineates the overarching methodology employed for the dataset's transcription. This table includes a comprehensive account of the number of audio files processed, the aggregate duration of audio content, and the salient features of the transcription verification approach, thereby providing a succinct overview of the transcription methodology.

Table 4. Dataset transcription and verification overview.

Attribute	Detail
Total Audio Duration	240 h and 21 min
Number of Audio Files	69,643
Transcription Verification	Automated correction with Checkspeller library and custom script for medical terms

It is essential to clarify that the entire dataset underwent transcription through the selected Whisper model, which processes audio in segments from 2 to 30 s. This segmentation ensured detailed and accurate transcription for each segment, which were then cohesively assembled to form the complete transcription for each audio file. This methodology was chosen for its effectiveness in managing the extensive audio dataset and for its ability to capture the nuanced variations in medical dialogue.

Table 4 provides an overview of the transcription and verification process, detailing the total audio duration transcribed, the number of audio files processed, and the transcription verification methods employed.

2.1.4. Feature Extraction

The preparation of audio data for the ASR system involved comprehensive preprocessing and feature extraction. Using the librosa library, steps such as noise reduction, silence trimming, resampling, and compression were implemented to ensure the audio quality met the transcription requirements. The process also incorporated the Whisper Feature Extractor class from the Hugging Face's Transformers module. This stage focused on adjusting parameters like chunk length, feature size, hop length, and sampling rate, aligning them with the specific demands of the research. These modifications were essential for transforming the raw audio into a format suitable for machine learning models, laying the groundwork for model training and evaluation in this study.

2.2. Model Selection and Benchmarking

In developing an Automatic Speech Recognition (ASR) system tailored for radiological applications, a pivotal step involved selecting the most suitable model to ensure high transcription accuracy. Given the critical nature of radiological reports, where precision in medical terminology is paramount, the choice of the ASR model was approached with rigorous benchmarking criteria.

2.2.1. Benchmarking Strategy and Datasets

The benchmarking strategy was meticulously designed to evaluate various ASR models across multiple dimensions, including the Word Error Rate (WER), computational efficiency, and adaptability to diverse speech contexts. This comprehensive approach was essential to ascertain the models' performance in accurately transcribing radiological speech content, which is often laden with specialized terminology and presented in varied accents and background noises.

To facilitate a thorough comparison, a selection of datasets known for their relevance and complexity in speech recognition tasks was used. These included Common Voice, Multilingual LibriSpeech, VoxPopuli, African Accented French, and Fleur. Each dataset offered a unique set of challenges and speech characteristics, thereby providing a robust framework for evaluating the models' effectiveness across a wide spectrum of real-world applications.

2.2.2. Comparative Analysis and Model Selection

Our comparative analysis of ASR models, particularly focusing on the variants of the Whisper model, was grounded on a comprehensive benchmarking study utilizing datasets extracted from the Hugging Face Model Hub [27]. This approach, leveraging the platform's extensive repository of machine learning models, provided significant insights into each model's capabilities across a variety of speech recognition contexts. The Whisper Large-v2 model consistently outperformed its counterparts in terms of the WER across all datasets, underscoring its superior transcription accuracy. This was particularly evident in the handling of medical terminologies and in environments with diverse acoustic profiles, making it highly suitable for the project's requirements.

For instance, in the Common Voice dataset, Whisper Large-v2 achieved a remarkable WER of 7.67%, significantly lower than the other models evaluated. Similar trends were observed across other datasets, with Whisper Large-v2 maintaining the lowest WER, affirming its exceptional performance in diverse speech recognition contexts.

These findings are encapsulated in the comprehensive benchmarking shown in Table 5, which presents a side-by-side comparison of the Whisper Large-v2 model against other leading ASR models across various datasets used in our analysis. This consolidated table underscores the consistent superiority of the Whisper Large-v2 model in terms of the Word Error Rate (WER) across all datasets, affirming its exceptional capability to meet the intricate requirements of radiological speech transcription.

Table 5. Benchmarking using various datasets.

Fine-Tuned Model	Common Voice WER (%)	LibriSpeech WER (%)	VoxPopuli WER (%)	African Accented French WER (%)	Fleur WER(%)
bofenghuang/asr-wav2vec2-ctc-french	11.440	5.130	9.330	16.220	10.100
bofenghuang/whisper-large-v2-french	7.670	4.030	8.660	4.310	4.980
jonatasgrosman/whisper-large-fr-cv11	9.087	–	–	–	8.686
bofenghuang/asr-wav2vec2-xls-r-1b-ctc-french	14.800	9.390	11.800	22.980	–
bofenghuang/whisper-medium-cv11-french	8.540	5.860	11.350	7.020	6.850
bofenghuang/deprecated-whisper-large-v2-cv11- french-punct-plus	8.030	–	–	–	5.260
bofenghuang/whisper-medium-french	8.730	4.440	9.460	4.560	5.940
bofenghuang/whisper-small-cv11-french	10.990	8.910	–	9.260	9.830
pierreguillou/whisper-medium-french	11.141	–	–	–	–
sanchit-gandhi/whisper-small-fr-1k-steps	16.998	–	–	–	–

This rigorous selection and benchmarking process guaranteed that the foundation of the ASR system proposed in this study rests on a model surpassing the stringent requirements of medical speech transcription, setting the stage for notable progress in radiological diagnostics.

2.3. Implementation

2.3.1. Hardware Assessment and Initial Setup

Before embarking on the fine-tuning process, a thorough assessment of the computational resources was essential. This step is critical when dealing with advanced machine learning models like the Whisper Large-V2, which boasts 1.55 billion parameters, a testament to its complexity and capability. The hardware assessment centered on the GPU's specifications, which play a pivotal role in a model's training efficiency and speed.

The GPU, or Graphics Processing Unit, is a specialized electronic circuit designed to accelerate the creation and rendering of images, videos, and animations. It is also highly effective for the complex mathematical calculations often found in machine learning tasks, making it an indispensable resource in the setup.

For this study, a Tesla T4 GPU was used, known for its high performance in deep learning and AI applications. Below, Table 6 outlines the key specifications of the hardware setup.

Table 6. Hardware specifications.

Attribute	Detail
GPU	Tesla T4
GPU Memory	14.61 GB
GPU Computing Power	7.5 TFLOPs

- Tesla T4: This GPU is part of NVIDIA's Turing family, optimized for deep learning inference. The T4 is specifically designed to accelerate diverse cloud workloads, including high-performance computing, deep learning training and inference, machine learning, data analytics, and graphics.
- GPU Memory: The 14.61 GB of memory available on the Tesla T4 GPU is crucial for handling large datasets and complex neural networks. In deep learning tasks, the GPU memory needs to accommodate the model's parameters, gradients, and intermediate data generated during training. The Whisper model's vast number of parameters necessitates a GPU with substantial memory to ensure smooth and efficient training.
- GPU Computing Power: Measured in TFLOPs (Tera Floating-Point Operations per Second), its computing power of 7.5 TFLOPs indicates this GPU's capability to perform 7.5 trillion floating-point calculations per second. This high level of computational power is necessary to process the numerous operations involved in training the Whisper Large-V2 model, including matrix multiplications and other tensor operations fundamental to deep learning.

These specifications underpin the model's training process, providing the necessary computational resources to handle the intricate tasks associated with fine-tuning a state-of-the-art ASR system like Whisper Large-V2. The robustness of the Tesla T4, combined with its ample memory and computing power, ensures that the model can be trained efficiently, paving the way for the successful implementation of the speech recognition application.

2.3.2. Model Loading and Memory Optimization

To mitigate potential memory constraints, the Whisper Large-V2 model was loaded using an 8-bit precision for weights through quantization instead of 32-bit, a strategy that significantly reduced the memory footprint while preserving the accuracy of computations. This approach allowed for efficient use of the GPU memory, facilitating smoother model training sessions.

2.3.3. Optimization and Fine-Tuning Strategy

In optimizing the model architecture for computational constraints, the technique of Low-Rank Adaptation (LORA) was employed. Initially, the Whisper Large-V2 model, with its 1.55 billion parameters, posed a substantial demand on computational resources. To reconcile the model's complexity with the available hardware capabilities, a strategic reduction in trainable parameters was imperative.

Through the application of LORA, the parameter count was efficiently reduced from approximately 74.5 million to 15.7 million. This adjustment not only rendered the model more compatible with the hardware limitations but also streamlined the fine-tuning process by ensuring resource efficiency.

Text normalization was applied using the BasicTextNormalizer module, standardizing the inputs to improve the Word Error Rate (WER) evaluation consistency. This process included lowercasing, removing punctuation, and normalizing spaces.

The fine-tuning process was characterized by the strategic adjustment of training parameters, such as the batch size, learning rate, and warmup steps, optimizing the model's performance. Table 7 presents the fine-tuning parameters and LORA configuration, for which each parameter was meticulously chosen to guide the fine-tuning process towards achieving the best possible performance from the model under the constraints of the computational resources. This careful configuration ensured that the model's training was both effective and efficient, paving the way for its application in speech recognition tasks.

Table 7. Fine-tuning parameters and LORA configuration for model optimization.

Parameter	Description
Num_train_epochs = 3	The total number of times the training dataset is passed through the model. Three epochs mean the entire dataset is used thrice for training the model, enhancing its learning.
train_batch_size = 8	The number of training examples processed together in one iteration. A batch size of 8 allows for a balanced trade-off between learning efficiency and memory usage.
eval_batch_size = 8	Similar to train_batch_size, but used during the model evaluation phase. It determines the data chunk size for each evaluation step.
Warmup_steps = 500	The initial steps where the learning rate gradually increases to its peak, reducing the risk of training instability in the early phases.
lora_model configuration	Adjustments specific to the LORA approach:
R = 32	The rank parameter for LORA, impacting the model's approximation accuracy and the complexity of the adaptation.
Alpha = 64	Controls the scale of the Low-Rank Adaptation, influencing the balance between the original and adapted model components.
Lora_dropout = 0.05	The dropout rate used within the LORA adaptation to prevent overfitting by randomly omitting a fraction of the adaptation units during training.
Optimizer AdamW	Specifies the optimizer settings:
Adam-epsilon = 10^{-8}	A small constant for numerical stability in the AdamW optimization algorithm.
Beta-1 = 0.9	The exponential decay rate for the first-moment estimates in AdamW, balancing the influence of past gradients.
Beta-2 = 0.98	The exponential decay rate for the second-moment estimates in AdamW, controlling the moving average of the squared gradients.

2.3.4. System Pipeline and Deployment

The deployment of the "WhisperMed Radiology Transcriber", a specialized speech recognition application tailored for radiologists, involved configuring a server environment on Amazon Web Services (AWS). Flask was utilized for back-end management, while Nginx facilitated front-end integration, as depicted in Figure 4. The architecture of this application supports audio recording through a web interface, processes the recordings on a remote server, and displays transcriptions in real-time. Designed with an emphasis on real-time transcription and an intuitive user interface, the "WhisperMed Radiology Transcriber" aims to meet the precise needs of medical professionals within French-speaking clinical settings.

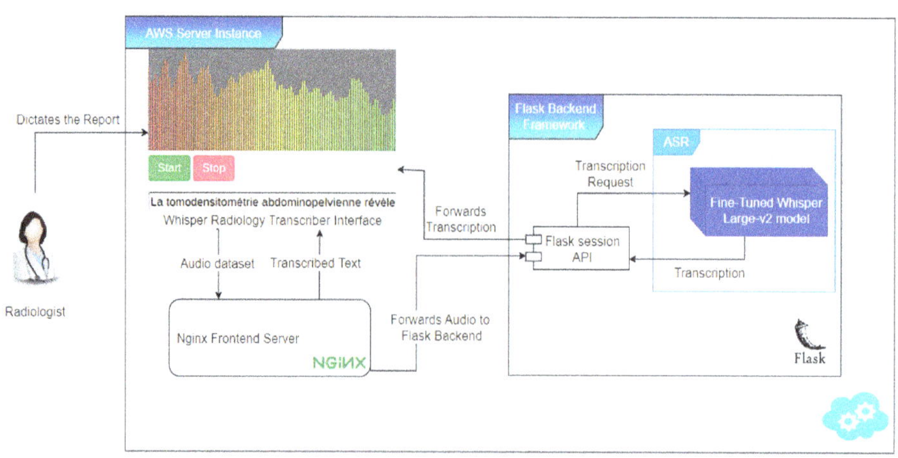

Figure 4. System deployment and operational flowchart.

3. Results

The comprehensive fine-tuning process of the Whisper Large-v2 model revealed significant insights into the model's performance under various training configurations. Initially, the training parameters were meticulously configured using the Seq2SeqTrainingArguments object from the Transformers library. Key parameters such as the batch size, learning rate, and warmup steps were strategically selected to optimize the model's performance. Notably, a learning rate of 10^{-3} was employed, which emerged as the most effective in enhancing the model's accuracy, as evidenced by a notable decrease in both the Word Error Rate (WER) and Normalized Word Error Rate (Normalized WER).

In the evaluation metrics, both the Word Error Rate (WER) and Normalized Word Error Rate (Normalized WER) are reported. The inclusion of the Normalized WER offers insights into the transcription accuracy post the application of text normalization techniques. Such a metric serves as an adjusted measure, more reflective of the model's ability to accurately decipher and transcribe medical radiology speech content. The Normalized WER evaluates the transcription's core content fidelity, discounting variations due to punctuation, capitalization, and whitespace. This adjusted metric is crucial in a medical context where precise terminology is paramount. The observed consistent improvement in the Normalized WER over the standard WER underscores the model's enhanced performance in transcribing detailed medical terminologies accurately.

The impact of different learning rates on the model's performance was systematically evaluated (Table 8). Our findings indicated that a learning rate of 10^{-3} led to promising results, particularly with a Normalized WER of 18.774% and a Normalized Character Error Rate (CER) of 12.103%. Additionally, the application of text normalization techniques significantly reduced the WER, underscoring the importance of this preprocessing step.

Table 8. Learning rate performance results.

Learning Rate	WER (%)	Normalized WER (%)	CER (%)	Normalized CER (%)	Training Loss	Validation Loss
10^{-2}	50.634	45.321	26.198	22.566	5.824	5.533
10^{-3}	25.781	18.774	15.337	12.103	0.378	0.510
10^{-4}	43.634	35.321	26.198	22.566	2.824	2.533

Further experiments were conducted to assess the influence of warmup steps on the model's performance. The results showed that a warmup step of 1000 yielded the best performance, achieving a Normalized WER of 18.504% (Table 9). This optimal configuration was thus subsequently adopted for further experimentation.

Table 9. Warmup steps performance results.

Warmup Steps	Normalized WER (%)	Normalized CER (%)	Training Loss	Validation Loss
250	21.563	18.235	0.499	0.667
500	18.774	15.337	0.288	0.510
750	18.720	15.349	0.270	0.499
1000	18.504	15.320	0.235	0.487
1250	23.757	19.813	0.507	0.689

In addition to these parameters, this study delved into the optimization settings, particularly focusing on the Adam epsilon parameter. The optimizer's configuration plays a crucial role in a model's ability to converge to an optimal solution. Our experiments with different Adam epsilon values revealed significant variations in performance, as summarized in Table 10. This table illustrates how subtle changes in the optimizer settings markedly influenced the model's effectiveness, guiding us to select the most suitable configuration for our specific needs.

Table 10. Model performance with different optimizer parameters.

Adam Epsilon	Normalized WER (%)	Training Loss	Validation Loss
10^{-7}	18.273	0.229	0.477
10^{-9}	17.640	0.219	0.457

The exploration of the LORA model's "R" parameter further demonstrated the impact of model configuration on performance. The configuration with R = 42 improved the model's performance, indicating its effectiveness in enhancing the model's transcription accuracy (Table 11).

Table 11. Model performance with different LORA configurations.

LORA Configuration (R)	Normalized WER (%)	Training Loss	Validation Loss
R = 42	17.660	0.223	0.467
R = 52	20.298	0.491	0.649

An additional layer of optimization focused on the Low-Rank Adaptation (LORA) technique's dropout parameter, Lora_dropout. A systematic comparison was undertaken to determine the most effective Lora_dropout value for the model, with the objective being to optimize the balance between reducing overfitting and preserving model performance. The comprehensive results of this comparison are presented in Table 12, illustrating that a Lora_dropout value of 0.04 resulted in the most favorable performance, evidenced by a Normalized Word Error Rate (WER) of 17.121%. This optimal Lora_dropout setting contributed significantly to the model's enhanced transcription accuracy.

Table 12. Performance comparison across different Lora_dropout configurations.

Lora_Dropout	Normalized WER (%)	Training Loss	Validation Loss
0.05	17.866	0.263	0.491
0.06	19.176	0.413	0.556
0.04	17.121	0.210	0.448
0.03	19.968	0.472	0.589

The final chosen configuration, achieving a Normalized WER of 17.121%, represents the culmination of the fine-tuning efforts, incorporating the ideal Lora_dropout value. This refined configuration underscores the effectiveness of the fine-tuning strategy in enhancing the transcription accuracy for medical radiology terms.

The fine-tuning of the Whisper Large-v2 model yielded significant improvements in the transcription accuracy. This process culminated in a final Word Error Rate (WER) of 17.121%, accompanied by a training loss of 0.210 and a validation loss of 0.448.

These metrics demonstrate the effectiveness of the fine-tuning strategy in enhancing the model's performance for medical radiology term transcription. The progression of the training and validation loss over the fine-tuning period is illustrated in the loss curves shown in Figure 5, providing a visual representation of the model's learning trajectory.

Concurrently, we deployed the "WhisperMed Radiology Transcriber", a speech recognition application, on an Amazon Web Services (AWS) server. This application utilizes the fine-tuned Whisper Large-v2 model to provide high-accuracy transcriptions of medical radiology terms. Key features of this application include real-time transcription capabilities and an intuitive user interface, designed to meet the specific needs of medical professionals.

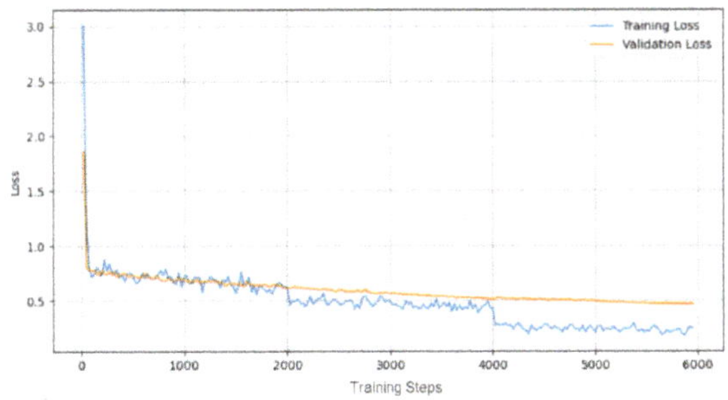

Figure 5. Loss curves.

4. Discussion

This study's integration of the Whisper Large-v2 model into radiological applications marks a significant advancement in medical Automatic Speech Recognition (ASR) systems. Demonstrating high accuracy in transcribing complex medical terminology, the model's effectiveness across diverse audio environments is a testament to its adaptability in various medical settings. This adaptability is crucial considering the acoustic complexities inherent in different medical fields. The success of AI-driven speech recognition systems in both general healthcare communication and specialized areas like radiation oncology ([28,29]) underscores their potential to revolutionize medical data processing across a spectrum of clinical contexts [30].

In clinical practices, the application of the proposed ASR system holds immense promise. The traditional process of transcribing diagnostic reports is often fraught with human error and inefficiency. By enhancing the accuracy and efficiency of medical documentation, this system stands to significantly improve the quality of patient care, as accurate records are vital for effective treatment planning [31]. Within the context of real-world application, the "WhisperMed Radiology Transcriber" stands as a Minimum Viable Product (MVP) designed specifically for radiologists. The development of this application is a direct response to the need for efficient, accurate medical transcription in radiology, aiming to minimize the time spent on generating reports while maximizing the accuracy of reports. Although the application is in its early stages, preliminary feedback from a selected group of radiologists has been promising, indicating a strong potential for integration into daily clinical practices. Future iterations of this application will focus on extensive testing with a larger cohort of medical professionals to fine-tune its functionalities and ensure seamless integration with existing hospital information systems.

Recognizing the need for a deeper analysis of our model's performance, we acknowledge that a comprehensive error analysis, particularly focusing on different types of data within the radiological domain, would provide valuable insights into the model's specific strengths and areas in need of improvement. Additionally, while our study highlights the model's effectiveness in transcribing complex medical terminology, a direct comparison with established French ASR baseline models, especially those previously applied in medical contexts, remains an area for future exploration. These comparisons would not only benchmark the Whisper Large-v2 model's performance but also pave the way for more targeted improvements, especially in handling the unique challenges presented by French medical terminology and diverse accents. Future research will aim to fill these gaps, offering a more detailed understanding of the model's performance nuances and its standing relative to existing French ASR solutions in healthcare. Additionally, integrating ASR systems with electronic health records (EHRs) could transform healthcare data management, reducing the administrative load on medical professionals and enabling a greater focus on patient care [32].

However, the implementation of ASR in healthcare is challenging. The system must navigate a vast array of medical terminologies, accents, and speech nuances. This research represents progress in this area, but ongoing refinement is essential to meet the stringent accuracy requirements of medical data transcription [33]. Addressing these challenges, particularly in non-English languages, remains a key area for future development. Studies on language-specific medical ASR solutions, such as those in Korean and French, highlight both the challenges and opportunities in creating effective multilingual medical ASR system [28–30].

The "WhisperMed Radiology Transcriber" serves as the tangible outcome of this research, specifically addressing the requirements of the radiological sector. As a Minimum Viable Product (MVP), this tool seeks to enhance report generation efficiency by providing accurate medical transcriptions tailored for radiology. Initial evaluations by a select cohort of radiologists have indicated positive reception, suggesting its potential for broader applications in clinical routines. Future developments will concentrate on comprehensive real-world evaluations to refine the application, ensuring its seamless integration with existing hospital information infrastructures and compliance with stringent medical documentation standards.

Beyond its clinical applications, this ASR system offers significant benefits in medical education. By facilitating the transcription of educational materials, it enhances accessibility and inclusivity, particularly for non-native speakers. This aligns with the digitalization trend in medical education, where technology is becoming increasingly pivotal in enriching learning experiences [33].

Future research avenues are abundant. Tailoring ASR systems to specific medical specialties or languages could greatly expand their utility. Exploring their integration with voice-activated medical devices and telemedicine platforms presents opportunities to further leverage ASR technology in healthcare [34].

The current study, despite its successes, encountered limitations due to resource constraints, which restricted the dataset size and prolonged the training period. Future studies should aim to utilize larger datasets and more robust computational resources to improve accuracy and efficiency. Real-world testing in clinical settings is also crucial to assess the system's practicality and identify areas for improvement.

The findings of this research contribute significantly to the medical ASR field, particularly in radiology transcription. The potential impact of this work on clinical practices, healthcare efficiency, and medical education underscores the vital role of technology in advancing healthcare solutions. Addressing the identified limitations, such as dataset diversity and practical application, will be essential in future research to fully realize the potential of ASR systems in healthcare.

5. Conclusions

This study's development of an Automatic Speech Recognition (ASR) system specifically designed for radiological applications represents a significant advancement in the application of technology within the healthcare sector. Our successful integration of the Whisper Large-v2 model into the ASR system has led to a notable achievement: a Word Error Rate (WER) of 17.121%. This achievement underscores the system's proficiency in accurately transcribing complex medical terminology and adapting to diverse accents, which are critical in radiological contexts.

The practical implications of this research are particularly significant in clinical settings. By automating the transcription of diagnostic reports, this ASR system addresses a key challenge in radiology—the need for accurate and efficient documentation. In light of our findings and the development of the "WhisperMed Radiology Transcriber", this research contributes significantly to the field of medical Automatic Speech Recognition (ASR) systems. The proposed application, although currently a prototype, embodies the practical application of our research findings. It is designed to be a foundational step towards creating a more robust and comprehensive tool that can be integrated into radiology departments worldwide. Moving forward, the focus will be on expanding the application's testing in real-world clinical environments. This will involve a series of pilot studies aimed at evaluating the application's effectiveness in live radiological settings, thereby ensuring that the final product is both user-friendly and highly accurate, meeting the exacting standards of medical documentation.

This improvement is not just a matter of convenience; it plays a vital role in enhancing patient care by supporting informed decision making based on precise and reliable medical records.

Moreover, the potential integration of the ASR system with electronic health records (EHRs) could be a game changer in healthcare administration. Such integration promises to streamline data entry processes, reduce the administrative burden on healthcare professionals, and improve the accuracy of patient records. This aligns with the broader goal of effective healthcare delivery, where accuracy and efficiency are paramount.

While this study has achieved its primary objectives, it also highlights areas for future exploration. The potential of tailoring ASR systems to specific medical specialties or languages, and integrating them with voice-activated medical devices and telemedicine platforms [35], presents exciting avenues for expanding the utility and impact of ASR in healthcare.

Despite its successes, this study faced limitations, primarily due to resource constraints. These limitations necessitated a training dataset of 20,000 examples and extended the training period to 14 days. Future research could benefit from larger datasets and more advanced computational resources to further enhance the accuracy and efficiency of ASR systems. Real-world testing in clinical environments is also crucial to validate the practical applicability of the system and to identify areas for improvement.

In summary, this research makes a significant contribution to the field of medical ASR systems, particularly in radiology. It offers a robust and efficient tool for medical transcription, with the potential to significantly impact clinical practices and the efficiency of healthcare services. Our findings pave the way for future innovations in technology-enhanced healthcare solutions.

Author Contributions: Conceptualization, M.J. and J.D.; methodology, M.J.; investigation, M.J., O.J. and J.D.; data curation, M.J. and O.J.; writing—original draft preparation, M.J.; writing—review and editing, M.J., O.J. and J.D. All authors have read and agreed to the published version of the manuscript.

Funding: This research received no external funding.

Institutional Review Board Statement: Not applicable.

Informed Consent Statement: Not applicable.

Data Availability Statement: The data presented in this study are available on request from the corresponding author due to privacy.

Conflicts of Interest: Authors Mariem Jelass and Oumaima Jemai were employed by the company Health Tech Innovation Systems Inc. The remaining authors declare that the research was conducted in the absence of any commercial or financial relationships that could be construed as a potential conflict of interest.

References

1. Zapata, J.; Kirkedal, A.S. Assessing the performance of automatic speech recognition systems when used by native and non-native speakers of three major languages in dictation workflows. In Proceedings of the 20th Nordic Conference of Computational Linguistics (NODALIDA 2015), Vilnius, Lithuania, 11–13 May 2015; pp. 201–210. Available online: https://aclanthology.org/W15-1825.pdf (accessed on 18 December 2023).
2. Jelassi, M.; Matteli, K.; Khalfallah, H.B.; Demongeot, J. Enhancing Mental Health Support through Artificial Intelligence: Advances in Speech and Text Analysis within Online Therapy Platforms. *Preprints* **2024**, 2024021585. [CrossRef]
3. Jiang, Y.; Poellabauer, C. A Sequence-to-sequence Based Error Correction Model for Medical Automatic Speech Recognition. In Proceedings of the 2021 IEEE International Conference on Bioinformatics and Biomedicine (BIBM), Houston, TX, USA, 9–12 December 2021; pp. 3029–3035. Available online: https://ieeexplore.ieee.org/abstract/document/9669554/ (accessed on 18 December 2023).

4. Essaid, B.; Kheddar, H.; Batel, N.; Lakas, A.; Chowdhury, M.E. Advanced Artificial Intelligence Algorithms in Cochlear Implants: Review of Healthcare Strategies, Challenges, and Perspectives. *arXiv* **2024**, arXiv:2403.15442.
5. Adedeji, A.; Joshi, S.; Doohan, B. The Sound of Healthcare: Improving Medical Transcription ASR Accuracy with Large Language Models. *arXiv* **2024**, arXiv:2402.07658.
6. Salimbajevs, A.; Kapočiūtė-Dzikienė, J. Automatic Speech Recognition Model Adaptation to Medical Domain Using Untranscribed Audio. In *Digital Business and Intelligent Systems*; Ivanovic, M., Kirikova, M., Niedrite, L., Eds.; Communications in Computer and Information Science; Springer International Publishing: Cham, Switzerland, 2022; Volume 1598, pp. 65–79, ISBN 978-3-031-09849-9.
7. Zielonka, M.; Krasiński, W.; Nowak, J.; Rośleń, P.; Stopiński, J.; Żak, M.; Górski, F.; Czyżewski, A. A survey of automatic speech recognition deep models performance for Polish medical terms. In Proceedings of the 2023 Signal Processing: Algorithms, Architectures, Arrangements, and Applications (SPA), Poznan, Poland, 20–22 September 2023; pp. 19–24. Available online: https://ieeexplore.ieee.org/abstract/document/10274442/ (accessed on 18 December 2023).
8. Mroz, A. Seeing how people hear you: French learners experiencing intelligibility through automatic speech recognition. *Foreign Lang. Ann.* **2018**, *51*, 617–637. [CrossRef]
9. Pascual, R.; Azcarraga, J.; Cheng, C.; Ing, J.A.; Wu, J.; Lim, M.L. Filipino and Bisaya Speech Corpus and Baseline Acoustic Models for Healthcare Chatbot ASR. In Proceedings of the 2023 3rd International Conference on Electrical, Computer, Communications and Mechatronics Engineering (ICECCME), Tenerife, Canary Islands, Spain, 19–21 July 2023; pp. 1–5. [CrossRef]
10. Chatzoudis, G.; Plitsis, M.; Stamouli, S.; Dimou, A.-L.; Katsamanis, A.; Katsouros, V. Zero-Shot Cross-lingual Aphasia Detection using Automatic Speech Recognition. *arXiv* **2022**, arXiv:2204.00448. Available online: http://arxiv.org/abs/2204.00448 (accessed on 18 December 2023).
11. Sunkara, M.; Ronanki, S.; Dixit, K.; Bodapati, S.; Kirchhoff, K. Robust Prediction of Punctuation and Truecasing for Medical ASR. *arXiv* **2020**, arXiv:2007.02025. Available online: http://arxiv.org/abs/2007.02025 (accessed on 18 December 2023).
12. Vase, S. The maturing of automatic speech recognition in healthcare practices. In *Joint Proceedings of Interactive Experiences and Doctoral Consortium at CHItaly 202, Bolzano-Bozen, Italy, 11–13 July 2021*; CEUR Workshop Proceedings: Tenerife, Spain, 2021; Available online: https://ceur-ws.org/Vol-2892/paper-13.pdf (accessed on 18 July 2023).
13. Scholz, M.L.; Collatz-Christensen, H.; Blomberg, S.N.F.; Boebel, S.; Verhoeven, J.; Krafft, T. Artificial intelligence in Emergency Medical Services dispatching: Assessing the potential impact of an automatic speech recognition software on stroke detection taking the Capital Region of Denmark as case in point. *Scand. J. Trauma Resusc. Emerg. Med.* **2022**, *30*, 36. [CrossRef] [PubMed]
14. Hacking, C.; Verbeek, H.; Hamers, J.P.; Aarts, S. The development of an automatic speech recognition model using interview data from long-term care for older adults. *J. Am. Med. Inform. Assoc.* **2023**, *30*, 411–417. [CrossRef] [PubMed]
15. Sezgin, E.; Oiler, B.; Abbott, B.; Noritz, G.; Huang, Y. "Hey Siri, Help Me Take Care of My Child": A Feasibility Study With Caregivers of Children With Special Healthcare Needs Using Voice Interaction and Automatic Speech Recognition in Remote Care Management. *Front. Public Health* **2022**, *10*, 366. [CrossRef] [PubMed]
16. Donnelly, L.F.; Grzeszczuk, R.; Guimaraes, C.V. Use of natural language processing (NLP) in evaluation of radiology reports: An update on applications and technology advances. In *Seminars in Ultrasound, CT and MRI*; Elsevier: Amsterdam, The Netherlands, 2022; pp. 176–181. Available online: https://www.sciencedirect.com/science/article/pii/S0887217122000191 (accessed on 18 December 2023).
17. Vatandoost, M.; Litkouhi, S. The future of healthcare facilities: How technology and medical advances may shape hospitals of the future. *Hosp. Pract. Res.* **2019**, *4*, 1–11. [CrossRef]
18. Ruby, J.; Daenke, S.; Yuan, Y. Automatic Speech Recognition and Machine Learning for Robotic Arm in Surgery. *Am. J. Clin. Surg.* **2020**, *2*, 10–18.
19. Schulte, A.; Suarez-Ibarrola, R.; Wegen, D.; Pohlmann, P.F.; Petersen, E.; Miernik, A. Automatic speech recognition in the operating room. *Ann. Med. Surg.* **2020**, *59*, 81–85. [CrossRef] [PubMed]
20. Brink, J.A.; Arenson, R.L.; Grist, T.M.; Lewin, J.S.; Enzmann, D. Bits and bytes: The future of radiology lies in informatics and information technology. *Eur. Radiol.* **2017**, *27*, 3647–3651. [CrossRef] [PubMed]
21. Latif, S.; Qadir, J.; Qayyum, A.; Usama, M.; Younis, S. Speech technology for healthcare: Opportunities, challenges, and state of the art. *IEEE Rev. Biomed. Eng.* **2020**, *14*, 342–356. [CrossRef] [PubMed]
22. Kumar, V.; Singh, H.; Mohanty, A. Real-Time Speech-To-Text/Text-To-Speech Converter with Automatic Text Summarizer Using Natural Language Generation and Abstract Meaning Representation. *Int. J. Eng. Adv. Technol. (IJEAT)* **2020**, *9*, 2361–2365.
23. Dua, M.; Akanksha; Dua, S. Noise robust automatic speech recognition: Review and analysis. *Int. J. Speech Technol.* **2023**, *26*, 475–519. [CrossRef]
24. Rista, A.; Kadriu, A. Automatic Speech Recognition: A Comprehensive Survey. *SEEU Rev.* **2020**, *15*, 86–112. [CrossRef]
25. Raclin, T.; Price, A.; Stave, C.; Lee, E.; Reddy, B.; Kim, J.; Chu, L. Combining Machine Learning, Patient-Reported Outcomes, and Value-Based Health Care: Protocol for Scoping Reviews. *JMIR Res. Protoc.* **2022**, *11*, e36395. [CrossRef] [PubMed]
26. Radford, A.; Kim, J.W.; Xu, T.; Brockman, G.; McLeavey, C.; Sutskever, I. Robust speech recognition via large-scale weak supervision. In Proceedings of the 40th International Conference on Machine Learning, Honolulu, HI, USA, 23–29 July 2023; pp. 28492–28518. Available online: https://proceedings.mlr.press/v202/radford23a.html (accessed on 20 December 2023).
27. Huging Face Model Hub. Available online: https://huggingface.co/docs/hub/models-the-hub (accessed on 6 April 2023).

28. Chun, S.-J.; Park, J.B.; Ryu, H.; Jang, B.-S. Development and benchmarking of a Korean audio speech recognition model for Clinician-Patient conversations in radiation oncology clinics. *Int. J. Med. Inform.* **2023**, *176*, 105112. [CrossRef] [PubMed]
29. Zhang, T.; Feng, T. Application and technology of an open source AI large language model in the medical field. *Radiol. Sci.* **2023**, *2*, 96–104. [CrossRef]
30. Jia, X.; Cunha, J.A.M.; Rong, Y. Artificial intelligence can overcome challenges in brachytherapy treatment planning. *J. Appl. Clin. Med. Phys.* **2022**, *23*, e13504. Available online: https://www.ncbi.nlm.nih.gov/pmc/articles/PMC8803284 (accessed on 24 December 2023). [CrossRef] [PubMed]
31. Cruz Rivera, S.; Dickens, A.P.; Aiyegbusi, O.L.; Flint, R.; Fleetcroft, C.; McPherson, D.; Collis, P.; Calvert, M.J. Patient-reported outcomes in the regulatory approval of medical devices. *Nat. Med.* **2021**, *27*, 2067–2068. [CrossRef] [PubMed]
32. Elsokah, M.M.; Zerek, A.R. Design and development Intelligent Medical Care Bed Using Voice Recognition. In Proceedings of the 2022 IEEE 2nd International Maghreb Meeting of the Conference on Sciences and Techniques of Automatic Control and Computer Engineering (MI-STA), Sabratha, Libya, 23–25 May 2022; pp. 299–304.
33. Czyzewski, A. Optimizing medical personnel speech recognition models using speech synthesis and reinforcement learning. *J. Acoust. Soc. Am.* **2023**, *154* (Suppl. S4), A202–A203. [CrossRef]
34. Davari, M.H.; Kazemi, T.; Saberhosseini, M. The status of Clinical education in ophthalmology surgery ward of Vali-e-Asr Hospital affiliated with Birjand University of Medical Science before and after intervention. *J. Surg. Trauma* **2018**, *6*, 30–34. Available online: https://jsurgery.bums.ac.ir/article-1-127-.pdf (accessed on 24 December 2023).
35. Chung, A.E.; Griffin, A.C.; Selezneva, D.; Gotz, D. Health and Fitness Apps for Hands-Free Voice-Activated Assistants: Content Analysis. *JMIR mHealth uHealth* **2018**, *6*, e9705. [CrossRef] [PubMed]

cancers

MDPI

Article

Prediction of Lymph Node Metastasis in T1 Colorectal Cancer Using Artificial Intelligence with Hematoxylin and Eosin-Stained Whole-Slide-Images of Endoscopic and Surgical Resection Specimens

Joo Hye Song [1], Eun Ran Kim [2,*], Yiyu Hong [3,*], Insuk Sohn [3], Soomin Ahn [4], Seok-Hyung Kim [4] and Kee-Taek Jang [4]

1 Department of Internal Medicine, Konkuk University Medical Center, Konkuk University School of Medicine, Seoul 05030, Republic of Korea; 20230514@kuh.ac.kr

2 Department of Medicine, Samsung Medical Center, Sungkyunkwan University School of Medicine, Seoul 06351, Republic of Korea

3 Department of R&D Center, Arontier Co., Ltd., Seoul 06735, Republic of Korea; insuks@gmail.com

4 Department of Pathology, Samsung Medical Center, Sungkyunkwan University School of Medicine, Seoul 06351, Republic of Korea; soomin17.ahn@samsung.com (S.A.); parmenides.kim@samsung.com (S.-H.K.); kt12.jang@samsung.com (K.-T.J.)

* Correspondence: erkim75@gmail.com (E.R.K.); yyhong@arontier.co (Y.H.); Tel.: +82-2-3410-1182 (E.R.K.); +82-2-597-0365 (Y.H.)

Simple Summary: We developed an attention-based whole slide image (WSI)-level classification deep learning model employing surgically and endoscopically resected specimens to predict LNM in T1 CRC. Our AI model with H&E-stained WSIs and without annotations showed good performance power with the validation of an independent cohort in a single center. The area under the curve of our model was 0.781–0.824, higher than that of previous artificial intelligence (AI) studies with only WSIs. Our AI model, which showed the highest sensitivity (92.9%), reduced unnecessary additional surgery by 14.2% more than using the current JSCCR guidelines (68.3% vs. 82.5%). This revealed the feasibility of using an AI model with only H&E-stained WSIs to predict LNM in T1 CRC.

Abstract: According to the current guidelines, additional surgery is performed for endoscopically resected specimens of early colorectal cancer (CRC) with a high risk of lymph node metastasis (LNM). However, the rate of LNM is 2.1–25.0% in cases treated endoscopically followed by surgery, indicating a high rate of unnecessary surgeries. Therefore, this study aimed to develop an artificial intelligence (AI) model using H&E-stained whole slide images (WSIs) without handcrafted features employing surgically and endoscopically resected specimens to predict LNM in T1 CRC. To validate with an independent cohort, we developed a model with four versions comprising various combinations of training and test sets using H&E-stained WSIs from endoscopically (400 patients) and surgically resected specimens (881 patients): Version 1, Train and Test: surgical specimens; Version 2, Train and Test: endoscopic and surgically resected specimens; Version 3, Train: endoscopic and surgical specimens and Test: surgical specimens; Version 4, Train: endoscopic and surgical specimens and Test: endoscopic specimens. The area under the curve (AUC) of the receiver operating characteristic curve was used to determine the accuracy of the AI model for predicting LNM with a 5-fold cross-validation in the training set. Our AI model with H&E-stained WSIs and without annotations showed good performance power with the validation of an independent cohort in a single center. The AUC of our model was 0.758–0.830 in the training set and 0.781–0.824 in the test set, higher than that of previous AI studies with only WSI. Moreover, the AI model with Version 4, which showed the highest sensitivity (92.9%), reduced unnecessary additional surgery by 14.2% more than using the current guidelines (68.3% vs. 82.5%). This revealed the feasibility of using an AI model with only H&E-stained WSIs to predict LNM in T1 CRC.

Keywords: lymph node metastasis; artificial intelligence; whole slide image; T1 colorectal cancer

1. Introduction

Colorectal cancer (CRC) is the second most fatal and the third most commonly diagnosed cancer worldwide [1,2]. However, CRC incidence and mortality have decreased due to colonoscopy screening, surveillance, and high-quality endoscopic treatment [3–5]. Endoscopic resection is recommended as the first-line treatment for early CRC without distant or lymph node metastasis (LNM). Although intramucosal CRC is not associated with LNM, submucosal CRC exhibits LNM in approximately 10% of cases [6–10]. Therefore, additional surgical resection is performed only when endoscopically resected specimens show high-risk features (deep submucosal (SM) invasion, lymphovascular invasion (LVI), tumor budding, or poorly differentiated histology) related to LNM [7,11–15]. However, even though additional surgery is recommended based on the current guidelines, LNM occurs in 2.1–25.0% of cases treated endoscopically and then surgically. In other words, 75–98% of additional surgeries are unnecessary [9,16–19]. The main challenge is to figure out LNM before undergoing surgery. Several studies have attempted to identify a method to predict LNM in patients with T1 CRC (tumor-invaded submucosa, according to the Japanese Society for Cancer of the Colon and Rectum (JSCCR) and American Joint Committee on Cancer) to reduce the number of unnecessary surgeries and minimize the risk of LNM. However, since low inter-observer agreement and limited indications of current guidelines, it is nearly impossible to predict LNM through pathologic examination based on Hematoxylin and eosin(H&E)-stained endoscopically resected specimen [20–22].

Recent studies have attempted to solve these problems using artificial intelligence (AI) [23–27]. The two strategical approaches for AI-assisted assessment of the risk of LNM in T1 CRC were pathologist-dependent and independent [28,29]. The pathologist-dependent strategy used text-based data, which included the histologic features obtained by a pathologist, such as depth of SM invasion, tumor differentiation, and LVI [23,25,30]. These test data-based AI models proved sufficient evidence with large cohorts and external validation, outperforming the current guidelines. Nevertheless, there were still limitations, such as varying pathologic criteria and standards among different guidelines and diagnostic disagreement among pathologists. To address these issues, a pathologist-independent AI model utilizing whole slide images (WSIs) has been reported. WSI-based AI models with hematoxylin and eosin staining alone, including our previous study, were simplified and less disruptive than current clinical best practices [26,27,31]. This strategy appears to be ideal for overcoming inter-observer discrepancy, but a relatively low area under the curve (AUC) compared to the pathologist-dependent method and external validation remain a challenge.

Even though our previous study demonstrated the potential of using an AI with H&E-stained WSIs from endoscopically resected specimens without handcrafted features to predict LNM in patients with T1 CRC, our model had certain limitations [31]. WSIs from endoscopically resected specimens had high-risk histological features of LNM because they belonged to patients who underwent additional surgery after endoscopic treatment. So, the previous model was unsuitable for predicting LNM in low-risk patients with T1 CRC. Also, the study population was small (n = 400), and AUC was relatively low. To increase the number of patients and WSIs from patients with low risk of LNM, we conducted a study with AI training and testing by expanding the scope to include previously endoscopically resected specimens from patients who underwent additional surgery due to the high risk of LNM, as well as surgical specimens from patients who underwent surgery for T1 CRC. Since the previous model lacked external validation with an independent cohort, we wanted to perform extensive external validation with WSIs from multi-centers and apply it to WSIs from T1 CRC patients who underwent endoscopic treatment. However, it takes a lot of time to prepare WSI from multicenter and obtain a 5-year overall survival rate in patients who have only undergone endoscopic treatment for T1 CRC. So, we conducted a study using an alternative method instead of external validation. To validate with an independent cohort in a single center, we aimed to develop an AI model with four versions comprising various combinations of training and test sets using H&E-stained WSIs from surgical and endoscopically resected specimens. Because endoscopic resected specimens contained only part of the SM layer while surgical specimens contained the entire layer of the intestine, the two cohorts were independent of each other. Additionally, we aimed to apply our AI program to predict LNM in T1 CRC samples.

2. Materials and Methods

2.1. Study Population

The inclusion criteria were (1) patients who underwent surgical resection for newly diagnosed T1 CRC between 2003 and 2020 at the Samsung Medical Center or (2) patients who underwent endoscopic treatment including endoscopic mucosal resection (EMR) and endoscopic submucosal dissection (ESD) for newly diagnosed T1 CRC, and those who underwent additional surgery based on the JSCCR guidelines [14] due to high risk of LNM indicated by at least one of the following histologic features: positive resection margin, deep SM invasion (SM depth > 1 mm, Sm2/Sm3 for sessile T1, and Haggitt 4 for pedunculated T1 CRC), presence of LVI, poorly differentiated histology, or tumor budding: within 3 months after EMR/ESD from 2010 to 2018 at the Samsung Medical Center. The exclusion criteria were as follows: (1) unavailable H&E-stained slide, (2) unclear H&E-stained slide image for analysis, (3) no LN dissection, or (4) presence of synchronous invasive carcinoma. The study protocol was approved by the Institutional Review Board of Samsung Medical Center (2021-01-042-005). The requirement for informed consent from the patients was waived due to the use of de-identified data routinely collected during hospital visits.

2.2. Clinicopathologic Features and Preparation of Whole Slide Images for the Study Population

Clinical data such as age at diagnosis, sex, body mass index, family history of CRC, presence of comorbidities, smoking status, alcohol consumption, and tumor location were reviewed. Additionally, pathologic features, such as the tumor size (length of cancer component measured by excluding adenoma component), positive resection margin, depth of SM invasion, LVI, histologic differentiation (based on the least differentiated component), tumor budding, and microsatellite instability, were reviewed by a pathologist and used only for comparison with the predictive performance of our model. Assessment of histological differentiation was based on the least high-grade pattern of the carcinoma, which often co-exists with dominant elements of low-grade patterns. Immunostaining with D2–40 was occasionally performed for lymphatic vessel to determine whether it was a true lymphatic or an iatrogenic empty space caused by tissue being pushed in the process of specimen fixing in formaldehyde and making into slide.

Surgical and endoscopically resected specimens were fixed in formaldehyde and embedded in paraffin. Tissue specimens were cut into sections with 3 μm that were placed on the slides. During preparation, the artifact was removed from ethanol and a 50 °C floating hot water tank. H&E-stained specimen slides were scanned using a VENTANA iScan HT scanner (Roche Diagnostics, Basel, Switzerland) at ×20 magnification.

2.3. Deep Learning Artificial Intelligence Model Development

The deep learning method used in this study is the same as that employed in our previous study [31]. We developed an attention-based WSI-level classification deep learning model to predict whether a WSI is LNM positive or negative (Figure 1). The model was trained for a binary classification task, where the input was a WSI, and the output was the probability of the WSI being LNM-positive.

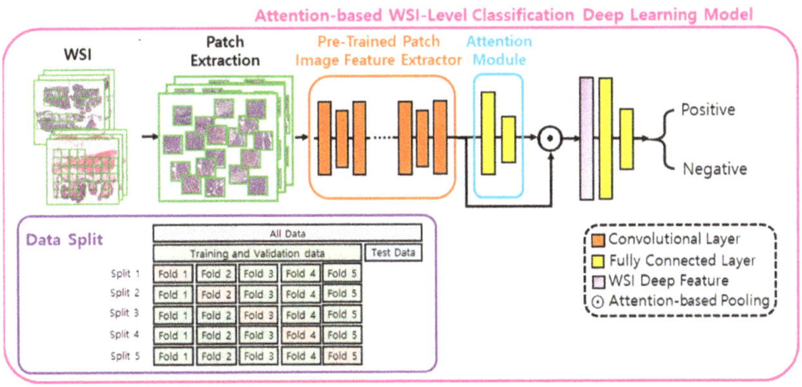

Figure 1. Pipeline of the approach for classifying lymph node metastasis. WSI, whole slide image.

The model is an end-to-end neural network comprising a deep convolutional neural network (DCNN), attention module (AM), and classification module (CM) [32,33]. The DCNN was pre-trained with patches labeled as positive (patches from LNM positive WSIs) or negative (patches from LNM negative WSIs) to learn features in histopathological images in advance and to function as a patch image feature extractor (FE) [34]. The AM computes an attention score (AS), between 0 and 1, for each patch image in a WSI; the sum of these scores is equal to 1. An attention mechanism was used to visualize the spatial distribution of ASs of the WSIs. A higher AS indicates that the patch image is relatively more informative and has a greater influence on the final classification decision.

The model's inferencing details are as follows: For a given WSI, all tissue regions are patched in a tiling manner and used as input for the DCNN FE, which compresses and encodes each patch image into a 512-dimensional feature vector (FV). The FVs are further aggregated into a single WSI-level FV (WSI deep feature) with 512 dimensions using their weighted average determined by the AS, computed by the AM [32]. The final WSI deep feature is then input into the CM to obtain the final prediction for LNM.

2.4. Statistical Analysis

Continuous variables are expressed as medians with interquartile ranges (IQRs) and analyzed using Student's *t*-test and the Mann–Whitney U test. Statistical significance was set at $p < 0.05$. All statistical analyses were performed using SPSS software version 28 for Windows (SPSS Inc., Chicago, IL, USA).

The AI performance was evaluated using the AUC receiver operating characteristic curve (ROC). ROC is a probability curve, and AUC represents the degree or measure of separability. It showed how much the model was capable of distinguishing between classes.

To validate our model in case of a lack of other hospital WSI, we developed a model with four versions of training and test set combinations using endoscopically and surgically resected specimens: Version 1, Train and Test: surgical specimens; Version 2, Train and Test: endoscopic and surgically resected specimens; Version 3, Train: endoscopic and surgical specimens and Test: surgical specimens; and Version 4, Train: endoscopic and surgical specimens and Test: endoscopic specimens.

We performed a five-fold cross-validation (CV) on the training set, preserving the percentage of each class to determine how well our approach worked on each fold. Consequently, each of the five models trained in CV was applied to the held-out test set, and the results were obtained by averaging the output predictions. By comparing our AI model with a model using clinicopathological features, we trained a random forest (RF) classifier with 500 trees to predict LNM [35]. RF is a versatile and widely used machine learning algorithm that constructed multiple decision trees and combined their outputs for robust and accurate predictions.

The optimal cut-off sensitivity and specificity of each model were evaluated using the Youden index, the maximum potential effectiveness of a diagnostic biomarker, and a common summary measure of the ROC curve [36]. And we used McNemar's tests, non-parametric test used to analyze paired nominal data, to compare predictive performances between our model and JSCCR guidelines, the most widely used guidelines in Asia.

3. Results

3.1. Baseline Characteristics of the Study Population

A total of 1737 patients with T1 CRCs (1046 surgical resections and 691 endoscopic resections followed by surgery) were eligible for this study, and 456 patients were excluded. Thus, 1281 patients (881 surgical resections and 400 endoscopic resections followed by surgery) were analyzed (Figure 2). Their baseline clinicopathological characteristics are presented in Table 1. The median age at CRC diagnosis was much younger in patients with endoscopic resection followed by additional surgery (59.0; IQR, 52.0–65.0) than in patients with surgical resection (60.0; IQR, 52.0–69.0). Men accounted for 59.6% of the total population. The percentage of patients with a family history of CRC, ex-/current smoker, or alcohol ex-/current drinker was higher in endoscopic resection followed by additional surgery. Patients without a family history of CRC accounted for 89.2% of the patients. High-risk pathologic features related to LNM, including LVI, tumor budding, positive resection margin, and microsatellite instability, were more in patients with endoscopic resection followed by additional surgery than surgical resection.

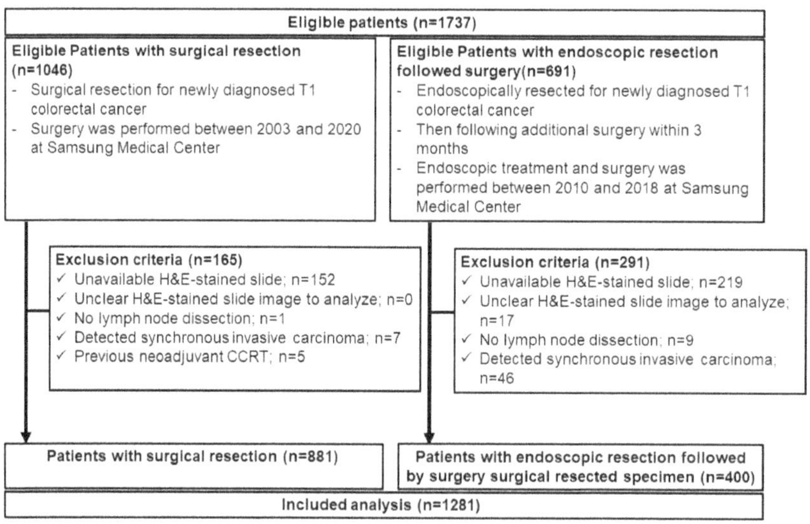

Figure 2. Flow chart of study population. CCRT, concurrent chemoradiotherapy.

Patients with CRC and LNM accounted for 6.6% (n = 58) of patients with surgical resection and 17.8% (n = 71) of patients with endoscopic resection followed by additional surgery. LN yield, the total number of LNs retrieved after surgery was 22,022. The LN ratio, the ratio of positive LNs out of the total removed, was 1.24% (273/22,022). In our study, an average of 17 LNs were retrieved in each surgery. When we compared the past group (patients who underwent surgery in 2003–2010) and the recent group (2011–2020), an average of 16 LNs were retrieved per surgery in the past group, and 18 LNs were retrieved per surgery in the recent group.

Table 1. Baseline characteristics of study population.

			Endoscopic Resection Followed by Additional Surgery (*n* = 400)		Surgical Resection (*n* = 881)		
		Total	Negative LNM (*n* = 329)	Positive LNM (*n* = 71)	Negative LNM (*n* = 780)	Positive LNM (*n* = 101)	*p* Value *
Clinical features							
Age at diagnosis	Year (IQR)	60.0 (52.0–68.0)	59.0 (52.0–65.0)	60.0 (52.0–68.0)	60.0 (52.0–69.0)	59.0 (52.0–67.0)	0.041
Sex	Male	764 (59.6)	193 (58.7)	46 (64.8)	467 (59.9)	58 (57.4)	0.504
	Female	517 (40.4)	136 (41.3)	25 (35.2)	313 (40.1)	43 (42.6)	
Body mass index	kg/m^2 (IQR)	24.1 (22.2–26.1)	23.9 (22.0–26.1)	24.8 (23.3–27.4)	24.1 (22.2–26.0)	24.8 (23.0–26.0)	0.704
Presence of comorbidity	No	795 (62.1)	217 (66.0)	36 (50.7)	477 (61.2)	65 (64.4)	0.299
	Yes	486 (37.9)	112 (34.0)	35 (49.3)	302 (38.7)	36 (35.6)	
Family history of CRC	No	1143 (89.2)	294 (86.3)	61 (85.9)	708 (90.8)	90 (89.1)	0.014
	yes	138 (10.8)	45 (13.7)	10 (14.1)	72 (9.2)	11 (10.9)	
Smoking status	No	912 (71.2)	214 (65.0)	43 (60.6)	588 (75.4)	67 (66.3)	<0.001
	Ex-smoker	201 (15.7)	59 (17.9)	10 (14.1)	104 (13.3)	23 (22.8)	
	Yes	168 (13.1)	56 (17.0)	18 (25.4)	88 (11.3)	11 (10.9)	
Alcohol consumption	No	809 (63.2)	192 (58.4)	31 (43.7)	523 (67.1)	63 (62.4)	<0.001
	Ex-drinker	71 (5.5)	27 (8.2)	9 (12.7)	29 (3.7)	6 (5.9)	
	Yes	401 (31.3)	110 (33.4)	31 (43.7)	228 (29.2)	32 (21.7)	
Tumor location	Left side	913 (71.3)	241 (73.3)	50 (70.4)	542 (69.5)	80 (79.2)	0.236
	Right side	368 (28.7)	88 (26.7)	21 (29.6)	238 (30.5)	21 (20.8)	
Pathologic features							
Size of cancer	mm (IQR)	15.0 (10.0–22.0)	10.0 (7.3–14.0)	8.0 (7.0–12.0)	20.0 (15.0–25.0)	16.5 (14.3–25.0)	<0.001
Depth of SM invasion	µm (IQR)	1775.0 (1000.0–2200.0)	1800.0 (1075.0–2300.0)	1500.0 (1000.0–2000.0)			N/A
	SM1	340 (38.6)			318 (40.8)	22 (21.8)	N/A
	SM2	218 (24.7)			185 (23.7)	33 (32.7)	
	SM3	323 (36.7)			277 (35.5)	46 (45.5)	
Differentiation	Well	760 (59.3)	182 (55.3)	55 (77.5)	480 (61.5)	43 (42.6)	0.210
	Moderate	485 (37.9)	133 (40.4)	14 (19.7)	286 (36.7)	52 (51.5)	
	Poorly	36 (2.8)	14 (4.3)	2 (2.8)	14 (1.8)	6 (5.9)	
Lympho-vascular invasion	No	1030 (80.4)	243 (73.9)	49 (69.0)	691 (89.6)	47 (46.5)	<0.001
	Yes	251 (19.6)	86 (26.1)	22 (31.0)	89 (11.4)	54 (53.5)	
Tumor budding	No	1084 (84.6)	289 (87.8)	62 (87.3)	667 (85.5)	66 (65.3)	0.021
	Yes	197 (15.4)	40 (12.2)	9 (12.7)	113 (14.5)	35 (34.7)	
Positive resection margin	No	1167 (91.1)	235 (71.4)	51 (71.8)	780 (100)	101 (100)	<0.001
	Yes	114 (8.9)	94 (28.6)	20 (28.2)	0	0	
Microsatellite stability	Stable	915 (71.5)	82 (25.0)	28 (39.4)	667 (85.5)	89 (88.1)	<0.001
	Unstable	86 (6.7)	8 (2.4)	2 (2.8)	69 (8.8)	7 (6.9)	
	Unknown	279 (21.8)	238 (72.6)	41 (57.7)	44 (5.6)	5 (5.0)	

* *p*-value: difference between endoscopic resection followed by additional surgery (*n* = 400) and surgical resection (*n* = 881). LN, lymph node; IQR, interquartile range; CRC, colorectal cancer; SM, submucosal; N/A; not applicable; SM1, upper third, if depth of submucosal invasion was pragmatically divided in equal thirds according to Kudo classification; SM2, middle third; SM3, lower third.

3.2. Train and Test Set in Model with Four Versions

A total of 2604 WSIs (184 positive LNM and 1139 negative LNM) from 881 surgical specimens (102 positive LNM and 791 negative LNM) and 400 endoscopically resected specimens (82 positive LNM and 348 negative LNM) were used to develop the model. A summary of the four versions is presented in Table 2.

In Version 1, 893 WSIs (102 positive LNM and negative 791 LNM) from 881 surgical specimens were randomly split into training and test sets in a ratio of 4:1 at the patient level. Accordingly, 80 and 21 patients with positive LNM and 624 and 156 with negative LNM were assigned to the training and test sets, respectively.

Table 2. Composition of number of patients and WSI according to lymph node metastasis in the training and test set of artificial intelligence model with four versions.

	LNM		Previous Study	Version 1	Version 2	Version 3	Version 4
Training (5 fold) set	+	No of patients	57	80	137	137	137
	+	No of WSI	63	81	144	144	144
	−	No of patients	263	624	887	887	887
	−	No of WSI	277	634	911	911	911
Test set	+	No of patients	14	21	35	21	14
	+	No of WSI	19	21	40	21	19
	−	No of patients	66	156	222	156	66
	−	No of WSI	71	157	228	157	71

WSI, whole slide image; LNM, lymph node metastasis; Version 1, train and test: surgical specimen; Version 2, train and test: endoscopic and surgical specimen; Version 3, train: endoscopic and surgical specimen and test: surgical specimen; Version 4, train: endoscopic and surgical specimen and test: endoscopic specimen.

In Version 2, 1323 WSIs (184 positive LNM and negative 1139 LNM) from 881 surgical specimens and 400 endoscopically resected specimens were randomly split into training and test sets in a ratio of 4:1 at the patient level. Accordingly, 137 and 35 patients with positive LNM and 887 and 222 patients with negative LNM were assigned to the training and test sets, respectively.

In version 3, 1144 WSIs (165 positive LNM and negative 1068 LNM) from 881 surgical specimens and 400 endoscopically resected specimens were randomly split into the training set and surgical specimens were randomly split into the test set in a ratio of 6:1 at the patient level. Accordingly, 137 and 21 patients with positive LNM and 887 and 156 patients with negative LNM were assigned to the training and test sets, respectively.

In Version 4, 1145 WSIs (163 positive LNM and 982 negative LNM) from 881 surgical specimens and 400 endoscopically resected specimens were randomly split into the training set and endoscopically resected specimens were randomly split into the test set in a ratio of 13:1 at the patient level. Accordingly, 137 and 14 patients with positive LNM and 887 and 66 patients with negative LNM were assigned to the training and test sets, respectively.

3.3. *Area under the Curve for Predicting Lymph Node Metastasis*

The AUCs for predicting LNM in T1 CRC using the AI model with histopathological images of endoscopic and surgical specimens and RF with clinicopathological features are shown in Table 3. Our model showed better prediction performance, with an AUC of 0.758–0.830 for the training set and 0.781–0.824 for the test set, than that of the model with clinicopathological features (AUC 0.516–0.683 in the test set). The ROC curves of the AI model are shown in Figure 3. The sensitivity and specificity of each version were 71.4% and 92.9% for version 1, 71.4% and 84.2% for version 2, 76.2% and 85.9% for version 3, and 92.9% and 57.6% for version 4 respectively.

Table 3. Area under the curve of artificial intelligence model, compared to random forest with clinicopathologic features predicting of lymph node metastasis in in T1 CRC.

	Cross-Validation on Train Set	Previous Study	Version 1	Version 2	Version 3	Version 4
Attention-base WSI-level classification deep learning model	1	0.772	0.829	0.780	0.770	0.766
	2	0.781	0.901	0.863	0.904	0.789
	3	0.683	0.827	0.771	0.779	0.741
	4	0.780	0.723	0.783	0.803	0.736
	5	0.724	0.882	0.836	0.890	0.760
	Average of five-folds	0.747	0.830	0.806	0.828	0.758
	Test set	0.764	0.814	0.822	0.824	0.781

Table 3. *Cont.*

	Cross-Validation on Train Set	Previous Study	Version 1	Version 2	Version 3	Version 4
RF with clinicopathologic features *	1	0.598	0.659	0.653	0.728	0.512
	2	0.574	0.713	0.722	0.704	0.712
	3	0.703	0.710	0.739	0.728	0.746
	4	0.631	0.729	0.725	0.712	0.721
	5	0.623	0.670	0.647	0.666	0.593
	Average of five-folds	0.626	0.696	0.697	0.708	0.657
	Test set	0.598	0.701	0.635	0.683	0.516

WSI, whole slide image; RF, random forest; Version 1, train and test: surgical specimen; Version 2, train and test: endoscopic and surgical specimen; Version 3, train: endoscopic and surgical specimens and test: surgical specimen; Version 4, train: endoscopic and surgical specimens and test: endoscopic specimen. * Clinicopathological features included age at diagnosis, sex, body mass index, presence of comorbidities, family history of CRC, smoking status, alcohol consumption, tumor location, size of cancer, depth of submucosal invasion, lymphovascular invasion, histologic differentiation, tumor budding, and microsatellite instability.

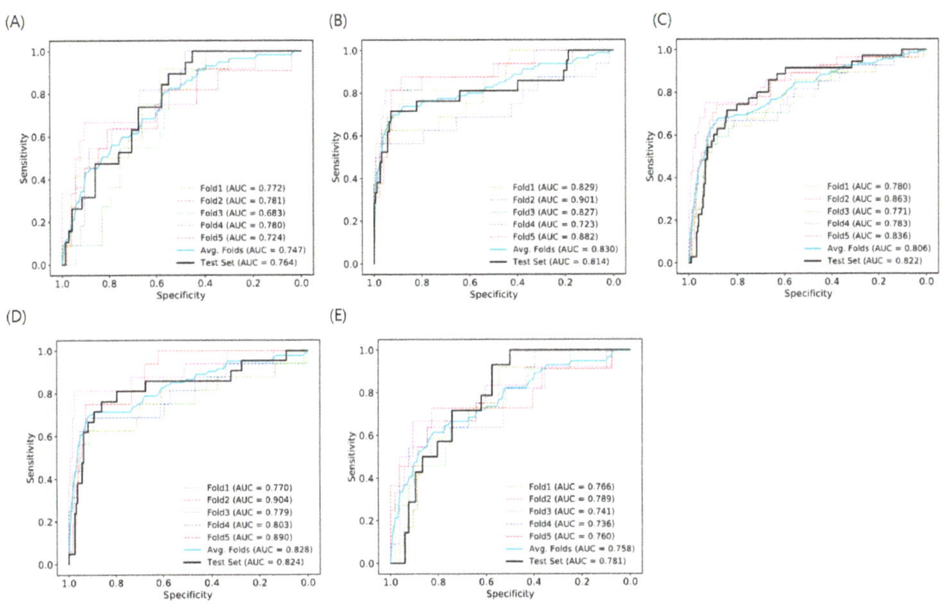

Figure 3. Area under the ROC curve for attention-based WSI-level classification deep learning model for predicting lymph node metastasis in T1 colorectal cancer. (**A**) Previous model, (**B**) Version 1, (**C**) Version 2, (**D**) Version 3, (**E**) Version 4 ROC, receiver operating characteristic; WSI, whole-slide image; Version 1, train and test: surgical specimen; Version 2, train and test: endoscopic and surgical specimen; Version 3, train: endoscopic and surgical specimens and test: surgical specimen; Version 4, train: endoscopic and surgical specimens and test: endoscopic specimen; AUC: area under the curve; Avg: average.

3.4. Predictive Performance of Model with Four Versions vs. That of JSCCR Guidelines

We compared the performance of our model (four versions) with that of JSCCR guidelines using the test set (Table 4). JSCCR guidelines recommend that additional colorectal surgery be performed when endoscopically resected specimens show at least one of the high-risk features of LNM. JSCCR guideline did not allow any LNM of T1 CRC, which resulted in unnecessary additional surgery. It meant that this strategy showed 100% sensitivity and 0% specificity. On the other hand, to reflect reality as much as possible, we used the sensitivity and specificity of our model determined through the Youden index instead of setting it at 100% sensitivity to not allowing false negatives. The rate of unnecessary additional surgery attributable to misdiagnosing patients with negative LNM as having positive LNM was anticipated to be from 42.3% to 68.3% by our model with four versions and 82.5 to 88.1% by the JSCCR guidelines. Based on the results of the analysis, our model avoided at least 14.2% of unnecessary additional surgeries than predicted using the current JSCCR guidelines.

Table 4. Predictive value of our artificial intelligence model with four versions and JSCCR guideline for lymph node metastasis in patients with T1 colorectal cancer.

		Artificial Intelligence	JSCCR	*p* Value
Version 1	Sensitivity (%)	71.4	100	<0.001
	Specificity (%)	92.9	0	<0.001
	PPV (%)	57.7	11.9	<0.001
	Accuracy (%)	90.4	11.9	<0.001
	Unnecessary additional Surgery (%)	42.3	88.1	<0.001
	Missed LNM (%)	28.6	0	<0.001
	Reduced unnecessary additional surgery (%) *	45.8		
Version 2	Sensitivity (%)	71.4	100	<0.001
	Specificity (%)	84.2	0	<0.001
	PPV (%)	41.7	13.6	<0.001
	Accuracy (%)	82.5	13.6	<0.001
	Unnecessary additional Surgery (%)	58.3	86.4	<0.001
	Missed LNM (%)	28.6	0	<0.001
	Reduced unnecessary additional surgery (%)	28.1		
Version 3	Sensitivity (%)	76.2	100	<0.001
	Specificity (%)	85.9	0	<0.001
	PPV (%)	42.1	11.9	<0.001
	Accuracy (%)	84.7	11.9	<0.001
	Unnecessary additional Surgery (%)	57.9	88.1	<0.001
	Missed LNM (%)	23.8	0	<0.001
	Reduced unnecessary additional surgery (%)	30.2		
Version 4	Sensitivity (%)	92.9	100	<0.001
	Specificity (%)	57.6	0	<0.001
	PPV (%)	31.7	17.5	<0.001
	Accuracy (%)	63.8	17.5	<0.001
	Unnecessary additional Surgery (%)	68.3	82.5	<0.001
	Missed LNM (%)	7.1	0	<0.001
	Reduced unnecessary additional surgery (%)	14.2		

* Reduced unnecessary additional surgery when using the artificial intelligence model, compared to JSCCR guidelines. JSCCR, Japanese Society for Cancer of the Colon and Rectum; Version 1, train and test: surgical specimen; Version 2, train and test: endoscopic and surgical specimen; Version 3, train: endoscopic and surgical specimens and test: surgical specimen; Version 4, train: endoscopic and surgical specimens and test: endoscopic specimen; PPV, positive predictive value; LNM, lymph node metastasis

3.5. Attention Score

The attention mechanism interprets the effect of each patch on the final WSI-level decision using a scoring system. The calculated ASs of WSIs for positive LNM are displayed as a heatmap, highlighting regions of interest (ROIs), where ASs were normalized using a simple min-max normalization method (Figure 4). Sample patch images of LNM-positive WSIs are shown in Figure 4B. The prominent features of the sample patch images with high ASs were tumor budding and micropapillary patterns.

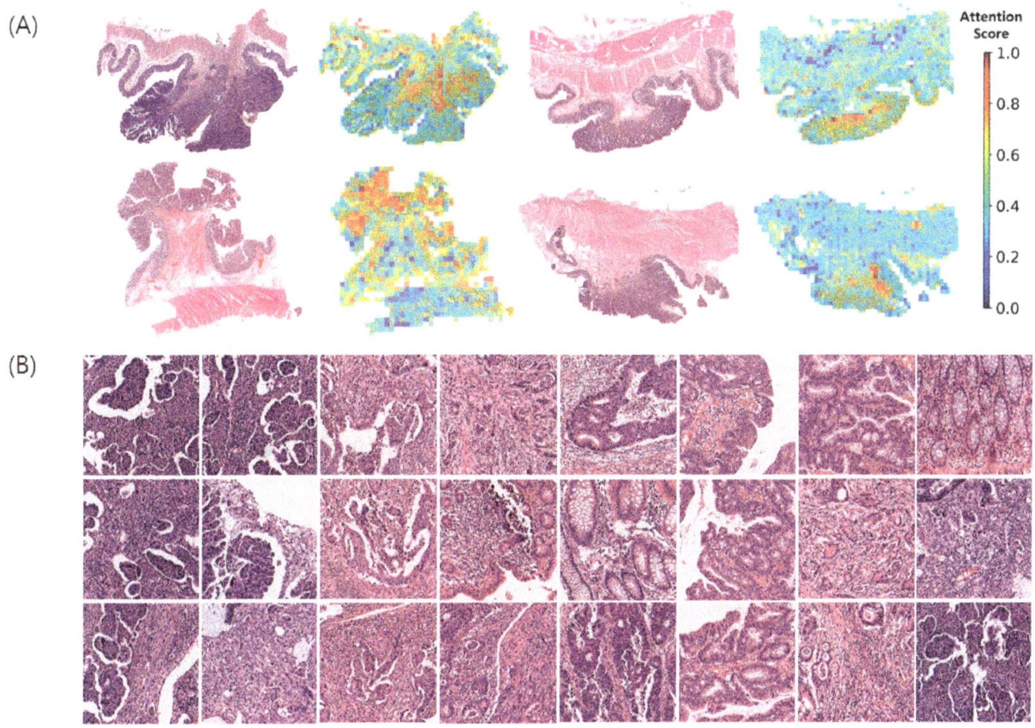

Figure 4. Attention score visualization in WSIs of positive lymph node metastasis. (**A**) Spatial distribution of attention scores on the WSIs, (**B**) Patch-images stratified by high attention scores WSIs, whole slide images.

4. Discussion

The risk of LNM in T1 CRC is associated with the following histological risk factors in endoscopically resected specimens: LVI, tumor budding, histological grade, and depth of SM invasion. In cases of high-risk LNM, additional surgery is recommended based on the current guidelines. However, the risk of LNM in T1 CRC after additional surgery with LN dissection is estimated to be 6–14% [37]. Therefore, to avoid unnecessary surgery, it is important to predict LNM using endoscopically resected specimens before surgery. However, it is almost impossible to predict LNM based on pathological evaluation using only H&E-stained, endoscopically resected specimens. To address this issue, several recent studies have used AI models to determine the histological risk of LNM [23,24,26,38,39]. However, these DL models are still in the early stages of development and require extensive external validation [28,29,40].

In our previous study, we developed a prediction model analyzing H&E-stained WSIs for LNM in T1 CRC using DL without manual pixel-level annotation. Compared to existing studies, this study had the strengths of a relatively large target group that underwent additional surgery after endoscopic resection, resulting in better AUCs for predicting LNM with H&E-stained WSI information alone. Although the previous study included high-risk histological features of LNM, the absolute number of enrolled patients was small. Moreover, as it was difficult to perform an external validation using scanned WSIs from other hospitals in a relatively short time, no external validation was performed. Consequently, we planned to validate our model using not only endoscopic specimens but also surgical specimens. To increase the number of patients and WSIs from patients with low risk of LNM, we included patients who underwent surgery between 2003–2020, a longer study period than those who underwent endoscopic resection followed by surgery (2010–2018). Massive surgical specimens that were performed when surgery was the only treatment option for T1 CRC showed a lower risk of LNM compared to endoscopic resected specimens. Indeed, pathologic characteristics of patients with surgical resection showed a lower risk of LNM than in patients with endoscopic resection, followed by surgery. Therefore, as an alternative to the independent cohort, we trained and tested the model in four versions and assessed its performance.

We developed an AI model with a DL program to predict LNM in T1 CRC using surgical and endoscopic specimens. The AUCs of our DL model were 0.758–0.830 for the training set and 0.781–0.824 for the test set, which were improved compared with the previous model (AUC: 0.747 in training and 0.767 in testing sets). This could be explained by the fact that surgical specimens contained much more tissue and information than endoscopically resected specimens, and over 1000 WSIs were used for analysis compared with previous studies. Among four versions, Version 3 (train: endoscopic and surgical specimens, test: surgical specimens), which contained surgical specimens in both training and test sets, had the highest performance power. However, all versions of the AI model showed acceptable AUC ranges for predicting LNM in patients with T1 CRC. On the other hand, RF with clinicopathological features showed a lower AUC (0.516–0.701) than the AI model. Only Version 1 (training and test: surgical specimen) had an AUC barely greater than 0.7.

Among four versions, Version 4 (train: endoscopic and surgical specimens, test: endoscopic specimens) was the closest to the actual prediction target. Because the ultimate goal of the AI model was to predict LNM in patients who were only treated with endoscopic treatment for T1 CRC, however, considering the study results, it could be assumed that test with endoscopic resected specimen was difficult to predict LNM. The AUC of RF with clinicopathologic features was the lowest (0.516) in Version 4. The AUC of Version 4 was the lowest among the four versions, even though the difference was not significant. However, it was remarkable that the AI model with Version 4 had the greatest improvement of AUC (0.265), compared to RF with clinicopathologic features, among the four versions. Thus, our newly developed model showed the possibility of application in clinical practice for LNM prediction.

In a previous study, when we compared the AI model with JSCCR guidelines, we ideally set the cutoff threshold of the AI model at 100% sensitivity not to allow missed LNM, like JSCCR guidelines. As a result, the previous model reduced unnecessary additional surgeries by 15.1% than the current JSCCR guidelines. However, setting the cutoff threshold at 100% sensitivity might not reflect reality, so we used the Youden index for setting the cutoff in our present study. The present model avoided 14.2–45.8% of unnecessary additional surgeries than predicted using the current JSCCR guidelines while allowing missed LNM, which ranged from 7.1 to 28.6%. The AI model that reduced unnecessary additional surgery allowed more missed LNM. So, careful interpretation of results was needed. Considering, acceptable the lowest rate of missed LNM, the ultimate target population, and the improvement of AUC using the AI model, the AI model with Version 4 was compatible with clinical practice to predict LNM in T1 CRC. It reduced 14.2% of unnecessary additional surgeries than predicted using the current JSCCR guidelines while allowing 7% of missed LNM.

Previous studies using AI to determine the risk of LNM on histology showed AUC ranging between 0.567 and 0.938, consistent with our results (0.781–0.824) [26,27,31,38,39,41]. Most studies included clinicopathologic variables and/or additional immunohistochemistry performed by pathologists. However, several recent studies have demonstrated the potential of applying DL to predict LNM in T1 CRC using H&E-stained WSIs without a histological assessment [26,27,31]. This pathologist-independent strategy may be the focus of the next era of T1 CRC management [29]. Similarly, our AI model also used WSIs without annotation and included a large number of T1 CRC cases (n = 1281). The model was validated using an independent cohort at the same institution and showed the best AUC among the AI models using only WSI.

In contrast to previous studies, Kasahara et al. developed an AI model with 80–85% accuracy using biopsy specimens and mucosal layer of the surgical specimens in the absence of biopsy specimens to predict patients with T1 CRC without LNM and their LNM risk before treatment, and select appropriate procedure before treatment [41]. The study suggests that biopsy specimen characteristics are associated with LNM risk. However, they implemented a weakly supervised model with a small number of patients and images of the site of choice for each ROI selected by the pathologist. Our previous study was conducted using high-risk histological features of LNM and was unsuitable for predicting LNM in low-risk patients with T1 CRC. However, 10.1% of the present study population had LNM, consistent with previous Japanese studies on long-term outcomes of CRC (10.8–12.4%) [42,43]. Additionally, the sensitivity and specificity of the present model were improved compared to our previous study. Therefore, it might be acceptable to apply our AI model to predict LNM in patients with low-risk T1 CRC.

Even though depth of SM invasion and tumor budding were risk factors of LNM, the meaning of these is controversial, and inter-observer variation for measurement existed. According to JSCCR guidelines, SM depth >1000 μm was one of the risk factors for LNM, but several studies showed differences in SM invasion depth related to LNM [44–46]. The International Tumor Budding Consensus Conference guidelines recommended the use of a three-tier system for risk stratification: Bd 1, low budding (0–4 buds); Bd 2, intermediate budding (5–9 buds); Bd 3, high budding (10 or more buds) [47]. In p1 CRC, Bd 2 and Bd 3 were associated with an increased risk of LNM, whereas in stage II CRC, Bd 3 is associated with an increased risk of recurrence and mortality. Moreover, the current tumor bud assessment system focused only on the tumor bud count and did not account for other features [48]. So, we wanted to figure out the meaning of depth of invasion for LNM and tumor budding using an attention-based WSI-level classification deep learning model. Patch images with high ASs appeared to be located in the transformation zone, which is the boundary between normal and cancerous tissues. In our study, the prominent features of the patch images with high ASs were poorly differentiated histological grades, tumor budding and micropapillary patterns, well-known pathological factors associated with poor prognosis [49,50]. Additionally, Brockmoeller et al. demonstrated an association between inflamed fat in CRC and LNM and that AI had the potential to discover new mechanisms in cancer progression [26]. However, unlike their study, our patch images with high AS did not contain inflamed fat.

Nevertheless, our study had some limitations. First, it was a single tertiary center retrospective study, which has a potential for bias. Second, the AUC of our method was relatively low to use as a prediction model despite the improvement achieved by increasing the study population and using various training and test sets for endoscopic and surgical specimens. Additionally, the DL model was influenced by class balance, and intrinsic LNM in T1 CRC was low. Nonetheless, among the AI models that used only WSIs, our study showed the best performance. Third, extensive external validation was lacking. We performed validation with an independent cohort in a single center; however, staining using H&E, variations in WSI color, and clinicopathological characteristics in a single center were similar. Therefore, the discriminating power may have been overestimated [29,40]. However, our study enrolled a relatively large number of patients compared with previous studies. Moreover, the clinicopathological features did not seem to be important in predicting LN metastasis in our AI model with H&E-stained WSI. Finally, our model was not validated in a cohort that underwent endoscopic resection of T1 CRC without additional surgery, which is a part of the model's real target.

5. Conclusions

In conclusion, our AI model with H&E-stained WSIs and without pathologists showed higher performance power (AUC, 0.782–0.824) with validation of an independent cohort in a single center than previous studies. Since WSIs from 1281 patients with low to high risk of LNM were used to develop the present AI model, it was suitable for predicting LNM even in low-risk patients with T1 CRC. Moreover, this model reduced 14.2% of unnecessary additional surgeries than predicted using the current JSCCR guidelines while allowing 7% of missed LNM. This revealed the feasibility of using an AI model with only H&E-stained WSIs to predict LNM in T1 CRC. However, to apply our model to real-world clinical practice, extensive external validation with WSI from multiple centers and patients who undergo only endoscopic treatment is warranted.

Author Contributions: Conceptualization, J.H.S., E.R.K. and Y.H.; methodology, J.H.S., E.R.K. and Y.H.; software, Y.H.; validation, Y.H. and I.S.; formal analysis, J.H.S.; investigation, J.H.S. and Y.H.; resources, J.H.S. and Y.H.; data curation, J.H.S.; writing—original draft preparation, J.H.S.; writing—review and editing, E.R.K. and Y.H.; visualization, J.H.S. and Y.H.; supervision, E.R.K., Y.H., I.S., S.A., S.-H.K. and K.-T.J.; funding acquisition, J.H.S. and K.-T.J. All authors have read and agreed to the published version of the manuscript.

Funding: This study was supported by the Research Supporting Program of the Korean Association for the Study of Intestinal Diseases for 2023 (2023-8). This research was supported by a grant of the Korea Health Technology R&D Project through the Korea Health Industry Development Institute (KHIDI), funded by the Ministry of Health and Welfare, Republic of Korea (grant number: HI21C1137).

Institutional Review Board Statement: The study was conducted in accordance with the Declaration of Helsinki and approved by the Institutional Review Board of Samsung Medical Center (2021-01-042-005, 17 November 2021).

Informed Consent Statement: Patient consent was waived due to the use of de-identified data routinely collected during hospital visits.

Data Availability Statement: The raw data supporting the conclusions of this article will be made available by the authors on request.

Acknowledgments: We thank all the patients who participated in this study.

Conflicts of Interest: Insuk Sohn was employed by the company Arontier Co., Ltd. The remaining authors declare no conflicts of interest.

Abbreviations

CRC	colorectal cancer
LNM	lymph node metastasis
SM	submucosal
LVI	lymphovascular invasion
JSCCR	Japanese Society for Cancer of the Colon and Rectum
H&E	Hematoxylin and eosin
AI	artificial intelligence
WSI	whole slide images
AUC	area under the curve
EMR	endoscopic mucosal resection
ESD	endoscopic submucosal dissection
DCNN	a deep convolutional neural network
AM	attention module
CM	classification module
AS	attention score
FV	feature vector

IQR	interquartile ranges
ROC	receiver operating characteristic curve
CV	cross-validation
RF	random forest
ROI	regions of interest

References

1. Wong, M.C.S.; Ding, H.; Wang, J.; Chan, P.S.F.; Huang, J. Prevalence and risk factors of colorectal cancer in Asia. *Intest. Res.* **2019**, *17*, 317–329. [CrossRef]
2. Sung, H.; Ferlay, J.; Siegel, R.L.; Laversanne, M.; Soerjomataram, I.; Jemal, A.; Bray, F. Global Cancer Statistics 2020: GLOBOCAN Estimates of Incidence and Mortality Worldwide for 36 Cancers in 185 Countries. *CA Cancer J. Clin.* **2021**, *71*, 209–249. [CrossRef] [PubMed]
3. Winawer, S.J.; Zauber, A.G. The advanced adenoma as the primary target of screening. *Gastrointest. Endosc. Clin. N. Am.* **2002**, *12*, 1–9. [CrossRef] [PubMed]
4. Wook, H.S.; Jeong-Sik, B. Endoscopic diagnosis and treatment of early colorectal cancer. *Intest. Res.* **2022**, *20*, 281–290.
5. Kim, S.Y.; Kwak, M.S.; Yoon, S.M.; Jung, Y.; Kim, J.W.; Boo, S.-J.; Oh, E.H.; Jeon, S.R.; Nam, S.-J.; Park, S.-Y.; et al. Korean Guidelines for Postpolypectomy Colonoscopic Surveillance: 2022 revised edition. *Intest. Res.* **2023**, *21*, 20–42. [CrossRef] [PubMed]
6. Fujimori, T.; Kawamata, H.; Kashida, H. Precancerous lesions of the colorectum. *J. Gastroenterol.* **2001**, *36*, 587–594. [CrossRef]
7. Morson, B.C.; Whiteway, J.E.; Jones, E.A.; Macrae, F.A.; Williams, C.B. Histopathology and prognosis of malignant colorectal polyps treated by endoscopic polypectomy. *Gut* **1984**, *25*, 437–444. [CrossRef] [PubMed]
8. Minamoto, T.; Mai, M.; Ogino, T.; Sawaguchi, K.; Ohta, T.; Fujimoto, T.; Takahashi, Y. Early invasive colorectal carcinomas metastatic to the lymph node with attention to their nonpolypoid development. *Am. J. Gastroenterol.* **1993**, *88*, 1035–1039. [PubMed]
9. Kitajima, K.; Fujimori, T.; Fujii, S.; Takeda, J.; Ohkura, Y.; Kawamata, H.; Kumamoto, T.; Ishiguro, S.; Kato, Y.; Shimoda, T. Correlations between lymph node metastasis and depth of submucosal invasion in submucosal invasive colorectal carcinoma: A Japanese collaborative study. *J. Gastroenterol.* **2004**, *39*, 534–543. [CrossRef]
10. Kyzer, S.; Begin, L.R.; Gordon, P.H.; Mitmaker, B. The care of patients with colorectal polyps that contain invasive adenocarcinoma. Endoscopic polypectomy or colectomy? *Cancer* **1992**, *70*, 2044–2050. [CrossRef]
11. Nivatvongs, S.; Rojanasakul, A.; Reiman, H.M.; Dozois, R.R.; Wolff, B.G.; Pemberton, J.H.; Beart, R.W., Jr.; Jacques, L.F. The risk of lymph node metastasis in colorectal polyps with invasive adenocarcinoma. *Dis. Colon Rectum* **1991**, *34*, 323–328. [CrossRef] [PubMed]
12. Netzer, P.; Forster, C.; Biral, R.; Ruchti, C.; Neuweiler, J.; Stauffer, E.; Schönegg, R.; Maurer, C.; Hüsler, J.; Halter, F.; et al. Risk factor assessment of endoscopically removed malignant colorectal polyps. *Gut* **1998**, *43*, 669–674. [CrossRef] [PubMed]
13. Watanabe, T.; Muro, K.; Ajioka, Y.; Hashiguchi, Y.; Ito, Y.; Saito, Y.; Hamaguchi, T.; Ishida, H.; Ishiguro, M.; Ishihara, S.; et al. Japanese Society for Cancer of the Colon and Rectum (JSCCR) guidelines 2016 for the treatment of colorectal cancer. *Int. J. Clin. Oncol.* **2018**, *23*, 1–34. [CrossRef] [PubMed]
14. Ramirez, M.; Schierling, S.; Papaconstantinou, H.T.; Thomas, J.S. Management of the malignant polyp. *Clin. Colon Rectal Surg.* **2008**, *21*, 286–290. [CrossRef] [PubMed]
15. Aarons, C.B.; Shanmugan, S.; Bleier, J.I. Management of malignant colon polyps: Current status and controversies. *World J. Gastroenterol.* **2014**, *20*, 16178–16183. [CrossRef] [PubMed]
16. Cooper, H.S. Surgical pathology of endoscopically removed malignant polyps of the colon and rectum. *Am. J. Surg. Pathol.* **1983**, *7*, 613–623. [CrossRef] [PubMed]
17. Coverlizza, S.; Risio, M.; Ferrari, A.; Fenoglio-Preiser, C.M.; Rossini, F.P. Colorectal adenomas containing invasive carcinoma. Pathologic assessment of lymph node metastatic potential. *Cancer* **1989**, *64*, 1937–1947. [CrossRef]
18. Colacchio, T.A.; Forde, K.A.; Scantlebury, V. Endoscopic Polypectomy: Inadequate Treatment for Invasive Colorectal Carcinoma. *Ann. Surg.* **1982**, *194*, 704–707. [CrossRef]
19. Choi, Y.S.; Kim, W.S.; Hwang, S.W.; Park, S.H.; Yang, D.-H.; Ye, B.D.; Myung, S.-J.; Yang, S.-K.; Byeon, J.-S. Clinical outcomes of submucosal colorectal cancer diagnosed after endoscopic resection: A focus on the need for surgery. *Intest. Res.* **2020**, *18*, 96–106. [CrossRef]
20. Kojima, M.; Puppa, G.; Kirsch, R.; Basturk, O.; Frankel, W.L.; Vieth, M.; Lugli, A.; Sheahan, K.; Yeh, M.; Lauwers, G.Y.; et al. Blood and lymphatic vessel invasion in pT1 colorectal cancer: An international concordance study. *J. Clin. Pathol.* **2015**, *68*, 628–632. [CrossRef]
21. Kouyama, Y.; Kudo, S.E.; Miyachi, H.; Ichimasa, K.; Hisayuki, T.; Oikawa, H.; Matsudaira, S.; Kimura, Y.J.; Misawa, M.; Mori, Y.; et al. Practical problems of measuring depth of submucosal invasion in T1 colorectal carcinomas. *Int. J. Color. Dis.* **2016**, *31*, 137–146. [CrossRef]
22. Barel, F.; Auffret, A.; Cariou, M.; Kermarrec, T.; Samaison, L.; Bourhis, A.; Badic, B.; Jézéquel, J.; Cholet, F.; Bail, J.P.; et al. High reproducibility is attainable in assessing histoprognostic parameters of pT1 colorectal cancer using routine histopathology slides and immunohistochemistry analyses. *Pathology* **2019**, *51*, 46–54. [CrossRef]

23. Ichimasa, K.; Kudo, S.E.; Mori, Y.; Misawa, M.; Matsudaira, S.; Kouyama, Y.; Baba, T.; Hidaka, E.; Wakamura, K.; Hayashi, T.; et al. Artificial intelligence may help in predicting the need for additional surgery after endoscopic resection of T1 colorectal cancer. *Endoscopy* **2018**, *50*, 230–240. [PubMed]
24. Takamatsu, M.; Yamamoto, N.; Kawachi, H.; Chino, A.; Saito, S.; Ueno, M.; Ishikawa, Y.; Takazawa, Y.; Takeuchi, K. Prediction of early colorectal cancer metastasis by machine learning using digital slide images. *Comput. Methods Programs Biomed.* **2019**, *178*, 155–161. [CrossRef]
25. Kudo, S.E.; Ichimasa, K.; Villard, B.; Mori, Y.; Misawa, M.; Saito, S.; Hotta, K.; Saito, Y.; Matsuda, T.; Yamada, K. Artificial Intelligence System to Determine Risk of T1 Colorectal Cancer Metastasis to Lymph Node. *Gastroenterology* **2021**, *160*, 1075–1084.e2. [CrossRef]
26. Brockmoeller, S.; Echle, A.; Ghaffari Laleh, N.; Eiholm, S.; Malmstrøm, M.L.; Plato Kuhlmann, T.; Levic, K.; Grabsch, H.I.; West, N.P.; Saldanha, O.L.; et al. Deep learning identifies inflamed fat as a risk factor for lymph node metastasis in early colorectal cancer. *J. Pathol.* **2022**, *256*, 269–281. [CrossRef]
27. Takamatsu, M.; Yamamoto, N.; Kawachi, H.; Nakano, K.; Saito, S.; Fukunaga, Y.; Takeuchi, K. Prediction of lymph node metastasis in early colorectal cancer based on histologic images by artificial intelligence. *Sci. Rep.* **2022**, *12*, 2963. [CrossRef] [PubMed]
28. Ichimasa, K.; Kudo, S.-e.; Lee, J.W.J.; Nemoto, T.; Yeoh, K.G. Artificial intelligence–assisted treatment strategy for T1 colorectal cancer after endoscopic resection. *Gastrointest. Endosc.* **2023**, *97*, 1148–1152. [CrossRef]
29. Ichimasa, K.; Kudo, S.-E.; Lee, J.W.J.; Yeoh, K.G. "Pathologist-independent" strategy for T1 colorectal cancer after endoscopic resection. *J. Gastroenterol.* **2022**, *57*, 815–816. [CrossRef] [PubMed]
30. Ahn, J.H.; Kwak, M.S.; Lee, H.H.; Cha, J.M.; Shin, H.P.; Jeon, J.W.; Yoon, J.Y. Development of a novel prognostic model for predicting lymph node metastasis in early colorectal cancer: Analysis based on the surveillance, epidemiology, and end results database. *Front. Oncol.* **2021**, *11*, 614398. [CrossRef]
31. Song, J.H.; Hong, Y.; Kim, E.R.; Kim, S.-H.; Sohn, I. Utility of artificial intelligence with deep learning of hematoxylin and eosin-stained whole slide images to predict lymph node metastasis in T1 colorectal cancer using endoscopically resected specimens; prediction of lymph node metastasis in T1 colorectal cancer. *J. Gastroenterol.* **2022**, *57*, 654–666.
32. Ilse, M.; Tomczak, J.; Welling, M. Attention-based deep multiple instance learning. In Proceedings of the International Conference on Machine Learning (PMLR), Stockholm, Sweden, 10–15 July 2018.
33. Lu, M.Y.; Zhao, M.; Shady, M.; Lipkova, J.; Chen, T.Y.; Williamson, D.F.; Mahmood, F. Deep learning-based computational pathology predicts origins for cancers of unknown primary. *arXiv* **2020**, arXiv:2006.13932.
34. He, K.; Zhang, X.; Ren, S.; Sun, J. Deep residual learning for image recognition. In Proceedings of the IEEE Conference on Computer Vision and Pattern Recognition, Las Vegas, NV, USA, 27–30 June 2016.
35. Pedregosa, F.; Varoquaux, G.; Gramfort, A.; Michel, V.; Thirion, B.; Grisel, O.; Blondel, M.; Prettenhofer, P.; Weiss, R.; Dubourg, V. Scikit-learn: Machine learning in Python. *J. Mach. Learn. Res.* **2011**, *12*, 2825–2830.
36. Ruopp, M.D.; Perkins, N.J.; Whitcomb, B.W.; Schisterman, E.F. Youden Index and optimal cut-point estimated from observations affected by a lower limit of detection. *Biom. J.* **2008**, *50*, 419–430. [CrossRef] [PubMed]
37. Ebbehøj, A.L.; Jørgensen, L.N.; Krarup, P.M.; Smith, H.G. Histopathological risk factors for lymph node metastases in T1 colorectal cancer: Meta-analysis. *Br. J. Surg.* **2021**, *108*, 769–776. [CrossRef] [PubMed]
38. Kwak, M.S.; Lee, H.H.; Yang, J.M.; Cha, J.M.; Jeon, J.W.; Yoon, J.Y.; Kim, H.I. Deep Convolutional Neural Network-Based Lymph Node Metastasis Prediction for Colon Cancer Using Histopathological Images. *Front. Oncol.* **2020**, *10*, 619803. [CrossRef] [PubMed]
39. Kang, J.; Choi, Y.J.; Kim, I.K.; Lee, H.S.; Kim, H.; Baik, S.H.; Kim, N.K.; Lee, K.Y. LASSO-Based Machine Learning Algorithm for Prediction of Lymph Node Metastasis in T1 Colorectal Cancer. *Cancer Res. Treat.* **2021**, *53*, 773–783. [CrossRef]
40. Li, J.W.; Wang, L.M.; Ichimasa, K.; Lin, K.W.; Ngu, J.C.-Y.; Ang, T.L. Use of artificial intelligence in the management of T1 colorectal cancer: A new tool in the arsenal or is deep learning out of its depth? *Clin. Endosc.* **2023**, *57*, 24–35. [CrossRef]
41. Kasahara, K.; Katsumata, K.; Saito, A.; Ishizaki, T.; Enomoto, M.; Mazaki, J.; Tago, T.; Nagakawa, Y.; Matsubayashi, J.; Nagao, T.; et al. Artificial intelligence predicts lymph node metastasis or risk of lymph node metastasis in T1 colorectal cancer. *Int. J. Clin. Oncol.* **2022**, *27*, 1570–1579. [CrossRef]
42. Yoda, Y.; Ikematsu, H.; Matsuda, T.; Yamaguchi, Y.; Hotta, K.; Kobayashi, N.; Fujii, T.; Oono, Y.; Sakamoto, T.; Nakajima, T.; et al. A large-scale multicenter study of long-term outcomes after endoscopic resection for submucosal invasive colorectal cancer. *Endoscopy* **2013**, *45*, 718–724. [CrossRef]
43. Ikematsu, H.; Yoda, Y.; Matsuda, T.; Yamaguchi, Y.; Hotta, K.; Kobayashi, N.; Fujii, T.; Oono, Y.; Sakamoto, T.; Nakajima, T.; et al. Long-term Outcomes After Resection for Submucosal Invasive Colorectal Cancers. *Gastroenterology* **2013**, *144*, 551–559. [CrossRef] [PubMed]
44. Nakadoi, K.; Tanaka, S.; Kanao, H.; Terasaki, M.; Takata, S.; Oka, S.; Yoshida, S.; Arihiro, K.; Chayama, K. Management of T1 colorectal carcinoma with special reference to criteria for curative endoscopic resection. *J. Gastroenterol. Hepatol.* **2012**, *27*, 1057–1062. [CrossRef] [PubMed]
45. Tanaka, S.; Haruma, K.; Oh, E.H.; Nagata, S.; Hirota, Y.; Furudoi, A.; Amioka, T.; Kitadai, Y.; Yoshihara, M.; Shimamoto, F. Conditions of curability after endoscopic resection for colorectal carcinoma with submucosally massive invasion. *Oncol. Rep.* **2000**, *7*, 783–788. [CrossRef] [PubMed]

46. Egashira, Y.; Yoshida, T.; Hirata, I.; Hamamoto, N.; Akutagawa, H.; Takeshita, A.; Noda, N.; Kurisu, Y.; Shibayama, Y. Analysis of pathological risk factors for lymph node metastasis of submucosal invasive colon cancer. *Mod. Pathol.* **2004**, *17*, 503–511. [CrossRef] [PubMed]
47. Lugli, A.; Kirsch, R.; Ajioka, Y.; Bosman, F.; Cathomas, G.; Dawson, H.; El Zimaity, H.; Fléjou, J.-F.; Hansen, T.P.; Hartmann, A.; et al. Recommendations for reporting tumor budding in colorectal cancer based on the International Tumor Budding Consensus Conference (ITBCC) 2016. *Mod. Pathol.* **2017**, *30*, 1299–1311. [CrossRef] [PubMed]
48. Chen, L.; Yang, F.; Qi, Z.; Tai, J. Predicting lymph node metastasis and recurrence in patients with early stage colorectal cancer. *Front. Med.* **2022**, *9*, 991785. [CrossRef]
49. Pyo, J.-S.; Park, M.J.; Kang, D.-W. The clinicopathological significance of micropapillary pattern in colorectal cancers. *Hum. Pathol.* **2018**, *77*, 159–165. [CrossRef]
50. Zhang, S.; Zhang, D.; Yang, Z.; Zhang, X. Tumor Budding, Micropapillary Pattern, and Polyploidy Giant Cancer Cells in Colorectal Cancer: Current Status and Future Prospects. *Stem Cells Int.* **2016**, *2016*, 4810734. [CrossRef]

Journal of
Clinical Medicine

MDPI

Article

Anomaly Detection and Biomarkers Localization in Retinal Images

Liran Tiosano [1,*,†], Ron Abutbul [2,†], Rivkah Lender [1], Yahel Shwartz [1], Itay Chowers [1], Yedid Hoshen [1] and Jaime Levy [1]

1 Department of Ophthalmology, Hadassah-Hebrew University Medical Center, Hadassah School of Medicine, Hebrew University, Jerusalem 9574409, Israel; levjaime@gmail.com (J.L.)
2 School of Computer Science and Engineering, Hebrew University of Jerusalem, Jerusalem 9574409, Israel
* Correspondence: tiosano@hadassah.org.il
† These authors contributed equally to this work.

Abstract: Background: To design a novel anomaly detection and localization approach using artificial intelligence methods using optical coherence tomography (OCT) scans for retinal diseases. **Methods**: High-resolution OCT scans from the publicly available Kaggle dataset and a local dataset were used by four state-of-the-art self-supervised frameworks. The backbone model of all the frameworks was a pre-trained convolutional neural network (CNN), which enabled the extraction of meaningful features from OCT images. Anomalous images included choroidal neovascularization (CNV), diabetic macular edema (DME), and the presence of drusen. Anomaly detectors were evaluated by commonly accepted performance metrics, including area under the receiver operating characteristic curve, F1 score, and accuracy. **Results**: A total of 25,315 high-resolution retinal OCT slabs were used for training. Test and validation sets consisted of 968 and 4000 slabs, respectively. The best performing across all anomaly detectors had an area under the receiver operating characteristic of 0.99. All frameworks were shown to achieve high performance and generalize well for the different retinal diseases. Heat maps were generated to visualize the quality of the frameworks' ability to localize anomalous areas of the image. **Conclusions**: This study shows that with the use of pre-trained feature extractors, the frameworks tested can generalize to the domain of retinal OCT scans and achieve high image-level ROC-AUC scores. The localization results of these frameworks are promising and successfully capture areas that indicate the presence of retinal pathology. Moreover, such frameworks have the potential to uncover new biomarkers that are difficult for the human eye to detect. Frameworks for anomaly detection and localization can potentially be integrated into clinical decision support and automatic screening systems that will aid ophthalmologists in patient diagnosis, follow-up, and treatment design. This work establishes a solid basis for further development of automated anomaly detection frameworks for clinical use.

Keywords: age-related macular degeneration; deep learning; anomaly detection; optical coherence tomography angiography

1. Introduction

Retinal diseases affect millions of people worldwide, resulting in reduced visual acuity and blindness. Clinical diagnosis and follow-up exams rely extensively on optical coherence tomography (OCT) scans, which provide high-resolution, cross-sectional imaging of the retina layers [1]. Timely diagnosis is crucial for optimal treatment; however, at the earlier stages of the diseases, imaging biomarkers and lesions are more difficult to detect. Furthermore, due to the subjective nature of the task, often there is a disagreement even among domain experts when describing the features in retinal scans. Therefore, there is a need for an automated clinical decision support system that will aid ophthalmologists in the early detection of biomarkers for the development and progression of the disease.

Anomaly detection (AD) is a subclass of machine learning methods based on a binary classification between normal and anomalous classes. Although visual anomaly detection is highly valuable, it also poses significant challenges. One major challenge is that it is not always possible to train a model with full supervision for a given task due to the wide variety of anomalies and the lack of classified anomalous data. Hence, retinal datasets often contain annotation at the disease stage, but not particularly for biomarkers and lesion levels. The field of image anomaly detection has transformed in recent years due to the emergence of deep networks [2]. The strength of these networks lies in their ability to learn meaningful representations of images. Similar semantic images are typically assigned close numerical representation. In contrast, raw image pixels provide a much weaker representation. The latest state-of-the-art anomaly detection methods use a simple three-step paradigm: (1) compute a numerical representation for each image in the normal dataset using a deep neural network; (2) estimate the normal data distribution with a probabilistic model; (3) calculate the likelihood for every test sample employing the probabilistic model [2]. If the model considers an image unlikely, it is labeled anomalous. Despite training on non-medical datasets, these methods performed well on retinal images. Burlina et al. validated that such methods achieve state-of-the-art performance for retinal fundus images [3]. Retinal pathologies such as choroidal neovascularization (CNV), diabetic macular edema (DME), and drusen create a diverse set of anomalous images. CNV severely disrupts the retinal structure, DME results in swelling of the retinal layers, and drusen appears as localized elevation of the retina and is the hallmark of age-related macular degeneration (AMD), the leading cause of blindness in the elderly population in the Western world.

Thus, the aim of this study was to identify those common retinal pathologies using novel self-supervised anomaly detection deep learning methods.

2. Methods

This retrospective study used the Kaggle dataset, a public domain dataset of 84,495 OCT slabs (Spectralis OCT, Heidelberg Engineering, Heidelberg, Germany) from 44,346 individuals and a second local real-world dataset—the Hadassah Imaging Dataset—which consists of OCT volume scans (Spectralis OCT, Heidelberg Engineering, Heidelberg, Germany) of 348,657 OCT scans from 4663 patients diagnosed with age-related macular degeneration. Four categories were used for the model training: normal retinal structure, CNV, DME, and early or intermediate AMD with the presence of drusen. The study adhered to the tenets of the Declaration of Helsinki. Institutional review board (IRB) approval was obtained from the Hadassah Medical Center (0382-19). As this was a retrospective data collection study, a waiver of informed consent was granted. The dataset was divided into training, validation, and test sets. We used the test and validation sets for evaluation. In addition, we used a validation set as suggested in Sparse-GAN [4]. The validation set comprised 4000 normal and 1000 anomalous image slabs that were randomly chosen from each of the categories. This dataset presents a challenge for anomaly detection as the retinal scans are not aligned, not centered, and contain significant noise. Additionally, and most challenging, the anomalies are diverse in their characteristics and location through the different layers of the retina.

Our novel approach follows the latest state-of-the-art (SOTA) methods paradigm and utilizes local region representations of healthy scans. We first employ the pre-trained neural network over a healthy retinal scans dataset to obtain a local representation bank. Then, we fit a probabilistic model for the local representations. The probabilistic model was applied to new OCT scans to estimate the likelihood of their local regions. Local regions with low likelihood scores were deemed abnormal. Finally, retinal scans that consist of one or more abnormal regions were classified as anomalous. Additionally, we used the regions' likelihood scores for the localization of anomalous patches. An initial self-supervised fine-tuning step could be performed on the pre-trained neural network. This step adapts the neural network to the normal retinal dataset and enhances the method's performance.

We use center loss adaptation, as suggested in PANDA, to fine-tune the pre-trained neural network and achieve better results [2].

We compared four SOTA frameworks for anomaly detection and segmentation in images. All the frameworks in this work used pre-trained CNNs for feature extraction and embedding creation. The four SOTA frameworks are: (1) Pretrained anomaly detection adaptation (PANDA) [2]. This framework consists of several stages: (i) Feature extraction using a pre-trained deep neural network and adaptation, (ii) retrieval of the nearest K normal neighbors to the target, and calculation of anomaly scoring. (2) Semantic Pyramid Anomaly Detection (SPADE) [5]. This framework consists of several stages: (i) Image embedding extraction using a pre-trained deep neural network, (ii) retrieval of the nearest K normal neighbors (kNN) to the target, and (iii) calculation of dense pixel level correlation between the target and the normal images. (3) Patch Distribution Modeling (PaDiM) framework [6]. Stages included (i) Image embedding extraction using a pre-trained deep neural network, (ii) fitting a multivariate Gaussian distribution to every patch using the normal image embedding, and (iii) estimation of the plausibility of every patch in the target image using the Mahalanobis distance between the target patches and the corresponding multivariate Gaussian distribution. (4) PatchCore framework [7]. This framework consists of several stages: (i) Creating patch embedding for every image in the training set, (ii) sub-sampling the patch embeddings using the coreset mechanism, (iii) calculating segmentation maps and image-level anomaly scores for each sample from the test set using the normal images patch embeddings sub-set.

Implementation details: an initial preprocessing stage included black-and-white margin removal using classical image processing algorithms. Specifically, a contour detector was applied to find white and black margins. In cases where the corners were part of a contour, we checked if each row or column held more than a quarter of white or black pixels and removed them in such cases. Then, the images were resized to 224 × 224. ResNet152 pre-trained on ImageNet 1 k was used as a deep neural network for the representation extraction [8]. We evaluated both local region and image-level representation methods. We represent each local region by combining the features of the second and third residual blocks of the ResNet152 model. In addition, the features after global average pooling are used as image-level representations. K nearest neighbors were utilized for the density estimation with $k = 5$ [9]. For the local region approach, the density estimation takes a global approach. A local region's density was estimated against all local regions within the nominal bank, regardless of their spatial location. In order to reduce the size of the local region bank and lower the computational cost, we used a greedy coreset. The nominal bank keeps 1% of healthy local regions for the open source and 10% for the clinical dataset. In the fine-tuning step, we used PANDA for feature adaptation over the training data for 40 epochs [2].

After training the model on normal-only training OCT scans, a nominal local bank was extracted. The model was operated to score each of the OCT scans in the test set using kNN. The ROC AUC was used as a parameter-free criterion for scoring the model. Every experiment was conducted with 3 different random seeds. All studies were performed on NVIDIA RTX 2080 GPU cards using Pytorch 2.3.0.

3. Local Retinal Region Anomaly Detection

Data representation: numerical representations of local regions are extracted using a deep neural network from healthy retinal scans. The neural network is pre-trained on non-medical images but has been shown to learn effective representation for medical images, including color fundus photos [10–12]. The representations need to satisfy the following property: regions with similar properties should be mapped to numerically similar representations, while dissimilar local retinal regions should be mapped to dissimilar numerical representations. For example, OCT regions that contain drusen should map to the same deep representation, which should differ from fluid-presented OCT representation (Figure 1).

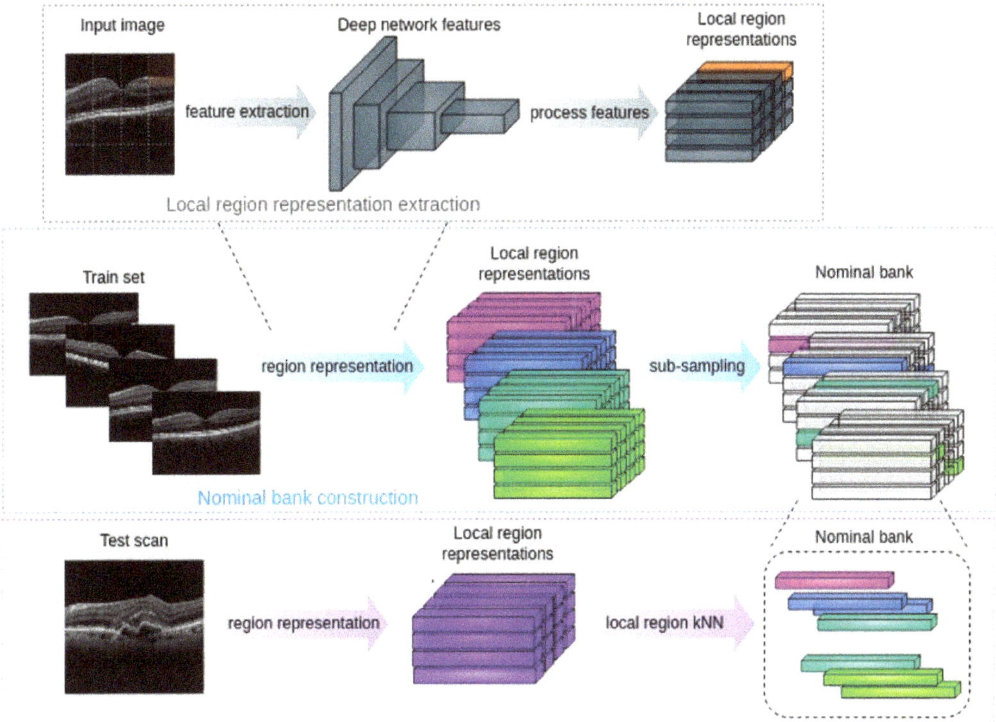

Figure 1. Demonstration of local region anomaly detection workflow. The non-medical pre-trained neural network learns local region representations. Regions with similar properties are mapped to numerically similar representations, while dissimilar local retinal regions are mapped to dissimilar representations. The last row presents a test scan with choroidal neovascularization which the fluid representation differs from the present of the pigment epithelial detachment and drusen.

Density estimation: following representation extraction, we estimate the distribution of nominal retinal regions. To represent the normal data, we train a probabilistic model. Models typically fall under two categories: parametric (following a simple, mathematically specified function) and non-parametric models. Unfortunately, the appearance of local retinal regions is complex and highly variable and, therefore, does not fit a simple mathematical form. Instead, we opted for a well-known non-parametric model, the K nearest neighbors (kNN) distance [9]. For a target image, the model specifies the likelihood of a region by first retrieving the K nominal local region with the most similar representation using the nominal region bank. We then record the average of the distances between the numerical representation of the target local region and each of the representations of the k nearest local regions. The kNN distance measures the likelihood of the local region being anomalous. Regions with high kNN distance are very atypical, i.e., their representation is not like the representation of any previously observed normal region. These regions have a very low likelihood and are classified as anomalous. Conversely, representations of regions with low kNN distance are similar to those observed as normal; hence, these regions are expected to be normal. Note that the kNN distance is not a calculation of probability calculation [13,14]. However, their results are highly correlated to kNN results, and the kNN has less computational starving.

Efficient nearest neighbors: we reduce the number of healthy local regions in the nominal bank to make the similarity search more efficient. The computation of the kNN can be slow for large datasets due to neighbor retrieval. We encounter the same case in retinal localization, where each training image consists of many local retinal regions. The train set contains thousands of normal scans that enlarge the amount of local retinal regions. The likelihood is estimated over local regions and may be computation-consuming. In order to speed up the computation of the kNN, most approaches typically attempt to reduce the number of potential matches without removing the likely matches. We follow previous methods in choosing a reduced number of prototypical regions that provide a compressed representation of all the nominal regions observed during training. The prominent approaches for performing this compression are K means and coreset methods, and in this work, we followed PatchCore in using an approximation algorithm of the core set for normal region dataset compression [7,9].

Representation fine-tuning on retinal data: neural networks pre-trained on external non-medical datasets extract powerful representations even for ophthalmic data. They may be further improved by another training stage on the healthy retinal scan data. We employ the deep network and extract image-level representations for the healthy training set. Then, we compute the center of the numerical representations using their average. A center loss is used to fine-tune the network over the healthy scans. It demands that the representations of normal scans would be close to the calculated center. As a result, we hoped that the normal scan representations would be closer to the center than the anomalous scans. To prevent catastrophic forgetting, we include an elastic weight consolidation regularization loss in addition to representation center loss as advocated by PANDA [2].

Full retinal scan anomaly detection: after extracting anomaly scores for each local region of a retinal scan, the next step was to classify the scan as normal or abnormal. Our approach defines the anomaly score as the maximum of the anomaly scores of all local regions within the retinal scan. The underlying logic was that an anomaly is of interest even if it lies in a small region of the retina. Such an approach can help detect even small lesions and changes in the retina structure.

4. Results

The study was designed to answer several questions: (i) Should anomaly detection be performed at the local region or image level? (ii) Are representations learned using non-medical images effective for anomaly detection on OCT retinal scans? (iii) Given the effectiveness of pre-trained features, are there benefits to self-supervised training over the normal data? (iv) Can inter-scan alignment assumptions be used in the nearest neighbor procedure? (v) Are the local region anomaly scores informative for humans?

The local region approach had generally greater accuracy, sensitivity, specificity and F1 score comparing the tested SOTA methods, with averages of 94.8, 94.4, 95.9, and 0.95, respectively. Table 1 presents the comparison between the different methods.

Table 1. Quantitative comparison with the state-of-the-art methods.

	Validation Set		Local Region	
	AUC	**Sensitivity**	**AUC**	**Sensitivity**
Auto-Encoder	72.9	78.3	75.1	83.4
AnoGAN	81.5	84.6	78.9	91.7
F-AnoGAN	84.9	88.2	80.8	87.1
Pix2pix	83.7	87.4	81.5	90
Sparse-GAN	88.5	92.5	84.1	95.1
Local region	98.6	99.7	97.8	98.1

AUC: area under the curve, GAN: Generative Adversarial Networks.

5. Image-Level vs. Local Region Representation

In the approach presented by Burlina et al. [3]. Anomaly scoring is performed using image-level features. A representation is computed for the entire retinal scan, and an anomaly score is assigned to the image based on the extracted representation. In contrast, we advocate a local approach, which scores regions rather than the entire retinal scan. Local region representations were computed using a deep network followed by a region anomaly scoring stage. The set of region scores is used to compute an image-level anomaly score. The two approaches are compared in Table 2.

Table 2. Comparison of local region and image-level anomaly detection methods (ROC AUC%).

	Validation Set		Test Set	
	Image-Level	**Local-Level**	**Image-Level**	**Local-Level**
CNV	98.7	99.9	99.4	100
DME	95.4	99.1	97.9	100
Drusen	92.1	96.7	93.6	99
Average	95.4	98.6	97	99.7

AUC: area under the curve, CNV: choroidal neovascularization, DME: diabetic macular edema.

6. Self-Supervised vs. Auxiliary Pre-Trained Feature Representations

We compare two approaches for learning representations. The first is self-supervised representation learning, which only uses the training data consisting of healthy OCT retinal scans. The second approach uses a feature representation trained on an auxiliary, non-medical dataset—ImageNet. Note that the ImageNet dataset contains a label for every image indicating its object category (e.g., dog, cat, car, etc.). ImageNet images are very different from OCT scans, apart from the obvious difference of not containing retinas, they also consist of color images and are relatively noise-free. The comparison between the approaches is presented in Table 3. We can observe that ImageNet-pretrained representations outperform the self-supervised representation. This is non-trivial, as during training, the model does not observe any retinal OCT scans.

Table 3. Comparison of pre-trained and self-supervised (CutPaste) features ROC AUC%.

	Validation Set		Test Set	
	Self-Supervised	**Pre-Trained**	**Self-Supervised**	**Pre-Trained**
CNV	96.7	99.8	97.4	100
DME	96.7	98.9	98.6	100
Drusen	81.9	97	82.1	99.1
Average	91.8	98.6	92.7	99.7

CNV: choroidal neovascularization, DME: diabetic macular edema.

7. Representation Fine-Tuning

Although representations pre-trained on non-retinal images are clearly effective for retinal OCT anomaly detection, it begs the question of whether incorporating retinal scans into the training images will result in further improvements. To test this hypothesis, we fine-tuned the ImageNet-pre-trained representation on the training set, which consists of healthy OCT scans. Specifically, we used the procedure introduced in PANDA [2]. We present the results in Table 4. It can be observed that the proposed adaptation stage improved both image-level and local-level anomaly detection approaches. The performance is particularly significant for OCT scans containing drusen. This demonstrates that using both auxiliary non-retinal data as well as the normal OCT scans provided for training is more effective than merely the auxiliary pre-training dataset.

Table 4. An evaluation of feature adaptation (ROC AUC%).

	Image-Level		Local-Level	
	Pre-Trained	Adapted	Pre-Trained	Adapted
CNV	98.7	99.1	99.8	100
DME	95.4	95.9	98.9	99.9
Drusen	92.1	93	97	99.4
Average	95.4	96	98.6	99.8

CNV: choroidal neovascularization, DME: diabetic macular edema, AUC: area under the curve.

8. Slice Alignment Assumptions

Previous local region anomaly detection approaches (e.g., PaDiM) have suggested that the anomaly score for each local region may be computed by comparing its representation to those of other regions having the same spatial location in the image [6]. In other words, a region centered around the (x, y) pixel location is compared with other regions across different slices and scans that are also centered around the (x, y) pixel. This assumes that different scans are aligned. This approach has multiple benefits when the slices are aligned, including faster runtime and higher accuracy. However, these advantages are only beneficial when the scans are indeed well aligned. This approach was compared to the standard, global approach of comparing all local regions regardless of their center location. The results are presented in Table 5. We can observe that the alignment assumption is not effective for unaligned retinal scans and results in inferior performance relative to the global search.

Table 5. Evaluation of the alignment assumption ROC AUC%.

	Aligned	Global
CNV	84.3	98.3
DME	85.1	93.7
Drusen	74.2	86.7
Average	81.2	92.9

CNV: choroidal neovascularization, DME: diabetic macular edema.

9. Discussion

In this paper, we present a novel approach for anomaly detection for retinal OCT scans. Our approach is based on local region anomaly detection and localization. First, a numerical representation was computed for each local region of the retinal scan. We then fit a model for the local representations—estimating the likelihood that each local region of the retinal scan is normal. We used this model to localize the normal and anomalous regions of the retina scans. Finally, retinal scans that contained one or more anomalous regions were classified as anomalous. Furthermore, our method represents data using a neural network that was pre-trained on an external, non-medical dataset. Our method was shown to perform well on two datasets, a popular public dataset as well as a local real-world clinical dataset.

Anomaly detection and localization are vital fields in visual machine learning. The methods in the fields can be categorized into several categories: reconstruction-based, distribution-based, and classification-based.

Reconstruction-based methods learn to reconstruct the normal training data using a set of basis functions. During the reconstruction process, these methods use a bottleneck to create a compressed representation, which is, in turn, used to reconstruct the input sample. The main idea is that normal samples should be reconstructed accurately, while anomalous data will not. Therefore, the reconstruction loss is used as the anomaly criterion. Classical reconstruction-based methods are k nearest neighbors (kNN) [9], K-means [15], and principal component analysis (PCA). In recent years, the use of deep learning methods has expanded to the field of reconstruction-based methods. Deep learning architectures such as Auto-Encoder (AE) [4,16], Variational Auto-Encoder (VAE) [17], and Generative Adversarial Networks (GAN) [18] are all trained to reconstruct normal images. The common reconstruction loss functions are Euclidean distance, L1, and structural similarity (SSIM) [14]. Deep learning architectures also use deep perceptual loss and discriminators as adversarial loss functions [13].

Distribution-based methods attempt to learn the probability density function (PDF) of the distribution of normal samples. The anomaly score for every given image from the test set is calculated by the PDF. The expectation is that normal images will be mapped to dense areas using the PDF so that their likelihood will be low compared to anomalous images. Therefore, in cases where the anomaly score of an image is larger than a given threshold, the image is deemed anomalous. Distribution-based methods differ in the distributional assumptions that they adopt. Such methods include parametric models such as multivariate Gaussian and Gaussian mixture models and non-parametric models such as kernel density estimation, robust kernel density estimation, and KNN, which also performs density estimation [5,6].

There is a known difficulty in achieving good results with this approach when handling high-dimensional data due to the PDF estimation. To mitigate this problem, deep learning methods are used to project the high-dimensional data to lower-dimensional space. Works such as PANDA [5], SPADE [6], and PatchCore [7] use pre-trained CNNs to extract embedding and use kNN to evaluate the anomaly score for a sample in the test set. Other approaches use AE or GAN architectures, such as DAGMM, which employs a combination of distribution and reconstruction loss [19].

Classification-based methods are another paradigm for anomaly detection. These methods find a separate manifold between the normal and the anomalous data in a given representation space. Such methods are one-class support vector machines (OC-SVM) and their variants, such as support vector data description (SVDD), which obtain a spherically shaped boundary around a given dataset. Recently, deep learning methods have been used to improve classical approaches. Examples of such methods are Deep SVDD and deep OC-SVM. An additional set of deep learning methods uses the self-supervised training approach, in which models attempt to solve an auxiliary task with either pre-existing or easily obtained data. Golan and El-Yaniv devised the Rot-Net-based method, a self-supervised method that utilizes rotation transformations to classify test samples. The method was later improved and expanded [7,20].

Another unique challenge that visual anomaly detection presents is anomaly localization. For every detected anomalous scan, the anomaly detection algorithm segments all the areas that were identified as anomalous. This setting is important for algorithm explainability (Figure 2), as it sheds light on the algorithm's decision. Additionally, in the field of medical images, anomaly segmentation can help detect disease biomarkers and lesions in the scans. These algorithms have the potential to reveal new biomarkers and thereby improve diagnosis. This might also be a significant step in evaluating the clinical-pathological correlation between known or new biomarkers and visual acuity.

Drusen, for example, is the hallmark of AMD which represents pathological proteinaceous and lipids accumulation between the choroid and the retinal pigment epithelium.

Drusen is supposed to be a pathogenic trigger of the disorder. In fact, drusen may mechanically alter retinal function. A novel hypothesis exists, suggesting that a metabolic defect (systemic or focal within the retinal pigment epithelium) may be the real determinant of visual impairment while causing the concomitant accumulation of the drusen. Pinelli et al. did not find a clear correlation between visual impairment and the occurrence of drusen number, size, and the extent of a drusenoid area in the foveal region in 120 AMD patients. The authors concluded that drusen and visual deterioration develop because of similar upstream biochemical alterations, but it is likely that drusen by itself does not produce visual deterioration [21]. Accurate localization of biomarkers like drusen and its geometry features, especially in the macular cube using AD algorithms, might obtain insight into analyzing a quantitative correlation between drusen (or other anomalous regions) and visual impairment in a specific macular zone.

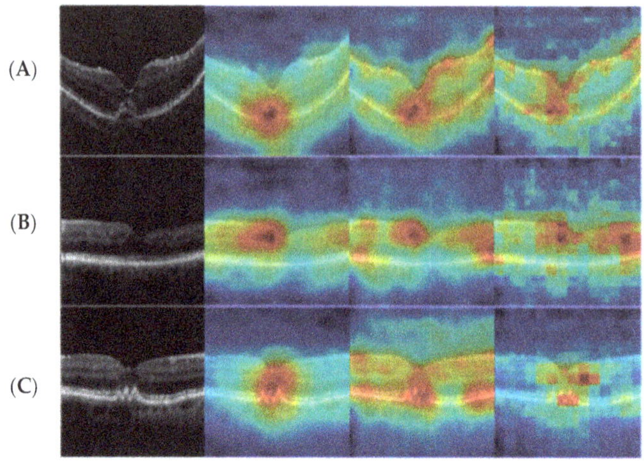

Figure 2. Heat maps of anomalous retinal OCT scans containing (**A**) choroidal neovascularization, (**B**) diabetic macular edema, and (**C**) drusen. Column 1 presents the original OCT scan. Heat-maps were extracted by local region using aligned density estimation (column 2) and local region with global density estimation (column 3).

Anomaly segmentation has received less attention compared to image-level anomaly detection. Early works proposed patch-based localization using classical approaches [22,23]. Later works expanded these patch-based methods and used pre-trained CNNs as a feature extractor for a K-means classifier [24]. Bergmann et al. introduced the MVTec dataset and evaluated GAN, AE, and classical methods with this dataset. Bergmann et al. followed up on this work with a student-teacher approach, which uses a pre-trained CNN [25]. Venkataramanan et al. introduced an attention-guided anomaly localization framework that uses VAE and other methods, such as GradCAM and adversarial loss [26]. Recently, a number of distribution-based frameworks achieved SOTA performance in the task of anomaly localization, namely PANDA, SPADE, PaDiM, and PatchCore. These frameworks utilize pre-trained CNNs for feature extraction and embedding creation and use density estimations for anomaly scoring.

In this work, four SOTA frameworks for visual anomaly detection were adapted to the domain of retinal OCT scans. Anomaly detection and localization frameworks have the potential to detect disease biomarkers and lesions, creating the ability to diagnose retinal pathologies using OCT scans. We showed that with the use of pre-trained feature extractors, these frameworks can generalize to the domain of retinal OCT scans and achieve high image-level ROCAUC scores. Additionally, adapting the feature extractor to the OCT scan domain can cause the framework to outperform the "raw" baseline. The localization results of these frameworks are promising and successfully capture areas that indicate the presence of retinal pathology. In this research, we have evaluated OCT sections obtained from eyes affected by AMD and DME, which comprise the most common cause of blindness in older people and in the working age group, respectively. There are multiple other sigh-threatening retinal pathologies, and the fact that such unsupervised anomaly detection frameworks obtained clinical-level performance suggests that other retinal pathologies may also be readily identified in OCT sections. Such frameworks for anomaly detection and localization can be integrated into clinical decision support systems that will aid ophthalmologists in patient screening, diagnosis, follow-up, and treatment design.

Caveats of our study include a relatively lower number of scans and different image quality parameters like different scan numbers in each B-scan volume, different ART values, and different alignment of the image. Yet, the OCT images studied where from a commonly used OCT devise which produces high-quality sections. Furthermore, we have applied an unsupervised approach, which reduces the risk of bias generated by training.

This preliminary work establishes a solid basis for further development of automated anomaly detection frameworks for clinical use. Future works should focus on exploiting information that exists beyond a given OCT scan, such as diagnosis or patient medical history, to improve the clinical performance of the automatic anomalous detection algorithm. This direction has great potential for groundbreaking results with far-reaching implications.

Author Contributions: L.T., J.L., R.L. and I.C. contributed to the study concept and design, acquisition, analysis, or interpretation of data, drafting of the manuscript, and critical revision of the manuscript. Y.S. contributed to the acquisition, analysis, or interpretation of data. R.A. and Y.H. contributed to the analysis or interpretation of data, drafting of the manuscript, and critical revision of the manuscript. All authors have read and agreed to the published version of the manuscript.

Funding: This work was supported in part by the Israel Science Foundation under Grant 3485-19.

Institutional Review Board Statement: The study adhered to the tenets of the Declaration of Helsinki. Institutional review board (IRB) approval was obtained from the Hadassah Medical Center (0382-19) from 13 October 2021.

Informed Consent Statement: Not applicable.

Data Availability Statement: The data presented in this study are available on request from the corresponding author.

Conflicts of Interest: The authors declare no conflict of interest.

References

1. Adhi, M.; Duker, J.S. Optical Coherence Tomography—Current and Future Applications. *Curr. Opin. Ophthalmol.* **2013**, *24*, 213–221. [CrossRef]
2. Reiss, T.; Cohen, N.; Bergman, L.; Hoshen, Y. PANDA: Adapting Pretrained Features for Anomaly Detection and Segmentation. In Proceedings of the IEEE/CVF Conference on Computer Vision and Pattern Recognition, Nashville, TN, USA, 20–25 June 2021; pp. 2805–2813. [CrossRef]
3. Burlina, P.; Paul, W.; Liu, T.Y.A.; Bressler, N.M. Detecting Anomalies in Retinal Diseases Using Generative, Discriminative, and Self-Supervised Deep Learning. *JAMA Ophthalmol.* **2022**, *140*, 185–189. [CrossRef] [PubMed]
4. Akcay, S.; Atapour-Abarghouei, A.; Breckon, T.P. Ganomaly: Semi-Supervised Anomaly Detection via Adversarial Training. In *Computer Vision—ACCV 2018, Proceedings of the 14th Asian Conference on Computer Vision, Perth, Australia, 2–6 December 2018*; Revised Selected Papers, Part III 14; Springer: Berlin/Heidelberg, Germany, 2019; pp. 622–637.
5. Cohen, N.; Hoshen, Y. Sub-Image Anomaly Detection with Deep Pyramid Correspondences. *arXiv* **2020**, arXiv:2005.02357.
6. Defard, T.; Setkov, A.; Loesch, A.; Audigier, R. PaDiM: A Patch Distribution Modeling Framework for Anomaly Detection and Localization. In *Pattern Recognition, ICPR International Workshops and Challenges, Proceedings of the ICPR 2021, Virtual Event, 10–15 January 2021*; Proceedings, Part IV; Springer: Berlin/Heidelberg, Germany, 2021; pp. 475–489.
7. Roth, K.; Pemula, L.; Zepeda, J.; Schölkopf, B.; Brox, T.; Gehler, P. Towards Total Recall in Industrial Anomaly Detection. In Proceedings of the IEEE/CVF Conference on Computer Vision and Pattern Recognition, New Orleans, LA, USA, 18–24 June 2022; pp. 14318–14328.
8. He, K.; Zhang, X.; Ren, S.; Sun, J. Deep Residual Learning for Image Recognition. In Proceedings of the 2016 IEEE Conference on Computer Vision and Pattern Recognition (CVPR), Las Vegas, NV, USA, 27–30 June 2016.
9. Eskin, E.; Arnold, A.; Prerau, M.; Portnoy, L.; Stolfo, S. *A Geometric Framework for Unsupervised Anomaly Detectio*; Applicatio; Springer: Boston, MA, USA, 2002.
10. Seeböck, P.; Waldstein, S.M.; Klimscha, S.; Bogunovic, H.; Schlegl, T.; Gerendas, B.S.; Donner, R.; Schmidt-Erfurth, U.; Langs, G. Unsupervised Identification of Disease Marker Candidates in Retinal OCT Imaging Data. *IEEE Trans. Med. Imaging* **2019**, *38*, 1037–1047. [CrossRef]
11. Han, Y.; Li, W.; Liu, M.; Wu, Z.; Zhang, F.; Liu, X.; Tao, L.; Li, X.; Guo, X. Application of an Anomaly Detection Model to Screen for Ocular Diseases Using Color Retinal Fundus Images: Design and Evaluation Study. *J. Med. Internet Res.* **2021**, *23*, e27822. [CrossRef]
12. Zhao, H.; Li, Y.; He, N.; Ma, K.; Fang, L.; Li, H.; Zheng, Y. Anomaly Detection for Medical Images Using Self-Supervised and Translation-Consistent Features. *IEEE Trans. Med. Imaging* **2021**, *40*, 3641–3651. [CrossRef] [PubMed]

13. Kim, J.; Scott, C.D. Robust Kernel Density Estimation. *J. Mach. Learn. Res.* **2012**, *13*, 2529–2565.
14. Latecki, L.J.; Lazarevic, A.; Pokrajac, D. *Outlier Detection with Kernel Density Functions BT—Machine Learning and Data Mining in Pattern Recognition*; Perner, P., Ed.; Springer: Berlin/Heidelberg, Germany, 2007; pp. 61–75.
15. Hartigan, J.A.; Wong, M.A. A K-Means Clustering Algorithm. *R. Stat. Soc. Ser. C* **1979**, *28*, 100–108. [CrossRef]
16. Liu, W.; Li, R.; Zheng, M.; Karanam, S.; Wu, Z.; Bhanu, B.; Radke, R.J.; Camps, O. Towards Visually Explaining Variational Autoencoders. In Proceedings of the 2020 IEEE/CVF Conference on Computer Vision and Pattern Recognition (CVPR), Seattle, WA, USA, 13–19 June 2020; pp. 8639–8648.
17. Wang, Z.; Bovik, A.C.; Sheikh, H.R.; Simoncelli, E.P. Image Quality Assessment: From Error Visibility to Structural Similarity. *IEEE Trans. Image Process.* **2004**, *13*, 600–612. [CrossRef]
18. Zhang, R.; Isola, P.; Efros, A.A. *Colorful Image Colorization BT—Computer Vision—ECCV 2016*; Leibe, B., Matas, J., Sebe, N., Welling, M., Eds.; Springer International Publishing: Cham, Switzerland, 2016; pp. 649–666.
19. Zong, B.; Song, Q.; Min, M.R.; Cheng, W.; Lumezanu, C.; Cho, D.; Chen, H. Deep Autoencoding Gaussian Mixture Model for Unsupervised Anomaly Detection. In Proceedings of the International Conference on Learning Representations, Vancouver, BC, Canada, 30 April–3 May 2018.
20. Golan, I.; El-Yaniv, R. Deep Anomaly Detection Using Geometric Transformations. *Adv. Neural Inf. Process. Syst* **2018**, *31*.
21. Pinelli, R.; Bertelli, M.; Scaffidi, E.; Fulceri, F.; Busceti, C.L.; Biagioni, F.; Fornai, F. Measurement of Drusen and Their Correlation with Visual Symptoms in Patients Affected by Age-Related Macular Degeneration. *Arch. Ital. Biol.* **2020**, *158*, 82–104. [CrossRef]
22. Boracchi, G.; Carrera, D.; Wohlberg, B. Novelty Detection in Images by Sparse Representations. In Proceedings of the 2014 IEEE Symposium on Intelligent Embedded Systems (IES), Orlando, FL, USA, 9–12 December 2014; pp. 47–54.
23. Carrera, D.; Manganini, F.; Boracchi, G.; Lanzarone, E. Defect Detection in SEM Images of Nanofibrous Materials. *IEEE Trans. Industr. Inform.* **2017**, *13*, 551–561. [CrossRef]
24. Napoletano, P.; Piccoli, F.; Schettini, R. Anomaly Detection in Nanofibrous Materials by CNN-Based Self-Similarity. *Sensors* **2018**, *18*, 209. [CrossRef] [PubMed]
25. Bergmann, P.; Fauser, M.; Sattlegger, D.; Steger, C. Uninformed Students: Student-Teacher Anomaly Detection With Discriminative Latent Embeddings. In Proceedings of the 2020 IEEE/CVF Conference on Computer Vision and Pattern Recognition (CVPR), Seattle, WA, USA, 13–19 June 2020; pp. 4182–4191.
26. Venkataramanan, S.; Peng, K.-C.; Singh, R.V.; Mahalanobis, A. *Attention Guided Anomaly Localization in Images BT—Computer Vision—ECCV 2020*; Vedaldi, A., Bischof, H., Brox, T., Frahm, J.-M., Eds.; Springer International Publishing: Cham, Switzerland, 2020; pp. 485–503.

diagnostics

Article

Evaluating Cellularity Estimation Methods: Comparing AI Counting with Pathologists' Visual Estimates

Tomoharu Kiyuna [1,*], Eric Cosatto [2], Kanako C. Hatanaka [3,*], Tomoyuki Yokose [4], Koji Tsuta [5], Noriko Motoi [6], Keishi Makita [7], Ai Shimizu [8], Toshiya Shinohara [9], Akira Suzuki [10], Emi Takakuwa [8], Yasunari Takakuwa [11], Takahiro Tsuji [12], Mitsuhiro Tsujiwaki [13], Mitsuru Yanai [14], Sayaka Yuzawa [15], Maki Ogura [1] and Yutaka Hatanaka [3]

1 Healthcare Life Science Division, NEC Corporation, Tokyo 108-8556, Japan; maki.ogura@nec.com
2 Department of Machine Learning, NEC Laboratories America, Princeton, NJ 08540, USA; cosatto@nec-labs.com
3 Center for Development of Advanced Diagnostics (C-DAD), Hokkaido University Hospital, Sapporo 060-8648, Japan; yhatanaka@huhp.hokudai.ac.jp
4 Department of Pathology, Kanagawa Cancer Center, Yokohama 241-8515, Japan; kamaboko8ty@gmail.com
5 Department of Pathology, Kansai Medical University, Osaka 573-1010, Japan; tsutakoj@hirakata.kmu.ac.jp
6 Department of Pathology, Saitama Cancer Center, Saitama 362-0806, Japan; motoi.noriko@saitama-pho.jp
7 Department of Pathology, Oji General Hospital, Tomakomai 053-8506, Japan
8 Department of Surgical Pathology, Hokkaido University Hospital, Sapporo 060-8648, Japan; aishimizu@huhp.hokudai.ac.jp (A.S.); emitaka@huhp.hokudai.ac.jp (E.T.)
9 Department of Pathology, Teine Keijinkai Hospital, Sapporo 006-0811, Japan
10 Department of Pathology, KKR Sapporo Medical Center, Sapporo 062-0931, Japan
11 Department of Pathology, NTT Medical Center Sapporo, Sapporo 060-0061, Japan; yasunari.takakuwa@east.ntt.co.jp
12 Department of Pathology, Sapporo City General Hospital, Sapporo 060-8604, Japan; tsuji.takahiro@gmail.com
13 Department of Surgical Pathology, Sapporo Medical University Hospital, Sapporo 060-8543, Japan; tsujiwaki@sapmed.ac.jp
14 Department of Pathology, Sapporo Tokushukai Hospital, Sapporo 004-0041, Japan; mitsuruyanai.md@gmail.com
15 Department of Diagnostic Pathology, Asahikawa Medical University Hospital, Asahikawa 078-8510, Japan
* Correspondence: kiyuna@nec.com (T.K.); kyanack@huhp.hokudai.ac.jp (K.C.H.)

Abstract: The development of next-generation sequencing (NGS) has enabled the discovery of cancer-specific driver gene alternations, making precision medicine possible. However, accurate genetic testing requires a sufficient amount of tumor cells in the specimen. The evaluation of tumor content ratio (TCR) from hematoxylin and eosin (H&E)-stained images has been found to vary between pathologists, making it an important challenge to obtain an accurate TCR. In this study, three pathologists exhaustively labeled all cells in 41 regions from 41 lung cancer cases as either tumor, non-tumor or indistinguishable, thus establishing a "gold standard" TCR. We then compared the accuracy of the TCR estimated by 13 pathologists based on visual assessment and the TCR calculated by an AI model that we have developed. It is a compact and fast model that follows a fully convolutional neural network architecture and produces cell detection maps which can be efficiently post-processed to obtain tumor and non-tumor cell counts from which TCR is calculated. Its raw cell detection accuracy is 92% while its classification accuracy is 84%. The results show that the error between the gold standard TCR and the AI calculation was significantly smaller than that between the gold standard TCR and the pathologist's visual assessment ($p < 0.05$). Additionally, the robustness of AI models across institutions is a key issue and we demonstrate that the variation in AI was smaller than that in the average of pathologists when evaluated by institution. These findings suggest that the accuracy of tumor cellularity assessments in clinical workflows is significantly improved by the introduction of robust AI models, leading to more efficient genetic testing and ultimately to better patient outcomes.

Keywords: tumor content ratio (TCR); next generation sequencing (NGS); artificial intelligence (AI); U-Net model; domain shift; site dependency

1. Introduction

Genetic panel testing is a fundamental tool for diagnosis and treatment selection in cancer medicine. Since genetic panel testing analyzes the DNA contained in individual cells, accurate sample collection is essential for its success, and a sample with a higher number of tumor cells is considered to be a better specimen. For example, in FDA-approved FoundationOne [1] and OncomineDx Target Test [2], the overall cellularity, or tumor content ratio (TCR) should be more than 20%. For tissues where the overall TCR is between 10% and 20%, micro-dissection and enrichment should be performed to bring up the overall ratio.

In a typical clinical workflow, TCR is estimated manually by pathologists examining H&E-stained slides and is a subjective and error-prone process. Several factors affect the accuracy of counting cells by pathologists: (1) distinguishing individual cells in crowded areas, (2) distinguishing between tumor and non-tumor cells in heterogeneous areas, (3) integrating counts over a large area. Visual estimation is indeed inherently subjective and varies significantly by the examiner as reported in a widely cited study [3].

The automation of cell counting on images of H&E-stained slides using artificial intelligence (AI) is expected to not only reduce the workload of pathologists, but also to improve accuracy. AI-based methods help reduce errors by using image analysis and machine learning techniques to identify and count cells more accurately and objectively.

AI has been increasingly applied to digital pathology in recent years, with a wide range of applications in cell segmentation [4–6], cell counting [7,8], cell classification [9], tumor detection [10], patient outcome prediction [11–14], and image generation [15]. In particular, AI is expected to provide tools that can improve examiners' efficacy by reducing the time they spend in tedious tasks such as identifying metastatic or mitotic cells, counting tumor cells, or searching for rare types such as signet ring cells. Additionally, AI is also expected to bring a measure of objectivity and reduce the typically large variations observed across examiners on those tasks. Finally, recent advances in deep learning models as well as the availability of fast, low-cost GPUs have pushed the boundary of what AI is capable of to the point of surpassing human accuracy [16], while keeping costs in check.

However, although AI has shown potential in a wide range of pathology at the research level, only a small number of AI-based systems are routinely used in clinical settings, especially AI systems that have been approved as medical device software [17,18].

One of the reasons why AI is not widely used in clinical pathology is that it does not adequately address the variability in image quality of input images. Specifically, after training and evaluating an AI model on a dataset collected from one site, its performance is often degraded when applied to a dataset collected from a different site.

Pathology images are affected by various factors, such as the fixation method of the pathology specimen, the thickness of the slice, the light source of the imaging device, the characteristics of the objective lens, the characteristics of the charge coupled devices (CCD) image sensor, the degree of focus at the time of scanning, as well as image postprocessing on the scanner. As a result, significant variations in color, brightness, and sharpness do occur [19]. To be truly useful in a clinical setting, AI must be robust to such variations in data source sites and imaging devices. However, it is generally difficult to collect pathology images with precise annotations from a variety of facilities using a variety of imaging devices.

Several AI approaches have been reported to address these robustness issues. One approach is to normalize the input images. This can be performed by matching the input images to the spectrum of a reference template image, or by using generative adversarial networks (GANs) to convert the input images to a target quality [20]. However, the performance of such approaches tend to deteriorate for input images that are significantly different from the template images. In addition, for GAN-based normalization, the GAN model itself also requires a large amount of computational cost to learn and may suffer from hallucinations that change the semantic content of the image, therefore introducing label-noise.

An effective method to improve the robustness of AI models from limited data is data augmentation (DA) [21,22]. This method randomly adds variations in positional information (rotation, flipping) and color, brightness, etc., to the original input images to increase the diversity of the dataset without changing the semantics of the data (location, number and type of cells). By constructing AI models from these augmented datasets, the robustness of AI to variations in image quality is improved. In [23], DA is reported to be more effective than normalization of input images for improving the robustness of AI models to staining variations.

To develop a practical AI-powered TCR calculation software, it is essential to perform cell detection and classification accurately and efficiently. Chen et al. [24] developed a method for identifying the cell cycle phase of cells based on fluorescence images. Their approach utilizes k-means clustering and rule-based heuristics to classify cells into different phases; while this method may be effective for limited datasets, its generalization performance to datasets from different institutions or acquired using different imaging devices is likely to be constrained. Ghani et al. [25] proposed a method for accelerating cell detection using a convolutional neural network embedded on an FPGA device. This approach offers significant speedups compared to software-based implementations. The authors demonstrated the effectiveness of their method in detecting different types of damaged kidney cells with an accuracy of nearly 100%. However, the limited size of their test dataset raises concerns about the generalizability of their results. Further validation with a larger and more diverse dataset is recommended.

Addressing these challenges, we leverage a previously-developed deep-learning model [26] for TCR counting and use it in this study to predict TCR for a cohort (see Section 2.1) of 41 non-small cell lung cancer patients from four different medical institutions (sites). In other reported experiments on TCR counting [27], the "gold standard" ground truth is established by first defining a tumor area and then counting all cells within that area as tumor cells. In contrast, our approach is more fine-grained and classifies each cell independently as tumor or non-tumor.

In Section 2.2, we first establish a "gold standard" (GS) set of exhaustive cell-level annotations by three pathologists in regions of interests of the cohort. We also ask 13 pathologists to visually estimate the TCR on these regions (see Section 2.3). In Section 2.4, we detail the model architecture, training partition, and data augmentation we use to create our AI model. Finally, to evaluate the real-world robustness of the AI model, we devised a leave-one-hospital-out cross-validation scheme, where we test it on images from sites unseen during training. In Section 3, we report our findings, comparing the TCR predictions by the AI model to the gold standard and to the pathologists' visual estimate.

2. Materials and Methods

2.1. Cohort

The cohort in this study consists of 41 patient at various stages of non-small cell lung cancer (NSCLC) and considered for genetic panel testing. The specimens were collected between 2018 and 2022 from 4 sites: Hokkaido University Hospital (HUH), Kansai Medical University Hospital (KMU), Kanagawa Cancer Center (KCC), and Saitama Cancer Center (SCC). A total of 11 specimens were extracted with trans-bronchial biopsy (TBB), 9 were extracted with trans-bronchial needle aspiration (TBNA), 9 were extracted with core-needle biopsy (CNB), and 12 were extracted with surgical resections. These specimens were then prepared into blocks using the formalin-fixed paraffin-embedded (FFPE) method, sectioned, stained with hematoxylin and eosin (H&E), and scanned in bright-field at 40× magnification (0.25 microns/pixel) with a whole slide device (Philips UFS with Philips IntelliSite Pathology Solution, Philips, Amsterdam, The Netherlands) to generate WSI images.

Immunostained images from the same blocks were used during case selection for histological type differentiation but were not subsequently used for TCR estimation by pathologists nor by AI. Specimens with a high number of crushed necrotic cells were excluded. Specimen in the cohort exhibited adenocarcinoma (27) and squamous cell carcinoma (14). Care was taken that both cancer subtypes and sample extraction methods were split among sites to avoid site biases.

2.2. Gold Standard Labels

In a first step, we define, for each WSI slide a region of interest (ROI) where the labeling will take place (Figure 1). To eliminate bias in selecting the ROIs from the WSI slides, we employed the following procedure:

1. A pathologist manually traces a target area on a WSI slide (typically, the tumor area).
2. A program divides the area into square tiles of 400 microns (1760 × 1760 pixels at 40× magnification) and randomly selects a tile.
3. The pathologist examines the selected tile. If it does not contain tumor cells or has an image quality issue (e.g., blurriness, artifacts), it is excluded, and another tile is randomly selected by the program. If the selected tile has none of the aforementioned issues, it is finalized as the representative ROI for the WSI.

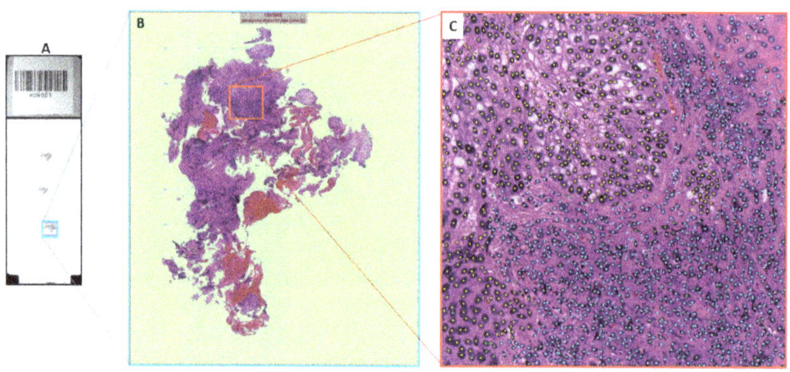

Figure 1. Region of interest (ROI) selection over WSI slide. In (**A**), a tissue is selected on the WSI slide. In (**B**), the tissue is tiled and one tile is selected as ROI. In (**C**), the cells of the ROI are exhaustively labeled.

In this manner, a representative ROI was selected from each WSI of the 41 cases, resulting in a total of 41 ROIs.

Three pathologists were then independently instructed to exhaustively identify the location of every cell in the ROI and to label them as either tumor cells (tCells), non-tumor cells (nCells), or indistinguishable cells (iCells). iCells are cells within an ROI that cannot be definitively classified as either tCells, nCells, or cells that should not be labeled. These cells may also be excluded from tumor cell content calculations by pathologists if DNA nucleic acids cannot be extracted due to crush, necrosis, degeneration, or keratinization.

In addition, cells that are not used for tumor cell content calculations by pathologists, such as red blood cells and cells whose nuclei cannot be recognized due to necrosis or degeneration, are excluded from the labeling process.

For each cell, the labels given by the three pathologists were combined into a single final label using a majority rule. Cells are initially matched using a distance-based matching algorithm thus resulting in a 3-cell match (all 3 pathologists annotated that cell), a 2-cell match, or a 1-cell match. Then, the final label was established following the rules shown in Table 1.

Table 1. Results of majority aggregation of three pathologists. In the first three rows, full agreement is reached, while in the bottom three rows, a tie was resolved by setting a cell to 'i' (indistinguishable) or a cell was discarded because only one annotator labeled it. The last column indicate the number of times each situation was encountered (asterisk "*" means any label).

Matched Annotations	Agreement	Final Label	Number of Cells
3	n, n, n	n	10,040
3	t, t, t	t	14,587
3	i, i, i	i	2824
3	n, n, NOT-n	n	949
3	t, t, NOT-t	t	1047
3	i, i, NOT-i	i	1591
2	t, t	t	21
2	n, n	n	24
2	i, i	i	20
3	n, t, i	i	92
2	*, NOT-*	i	8
1	n OR t OR i	discard	93 + 78 + 132 = 303

The annotations provided by the three pathologist labelers were then aggregated into a single final set of labels using a distance-based algorithm:

1. For each cell on the ROI, the labels from the three pathologists are gathered. Starting with a labeled cell from one labeler, the cell closest in distance from each other labeler is selected. Cells which are further than 4 microns are discarded. The resulting set of one, two or three cells are considered in the next step.
2. The final label for the set is established following the rules shown in Table 1.

In total, for the 41 ROIs, we collected approximately 40K cell labels. From those cell-level labels, the gold-standard TCR can be computed as the ratio of tCells over all cells, ignoring iCells.

$$TCR_{GS} = \frac{tCells_{GS}}{(tCells_{GS} + nCells_{GS})} \tag{1}$$

2.3. *Estimate of Tumor Content Ratio*

Before annotating the cells of the gold standard ROIs, 13 pathologists, including the three pathologists who created the gold standard labels, participated in a visual assessment of TCR. There was no time limit for the visual assessment, and iCells were instructed to be excluded from the estimation. Estimates were given in % with increments of 5%. Hence, for each of the 41 ROIs, we collected 13 pathologist estimates of the TCR.

2.4. *AI Model*

We developed an efficient and accurate AI model capable of processing an entire WSI slide in about a minute, counting several thousand cells per second. The model is based on the fully convolutional deep learning approach and uses the U-Net neural network architecture [28]. We have described such a model in a previous publication [26], and here we only highlight the main differences with that implementation. In particular, instead of using a multi-scale approach, we use an intermediate magnification (15×) that offers a good compromise between the ability to distinguish individual cells in densely packed areas and a sufficiently large field of view (300×300 pixels at 15× magnification or 200×200 microns) that provides enough context for the model to make an educated classification of normal and tumor cells. In another departure, our memory-compact U-Net model predicts simultaneously two density maps, one for normal cells and one for tumor cells, from which a simple peak detector with a cutoff threshold and max function can efficiently return two lists of coordinates. Our approach is memory-efficient on the GPU (compact model) and minimizes CPU post-processing, allowing an entire WSI with a tissue sample of 20×20 mm to be processed under 2 minutes on a single 12 GB GPU. Figure 2 (left) illustrates the overall system and Figure 2 (right) shows the neural network layered architecture of our model.

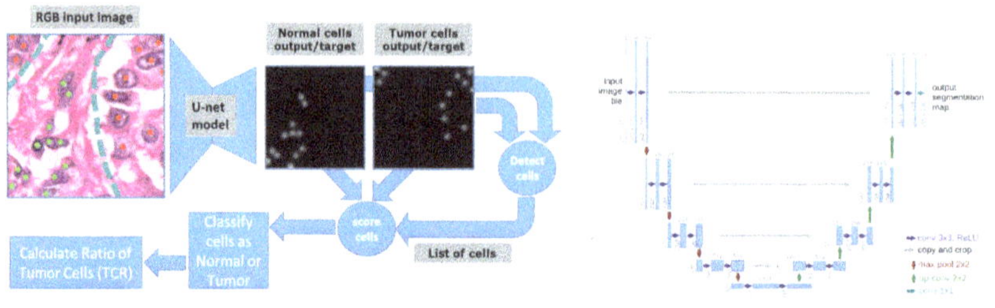

Figure 2. The left panel shows the overall workflow of the TCR system. An RGB image patch is the input to the model, which outputs two density maps. Annotations marking the centroid of cells (also shown as green and red overlay dots on the input image) are used to generate the two target density maps (by drawing Gaussian peaks at the location of annotated cells) which are used to train the model by back-propagating the difference (loss) between them and the maps generated by the model. The right panel shows a graphical representation of the architecture of the U-Net fully convolutional model. The numbers illustrate a 572 × 572 input image. For an 800 × 800 input image and two output maps, the total number of parameters is 28,942,850 and the total size of the model for inference (not counting training gradients) is about 3 GB.

2.5. AI Model Training and Evaluation Data

To establish that our model is robust to data samples collected from different hospital sites, we follow a 4-way hospital-wise cross-validation protocol. We train a model with data collected from three hospitals and test it on the data from remaining fourth hospital. The test cohort of 41 patients described in Section 2.1 provides the test data and part of the training data. Additional training data from three of the same four hospitals are used to enrich the training set. Those data are from distinct patients and are annotated by a distinct pathologist annotator following the same procedure as the test set. Those data consist of 131 ROIs from 34 patients from HUH (labeled HUNEC in Table 2), 16 ROIs from seven patients from KCC, and 3 ROIs from one patient from KMU. The 131 ROIs from HUH were collected for our initial study [26] and consist of TBB and TBNA tissue samples. Table 2 shows the 4 partitions of the data used to train and test each model. Each of the 4 partitions include training, validation, and testing partitions. We note that the training data of partition 2 technically contain HUH samples in both training (HUNEC) and test sets; however, these sets are completely different and were collected more than a year apart. Hence, we deemed it was sufficiently distinct as to not disqualify partition 2.

The scanner used for all the training data is a Nanozoomer (Hamamatsu Photonics, Hamamatsu, Japan). Note that the cohort of 41 cases has been scanned with both Nanozoomer and Philips UFS (Philips, Amsterdam, The Netherlands) scanners, with the Nanozoomer-scanned images used for with training and the Philips-scanned images used for testing. In total, the number of annotated cells for training was 212,180, roughly balanced between tumor and non-tumor cells.

Table 2. Four partitions used for the leave-one-hospital-out cross-validation. The number in parenthesis represent the number of images used for each institution and each task.

Partition	Test Set	Training Set	Validation Set
1	SCC (10)	HUNEC (75) + HUH (11) + KMU (12) + KCC (27) = 125	HUNEC (56)
2	HUH (11)	HUNEC (75) + SCC (10) + KMU (12) + KCC (27) = 124	HUNEC (56)
3	KMU (9)	HUNEC (75) + SCC (10) + KCC (27) + HUH (11) = 123	HUNEC (56)
4	KCC (11)	HUNEC (75) + SCC (10) + KMU (12) + HUH (11) = 108	HUNEC (56)
total	41	135	56

2.6. AI Model Data Augmentation

Since the model is trained from images coming from a limited number of only 4 hospitals and scanned on only one model of WSI scanner (Hamamatsu Nanozoomer), we deemed that it would not be robust enough to variations encountered in samples from unseen institutions or scanners devices. Indeed, deep-learning neural-networks have a strong tendency to overlearn biases found in particular datasets. For example, image corrections applied by scanner devices for aesthetic purposes may move an image outside of the range that a model has seen during training and result in significant degradation in accuracy. Similarly, an institution may use H&E staining chemicals from different manufacturers in different quantities, resulting in variations in colors and intensity that may also fall outside the range that was seen during training. To counter this issue, data augmentation has been used almost ever since neural networks were invented. Data augmentation consists of creating new training examples automatically from existing examples. The new created images preserve the semantics of the originals and annotations obtained on the originals can still be used with the created images to train the model. Here, we simulate variations in scanner light and focusing as well as variations in staining protocols. To simulate shifts in the stain intensity of H&E, we apply color deconvolution in the optical density color space and random shift along the H (hematoxylin stain) and E (eosin stain) basis (see Figure 3). To simulate color shifts due to the scanner light, we apply intensity random shifts in the RGB color space. To simulate variations in scanner optics and the focusing mechanism, we apply random small amounts of pixel blur and sharpening. Finally, to simulate software image processing by the scanner, we apply gamma correction, brightness, contrast, and saturation shifts. We summarize the augmentations and their respective range of parameters in Table 3.

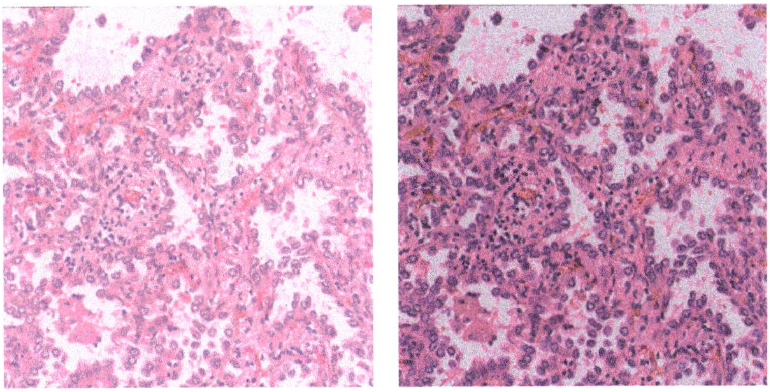

Figure 3. Example of data augmentation. The left image is the original, while the right image is generated by applying a gamma correction of 2.4.

Table 3. Data augmentation parameters for color and blurriness/sharpness. The algorithm first randomly decides to apply either HE or RGB color shift, then randomly decides either gamma or BCS, and finally randomly decides between blur, sharpen, and nothing.

Augmentation	Parameters
Hematoxylin and Eosin (HE)	random add ±16% of range
Red, Green Blue	random add ±12% of range
Gamma	random apply Gamma correction within [0.4; 1.5]
Brightness	random subtract 15% of range
Contrast and Saturation	multiply by a random value within [70%; 130%]
Blur (Gaussian)	Convolve with Gaussian kernel sigma = random {0.3, 0.5}
Sharpen	Apply sharpen filter with random intensity in [1.0; 1.2]

2.7. AI Model Training

During training, patches of image pixels (300 × 300) are extracted at random locations from the training ROIs, a random data augmentation is applied to the patch, as described in Section 2.6, and the patch is presented to the model. The model's output is compared to the target maps generated from the annotations (by drawing Gaussian peaks at the location of annotated cells into the map corresponding to the annotation label—tumor or non-tumor) and a loss is calculated and backpropagated to update the model's weights. The binary cross-entropy loss combined with a sigmoid layer $\sigma(x)$ is used:

$$L_{\mathrm{BCE}} = -\frac{1}{N}\sum_{n}^{N}[y_n \ln \sigma(x_n) + (1 - y_n)\ln(1 - \sigma(x_n))] \tag{2}$$

where N is the number of pixels in the output map, x_n an output pixel, and y_n a target pixel.

Batch normalization is used at each layer of the model to provide a smooth learning curve. To avoid overfitting the model on the training set, training is stopped when the loss on the validation set (see partition on Table 2) stops to decrease for 4 epochs. At each epoch, the model is trained with 4000 examples and achieves convergence in about 50 epochs. Figure 4 shows the behavior of the loss during the first 27 epochs.

We use the PyTorch (version 1.10.2+cu113) [29] toolchain to train our models using the Adam [30] optimizer and a learning rate of 1×10^{-4}. Training a model takes about 3 hours on a NVIDIA RTX3090 GPU.

Figure 4. The training curve shows the cross-entropy loss as a function of the epoch. The training loss is shown in red, and the blue curve shows the validation loss.

2.8. AI Model Tuning of Detection Threshold and Evaluation Protocol

On the validation set, we then search for the optimal threshold for detecting cells on the output maps produced by the trained models using sequential domain reduction. A detection map is first obtained by combining the 'normal' and 'tumor' maps with the max operator. Peaks are then detected on the detection map when a pixel has a higher intensity than its eight neighbors and peaks with values below the detection threshold are discarded. To evaluate the accuracy of the model, we match detections with annotation labels using bipartite matching of cells within 4 microns of each other and obtain the F1-score. We then search for the threshold that maximizes the F1-score. Applying the four models with their respective detection thresholds to the test set yielded an average detection-only accuracy of 92% (balanced F1-score).

For each detected cells, a class is assigned based on the softmax of the values from the original tumor and non-tumor density maps. On the test set of 41 ROIs, we report the cell-level raw confusion matrix of the combined four leave-one-hospital-out cross-validation classification results on Table 4. We then evaluate the cell-level classification accuracy from the confusion matrix and report it on Table 5. On the same table, we also report on the third row the per-ROI classification accuracy of matched cells. Figure 5 shows an example of the output of the AI model.

Table 4. Cell-level confusion matrix of the combined 4 leave-one-hospital-out cross-validation classification results on 41 ROIs.

	Prediction Non-Tumor	Prediction Tumor	Unmatched Label	Total Labels
Label Non-Tumor	NN = 10,762 (26%)	NT = 2044 (5%)	ULN = 1408 (3%)	14,214 (34%)
Label Tumor	TN = 3171 (7%)	TT = 17,174 (42%)	ULT = 1644 (4%)	21,989 (53%)
Label Indistinguishable	IN = 2541 (6%)	IT = 1535 (3%)	ULI = 664 (1%)	4740 (11%)
Unmatched Predictions	UPN = 1678 (4%)	UPT = 1430 (3%)	N/A	3108 (7%)
Total Predictions	18,152 (45%)	22,183 (54%)	3716 (9%)	40,335;40,943

Table 5. Cell-level sensitivity and specificity of the combined 4 leave-one-hospital-out cross-validation classification results on 41 ROIs calculated from the confusion matrix of Table 4. The first row reports the accuracies for only the predicted cells that were matched to a label: $SEN = \frac{TT}{TT+TN}$ $SPE = \frac{NN}{NN+NT}$. The second row reports accuracies that also include the predicted cells that were not matched to a label (false positives) as well as the labels that were not matched to a prediction (false negatives): $SEN = \frac{TT}{TT+TN+ULT}$ $SPE = \frac{NN}{NN+NT+ULN}$. The third row reports the per-ROI matched cells performance averaged over the 41 ROIs.

	Sensitivity	Specificity
Matched Cells Only	84.4%	84.0%
All Cells	78.1%	75.7%
ROI-level	80.8%	79.0%

Finally, we define the predicted TCR by the AI model as:

$$TCR_{\mathrm{AI}} = \frac{tCells_{\mathrm{AI}}}{(tCells_{\mathrm{AI}} + nCells_{\mathrm{AI}})} \tag{3}$$

where $tCells_{\mathrm{AI}}$ is the number of cells predicted by AI as tumor and matched to annotated tCells, and $nCells_{\mathrm{AI}}$ is the number of cells predicted as non-tumor by AI and matched to annotated nCells. In the calculation of TCR_{AI}, we discarded predictions that were matched to iCells as a way to fairly compare the AI TCR with that of the pathologists' visual estimates.

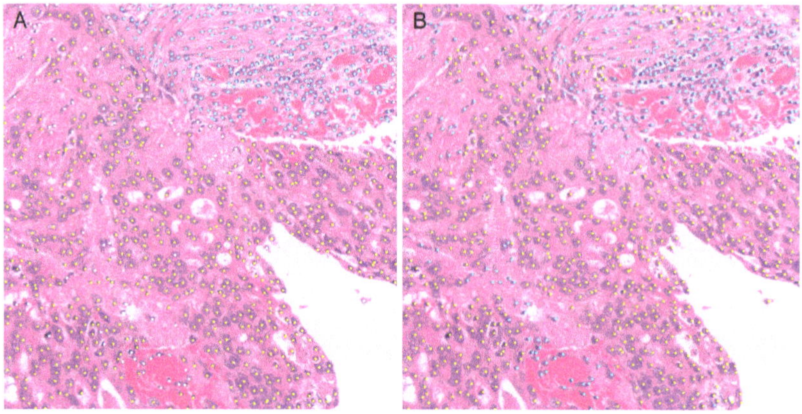

Figure 5. Example of tumor detection using AI. (**A**) Gold standard label. Yellow indicates tumor cells, cyan indicates non-tumor cells, and green indicates indistinguishable cells. (**B**) Predictions by the AI model. Yellow indicates tumor cells and cyan indicates non-tumor cells.

3. Results

We evaluated both the absolute errors of visual estimations by pathologists and of AI predictions to the gold standard TCR using the 41 annotated test cases' ROIs. The gold standard TCR values ranged from a minimum of 1.71% to a maximum of 100%, with a mean of 62.0 ± 28.6%. The proportion of iCells (the number of iCells relative to the total number of labeled cells) ranged from 0.5% to 48.0% (mean: 17.5 ± 6.5%).

In Figure 6, we can appreciate the wide variation in the visual TCR values measured by pathologists (the largest variation is 65 %). In contrast, the largest difference between the AI's TCR (TCR_{AI}) and the gold standard TCR (TCR_{GS}) is only 40%, with two cases with a difference of more than 30%. We also notice that, for both the pathologists' visual estimate and the AI, a few ROIs with a large error strongly affect the mean error.

The mean absolute error of pathologists is defined as:

$$\varepsilon_{\mathrm{PV}} = \frac{1}{N_{\mathrm{ROI}}} \sum_{i=1}^{N_{\mathrm{ROI}}} \sum_{j=1}^{N_P(i)} \left| TCR^{j}_{\mathrm{PV}}(i) - TCR_{\mathrm{GS}}(i) \right|, \quad (4)$$

where $TCR^{j}_{\mathrm{PV}}(i)$ is the TCR visually estimated by the j-th pathologist for the i-th ROI, $TCR_{GS}(i)$ is the gold standard TCR for the i-th ROI, N_{ROI} is the number of ROIs, and $N_P(i)$ represents the number of pathologists who performed visual estimation for the i-th ROI (which varies depending on the ROI, as some pathologists were unable to participate in the visual estimation experiment for data obtained from a site). The absolute error of AI is defined as follows:

$$\varepsilon_{\mathrm{AI}} = \frac{1}{N_{\mathrm{ROI}}} \sum_{i=1}^{N_{\mathrm{ROI}}} |TCR_{\mathrm{AI}}(i) - TCR_{\mathrm{GS}}(i)|, \quad (5)$$

where $TCR_{\mathrm{AI}}(i)$ is TCR calculated from AI predictions for the i-th ROI.

The mean absolute errors (MAEs) of the AI-predicted and pathologist-estimated TCRs for the 41 ROIs were compared against the gold standard TCR. The AI had a mean absolute error of 10.9 ± 9.5, while the pathologist had a mean absolute error of 13.2 ± 9.7. The AI's predictions were significantly closer to the GS TCR than the pathologist's estimates (p = 0.028, with signed rank test, see Figure 7).

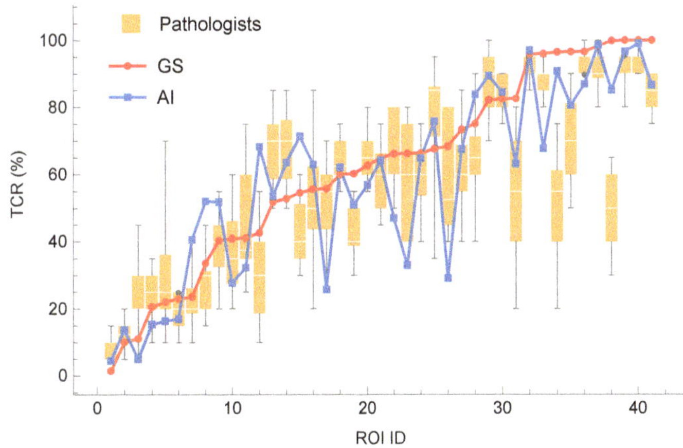

Figure 6. Box and whisker plot of tumor content ratio (TCR) estimated visually by 13 pathologists (yellow) together with predicted TCR by AI (solid blue line). The red solid line represent the gold standard TCR. Boxes show medians, quartiles, and outliers for each group. The boxes extend from the 25th to the 75th percentile, and the whiskers extend from the minimum to the maximum TCR within a group.

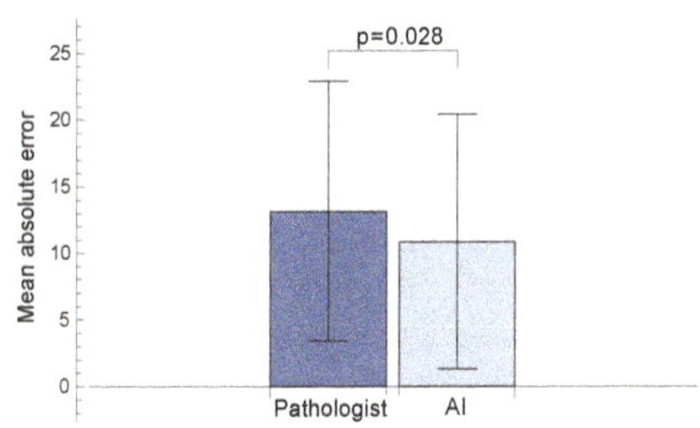

	MAE±SD
Pathologists	13.2 ± 9.7
AI	10.9 ± 9.5

Figure 7. Comparison of mean absolute errors of pathologist and AI predictions to gold standard TCR.

Figure 8 shows ROIs that exhibited good agreement and significant deviations from the gold standard in both pathologists' estimations and AI predictions. Figure 8A is an ROI where pathologists' estimations exhibited good agreement with the gold standard TCR. The pathologists' estimations ranged from 75% to 90% for $TCR_{GS} = 82.5\%$ (MAE = 5.0%). AI's prediction for this ROI was also in good agreement ($TCR_{AI} = 84.6\%$, with an absolute error of 2.1%). Figure 8B shows an ROI where pathologists' estimations exhibited significant deviation from the gold standard. The pathologists' estimations ranged from 20% to 80% for $TCR_{GS} = 82.6\%$ (MAE = 29.3%). AI's prediction for this ROI was $TCR_{AI} = 63.3\%$ with an absolute error of 19.3%).

Figure 8C shows an ROI where AI's prediction was in good agreement with the gold standard TCR ($TCR_{AI} = 64.3\%$ and $TCR_{GS} = 64.9\%$, with an absolute error of 0.6%). For this ROI, pathologists' estimations ranged from 45% to 75%, resulted in MAE = 9.2%. Figure 8D shows an ROI where AI's prediction exhibited significant deviation from the gold standard TCR ($TCR_{AI} = 33.0\%$ and $TCR_{GS} = 66.3\%$, with an absolute error of 33.3%). For this ROI, pathologists' estimations ranged from 40% to 80%, resulted in MAE = 14.6%.

There was little overlap between the ROIs with large errors estimated by the pathologist and the ROIs with large errors calculated by the AI. In fact, as shown in Figure 9, the correlation between the absolute errors of the pathologist and the AI was small ($\tau = 0.265$, $p = 0.014$, Kendall's τ correlation).

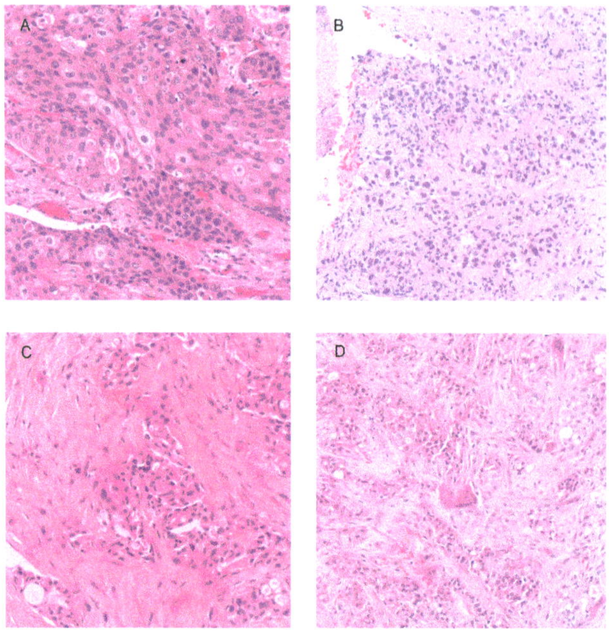

Figure 8. Examples of ROIs with small and large errors of pathologist's estimation (**A**,**B**) and AI's prediction (**C**,**D**). Pathologists' estimations ranged from 75 to 90% for $TCR_{GS} = 82.5\%$ with a mean absolute error of 5.0% (**A**), and ranged from 20 to 80% for $TCR_{GS} = 82.6\%$ with a mean absolute error of 29.3% (**B**). AI's prediction was 64.3% for $TCR_{GS} = 98.4\%$ with an absolute error of 0.2% (**C**) and 33.0% for $TCR_{GS} = 66.3\%$ with an absolute error of 33.3% (**D**).

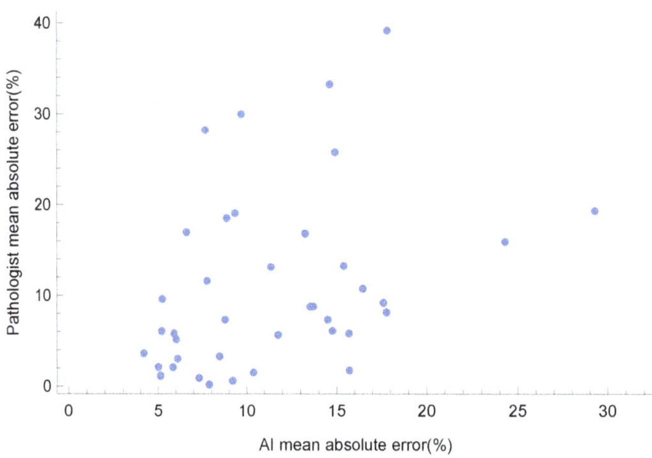

Figure 9. Scatter plot of the mean absolute error of the pathologist's estimation and the AI's prediction.

Site Dependency

Figure 10 shows the mean absolute error for each pathologist by sites. Surprisingly, MAE varies significantly for most pathologists based on the site. To investigate this site dependence on the performance of pathologists, we define the site dependence index (SDI) as follows:

$$\text{SDI} = \text{Max}_i(\varepsilon_i) - \text{Min}_i(\varepsilon_i), \quad (6)$$

where ε_i is the mean absolute error within the i-th site, and Max_i (Min_i) is the maximum (minimum) MAE among four sites. In other words, the site dependency of each evaluator is assessed based on the difference between the site with the largest error and the smallest error. Table 6 shows the combined results of each pathologist and AI.

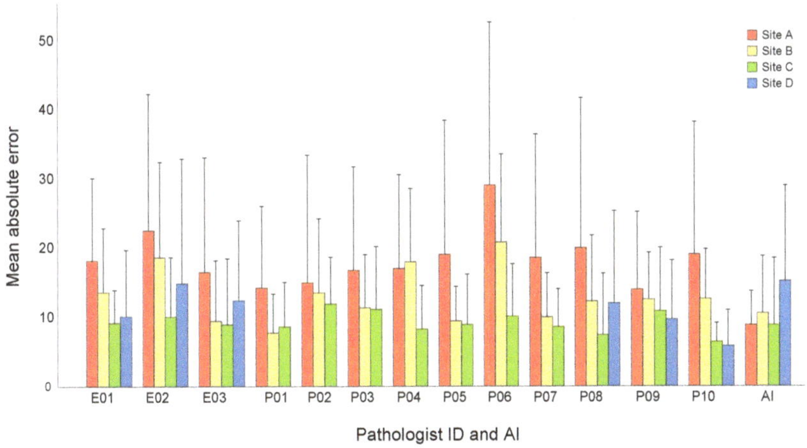

Figure 10. Visualization of mean absolute error of each pathologist and AI against the gold standard per site. The length of the line above the bar represents the standard deviation.

Table 6. Site dependency indices and mean absolute error of each pathologist and AI against the gold standard per site. Data for 7 pathologists (ID = P01–P07) are missing because they did not participate in the visual estimation of cases for Site D.

Site	Pathologist														AI
	E01	E02	E03	P01	P02	P03	P04	P05	P06	P07	P08	P09	P10	Mean ± SD	
A	18.2	22.6	16.5	14.3	15.0	16.8	17.0	19.1	29.1	18.6	20.0	14.0	19.1	18.5 ±4.0	8.9
B	13.6	18.6	9.5	7.8	13.5	11.4	18.0	9.5	20.8	10.0	12.3	12.6	12.7	13.1 ± 3.9	10.6
C	9.2	10.1	9.0	8.7	11.9	11.1	8.3	9.0	10.1	8.6	7.5	10.9	6.5	9.3 ± 1.5	8.9
D	10.2	14.9	12.4								12.0	9.7	5.9	10.6 ± 3.0	15.2
SDI	9.0	12.5	7.6	6.5	3.0	5.6	9.7	10.1	19.0	10	12.5	4.3	13.2	9.5 ± 4.7	6.3

4. Discussion

In this study, we first established a gold standard tumor content ratio for a cohort of 41 cases (ROIs) from four hospitals. Three pathologists exhaustively labeled all cells on the ROIs and we used the consensus label of the three pathologists as the gold standard. We allowed the pathologists to label cells that they were not able to distinguish between tumor and non-tumor as iCells (i for indistinguishable). Since the AI model is trained to predict only between tumor and non-tumor cells, we decided to discard predictions that were matched to iCells as a way to fairly compare the AI TCR with that of the pathologists visual estimates (who were instructed to ignore them as well).

We then contrasted the accuracy of an AI model that counts and classifies every cell with that of pathologists' visual estimation. As a result, we found that the absolute error of the AI was smaller than the mean absolute error of pathologists. This suggests that AI-based TCR measurement is useful for accurate estimation of TCR.

Figure 8 shows examples of ROIs with low and high errors for both 'pathologist visual estimation' and 'AI counting'. In ROIs with low error, concordance was typically high between visual estimation by pathologists and AI counting. On the other hand, different trends were observed for ROIs with large errors. Visual estimation by pathologists showed large errors for tissue patterns with strong tissue degeneration and unclear nuclear borders. However, AI did not show particularly large errors for the same images. In contrast, AI showed a tendency to count small tumor cells scattered between large tumor cells as non-tumor. This is likely due to the fact that AI cannot easily identify benign-looking cells that pathologists judge to be part of a tumor nest based on a large surrounding context, as AI model makes judgments based on relatively limited input field of view of 200 square microns, encompassing only a few dozen cells. This problem could be alleviated by adopting more complex models that can consider a larger context or use attention mechanisms [31,32].

The study also evaluated the site dependency of TCR estimation error. We used the difference between the site with the largest error and the site with the smallest error as the site dependency index for each pathologist and AI. Based on this index, we found that the dependency of the pathologist was overall significantly larger than that of AI.

We observed that pathologists' estimations were worse on site A and it was reported during post-test interviews that the staining from site A was more reddish than at other sites. Since site A was the main data collection site for the AI training, we investigated whether the AI could have been advantaged by better adapting to site A. However, such an adaptation would have resulted in significantly worse performance on other sites, which was not observed in the results.

In general, AI models are known to degrade in performance when tested on data collected from a different site than the one where the training data were collected, a phenomenon known as domain shift. Here, we observe a similar phenomenon with pathologists' visual TCR estimation, and we show that an AI model trained with data augmentation is made robust to domain shifts encountered in the variations in sample preparation across sites. Based on these results, it is expected that the use of AI for TCR quantification will be beneficial compared to today's pathologist visual estimation. The use of an AI model trained with data augmentation will lead to a robust TCR quantification that is resistant to differences in assessors, data collection sites (hospitals or cancer centers), and imaging devices.

The AI model used in this study is part of a software program developed by our group. The software takes a WSI file as input, detects all cells within one or more areas indicated by the user through the graphical user interface, classifies them as tumor or non-tumor cells, and reports the total TCR for all areas and as a heatmap on the WSI. In our experimental environment explained in Section 2.4, the processing time for a large surgical specimen slide of 400 mm^2 is less than 3 min, which is very fast considering that more than a million cells are processed. Although the use of AI does not lead to a shorter examination time because the visual judgment by the pathologist is completed in a short time, it is within competitive range and has the major advantages of improved accuracy and reduced variations.

The introduction of AI to the clinical practice is not without challenges and brings fundamental changes to the workflow. Whether on-premises or in the cloud, AI computational assays will need to be competitively priced and their turnaround times will need to be clearly established. Clinical workflows will need to be adapted to use all resources optimally such that overall turnaround times from sample preparation to final diagnosis can be reduced. For example, some basic AI assays such as cell detection/classification/counting/segmentation can be systematically pre-ordered along with sample preparation and be delivered to the pathologist along with the WSI. Visualization and interpretation of those assays can happen hand-in-hand with clinical diagnosis on graphical user interface browsers and significantly increase pathologists' productivity and accuracy.

5. Conclusions

The results of this study demonstrate the usefulness of AI for measuring tumor cellularity. We found that AI can calculate TCR with smaller errors than visual estimation by a pathologist by comparing both against a gold standard TCR established by exhaustively labeling each cell. In addition, the evaluation results using data obtained from different institutions showed that AI has a lower site dependency compared to the visual estimation by the pathologist. Moreover, the trend of errors between the pathologist and AI showed a small correlation, suggesting that the combined use of AI and visual estimation would be useful for high-accuracy TCR calculation.

Author Contributions: Conceptualization, Y.H.; methodology, E.C.; software, E.C.; validation, T.K., K.C.H., and M.O.; formal analysis, T.K. and E.C.; investigation, T.K. and E.C.; resources, K.C.H., T.Y., K.T. and N.M.; data curation, K.C.H., T.Y., K.T. and N.M.; experimental measurement, K.C.H., T.Y., K.T., N.M., K.M., A.S. (Ai Shimizu), T.S., A.S. (Akira Suzuki), E.T., Y.T., T.T., M.T., M.Y. and S.Y.; writing—original draft preparation, T.K. and E.C.; writing—review and editing, T.K. and E.C.; visualization, T.K. and E.C.; supervision, Y.H.; project administration, M.O. All authors have read and agreed to the published version of the manuscript.

Funding: This research received no external funding.

Institutional Review Board Statement: The study was conducted according to the guidelines of the Declaration of Helsinki, and approved by the Hokkaido University Institutional Review Board in 15 November 2017 (016-0222).

Informed Consent Statement: Informed consent was obtained from all subjects involved in the study.

Data Availability Statement: The datasets presented in this article are not readily available because the data are part of an ongoing study.

Conflicts of Interest: K.C.H. and Y.H. have received research grants from NEC Corporation. T.K. and M.O. are employees of NEC Corporation. E.C. is an employee of NEC Laboratories America, Inc. The other authors report no conflicts of interest.

Abbreviations

AI	artificial intelligence
NGS	next-generation sequencing
TCR	tumor content ratio
H&E	hematoxylin and eosin
GANs	generative adversarial networks
DA	data augmentation
ROI	region of interest
GS	gold standard
NSCLC	non-small cell lung cancer
TBB	trans-bronchial biopsy
TBNA	trans-bronchial needle aspiration
CNB	core-needle biopsy
FFPE	formalin-fixed paraffin-embedded
WSI	whole-slide image
tCell	tumor cell
nCell	non-tumor cell
iCell	indistinguishable cell
MAE	mean absolute errors
SDI	site dependency index

References

1. Foundation Medicine Inc. FoundationOne CDx. 2020. Available online: https://www.foundationmedicine.com/test/foundationone-cdx (accessed on 24 July 2020).
2. ThermoFisher Scientific. Oncomine Dx Target Test. 2018. Available online: https://www.oncomine.com/hubfs/Discussion%20Guide:%20In-House%20Testing%20with%20ODxTT.pdf (accessed on 24 July 2020).
3. Smits, A.J.; Kummer, J.A.; De Bruin, P.C.; Bol, M.; Van Den Tweel, J.G.; Seldenrijk, K.A.; Willems, S.M.; Offerhaus, G.J.A.; De Weger, R.A.; Van Diest, P.J.; et al. The estimation of tumor cell percentage for molecular testing by pathologists is not accurate. *Mod. Pathol.* **2014**, *27*, 168–174. [CrossRef] [PubMed]

4. Graham, S.; Vu, Q.D.; Raza, S.E.A.; Azam, A.; Tsang, Y.W.; Kwak, J.T.; Rajpoot, N. Hover-net: Simultaneous segmentation and classification of nuclei in multi-tissue histology images. *Med. Image Anal.* **2019**, *58*, 101563. [CrossRef] [PubMed]
5. Lal, S.; Das, D.; Alabhya, K.; Kanfade, A.; Kumar, A.; Kini, J. NucleiSegNet: Robust deep learning architecture for the nuclei segmentation of liver cancer histopathology images. *Comput. Biol. Med.* **2021**, *128*, 104075. [CrossRef] [PubMed]
6. Natarajan, V.A.; Kumar, M.S.; Patan, R.; Kallam, S.; Mohamed, M.Y.N. Segmentation of nuclei in histopathology images using fully convolutional deep neural architecture. In Proceedings of the 2020 International Conference on Computing and Information Technology (ICCIT-1441), Tabuk, Saudi Arabia, 9–10 September 2020; IEEE: New York, NY, USA; pp. 1–7.
7. Falk, T.; Mai, D.; Bensch, R.; Çiçek, Ö.; Abdulkadir, A.; Marrakchi, Y.; Böhm, A.; Deubner, J.; Jäckel, Z.; Seiwald, K.; et al. U-Net: deep learning for cell counting, detection, and morphometry. *Nat. Methods* **2019**, *16*, 67–70. [CrossRef] [PubMed]
8. Morelli, R.; Clissa, L.; Amici, R.; Cerri, M.; Hitrec, T.; Luppi, M.; Rinaldi, L.; Squarcio, F.; Zoccoli, A. Automating cell counting in fluorescent microscopy through deep learning with c-ResUnet. *Sci. Rep.* **2021**, *11*, 22920. [CrossRef] [PubMed]
9. Sirinukunwattana, K.; Raza, S.E.A.; Tsang, Y.W.; Snead, D.R.; Cree, I.A.; Rajpoot, N.M. Locality sensitive deep learning for detection and classification of nuclei in routine colon cancer histology images. *IEEE Trans. Med. Imaging* **2016**, *35*, 1196–1206. [CrossRef] [PubMed]
10. Cosatto, E.; Laquerre, P.F.; Malon, C.; Graf, H.P.; Saito, A.; Kiyuna, T.; Marugame, A.; Kamijo, K. Automated gastric cancer diagnosis on h&e-stained sections; ltraining a classifier on a large scale with multiple instance machine learning. In Proceedings of the Medical Imaging 2013: Digital Pathology, Lake Buena Vista, Fl, USA, 9–14 February 2013; SPIE: Bellingham, WA , USA, 2013; Volume 8676, pp. 51–59.
11. Wang, X.; Janowczyk, A.; Zhou, Y.; Thawani, R.; Fu, P.; Schalper, K.; Velcheti, V.; Madabhushi, A. Prediction of recurrence in early stage non-small cell lung cancer using computer extracted nuclear features from digital H&E images. *Sci. Rep.* **2017**, *7*, 13543. [PubMed]
12. Qaiser, T.; Lee, C.Y.; Vandenberghe, M.; Yeh, J.; Gavrielides, M.A.; Hipp, J.; Scott, M.; Reischl, J. Usability of deep learning and H&E images predict disease outcome-emerging tool to optimize clinical trials. *NPJ Precis. Oncol.* **2022**, *6*, 37.
13. Farahmand, S.; Fernandez, A.I.; Ahmed, F.S.; Rimm, D.L.; Chuang, J.H.; Reisenbichler, E.; Zarringhalam, K. Deep learning trained on hematoxylin and eosin tumor region of Interest predicts HER2 status and trastuzumab treatment response in HER2+ breast cancer. *Mod. Pathol.* **2022**, *35*, 44–51. [CrossRef]
14. Kiyuna, T.; Motoi, N.; Yoshida, H.; Horinouchi, H.; Yoshida, T.; Kohno, T.; Watanabe, S.i.; Ohe, Y.; Ochiai, A. Drug response prediction using deep neural network trained by adaptive resampling of histopathological images. In Proceedings of the Medical Imaging 2022: Computer-Aided Diagnosis, San Diego, CA, USA, 20–24 February 2022; SPIE: Bellingham, WA , USA, 2022; Volume 12033, pp. 769–774.
15. Cheng, J.; Ye, J.; Deng, Z.; Chen, J.; Li, T.; Wang, H.; Su, Y.; Huang, Z.; Chen, J.; Jiang, L.; et al. Sam-med2d. *arXiv* **2023**, arXiv:2308.16184.
16. Bejnordi, B.E.; Veta, M.; Van Diest, P.J.; Van Ginneken, B.; Karssemeijer, N.; Litjens, G.; Van Der Laak, J.A.; Hermsen, M.; Manson, Q.F.; Balkenhol, M.; et al. Diagnostic assessment of deep learning algorithms for detection of lymph node metastases in women with breast cancer. *JAMA* **2017**, *318*, 2199–2210. [CrossRef] [PubMed]
17. Homeyer, A.; Lotz, J.; Schwen, L.O.; Weiss, N.; Romberg, D.; Höfener, H.; Zerbe, N.; Hufnagl, P. Artificial intelligence in pathology: From prototype to product. *J. Pathol. Inform.* **2021**, *12*, 13. [CrossRef] [PubMed]
18. Yoshida, H.; Kiyuna, T. Requirements for implementation of artificial intelligence in the practice of gastrointestinal pathology. *World J. Gastroenterol.* **2021**, *27*, 2818–2833. [CrossRef] [PubMed]
19. Hanna, M.G.; Pantanowitz, L. Digital Pathology. In *Encyclopedia of Biomedical Engineering*; Narayan, R., Ed.; Elsevier: Oxford, UK, 2019; pp. 524–532.
20. Shaban, M.T.; Baur, C.; Navab, N.; Albarqouni, S. Staingan: Stain style transfer for digital histological images. In Proceedings of the 2019 IEEE 16th International Symposium on Biomedical Imaging (ISBI 2019), Venice, Italy, 8–11 April 2019; IEEE: New York, NY, USA, 2019; pp. 953–956.
21. Marini, N.; Otalora, S.; Wodzinski, M.; Tomassini, S.; Dragoni, A.F.; Marchand-Maillet, S.; Morales, J.P.D.; Duran-Lopez, L.; Vatrano, S.; Müller, H.; et al. Data-driven color augmentation for H&E stained images in computational pathology. *J. Pathol. Inform.* **2023**, *14*, 100183. [PubMed]
22. Tellez, D.; Litjens, G.; Bándi, P.; Bulten, W.; Bokhorst, J.M.; Ciompi, F.; Van Der Laak, J. Quantifying the effects of data augmentation and stain color normalization in convolutional neural networks for computational pathology. *Med. Image Anal.* **2019**, *58*, 101544. [CrossRef] [PubMed]
23. Michielli, N.; Caputo, A.; Scotto, M.; Mogetta, A.; Pennisi, O.A.M.; Molinari, F.; Balmativola, D.; Bosco, M.; Gambella, A.; Metovic, J.; et al. Stain normalization in digital pathology: Clinical multi-center evaluation of image quality. *J. Pathol. Inform.* **2022**, *13*, 100145. [CrossRef] [PubMed]
24. Chen, X.; Zhou, X.; Wong, S.T. Automated segmentation, classification, and tracking of cancer cell nuclei in time-lapse microscopy. *IEEE Trans. Biomed. Eng.* **2006**, *53*, 762–766. [CrossRef] [PubMed]
25. Ghani, A.; Hodeify, R.; See, C.H.; Keates, S.; Lee, D.J.; Bouridane, A. Computer vision-based Kidney's (HK-2) damaged cells classification with reconfigurable hardware accelerator (FPGA). *Electronics* **2022**, *11*, 4234. [CrossRef]

26. Cosatto, E.; Gerard, K.; Graf, H.P.; Ogura, M.; Kiyuna, T.; Hatanaka, K.C.; Matsuno, Y.; Hatanaka, Y. A multi-scale conditional deep model for tumor cell ratio counting. In Proceedings of the Medical Imaging 2021: Digital Pathology, online, 15–20 February 2021; SPIE: Bellingham, WA, USA, 2021; Volume 11603, pp. 31–42.
27. Sakamoto, T.; Furukawa, T.; Pham, H.H.; Kuroda, K.; Tabata, K.; Kashima, Y.; Okoshi, E.N.; Morimoto, S.; Bychkov, A.; Fukuoka, J. A collaborative workflow between pathologists and deep learning for the evaluation of tumour cellularity in lung adenocarcinoma. *Histopathology* **2022**, *81*, 758–769. [CrossRef]
28. Ronneberger, O.; Fischer, P.; Brox, T. U-Net: Convolutional networks for biomedical image segmentation. In Proceedings of the International Conference on Medical Image Computing and Computer-Assisted Intervention, Munich, Germany, 5–9 October 2015; Springer: Berlin/Heidelberg, Germany, 2015; pp. 234–241.
29. Paszke, A.; Gross, S.; Massa, F.; Lerer, A.; Bradbury, J.; Chanan, G.; Killeen, T.; Lin, Z.; Gimelshein, N.; Antiga, L.; et al. Pytorch: An imperative style, high-performance deep learning library. In Proceedings of the Advances in Neural Information Processing Systems, Vancouver, BC, Canada, 8–14 December 2019; pp. 8026–8037.
30. Zhang, Z. Improved adam optimizer for deep neural networks. In Proceedings of the 2018 IEEE/ACM 26th International Symposium on Quality of Service (IWQoS), Banff, AB, Canada, 4–6 June 2018; IEEE: New York, NY, USA, 2018; pp. 1–2.
31. Vaswani, A.; Shazeer, N.; Parmar, N.; Uszkoreit, J.; Jones, L.; Gomez, A.N.; Kaiser, Ł.; Polosukhin, I. Attention is all you need. *Adv. Neural Inf. Process. Syst.* **2017**, *30*.
32. Dosovitskiy, A.; Beyer, L.; Kolesnikov, A.; Weissenborn, D.; Zhai, X.; Unterthiner, T.; Dehghani, M.; Minderer, M.; Heigold, G.; Gelly, S.; et al. An image is worth 16 × 16 words: Transformers for image recognition at scale. *arXiv* **2020**, arXiv:2010.11929.

tomography MDPI

Article

Breast Cancer Diagnosis Method Based on Cross-Mammogram Four-View Interactive Learning

Xuesong Wen, Jianjun Li * and Liyuan Yang

School of Mechanical and Electrical Engineering, China Jiliang University, Hangzhou 310018, China; s21010811030@cjlu.edu.cn (X.W.); p21010854118@cjlu.edu.cn (L.Y.)
* Correspondence: 13a0104121@cjlu.edu.cn

Abstract: Computer-aided diagnosis systems play a crucial role in the diagnosis and early detection of breast cancer. However, most current methods focus primarily on the dual-view analysis of a single breast, thereby neglecting the potentially valuable information between bilateral mammograms. In this paper, we propose a Four-View Correlation and Contrastive Joint Learning Network (FV-Net) for the classification of bilateral mammogram images. Specifically, FV-Net focuses on extracting and matching features across the four views of bilateral mammograms while maximizing both their similarities and dissimilarities. Through the Cross-Mammogram Dual-Pathway Attention Module, feature matching between bilateral mammogram views is achieved, capturing the consistency and complementary features across mammograms and effectively reducing feature misalignment. In the reconstituted feature maps derived from bilateral mammograms, the Bilateral-Mammogram Contrastive Joint Learning module performs associative contrastive learning on positive and negative sample pairs within each local region. This aims to maximize the correlation between similar local features and enhance the differentiation between dissimilar features across the bilateral mammogram representations. Our experimental results on a test set comprising 20% of the combined Mini-DDSM and Vindr-mamo datasets, as well as on the INbreast dataset, show that our model exhibits superior performance in breast cancer classification compared to competing methods.

Keywords: bilateral mammograms; deep learning; breast cancer; computer-aided diagnosis; interpretable classifier

1. Introduction

According to 2023 statistics, breast cancer is the most prevalent cancer type among women in the United States, with an estimated 297,790 new cases, accounting for 31% of all new cancer cases, and an expected death toll of 43,170 [1]. These figures highlight the significant threat that breast cancer poses to women's health, underscoring the importance of its prevention and early screening. Mammography screening, essential for breast cancer prevention, typically comprises two ipsilateral views of each breast: the bilateral cranio-caudal (CC) view, a top-down perspective, and the mediolateral oblique (MLO) view, angled from the chest center toward the armpit at 45 to 50 degrees [2,3]. In addition to analyzing and comparing these two views, radiologists also compare ipsilateral views (the CC view and MLO view of the same breast) and bilateral views (the same view of both breasts), as such comparisons provide a richer set of feature information [4], facilitating the search for global structural distortions, local tumors, and calcifications, thereby enabling a comprehensive analysis of each breast [5]. For each patient, four high-resolution mammographic images of the left and right breasts are taken. Any detected abnormalities will require further diagnostic imaging and tissue biopsy for confirmation. Based on the standards of the American College of Radiology's Breast Imaging Reporting and Data System (BI-RADS), radiologists perform a standardized assessment for each screening mammogram, providing specific follow-up recommendations based on the BI-RADS score for each patient [6].

In contemporary practice, deep learning methods have rapidly evolved in the field of medical image analysis and have achieved significant results [7]. Many medical fields now employ Computer-Aided Detection (CAD) systems, providing radiologists with rapid, objective recommendations that enhance clinical decision-making during large-scale breast cancer screenings. The prevailing approach involves using multi-view image information as the input for models. For works that use ipsilateral views as model inputs, the CC and MLO views are used for feature extraction for cancer diagnosis [8,9], but each view extracts features independently and then combines them, resulting in a lack of information interaction between views, leading to the loss of inter-view information relationships. In 2021, van Tulder et al. [10] introduced an inter-view attention mechanism for information transfer between views. This method allows the model to connect different views at a more detailed spatial feature level, rather than merely concatenating at a global feature level. In 2022, Chen et al. [5] proposed the Local Co-occurrence and Global Consistency method, which not only completed the information interaction between views but also introduced inter-view similarity learning. In 2023, the CVR-RCNN network framework [11] was proposed. It aims to transfer visual and geometric information between two views, thereby enhancing tumor detection in one view. In 2023, Wang et al. [12] introduced DCHA-Net, employing Hybrid Attention in their Hybrid Attention modules for feature interaction and registration between views, thereby mitigating the feature misalignment problem between dual views. Nguyen et al. [13] introduced DIVF-Net, a network that first fuses features from bilateral views of the same breast. This process is followed by the element-wise addition of the resultant fused features to the feature map of the primary view, thereby enhancing the information of the primary view. In 2021, Yan et al. [14] proposed a unified Siamese network for simultaneous patch-level mass or non-mass classification and dual-view mass matching. In 2018, Wang et al. [15] introduced the MV-DNN approach, in which LSTM is utilized to effectively aggregate data from dual views of a unilateral breast, integrating contextual information from both views. In 2016, Bekker et al. [16] proposed the MV-NN method, which employs view-level classifiers for individual view classification judgments, followed by a neural network layer to integrate decisions from the two view levels. Although these methods demonstrated good performance, they only utilized information from dual views, neglecting the feature information of the patient's contralateral breast and the interactive information between breasts.

Regarding the work using bilateral four-view mammograms as model inputs, in 2021, Li et al. [17] developed a multi-stream network architecture to integrate four views from bilateral breasts, enabling the network to independently learn features from each view. In the network's later stages, features from different views are concatenated, thereby enhancing classification performance. While this approach demonstrates good performance, it does not fully exploit the latent relationships between bilateral breasts. Nguyen et al. [18] proposed a two-stage multi-view model for breast imaging. In the first stage, features are extracted separately from the left and right breasts. In the second stage, these features are averaged and input into separate BI-RADS and density classifiers using LightGBM. The final classification output is determined by taking the maximum value of the predictions from both breasts. Chen et al. [19] introduced the MVT model, which utilizes four views of bilateral mammograms as inputs. This model segments the four views into multiple patches, extracts features independently from each patch, and employs Global Transformer blocks to analyze the relationships between patches. However, due to the non-rigid nature of breasts, morphological variations across different views present significant challenges, making it difficult for the model to capture features directly related to cancer. In 2022, Lopez et al. [4] proposed the PHYSEnet model. They employed a parameterized hypercomplex neural network capable of handling breast cancer classification by capturing the intrinsic correlations between different views and using a shared encoder to analyze all four views (left and right CC and MLO), thus achieving inter-breast feature interaction. However, simply inputting all four views into a shared backbone without feature registration and contrastive work can lead to feature misalignment learning in the model.

Inspired by the limitations of these previous works, we have pioneered an approach to perform correlation and contrastive learning between the features of bilateral mammogram views. Our method requires only image-level labels to achieve accurate and robust classification of the entire mammograms of both the left and right breasts. Additionally, our approach utilizes the four-view feature information from bilateral mammograms. We have also successfully addressed the issue of incorrect feature matching between the left and right mammograms. Furthermore, our approach integrates joint and contrastive learning of cancerous and normal tissue features. This method enhances the similarity between corresponding features in the left and right mammograms while amplifying the differences between dissimilar features. Consequently, the model more effectively distinguishes between normal tissue and malignant breast lesions. Moreover, our model facilitates local feature interaction learning with the global region of the contralateral feature map, improving the classification of benign and malignant breasts. This four-view diagnostic method aligns with the practice of physicians who both analyze ipsilateral views and compare contralateral views during the diagnostic process. Our model demonstrates excellent classification performance, greatly enhancing the model's robustness and generalizability, and achieves competitive results. In summary, our contributions are as follows:

1. We propose a novel approach to the associative matching learning of local features across global regions of bilateral mammograms, achieving feature interaction consistency and complementarity between them, effectively alleviating the issue of misaligned feature matching, and significantly enriching the information content of the related features.
2. We devised a novel joint contrastive learning strategy for bilateral mammograms capable of capturing the correlational characteristics of each local region between bilateral breast feature maps to maximize similarity. Concurrently, it facilitates the contrastive learning of distinct features to maximize feature disparity. This approach aids the model in identifying the features of cancerous regions and distinguishing them from those of normal tissue, and furthermore, it precludes the occurrence of misaligned feature learning.
3. We evaluated the performance of our proposed FV-Net model on a 20% test set of a combined dataset comprising Mini-DDSM [20] and Vindr-mamo [21], as well as on the INbreast dataset [22]. The experimental results confirm that our method outperforms competing methods on multiple datasets.

2. Related Work

Deep learning models are now widely used in the diagnosis of breast cancer, with two primary approaches to classification. The first approach requires a binary segmentation mask during training. Ru et al. [23] proposed the Att-U-Node for automatically segmenting breast tumors. This network utilizes an attention module to guide a framework based on neural ODEs, addressing several challenges faced by popular deep neural networks, such as large parameter counts, a lack of interpretability, and issues with overfitting. Tsochatzidis et al. [24] introduced a method that integrates tumor segmentation information from mammograms into a Convolutional Neural Network (CNN), aiming to improve the diagnosis of breast cancer in mammograms. Furthermore, Ghosh et al. [25] designed an innovative automatic mammogram segmentation method. This method employs Intuitionistic Fuzzy Soft Sets (IFSS) and multi-granularity rough sets. It introduces a novel hybrid soft computing approach, which is integrated into the segmentation process. This enhances the early detection of breast cancer. Sarangi et al. [26] developed a model using a single-layer Legendre neural network, which was trained with a Block-Based Normalized Sign-Sign Least Mean Square (BBNSSLMS) algorithm to enhance performance. However, the aforementioned methods require experienced radiologists to annotate regions of interest (ROIs) at the pixel level, significantly increasing data annotation costs. The second approach no longer requires pixel-level ROI annotations, and many of its methods employ CNN technology to diagnose breast cancer [27–31]. For instance, Albashish et al. [30] employed a transfer learning model based on the Visual Geometry Group's 16-layer deep model architecture (VGG16), outperforming the latest classical machine learning algorithms in breast cancer diagnosis. Heenaye-Mamode Khan et al. [32] used a pretrained ResNet50 model to develop an enhanced deep learning model, achieving an accuracy of 88%. Although these methods have achieved significant success in medical image processing and play an important role in breast cancer screening, due to the limited receptive field of convolutional kernels, CNN methods struggle to capture the interactive information of bilateral mammograms and thus leverage their potentially valuable information. The limitations of CNNs make it difficult to utilize global information. Our proposed method not only employs CNNs to extract features from bilateral mammograms but also realizes local-to-global area feature attention correlation learning between the two breasts, overcoming the limitation of the CNN's local receptive field. Additionally, in terms of model design, current works [5,8–12,14,33–36] mainly focus on improving the diagnostic accuracy for individual breasts, with only a few methods designing models for four-view analysis [4,18,19,37]. However, these models fail to fully explore the relationship between bilateral mammograms. Therefore, it is both urgent and crucial to enhance the diagnostic capabilities of bilateral multi-view breast models for clinical decision-making. Our proposed method leverages information from four views to diagnose bilateral mammogram images simultaneously, enhancing the model's classification capability by utilizing the latent relationship between the bilateral mammary glands. This approach culminates in an end-to-end model capable of concurrently predicting the probability of breast cancer in both breasts.

3. Materials

3.1. Data Collection

The datasets used in this study include the Mini-DDSM dataset, the Vindr-mamo dataset, and the INbreast dataset. Each breast in the datasets has CC (cranio-caudal) and MLO (mediolateral oblique) mammographic X-ray views, with each case comprising four mammograms. Due to the insufficient number of cases and their label distribution in either Mini-DDSM or Vindr-mamo alone, which did not meet our requirements for various case types, we decided to merge these two datasets. Together, the Mini-DDSM and Vindr-mamo datasets include a total of 6952 cases of full-field digital mammographic X-ray images. However, two cases from the Vindr-mamo dataset are missing some mammograms, leading to a final count of 6950 cases. Figure 1 shows a few mammography images from the datasets we used.

Mini-DDSM: The Mini-DDSM dataset contains 7808 mammograms. The breast classification labels in this dataset are categorized as benign, cancer, and normal. In our study, we classify normal and benign cases as negative (label: 0) and cancer cases as positive (label: 1). The dataset includes 679 cancer cases, 671 benign cases, and 602 normal cases.

Vindr-mamo: The original Vindr-mamo dataset contains 5000 cases, but only 4998 cases are actually usable. This dataset does not directly provide breast classification labels but rather offers BI-RADS scores ranging from 1 to 5 for each full-field digital mammographic X-ray image. In our study, we consider cases with BI-RADS scores of 1 to 3 as negative and those with scores of 4 and 5 as positive.

INbreast: The INbreast dataset consists of 115 cases (410 images), of which only 75 cases are composed of four views from bilateral mammograms; thus, these 75 cases were used as the test set. This dataset provides various types of annotations, including BI-RADS classification scores, masks for the segmentation of masses or calcifications, and other data annotations. We primarily determine the labels based on the BI-RADS rating scale: BI-RADS levels 1–3 are considered negative, while 4–6 are deemed positive.

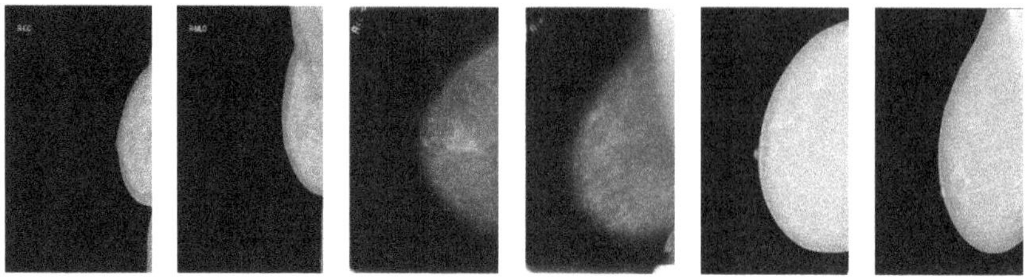

(a) (b) (c) (d) (e) (f)

Figure 1. Examples from the training and test datasets of mammography images. (**a**,**b**) Vindr-mamo mammography images; (**c**,**d**) Mini-DDSM mammography images; (**e**,**f**) INbreast mammography images.

3.2. Data Preprocessing

Given the abundance of irrelevant background information in mammograms and the fact that the lesion area occupies only a small part of the entire mammographic image, combined with the certain obscurity of the breast lesion area, it is necessary to preprocess the mammography images to enhance the contrast and recognizability of different features within the breast area. We employ various processing techniques, including Breast Region Detection (BRD), Contrast-Limited Adaptive Histogram Equalization (CLAHE), and truncated normalization.

3.2.1. Breast Region Detection (BRD)

As shown in Figure 2a, mammograms contain a large amount of irrelevant black background pixel information. Removing background pixels unrelated to classification allows the model to focus only on the features of the breast area. We employ our custom-designed Breast Region Detection (BRD) method to preprocess the mammograms. First, the module conducts orientation detection on all mammographic images to ensure all images are oriented toward the right-hand side, thus preventing the model from being influenced by varying image orientations during the learning process. It uses a GaussianBlur with a 5×5 kernel for image smoothing to reduce noise. It then utilizes OTSU thresholding to automatically determine the optimal threshold for the mammographic images and performs binarization, significantly separating the breast area from the background. The findContours function is used to detect the edges of the breast area in the binary image, eventually obtaining the rectangular area of the largest contour of the breast area, as shown in Figure 2b.

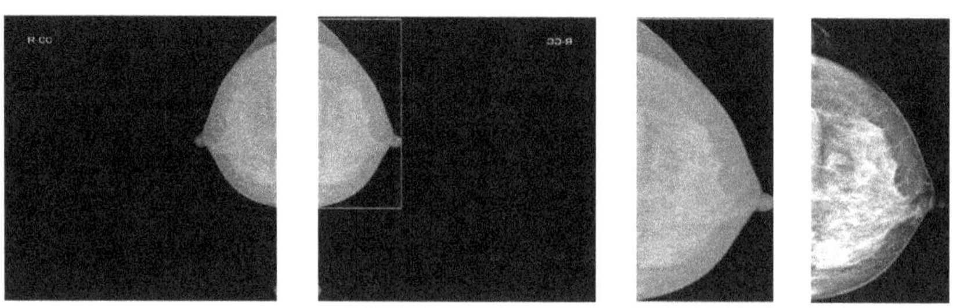

(a) (b) (c) (d)

Figure 2. The data preprocessing procedure. (**a**) The original image; (**b**) the image processed with BRD; (c) the image processed with BRD and cropping; (**d**) the image processed with BRD, cropping, CLAHE, and truncated normalization.

3.2.2. Contrast-Limited Adaptive Histogram Equalization and Truncated Normalization

Due to the extremely subtle differences between healthy and pathological tissues in the breast, we enhance local pixel contrast by applying Contrast-Limited Adaptive Histogram Equalization (CLAHE) [38]. After analysis and comparison, we set the clipLimit parameter value to 1.0. Additionally, considering the presence of extremely dark and bright areas within the breast, we empirically set two percentile thresholds at 5% and 99%. This means ignoring the lowest 5% and the highest 1% of all pixel values in the image. The clipped pixel values are then normalized, which reduces image variations caused by noise or non-representative features and further enhances image contrast. Figure 2d presents the final effect of data preprocessing.

3.3. Data Upsampling

Due to the significant imbalance in the dataset distribution, it is crucial to prevent the model from disproportionately focusing on the majority negative sample categories, thereby neglecting the minority positive categories. Therefore, it is necessary to upsample cases with cancer in both breasts as well as cases with cancer in only one breast. When integrating the Mini-DDSM and Vindr-mamo datasets, we do not simply merge them into a single dataset. Instead, we rearrange the data by individual cases to ensure a uniform distribution of different case categories, thereby better addressing the issue of data imbalance. Subsequently, we allocate 20% of the processed dataset to the test set and the remaining 80% to the training set, with the specific data distribution detailed in Table 1.

As shown in Table 2, after upsampling the data in the training set, we obtain data for 4629 patients with no cancer in either breast, 2749 patients with cancer in both breasts, and 1880 patients with cancer in only one breast. This approach ensures that the sum of the number of cases with cancer in both breasts and the number of cases with cancer in only one breast is equal to the number of cases where both breasts are normal.

Table 1. Distribution of data categories without upsampling.

Dataset Name	Number of Cases with Both Breasts Normal	Number of Cases with Both Breasts Cancerous	Number of Cases with Cancer in Only One Breast	Total
Original dataset	5790	692	468	6950
Training dataset	4629	555	376	5560
Test dataset	1161	137	92	1390

Table 2. Distribution of data categories after upsampling.

Dataset Name	Number of Cases with Both Breasts Normal	Number of Cases with Both Breasts Cancerous	Number of Cases with Cancer in Only One Breast	Total
Training dataset	4629	2749	1880	9258
Test dataset	1161	137	92	1390

4. Methods

4.1. Problem Statement

We established a training dataset that includes bilateral four-view mammographic images and applied weakly supervised learning to the dual views of each breast per case, indicating that the entire mammogram requires only an image-level label. The labels for different views of the same breast are identical, denoted by $\mathcal{D} = \{(R_i^m, R_i^c, L_i^m, L_i^c, y_i)\}_{i=1}^{|\mathcal{D}|}$, where R_i^m and R_i^c represent the MLO (mediolateral oblique) and CC (cranio-caudal) views of the patient's right breast, respectively, and L_i^m and L_i^c represent the MLO and CC views of the left breast for the same patient. The index i denotes the patient number. The label $y_i \in \mathcal{Y} = \{0, 1\}$, where 1 indicates cancer (positive) and 0 indicates normal (negative). Here, the label y_i refers to the annotations made by doctors indicating whether the mammogram is of a cancerous or normal breast. The test set is defined in the same manner. The ultimate goal is to accurately predict the probability of cancer in each patient's left and right breasts.

4.2. Motivation

Considering that most existing methods primarily focus on the analysis of dual-view mammography images of a single breast, only a few studies have explored feature learning across four-view mammography images of bilateral breasts. We have found that the existing four-view methods typically enable only simplistic and direct interactions of features between bilateral mammography images. These interactions are clearly insufficient for complex four-view analysis. Our approach addresses a critical issue in the analysis of bilateral breast four-view mammography: when extracting features using four-view mammography images of bilateral breasts, the uncertainty in the size and location of lesions in the bilateral breasts often leads to incorrect feature matching, as shown in Figure 3. This issue can make it difficult for the model to effectively distinguish between cancerous and non-cancerous tissues, thereby severely affecting the model's learning performance. We introduce a novel local-feature-matching learning mechanism for bilateral breasts. Additionally, we developed a contrastive joint learning method for bilateral breasts. These innovations effectively alleviate the issue of incorrect feature matching in bilateral breasts and significantly enhance the model's ability to differentiate between features.

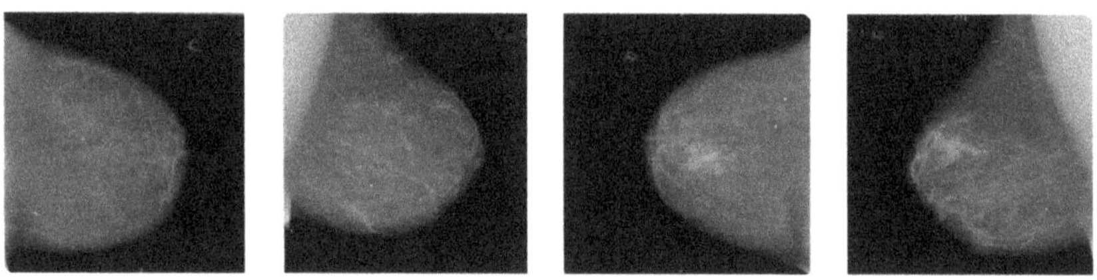

(a) (b) (c) (d)

Figure 3. (**a**) The left CC (cranio-caudal) view; (**b**) The left MLO (mediolateral oblique) view; (**c**) The right CC view; (**d**) The right MLO view. The areas within the red bounding boxes represent the lesion regions of the mammograms.

One potential solution is to employ semantic segmentation methods [39,40] to explicitly delineate the lesion areas' location and size in the breast for the model. However, this approach necessitates fine-grained pixel-level annotations of mammography images by doctors, implying substantial manual annotation costs and the risk of errors due to repetitive, intensive labor. Observing the characteristics of the dataset, we noted that the bilateral breast distribution in cases can be categorized into three scenarios: (1) both breasts are normal; (2) both breasts are cancerous; (3) only one breast is cancerous. Therefore, to address cross-breast feature learning in these distinct scenarios, we introduced a bilateral breast local-feature-matching learning mechanism and achieved inter-breast similarity feature correlation learning, as well as dissimilar feature contrastive learning, thus resolving the aforementioned issues. Our proposed Four-view Correlation and Contrastive Joint Learning Model (FV-Net) primarily comprises the following modules:

1. Pretrained truncated EfficientNet-b0: used for extracting features from both breasts.
2. Cross-Mammogram Dual-Pathway Attention Module: used for calculating local-feature-matching relationships between the left and right breast feature maps.
3. Bilateral-Mammogram Contrastive Joint Learning: used for the joint contrastive learning of the interaction feature maps.
4. Classifier and loss function: includes fully connected layers for the left and right breasts, BCE loss, and global average pooling.

4.3. Pretrained Truncated EfficientNet-b0 Module

In processing unilateral breast images, we first concatenate the CC (cranio-caudal)-view and MLO (mediolateral oblique)-view mammographic images of the left breast for each case, applying the same procedure for the right breast. The concatenated mammographic images of the left and right breasts are then fed into a shared feature extractor.

We opt for a truncated version of EfficientNet-b0, pretrained on ImageNet-1K [41], as our feature extractor; detailed information about its architecture can be found in the "shared weights" section in Figure 4. Diverging from the classic EfficientNet-b0, we removed the final fully connected layer and pooling layer, retaining only the feature extraction module to preserve more spatial information. The feature extractor reduces the size of the original image by 1024 times, outputting feature maps of the left and right breasts with dimensions of 40 × 20 and a feature channel count of 1280. Each pixel point corresponds to a receptive field of size 32 × 32 in the original image; this is specifically achieved through the following equations:

$$F_L = f(L_i^m, L_i^c) \tag{1}$$

$$F_R = f(R_i^m, R_i^c) \tag{2}$$

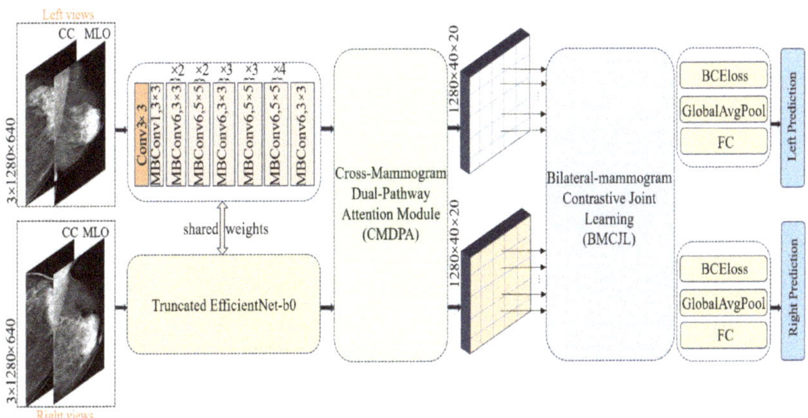

Figure 4. Our proposed FV-Net framework utilizes a shared modified truncated EfficientNet-b0 for feature extraction and employs the CMDPA to reshape the fea ture maps, along with the BMCJL module for four-view local feature joint contrastive learning.

4.4. Cross-Mammogram Dual-Pathway Attention Module

Our method incorporates an attention block [42] comprising three core elements: Q (Query vector), K (Key vector), and V (Value vector). The Query vector represents the feature item currently being processed, the Key vector is used for matching with the Query vector, and the Value vector contains the actual content of information. This content, after being weighted by attention, is used to construct the final output. Q, K, and V are typically represented as feature tensors of the shape $\mathbb{R}^{C \times D}$. The computation of relations is achieved by computing the dot product of the Query with all Key items, dividing by $\sqrt{C}$ (where C represents the dimension of the Key vector), and then applying the softmax function to obtain attention weights for the input elements. These weights are multiplied by the Value vector V to obtain a weighted summary containing information weighted based on the association between the Query and the Keys. The computation equation is as follows:

$$F(Q, K, V) = \text{softmax}\left(\frac{QK^T}{\sqrt{C}}\right)V \tag{3}$$

Next, we describe an innovative application of Equation (3) in our study, namely, the cross-mammogram local multi-head interaction relationship, as detailed in Figure 5. As illustrated in Figure 5, our proposed Cross-Mammogram Dual-Pathway Attention Module adopts a dual-path architecture, aiming to capture the feature correlation and matching information between bilateral mammograms. Taking the original high-dimensional feature maps of bilateral breast images, $F_L, F_R \in \mathbb{R}^{B \times C \times H \times W}$, as input, we first reshape the input features into the shape of (B, L, C), forming the feature matrices of the left and right breasts, $\mathbf{A}_L = [a_1^L, a_2^L, \ldots, a_n^L]$, $\mathbf{A}_R = [b_1^R, b_2^R, \ldots, b_n^R]$. Subsequently, through two linear transformation branches, A_L and A_R are mapped into $P_L, P_R \in \mathbb{R}^{B\times L\times 3C}$. By performing sliding segmentation on the channel dimension of the mapped P_L and P_R, the Query map, Key map, and Value map $\in (B, M, L, C')$ are generated. From these, we separate out M sets of Q_i, K_i, V_i, and $Q_i, K_i, V_i \in \mathbb{R}^{B\times L\times d}, i = 0, \ldots, M-1$, where the parameter M controls the number of feature attention heads in multi-head attention. Here, the parameter d represents the dimension of the features within each attention head. The value of d can be calculated by the following equation:

$$d = C' = \frac{3C}{M} \tag{4}$$

For each Q in the Query map, we compute its dot-product attention with all Ks in the Key map of the contralateral mammograms and employ the softmax function to obtain normalized bilateral breast local feature correlation attention weights. These attention weights are then used to weight the corresponding Vs in the Value map. This process is symmetrically applied to both breasts. Therefore, the relation maps for each attention head of the left and right mammography views are, respectively, calculated by the following equations:

$$F_{L_i}^{\text{mha}}(Q, K, V) = \text{softmax}\left(\frac{Q_{L_i} K_R^T}{\sqrt{C}}\right) V_R \tag{5}$$

$$F_{R_i}^{\text{mha}}(Q, K, V) = \text{softmax}\left(\frac{Q_{R_i} K_L^T}{\sqrt{C}}\right) V_L \tag{6}$$

In Equations (5) and (6), Q_{L_i} and Q_{R_i} represent the Query of each local feature attention head for the left and right mammography feature maps, respectively. K_L, K_R, V_L, and V_R correspond to all Keys and Values within the Key maps and Value maps of the mammographic feature representations. Finally, after linear projection and feature reshaping, the weighted feature matrix obtained from each attention head is recombined into a cohesive feature map. The resulting new feature maps, denoted by F_L'', $F_R'' \in \mathbb{R}^{C\times H\times W}$, maintain their complete spatial structure. This facilitates the associative matching of local feature information from each mammogram with the global feature regions of the contralateral breast.

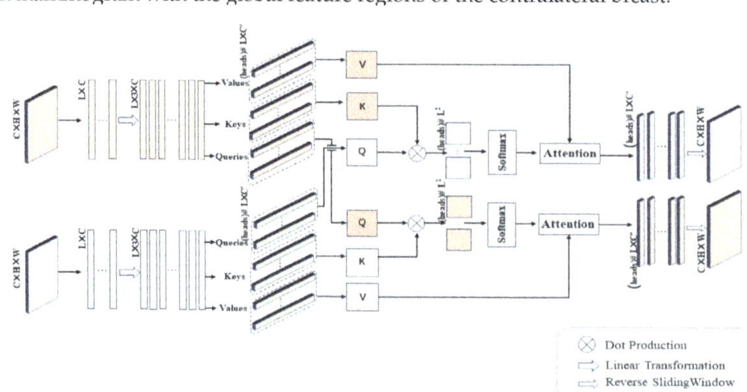

Figure 5. Detailed architecture of Cross-Mammogram Dual-Pathway Attention Module, (heads) # L × C′ represents numerical units with the total number of heads and a size of L × C′ , and the others are similarly defined.

4.5. Bilateral-Mammogram Contrastive Joint Learning

Inspired by the diverse distribution of label combinations in bilateral breast images, in FV-Net, we innovatively design a contrastive joint loss function, introducing a novel method for local feature interaction learning between bilateral mammographic feature maps. This method aims to maximize the similarity between the most similar local features and enhance the disparity between the most dissimilar local features. As shown on the right side of Figure 4, the recombined feature maps of the left and right mammograms, F_L'', F_R'', processed by the " Cross-Mammogram Dual-Pathway Attention Module", are divided into equally sized, non-overlapping patch blocks. Each block consists of $\frac{H \times W}{k^2}$ patches, where $\{F_{L_i}'', F_{R_i}''\} \in \mathbb{R}^{C \times k^2}$ for $i = 0, \ldots, \frac{H \times W}{k^2} - 1$. Each patch block size is (C, K, K), and the feature map is divided from (C, H, W) into (N, C, K, K), where N is the number of patches, and K is set to 5.

We calculate the similarity between the feature maps F_{L_i}'' of each left mammographic image and the feature maps F_{R_i}'' of the contralateral mammographic image. This process is accomplished by comparing similarity scores between different patch blocks to identify pairs of patches in F_L'' and all patch blocks in F_R'' with the highest and lowest similarity scores. The patch pairs with the highest similarity scores are considered positive samples, while those with the lowest scores are considered negative samples. Specifically, when the labels of the left and right breasts indicate unilateral or bilateral cancer, we need to determine the indices of the feature patch pairs with the highest and lowest similarity, that is, the positive and negative sample pairs. However, when both breasts are normal, we only need to identify the most similar patch index pairs, that is, the positive sample pairs.

More specifically, we first normalize the given feature vectors X_i and Y_j (representing two patch blocks from bilateral mammograms) separately. This step is achieved by dividing each feature vector by its L2 norm (adding a small constant $\epsilon = 1 \times 10^{-6}$). The normalized feature vectors X_i and Y_j ensure consistency in length, making the subsequently calculated similarity scores reflect only directional differences. The similarity score, Sim, is obtained by calculating the dot product of the normalized feature vectors as follows:

$$\text{Sim}(X_i, Y_j) = \frac{X_i}{\|X_i\| + \epsilon} \cdot \frac{Y_j}{\|Y_j\| + \epsilon} \tag{7}$$

The method for identifying positive and negative sample pairs is as follows: after calculating the similarity between all pairs of patches, we use the following Equation (8) to determine the indices of the most similar (positive sample pairs) and the least similar (negative sample pairs) patch pairs:

$$j(i) = \arg\max \text{Sim}(X_i, Y_j) \tag{8}$$

$$j'(i) = \arg\min \text{Sim}(X_i, Y_j') \tag{9}$$

Equation (8) implements the assignment of each index i to index j of the patch Y_j in the contralateral breast's feature map that is most similar to the patch X_i on this side of the breast's feature map, thereby establishing a positive sample pair between the feature maps of the left and right breasts. Similarly, the index of the patch pair with the lowest similarity score is determined through Equation (9), thereby establishing a negative sample pair.

After determining all positive and negative sample pairs, we employ the designed joint contrastive loss function L_{sim} for learning. This loss function aims to reward the similarity between positive sample pairs and penalize the similarity between negative sample pairs. Its expression is as follows:

$$\begin{aligned} L_{\text{sim}} = \frac{1}{2N} \sum_{i=0}^{N-1} (1 - I(y)) \left[\exp\left(-\frac{\text{Sim}(X_i, Y_{j(i)})}{t} \right) + \exp\left(\frac{\text{Sim}(X_i, Y'_{j'(i)})}{t} \right) \right] \\ + \frac{1}{N} \sum_{i=0}^{N-1} I(y) \exp\left(-\frac{\text{Sim}(X_i, Y_{j(i)})}{t} \right) \end{aligned} \tag{10}$$

Here, N represents the total number of patch blocks in the reconstructed feature map of a unilateral breast, and t represents the temperature parameter, which we set to 0.5. $I(y)$ is an indicator function that is true when the labels for a pair of mammographic images are both normal. In this scenario, the loss function primarily focuses on the similarity of the most similar patch pairs. When at least one image is labeled as abnormal, the loss function takes into account the similarity of both the most similar and the least similar patch pairs. We calculate the similarity L_{sim_i} for each pair of patch blocks in the model and then compute their average. Our proposed joint contrastive learning loss function encourages the model to reduce differences between positive sample pairs and increase differences between negative sample pairs. This strategy facilitates the model's ability to more easily differentiate between cancerous and non-cancerous features, thereby significantly enhancing the model's robust classification capabilities.

4.6. Classifier and Loss Function

In our proposed FV-Net framework, the ultimate goal is to concurrently classify bilateral mammogram images. To this end, on top of the extracted and reconstructed feature maps, we design a dual-path classifier with non-shared weights for the classification predictions of the left and right breasts, denoted by L_{cls} and R_{cls}, respectively. The shape of the reconstructed feature maps for the left and right breasts is (2, 1280, 40, 20). First, we perform global average pooling on each breast feature map to obtain a 1280-dimensional feature vector representation. Then, through their respective sequences of fully connected layers, followed by a sigmoid function, we predict the probability of cancer presence p for each breast, where p denotes the likelihood of malignant tumor lesions in the input images. The classification training loss functions for the left and right breasts are defined as follows:

$$L_{\text{cls\_loss}} = -\frac{1}{S}\sum_{i=1}^{S}\left[y_i \log(P_{L_i}) + (1-y_i)\log(1-P_{L_i})\right] \quad (11)$$

$$R_{\text{cls\_loss}} = -\frac{1}{S}\sum_{i=1}^{S}\left[y_i \log(P_{R_i}) + (1-y_i)\log(1-P_{R_i})\right] \quad (12)$$

During the training process, the BCE (Binary Cross-Entropy) loss is utilized to quantify the discrepancy between the predicted values P_{L_i} and P_{R_i} and the true value y_i. The total loss of the FV-Net model is calculated, as expressed in Equation (13), where u_1 and u_2 are the weighting coefficients, set to 5/6 and 1/6, respectively.

$$L_{\text{total\_loss}} = u_1 \cdot L_{\text{sim}} + u_2 \cdot (L_{\text{cls\_loss}} + R_{\text{cls\_loss}}) \quad (13)$$

5. Experiment

5.1. Implementation Details

First, we adjust the size of the mammography images, which consist of concatenated dual-view images of each breast for every case, to a resolution of 1280 × 640 pixels. In the dataset, 20% of the cases are allocated to a test set, while the remaining 80% are designated for the training set and are subjected to upsampling. Care is taken to ensure that data from the same patient do not appear in both the training and test sets concurrently. For the training set, we implement a series of data augmentation techniques, including the random horizontal and vertical flipping of images, applying RandomResizedCrop and adjusting the cropping area to a resolution of 1280 × 640 pixels, employing random affine transformations, conducting random color enhancement, and utilizing the RandomErasing technique. The proposed FV-Net model is implemented using the PyTorch library, with model training completed on an NVIDIA GeForce RTX 4090 GPU with 24 GB of memory. The Adam optimizer is employed, with the initial learning rate set to 1×10^{-4} and the weight decay at 5×10^{-4}. A ReduceLROnPlateau learning rate scheduler is used, reducing the learning rate by a factor of 10 if there is no improvement in the loss value over 3 consecutive epochs. The loss function for the classification head is BCEWithLogitsLoss, and the batch size is set to 8. Each batch is fed with upsampled training data using a custom sampler (PatientSampler), ensuring that an equal number of cases are randomly selected from each category (cancer and normal), thereby balancing the class ratio in each batch and effectively learning the features of breast lesion areas in each iteration.

5.2. Evaluation Metrics

Our proposed FV-Net model is employed to predict whether a mammographic image represents a malignant or normal breast, thus presenting a classification challenge. To evaluate the performance of the model, we utilize the commonly adopted evaluation metrics for classification models in most of the literature, namely, the Area Under the Receiver Operating Characteristic Curve (AUC-ROC) and accuracy (ACC). The Area Under the Curve (AUC) of the ROC, where the ROC curve's x-axis represents the False Positive Rate (FPR) and the y-axis represents the True Positive Rate (TPR), is a crucial metric for assessing the performance of a binary classification model. An AUC value closer to 1 indicates better model performance [43]. The calculation of accuracy (ACC) is as follows:

$$\text{Accuracy} = \frac{\text{TP} + \text{TN}}{\text{FP} + \text{FN} + \text{TP} + \text{TN}} \times 100\% \tag{14}$$

The True Positive Rate (TPR) and False Positive Rate (FPR) are defined, respectively, as follows:

$$\text{TPR} = \frac{\text{TP}}{\text{TP} + \text{FN}} \tag{15}$$

$$\text{FPR} = \frac{\text{FP}}{\text{FP} + \text{TN}} \tag{16}$$

In this context, TP (True Positive), TN (True Negative), FP (False Positive), and FN (False Negative), respectively, represent the number of malignant samples correctly identified, the number of normal samples correctly identified, the number of normal samples incorrectly identified as malignant, and the number of malignant samples incorrectly identified as normal.

5.3. Ablation Analysis

To evaluate the effectiveness of each component of our proposed FV-Net model, we conduct an ablation study on the well-known public mammographic X-ray image dataset INbreast. As shown in Table 3, we compare the performance of five different model variants on the INbreast dataset based on accuracy (ACC) and AUC-ROC results. These variants include (1) training on the baseline model efficientnet-b0 using raw data without preprocessing (first row); (2) training on the efficientnet-b0 baseline model with data processed by the preprocessing module (second row); (3) combining the preprocessing module with the Cross-Mammogram Dual-Pathway Attention Module (CMDPA) (third row); (4) combining the preprocessing module with Bilateral-Mammogram Contrastive Joint Learning (BMCJL) (fourth row); (5) using FV-Net, which both employs the preprocessing module and integrates the CMDPA and BMCJL (fifth row).

Table 3. Model variants' performance on INbreast dataset.

Preprocessing Module	CMDPA	BMCJL	ACC (%)	AUC
×	×	×	68.00	0.7818
✓	×	×	80.00	0.8627
✓	✓	×	84.67	0.8877
✓	×	✓	86.67	0.8848
✓	✓	✓	87.34	0.9322

The results of the ablation experiments demonstrate that the baseline model without preprocessing exhibits the poorest performance, whereas the model incorporating the preprocessing module, CMDPA, and BMCJL concurrently manifests superior performance. Compared to the original baseline model, our proposed FV-Net significantly enhances the accuracy by 19.34% and the Area Under the Curve (AUC) by 0.1504. This highlights the combined efficacy of the three components: the preprocessing module, the CMDPA, and BMCJL. Specifically, the implementation of the preprocessing module alone results in an increase of 12% in accuracy and 0.0809 in AUC. Furthermore, the combined use of the preprocessing module and CMDPA, in contrast to the baseline model, leads to a 16.67% rise in accuracy and a 0.1059 boost in AUC. On the other hand, the integration of the preprocessing module and BMCJL compared to the baseline model increases the accuracy by 18.67% and the AUC by 0.103. It is noteworthy that adding the CMDPA alone leads to an increase of 4.67% in accuracy and an enhancement of 0.025 in AUC. Similarly, incorporating only the BMCJL module results in an improvement of 6.67% in accuracy and a rise of 0.0221 in AUC. When the preprocessing module, the CMDPA, and BMCJL are employed simultaneously, there is an additional improvement of 7.34% in accuracy and 0.0695 in AUC compared to the model that incorporates only the preprocessing module. The above experimental data clearly demonstrate that the data preprocessing module effectively addresses the issue of poor image quality in the original training dataset. It trims the background areas and highlights the pixels of the lesion areas, allowing the model to focus solely on the features of the breast region. Secondly, the CMDPA effectively facilitates the matching learning of local feature correlations across global regions of the breast, significantly mitigating potential misalignment issues between the features of bilateral mammogram views. Additionally, the experimental results demonstrate that the contrastive joint loss function applied by the BMCJL module effectively enables the model to learn the differences between lesion area features and normal tissue features, as well as the similarities among features within the same category. This not only facilitates the model's ability to distinguish between lesion areas and normal tissue regions in the breast but also allows it to acquire a more comprehensive set of similar feature information.

To visualize our experimental results, we plot ROC-AUC curves for five model variants on the INbreast dataset. As shown in Figure 6, these variants include (1) the Vanilla Baseline Model, corresponding to the first row on the bottom right of the graph; (2) the Preprocessed Baseline Model, corresponding to the second row; (3) the Preprocessed Baseline Model with the CMDPA, corresponding to the third row; (4) the Preprocessed Baseline Model with BMCJL, corresponding to the fourth row; (5) the complete FV-Net model, corresponding to the fifth row. These ROC-AUC curves clearly demonstrate that our experimental results are entirely consistent with the above analysis, unequivocally confirming the effectiveness of the preprocessing module, the CMDPA, and BMCJL.

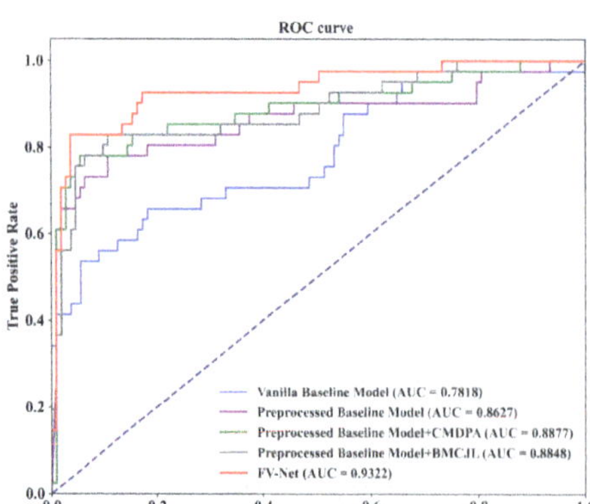

Figure 6. ROC curves graph from ablation study on the public INbreast dataset.

To further demonstrate the role of the components that we propose in the process of predicting the probability of breast cancer through our model, clarify the extent to which our method enhances the model's ability to identify tumor regions, and improve the model's credibility by visualizing and explaining the rationale behind model predictions, we utilized Grad-CAM [44] to visualize the most suspicious cancerous areas predicted by different method groups. Grad-CAM, which is used as a visualization explanation method to generate model focus areas, highlights key areas for classification decisions by computing the gradient of the cancer probability prediction relative to the feature maps of the last convolutional layer. These gradients indicate the contribution of each unit (i.e., each pixel or region) within the feature map to the final cancer probability prediction, with the brightest areas representing the most suspicious tumor regions contributing the most to the final cancer probability prediction. As shown in Figure 7b, when using only the Preprocessed Baseline Model for predicting the probability of cancer, the absence of interactive learning of bilateral breast feature maps prevents the association and comparative learning of bilateral mammogram views, and thus, the model is easily distracted by some irrelevant features, with the model's attention only focused on small areas at the tumor edge. As shown in Figure 7c, after solely incorporating the joint contrastive learning module, the model focuses on the local area of the tumor rather than the peripheral areas. Moreover, compared to Figure 7b, the area of attention of the model is more comprehensive, covering a larger extent of the tumor area. This is attributed to the joint contrastive learning of the features of bilateral mammogram views. As shown in Figure 7d through Grad-CAM, by integrating the joint contrastive module (BMCJL) with the Cross-Mammogram Dual-Pathway Attention Module (CMDPA), the model is capable of more comprehensively and accurately focusing on and identifying tumor regions in both CC and MLO views. This not only enables the model to effectively distinguish between cancerous regions and normal tissue areas but also mitigates the issue of incorrect feature space matching.

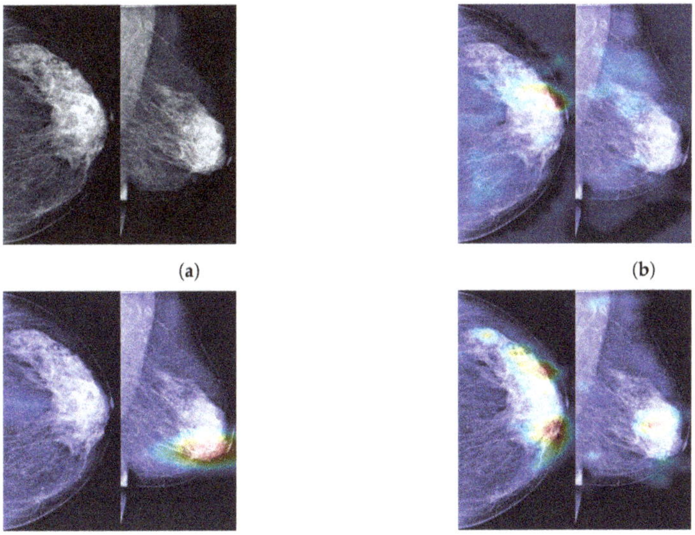

(a) (b) (c) (d)

Figure 7. A comparison of visualization results for the most suspicious malignant tumor areas in paired CC and MLO views of the same case predicted by different method groups. (**a**) Raw image; (**b**) Preprocessed Baseline; (**c**) Preprocessed Baseline Model with BMCJL; (**d**) FV-Net.

5.4. Comparison with Other Methods

As demonstrated in Table 4, we first conduct a comparison on the well-known public INbreast dataset against eight competing methodologies. These methods include

ConvNext-small, proposed by Liu et al. [45] in 2022; RegNet_x_1_6gf, introduced by Xu et al. [46] in 2021; MobileNet-v2, presented by Sandler et al. [47] in 2019; EfficientNet-b0 and EfficientNet-b3, proposed by Tan et al. [48] in 2019; ResNext101_32×8d, introduced by Xie et al. [49] in 2017; and ResNet50 and ResNet101, proposed by He et al. [50] in 2016. Additionally, we plot Figure 8, which illustrates the ROC (Receiver Operating Characteristic) curves of our FV-Net model compared with these eight competing approaches, visually representing the classification performance of each method. To ensure fairness, the comparison of all models is conducted under uniform conditions involving data augmentation, data preprocessing techniques, training strategies, and Data Division methods. Notably, our proposed FV-Net model excels over all compared methods in terms of both accuracy and AUC, achieving an accuracy of 87.34% and an AUC of 0.9322. This further substantiates the effectiveness of our proposed Cross-Mammogram Dual-Pathway Attention Module and Bilateral-Mammogram Contrastive Joint Learning in proficiently mining the latent correlative and distinctive features across bilateral mammogram views.

Additionally, we conduct evaluations on a 20% independent test set, as shown at the bottom of Table 4. In comparison with the other eight methods, our proposed FV-Net model achieves the best performance in both accuracy and AUC, reaching 98.02% and 0.9664, respectively. To more clearly demonstrate the comparative performance of all models, Figure 9 presents the ROC curves of our method against the other competitors on the 20% independent test set.

Table 4. Quantitative comparison of different methods on the INbreast dataset and a 20% test set.

Methods	View Approach	Data Division	#Params (M)	ACC (%)	AUC
Dataset: INbreast					
ResNet-50 [50]	Four-view	patient	105.69	72.00	0.7075
ResNet-101 [50]	Four-view	patient	178.14	74.00	0.6657
ConvNext-small [45]	Four-view	patient	190.90	72.67	0.7245
ResNext101_32x8d [49]	Four-view	patient	346.91	70.00	0.6699
EfficientNet-b0 [48]	Four-view	patient	21.55	80.00	0.8627
EfficientNet-b3 [48]	Four-view	patient	49.81	86.67	0.8823
MobileNet-v2 [47]	Four-view	patient	14.74	80.00	0.8841
RegNet_x_1_6gf [46]	Four-view	patient	34.75	74.00	0.9029
Ours	Four-view	patient	71.57	**87.34**	**0.9322**
Dataset: 20% test set					
ResNet-50 [50]	Four-view	patient	105.69	96.22	0.7140
ResNet-101 [50]	Four-view	patient	178.14	96.19	0.6363
ConvNext-small [45]	Four-view	patient	190.90	96.15	0.6996
EfficientNet-b0 [48]	Four-view	patient	21.55	96.94	0.9463
EfficientNet-b3 [48]	Four-view	patient	49.81	97.01	0.9343
MobileNet-v2 [47]	Four-view	patient	14.74	95.83	0.8572
RegNet_x_1_6gf [46]	Four-view	patient	34.75	95.97	0.9481
ResNext101_32x8d [49]	Four-view	patient	346.91	94.96	0.6859
Ours	Four-view	patient	71.57	**98.02**	**0.9664**

Furthermore, as clearly demonstrated in Table 4, compared with some of the other competing methods, our proposed FV-Net model has a smaller number of parameters (71.57 M), yet it still maintains the best performance on two different test sets. This underscores the efficacy of our meticulously designed Cross-Mammogram Dual-Pathway Attention Module and Bilateral-Mammogram Contrastive Joint Learning module, which significantly optimize model performance even with a smaller parameter count, thus confirming the superior efficiency of our model in terms of parameter utilization. This advantage is particularly valuable in clinical settings with limited computational resources, as it reduces the computational burden without sacrificing diagnostic accuracy.

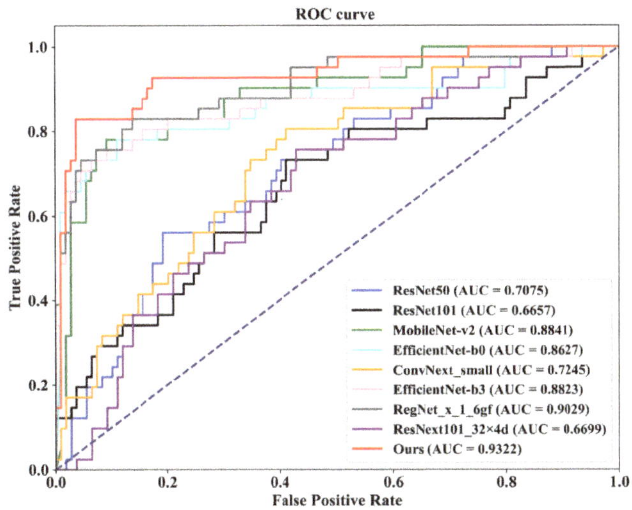

Figure 8. The ROC curves comparison of the classification performance of FV-Net and eight competing methods on the INbreast dataset.

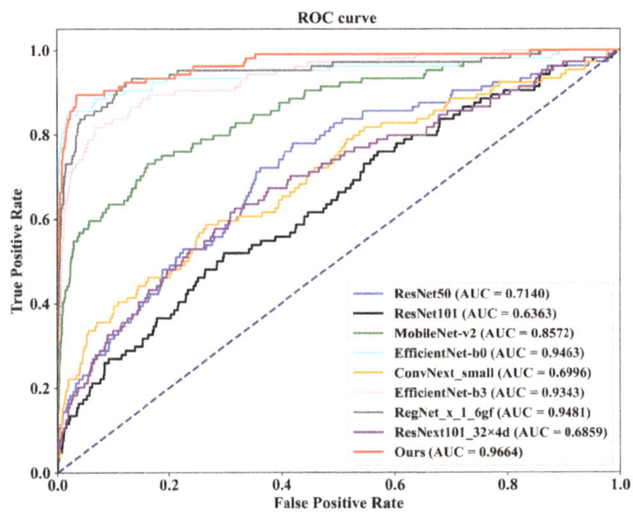

Figure 9. The comparison of ROC curves for the classification performance of FV-Net and eight competing methods on a 20% independent test set.

To further present the experimental results, as illustrated in Figure 10, we plot a visual comparison of the confusion matrix on the INbreast dataset for the FV-Net model versus the other eight methods. It is evident that our model outperforms in effective classification capability when compared to the others. This outstanding classification performance can be attributed to the effective combination of the CMDPA and BMCJL. Moreover, across both datasets, our methodology yields significant performance enhancements relative to the baseline model and consistently outperforms all other methodologies assessed. This unequivocally demonstrates that our approach not only elevates the model's capacity for classification but also exhibits certain generalization capabilities.

To demonstrate that our proposed FV-Net model has higher lesion area recognition accuracy compared to other assessed model methods, we employ Grad-CAM technology. This technique generates heatmaps based on the output feature maps of the last convolutional layers of different models and is used to conduct comparisons on the INbreast test set. The comparison results in Figure 11 clearly show the heatmaps of different models: models such as ResNet101, ConvNext_small, MobileNet-v2, and RegNet_x_1_6gf mainly focus on the edges or background areas of the breast; the EfficientNet-b0 and EfficientNet-b3 models perform slightly better, focusing on the edges of the lesion; additionally, the attention of ResNext101_32×4d widely disperses across normal breast tissue areas, while the focal areas of ResNet50 sporadically concentrate within normal breast tissue areas. In contrast, the FV-Net model identifies breast lesion areas more concentratedly and comprehensively, with its focus area almost overlapping with the entire lesion area, thereby achieving a more reasonable and precise diagnosis of breast cancer.

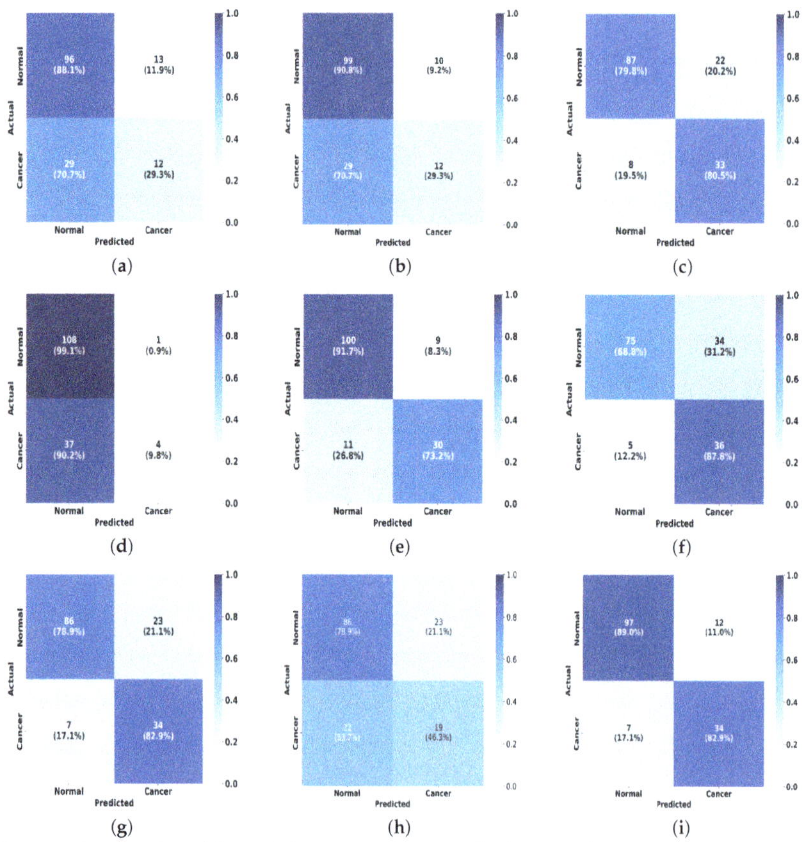

Figure 10. A comparison of the confusion matrices for our method against other methods on the INbreast dataset. (**a**) ResNet50; (**b**) ResNet101; (**c**) EfficientNet-b0; (**d**) ConvNext_small; (**e**) EfficientNet-b3; (**f**) RegNet_x_1_6gf; (**g**) MobileNet-v2; (**h**) ResNext101_32×4d; (**i**) Ours.

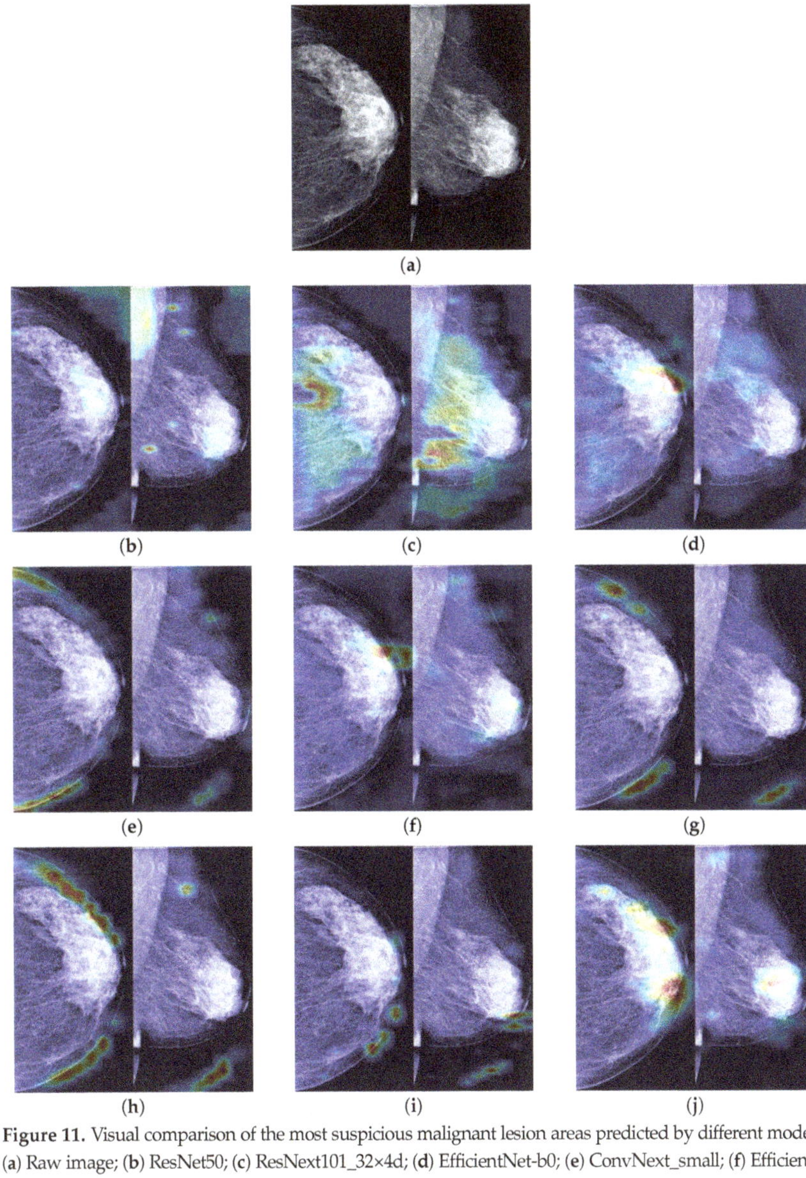

Figure 11. Visual comparison of the most suspicious malignant lesion areas predicted by different models. (**a**) Raw image; (**b**) ResNet50; (**c**) ResNext101_32×4d; (**d**) EfficientNet-b0; (**e**) ConvNext_small; (**f**) EfficientNet-b3; (**g**) RegNet_x_1_6gf; (**h**) MobileNet-v2; (**i**) ResNet101; (**j**) Ours.

6. Conclusions

In this paper, we employ deep learning techniques to classify and diagnose normal and cancerous cases using bilateral mammograms. We preprocess the original dataset to obtain updated samples, which enhances the model's performance in early breast cancer screening and better conforms to actual clinical diagnostics. We innovatively propose a bilateral breast four-view feature interaction model named FV-Net, containing two key components aimed at enhancing the classification capabilities of mammographic images. First, the Cross-Mammogram Dual-Pathway Attention Module (CMDPA) method achieves the association matching of the local features of each breast with the local features of the contralateral breast's global region. This approach not only effectively mitigates the negative impact of misalignment issues in inter-breast feature matching but also captures the consistency and complementarity information between the bilateral breasts. Furthermore, the Bilateral-Mammogram Contrastive Joint Learning (BMCJL) module, by processing the recombined feature maps after bilateral breast associative learning, further enhances the correlation between similar features and increases the distinguishability of dissimilar features. This module significantly enhances the model's ability to recognize distinct features and learn richer information on similar features. Extensive experiments conducted on test sets show that each key component of our proposed FV-Net model effectively enhances the model's performance. Furthermore, we use Grad-CAM to conduct an interpretability analysis of the proposed method and the compared models, visualizing the regions of interest during the models' decision-making process. This not only demonstrates the credibility and accuracy of our proposed model in identifying lesion areas but also more fully illustrates the effectiveness of the component methods we propose. The study results indicate that on a 20% independent test set, the accuracy reaches 98.02% with an AUC of 0.9664; on the INbreast test set, the accuracy reaches 87.34% with an AUC of 0.9322. Notably, our method surpasses the performance of various existing competing approaches.

Author Contributions: Conceptualization, X.W. and J.L.; methodology, X.W.; software, X.W.; validation, X.W., J.L., and L.Y.; formal analysis, X.W.; investigation, X.W.; resources, J.L.; data curation, L.Y.; writing—original draft preparation, X.W.; writing—review and editing, X.W. and J.L.; visualization, L.Y.; supervision, J.L. All authors have read and agreed to the published version of the manuscript.

Funding: This research received no external funding.

Institutional Review Board Statement: Not applicable.

Informed Consent Statement: Not applicable.

Data Availability Statement: The raw datasets utilized in this study include Vindr-mammo (https://physionet.org/content/vindr-mammo/1.0.0/ (accessed on 15 April 2023)), Mini-DDSM (https://www.kaggle.com/datasets/cheddad/miniddsm2?select=MINI-DDSM-Complete-PNG-16 (accessed on 15 April 2023)), and INbreast (https://www.kaggle.com/datasets/tommyngx/inbreast2012 (accessed on 10 November 2023)).

Conflicts of Interest: The authors declare no conflicts of interest.

References

1. Siegel, R.L.; Miller, K.D.; Wagle, N.S.; Jemal, A. Cancer statistics, 2023. *Ca Cancer J. Clin.* **2023**, *73*, 17–48. [CrossRef] [PubMed]
2. Liu, Y.; Zhang, F.; Chen, C.; Wang, S.; Wang, Y.; Yu, Y. Act like a radiologist: Towards reliable multi-view correspondence reasoning for mammogram mass detection. *IEEE Trans. Pattern Anal. Mach. Intell.* **2021**, *44*, 5947–5961. [CrossRef] [PubMed]
3. Walton, W.C.; Kim, S.J.; Mullen, L.A. Automated registration for dual-view x-ray mammography using convolutional neural networks. *IEEE Trans. Biomed. Eng.* **2022**, *69*, 3538–3550. [CrossRef]
4. Lopez, E.; Grassucci, E.; Valleriani, M.; Comminiello, D. Hypercomplex Neural Architectures for Multi-View Breast Cancer Classification. *arXiv* **2022**, arXiv:2204.05798.
5. Chen, Y.; Wang, H.; Wang, C.; Tian, Y.; Liu, F.; Liu, Y.; Elliott, M.; McCarthy, D.J.; Frazer, H.; Carneiro, G. Multi-view local co-occurrence and global consistency learning improve mammogram classification generalisation. In Proceedings of the International Conference on Medical Image Computing and Computer-Assisted Intervention, Vancouver, BC, Canada, 8–12 October 2022; Springer: Berlin/Heidelberg, Germany, 2022; pp. 3–13.
6. Liberman, L.; Menell, J.H. Breast imaging reporting and data system (BI-RADS). *Radiol. Clin.* **2002**, *40*, 409–430. [CrossRef] [PubMed]
7. Galić, I.; Habijan, M.; Leventić, H.; Romić, K. Machine learning empowering personalized medicine: A comprehensive review of medical image analysis methods. *Electronics* **2023**, *12*, 4411. [CrossRef]
8. Xia, L.; An, J.; Ma, C.; Hou, H.; Hou, Y.; Cui, L.; Jiang, X.; Li, W.; Gao, Z. Neural network model based on global and local features for multi-view mammogram classification. *Neurocomputing* **2023**, *536*, 21–29. [CrossRef]
9. Seyyedi, S.; Wong, M.J.; Ikeda, D.M.; Langlotz, C.P. SCREENet: A Multi-view Deep Convolutional Neural Network for Classification of High-resolution Synthetic Mammographic Screening Scans. *arXiv* **2020**, arXiv:2009.08563.
10. Van Tulder, G.; Tong, Y.; Marchiori, E. Multi-view analysis of unregistered medical images using cross-view transformers. In *Proceedings of the Medical Image Computing and Computer Assisted Intervention—MICCAI 2021: 24th International Conference, Strasbourg, France, 27 September–1 October 2021*; Proceedings, Part III 24; Springer: Berlin/Heidelberg, Germany, 2021; pp. 104–113.

11. Ma, J.; Li, X.; Li, H.; Wang, R.; Menze, B.; Zheng, W.S. Cross-view relation networks for mammogram mass detection. In Proceedings of the 2020 25th International Conference on Pattern Recognition (ICPR), Milan, Italy, 10–15 January 2021; IEEE: New York, NY, USA, 2021; pp. 8632–8638.
12. Wang, Z.; Xian, J.; Liu, K.; Li, X.; Li, Q.; Yang, X. Dual-view Correlation Hybrid Attention Network for Robust Holistic Mammogram Classification. *arXiv* **2023**, arXiv:2306.10676.
13. Nguyen, T.H.; Kha, Q.H.; Truong, T.N.T.; Lam, B.T.; Ngo, B.H.; Dinh, Q.V.; Le, N.Q.K. Towards robust natural-looking mammography lesion synthesis on ipsilateral dual-views breast cancer analysis. In Proceedings of the IEEE/CVF International Conference on Computer Vision, Paris, France, 2–6 October 2023; pp. 2564–2573.
14. Yan, Y.; Conze, P.H.; Lamard, M.; Quellec, G.; Cochener, B.; Coatrieux, G. Towards improved breast mass detection using dual-view mammogram matching. *Med. Image Anal.* **2021**, *71*, 102083. [CrossRef]
15. Wang, H.; Feng, J.; Zhang, Z.; Su, H.; Cui, L.; He, H.; Liu, L. Breast mass classification via deeply integrating the contextual information from multi-view data. *Pattern Recognit.* **2018**, *80*, 42–52. [CrossRef]
16. Bekker, A.J.; Greenspan, H.; Goldberger, J. A multi-view deep learning architecture for classification of breast microcalcifications. In Proceedings of the 2016 IEEE 13th International Symposium on Biomedical Imaging (ISBI), Prague, Czech Republic, 13–16 April 2016; IEEE: New York, NY, USA, 2016; pp. 726–730.
17. Li, C.; Xu, J.; Liu, Q.; Zhou, Y.; Mou, L.; Pu, Z.; Xia, Y.; Zheng, H.; Wang, S. Multi-view mammographic density classification by dilated and attention-guided residual learning. *IEEE/ACM Trans. Comput. Biol. Bioinform.* **2020**, *18*, 1003–1013. [CrossRef] [PubMed]
18. Nguyen, H.T.; Tran, S.B.; Nguyen, D.B.; Pham, H.H.; Nguyen, H.Q. A novel multi-view deep learning approach for BI-RADS and density assessment of mammograms. In Proceedings of the 2022 44th Annual International Conference of the IEEE Engineering in Medicine & Biology Society (EMBC), Scotland, UK, 11–15 July 2022; IEEE: New York, NY, USA, 2022; pp. 2144–2148.
19. Chen, X.; Zhang, K.; Abdoli, N.; Gilley, P.W.; Wang, X.; Liu, H.; Zheng, B.; Qiu, Y. Transformers improve breast cancer diagnosis from unregistered multi-view mammograms. *Diagnostics* **2022**, *12*, 1549. [CrossRef] [PubMed]
20. Lekamlage, C.D.; Afzal, F.; Westerberg, E.; Cheddad, A. Mini-DDSM: Mammography-based automatic age estimation. In Proceedings of the 2020 3rd International Conference on Digital Medicine and Image Processing, Kyoto, Japan, 6–9 November 2020; pp. 1–6.
21. Nguyen, H.T.; Nguyen, H.Q.; Pham, H.H.; Lam, K.; Le, L.T.; Dao, M.; Vu, V. VinDr-Mammo: A large-scale benchmark dataset for computer-aided diagnosis in full-field digital mammography. *Sci. Data* **2023**, *10*, 277. [CrossRef] [PubMed]
22. Moreira, I.C.; Amaral, I.; Domingues, I.; Cardoso, A.; Cardoso, M.J.; Cardoso, J.S. Inbreast: toward a full-field digital mammographic database. *Acad. Radiol.* **2012**, *19*, 236–248. [CrossRef] [PubMed]
23. Ru, J.; Lu, B.; Chen, B.; Shi, J.; Chen, G.; Wang, M.; Pan, Z.; Lin, Y.; Gao, Z.; Zhou, J.; et al. Attention guided neural ODE network for breast tumor segmentation in medical images. *Comput. Biol. Med.* **2023**, *159*, 106884. [CrossRef] [PubMed]
24. Tsochatzidis, L.; Koutla, P.; Costaridou, L.; Pratikakis, I. Integrating segmentation information into CNN for breast cancer diagnosis of mammographic masses. *Comput. Methods Programs Biomed.* **2021**, *200*, 105913. [CrossRef] [PubMed]
25. Ghosh, S.K.; Mitra, A.; Ghosh, A. A novel intuitionistic fuzzy soft set entrenched mammogram segmentation under multigranulation approximation for breast cancer detection in early stages. *Expert Syst. Appl.* **2021**, *169*, 114329. [CrossRef]
26. Sarangi, S.; Rath, N.P.; Sahoo, H.K. Mammogram mass segmentation and detection using Legendre neural network-based optimal threshold. *Med. Biol. Eng. Comput.* **2021**, *59*, 947–955. [CrossRef] [PubMed]
27. Ting, F.F.; Tan, Y.J.; Sim, K.S. Convolutional neural network improvement for breast cancer classification. *Expert Syst. Appl.* **2019**, *120*, 103–115. [CrossRef]
28. Ribli, D.; Horváth, A.; Unger, Z.; Pollner, P.; Csabai, I. Detecting and classifying lesions in mammograms with deep learning. *Sci. Rep.* **2018**, *8*, 4165. [CrossRef]
29. Li, L.; Xie, N.; Yuan, S. A Federated Learning Framework for Breast Cancer Histopathological Image Classification. *Electronics* **2022**, *11*, 3767. [CrossRef]
30. Albashish, D.; Al-Sayyed, R.; Abdullah, A.; Ryalat, M.H.; Almansour, N.A. Deep CNN model based on VGG16 for breast cancer classification. In Proceedings of the 2021 International conference on information technology (ICIT), Amman, Jordan, 14–15 July 2021; IEEE: New York, NY, USA, 2021; pp. 805–810.
31. Alzubaidi, L.; Al-Shamma, O.; Fadhel, M.A.; Farhan, L.; Zhang, J.; Duan, Y. Optimizing the performance of breast cancer classification by employing the same domain transfer learning from hybrid deep convolutional neural network model. *Electronics* **2020**, *9*, 445. [CrossRef]
32. Heenaye-Mamode Khan, M.; Boodoo-Jahangeer, N.; Dullull, W.; Nathire, S.; Gao, X.; Sinha, G.; Nagwanshi, K.K. Multi-class classification of breast cancer abnormalities using Deep Convolutional Neural Network (CNN). *PLoS ONE* **2021**, *16*, e0256500. [CrossRef]
33. Dhungel, N.; Carneiro, G.; Bradley, A.P. A deep learning approach for the analysis of masses in mammograms with minimal user intervention. *Med. Image Anal.* **2017**, *37*, 114–128. [CrossRef]
34. Cao, Z.; Yang, Z.; Zhuo, X.; Lin, R.S.; Wu, S.; Huang, L.; Han, M.; Zhang, Y.; Ma, J. Deeplima: Deep learning based lesion identification in mammograms. In Proceedings of the IEEE/CVF International Conference on Computer Vision Workshops, Seoul, Republic of Korea, 27 October–2 November 2019.

35. Kooi, T.; Litjens, G.; Van Ginneken, B.; Gubern-Mérida, A.; Sánchez, C.I.; Mann, R.; den Heeten, A.; Karssemeijer, N. Large scale deep learning for computer aided detection of mammographic lesions. *Med. Image Anal.* **2017**, *35*, 303–312. [CrossRef]
36. Yang, Z.; Cao, Z.; Zhang, Y.; Tang, Y.; Lin, X.; Ouyang, R.; Wu, M.; Han, M.; Xiao, J.; Huang, L.; et al. MommiNet-v2: Mammographic multi-view mass identification networks. *Med. Image Anal.* **2021**, *73*, 102204. [CrossRef]
37. Khan, H.N.; Shahid, A.R.; Raza, B.; Dar, A.H.; Alquhayz, H. Multi-view feature fusion based four views model for mammogram classification using convolutional neural network. *IEEE Access* **2019**, *7*, 165724–165733. [CrossRef]
38. Muniyappan, S.; Allirani, A.; Saraswathi, S. A novel approach for image enhancement by using contrast limited adaptive histogram equalization method. In Proceedings of the 2013 Fourth International Conference on Computing, Communications and Networking Technologies (ICCCNT), Tiruchengode, India, 4–6 July 2013; IEEE: New York, NY, USA, 2013; pp. 1–6.
39. Ahmed, L.; Iqbal, M.; Aldabbas, H.; Khalid, S.; Saleem, Y.; Saeed, S. Images data practices for semantic segmentation of breast cancer using deep neural network. *J. Ambient Intell. Humaniz. Comput.* **2020**, *14*, 15227–15243. [CrossRef]
40. Salama, W.M.; Aly, M.H. Deep learning in mammography images segmentation and classification: Automated CNN approach. *Alex. Eng. J.* **2021**, *60*, 4701–4709. [CrossRef]
41. Deng, J.; Dong, W.; Socher, R.; Li, L.J.; Li, K.; Fei-Fei, L. Imagenet: A large-scale hierarchical image database. In Proceedings of the 2009 IEEE Conference on Computer Vision and Pattern Recognition, Miami, FL, USA, 20–25 June 2009; IEEE: New York, NY, USA, 2009; pp. 248–255.
42. Vaswani, A.; Shazeer, N.; Parmar, N.; Uszkoreit, J.; Jones, L.; Gomez, A.N.; Kaiser, Ł.; Polosukhin, I. Attention is all you need. *Adv. Neural Inf. Process. Syst.* **2017**, *30*, 5998–6008.
43. Narasimhan, H.; Agarwal, S. Support vector algorithms for optimizing the partial area under the ROC curve. *Neural Comput.* **2017**, *29*, 1919–1963. [CrossRef] [PubMed]
44. Selvaraju, R.R.; Cogswell, M.; Das, A.; Vedantam, R.; Parikh, D.; Batra, D. Grad-cam: Visual explanations from deep networks via gradient-based localization. In Proceedings of the IEEE International Conference on Computer Vision, Venice, Italy, 22–29 October 2017; pp. 618–626.
45. Liu, Z.; Mao, H.; Wu, C.Y.; Feichtenhofer, C.; Darrell, T.; Xie, S. A convnet for the 2020s. In Proceedings of the IEEE/CVF Conference on Computer Vision and Pattern Recognition, New Orleans, LA, USA, 19–24 June 2022; pp. 11976–11986.
46. Xu, J.; Pan, Y.; Pan, X.; Hoi, S.; Yi, Z.; Xu, Z. RegNet: Self-regulated network for image classification. *IEEE Trans. Neural Netw. Learn. Syst.* **2022**, *34*, 9562–9567. [CrossRef] [PubMed]
47. Sandler, M.; Howard, A.; Zhu, M.; Zhmoginov, A.; Chen, L.C. Mobilenetv2: Inverted residuals and linear bottlenecks. In Proceedings of the IEEE Conference on Computer Vision and Pattern Recognition, Salt Lake, UT, USA, 18–23 June 2018; pp. 4510–4520.
48. Tan, M.; Le, Q. Efficientnet: Rethinking model scaling for convolutional neural networks. In Proceedings of the International Conference on Machine Learning, PMLR, Long Beach, CA, USA, 9–15 June 2019; pp. 6105–6114.
49. Xie, S.; Girshick, R.; Dollár, P.; Tu, Z.; He, K. Aggregated residual transformations for deep neural networks. In Proceedings of the IEEE Conference on Computer Vision and Pattern Recognition, Honolulu, HI, USA, 21–26 July 2017; pp. 1492–1500.
50. He, K.; Zhang, X.; Ren, S.; Sun, J. Deep residual learning for image recognition. In Proceedings of the IEEE Conference on Computer Vision and Pattern Recognition, Las Vegas, NV, USA, 27–30 June 2016; pp. 770–778.

tomography

MDPI

Article

Causal Forest Machine Learning Analysis of Parkinson's Disease in Resting-State Functional Magnetic Resonance Imaging

Gabriel Solana-Lavalle [1,2], Michael D. Cusimano [3,4], Thomas Steeves [5], Roberto Rosas-Romero [1] and Pascal N. Tyrrell [2,3,6,*]

1 Department of Computing, Electronics, and Mechatronics, Universidad de las Américas Puebla Santa Catarina Mártir, San Andrés Cholula, Puebla 78210, Mexico; gabriel.solanale@udlap.mx (G.S.-L.); roberto.rosas@udlap.mx (R.R.-R.)
2 Department of Medical Imaging, University of Toronto, Toronto, ON M5S 1A1, Canada
3 Institute of Medical Science, University of Toronto, Toronto, ON M5S 1A1, Canada; michael.cusimano@unityhealth.to
4 Division of Neurosurgery, Unity Health Toronto, St. Michael's Hospital, Toronto, ON M5B 1W8, Canada
5 Division of Neurology, Unity Health Toronto, St. Michael's Hospital, Toronto, ON M5B 1W8, Canada; thomas.steeves@unityhealth.to
6 Department of Statistical Sciences, University of Toronto, Toronto, ON M5S 1A1, Canada
* Correspondence: pascal.tyrrell@utoronto.ca

Abstract: In recent years, Artificial Intelligence has been used to assist healthcare professionals in detecting and diagnosing neurodegenerative diseases. In this study, we propose a methodology to analyze functional Magnetic Resonance Imaging signals and perform classification between Parkinson's disease patients and healthy participants using Machine Learning algorithms. In addition, the proposed approach provides insights into the brain regions affected by the disease. The functional Magnetic Resonance Imaging from the PPMI and 1000-FCP datasets were pre-processed to extract time series from 200 brain regions per participant, resulting in 11,600 features. Causal Forest and Wrapper Feature Subset Selection algorithms were used for dimensionality reduction, resulting in a subset of features based on their heterogeneity and association with the disease. We utilized Logistic Regression and XGBoost algorithms to perform PD detection, achieving 97.6% accuracy, 97.5% F_1 score, 97.9% precision, and 97.7%recall by analyzing sets with fewer than 300 features in a population including men and women. Finally, Multiple Correspondence Analysis was employed to visualize the relationships between brain regions and each group (women with Parkinson, female controls, men with Parkinson, male controls). Associations between the Unified Parkinson's Disease Rating Scale questionnaire results and affected brain regions in different groups were also obtained to show another use case of the methodology. This work proposes a methodology to (1) classify patients and controls with Machine Learning and Causal Forest algorithm and (2) visualize associations between brain regions and groups, providing high-accuracy classification and enhanced interpretability of the correlation between specific brain regions and the disease across different groups.

Keywords: computer-assisted; Causal Forest; functional Magnetic Resonance Imaging; Machine Learning; Multiple Correspondence Analysis; Parkinson's disease detection

1. Introduction

Parkinson's disease (PD) is a synucleinopathy that affects various regions of the brain as it progresses [1]. It is characterized by dopamine depletion and alterations in different neural structures and neurochemical systems of the brain [2]. Functional Magnetic Resonance Imaging (fMRI) is a non-invasive neuroimaging technique that medical experts have used to assess the functional state of brain regions implicated in the motor and non-motor symptoms of PD [3]. This imaging modality has been useful to (1) detect functional abnormalities across the whole brain using connectivity and graph analysis, (2) distinguish between PD patients and healthy controls, and (3) track the progression of the disease in longitudinal studies [4].

In recent years, Artificial Intelligence (AI) has assisted healthcare professionals (HP) in the detection of neurological diseases through the early detection pathological areas [5]. To analyze the fluctuations in blood flow in the brain, shown on resting-state functional MRI (rs-fMRI), machine learning (ML) algorithms have proven to be valuable tools to (1) discover spatial patterns, (2) find dynamic functional connectivity patterns, and (3) develop diagnostics or forecasting tools [6].

One of the challenges when using ML with medical images is the high number of features available to train these algorithms. Reducing the number of features, also known as feature selection or dimensionality reduction, offers models of lower complexity and easier to interpret. Dimensionality reduction applied to medical image analysis can lead to a better understanding of the relationships between features and the Regions of Interest (ROIs) that contribute the most to the decision-making process during ailment detection. Approaches such as Radiomics are based on extracting many descriptors and then selecting the most useful ones to train the ML algorithms [7]. During rs-fMRI analysis, some of the most used techniques to reduce dimensionality and enhance ML performance include linear dimensionality reduction like PCA [8], non-linear dimensionality reduction like Laplacian eigenmaps [9], and ML-based dimensionality reduction like Support Vector Machines [10,11], LASSO [12–14], and tree-based algorithms [15].

In recent years, comparisons between correlation-based and causal-based feature selection have been of interest, as the latter techniques present different advantages over traditional correlation-based feature selection. Some advantages of causal-based methods include their ability to select the most relevant features that have a meaningful impact on the outcome, improve the generalization of the model with unseen data, and provide more consistent results, sometimes at the expense of accuracy and computational complexity [16].

In this work, we propose a methodology that leverages causal-based and correlation-based feature selection along with ML to detect PD in fMRI signals. First, we use a recent technique named Causal Forest (CF) [17], which has been used for estimating causal effects in multiple areas including medicine [18], education [19], finance [20], and software simulations [21] among others. CF is an efficient algorithm capable to rank features based on the frequency with which features are used to split data across trees. The goal is to reduce the dimensionality of the dataset and select only the features that most affect the outcome (PD or healthy). Once we have a smaller subset of features, we use the traditional correlation-based Wrapper Feature Subset Selection (WFSS) algorithm, which is a resource-intensive algorithm, to identify the best subset for a specific classifier.

To assist the interpretability of the results, we leverage statistical tools to visualize and interpret the results and provide an analysis of the Regions of Interest (ROIs) in the brain that have a strong association with the disease, according to a data-based analysis of the extracted features. Therefore, expert analysis can focus on these regions.

The objectives of this work included providing a set of features to describe the activations in the brain of PD patients, thereby achieving (1) high accuracy and (2) interpretability of PD detection with ML, and (3) the ability to visualize the ROIs and scores associated with the disease according to the Unified Parkinson's Disease Rating Scale.

2. Materials and Methods

Figure 1 shows an overview of the proposed approach, which consists of eight stages: (1) image pre-processing, (2) generation of a 200-time series that describes the temporal variations of the average gray level content in each region, (3) a bank of band-pass filters that separate each time series into 10 bands, (4) feature extraction from each filtered time series, (5) selection of the most relevant features with CF, (6) selection of the features that achieve the best classification performance with the Wrapper Feature Subset Selection (WFSS) algorithm, (7) classification to identify an individual as PD positive or negative, and (8) Multiple Correspondence Analysis (MCA) to associate each group with those brain regions with the highest average causal effect. This methodology was implemented in Python version 3.10.9. The code for this publication is publicly available at the GitHub page: https://github.com/GabrielSolana29/fmri_causalForest (accessed on 2 June 2024).

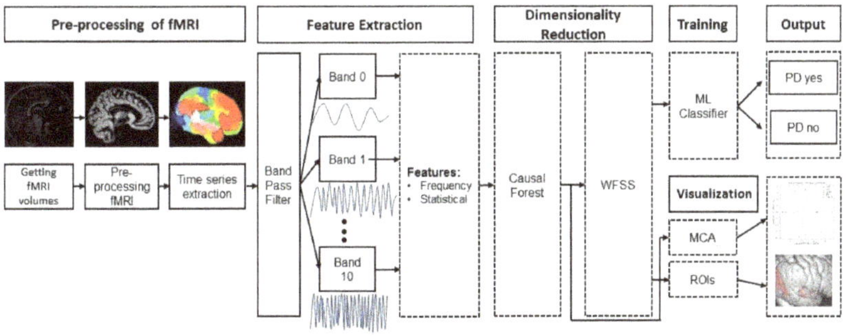

Figure 1. Methodology for PD detection and subsequent interpreting analysis of PD with rs-fMRI.

2.1. Data Set

The rs-fMRI images from PD patients and controls were obtained from the Parkinson's Progression Markers Initiative (PPMI) data set [22]. Initially, 217 PPMI fMRI images were selected for this study, coming from 46 male and 22 female patients. The Unified Parkinson's Disease Rating Scale (UPDRS) test, available on the PPMI site, was used to rate the severity and progression in 68 PD patients. Since the PPMI data set does not contain enough fMRI images from controls for a balanced study, different public data sets were used to obtain additional fMRI images. The additional data sets were obtained from the 1000 Functional Connectomes project (FCP), which contains rs-fMRI images from 33 sites [23]. Both datasets are publicly available. Some patients contributed various images to the data set since they participated in different stages of the disease. Table 1 shows the distribution of images in different groups. Each data set was categorized by sex, age range, and repetition time (TR). The voxel size ranged from 3 to 4 mm, and the number of fMRI frames ranged from 175 to 265, which accounts for 6.3 to 8.8 minutes of scanning time. Data from each of the individual datasets from the 1000 FCP that were used in this work can be found in Table S1 of the Supplementary Material.

Table 1. Distribution of images used for PD detection and analysis. The images are grouped in terms of data sets, number of patients, sex, age range, and repetition time.

Data Set	PD		Control			
	Female	Male	Female	Male	Age	TR
PPMI	70	147	4	18	38–77	2.4
1000 Functional Connectome Project	0	0	103	101	19–65	2–2.3
Total	70	147	107	119	19–77	2–2.4

To handle variations in data quality, resolution, and acquisition methods, crucial in machine learning applications, four data processing strategies were incorporated to obtain a reliable and robust method. (1) *Standardization* is a preprocessing technique that was used to make the data more uniform by centering data around the mean and scaling data to obtain a unit variance. (2) *Image registration* applies transformations like rotation, scaling and flipping to align images taken with different sensors. (3) Instead of using raw image voxel values, *feature extraction* involves the generation of relevant features from images under different domains (time, frequency), which can be more robust to image variations. (4) An *ensemble of feature selection methods* was used to reduce the impact of image variations and improve performance and robustness.

2.2. Image Pre-Processing

The fMRI volumes from the PPMI dataset were transformed to the BIDS format to standardize them. The tools used to pre-process images were fMRI-prep version 21.0.2 and Nipype version 1.6.1 [24], which create a robust and reproducible pre-processing pipeline that uses different packages such as FSL, FreeSurfer, and AFNI. The pipeline can perform co-registration, normalization, warping, noise component extraction, segmentation, and skull stripping with state-of-the-art techniques [25]. The output of the fMRI-prep pipeline includes the anatomical and the BOLD files.

The first step in the pipeline was to pre-process and skull-strip anatomical T1w structural MRI. Then, the tissues were segmented, and spatial normalization was performed. Finally, the T1w images underwent surface reconstruction to accurately map functional activations from fMRI onto the participant's brain surface [25]. BOLD images underwent reference image estimation to create a brain mask for the BOLD signals, head motion estimation, and slice time correction, where the slices were re-aligned in time to the middle of each repetition time. Susceptibility distortion correction was performed to account for the differences in the field inside the scanners. The surface created with the T1w image was used to calculate the alignment with the Echo Planar Image (EPI), then it was mapped to the standard spaces of the T1w mask, and the surfaces are generated based on the template space [25].

2.3. Generation of Time Series and Feature Extraction

For each individual, the cerebral cortex was divided into 200 regions according to the partition in the atlas generated by Schaefer et al. [26]. A time series was extracted from each brain region, which carried the temporal variation of the voxel gray intensity within the brain region. The total number of features extracted was 11,600 features per participant. These features were categorized into three groups: voxel gray intensity, frequency and connectivity.

The voxel gray intensity carried within the time series extracted from a brain region was analyzed to calculate six features that represent the brightness levels of voxels in an image, making them easy to interpret: (1) *mean value*, (2) *variance*, (3) *skewness*, (4) *kurtosis*, (5) *average auto-correlation*, and (6) *maximum wave height* of the time series, which is the vertical distance between the crest and the trough. The total number of *voxel gray intensity features* was 200 brain time series per participant × six features per time series = 1200 features per participant.

The Fourier Transform of each time series was computed to generate its frequency spectrum and extract frequency features, which provide information about the spatial distribution of voxel gray intensities at different frequency scales indicating differences in brain tissue density. The spectrum of each time series was analyzed within a bandwidth ranging from 0.01 to 0.15 Hz, where there is a significant presence of neural fluctuations and an absence of higher frequencies that contain noise from respiration and cardiac signals [27]. The frequency spectrum of a brain time series was divided into ten bands, each of 0.014 Hz. From each band, four frequency features were calculated: (1) band energy, (2) band dominant frequency, (3) variance, (4) average auto-correlation. In addition to the extraction of four features from each spectrum band, two global features were calculated by considering the entire frequency range (from 0.01 to 0.15 Hz) that includes the ten bands: (1) *dominant frequency*, (2) *energy percentage of dominant frequency*. Thus, the total number of frequency features was *200 signal spectra per participant* × (*ten bands per spectrum* × *four features per band* + *two features per entire spectrum*) = *8400 features per participant*.

At each brain region, a connectivity analysis was conducted to calculate the average correlation between each band and a baseline sinusoidal signal with a frequency corresponding to the central frequency of the band under analysis. The maximum overlap between the baseline sinusoidal and each band's time series was determined. The total number of connectivity features was *2000 connectivity features* per participant.

2.4. Feature Selection with Causal Forest

Feature selection was used to obtain a subset from the original set of 11,600 features. Feature selection reduces computational complexity, improves classification performance and enhances interpretability by finding the most relevant features while discarding noisy, redundant, or irrelevant features [17,28,29]. Classification performance is improved by removing irrelevant features that introduce noise and decrease accuracy. In addition, fewer features make it easier to understand and interpret the relationships between inputs and outputs. In this research Causal Forests (CF) and Wrappers Feature Subset Selection (WFSS) were combined to provide a stable and reliable feature subset.

Causal forests (CF) use the same principles for Random Forests (RF) [30,31], which are based on various nested binary decisions implemented with if-then-else statements that recursively split data into smaller subsets based on the values of features. The hierarchical structure of a single binary decision-making process consists of nodes and branches and that is why it is named decision tree. RFs consist of an ensemble of decision trees, where each tree is trained independently on a subset of the training data and a random subset of features [32]. RFs aggregate the decisions taken by various decision trees to make a final one, reduce overfitting, and improve generalization performance if compared to a single decision tree.

Causal forests (CF) train each tree on a random subset of features at each split in the same manner as RF. This randomization allows growing diverse trees and reduces the chance of overfitting to specific features. CFs use splitting criteria based on causal inference rather than entropy, which is used as criterion in RF. CF splitting criteria assess the relationship between features and outcomes. Thus, CFs grow more effective trees and focus on relevant features for estimating causal inference. After determining the relevance of each feature, these are ranked based on their contribution to the average contribution to Causal Forest. CFs were implemented using the open-source software developed by Microsoft Research [33].

CFs handle data heterogeneity that refers to the presence of a diversity of features within the data. CFs effectively capture heterogeneity in features across different groups, identifying specific features and allowing an understanding of how features vary across different classes.

After feature set reduction with CF, the number of features still remained high, so further reduction was conducted by using WFSS [34], an algorithm that searches for the optimal feature subset to achieve optimum PD detection. WFSS starts with an empty set of selected features. It then generates candidate feature subsets using a heuristic search method. Each candidate feature subset is used to train a classifier. The classification performance of the classifier is evaluated using a performance metric to select the subset that achieves the best performance.

2.5. Classification

The participant's features were fed to a classifier to classify an fMRI as corresponding to a PD patient or a control individual. In this research, PD detection was implemented using two classification models: the logistic classifier [35] and extreme gradient boosting (XGBoost) [36]. These two classification models have been used in various computer-assisted diagnosing applications [37–39].

The logistic classifier is a classification model that is built using a conditional probability function $P(y=1|x,\omega) = \frac{1}{1+e^{-\omega^T x}}$ and its complement $P(y=1|x,\omega) = 1 - P(y=0|x,\omega)$, where x is the feature vector extracted from one participant, $y=1$ corresponds to the outcome "PD positive", $y=0$ corresponds to the outcome "PD negative", and ω is a vector that contains the model parameters. To train the logistic classifier, a loss function was defined and maximized using the maximum likelihood algorithm.

Extreme Gradient Boosting (XGBoost) builds an ensemble of decision trees by starting with weak trees. Each decision tree is trained sequentially to correct the errors from previous trees using a gradient boosting strategy so that the new tree is stronger than the previous ones. Each new tree is trained by minimizing the residuals from previous trees, where the residuals are the difference between the predicted values and the desired ones. XGBoost optimizes the parameters of decision trees using gradient descent optimization techniques. Once individual decision trees are trained, their classification outcomes are aggregated using a weighted voting scheme to obtain the final outcome.

2.6. PD Detection Performance Assessment

PD detection performance was evaluated with k-fold cross-validation [40]. The data set was divided into k subsets or folds so that the classifier is trained and tested k times, an important strategy when the dataset is relatively small. Each time, a different fold is used for evaluation and the remaining folds are used for training. In k-fold cross-validation, all the feature vectors are used for training and testing, which leads to a more reliable evaluation of the classification performance. The performance metrics used to assess classification performance were accuracy, recall, F_1 score, and precision. These metrics were averaged across k iterations to obtain a more reliable estimate of the classification performance. In addition, k-fold cross-validation can be used to select the optimal set of model parameters while providing a reliable estimate of the classification performance.

Nested cross-validation uses a double loop: an outer loop to assess the quality of the model, and an inner loop for model selection. The outer loop is repeated ℓ times to generate ℓ different outer test sets and ℓ different outer test sets. At each iteration of the outer loop, the outer training set is further divided into k folds. Thus, the total number of trained models is $\ell \times k$. At each iteration of the outer loop, only the best inner model is evaluated on the outer test set. The total number of performance estimates is ℓ, and these are are averaged to assess the quality of the classification model.

Since some patients contributed with various images at different stages of the disease, using the same patient for training and testing was avoided. All the studies coming from one patient were in the same fold so that the information of that patient was only used for training or for testing at each of the k iterations.

2.7. Multiple Correspondence Analysis

Multiple Correspondence Analysis (MCA) is a statistical technique used to uncover associations and dependencies between characteristics or variables and groups or populations [41–43]. Medical images are characterized by features of high dimension and MCA helps in reducing the dimensionality of these variables while preserving relevant information and allowing visualization and interpretation. Visualization in a lower dimensional space enables the exploration of relationships between variables and populations simultaneously. This leads to insights into brain regions associated with PD patients.

Since features may have different scales and levels of variability, these data is normalized, ensuring that each variable contributes equally to the analysis. For each brain region, MCA computes the frequency or number of occurrences of each particular characteristic. MCA then performs a transformation on the data to retain only the two most significant dimensions based on their inertia values, which captures the maximum amount of variance. MCA calculates the (x, y) coordinates in the reduced-dimensional space. These coordinates represent the positions of brain regions and groups (male PD patients, male controls, female PD patients, female controls) along the MCA dimensions so that data can be visualized in the reduced-dimensional space using points to represent populations and brain regions and their positions reflect their similarities. MCA can assist in categorizing images into distinct groups, which corresponds to PD patients and controls, men and women.

3. Results

3.1. Parkinson Disease Detection Performance Assessment

Figure 2 shows the PD detection performance in six experiments conducted using two classifiers (XGBoost and logistic regression) in three populations: women, men, and mixed. For each set of experiments, four metrics were used to assess PD detection performance: accuracy, F1 score, precision, and recall. These results are shown in Figure 2. The complete set of experiments using nested cross-validation for each group can be found in Tables S2–S7 of the Supplementary Material.

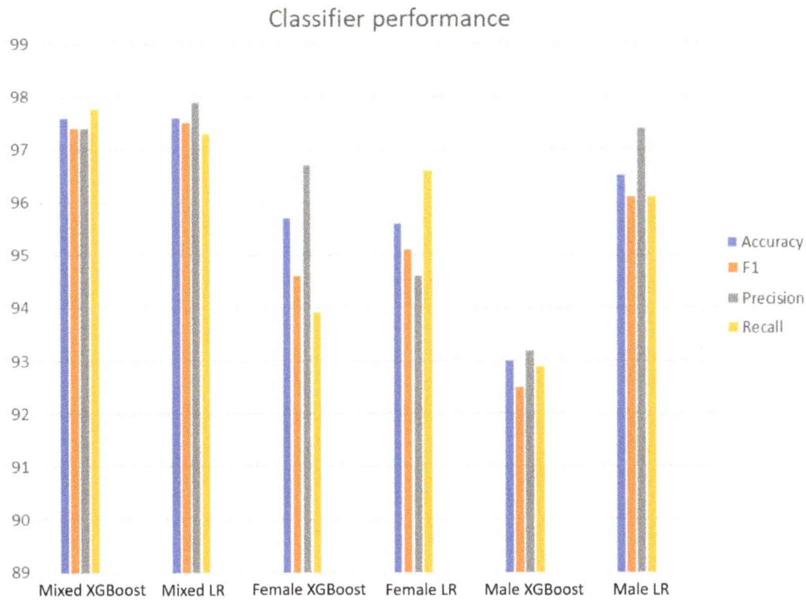

Figure 2. PD detection performance in three populations: female, male, and mixed. For each population, PD detection was implemented using two classifiers, XGBoost and logistic regression (LR), using nested cross-validation. Four metrics were used to measure detection performance: accuracy, F1 score, precision and recall.

3.2. Identification of the Most Relevant Characteristics for PD Detection

Feature extraction provided a set of 11,600 features per participant. However, the use of all the features provided classifiers with little discriminative power for PD detection. The selection of the most relevant features helped to improve classification performance and reduce model complexity. The number of features was reduced with CF, which kept the most relevant features in terms of impact across two groups, PD patients and controls. Once CF reduction was conducted, the feature set was further reduced for each classifier by running WFSS. Finally, PD detection performance was evaluated and the results are shown in Figure 2. CF and WFSS considerably reduced the feature set as shown in Table 2 that specifies (1) reduction percentage of the feature set, (2) number of features, and (3) PD detection accuracy for three population (female, male, mixed) using two classifiers (logistic regression, XGBoost).

A 98% reduction means that only 2% of the top-ranked features by CF were chosen. CF was run five times during the PD detection evaluation, setting the feature set reduction percentage to 99.9%, 99.5%, 99%, 98%, and 96%. Table 2 shows the reduction percentage and the number of features corresponding to the highest PD detection performances in six experiments. The most predominant group of features for PD detection corresponded to voxel gray intensity, followed by frequency features. Once features were selected with CF and WFSS, 56% (based on the XGBoost classifier) and 60.4% (LR) of the selected features corresponded to gray intensity, 39.2% (XGBoost) and 36.3% (LR) corresponded to frequency, 4.8% (XGBoost) and 3.3% (LR) corresponded to connectivity.

Table 2. Feature set reductions that correspond to the best PD detection accuracy using nested cross-validation. The original number of features per patient was 11,600. After CF reduction, WFSS was used to tailor the subset to each classification model.

Dataset	CF Reduction	Number of Features	PD Detection Accuracy
Mixed XGBoost	98%	192	0.976
Mixed LR	96%	26	0.976
Female XGBoost	99%	445	0.957
Female LR	96%	55	0.956
Male XGBoost	96%	16	0.930
Male LR	96%	37	0.965

3.3. *Brain Regions with the Highest Average Contribution to Causal Forest in Four Populations*

To interpret fMRI data from each participant, 11,600 features were extracted from 200 brain regions that were localized according to the partition in the atlas generated by Schaefer et al. [26]. Thus, 58 features were extracted from each brain region. Causal forest assigned a score to each feature and ranked it according to its contribution during the split of decision trees. Since causal forest build binary trees in a random manner, causal forest was run ten times to select those features that were highly ranked at least during four runs. Once CF ranked all the features, the top 4% were selected. Table 3 shows the percentage of selected features by CF from each group of features (gray intensity, frequency and connectivity) and for each population (female contro, female PD patient, male control, male PD patient).

Table 3. Percentage of features selected by CF from each group of features (voxel gray intensity, frequency, and connectivity) for each population (female control, male control, female PD patient, male PD patient).

Family of Features	CF Female Control	CF Male Control	CF Female PD	CF Male PD
Voxel gray intensity	59.21%	31.41%	43.05%	31.5%
Frequency	35.43%	65.52%	56.53%	64.82%
Connectivity	5.36%	3.07%	0.41%	3.67%

Since features were extracted from 200 brain regions, each brain region is characterized by a specific set of highly ranked features. In each brain region, the average of the scores assigned by CF to the top-ranked features was calculated. These average rankings were used to determine the regions with the highest average contribution to CF. The complete list of ROIs selected by CF, their ranking, and frequency of appearance in each group are shown in Figure S1 of the Supplementary Material.

Bubble plots are a useful tool to visually identify brain regions with the highest average contribution to causal forest in each group (female PD patients, female controls, male PD patients, and male controls). The bubble plots in Figure 3 assist in visualizing those brain regions from which highly ranked features come from. These plots show the average ranking (y axis) and the number of relevant features (bubble size) in various brain regions for two groups: female PD patients (left panel) and female controls (right panel). For each brain region, a bubble plot shows the relationship between (1) the index of the brain region, represented by the x axis; (2) its corresponding average ranking, represented by the y axis; and (3) the number of top-ranked features, represented by the dot size and color intensity. The greater the y coordinate the higher the region average ranking. The larger the bubble size the larger the number of top-ranked features in the brain region. Each brain region was assigned an integer index (x axis) that takes values from 1 to 200 since the cerebral cortex was divided into 200 regions. Figure 4 shows the corresponding bubble plots for PD male patients (left panel) and male controls (right panel). The brain regions shown in the bubble plots correspond to the top-ranked regions which were later used to conduct multiple correspondence analysis.

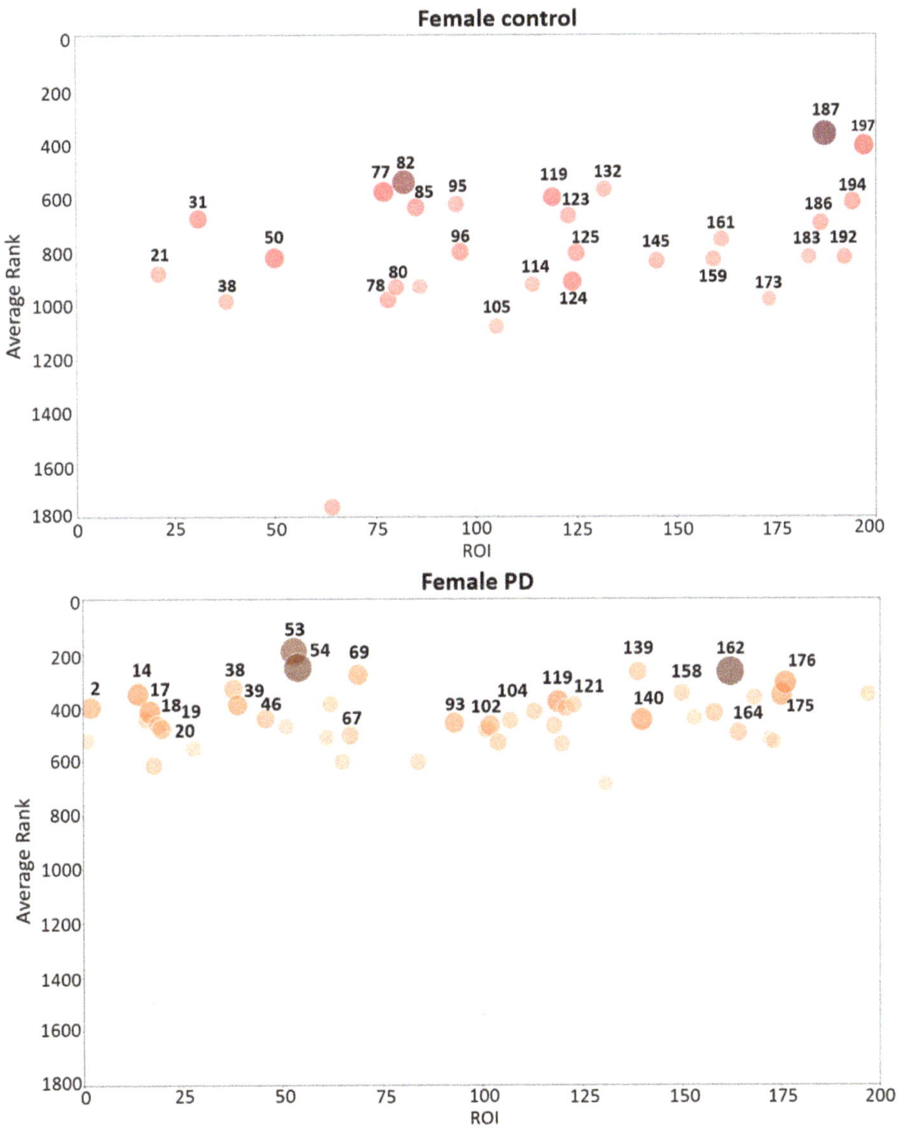

Figure 3. Bubble plot that shows brain region indexes (*X*-axis), region average rankings (*Y*-axis), and number brain features (bubble size and color intensity) for female PD patients (lower panel) and female controls (upper panel). The parcellation of the ROIs shown in the figure come from the Schaefer 2018 atlas [26].

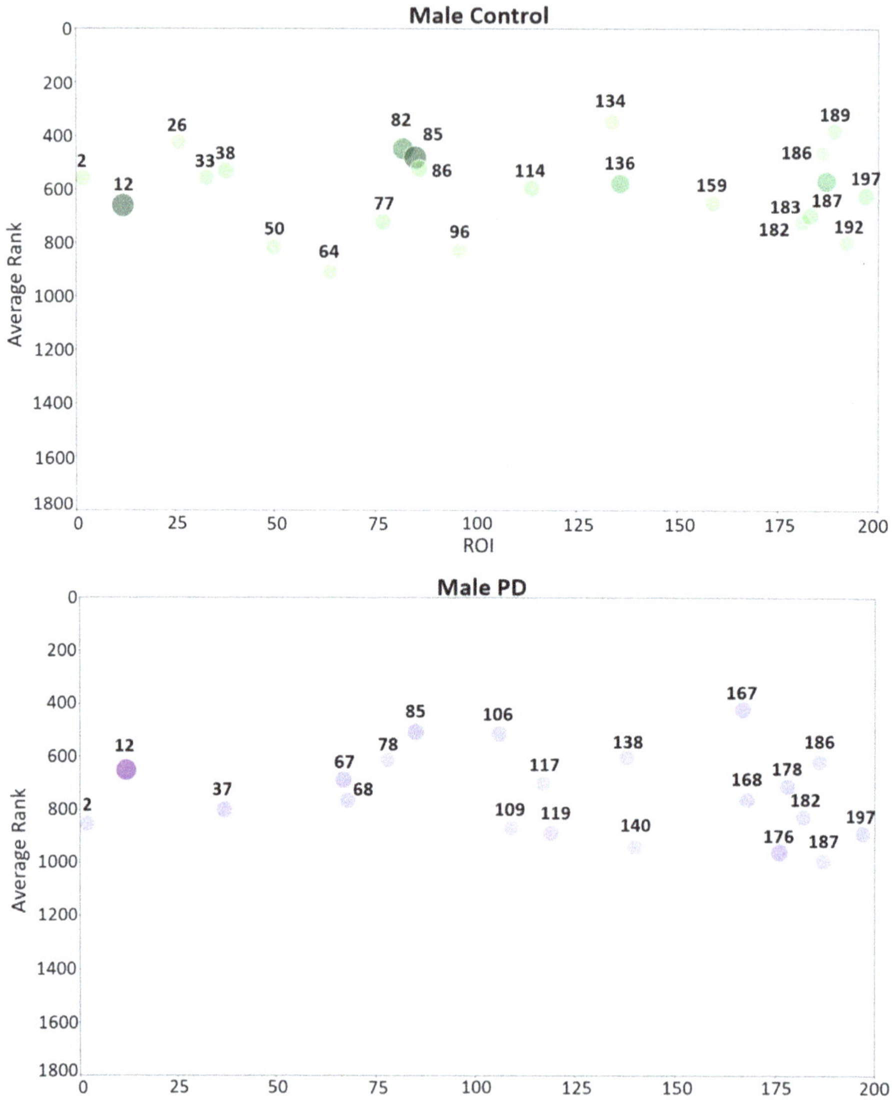

Figure 4. Bubble plot that shows brain region indexes (*X*-axis), region average rankings (*Y*-axis), and number of region features (bubble size and color intensity), for male PD patients (lower panel) and male controls (upper panel). The parcellation of the regions shown in this figure comes from the Schaefer 2018 atlas [26].

3.4. Association between Brain Regions and Populations

Causal forests provided an understanding of the relationship among features, brain regions and each specific group (female PD patients, female controls, male PD patients, male controls). MCA was then used to identify and visually interpret associations between each group and brain regions (200 brain regions were localized according to the atlas generated by Schaefer et al. [26]) by projecting these variables as points on a two-dimensional space, as shown in Figure 5. This information is valuable to understanding the conditions under which a specific brain region is more informative about a group. The bubble plots of Figures 3 and 4 show associations between brain regions and each group separately; however, interdependencies among groups are not shown. On the other hand, MCA can handle all the groups simultaneously in a single graph.

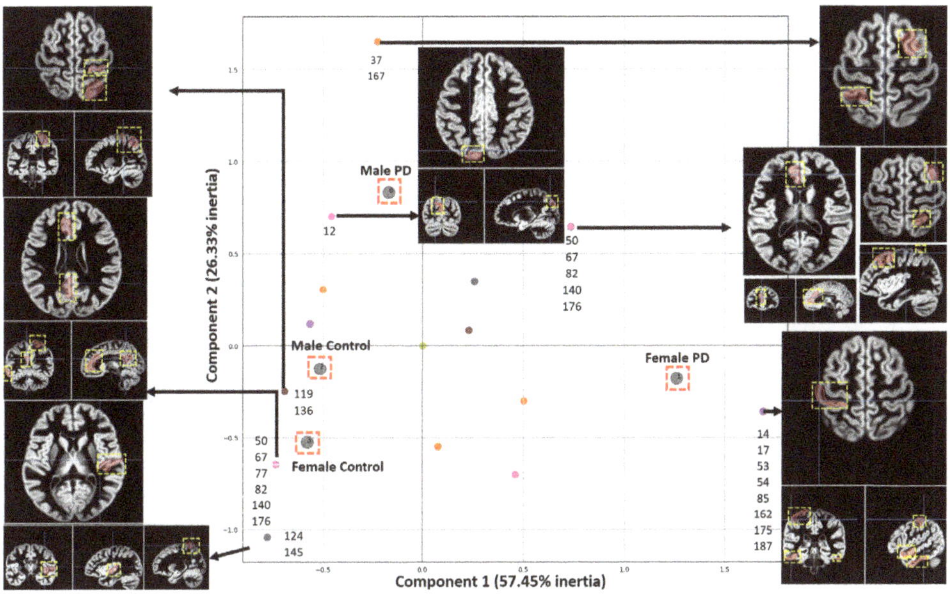

Figure 5. Associations between brain regions and groups. Each point represents an association between a group and the regions. The two most important Principal Dimensions are shown, which account for 83.78% of the total inertia. Each axis accounts for a different amount of inertia, where the weight of the *X*-axis is higher than the one of the *Y*-axis. The parcellation of the regions shown in this figure comes from the Schaefer 2018 atlas [26]. The ROIs are shown as red areas inside the yellow dashed box.

Each point enclosed in a red square in the MCA plot of Figure 5 represents a specific group. The position of each point in the MCA plot is determined by the relationships among groups and brain regions with the highest average contribution to causal forest. Points closer to each other indicate that these points are associated with similar brain regions. Since the x axis contains more inertia, the higher the separation from the center on this axis, the more relevant the associations. In some points, a list of the associated brain regions is shown. For some brain regions their corresponding fMRI views are shown. The usefulness of MCA is based upon closeness between points from the same set in a low-dimensional space since proximity between points means that observations associated with these points are themselves similar.

MCA was also used to visualize the associations between brain regions and groups (female PD patients, female controls, male PD patients, PD controls) by considering patients with a total score above 23.7 (threshold) in the third section of the UPDRS scale, as shown in Figure 6. This scale was used to correlate regions for each group based on the rankings given by causal forest. The criterion for obtaining the threshold was based on the work of [44], which specifies that the second stage of the Hoehn and Yahr scale (HYS) is met approximately at that score.

The following steps were done to find associations between the fMRI regions and the UPDRS scores using CF and MCA: (1) Features were extracted from the fMRI of each patient. (2) Data was labelled into one of four classes or groups, including female PD patients with scores below and above the threshold and male PD patients with scores below and above the threshold. (3) The CF algorithm was run to obtain the scores for each feature. (4) MCA was performed to visualize the results.

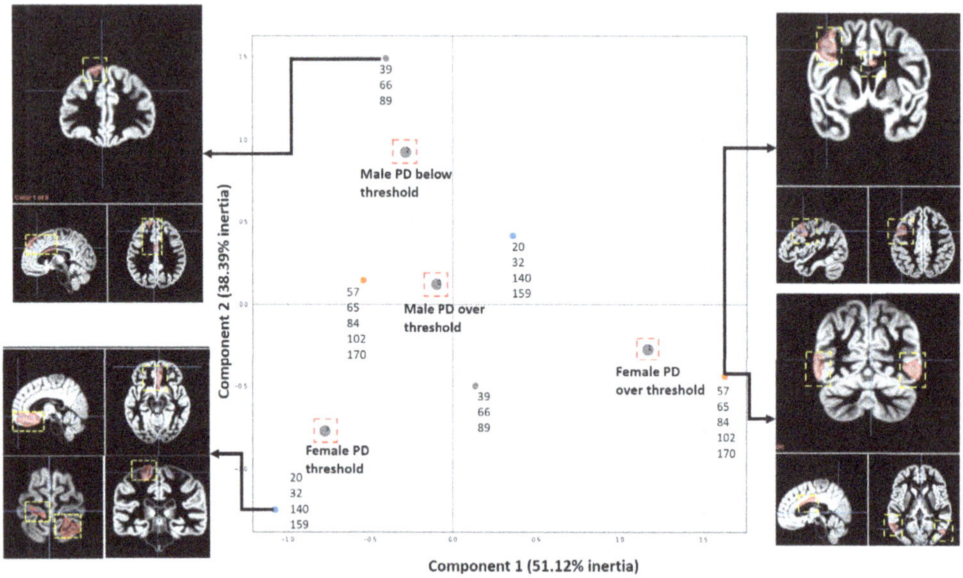

Figure 6. MCA analysis shows the associations between the scores of the motor section of the UPDRS test and the most relevant ROI resulting from running CF with the data from the patients with PD from the PPMI. Four groups were studied, including Males and Females with positive results from the third section UPDRS and Males and Females with negative results from the motor test. The most relevant regions are shown in the brain illustrations. The two Principal Dimensions with the highest inertia are shown, which account for 89.51% of the total inertia. Since each axis accounts for different amount of inertia, the weight of the *X*-axis is bigger than the one of the *Y*-axis. The ROIs are shown as red areas inside the yellow dashed box.

4. Discussion

This paper presents a new methodology to (1) assist PD detection by analyzing fMR images and (2) find relationships between brain regions and each of four groups: female PD patients, female controls, male PD patients, male controls. The fMRI studies for these groups were obtained from the PPMI and FCP public datasets. Although this research was focused on PD, the same methodology can be applied to assist the diagnosis of other neurodegenerative disorders by analyzing fMRI data.

4.1. Data Set

The majority of control images come from data sets different to the one with images from PD patients since capturing fMRI scans from controls with the same acquisition system can be very difficult due to lack of interest in participating in such studies, time or cost. In such cases, the use of different control data sets that are representative can be a practical alternative. Pre-processing was applied to images from different data sets, mainly standardization and image registration. Data pre-processing helps a classification model not to detect differences in data quality, resolution, and acquisition methods as differences between PD patients and controls. The incorporation of control data acquired from diverse settings strengthens the statistical validity of the analysis.

4.2. Selection of the Most Relevant Causal Characteristics in Each Group for PD Detection

The first step towards a reduction of the feature set and an increase in PD detection performance consisted of ranking and selecting features according to their contribution to causal forest during the split of decision trees. This ranking process mainly depends on feature relevance, which corresponds to feature heterogeneity. Once the feature set is reduced to keep a small percentage of the top ranked features by CF, WFSS was used to select the best feature subset for each classifier, resulting in dimensionality reduction and an increased PD classification performance. The reason for conducting CF followed by wrappers to reduce the feature set is that WFSS is much more time consuming than CF, where the latter is faster and requires a smaller amount of memory.

From the three families of features utilized in this work (voxel gray intensity, frequency-based, and connectivity-based features), gray intensity features were the most predominant according to CF. The WFSS algorithm mostly tends to choose frequency features.

4.3. PD Detection

Two ML models (LR and XGBoost) were used to implement PD detection, which reached the highest accuracy when using feature subsets that contained at most 4% of the original feature set, as shown in Table 2. The highest PD detection accuracy (97.6%) was reached in a mixed population. The lowest accuracy was reached when detecting PD in men (93%).

Table 4 shows the performance of various methods, including the proposed one. The Table describes these methodologies in terms of dataset, framework, and the corresponding results. The PPMI dataset is the most used one by the scientific community and it is mostly used to predict PD progression.

None of the other methods conducted experiments on male and female populations. The size of the PPMI dataset (70 female and 147 male patients) allowed for experiments to be conducted on separate populations, women and men. However, a limitation is the reduced number of fMRI studies coming from controls (4 female and 18 male controls). The use of data from the 1000 FCP allowed the generation of two balanced datasets: The data for women consisted of (1) PPMI studies from 22 patients and 4 controls and (2) 1000 FCP studies from 18 controls. The data for men consisted of (1) PPMI studies from 46 patients and 18 controls and (2) 1000 FCP studies from 28 controls.

PD detection performance was higher in women than in men. This result coincides with those obtained with MCA since the correspondence analysis indicates that the main characteristics of the female population have a discriminative power (PD patient vs. control) greater than that of the characteristics extracted from men.

Table 4. A comparison with other PD detection methods.

Author and Year	Dataset	Framework	Performance
Kazeminejad et al., 2017 [45]	Resting state fMRI data from 18 healthy controls and 19 patients	Global graph theoretical metrics were extracted and used as features to a support vector machine classifier	Accuracy of 95% with leave-one-out cross-validation
Guo et al., 2022 [46]	84 subjects (56 in stage 2 and 28 in stage 1) from PPMI data set	Long short-term memory (LSTM) network to characterize early stages of PD	Accuracy of 71.63% with 10-fold stratified cross-validation
Nguyen et al., 2020 [47]	PPMI data from 82 PD subjects are used to predict clinical severity and progression at 1 year, 2 years, and 4 years	High- and low-progression is classified with Gradient Boosting, ElasticNet and SVM	Positive predictive values up to 71% and negative predictive values up to 84%
Cao et al., 2020 [12]	Private data from fifty healthy controls and 70 PD patients	6664 features are extracted and fed to SVM	Accuracy 100%
Rubbert et al., 2019 [48]	Private data from 42 PD patients and 47 controls	Boosted Logistic Regression models were trained with correlation matrices	Accuracy 76.2%, sensitivity 81%, specificity 72.7%

Table 4. *Cont.*

Author and Year	Dataset	Framework	Performance
Fariah Haq et al., 2020 [49]	University of British Columbia data from fifteen control participants and seventeen PD patients	Graph theoretic features were extracted and fed to an SVM classifier	Sensitivity 94%
Proposed method	PPMI data from 46 male and 22 female patients. PPMI data from 18 male and 4 controls. Data from the 1000 Functional Connectcomes project dataset: 28 male and 18 female controls	Logistic Classifier and XGBoost, gray intensity and frequency features, feature selection	Accuracy 95.7% (women), 96.5% (men) and 97.6% (mixed). Precision 96.7% (women), 97.4% (men) and 97.4% (mixed). Recall 96.6% (women), 96.1% (men) and 97.7% (mixed). F_1 score 95.1% (women), 96.1% (men), 97.5% (mixed)

4.4. Associations between Brain Regions and Groups of Participants

To interpret fMRI data from 200 brain regions, MCA projects the relationships between brain regions and each of four groups (female PD patients, female controls, male PD patients, male controls) into a two-dimensional space containing the two most important principal dimensions. MCA highlights for each group those brain regions with the highest average contribution to Causal Forest. The associations along the x axis are the most relevant due to the higher inertia. MCA shows the brain regions associated with each group according to CF. Figure 5 shows that some of the regions, relevant and indicative in male PD patients, include the left hemisphere visual peripheral extrastriate superior cortex, the right hemisphere lateral dorsal prefrontal cortex, and different regions from the left hemisphere temporal parietal. In female PD patients, the most relevant and indicative regions are located in the right second quadrant of the MCA plot as shown in Figure 5 and these regions include the right and left hemisphere limbic temporal pole, the right hemisphere lateral dorsal prefrontal cortex, and multiple regions from the right and left hemisphere somatomotor region.

Figure 6 shows the associations between brain regions and each group of participants according to the UPDRS scores. These results show that the proposed approach can identify the relationships between features extracted from fMRI studies and the scores of the progression of the disease's motor symptoms. Figure 6 illustrates the ROIs most associated with one group (female above/below threshold or male below/above threshold) according to the CF ranking when compared to the other three groups. We are visualizing only the regions that are characteristic of one group; for example, the group of females above threshold shows that the right central visual cortex was selected as a ROI. This does not mean that other regions, such as the left hemisphere's somatomotor network in the group of females below the threshold, are unaffected.

4.5. Limitations

A valid concern exists where nested cross-validation does not increase confidence in the PD detection results and introduces additional parameters that may be over-tuned to the training data without proper held-out validation on unseen data. This may lead to limited ability to reveal generalizing patterns about the disease state. The controls that provided data for this work are substantially younger than the patients, and AI models are well-known to be sensitive to age-related changes in MR imaging. Distinguishing between younger and older patients could account for a substantial portion of the contrast between PD patients and controls. For these reasons, this is a proof of concept that remains to be validated.

4.6. Parkinsonism vs. Parkinson as Future Work

The proposed method could be used to discriminate between patients with PD and patients with Parkinsonism, which is a more complex problem. As more studies from

PD patients become available, applying the proposed method to a longitudinal study with multiple images from each patient could shed some light on the progression of brain affectations from the disease.

Understanding subtypes of PD (tremor-dominant and akinetic-rigid) can be enhanced with machine learning techniques to provide insights into the neural mechanisms underlying the different manifestations of PD [50]. Causal forest along with multiple correspondence analysis might facilitate the differentiation between akinetic-rigid and tremor-dominant subtypes, which differ in symptomatology and progression by selecting and identifying features in imaging data for identification of PD subtypes.

5. Conclusions

This work proposes a method for (1) classifying fMRI studies as PD positives or negatives and (2) visualizing the relationships between brain regions and four groups in a two-dimensional plot. The four groups include fMRI from women with and without PD, and men with and without PD. The characteristics extracted from the fMRI included voxel gray intensity, frequency-based, and connectivity features extracted from 200 regions. CF was used for dimensionality reduction by selecting those features that contribute the most to the representation of each particular group (male PD patients, male controls, female PD patients, female controls). The results showed that different brain regions are associated with a specific population. In addition, the results showed that regions that contributed the most in PD patients with a high UPDRS motor score are different from those that corresponded to patients with low scores. The classification of fMRI studies achieved a performance above 92% in four metrics (accuracy, F_1 score and recall) by analyzing a reduced number of features and maintaining a high level of interpretability.

Supplementary Materials: The following supporting information can be downloaded at: https://www.mdpi.com/article/10.3390/tomography10060068/s1.

Author Contributions: G.S.-L.: Conceptualization, Methodology, Software, Formal Analysis, Investigation, Writing—Original Draft, Visualization. M.D.C.: Writing—Review & Editing. T.S.: Writing—Review & Editing, R.R.-R.: Writing—Original Draft, Visualization. P.N.T.: Conceptualization, Methodology, Formal analysis, Writing—Review & Editing, Project administration. All authors have read and agreed to the published version of the manuscript.

Funding: This research received no external funding.

Institutional Review Board Statement: The Institutional Review Board approved the PPMI program of each participating site and all participants gave their written informed consent to participate in the program. The ethics board for PPMI Clinical study from WCG with approval number 20200597I. The University of Rochester Institutional Review Board oversaw the resting-state functional Magnetic Resonance Imaging studies for the PPMI.

Informed Consent Statement: All participants provided written informed consent to participate under the PPMI consent. PPMI is registered in ClinicalTrials.gov as NCT01141023 (accessed on 2 June 2024).

Data Availability Statement: This analysis used data openly available from PPMI. Data from Parkinson's disease patients used in the preparation of this article were obtained from the Parkinson's Progression Markers Initiative (PPMI) database (accessed on 25 June 2022) (www.ppmi-info.org/access-dataspecimens/download-data), RRID:SCR 006431. For up-to-date information on the study, visit www.ppmi-info.org; Data for healthy controls were obtained from the 1000 Functional Connectomes Project (accessed on 3 July 2022) (http://fcon_1000.projects.nitrc.org).

Acknowledgments: PPMI—a public-private partnership—is funded by the Michael J. Fox Foundation for Parkinson's Research and funding partners, including 4D Pharma, Abbvie, AcureX, Allergan, Amathus Therapeutics, Aligning Science Across Parkinson's, AskBio, Avid Radiopharmaceuticals, BIAL, BioArctic, Biogen, Biohaven, BioLegend, BlueRock Therapeutics, Bristol-Myers Squibb, Calico Labs, Capsida iotherapeutics, Celgene, Cerevel Therapeutics, Coave Therapeutics, DaCapo Brainscience, Denali, Edmond J. Safra Foundation, Eli Lilly, Gain Therapeutics, GE HealthCare, Genentech, GSK, Golub Capital, Handl Therapeutics, Insitro, Jazz Pharmaceuticals, Johnson & Johnson Innovative Medicine, Lundbeck, Merck, Meso cale Discovery, Mission Therapeutics, Neurocrine Biosciences, Neuron23, Neuropore, Pfizer, Piramal, Prevail Therapeutics, Roche, Sanofi, Servier, Sun Pharma Advanced Research Company, Takeda, Teva, UCB, Vanqua Bio, Verily, Voyager Therapeutics, the Weston Family Foundation and Yumanity Therapeutics.

Conflicts of Interest: The authors declare no conflicts of interest.

Abbreviations

The following abbreviations are used in this manuscript:

AI	Artificial Intelligence
CF	Causal Forest
EPI	Echo Planar Image
FCP	1000 Functional Connectomes Project
fMRI	Functional Magnetic Resonance Imaging
HP	Healthcare Professionals
HYS	Hoehn and Yahr scale
LASSO	Least Absolute Shrinkage and Selection Operator
MCA	Multiple Correspondence Analysis
ML	Machine Learning
PD	Parkinson's Disease
PPMI	Parkinson's Progression Markers Initiative
RF	Random Forest
ROI	Region of Interest
rs-fMRI	Resting-State Functional Magnetic Resonance Imaging
TR	Repetition Time
UPDRS	Unified Parkinson's Disease Rating Scale
WFSS	Wrapper Feature Subset Selection
XGBoost	Extreme Gradient Boosting

References

1. Braak, H.; Ghebremedhin, E.; Rüb, U.; Bratzke, H.; Del Tredici, K. Stages in the development of Parkinson's disease-related pathology. *Cell Tissue Res.* **2004**, *318*, 121–134. [CrossRef] [PubMed]
2. Moustafa, A.A.; Chakravarthy, S.; Phillips, J.R.; Gupta, A.; Keri, S.; Polner, B.; Frank, M.J.; Jahanshahi, M. Motor symptoms in Parkinson's disease: A unified framework. *Neurosci. Biobehav. Rev.* **2016**, *68*, 727–740. [CrossRef] [PubMed]
3. Ryman, S.G.; Poston, K.L. MRI biomarkers of motor and non-motor symptoms in Parkinson's disease. *Park. Relat. Disord.* **2020**, *73*, 85–93. [CrossRef] [PubMed]
4. Tahmasian, M.; Bettray, L.M.; van Eimeren, T.; Drzezga, A.; Timmermann, L.; Eickhoff, C.R.; Eickhoff, S.B.; Eggers, C. A systematic review on the applications of resting-state fMRI in Parkinson's disease: Does dopamine replacement therapy play a role? *Cortex* **2015**, *73*, 80–105. [CrossRef] [PubMed]
5. Nawaz, A.; Rehman, A.U.; Ali, T.M.; Hayat, Z.; Khaleeq, U.; Zaman, U.; Ali, A.R. A Comprehensive Literature Review of Application of Artificial Intelligence in Functional Magnetic Resonance Imaging for Disease Diagnosis ABSTRACT. *Appl. Artif. Intell.* **2021**, *35*, 1420–1438. [CrossRef]
6. Khosla, M.; Jamison, K.; Ngo, G.H.; Kuceyeski, A.; Sabuncu, M.R. Machine learning in resting-state fMRI analysis. *Magn. Reson. Imaging* **2019**, *64*, 101–121. [CrossRef] [PubMed]
7. van Timmeren, J.E.; Cester, D.; Tanadini-Lang, S.; Alkadhi, H.; Baessler, B. Radiomics in medical imaging—"How-to" guide and critical reflection. *Insights Imaging* **2020**, *11*, 91. [PubMed]
8. Calesella, F.; Testolin, A.; De Filippo De Grazia, M.; Zorzi, M. A comparison of feature extraction methods for prediction of neuropsychological scores from functional connectivity data of stroke patients. *Brain Inform.* **2021**, *8*, 8. [CrossRef] [PubMed]
9. Pospelov, N.; Tetereva, A.; Martynova, O.; Anokhin, K. The Laplacian eigenmaps dimensionality reduction of fMRI data for discovering stimulus-induced changes in the resting-state brain activity. *Neuroimage Rep.* **2021**, *1*, 100035. [CrossRef]
10. Shi, D.; Yao, X.; Li, Y.; Zhang, H.; Wang, G.; Wang, S.; Ren, K. Classification of Parkinson's disease using a region-of-interest- and resting-state functional magnetic resonance imaging-based radiomics approach. *Brain Imaging Behav.* **2022**, *16*, 2150–2163. [CrossRef]
11. Liu, G.; Lu, W.; Qiu, J.; Shi, L. Identifying individuals with attention-deficit/hyperactivity disorder based on multisite resting-state functional magnetic resonance imaging: A radiomics analysis. *Hum. Brain Mapp.* **2023**, *44*, 3433–3445. [CrossRef] [PubMed]
12. Cao, X.; Wang, X.; Xue, C.; Zhang, S.; Huang, Q.; Liu, W. A Radiomics Approach to Predicting Parkinson's Disease by Incorporating Whole-Brain Functional Activity and Gray Matter Structure. *Front. Neurosci.* **2020**, *14*, 751. [PubMed]
13. Zhang, X.; Cao, X.; Xue, C.; Zheng, J.; Zhang, S.; Huang, Q.; Liu, W. Aberrant functional connectivity and activity in Parkinson's disease and comorbidity with depression based on radiomic analysis. *Brain Behav.* **2021**, *11*, e02103. [CrossRef] [PubMed]

14. Shi, D.; Zhang, H.; Wang, G.; Wang, S.; Yao, X.; Li, Y.; Guo, Q.; Zheng, S.; Ren, K. Machine learning for detecting parkinson's disease by resting-state functional magnetic resonance imaging: A multicenter radiomics analysis. *Front. Aging Neurosci.* **2022**, *14*, 806828. [CrossRef] [PubMed]
15. Shi, C.; Zhang, J.; Wu, X. An fMRI feature selection method based on a minimum spanning tree for identifying patients with autism. *Symmetry* **2020**, *12*, 1995. [CrossRef]
16. Yu, K.; Liu, L.; Li, J. A unified view of causal and non-causal feature selection. *ACM Trans. Knowl. Discov. Data (TKDD)* **2021**, *15*, 63. [CrossRef]
17. Athey, S.; Tibshirani, J.; Wager, S. Generalized random forests. *Ann. Stat.* **2019**, *47*, 1179–1203. [CrossRef]
18. Venkatasubramaniam, A.; Mateen, B.A.; Shields, B.M.; Hattersley, A.T.; Jones, A.G.; Vollmer, S.J.; Dennis, J.M. Comparison of causal forest and regression-based approaches to evaluate treatment effect heterogeneity: An application for type 2 diabetes precision medicine. *BMC Med. Inform. Decis. Mak.* **2023**, *23*, 110. [CrossRef]
19. Suk, Y.; Kang, H.; Kim, J.S. Random forests approach for causal inference with clustered observational data. *Multivar. Behav. Res.* **2021**, *56*, 829–852. [CrossRef]
20. Gulen, H.; Jens, C.; Page, T.B. Balancing External vs. Internal Validity: An Application of Causal Forest in Finance. October 2022. Available online: https://ssrn.com/abstract=3583685 (accessed on 2 June 2024). [CrossRef]
21. Clark, A.G.; Foster, M.; Prifling, B.; Walkinshaw, N.; Hierons, R.M.; Schmidt, V.; Turner, R.D. Testing Causality in Scientific Modelling Software. *ACM Trans. Softw. Eng. Methodol.* **2023**, *33*, 10. [CrossRef]
22. Michael, J. Fox Foundation for Parkinson Research Data Resources. 2018. Available online: https://www.michaeljfox.org/data-resources (accessed on 2 June 2024).
23. Nueroimaging Tools and Resources Collaboratory. Neuroimaging Data Repository. 2023. Available online: https://www.nitrc.org/xnat/index.php (accessed on 2 June 2024).
24. Esteban, O.; Markiewicz, C.J.; Blair, R.W.; Moodie, C.A.; Isik, A.I.; Erramuzpe, A.; Kent, J.D.; Goncalves, M.; DuPre, E.; Snyder, M.; et al. fMRIPrep: A robust preprocessing pipeline for functional MRI. *Nat. Methods* **2019**, *16*, 111–116. [CrossRef] [PubMed]
25. The fMRIPrep Developers fMRIPrep: A Robust Preprocessing Pipeline for fMRI Data. 2023. Available online: https://fmriprep.org/en/stable/ (accessed on 2 June 2024).
26. Schaefer, A.; Kong, R.; Gordon, E.M.; Laumann, T.O.; Zuo, X.N.; Holmes, A.J.; Eickhoff, S.B.; Yeo, B.T.T. Local-global parcellation of the human cerebral cortex from intrinsic functional connectivity MRI. *Cereb Cortex* **2018**, *28*, 3095–3114. [CrossRef]
27. Gohel, S.R.; Biswal, B.B. Functional integration between brain regions at rest occurs in multiple-frequency bands. *Brain Connect.* **2015**, *5*, 23–34. [CrossRef] [PubMed]
28. Jawadekar, N.; Kezios, K.; Odden, M.C.; Stingone, J.A.; Calonico, S.; Rudolph, K.; Hazzouri, A.Z.A. Practical Guide to Honest Causal Forests for Identifying Heterogeneous Treatment Effects. *Am. J. Epidemiol.* **2023**, *192*, 1155–1165. [CrossRef]
29. Spirtes, P. Introduction to causal inference. *J. Mach. Learn. Res.* **2010**, *11*, 1643–1662.
30. Ho, T.K. Random Decision Forests. In Proceedings of the 3rd International Conference on Document Analysis and Recognition, San Jose, CA, USA, 14–16 August 1995; pp. 278–282.
31. Ho, T.K. The Random Subspace Method for Constructing Decision Forests. *IEEE Trans. Pattern Anal. Mach. Intell.* **1998**, *20*, 832–844. [CrossRef]
32. Roobaert, D.; Karakoulas, G.; Chawla, N.V. Information gain, correlation and support vector machines. *Stud. Fuzziness Soft Comput.* **2006**, *207*, 463–470.
33. Oprescu, M.; Syrgkanis, V.; Battocchi, K.; Hei, M.; Lewis, G. EconML: A Python Package for ML-Based Heterogeneous Treatment Effects Estimation. In Proceedings of the 33rd Conference on Neural Information Processing Systems (NeurIPS 2019), Vancouver, BC, Canada, 8–14 December 2019. Available online: https://cpb-us-w2.wpmucdn.com/sites.coecis.cornell.edu/dist/a/238/files/2019/12/Id_112_final.pdf (accessed on 2 June 2024).
34. Kohavi, R.; John, G.H. Wrappers for feature subset selection. *Artif. Intell.* **1997**, *97*, 273–324. [CrossRef]
35. James, G.; Witten, D.; Hastie, T.; Tibshirani, R. *An Introduction to Statistical Learning with Applications in R*; Springer Texts in Statistics; Springer: New York, NY, USA, 2013.
36. Chen, T.; Guestrin, C. XGBoost: A Scalable Tree Boosting System. In Proceedings of the 22nd ACM SIGKDD International Conference on Knowledge Discovery and Data Mining (KDD '16), San Francisco, CA, USA, 13–17 August 2016; pp. 1–13.
37. Budholiya, K.; Shrivastava, S.K.; Sharma, V. An Optimized XGBoost Based Diagnostic System for Effective Prediction of Heart Disease. *J. King Saud Univ. Comput. Inf. Sci.* **2022**, *34*, 4514–4523. [CrossRef]
38. Farzipour, A.; Elmi, R.; Nasiri, H. Detection of Monkeypox Cases Based on Symptoms Using XGBoost and Shapley Additive Explanations Methods. *Diagnostics* **2023**, *13*, 2391. [CrossRef]
39. Guan, X.; Du, Y.; Ma, R.; Teng, N.; Ou, S.; Zhao, H.; Li, X. Construction of the XGBoost model for early lung cancer prediction based on metabolic indices. *BMC Med. Inform. Decis. Mak.* **2023**, *23*, 107. [CrossRef]
40. Dutschmann, T.M.; Kinzel, L.; ter Laak, A.; Baumann, K. Large-scale evaluation of k-fold cross-validation ensembles for uncertainty estimation. *J. Cheminform.* **2023**, *15*, 832–844. [CrossRef] [PubMed]
41. Soares-Costa, P.; Correia-Santos, N.; Cunha, P.; Cotter, J.; Sousa1, N. The use of multiple correspondence analysis to explore associations between categories of qualitative variables in Healthy ageing. *J. Aging Res.* **2013**, *2013*, 302163. [CrossRef]
42. Ayele, D.; Zewotir, T.; Mwambi, H. Multiple correspondence analysis as a tool for analysis of large health surveys in African settings. *Afr. Health Sci.* **2014**, *14*, 1036–1045. [CrossRef]

43. Alhuzali, T.; Beh, E.; Stojanovski, E. Multiple correspondence analysis as a tool for examining Nobel Prize data from 1901 to 2018. *PLoS ONE* **2022**, *14*, e0265929. [CrossRef]
44. Shulman, L.M.; Gruber-Baldini, A.L.; Anderson, K.E.; Fishman, P.S.; Reich, S.G.; Weiner, W.J. The clinically important difference on the unified Parkinson's disease rating scale. *Arch. Neurol.* **2010**, *67*, 64–70. [CrossRef]
45. Kazeminejad, A.; Golbabaei, S.; Soltanian-Zadeh, H. Graph theoretical metrics and machine learning for diagnosis of Parkinson's disease using rs-fMRI. In Proceedings of the 2017 Artificial Intelligence and Signal Processing Conference (AISP), Shiraz, Iran, 25–27 October 2017; pp. 134–139.
46. Guo, X.; Tinaz, S.; Dvornek, N.C. Characterization of Early Stage Parkinson's Disease From Resting-State fMRI Data Using a Long Short-Term Memory Network. *Front. Neuroimaging* **2022**, *1*, 952084. [CrossRef] [PubMed]
47. Nguyen, K.P.; Raval, V.; Treacher, A.; Mellema, C.; Yu, F.; Pinho, M.C.; Subramaniam, R.M.; Richard B. Dewey, J.; Montillo, A. Predicting Parkinson's disease trajectory using clinical and neuroimaging baseline measures. *Park. Relat. Disord.* **2021**, *84*, 44–51 [CrossRef]
48. Rubbert, C.; Mathys, C.; Jockwitz, C.; Hartmann, C.J.; Eickhoff, S.B.; Hoffstaedter, F.; Caspers, S.; Eickhoff, C.R.; Sigl, B.; Teichert, N.A.; et al. Machine-learning identifies Parkinson's disease patients based on resting-state between-network functional connectivity. *Br. J. Radiol.* **2019**, *92*, 20180886. [CrossRef]
49. Haq, N.F.; Cai, J.; Yu, T.; McKeown, M.J.; Wang, Z.J. *Parkinson's Disease Detection from fMRI-Derived Brainstem Regional Functional Connectivity Networks*; Springer: Berlin/Heidelberg, Germany, 2020; pp. 33–43.
50. Ram, A. Analysis, Identification and Prediction of Parkinson's disease sub-types and progression through Machine Learning. *Open Access Libr. J.* **2024**, *11*, 1–15. [CrossRef]

Journal of
Clinical Medicine

MDPI

Review

Artificial Intelligence in Coronary Artery Calcium Scoring

Afolasayo A. Aromiwura [1] and Dinesh K. Kalra [2,*]

[1] Department of Medicine, University of Louisville, Louisville, KY 40202, USA
[2] Division of Cardiology, Department of Medicine, University of Louisville, Louisville, KY 40202, USA
* Correspondence: dinesh.kalra@louisville.edu; Tel.: +1-502-852-9505; Fax: +1-502-852-6233

Abstract: Cardiovascular disease (CVD), particularly coronary heart disease (CHD), is the leading cause of death in the US, with a high economic impact. Coronary artery calcium (CAC) is a known marker for CHD and a useful tool for estimating the risk of atherosclerotic cardiovascular disease (ASCVD). Although CACS is recommended for informing the decision to initiate statin therapy, the current standard requires a dedicated CT protocol, which is time-intensive and contributes to radiation exposure. Non-dedicated CT protocols can be taken advantage of to visualize calcium and reduce overall cost and radiation exposure; however, they mainly provide visual estimates of coronary calcium and have disadvantages such as motion artifacts. Artificial intelligence is a growing field involving software that independently performs human-level tasks, and is well suited for improving CACS efficiency and repurposing non-dedicated CT for calcium scoring. We present a review of the current studies on automated CACS across various CT protocols and discuss consideration points in clinical application and some barriers to implementation.

Keywords: artificial intelligence; computed tomography; cardiac; coronary artery calcium scoring

1. Introduction

Coronary heart disease (CHD) is the most common type of cardiovascular disease (CVD) in the United States, and it accounted for 696,937 deaths in 2020 [1]. In addition, approximately USD 407.3 billion in CVD-associated costs were incurred in the US between 2018 and 2019. Considering the fact that around 50% of CVD-associated deaths occur in asymptomatic individuals or patients without prior CVD diagnoses, atherosclerotic CVD (ASCVD) risk stratification and modification are essential aspects for ensuring CVD prevention and subsequent disease cost reduction, early diagnosis, and the reduction of mortality and major adverse cardiovascular events (MACE) [2]. Coronary artery calcium (CAC) is an established indicator of coronary artery disease (CAD) that is associated with disease burden and ASCVD risk and is quantified by ECG-gated non-contrast computed tomography (NCCT) [3,4]. CAC scoring (CACS) by ECG-gated NCCT is a total measure of calcium density and plaque attenuation, which may be used to inform the decision for therapy initiation [4]. The Agatston method for CACS estimates coronary artery calcium lesion scores, defined as the product of the total area of calcified plaque (in squared millimeters) and the peak calcium density weighing score [5]. Absolute CAC scores are then assigned to each coronary vessel based on the maximal Hounsfield units (HU) and may be associated with a visual score such that 0 = none, 1–10 = minimal, 11–100 = mild, 101–400 = moderate, and >400 = severe. Visual scores are subjective estimations of CAC based on visual analysis of non-ECG-gated scans [6].

Several society guidelines including the American College of Cardiology/American Heart Association (ACC/AHA), European Society of Cardiology, and National Lipid Association have recommended the use of CACS to guide preventive therapy initiation in specific populations [7]. The ACC/AHA recommends CACS in patients with intermediate risk and some with borderline risk and uncertainty regarding risk-based preventive therapy; statin initiation is recommended when CACS $\geq$ 100 [8]. Other risk stratification tools, such as the Multi-Ethnic Study of Atherosclerosis (MESA) risk score, a race-, age-, and sex-adjusted score that incorporates CACS with other known CAD risk factors, have been shown to improve the estimation of 10-year CVD risk. However, the extensive use of CACS is still limited by several factors including its lack of insurance coverage, the need for a dedicated ECG-gated NCCT protocol, and the need for specialized imaging lab personnel, particularly in high-volume imaging labs and institutions. Although the application of non-dedicated CTs (CTs acquired for other purposes besides coronary artery calcium scoring) to manual CACS and calcium visual estimation has been described by several authors to have good correlation to Agatston scoring, it is not the current standard of practice [9–11].

As artificial intelligence (AI) continues to play an increasing role in medicine and radiology, it offers unique advantages to CACS and CVD risk estimation [12–14]. Beyond improving the time-consuming, labor-intensive, and repetitive tasks of calcium segmentation and quantification, AI offers the possibility of acquiring quantitative CACS from non-dedicated routine chest CT protocols acquired for other purposes, including low-dose CT (LDCT), cardiac CT angiography (CCTA), and positron emission tomography (PET)/CT attenuation scans. Non-dedicated CT use also has the advantage of decreased summative radiation exposure. There are a few existing commercially available semiautomatic and automatic CACS software products, some of which were utilized in the studies discussed below (Table 1). Although semi-automatic tools are useful, they still require manual allocation of automatically segmented and detected calcium; therefore, they are user-dependent and time-consuming.

Table 1. Commercially available systems for automatic CACS.

Company	Software	Applications
General Electric Healthcare, IL, United States	CardIQ Suite	Coronary calcium segmentation and coronary artery labeling with total and per-region scoring.
Arytra Ltd., West Perth, Australia	DeepC architecture	Coronary artery calcium detection and plaque volume measurement.
Coreline Soft, Seoul, Korea	AVIEW CAC	Coronarartery segmentation, calcium analysis, and automatic report generation.
Nanox AI, Petah Tikva, Israel	HealthCCSng	Coronary calcium quantification and categorization.
Siemens Healthineers, PA, United State	AI-Rad Companion (Cardiovascular)	Coronary calcium and heart volume quantification in gated and non-gated NCCT. Does not perform Agatston scoring [15].

2. Deep Learning and Artificial Neural Networks

The multi-layered neural networks of deep learning (DL) algorithms learn from inputs of complex datasets and automatically produce outputs by recognizing intricate data relationships that might otherwise be missed at a human level. DL techniques are widespread and commonly applied in speech recognition, computer vision, and language processing. In recent years, DL has been increasingly applied across various cardiovascular imaging modalities for various tasks including image acquisition, reconstruction, segmentation, analysis, and prognosis [16]. In particular, convolutional neural networks (CNNs) are the most commonly used in cardiovascular imaging and automated CACS. CNNs comprise several specialized network layers that identify image-based features and can create feature maps that aid the prediction of the final model output [17].

3. Studies of CACS Automation

A fully automated CACS software product should be able to perform coronary artery segmentation, coronary calcium analysis, and coronary artery labeling (Figure 1). Given the role of CACS as a risk stratification tool, the process of automatic CACS model development and testing should demonstrate excellent generalizability and ability to assess the risk of ASCVD across a diverse population. Models that are limited in dataset size and diversity tend to have overfitting and poor generalizability, a situation where they perform well with training data, but are unable to make accurate predictions with test data; these models underperform in the real world [17,18]. The training data typically form the majority of the entire dataset and are utilized for model development, while the test data are used to assess model performance after model training [17]. Some of the consequences of poor generalizability are reductions in accuracy and greater variability in model sensitivity and specificity when tested against external datasets. For instance, one CNN algorithm was developed for hepatic fibrosis categorization on ultrasound images and demonstrated an accuracy of 83.5% when tested against the internal dataset; however, the model accuracy reduced to 76.4% with external testing, reflecting the model's inability to generate a reliable output when small changes were made to its input data such as a new or external testing dataset [19]. Therefore, the assessment of model generalizability through external validation is essential. The development of diverse multi-detector and multi-institutional data banks will be necessary for building clinically relevant AI risk assessment models.

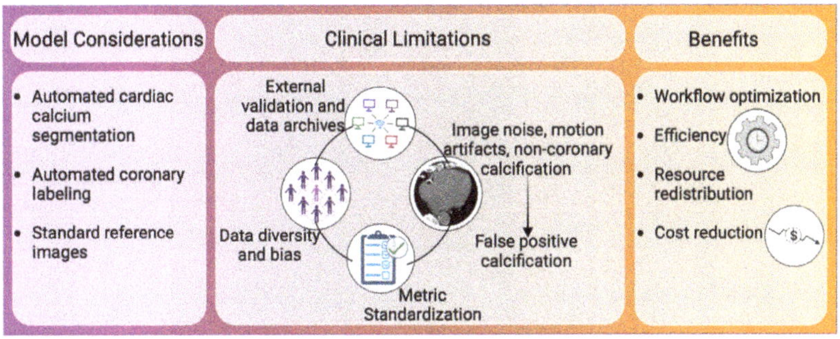

Figure 1. Overview of Artificial Intelligence in Coronary Artery Calcium Scoring. Automatic cardiac segmentation and coronary labeling are hallmarks of proposed models. Improvement of data diversity, data repositories, external validation, image artifacts, and metric standardization will enhance the proposed models. CACS automation optimizes workflow, reduces cost, and allows redistribution of resources in image post-processing labs.

Beyond the major task performances, the reduction of false positives and appropriate reference standards are necessary for reliable model development. Proposed models should have the ability to focus on target coronary anatomy to avoid misclassification of aortic and valvular calcifications as coronary calcifications [20–22]. Various approaches have been described for region-of-interest localization and segmentation including conventional manual segmentation methods, bounding boxes with manual lesion localization via coordinates, and automatic coronary extraction [20,23,24]. Additionally, though gated and non-gated NCCT CACS have been shown to have good agreement, they may differ in mean absolute scores, so manually derived gated CACS are preferred as a reference standard for comparing automated scores. However, in models trained on non-dedicated CT, reference manual scores from non-dedicated CT also allow the independent evaluation of model accuracy.

3.1. ECG-Gated and Non-Gated NCCT

Over time, various approaches, model types, and datasets have been proposed for CACS automation with varying results (Table 2). One study, by Eng et al., proposed two CNN-based models for automatic scoring using gated coronary CT and non-gated chest CT, respectively (Figure 2) [25]. Automatic scores from both models demonstrated an almost-perfect correlation with manual scoring (Cohen's kappa 0.89, $p < 0.0001$). The non-gated model also had very good sensitivity (71–94%) and positive predictive value (PPV) (88–100%) and the gated model had a faster average scoring time (3.5 ± 2.1 s vs. 261 s).

Other researchers have proposed models trained on gated CT images and compared them to gated CT-derived reference manual scores. For instance, Ihdayhid et al. used a CNN-based model developed by Artrya Ltd. for automatic CACS in gated NCCT scans [22]. The model included separate CNNs for aortic and cardiac segmentation to distinguish aortic from coronary calcifications and decrease the false positive rate of the proposed model. Overall, the proposed model efficiently produced automatic scores that had excellent agreement with manual scoring (κ = 0.90 [95 CI, 0.88–0.9], $p < 0.001$).

Table 2. Artificial intelligence in CACS.

Author	N	Test Image Type/Protocol	Reference Image	Results	Model
Eng et al., 2021 [25]	Gated CT model (retrospective 866 scans, prospective test 55 scans) Non-gated routine chest CT (341 training, Stanford total 215 scans [42 test], MESA total 232 scans [46 test], external validation 303 scans)	- Gated NCCT - Non-gated routine chest CT	- Gated NCCT manual - Non-gated manual NCCT	For CACS ≥ 100 in non-gated CT model: - Sensitivity = 71–94% - PPV = 88–100% For gated NCCT: - Cohen's kappa = 0.89, p <0.0001 - AI processing time vs. manual scoring = 3.5 ± 2.1 s vs. 261 s	CNN
Ihdayhid et al., 2023 [22]	Training 2439 cardiac CT scans Validation 771 scans Test set 1849 cardiac CT scans	- ECG-gated NCCT scans	- ECG-gated NCCT	AI vs. Manual CACS: - Spearman's r = 0.90 [95% CI, 0.89–0.91], $p < 0.001$ - ICC = 0.98 [95% CI, 0.98–0.99], $p < 0.001$ - Bland–Altman = 1.69 - κ = 0.90 [95 CI, 0.88–0.9], $p < 0.001$ - Analysis time = 13.1 ± 3.2 s/scan	DeepC Architecture (3D-CNN)
Pieszko et al., 2023 [26]	Training and internal testing 9543 (1827 gated CT and 7716 CTAC) External validation 4331 (2737 had ECG-gated NCCT)	- CT attenuation correction scans for AI - ECG-gated NCCT	- ECG-gated NCCT	- Automated scoring time = <6 s/scan - Net reclassification improvement = −0.02 [95% CI, −0.11–0.07] - NPV of DL CTAC = 83%	DL
Morf et al., 2022 [27]	Test set 100 patients	- non-gated NCCT for AI - ECG-gated CT	- ECG-gated NCCT	Per-patient AI CACS: - sensitivity = 85% - specificity = 90% Inter-score agreement = 0.88 [95% CI: 0.827, 0.918] κ = 0.9 Interscore agreement per-vessel = 0.716	AVIEW CAC (U-Net)
Wolterink et al., 2016 [24]	250 CCTA and 250 gated NCCT scans	- CCTA - ECG-gated NCCT	- Manual CCTA and ECG-gated NCCT	Pearson's = 0.950 ICC = 0.944 CVD risk accuracy = 83% κ = 0.83 Sensitivity/FP = 0.72/0.48 Bland–Altmann = −0.2 (−38.7–38.3)	ConvPairs (CNN)
Suh et al., 2023 [28]	452 subjects (across 3 institutions)	- LDCT - ECG-gated NCCT	- Manual ECG-gated NCCT - Manual LDCT	Comparison of automatic and manual LDCT: κ = 0.972–0.918 Comparison of automatic and manual gated NCCT κ = 0.748–0.924	AVIEW CAC, Coreline Soft
Sabia et al., 2022 [29]	1129 subjects (Multicenter Italian Lung Disease Trial)	- LDCT	- Manual LDCT scoring	All-cause mortality CAC > 400: Hazard ratio = 5.75 [95% CI, 2.08–15.92]	AViEW, Coreline Soft (U-Net structure)

Table 2. *Cont.*

Author	N	Test Image Type/Protocol	Reference Image	Results	Model
Yuan et al., 2023 [30]	2831 TTE videos paired with gated NCCT	- 32-frame TTEs in parasternal long-axis view	- Manual CACS by gated NCCT	AI TTE zero CACS vs. high CACS - AUC = 0.81 [95% CI, 0.74–0.88] vs. 0.74 [0.68–0.8] - F1 score = 0.95 vs. 0.74	CNN
Zeleznik at al., 2021 [31]	Test set 1857 ECG-gated CTs and LDCT NLST 14,959 patients FHS-CT2 663 PROMISE 4021 ROMICAT-II 441	- LD chest CT (NLST) - ECG-gated (FHS-CT2, PROMISE and ROMICAT-II)	- Manual CACS by LDCT and gated NCCT	Automatic = 1.938 s per scan κ = 0.70	U-Net
Xu at al., 2022 [22]	Training set 150 (group A—1 mm slice thickness) and 170 (group B—3 mm) chest CTs Test set 144 (1 mm) and 144 (3 mm) chest CTs External validation 344 paired scans	- ECG-gated NCCT - non-gated chest CT	- manual CACS by gated NCCT	Agreement between AI and gold standard manual CACS: - ICC Group A = 0.9 [95% CI, 0.85–0.93] - ICC Group B = 0.94 [95% CI, 0.92–0.96] Risk category classification: κ Group A = 0.72 κ Group B = 0.82 PPV, NPV, and accuracy: Group A = 90%, 83%, and 88% Group B = 93%, 98%, and 94%	U-Net
Sandhu et al., 2023 [32]	Test set 173 patients	Non-gated NCCT	Manual non-gated NCCT	Statin prescription in notification group vs. usual care group: 51.2% vs. 6.9%	DL
Peng et al., 2023 [33]	Test set 5678 adults	Non-gated NCCT	N/A	DL-CAC ≥ 100: - Mean 10 yrs ASCVD = 24% - 26% pts on statins DL-CAC ≥ 100 vs. DL-CAC = 0: - HR death = 1.51 [95% CI, 1.28–1.79] - HR death/MI/stroke = 1.57 [95% CI, 1.33–1.84] - HR death/MI/stroke/revascularization = 1.69 [95% CI, 1.45–1.98]	CNN
Van Velzen et al., 2020 [34]	Total 7240 ECG-gated standard CAC CT 902, CTAC 399, 1409 CTs radiation treatment planning (RadTherapy) 1409, 470 diagnostic Chest CTs, 2879 ECG-gated from JHS, 1181 NLST	LDCT ECG-gated CTAC	- Semi-automatic	Data for CAC CT, CTAC, diagnostic CT, and RadTherapy: ICC for CAC volume = 0.98, 0.97, 0.98, and 0.92, respectively Overall κ = 0.92 (95% CI, 0.91–0.93)	CNN
Yu et al., 2022 [35]	405 LDCT and 405 gated CT	LDCT Gated NCCT	LDCT and gated NCCT	Comparison with LDCT:	CACScoreDoc
Hong et al., 2022 [36]	1811 cases Training 754 Test 1 = 215 Test 2 = 744 Validation = 98	Gated NCCT	Semi-automated clinical software (syngo.CT CaScoring, Siemens)	Data for training dataset 1 ICC 1.00, $p < 0.001$ κ = 0.931 U-Net vs. U-Net++ - Dice = 0.54 vs. 0.86 - IoU = 0.54 vs. 0.84 - Precision = 0.54 vs. 0.88 Analysis time 50 ms per scan	U-Net++ (U-Net with immediate upsampling after downsampling)

Table 2. *Cont.*

Author	N	Test Image Type/Protocol	Reference Image	Results	Model
Gogin et al., 2021 [37]	Test set 783 CT (SFR data challenge set) External validation 98 CTs (orCaScore challenge set)	Gated NCCT	- Manual CACS by gated NCCT	A five-ensemble model trained on all datasets: ICC = 0.970 κ = 0.894 Accuracy = 85.7%	CNN with 3D U-Net structure
Sandstedt et al., 2020 [38]	315 scans from SWEDEHEART registry	Gated NCCT	Semiautomatic and manual CACS	Correlation for CACS: Pearson's = 0.935 ICC = 0.996 Bland–Altman = −8.2 (−115.1 to 98.2) κ = 0.919 Median analysis time: - semi-automatic = 59 s - automatic = 36 s	-

CTAC = Computed Tomography Attenuation Correction, FHS-CT2 = Framingham Heart Study, NLST = National Lung Screening Trial, PROMISE = Prospective Multicenter Imaging Study for Evaluation of Chest Pain, ROMICAT-II = Rule Out Myocardial Infarction using Computer Assisted Tomography II, JHS = Jackson Heart Study, LDCT = Low dose CT, NCCT = Non-contrast CT, ICC = Intraclass correlation.

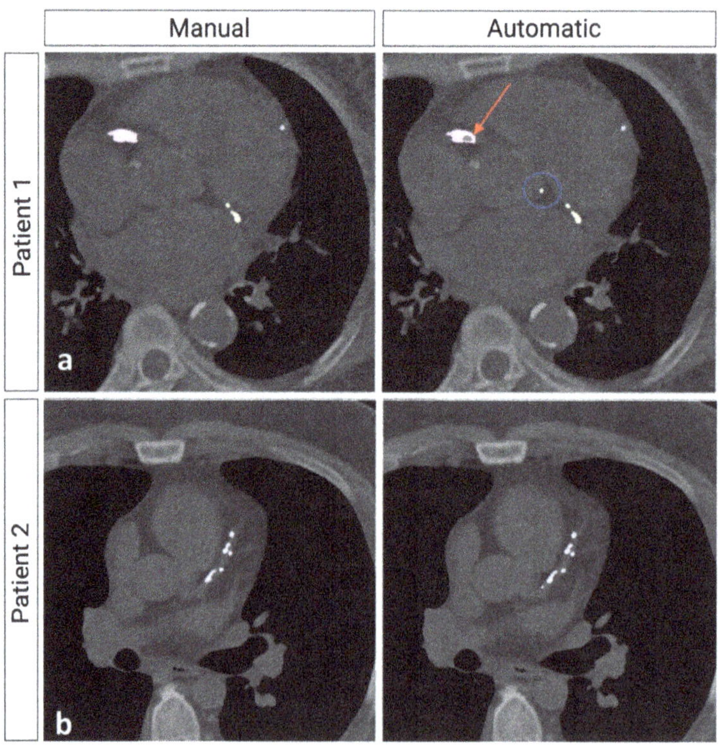

Figure 2. Comparison of Manual and Automatic CAC Identification. Image adapted from Eng et al. [25] Manual and automatic CACS comparison in two patients. The automatic model excludes calcifications in the descending aorta and some in the aortic root. (**a**) False negative calcium analysis by the automatic model in the right coronary artery (red arrow). False positive aortic root calcification is present (blue circle). (**b**) Comparison of automatic and manual coronary calcifications in another patient.

While most studies used one or two CNN-based models, a multicenter, multi-scanner, and multivendor study trained and tested an ensemble of five 3D U-Net models [37]. The ensemble model trained on all data subsets achieved the best Cohen's kappa (0.894), accuracy (85.7%), and intraclass correlation coefficient (ICC) (0.970) relative to single models and the ensemble model trained on partial data subsets. This study further highlighted the benefit of a large training dataset size on model performance. Two separate studies compared their suggested automatic tools with established semi-automatic software and had good outcomes. The first report compared a proposed automatic software product with a reference semi-automatic software product, syngo.via, and showed excellent correlation by Pearson's coefficient (0.935) and ICC (0.996); furthermore, good risk category assignment was also achieved ($\kappa = 0.919$) [38]. Similarly, another study proposed a model based on an improved U-Net structure, known as U-Net++, and compared it to syngo.CT CaScoring, a semiautomatic software product [36]. The model was tested on two datasets, with and without clinically detected CAC. The model achieved excellent ICC (1.0) for Agatston, volume, and mass scores relative to semi-automated CACS and kappa for risk categorization.

A 2021 study by Xu et al. was unique in its comparison of automatic scoring from non-gated chest CTs of varying slice thicknesses, 1 mm and 3 mm [23]. Manual gated NCCT was used as a reference, and though both slice thicknesses had good ICC (1 mm = 0.9 [95% CI, 0.85–0.93] and 3 mm = 0.94 [95% CI, 0.92–0.96]), PPV (1 mm = 90% vs. 3 mm = 93%), accuracy (1 mm = 88% vs. 3 mm = 94%), and κ (1 mm = 0.72 and 3 mm = 0.82), automatic scores from the 3 mm scans demonstrated slightly better values overall. Although this study showed improved accuracy with thicker slice scans, further analyses are required to determine the optimal thickness for model accuracy and noise reduction considering that noise increases with thickness and contributes to calcium score misclassification.

A quality improvement project by Sandhu et al. derived automated CACS from previously acquired non-gated NCCT and showed 51% statin prescription for primary prevention at 6 months when primary care physicians were notified of CAC presence, versus 7% without notification [32]. The study also demonstrated a significant decrease in low-density lipoprotein and an increase in further non-invasive CAD testing in the notification arm. The study highlights the potential for improved preventative care with AI, non-dedicated CT, and results notification; further studies on its impact on MACE would be enlightening. A cardiovascular outcomes study utilized automated CAC derived from non-gated NCCT and determined that CAC $\geq$ 100 was associated with a higher risk of death, as well as a composite of death/MI/stroke and death/MI/stroke/revascularization, relative to CAC = 0 [33]. Furthermore, patients were being undertreated with statins.

3.2. PET/CT Attenuation Correction

Non-gated CT attenuation correction scans in PET imaging have also been used for automatic CACS. Pieszko et al. proposed a DL model for automated CACS from CT attenuation correction (CTAC) scans acquired with cardiac PET imaging [26]. There were no significant differences in net reclassification and the model showed a stepwise increase in MACE in the CACS groups. Similarly, standard CACS and DL-based CTAC scores had similar negative predictive values (NPV) for MACE at 85% and 83%, respectively.

One study used a U-Net-based model, AVIEW CAC by Coreline Soft, for automatic CACS in ungated CT scans from 100 patients who underwent 18-FDG PET/CT [27]. Patients in this study also underwent ECG-gated CT scans within 6 months of PET/CT that were manually scored and compared to the AI-based CACS from ungated CT. Though the model had almost perfect risk categorization κ, it underestimated the CAC category in 42% of cases and 44% had to be recategorized.

Another group presented a model for automatic CAC quantification in CCTA scans [24]. The volume of interest was first automatically determined by placing a "bounding box" around the heart for extracardiac calcification exclusion. Four ConvPairs were generated based on dimensionality (2.5D and 3D) and input patch size (15 or 25 voxels) and used for voxel classification; overall, the best-performing ensemble had a 71% sensitivity and 0.48 FP errors per scan. The model also had excellent ICC and an almost perfect κ relative to the reference, gated NCCT mass score.

3.3. Low-Dose Chest CT and Transthoracic Echocardiogram

LDCT has also been applied towards automatic CAC scoring with good outcomes. One study analyzed automatic CACS using AVIEW CAC by Coreline Soft in LDCT and gated CT across three institutions [28]. Compared to manual scores from both scan types, the LDCT scores were substantial to almost-perfect κ, while gated CT scores were almost perfect κ across all institutions. LDCT also had a higher false positive rate which may have been contributed by more noise and artifacts or poorer model performance due to lymph node calcifications. Another study assessed automated CACS, using AVIEW by Coreline, as a predictor of 12-yr all-cause mortality in LDCT and showed an incremental association between CACS and all-cause mortality [29].

Yu et al. used a commercially available automatic CACS software product, CAC-Score Doc by ShuKun technology, that was trained and tested on non-gated chest CT for CAC quantification [35]. Automatic software was compared to semiautomatic software, CaScoring, Syngo by Siemens, and manual scoring.

Interestingly, a study by Yuan et al. employed a video-based CNN model for binary CACS prediction from transthoracic echocardiograms (TTE) [30]. The model was able to discriminate zero CAC from high CAC (≥400 Agatston units) with very good AUC and F1 scores for zero and high CAC. Though binary CACS is less informative in guiding therapy initiation due to the loss of information on patients with CACS between >0 to <400, the study shows promise for a potential role for TTE in automated CACS.

3.4. Multiple CT Protocols

Using data from four large cohort studies, Zeleznik et al. trained a model for cardiac segmentation and CAC quantification using manually segmented ECG-gated CTs and tested the model with both gated and low-dose chest CTs [31]. There was excellent correlation between the automatic and manual calcium score groups; however, the AUC for event prediction between the two was not statistically significant. A CNN-based algorithm suggested by Van Velzen et al. was tested on a diverse set of CT protocols including standard ECG-gated CT, LDCT, CTAC, diagnostic chest CT, and radiation therapy planning CTs with excellent ICC for CAC volume and overall κ [34].

4. Towards Clinical Implementation

4.1. Workflow Optimization

Presently, several institutions are employing CACS automation algorithms in clinical settings for use in routine non-dedicated CTs and standard, gated NCCTs. AI is able to improve the workflow in 3D imaging post-processing labs, particularly at high-volume centers. Automatic CACS models can improve efficiency and resource utilization by decreasing time spent on segmentation and coronary annotation. Though manual double-checks will be required to prevent oversight, the combined time for automatic scoring and double-checking has been shown to be shorter than manual scoring. Consequently, radiologists can use less time overall by mainly verifying the automated results, and radiology technicians can be repurposed for other post-processing tasks. This will also aid in cost reduction in imaging labs. In addition, high inter-observer variability in lower-quality non-dedicated scans can also be reduced by AI.

4.2. Image Considerations

Overall, the problem of miscategorization and false positive calcifications persists in CACS automation and has been attributed to artifacts, noise, and non-coronary calcifications (aortic, valvular, and lymph node calcifications) [20,22]. Denoising, region-of-interest localization, and segmentation are potential areas of intervention to improve image quality and reduce false positive calcifications. Multiple studies have demonstrated the superiority of iterative reconstruction (IR) over filtered back projection (FBP) for noise reduction during image reconstruction [39,40]. One study showed decreased radiation dose, higher signal-to-noise ratio (SNR), and fewer false positive calcifications with low-dose iterative reconstruction by establishing noise thresholds; low-dose IR exhibited better performance than filtered back projection [41]. Furthermore, DL-based image reconstruction (DLIR) may be an even better alternative to IR and FBP. However, a study showed that while incremental DLIR was associated with a stepwise decrease in noise and an increase in SNR, there was a tendency for significant incremental decreases in CACS and CAC volume [42]. As such, further research should be conducted in applying noise reduction to DL reconstruction to identify the optimal noise reduction level through DLIR without compromising quantitative CACS.

4.3. External Validation and Data Diversity

Training dataset diversity and external validation are essential for AI algorithm generalizability. Studies have shown the importance of large databases in model training and demonstrated inferior ICC and Cohen's kappa when a model is trained with a smaller dataset [36]. Poorly generalizable models perform well with training datasets and poorly with test sets that differ from their training sets, a phenomenon known as overfitting. As such, AI models need diverse training datasets to excel in realistic clinical settings and prevent the propagation of real-world biases [43]. This goal can be attained through the creation of large multicenter, multivendor, multi-detector, and multi-phenotype databases, achievable through cross-institutional collaboration. For instance, BunkerHill Health has an existing research consortium including several academic institutions to facilitate faster multicenter cooperation by aiding AI algorithm training and validation, clinical deployment, and addressing the legal implications of multicenter partnerships [44]. Large dataset repositories exist for other imaging modalities including CMR and SPECT. Current research endeavors in model development can contribute to data archives by publicizing their annotated datasets and permitting their collation by research consortiums.

4.4. Metrics Standardization

During study evaluation, metric selection is essential for appropriate criteria evaluation and optimization during model training. Cohen's kappa, concordance index, and ICC scores are ideal for assessing the risk category allocation, accuracy, and reliability; as such, they are commonly used metrics in automated CACS [45,46]. The Proposed Requirements for Cardiovascular Imaging-Related Machine Learning Evaluation (PRIME) checklist provides a guideline for reporting model evaluation measures including Bland–Altmann plots, misclassification risk, accuracies, and inter-/intra-observer variability; however, specific and standard acceptable parameter thresholds are undefined [47]. For example, Cohen's kappa ranges from 0–1.0 with six different subgroups, the best of which is between 0.81–1.00, and is indicative of almost-perfect risk categorization [48]. However, there is no standard minimum acceptable value for automated models. A minimum requirement of almost-perfect categorization would be acceptable for proposed models; nevertheless, the requirement needs to be defined for Cohen's kappa and other metrics to give more meaning to each model's clinical adequacy.

5. Conclusions

AI application in CACS has the potential to produce precise, efficient, and accurate scores from dedicated and non-dedicated CT. While most studies presented so far have produced fast and accurate automatic scores, the challenges of data homogeneity, inadequate dataset size, and calcium mis-categorization due to noise artifacts and aortic/valvular calcifications remain persistent. Although a certain degree of false positive rates is expected with imaging tests, it is essential to minimize this in the higher CAC risk groups (>100 AU) where results significantly impact medical decision-making, to avoid over-utilization of resources for primary prevention and further diagnostic testing. Furthermore, creating data consortiums will support large-scale studies, facilitate accurate model development, and aid clinical implementation; however, an equal representation of samples from various demographics is essential to prevent the proliferation of real-world biases and disparities through biased datasets and AI models.

Author Contributions: Conceptualization, A.A.A. and D.K.K.; methodology, A.A.A. and D.K.K.; formal analysis, A.A.A. and D.K.K.; investigation, A.A.A. and D.K.K.; resources, A.A.A. and D.K.K.; data curation, A.A.A. and D.K.K.; writing—original draft preparation, A.A.A.; writing—review and editing, A.A.A. and D.K.K.; visualization, A.A.A.; supervision, D.K.K.; project administration, D.K.K. All authors have read and agreed to the published version of the manuscript.

Funding: This research received no external funding.

Conflicts of Interest: The authors declare no conflict of interest.

Abbreviations

ACC/AHA = American College of Cardiology/American Heart Association, AI = Artificial Intelligence, ASCVD = Atherosclerotic Cardiovascular Disease, CCTA = Cardiac Computed Tomography Angiography, CT = Computed Tomography, CTAC = Computed Tomography Attenuation Correction, CNN = Convolutional Neural Network, CAC = Coronary Artery Calcium, CACS = Coronary Artery Calcium Score, CAD = Coronary Artery Disease, CHD = Coronary Heart Disease, DL = Deep Learning, DLIR = Deep Learning Image Reconstruction, FBP = Filtered Back Projection, IR = Iterative Reconstruction, ICC = Intraclass Correlation Coefficient, LDCT = Low-Dose Computed Tomography, MACE = Major Adverse Cardiovascular Event, MESA = Multi-Ethnic Study of Atherosclerosis, NPV = Negative Predictive Value, NCCT = Non-Contrast Computed Tomography, PPV = Positive Predictive Value, PET = Positron Emission Tomography, PRIME = Proposed Requirements for Cardiovascular Imaging-Related Machine Learning Evaluation, SNR = Signal-to-Noise Ratio, TTE = Transthoracic Echocardiogram.

References

1. Tsao, C.W.; Aday, A.W.; Almarzooq, Z.I.; Anderson, C.A.M.; Arora, P.; Avery, C.L.; Baker-Smith, C.M.; Beaton, A.Z.; Boehme, A.K.; Buxton, A.E.; et al. Heart Disease and Stroke Statistics-2023 Update: A Report from the American Heart Association. *Circulation* **2023**, *147*, e93–e621. [CrossRef]
2. Greenland, P.; Alpert, J.S.; Beller, G.A.; Benjamin, E.J.; Budoff, M.J.; Fayad, Z.A.; Foster, E.; Hlatky, M.A.; Hodgson, J.M.; Kushner, F.G.; et al. 2010 ACCF/AHA Guideline for Assessment of Cardiovascular Risk in Asymptomatic Adults. *J. Am. Coll. Cardiol.* **2010**, *56*, e50–e103. [CrossRef]
3. Mori, H.; Torii, S.; Kutyna, M.; Sakamoto, A.; Finn, A.V.; Virmani, R. Coronary Artery Calcification and Its Progression. *JACC Cardiovasc. Imaging* **2018**, *11*, 127–142. [CrossRef]
4. Razavi, A.C.; Agatston, A.S.; Shaw, L.J.; De Cecco, C.N.; Van Assen, M.; Sperling, L.S.; Bittencourt, M.S.; Daubert, M.A.; Nasir, K.; Blumenthal, R.S.; et al. Evolving Role of Calcium Density in Coronary Artery Calcium Scoring and Atherosclerotic Cardiovascular Disease Risk. *JACC Cardiovasc. Imaging* **2022**, *15*, 1648–1662. [CrossRef]
5. Agatston, A.S.; Janowitz, W.R.; Hildner, F.J.; Zusmer, N.R.; Viamonte, M.; Detrano, R. Quantification of Coronary Artery Calcium Using Ultrafast Computed Tomography. *J. Am. Coll. Cardiol.* **1990**, *15*, 827–832. [CrossRef]
6. Kumar, P.; Bhatia, M. Coronary Artery Calcium Data and Reporting System (CAC-DRS): A Primer. *J. Cardiovasc. Imaging* **2023**, *31*, 1–17. [CrossRef]
7. Obisesan, O.H.; Osei, A.D.; Uddin, S.M.I.; Dzaye, O.; Blaha, M.J. An Update on Coronary Artery Calcium Interpretation at Chest and Cardiac CT. *Radiol. Cardiothorac. Imaging* **2021**, *3*, e200484. [CrossRef]
8. Arnett, D.K.; Blumenthal, R.S.; Albert, M.A.; Buroker, A.B.; Goldberger, Z.D.; Hahn, E.J.; Himmelfarb, C.D.; Khera, A.; Lloyd-Jones, D.; McEvoy, J.W.; et al. 2019 ACC/AHA Guideline on the Primary Prevention of Cardiovascular Disease: A Report of the American College of Cardiology/American Heart Association Task Force on Clinical Practice Guidelines. *Circulation* **2019**, *140*, e596–e646. [CrossRef]
9. Einstein, A.J.; Johnson, L.L.; Bokhari, S.; Son, J.; Thompson, R.C.; Bateman, T.M.; Hayes, S.W.; Berman, D.S. Agreement of Visual Estimation of Coronary Artery Calcium from Low-Dose CT Attenuation Correction Scans in Hybrid PET/CT and SPECT/CT with Standard Agatston Score. *J. Am. Coll. Cardiol.* **2010**, *56*, 1914–1921. [CrossRef]
10. Chiles, C.; Duan, F.; Gladish, G.W.; Ravenel, J.G.; Baginski, S.G.; Snyder, B.S.; DeMello, S.; Desjardins, S.S.; Munden, R.F.; NLST Study Team. Association of Coronary Artery Calcification and Mortality in the National Lung Screening Trial: A Comparison of Three Scoring Methods. *Radiology* **2015**, *276*, 82–90. [CrossRef]

11. Huang, Y.-L.; Wu, F.-Z.; Wang, Y.-C.; Ju, Y.-J.; Mar, G.-Y.; Chuo, C.-C.; Lin, H.-S.; Wu, M.-T. Reliable Categorisation of Visual Scoring of Coronary Artery Calcification on Low-Dose CT for Lung Cancer Screening: Validation with the Standard Agatston Score. *Eur. Radiol.* **2013**, *23*, 1226–1233. [CrossRef]
12. Pinto-Coelho, L. How Artificial Intelligence Is Shaping Medical Imaging Technology: A Survey of Innovations and Applications. *Bioengineering* **2023**, *10*, 1435. [CrossRef]
13. Makimoto, H.; Kohro, T. Adopting Artificial Intelligence in Cardiovascular Medicine: A Scoping Review. *Hypertens. Res.* **2024**, *47*, 685–699. [CrossRef]
14. Van den Eynde, J.; Lachmann, M.; Laugwitz, K.-L.; Manlhiot, C.; Kutty, S. Successfully Implemented Artificial Intelligence and Machine Learning Applications in Cardiology: State-of-the-Art Review. *Trends Cardiovasc. Med.* **2023**, *33*, 265–271. [CrossRef]
15. Siemen Healthineers. Computed Tomography. Available online: https://www.siemens-healthineers.com/en-us/computed-tomography (accessed on 25 February 2023).
16. Litjens, G.; Ciompi, F.; Wolterink, J.M.; de Vos, B.D.; Leiner, T.; Teuwen, J.; Išgum, I. State-of-the-Art Deep Learning in Cardiovascular Image Analysis. *JACC Cardiovasc. Imaging* **2019**, *12*, 1549–1565. [CrossRef]
17. Alzubaidi, L.; Zhang, J.; Humaidi, A.J.; Al-Dujaili, A.; Duan, Y.; Al-Shamma, O.; Santamaría, J.; Fadhel, M.A.; Al-Amidie, M.; Farhan, L. Review of Deep Learning: Concepts, CNN Architectures, Challenges, Applications, Future Directions. *J. Big Data* **2021**, *8*, 53. [CrossRef]
18. Recht, M.P.; Dewey, M.; Dreyer, K.; Langlotz, C.; Niessen, W.; Prainsack, B.; Smith, J.J. Integrating Artificial Intelligence into the Clinical Practice of Radiology: Challenges and Recommendations. *Eur. Radiol.* **2020**, *30*, 3576–3584. [CrossRef]
19. Lee, J.H.; Joo, I.; Kang, T.W.; Paik, Y.H.; Sinn, D.H.; Ha, S.Y.; Kim, K.; Choi, C.; Lee, G.; Yi, J.; et al. Deep Learning with Ultrasonography: Automated Classification of Liver Fibrosis Using a Deep Convolutional Neural Network. *Eur. Radiol.* **2020**, *30*, 1264–1273. [CrossRef]
20. Lessmann, N.; van Ginneken, B.; Zreik, M.; de Jong, P.A.; de Vos, B.D.; Viergever, M.A.; Isgum, I. Automatic Calcium Scoring in Low-Dose Chest CT Using Deep Neural Networks with Dilated Convolutions. *IEEE Trans. Med. Imaging* **2018**, *37*, 615–625. [CrossRef]
21. Wolterink, J.M.; Leiner, T.; Takx, R.A.P.; Viergever, M.A.; Isgum, I. Automatic Coronary Calcium Scoring in Non-Contrast-Enhanced ECG-Triggered Cardiac CT with Ambiguity Detection. *IEEE Trans. Med. Imaging* **2015**, *34*, 1867–1878. [CrossRef]
22. Ihdayhid, A.R.; Lan, N.S.R.; Williams, M.; Newby, D.; Flack, J.; Kwok, S.; Joyner, J.; Gera, S.; Dembo, L.; Adler, B.; et al. Evaluation of an Artificial Intelligence Coronary Artery Calcium Scoring Model from Computed Tomography. *Eur. Radiol.* **2023**, *33*, 321–329. [CrossRef]
23. Xu, C.; Guo, H.; Xu, M.; Duan, M.; Wang, M.; Liu, P.; Luo, X.; Jin, Z.; Liu, H.; Wang, Y. Automatic Coronary Artery Calcium Scoring on Routine Chest Computed Tomography (CT): Comparison of a Deep Learning Algorithm and a Dedicated Calcium Scoring CT. *Quant. Imaging Med. Surg.* **2022**, *12*, 2684–2695. [CrossRef]
24. Wolterink, J.M.; Leiner, T.; De Vos, B.D.; Van Hamersvelt, R.W.; Viergever, M.A.; Išgum, I. Automatic Coronary Artery Calcium Scoring in Cardiac CT Angiography Using Paired Convolutional Neural Networks. *Med. Image Anal.* **2016**, *34*, 123–136. [CrossRef]
25. Eng, D.; Chute, C.; Khandwala, N.; Rajpurkar, P.; Long, J.; Shleifer, S.; Khalaf, M.H.; Sandhu, A.T.; Rodriguez, F.; Maron, D.J.; et al. Automated Coronary Calcium Scoring Using Deep Learning with Multicenter External Validation. *npj Digit. Med.* **2021**, *4*, 88. [CrossRef]
26. Pieszko, K.; Shanbhag, A.; Killekar, A.; Miller, R.J.H.; Lemley, M.; Otaki, Y.; Singh, A.; Kwiecinski, J.; Gransar, H.; Van, K.S.D.; et al. Deep Learning of Coronary Calcium Scores from PET/CT Attenuation Maps Accurately Predicts Adverse Cardiovascular Events. *JACC Cardiovasc. Imaging* **2023**, *16*, 675–687. [CrossRef]
27. Morf, C.; Sartoretti, T.; Gennari, A.G.; Maurer, A.; Skawran, S.; Giannopoulos, A.A.; Sartoretti, E.; Schwyzer, M.; Curioni-Fontecedro, A.; Gebhard, C.; et al. Diagnostic Value of Fully Automated Artificial Intelligence Powered Coronary Artery Calcium Scoring from 18F-FDG PET/CT. *Diagnostics* **2022**, *12*, 1876. [CrossRef]
28. Suh, Y.J.; Kim, C.; Lee, J.-G.; Oh, H.; Kang, H.; Kim, Y.-H.; Yang, D.H. Fully Automatic Coronary Calcium Scoring in Non-ECG-Gated Low-Dose Chest CT: Comparison with ECG-Gated Cardiac CT. *Eur. Radiol.* **2023**, *33*, 1254–1265. [CrossRef]
29. Sabia, F.; Balbi, M.; Ledda, R.E.; Milanese, G.; Ruggirello, M.; Valsecchi, C.; Marchianò, A.; Sverzellati, N.; Pastorino, U. Fully Automated Calcium Scoring Predicts All-Cause Mortality at 12 Years in the MILD Lung Cancer Screening Trial. *PLoS ONE* **2023**, *18*, e0285593. [CrossRef]
30. Yuan, N.; Kwan, A.C.; Duffy, G.; Theurer, J.; Chen, J.H.; Nieman, K.; Botting, P.; Dey, D.; Berman, D.S.; Cheng, S.; et al. Prediction of Coronary Artery Calcium Using Deep Learning of Echocardiograms. *J. Am. Soc. Echocardiogr.* **2023**, *36*, 474–481.e3. [CrossRef]
31. Zeleznik, R.; Foldyna, B.; Eslami, P.; Weiss, J.; Alexander, I.; Taron, J.; Parmar, C.; Alvi, R.M.; Banerji, D.; Uno, M.; et al. Deep Convolutional Neural Networks to Predict Cardiovascular Risk from Computed Tomography. *Nat. Commun.* **2021**, *12*, 715. [CrossRef]
32. Sandhu, A.T.; Rodriguez, F.; Ngo, S.; Patel, B.N.; Mastrodicasa, D.; Eng, D.; Khandwala, N.; Balla, S.; Sousa, D.; Maron, D.J. Incidental Coronary Artery Calcium: Opportunistic Screening of Previous Nongated Chest Computed Tomography Scans to Improve Statin Rates (NOTIFY-1 Project). *Circulation* **2023**, *147*, 703–714. [CrossRef]
33. Peng, A.W.; Dudum, R.; Jain, S.S.; Maron, D.J.; Patel, B.N.; Khandwala, N.; Eng, D.; Chaudhari, A.S.; Sandhu, A.T.; Rodriguez, F. Association of Coronary Artery Calcium Detected by Routine Ungated CT Imaging with Cardiovascular Outcomes. *J. Am. Coll. Cardiol.* **2023**, *82*, 1192–1202. [CrossRef]

34. van Velzen, S.G.M.; Lessmann, N.; Velthuis, B.K.; Bank, I.E.M.; van den Bongard, D.H.J.G.; Leiner, T.; de Jong, P.A.; Veldhuis, W.B.; Correa, A.; Terry, J.G.; et al. Deep Learning for Automatic Calcium Scoring in CT: Validation Using Multiple Cardiac CT and Chest CT Protocols. *Radiology* **2020**, *295*, 66–79. [CrossRef]
35. Yu, J.; Qian, L.; Sun, W.; Nie, Z.; Zheng, D.; Han, P.; Shi, H.; Zheng, C.; Yang, F. Automated Total and Vessel-Specific Coronary Artery Calcium (CAC) Quantification on Chest CT: Direct Comparison with CAC Scoring on Non-Contrast Cardiac CT. *BMC Med. Imaging* **2022**, *22*, 177. [CrossRef]
36. Hong, J.-S.; Tzeng, Y.-H.; Yin, W.-H.; Wu, K.-T.; Hsu, H.-Y.; Lu, C.-F.; Liu, H.-R.; Wu, Y.-T. Automated Coronary Artery Calcium Scoring Using Nested U-Net and Focal Loss. *Comput. Struct. Biotechnol. J.* **2022**, *20*, 1681–1690. [CrossRef]
37. Gogin, N.; Viti, M.; Nicodème, L.; Ohana, M.; Talbot, H.; Gencer, U.; Mekukosokeng, M.; Caramella, T.; Diascorn, Y.; Airaud, J.-Y.; et al. Automatic Coronary Artery Calcium Scoring from Unenhanced-ECG-Gated CT Using Deep Learning. *Diagn. Interv. Imaging* **2021**, *102*, 683–690. [CrossRef]
38. Sandstedt, M.; Henriksson, L.; Janzon, M.; Nyberg, G.; Engvall, J.; De Geer, J.; Alfredsson, J.; Persson, A. Evaluation of an AI-Based, Automatic Coronary Artery Calcium Scoring Software. *Eur. Radiol.* **2020**, *30*, 1671–1678. [CrossRef]
39. Willemink, M.J.; Leiner, T.; de Jong, P.A.; de Heer, L.M.; Nievelstein, R.A.J.; Schilham, A.M.R.; Budde, R.P.J. Iterative Reconstruction Techniques for Computed Tomography Part 2: Initial Results in Dose Reduction and Image Quality. *Eur. Radiol.* **2013**, *23*, 1632–1642. [CrossRef]
40. Den Harder, A.M.; Willemink, M.J.; De Ruiter, Q.M.B.; De Jong, P.A.; Schilham, A.M.R.; Krestin, G.P.; Leiner, T.; Budde, R.P.J. Dose Reduction with Iterative Reconstruction for Coronary CT Angiography: A Systematic Review and Meta-Analysis. *Br. J. Radiol.* **2016**, *89*, 20150068. [CrossRef]
41. Garmer, M.; Lehrenfeld, C.; Metz, F.; Klein-Wiele, O.; Brandts, B.; Grönemeyer, D. False-Positive Calcifications and Radiation Dose in Coronary Artery Calcium Scoring Using Iterative Reconstruction on the Basis of a Noise Threshold. *Radiol. Med. Diagn. Imaging* **2019**, *2*, 1–6. [CrossRef]
42. Rossi, A.; Gennari, A.G.; Etter, D.; Benz, D.C.; Sartoretti, T.; Giannopoulos, A.A.; Mikail, N.; Bengs, S.; Maurer, A.; Gebhard, C.; et al. Impact of Deep Learning Image Reconstructions (DLIR) on Coronary Artery Calcium Quantification. *Eur. Radiol.* **2023**, *33*, 3832–3838. [CrossRef]
43. Gong, Z.; Zhong, P.; Hu, W. Diversity in Machine Learning. *IEEE Access* **2019**, *7*, 64323–64350. [CrossRef]
44. Bunkerhill Health | Advancing AI Healthcare from Concept to Clinic. Available online: https://www.bunkerhillhealth.com/ (accessed on 2 June 2024).
45. Kalderstam, J.; Edén, P.; Bendahl, P.-O.; Strand, C.; Fernö, M.; Ohlsson, M. Training Artificial Neural Networks Directly on the Concordance Index for Censored Data Using Genetic Algorithms. *Artif. Intell. Med.* **2013**, *58*, 125–132. [CrossRef]
46. Li, M.; Gao, Q.; Yu, T. Kappa Statistic Considerations in Evaluating Inter-Rater Reliability between Two Raters: Which, When and Context Matters. *BMC Cancer* **2023**, *23*, 799. [CrossRef]
47. Sengupta, P.P.; Shrestha, S.; Berthon, B.; Messas, E.; Donal, E.; Tison, G.H.; Min, J.K.; D'hooge, J.; Voigt, J.-U.; Dudley, J.; et al. Proposed Requirements for Cardiovascular Imaging-Related Machine Learning Evaluation (PRIME): A Checklist. *JACC Cardiovasc. Imaging* **2020**, *13*, 2017–2035. [CrossRef]
48. McHugh, M.L. Interrater Reliability: The Kappa Statistic. *Biochem. Med.* **2012**, *22*, 276–282. [CrossRef]

cancers

MDPI

Article

Breast Cancer Screening Using Inverse Modeling of Surface Temperatures and Steady-State Thermal Imaging

Nithya Sritharan [1], Carlos Gutierrez [2], Isaac Perez-Raya [2,3], Jose-Luis Gonzalez-Hernandez [2], Alyssa Owens [2], Donnette Dabydeen [1], Lori Medeiros [1], Satish Kandlikar [2,3] and Pradyumna Phatak [1,3,*]

[1] Department of Hematology-Oncology, Rochester Regional Health, Rochester, NY 14621, USA; nithya.sritharan@rochesterregional.org (N.S.); donnette.dabydeen@rochesterregional.org (D.D.); lori.medeiros@rochesterregional.org (L.M.)

[2] Department of Mechanical Engineering, Rochester Institute of Technology, Rochester, NY 14623, USA; cg9804@rit.edu (C.G.); iperez@biredimaging.com (I.P.-R.); jlgh1188@gmail.com (J.-L.G.-H.); anr493@gmail.com (A.O.); skandlikar@biredimaging.com (S.K.)

[3] BiRed Imaging Inc., Rochester, NY 14609, USA

* Correspondence: pradyumna.phatak@rochesterregional.org

Simple Summary: Early cancer detection is crucial for favorable patient outcomes, with mammography playing a central role in breast cancer detection. However, challenges persist, such as limited sensitivity in dense breast tissue and low specificity leading to excessive invasive testing. Leveraging the distinct biological characteristics of malignant tumors, we employed high-sensitivity thermal imaging to identify temperature changes associated with cancer. This innovative approach integrates a novel imaging technique and a physics-based prediction model to accurately ascertain the presence of breast cancer, regardless of size, location, and breast density. Our goal is to develop this technique as a complementary tool to mammography for widespread screening and as a cost-effective, stand-alone method for specific populations underserved by mammography.

Abstract: Cancer is characterized by increased metabolic activity and vascularity, leading to temperature changes in cancerous tissues compared to normal cells. This study focused on patients with abnormal mammogram findings or a clinical suspicion of breast cancer, exclusively those confirmed by biopsy. Utilizing an ultra-high sensitivity thermal camera and prone patient positioning, we measured surface temperatures integrated with an inverse modeling technique based on heat transfer principles to predict malignant breast lesions. Involving 25 breast tumors, our technique accurately predicted all tumors, with maximum errors below 5 mm in size and less than 1 cm in tumor location. Predictive efficacy was unaffected by tumor size, location, or breast density, with no aberrant predictions in the contralateral normal breast. Infrared temperature profiles and inverse modeling using both techniques successfully predicted breast cancer, highlighting its potential in breast cancer screening.

Keywords: inverse modeling; breast cancer screening; heat generation map; physics-informed neural network

1. Introduction

Breast cancer is the most prevalent cancer affecting women in the United States and stands as the second-leading cause of death among them [1]. While it predominantly impacts women aged 50 years or older, presenting at a median age of 62 years [2], breast cancer also poses challenges for younger women, often manifesting at advanced stages. Mammogram screening exhibits limited sensitivity in younger women, stemming from challenges posed by dense breast tissue that conceals underlying lesions and in cases of lobular carcinomas where discrete tumors are often not readily apparent [3,4]. It is estimated that more than 40% of women have dense breast tissue, which are four to six times more at risk of developing cancer [4–7]. Despite the advancements offered by 3D digital breast mammograms to address this issue, they come with increased radiation exposure [8,9]. Various adjunctive methods, including ultrasound, magnetic resonance imaging (MRI), and contrast-enhanced mammography, have shown promise in enhancing breast cancer detection. Computer aided detection (CAD) programs have been developed to aid and improve mammography, utilizing tools such as artificial intelligence and other computation techniques [10–15]. However, these methods also present challenges, leading to high false positives and unnecessary invasive testing, with less than 1% of these women eventually diagnosed with breast cancer [16–19]. Consequently, there is a persistent demand for cost-effective screening methods, both as complements to mammography and as potential stand-alone techniques, especially for specific patient populations not optimally served with mammography, with a simultaneous focus on minimizing cumulative radiation exposure.

Thermal Imaging Background

Thermal imaging is a method that captures the infrared radiation emitted from the body captured by an infrared camera as surface temperature measurements [20]. Strąkowska et al. [21] has shown the ability of utilizing thermal imaging in the detection of skin diseases. In 1956, Lawson [22–25] showed that malignant tumors generated an increase in temperature measurements that can be captured through thermal imaging. Our research endeavors in thermal imaging for breast cancer detection have been ongoing since 2015 [26–32], with a focus on overcoming the limitations of traditional approaches. Malignant tumors are characterized by increased angiogenesis and metabolic rates to sustain rapid cell proliferation [33–35]. Traditional thermal imaging techniques have historically faced challenges in detecting malignant tumors, with contributing factors including low-sensitivity cameras unable to detect subtle temperature changes, the influence of body temperature transmitted through the chest wall, and a lack of a clear methodology for translating identified hot spots on breast surfaces [30–32]. To address these issues, we developed a novel steady-state prone position imaging method, eliminating the impact of chest wall motion and variability in breast temperatures associated with imaging in the supine position. The relation between the emissive power of a body and its temperature is based on the Stefan–Boltzmann Law and, in the human body, is noted to be independent of skin color [36–38]. This characteristic can be used to obtain the surface temperature of breasts as previously described by Lahiri et al. [39] and to detect abnormalities that would alter this temperature distribution. Gautherie [40–42] correlated thermal conductivity and surface temperature measurements to increased vasculatures and metabolic activity in tumor tissues. He developed a model that encapsulated the thermal effect from the metabolic activity as a heat source dependent on the tumor volume and doubling time [43–45]. This allowed researchers to model the tumor as a heat source dependent on the tumor size. We developed an algorithm leveraging the well-established Pennes' bioheat transfer model [46–50], which helps accurately predict hot spots located deep within breast tissue using surface temperature measurements, along with 3D modeling of the breasts using MRI images.

By enhancing the precision of thermal imaging in breast cancer diagnosis, we aspire to contribute significantly to early detection efforts and ultimately improve patient outcomes.

2. Materials and Methods

We conducted a prospective, non-invasive study at Rochester General Hospital (RGH) between March 2018 and September 2019, after approval by the Institutional Review Board (IRB) at RGH. This study was conducted in collaboration with researchers at the Rochester Institute of Technology (RIT).

Inclusion criteria incorporated all of the following:

- Women 21 years or older;
- Able to provide informed consent;

- Breast lesions identified as BIRADS 4 or BIRADS 5, or detected clinically on physical exam;
- Malignancy confirmed by biopsy of the lesion.

A total of 30 women were recruited to undergo the study protocol. Informed consent was obtained from the subjects regarding the procedure and effects of infrared imaging.

MRI images of bilateral breasts of the patients were captured in the prone position with a GE 3T MRI scanner (GE Healthcare, Chicago, IL, USA) under an IRB-approved protocol prior to biopsy [51]. Axial, coronal, and sagittal imaging were captured pre- and post-contrast with GE 3T MRI. Multi-view infrared images, which included 8 viewed at 45° intervals around the bilateral breasts, were captured in the same prone position as the MRI, using an FLIR (Wilsonville, OR, USA) SC6700 IR camera with a thermal sensitivity of 0.02 °C. Capturing infrared images of the breast in the prone position allowed for a full 360° view, with each breast being imaged and analyzed separately for each patient. Figure 1 shows an illustration of the infrared imaging procedure and the multi-view infrared data of a patient [52]. The patients were imaged after about 10 min of acclimation to the room to ensure the body reached a steady-state temperature.

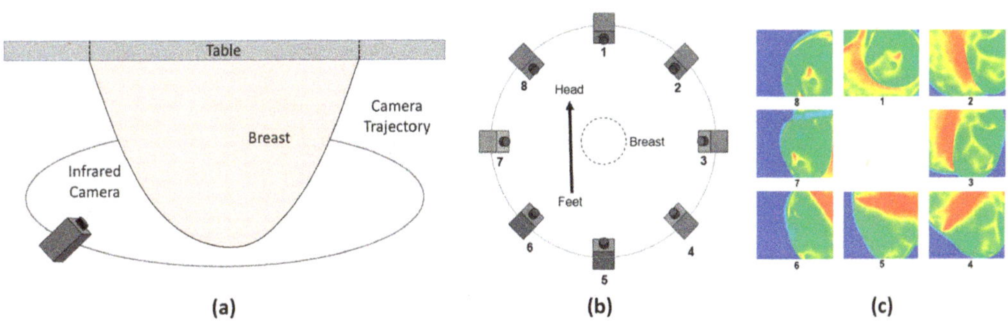

Figure 1. Illustration of infrared imaging procedure of (**a**) a breast under an imaging table in the prone position and (**b**) eight positions to extract multi-view infrared images. (**c**) Example of a patient's infrared images obtained using infrared imaging in the prone position [52].

The following steps were conducted for each patient by the RIT researchers with the obtained images, with no transmission of patient identifiers:

- Patient-specific digital breast models of both breasts generated using MRI images through image processing and 3D reconstruction techniques with ImageJ 1.51n software as described in Gonzalez-Hernandez et al. [53];
- Simulated breast surface temperatures of each breast generated using the patient-specific breast model with Ansys Fluent 2019 R2 thermal modeling software for thermal modeling of breast cancer;
- Tumor size and location predicted through inverse modeling using the Levenberg–Marquard algorithm (LMA) for inverse modeling [54].
- Infrared imaging data integrated with the above software and algorithm to accurately predict the presence or absence of breast cancer.

Figure 2 shows a process flowchart for detecting the presence or absence of breast cancer using infrared imaging, thermal modeling, and inverse modeling. This process relies on three primary inputs: (i) initial tumor parameters, including size and location, (ii) a patient-specific breast model, and (iii) infrared temperatures from multi-view images. Initial tumor parameters, set to a diameter of 1.8 cm and placed centrally within the breast geometry, along with the patient-specific breast model, are fed into the thermal modeling software to generate simulated surface temperatures. These simulated temperatures, alongside actual IR temperatures, are inputted simultaneously into the LMA detection algorithm for alignment and comparison. If disparities arise between simulated and actual temperatures, the algorithm iterates, updating tumor parameters until a best match is achieved, signaling either tumor detection or its absence. In the case of detection, the algorithm predicts tumor size and location within the breast. Conversely, if no tumor is detected, the algorithm positions it in areas minimally impacting surface temperature, such as outside the breast or at the chest wall, as illustrated in Figure 2. This iterative process is applied to each patient and each breast individually.

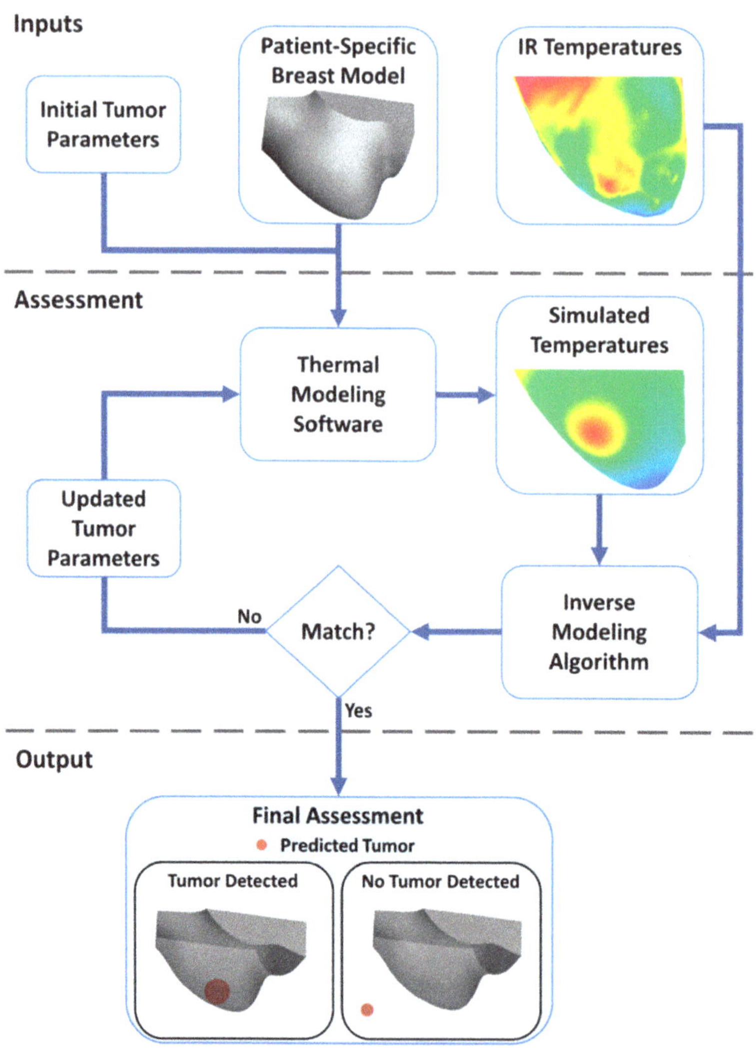

Figure 2. Flowchart of the developed breast cancer detection algorithm that utilizes thermal modeling and inverse modeling with patient-specific breast models and infrared surface temperatures. The inverse model provides a final assessment that indicates the presence or absence of a tumor heat source.

Gonzalez-Hernandez et al. [54] provide a detailed account of the inverse modeling process employed for breast cancer detection using surface temperatures. This methodology underwent initial validation on seven biopsy-proven breast cancer patients, detailed in both Gonzalez-Hernandez et al. [54] and Recinella et al. [51]. Gutierrez et al. [52] subsequently automated the algorithm to accommodate a larger volume of cases, implementing enhancements to optimize its runtime. In this investigation, ANSYS Fluent and the LMA algorithm were utilized for patients with accessible MRI data.

Clinical data, encompassing patient age, breast tissue density, tumor location, breast tissue composition evaluated via mammography, and tumor histology, were extracted from the electronic medical record (EMR) and deidentified prior to analysis. All patients included in this study underwent surgical resection of tumors with curative intent. Surgical pathology findings were categorized based on histological types, tumor grade, and estrogen receptor (ER) and progesterone receptor (PR) expression, as well as Her2/neu status. The actual tumor diameter was approximated by the volume calculated from MRI image dimensions. Statistical analysis using ANOVA was conducted to compare estimated and actual tumor sizes. Additionally, all enrolled patients received clinical follow-up for a minimum of two years to monitor for any instances of recurrent breast cancer in close proximity to the initial tumors. In this work, the positive control was breasts with verified malignancy, while the negative control was the contralateral healthy breasts.

3. Results

The final analysis included 24 patients diagnosed with breast tumors who underwent both MRI and infrared imaging, yielding a total of 25 breast tumors and 23 contralateral breasts devoid of tumors. Demographic and tumor specifics are outlined for each individual patient in Table 1.

All patients were biologically female, aged between 42 and 72 years, with a median age of 67 years. Among them, 12 patients presented with left-sided tumors, 11 presented with right-sided tumors, and 1 patient exhibited bilateral breast tumors. Breast tissue density was classified into categories: predominantly fatty (PF), scattered fibro-glandular (SF), heterogeneously dense (HD), and extremely dense tissue (ED). The majority of patients had fibro-glandular breast tissue, with 5 patients having heterogeneously dense breasts and 1 with extremely dense breast tissue. Quadrant division delineated breast tissue involvement, specifically in the upper outer (UOQ), upper inner (UIQ), lower outer (LOQ), and lower inner (LIQ) quadrants, with most tumors located in the UOQ and fewest in the LIQ, consistent with epidemiological expectations. Histological analysis revealed various tumor types including atypical ductal hyperplasia (ADH), ductal carcinoma in situ (DCIS), invasive ductal carcinoma (IDC), invasive lobular carcinoma (ILC), and lobular carcinoma in situ, with tumor grades ranging from 1 to 3. Tumors were further examined for the presence of estrogen (ER), progesterone (PR), and HER2 receptors.

The algorithm demonstrated the successful detection of all biopsy-confirmed breast cancers, as depicted in Figure 3. Furthermore, none of the 23 contralateral breasts exhibited predicted tumors. Accurate estimation of tumor sizes was achieved, with a maximum error of 7 mm observed between actual and estimated tumor sizes, accompanied by variability in size differences. The sensitivity of tumor detection extended to tumors as small as 5 mm. A trend towards larger estimated thermal signatures compared to actual tumor sizes was noted in high-grade tumors ($p = 0.181$), as well as in cases with concomitant in situ carcinoma and invasive carcinoma ($p = 0.466$) and triple-negative breast cancer ($p = 0.784$).

Table 1. Demographic and clinical data for the 25 malignant breast tumors: laterality designed as right (R) and left (L) location within the breast—upper outer quadrant (UOQ), upper inner quadrant (UIQ), lower outer quadrant (LOQ), and lower inner quadrant (LIQ); tumor grade indeterminate (X)—low (1), intermediate (2), and high-grade (3); presence of additional DCIS/ LCIS with invasive carcinoma; and TNM staging and the presence of prognostic markers including estrogen receptor (ER), progesterone receptor (PR), and HER2 receptor. Tumor depth was calculated using both the infrared images and MRI images.

Age	Laterality	Location	Breast Tissue Density	Histology	Grade	Actual Size (cm)	Estimated Size (cm)	DCIS/ LCIS	Staging	ER	PR	HER2	Depth of Tumor Based on MRI (cm)
68	L	UOQ	SF	ADH	X	0.5	1	None	—	—	—	—	2.91
60	R	UOQ	HD	DCIS	2	1.4	1.3	DCIS	T1c N0 Mx	+	+	—	1.18
71	R	UOQ	PF	IDC	1	0.9	1	None	T1c N0 Mx	+	-	1+	2.26
67	L	UIQ	ED	IDC	1	1.7	1.9	None	T1c N0 Mx	+	+	1+	2.4
67	L	UOQ	SF	IDC	1	1.1	1.2	None	T1c N0 Mx	+	+	2+	2.28
48	R	UOQ	SF	IDC	1	1.1	1	DCIS	T1c N0 Mx	+	+	1+	2.23
64	R	UOQ	SF	IDC	1	1.2	1	None	T1c N0 Mx	+	+	1+	4.95
65	L	UOQ	HD	IDC	1	1.6	1.4	None	T1c N0 Mx	+	+	1+	—
70	R	UOQ	SF	IDC	2	0.8	1	DCIS	T1c N0 Mx	+	+	1+	2.14
51	L	UOQ	SF	IDC	2	1.9	1.9	LCIS	T2 N1a M0	+	+	1+	0.95
46	R	LIQ	HD	IDC	2	1.1	1.5	DCIS	T1c N0 Mx	+	+	1+	2.96
72	R	UOQ	SF	IDC	2	1.1	1	DCIS	T1c N0 Mx	+	+	2+	2.74
64	L	UOQ	PF	IDC	2	1.5	1	DCIS	T1c N1a M0	+	+	2+	2.93
63	L	UIQ	SF	IDC	2	0.5	1	DCIS	T1b N0 Mx	+	+	0+	3.9
57	L	UIQ	SF	IDC	2	1.2	1	None	T1c N0 Mx	+	+	2+	2
52	R	UOQ	SF	IDC	3	1.2	1	DCIS	T1a N0 Mx	—	—	0+	5.45
68	R	UOQ	SF	IDC	3	2.7	2.7	DCIS	T2 N1a Mx	+	+	1+	2.72
68	L	UOQ	HD	IDC	3	1.3	1	None	T2 N0 Mx	—	—	0+	2.43
70	R	LIQ	SF	IDC	3	0.5	1	DCIS	T1b N0 Mx	—	—	0+	3.76
42	R	UOQ	HD	IDC	3	0.5	1	DCIS	T1b N0 Mx	—	—	0+	2.42
49	R	LOQ	SF	IDC	3	2.6	2.7	DCIS	T2 N0 Mx	—	—	0+	4.3
72	L	UIQ	SF	IDC	3	0.9	1	DCIS	T1b N0 Mx	—	—	0+	1.14
68	L	UOQ	SF	ILC	1	0.8	1	DCIS	T1c N1a M0	+	+	1+	2.93
70	L	UOQ	SF	ILC	2	2.1	2.3	LCIS	T2 N0 Mx	+	+	2+	2.27
67	L	UIQ	SF	LCIS	X	0.5	1	LCIS	—	—	—	—	1.29

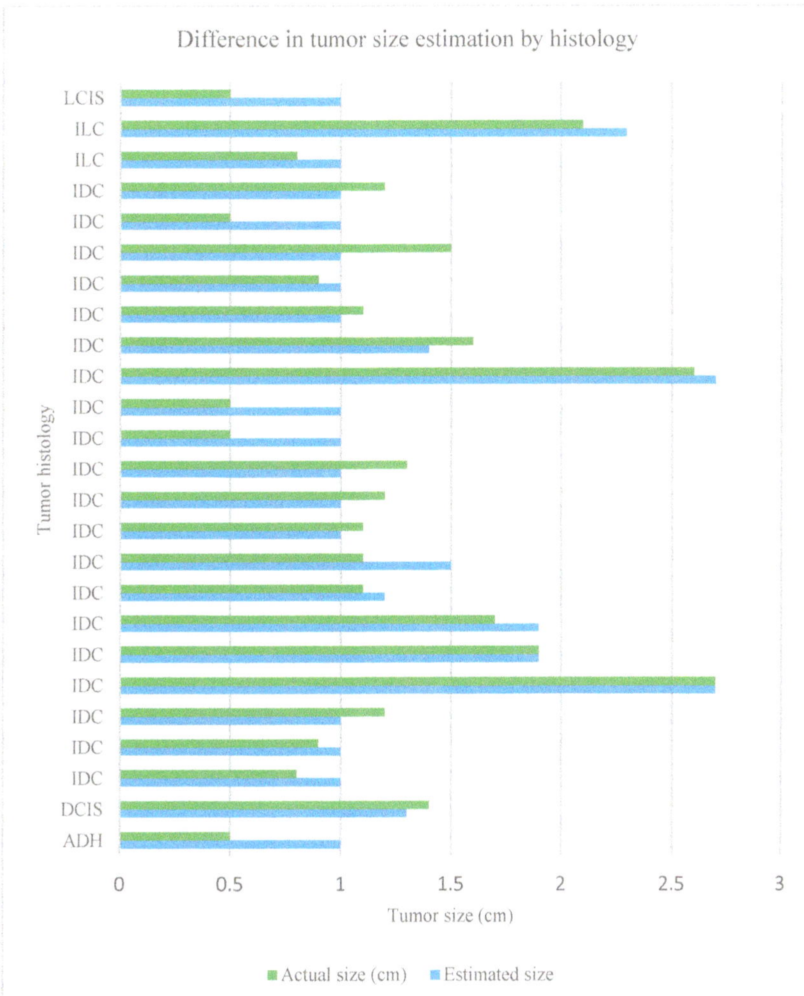

Figure 3. All 25 breast tumors with a comparison of the actual and estimated tumor size by histological subtype. Histology subtypes included invasive ductal carcinoma (IDC), invasive lobular carcinoma (ILC), ductal carcinoma in situ (DCIS), lobular carcinoma in situ (LCIS) and atypical ductal hyperplasia (ADH).

4. Discussion

Breast cancer screening has played a pivotal role in reducing mortality rates associated with the disease by facilitating early tumor detection and improving cure rates. Despite the central role of mammograms in routine screening, challenges such as discomfort during procedures, radiation exposure, and limited efficacy in dense breast tissue persist. To address these challenges, various adjunct techniques have been explored. In our study, we leveraged infrared technology, extensively researched for decades, in combination with advanced computational fluid dynamics software. This innovative approach yielded significant success in accurately predicting the presence of cancerous tumors.

Our algorithm leverages the principle that metabolically active, well-perfused malignant tumors serve as heat sources, influencing breast surface temperature. It reliably and accurately predicted breast cancer regardless of tumor location, tissue density, histological subtype, prognostic receptor status, or tumor depth by analyzing breast surface temperature data. This comprehensive predictive capability extends to precancerous lesions, including atypical ductal hyperplasia. The patient cohort encompassed commonly encountered histological subtypes such as IDC, ILC, DCIS, and LCIS, confirming the technique's broad applicability. The precision in predicting tumor sizes, with errors consistently below 1 cm, further highlights the robustness of our approach. Further studies on the minimal tumor size and other factors that affect the detectability of breast cancer using our algorithm are in development. Gutierrez and Kandlikar [55] have identified the detectability of the algorithm through numerical studies.

The observed correlation between thermal signatures and tumor characteristics aligns with known attributes of malignant tumors, characterized by heightened metabolic rates and increased vascularity. Notably, our method identified larger thermal signatures in high-grade and triple-negative tumors, both known for their rapid growth and expected elevation in angiogenesis and metabolism. Although the small sample size may limit the statistical significance of these findings, the observed trends hint at the potential to gain valuable insights into tumor behavior even before biopsy, thereby influencing patient care decisions.

The absence of false positives in contralateral breasts enhances the credibility of our method for detecting malignant lesions. Encouraged by these promising outcomes, our next step involves expanding our investigations through larger clinical studies. This will enable a more comprehensive evaluation of the sensitivity and specificity of infrared imaging using physics-based inverse modeling with breast surface temperatures as a robust technique for breast cancer detection. The implications of our findings suggest a potential paradigm shift in early cancer detection, paving the way for enhanced patient care and management strategies.

5. Conclusions

In a promising pilot study involving 24 patients, our approach exhibited a remarkable 100% sensitivity and specificity rate in detecting all malignant breast tumors, without any false positive results observed in the contralateral breasts, irrespective of tumor size, location, and breast tissue density. Larger studies are in process to further illuminate the pathway for this new technology in breast cancer detection.

Author Contributions: Conceptualization, N.S. and P.P.; Methodology, C.G., I.P.-R., J.-L.G.-H., A.O., L.M., S.K. and P.P.; Software, C.G., I.P.-R. and J.-L.G.-H.; Validation, C.G. and I.P.-R.; Formal analysis, N.S.; Investigation, A.O., D.D. and S.K.; Resources, I.P.-R., A.O., D.D., L.M. and P.P.; Data curation, N.S.; Writing—original draft, N.S.; Writing—review and editing, N.S., C.G., I.P.-R., S.K. and P.P.; Visualization, S.K.; Supervision, S.K. and P.P.; Project administration, D.D., L.M., S.K. and P.P. All authors have read and agreed to the published version of the manuscript.

Funding: This research received no external funding.

Institutional Review Board Statement: The Rochester Regional Health Clinical Investigation Committee reviewed the protocol NSF CBT-1511314 (A thermal imaging technique for the detection of breast cancer based on computational simulations), and it received approval as a minimal-risk new study on 24 October 2017, with extended approval until December 2019. IRB 1788-A Dabydeen.

Informed Consent Statement: Informed consent was obtained from all subjects involved in this study.

Data Availability Statement: The original contributions presented in this study are included in the article; further inquiries can be directed to the corresponding author.

Conflicts of Interest: Five of the authors, Pradyumna Phatak, Jose-Luis Gonzalez, Alyssa Owens, Donnette Dabydeen, Lori Madeiros, and Satish Kandlikar, have equity interest in BiRed, a company specializing in innovative breast cancer detection. The remaining authors declare that the research was conducted in the absence of any commercial or financial relationships that could be construed as a potential conflict of interest.

References

1. Sung, H.; Ferlay, J.; Siegel, R.L.; Laversanne, M.; Soerjomataram, I.; Jemal, A.; Bray, F. Global Cancer Statistics 2020: GLOBOCAN Estimates of Incidence and Mortality Worldwide for 36 Cancers in 185 Countries. *CA Cancer J. Clin.* **2021**, *71*, 209–249. [CrossRef]
2. Cancer Facts & Figures 2022. Available online: https://www.cancer.org/research/cancer-facts-statistics/all-cancer-facts-figures/cancer-facts-figures-2022.html (accessed on 20 December 2023).
3. Freer, P.E. Mammographic Breast Density: Impact on Breast Cancer Risk and Implications for Screening. *Radiographics* **2015**, *35*, 302–315. [CrossRef]
4. Lian, J.; Li, K. A Review of Breast Density Implications and Breast Cancer Screening. *Clin. Breast Cancer* **2020**, *20*, 283–290. [CrossRef]
5. Massat, M.B. Breast Imaging Update: Guidelines, Recall Rates and Personalized Care. *Appl. Radiol.* **2017**, *46*, 28–31. [CrossRef]
6. Hussein, H.; Abbas, E.; Keshavarzi, S.; Fazelzad, R.; Bukhanov, K.; Kulkarni, S.; Au, F.; Ghai, S.; Alabousi, A.; Freitas, V. Supplemental Breast Cancer Screening in Women with Dense Breasts and Negative Mammography: A Systematic Review and Meta-Analysis. *Radiology* **2023**, *306*, e221785. [CrossRef]
7. Choi, Y.; Woo, O.-H.; Shin, H.-S.; Cho, K.R.; Seo, B.K.; Choi, G.-Y. Quantitative Analysis of Radiation Dosage and Image Quality between Digital Breast Tomosynthesis (DBT) with Two-Dimensional Synthetic Mammography and Full-Field Digital Mammography (FFDM). *Clin. Imaging* **2019**, *55*, 12–17. [CrossRef]
8. Gennaro, G.; Bernardi, D.; Houssami, N. Radiation Dose with Digital Breast Tomosynthesis Compared to Digital Mammography: Per-View Analysis. *Eur. Radiol.* **2018**, *28*, 573–581. [CrossRef]
9. Christiansen, C.L.; Wang, F.; Barton, M.B.; Kreuter, W.; Elmore, J.G.; Gelfand, A.E.; Fletcher, S.W. Predicting the Cumulative Risk of False-Positive Mammograms. *JNCI J. Natl. Cancer Inst.* **2000**, *92*, 1657–1666. [CrossRef]
10. Ramadan, S.Z. Methods Used in Computer-Aided Diagnosis for Breast Cancer Detection Using Mammograms: A Review. *J. Healthc. Eng.* **2020**, *2020*, e9162464. [CrossRef]
11. Zebari, D.A.; Ibrahim, D.A.; Zeebaree, D.Q.; Haron, H.; Salih, M.S.; Damaševičius, R.; Mohammed, M.A. Systematic Review of Computing Approaches for Breast Cancer Detection Based Computer Aided Diagnosis Using Mammogram Images. *Appl. Artif. Intell.* **2021**, *35*, 2157–2203. [CrossRef]
12. Bai, J.; Posner, R.; Wang, T.; Yang, C.; Nabavi, S. Applying Deep Learning in Digital Breast Tomosynthesis for Automatic Breast Cancer Detection: A Review. *Med. Image Anal.* **2021**, *71*, 102049. [CrossRef]
13. Jones, M.A.; Islam, W.; Faiz, R.; Chen, X.; Zheng, B. Applying Artificial Intelligence Technology to Assist with Breast Cancer Diagnosis and Prognosis Prediction. *Front. Oncol.* **2022**, *12*, 980793. [CrossRef]
14. Nassif, A.B.; Talib, M.A.; Nasir, Q.; Afadar, Y.; Elgendy, O. Breast Cancer Detection Using Artificial Intelligence Techniques: A Systematic Literature Review. *Artif. Intell. Med.* **2022**, *127*, 102276. [CrossRef]
15. Henriksen, E.L.; Carlsen, J.F.; Vejborg, I.M.; Nielsen, M.B.; Lauridsen, C.A. The Efficacy of Using Computer-Aided Detection (CAD) for Detection of Breast Cancer in Mammography Screening: A Systematic Review. *Acta Radiol.* **2019**, *60*, 13–18. [CrossRef]
16. Giess, C.S.; Wang, A.; Ip, I.K.; Lacson, R.; Pourjabbar, S.; Khorasani, R. Patient, Radiologist, and Examination Characteristics Affecting Screening Mammography Recall Rates in a Large Academic Practice. *J. Am. Coll. Radiol.* **2019**, *16*, 411–418. [CrossRef]
17. Veenhuizen, S.G.A.; de Lange, S.V.; Bakker, M.F.; Pijnappel, R.M.; Mann, R.M.; Monninkhof, E.M.; Emaus, M.J.; de Koekkoek-Doll, P.K.; Bisschops, R.H.C.; Lobbes, M.B.I.; et al. Supplemental Breast MRI for Women with Extremely Dense Breasts: Results of the Second Screening Round of the DENSE Trial. *Radiology* **2021**, *299*, 278–286. [CrossRef]
18. Vourtsis, A.; Berg, W.A. Breast Density Implications and Supplemental Screening. *Eur. Radiol.* **2019**, *29*, 1762–1777. [CrossRef]
19. Mullen, L.A.; Panigrahi, B.; Hollada, J.; Panigrahi, B.; Falomo, E.T.; Harvey, S.C. Strategies for Decreasing Screening Mammography Recall Rates While Maintaining Performance Metrics. *Acad. Radiol.* **2017**, *24*, 1556–1560. [CrossRef]
20. Vollmer, M.; Möllmann, K.-P. *Infrared Thermal Imaging: Fundamentals, Research and Applications*, 2nd ed.; Wiley-VCH Verlag GmbH & Co. KGaA: Weinheim, Germany, 2018; ISBN 978-3-527-41351-5.
21. Strąkowska, M.; Strąkowski, R.; Strzelecki, M.; De Mey, G.; Więcek, B. Thermal Modelling and Screening Method for Skin Pathologies Using Active Thermography. *Biocybern. Biomed. Eng.* **2018**, *38*, 602–610. [CrossRef]
22. Lawson, R. Implications of Surface Temperatures in the Diagnosis of Breast Cancer. *Can. Med. Assoc. J.* **1956**, *75*, 309.
23. Lawson, R.N. A New Infrared Imaging Device. *Can. Med. Assoc. J.* **1958**, *79*, 402–403.
24. Lawson, R.N.; Chughtai, M.S. Breast Cancer and Body Temperature. *Can. Med. Assoc. J.* **1963**, *88*, 68–70.
25. Lawson, R.N.; Saunders, A.L.; Cowen, R.D. Breast Cancer and Heptaldehyde. *Can. Med. Assoc. J.* **1956**, *75*, 486–488.
26. Kandlikar, S.G.; Perez-Raya, I.; Raghupathi, P.A.; Gonzalez-Hernandez, J.-L.; Dabydeen, D.; Medeiros, L.; Phatak, P. Infrared Imaging Technology for Breast Cancer Detection—Current Status, Protocols and New Directions. *Int. J. Heat. Mass. Transf.* **2017**, *108*, 2303–2320. [CrossRef]
27. Singh, D.; Singh, A.K. Role of Image Thermography in Early Breast Cancer Detection—Past, Present and Future. *Comput. Methods Programs Biomed.* **2020**, *183*, 105074. [CrossRef]
28. Collett, A.E.; Guilfoyle, C.; Gracely, E.J.; Frazier, T.G.; Barrio, A.V. Infrared Imaging Does Not Predict the Presence of Malignancy in Patients with Suspicious Radiologic Breast Abnormalities. *Breast J.* **2014**, *20*, 375–380. [CrossRef]
29. Gonzalez-Hernandez, J.-L.; Recinella, A.N.; Kandlikar, S.G.; Dabydeen, D.; Medeiros, L.; Phatak, P. Technology, Application and Potential of Dynamic Breast Thermography for the Detection of Breast Cancer. *Int. J. Heat. Mass. Transf.* **2019**, *131*, 558–573. [CrossRef]

30. Owens, A.; Kandlikar, S.G.; Phatak, P. Potential of Infrared Imaging for Breast Cancer Detection: A Critical Evaluation. *J. Eng. Sci. Med. Diagn. Ther.* **2021**, *4*, 041005. [CrossRef]
31. Mashekova, A.; Zhao, Y.; Ng, E.Y.K.; Zarikas, V.; Fok, S.C.; Mukhmetov, O. Early Detection of the Breast Cancer Using Infrared Technology—A Comprehensive Review. *Therm. Sci. Eng. Prog.* **2022**, *27*, 101142. [CrossRef]
32. Lozano, A.; Hassanipour, F. Infrared Imaging for Breast Cancer Detection: An Objective Review of Foundational Studies and Its Proper Role in Breast Cancer Screening. *Infrared Phys. Technol.* **2019**, *97*, 244–257. [CrossRef]
33. Hanahan, D.; Weinberg, R.A. The Hallmarks of Cancer. *Cell* **2000**, *100*, 57–70. [CrossRef]
34. Hanahan, D.; Weinberg, R.A. Hallmarks of Cancer: The Next Generation. *Cell* **2011**, *144*, 646–674. [CrossRef]
35. Castañeda-Gill, J.M.; Vishwanatha, J.K. Antiangiogenic Mechanisms and Factors in Breast Cancer Treatment. *J. Carcinog.* **2016**, *15*, 1. [CrossRef]
36. Watmough, D.J.; Oliver, R. Emissivity of Human Skin in the Waveband between 2μ and 6μ. *Nature* **1968**, *219*, 622–624. [CrossRef]
37. Steketee, J. Spectral Emissivity of Skin and Pericardium. *Phys. Med. Biol.* **1973**, *18*, 686. [CrossRef]
38. Charlton, M.; Stanley, S.A.; Whitman, Z.; Wenn, V.; Coats, T.J.; Sims, M.; Thompson, J.P. The Effect of Constitutive Pigmentation on the Measured Emissivity of Human Skin. *PLoS ONE* **2020**, *15*, e0241843. [CrossRef]
39. Lahiri, B.B.; Bagavathiappan, S.; Jayakumar, T.; Philip, J. Medical Applications of Infrared Thermography: A Review. *Infrared Phys. Technol.* **2012**, *55*, 221–235. [CrossRef]
40. Gautherie, M. Thermopathology of Breast Cancer: Measurement and Analysis of in Vivo Temperature and Blood Flow. *Ann. N. Y. Acad. Sci.* **1980**, *335*, 383–415. [CrossRef]
41. Gautherie, M. Temperature and Blood Flow Patterns in Breast Cancer during Natural Evolution and Following Radiotherapy. *Prog. Clin. Biol. Res.* **1982**, *107*, 21–64.
42. Gautherie, M. Thermobiological Assessment of Benign and Malignant Breast Diseases. *Am. J. Obstet. Gynecol.* **1983**, *147*, 861–869. [CrossRef]
43. Gullino, P.M. Natural History of Breast Cancer: Progression from Hyperplasia to Neoplasia as Predicted by Angiogenesis. *Cancer* **1977**, *39*, 2697–2703. [CrossRef]
44. Gullino, P.M.; Yi, P.-N.; Grantham, F.H. Relationship Between Temperature and Blood Supply or Consumption of Oxygen and Glucose by Rat Mammary Carcinomas. *JNCI J. Natl. Cancer Inst.* **1978**, *60*, 835–847. [CrossRef]
45. Gullino, P.M. Influence of Blood Supply on Thermal Properties and Metabolism of Mammary Carcinomas. *Ann. N. Y. Acad. Sci.* **1980**, *335*, 1–21. [CrossRef]
46. Etehadtavakol, M.; Ng, E.Y.K. Survey of Numerical Bioheat Transfer Modelling for Accurate Skin Surface Measurements. *Therm. Sci. Eng. Prog.* **2020**, *20*, 100681. [CrossRef]
47. Pennes, H.H. Analysis of Tissue and Arterial Blood Temperatures in the Resting Human Forearm. *J. Appl. Physiol.* **1948**, *1*, 93–122. [CrossRef]
48. Shrivastava, D. *Theory and Applications of Heat Transfer in Humans*; John Wiley & Sons, Incorporated: Newark, UK, 2018; ISBN 978-1-119-12731-4.
49. Lozano, A.; Hayes, J.C.; Compton, L.M.; Azarnoosh, J.; Hassanipour, F. Determining the Thermal Characteristics of Breast Cancer Based on High-Resolution Infrared Imaging, 3D Breast Scans, and Magnetic Resonance Imaging. *Sci. Rep.* **2020**, *10*, 10105. [CrossRef]
50. Mukhmetov, O.; Igali, D.; Mashekova, A.; Zhao, Y.; Ng, E.Y.K.; Fok, S.C.; Teh, S.L. Thermal Modeling for Breast Tumor Detection Using Thermography. *Int. J. Therm. Sci.* **2021**, *161*, 106712. [CrossRef]
51. Recinella, A.N.; Gonzalez-Hernandez, J.-L.; Kandlikar, S.G.; Dabydeen, D.; Medeiros, L.; Phatak, P. Clinical Infrared Imaging in the Prone Position for Breast Cancer Screening—Initial Screening and Digital Model Validation. *J. Eng. Sci. Med. Diagn. Ther.* **2020**, *3*, 011005. [CrossRef]
52. Gutierrez, C.; Owens, A.; Medeiros, L.; Dabydeen, D.; Sritharan, N.; Phatak, P.; Kandlikar, S.G. Breast Cancer Detection Using Enhanced IRI-Numerical Engine and Inverse Heat Transfer Modeling: Model Description and Clinical Validation. *Sci. Rep.* **2024**, *14*, 3316. [CrossRef]
53. Gonzalez-Hernandez, J.-L.; Kandlikar, S.G.; Dabydeen, D.; Medeiros, L.; Phatak, P. Generation and Thermal Simulation of a Digital Model of the Female Breast in Prone Position. *J. Eng. Sci. Med. Diagn. Ther.* **2018**, *1*, 041006. [CrossRef]
54. Gonzalez-Hernandez, J.-L.; Recinella, A.N.; Kandlikar, S.G.; Dabydeen, D.; Medeiros, L.; Phatak, P. An Inverse Heat Transfer Approach for Patient-Specific Breast Cancer Detection and Tumor Localization Using Surface Thermal Images in the Prone Position. *Infrared Phys. Technol.* **2020**, *105*, 103202. [CrossRef]
55. Gutierrez, C.; Kandlikar, S.G. Detectability of Breast Cancer through Inverse Heat Transfer Modeling Using Patient-Specific Surface Temperatures. *J. Eng. Sci. Med. Diagn. Ther.* 2024, *submitted*.

diagnostics

MDPI

Article

Lung Disease Detection Using U-Net Feature Extractor Cascaded by Graph Convolutional Network

Pshtiwan Qader Rashid and İlker Türker *

Department of Computer Engineering, Karabuk University, 78050 Karabuk, Turkey; pshtiwan572@gmail.com
* Correspondence: iturker@karabuk.edu.tr

Abstract: Computed tomography (CT) scans have recently emerged as a major technique for the fast diagnosis of lung diseases via image classification techniques. In this study, we propose a method for the diagnosis of COVID-19 disease with improved accuracy by utilizing graph convolutional networks (GCN) at various layer formations and kernel sizes to extract features from CT scan images. We apply a U-Net model to aid in segmentation and feature extraction. In contrast with previous research retrieving deep features from convolutional filters and pooling layers, which fail to fully consider the spatial connectivity of the nodes, we employ GCNs for classification and prediction to capture spatial connectivity patterns, which provides a significant association benefit. We handle the extracted deep features to form an adjacency matrix that contains a graph structure and pass it to a GCN along with the original image graph and the largest kernel graph. We combine these graphs to form one block of the graph input and then pass it through a GCN with an additional dropout layer to avoid overfitting. Our findings show that the suggested framework, called the feature-extracted graph convolutional network (FGCN), performs better in identifying lung diseases compared to recently proposed deep learning architectures that are not based on graph representations. The proposed model also outperforms a variety of transfer learning models commonly used for medical diagnosis tasks, highlighting the abstraction potential of the graph representation over traditional methods.

Keywords: lung disease detection; graph convolutional networks; COVID-19; graph representative learning; deep learning

1. Introduction

Lung diseases are assumed to be a major global health concern, affecting millions of lives and placing a significant burden on healthcare systems worldwide [1]. Coronavirus disease (COVID-19), an infectious disease caused by the SARS-CoV-2 virus, significantly impacts human health, particularly those with lung disease, causing respiratory symptoms, pneumonia, acute respiratory distress syndrome (ARDS), and other conditions [2]. The early detection and accurate diagnosis of lung diseases are critical for effective treatment and improved patient health outcomes. Traditional diagnostic methods often rely on the human interpretation of medical images, leading to time-consuming and subjective assessments. However, the intersection of cutting-edge technology and medical science is opening new avenues to increase the precision and effectiveness of the early diagnosis of respiratory diseases [3].

Baratella et al. performed a study to compare how well traditional chest X-rays (CXR) and digital tomosynthesis (DTS) could find changes in the pulmonary interstitial spaces in people who had recovered from severe COVID-19. Two radiologists, each with 16 and 10 years of experience in chest imaging, independently assessed the DTS images to compare them with computed tomography (CT). The diagnostic accuracy of DTS was markedly superior to that of CXR in identifying interstitial lung abnormalities [4]. Bellini et al. conducted a study to assess the potential reduction in the lung volume in long-term COVID-19 patients with mild respiratory symptoms using the quantitative analysis of chest

CT images. In patients with long COVID symptoms and no visible abnormalities on chest CT, quantitative volume analysis revealed an average reduction in the lung volume of 10% compared to individuals of the same age who had never had COVID-19. If a chest CT scan shows no signs of inflammation, doctors may mistakenly attribute moderate respiratory symptoms in young COVID-19 patients to anxiety. Upon examination, a chest CT scan revealed no evidence of inflammatory abnormalities [5]. Thoracic imaging is a multimodal technique that utilizes many types of waves to generate images of the organs located in the thorax. The medical imaging techniques used include chest X-rays, computed tomography (CT), lung ultrasonography, and magnetic resonance imaging (MRI). Modalities such as thoracic imaging techniques have proven to be valuable in diagnosing and predicting the outcomes of COVID-19. These imaging techniques are also effective in monitoring the health of COVID-19 survivors who experience long-term symptoms [6].

To train the CompLung structure, Pardyl, Adam et al. used the publicly available LIDC-IDRI dataset along with lung segmentation masks to improve the performance and interpretability of CompLung in comparison to prior techniques used to diagnose lung cancer [7]. Garstka et al. (2020) trained a self-constructed convolutional neural network on a relatively short dataset to classify lung X-ray images. They conducted a comparative analysis to evaluate the impact of data augmentation on the model's performance and its ability to prevent overfitting. The categorization procedure achieved 85% accuracy with sensitivity of 0.95 [8]. Nurzynska et al. proposed a parameterized pipeline for the classification of whole slide images (WSI) in order to determine whether using many layers of imaging enhances the accuracy in classifying slides. The pipeline integrated a convolutional neural network (CNN) to categorize tiles within each image layer, leading to the creation of an AFB possibility score heatmap. They subsequently input the features generated from the heatmap into a whole slide image (WSI) classifier. The findings suggested that the process of acquiring a single layer can generate bias, also known as a sampling error, in the whole slide image (WSI). Either multilayer or extended-focus acquisition can reduce this bias [9]. Certain measures were employed to mitigate the spread of tuberculosis, a prevalent mycobacterial infection that impacts human health, typically using Ziehl–Neelsen (ZN)-stained slides to identify acid-fast mycobacteria (AFB) in tissue sections. These slides display vibrant red AFB against a blue background. Yang, Mu et al. suggested a machine learning pipeline that can correctly label digitized ZN-stained slides as either AFB-positive or AFB-negative. For tile recognition, the pipeline consists of two convolutional neural network (CNN) models. They assessed the work on a distinct set of tiles, yielding F1 ratings of 99.03% and 98.75%, respectively [10].

Artificial intelligence (AI) and machine learning (ML) have enabled significant advances in recent years, offering promising solutions to address the challenges associated with respiratory diseases. Among these advances, graph neural networks (GNNs) have emerged as a revolutionary system in medical image classification tasks. GNNs, originally designed for the analysis of graph-structured data, have emerged as a powerful type of network in medical imaging, where the relationships and connections within the data significantly improve the accuracy of diagnosis [11]. GCNs, or graph convolutional networks, go beyond traditional graph embedding techniques like Deepwalk in that they focus on creating a low-dimensional network representation while excluding node features [12,13]. Graph representative learning techniques are proven to represent comparable or superior classification performance for various medical tasks, including the signal and image domains [14–16].

Automatic diagnosis methods often use deep learning algorithms instead of reverse transcription polymerase chain reaction (RT-PCR) to diagnose chest X-ray images [17]. Chest scans are effective in identifying COVID-19 through visual markers such as the ground-glass opacity or hazy dark patches on the lungs, helping to distinguish affected individuals from healthy control individuals [18]. In this context, automated diagnosis systems frequently use chest computed tomography (CT) scans because of their high sensitivity and speed [19,20].

In contrast to traditional classification models, convolutional neural networks (CNNs) can work in the original high-dimensional space because they can be abstract. This implies that the preprocessing of the input image is not necessary [21,22].

Yang et al. [23] investigated and compared several deep learning-based methods using X-ray and CT scan images in the medical field to detect COVID-19 infection. The researchers employed four powerful pre-trained CNN models, DenseNet121, VGG16, ResNet50, and ResNet152, for the binary classification of COVID-19 from CT scan images. The F1-score and accuracy achieved were over 96%, indicating that the listed transfer learning techniques supported tasks with relatively limited data and reduced the training time.

Alrahhal and Supreethi [24] have developed a diagnostic system designed for the identification of COVID-19 based on CT scan images. The ResNet50 architecture improves feature extraction by producing a graphical representation of oriented gradient descriptors based on the visual phrases' content. Subsequently, they employed an adaptive boosting classification model to identify the existence of COVID-19. They implemented this methodology on CT scans and an X-ray database, and the results were better when compared to other similar methods.

Xu et al. [25] preprocessed CT scan images to segment them into several image cubes using a 3D-CNN model. Then, using the extracted features from the ResNet18 model, a Bayesian learner categorized all of the image patches as COVID-19, influenza, and normal. They described their database, which featured 175 images in the normal category, 224 images in the viral pneumonia category, and 219 images in the COVID-19 category.

Yang et al. [26] used data augmentation and transfer learning to address the issue of overfitting that can easily emerge from the training of deep learning (DL) models on a limited dataset. They trained a DenseNet model on sample images from chest X-ray scans and then improved the pre-trained network on the COVID-19 dataset. Their supplied dataset featured 195 images in the normal category and 275 images in the COVID-19 category.

Song et al.'s method [27] offered three primary steps. In the first step, they extracted the major lung areas, and then they executed the segmentation process with the lungs themselves. To obtain the top-K data from the CT scans and provide image-level predictions, in the second step, they created a Detail Relation Extraction Neural Network (DRE-Net). Third, they combined the image-level predictions to achieve patient-level diagnoses. Their database consisted of 86 images for the normal group, 101 images for viral pneumonia, and 88 images for the COVID-19 category.

Zheng et al. [28] proposed a DeCoVNet with three steps. The first step was the network branch, and the second step comprised two 3D residual blocks (ResBlocks). The third step employed a progressive classifier (ProClf), utilizing a softmax activation function in the fully connected layer and 3D convolution layers. Their CT scan database consisted of 229 and 313 images for the normal and COVID-19 categories, respectively. Li et al. proposed COVNet, a method based on the RestNet-50 architecture [29]. This model generates features from the required CT slices. They then employed a max-pooling strategy to combine the features obtained from each individual slice. They utilized the softmax activation and a fully connected layer to provide a probability score based on the finalized feature map. Their dataset contained 1325, 1296, and 1736 images categorized as normal, COVID-19, and pneumonia, respectively.

Ucar et al. have suggested a deep learning method with a segmentation-based approach for COVID-19 disease detection based on CT scans [30]. To construct the suggested model, they changed the encoder part of the segmentation from the U-Net model. They used the deep learning models ResNet101, VGG16, DenseNet121, EfficientNetB5, and InceptionV3 in the encoder section. Then, using the majority voting rule, they combined the results of each updated U-Net model to determine a final conclusion. The experimental results showed that the suggested model had 99.38% specificity, 89.13% sensitivity, and an 85.03% segmentation Dice score.

A variety of studies aiming to detect lung disease, especially COVID-19 cases, use graph-induced approaches, such as graph convolutional networks (GCNs) [31]. Specifically applicable to 3D-CT images, a 3D-CNN architecture extracts visual features that enable the construction of COVID-19 graphs, designated as inputs to GCNs. However, due to its high computational complexity, the 3D-CNN is found to be less accurate, use significantly more memory, and require large datasets.

In the current study, we propose a COVID-19 diagnosis framework that combines the U-Net architecture with a feature-extracted GCN. With this, we attempted to reduce the high level of complexity in the data and explore higher-order patterns, which would improve the classification performance. By merging a graph convolution network with a U-Net model that is input with CT scan images, we aimed to extract pixel-level connectivity information based on their neighboring patterns to improve the predictions for the detection and classification of lung diseases. The graph-induced approach gives promising results and is applicable to imagery tasks related to medical or spectral images in future works.

2. Data and Methods

2.1. Dataset

We validate the proposed approach by employing a publicly accessible repository of SARS-CoV-2 CT scan images. The dataset, available on Kaggle, has a total of 2482 CT scans, each taken from a single patient, containing 1252 CT scans that are positive for SARS-CoV-2 infection and 1230 CT scans for patients not affected by SARS-CoV-2. The whole dataset is reported to be collected from real patients in hospitals from Sao Paulo, Brazil [32–34]. Figure 1 exhibits a selection of CT scan images depicting both COVID-19 and non-COVID-19 instances.

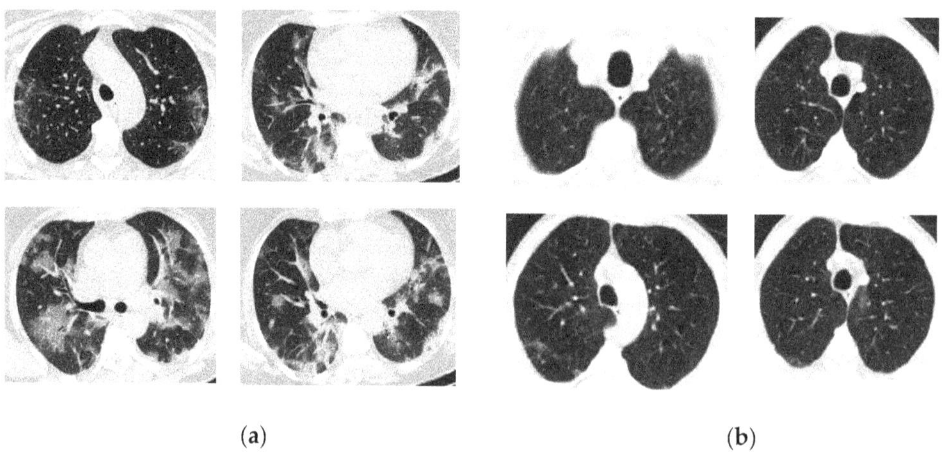

Figure 1. (**a**) COVID-19 and (**b**) non-COVID-19 samples [32].

2.2. Overview

We briefly explain the current study's methodology as follows. Initially, we run a preprocessing procedure for each input CT scan image, which includes filtering, normalization, and data augmentation, to enhance the abstraction capacity of the 3D-CT image. Next, we detect images using nuclei and train the U-Net model on the dataset. The U-Net model performs the feature extraction and segmentation of the input CT images, yielding a graph-based feature map for each patient. We classify the 3D-CT images for diagnosis by feeding the modified GCN, known as the "feature-extracted GCN" (FGCN), with the graph-structured input. Figure 2 presents the block diagram of the proposed method.

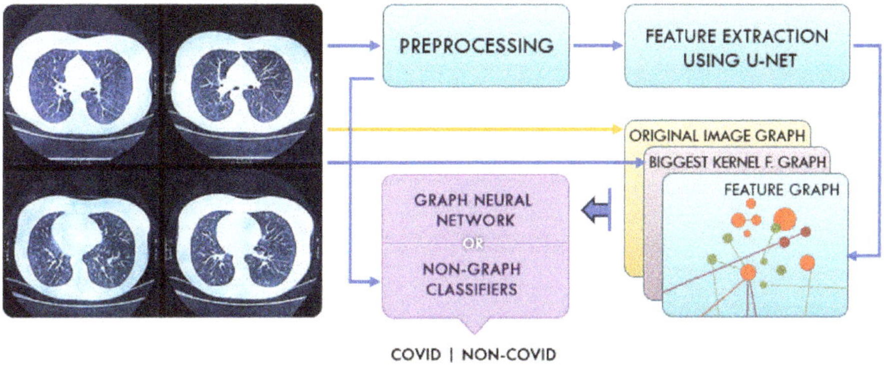

Figure 2. Block diagram of the proposed method.

2.3. Preprocessing

The preprocessing steps aim to enhance the abstraction of the 3D-CT images obtained from patients. Preprocessing includes three phases, listed as follows.

- Filtering: This process enhances or improves the quality of the 3D-CT scan images. Therefore, during filtering, a set of rules determines the value of any given pixel within the output image by calculating the values of the pixels in its vicinity.
- Normalization: This process modifies the range of pixel intensity levels. We also refer to it as "contrast stretching" because it enhances the image's contrast.
- Data Augmentation: This is considered the most commonly used preprocessing technique for the U-Net model, aiming to improve the size of the training dataset by applying many modifications, e.g., rotation, translation, several types of symmetry, etc. Accordingly, it reduces the training's sensitivity to noise and overfitting compared to the original input.

2.4. Feature Extraction Using the U-Net Model

Feature extraction strategies are critical in developing capabilities that will be useful in classifying and popularizing images. Using the U-Net model, we extract features from 3D-CT scan images. For biological image segmentation, U-Net primarily uses a straightforward structure with high flexibility and excellent pixel-level segmentation results. We intentionally chose the symmetrical architecture of U-Net to assist in image processing and computer vision tasks that require feature extraction and localization, context modeling, and precise resolution recovery. It leverages the benefits of both the encoder and decoder pathways to produce accurate and detailed output predictions. This model includes an encoder part (also called a contracting path; left side in Figure 3) and a decoder part (also called an expanding path; right side in Figure 3). Each of the boxes in the U-Net structure is a multi-channel feature map. The arrows represent various operations, such as max pooling, convolution, and copy and crop [35].

2.5. Classification Using FGCN

2.5.1. Graph Conversion

The formula $G = (N, E, A)$ represents a graph formula, with N denoting the collection of nodes, (E) is the edges between nodes, and (A) is the adjacency matrix. The adjacency matrix A_{ij} represents the connections between each node pair, with an entry indicating the weight of the link between i and the j-th node, which is the intersection of the i-th row and the j-th column. We can construct the graph using the Pearson correlation, the k-nearest neighbor (KNN) algorithm, or distance-based approaches to calculate the entries [36]. Figure 4 represents a sample of a graph with six nodes and the edges bridging them. We also provide the matrix that represents the adjacency of the graph nodes.

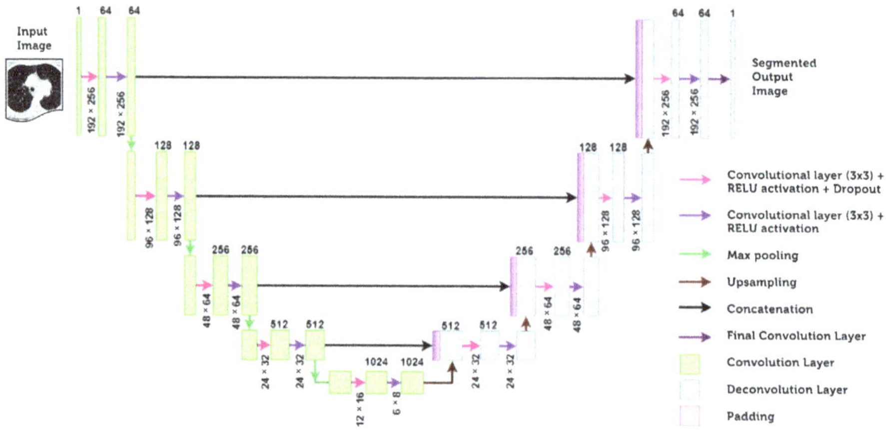

Figure 3. Feature extraction in U-Net architecture.

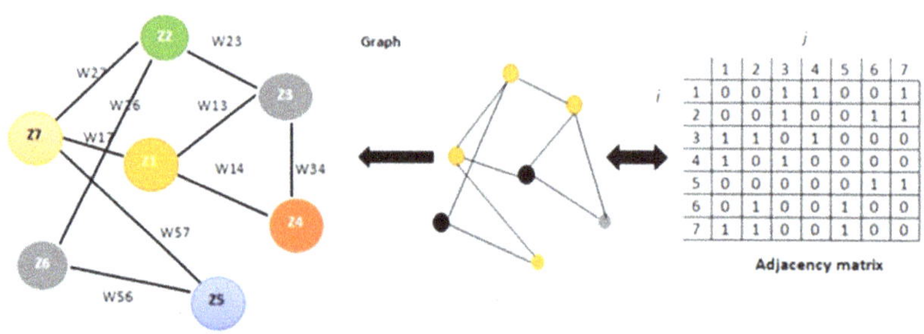

Figure 4. Directed graph example and its accompanying adjacency matrix modified from an image.

The convolution process for spectral-based GCNs is constructed with the Fourier transform by calculating the graph Laplacian's eigen-decomposition [37]. The description of graph Laplacian normalization is $L = \left(I_N - D^{-\frac{1}{2}} A D^{-\frac{1}{2}} = U \wedge U^T\right)$, where D is the degree matrix and A is the adjacency matrix. The columns of U constitute the eigenvector matrix and $\wedge$ is the diagonal matrix, which contains its eigenvalues. This operation is described as the multiplication of a signal $\left(X \in R^N\right)$, and the scalar for every node with a filter $(g_\theta = diag(\theta))$ is parameterized by $\left(\theta \in R^N\right)$.

$$g_\theta * x = U g_\theta(\wedge) U^T x \quad (1)$$

Defferrard et al. proposed ChebNet, which avoids computing the Fourier basis by approximating the spectrum filters by shortened Chebyshev polynomials. The procedure is defined as using a Chebyshev polynomial $T_m(x)$ of order m [38].

$$g_\theta * x \approx \sum_{m=0}^{M-1} \theta_m T_m\left(\overline{L}\right)_x \quad (2)$$

In Equation (2), $\overline{L}$ is the diagonal matrix of a scaled eigenvalue with a formula $\overline{L} = 2L/\lambda\text{max} - \text{I}_\text{N}$. The largest eigenvalue of L is indicated by the symbol max. The Chebyshev polynomials are denoted by $T_m(x) = 2xT_{k-1}(x) - T_{k-2}(x)$, where $T_0(x) = 1$ and $T_1(x) = x$.

ChebNet uses Chebyshev polynomials, eliminating the need to compute the Laplacian matrix's eigenvectors and reducing the computational cost. A graph pooling layer in the GCN decreases the size of the graph and increases the receptive field of the graph filters. The graph convolutional network's preceding layer combines the feature vectors to create a singular vector, which then feeds into a fully connected layer to produce the classification results.

2.5.2. Graph Convolutional Network (GCN)

A spectral GNN with mean pooling accumulation is referred to as a GCN. Kipf and Welling [39] proposed the GCN using a limited first-order estimate of the spectral convolution layers on graphs. Figure 5 illustrates a straightforward layer-wise propagation algorithm that converts the connections between the nodes in the graph design into node features. By assuming a $\lambda \approx 2$ reduction in the size of the convolutional filter to K = 1, we can simplify Equation (2) and address the issue of overfitting in graphs with a large degree distribution of nodes in their local neighborhood structure [39].

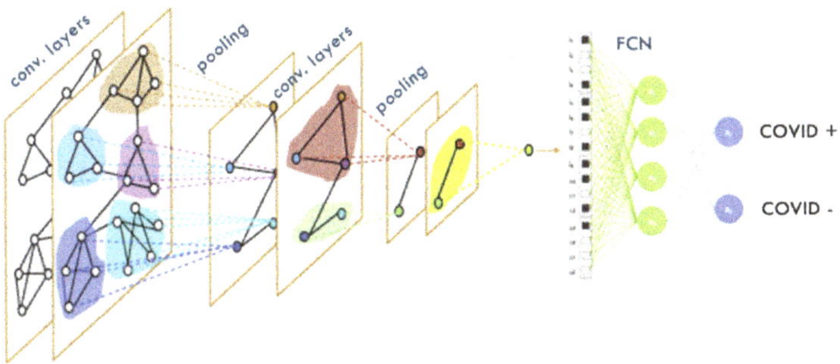

Figure 5. Evaluation of graph input data with a graph convolutional network.

$$g_\theta * x \approx \theta_0 + \theta_1 (L - I_N)_x = \theta_{0x} + \theta_1 D^{-\frac{1}{2}} A D^{-\frac{1}{2}} x \quad (3)$$

The values of θ_0 and θ_1 are not limited in Equation (3). The GCN additionally assumes that $\theta = \theta_0 - \theta_1$ so as to restrict the number of parameters and prevent overfitting. This results in the formulation of a graph convolution as follows:

$$g_\theta * x \approx \theta\left(I_N + D^{-\frac{1}{2}}\ A\ D^{-\frac{1}{2}}\right) x \quad (4)$$

This process will result in numerical instability and the explosion or disappearance of the gradients if it is stacked.

In order to apply the signal definition, we require $x \in R^{F*C}$ with C input channels and F filters for feature extraction. Kipf and Welling [39] expand this formula as follows:

$$Z = D^{-\frac{1}{2}} A D^{-\frac{1}{2}} x_\theta \quad (5)$$

where $\Theta \in R^{N*F}$ is the signal matrix formed via convolution and $\Theta \in R^{CXF}$ is the matrix formed by filterbank settings.

The classification task is performed using the modified version of the GCN, labeled the feature-extracted GCN (FGCN) in the current study. The steps involved in the FGCN are given below.

Step 1: The pyramid features are extracted from the CT scan images using a U-Net model at different layers and with different sizes of kernels.
Step 2: These extracted features are combined to form an adjacency matrix.
Step 3: The COVID-19 CT scan images are converted into a graph, which is formed using a combined adjacency matrix representing the edges and extracted features.
Step 4: The original CT scan graphs and the largest kernel graph are formed.
Step 5: These three graphs are combined to form one block of graph input, which is passed through the GCN with an extra dropout layer to reduce overfitting.
Step 6: Finally, image classification is performed to detect whether the patient is affected by COVID-19.

2.6. Baseline Learning Models

Deep learning has employed several CNN models to tackle significant tasks in image processing, like medical image classification and object detection. Medical image classification tasks employ an extensive variety of customized CNN models, and we also examined some CNN-based deep learning models on the same dataset with the same FGCN model; we provide a brief explanation below.

DenseNet201: This is a convolutional neural network (CNN) model that has been specifically designed with 201 layers. We utilized a previous version of the model that experienced training on a dataset including more than one million images taken from the ImageNet database. The pre-trained network employs a feed-forward connection between the layers and possesses the capability to categorize images into 1000 different classes. This includes the identification of various items, as well as the diagnosis of diseases in medical image classification [40].

VGG16: This is a widely used transfer learning model that consists of 13 convolutional layers and three fully connected layers. Each convolutional layer has 3×3 kernels, while the pooling layers have 2×2 parameters. Blocks 1 to 5 consist of many convolutional layers and one pooling layer, which together form the convolutional and pooling layers of VGG16. Block $1'$s two convolutional layers use 16 kernels to extract features, while the pooling layer reduces the image size. The design of subsequent blocks is uniform, except for the fact that blocks 1 and 2 utilize two convolutional layers, while blocks 3–5 utilize three convolutional layers, each with a distinct kernel size. This serves to deepen the network and boost its accuracy. Three fully interconnected layers are combined in the last stage to provide features classified into two distinct classes [41].

InceptionV3: This is a convolutional neural network model that has 48 layers and can learn to detect difficult patterns as well as features in medical images. This model's capacity to adjust a huge amount of data and manage images of different shapes and qualities is one of its primary strengths. This is critical in the field of medical image processing because of the wide range of image sizes, quality levels, and resolutions. This model typically has three convolutions of varying shapes and a maximum of one pooling layer [42].

ResNet50: This convolutional neural network model specifically tackles the problems of vanishing or expanding gradients. ResNet50 presents the idea of a residual neural network, which is a convolutional neural network consisting of 50 layers that emphasizes the acquisition of residuals rather than features [42].

NASNet Mobile: Google introduced NASNet Mobile, a powerful and well-designed solution that utilizes extensive processing capabilities. It treats the task of finding the optimal structure for a convolutional neural network (CNN) as a problem to solve through reinforcement learning. The primary objective of this model is to determine the most efficient configuration for each parameter in the search space, such as the filter sizes, output channels, strides, and number of layers. We designed every search operation in the reinforcement learning framework to evaluate and reward the correctness of this model on the given dataset.

NASNet achieved a cutting-edge outcome in the ImageNet competition. Nevertheless, the model's extensive computational requirements restrict its applicability to a limited number of classification tasks, while simultaneously enhancing the efficiency of the model's architecture [43].

EfficientNet: This is a convolutional neural network (CNN) approach that uses a compound coefficient to appropriately scale the dimensions of depth, breadth, and resolution. EfficientNet's scaling technique uniformly scales the depth, width, and resolution of the network by using a predefined set of scaling coefficients. This is different from the conventional approach, where these variables are scaled without a specific pattern. EfficientNet employs a compound coefficient to consistently scale all dimensions and resolutions of the network. The mixed scaling approach operates on the principle that larger input images require an increase in the number of layers to expand the network's receptive field and a greater number of channels to capture more intricate shapes within the entire image [44].

2.7. Experimental Environment

The experimental setup employs the Python environment, Torch package, SciPy, and NumPy to train the proposed deep learning models. The FGCNs were executed on a standard system, which included 64 GB of RAM, an Intel Core i7-12700HQ CPU operating at a frequency of 2.8 GHz, and an RTX 3080 GPU with 8 GB of memory.

2.8. Hyperparameters

The recommended specifications for the GCN structure include 50 epochs each with 64 neurons per layer. We set the learning rate at 0.0001 and used a dropout rate of 0.1. Concretely, we resized each image to a fixed resolution of 512 × 512 pixels. To mitigate overfitting in all pre-trained models using a particular dataset, we employed a random 80–20 split, allocating 80% for training and 20% for testing. The software environment for the execution of the Python 3.11 code included Spyder and Jupyter Notebook, both of which are part of the Anaconda distribution.

We used the Rectified Linear Unit (ReLU) [45] with the Adam optimizer [46] to activate each of the convolutional layers in the transfer learning models examined in this study. In addition, we incorporated a dropout layer with a rate of 0.3, which randomly deactivated thirty percent of the neurons throughout each training session. This mitigated the risk of overfitting on the training dataset.

3. Results and Discussion

This section shows the success of our suggested method (FGCN) in classification using different general DL models, such as VGG16, InceptionV3, NasNet Mobile, ResNet50, and DenseNet201. Table 1 displays several metrics, including the sensitivity, precision, specificity, F1-score, and accuracy, used to evaluate the performance of each model.

Table 1. Classification results achieved for SARS-CoV-2 CT dataset using several pre-trained deep learning models.

DL Model	Sensitivity	Precision	Specificity	F1-Score	Accuracy
DenseNet201	0.9715	0.9522	0.9522	0.9618	0.9618
EfficientNetB0	0.8880	0.8949	0.8866	0.8914	0.8873
InceptionV3	0.9062	0.9355	0.9336	0.9206	0.9195
NasNet Mobile	0.7887	0.8196	0.8017	0.8039	0.7948
ResNet50	0.9574	0.9657	0.9693	0.9615	0.9637
VGG16	0.9667	0.9789	0.9805	0.9728	0.9738
FGCN	0.9967	0.9905	0.9845	0.9936	0.9919

Based on the findings, the suggested model (FGCN) demonstrates classification accuracy of 99.19%, outperforming the other examined models. The models that achieved the highest levels of success were VGG16, ResNet50, and DenseNet201, with accuracy of 97.38%, 96.37%, and 96.18%, respectively. InceptionV3 and EfficientNetB0 were unable to compete with the other models because their accuracy values were below 92%. The NASNet Mobile model had the lowest capabilities, with scores of approximately 80%. The suggested model exhibits exceptional sensitivity, precision, specificity, and F1-score metrics, all over 99%, as demonstrated.

Figure 6 provides a detailed overview of the classification metrics mentioned in Table 1 by displaying the confusion matrices for all of the examined models. The proposed FGCN model incorrectly classified only one and four cases into the positive and negative classes, respectively. The models that had the most similar performance were DenseNet, which misclassified seven positive cases, and VGG16, which misclassified five negative cases. The models with the lowest accuracy demonstrated a balanced distribution of misclassifications between the two classes.

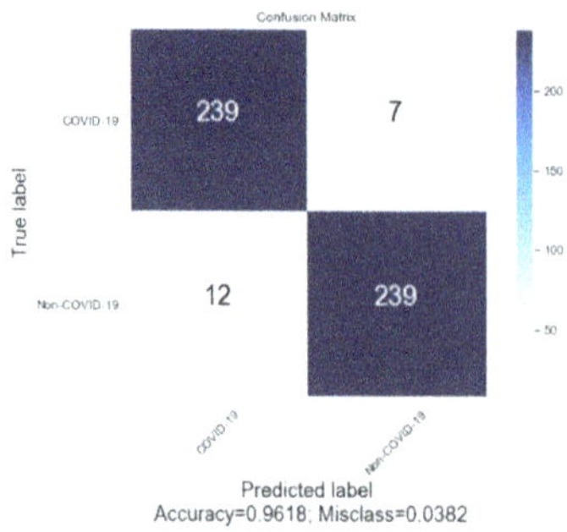

(**a**) DenseNet201

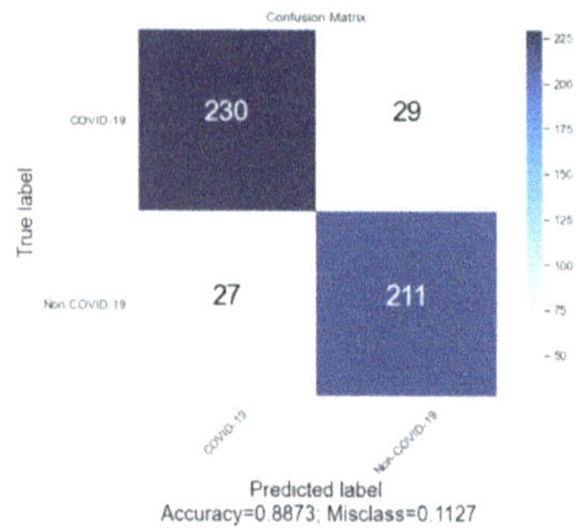

(**b**) EfficientNetB0

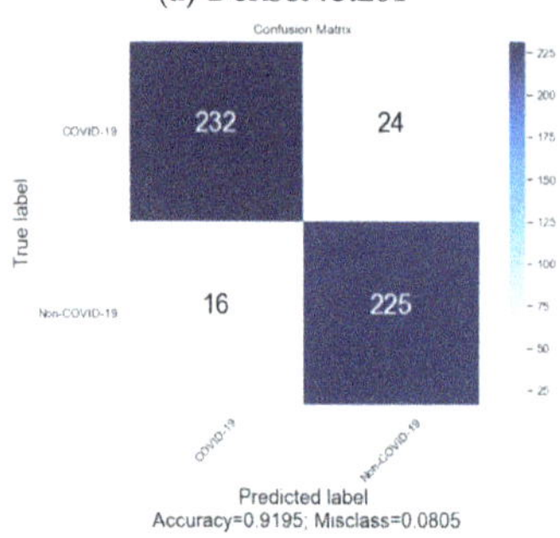

(**c**) InceptionV3

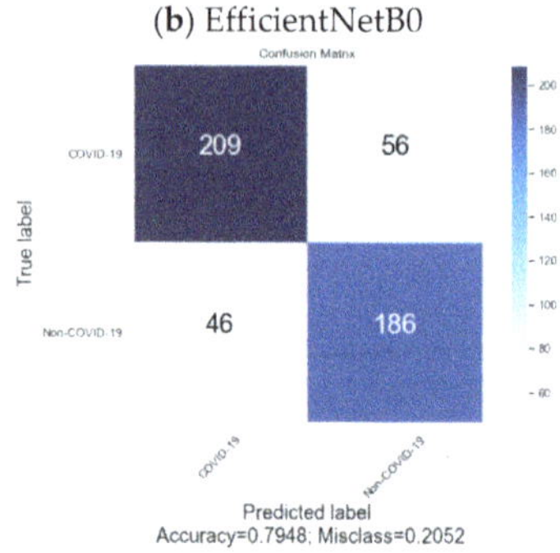

(**d**) NasNet Mobile

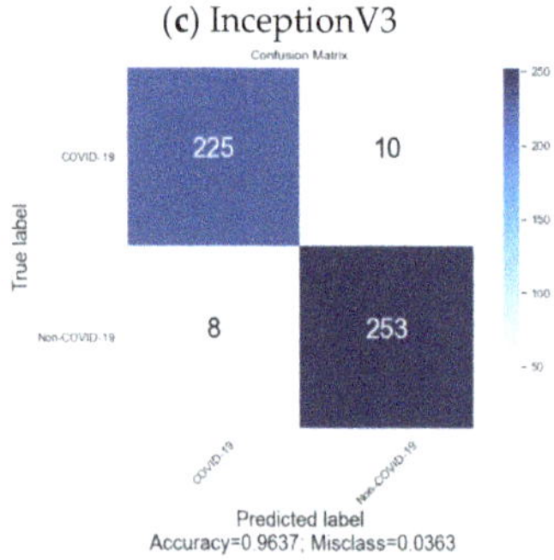

(**e**) ResNet50

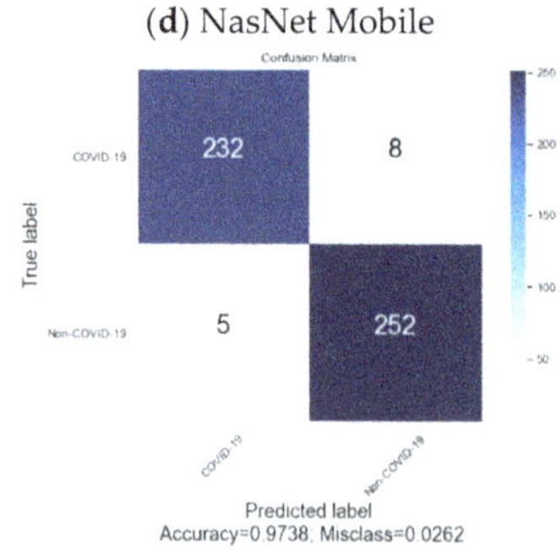

(**f**) VGG16

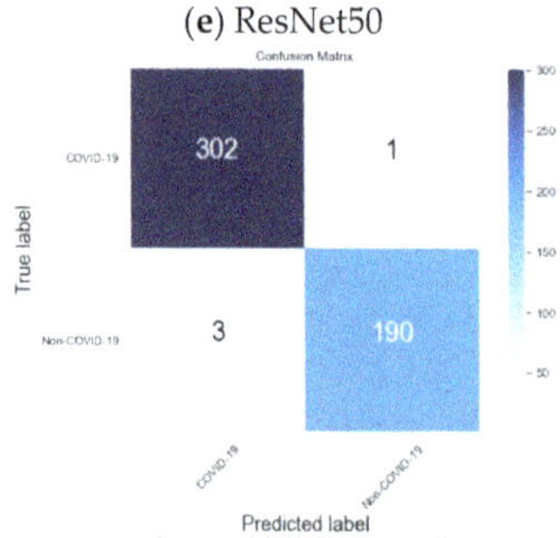

(**g**) FGCN

Figure 6. Confusion matrices for the models tested.

Table 2 provides a brief description of the most recent deep learning algorithms used to detect COVID-19 through the analysis of computerized X-ray (CXR) or CT images. Compared to previous research, the proposed FGCN model provides similarly excellent performance, characterized by its unique feature of integrating the U-Net architecture with a GCN. Furthermore, it demonstrates the efficacy of a graph-based method for the diagnosis and identification of complex patterns associated with lung diseases.

Table 2. Comparison some of DL models based on performance on various image datasets for COVID-19 detection.

Reference	Dataset	Model	Accuracy	Sensitivity	Precision	Specificity	F1-Score	AUC
[47]	CT scans (4382 COVID-19, and 9369 non-COVID-19)	U-Net++	95.2	100	-	93.6	-	
[48]	Total of 1918 CT scans	DCN	95.99	89.14	-	98.04	-	97.55
[49]	CT scans (449 COVID-19 and 595 non-COVID-19)	Two U-Nets	86	94	-	79	-	93
[50]	COVID-19 CT scans	U-Net+	82.9	97.4	-	92.2	-	-
[51]	CT scans (521 COVID-19 and 665 non-COVID-19)	EfficientNetB4	87	89	-	87	-	90
[52]	CT scans (1262 COVID-19 and 1230 non-COVID-19)	DenseNet201	96.25	96.29	96.29	96.21	96.29	-
[53]	CT scans (108 COVID-19 and 912 non-COVID-19)	Xception	99.02	96.29	96.29	96.21	96.29	-
[29]	CT scans (468 COVID-19 and 2996 non-COVID-19)	ResNet50	89.5	87	-	92	-	95
[50]	CT scans (723 COVID-19 and 413 non-COVID-19)	U-Net and ResNet50	94.8	97.4	-	92.2	-	-
[54]	CT scans (360 COVID-19 and 34 non-COVID-19)	VGG16	91	94	100	-	97	-
[27]	CT scans (219 COVID-19 and 399 non-COVID-19)	ResNet50	86	96	79	-	-	9596
[55]	Consists of 1065 CT scans	CNN	83	84	-	80.5	-	-
[56]	CT scans (1493 COVID-19 and 4594 non-COVID-19)	Inception-ResNetV2	92.18	92.11	92.38	96.06	-	-
[57]	CT scans (260 COVID-19 and 600 non-COVID-19)	VGG19	89.3	89	90	-	90	-
[58]	CT scans (1252 COVID-19 and 1230 non-COVID-19)	DarkNet19 with repeated holdout 10FCV	98.91	98.96	-	98.86	0.99	-
[59]	CT scans (313 COVID-19 and 229 non-COVID-19)	U-Net and CNN	90.9	90.7	-	91.1	-	95.9
[60]	CT scans (192 COVID-19 and 145 non-COVID-19)	nCOVnet	97.62	97.62	-	78.57	-	-
[61]	CT scans (347 COVID-19 and 397 non-COVID-19)	ResNet18	78.29	76.9	81	79.9	78.9	83.82
Current study	**CT scans (1252 COVID-19 and 1230 non-COVID-19)**	**FGCN**	**99.19**	**99.67**	**99.05**	**98.45**	**99.36**	

4. Conclusions

This paper introduces a novel approach to COVID-19 detection by combining the U-Net model with a GCN to create a feature-extracted GCN (FGCN). We employ the U-Net model for both image segmentation and feature extraction. We use the generated features to create an adjacency matrix holding the graph structure. The GCN also receives the original image graph and the largest kernel graph. To establish unified input graph data, we combine these graphs and pass them through a graph convolutional network (GCN) along with a dropout layer. This helps to reduce overfitting while diagnosing COVID-19. The resulting model diverges from the existing works as being the first approach to evaluate CT images of lungs structured as a graph representation of features, classified by a graph neural network model, also outperforming the most recent models proposed for COVID-19 detection in the literature.

Moreover, the proposed FGCN model is compared with six commonly used transfer learning models, namely DenseNet201, EfficientNetB0, InceptionV3, NasNet Mobile, ResNet50, and VGG16. The FGCN is found to overperform these transfer learning models. These outcomes underscore the abstraction potential of the graph-induced technique, making it suitable for similar medical diagnosis tasks.

Author Contributions: Methodology, Software, Validation, Resources, Writing, Visualization, P.Q.R.; Conceptualization, Writing, Supervision, Methodology, İ.T. All authors have read and agreed to the published version of the manuscript.

Funding: This research received no external funding.

Institutional Review Board Statement: Not applicable.

Informed Consent Statement: Not applicable.

Data Availability Statement: The original contributions presented in the study are included in the article, further inquiries can be directed to the corresponding author.

Conflicts of Interest: The authors declare no conflict of interest.

References

1. Okereke, M.; Ukor, N.A.; Adebisi, Y.A.; Ogunkola, I.O.; Favour Iyagbaye, E.; Adiela Owhor, G.; Lucero-Prisno, D.E., III. Impact of COVID-19 on access to healthcare in low-and middle-income countries: Current evidence and future recommendations. *Int. J. Health Plan. Manag.* **2021**, *36*, 13–17. [CrossRef] [PubMed]
2. Karmouty-Quintana, H.; Thandavarayan, R.A.; Keller, S.P.; Sahay, S.; Pandit, L.M.; Akkanti, B. Emerging mechanisms of pulmonary vasoconstriction in SARS-CoV-2-induced acute respiratory distress syndrome (ARDS) and potential therapeutic targets. *Int. J. Mol. Sci.* **2020**, *21*, 8081. [CrossRef] [PubMed]
3. Shorten, C.; Khoshgoftaar, T.M.; Furht, B. Deep Learning applications for COVID-19. *J. Big Data* **2021**, *8*, 18. [CrossRef] [PubMed]
4. Baratella, E.; Ruaro, B.; Marrocchio, C.; Poillucci, G.; Pigato, C.; Bozzato, A.M.; Salton, F.; Confalonieri, P.; Crimi, F.; Wade, B. Diagnostic Accuracy of Chest Digital Tomosynthesis in Patients Recovering after COVID-19 Pneumonia. *Tomography* **2022**, *8*, 1221–1227. [CrossRef] [PubMed]
5. Bellini, D.; Capodiferro, P.; Vicini, S.; Rengo, M.; Carbone, I. Long COVID in Young Patients: Impact on Lung Volume Evaluated Using Multidetector CT. *Tomography* **2023**, *9*, 1276–1285. [CrossRef] [PubMed]
6. Alqahtani, J.S.; Alghamdi, S.M.; Aldhahir, A.M.; Althobiani, M.; Raya, R.P.; Oyelade, T. Thoracic imaging outcomes in COVID-19 survivors. *World J. Radiol.* **2021**, *13*, 149. [CrossRef] [PubMed]
7. Pardyl, A.; Rymarczyk, D.; Jaworek-Korjakowska, J.; Kucharski, D.; Brodzicki, A.; Lasek, J.; Schneider, Z.; Kucybała, I.; Urbanik, A.; Obuchowicz, R. CompLung: Comprehensive Computer-Aided Diagnosis of Lung Cancer. In Proceedings of the ECAI 2023, Kraków, Poland, 30 September–5 October 2023; pp. 1835–1842.
8. Garstka, J.; Strzelecki, M. Pneumonia detection in X-ray chest images based on convolutional neural networks and data augmentation methods. In Proceedings of the 2020 Signal Processing: Algorithms, Architectures, Arrangements, and Applications (SPA), Poznan, Poland, 23–25 September 2020; pp. 18–23.
9. Nurzynska, K.; Li, D.; Walts, A.E.; Gertych, A. Multilayer outperforms single-layer slide scanning in AI-based classification of whole slide images with low-burden acid-fast mycobacteria (AFB). *Comput. Methods Programs Biomed.* **2023**, *234*, 107518. [CrossRef] [PubMed]
10. Yang, M.; Nurzynska, K.; Walts, A.E.; Gertych, A. A CNN-based active learning framework to identify mycobacteria in digitized Ziehl-Neelsen stained human tissues. *Comput. Med. Imaging Graph.* **2020**, *84*, 101752. [CrossRef]
11. Zhang, X.-M.; Liang, L.; Liu, L.; Tang, M.-J. Graph neural networks and their current applications in bioinformatics. *Front. Genet.* **2021**, *12*, 690049. [CrossRef]
12. Perozzi, B.; Al-Rfou, R.; Skiena, S. Deepwalk: Online learning of social representations. In Proceedings of the 20th ACM SIGKDD International Conference on Knowledge Discovery and Data Mining, New York, NY, USA, 24–27 August 2014; pp. 701–710.
13. Grover, A.; Leskovec, J. node2vec: Scalable feature learning for networks. In Proceedings of the 22nd ACM SIGKDD International Conference on Knowledge Discovery and Data Mining, San Francisco, CA, USA, 13–17 August 2016; pp. 855–864.
14. Türker, I.; Aksu, S. Connectogram–A graph-based time dependent representation for sounds. *Appl. Acoust.* **2022**, *191*, 108660. [CrossRef]
15. Kutluana, G.; Türker, İ. Classification of cardiac disorders using weighted visibility graph features from ECG signals. *Biomed. Signal Process. Control* **2024**, *87*, 105420. [CrossRef]
16. Turker, I.; Tan, S.O. Scientific Impact of Graph-Based Approaches in Deep Learning Studies—A Bibliometric Comparison. *arXiv* **2022**, arXiv:2210.07343.

17. Corman, V.M.; Landt, O.; Kaiser, M.; Molenkamp, R.; Meijer, A.; Chu, D.K.; Bleicker, T.; Brünink, S.; Schneider, J.; Schmidt, M.L. Detection of 2019 novel coronavirus (2019-nCoV) by real-time RT-PCR. *Eurosurveillance* **2020**, *25*, 2000045. [CrossRef] [PubMed]
18. Bernheim, A.; Mei, X.; Huang, M.; Yang, Y.; Fayad, Z.A.; Zhang, N.; Diao, K.; Lin, B.; Zhu, X.; Li, K. Chest CT findings in coronavirus disease-19 (COVID-19): Relationship to duration of infection. *Radiology* **2020**, *295*, 685–691. [CrossRef] [PubMed]
19. Li, M. Chest CT features and their role in COVID-19. *Radiol. Infect. Dis.* **2020**, *7*, 51–54. [CrossRef] [PubMed]
20. Han, B.; Davis, L.S. Density-based multifeature background subtraction with support vector machine. *IEEE Trans. Pattern Anal. Mach. Intell.* **2011**, *34*, 1017–1023.
21. Wu, J. Efficient HIK SVM learning for image classification. *IEEE Trans. Image Process.* **2012**, *21*, 4442–4453. [PubMed]
22. Arunadevi, S.; Raja, S.D.M. A Survey on Image Classification Algorithm Based on Per-pixel. *Int. J. Eng. Res. Gen. Sci.* **2014**, *2*, 387–392.
23. Yang, D.; Martinez, C.; Visuña, L.; Khandhar, H.; Bhatt, C.; Carretero, J. Detection and analysis of COVID-19 in medical images using deep learning techniques. *Sci. Rep.* **2021**, *11*, 19638. [CrossRef]
24. Alrahhal, M.; KP, S. COVID-19 diagnostic system using medical image classification and retrieval: A novel method for image analysis. *Comput. J.* **2022**, *65*, 2146–2163. [CrossRef]
25. Xu, X.; Jiang, X.; Ma, C.; Du, P.; Li, X.; Lv, S.; Yu, L.; Ni, Q.; Chen, Y.; Su, J. A deep learning system to screen novel coronavirus disease 2019 pneumonia. *Engineering* **2020**, *6*, 1122–1129. [CrossRef] [PubMed]
26. Yang, X.; He, X.; Zhao, J.; Zhang, Y.; Zhang, S.; Xie, P. COVID-CT-dataset: A CT scan dataset about COVID-19. *arXiv* **2020**, arXiv:2003.13865.
27. Song, Y.; Zheng, S.; Li, L.; Zhang, X.; Zhang, X.; Huang, Z.; Chen, J.; Wang, R.; Zhao, H.; Chong, Y. Deep learning enables accurate diagnosis of novel coronavirus (COVID-19) with CT images. *IEEE/ACM Trans. Comput. Biol. Bioinform.* **2021**, *18*, 2775–2780.
28. Zhang, J.; Chu, Y.; Zhao, N. Supervised framework for COVID-19 classification and lesion localization from chest CT. *Ethiop. J. Health Dev.* **2020**, *34*, 236–242.
29. Li, L.; Qin, L.; Xu, Z.; Yin, Y.; Wang, X.; Kong, B.; Bai, J.; Lu, Y.; Fang, Z.; Song, Q. Using artificial intelligence to detect COVID-19 and community-acquired pneumonia based on pulmonary CT: Evaluation of the diagnostic accuracy. *Radiology* **2020**, *296*, E65–E71. [CrossRef] [PubMed]
30. Uçar, M. Automatic segmentation of COVID-19 from computed tomography images using modified U-Net model-based majority voting approach. *Neural Comput. Appl.* **2022**, *34*, 21927–21938. [CrossRef]
31. Liang, X.; Zhang, Y.; Wang, J.; Ye, Q.; Liu, Y.; Tong, J. Diagnosis of COVID-19 pneumonia based on graph convolutional network. *Front. Med.* **2021**, *7*, 612962. [CrossRef]
32. Soares, E.; Angelov, P.; Biaso, S.; Froes, M.H.; Abe, D.K. SARS-CoV-2 Ct-Scan Dataset. *medRxiv* **2020**. Available online: https://www.medrxiv.org/content/10.1101/2020.04.24.20078584v3 (accessed on 1 April 2024).
33. Angelov, P.; Soares, E. Explainable-by-design approach for COVID-19 classification via CT-scan. *medRxiv* **2020**. Available online: https://www.medrxiv.org/content/10.1101/2020.04.24.20078584v1 (accessed on 1 April 2024).
34. Angelov, P.; Soares, E. Towards explainable deep neural networks (xDNN). *Neural Netw.* **2020**, *130*, 185–194. [CrossRef]
35. Ronneberger, O.; Fischer, P.; Brox, T. U-net: Convolutional networks for biomedical image segmentation. In *Medical Image Computing and Computer-Assisted Intervention–MICCAI 2015: 18th International Conference, Munich, Germany, 5–9 October 2015*; Proceedings, Part III 18; Springer: Cham, Switzerland, 2015; pp. 234–241.
36. Shuman, D.I.; Narang, S.K.; Frossard, P.; Ortega, A.; Vandergheynst, P. The emerging field of signal processing on graphs: Extending high-dimensional data analysis to networks and other irregular domains. *IEEE Signal Process. Mag.* **2013**, *30*, 83–98. [CrossRef]
37. Bruna, J.; Zaremba, W.; Szlam, A.; LeCun, Y. Spectral networks and locally connected networks on graphs. *arXiv* **2013**, arXiv:1312.6203.
38. Defferrard, M.; Bresson, X.; Vandergheynst, P. Convolutional neural networks on graphs with fast localized spectral filtering. In Proceedings of the Advances in Neural Information Processing Systems 29 (NIPS 2016), Barcelona, Spain, 5–10 December 2016.
39. Kipf, T.N.; Welling, M. Semi-supervised classification with graph convolutional networks. *arXiv* **2016**, arXiv:1609.02907.
40. Huang, G.; Liu, Z.; Van Der Maaten, L.; Weinberger, K.Q. Densely connected convolutional networks. In Proceedings of the IEEE Conference on Computer Vision and Pattern Recognition, Honolulu, HI, USA, 21–26 July 2017; pp. 4700–4708.
41. Jiang, Z.-P.; Liu, Y.-Y.; Shao, Z.-E.; Huang, K.-W. An improved VGG16 model for pneumonia image classification. *Appl. Sci.* **2021**, *11*, 11185. [CrossRef]
42. Pan, Y.; Liu, J.; Cai, Y.; Yang, X.; Zhang, Z.; Long, H.; Zhao, K.; Yu, X.; Zeng, C.; Duan, J. Fundus image classification using Inception V3 and ResNet-50 for the early diagnostics of fundus diseases. *Front. Physiol.* **2023**, *14*, 1126780. [CrossRef] [PubMed]
43. Yanhui, C. From AlexNet to NASNet: A Brief History and Introduction of Convolutional Neural Networks. 2021. Available online: https://towardsdatascience.com/from-alexnet-to-nasnet-a-brief-history-and-introduction-of-convolutional-neural-networks-cf63bf3320e1 (accessed on 1 April 2024).
44. Tan, M.; Le, Q. Efficientnet: Rethinking model scaling for convolutional neural networks. In Proceedings of the 36th International Conference on Machine Learning, Long Beach, CA, USA, 9–15 June 2019; pp. 6105–6114.
45. Nair, V.; Hinton, G.E. Rectified linear units improve restricted boltzmann machines. In Proceedings of the 27th International Conference on Machine Learning (ICML-10), Haifa, Israel, 21–24 June 2010; pp. 807–814.
46. Kingma, D.P.; Ba, J. Adam: A method for stochastic optimization. *arXiv* **2014**, arXiv:1412.6980.

47. Chen, J.; Wu, L.; Zhang, J.; Zhang, L.; Gong, D.; Zhao, Y.; Chen, Q.; Huang, S.; Yang, M.; Yang, X. Deep learning-based model for detecting 2019 novel coronavirus pneumonia on high-resolution computed tomography. *Sci. Rep.* **2020**, *10*, 19196. [CrossRef] [PubMed]
48. Gao, K.; Su, J.; Jiang, Z.; Zeng, L.-L.; Feng, Z.; Shen, H.; Rong, P.; Xu, X.; Qin, J.; Yang, Y. Dual-branch combination network (DCN): Towards accurate diagnosis and lesion segmentation of COVID-19 using CT images. *Med. Image Anal.* **2021**, *67*, 101836. [CrossRef] [PubMed]
49. Amyar, A.; Modzelewski, R.; Li, H.; Ruan, S. Multi-task deep learning based CT imaging analysis for COVID-19 pneumonia: Classification and segmentation. *Comput. Biol. Med.* **2020**, *126*, 104037. [CrossRef] [PubMed]
50. Jin, S.; Wang, B.; Xu, H.; Luo, C.; Wei, L.; Zhao, W.; Hou, X.; Ma, W.; Xu, Z.; Zheng, Z. AI-assisted CT imaging analysis for COVID-19 screening: Building and deploying a medical AI system in four weeks. *medRxiv* **2020**. [CrossRef]
51. Bai, H.X.; Wang, R.; Xiong, Z.; Hsieh, B.; Chang, K.; Halsey, K.; Tran, T.M.L.; Choi, J.W.; Wang, D.-C.; Shi, L.-B. Artificial intelligence augmentation of radiologist performance in distinguishing COVID-19 from pneumonia of other origin at chest CT. *Radiology* **2020**, *296*, E156–E165. [CrossRef] [PubMed]
52. Jaiswal, A.; Gianchandani, N.; Singh, D.; Kumar, V.; Kaur, M. Classification of the COVID-19 infected patients using DenseNet201 based deep transfer learning. *J. Biomol. Struct. Dyn.* **2021**, *39*, 5682–5689. [CrossRef]
53. Ardakani, A.A.; Kanafi, A.R.; Acharya, U.R.; Khadem, N.; Mohammadi, A. Application of deep learning technique to manage COVID-19 in routine clinical practice using CT images: Results of 10 convolutional neural networks. *Comput. Biol. Med.* **2020**, *121*, 103795. [CrossRef]
54. Dansana, D.; Kumar, R.; Bhattacharjee, A.; Hemanth, D.J.; Gupta, D.; Khanna, A.; Castillo, O. Early diagnosis of COVID-19-affected patients based on X-ray and computed tomography images using deep learning algorithm. *Soft Comput.* **2020**, *27*, 2635–2643. [CrossRef] [PubMed]
55. Wang, S.; Kang, B.; Ma, J.; Zeng, X.; Xiao, M.; Guo, J.; Cai, M.; Yang, J.; Li, Y.; Meng, X. A deep learning algorithm using CT images to screen for Corona Virus Disease (COVID-19). *Eur. Radiol.* **2021**, *31*, 6096–6104. [CrossRef] [PubMed]
56. El Asnaoui, K.; Chawki, Y. Using X-ray images and deep learning for automated detection of coronavirus disease. *J. Biomol. Struct. Dyn.* **2021**, *39*, 3615–3626. [CrossRef] [PubMed]
57. Rahaman, M.M.; Li, C.; Yao, Y.; Kulwa, F.; Rahman, M.A.; Wang, Q.; Qi, S.; Kong, F.; Zhu, X.; Zhao, X. Identification of COVID-19 samples from chest X-Ray images using deep learning: A comparison of transfer learning approaches. *J. X-ray Sci. Technol.* **2020**, *28*, 821–839.
58. Gupta, K.; Bajaj, V. Deep learning models-based CT-scan image classification for automated screening of COVID-19. *Biomed. Signal Process. Control* **2023**, *80*, 104268.
59. Zheng, C.; Deng, X.; Fu, Q.; Zhou, Q.; Feng, J.; Ma, H.; Liu, W.; Wang, X. Deep learning-based detection for COVID-19 from chest CT using weak label. *medRxiv* **2020**. [CrossRef]
60. Panwar, H.; Gupta, P.; Siddiqui, M.K.; Morales-Menendez, R.; Singh, V. Application of deep learning for fast detection of COVID-19 in X-Rays using nCOVnet. *Chaos Solitons Fractals* **2020**, *138*, 109944. [CrossRef]
61. Attallah, O.; Ragab, D.A.; Sharkas, M. MULTI-DEEP: A novel CAD system for coronavirus (COVID-19) diagnosis from CT images using multiple convolution neural networks. *PeerJ* **2020**, *8*, e10086. [CrossRef]

diagnostics

MDPI

Article

Augmenting Radiological Diagnostics with AI for Tuberculosis and COVID-19 Disease Detection: Deep Learning Detection of Chest Radiographs

Manjur Kolhar [1,*], Ahmed M. Al Rajeh [2] and Raisa Nazir Ahmed Kazi [2]

1 Department Health Informatics, College of Applied Medical Sciences, King Faisal University, Al-Hofuf 31982, Saudi Arabia
2 College of Applied Medical Sciences, King Faisal University, Al-Hofuf 31982, Saudi Arabia; amalrajeh@kfu.edu.sa (A.M.A.R.); rnahmed@kfu.edu.sa (R.N.A.K.)
* Correspondence: mkolhar@kfu.edu.sa

Abstract: In this research, we introduce a network that can identify pneumonia, COVID-19, and tuberculosis using X-ray images of patients' chests. The study emphasizes tuberculosis, COVID-19, and healthy lung conditions, discussing how advanced neural networks, like VGG16 and ResNet50, can improve the detection of lung issues from images. To prepare the images for the model's input requirements, we enhanced them through data augmentation techniques for training purposes. We evaluated the model's performance by analyzing the precision, recall, and F1 scores across training, validation, and testing datasets. The results show that the ResNet50 model outperformed VGG16 with accuracy and resilience. It displayed superior ROC AUC values in both validation and test scenarios. Particularly impressive were ResNet50's precision and recall rates, nearing 0.99 for all conditions in the test set. On the hand, VGG16 also performed well during testing—detecting tuberculosis with a precision of 0.99 and a recall of 0.93. Our study highlights the performance of our deep learning method by showcasing the effectiveness of ResNet50 over traditional approaches like VGG16. This progress utilizes methods to enhance classification accuracy by augmenting data and balancing them. This positions our approach as an advancement in using state-of-the-art deep learning applications in imaging. By enhancing the accuracy and reliability of diagnosing ailments such as COVID-19 and tuberculosis, our models have the potential to transform care and treatment strategies, highlighting their role in clinical diagnostics.

Keywords: ResNet50; VGG16. augmenting; lung; disease; deep learning

1. Introduction

Tuberculosis, commonly known as TB, is an illness that primarily targets the lungs and is triggered by a strain of bacteria by the name Mycobacterium tuberculosis. The disease is transmitted through the air when individuals who are infected cough, sneeze or spit. Coronavirus disease (COVID-19) is an infectious disease caused by the SARS-CoV-2 virus. Most people infected with the virus will experience mild to moderate respiratory illness and recover without requiring special treatment. Given the substantial global impact of TB as the leading cause of mortality from infectious diseases before the advent of COVID-19, projections by the Stop TB Partnership suggest that the COVID-19 pandemic could exacerbate TB's burden [1,2]. Specifically, from 2020 to 2025, an estimated increase of 6.3 million TB cases and 1.4 million TB-related deaths is anticipated [3,4], predominantly affecting the 30 countries with the highest disease burden. Early diagnosis is not just crucial but a matter of utmost importance for both COVID-19 and tuberculosis. Timely detection of these illnesses is crucial for treatment and to stop them from spreading further. Early identification, proactive care, and regular monitoring are not just important [5] but are key to achieving the best possible outcomes in treatment and preventing complications linked with both COVID-19 and tuberculosis [6]. The integration of intelligence (AI) in recent times has significantly advanced the healthcare field, mainly because of the increased access to medical data [7]. These data, comprising an extensive collection of chest X-ray images, have played a role in training AI systems that can accurately spot diseases, predict results, and determine the most suitable treatments [8]. The promise of AI to greatly improve the diagnosis of diseases such as tuberculosis and COVID-19 is a source of optimism, as it can swiftly and precisely analyze images and vast datasets to identify subtle irregularities and assess risk factors, resulting in earlier discovery and treatment. The rapid progress of AI technology has notably expanded the use of AI tools in imaging, significantly improving the assistance these tools offer to healthcare professionals in diagnosing and caring for patients. In our research project, we utilized two learning models, VGG16 and ResNet50, to examine a set of chest X-ray images. We utilized these models to conduct training, validation, and testing for COVID-19 (coronavirus disease), tuberculosis, and cases without any disease (normal condition). Furthermore, we fine-tuned their design to enhance accuracy.

This study presents a deep learning model created for the identification of lung ailments from chest X-ray images with a specific focus on COVID-19 (coronavirus disease), tuberculosis, and cases displaying normal (no disease) conditions. Lung-related diseases pose a public health challenge in the United States, resulting in millions of deaths annually. The lungs are organs that are prone to various illnesses that impact their components. In our investigation, we employed two known deep learning architectures, the VGG16 and ResNet50 models, to examine our collection of chest X-ray images. These models play a role in image recognition and have exhibited exceptional precision in detecting features that are crucial for diagnosing diseases like COVID-19 and tuberculosis as well as conditions indicating a normal lung function.

Section 2 of this paper commences with a review of the literature that places our research within the context of existing knowledge, emphasizing the advancements and prior studies that guided our methodology. Section 3 outlines the approach used to collect and analyze the data, ensuring the transparency and reproducibility of our findings.

In Section 4, we examine the results, delving into the important discoveries and what they mean for the field. Section 5 links these results back to our research goals, offering a profound insight into the studies' significance. The discussion offers a thorough interpretation of how our findings align with or diverge from the established theories and practices. This analysis helps to clarify the significance of our results within the broader context of the field. Finally, the paper concludes by summarizing the principal conclusions drawn from the research across these sections and suggesting potential directions for future work.

2. Literature Review

The study introduces the COVLIAS 1.0 system, a hybrid deep learning model featuring SegNet, VGG-SegNet, and ResNet-SegNet. The model demonstrates superior performance in COVID-19 lung segmentation using CT scans, with significant improvements over the NIH benchmark, achieving high accuracy (AUCs ~0.96 to ~0.98) and rapid processing times (<1 s per image), making it viable for real-time use in clinical settings [9]. The ResNet50-Ensemble Voting model demonstrated excellent accuracy in distinguishing benign from malignant small pulmonary nodules on CT scans, showing great potential for enhancing early-stage lung nodule diagnosis in clinical settings [10]. Ali et al. significantly enhanced lung nodule classification in CT images by employing a decision-level fusion technique with SVM and AdaBoostM2 classifiers and leveraging deep features from advanced architectures, achieving an impressive accuracy of 90.46 $\pm$ 0.25% on the LUNGx dataset and outperforming existing methods [11]. The study [12] demonstrated that the BDCNet model, integrating VGG-19 and CNN, significantly outperformed conventional deep learning models in diagnosing COVID-19, pneumonia, and lung cancer from chest radiographs, achieving remarkable classification accuracy and supporting effective early diagnosis. The study [13] revealed that the AlexNet architecture, combined with the SGD optimizer, outperformed other state-of-the-art CNN architectures like LeNet, VGG16, ResNet50, and Inception-V1 in detecting lung cancer on LUNA16 datasets, achieving the highest validation accuracy and overall performance metrics. The study by Dina M. Ibrahim et al. [14]. demonstrated that the VGG19+CNN model excelled in diagnosing COVID-19, pneumonia, and lung cancer from combined chest X-ray and CT images, outperforming other advanced models with exceptionally high accuracy and comprehensive performance metrics across various evaluation criteria. The study [15] highlighted that the integration of Wiener filter preprocessing, GAN segmentation with SSSOA, and CNN classification using VGG16 effectively predicts lung cancer in early stages, achieving an impressive accuracy of 97%, thereby enhancing the potential for early diagnosis and treatment. The study [16] utilized 11 well-known convolutional neural networks to classify COVID-19 and non-COVID-19 lung images, providing critical insights into model performance across varying batch sizes and epochs, thus aiding in the selection of optimal models for enhancing the diagnosis and management of lung-related diseases. Upasana Chutia et al. presented a DenseNet201 model enhanced with CLAHE and a hybrid mechanism that significantly surpasses traditional models in lung disease diagnosis from X-ray images, achieving high accuracy and providing crucial visual insights to support radiological assessments [17]. The study by the authors [18] demonstrated that their proposed deep learning architecture, combining VGG19 with additional CNN layers, excels in classifying various lung diseases, including COVID-19, from CXR images. Achieving an accuracy of 96.48%, a recall of 93.75%, a precision of 97.56%, an F1 score of 95.62%, and an AUC of 99.82%, the model significantly outperformed existing methods, enhancing diagnostic speed and efficiency for healthcare practitioners. Malik, H., Anees, T., Din, M., & Naeem et al. [19], demonstrated that their CDC Net model, utilizing DL techniques, outperformed standard CNN-based models like Vgg-19, ResNet50, and Inception v3 in classifying multiple chest diseases from X-rays, achieving superior accuracy and robustness with an AUC of 0.9953, confirming its efficacy in early and accurate disease diagnosis.

Table 1, below, summarizes the methodologies and key results of various studies focusing on the application of deep learning models for the diagnosis of lung diseases using imaging data: In conclusion, the studies listed in Table 1 explore various deep learning architectures and methodologies to diagnose lung diseases from imaging data effectively. Each model brings advancements in classification accuracy, speed, and diagnostic efficiency, showing potential for real-world clinical application. The results indicate a significant progression towards automating the diagnosis process, thereby enhancing the capability to detect and treat lung diseases at earlier stages.

Table 1. Summary of Deep Learning Models Used for Lung Disease Diagnosis from Imaging Data.

Reference	Model Name	Methodology	Key Results
[9]	COVLIAS 1.0	Hybrid deep-learning model combining SegNet, VGG-SegNet, and ResNet-SegNet for lung segmentation.	AUCs ~0.96 to ~0.98, processing times <1 s, superior to NIH benchmarks.
[10]	ResNet50-Ensemble	Machine learning model for malignant–benign small pulmonary nodule classification on CT images.	High accuracy in classifying nodules, demonstrating potential for early diagnosis.
[11]	Decision Level Fusion	Deep feature selection with SVM and AdaBoostM2 for lung nodule classification.	Achieved 90.46 ± 0.25% accuracy on the LUNGx dataset.
[12]	BDCNet	Multi-classification CNN for COVID-19, pneumonia, and lung cancer diagnosis from chest radiographs.	Remarkable classification accuracy, enhancing early diagnosis.
[13]	AlexNet with SGD	Analysis of CNN architectures for lung cancer detection on LUNA16 datasets.	Highest validation accuracy and performance metrics among tested models.

Table 1. *Cont.*

Reference	Model Name	Methodology	Key Results
[14]	VGG19+CNN	Deep-chest: Multi-classification model for diagnosing COVID-19, pneumonia, and lung cancer.	Exceptionally high accuracy and comprehensive performance metrics.
[15]	GAN-VGG16	GAN based segmentation and VGG16 for classification to predict lung cancer.	Predicted lung cancer with 97% accuracy, effective for early stages.
[16]	Eleven CNN Comparison	Comparative analysis of eleven neural networks for small datasets of lung images of COVID-19 patients.	Provided insights into model performance, aiding in optimal model selection.
[17]	Modified DenseNet	Classification of lung diseases using an attention-based modified DenseNet model.	High accuracy, providing crucial visual insights for radiological assessments.
[18]	Deep-CXR	Deep learning architecture for multi-class lung diseases classification using CXR images.	Achieved high classification accuracy across various lung diseases.
[19]	CDC_Net	Multi-classification CNN for detection of COVID-19, pneumothorax, pneumonia, lung cancer, and tuberculosis using chest X-rays.	Superior accuracy and robustness with an AUC of 0.9953.

Our research focuses on enhancing image augmentation techniques to optimize the performance of deep learning models, aimed at improving the diagnosis of significant lung diseases such as COVID-19, tuberculosis, and others. By integrating advanced augmentation strategies, we aim to boost the robustness and generalizability of our models. Future efforts will involve validating these optimized models on unseen data, demonstrating their efficacy in real-world settings, and ensuring they can reliably aid in early and accurate diagnosis across diverse clinical environments. This approach not only pushes forward the boundaries of medical imaging analysis but also promises to enhance diagnostic accuracy, thereby improving patient outcomes in the fight against lung-related illnesses.

3. Methodology

In the initial phase of the study, data preprocessing was crucial for the preparation of image data for model ingestion. The dataset was systematically curated into stratified subsets, encompassing training, validation, and testing partitions. The images underwent a resizing process to conform to the input specifications required by the models, which for VGG16 and ResNet50 architectures, is generally set at 224 $\times$ 224 pixels. Additionally, an essential preprocessing step involved the normalization of image pixel intensities to a standardized scale, typically normalized to a range between 0 and 1 or standardized to have a mean of 0 and a standard deviation of 1, in accordance with the model's architectural preconditions. Table 2 outlines how the dataset is distributed across the categories specified by the columns in the table. The table in the image provides information about three types of medical images: tuberculosis, normal, and coronavirus disease. It lists the format, size, and mode of these images. Joint Photographic Experts Group (JPEG) a commonly used method of lossy compression for digital images, particularly for those images produced by digital photography, was used. Tuberculosis is 512 $\times$ 512 pixels, which means the image is 512 pixels wide and 512 pixels tall. Normal is 1580 $\times$ 1410 pixels, which means the image is 1580 pixels wide and 1410 pixels tall. Coronavirus disease is 2000 $\times$ 2000 pixels, which means the image is 2000 pixels wide and 2000 pixels tall.

Additionally, in Figure 1 and Tables 3 and 4, we employed the VGG16 and ResNet50 models, enhancing the data.

The model summary, provided in the Table 3, describes a neural network architecture based on VGG16 with additional custom layers for classification. The VGG16 functional layer extracts features from input images, resulting in an output shape of (7, 7, 512) with 14,714,688 parameters. The VGG16 functional layer is a pre-trained convolutional neural network that extracts features from input images. It processes the images through multiple convolutional layers, producing a feature map with the shape (7, 7, 512). This means that the network outputs a 7 × 7 grid for each image with 512 feature channels. The layer has 14,714,688 parameters, weights, and biases learned during training. These parameters help the network recognize various features like edges, textures, and objects within the images. The flattening process takes 3D tensor and converts it into a 1D vector. It unrolls all the values in the 7 × 7 × 512 feature map into a single continuous vector. Hence, flattening the 3D output from VGG16 prepares the feature map for the following layers in the neural network, typically fully connected (dense) layers, which require a 1D input. This layer is crucial in learning and mapping the extracted features from the VGG16 output to the final classification or regression task. The dropout layer is a regularization technique used to prevent overfitting in neural networks. It randomly "drops out" (sets to zero) a fraction of the neurons during training, which helps the model generalize better. The VGG16 functional layer is crucial for extracting meaningful features from medical images. It learns from many parameters to help identify patterns such as lesions, tumors, and other anomalies.

Table 2. Dataset distribution of the images.

Diseases	Image Description	Image
Tuberculosis	Image Format: JPEG, Image Size: (512, 512) Image Mode: RGB	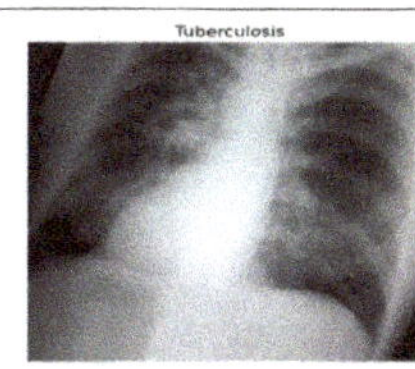
Normal	Image Format: JPEG, Image Size: (1580, 1410) and Image Mode: L	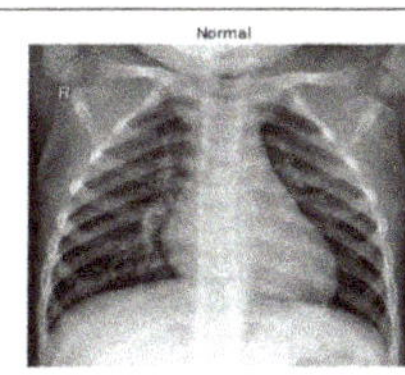
Corona Virus Disease	Image Format: JPEG, Image Size: (2000, 2000) and Image Mode: RGB	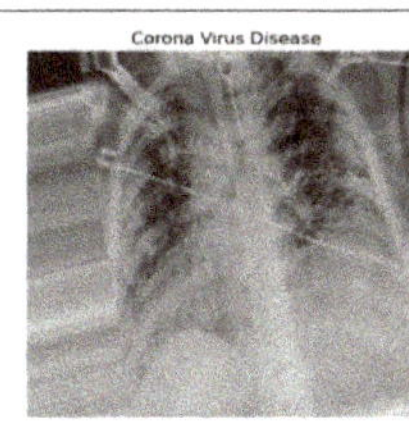

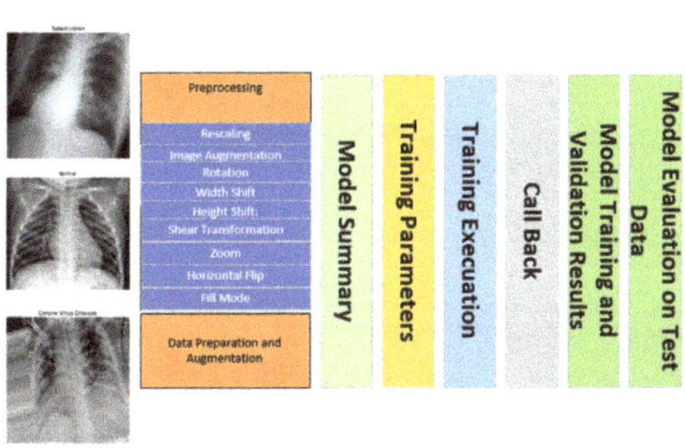

Figure 1. Working model under training and validation along with data preparation and augmentation.

Table 3. Model Summary of the VGG16 with data preparation and Augmentation.

Layer (Type)	Output Shape	Param #
vgg16 (Functional)	(None, 7, 7, 512)	14,714,688
flatten_2 (Flatten)	(None, 25,088)	0
dense_4 (Dense)	(None, 256)	6,422,784
dropout_2 (Dropout)	(None, 256)	0
dense_5 (Dense)	(None, 3)	771
Total params: 33,985,355 (129.64 MB)		
Trainable params: 6,423,555 (24.50 MB)		
Non-trainable params: 14,714,688 (56.13 MB)		
Optimizer params: 12,847,112 (49.01 MB)		

Table 4. Model Summary of the ResNet50 with data preparation and Augmentation.

Layer (Type)	Output	Shape Param #
Conv2d-1	[−1, 64, 112, 112]	9408
BatchNorm2d-2	[−1, 64, 112, 112]	128
ReLU-3	[−1, 64, 112, 112]	0
MaxPool2d-4	[−1, 64, 56, 56]	0
Conv2d-5	[−1, 64, 56, 56]	4096
BatchNorm2d-6	[−1, 64, 56, 56]	128
ReLU-7	[−1, 64, 56, 56]	0
Conv2d-8	[−1, 64, 56, 56]	36,864
BatchNorm2d-9	[−1, 64, 56, 56]	128
ReLU-10	[−1, 64, 56, 56]	0
Conv2d-11	[−1, 256, 56, 56]	16,384
BatchNorm2d-12	[−1, 256, 56, 56]	512
Conv2d-13	[−1, 256, 56, 56]	16,384
BatchNorm2d-14	[−1, 256, 56, 56]	512
ReLU-15	[−1, 256, 56, 56]	0
Bottleneck-16	[−1, 256, 56, 56]	0
Conv2d-17	[−1, 64, 56, 56]	16,384
ReLU-171	[−1, 2048, 7, 7]	0
Bottleneck-172	[−1, 2048, 7, 7]	0
AdaptiveAvgPool2d-173	[−1, 2048, 1, 1]	0
Linear-174	[−1, 3]	6147
Total params: 23,514,179		
Trainable params: 23,514,179		
Non-trainable params: 0		
Input size (MB): 0.57		
Forward/backward pass size (MB): 286.55		
Params size (MB): 89.70		
Estimated Total Size (MB): 376.82		

Table 4 outlines the layers and parameters of the ResNet50 model, which is also a deep convolutional neural network used for image classification and feature extraction. The model contains many parameters, each contributing to its ability to learn and extract meaningful features from medical images. The Conv2d-1 layer uses 64 filters to scan the input image. Each filter detects specific features in the image, such as edges, textures, or other patterns. Unlike fully connected layers, Conv2d layers are locally connected, meaning each neuron is connected only to a small region of the input image (receptive field), making the layer efficient in capturing spatial hierarchies. The Conv2d-1 layer is foundational in building the network's ability to understand and analyze images by breaking down the visual data into fundamental components. The BatchNorm2d-2 layer normalizes the inputs for each mini-batch, ensuring that the mean output is close to 0 and the standard deviation is close to 1. Batch normalization reduces the internal covariate shift, making the training process more stable and allowing for higher learning rates. By normalizing the inputs, it helps the model converge faster and can also improve the overall performance and generalization. By introducing non-linearity, the Rectified Linear Unit (ReLU) enables the network to learn and model more complex relationships within the data. Unlike sigmoid or tanh functions, ReLU does not saturate in the positive domain, helping to mitigate the vanishing gradient problem. ReLU is computationally efficient, making it a popular choice for deep neural networks. The Bottleneck-16 layer is a specialized block in the ResNet architecture designed to deepen the network while maintaining computational efficiency. It allows for efficient feature extraction and learning by reducing and then expanding the dimensionality of the feature maps. This layer is fundamental to the ResNet architecture, enabling deep networks to be trained efficiently and effectively by combining dimensionality reduction, convolution operations, and residual connections.

The VGG16 model, known for its simplicity and depth, was characterized by its sequential convolutional layers that effectively captured the textures and patterns in medical images. Using a pre-trained ResNet50 architecture was a strategic choice to classify lung images efficiently. ResNet50 is highly respected for its performance in handling image classification tasks initially created for the extensive ImageNet dataset. It excels at overcoming learning obstacles like vanishing gradients that can impede learning in deep neural networks. We customized ResNet50 to suit our needs precisely. We substituted its layer with a new one tailored to our project requirements. This adjustment maintained the structure of the model, which had undergone training on ImageNet. By keeping the trained layers fixed and concentrating on training the new output layer, we captured the nuances of lung imaging. This approach not only proved effective but efficient in saving resources addressing the unique challenges encountered in medical research environments. By utilizing the knowledge acquired by ResNet50, our model could accurately differentiate between lung conditions. This meticulous adaptation of a known architecture conserved resources and optimized its significant capabilities making it an excellent option, for analyzing medical images.

Furthermore, we applied, augmenting techniques for dataset (images) were applied to artificially expand the variety of data available for training models, particularly when using advanced neural networks like ResNet50 and VGG16, to achieve better results. These procedures involved making systematic modifications to images in a dataset to create new, altered versions of the same images. Common augmentations included rotations, scaling, cropping, flipping, and adjustments to the brightness, contrast, or color saturation of images. The primary purpose of these techniques was to enhance the robustness and generalization capability of image-processing algorithms. By exposing models like ResNet50 and VGG16 to a broader range of variations of the same image, these techniques helped prevent overfitting, where a model performs well on training data but poorly on unseen data.

3.1. Dataset

The dataset contains X-ray images of the chest created by merging and organizing datasets to include four types of lung diseases. Additionally, there is a folder dedicated to lung images. To expand the dataset, augmentation was used, resulting in a total of 10,000 images. In our study we specifically examined two diseases—COVID-19 and tuberculosis—and normal lungs. These diseases are separated into folders for training, validation, and testing datasets. For details, please refer to the hyperlink provided below.

https://www.kaggle.com/datasets/omkarmanohardalvi/lungs-disease-dataset-4-types, accessed on 20 November 2023.

3.2. Augmentation

Image augmentation and normalization are crucial in familiarizing DL models [20–22], especially for image classification. DL models require that all input images be of the same size [23,24]. Resizing and cropping are necessary to ensure that each image fed into the model has the exact dimensions. If the images vary in size, the model will not be able to handle them in batches, which can lead to errors or require more complex preprocessing [25–27]. Utilizing methods such as cropping can assist the model in improving its attention on areas of an image while undergoing training, ultimately enhancing its capacity to identify objects regardless of their placement within the image. This results in improved adaptability when the model is presented with images. Standardizing the image data when using models pre-trained on a dataset like ImageNet is essential [28,29]. Many COVID-19 radiography image datasets come in various formats, standards, sizes, and quality levels. These variations pose challenges for researchers looking to advance AI research related to COVID-19. Moving forward, it would be beneficial to establish operating procedures for COVID-19 radiography images [30]. These models are fine-tuned to work with input distributions characterized by values and standard deviations for each color channel. Applying the standardization process ensures that the feature distribution of the input image aligns with that of the dataset used for pre-training, helping the pre-trained model perform effectively. We applied resizing and cropping, then conversion to Totensor, and finally, normalization was applied; refer to the programming code that is supplied with this manuscript.

We used the following evaluation metric for our proposed models. Precision refers to the ratio of correctly predicted positive observations to the total predicted positives. It indicates the accuracy of the positive predictions.

$$\text{Precision} = \frac{True\ Positives\ (TP)}{True\ positive\ (TP) + False\ positive\ (FP)}$$

Recall (Sensitivity) refers to the ratio of correctly predicted positive observations to all observations in the actual class. It measures the model's ability to capture positive cases.

$$\text{Recall} = \frac{True\ Positives\ (TP)}{True\ positive\ (TP) + False\ negative\ (FN)}$$

The F1-Score is the harmonic means of precision and recall, providing a balance between the two. It is useful when you need to seek a balance between precision and recall.

$$\text{F1-Score} = 2 \times \frac{precision \times recall}{precision + Recall}$$

An ROC Curve (Receiver Operating Characteristic Curve) is a graphical representation of a classifier's performance. It plots the true positive rate (recall) against the false positive rate (1—specificity) at various threshold settings. It shows the trade-off between sensitivity and specificity. The AUC (Area Under the ROC Curve) is a single scalar value to summarize the performance of a classifier. It ranges from 0 to 1, with a value closer to 1 indicating a better-performing model.

4. Results and Discussion

Based on the results and evaluation metrics, a radiologist can conclude that the ResNet50 model exhibits outstanding performance in diagnosing COVID-19 and normal lung conditions, with near-perfect precision, recall, and F1-scores, and a high ability to detect tuberculosis, though with some room for improvement. The ROC curves and AUC values confirm the model's high discriminatory power. The benefits of the model include providing high diagnostic accuracy, reducing misdiagnosis, and ensuring appropriate patient care while preventing unnecessary procedures for healthy patients. It enhances efficiency in clinical settings by providing rapid, consistent diagnoses, which is crucial during high-demand periods like pandemics. It supports radiologists by serving as a second opinion, reducing their cognitive load. The model optimizes resource allocation by accurately identifying cases without disease, improving radiology department workflow and patient management. Additionally, the model can be continuously improved with more data and fine-tuning, providing a platform for training new radiologists in AI-supported diagnostics. Implementing the ResNet50 model in clinical settings can significantly enhance diagnostic accuracy, efficiency, and resource management, benefiting healthcare providers and patients.

In the evaluation of lung imaging using the ResNet50 deep learning model, the classification reports and visual results from various sets demonstrate the model's excellent diagnostic precision. This model has proved its capability in effectively distinguishing between normal lung scans and those showing signs of tuberculosis and coronavirus disease.

The initial graph as shown in the Figure 2, depicting training and validation accuracy, reveals significant fluctuations in the training accuracy, suggesting variability in the learning process—potentially due to factors like mini-batch selection or adjustments in learning rates. It also illustrates training and validation losses, both tapering off over time yet marked by noticeable volatility. The pronounced decline in training loss, consistently lower than the validation loss, suggests effective learning, as evidenced by the less smooth reduction in validation loss.

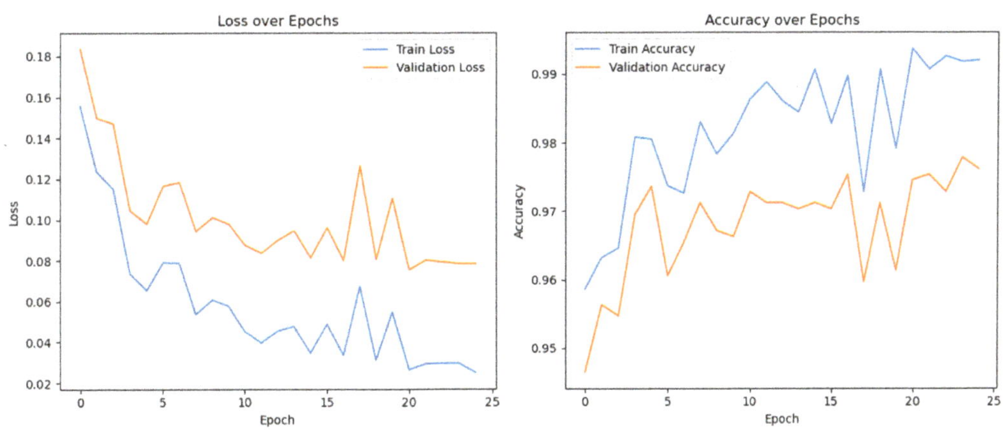

Figure 2. Training and Validation result in terms of loss and accuracy of ResNet50 model.

Table 5 shows the classification report for the validation set and reveals excellent performance of the model across three categories: coronavirus disease, normal, and tuberculosis. Each category shows high precision, recall, and F1-scores, with values nearly or exactly at 0.97 and 0.99, indicating the model's robust capability in accurately diagnosing and distinguishing these conditions. Specifically, the model achieves nearly perfect results for 'normal' conditions, demonstrating its effectiveness in accurately identifying cases without disease, which is crucial for preventing false diagnoses in clinical settings. For 'coronavirus disease' and 'tuberculosis', the model also shows high effectiveness with scores around 0.97, underscoring its utility as a reliable diagnostic tool in detecting these significant pulmonary diseases with minimal error rates. Table 5 showcases how well our model performs in identifying COVID-19, normal lung conditions and tuberculosis. The precision and recall rates are impressively high, ranging from 0.98 to 1.00 with F1 scores reflecting these results. This demonstrates the reliability and accuracy of the model. Notably, the flawless recall rate for lung conditions underscores its ability to accurately detect cases without any illness present, which is crucial for avoiding procedures and treatments for patients. The model also shows high performance in diagnosing tuberculosis, with errors highlighting its efficiency in identifying this condition. In summary, our model proves to be a tool with the accuracy and precision that are particularly beneficial in settings where accurate disease detection is essential for optimal patient care and treatment.

Table 5. Validation and test dataset classification report of 3 conditions by ResNet50.

Validation Classification Report				
Class	**Precision**	**Recall**	**F1-Score**	**Support**
Coronavirus Disease	0.97	0.97	0.97	406
Normal	0.99	0.99	0.99	402
Tuberculosis	0.98	0.97	0.97	406
Test Classification Report on				
Coronavirus Disease	0.98	0.97	0.98	407
Normal	0.98	1.00	0.99	404
Tuberculosis	0.99	0.99	0.99	408

The confusion matrices for both training and validation sets illuminate the model's adeptness at accurately classifying the conditions, as shown in the Figure 3. The left graph displays the confusion matrix from the training dataset, where the model achieves high accuracy in classifying COVID-19, normal, and tuberculosis (TB) cases, with minimal misclassifications. The right graph represents the validation dataset, showing how the model performs with new, unseen data, with slightly higher misclassification rates for TB and COVID-19, indicating areas for improvement in model generalization. This comparison underscores the model's robust training performance while highlighting the need for further optimization to improve validation accuracy. The confusion matrices illustrate the ResNet50 model's strong performance in classifying COVID-19, with high true positive rates and low misclassification rates. The model's reliability and accuracy make it a valuable tool for assisting radiologists in diagnosing COVID-19 from medical images. Continuous monitoring and refinement based on confusion matrix insights can further enhance the model's clinical utility.

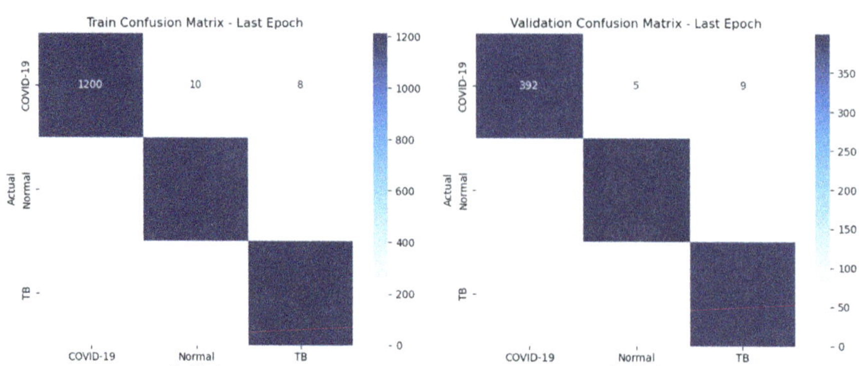

Figure 3. Train and validation confusion matrices for the ResNet50 model at the last epoch.

The ROC curve and associated AUC values provide robust evidence that the ResNet50 model performs exceptionally well across all three conditions in the test data, as shown in Figure 4. It shows nearly perfect or perfect discriminatory ability to distinguish between normal conditions, COVID-19, and tuberculosis, which is consistent with the high precision, recall, and F1-scores noted earlier.

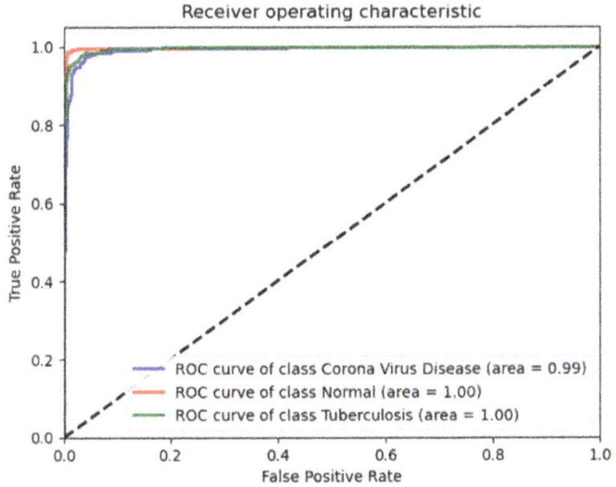

Figure 4. Receiver operating characteristic (ROC) curves for the ResNet50 model in diagnosing lung conditions, on validation dataset.

Figure 5 shows the ROC curves for the ResNet50 model, assessing its diagnostic accuracy across three classes: coronavirus disease (blue line, AUC = 1.00), normal lung conditions (green line, AUC = 1.00), and tuberculosis (red line, AUC = 1.00). The curves demonstrate the model's exceptional ability to correctly classify each condition with minimal false positives, highlighting its robustness in clinical diagnostic settings.

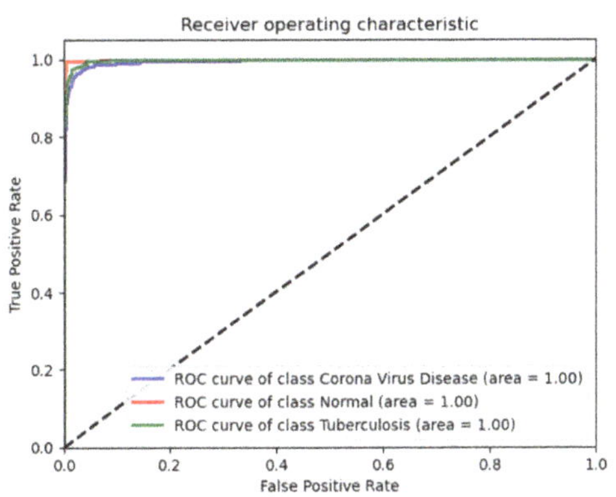

Figure 5. Receiver operating characteristic (ROC) curves for the ResNet50 model in diagnosing lung conditions, on test dataset.

The test set confusion matrix shows an outstanding ability of the model to correctly diagnose coronavirus disease, with 399 true positives out of 406, and only eight cases misclassified as tuberculosis, showing a robust sensitivity for this condition, as shown in Figure 6. The model performed flawlessly in identifying all cases without errors, a crucial factor in avoiding false alarms in medical environments. The ROC curves of the Res model showcase its ability to detect lung ailments, achieving perfect AUC scores for COVID-19, normal cases, and tuberculosis instances. This means that the model is highly dependable and efficient, serving as an aid for radiologists in diagnosing these conditions based on images. With its sensitivity and specificity, the model ensures detection and categorization, leading to improved diagnostic precision and effectiveness in clinical practice.

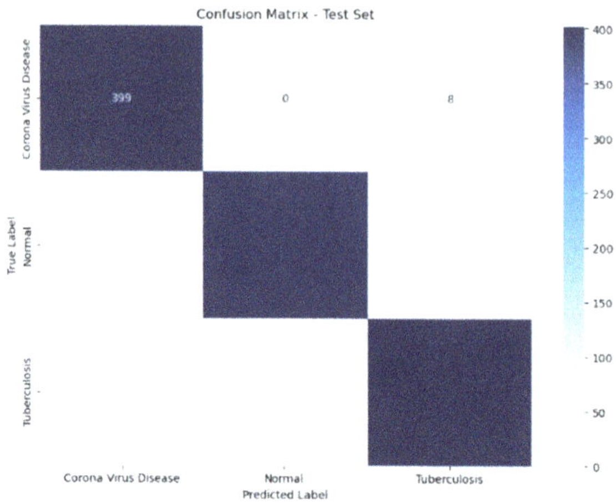

Figure 6. Confusion matrix of testing optimized using augmentation techniques.

The ResNet50 model is most effective in diagnosing COVID-19 and identifying normal lung conditions, showing excellent performance that slightly improves or maintains in validation. However, the model needs improvement in tuberculosis detection for better generalization to unseen data. Enhancing its ability to detect tuberculosis without sacrificing accuracy for other conditions would make it more robust and reliable for broader clinical use.

The provided figures, bar charts, and confusion matrices illustrate the performance of the VGG16 model in diagnosing lung conditions such as COVID-19, normal lung conditions, and tuberculosis. Furthermore, they have provided a clear and comprehensive understanding of the VGG16 model's performance, highlighting its strengths and areas for further development. This ensures that it is a reliable diagnostic tool in clinical settings.

Based on the findings and assessment criteria, a radiologist can determine that the ResNet50 model shows performance in diagnosing COVID-19 and normal lung conditions. It demonstrates near precision, recall, and F1 scores, along with an ability to detect tuberculosis, though there is room for enhancement. The ROC curves and AUC values validate the model's capability. The advantages of this model include diagnostics, reducing misdiagnoses for patient care, and avoiding unnecessary procedures for healthy individuals. It streamlines processes by delivering consistent diagnoses, especially during times of high demand, like pandemics. Furthermore, it helps radiologists ease their workload. The model optimizes resource allocation by pinpointing disease cases and improving workflow in radiology departments and patient care. Moreover, continuous refinement with data and adjustments offers a platform for training radiologists in AI-assisted diagnostics. Integration of the model in clinical environments can significantly boost diagnostic precision, operational efficiency, and resource utilization to benefit both healthcare providers and patients.

Table 6 shows the classification reports for the VGG16 model on both validation and test datasets, demonstrating its effectiveness in diagnosing three specific conditions: coronavirus disease, normal lung conditions, and tuberculosis. In the validation dataset, the model shows a commendable performance with high precision and recall, particularly excelling in identifying normal conditions, with nearly perfect scores (0.99 for both precision and recall). However, our model does show some room for improvement in identifying tuberculosis, as indicated by a slightly lower recall rate of 0.89. This suggests that while the model is highly effective, it can sometimes miss cases of tuberculosis. In contrast, when tested on a new dataset, the model demonstrates enhanced performance, showing higher precision and recall across all conditions. Specifically, for COVID-19, the model achieves an impressive precision of 0.92 and a recall of 0.98, maintaining high accuracy for normal lung conditions as well. Our model has made significant progress in detecting tuberculosis, with precision reaching 0.99 and recall increasing to 0.93. These advancements demonstrate the model's improved capacity to identify tuberculosis in datasets accurately. In general, these findings emphasize the capabilities of the VGG16 model, especially its ability to apply knowledge gained from validation scenarios to real-world testing situations. Hence, our model underscores its potential utility in clinical settings, where the model's accurate and reliable disease identification can be crucial for effective patient management and treatment planning. The VGG16-based model demonstrates high accuracy and robustness in classifying medical images for coronavirus disease, normal, and tuberculosis. The high precision and recall values indicate that the model can consistently distinguish between disease and normal cases, making it an effective tool in medical diagnostics. For coronavirus disease and normal cases, the model shows exceptional performance. While the model is slightly less precise in detecting tuberculosis during validation, it performs better on the test set, indicating its potential for clinical application in identifying these conditions.

Table 6. Validation and test dataset classification report of 3 conditions by VGG16.

Validation Classification Report				
Class	**Precision**	**Recall**	**F1-Score**	**Support**
Coronavirus Disease	0.88	0.97	0.93	406
Normal	0.99	0.98	0.99	402
Tuberculosis	0.98	0.89	0.93	406
Test Classification Report on				
Coronavirus Disease	0.92	0.98	0.95	407
Normal	0.99	99	0.99	404
Tuberculosis	0.99	0.93	0.96	408

Figure 7 in our report presents the confusion matrix for the validation set, showcasing the VGG16 model's performance in classifying COVID-19, normal lung conditions, and tuberculosis. The model performs exceptionally well in identifying COVID-19, correctly diagnosing 395 cases, though it does misclassify nine cases as tuberculosis and two as normal. This highlights the model's strong capability to detect COVID-19, albeit with some confusion when it comes to distinguishing it from tuberculosis. For cases categorized as normal, the precision is very high, indicating that the model is extremely effective at identifying non-diseased conditions with minimal error, though the exact number of true positives is not shown in the figure. However, the issue of misclassifying COVID-19 as tuberculosis is a point of concern, pinpointing an area where the model needs improvement. Enhancing the model's ability to differentiate more effectively between these two conditions is crucial to prevent potential false diagnoses in a clinical setting. This improvement could lead to more accurate treatment decisions and better patient outcomes.

Figure 8 displays the confusion matrix related to the classification of COVID-19, normal lung conditions, and tuberculosis. The matrix reveals that the model performs highly in identifying COVID-19, as evidenced by 400 true positive cases, showcasing a high level of precision with minimal confusion regarding other conditions. Nonetheless, there are some inaccuracies observed in the model's performance, such as misclassifying four COVID-19 cases as tuberculosis and three as normal cases. These findings suggest that our model may face challenges in distinguishing between these diseases. On a note, the model demonstrates a capability in recognizing cases classified as normal despite a slight overlap with COVID-19 in certain misclassifications. However, the slight misclassifications between COVID-19 and tuberculosis underscores an area where further refinement is warranted. Improving the model's accuracy in distinguishing between these diseases could significantly enhance its practicality, in settings leading to decision-making processes and better patient outcomes. The model also demonstrates a strong ability to recognize cases categorized as normal, although there is a slight overlap with COVID-19 in some misclassifications. Despite these minor issues, the overall results affirm the model's robust diagnostic capabilities for identifying these conditions. The ResNet50 model was enhanced using augmentation methods, demonstrating the ResNet50 model's accuracy and dependability in identifying COVID-19, normal conditions, and tuberculosis cases. Utilizing this model results in a greater number of diagnoses compared to manual image analysis, leading to better patient outcomes. Integrating this technology into settings enables radiologists to provide precise diagnoses, ultimately improving patient care and optimizing healthcare resources.

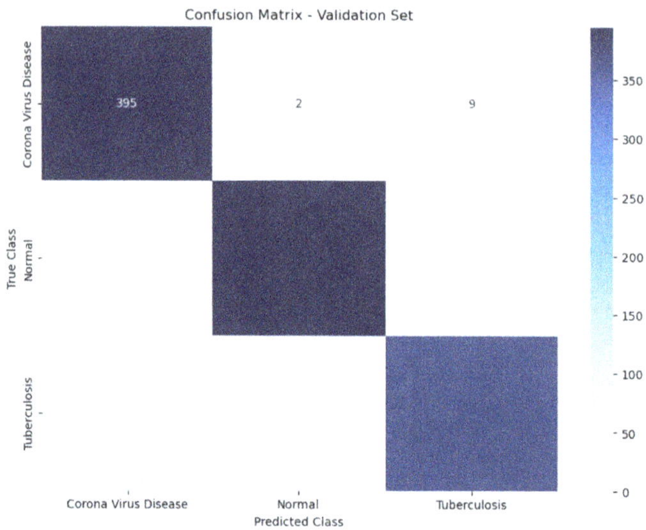

Figure 7. Confusion matrix of validation optimized using augmentation techniques.

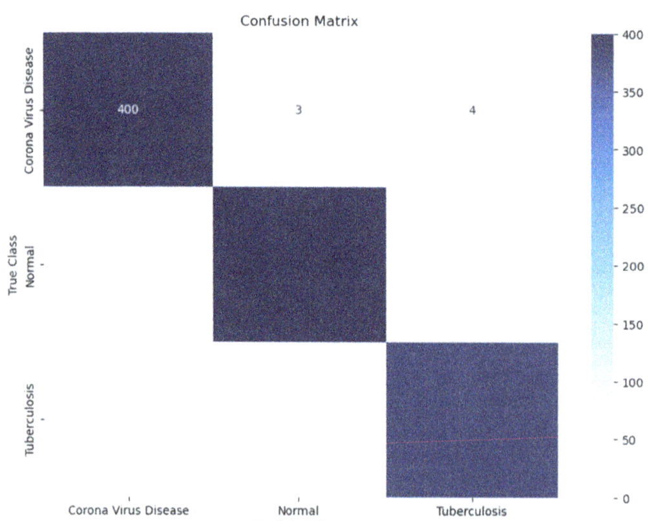

Figure 8. Confusion matrix of test dataset optimized using augmentation techniques.

Figure 9 depicts the ROC (receiver operating characteristic) curves for a multi-class classifier designed to identify three distinct conditions: COVID-19, normal (healthy state), and tuberculosis. Each curve represents one of the classes, and they all show perfect classification performance, with an area under the curve (AUC) of 1.00. This perfect AUC score means that the classifier is exceptionally effective at distinguishing between affected and unaffected individuals for all the categories. It achieves high levels of both sensitivity (the ability to detect positive cases) and specificity (the ability to avoid false alarms) across the board, without any increase in false positive rates even in the regions where sensitivity is highest. This level of accuracy indicates that the classifier is highly reliable for medical diagnostics, providing confidence in its use for disease detection without misclassifying healthy or diseased individuals.

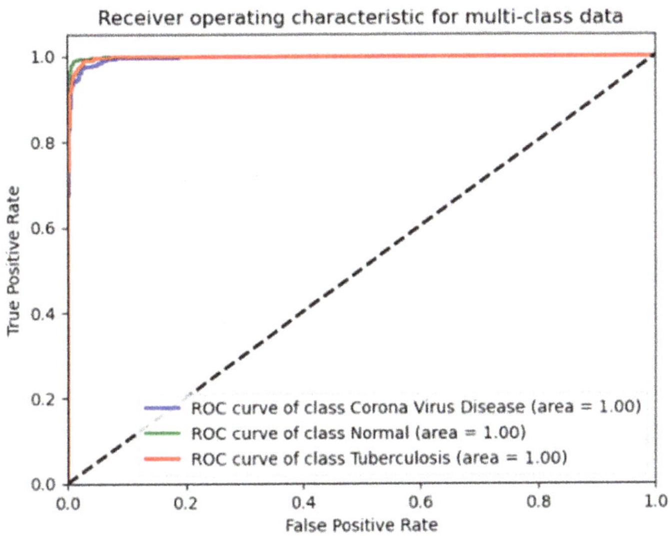

Figure 9. Receiver operating characteristic (ROC) curves for the VGG16 model in diagnosing lung conditions, on test dataset.

Figure 10 shows a comparison of AUC (area under the curve) outcomes among cutting edge techniques, including a recently introduced method for identifying lung ailments from chest X-ray images. Each bar on the x axis is tagged with a reference number. The y axis illustrates the range of AUC results, spanning from 0.75 to 1.00. A higher AUC score indicates a higher performance of a model in distinguishing between diseased and healthy states. In this assessment, our proposed method exhibits superiority over numerous existing approaches, underscoring the effectiveness of the novel strategy employed in this research. This strategy harnesses methodologies like data augmentation and balancing to enhance the classification process. ResNet50 stands out for its results, indicating its potential as a choice for assisting in clinical diagnoses of illnesses such as pneumonia, COVID-19, and tuberculosis. It positions the proposed approach as a step in ongoing efforts to improve the accuracy and dependability of diagnosing lung diseases. This advancement aims to contribute to patient care and treatment strategies.

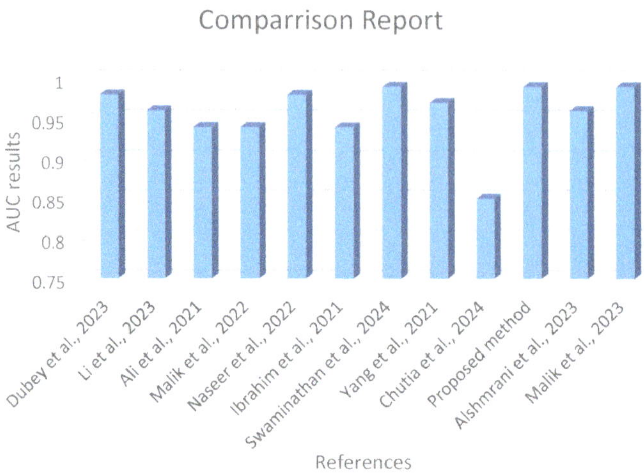

Figure 10. Comparison of AUC results for state-of-the-art lung disease detection models [9–19].

5. Conclusions

The VGG16 and ResNet50 models have shown accuracy when identifying lung conditions like tuberculosis, COVID-19 and normal lung states. Overall, ResNet50 tends to perform better than VGG16. These models have proven to be effective thanks to data augmentation, demonstrating their ability to generalize well on data. Their high precision and recall rates highlight their potential for use in diagnostics, marking a significant advancement in automated disease detection through image analysis. While VGG16 initially lagged behind ResNet50 in validation, it showed improvement during testing. In the validation phase, the model achieved precision rates ranging from 0.88 to 0.99 and recall rates from 0.89 to 0.98. During the testing phase, we observed a notable increase in both precision and recall rates. The model achieved a commendable score of 0.99 for detecting tuberculosis, indicating progress in diagnosing this condition. Our future efforts will be dedicated to improving the model's reliability by expanding its range to cover more conditions and seamlessly integrating them into real-time clinical diagnostic systems. Additionally, our exploration of data integration and advanced data augmentation techniques will further enhance accuracy. However, it is crucial to underline the urgency of addressing biases and ensure that these models perform consistently across diverse populations as they approach clinical use.

Future work aims to enhance the models' resilience by expanding the range of conditions it can detect and integrating them into real-time diagnostic systems. Exploring data integration and employing data augmentation strategies will also boost diagnostic accuracy. Ensuring performance across populations becomes critical as these models approach clinical implementation.

Author Contributions: Methodology, M.K., A.M.A.R. and R.N.A.K.; Software, M.K.; Validation, M.K., A.M.A.R. and R.N.A.K.; Formal analysis, M.K. and R.N.A.K.; Investigation, M.K.; Resources, M.K. and R.N.A.K.; Data curation, M.K. and R.N.A.K.; Writing—original draft, M.K.; Writing—review & editing, M.K., A.M.A.R. and R.N.A.K.; Visualization, M.K., A.M.A.R. and R.N.A.K.; Supervision, M.K. and A.M.A.R.; Project administration, M.K. and A.M.A.R.; Funding acquisition, M.K. and A.M.A.R. All authors have read and agreed to the published version of the manuscript.

Funding: This work was supported by the Deanship of Scientific Research, Vice Presidency for Graduate Studies and Scientific Research, King Faisal University, Saudi Arabia Grant No. KFU241219.

Institutional Review Board Statement: Not applicable.

Informed Consent Statement: Not applicable.

Data Availability Statement: Data available in a publicly accessible repository https://www.kaggle.com/datasets/omkarmanohardalvi/lungs-disease-dataset-4-types, accessed on 20 November 2023.

Conflicts of Interest: The authors declare no conflict of interest.

References

1. Ledesma, J.R.; Ma, J.; Zhang, M.; Basting, A.V.; Chu, H.T.; Vongpradith, A.; LeGrand, K.E.; Xu, Y.Y.; Dai, X.; Nicholson, S.I.; et al. Global, regional, and national age-specific progress towards the 2020 milestones of the WHO End TB Strategy: A systematic analysis for the Global Burden of Disease Study 2021. *Lancet Infect. Dis.* **2024**. [CrossRef] [PubMed]
2. Khanna, A.; Saha, R.; Ahmad, N. National TB elimination programme-What has changed. *Indian J. Med. Microbiol.* **2023**, *42*, 103–107. [CrossRef] [PubMed]
3. Migliori, G.B.; Dowdy, D.; Denholm, J.T.; D'Ambrosio, L.; Centis, R. The path to tuberculosis elimination: A renewed vision. *Eur. Respir. J.* **2023**, *61*, 2300499. [CrossRef] [PubMed]
4. Alsayed, S.S.; Gunosewoyo, H. Tuberculosis: Pathogenesis, current treatment regimens and new drug targets. *Int. J. Mol. Sci.* **2023**, *24*, 5202. [CrossRef] [PubMed]
5. Roure, S.; Vallès, X.; Sopena, N.; Benítez, R.M.; Reynaga, E.A.; Bracke, C.; Loste, C.; Mateu, L.; Antuori, A.; Baena, T.; et al. Disseminated tuberculosis and diagnosis delay during the COVID-19 era in a Western European country: A case series analysis. *Front. Public Health* **2023**, *11*, 1175482.
6. Global Tuberculosis Network and TB/COVID-19 Global Study Group; Casco, N.; Jorge, A.L.; Palmero, D.J.; Alffenaar, J.W.; Fox, G.J.; Ezz, W.; Cho, J.G.; Denholm, J.; Skrahina, A.; et al. Long-term outcomes of the global tuberculosis and COVID-19 co-infection cohort. *Eur. Respir. J.* **2023**, *62*, 2300925.
7. Boutet, A.; Haile, S.S.; Yang, A.Z.; Son, H.J.; Malik, M.; Pai, V.; Nasralla, M.; Germann, J.; Vetkas, A.; Khalvati, F.; et al. Assessing the Emergence and Evolution of Artificial Intelligence and Machine Learning Research in Neuroradiology. *Am. J. Neuroradiol.* 2024, *online ahead of print*. [CrossRef]
8. Chafai, N.; Bonizzi, L.; Botti, S.; Badaoui, B. Emerging applications of machine learning in genomic medicine and healthcare. *Crit. Rev. Clin. Lab. Sci.* **2024**, *61*, 140–163. [CrossRef]
9. Dubey, A.K.; Chabert, G.L.; Carriero, A.; Pasche, A.; Danna, P.S.; Agarwal, S.; Mohanty, L.; Nillmani; Sharma, N.; Yadav, S.; et al. Ensemble deep learning derived from transfer learning for classification of COVID-19 patients on hybrid deep-learning-based lung segmentation: A data augmentation and balancing framework. *Diagnostics* **2023**, *13*, 1954. [CrossRef]
10. Li, W.; Yu, S.; Yang, R.; Tian, Y.; Zhu, T.; Liu, H.; Jiao, D.; Zhang, F.; Liu, X.; Tao, L.; et al. Machine Learning Model of ResNet50-Ensemble Voting for Malignant–Benign Small Pulmonary Nodule Classification on Computed Tomography Images. *Cancers* **2023**, *15*, 5417. [CrossRef]
11. Ali, I.; Muzammil, M.; Haq, I.U.; Amir, M.; Abdullah, S. Deep feature selection and decision level fusion for lungs nodule classification. *IEEE Access* **2021**, *9*, 18962–18973. [CrossRef]
12. Malik, H.; Anees, T. BDCNet: Multi-classification convolutional neural network model for classification of COVID-19, pneumonia, and lung cancer from chest radiographs. *Multimed. Syst.* **2022**, *28*, 815–829. [CrossRef] [PubMed]
13. Naseer, I.; Akram, S.; Masood, T.; Jaffar, A.; Khan, M.A.; Mosavi, A. Performance analysis of state-of-the-art cnn architectures for luna16. *Sensors* **2022**, *22*, 4426. [CrossRef] [PubMed]
14. Ibrahim, D.M.; Elshennawy, N.M.; Sarhan, A.M. Deep-chest: Multi-classification deep learning model for diagnosing COVID-19, pneumonia, and lung cancer chest diseases. *Comput. Biol. Med.* **2021**, *132*, 104348. [CrossRef] [PubMed]
15. Swaminathan, V.P.; Balasubramani, R.; Parvathavarthini, S.; Gopal, V.; Raju, K.; Sivalingam, T.S.; Thennarasu, S.R. GAN Based Image Segmentation and Classification Using Vgg16 for Prediction of Lung Cancer. *J. Adv. Res. Appl. Sci. Eng. Technol.* **2024**, *35*, 45–61.
16. Yang, Y.; Zhang, L.; Du, M.; Bo, J.; Liu, H.; Ren, L.; Li, X.; Deen, M.J. A comparative analysis of eleven neural networks architectures for small datasets of lung images of COVID-19 patients toward improved clinical decisions. *Comput. Biol. Med.* **2021**, *139*, 104887. [CrossRef] [PubMed]
17. Chutia, U.; Tewari, A.S.; Singh, J.P.; Raj, V.K. Classification of lung diseases using an attention-based modified DenseNet model. *J. Imaging Inform. Med.* **2024**. *online ahead of print*. [CrossRef]
18. Alshmrani GM, M.; Ni, Q.; Jiang, R.; Pervaiz, H.; Elshennawy, N.M. A deep learning architecture for multi-class lung diseases classification using chest X-ray (CXR) images. *Alex. Eng. J.* **2023**, *64*, 923–935. [CrossRef]
19. Malik, H.; Anees, T.; Din, M.; Naeem, A. CDC_Net: Multi-classification convolutional neural network model for detection of COVID-19, pneumothorax, pneumonia, lung Cancer, and tuberculosis using chest X-rays. *Multimed. Tools Appl.* **2023**, *82*, 13855–13880. [CrossRef]
20. Ullah, F.; Ansari, S.U.; Hanif, M.; Ayari, M.A.; Chowdhury ME, H.; Khandakar, A.A.; Khan, M.S. Brain MR image enhancement for tumor segmentation using 3D U-Net. *Sensors* **2021**, *21*, 7528. [CrossRef]
21. Zadeh Shirazi, A.; Fornaciari, E.; McDonnell, M.D.; Yaghoobi, M.; Cevallos, Y.; Tello-Oquendo, L.; Inca, D.; Gomez, G.A. The application of deep convolutional neural networks to brain cancer images: A survey. *J. Pers. Med.* **2020**, *10*, 224. [CrossRef]

22. Amirrajab, S.; Al Khalil, Y.; Lorenz, C.; Weese, J.; Pluim, J.; Breeuwer, M. Label-informed cardiac magnetic resonance image synthesis through conditional generative adversarial networks. *Comput. Med. Imaging Graph.* **2022**, *101*, 102123. [CrossRef] [PubMed]
23. Li, Y.; Zhang, H.; Xue, X.; Jiang, Y.; Shen, Q. Deep learning for remote sensing image classification: A survey. *Wiley Interdiscip. Rev. Data Min. Knowl. Discov.* **2018**, *8*, e1264. [CrossRef]
24. Tai, Y.; Yang, J.; Liu, X. Image super-resolution via deep recursive residual network. In Proceedings of the IEEE Conference on Computer Vision and Pattern Recognition, Honolulu, HI, USA, 21–26 July 2017; pp. 3147–3155.
25. Ray, S. A quick review of machine learning algorithms. In Proceedings of the 2019 International Conference on Machine Learning, Big Data, Cloud and Parallel Computing (COMITCon), Faridabad, India, 14–16 February 2019; pp. 35–39.
26. Shen, H.; Chen, L.; Jin, Y.; Zhao, L.; Kong, B.; Philipose, M.; Sundaram, R. Nexus: A GPU cluster engine for accelerating DNN-based video analysis. In Proceedings of the 27th ACM Symposium on Operating Systems Principles, Huntsville, ON, Canada, 27–30 October 2019; pp. 322–337.
27. Liu, W.; Wang, Z.; Liu, X.; Zeng, N.; Liu, Y.; Alsaadi, F.E. A survey of deep neural network architectures and their applications. *Neurocomputing* **2017**, *234*, 11–26. [CrossRef]
28. Morid, M.A.; Borjali, A.; Del Fiol, G. A scoping review of transfer learning research on medical image analysis using ImageNet. *Comput. Biol. Med.* **2021**, *128*, 104115. [CrossRef]
29. Rippel, O.; Mertens, P.; Merhof, D. Modeling the distribution of normal data in pre-trained deep features for anomaly detection. In Proceedings of the 2020 25th International Conference on Pattern Recognition (ICPR), Milan, Italy, 10–15 January 2021; pp. 6726–6733.
30. Serena Low, W.C.; Chuah, J.H.; Tee, C.A.T.; Anis, S.; Shoaib, M.A.; Faisal, A.; Khalil, A.; Lai, K.W. An overview of deep learning techniques on chest X-ray and CT scan identification of COVID-19. *Comput. Math. Methods Med.* **2021**, *2021*, 5528144. [CrossRef]

Journal of
Clinical Medicine

MDPI

Article

Developing the Benchmark: Establishing a Gold Standard for the Evaluation of AI Caries Diagnostics

Julian Boldt [1,†], Matthias Schuster [1,*,†], Gabriel Krastl [2], Marc Schmitter [1], Jonas Pfundt [1], Angelika Stellzig-Eisenhauer [3] and Felix Kunz [3]

[1] Department of Prosthetic Dentistry, University Hospital Würzburg, 97070 Würzburg, Germany; schmitter_m@ukw.de (M.S.); pfundt.jonas@stud-mail.uni-wuerzburg.de (J.P.)
[2] Center of Dental Traumatology, Department of Conservative Dentistry and Periodontology, University Hospital Würzburg, 97070 Würzburg, Germany; krastl_g@ukw.de
[3] Department of Orthodontics, University Hospital Würzburg, 97070 Würzburg, Germany; stellzig_a@ukw.de (A.S.-E.); kunz_f@ukw.de (F.K.)
* Correspondence: schuster_m3@ukw.de
† These authors contributed equally to this work.

Abstract: Background/Objectives: The aim of this study was to establish a histology-based gold standard for the evaluation of artificial intelligence (AI)-based caries detection systems on proximal surfaces in bitewing images. **Methods**: Extracted human teeth were used to simulate intraoral situations, including caries-free teeth, teeth with artificially created defects and teeth with natural proximal caries. All 153 simulations were radiographed from seven angles, resulting in 1071 in vitro bitewing images. Histological examination of the carious lesion depth was performed twice by an expert. A total of thirty examiners analyzed all the radiographs for caries. **Results**: We generated in vitro bitewing images to evaluate the performance of AI-based carious lesion detection against a histological gold standard. All examiners achieved a sensitivity of 0.565, a Matthews correlation coefficient (MCC) of 0.578 and an area under the curve (AUC) of 76.1. The histology receiver operating characteristic (ROC) curve significantly outperformed the examiners' ROC curve ($p < 0.001$). All examiners distinguished induced defects from true caries in 54.6% of cases and correctly classified 99.8% of all teeth. Expert caries classification of the histological images showed a high level of agreement (intraclass correlation coefficient (ICC) = 0.993). Examiner performance varied with caries depth ($p \leq 0.008$), except between E2 and E1 lesions ($p = 1$), while central beam eccentricity, gender, occupation and experience had no significant influence (all $p \geq 0.411$). **Conclusions**: This study successfully established an unbiased dataset to evaluate AI-based caries detection on bitewing surfaces and compare it to human judgement, providing a standardized assessment for fair comparison between AI technologies and helping dental professionals to select reliable diagnostic tools.

Keywords: dental caries; artificial intelligence; diagnostics; bitewing; radiography; benchmarking

1. Introduction

With the exponential growth in computational power across virtually all semiconductor-based devices, artificial intelligence (AI) is finding its way into medical sciences, driven by the desire to increase diagnostic accuracy, improve treatment outcomes and optimize workflow efficiency [1–3]. The increasing prevalence of articles on this subject in literature is evidence of this [4]. From identifying anatomical or pathological structures to assisting with logistical challenges, AI promises to save time and reduce costs [5–7].

In human medical imaging, AI applications show promising potential in several areas, particularly in oncology [8]. A major advantage of these AI applications is that their training is based on verified histopathological findings, thus relying on a reliable reference.

In dentistry AI, algorithms have already been developed for automated analysis of radiographs for caries diagnosis [9–12]. Image recognition in regard to caries detection has been approached using a variety of techniques [13]. However, the traditional comprehensive analysis of X-rays by the dentist is time-consuming and limited by the possibility of human error, which AI promises to largely eliminate [14–17].

In 2022, Mohammad-Rahimi et al. conducted a systematic review to evaluate the accuracy of automated caries detection systems and showed that the majority of the models included were able to deliver results with clinically acceptable performance parameters, although the quality of studies is often currently low [18]. In particular, in a systematic review and meta-analysis, Ammar and Kühnisch reported acceptable diagnostic accuracy of AI models for caries detection and classification on bitewing radiographs [19]. These radiographs are the most reliable and widely used clinical imaging method for caries diagnosis [20,21]. Despite some promising results, it has also been criticized that AI-based caries diagnostic studies often neither include an appropriate definition of caries nor provide information on the type of carious lesion detected and have limitations in regard to size and heterogeneity of the reported datasets [22–24].

The advancement of AI applications for caries detection in bitewing images relies primarily on the use of deep learning networks, primarily convolutional neural networks [25]. This iterative process begins with the compilation of large datasets of annotated bitewing radiographs, in which dental professionals delineate regions of interest corresponding to caries, healthy tooth structure and other anatomical structures [4]. These annotated images are then divided into distinct training and test sets. Using machine learning algorithms, AI-driven methods analyze the training dataset, identifying intricate patterns and extrapolating the desired results [4]. The integrity of the trained model is then evaluated against the separate test dataset, assessing its ability to analyze novel, unseen data. The accuracy of the model is quantified by comparing the predictions derived from the test dataset with the actual annotations. This dichotomy between training and test datasets is crucial to ensure that the AI model goes beyond simply memorizing specific instances from the training dataset, and instead acquires a robust understanding of the general patterns and features that are essential for accurate caries detection.

However, a fundamental limitation arises in the whole training process, which lies in the annotation of radiographs by dentists, representing the AI training gold standard. According to the Standards for Reporting Diagnostic Accuracy Studies (STARD), a gold standard is defined as an error-free reference standard that represents the best available method for determining the presence or absence of the target condition [26]. Although dentists are trained in clinical diagnosis, their sensitivity and specificity for detecting carious lesions on radiographs is somewhat limited [27–30], in particular for subtle or early stages of lesions. In addition, various factors, such as experience, knowledge, technical skills and time pressure, may influence diagnostic accuracy [31]. While it is undeniable that deep learning can identify features indicative of caries, the underlying methodology has potentially serious practical implications as the predictions only reflect sensitivity and specificity within the training and test data. This concern is exacerbated by the existence of commercial automated dental radiograph analysis software solutions, most of which lack transparency regarding the scientific basis of their AI models.

The aim of this study was, therefore, to develop reliable in vitro simulations of bitewing radiographs based on the histological gold standard to provide a basis for evaluating the performance of AI-based software currently offered by commercial vendors for the automated analysis of caries in bitewing radiographs. In addition, a reference dataset of caries diagnoses from in vitro bitewing radiographs by different examiners was created to serve as a benchmark for predicting whether AI applications can provide a diagnostic advantage to dental examiners.

2. Materials and Methods

2.1. Ethical Aspects

This study was approved by the Ethics Committee of the Medical Faculty of the University of Würzburg (15/15, 9 February 2015) and was carried out in compliance with the

Declaration of Helsinki. All teeth used were extracted for existing clinical indications, with ethical approval, voluntarily and without coercion, and were anonymized. Information provided to patients still allowed for patient withdrawal but excluded the possibility of targeted destruction of donated teeth.

2.2. Trial Profile

The trial profile is depicted in Figure 1.

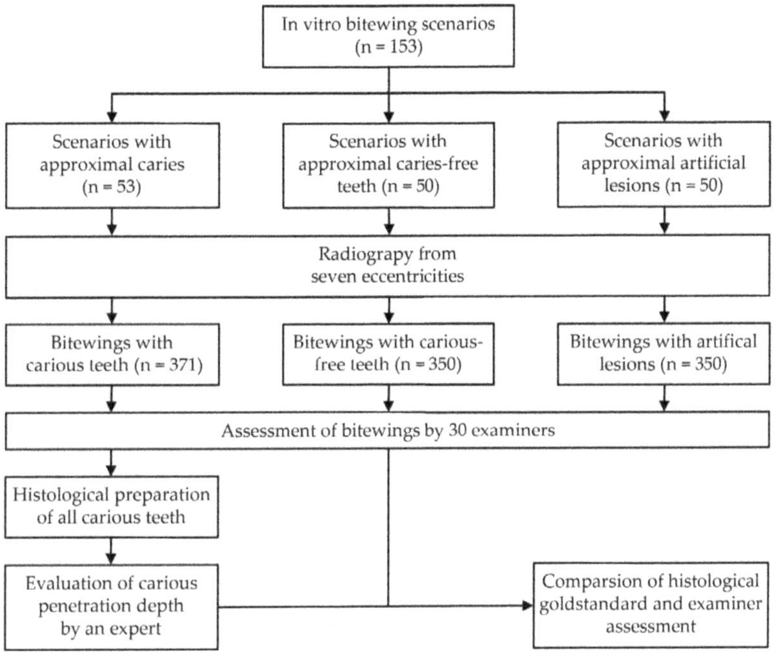

Figure 1. Trial profile.

2.3. Tooth Selection

This study used 179 extracted permanent human teeth that were preserved in a 1% tosylchloramide–sodium solution immediately after extraction. All teeth were obtained from various dental clinics and hospitals, ensuring a diverse representation of carious and caries-free conditions. Inclusion criteria were visually and radiographically normal and properly formed permanent teeth with restorative measures that did not significantly interfere with or prevent radiographic caries diagnosis of proximal surfaces. Exclusion criteria comprised completely decayed teeth or root remains, and teeth whose clinical appearance matched hereditary anomalies. All teeth were examined for possible carious lesions by visual inspection using a 2.5× close-up magnification loupe (GTX 2 telescope loupe system; Carl Zeiss Vision GmbH, Aalen, Germany) and tactile examination using a dental probe (EXS3A; Henry Schein Dental Deutschland GmbH, Langen, Germany). A digital single-lens reflex camera (Olympus E-400; Olympus Europa SE & Co. KG, Hamburg, Germany) with 50 mm macro lens (four thirds standard) was used to photograph each tooth from five directions (occlusal, vestibular, oral, mesial, distal). In addition, each tooth was radiographed in the vestibulo-oral and mesiodistal directions (Sirona Heliodent DS; Dentsply Sirona Deutschland GmbH, Bensheim, Germany) (Figure 2). Based on the visual, tactile and radiographic findings, two dentists classified all teeth as carious or caries-free.

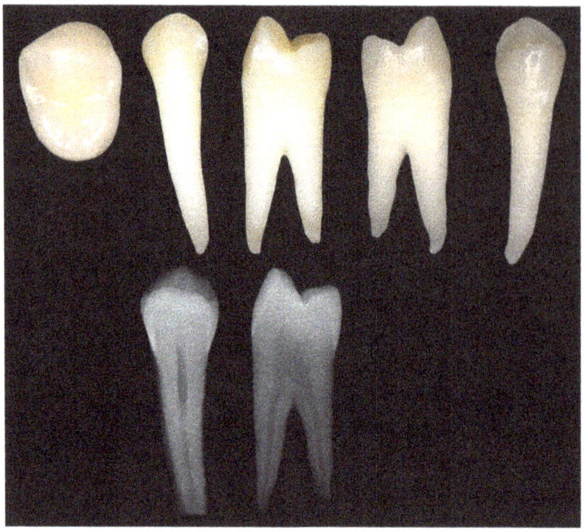

Figure 2. Photographic and radiological documentation of all teeth.

2.4. Preparation of Artificial Defects

A total of 50 caries-free teeth were used to test the ability to discriminate between carious lesions and artificial defects. The artificial defects were created on the proximal surfaces using 1 mm, 2 mm, 3 mm and 4 mm spherical diamond burs (Gebr. Brasseler GmbH & Co. KG, Lemgo, Germany). During the preparation process, the burs were inserted into the teeth, creating artificial defects half the size of the drill's diameter.

The selection of diameters ranging from 1 mm to 4 mm was based on findings of Stroud et al. on the mean enamel thickness of permanent posterior teeth [32]. This allowed for clinically accurate lesion simulations.

2.5. Bitewing Design

An occlusal holder (Split-Fixator; Scheu-Dental GmbH, Iserlohn, Germany) was fitted with Plexiglas blocks attached at the top and bottom by means of a milled groove. The teeth were embedded in Periphery Wax (Sigma Dental, Handewitt, Germany) and mounted in an anatomically and physiologically accurate configuration to standardize their position for radiographic imaging of the bitewings (Figure 3).

Despite clinical best efforts to use the parallel technique, obtaining superposition-free images of the region of interest in bitewing radiographs remains challenging. Factors such as relative positioning of the teeth, superimpositions, the curvature of the dental arch, the orientation and spatial distortion of the film during exposure and the alignment of the X-ray tube all contribute to the superposition of dental tissue in the interproximal region [33,34]. To mimic clinically relevant situations and improve data quality, the study included not only orthoradial images, but also mesial and distal eccentric images at varying angles. For this purpose, the model was fixed in a rotating vice with a graduated scale that allowed precise angular adjustments in 2-degree increments.

Each examination series yielded a total of seven radiographs, all taken with the same X-ray unit (Sirona Heliodent DS; Dentsply Sirona Deutschland GmbH, Bensheim, Germany; 60 kV, 7 mA, 0,06 ms). These included a 0° orthogonal image and 4°, 6° and 8° mesial and distal eccentric images (totaling 7 images per series) (Figure 4).

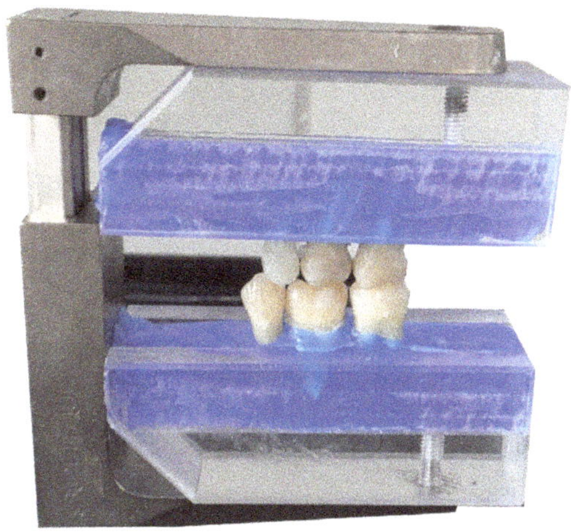

Figure 3. Occlusion holder with fixed teeth simulating clinical bitewing scenarios.

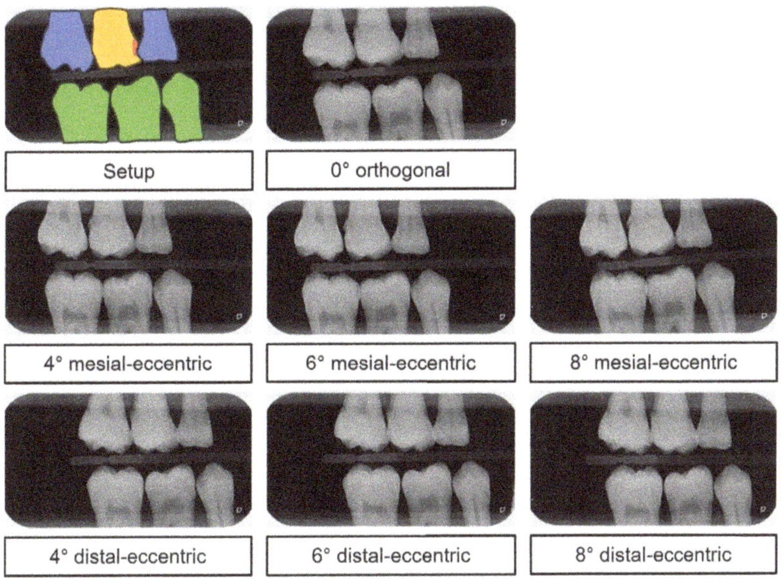

Figure 4. Digital in vitro bitewing images. Top: color-coded setup—yellow: examination tooth, red: carious lesion, blue: adjacent tooth, green: antagonistic tooth. Below: The mesial-eccentric series shows increased superimposition as the ray path becomes increasingly eccentric in the proximal region of teeth 46 and 47. Conversely, the distal-eccentric series shows increased superimposition as the ray path becomes increasingly eccentric in the interproximal region of teeth 15 and 16.

2.6. Preparation of Histological Samples

The sample preparation steps are shown in Figure 5.

After radiography, all carious teeth were subjected to an adapted standardized histological examination procedure (Figure 5) [35]. This was an elaborate process, beginning with a six-day ascending dehydration series with increasing concentrations of ethanol, followed by a six-day resin infiltration (Technovit 7200 VLC; Kulzer GmbH & Co. KG, Wehrheim, Germany) to effectively preserve carious lesions for subsequent processing (Table 1).

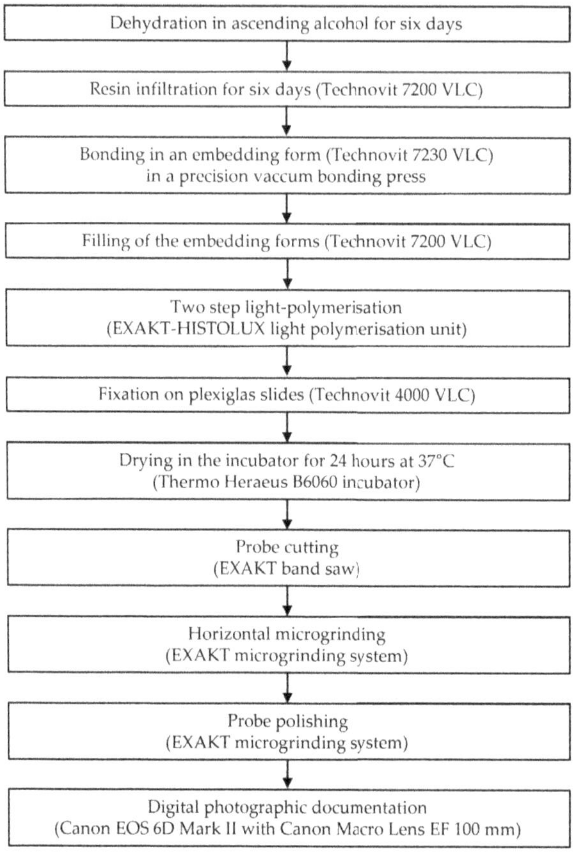

Figure 5. Sample preparation steps.

Table 1. Schematic overview of tooth dehydration and resin infiltration.

Time	Chemical Solution	Volume Ratio	Storage
Day 1	EtOH 70%/purif. H_2O	100	50 mL plastic flacons
Day 2	EtOH 80%/purif. H_2O	100	50 mL plastic flacons
Day 3	EtOH 90%/purif. H_2O	100	50 mL plastic flacons
Day 4	EtOH 96%/purif. H_2O	100	50 mL plastic flacons
Day 5 and 6	EtOH 99%	100	50 mL plastic flacons
Day 7	EtOH 99%/Technovit 7200 VLC	50/50	50 mL plastic flacons (in darkness)
Day 8	Technovit 7200 VLC	100	Snap-on lid tablet glass (in darkness)
Day 9	Technovit 7200 VLC	100	Snap-on lid tablet glass (in darkness)
Day 10	Technovit 7200 VLC	100	Snap-on lid tablet glass (in darkness)
Day 11	Technovit 7200 VLC	100	Snap-on lid tablet glass (in darkness)
Day 12	Technovit 7200 VLC	100	Snap-on lid tablet glass (in darkness)

purif. = purified, EtOH = ethanol.

The (carious) teeth were then bonded (Technovit 7230 VLC; Kulzer GmbH & Co. KG, Wehrheim, Germany), vestibular side down, to an embedding form (Kulzer GmbH & Co. KG, Wehrheim, Germany) using a disposable spatula and cured with UV light for 10 min in a precision vacuum bonding press (EXAKT Apparatebau GmbH & Co. KG, Norderstedt, Germany). The forms were filled with embedding resin (Technovit 7200 VLC; Kulzer GmbH & Co. KG, Wehrheim, Germany) using a disposable pipette. Pre-polymerization was performed in an EXAKT-HISTOLUX light polymerization unit (Exakt Apparatebau GmbH & Co. KG, Nordstedt) with two UV lamps for two hours, followed by the actual polymerization with eight UV lamps for a further eight hours. The polymerized blocks were fixed to Plexiglas slides (Walter-Messner GmbH, Oststeinbek, Germany) using mixed Technovit 4000 (Kulzer GmbH & Co. KG, Wehrheim, Germany) and cured with UV light for 10 min in the precision vacuum bonding press (EXAKT Apparatebau GmbH & Co. KG, Norderstedt, Germany). Before further processing, the samples were dried in an incubator (Thermo Heraeus B6060 incubator; Heraeus Holding GmbH, Hanau, Germany) for 24 h at 37 °C.

The (carious) teeth were sectioned directly in front of the lesion using a saw with a diamond-coated band 100 µm wide (EXAKT Apparatebau GmbH & Co. KG, Norderstedt, Germany) under constant water cooling. Due to inherent vibrations and the cutting width of the saw blade, a loss of tooth substance of approximately 300 µm per cut (slice) was assumed. During the cutting process, the block was fixed to the machine by a vacuum pump at 680 mbar and pulled through the saw blade by a constant force of 400 g (40 N). The hard-cut method was used to divide the carious teeth before the lesion reached its maximum extent.

This was followed by a meticulous, progressive approach to the carious defect using the wet grinding technique with the EXAKT horizontal microgrinding system and a 400 g press weight (EXAKT Apparatebau GmbH & Co. KG, Norderstedt, Germany) (Figure 6). The microgrinding unit was calibrated by grinding a microscope slide with 1200 grit Al_2O_3 sandpaper for two minutes. A difference in the slide of no more than 5 µm at four different measuring points was considered acceptable. The final step was polishing with the EXAKT horizontal microgrinding system using 2400 and 4000 grit Al_2O_3 sandpaper, with each incremental step documented by digital photographic records with a digital single-lens reflex camera (Canon EOS 6D Mark II; Canon Deutschland GmbH, Krefeld, Germany) and a macro lens (Canon Macro Lens EF 100 mm, Canon Deutschland GmbH, Krefeld, Germany) to illustrate the maximum extent of the lesion in the mesiodistal direction. The removal of tooth material between grinding was determined by measuring the thickness with a micrometer screw (EXAKT Apparatebau GmbH & Co. KG, Norderstedt, Germany).

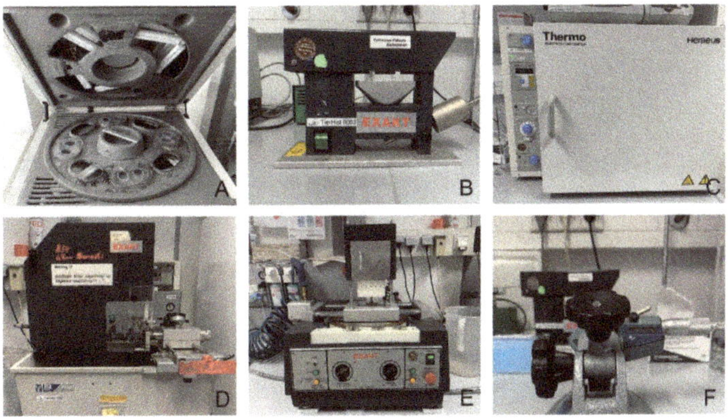

Figure 6. Equipment for the preparation of histological specimens. (**A**): EXAKT-HISTOLUX light polymerization unit, (**B**) EXAKT precision vacuum bonding press, (**C**): Thermo Heraeus B6060 Incubator, (**D**): EXAKT band saw, (**E**): EXAKT horizontal microgrinding system, (**F**): EXAKT micrometer screw.

2.7. Lesion Classification of the Histological Samples

All histological specimens, with the maximum extent of the carious lesion in mesio-distal direction, were digitally photographed and displayed on a diagnostic monitor (Nio Color 2 MP LED; Barco, Kortrijk, Brussels, Belgium) with no time limit (Figure 7). A review was performed twice at three-month intervals by an expert with extensive professional and scientific experience, following the common radiographic classification scheme (Table 2).

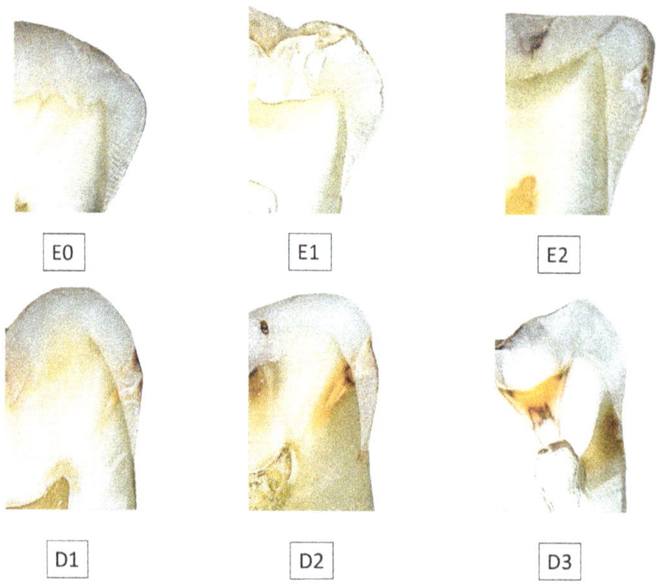

Figure 7. Histological specimen with different proximal carious lesion depths. E0 = Caries-free, E1 = Caries limited to the outer half of the enamel, E2 = Caries extending to the inner half of the enamel, D1 = Caries in the outer third of dentin, D2 = Caries in the middle third of dentin, D3 = Caries in the dentinal third close to the pulp or up to the pulp.

Table 2. Caries classification scheme.

Classification of Caries	Carious Lesion Extension
E1	Caries limited to the outer half of the enamel
E2	Caries extending to the inner half of the enamel
D1	Caries in the outer third of dentin
D2	Caries in the middle third of dentin
D3	Caries in the dentinal third close to the pulp or up to the pulp

The characteristics of the histological analysis are summarized in Table 3.

Table 3. Number of histologically confirmed carious lesions and their categorization according to the caries classification scheme.

Caries Classification	Proximal Surfaces	Percentage
E1	15	22.1%
E2	8	11.8%
D1	8	11.8%
D2	18	26.4%
D3	19	27.9%
	68	100%

2.8. Radiographic Caries Diagnostic by Dental Examiners

To benchmark dental examiners when analyzing in vitro bitewing images, 10 clinicians, 10 private practitioners and 10 students were asked to evaluate these radiographs.

Clinicians were defined as dentists providing care in a hospital setting, whereas private practitioners were defined as dentists working independently outside an institutional setting, usually in their own private practice. As a baseline, all participants were informed that all teeth would be examined for the presence or absence of proximal caries. Each participant evaluated a random selection of 35 to 36 bitewing images on a dental diagnostic monitor (Nio Color 2 MP LED; Barco, Kortrijk, Brussels, Belgium) without a time limit. All examiners were categorized according to gender, occupation and professional experience to assess respective influence on the quality of caries findings in bitewing radiographs.

2.9. Statistical Analysis and Performance Metrics

Statistical analyses were performed using R (version 4.3.2). Quality of carious lesion classification was determined by assessing the intrarater reliability using the intraclass correlation coefficient (ICC). The performance of the combined examiners was assessed using several metrics, including sensitivity, specificity, accuracy, positive and negative predictive values (PPV/NPV), area "under the curve" (AUC), F1 score and Matthews correlation coefficient (MCC).

The F1 score, a harmonic mean of precision and sensitivity, is a commonly used metric for binary classifier evaluation and ranges from 0 to 1, with higher values indicating superior classifier performance. It is defined as $2 \times \frac{(\mathrm{PPV} \times \mathrm{sensitivity})}{(\mathrm{PPV} + \mathrm{sensitivity})}$.

The Matthews Correlation Coefficient (MCC) is another key parameter for evaluating predictions against actual values and provides a reliable assessment of performance. The MCC is defined as $\frac{(\mathrm{TN} \times \mathrm{RP}) - (\mathrm{FN} \times \mathrm{FP})}{\sqrt{(\mathrm{TP}+\mathrm{FP}) \times (\mathrm{TP}+\mathrm{FN}) \times (\mathrm{TN}+\mathrm{FP}) \times (\mathrm{TN}+\mathrm{FN})}}$. An MCC value of 1 indicates a perfect prediction, while -1 indicates a complete disagreement between prediction and observation, and 0 indicates a random prediction. By including true negatives, false positives, false negatives and true positives, the MCC provides a comprehensive assessment of the predictive accuracy of the system or examiner under investigation.

De Long's test was used to compare the receiver operating characteristic (ROC) curves of histology and examiners. In addition, MCC scores were tested for differences in correlation using Bonferroni correction to compare performance across varying eccentricities of the central X-ray beam, the different carious lesion depths, gender, occupation and experience. The ability of the examiners to discriminate between artificially induced defects and true caries was investigated by comparing correct and incorrect predictions.

2.10. Sample Sice Planning

Our sample size planning was based on the number of bitewing radiographs required for accurate and reliable AI-assisted caries detection. We reviewed recent studies in this area and found that the number of bitewing radiographs used ranged from 45 to 252, with an average of 114 [9,36–40]. Due to the wide variation in the number of bitewing radiographs used in the literature, we used significantly more radiographs for testing in our study, with a total of 371 bitewing radiographs of 53 carious teeth. It can, therefore, be concluded that our sample size provides a robust dataset for evaluation.

3. Results

3.1. Examiner Characteristics

The metrics for all examiners are shown in Table 4. Private practitioners, clinicians and students were equally represented with ten examiners each. The private practitioners were almost equally divided between six examiners with less than five years' experience and four examiners with five or more years' experience. However, there was some imbalance between the two groups, with four male and six female private practitioners. All ten clinicians were evenly split between those with less than five years' experience and those with five or more years' experience, as was the gender split with five males and five females. There were eight female students compared to two males. Eight of the eleven examiners with less than five years' experience were male, followed by three female examiners in this group. In the group of nine examiners with five or more years' experience, there were three male and six female examiners. Of the thirty examiners, thirteen were male and seven were female.

Table 4. Examiner characteristics.

	Occupation			Experience		Gender	
	Private Practitioners	**Clinicians**	**Students**	**<5 Years**	**≥5 Years**	**Male**	**Female**
Occupation							
Private practitioners	10	-	-	6	4	6	4
Clinicians	-	10	-	5	5	5	5
Students	-	-	10	-	-	2	8

3.2. *Reliability of Histological Lesion Classification*

Intrarater reliability was very high throughout both assessment rounds (ICC: 0.993; 95%-CI [0.990; 0.995]). In two cases where the expert's categorization of carious lesions differed between the two rounds of examination, a second expert was consulted to determine the final lesion class.

3.3. *Examiners Performance Metrics*

All examiners reached a combined accuracy of 0.799, a sensitivity of 0.565, a specificity of 0.956, a PPV of 0.896, a NPV of 0.765, an AUC of 76.1, a F1 score of 0.693 and a MCC of 0.578 (Table 5).

Table 5. Combined examiners' performance metrics for caries detection.

Parameter	
Accuracy	0.799
Sensitivity	0.565
Specificity	0.956
PPV	0.896
NPV	0.765
F1 score	0.693
MCC	0.578
AUC	76.1

Note. AUC = area under the curve, MCC = Matthews correlation coefficient, NPV = negative predictive value, PPV = positive predictive value.

3.4. *AUC*

All examiners achieved a combined AUC of 76.1, whereas histology, serving as the gold standard method in caries diagnostic research, was assigned an AUC of 100 (Figure 8). Statistical analysis using De Long's test to compare the two ROC curves revealed a significantly higher performance for histology compared to the examiners' assessments ($p < 0.001$).

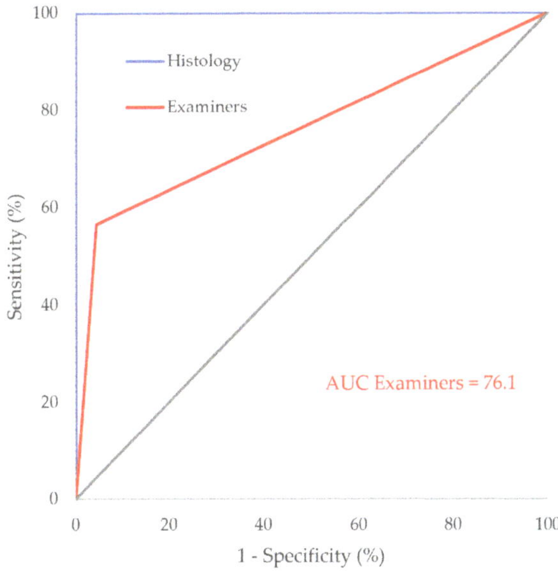

Figure 8. AUC of examiners and histology.

3.5. MCC by Lesion Class

The MCC showed variation according to the penetration depth of the carious lesions, with the best performance observed for D3 lesions (0.814), whereas E2 lesions showed the least favorable result (0.236) (Figure 9). The aggregated MCC for all lesion categories was 0.587.

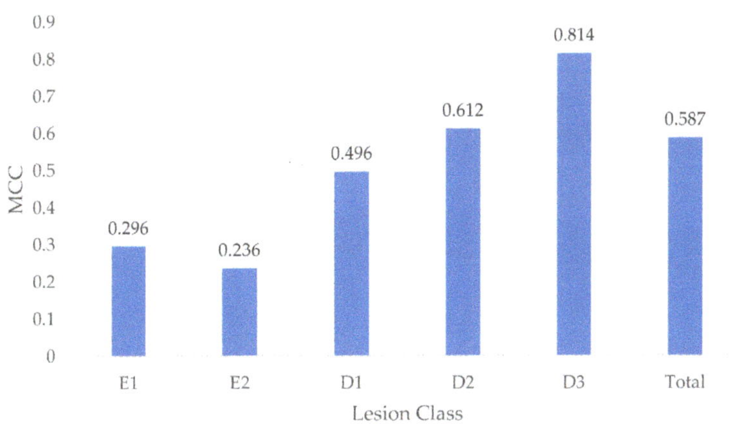

Figure 9. MCC by lesion class.

Testing for differences in MCC between different caries classifications revealed significant differences between all lesion classes ($p < 0.008$) except between E1 and E2 lesions ($p = 1$) (Table 6).

Table 6. Adjusted p-values for MCC comparison between lesion classes.

	Lesion Classification				
	E1	**E2**	**D1**	**D2**	**D3**
Lesion classification					
E1	-	1	<0.001 *	<0.001 *	<0.001 *
E2	1	-	<0.001 *	<0.001 *	<0.001 *
D1	<0.001 *	<0.001 *	-	0.008 *	<0.001 *
D2	<0.001 *	<0.001 *	0.008 *	-	<0.001 *
D3	<0.001 *	<0.001 *	<0.001 *	<0.001 *	-

Note. * Indicates significance (adjusted $p < 0.05$).

3.6. Gender Specific MCC

The MCC of male examiners was higher at 0.605 compared to the MCC of female examiners at 0.575 (Figure 10). However, testing for differences in MCC showed no significant effect of gender ($p = 0.44$).

Figure 10. MCC by gender.

3.7. MCC by Occupation

Private practitioners had the highest MCC (0.595), followed by students (0.593) and clinical practitioners (0.571) (Figure 11).

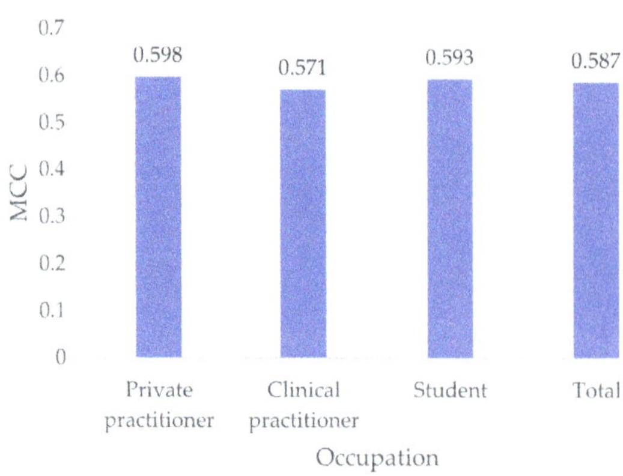

Figure 11. MCC by occupation.

Testing for differences in MCC showed no significant differences between all occupations ($p \geq 0.556$).

3.8. MCC by Experience

Dentists with less than 5 years of experience showed the best MCC (0.611), followed by students (0.593) and dentists with 5 or more years of experience (0.551) (Figure 12).

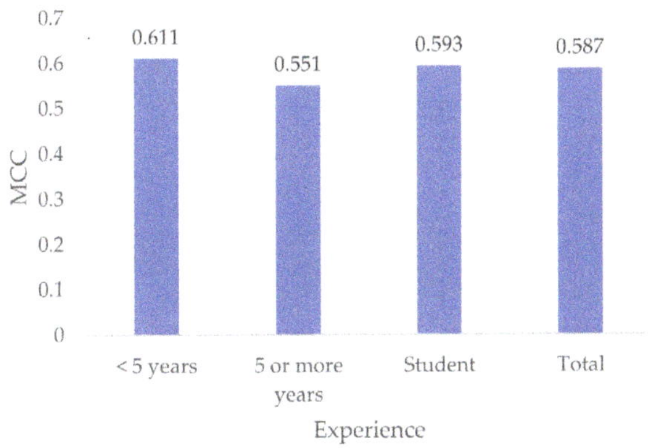

Figure 12. MCC by experience.

No significant differences were found by testing for differences in MCC according to experience ($p = 1$).

3.9. Influence of Eccentricity on MCC

Different eccentricity angles resulted in different MCC values (Figure 13).

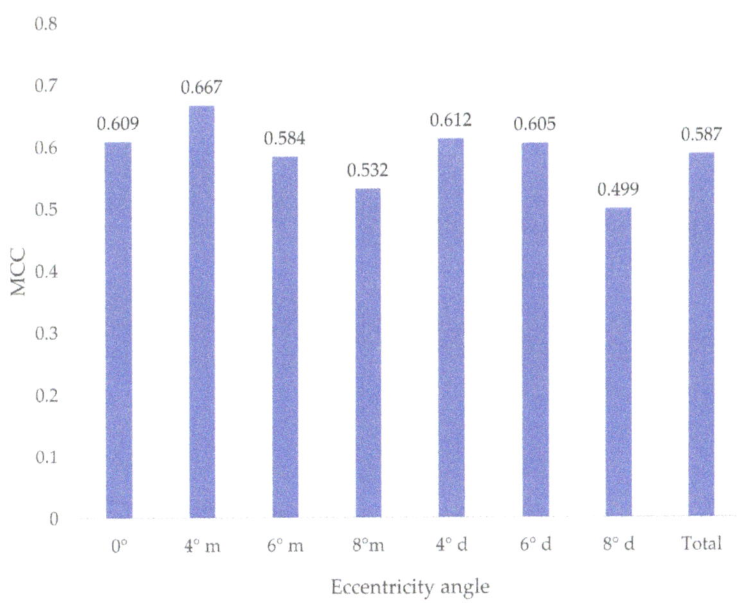

Figure 13. MCC by eccentricity angle. m = mesial-eccentric, d = distal-eccentric.

No statistically significant difference between the groups could be found ($p \geq 0.411$).

3.10. Differentiation between Carious Lesions and Artifically Induced Lesions

Out of a total of 350 artificial defects presented, 159 defects (45.4%) were identified as carious lesions by all examiners and 191 defects (54.6%) were identified as atypical for caries (Figure 14).

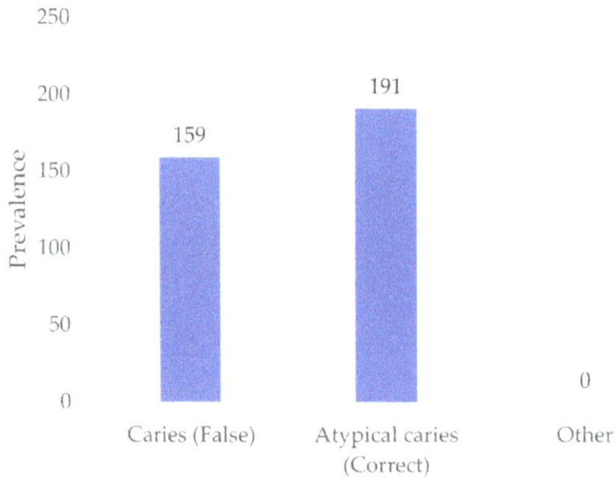

Figure 14. Assessment of artificially induced lesions.

3.11. Tooth Classification

The results indicate that 99.8% of the examiners correctly positioned the teeth depicted in the bitewing simulations according to the World Dental Federation (FDI) tooth numbering system (Figure 15).

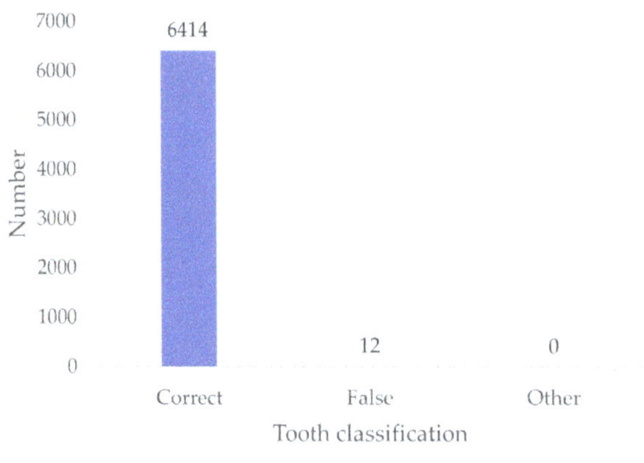

Figure 15. Tooth classification according to the FDI scheme.

4. Discussion

The European Medical Device Regulation (MDR) classifies medical imaging software as a medical device and, therefore, imposes several requirements on manufacturers to ensure safety and quality. Among other things, manufacturers are required to conduct a comprehensive clinical evaluation of their medical devices. As AI-based imaging software for caries diagnosis has been approved as a medical device, the underpinnings deserve scrutiny. The aim of this study was, therefore, to create a pool of histology-based radiographs to provide a scientifically sound testbed for such software. We are currently unaware of the existence of such a dataset.

In the context of fuzzy gold standards, several mitigation strategies have been proposed. One approach aims to supplement existing datasets with additional data from external sources [41]. By incorporating different perspectives, especially in cases where the gold standard may be imperfect, this strategy aims to improve the robustness of AI models and mitigate bias. The use of multiple diagnostic tests is also encouraged, as this can increase the transparency and reliability of diagnostic results [41]. Despite these efforts, the almost complete elimination of bias in AI-based dental caries diagnostics will, at least for an extended period, remain an elusive goal.

In general, in vitro studies provide a robust method for validating new caries diagnostic methods because they can refer to a reliable gold standard by means of histological analysis. Also, literature states that histological examination shall serve as the basis for a gold standard for the evaluation of new caries diagnostic methods [42]. Therefore, the ideal, albeit theoretical, method for evaluating diagnostic accuracy would be to first assess the diagnoses in vivo and then re-examine the same surfaces in vitro after tooth extraction using the histological gold standard [43]. However, logistical constraints and ethical considerations associated with invasive procedures, particularly the need for extraction, make this approach infeasible. Furthermore, it has been argued that differences between in vivo and in vitro results may cast doubt on the generalizability of in vitro data [43]. Nevertheless, previous studies have confirmed that no significant difference in the diagnostic accuracy of proximal carious lesions on digital radiographs can be demonstrated between in vivo and in vitro settings [44,45].

To further ensure the applicability of our results to the clinical situation, we attempted to create clinical simulations of the orofacial region on bitewing radiographs that are as realistic as possible. Nevertheless, given the complexity of the human body, accurate reproduction of anatomical structures remains difficult. To account for potential uncertainties, only findings within the coronal region were considered. This approach was intended to reduce possible distortions caused by the setup, particularly the fixation material. A limitation concerns the in vitro radiographs that did not consider external factors that could have influenced the accuracy of the radiographic diagnosis, such as the influence of metal artefacts, patient movement or incorrect positioning of the film holder on the analysis results. For reasons of standardization, all bitewing radiographs were taken on a single X-ray unit, to account for unintended variations.

For the purpose of disinfection and protection against dehydration, all extracted teeth were immersed in 1% tosylchloramide. Previous studies have shown that tosylchloramide has no discernible effect on tooth hard tissue [46–49]. A possible influence of tosylchloramide storage on the infiltration behavior of Technovit cannot be completely excluded, however it seems unlikely in view of the high success rate of histological preparations. All teeth were obtained from a variety of sources, including dental, oral and maxillofacial surgery practices and clinics. This diverse selection supports the assumption of a representative assortment of teeth across different population groups.

As already mentioned, histological examination serves as the most widely used gold standard for the validation of new caries diagnostic methods [42]. Its substantial diagnostic quality and value have been highlighted in many publications [50,51]. A major criticism of histological examinations is the frequent bisection of teeth through an arbitrary centerline [52]. This carries the risk of irreversibly destroying the presumed maximum extent of the carious lesion, thereby obscuring the true maximum depth. To overcome this, the incision was positioned anterior to the carious lesion, and the wet grinding technique was used to approach the maximum extent of the lesion. This approach ensured that the deepest carious extension was accurately identified with a high degree of confidence. The use of final multi-stage polishing ensured a consistent surface quality for subsequent expert analysis.

In our study, all 30 examiners showed a combined accuracy, sensitivity, specificity and AUC of 0.799, 0.565, 0.956 and 76.1, respectively, for the detection of carious lesions on bitewing radiographs. The literature shows a wide range of results. Kay and Knill-Jones observed a dentist sensitivity of 0.26 for the detection of dentin caries on in vitro bitewing radiographs [53]. Devlin et al. showed a sensitivity of 44% for enamel-limited lesions on bitewing radiographs among 23 examiners [54]. Mileman and van der Welle reported an

AUC of 0.88 with a sensitivity of 0.54 and specificity of 0.97 for dentin caries on bitewing radiographs. Similarly, Peers et al. demonstrated a comparable sensitivity of 0.59 for the detection of dentin caries on bitewing radiographs [55]. It, therefore, can be assumed that the results of our study are consistent with the literature, as we also could demonstrate that carious lesion depth had a significant effect on the MCC of all examiners between all lesion classes, except between enamel-limited E1 and E2 lesions. We support the assumption that in vitro radiographs provide diagnostic quality parameters similar to studies using in vivo radiographs.

Our results also showed that, contrary to expectations, the eccentricity of the central X-ray beam up to 8°, whether mesial or distal, did not appear to have a significant effect on the examiner's judgement of the presence or absence of caries. The lack of significant impact from minor eccentricities humbly suggests that clinicians may not need to be overly concerned about small variations in radiographic positioning when assessing for caries. Like our results, the study by Deprá et al. investigated the influence of the central opening angle on the diagnosis of secondary caries and also concluded that it had no influence [56]. On the other hand, Chadwick et al. investigated the influence of different central irradiation angles on visualization of proximal cavities in bitewing radiographs and found that lesions are typically diagnosed, often resulting in overtreatment [57]. However, as both comparative studies do not provide information on the size of the eccentricity examined, we are, to the best of our knowledge, the first study to provide results with tangible values.

In the present study, no significant effect of examiner experience could be demonstrated. The results, thus, contradict the findings of Geibel et al., which have shown that experienced examiners detect proximal lesions up to four times more frequently than less experienced examiners [58]. A plausible explanation for this difference could be that dental students and practicing dentists with less than five years of professional experience in our study took more time to analyze in vitro bitewing images than their colleagues with five or more years of clinical experience, as the time factor has been demonstrated to influence diagnostic accuracy significantly [31].

It was found that just over half (54.6%) of the artificial lesions were judged by the examiners to be atypical for caries, effectively distinguishing them from true carious lesions. This observation highlights the ability of human examiners to differentiate iatrogenic defects, such as those resulting from invasive treatments resulting from treatments of the adjacent teeth, from true caries cases, primarily through the assessment of lesion morphology. To the best of our knowledge, this study represents the first attempt to establish a framework for evaluating AI algorithms in this regard and to compare their performance with human judgement.

The empirical evaluation of binary classification tasks, such as the distinction between caries and healthy tooth structure, is subject of discussion. It must be noted that accuracy, as a metric, comes with the significant limitation of sensitivity to unbalanced datasets, potentially limiting the validity of the results. As the Fifth German Oral Health Study has already confirmed, caries prevalence is decreasing in all age groups, increasing the imbalance between carious and non-carious teeth on radiographs. Therefore, the suitability of accuracy to determine diagnostic quality must strongly be questioned [59]. Furthermore, Dinga et al. recommend completely omitting accuracy as sole criterion for evaluating clinical models, as it fails to take into account clinically relevant information [60]. Nevertheless, accuracy is still somewhat stubbornly used as the main parameter for performance evaluation in the literature. For the sake of comparability, we have included this metric, but explicitly point out its shortcomings. Positive predictive value (PPV), sensitivity, specificity and the F1 score, which is the harmonic mean of precision and recall, are commonly used parameters to evaluate binary classifiers [61]. However, these metrics assume that the "positive" class (in this case a detection of caries) is of primary interest, while true negatives are omitted in their calculation. Consequently, PPV, sensitivity and F1 scores are unaffected by variations in the number of true negatives, whether their value is extremely high or low. To overcome this limitation, we made use of Matthews correlation coefficient (MCC). MCC gives high values only when the predictions of all categories (true positives, true negatives, false positives and false negatives) show good performance, also considering the proportions of the positive and negative classes. As a result, the MCC is a statistically robust measure, even in the presence of unbalanced datasets.

5. Conclusions

The aim of this study was to establish a histology-based gold standard for the unbiased evaluation of AI-based caries detection systems on proximal surfaces in bitewing radiographs. Through meticulous in vitro simulations and histological analyses, we created a robust dataset to evaluate the performance of AI algorithms in caries detection and compare it to human judgement. Although AI promises to improve diagnostic accuracy and workflow efficiency, its effectiveness depends primarily on the quality of the training data and validation processes. Future research should be designed to accurately reflect the true performance of AI models using histological analysis as a benchmark. In doing so, we have laid the foundation for evaluating the real-world performance of AI systems, thereby advancing evidence-based dentistry. Ongoing advances in AI technology and regulatory frameworks require continuous refinement and validation of diagnostic tools to ensure patient safety and clinical effectiveness. The creation of a standardized database of reference histological specimens and associated radiographs could serve as a benchmark for the development and validation of new AI-based caries detection systems. This database would allow different AI systems to be compared and their performance tested against an established gold standard, helping to identify and develop the most accurate models. However, generating a histology-based dataset is time consuming and requires resources and equipment. Therefore, a simple histology-based implementation will not be readily available in the future. In addition, it remains to be seen whether newer intraoral caries detection techniques will provide higher sensitivity, which could serve as a solid basis for training dental AI systems. In conclusion, our study is an important step towards the creation of standardized evaluation protocols for AI-based caries detection, thereby promoting transparency, reliability and confidence in dental diagnostics.

Author Contributions: M.S. (Matthias Schuster), J.B., J.P. and F.K. contributed to the conception, design, data acquisition, statistical analyses and interpretation, drafting and critical revision of the manuscript; G.K., M.S. (Marc Schmitter) and A.S.-E. contributed to conception, data interpretation, drafting and critical revision of the manuscript. All authors have read and agreed to the published version of the manuscript.

Funding: The authors received no financial support for the research, authorship and/or publication of this article. This work was entirely self-funded by Matthias Schuster and Julian Boldt.

Institutional Review Board Statement: The study was conducted in accordance with the Declaration of Helsinki, and approved by the Ethics Committee of the University of Würzburg (protocol code 15/15, 9 February 2015).

Informed Consent Statement: Informed consent was obtained from all subjects involved in the study.

Data Availability Statement: The data presented in this study are available on request from the corresponding author due to ethical restrictions.

Conflicts of Interest: The authors declare no potential conflicts of interest concerning the research, authorship and/or publication of this article.

Abbreviations

AI	Artificial intelligence
AUC	Area under the curve
EtOH	Ethanol
ICC	Intraclass correlation coefficient
NPV	Negative predictive value
MCC	Matthews correlation coefficient
PPV	Positive predictive value
ROC	Receiver operating characteristics
STARD	Standards for Reporting of Diagnostic Accuracy Studies
UV	Ultraviolet

References

1. Schwendicke, F.; Samek, W.; Krois, J. Artificial Intelligence in Dentistry: Chances and Challenges. *J. Dent. Res.* **2020**, *99*, 769–774. [CrossRef] [PubMed]
2. Ahmed, N.; Abbasi, M.S.; Zuberi, F.; Qamar, W.; Halim, M.S.B.; Maqsood, A.; Alam, M.K. Artificial Intelligence Techniques: Analysis, Application, and Outcome in Dentistry-A Systematic Review. *Biomed Res. Int.* **2021**, *2021*, 9751564. [CrossRef]
3. Jiang, F.; Jiang, Y.; Zhi, H.; Dong, Y.; Li, H.; Ma, S.; Wang, Y.; Dong, Q.; Shen, H.; Wang, Y. Artificial intelligence in healthcare: Past, present and future. *Stroke Vasc. Neurol.* **2017**, *2*, 230–243. [CrossRef]
4. Khanagar, S.B.; Al-Ehaideb, A.; Maganur, P.C.; Vishwanathaiah, S.; Patil, S.; Baeshen, H.A.; Sarode, S.C.; Bhandi, S. Developments, application, and performance of artificial intelligence in dentistry—A systematic review. *J. Dent. Sci.* **2021**, *16*, 508–522. [CrossRef]
5. Schwendicke, F.; Rossi, J.G.; Göstemeyer, G.; Elhennawy, K.; Cantu, A.G.; Gaudin, R.; Chaurasia, A.; Gehrung, S.; Krois, J. Cost-effectiveness of Artificial Intelligence for Proximal Caries Detection. *J. Dent. Res.* **2021**, *100*, 369–376. [CrossRef]
6. Schwendicke, F.; Paris, S.; Stolpe, M. Detection and treatment of proximal caries lesions: Milieu-specific cost-effectiveness analysis. *J. Dent.* **2015**, *43*, 647–655. [CrossRef]
7. Alam, M.K.; Alftaikhah, S.A.A.; Issrani, R.; Ronsivalle, V.; Lo Giudice, A.; Cicciù, M.; Minervini, G. Applications of artificial intelligence in the utilisation of imaging modalities in dentistry: A systematic review and meta-analysis of in-vitro studies. *Heliyon* **2024**, *10*, e24221. [CrossRef]
8. Obuchowicz, R.; Strzelecki, M.; Piórkowski, A. Clinical Applications of Artificial Intelligence in Medical Imaging and Image Processing—A Review. *Cancers* **2024**, *16*, 1870. [CrossRef]
9. Bayraktar, Y.; Ayan, E. Diagnosis of interproximal caries lesions with deep convolutional neural network in digital bitewing radiographs. *Clin. Oral Investig.* **2022**, *26*, 623–632. [CrossRef] [PubMed]
10. Zhu, H.; Cao, Z.; Lian, L.; Ye, G.; Gao, H.; Wu, J. CariesNet: A deep learning approach for segmentation of multi-stage caries lesion from oral panoramic X-ray image. *Neural Comput. Appl.* **2022**, *35*, 1–9. [CrossRef]
11. Park, E.Y.; Cho, H.; Kang, S.; Jeong, S.; Kim, E.-K. Caries detection with tooth surface segmentation on intraoral photographic images using deep learning. *BMC Oral Health* **2022**, *22*, 573. [CrossRef] [PubMed]
12. Chen, X.; Guo, J.; Ye, J.; Zhang, M.; Liang, Y. Detection of Proximal Caries Lesions on Bitewing Radiographs Using Deep Learning Method. *Caries Res.* **2022**, *56*, 455–463. [CrossRef] [PubMed]
13. Obuchowicz, R.; Nurzynska, K.; Obuchowicz, B.; Urbanik, A.; Piórkowski, A. Caries detection enhancement using texture feature maps of intraoral radiographs. *Oral Radiol.* **2020**, *36*, 275–287. [CrossRef] [PubMed]
14. Anil, S.; Porwal, P.; Porwal, A. Transforming Dental Caries Diagnosis Through Artificial Intelligence-Based Techniques. *Cureus* **2023**, *15*, e41694. [CrossRef] [PubMed]
15. Roosanty, A.; Widyaningrum, R.; Diba, S.F. Artificial intelligence based on Convolutional Neural Network for detecting dental caries on bitewing and periapical radiographs. *J. Radiol. Dentomaksilofasial Indones. (JRDI)* **2022**, *6*, 89–94. [CrossRef]
16. Kunz, F.; Stellzig-Eisenhauer, A.; Zeman, F.; Boldt, J. Artificial intelligence in orthodontics: Evaluation of a fully automated cephalometric analysis using a customized convolutional neural network. *J. Orofac. Orthop.* **2020**, *81*, 52–68. [CrossRef] [PubMed]
17. Kunz, F.; Stellzig-Eisenhauer, A.; Boldt, J. Applications of Artificial Intelligence in Orthodontics—An Overview and Perspective Based on the Current State of the Art. *Appl. Sci.* **2023**, *13*, 3850. [CrossRef]
18. Mohammad-Rahimi, H.; Motamedian, S.R.; Rohban, M.H.; Krois, J.; Uribe, S.E.; Mahmoudinia, E.; Rokhshad, R.; Nadimi, M.; Schwendicke, F. Deep learning for caries detection: A systematic review. *J. Dent.* **2022**, *122*, 104115. [CrossRef] [PubMed]
19. Ammar, N.; Kühnisch, J. Diagnostic performance of artificial intelligence-aided caries detection on bitewing radiographs: A systematic review and meta-analysis. *Jpn. Dent. Sci. Rev.* **2024**, *60*, 128–136. [CrossRef]
20. Gomez, J. Detection and diagnosis of the early caries lesion. *BMC Oral Health* **2015**, *15* (Suppl. 1), S3. [CrossRef]
21. Grieco, P.; Jivraj, A.; Da Silva, J.; Kuwajima, Y.; Ishida, Y.; Ogawa, K.; Ohyama, H.; Ishikawa-Nagai, S. Importance of bitewing radiographs for the early detection of interproximal carious lesions and the impact on healthcare expenditure in Japan. *Ann. Transl. Med.* **2021**, *10*, 2. [CrossRef] [PubMed]
22. Prados-Privado, M.; García Villalón, J.; Martínez-Martínez, C.H.; Ivorra, C.; Prados-Frutos, J.C. Dental Caries Diagnosis and Detection Using Neural Networks: A Systematic Review. *J. Clin. Med.* **2020**, *9*, 3579. [CrossRef]

23. Khanagar, S.B.; Alfouzan, K.; Awawdeh, M.; Alkadi, L.; Albalawi, F.; Alfadley, A. Application and Performance of Artificial Intelligence Technology in Detection, Diagnosis and Prediction of Dental Caries (DC)-A Systematic Review. *Diagnostics* **2022**, *12*, 1083. [CrossRef] [PubMed]
24. Albano, D.; Galiano, V.; Basile, M.; Di Luca, F.; Gitto, S.; Messina, C.; Cagetti, M.G.; Del Fabbro, M.; Tartaglia, G.M.; Sconfienza, L.M. Artificial intelligence for radiographic imaging detection of caries lesions: A systematic review. *BMC Oral Health* **2024**, *24*, 274. [CrossRef] [PubMed]
25. Alzubaidi, L.; Zhang, J.; Humaidi, A.J.; Al-Dujaili, A.; Duan, Y.; Al-Shamma, O.; Santamaría, J.; Fadhel, M.A.; Al-Amidie, M.; Farhan, L. Review of deep learning: Concepts, CNN architectures, challenges, applications, future directions. *J. Big Data* **2021**, *8*, 53. [CrossRef]
26. Bossuyt, P.M.; Reitsma, J.B.; Bruns, D.E.; Gatsonis, C.A.; Glasziou, P.P.; Irwig, L.; Lijmer, J.G.; Moher, D.; Rennie, D.; Vet, H.C.W.d.; et al. STARD 2015: An Updated List of Essential Items for Reporting Diagnostic Accuracy Studies. *Radiology* **2015**, *277*, 826–832. [CrossRef] [PubMed]
27. Schwendicke, F.; Göstemeyer, G. Conventional Bitewing Radiographs. In *Detection and Assessment of Dental Caries: A Clinical Guide*, 1st ed.; Ferreira Zandona, A., Longbottom, C., Eds.; Springer International Publishing: Cham, Switzerland, 2019; pp. 109–117. [CrossRef]
28. Devlin, H.; Williams, T.; Graham, J.; Ashley, M. The ADEPT study: A comparative study of dentists' ability to detect enamel-only proximal caries in bitewing radiographs with and without the use of AssistDent artificial intelligence software. *Br. Dent. J.* **2021**, *231*, 481–485. [CrossRef]
29. Vaarkamp, J.; Ten Bosch, J.J.; Verdonschot, E.H.; Bronkhorst, E.M. The Real Performance of Bitewing Radiography and Fiber-Optic Transillumination in Approximal Caries Diagnosis. *J. Dent. Res.* **2000**, *79*, 1747–1751. [CrossRef] [PubMed]
30. Bader, J.D.; Shugars, D.A.; Bonito, A.J. Systematic reviews of selected dental caries diagnostic and management methods. *J. Dent. Educ.* **2001**, *65*, 960–968. [CrossRef]
31. Hegde, S.; Gao, J.; Vasa, R.; Cox, S. Factors affecting interpretation of dental radiographs. *Dentomaxillofacial Radiol.* **2022**, *52*, 20220279. [CrossRef]
32. Stroud, J.L.; English, J.; Buschang, P.H. Enamel thickness of the posterior dentition: Its implications for nonextraction treatment. *Angle Orthod.* **1998**, *68*, 141–146. [PubMed]
33. Kamburoglu, K.; Kolsuz, E.; Murat, S.; Yüksel, S.; Ozen, T. Proximal caries detection accuracy using intraoral bitewing radiography, extraoral bitewing radiography and panoramic radiography. *Dentomaxillofacl Radiol.* **2012**, *41*, 450–459. [CrossRef]
34. Wenzel, A. Bitewing and digital bitewing radiography for detection of caries lesions. *J. Dent. Res.* **2004**, *83*, 72–75. [CrossRef]
35. Donath, K. *Die Trenn-Dünnschliff-Technik zur Herstellung Histologischer Präparate von nicht schneidbaren Geweben und Materialien: Apparate- und Methodenbeschreibung*; EXAKT-Kulzer-Druckschriften: Norderstedt, Germany, 1988.
36. Cantu, A.G.; Gehrung, S.; Krois, J.; Chaurasia, A.; Rossi, J.G.; Gaudin, R.; Elhennawy, K.; Schwendicke, F. Detecting caries lesions of different radiographic extension on bitewings using deep learning. *J. Dent.* **2020**, *100*, 103425. [CrossRef]
37. Bayrakdar, I.S.; Orhan, K.; Akarsu, S.; Çelik, Ö.; Atasoy, S.; Pekince, A.; Yasa, Y.; Bilgir, E.; Sağlam, H.; Aslan, A.F.; et al. Deep-learning approach for caries detection and segmentation on dental bitewing radiographs. *Oral Radiol.* **2022**, *38*, 468–479. [CrossRef]
38. Moran, M.; Faria, M.; Giraldi, G.; Bastos, L.; Oliveira, L.; Conci, A. Classification of Approximal Caries in Bitewing Radiographs Using Convolutional Neural Networks. *Sensors* **2021**, *21*, 5192. [CrossRef]
39. Lee, S.; Oh, S.I.; Jo, J.; Kang, S.; Shin, Y.; Park, J.W. Deep learning for early dental caries detection in bitewing radiographs. *Sci. Rep.* **2021**, *11*, 16807. [CrossRef]
40. Mao, Y.-C.; Chen, T.-Y.; Chou, H.-S.; Lin, S.-Y.; Liu, S.-Y.; Chen, Y.-A.; Liu, Y.-L.; Chen, C.-A.; Huang, Y.-C.; Chen, S.-L.; et al. Caries and Restoration Detection Using Bitewing Film Based on Transfer Learning with CNNs. *Sensors* **2021**, *21*, 4613. [CrossRef] [PubMed]
41. Walsh, T. Fuzzy gold standards: Approaches to handling an imperfect reference standard. *J. Dent.* **2018**, *74*, 47–49. [CrossRef]
42. Jablonski-Momeni, A.; Stachniss, V. Serial sectioning of teeth and microscopy in cariology research. In *Microscopy: Science, Technology, Applications and Education*, 4th ed.; Méndez-Vilas, A., Díaz, J., Eds.; FORMATEX: Badajoz, Spain, 2010; Volume 3, pp. 785–791.
43. Pitts, N.B. Clinical diagnosis of dental caries: A European perspective. *J. Dent. Educ.* **2001**, *65*, 972–978. [CrossRef]
44. Li, G.; Qu, X.-m.; Chen, Y.; Zhang, J.; Zhang, Z.-y.; Ma, X.-c. Diagnostic accuracy of proximal caries by digital radiographs: An in vivo and in vitro comparative study. *Oral Surg. Oral Med. Oral Pathol. Oral Radiol. Endodontology* **2010**, *109*, 463–467. [CrossRef]
45. Hintze, H.; Wenze, A. Clinical and laboratory radiographic caries diagnosis. A study of the same teeth. *Dentomaxillofacl Radiol.* **1996**, *25*, 115–118. [CrossRef] [PubMed]
46. Suzuki, T.; Finger, W.J. Dentin adhesives: Site of dentin vs. bonding of composite resins. *Dent. Mater.* **1988**, *4*, 379–383. [CrossRef]
47. O'Brien, J.A., 3rd; Retief, D.H.; Bradley, E.L.; Denys, F.R. Shear bond strength of a new dentin bonding restorative system. *Dent. Mater.* **1988**, *4*, 179–183. [CrossRef]
48. Haller, B.; Hofmann, N.; Klaiber, B.; Bloching, U. Effect of storage media on microleakage of five dentin bonding agents. *Dent. Mater.* **1993**, *9*, 191–197. [CrossRef]
49. Söderholm, K.J.M. Correlation of in vivo and in vitro performance of adhesive restorative materials: A report of the ASC MD156 task group on test methods for the adhesion of restorative materials. *Dent. Mater.* **1991**, *7*, 74–83. [CrossRef]

50. Wenzel, A.; Hintze, H. Comparison of microscopy and radiography as gold standards in radiographic caries diagnosis. *Dentomaxillofacl Radiol.* **1999**, *28*, 182–185. [CrossRef] [PubMed]
51. Rodrigues, J.A.; Neuhaus, K.W.; Diniz, M.B.; Hug, I.; Stich, H.; Karlsson, L.; Lussi, A. Comparison among gold standard techniques used for the validation of methods for occlusal caries detection. *Microsc. Res. Tech.* **2012**, *75*, 605–608. [CrossRef] [PubMed]
52. Schulze, R.K.; Nackat, D.; D'Hoedt, B. In vitro carious lesion detection on D-, E-, and F-speed radiographic films. *Oral Surg. Oral Med. Oral Pathol. Oral Radiol. Endodontology* **2004**, *97*, 529–534. [CrossRef]
53. Kay, E.J.; Knill-Jones, R. Variation in restorative treatment decisions: Application of Receiver Operating Characteristic curve (ROC) analysis. *Community Dent. Oral Endodontology* **1992**, *20*, 113–117. [CrossRef]
54. Mileman, P.A.; van der Weele, L.T. Accuracy in radiographic diagnosis: Dutch practitioners and dental caries. *J. Dent.* **1990**, *18*, 130–136. [CrossRef] [PubMed]
55. Peers, A.; Hill, F.J.; Mitropoulos, C.M.; Holloway, P.J. Validity and reproducibility of clinical examination, fibre-optic transillumination, and bite-wing radiology for the diagnosis of small approximal carious lesions: An in vitro study. *Caries Res.* **1993**, *27*, 307–311. [CrossRef]
56. Deprá Lde, C.; Vessoni Iwaki, L.C.; Chicarelli, M.; Takeshita, W.M. Influence of Image Filters and Variation in Horizontal Angle of Incidence of X-ray Beam in Digital Interproximal Radiographs for Diagnosis of Secondary Caries in Esthetic Restorations. *J. Contemp. Dent. Pract.* **2015**, *16*, 805–812. [CrossRef] [PubMed]
57. Chadwick, B.L.; Dummer, P.M.; van der Stelt, P.F. The effect of alterations in horizontal X-ray beam angulation and bucco-lingual cavity width on the radiographic depth of approximal cavities. *J. Oral Rehabil.* **1999**, *26*, 292–301. [CrossRef] [PubMed]
58. Geibel, M.-A.; Carstens, S.; Braisch, U.; Rahman, A.; Herz, M.; Jablonski-Momeni, A. Radiographic diagnosis of proximal caries—Influence of experience and gender of the dental staff. *Clin. Oral Investig.* **2017**, *21*, 2761–2770. [CrossRef]
59. Jordan, A.; Micheelis, W.; Cholmakow-Bodechtel, C.; Füßl-Grünig, E.; Geyer, S.; Hertrampf, K.; Hoffmann, T.; Holtfreter, B.; Kocher, T.; Nitschke, I.; et al. *Fünfte Deutsche Mundgesundheitsstudie (DMS V)*; Deutscher Zahnärzteverlag: Köln, Germany, 2016.
60. Dinga, R.; Penninx, B.W.J.H.; Veltman, D.J.; Schmaal, L.; Marquand, A.F. Beyond accuracy: Measures for assessing machine learning models, pitfalls and guidelines. *bioRxiv* **2019**. [CrossRef]
61. Chicco, D.; Jurman, G. The advantages of the Matthews correlation coefficient (MCC) over F1 score and accuracy in binary classification evaluation. *BMC Genom.* **2020**, *21*, 6. [CrossRef]

Journal of
Clinical Medicine

MDPI

Article

Development and Validation of an Artificial Intelligence Model for Detecting Rib Fractures on Chest Radiographs

Kaehong Lee [1], Sunhee Lee [1], Ji Soo Kwak [1], Heechan Park [1], Hoonji Oh [2] and Jae Chul Koh [1,*]

1 Department of Anesthesiology and Pain Medicine, Korea University College of Medicine, Seoul 02841, Republic of Korea; carrot809@korea.ac.kr (K.L.); sunfanooo@kumc.or.kr (S.L.); calorie@korea.ac.kr (J.S.K.); qgc9461@korea.ac.kr (H.P.)

2 Department of Biostatistics, College of Medicine, Korea University, Seoul 02841, Republic of Korea; hchavi531@korea.ac.kr

* Correspondence: jaykoh@korea.ac.kr; Tel.: +82-2-920-5632

Abstract: Background: Chest radiography is the standard method for detecting rib fractures. Our study aims to develop an artificial intelligence (AI) model that, with only a relatively small amount of training data, can identify rib fractures on chest radiographs and accurately mark their precise locations, thereby achieving a diagnostic accuracy comparable to that of medical professionals. **Methods**: For this retrospective study, we developed an AI model using 540 chest radiographs (270 normal and 270 with rib fractures) labeled for use with Detectron2 which incorporates a faster region-based convolutional neural network (R-CNN) enhanced with a feature pyramid network (FPN). The model's ability to classify radiographs and detect rib fractures was assessed. Furthermore, we compared the model's performance to that of 12 physicians, including six board-certified anesthesiologists and six residents, through an observer performance test. **Results**: Regarding the radiographic classification performance of the AI model, the sensitivity, specificity, and area under the receiver operating characteristic curve (AUROC) were 0.87, 0.83, and 0.89, respectively. In terms of rib fracture detection performance, the sensitivity, false-positive rate, and free-response receiver operating characteristic (JAFROC) figure of merit (FOM) were 0.62, 0.3, and 0.76, respectively. The AI model showed no statistically significant difference in the observer performance test compared to 11 of 12 and 10 of 12 physicians, respectively. **Conclusions**: We developed an AI model trained on a limited dataset that demonstrated a rib fracture classification and detection performance comparable to that of an experienced physician.

Keywords: artificial intelligence (AI); rib fractures; chest radiograph; rib fracture AI model; rib fracture detection; rib fracture localization; radiograph classification; convolutional neural network (CNN); deep learning model; Detectron2

1. Introduction

Rib fractures are among the most frequently encountered injuries by trauma teams, operating room staff, and pain medicine clinics, highlighting the need for effective diagnostic techniques. They are the most common thoracic injuries, occurring in 10% of all traumatic injuries and in almost 40% of patients who have suffered severe injuries or blunt chest trauma [1]. Chest radiography and computed tomography (CT) are the two main modalities used to detect rib fractures [2,3]. Although there are more accurate methods for diagnosing rib fractures, such as CT, thoracic CT can expose patients to radiation equivalent to 50–450 chest radiographs [4]. Moreover, because of the cost and time required, CT is not universally administered, especially in patients with minor blunt trauma. Conversely, chest radiography, which has a relatively lower sensitivity, is a routine examination that offers significant economic and clinical advantages beyond health screening [5,6]. The American College of Radiology recommends plain chest radiography as the initial test for suspected rib fractures after minor trauma, establishing it as the first-line imaging modality [2]. However, up to 50% of rib fractures may be missed on standard X-rays [7]. The low detection rate may be attributable to various factors. First, rib fractures can be identified incidentally on chest radiography. Among the various diagnoses detectable on chest radiography, the identification of rib fractures can be challenging for clinicians. Rib fractures may not be easily suspected in patients with communication difficulties, such as older individuals or those with cerebrovascular disease. Additionally, the ambiguity resulting from overlapping anatomical structures, as well as the varying locations and sizes of fractures on radiographs, contributes to this challenge [8]. However, image interpretation requires considerable experience and training. While ultrasound can be helpful, it requires applying pressure with the probe on suspected rib fractures, can produce artifacts, demands operator proficiency, and is time-consuming, which limits its use [9]. Therefore, developing a rapid, accurate, and accessible automatic detection system for rib fractures on chest radiographs is crucial for improving diagnostic precision, assisting clinicians, and establishing cost-effective tools.

Advances in artificial intelligence (AI) and automatic medical image processing technologies have opened promising avenues for development and innovation in various medical fields [10,11]. Research has been conducted on the development of AI to analyze medical images using neural networks, which are mostly composed of convolutional neural networks. In these studies, attempts were made to develop algorithms with better performance by combining layers of different configurations. Through this process, algorithms that exhibit excellent performance in most image analyses have been introduced [12–14]. However, it is difficult to analyze medical images of various resolutions and present the desired results with a combination of these neural networks alone. Therefore, it has become important to use an algorithm that can automatically change images that exist in various forms into a form suitable for application in neural networks.

The purpose of our study was to develop an AI platform specifically designed to detect rib fractures on chest radiographs, implement an intuitive interface for clinician review, and validate its detection performance with that of experienced clinicians.

2. Materials and Methods

2.1. Dataset Preparation

For the AI model development, 1080 chest antero-posterior or posteroanterior view radiographs with rib fracture findings based on radiology reports were retrospectively collected between January 2017 and November 2023 from the anonymized picture archiving and communication system (PACS) database at our institution (Korea University Anam Hospital) (Figure 1). Chest radiographs were excluded from the training dataset if rib fractures were not distinctly identifiable even after verification with the associated CT scans, if the image quality was compromised due to factors such as underexposure, motion blur, or insufficient resolution, or if the radiographs were duplicates of cases already included. After these exclusions, the dataset included 300 chest radiographs of patients with rib fractures. To ensure comparability, we matched these with 300 normal chest radiographs, selecting images from 300 different patients who had no recorded abnormalities in their radiology reports during the same period, using the PACS system. Subsequently, the chest radiographic data were randomly allocated to one of three distinct datasets to assess the classification and detection performance of the trained AI model: a training dataset consisting of 480 chest radiographs (240 normal and 240 with rib fractures), a validation dataset containing 60 chest radiographs (30 normal and 30 with rib fractures), and a test dataset containing 60 chest radiographs (30 normal and 30 with rib fractures). The training dataset included 240 chest radiographs of 771 rib fractures, the validation dataset comprised 30 chest radiographs of 77 rib fractures, and the test dataset contained 30 chest radiographs of 73 rib fractures. The validation dataset was used to assess model performance and fine-tune hyperparameters during the training process to prevent overfitting before applying the model to unseen data. Conversely, the test dataset was used to evaluate the performance of the final model after optimization of these hyperparameters. Additionally, an observer performance test using the same test dataset was conducted to compare the performances. All chest radiographs in each dataset were obtained from different patients to ensure exclusivity among datasets.

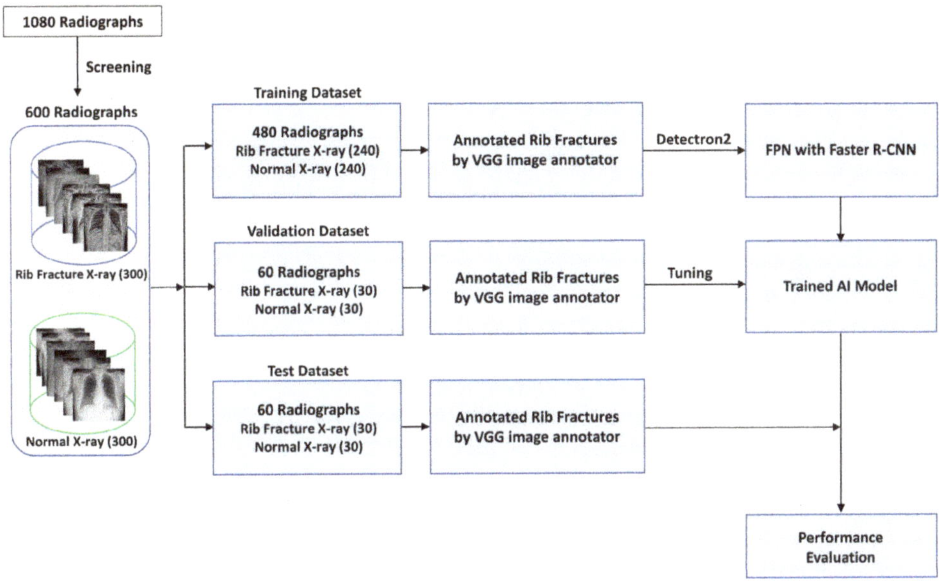

Figure 1. Study flowchart for the development and evaluation of an artificial intelligence model for rib fracture detection and localization on chest radiographs. AI = Artificial Intelligence, VGG = Visual Geometry Group, Faster R-CNN = Faster Region-Convolutional Neural Network.

2.2. Rib Fracture Annotation on Chest Radiographs

Chest radiographs from the training, validation, and test datasets were labeled as either normal or rib fracture at the image level, and the location of rib fractures on rib fracture chest radiographs was annotated at the pixel level (Figure 2A). The labeling for each radiograph and annotation for each rib fracture were performed based on interpretations by radiologists using the basic annotator (https://www.robots.ox.ac.uk/~vgg/software/via/via_demo.html (accessed on 17 October 2022)) provided by the Visual Geometry Group (University of Oxford, Department of Engineering). The pixel area containing rib fracture lesions was annotated by placing it at the center of the bounding box, ensuring that it was minimized in size yet sufficient to fully encompass both cross-sections of the fractured rib. Chest CT scans and rib series radiographs were used as reference standards, and annotations were based on comparisons with these imaging modalities as well as radiology reports. Annotations included up to seven multiple rib fractures per chest radiograph, encompassing clear displacement cases, non-displacement cases with intact alignment, and rib fractures in a healing state characterized by the presence of bony calluses.

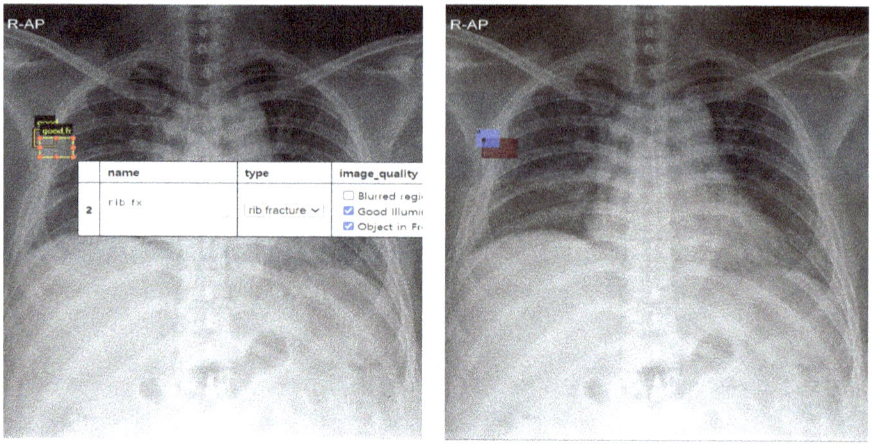

(A) (B)

Figure 2. Annotation and preprocessing of rib fracture radiographs for AI training (**A**) Annotated rib fractures placed in the middle of the bounding box using Visual Geometry Group (VGG) annotator. (**B**) Converted region of interest as a bounding box to be prepared for artificial intelligence training.

2.3. Development of AI Model

After completing labeling and annotation, the generated file included the coordinates of the center point and the horizontal and vertical dimensions of the rectangle around the rib fractures. To translate this information into a trainable format, we created a program that automatically designated each annotated rectangle as a bounding box and the region within it for segmentation in preparation for training (Figure 2B).

Detectron2, an open-source platform created by Facebook AI Research (FAIR), was used for model development [15]. This platform efficiently combines neural networks, feature pyramid networks, and region proposal networks, enabling superior performance with less training data compared to previous medical AI developments. Based on this library, we applied the Faster_R-CNN_R_101_FPN_3x model to develop the AI model. This architecture utilizes preconfigured Faster Regions with Convolutional Neural Networks (Faster R-CNN) by applying a ResNet-101 backbone and a Feature Pyramid Network (FPN) [16]. To optimize the model, hyperparameters were fine-tuned during the training process as follows: the batch size was set to 512, the base learning rate was set to 0.00025, and 4 images per batch were used up to 30,000 iterations. We adopted this platform and programmed it so that the transformed trainable data mentioned above could be subsequently applied.

The Python Tkinter library was used to develop an executable program that can be easily applied in clinical settings. By creating this program, we built a system designed to operate seamlessly in real clinical environments. This system enables clinicians to capture X-ray images while seeing patients, which are then imported into the program as image files. This approach bypasses the need for direct integration with electronic health records. Additionally, we implemented an intuitive interface that allows clinicians to quickly review and verify the AI's findings. Using a pre-trained model, the system promptly identifies and reports potential rib fractures (Figure 3).

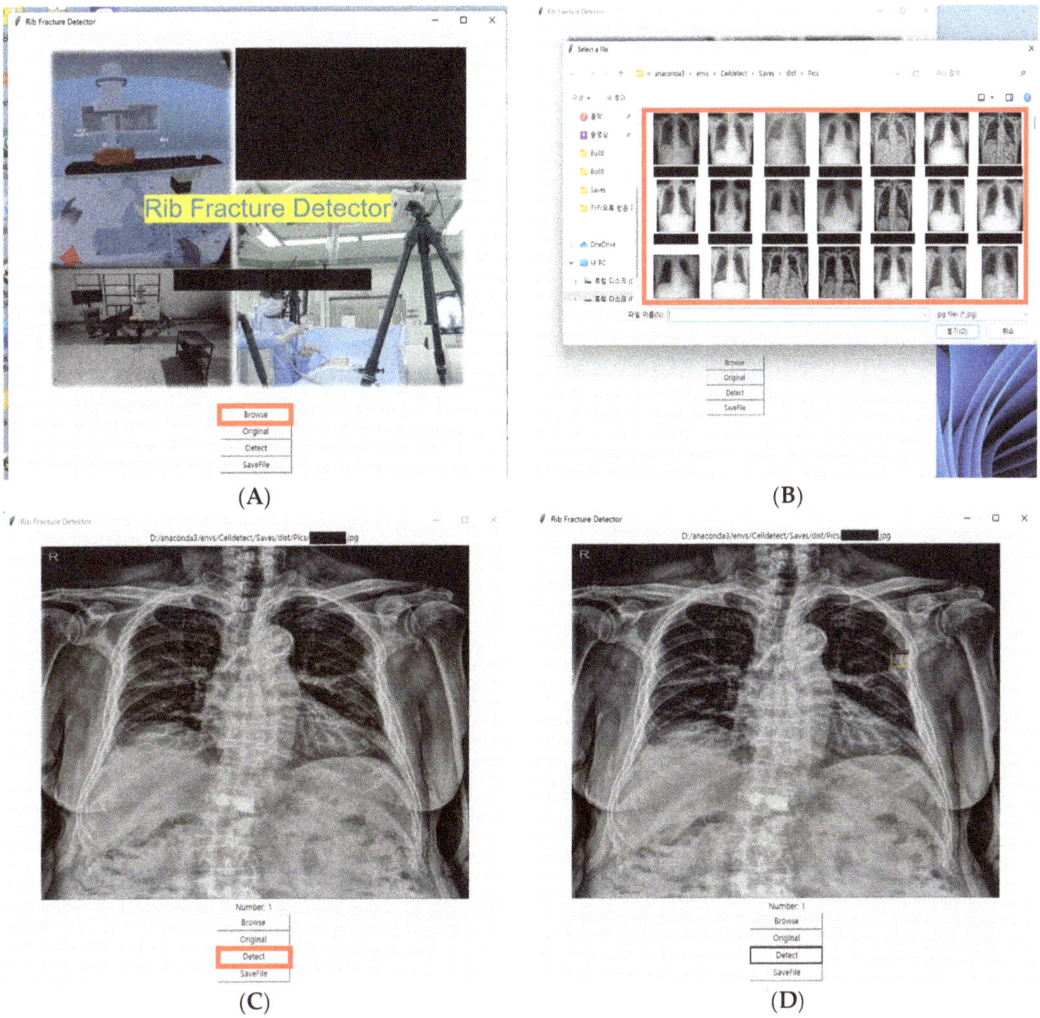

Figure 3. AI-powered rib fracture detection system interface and diagnostic output (**A**) The initial interface of the program is designed for convenient execution in a clinical setting. (**B**) A user-friendly interface is designed to facilitate easy selection of a file/image to be analyzed. (**C**) The original chest radiograph before the site of the fracture is identified. (**D**) The image with the site of the rib fracture identified and marked by the AI model. AI: Artificial Intelligence.

2.4. Evaluation of AI Model

The AI model identified suspected rib fracture sites on radiography with a confidence level greater than 5%, marking these areas as potential fractures with boxes, and generating continuous numeric values between 0 and 1 alongside them to indicate the probability of a fracture. In cases in which multiple fracture probabilities were identified on a single chest radiograph, the highest value was designated as the fracture probability. Conversely, if no areas were marked, the chest radiograph showed a 0% probability of rib fracture. Radiograph classification and fracture detection performance were assessed on a per-case basis for the validation and test datasets, and on a per-fracture basis, respectively. An observer performance test was conducted using the test dataset to compare the radiographic classification and fracture detection performance of the AI model with those of physicians. Twelve physicians, divided into two subgroups (six board-certified anesthesiologists, specifically pain medicine specialists who are experienced in both radiographic interpretation and patient care, and six anesthesiology residents training in pain medicine), participated as observers. During the residency program, trainees receive comprehensive training in both fields, including the ability to interpret and analyze imaging studies for patients with various types of pain, such as diagnosing rib fractures. Each observer independently reviewed each chest radiograph to distinguish normal chest radiographs from those with rib fractures (radiograph classification) and to identify the location of rib fractures (fracture detection) using a four-staged confidence scale: 25% indicated a potential lesion with a low degree of suspicion, 50% indicated a dubious lesion, 75% indicated a probable lesion with high confidence, and 100% indicated a definite lesion.

2.5. Statistical Analysis

The performance of the AI model in the radiograph classification task, which involves determining the presence or absence of rib fractures on each chest radiograph, was evaluated using the AUROC curve as a measure of probability. For the fracture detection task, which entailed localizing rib fracture lesions on a chest radiograph, the assessment was conducted using figures of merit (FOMs) obtained from the jackknife alternative free-response receiver operating characteristic analysis (JAFROC version 4.2.1; available at https://github.com/dpc10ster/WindowsJAFROC (accessed on 11 October 2023)). This method evaluates the diagnostic accuracy of imaging techniques by analyzing their efficacy in detecting and localizing abnormalities in images. In JAFROC, the FOM represents the likelihood that true lesions are rated higher than the highest-rated non-lesion mark on a normal chest radiograph, with higher values indicating better performance. A prediction was deemed accurate if there was an overlap between the predicted and annotated bounding boxes. A true positive was defined when the overlapping area between the annotated and predicted boxes exceeded 30%; otherwise, any predicted box marked outside this criterion was defined as a false positive. When the overlap between the annotated and predicted boxes was less than 30%, the fracture was classified as a false negative. Examples of rib fractures detected on chest radiographs using the AI model are shown in Figure 4.

Regarding the observer performance test, we compared the performance of our AI model with that of experienced clinicians by conducting a test where both the AI system and the clinicians were given the same test dataset of anonymized chest radiographs. The results were evaluated based on sensitivity, specificity, false positive ratio, and metrics such as the area under the receiver operating characteristic (AUROC) and the Free-response Receiver Operating Characteristic (FROC). The radiographic classification and rib fracture detection capabilities of the AI model and 12 physicians (six board-certified anesthesiologists and six anesthesiology residents) were assessed and compared using the pairwise comparison AUROC and JAFROC FOMs, respectively. To compare AUC between an individual observer and the AI model, DeLong's test was conducted [17]. To compare JAFROC FOMs between an individual observer and the AI model, a fixed-reader random-case method was used [18]. The random-case, random-reader method was used to average the performances of the two subgroups: a board-certified anesthesiologist subgroup and an anesthesiology resident group. p-value < 0.05 was considered statistically significant.

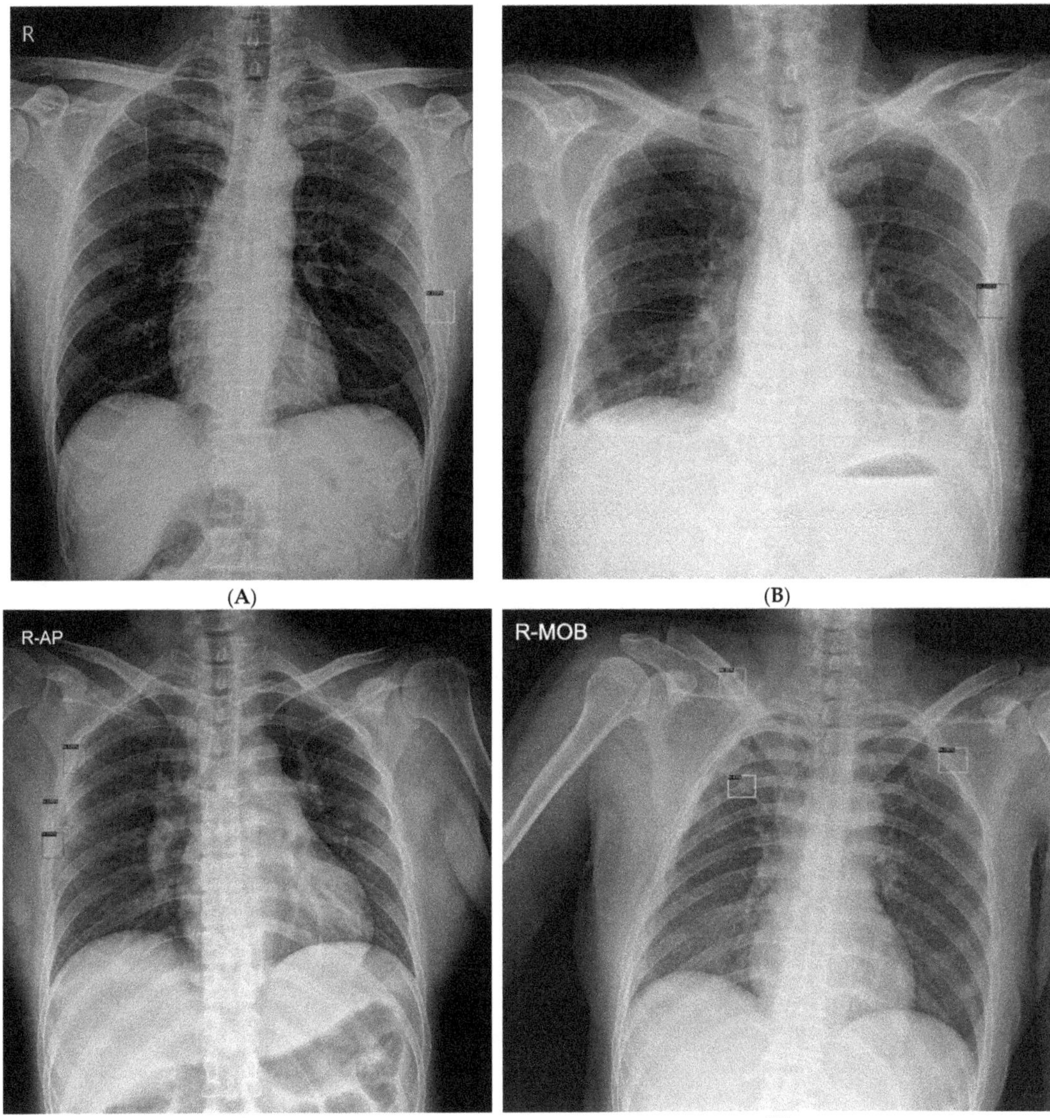

Figure 4. Examples of rib fractures detected on chest radiographs using the AI model (**A**) Single rib fracture: The AI model's correct identification of a rib fracture is demonstrated on the left lateral side, marked with a predicted box and assigned a 100% probability of fracture. (**B**) Single rib fracture in low resolution shows the AI model's capacity to precisely mark a rib fracture location on a low-resolution image. (**C**) Multiple rib fractures: This image displays the AI model's marking of several rib fracture sites, with each predicted box accompanied by a respective estimated probability of fracture. (**D**) Accurate and erroneous marking: This image features the AI model's accurate marking of a rib fracture on the left side and a false-positive marking on the right side. Additionally, it includes an unintended marking of a clavicle fracture, not originally part of the training data. AI: Artificial Intelligence.

3. Results

3.1. Training Iterations Experiment

To determine a sufficient number of learning iterations, we varied the number of training iterations in the dataset from 500 to 30,000 and then evaluated the performance of the developed AI model in terms of accuracy and false-negative ratio. When comparing the AI models developed with 10,000 and 30,000 learning iterations, there was only a 0.01 increase in the accuracy and a 0.01 decrease in the false-negative ratio (Figure 5).

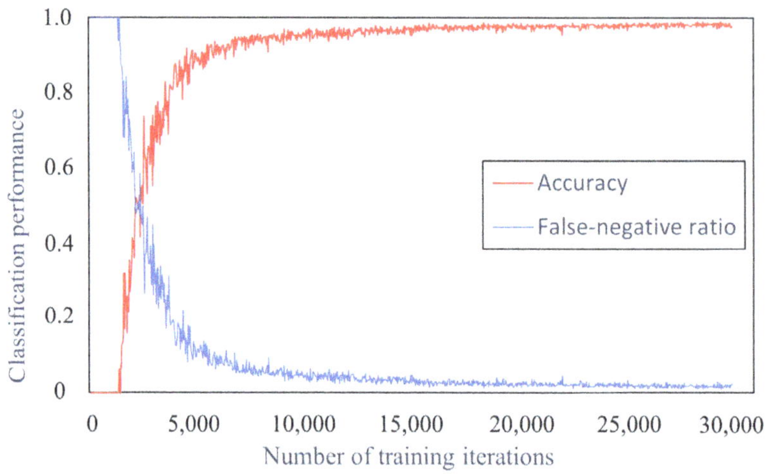

Figure 5. Classification performance of the AI model with machine learning training iterations. After reaching 10,000 training iterations, improvement in both the accuracy and the false-negative ratio tends to plateau.

3.2. Classification Performance of AI Model

The performance of the AI model is assessed using validation and test datasets. For the validation data set of 60 chest radiographs (30 normal and 30 with rib fractures), the sensitivity and specificity analyses resulted in values of 0.7 and 0.93, respectively. The AI model achieved an AUROC of 0.83. In the test dataset (30 normal subjects and 30 patients with rib fractures), the sensitivity, specificity, and AUROC were 0.87, 0.83, and 0.89, respectively (Table 1).

Table 1. Radiograph classification and rib fracture detection performance of the artificial intelligence (AI) model with the test dataset.

	Radiograph Classification Performance			Rib Fracture Detection Performance		
	AUROC	Sensitivity [1] (%)	Specificity (%)	JAFROC FOM	Sensitivity [2] (%)	Rate of FP [3] (%)
AI model	0.89	0.87 (26/30)	0.83 (25/30)	0.76	0.62 (45/73)	0.3 (18/60)

The data in parentheses are the numerators and denominators. AUROC = area under the receiver operating characteristic curve. JAFROC = jackknife alternative free-response receiver operating characteristic; FOM = figure of merit. [1] Sensitivity indicates the number of radiographs detected correctly divided by the number of radiographs showing fractures. [2] Sensitivity was calculated as the number of correctly detected rib fractures divided by the total number of rib fractures, for which the threshold value was set at 0.05. [3] The false-positive rate was calculated as the total number of fractures with false-positive findings divided by the total number of chest radiographs, for which the threshold value was set at 0.05.

3.3. Rib Fracture Detection Performance of AI Model

For the validation dataset, the sensitivity and false-positive rate were 0.49 and 0.27, respectively. The JAFROC FOM was 0.72. In the test dataset, the sensitivity, specificity, and JAFROC FOM were 0.62, 0.3, and 0.76, respectively (Table 1).

3.4. Comparison of Radiograph Classification and Fracture Detection Performance between AI Model and Observers

In the radiographic classification, the sensitivity of the AI model (0.87) was equal to or higher than that of seven out of 12 physicians (three board-certified anesthesiologists and four anesthesiology residents). Additionally, the specificity of the AI model (0.83) matched or exceeded that of five out of 12 physicians (one board-certified anesthesiologist and four anesthesiology residents). In rib fracture detection, the sensitivity of the AI model (0.62) surpassed that of seven out of 12 physicians (two board-certified anesthesiologists and five anesthesiology residents). Moreover, the AI model's false-positive rate (0.3) was lower than that of three out of 12 physicians (two board-certified anesthesiologists and one anesthesiology resident) (Table 2).

Table 2. Classification and rib fracture detection performance of observers with the test dataset.

	Radiograph Classification Performance		Rib Fracture Detection Performance	
Observer [1]	**Sensitivity**	**Specificity**	**Sensitivity** [2]	**Rate of FP** [3]
Board-certified anesthesiologists				
Observer 1	0.97 (29/30)	0.97 (29/30)	0.84 (61/73)	0.12 (7/60)
Observer 2	0.90 (27/30)	0.93 (28/30)	0.74 (54/73)	0.18 (11/60)
Observer 3	0.63 (19/30)	1.00 (30/30)	0.48 (35/73)	0.02 (2/60)
Observer 4	0.90 (27/30)	0.80 (24/30)	0.81 (59/73)	0.57 (34/60)
Observer 5	0.87 (26/30)	0.93 (28/30)	0.59 (43/73)	0.13 (8/60)
Observer 6	0.87 (26/30)	0.93 (28/30)	0.71 (52/73)	0.33 (20/60)
Anesthesiology residents				
Observer 7	0.77 (23/30)	0.93 (28/30)	0.59 (43/73)	0.17 (10/60)
Observer 8	0.90 (27/30)	0.80 (24/30)	0.70 (51/73)	0.35 (21/60)
Observer 9	0.93 (28/30)	0.70 (21/30)	0.58 (42/73)	0.25 (15/60)
Observer 10	0.87 (26/30)	0.77 (23/30)	0.55 (40/73)	0.20 (12/60)
Observer 11	0.87 (26/30)	0.77 (23/30)	0.56 (41/73)	0.25 (15/60)
Observer 12	0.87 (26/30)	0.90 (27/30)	0.60 (44/73)	0.22 (13/60)

Data in parentheses are the numerators and denominators. [1] Experience, Observer 1–6: 6 to 12 years of clinical experience after obtaining board, Observer 7–12: 1 to 4 years of residency. [2] Sensitivity was calculated as the number of correctly detected rib fractures divided by the total number of rib fractures, for which the threshold value was set at 0.05. [3] The false-positive rate was calculated as the total number of fractures with false-positive findings divided by the total number of chest radiographs, for which the threshold value was set at 0.05.

In assessing radiographic classification performance, the AI model demonstrated an AUROC of 0.89, which was higher than the results for five out of 12 physicians (one board-certified anesthesiologist and four anesthesiology residents). However, no statistically significant difference was found when compared with 11 of the 12 physicians ($p > 0.05$). Concerning rib fracture detection performance, the AI model exhibited a JAFROC FOM of 0.76, exceeding the performance of five out of 12 physicians (one board-certified anesthesiologist and four anesthesiology residents). Again, there was no statistically significant difference compared to 10 of the 12 physicians ($p > 0.05$). The JAFROC FOMs for the board-certified anesthesiologists and anesthesiology resident subgroups were 0.83 and 0.74, respectively. Random-reader analysis from JAFROC indicated that the difference in JAFROC FOM between the AI model and the group of six board-certified anesthesiologists was 0.07 ($p = 0.051$). The difference between the AI model's JAFROC FOM and that of the six anesthesiology residents was 0.02 ($p = 0.6$) (Table 3).

Table 3. Classification and rib fracture detection at the observer performance test.

	Test		AI Model versus Observer (p Value)	
	Radiograph Classification (AUROC)	Rib Fracture Detection (JAFROC FOM)	Radiograph Classification	Rib Fracture Detection
Board-certified anesthesiologists				
Observer 1	0.98	0.91	0.013	<0.001
Observer 2	0.95	0.86	0.054	0.028
Observer 3	0.82	0.74	0.2	0.7
Observer 4	0.90	0.85	0.9	0.050
Observer 5	0.93	0.78	0.4	0.6
Observer 6	0.93	0.85	0.4	0.059
Group		0.83		0.051
Anesthesiology residents				
Observer 7	0.87	0.73	0.7	0.6
Observer 8	0.90	0.84	0.8	0.093
Observer 9	0.88	0.68	0.9	0.079
Observer 10	0.88	0.70	0.9	0.2
Observer 11	0.88	0.71	0.8	0.3
Observer 12	0.92	0.78	0.4	0.6
Group		0.74		0.6
AI model	0.89	0.76		

Radiograph classification performance was described using the area under the receiver operating characteristic curve analysis, and associated p-values were calculated using comparison receiver operating characteristic analysis. Rib fracture detection performance was described using a figure of merit from jackknife free-response receiver operating characteristic analysis, and associated p values were calculated using the fixed readers and random cases method for the AI model for observer comparison using jackknife free-response receiver operating characteristic analysis. AI model, artificial intelligence model; AUROC, area under the receiver operating characteristic curve; JAFROC, jackknife alternative free-response receiver operating characteristic; FOM, figure of merit.

4. Discussion

In this study, we developed an AI model to detect rib fractures on chest radiographs, achieving performance levels in chest radiograph classification and detection comparable to those of board-certified anesthesiologists and anesthesiology residents, even with a relatively small dataset.

CNNs have become a cornerstone in the field of AI applications within medical imaging, and their use is progressively expanding into the realm of medical diagnosis [19,20]. Studies have shown that multiple rib fractures are associated with significant morbidity and mortality particularly due to pulmonary complications [21]. This AI model can selectively classify chest radiographs with rib fractures with a sensitivity of 0.87 (26 out of 30), and an AUROC of 0.89. It also possesses multi-lesion detection capabilities, marking multiple rib fractures on chest radiographs with a sensitivity of 0.62 (45 out of 73) and a JAFROC of 0.76. However, traditional evaluations of radiographs have only been able to detect a small percentage of rib fractures, often less than 50% [22]. These results suggest that utilizing AI can enable clinicians to more effectively interpret chest radiographs alone, reducing the dependency on additional diagnostic procedures. Despite their high cost and increased patient exposure to radiation, advanced imaging is generally used, in cases with associated lesions of the thorax that have to be addressed or when there is a discrepancy between clinical findings and radiology. Plain X-rays remain the best method for detecting rib fractures [23].

The development of an AI model for diagnosing rib fractures was previously introduced [24]. Image classification studies were conducted to determine the presence or absence of rib fracture lesions on radiographs, and these image classification models can serve as screening tests to determine the necessity of more precise diagnostic examinations.

However, it has been observed that doctors find it challenging to rely on these classification models, which do not indicate suspected areas but only suggest whether additional tests are recommended [25]. Typically, they prefer to directly confirm the basis of the AI judgment [26]. Meanwhile, the Faster R-CNN algorithm used in this study can identify a region of interest with a bounding box, along with classification, through a region proposal network. This detection allows clinicians to evaluate the soundness of the AI judgment and gain greater credibility from the results. Furthermore, the model may be useful for correlating patient symptoms with clinical outcomes, explaining them to patients, and establishing a treatment plan.

Training CT images have been used to create models that locate rib fracture sites [27–29]. However, chest CT is not used in routine practice because of its longer duration, higher economic costs, and potential risks associated with radiation exposure compared to plain chest radiography. It is commonly performed after diagnostic chest radiography. Therefore, the development of an AI model based on the widely used plain chest radiography would be more clinically useful. In particular, plain chest radiography is often used for basic screening purposes, allowing the detection of fractures, even in individuals who have difficulty communicating or are unconscious. Although fractures are easily missed, few attempts have been made to address this issue [30].

Recently, attempts have been made to diagnose rib fractures using chest radiography, as in this study [31–33]. Sun et al. [32] reported a sensitivity of 0.82 and an FROC of 0.87 with a false-positive count of 5 per image using their Fully Convolutional One-Stage system. However, when the false-positive count was reduced to 1, the sensitivity dramatically dropped to 0.60, and the FROC to 0.70. In comparison, our study achieved a sensitivity of 0.62 and a JAFROC FOM of 0.76, despite a much lower false-positive count of 0.3 per image. This result suggests that the lower false-positive count is a significant factor, especially considering that increasing sensitivity often requires sacrificing specificity. Huang et al. [31] achieved an accuracy range of 0.91–0.93 and an AUROC of 0.97–0.99 with their multi-CNN approach. However, their assessment used fixed pixel resolutions of 128×128, which differs from our study that evaluated performance using entire chest radiographs, precluding a direct comparison using FROC. Additionally, previous studies often involved image processing techniques that may not be practical in clinical settings. For example, Huang et al. employed data augmentation techniques such as flipping, rotation, and parallel shifting, and Wu et al. [33] standardized their images through multiscale image contrast amplification (MUSICA). In contrast, our study used unprocessed chest radiographs. Therefore, it is possible that our study's observers applied more stringent criteria compared with previous studies. Furthermore, these studies required datasets ranging from several thousand to tens of thousands of images for effective training. In contrast, this study utilized a dataset of 540 images, which is relatively small compared with that of other studies. This is important because most medical settings may not have access to vast amounts of medical data. Hence, obtaining results that can be applied in clinical practice using only a limited dataset has meaningful implications. Selection of inputs and determination of expected outputs, even within a pre-established neural network architecture, are crucial for effective AI training. Simulating various data types is essential to ensure that clinicians can achieve the intended outcomes and make the necessary adjustments. We believe that the efficiency of our approach can be attributed to the involvement of a practicing clinician who tailored the AI training environment for optimization and closely monitored the training process to ensure its effectiveness. This AI training model is believed to be pivotal to achieving the desired efficiency without compromising the model performance in a clinical setting.

Previously introduced image analysis AI often required input images with a fixed resolution [33]. However, in this case, image downscaling is necessary to transform the image into a form for training artificial intelligence. When applying AI in clinical practice, models trained in this manner are often inconvenient. The chest radiographs used in clinical settings typically have different resolutions. If images with these various resolutions are not analyzed as they are and downscaling is performed, the quality of the images may deteriorate [34]. Additionally, performing this extra task in a busy clinical setting can be burdensome for clinicians. In this study, using an algorithm that integrates the ResNet-101-based Feature Pyramid Network into the program made it possible to optimize the training and detection performances while performing these processes conveniently and automatically [35].

The observer performance test showed that our AI model could detect rib fractures on chest radiographs with an accuracy comparable to that of physicians. Compared with a previous study that reported detection sensitivity with a false-positive rate of 1–5 per image [32], our AI model demonstrated a substantially decreased rate of false positives while preserving the AUROC and JAFROC values, similar to the performance of board-certified anesthesiologists. This significant reduction in false positives could lead to fewer unnecessary follow-up procedures, thereby minimizing patient exposure to radiation [36]. Although not assessed in this study, we postulate that providing observers with suspected rib fracture sites identified by AI could enhance diagnostic performance. This collaborative approach between AI and medical professionals is likely to further improve the diagnostic accuracy and efficiency of the clinical workflow [37].

To analyze images using AI, even after training, it is necessary to apply image data through various complex processes in a programming environment. However, it may present time and hardware challenges for use in the clinical environment [10]. Therefore, for convenience, a program should be created in such a way that it can be easily run on commonly used operating systems. However, the functions and interfaces that users require can differ from the developer's configuration, which often causes inconvenience for users.

In the meantime, many developments in AI have been carried out by programmers specializing in AI rather than by users. However, in this study, all data preparation and training processes, including coding, were conducted directly by practicing clinicians. Therefore, we were able to develop a program that could be easily executed on Windows, which is a common operating system used on personal computers. Additionally, creating a program tailored to the needs of individual clinicians, which is convenient and efficient in clinical practice, is feasible. This was achieved by adopting a predetermined neural network architecture that has been previously developed and published. The use of predetermined neural networks offers several benefits to medical professionals. First, the time and effort required to construct a neural network can be reduced using an algorithm already optimized for image detection. Most image detection methods can perform well with a standardized algorithm without regenerating the neural network configuration. Even if a clinician has excellent coding skills, in most cases, sufficient time cannot be spent on coding because of the clinical work and the need to guide junior doctors. Second, the use of a predetermined neural network provides a standardized framework for image analysis, which can improve the consistency and reproducibility of the results across different medical centers and practitioners.

The demand for AI in healthcare is rapidly evolving and is seemingly endless. The AI model created in this study can be applied to any image analysis because it was performed according to the needs of clinicians, from training data generation to coding. Therefore, this model will be of great help in quickly meeting the increasing demand for AI in the medical field. Further advances in these technologies will help accelerate the advent of precision medicine, leading to pre-treatment simulations and intra-treatment guidance.

Our study has several limitations that should be considered. First, the relatively small dataset used for training may have impacted the accuracy of our rib fracture detection model. Additionally, the small validation sample size may have limited our ability to perform a detailed analysis of the diagnostic accuracy between physicians and the AI model. If we had validated interpretation skills against radiologists specializing in more advanced imaging interpretation, we might have obtained more objective and meaningful results. However, in this study, we consider that we have obtained meaningful data by comparing the interpretation abilities of AI with those of specialists who actively interpret imaging studies of real patients, as well as trainees who are training to interpret them. Moreover, if there had been comparisons with other AI models, this study could have produced more informative results. Lastly, the generalizability of our findings may be limited since the dataset was obtained from a single hospital. To improve the model's applicability and robustness, future studies should incorporate datasets from multiple institutions into the AI training process.

5. Conclusions

We developed an AI model utilizing Detectron2 and trained on a limited dataset that achieved performances comparable to those of experienced physicians in radiograph classification and rib fracture detection.

Author Contributions: Conceptualization, K.L. and J.C.K.; methodology, K.L.; software, J.C.K.; validation, K.L. and S.L.; formal analysis, K.L. and H.O.; investigation, K.L.; resources, K.L. and H.P.; data curation, K.L. and J.C.K.; writing—original draft preparation, K.L.; writing—review and editing, K.L. and J.C.K.; visualization, J.S.K.; supervision, K.L. and J.C.K.; project administration, J.C.K.; funding acquisition, J.C.K. All authors have read and agreed to the published version of the manuscript.

Funding: This research was supported by a grant of the Korea Health Technology R&D Project 449 through the Korea Health Industry Development Institute (KHIDI), funded by the Ministry of 450 Health & Welfare, Republic of Korea (grant number: HR22C1302).

Institutional Review Board Statement: The study was conducted in accordance with the Declaration of Helsinki, and approved by the Institutional Review Board of Korea University Anam Hospital (approval no: 2022AN0553 and date of approval: 1 December 2022).

Informed Consent Statement: The requirement to obtain informed consent was waived due to the retrospective nature of this study.

Data Availability Statement: The data presented in this study are available on request from the corresponding author.

Conflicts of Interest: The authors declare no conflicts of interest.

References

1. Alkadhi, H.; Wildermuth, S.; Marincek, B.; Boehm, T. Accuracy and time efficiency for the detection of thoracic cage fractures: Volume rendering compared with transverse computed tomography images. *J. Comput. Assist. Tomogr.* **2004**, *28*, 378–385. [CrossRef]
2. Henry, T.S.; Donnelly, E.F.; Boiselle, P.M.; Crabtree, T.D.; Iannettoni, M.D.; Johnson, G.B.; Kazerooni, E.A.; Laroia, A.T.; Maldonado, F.; Olsen, K.M.; et al. ACR Appropriateness Criteria(®) Rib Fractures. *J. Am. Coll. Radiol.* **2019**, *16*, S227–S234. [CrossRef] [PubMed]
3. Talbot, B.S.; Gange, C.P., Jr.; Chaturvedi, A.; Klionsky, N.; Hobbs, S.K.; Chaturvedi, A. Traumatic Rib Injury: Patterns, Imaging Pitfalls, Complications, and Treatment. *Radiographics* **2017**, *37*, 628–651. [CrossRef]
4. Kalra, M.K.; Maher, M.M.; Rizzo, S.; Kanarek, D.; Shepard, J.A. Radiation exposure from chest CT: Issues and strategies. *J. Korean Med. Sci.* **2004**, *19*, 159–166. [CrossRef]
5. Assi, A.A.; Nazal, Y. Rib fracture: Different radiographic projections. *Pol. J. Radiol.* **2012**, *77*, 13–16. [CrossRef] [PubMed]
6. Awais, M.; Salam, B.; Nadeem, N.; Rehman, A.; Baloch, N.U. Diagnostic Accuracy of Computed Tomography Scout Film and Chest X-ray for Detection of Rib Fractures in Patients with Chest Trauma: A Cross-sectional Study. *Cureus* **2019**, *11*, e3875. [CrossRef] [PubMed]
7. Dubinsky, I.; Low, A. Non-life-threatening blunt chest trauma: Appropriate investigation and treatment. *Am. J. Emerg. Med.* **1997**, *15*, 240–243. [CrossRef]
8. Sano, A. Rib Radiography versus Chest Computed Tomography in the Diagnosis of Rib Fractures. *Thorac. Cardiovasc. Surg.* **2018**, *66*, 693–696. [CrossRef]
9. Weingrow, D. Under What Situations Is Ultrasound Beneficial for the Detection of Rib Fractures? *Ann. Emerg. Med.* **2022**, *79*, 540–542. [CrossRef]
10. Chen, X.; Wang, X.; Zhang, K.; Fung, K.M.; Thai, T.C.; Moore, K.; Mannel, R.S.; Liu, H.; Zheng, B.; Qiu, Y. Recent advances and clinical applications of deep learning in medical image analysis. *Med. Image Anal.* **2022**, *79*, 102444. [CrossRef]
11. Seong, H.; Yun, D.; Yoon, K.S.; Kwak, J.S.; Koh, J.C. Development of pre-procedure virtual simulation for challenging interventional procedures: An experimental study with clinical application. *Korean J. Pain* **2022**, *35*, 403–412. [CrossRef] [PubMed]

12. Nam, J.G.; Park, S.; Hwang, E.J.; Lee, J.H.; Jin, K.N.; Lim, K.Y.; Vu, T.H.; Sohn, J.H.; Hwang, S.; Goo, J.M.; et al. Development and Validation of Deep Learning-based Automatic Detection Algorithm for Malignant Pulmonary Nodules on Chest Radiographs. *Radiology* **2019**, *290*, 218–228. [CrossRef] [PubMed]
13. Wang, S.; Wu, D.; Ye, L.; Chen, Z.; Zhan, Y.; Li, Y. Assessment of automatic rib fracture detection on chest CT using a deep learning algorithm. *Eur. Radiol.* **2023**, *33*, 1824–1834. [CrossRef] [PubMed]
14. Wu, M.; Chai, Z.; Qian, G.; Lin, H.; Wang, Q.; Wang, L.; Chen, H. Development and Evaluation of a Deep Learning Algorithm for Rib Segmentation and Fracture Detection from Multicenter Chest CT Images. *Radiol. Artif. Intell.* **2021**, *3*, e200248. [CrossRef] [PubMed]
15. Wu, Y.K.A.; Massa, F.; Lo, W.Y.; Girshick, R. Detectron2: A PyTorch-Based Modular Object Detection Library. Available online: https://ai.facebook.com/blog/-detectron2-a-pytorch-based-modular-object-detection-library-/ (accessed on 17 October 2022).
16. Lin, T.Y.; Dollár, P.; Girshick, R.; He, K.; Hariharan, B.; Belongie, S. Feature Pyramid Networks for Object Detection. In Proceedings of the 2017 IEEE Conference on Computer Vision and Pattern Recognition (CVPR), Honolulu, HI, USA, 21–26 July 2017; pp. 936–944.
17. DeLong, E.R.; DeLong, D.M.; Clarke-Pearson, D.L. Comparing the areas under two or more correlated receiver operating characteristic curves: A nonparametric approach. *Biometrics* **1988**, *44*, 837–845. [CrossRef] [PubMed]
18. Fletcher, J.G.; Yu, L.; Li, Z.; Manduca, A.; Blezek, D.J.; Hough, D.M.; Venkatesh, S.K.; Brickner, G.C.; Cernigliaro, J.C.; Hara, A.K.; et al. Observer Performance in the Detection and Classification of Malignant Hepatic Nodules and Masses with CT Image-Space Denoising and Iterative Reconstruction. *Radiology* **2015**, *276*, 465–478. [CrossRef] [PubMed]
19. Chassagnon, G.; Vakalopoulou, M.; Paragios, N.; Revel, M.P. Artificial intelligence applications for thoracic imaging. *Eur. J. Radiol.* **2020**, *123*, 108774. [CrossRef]
20. Fourcade, A.; Khonsari, R.H. Deep learning in medical image analysis: A third eye for doctors. *J. Stomatol. Oral Maxillofac. Surg.* **2019**, *120*, 279–288. [CrossRef] [PubMed]
21. Martin, T.J.; Eltorai, A.S.; Dunn, R.; Varone, A.; Joyce, M.F.; Kheirbek, T.; Adams, C., Jr.; Daniels, A.H.; Eltorai, A.E.M. Clinical management of rib fractures and methods for prevention of pulmonary complications: A review. *Injury* **2019**, *50*, 1159–1165. [CrossRef]
22. Crandall, J.; Kent, R.; Patrie, J.; Fertile, J.; Martin, P. Rib fracture patterns and radiologic detection—A restraint-based comparison. *Annu. Proc. Assoc. Adv. Automot. Med.* **2000**, *44*, 235–259.
23. Shuaib, W.; Vijayasarathi, A.; Tiwana, M.H.; Johnson, J.O.; Maddu, K.K.; Khosa, F. The diagnostic utility of rib series in assessing rib fractures. *Emerg. Radiol.* **2014**, *21*, 159–164. [CrossRef] [PubMed]
24. Tieu, A.; Kroen, E.; Kadish, Y.; Liu, Z.; Patel, N.; Zhou, A.; Yilmaz, A.; Lee, S.; Deyer, T. The Role of Artificial Intelligence in the Identification and Evaluation of Bone Fractures. *Bioengineering* **2024**, *11*, 338. [CrossRef] [PubMed]
25. Hosny, A.; Parmar, C.; Quackenbush, J.; Schwartz, L.H.; Aerts, H. Artificial intelligence in radiology. *Nat. Rev. Cancer* **2018**, *18*, 500–510. [CrossRef] [PubMed]
26. Chaddad, A.; Peng, J.; Xu, J.; Bouridane, A. Survey of Explainable AI Techniques in Healthcare. *Sensors* **2023**, *23*, 634. [CrossRef] [PubMed]
27. Kaiume, M.; Suzuki, S.; Yasaka, K.; Sugawara, H.; Shen, Y.; Katada, Y.; Ishikawa, T.; Fukui, R.; Abe, O. Rib fracture detection in computed tomography images using deep convolutional neural networks. *Medicine* **2021**, *100*, e26024. [CrossRef]
28. Niiya, A.; Murakami, K.; Kobayashi, R.; Sekimoto, A.; Saeki, M.; Toyofuku, K.; Kato, M.; Shinjo, H.; Ito, Y.; Takei, M.; et al. Development of an artificial intelligence-assisted computed tomography diagnosis technology for rib fracture and evaluation of its clinical usefulness. *Sci. Rep.* **2022**, *12*, 8363. [CrossRef]
29. Zhou, Z.; Fu, Z.; Jia, J.; Lv, J. Rib Fracture Detection with Dual-Attention Enhanced U-Net. *Comput. Math. Methods Med.* **2022**, *2022*, 8945423. [CrossRef]
30. Guermazi, A.; Tannoury, C.; Kompel, A.J.; Murakami, A.M.; Ducarouge, A.; Gillibert, A.; Li, X.; Tournier, A.; Lahoud, Y.; Jarraya, M.; et al. Improving Radiographic Fracture Recognition Performance and Efficiency Using Artificial Intelligence. *Radiology* **2022**, *302*, 627–636. [CrossRef] [PubMed]
31. Huang, S.T.; Liu, L.R.; Chiu, H.W.; Huang, M.Y.; Tsai, M.F. Deep convolutional neural network for rib fracture recognition on chest radiographs. *Front. Med.* **2023**, *10*, 1178798. [CrossRef]
32. Sun, H.; Wang, X.; Li, Z.; Liu, A.; Xu, S.; Jiang, Q.; Li, Q.; Xue, Z.; Gong, J.; Chen, L.; et al. Automated Rib Fracture Detection on Chest X-Ray Using Contrastive Learning. *J. Digit. Imaging* **2023**, *36*, 2138–2147. [CrossRef]
33. Wu, J.; Liu, N.; Li, X.; Fan, Q.; Li, Z.; Shang, J.; Wang, F.; Chen, B.; Shen, Y.; Cao, P.; et al. Convolutional neural network for detecting rib fractures on chest radiographs: A feasibility study. *BMC Med. Imaging* **2023**, *23*, 18. [CrossRef] [PubMed]
34. Sabottke, C.F.; Spieler, B.M. The Effect of Image Resolution on Deep Learning in Radiography. *Radiol. Artif. Intell.* **2020**, *2*, e190015. [CrossRef] [PubMed]
35. Satheesh Kumar, K.G.; Arunachalam, V. Depthwise convolution based pyramid ResNet model for accurate detection of COVID-19 from chest X-Ray images. *Imaging Sci. J.* **2024**, *72*, 540–556. [CrossRef]

36. Iyeke, L.; Moss, R.; Hall, R.; Wang, J.; Sandhu, L.; Appold, B.; Kalontar, E.; Menoudakos, D.; Ramnarine, M.; LaVine, S.P.; et al. Reducing Unnecessary 'Admission' Chest X-rays: An Initiative to Minimize Low-Value Care. *Cureus* **2022**, *14*, e29817. [CrossRef]
37. Zhang, B.; Jia, C.; Wu, R.; Lv, B.; Li, B.; Li, F.; Du, G.; Sun, Z.; Li, X. Improving rib fracture detection accuracy and reading efficiency with deep learning-based detection software: A clinical evaluation. *Br. J. Radiol.* **2021**, *94*, 20200870. [CrossRef]

diagnostics

MDPI

Article

Attention-Based Deep Learning Approach for Breast Cancer Histopathological Image Multi-Classification

Lama A. Aldakhil, Haifa F. Alhasson * and Shuaa S. Alharbi

Department of Information Technology, College of Computer, Qassim University, Buraydah 52571, Saudi Arabia; 441212544@qu.edu.sa (L.A.A.); shuaa.s.alharbi@qu.edu.sa (S.S.A.)
* Correspondence: hhson@qu.edu.sa

Abstract: Breast cancer diagnosis from histopathology images is often time consuming and prone to human error, impacting treatment and prognosis. Deep learning diagnostic methods offer the potential for improved accuracy and efficiency in breast cancer detection and classification. However, they struggle with limited data and subtle variations within and between cancer types. Attention mechanisms provide feature refinement capabilities that have shown promise in overcoming such challenges. To this end, this paper proposes the Efficient Channel Spatial Attention Network (ECSAnet), an architecture built on EfficientNetV2 and augmented with a convolutional block attention module (CBAM) and additional fully connected layers. ECSAnet was fine-tuned using the BreakHis dataset, employing Reinhard stain normalization and image augmentation techniques to minimize overfitting and enhance generalizability. In testing, ECSAnet outperformed AlexNet, DenseNet121, EfficientNetV2-S, InceptionNetV3, ResNet50, and VGG16 in most settings, achieving accuracies of 94.2% at 40×, 92.96% at 100×, 88.41% at 200×, and 89.42% at 400× magnifications. The results highlight the effectiveness of CBAM in improving classification accuracy and the importance of stain normalization for generalizability.

Keywords: breast cancer; breast tumors; convolutional neural networks; deep learning; diagnosis; transfer learning; histopathological images; image classifier

1. Introduction

The global incidence of breast cancer reached a concerning rate of 2.3 million diagnosed cases in 2022, tragically claiming the lives of 670,000 individuals [1]. Breast cancer occurs when breast cells mutate and grow uncontrollably. Early detection is vital for effective treatment. Visible indicators that warrant breast cancer screening include a palpable lump in the breast, dimpling in the breast skin texture, redness or swelling of the breast skin, blisters or sores on the breast surface, abnormal nipple discharge, and nipple inversion or flattening [2].

Early and precise diagnosis of breast tumors significantly improves prognosis and is primarily achieved through histopathology. This procedure involves a biopsy, which entails extracting soft tissue samples from suspicious areas using techniques such as fine-needle aspiration, core needle biopsy, vacuum-assisted biopsy, and surgical biopsy [3]. After extraction, the samples are affixed to microscopic slides. Before examination, the tissues undergo staining with hematoxylin and eosin (H&E), which helps distinguish and highlight particular features of the translucent tissue composition and cellular details [4].

Expert pathologists analyze the histological characteristics of the H&E-stained tissue sections, scanning for cancerous cells and abnormalities within the typical structures of the breast throughout the examination process [5]. However, histopathological slides present inherent challenges due to their high complexity and the diversity of tumor tissues. The complexity arises from the pronounced coherency of cancerous cells, substantial intra-class differences, and limited inter-class distinctions within the images. Additionally, images of the same class often exhibit significant resolution variations. Due to this, accurate diagnosis using this type of imaging modality is considered difficult and time consuming [6].

Deep learning (DL) has emerged as a groundbreaking innovation in artificial intelligence. Positioned as a subset of machine learning (ML), the study of DL revolves around training artificial neural networks to discern complex patterns within expansive datasets for various applications. The process of DL mirrors the functioning of the human brain, where interconnected neurons process and store information. DL employs models consisting of multiple layers of processing to acquire data representations at varying levels of abstraction. A crucial characteristic of DL is the ability to swiftly and accurately process copious amounts of data without necessitating explicit programming. As a result, DL models have established new benchmarks for state-of-the-art performance, opening up many possibilities of advancements across various disciplines, including natural language processing, image recognition, and autonomous vehicles [7].

Over the years, DL has seen substantial growth, receiving significant attention in the medical imaging research field [8]. The most popular DL architecture is the convolutional neural network (CNN). CNNs have achieved outstanding results in diagnostic applications of breast cancer from histopathological images [6,9]. These diagnostic applications include tumor detection [10], breast cancer grading [11], breast cancer sub-type classification [12], assessment of tumor heterogeneity and micro-environment [13], and assessment of receptor status and intrinsic sub-type [14].

While numerous DL-based approaches have been proposed in the literature, there is still room for improvement. Among the challenges that negatively affect the generalization of DL approaches for breast cancer diagnosis are the lack of sufficient representative images, the complexity of histology images captured at different magnifications, and the variability in laboratory H&E tissue-staining methods [15,16]. Hence, there is a need to develop an improved approach capable of extracting deep representative features effectively and accurately from breast histopathology images and classifying them into their respective sub-types while utilizing the currently available datasets. This paper aims to address this issue by proposing an attention-based DL approach while utilizing stain normalization and data augmentation techniques to address the diagnostic challenges of multi-class classification of breast tumors, which is crucial for ensuring timely and appropriate patient treatment.

The contributions of our paper are as follows:

1. We proposed the Efficient Channel-Spatial Attention Network (ECSAnet), which is an improved EfficientNetV2 architecture [17]. Our model integrates a convolutional block attention module (CBAM) [18] that efficiently captures features in both the channel and spatial dimensions. It refines the learned features by discerning the most discriminative features, focusing on what is important and where it is located within an image. Moreover, our model incorporates two additional fully connected layers for increased learning capacity.
2. We proposed an approach for creating an oversampled balanced dataset using data augmentation techniques to minimize the data imbalance and increase diversity.
3. We verified that the CBAM, FC layers, and Reinhard stain normalization [19] components helped increase the accuracy and generalization of our proposed model through an ablation study.
4. We compared our proposed model against state-of-the-art models, including AlexNet, DenseNet121, EfficientNetV2-S, InceptionNetV3, ResNet50, and VGG-16. The analysis showed that our model is more accurate than the mentioned models at most magnification settings.

The paper is organized as follows: Section 2 surveys previous studies relevant to the research. Section 3 outlines the key elements of the methodology applied. Section 4 details the results achieved, while Section 5 discusses these results. Section 6 suggests directions for future work. Finally, Section 7 concludes the paper.

2. Literature Review

Many studies have previously addressed the essential problem of automated breast cancer classification using DL-based approaches for histopathological images. Generally, the classification of breast histopathological images is approached through two distinct methods: binary and multi-class. Binary classification distinguishes between benign and malignant tumors, while multi-class classification is a more challenging problem than binary classification, as it involves classifying images into distinct tumor sub-types.

In their comprehensive study, Nasser et al. [16] identified CNNs as the leading DL method for detecting breast cancer, making them a popular choice among researchers. Moreover, previous studies have reported that CNNs consistently outperform other methods regarding accuracy within this field. This outstanding performance is primarily due to the CNNs' innate ability to autonomously extract and classify essential, discriminative features from complex image data. There are two primary approaches to developing CNNs: "de novo", where the network is built and trained from scratch; and transfer learning, which makes use of CNNs that have been pre-trained on large datasets, such as AlexNet, ResNets, GoogLeNet, or VGGNets, as a baseline [16].

The significance of transfer learning approaches lies in their potential to avoid expensive data-labeling efforts and enhance learning performance by leveraging knowledge from related domains [20]. Among the studies that have applied transfer learning for breast cancer histopathological images are Yari et al.'s [21]. They used two pre-trained models: ResNet50 and DenseNet-121. They modified the last FC layers in the models differently for each classification type. Consequently, they set the number of output features to eight for multi-class and two for binary classification. They evaluated the models for magnification-dependent (MD) and -independent (MI) classification. The results in binary classification demonstrated high image-level accuracy with values ranging from 99.02% to 100% for MD binary classification and 99.26% for MI binary classification. Regarding multi-class classification, the approach yielded MD accuracies ranging from 94.95% to 97.96% and 95.57% for MI classification.

Similarly, another study by Boumaraf et al. [22] used the ResNet18 pre-trained model for binary and multi-class classification, distinguishing between MD and MI classification. Following a block-wise fine-tuning strategy, they adapted the model to the BreakHis dataset. Furthermore, they modified the ResNet18 classifier by incorporating an additional FC layer for more robust feature learning. Their reported results showcased high image-level average accuracies of 98.84% and 92.15% for MD binary and eight-class classification, respectively. As for MI classification, it achieved 98.42% and 92.03% accuracy for binary and eight-class classification, respectively.

To minimize the feature complexities of varied magnifications in histopathological images, Sheikh et al. [12] proposed a multi-scale input and multi-feature network (MSI-MFnet). Their proposed approach captures the tissue cells and texture features by fusing multi-scale hierarchical feature maps from different layers using image patches. MSI-MFnet was evaluated for both binary and multi-class classification using two datasets: BreakHis and ICIAR2018. The results highlighted the importance of fusing multi-scale inputs and the need to effectively use multi-feature maps to extract distinctive salient features while preserving coarse-scale features. For the ICIAR2018 dataset, they achieved patch-wise accuracies of 82% and 68% for binary and multi-class classifications, respectively. Moreover, for the BreakHis dataset, they achieved patch-wise accuracies of 98% and 87% for binary and multi-class classification, respectively.

The effectiveness of attention mechanisms in enhancing the performance of computer vision methods has garnered substantial empirical support in recent years. Fundamentally, attention mechanisms selectively concentrate on salient features within an image, similar to the human visual system's capacity to discern and prioritize regions of interest in complex visual scenes. These mechanisms can be characterized as dynamic selection processes that adaptively adjust weights based on the significance of different features [23].

Given their efficiency, attention mechanisms have been adopted into DL-based approaches for classifying histopathological images of breast cancer. For instance, Togacar et al. [24] incorporated a CBAM attention mechanism in their BreastNet architecture. The CBAM block was used to refine features adaptively by processing feature maps across spatial and channel dimensions, which enhanced model accuracy and computational efficiency. In addition to CBAM, BreastNet integrated various components, such as convolutional, dense, and residual blocks, alongside a hyper-column technique. Each component improved feature discrimination, strengthened the gradient flow, optimized feature selection, and lastly, enabled multi-scale analysis through the hyper-column approach. In comparative assessments against state-of-the-art models like AlexNet, VGG-16, and VGG-19, BreastNet showed improved performance, achieving accuracies ranging from 95.88% to 98.52% at different magnification factors.

Another study by Li et al. [25] proposed an approach of adapting the squeeze-and-excitation (SE) attention mechanism into the DenseNet121 architecture, which they referred to as the interleaved DenseNet with SENet (IDSnet). Additionally, their approach addresses computational resource constraints and network overfitting by incorporating global average pooling, which reduces the model's complexity. IDSnet uses a pre-trained and fine-tuned DenseNet-121 to extract feature maps from histopathological images, which are then refined using SENet modules to capture essential channel-wise global information. They evaluated IDSnet classification performance compared to VGG-16 and ResNet50 models, where it proved superior, achieving patient recognition rates between 84.6% and 90% and image recognition rates from 84.5% to 89.1% across different magnifications.

Zou et al. [26] utilized the efficient channel attention (ECA) module within their proposed attention high-order deep network (AHoNet), which enhances the ResNet18 architecture. With an integrated ECA module, their approach incorporated non-dimensionality reduction and local cross-channel interaction. In addition, they implemented matrix power normalization to compute second-order covariance statistics, which further improved AHoNet's ability to capture salient local and global features effectively. The AHoNet model was evaluated on two datasets: BreakHis and BACH. Using BreakHis, they achieved impressive accuracies of 99.09% at the image level and 99.29% at the patient level. Whereas using BACH, it achieved an accuracy of 85%.

3. Materials and Methods

This section will provide details of the study methodology, covering (i) an overview of CNNs, (ii) the EfficientNetV2 architecture, (iii) the CBAM attention mechanism, (iv) the proposed approach, (v) the dataset employed, (vi) the data pre-processing and augmentation techniques used, (vii) the experimental setup, and finally, (viii) the evaluation metrics that we have used. Figure 1 presents a summary of the study workflow.

3.1. Convolutional Neural Networks

The CNN architecture is a widely recognized DL architecture with diverse applications in computer vision, such as image classification, action recognition, pose estimation, object detection and tracking, text detection and recognition, and many more [27]. The CNN architecture has seen the development of various variants, including well-known ones like LeNet, AlexNet, and VGGNet, among others. Although specific architectures may introduce additional layers or modifications, the fundamental structure of a CNN can be said to consist of three layers: a convolutional layer, a pooling layer, and a fully connected layer [27,28]. Figure 2 illustrates the basic architecture of a CNN.

- The convolutional layer: This layer plays a major role in a CNN, as its name suggests. It includes convolution kernels, also called filters, which are responsible for generating feature maps. Each neuron within a feature map establishes connections with a neighboring region of neurons in the preceding layer. Through this process, the convolutional layer can learn representations from the spatial dimensions inherent in the input data [27].

- The pooling layer: This layer reduces the dimensionality of feature maps to decrease the number of parameters and computational complexity. Typically positioned between convolutional layers, each feature map within the pooling layer establishes connections with the corresponding feature map in the preceding convolutional layer [28].
- The fully connected layer: This layer helps capture complex relationships between the features and make predictions based on the learned representations. In this layer, each neuron is connected to every neuron in the preceding layer. Consequently, the output of each neuron in the previous layer is treated as an input for every neuron within the fully connected layer [27].

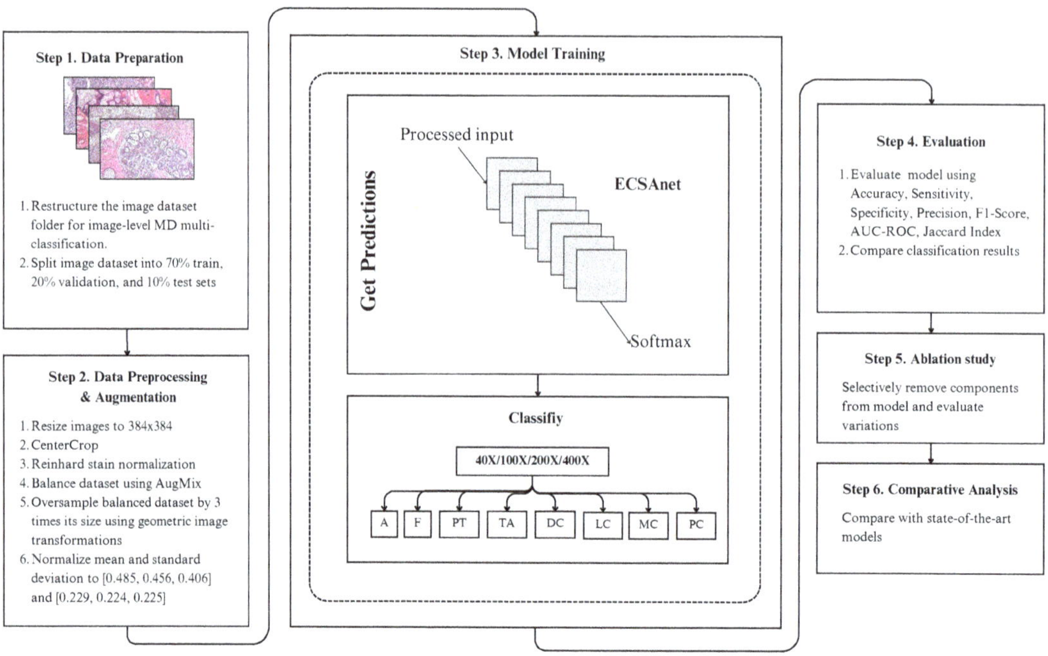

Figure 1. Workflow of the approach employed for breast histology image classification. Our approach begins with dataset processing steps, followed by training the ECSAnet model to extract features and obtain classification predictions, after which we move on to model evaluation and analysis steps.

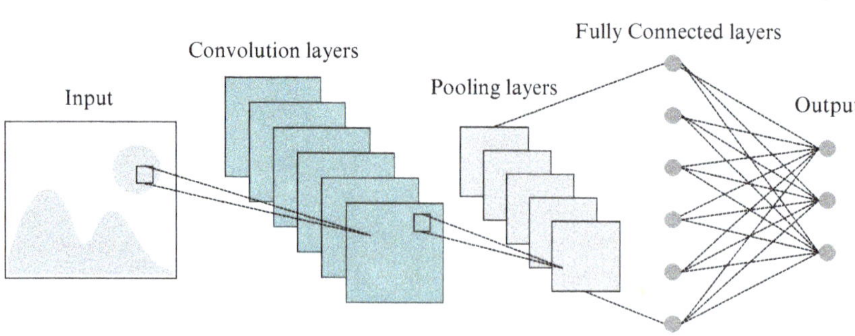

Figure 2. Basic architecture of a CNN [28].

3.2. *EfficientNetV2*

EfficientNetV2 [17] is an improved network of models (EfficientNetV2-S/M/L) built upon EfficientNet [29]. A distinctive characteristic of the EfficientNet architecture lies in its implementation of a compound scaling method. This method allows all model layers to be uniformly and effectively scaled by a constant ratio, optimizing the depth, width, and resolution of the layers for any resource constraint. Consequently, the models can allocate their computational resources to focus on more salient regions within an image, facilitating the learning of fine-grained features and ultimately enhancing accuracy. This scaling approach is achieved while maintaining fewer parameters and floating point operations, ensuring a favorable trade-off between model efficiency and performance. EfficientNetV2 improves upon EfficientNet in three ways. First, EfficientNetV2 enhances training speed by adopting a progressive learning technique. This technique dynamically adjusts the regularization parameters with the image size during training. Secondly, the architecture of EfficientNetV2 incorporates fused mobile inverted bottleneck convolution (Fused-MBConv) layers to replace the early layers. This replacement serves to enhance the training speed further. Thirdly, EfficientNetV2 introduces a modified scaling rule that constrains the maximum image size. This limitation mitigates the substantial memory consumption associated with larger image sizes. As a result, the training speed is improved, and computational resources are utilized more efficiently. Collectively, EfficientNetV2 excels in multiple dimensions in comparison to its predecessors. It surpasses previous models in terms of training speed, parameter efficiency, and overall accuracy. The architecture of EfficientNetV2 can be seen in Figure 3.

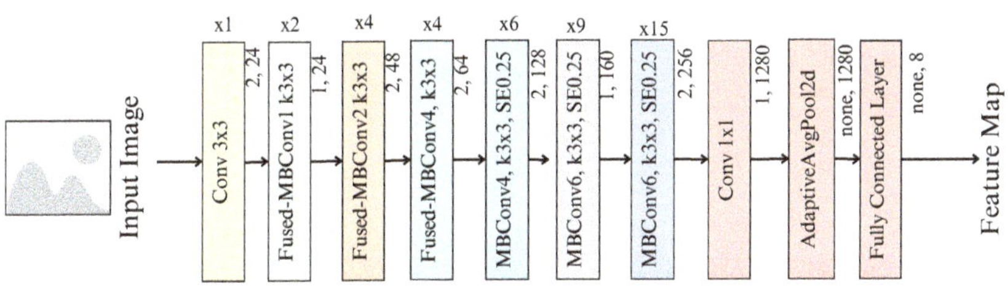

Figure 3. Architecture of EfficientNetV2 [17].

3.3. Convolutional Attention Block Module

The attention mechanism used in this paper is the CBAM. This module was first introduced in [18]. It is an efficient attention mechanism designed to work with feed-forward CNNs. This module combines the representative power of both channel attention (CAM) and spatial attention (SAM) modules with a small overhead. Essentially, it applies a CAM and SAM sequentially to focus on learning "what" and "where" to pay attention to along the channel and spatial dimensions. This process can efficiently learn salient features and suppress irrelevant ones.

When given a feature map tensor $F \in \mathbb{R}^{C\times H\times W}$, the CBAM module sequentially computes a 1D channel attention map $M_c \in \mathbb{R}^{C\times 1\times 1}$ and a 2D spatial attention $M_s \in \mathbb{R}^{1\times H\times W}$; in summary, the attention is computed using the following equation:

$$\begin{aligned} F' &= M_c(F) \otimes F \\ F'' &= M_s(F') \otimes F' \end{aligned} \quad (1)$$

where $\otimes$ indicates element-wise multiplication and F'' is the final refined feature map. Figure 4 depicts an overview of the computations of the CBAM and its sub-modules, SAM and CAM.

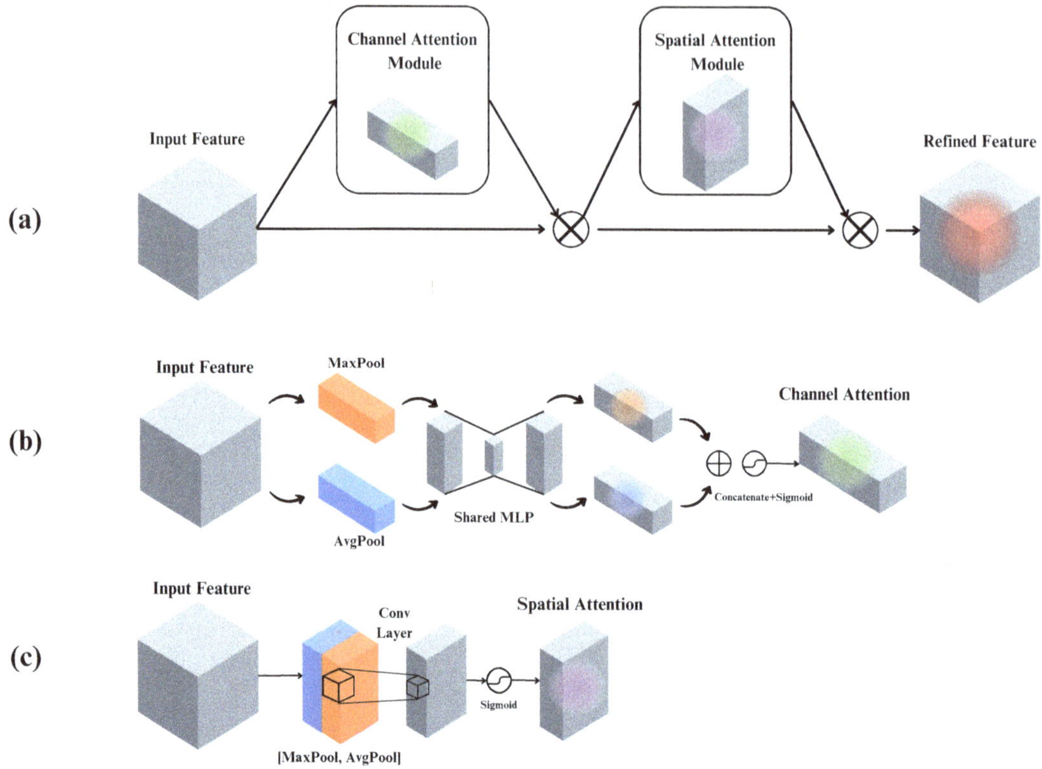

Figure 4. Computation processes of the attention modules: (**a**) CBAM, (**b**) CAM, and (**c**) SAM [18].

3.4. Proposed Approach

An improved model called ECSAnet is proposed to effectively extract discriminative features from histology images for breast cancer classification. ECSAnet adopts the EfficientNetV2-S architecture as its baseline. ECSAnet improves upon the baseline model in three ways:

1. It has an added CBAM block placed before the final classifier block.
2. The final classifier block has two additional fully connected layers.
3. The number of output features of the last FC layer is adjusted from 1000 to 8 to align with the eight tumor sub-types in the BreakHis dataset.

Following these changes, the ECSAnet model architecture summary is listed in Table 1 and illustrated in Figure 5.

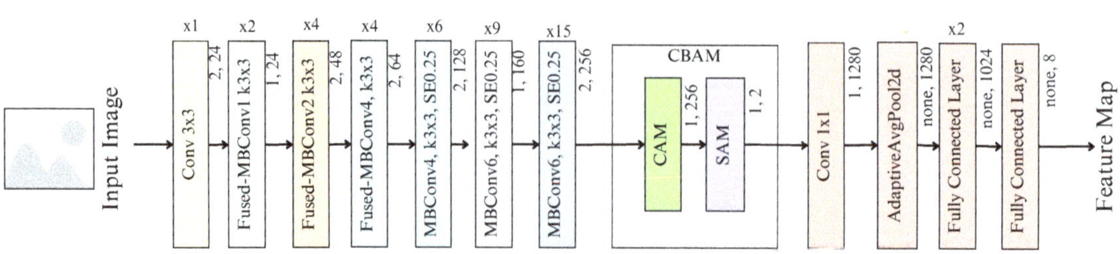

Figure 5. Architecture of ECSAnet.

Table 1. ECSAnet architecture summary.

No.	Block	Channel Reduction Ratio	Expansion Factor	Kernel Size	Stride	No. of Layers	Output Channels
0	Conv	-	-	3×3	2	1	24
1	Fused-MBConv	-	1	3×3	1	2	24
2	Fused-MBConv	-	4	3×3	2	4	48
3	Fused-MBConv	-	4	3×3	2	4	64
4	MBConv+SE	0.25	4	3×3	2	6	128
5	MBConv+SE	0.25	6	3×3	1	9	160
6	MBConv+SE	0.25	6	3×3	2	15	256
7	CBAM	16	-	3×3 CAM, 7×7 SAM	1	4	256
8	Conv + AdaptiveAvgPool2D + Fully Connected + Fully Connected	- - - -	- - - -	1×1 - - -	1 - - -	1 1 2 1	1280 1280 1024 8

The main building blocks of the architecture are the MBConv [30] and the Fused-MBConv [31] layers. The MBConv is a complex convolutional layer consisting of a squeeze-and-excitation module and a depth-wise convolutional layer. Meanwhile, the Fused-MBConv replaces the depth-wise convolutional layer with a 3×3 convolutional layer. The structures of these two layers are shown in Figure 6.

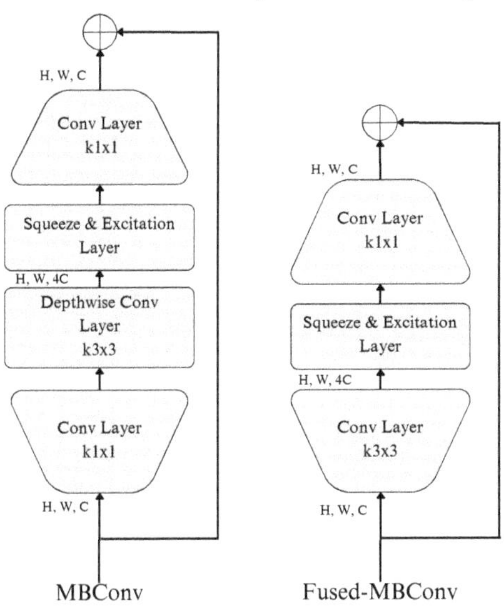

Figure 6. Structures of MBConv and Fused-MBConv [17,30,31].

The addition of FC layers in deep learning models is particularly useful for tasks that require complex relationships between inputs and outputs. FC layers connect all neurons between layers, allowing them to use all the information contained in the input layer. This makes FC layers a powerful tool for enhancing machine learning models, as they are capable of accurately identifying the complex relationships in the input data. However, this type of layer is more difficult to train than other layers because it is computationally inefficient. This issue can be solved by combining it with CBAM.

CBAM is designed to enhance convolutional neural networks by focusing on the most relevant parts of the input data. This selective focus enables networks to better handle large images or images containing complex details, which ultimately improves performance by refining the learned feature representations. Due to this, CBAM can be used to potentially reduce the amount of training time required with fully connected layers. Moreover, CBAM reduces the computational cost of training a network by avoiding the necessity of processing the entire input image each time.

The combination of CBAM with additional fully connected layers leverages the strengths of both components, which include CBAM's enhanced feature refinement capability and reduced model overhead and the FC layer's capability to identify complex relationships to improve model accuracy. The components can work synergistically as CBAM refines the features and reduces the amount of irrelevant information processed by the subsequent FC layers. Then, the additional FC layers add increased learning capacity, allowing them to learn and model complex relationships within refined feature representations more effectively. Additionally, the computational complexity associated with FC layers can be mitigated with fewer, more informative features.

3.5. Dataset

The dataset employed in this work is the Breast Cancer Histopathological Image Classification (BreakHis) dataset [32], which is publicly accessible online at this link: https://web.inf.ufpr.br/vri/databases/breast-cancer-histopathological-database-breakhis/ (accessed on 1 December 2023). This dataset comprises a total of 9109 microscopic images depicting breast tumor tissue. The images were collected from 82 patients and were captured at varying magnifications, specifically 40×, 100×, 200×, and 400×. Each image is stored in the PNG format and possesses the following specifications: a resolution of 700 × 460 pixels, a 3-channel RGB color space, and an 8-bit depth in each channel.

The BreakHis dataset is divided into two main groups: benign and malignant. Each group is then divided into sub-types. Benign tumor tissues are divided into four tumor classes: adenosis (A), fibroadenoma (F), phyllodes tumor (PT), and tubular adenoma (TA). On the other hand, malignant tumor tissues are divided into four tumor classes: ductal carcinoma (DC), lobular carcinoma (LC), mucinous carcinoma (MC), and papillary carcinoma (PC). Samples of a benign tumor and malignant tumor are shown in Figure 7. The class distribution of the BreakHis dataset is shown in Table 2.

The dataset has been reorganized for magnification-dependent image-level multi-classification and split into three parts: 70% for training, 20% for validation, and 10% for testing.

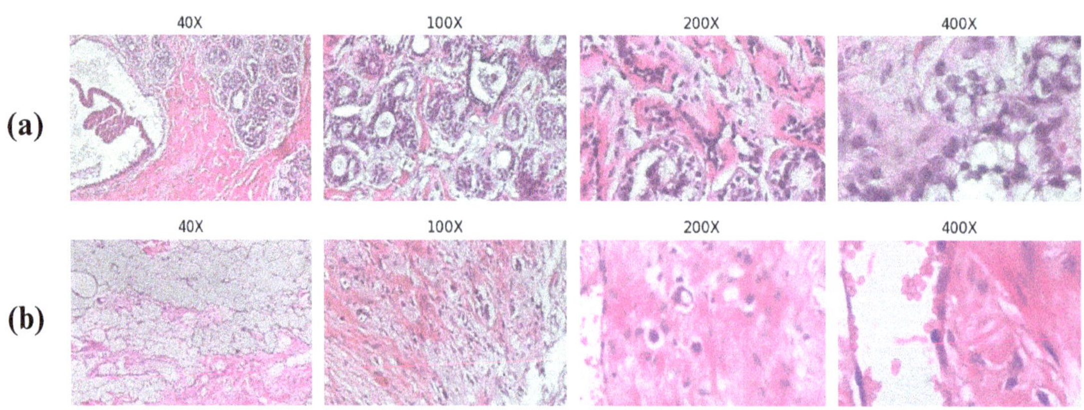

Figure 7. (**a**) Samples for benign tumor tissues; (**b**) samples for malignant tumor tissues [32].

Table 2. Class distribution of BreakHis.

Magnification	Benign				Malignant				Total
	A	F	PT	TA	DC	LC	MC	PC	
40×	114	253	109	149	864	156	205	145	1995
100×	113	260	121	150	903	170	222	142	2081
200×	111	264	108	140	896	163	196	135	2013
400×	106	237	115	130	788	137	169	138	1820
Sub-type total	444	1014	453	569	3451	626	792	560	7909
Type total	2480				5429				7909

3.6. Data Pre-Processing and Augmentation

Effectively preparing and enhancing data is a key contributor to successful DL models, particularly when dealing with task-specific requirements. In the context of breast histopathology and medical imagery, augmentation strategies must preserve essential image characteristics while introducing a diverse range of variations. This diversity is necessary to ensure models can generalize well when deployed in real-world diagnostic scenarios. Clinicians can interpret histopathology images irrespective of changes in angle, orientation, or scale, and this robustness should also be characteristic of DL models applied to the same task.

As outlined in Algorithm 1, three functions are present: pre-process, balance, and transform.

Algorithm 1 Constructing an oversampled balanced dataset

Input: *main_dir*: Directory containing class folders with images
Output: Oversampled balanced dataset

```
Identify and enumerate all classes in main_dir
Count the number of images per class
max_class_count ← maximum image count across classes
oversample_target ← 3 × max_class_count
for each class c do
    image_count ← count of images in class c
    if image_count < oversample_target then
        Oversample class c up to oversample_target using transform
    end if
    for i ← 1 to oversample_target do
        index ← (i − 1) mod image_count
        image_path ← path of index-th image in class c
        Load image from image_path
        Apply preprocess to the image
        if image_count < max_class_count then
            Apply balance to augment the image
        end if
        Apply transform to the image
        Return image and class label
    end for
end for
```

First, we have the pre-processing function, which is applied to all images, resizing and cropping them to dimensions of 384×384 pixels. To address variations in histopathological image staining, we employ the Reinhard color normalization technique [19]. This method adjusts the color distribution of a source image to match that of a target image, as expressed in Algorithm 2. Selecting an appropriate target image for this procedure requires expertise in the domain; therefore, we rely on an image identified in a previous study [33]. In that study, the authors collaborated with a pathologist to select a suitable image from the Mitosis-Atypia database [34]. For visual reference, the target image and an illustration of the stain normalization process are presented in Figure 8.

Algorithm 2 Reinhard Color Normalization

Input: Source image I_s in RGB, Target image I_t in RGB
Output: Normalized source image I_s' in RGB

Convert I_s from RGB to Lab color space to get L_s, a_s, b_s
Convert I_t from RGB to Lab color space to get L_t, a_t, b_t
Compute mean $\mu_{L_s}, \mu_{a_s}, \mu_{b_s}$ and standard deviation $\sigma_{L_s}, \sigma_{a_s}, \sigma_{b_s}$ of I_s
Compute mean $\mu_{L_t}, \mu_{a_t}, \mu_{b_t}$ and standard deviation $\sigma_{L_t}, \sigma_{a_t}, \sigma_{b_t}$ of I_t
for each channel $C \in \{L, a, b\}$ **do**
    Subtract mean from source: $C_s' \leftarrow C_s - \mu_{C_s}$
    Scale by standard deviation ratio: $C_s'' \leftarrow C_s' \times (\sigma_{C_t} / \sigma_{C_s})$
    Add target mean: $C_s''' \leftarrow C_s'' + \mu_{C_t}$
end for
Merge normalized channels to get Lab image $I_s' \leftarrow \{L_s''', a_s''', b_s'''\}$
Convert I_s' from Lab to RGB color space

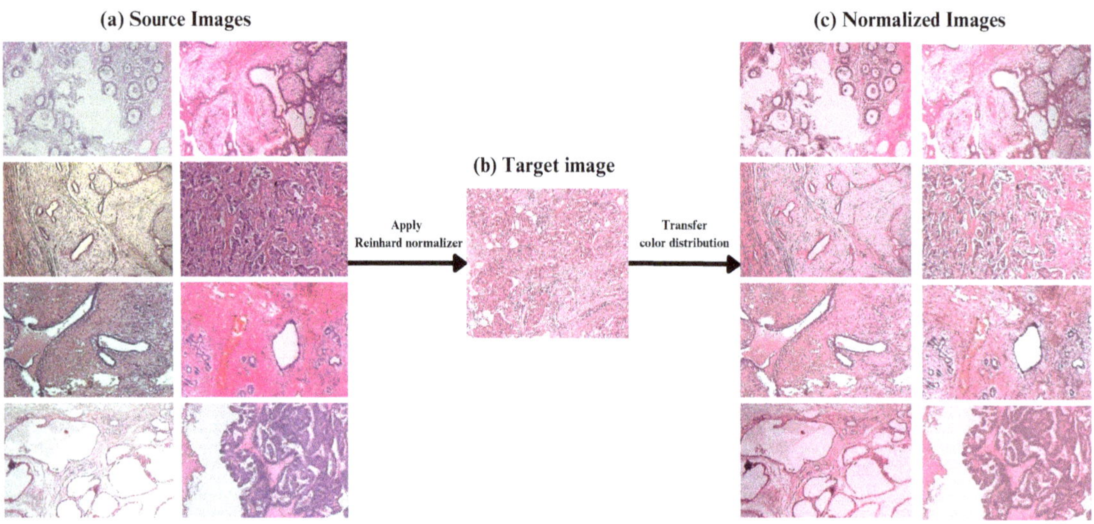

Figure 8. Demonstration of Reinhard stain normalization on breast histopathology images. (**a**) Source images before normalization. (**b**) The target image providing the reference color distribution. (**c**) Images after applying the Reinhard method for color normalization.

Next, we have the balancing function, which aims to equalize the number of samples across all classes. To achieve this, we oversample the minority classes to match the class with the maximum number of samples. This approach utilizes the AugMix [35] image augmentation technique, which produces new, augmented images. This process involves blending several images that have undergone traditional transformations, such as rotation and posterizing. The specific blending weights for each combination generated by AugMix are sampled from a Dirichlet distribution. The advantage of using AugMix is that it allows for the creation of a wide range of image variations. At the same time, it preserves the essential semantic features of the original images, resulting in more robust variations [35].

Finally, in order to artificially increase the training set, traditional augmentations are used to create modified versions of the images. This is particularly important for deep learning models, where the performance is highly dependent on the size and quality of the training data. Thus, we have the transform function, which serves to triple the size of the balanced image classes by geometrically augmenting their respective images using the following transformations:

- Random flips: Images are flipped horizontally and vertically with a probability of 0.5.
- Random rotations: Affine transformations include rotations at random angles from −45 to 45 degrees.
- Random translations: Images are translated vertically and horizontally by up to 10%.
- Random scaling: The size of the images is randomly adjusted by a scaling factor between 0.8 and 1.2.
- Random shearing: Images are sheared at random angles ranging from 0 to 10 degrees.

We also normalize the image tensors in this function to ensure standardized input data. This process adjusts the pixel values in each channel to have a standardized mean and standard deviation. Image normalization is an essential pre-processing step to stabilize the training process and increase convergence speed. When given an image tensor **X** with dimensions (H, W, C), in addition to a sequence of mean values $\mu = (\mu_1, \mu_2, \ldots, \mu_C)$ and standard deviation values $\sigma = (\sigma_1, \sigma_2, \ldots, \sigma_C)$, the normalized image tensor is computed as follows:

$$\mathbf{X}^{\text{norm}}[h, w, c] = \frac{\mathbf{X}[h, w, c] - \mu_c}{\sigma_c} \tag{2}$$

In this equation, $\mathbf{X}[h, w, c]$ denotes the original pixel value at height h, width w, and channel c. The term μ_c represents the mean of the pixel values for channel c, while σ_c stands for the standard deviation of the pixel values for channel c. The normalized tensor pixel values, $\mathbf{X}^{\text{norm}}[h, w, c]$, are acquired by subtracting the mean μ_c from the original value $\mathbf{X}[h, w, c]$, and then, dividing the result by the standard deviation σ_c.

The rationale behind using the two separate functions, balance and transform, is to address two issues in the dataset: class imbalance and limited data. The balance function allows us to apply a more aggressive augmentation strategy specifically to the minority classes, effectively increasing their representation in the dataset without introducing excessive duplication of the existing samples. The transform function then applies a consistent set of geometric transformations across the entire dataset, further expanding the diversity of the data and helping the model to generalize. This approach ensures that class imbalance is mitigated while the overall dataset benefits from a broad range of variations, reflecting the complexities of real-world data.

Some examples of the image augmentations that have been implemented are illustrated in Figure 9.

After applying the data augmentation approach for balancing and oversampling, the resulting training set size is presented in Table 3.

Table 3. Training set after balancing and oversampling.

Magnification	Benign				Malignant				Total
	A	F	PT	TA	DC	LC	MC	PC	
40×	1812	1812	1812	1812	1812	1812	1812	1812	14,496
100×	1896	1896	1896	1896	1896	1896	1896	1896	15,168
200×	1881	1881	1881	1881	1881	1881	1881	1881	15,048
400×	1653	1653	1653	1653	1653	1653	1653	1653	13,224
Sub-type total	7242	7242	7242	7242	7242	7242	7242	7242	57,936
Type total	28,968				28,968				57,936

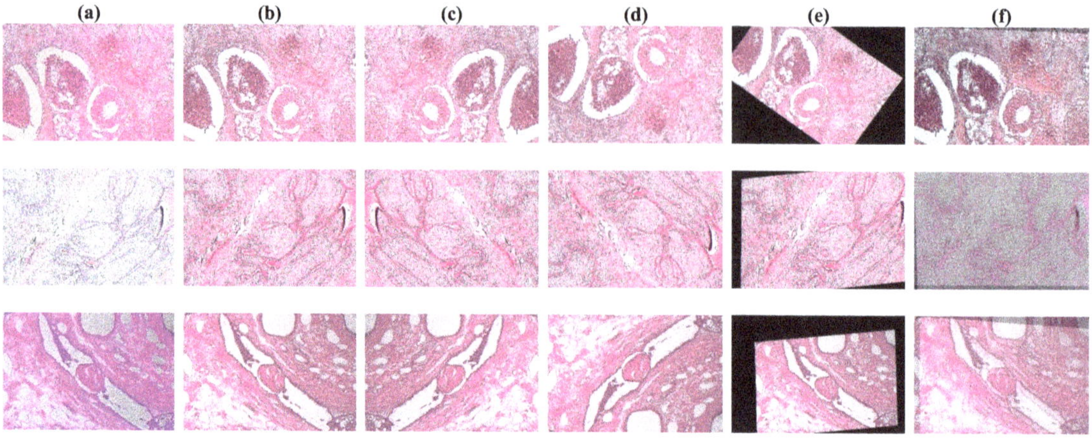

Figure 9. Demonstration of implemented data augmentations. Column (**a**) shows the images in their original state. Column (**b**) shows the images after stain normalization. Columns (**c**,**d**) show the images after horizontal and vertical flips, respectively. Column (**e**) shows the images after random affine transformations, which include scaling, rotation, and translation. Lastly, column (**f**) shows the images after AugMix augmentations.

3.7. Experimental Setup

All experiments were conducted on Google Colaboratory, a cloud-based service that offers computing resources through a hosted Jupyter Notebook environment built on the Python3.12.0 3 Google Compute Engine backend. A Colab Pro subscription was used to gain access to longer runtimes. The runtime resources used were a T4 GPU with 15 GB RAM, 12.7 GB system RAM, and 201.2 GB of disk space. Additionally, Colab enables easy integration of Google Drive, which was used to store and access the dataset, model weights, and log files. The code for this paper is available in the GitHub repository at this link: https://github.com/LamaAldakhil/ECSAnet (accessed on 1 June 2024).

The following sections will specify the Python libraries and training hyperparameters used in our proposed approach.

3.7.1. Python Libraries Used

This research relies on several Python libraries that provide tools for DL and data analysis. Listed in Table 4 are the libraries used, in addition to a brief description of their functions that were relevant to our research.

Table 4. Python libraries.

Library	Function Used
os	Handling file system, directory, and path operations.
time	Handling time-related tasks within code.
math	Computing basic mathematical operations.
torch	Creating the dataset classes and data loaders, loading the optimizer, criterion, and scheduler for model training, and logging model performance using Tensorboard.
torchvision	Access to V2 transforms for image data augmentations and loading pre-trained models.
PIL	Opening and manipulating images in the dataset.
collections	Counting the frequency of samples in dataset classes.
datetime	Access to the current date and time for model run logs.
uuid	Generating unique identifiers for model logs.
numpy	Handling data type conversions and mathematical operations.
sklearn [36]	Calculating different evaluation metrics and accessing data pre-processing tools.
seaborn [37]	Plotting confusion matrix.
matplotlib [38]	Plotting images and confusion matrix.
staintools	Reinhard stain normalizer.
grad-cam [39]	Model explainability methods to diagnose model predictions.

3.7.2. Model Fine-Tuning

The PyTorch library was utilized to build the DL models. PyTorch is a well-known library in the DL community and is widely used for many computer vision applications. It is a well-rounded library encompassing all the tools necessary for designing, building, and training DL models. Through this library, we built our pre-trained models, including our main baseline model, EfficientNetV2-S. To develop our proposed model, we created a subclass of the EfficientNetV2-S architecture. This approach enables building upon the existing model, incorporating the proposed improvements, and fine-tuning it for the task involving eight image classes.

Additionally, transfer learning was employed. Transfer learning reduces resource usage and training time compared to training from scratch. Moreover, it enables the model to effectively learn low-level features such as edges, textures, and colors, enhancing performance and minimizing the challenges associated with limited image data. The pre-trained weights were sourced from a model originally trained on the ImageNet dataset, which consists of 1000 image classes and contains over 14 million samples.

3.7.3. Training Hyperparameters

In ML, the performance of algorithms depends significantly on the training hyperparameters. We initiated the experiments with a batch size of 16 images. This number balances computational load and training efficiency, as it requires less memory than larger batches, making it suitable in environments with limited computing resources.

To avoid overfitting, where a model becomes too closely fitted to the training data and less able to generalize, we limited the training to 50 epochs. Additionally, an early stopping mechanism was used to halt training if the validation loss did not improve after 25 epochs, thereby preserving computational resources and model integrity.

For calculating loss during training and validation, we used the cross-entropy loss function as a criterion. In a multi-class classification task, this function is calculated using the following formula:

$$CrossEntropyLoss = -\sum_{c=1}^{M} y_{o,c} \log(p_{o,c}) \tag{3}$$

Here, M is the number of class categories, $y_{o,c}$ indicates the presence or absence of class c in observation o, and $p_{o,c}$ is the predicted probability of observation o belonging to class c.

As an optimizer for the loss function, stochastic gradient descent (SGD) was selected. SGD updates model parameters by calculating the gradient of the loss function based on a random data subset. The model's weights are adjusted iteratively according to the following rule:

$$w_{t+1} = w_t - \gamma_t \nabla_w Q(z_t, w_t) \tag{4}$$

In this equation, w represents the weights that are updated by a time step $t+1$ by taking the previous weights w_t and adjusting them in the direction opposite to the gradient of the loss function at the current step. This adjustment is scaled by a factor of γ_t, which is the learning rate at time t. The gradient, denoted as $\nabla_w Q(z_t, w_t)$, reflects the direction and magnitude of the steepest ascent of the loss function Q with respect to the weights, given the current input z_t [40].

The learning rate γ_t set for SGD is 0.001. This is a value used commonly for adapting pre-trained models that can help prevent rapid losses of previously learned information and increases in error rates.

Lastly, the ReduceLROnPlateau was chosen as a learning rate scheduler based on its effectiveness in decreasing the learning rate when progress stalls. It observes the validation loss and, after a specified 'patience' period without improvement, reduces the learning rate by a factor of 0.1, aiding the model's convergence toward better performance.

Table 5 gives a summary of the selected hyperparameters.

Table 5. Training hyperparameters.

Hyperparameter	Value
Learning Rate	0.001
Weight Decay	0.01
Batch Size	16
Number of Epochs	50
Loss Function	Cross-entropy loss
Optimizer	SGD
Learning Rate Scheduler	ReduceLROnPlateau
Early Stopping	Patience = 25 epochs

3.8. Evaluation Metrics

In our experiments, we assessed the different DL models using various evaluation metrics. These metrics are crucial for understanding various aspects of model performance, including precision, accuracy, F1 score, sensitivity, and specificity. Additionally, we utilize visual tools such as the ROC curve and its associated AUC value to gauge the model's discriminative ability. The Jaccard index and the confusion matrix provide further insights into the model's classification capabilities. The following is a detailed breakdown of each evaluation metric, along with their mathematical equations, if present:

- Precision: This performance metric evaluates the precision of predictions made by a model by computing the ratio of true positives to the total number of positive predictions made by the model, as shown in the following equation:

$$Precision = \frac{TP}{TP + FP} \tag{5}$$

- Accuracy: This metric measures the extent to which instances within a dataset are correctly classified, representing the ratio of accurately classified instances to the total number of instances in the dataset, as shown in the following equation:

$$Accuracy = \frac{TP + TN}{TP + TN + FP + FN} \tag{6}$$

- Sensitivity: This metric represents the true positive rate and evaluates a classification model's ability to identify positive instances correctly. It is equal to the recall metric, and it is also calculated using the same equation as recall:

$$Sensitivity = Recall = \frac{TP}{TP + FN} \tag{7}$$

- Specificity: This metric represents the true negative rate and evaluates the model's capability to identify negative instances correctly. It is calculated using the following equation:

$$Specificity = \frac{TN}{FP + TN} \tag{8}$$

- F1 score: This metric provides the harmonic mean of precision and recall to comprehensively evaluate the model's ability to achieve both high precision and recall simultaneously. It is calculated using the following equation:

$$F1 = \frac{2 \times Precision \times Recall}{Precision + Recall} = \frac{2 \times TP}{2 \times TP + FP + FN} \tag{9}$$

- AUC-ROC: The ROC curve is a graphical representation that depicts the association between the true positive rate ($Sensitivity$) and the false positive rate ($1 - Specificity$) at various classification thresholds. Meanwhile, the AUC is a scalar value that summarizes the overall performance of a classifier based on the ROC curve. Ranging from

0 to 1, a higher AUC indicates superior classifier performance. AUC is calculated as the area under the $Sensitivity$-$(1 - Specificity)$ curve.

- Jaccard index: This metric, which is also called the Jaccard similarity coefficient, measures the similarity between two sets by comparing a set of predicted labels for a sample to the corresponding set of labels in another sample [41]. The following equation calculates the similarity of two sets U and V:

$$Jaccard(U, V) = \frac{|U \cap V|}{|U \cup V|} \tag{10}$$

- Confusion matrix: The evaluation of an ML model's accuracy often involves the utilization of a confusion matrix, particularly in the context of classification problems. This matrix proves particularly valuable when dealing with imbalanced datasets [42]. Confusion matrices visually represent predicted versus true class labels by plotting instances of each category along matrix rows and columns. Row entries represent actual data classes, while column entries denote predicted classes, offering insights into true positives, false negatives, false positives, and true negatives.

4. Results

This section will present the quantitative results, the ablation study, and the comparative analysis.

4.1. Quantitative Results

In this paper, we proposed the ECSAnet model for the classification of multi-class breast histopathological images using the BreakHis dataset. The performance curves during model training and validation are illustrated in Figures 10 and 11. As seen in the figures, the model's performance during training reaches convergence around the 25th epoch and remains consistent thereafter. The dips observed in the validation curves are addressed by a learning rate reduction, which consequently improves performance in the following epochs. The highest validation accuracies, coupled with the lowest losses, were 94.2%, 91.8%, 91.5%, and 91.7% for the 40×, 100×, 200×, and 400× magnifications, respectively.

Whereas the highest testing accuracies achieved were, 94.2%, 92.96%, 88.41%, and 89.42% for 40×, 100×, 200×, and 400× magnification factors, respectively.

The model exhibited excellent generalization on the 40× and 100× magnifications test set. However, it experienced accuracy reductions of 3.09% and 2.28% for the 200× and 400× magnifications, respectively.

In Tables 6–9, the ECSAnet classification results using the test set are listed for each breast tissue sub-type and each magnification factor. Additionally, the confusion matrices for the classification are depicted in Figure 12.

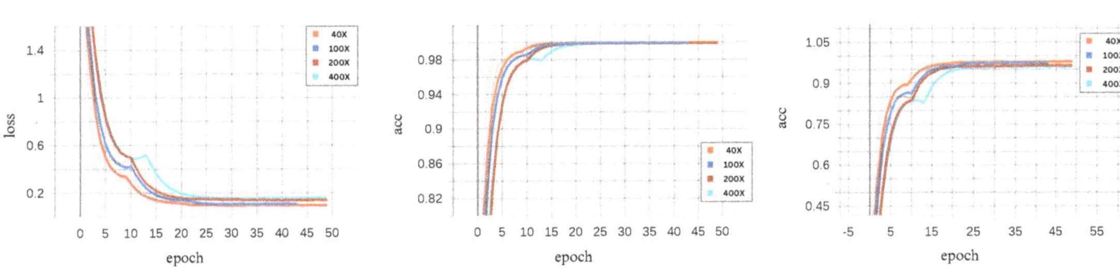

(a) Loss curve (b) ROC curve (c) Accuracy curve

Figure 10. ECSAnet performance on the training set across magnification factors.

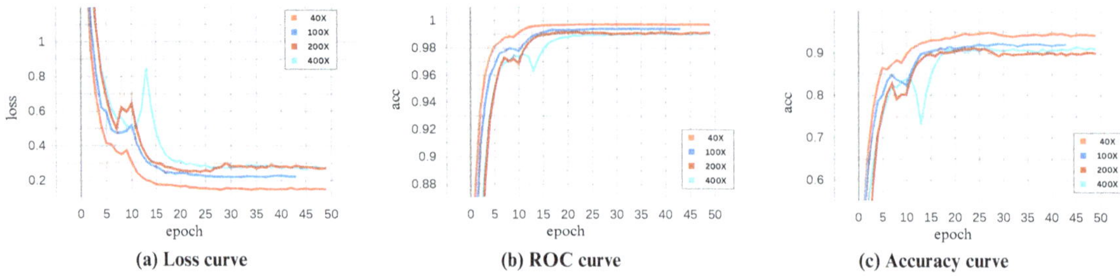

Figure 11. ECSAnet performance on the validation set across magnification factors.

Table 6. ECSAnet classification results for each class on the 40× magnification test set.

Class	Precision (%)	Sensitivity (%)	Specificity (%)	F1 Score (%)	Support
A	100	100	100	100	13
DC	96	92	97.48	94	88
F	96	100	99.45	98	26
LC	71	94	96.86	81	16
MC	95	95	99.46	95	21
PC	93	87	99.48	90	15
PT	100	92	100	96	12
TA	100	100	100	100	16
Accuracy				94	207
Macro Average	94	95	99.09	94	207
Weighted Average	95	94	98.23	94	207

Table 7. ECSAnet classification results for each class on the 100× magnification test set.

Class	Precision (%)	Sensitivity (%)	Specificity (%)	F1 Score (%)	Support
A	100	92	100	96	12
DC	93	96	94.26	94	91
F	96	88	99.47	92	26
LC	78	78	97.95	78	18
MC	95	91	99.47	93	23
PC	94	100	99.49	97	15
PT	92	92	99.50	92	13
TA	100	100	100	100	15
Accuracy				93	213
Macro Average	93	92	98.77	93	213
Weighted Average	93	93	96.08	93	213

Table 8. ECSAnet classification results for each class on the 200× magnification test set.

Class	Precision (%)	Sensitivity (%)	Specificity (%)	F1 Score (%)	Support
A	92	92	99.49	92	12
DC	89	94	90.6	91	90
F	86	86	97.77	86	28
LC	71	71	97.37	71	17
MC	88	75	98.93	81	20
PC	100	86	100	92	14
PT	100	83	100	91	12
TA	93	100	99.48	97	14
Accuracy				88	207
Macro Average	90	86	97.82	88	207
Weighted Average	89	88	90.49	88	207

Table 9. ECSAnet classification results for each class on the 400× magnification test set.

Class	Precision (%)	Sensitivity (%)	Specificity (%)	F1 Score (%)	Support
A	100	100	100	100	11
DC	89	95	91.74	92	80
F	85	88	97.56	86	25
LC	77	67	98.28	71	15
MC	89	94	98.83	92	18
PC	100	80	100	89	15
PT	100	83	100	91	12
TA	85	85	98.86	85	13
Accuracy				89	189
Macro Average	91	87	98.16	87	189
Weighted Average	90	89	95.8	89	189

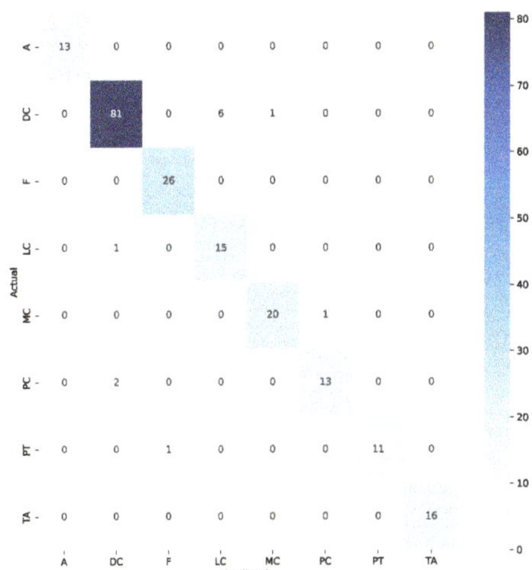

(**a**) 40×

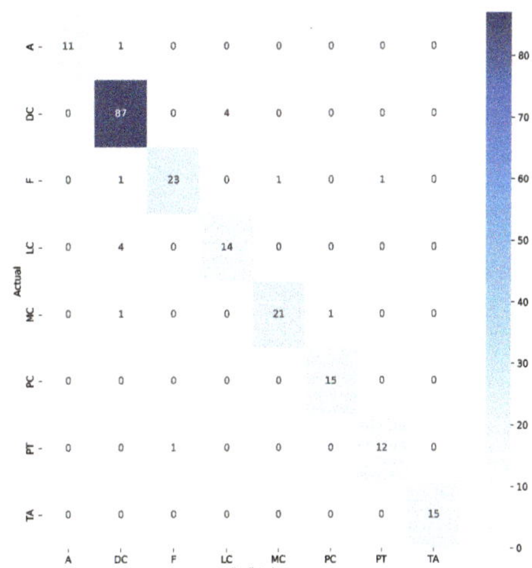

(**b**) 100×

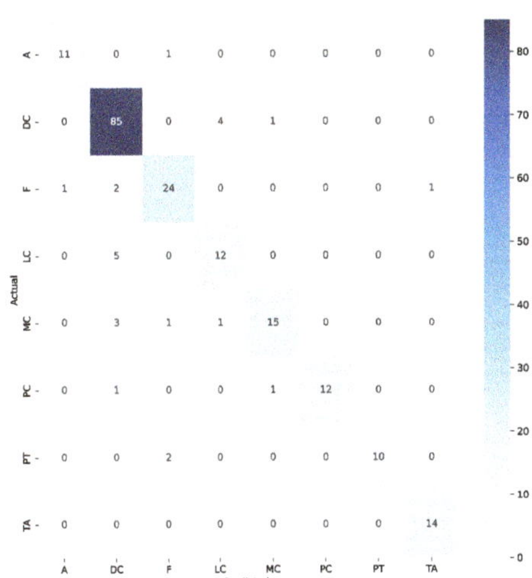

(**c**) 200×

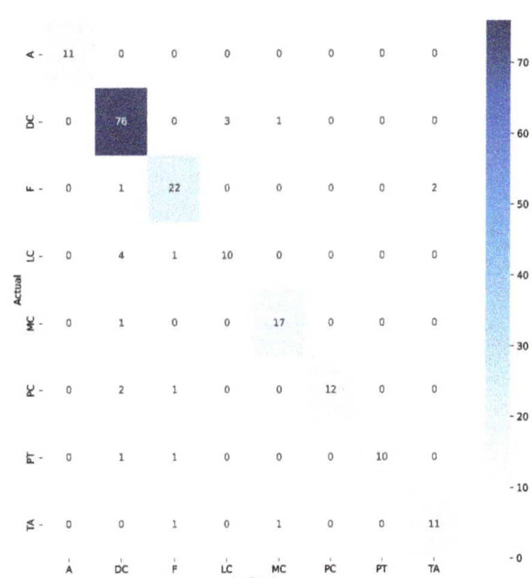

(**d**) 400×

Figure 12. Test set confusion matrices for ECSAnet across magnification factors.

Finally, we employed gradient-weighted class activation mapping (Grad-CAM) to generate visual explanations highlighting the regions within breast tissue images deemed most significant by the model in predicting tumor sub-types. Representative samples of these Grad-CAM visualizations are presented in Figure 13. Utilizing this technique, we can interpret the decision-making process of the model, which is particularly crucial in the classification of breast histopathology images.

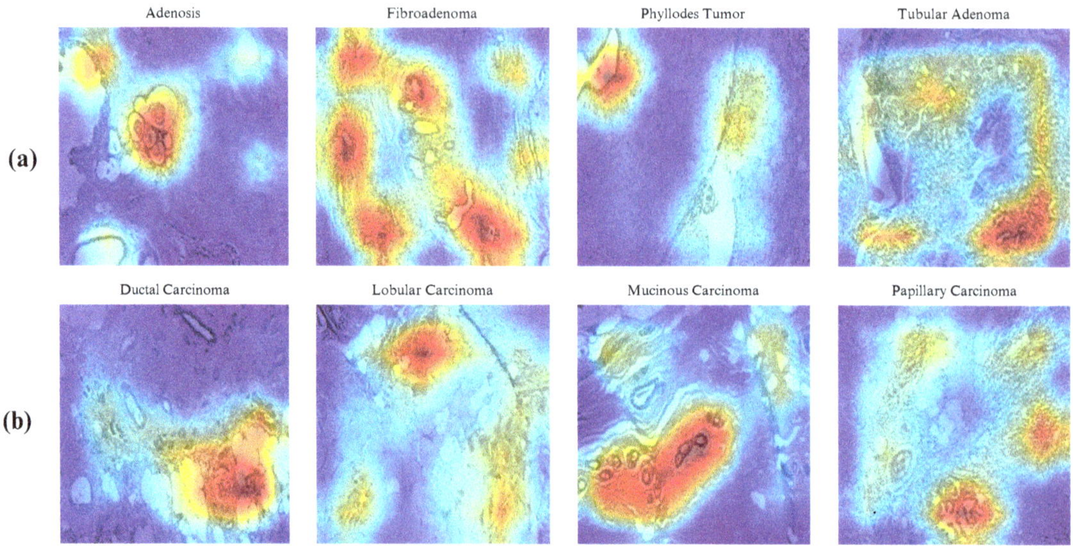

Figure 13. Regions of interest identified by the model using Grad-CAM. (**a**) shows example images of benign classes while (**b**) shows examples for the malignant classes.

4.2. Ablation Study

To understand the effects and interactions between the components we have added to ECSAnet, we conducted an ablation study. In this study, we conducted five experiments on the 40× magnification data, in which we achieved the best results. The five experiments were (i) ECSAnet without data augmentation, (ii) ECSAnet without balancing data augmentation, (iii) ECSAnet without the addition of the CBAM block, (iv) ECSAnet without the additional FC layers, and (v) ECSAnet without applying stain normalization as a pre-processing step.

The validation performance of each approach during training is compared to the ECSAnet model in Figure 14.

In addition, the metrics achieved are shown in Table 10, demonstrating each approach's performance on the test set.

The results indicate that without applying any data augmentation to the dataset during the training process, the model performance suffers drastically, by 17.87%. This shows that the data augmentation strategy was effective in reducing overfitting and increasing model prediction accuracy.

Subsequently, training the model without class-balancing augmentation showed a small decrease in accuracy, by 0.96%.

Additionally, we have found that adding FC layers to the model structure complements the CBAM block, enhancing the base model's accuracy in classifying breast tissue images. Specifically, the CBAM block improved the model's capability to select the most informative features, while the FC layers increased the model's learning capacity, allowing it to learn refined features more effectively. This synergy is evident by a notable reduction in accuracy when either component is excluded.

Without applying stain normalization, the model showed a validation accuracy of 95.5% during training, a value higher than we saw when we applied it, which was 94.2%. However, the impact of stain normalization becomes more apparent in the test set, where the normalized approach sustained its accuracy, while the non-normalized approach experienced a decrease of 2.75%. In this case, the stain normalization increased the model's generalization ability.

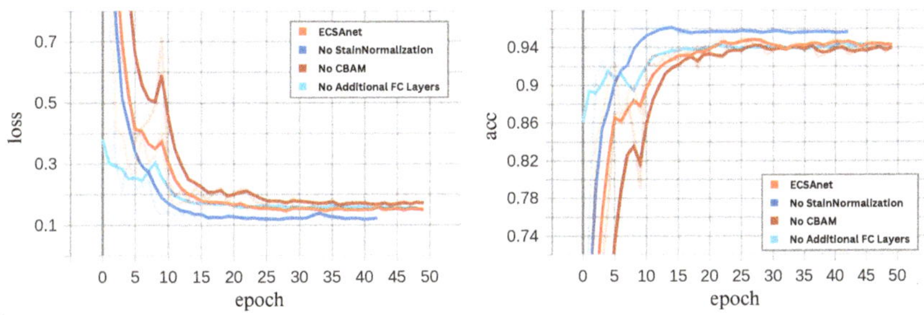

(a) Loss curve **(b) Accuracy curve**

Figure 14. Comparison of the ECSAnet's performance curves against variations with removed elements.

Table 10. Ablation results on the 40× magnification test set.

Model	Acc. (%)	Prec. (%)	F1 (%)	Jac. (%)	AUC (%)
ECSAnet+ No data augmentation	76.33	71.50	72.56	63.53	97.53
ECSAnet+ No balancing augmentations	93.24	93.82	93.35	87.98	99.39
ECSAnet+ No CBAM	92.75	93.58	92.96	87.46	99.67
ECSAnet+ No additional FC layers	91.79	92.25	91.93	85.69	99.70
ECSAnet+ No stain normalization	92.75	93.03	92.74	86.99	**99.85**
ECSAnet	**94.2**	**94.81**	**94.34**	**89.64**	99.62

Bold fonts indicate the best Values.

4.3. Comparative Analysis

As a final evaluation of our results, we conducted a comparative analysis using six state-of-the-art models: AlexNet, DenseNet121, InceptionV3, ResNet50, VGG16, and lastly, the base model EfficientNetV2-S. All models were trained under the same settings as ECSAnet. In Figures 15–18, the validation loss and accuracy of each model are compared with ECSAnet for each magnification factor: 40×, 100×, 200×, and 400×, respectively.

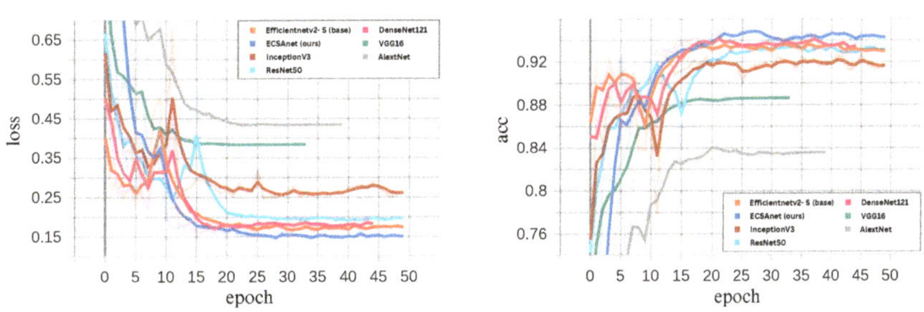

(a) Loss curve **(b) Accuracy curve**

Figure 15. ECSAnet validation performance compared to other state-of-the-art models on the 40× magnification.

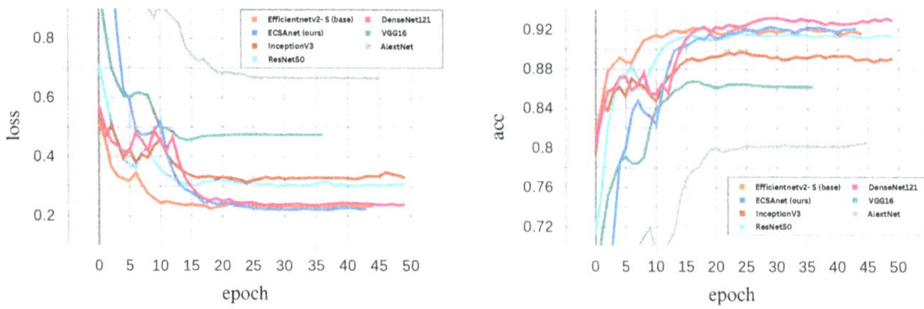

(a) Loss curve **(b) Accuracy curve**

Figure 16. ECSAnet validation performance compared to other state-of-the-art models on the 100× magnification.

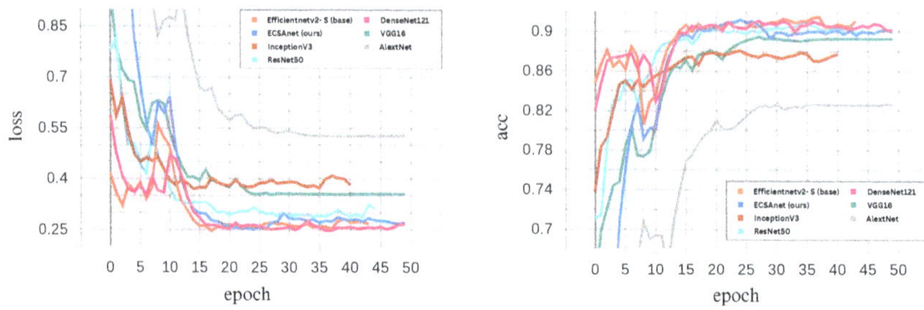

(a) Loss curve **(b) Accuracy curve**

Figure 17. ECSAnet validation performance compared to other state-of-the-art models on the 200× magnification.

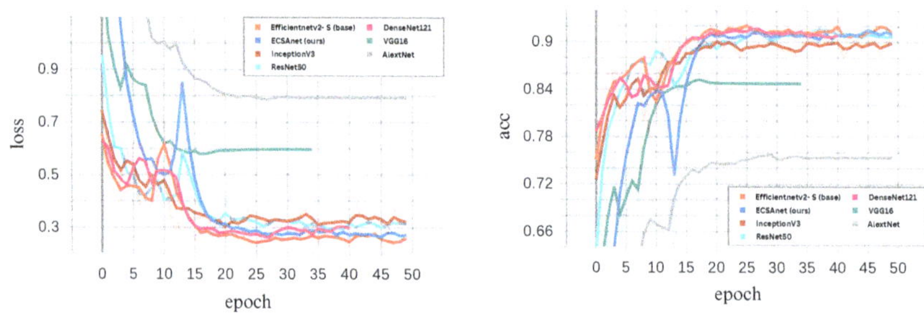

(a) Loss curve **(b) Accuracy curve**

Figure 18. ECSAnet validation performance compared to other state-of-the-art models on the 400× magnification.

The testing metrics of the models are detailed in Table 11. Our proposed model outperformed the other models at the 40×, 100×, and 400× magnifications across most metrics, whereas at 200×, DenseNet121 showed a minimal increase in accuracy of 0.48% compared to our model. Notably, InceptionNetV3 rivaled our model in accuracy at 100× but with a lower precision. In addition, at 200× magnification, our model's accuracy did not exceed that of the base model or ResNet50.

Table 11. ECSAnet performance on the test set compared to state-of-the-art models.

Model	Magnification	Acc. (%)	Prec. (%)	F1 (%)	Jac. (%)	AUC (%)
AlexNet	40×	82.13	84.42	82.50	70.81	98.46
	100×	78.40	80.36	78.52	64.93	97.70
	200×	77.29	79.82	77.96	64.92	96.28
	400×	74.07	74.36	73.67	59.79	95.91
DenseNet121	40×	91.30	92.15	91.53	85.09	**99.78**
	100×	92.02	92.18	92.05	85.75	99.44
	200×	**88.89**	**89.51**	**88.76**	**80.25**	**98.96**
	400×	86.77	87.38	86.30	76.63	98.85
InceptionNetV3	40×	90.82	91.89	91.09	84.21	99.60
	100×	**92.96**	92.97	92.92	**87.23**	99.20
	200×	87.44	87.63	87.32	78.38	98.10
	400×	84.13	84.58	83.24	72.57	98.13
ResNet50	40×	92.27	93.02	92.49	86.70	99.60
	100×	91.55	91.53	91.43	84.60	99.23
	200×	88.41	88.83	88.34	79.38	98.47
	400×	84.66	85.47	84.05	73.51	**99.25**
VGG16	40×	87.44	89.46	87.74	78.81	99.27
	100×	85.45	86.22	85.48	75.14	98.61
	200×	83.09	83.2	83.10	71.65	98.17
	400×	82.54	82.27	82.1	70.79	97.08
EfficientNetV2-S (base)	40×	93.24	93.94	93.41	88.07	99.70
	100×	90.61	91.02	90.68	83.55	99.44
	200×	88.41	88.38	88.32	79.73	98.28
	400×	87.30	87.89	87.09	77.53	99.09
ECSAnet (ours)	40×	**94.2**	**94.81**	**94.34**	**89.64**	99.62
	100×	**92.96**	**93.03**	**92.94**	87.19	**99.66**
	200×	88.41	88.6	88.32	79.65	98.34
	400×	**89.42**	**89.59**	**89.29**	**81.19**	99.1

Bold values indicate the highest values. Recall is omitted because it is equal to accuracy due to balanced image classes.

Furthermore, we compare the Grad-CAMs visual explanations for the same sample from each breast tumor sub-type across all models. In Figure 19, the Grad-CAM heat maps are presented. The decision-making interpretation of the models shows the most important regions of interest used for their decisions. With the incorporation of CBAM, the ECSAnet is capable of generating more accurate attention heat maps, making it more explainable than other models. Additionally, based on model performance, we assume that the features learned by ECSAnet were effective for correctly classifying the instances. However, the selection of regions made by each model needs to be assessed by domain experts to validate their accuracy and determine whether the ECSAnet model is truly effective.

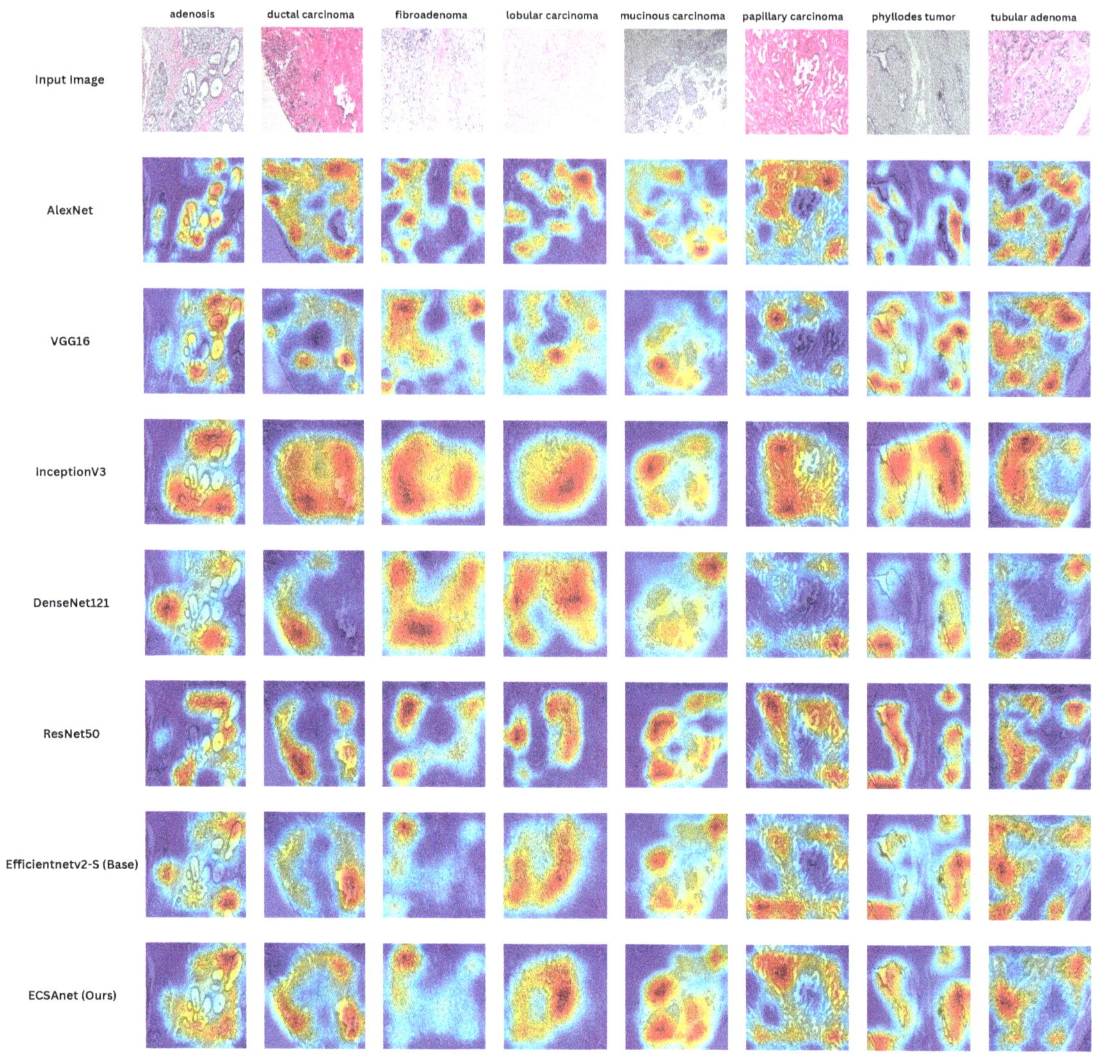

Figure 19. Grad-CAM visual explanations, illustrating the predictive focus areas for each class across models, descending vertically from the least accurate (AlexNet) to the most accurate (ECSAnet).

5. Discussion

5.1. Main Findings

From our experiments, three characteristics become clear, upon which we base our main findings:

- The impact of magnification: A trend in our results showed that as the magnification factor increases, the model's classification performance decreases; this observation can be seen in all the models that we have utilized. Similar results have been reported in other studies, such as Li et al.'s [25] binary classification and Boumaraf et al.'s [22] multi-class classification. Other studies have reported lower classification performance at 400× magnification specifically, such as [24,26]. Sheikh et al. [12] reported a counterpoint, saying that their approach performed better at higher magnifications. This contrast in findings indicates that the impact of magnification on classification accuracy is not yet fully understood and may be influenced by image processing techniques or specificities of model architectures, which require further investigation.

- Compatibility: Through our ablation study, we have found that the CBAM alone did not yield a performance improvement. When the CBAM was incorporated without additional FC layers, a decrease in model accuracy was noted. However, the model's performance improved when we combined the CBAM with the implemented FC layers. This indicates that while the CBAM is adept at directing attention to salient features in the input data, the subsequent learning within the FC layers capitalizes on this refined focus to enhance the model's accuracy. This suggests that there is a clear compatibility between our added components.
- Generalizability: Applying Reinhard stain normalization as a pre-processing step increased our model's generalization capabilities on unseen test images, as confirmed in our ablation study. This enhancement aligns with the positive outcomes reported in studies that utilized the Reinhard stain normalization technique, such as [12]. However, it is important to note that the mentioned study did not quantitatively assess the extent to which stain normalization contributes to the improved generalization of their model. Our study fills this gap by evaluating the impact of stain normalization on model performance.

5.2. Model Strengths and Limitations

Our model tended to misclassify instances of various classes as DC. As observed from the lower specificity recorded for the DC class and decreased precision for other classes, including F, LC, MC, and PC. The misclassifications indicate intra-class similarities between the features of these classes and the DC class that led to confusion by the model.

As observed from the confusion matrices in Figure 12, the confusion between LC and DC was particularly notable across different magnifications. Specifically, the model misclassified LC images as DC, with six occurrences at 40× magnification and four occurrences each at 100× and 200× magnifications, decreasing slightly to three at 400×. Conversely, DC images were also often misclassified as LC, occurring once at 40×, increasing to four times at 100×, peaking at five times at 200×, and then, slightly reducing to four times at 400× magnification.

On the other hand, the model could classify A and TA classes with high accuracy and, in most cases, showed perfect scores. Moreover, it exhibited high specificity for all classes across magnifications, indicating the model's ability to accurately identify true negatives and effectively minimize false positives.

6. Future Work

There are several ways to improve and expand our model's capabilities. Future work may include conducting clinical trials to test ECSAnet's effectiveness in real-world settings. Other key objectives involve enhancing classification accuracy for higher magnification settings and fine-tuning ECSAnet for benign vs. malignant binary classification. Moreover, we aim to develop the model's ability to classify images at the patient level and achieve magnification-independent breast tumor multi-classification. To further validate ECSAnet's robustness, we plan to test it on more extensive breast tumor histopathological datasets. Additionally, we will explore other attention mechanisms, experiment with different stain normalization techniques, such as Macenko and Vahadane, and investigate the effectiveness of various data augmentation methods, including patch generation and GANs.

7. Conclusions

Breast cancer remains one of the deadliest diseases worldwide, making the improvement of early diagnostic methods a critical area of research. In response to this challenge, we introduced the ECSAnet model architecture to enhance the accuracy and efficiency of multi-classification tasks in histopathological breast cancer image analysis. ECSAnet can extract discriminative breast cancer features efficiently along the spatial and channel dimensions using a CBAM attention mechanism with an increased learning capacity. The performance of ECSAnet has been evaluated on the BreakHis dataset at four magnification levels (40×, 100×, 200×, 400×). An ablation study has verified the importance of the added components in our model. Our model outperformed most state-of-the-art models in testing under the same training settings, attaining accuracies between 88.41% and 94.2% across magnification factors. The findings of this paper show positive outcomes that can help with the advancement of current clinical breast cancer diagnostic approaches, in addition to other cancers characterized by similar morphological cellular features [43].

Author Contributions: Conceptualization, H.F.A.; methodology, H.F.A. and L.A.A.; software, L.A.A.; validation, L.A.A.; formal analysis, L.A.A.; investigation, L.A.A.; resources, L.A.A.; data curation, L.A.A.; writing—original draft preparation, L.A.A.; writing—review and editing, H.F.A. and S.S.A.; visualization, L.A.A.; supervision, H.F.A.; project administration, H.F.A.; funding acquisition, H.F.A. All authors have read and agreed to the published version of the manuscript.

Funding: The researchers would like to thank the Deanship of Graduate Studies and Scientific Research at Qassim University for financial support (QU-APC-2024-9/1).

Institutional Review Board Statement: Not applicable.

Informed Consent Statement: Not applicable.

Data Availability Statement: The data presented in this study is available in the Breast Cancer Histopathological Database at: https://web.inf.ufpr.br/vri/databases/breast-cancer-histopathological-database-breakhis (accessed on 1 June 2024) [32].

Conflicts of Interest: The authors declare no conflicts of interest.

References

1. Breast Cancer. Available online: https://www.who.int/news-room/fact-sheets/detail/breast-cancer (accessed on 29 April 2024).
2. Breast Cancer Signs and Symptoms | Most Common Symptoms. Available online: https://www.cancer.org/cancer/types/breast-cancer/screening-tests-and-early-detection/breast-cancer-signs-and-symptoms.html (accessed on 15 December 2023).
3. Mahmood, T.; Li, J.; Pei, Y.; Akhtar, F.; Imran, A.; Rehman, K.U. A Brief Survey on Breast Cancer Diagnostic with Deep Learning Schemes Using Multi-Image Modalities. *IEEE Access* **2020**, *8*, 165779–165809. [CrossRef]
4. Shahidi, F.; Mohd Daud, S.; Abas, H.; Ahmad, N.A.; Maarop, N. Breast Cancer Classification Using Deep Learning Approaches and Histopathology Image: A Comparison Study. *IEEE Access* **2020**, *8*, 187531–187552. [CrossRef]
5. Mridha, M.F.; Hamid, M.A.; Monowar, M.M.; Keya, A.J.; Ohi, A.Q.; Islam, M.R.; Kim, J.M. A Comprehensive Survey on Deep-Learning-Based Breast Cancer Diagnosis. *Cancers* **2021**, *13*, 6116. [CrossRef]
6. Din, N.M.U.; Dar, R.A.; Rasool, M.; Assad, A. Breast cancer detection using deep learning: Datasets, methods, and challenges ahead. *Comput. Biol. Med.* **2022**, *149*, 106073. [CrossRef]
7. LeCun, Y.; Bengio, Y.; Hinton, G. Deep learning. *Nature* **2015**, *521*, 436–444. [CrossRef]
8. Anaya-Isaza, A.; Mera-Jiménez, L.; Zequera-Diaz, M. An overview of deep learning in medical imaging. *Inform. Med. Unlocked* **2021**, *26*, 100723. [CrossRef]
9. Deng, S.; Zhang, X.; Yan, W.; Chang, E.; Fan, Y.; Lai, M.; Xu, Y. Deep learning in digital pathology image analysis: A survey. *Front. Med.* **2020**, *14*, 470–487. [CrossRef]
10. Ragab, D.A.; Sharkas, M.; Marshall, S.; Ren, J. Breast cancer detection using deep convolutional neural networks and support vector machines. *PeerJ* **2019**, *7*, e6201. [CrossRef]
11. Wang, Y.; Acs, B.; Robertson, S.; Liu, B.; Solorzano, L.; Wählby, C.; Hartman, J.; Rantalainen, M. Improved breast cancer histological grading using deep learning. *Ann. Oncol.* **2022**, *33*, 89–98. [CrossRef]
12. Sheikh, T.S.; Lee, Y.; Cho, M. Histopathological Classification of Breast Cancer Images Using a Multi-Scale Input and Multi-Feature Network. *Cancers* **2020**, *12*, 2031. [CrossRef]
13. Chen, J.; Srinivas, C. Automatic Lymphocyte Detection in H&E Images with Deep Neural Networks. *arXiv* **2016**, arXiv:1612.03217. https://doi.org/10.48550/arXiv.1612.03217.
14. Couture, H.D.; Williams, L.A.; Geradts, J.; Nyante, S.J.; Butler, E.N.; Marron, J.S.; Perou, C.M.; Troester, M.A.; Niethammer, M. Image analysis with deep learning to predict breast cancer grade, ER status, histologic subtype, and intrinsic subtype. *npj Breast Cancer* **2018**, *4*, 30. [CrossRef]
15. van der Laak, J.; Litjens, G.; Ciompi, F. Deep learning in histopathology: The path to the clinic. *Nat. Med.* **2021**, *27*, 775–784. [CrossRef]

16. Nasser, M.; Yusof, U.K. Deep Learning Based Methods for Breast Cancer Diagnosis: A Systematic Review and Future Direction. *Diagnostics* **2023**, *13*, 161. [CrossRef]
17. Tan, M.; Le, Q. EfficientNetV2: Smaller models and faster training. In Proceedings of the 38th International Conference on Machine Learning, Virtual, 18–24 July 2021; Meila, M., Zhang, T., Eds.; PMLR: New York, NY, USA, 2021; Volume 139, pp. 10096–10106.
18. Woo, S.; Park, J.; Lee, J.Y.; Kweon, I.S. CBAM: Convolutional Block Attention Module. In Proceedings of the Computer Vision—ECCV, Munich, Germany, 8–14 September 2018; Ferrari, V., Hebert, M., Sminchisescu, C., Weiss, Y., Eds.; Springer: Cham, Switzerland, 2018; pp. 3–19. [CrossRef]
19. Reinhard, E.; Ashikhmin, M.; Gooch, B.; Shirley, P. Color Transfer between Images. *IEEE Comput. Graph. Appl.* **2001**, *21*, 34–41. [CrossRef]
20. Pan, S.J.; Yang, Q. A Survey on Transfer Learning. *IEEE Trans. Knowl. Data Eng.* **2010**, *22*, 1345–1359. [CrossRef]
21. Yari, Y.; Nguyen, T.V.; Nguyen, H.T. Deep Learning Applied for Histological Diagnosis of Breast Cancer. *IEEE Access* **2020**, *8*, 162432–162448. [CrossRef]
22. Boumaraf, S.; Liu, X.; Zheng, Z.; Ma, X.; Ferkous, C. A new transfer learning based approach to magnification dependent and independent classification of breast cancer in histopathological images. *Biomed. Signal Process. Control* **2021**, *63*, 102192. [CrossRef]
23. Guo, M.H.; Xu, T.X.; Liu, J.J.; Liu, Z.N.; Jiang, P.T.; Mu, T.J.; Zhang, S.H.; Martin, R.R.; Cheng, M.M.; Hu, S.M. Attention Mechanisms in Computer Vision: A Survey. *Comput. Vis. Media* **2022**, *8*, 331–368. [CrossRef]
24. Toğaçar, M.; Özkurt, K.B.; Ergen, B.; Cömert, Z. BreastNet: A novel convolutional neural network model through histopathological images for the diagnosis of breast cancer. *Phys. A Stat. Mech. Its Appl.* **2020**, *545*, 123592. [CrossRef]
25. Li, X.; Shen, X.; Zhou, Y.; Wang, X.; Li, T.Q. Classification of breast cancer histopathological images using interleaved DenseNet with SENet (IDSNet). *PLoS ONE* **2020**, *15*, e0232127. [CrossRef] [PubMed]
26. Zou, Y.; Zhang, J.; Huang, S.; Liu, B. Breast cancer histopathological image classification using attention high-order deep network. *Int. J. Imaging Syst. Technol.* **2022**, *32*, 266–279. [CrossRef]
27. Gu, J.; Wang, Z.; Kuen, J.; Ma, L.; Shahroudy, A.; Shuai, B.; Liu, T.; Wang, X.; Wang, G.; Cai, J.; et al. Recent advances in convolutional neural networks. *Pattern Recognit.* **2018**, *77*, 354–377. [CrossRef]
28. O'Shea, K.; Nash, R. An Introduction to Convolutional Neural Networks. *arXiv* **2015**, arXiv:1511.08458. https://doi.org/10.48550/arXiv.1511.08458.
29. Tan, M.; Le, Q.V. EfficientNet: Rethinking Model Scaling for Convolutional Neural Networks. In Proceedings of the 36th International Conference on Machine Learning, ICML 2019, Long Beach, CA, USA, 9–15 June 2019; Chaudhuri, K., Salakhutdinov, R., Eds.; PMLR: New York, NY, USA, 2019; Volume 97, pp. 6105–6114.
30. Sandler, M.; Howard, A.; Zhu, M.; Zhmoginov, A.; Chen, L.C. MobileNetV2: Inverted Residuals and Linear Bottlenecks. In Proceedings of the 2018 IEEE/CVF Conference on Computer Vision and Pattern Recognition, Salt Lake City, UT, USA, 18–22 June 2018; pp. 4510–4520. [CrossRef]
31. Gupta, S.; Akin, B. Accelerator-aware Neural Network Design using AutoML. *arXiv* **2020**, arXiv:2003.02838. https://doi.org/10.48550/arXiv.2003.02838.
32. Spanhol, F.A.; Oliveira, L.S.; Petitjean, C.; Heutte, L. A Dataset for Breast Cancer Histopathological Image Classification. *IEEE Trans. Biomed. Eng.* **2016**, *63*, 1455–1462. [CrossRef]
33. Gandomkar, Z.; Brennan, P.C.; Mello-Thoms, C. MuDeRN: Multi-category classification of breast histopathological image using deep residual networks. *Artif. Intell. Med.* **2018**, *88*, 14–24. [CrossRef] [PubMed]
34. MITOS-ATYPIA-14-Grand Challenge. Available online: https://mitos-atypia-14.grand-challenge.org/ (accessed on 1 December 2023).
35. Hendrycks, D.; Mu, N.; Cubuk, E.D.; Zoph, B.; Gilmer, J.; Lakshminarayanan, B. AugMix: A Simple Data Processing Method to Improve Robustness and Uncertainty. In Proceedings of the 8th International Conference on Learning Representations, ICLR 2020, Addis Ababa, Ethiopia, 26–30 April 2020.
36. Pedregosa, F.; Varoquaux, G.; Gramfort, A.; Michel, V.; Thirion, B.; Grisel, O.; Blondel, M.; Prettenhofer, P.; Weiss, R.; Dubourg, V.; et al. Scikit-learn: Machine Learning in Python. *J. Mach. Learn. Res.* **2011**, *12*, 2825–2830.
37. Waskom, M.L. seaborn: Statistical data visualization. *J. Open Source Softw.* **2021**, *6*, 3021. [CrossRef]
38. Hunter, J.D. Matplotlib: A 2D graphics environment. *Comput. Sci. Eng.* **2007**, *9*, 90–95. [CrossRef]
39. Gildenblat, J. PyTorch Library for CAM Methods. 2021. Available online: https://github.com/jacobgil/pytorch-grad-cam (accessed on 11 December 2023).
40. Bottou, L. Large-Scale Machine Learning with Stochastic Gradient Descent. In *Statistical Learning and Data Science*; Summa, M.G., Bottou, L., Goldfarb, B., Murtagh, F., Pardoux, C., Touati, M., Eds.; Chapman and Hall/CRC: Boca Raton, FL, USA, 2011; pp. 33–42. [CrossRef]
41. Jaccard Index. 2024. Available online: https://en.wikipedia.org/w/index.php?title=Jaccard_index&oldid=1220812875 (accessed on 2 May 2024).

42. Kulkarni, A.; Chong, D.; Batarseh, F.A. 5 - Foundations of data imbalance and solutions for a data democracy. In *Data Democracy*; Batarseh, F.A., Yang, R., Eds.; Academic Press: Cambridge, MA, USA, 2020; pp. 83–106. [CrossRef]
43. Dudzińska, D.; Piórkowski, A. Tissue Differentiation Based on Classification of Morphometric Features of Nuclei. In Proceedings of the Applied Informatics, Ota, Nigeria, 29–31 October 2020; Florez, H., Misra, S., Eds.; Springer: Cham, Switzerland, 2020; pp. 420–432. [CrossRef]

Journal of
Clinical Medicine

MDPI

Brief Report

Enhanced Diagnostic Precision: Assessing Tumor Differentiation in Head and Neck Squamous Cell Carcinoma Using Multi-Slice Spiral CT Texture Analysis

Lays Assolini Pinheiro de Oliveira [1,2], Diana Lorena Garcia Lopes [2], João Pedro Perez Gomes [3], Rafael Vinicius da Silveira [4,5], Daniel Vitor Aguiar Nozaki [6], Lana Ferreira Santos [7], Gabriela Castellano [4,5], Sérgio Lúcio Pereira de Castro Lopes [7] and Andre Luiz Ferreira Costa [1,2,6,*]

1 Department of Anesthesiology, Oncology and Radiology, Faculty of Medical Sciences, University of Campinas (UNICAMP), Campinas 13084-971, SP, Brazil; lays_08@hotmail.com
2 Postgraduate Program in Dentistry, Dentomaxillofacial Radiology and Imaging Laboratory, Department of Dentistry, Cruzeiro do Sul University (UNICSUL), São Paulo 01506-000, SP, Brazil; dilomagar@hotmail.com
3 Department of Stomatology, Division of Oral Radiology, School of Dentistry, University of São Paulo (USP), São Paulo 05508-000, SP, Brazil; joao.pedro@usp.br
4 Institute of Physics Gleb Wataghin, Universidade Estadual de Campinas (UNICAMP), Campinas 13084-971, SP, Brazil; r137382@dac.unicamp.br (R.V.d.S.); gabriela@unicamp.br (G.C.)
5 Brazilian Institute of Neuroscience and Neurotechnology (BRAINN), Campinas 13083-970, SP, Brazil
6 School of Dentistry of Paulista Association of Dentists (FAOA), São Paulo 02010-000, SP, Brazil; daniel.odontofaoa@gmail.com
7 Department of Diagnosis and Surgery, São José dos Campos School of Dentistry, São Paulo State University (UNESP), São José dos Campos, São Paulo 12245-000, SP, Brazil; lana.santos@unesp.br (L.F.S.); sergioluciolopes@gmail.com (S.L.P.d.C.L.)
* Correspondence: alfcosta@gmail.com

Abstract: This study explores the efficacy of texture analysis by using preoperative multi-slice spiral computed tomography (MSCT) to non-invasively determine the grade of cellular differentiation in head and neck squamous cell carcinoma (HNSCC). In a retrospective study, MSCT scans of patients with HNSCC were analyzed and classified based on its histological grade as moderately differentiated, well-differentiated, or poorly differentiated. The location of the tumor was categorized as either in the bone or in soft tissues. Segmentation of the lesion areas was conducted, followed by texture analysis. Eleven GLCM parameters across five different distances were calculated. Median values and correlations of texture parameters were examined in relation to tumor differentiation grade by using Spearman's correlation coefficient and Kruskal–Wallis and Dunn tests. Forty-six patients were included, predominantly female (87%), with a mean age of 66.7 years. Texture analysis revealed significant parameter correlations with histopathological grades of tumor differentiation. The study identified no significant age correlation with tumor differentiation, which underscores the potential of texture analysis as an age-independent biomarker. The strong correlations between texture parameters and histopathological grades support the integration of this technique into the clinical decision-making process.

Keywords: computed tomography; computer-assisted diagnosis; oral cancer; radiomics; tumor

1. Introduction

Head and neck squamous cell carcinoma (HNSCC), which includes both oropharyngeal squamous cell carcinoma (OPSCC) and oral cavity squamous cell carcinoma (OCSCC), is a malignant tumor originating from keratinocytes within the squamous epithelium of the head and neck region [1,2]. It typically presents as cell groups arranged in cords and nests or as individual cells invading the connective tissue [3].

The degree of differentiation of tumor cells varies according to four parameters based on the Broders histological classification [4] as follows: grade 1 (0 to 25% of undifferentiated cells), grade 2 (25 to 50% of undifferentiated cells), grade 3 (50 to 75% of undifferentiated cells), and grade 4 (75 to 100% of undifferentiated cells). Meanwhile, there is a grading system for invasive margins, in which factors such as nuclear pleomorphism, invasion pattern, and degree of keratinization are taken into account [5].

The clinical diagnosis of a lesion is established based on a series of data obtained through anamnesis and physical examination. If neoplasia is suspected, a biopsy is mandatory to define the case through histopathological examination [6]. Imaging exams (e.g., computed tomography) help with diagnosis and, most importantly, evaluation of the extent of the tumor. The clinical examination, associated with biopsy and study of the lesion by computed tomography (CT), allows us to determine the tumor extent and define the treatment for the lesion [7–10].

However, despite significant advancements in the diagnosis and histopathological classification of HNSCC, there are still important gaps regarding the use of quantitative imaging techniques to assess tumor cell differentiation non-invasively [11,12]. Although cellular differentiation is a critical factor for tumor behavior and prognosis, reliable and non-invasive methodologies for its evaluation are still being developed [11]. Previous studies [13] emphasize the importance of cellular differentiation in determining tumor behavior, with poorly differentiated carcinomas showing a higher propensity for metastasis. Furthermore, its potential as a reliable biomarker, particularly in distinguishing between various grades of cellular differentiation, has not been extensively studied.

Considering the profound impact of the degree of cellular differentiation on prognosis, it becomes imperative to deeply investigate its significance, particularly in the context ofHNSCC. Recent evidence, as highlighted by Kademani et al. [14], underscores the critical role of cellular differentiation in determining tumor behavior, with poorly differentiated carcinomas demonstrating a heightened propensity for metastasis. This observation not only highlights the importance of precise differentiation but also of the urgency for reliable, new methodologies. Such predictive tools could revolutionize the clinical practice by enabling clinicians to anticipate disease aggressiveness and tailor treatment strategies, ultimately enhancing patient outcomes.

Texture analysis, a quantitative imaging technique, has emerged as a promising tool for characterizing tissue properties and identifying subtle histological features associated with tumor behavior [15–18]. By quantifying texture features of imaging modalities such as CT or magnetic resonance imaging (MRI), texture analysis can potentially enhance diagnostic accuracy and prognostic stratification of HNSCC [16,18].

Therefore, the aim of this study was to determine, through texture analysis, the grade of cellular differentiation in HNSC. By correlating texture features extracted from preoperative multi-slice spiral CT imaging with histopathological findings, and we aimed to establish a non-invasive, objective method for evaluating tumor differentiation, with implications for prognosis and treatment planning.

2. Materials and Methods

2.1. Patients

The study was conducted according to the guidelines of the Declaration of Helsinki and approved by the Institutional Review Board (or Ethics Committee) of Faculty of Medical Sciences at the University of Campinas (UNICAMP) (protocol code: 33377320.0.0000.5404; date of approval: 16 October 2020). All subjects provided a signed written informed consent form.

In this retrospective study, a search was conducted in our institution's database in order to identify all patients with HNSCC according to the following inclusion criteria: histopathologically proven HNSCC, no radiotherapy or "making interpretation difficult" chemotherapy, and contrast-enhanced MSCT scans. Exclusion criteria were applied to patients with tumors of histological types other than OPSCC, images with artifacts hindering interpretation, neoplasia images acquired without intravenous contrast administration (iodine), and unclear medical records. HNSCC was histologically graded as moderately differentiated, well-differentiated, and poorly differentiated, whereas tumor location was categorized as either in the bone or in soft tissues.

The classification of tumor location in the bone or soft tissues was specifically designed to facilitate the image processing during texture analysis. This targeted approach not only streamlines the image processing workflow but also potentially increases the accuracy and reliability of the texture analysis. Furthermore, the separation into the bone or soft tissue categories acknowledges the distinct texture features between these two types of tissues [19].

Recognizing the biological and histopathological differences between OPSCC and OCSCC, including the differing role of human papillomavirus (HPV) infection, both types were included in the study. This decision was driven by the limited sample size and the retrospective nature of the study, as excluding OPSCC cases would have further reduced the statistical power of the analysis. Previous research, such as the study by Kuno et al. [20], has demonstrated the feasibility and relevance of including a mixed sample of HNSCC for texture analysis.

2.2. CT Image Acquisition

All patients underwent a 64-section contrast-enhanced MSCT scan (Aquilion TSX-101A model, Toshiba Medical Systems Corporation, Tokyo, Japan) preoperatively by using a multi-slice system and field of vision (FOV) of 320 mm, yielding slice thickness and reconstruction interval of 3 mm each and matrix size of 512 × 512. The scanner was operated at 120 kilovolts kVp and 400 mA.

2.3. Image Processing and Analysis

All images were acquired in Digital Imaging and Communications in Medicine (DICOM). MSCT scans were selected based on the identification of the largest area of the lesion. Two radiologists with 6 and 16 years of experience in interpreting MSCT scans were extensively involved in reviewing all the cases. They performed the segmentation with mutual agreement. The InVesalius® software (www.cti.gov.br/invesalius, accessed on 5 July 2023) was used for the initial image processing. Once all the lesions were segmented and similar areas identified, the DICOM files were converted into the NIfTI format by using the InVesalius® software toolbox [21]. Figure 1 shows the segmentation process before calculating the texture parameter values.

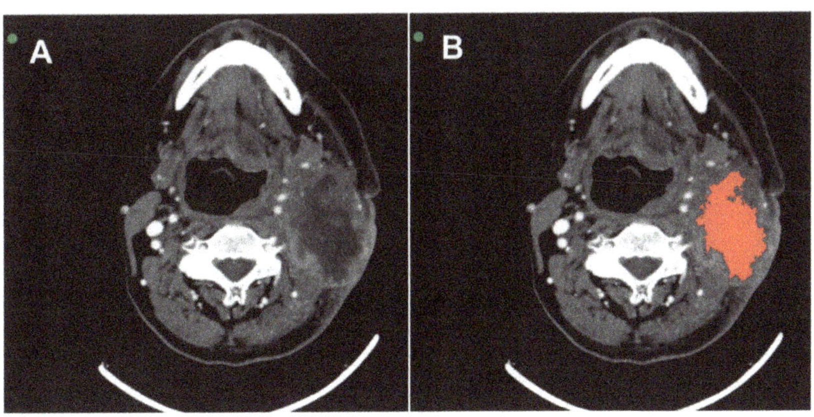

Figure 1. (**A**) Axial MSCT image shows squamous cell carcinoma located in the tonsillar pillar on the left side. (**B**) 3D VOI (red) segmentation process covering the lesion.

2.4. Texture Analysis

In this study, we assessed eleven gray-level co-occurrence matrix (GLCM) parameters from each segmented lesion volume by using texture analysis in the MATLAB software (MathWorks, Natick, MA, USA, www.mathworks.com, accessed on 19 July 2023). The GLCM is a matrix showing how many times a pair of pixel values appear at a specific distance and angle. The GLCM is used for capturing second-order statistical texture parameters such as contrast, correlation, entropy of difference, entropy, homogeneity, sum average, sum entropy, sum variance, uniformity, variance of difference, and variance. The mean value of the texture parameters was estimated on a volume of interest (VOI) basis. Hence, we opted for 128 levels as being the most suitable balance between GLCM shortage and amount of information extracted [22]. Previous studies have shown successful results by using Haralick parameters [21,23–25]. The number of slices used for GLCM calculation within the manually segmented VOI depending on the specific VOI being analyzed [22]. The texture parameters were assessed at five varying distances (q1, q2, q3, q4, and q5) and calculated similarly to the study by Gomes et al. [21].

2.5. Statistical Analysis

Spearman's correlation coefficient was used to assess the correlation between distances of the same texture analysis parameter. Tumor differentiation grades were compared by using the Kruskal–Wallis test, followed by the Dunn test (numerical variables) or the Chi-Square test (categorical variables). Statistical analysis was conducted by using the software R, version 3.6.0 (The R Foundation for Statistical Computing, Vienna, Austria), with a significance level set at 5%.

3. Results

After applying the criteria for inclusion and exclusion, 45 patients were included. There was a female predominance (87%), and the mean age was 66.7 years (range: 33–93 years). The results showed that five (11.1%) patients had a moderately differentiated tumor in the bones, seven (15.6%) had well-differentiated tumor in the soft tissues, 30 (66.7%) had moderately differentiated tumor in the soft tissues, and three (6.7%) had poorly differentiated tumor in the soft tissues.

Texture analysis with eleven parameters at five different distances generated a large number of variables, which significantly increased the chance of type I error. Therefore, the variables were reduced by using the mean of the five distances. Before calculating the mean of the five distances for each parameter, the Spearman's correlation coefficient between the distances was calculated and assessed. As a high correlation was observed in nine out of the eleven parameters, the mean value between the distances was used. In the correlation texture parameter, the distance 5 did not show a high correlation with the other distances. Therefore, this parameter was evaluated in two ways: the mean from 1 to 4 and 5 considered separately. A similar situation occurred with the texture parameter difference of entropy, where the mean of distances from 2 to 5 was used, and distance 1 was evaluated separately.

Table 1 shows the median of age and texture parameters according to tumor differentiation grade groups. Table 2 shows the comparison between tumor differentiation grade in relation to age and texture analysis. It is observed that no statistically significant difference was found between the groups in relation to age (p-value = 0.725). Figure 2 shows the tumor differentiation grade groups significant for texture parameters.

With regard to texture analysis, the observed results are as follows:

- Group BM (moderately differentiated tumor in bone) showed lower correlation compared to Group SM (moderately differentiated tumor in soft tissue);
- Group BM (moderately differentiated tumor in bone) showed lower uniformity compared to Group SM (moderately differentiated tumor in soft tissue) and Group SP (poorly differentiated tumor in soft tissue);

- Group BM (moderately differentiated tumor in bone) showed lower homogeneity compared to Group SM (moderately differentiated tumor in soft tissue) and Group SP (poorly differentiated tumor in soft tissue);
- Group BM (moderately differentiated tumor in bone) presented higher entropy and sum of entropy compared to Group SM (moderately differentiated tumor in soft tissue) and Group SP (poorly differentiated tumor in soft tissue);
- Group BM (moderately differentiated tumor in bone) presented higher entropy of difference (mean of distances from 2 to 5) compared to Group SM (moderately differentiated tumor in soft tissue) and Group SP (poorly differentiated tumor in soft tissue);
- Group SW (well-differentiated tumor in soft tissue) and Group SP (poorly differentiated tumor in soft tissue) showed lower entropy of difference (distance 1) compared to Group BM (moderately differentiated tumor in bone) and Group SM (moderately differentiated tumor in soft tissue).

Table 1. Median of age and texture parameters according to tumor differentiation.

Texture Parameters	Moderately Differentiated Bone (BM) (N = 5)	Well Differentiated Soft Tissue (SW) (N = 7)	Moderately Differentiated Soft Tissue (SM) (N = 30)	Poorly Differentiated Soft Tissue (SP) (N = 3)
Age	63.0 [59.0;85.0]	70.0 [59.0;89.0]	65.5 [33.0;93.0]	67.0 [63.0;73.0]
Uniformity	**0.06 [0.01;0.18]**	**0.18 [0.04;0.32]**	**0.20 [0.02;0.69]**	**0.69 [0.14;0.78]**
Contrast	76.8 [14.9;271]	24.8 [0.71;49.9]	9.63 [0.40;166]	0.97 [0.22;37.6]
Correlation M	0.75 [0.50;0.76]	0.86 [0.40;0.91]	0.73 [0.27;0.96]	0.63 [0.47;0.85]
Correlation q5	**0.50 [0.21;0.62]**	**0.76 [0.14;0.82]**	**0.84 [0.07;0.94]**	**0.40 [0.28;0.73]**
Variance	147 [24.2;243]	80.3 [2.67;125]	18.6 [0.47;279]	0.87 [0.27;109]
Homogeneity	**0.49 [0.36;0.64]**	**0.71 [0.54;0.88]**	**0.75 [0.39;0.91]**	**0.93 [0.65;0.93]**
Entropy	**2.12 [1.55;2.40]**	**1.29 [0.77;1.74]**	**1.08 [0.39;2.66]**	**0.39 [0.32;1.96]**
SumAverage	74.4 [59.0;126]	77.7 [58.4;131]	80.7 [24.5;137]	94.7 [77.7;98.2]
SumVariance	570 [82.0;702]	276 [9.98;473]	62.8 [1.19;951]	2.50 [0.88;399]
SumEntropy	**1.52 [1.15;1.63]**	**1.04 [0.68;1.26]**	**0.82 [0.33;1.80]**	**0.33 [0.26;1.17]**
DifferenceVariance	55.7 [6.81;212]	20.5 [0.61;40.4]	9.65 [0.35;141]	0.92 [0.20;31.9]
DifferenceEntropy M	**0.98 [0.79;1.19]**	**0.68 [0.31;0.84]**	**0.54 [0.24;1.22]**	**0.21 [0.21;0.78]**
DifferenceEntropy q1	0.71 [0.61;0.90]	0.50 [0.19;0.61]	0.64 [0.60;0.71]	0.19 [0.12;0.55]

CorrelationM = average of distances 1 to 4; DifferenceEntropyM = average of distances 2 to 5. Bold indicates significant p value.

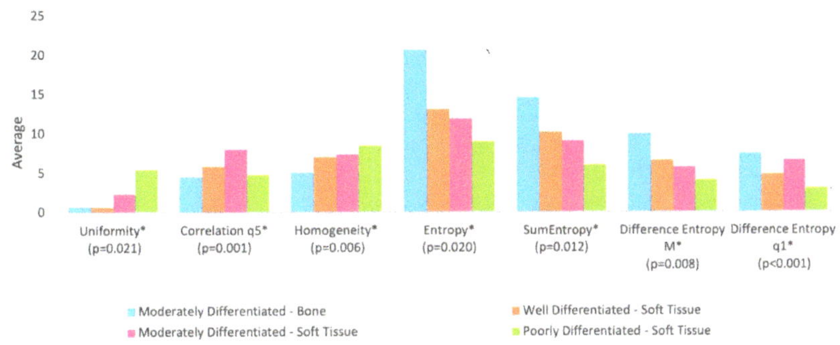

Figure 2. The groups are statistically different at 5% significance level regarding parameters followed by asterisk (*). All parameters were rescaled to be inserted into the graph in order to avoid distorting the scale for the other parameters.

Table 2. Comparison of tumor differentiation grade in relation to age and texture analysis.

Texture Parameters	Moderately Differentiated Bone (BM) (N = 5)	Well Differentiated Soft Tissue (SW) (N = 7)	Moderately Differentiated Soft Tissue (SM) (N = 30)	Poorly Differentiated Soft Tissue (SP) (N = 3)	p-Value
Age	67.0 (10.3)	71.1 (9.01)	65.5 (13.4)	67.7 (5.03)	0.725
Uniformity	**0.07 (0.07)**	**0.18 (0.10)**	**0.24 (0.16)**	**0.54 (0.35)**	**0.021**
Contrast	99.4 (104)	22.2 (16.5)	23.6 (39.5)	12.9 (21.4)	0.062
Correlation M	0.69 (0.11)	0.73 (0.21)	0.70 (0.20)	0.65 (0.19)	0.807
Correlation q5	**0.45 (0.15)**	**0.58 (0.28)**	**0.80 (0.16)**	**0.47 (0.23)**	**0.001**
Variance	127 (96.5)	59.0 (51.4)	52.1 (75.0)	36.7 (62.6)	0.123
Homogeneity	**0.50 (0.11)**	**0.70 (0.11)**	**0.73 (0.12)**	**0.84 (0.16)**	**0.006**
Entropy	**2.06 (0.34)**	**1.30 (0.36)**	**1.18 (0.53)**	**0.89 (0.93)**	**0.020**
SumAverage	84.7 (27.3)	83.6 (22.9)	85.3 (26.2)	90.2 (11.0)	0.836
SumVariance	445 (274)	214 (193)	184 (265)	134 (229)	0.092
SumEntropy	**1.45 (0.19)**	**1.01 (0.25)**	**0.90 (0.36)**	**0.59 (0.51)**	**0.012**
DifferenceVariance	75.6 (82.2)	18.1 (13.2)	19.7 (31.8)	11.0 (18.1)	0.096
DifferenceEntropy M	**0.99 (0.15)**	**0.65 (0.18)**	**0.57 (0.24)**	**0.40 (0.33)**	**0.008**
DifferenceEntropy q1	**0.74 (0.14)**	**0.47 (0.14)**	**0.65 (0.03)**	**0.29 (0.23)**	**<0.001**

CorrelationM = average distances 1 to 4; DifferenceEntropyM = average of distances 2 to 5. Bold indicates significant p value.

4. Discussion

The objective of this study was to assess the degree of cellular differentiation in HNSCC by relating texture parameters derived from preoperative MSCT scans with histopathological features. We endeavored to devise a non-invasive, objective technique for determining tumor differentiation. This approach has implications for prognosis and treatment planning, while also considering the location of the lesion in soft and bone tissues.

It is observed that the parameter of correlation indicated a statistically significant difference (p = 0.001) in the Group MD (moderately differentiated tumor in hard tissue) compared to Group SM (moderately differentiated tumor in soft tissue) and Group SP (poorly differentiated tumor in soft tissue), indicating lower values in Group BM. The parameter of correlation assesses the degree of interdependence between image pixels and higher values, which indicates a greater interdependence between pixels [26], that is, the uniformity of the tissue content represented by the pixel values would be greater. This indicates that there is no variation in tissue types comprising the region, with a consequently less complex internal pattern [27,28]. Thus, this finding means that tumors in hard tissue (BM) are less uniform than those in soft tissue, either poorly or moderately differentiated.

The parameters of uniformity and homogeneity obtained by texture analysis, which were statistically significant in Group SW compared to Groups SM and MP, corroborate what was previously indicated (i.e., correlation) for this same group. This reinforces that texture image values of patients with moderately differentiated tumor in bone indicate greater tissue organization [29].

Considering the parameters of entropy (i.e., entropy, entropy of difference, and sum of entropy), it can be observed that they all presented statistically significant differences between the Groups BM, SM, and SP, with the former having higher values than the others. These are complementary parameters and indicate disorganization of image pixels. In the previously cited study by Costa et al. [30], entropy was directly related to image disorganization, with lower values indicating a greater lack of uniformity in the tissue and a greater variation in shades of gray (i.e., internal components of the tissue), which often correlates with a higher degree of malignancy. This reflects the complexity and heterogeneity often seen in more aggressive tumors.

Moreover, the difference in entropy parameters between the groups further underscores the potential of texture analysis in discriminating between different degrees of tumor differentiation [31,32]. Specifically, higher entropy values in Group BM (moderately differentiated tumor in bone) suggest a more chaotic and less predictable tissue structure compared to the soft tissue groups. This aligns with the notion that bone tumors, due to their denser and more complex structure, may exhibit more pronounced texture irregularities in the images [33], which can be captured through advanced analytical techniques such as those used in this study.

The findings of this study support the use of texture analysis in the context of medical imaging, particularly in enhancing our understanding of tumor biology and behavior without the need for invasive procedures [16,34]. By incorporating a detailed set of textural parameters, this study adds to the current knowledge and suggests further areas for exploration in the use of imaging analysis in oncology. For instance, a recent study demonstrated the efficacy of automated analysis of CT scans by employing textural features and machine learning techniques, achieving high accuracy in their applications, highlighting the potential of texture analysis in diverse medical contexts [35].

It is important to acknowledge the limitations of this study. The sample size, although adequate for a preliminary analysis, is relatively small and could affect the generalizability of the findings. Additionally, our sample included both OPSCC and OCSCC cases. Although we recognize the significant biological and histopathological differences between these two types of squamous cell carcinoma, including the differing role of HPV infection, we opted to include both to maintain a robust sample size. Excluding the small number of OPSCC cases would have further reduced the statistical power of our analysis. This approach is supported by the study conducted by Kuno et al. [20], which demonstrated the feasibility and relevance of using CT texture analysis across different subtypes of head and neck squamous cell carcinoma. Their research showed that CT texture features could significantly predict treatment outcomes, underscoring the potential of texture analysis to provide valuable insights even when diverse tumor subtypes are included in the study population. However, future studies should aim to separate these groups or control for these differences more explicitly to validate and expand upon our findings, ensuring a more nuanced understanding of how texture features correlate with tumor differentiation and patient prognosis.

Another limitation is the gender distribution of our sample, which was predominantly female (87%). This contrasts with the typical gender distribution in head and neck cancers, where males are usually more affected. The convenience sampling method used in this retrospective study resulted in a gender imbalance. This could influence the generalizability of our results, and future studies should aim for a more balanced gender distribution to ensure more representative findings

Further research involving larger cohorts and multiple cancer types would be valuable in validating and expanding our findings. Additionally, future studies should consider including HPV status and its potential impact on the analyzed texture parameters, especially in OPSCC cases. We have an ongoing prospective study that aims to address these points by incorporating a larger sample size and including cross-validation to further validate our findings and examine the benefits of including both OPSCC and OCSCC.

5. Conclusions

In conclusion, this study highlights the potential of texture analysis of preoperative MSCT images as a non-invasive method to assess tumor differentiation in HNSCC. The significant correlations found between texture parameters and histopathological features suggest that this approach could serve as a valuable tool in the clinical setting, aiding in the prognosis and tailoring of treatment strategies for patients with different tumor types. As medical imaging technology and analytical methods continue to evolve, the integration of texture analysis into clinical practice could enhance the precision and effectiveness of cancer diagnosis and treatment planning.

Author Contributions: Conceptualization, L.A.P.d.O., S.L.P.d.C.L. and A.L.F.C.; investigation, J.P.P.G., D.L.G.L., D.V.A.N. and L.F.S.; formal analysis, L.A.P.d.O., J.P.P.G., R.V.d.S. and G.C.; data curation, S.L.P.d.C.L. and D.L.G.L.; methodology, A.L.F.C., R.V.d.S. and G.C.; project administration,

S.L.P.d.C.L.; supervision, A.L.F.C.; writing—original draft, L.A.P.d.O., S.L.P.d.C.L. and A.L.F.C.; writing—review and editing, L.A.P.d.O., D.L.G.L., J.P.P.G., D.V.A.N., R.V.d.S., L.F.S., G.C., S.L.P.d.C.L. and A.L.F.C.; funding acquisition, A.L.F.C. and D.V.A.N. All authors have read and agreed to the published version of the manuscript.

Funding: This research was funded by FAPESP (São Paulo Research Foundation), grant number 23/08428-1.

Institutional Review Board Statement: This study has been approved by the institutional review board (Ethical Committee of the Faculty of Medical Sciences at the University of Campinas (UNICAMP); no. 33377320.0.0000.5404).

Informed Consent Statement: Informed consent was obtained from all subjects involved in the study.

Data Availability Statement: The datasets generated and/or analyzed during the current study are available from the corresponding author upon reasonable request.

Conflicts of Interest: The authors declare no conflicts of interest.

References

1. Panarese, I.; Aquino, G.; Ronchi, A.; Longo, F.; Montella, M.; Cozzolino, I.; Roccuzzo, G.; Colella, G.; Caraglia, M.; Franco, R. Oral and Oropharyngeal squamous cell carcinoma: Prognostic and predictive parameters in the etiopathogenetic route. *Expert Rev. Anticancer Ther.* **2019**, *19*, 105–119. [CrossRef] [PubMed]
2. Scully, C.; Bagan, J. Oral squamous cell carcinoma: Overview of current understanding of aetiopathogenesis and clinical implications. *Oral. Dis.* **2009**, *15*, 388–399. [CrossRef] [PubMed]
3. Ribeiro, C.V.; Vasconcelos, A.C.; Andrade Filho Jde, S. Apoptosis and expression of argyrophilic nucleolus organizer regions in epithelial neoplasms of the larynx. *Braz. J. Otorhinolaryngol.* **2015**, *81*, 158–166. [CrossRef] [PubMed]
4. Broders, A.C. The microscopic grading of cancer. *Surg. Clin. N. Am.* **1941**, *21*, 947–962.
5. Bryne, M.; Koppang, H.S.; Lilleng, R.; Stene, T.; Bang, G.; Dabelsteen, E. New malignancy grading is a better prognostic indicator than Broders' grading in oral squamous cell carcinomas. *J. Oral. Pathol. Med.* **1989**, *18*, 432–437. [CrossRef] [PubMed]
6. Marocchio, L.S.; Lima, J.; Sperandio, F.F.; Correa, L.; de Sousa, S.O. Oral squamous cell carcinoma: An analysis of 1564 cases showing advances in early detection. *J. Oral. Sci.* **2010**, *52*, 267–273. [CrossRef] [PubMed]
7. Stoeckli, S.J.; Haerle, S.K.; Strobel, K.; Haile, S.R.; Hany, T.F.; Schuknecht, B. Initial staging of the neck in head and neck squamous cell carcinoma: A comparison of CT, PET/CT, and ultrasound-guided fine-needle aspiration cytology. *Head Neck* **2012**, *34*, 469–476. [CrossRef] [PubMed]
8. Pandeshwar, P.; Jayanthi, K.; Raghuram, P. Pre-operative contrast enhanced computer tomographic evaluation of cervical nodal metastatic disease in oral squamous cell carcinoma. *Indian J. Cancer* **2013**, *50*, 310–315. [CrossRef]
9. Sproll, K.C.; Leydag, S.; Holtmann, H.; Schorn, L.K.; Aissa, J.; Kropil, P.; Kaisers, W.; Toth, C.; Handschel, J.; Lommen, J. Is the prediction of one or two ipsilateral positive lymph nodes by computerized tomography and ultrasound reliable enough to restrict therapeutic neck dissection in oral squamous cell carcinoma (OSCC) patients? *J. Cancer Res. Clin. Oncol.* **2021**, *147*, 2421–2433. [CrossRef]
10. Dammann, F.; Horger, M.; Mueller-Berg, M.; Schlemmer, H.; Claussen, C.D.; Hoffman, J.; Eschmann, S.; Bares, R. Rational diagnosis of squamous cell carcinoma of the head and neck region: Comparative evaluation of CT, MRI, and 18FDG PET. *AJR Am. J. Roentgenol.* **2005**, *184*, 1326–1331. [CrossRef]
11. Aerts, H.J.; Velazquez, E.R.; Leijenaar, R.T.; Parmar, C.; Grossmann, P.; Carvalho, S.; Bussink, J.; Monshouwer, R.; Haibe-Kains, B.; Rietveld, D.; et al. Decoding tumour phenotype by noninvasive imaging using a quantitative radiomics approach. *Nat. Commun.* **2014**, *5*, 4006. [CrossRef] [PubMed]
12. Mittra, E.; Quon, A. Positron emission tomography/computed tomography: The current technology and applications. *Radiol. Clin. N. Am.* **2009**, *47*, 147–160. [CrossRef] [PubMed]
13. Fang, K.H.; Kao, H.K.; Cheng, M.H.; Chang, Y.L.; Tsang, N.M.; Huang, Y.C.; Lee, L.Y.; Yu, J.S.; Hao, S.P.; Chang, K.P. Histological differentiation of primary oral squamous cell carcinomas in an area of betel quid chewing prevalence. *Otolaryngol. Head Neck Surg.* **2009**, *141*, 743–749. [CrossRef]
14. Kademani, D.; Bell, R.B.; Bagheri, S.; Holmgren, E.; Dierks, E.; Potter, B.; Homer, L. Prognostic factors in intraoral squamous cell carcinoma: The influence of histologic grade. *J. Oral. Maxillofac. Surg.* **2005**, *63*, 1599–1605. [CrossRef]
15. Wu, W.; Ye, J.; Wang, Q.; Luo, J.; Xu, S. CT-Based Radiomics Signature for the Preoperative Discrimination between Head and Neck Squamous Cell Carcinoma Grades. *Front. Oncol.* **2019**, *9*, 821. [CrossRef] [PubMed]
16. Ren, J.; Yuan, Y.; Shi, Y.; Tao, X. Tumor heterogeneity in oral and oropharyngeal squamous cell carcinoma assessed by texture analysis of CT and conventional MRI: A potential marker of overall survival. *Acta Radiol.* **2019**, *60*, 1273–1280. [CrossRef]
17. Ren, J.; Qi, M.; Yuan, Y.; Duan, S.; Tao, X. Machine Learning-Based MRI Texture Analysis to Predict the Histologic Grade of Oral Squamous Cell Carcinoma. *AJR Am. J. Roentgenol.* **2020**, *215*, 1184–1190. [CrossRef]

18. Ranjbar, S.; Ning, S.; Zwart, C.M.; Wood, C.P.; Weindling, S.M.; Wu, T.; Mitchell, J.R.; Li, J.; Hoxworth, J.M. Computed Tomography-Based Texture Analysis to Determine Human Papillomavirus Status of Oropharyngeal Squamous Cell Carcinoma. *J. Comput. Assist. Tomogr.* **2018**, *42*, 299–305. [CrossRef]
19. Xu, R.; Kido, S.; Suga, K.; Hirano, Y.; Tachibana, R.; Muramatsu, K.; Chagawa, K.; Tanaka, S. Texture analysis on (18)F-FDG PET/CT images to differentiate malignant and benign bone and soft-tissue lesions. *Ann. Nucl. Med.* **2014**, *28*, 926–935. [CrossRef]
20. Kuno, H.; Qureshi, M.M.; Chapman, M.N.; Li, B.; Andreu-Arasa, V.C.; Onoue, K.; Truong, M.T.; Sakai, O. CT Texture Analysis Potentially Predicts Local Failure in Head and Neck Squamous Cell Carcinoma Treated with Chemoradiotherapy. *AJNR Am. J. Neuroradiol.* **2017**, *38*, 2334–2340. [CrossRef]
21. Gomes, J.P.P.; Ogawa, C.M.; Silveira, R.V.; Castellano, G.; De Rosa, C.S.; Yasuda, C.L.; Rocha, A.C.; Hasseus, B.; Orhan, K.; Braz-Silva, P.H.; et al. Magnetic resonance imaging texture analysis to differentiate ameloblastoma from odontogenic keratocyst. *Sci. Rep.* **2022**, *12*, 20047. [CrossRef]
22. Silveira, R.V.C.; Campos, B.M.; Li, L.M.; Castellano, G. Texture-based networks for DMN regions: A pilot study. *J. Epilepsy Clin. Neuroradiol.* **2020**, *26*, 34.
23. de Oliveira, M.S.; D'Abreu, A.; Franca, M.C., Jr.; Lopes-Cendes, I.; Cendes, F.; Castellano, G. MRI-texture analysis of corpus callosum, thalamus, putamen, and caudate in Machado-Joseph disease. *J. Neuroimaging* **2012**, *22*, 46–52. [CrossRef]
24. Oliveira, M.S.; Fernandes, P.T.; Avelar, W.M.; Santos, S.L.; Castellano, G.; Li, L.M. Texture analysis of computed tomography images of acute ischemic stroke patients. *Braz. J. Med. Biol. Res.* **2009**, *42*, 1076–1079. [CrossRef] [PubMed]
25. Mungai, F.; Verrone, G.B.; Pietragalla, M.; Berti, V.; Addeo, G.; Desideri, I.; Bonasera, L.; Miele, V. CT assessment of tumor heterogeneity and the potential for the prediction of human papillomavirus status in oropharyngeal squamous cell carcinoma. *Radiol. Med.* **2019**, *124*, 804–811. [CrossRef] [PubMed]
26. Haralick, R.M.; Shanmugam, K.; Dinstein, I.H. Textural Features for Image Classification. *IEEE Trans. Syst. Man Cybern.* **1973**, *SMC-3*, 610–621. [CrossRef]
27. Garpebring, A.; Brynolfsson, P.; Kuess, P.; Georg, D.; Helbich, T.H.; Nyholm, T.; Lofstedt, T. Density estimation of grey-level co-occurrence matrices for image texture analysis. *Phys. Med. Biol.* **2018**, *63*, 195017. [CrossRef]
28. Lofstedt, T.; Brynolfsson, P.; Asklund, T.; Nyholm, T.; Garpebring, A. Gray-level invariant Haralick texture features. *PLoS ONE* **2019**, *14*, e0212110. [CrossRef]
29. Reinert, C.P.; Krieg, E.; Esser, M.; Nikolaou, K.; Bosmuller, H.; Horger, M. Role of computed tomography texture analysis using dual-energy-based bone marrow imaging for multiple myeloma characterization: Comparison with histology and established serologic parameters. *Eur. Radiol.* **2021**, *31*, 2357–2367. [CrossRef]
30. Costa, A.L.F.; Fardim, K.A.C.; Ribeiro, I.T.; Jardini, M.A.N.; Braz-Silva, P.H.; Orhan, K.; de Castro Lopes, S.L.P. Cone-beam computed tomography texture analysis can help differentiate odontogenic and non-odontogenic maxillary sinusitis. *Imaging Sci. Dent.* **2023**, *53*, 43–51. [CrossRef]
31. Liu, S.; Zheng, H.; Pan, X.; Chen, L.; Shi, M.; Guan, Y.; Ge, Y.; He, J.; Zhou, Z. Texture analysis of CT imaging for assessment of esophageal squamous cancer aggressiveness. *J. Thorac. Dis.* **2017**, *9*, 4724–4732. [CrossRef] [PubMed]
32. Lisson, C.S.; Lisson, C.G.; Flosdorf, K.; Mayer-Steinacker, R.; Schultheiss, M.; von Baer, A.; Barth, T.F.E.; Beer, A.J.; Baumhauer, M.; Meier, R.; et al. Diagnostic value of MRI-based 3D texture analysis for tissue characterisation and discrimination of low-grade chondrosarcoma from enchondroma: A pilot study. *Eur. Radiol.* **2018**, *28*, 468–477. [CrossRef] [PubMed]
33. Fritz, B.; Muller, D.A.; Sutter, R.; Wurnig, M.C.; Wagner, M.W.; Pfirrmann, C.W.A.; Fischer, M.A. Magnetic Resonance Imaging-Based Grading of Cartilaginous Bone Tumors: Added Value of Quantitative Texture Analysis. *Investig. Radiol.* **2018**, *53*, 663–672. [CrossRef] [PubMed]
34. Alic, L.; Niessen, W.J.; Veenland, J.F. Quantification of heterogeneity as a biomarker in tumor imaging: A systematic review. *PLoS ONE* **2014**, *9*, e110300. [CrossRef]
35. Nurzynska, K.; Piórkowski, A.; Strzelecki, M.; Kociołek, M.; Banyś, R.P.; Obuchowicz, R. Differentiating age and sex in vertebral body CT scans—Texture analysis versus deep learning approach. *Biocybern. Biomed. Eng.* **2024**, *44*, 20–30. [CrossRef]

diagnostics

MDPI

Article

Optimizing GPT-4 Turbo Diagnostic Accuracy in Neuroradiology through Prompt Engineering and Confidence Thresholds

Akihiko Wada [1,*], Toshiaki Akashi [1], George Shih [2], Akifumi Hagiwara [1], Mitsuo Nishizawa [1], Yayoi Hayakawa [1], Junko Kikuta [1], Keigo Shimoji [1], Katsuhiro Sano [1], Koji Kamagata [1], Atsushi Nakanishi [1] and Shigeki Aoki [1]

[1] Department of Radiology, Juntendo University Graduate School of Medicine, Tokyo 113-8421, Japan
[2] Clinical Radiology, Weill Cornell Medical College, New York, NY 10065, USA
* Correspondence: a-wada@juntendo.ac.jp

Abstract: Background and Objectives: Integrating large language models (LLMs) such as GPT-4 Turbo into diagnostic imaging faces a significant challenge, with current misdiagnosis rates ranging from 30–50%. This study evaluates how prompt engineering and confidence thresholds can improve diagnostic accuracy in neuroradiology. Methods: We analyze 751 neuroradiology cases from the American Journal of Neuroradiology using GPT-4 Turbo with customized prompts to improve diagnostic precision. Results: Initially, GPT-4 Turbo achieved a baseline diagnostic accuracy of 55.1%. By reformatting responses to list five diagnostic candidates and applying a 90% confidence threshold, the highest precision of the diagnosis increased to 72.9%, with the candidate list providing the correct diagnosis at 85.9%, reducing the misdiagnosis rate to 14.1%. However, this threshold reduced the number of cases that responded. Conclusions: Strategic prompt engineering and high confidence thresholds significantly reduce misdiagnoses and improve the precision of the LLM diagnostic in neuroradiology. More research is needed to optimize these approaches for broader clinical implementation, balancing accuracy and utility.

Keywords: large language model (LLM); diagnostic imaging; neuroradiology; artificial intelligence in medicine; prompt engineering; confidence thresholds; GPT-4 Turbo; misdiagnosis reduction; AI diagnostic tools; clinical decision support

1. Introduction

Large language models (LLMs) have demonstrated significant potential in processing textual information, often achieving performance levels comparable to human expertise. These models are increasingly being applied in medicine and offer valuable help in interpreting complex medical data. In general internal medicine, Hirosawa et al. reported a promising 93.3% accuracy for GPT-3 in diagnosing clinical vignettes [1]. Similarly, Chen et al. found that GPT-3 achieved 78.8% accuracy in symptom checks on a multilabel classification task using patient-reported symptoms [2]. In ophthalmology, Antaki et al. found that GPT-4 achieved 55.8% accuracy on a diagnosis task using fundus images and 42.7% on a treatment recommendation task [3]. In dermatology, Lallas et al. demonstrated a 51.5% sensitivity to diagnose early-stage skin cancer, and the inverse approach with classic pattern analysis improved to 83.6% [4]. For medical licensing exams testing broad clinical knowledge, Yang et al. reported promising results, with GPT-4 achieving 86.2% on the USMLE, 62.0% on AMBOSS, and 73.1% on the DRQCE exam [5].

In radiology, LLM has been reported to be indicated in various areas [6–13]. In terms of diagnostic accuracy performance, it is more modest. Bhayana et al. assessed ChatGPT performance on a board-style radiology examination, finding an overall precision of 69% [14]. Ueda et al. compared ChatGPT's diagnostic performance from patient history and imaging findings, revealing a 61% diagnostic accuracy that supports its potential as a supplementary tool for clinicians [15]. Kottlors et al. explored the 68.8% feasibility of using ChatGPT for differential diagnosis based on imaging patterns [16]. Horiuchi et al. investigated the accuracy of ChatGPT-generated diagnoses from patient medical history and imaging findings in neuroradiology cases with a 50% lower accuracy than radiologists [17]. Suthar et al. conducted an in-depth evaluation of the accuracy of ChatGPT with the American Journal of Neuroradiology's "Case of the Month", reporting an overall diagnostic accuracy of 57.86% [18]. These reports suggest that LLM models achieve approximately 50–69% accuracy in identifying correct diagnoses from imaging findings. However, the 30–50% misdiagnosis rate is relatively high, which may be insufficient to assist healthcare professionals in making accurate clinical decisions. Physicians generally seek diagnostic tools that minimize the risks of misdiagnosis to ensure patient safety and effective treatment. The potential and limitations of LLM in medical applications highlight the need to improve accuracy and reduce misdiagnosis rates in clinical settings [19].

Prompt engineering, a method of giving precise instructions to LLMs, has shown effectiveness in eliciting desired responses and is reported to improve LLM performance in various applications [20]. This technique involves carefully crafting prompts that guide the LLM logically, ensuring that the model generates accurate and relevant outputs. Prompt engineering can help LLMs better understand complex queries and produce more useful responses by specifying the context, structure, and format of the response. In this study, we explore how prompt engineering can improve the diagnostic accuracy of LLM in medical imaging to reduce misdiagnosis rates.

In this study, we aim to utilize GPT-4 Turbo's diagnostic abilities in medical imaging with prompt engineering techniques, particularly focusing on reducing misdiagnosis rates. By adopting these advanced technologies, we seek to improve the precision of diagnostic suggestions, using the capabilities of GPT-4 Turbo to address the challenges of accurately interpreting medical images.

2. Materials and Methods

This study was carried out using the checklist for artificial intelligence in medical imaging. It was exempted from institutional review board oversight because it used publicly available data.

2.1. Data Collection

Our methodology examined 751 publicly available neuroradiological cases from 2012 to 2023 from the American Journal of Neuroradiology (AJNR) Case of the Week Archives (https://www.ajnr.org/cow/by/diagnosis, accessed on 18 March 2024) [21]. The AJNR Case of the Week site separates clinical information, images, and diagnoses/explanations into separate tabs. GPT-4 Turbo accessed the indicated URL to retrieve clinical information and image findings as textual information without knowing the diagnosis name.

2.2. AI Model and Platform

We employed GPT-4 Turbo, an advanced version of the LLM developed by OpenAI [22]. The selection of GPT-4 Turbo for this study was based on its demonstrated superior performance in recent evaluations compared to other LLMs. According to a recent study, GPT-4 achieved a higher accuracy rate in medical diagnostics compared to other LLMs, validating its suitability for our research aimed at improving diagnostic precision [23]. Furthermore, GPT-4 has been found to generate more coherent and contextually relevant responses, which is crucial for accurate medical diagnosis and effective communication with clinicians. Based on these findings, we introduce GPT-4 Turbo, known for its enhanced capabilities and a vast 128 k context window, allowing comprehensive analysis within a single prompt.

To implement this, we employed the MD.ai Reporting/Chat application, which provides direct URL access to extract relevant clinical and imaging information, omitting diagnoses to test the diagnostic accuracy of GPT-4 Turbo [24]. MD.ai Chat is a reporting/chat application within the MD.ai platform that leverages LLMs such as GPT-3.5, GPT-4, and GPT-4 Turbo. One of the key features of MD.ai Chat is its support for natural language interactions, allowing healthcare professionals to engage in spoken dialogue with the model. This facilitates efficient and intuitive communication, making it easier to extract and understand complex clinical information. MD.ai Chat also provides direct URL access, allowing the retrieval of textual information necessary for clinical and imaging data analysis. Users can create customizable prompts for report interactions, tailoring the chat interface to their specific needs. This flexibility allows healthcare professionals to design the most relevant prompts for their clinical scenarios, enhancing the application's utility.

2.3. *Prompt Instruction*

In this study, we employed three innovative prompt engineering strategies to improve the diagnostic precision of GPT-4 Turbo in neuroradiology. Drawing from cutting-edge engineering guides and research, we implemented role adoption, step-by-step thinking, and confidence level assessment [20,25]. Box 1 presents the detailed prompt used to guide the AI model in generating diagnostic suggestions.

2.3.1. Role-Playing

This strategy involved programming GPT-4 Turbo to act as an expert in medical imaging diagnostics. Adopting the specialist role, the model shifted its processing from general data analysis to more focused, knowledge-based decision-making. This role-centered approach allowed LLM to prioritize critical and relevant information for disease diagnosis from various medical imaging modalities, such as CT, MRI, and X-rays. We hypothesized that by concentrating the focus of LLM on a specific domain, the quality and relevance of its diagnostic output would improve significantly, leading to higher precision in response and better alignment with clinical expectations.

2.3.2. Step-by-Step Thinking

We directed GPT-4 Turbo to adopt a sequential diagnostic process that mirrors the decision-making steps that human experts typically take. The prompts guided the model in formulating an initial differential diagnosis based solely on clinical information, integrating imaging findings, and refining the initial diagnosis accordingly. This structured approach was designed to promote the gradual integration of data, improve the ability of the LLM to reason diagnostically, and increase the clarity and reliability of its diagnostic suggestions.

2.3.3. Multiple Diagnostic Suggestions

Previous studies evaluating the accuracy of LLMs in medical imaging diagnostics typically required the LLM to provide only the most likely diagnosis [6–13]. However, in this study, we designed the prompts to instruct the LLM to provide the most likely diagnosis and four additional possible diagnostic suggestions, making a total of five potential diagnoses. This approach aims to increase the probability that the correct diagnosis is included among the suggestions, thereby reducing the likelihood of misdiagnosis. This strategy ensures that the LLM's responses offer a broader spectrum of diagnostic possibilities, supporting the clinician's decision-making process and enhancing the overall reliability of the AI system in a clinical setting.

2.3.4. Confidence Assessment

The model was also instructed to perform self-monitoring by evaluating the confidence level of each diagnostic suggestion. This process involved the LLM evaluating its responses based on the difficulty of the task, the degree of consistency with the training data, and the consistency across its outputs. By quantitatively assessing confidence levels, we enabled a mechanism by which only high-confidence diagnostic suggestions were considered reliable. This method aimed to reduce misdiagnoses by ensuring that only the most probable and well-supported diagnoses were reported, improving the overall reliability of the diagnostic process.

These prompt engineering strategies were crucial to optimizing GPT-4 Turbo's performance in diagnosing complex neuroradiology cases. The goal was to balance diagnostic accuracy with practical usability in a clinical setting.

Box 1. Expert diagnostic prompt.

 # Role
You are an expert in medical imaging diagnosis with extensive experience interpreting various medical images, including CT, MRI, and X-rays. Your expertise includes identifying pathologies, understanding radiology clinical report contexts, and correlating to imaging findings with potential diagnoses proofread.

 # Request
Along with the following Regulation prompt, present a refined list of five differential diagnoses, including the most probable diagnosis and four alternatives.
Each diagnosis should have a corresponding confidence level based on your comprehensive analysis.

 # Regulation
Using the clinical information provided: {# URL of clinical information}, list five initial differential diagnoses.
Then, review the imaging findings: {# URL of image findings}, and update your diagnoses accordingly. Reflect on how the new data alters your assessment.
For each diagnosis in your updated list, assign a confidence level between 0% and 100%, considering the task's complexity and the extent to which clinical and imaging data support each diagnosis.

2.4. Evaluation of the Diagnostic Accuracy of GPT-4 Turbo

Two board-certified neuroradiologists with 15 and 28 years of clinical experience (T.A. and A.W) rigorously evaluated the diagnostic suggestions from GPT-4 Turbo. The evaluation involved a detailed review of GPT-4 Turbo's response list, where each response was classified into one of three categories based on diagnostic accuracy: "Excellent", "Good", and "Insufficient". This classification was performed post hoc by neuroradiologists who reviewed each response without prior knowledge of the AI confidence score or the difficulty level assessment provided by the model.

- Excellent: The top diagnostic suggestion matched the correct diagnosis exactly.
- Good: The correct diagnosis was among the top suggested candidates, indicating a useful but not precise match.
- Insufficient: The correct diagnosis was not listed among the suggested candidates, indicating a failure in the diagnostic process.

3. Results

3.1. Case Distribution Analysis

Figure 1 classifies the 751 challenge cases into various disease categories. From this graph, it is recognized that there is a high frequency of challenges for tumors and demyelinating and inflammatory diseases, as well as genetic and degenerative diseases.

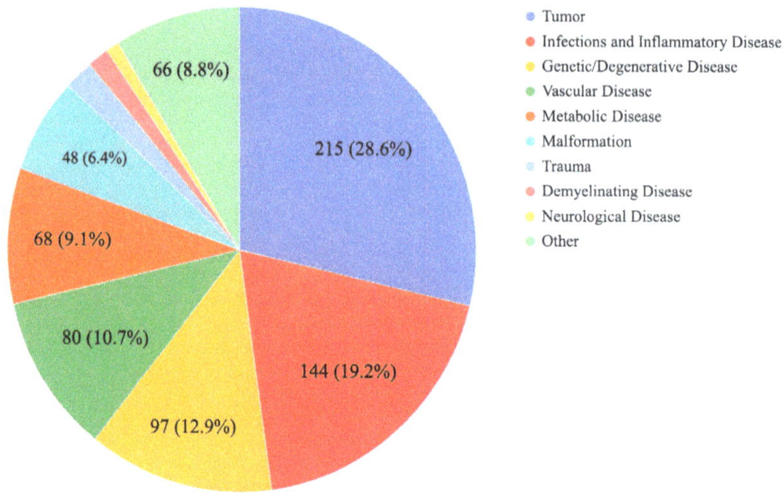

Figure 1. Proportion of total cases by disease category. This pie chart shows the distribution of 751 clinical cases in various disease categories.

3.2. Diagnostic Performance Overview

Figure 2 and Table 1 illustrate the baseline diagnostic accuracy of GPT-4 Turbo in an analysis of 751 neuroradiological cases. The 'Excellent' rating, where the predicted top diagnosis precisely matched the ground truth, was obtained in 55.1% of cases. Furthermore, the 'Good' category, where the correct diagnosis was included among the top five predictions, accounted for 15.5% of cases. The total frequency of GPT-4 Turbo responses that included the correct diagnosis and helped clinical decision-making was 70.6%. However, the model produced 'Insufficient' responses in 29.4% of cases, where it failed to provide a useful candidate diagnosis.

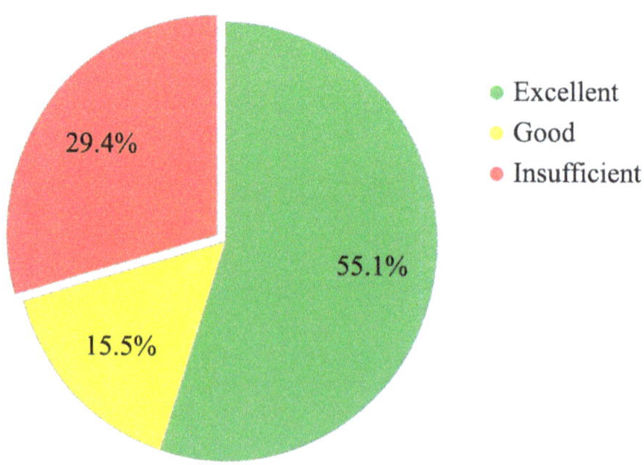

Figure 2. Evaluation of GPT-4 Turbo responses in 751 cases of neuroradiology.

Table 1. Breakdown of GPT-4 Turbo tasks in each disease category in neuroradiological cases.

Disease Category	GPT4-Turbo Response Results			Proportion of Total Cases
	Excellent	Good	Insufficient	
Tumor	0.442	0.191	0.367	0.29 (215)
Demyelinating Disease	0.727	0.000	0.273	0.01 (11)
Infections and Inflammatory Disease	0.535	0.153	0.313	0.19 (144)
Vascular Disease	0.688	0.150	0.163	0.11 (80)
Genetic/Degenerative Disease	0.515	0.134	0.351	0.13 (97)
Trauma	0.667	0.267	0.067	0.02 (15)
Metabolic Disease	0.735	0.088	0.176	0.09 (68)
Malformation	0.563	0.229	0.208	0.06 (48)
Neurological Disease	0.571	0.000	0.429	0.01 (7)
Other	0.576	0.106	0.318	0.09 (66)
Total	0.551	0.154	0.294	1.00 (751)

The 'Excellent' category represents cases where the top diagnostic prediction matches the correct diagnosis. 'Good' indicates cases where the correct diagnosis was included within the top five diagnostic predictions. 'Insufficient' marks cases where the correct diagnosis was not included in the diagnostic predictions.

3.3. *Impact of Confidence Thresholds on Diagnostic Accuracy*

Table 2 and Figure 3 show the effect of confidence threshold adjustments on diagnostic accuracy and acceptance rates. At the standard 60% confidence threshold, the 'Excellent' diagnoses rate remained steady at 55.1%, and the combined 'Excellent + Good' rate was 70.6%. In particular, the misdiagnosis rate was 29.4%. Increasing the confidence threshold to 90% markedly improved diagnostic precision: the misdiagnosis rate dropped to 14.1%, effectively halving the rate of diagnostic errors. During the same period, the rate of 'excellent' diagnoses increased to 72.9%. However, this rigorous threshold reduced the scope of the analysis to only 47% of the cases that met the high-confidence criteria.

Stacked bars represent the 'Excellent', 'Good', and 'Insufficient' diagnostic outcomes. This graph illustrates the diagnostic performance classified by confidence level threshold from 60 (all cases) to 90. At higher thresholds, the decay of 'Excellent' and 'Good' outcomes is slight. In contrast, 'Insufficient' decreases with increased thresholds, showcasing improved diagnostic reliability.

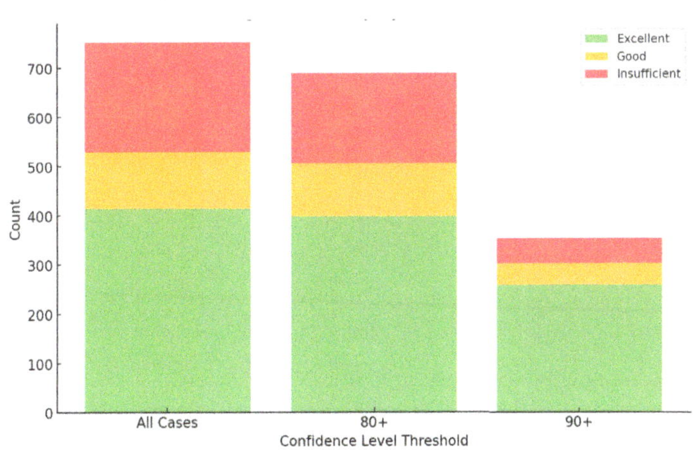

Figure 3. Impact of confidence thresholds on diagnostic performance.

Table 2. Diagnostic accuracy of GPT-4 Turbo at Varying Confidence Thresholds.

Confidence Threshold	Excellent (%)	Good (%)	Insufficient (%)	Adoption Rate
≥60%	55.1	15.5	29.4	100% (751/751)
≥70%	55.3	15.5	29.2	99% (746/751)
≥80%	57.9	15.8	26.3	92% (689/751)
≥90%	72.9	13.0	14.1	47% (354/751)
1	87.5	12.5	0.0	1% (8/751)

4. Discussion

The baseline precision of GPT-4 Turbo at 55.1% is in line with previous findings in this domain, underscoring the persistent challenge of improving diagnostic precision in complex medical fields. This study introduces innovative and prompt engineering strategies that reshape how LLMs process diagnostic data. Our prompt included three instructions: role-playing, step-by-step thinking, multiple diagnostic suggestions, and confidence assessment.

Role-playing is one of the fundamental techniques in prompt engineering. Tailored responses can be obtained by instructing the model to act as a specific entity, such as a historian or a scientist. For example, directing the model with "As a physician, evaluate the following treatment plan" can yield responses grounded in medical science.

Step-by-step prompt engineering is a crucial technique for optimizing AI performance. This approach, known as step-by-step thinking, involves guiding AI through a series of clear sequential steps to solve complex problems. By breaking down the problem-solving process, errors can be minimized at each stage, ultimately improving the accuracy of the final solution. Ye et al. demonstrated that prompt engineering is essential for enhancing the performance of LLMs [26]. They proposed using step-by-step reasoning templates to draw out complex inferential capabilities, thereby improving model performance.

Similarly, Sylvester and Reggia emphasized the importance of a step-by-step approach in high-level problem-solving with AI [27]. They developed a neural network framework that combines top-down and bottom-up approaches to achieve effective results, especially for tasks requiring ordered steps, such as card-matching problems. Scandura et al. highlighted the significance of step-by-step computational procedures in algorithm learning and problem-solving across various fields, showing how step-by-step methods contribute to effective problem resolution [28]. These studies underscore that step-by-step prompt engineering improves AI performance by facilitating structured and accurate problem-solving processes.

Providing multiple diagnostic suggestions instead of a single diagnosis is a technique that falls under adaptive prompting techniques. In the context of adaptive prompting, AI models are developed to adjust their responses based on the user's input style and preferences. This personalization approach aims to make AI interactions more natural and user-friendly. For instance, if a user tends to ask concise questions, the AI adapts to provide concise answers, and vice versa. This development is particularly promising for enhancing user experience in AI-driven applications such as virtual assistants and chatbots. Applying this concept to a medical diagnosis and providing multiple potential answers can be considered an adaptive prompting technique. By offering several diagnostic suggestions, the AI adapts to the clinician's needs, who may need various options for the best possible diagnosis. This method supports the clinician's decision-making process and improves the overall accuracy and reliability of the AI system in a clinical setting. By expanding from a single diagnostic prediction to a set of five, the probability of including the correct diagnosis increased to 70%, and the instances of insufficient responses were reduced to 30%. In medical diagnosis, where LLMs assist doctors, the risk of misdiagnosis can be reduced if LLMs provide five potential diagnoses rather than just one. Offering multiple diagnostic suggestions increases the probability of including the correct diagnosis, thus reducing the chance of misdiagnosis. Zheng et al. found that the accuracy of LLM responses greatly depends on the design of the prompts [29]. Using methods like Progressive-Hint Prompting, LLMs are guided through a series of steps, helping them to get closer to the correct answer. This approach involves generating multiple potential answers and using these as hints to refine subsequent responses, ultimately improving the final accuracy. Huang et al. showed that LLMs can improve their reasoning skills by using high-confidence answers that they generate themselves. By producing multiple answers and selecting the most reliable ones, LLMs improve their accuracy and reliability [30]. Savage et al. demonstrated that providing multiple diagnostic suggestions helps physicians better assess and understand LLM diagnoses. This approach makes it easier for physicians to review the LLM diagnostic process, improving diagnostic accuracy and gaining greater trust in the LLM [31].

Implementing systems that consider confidence thresholds is a key aspect of adaptive modeling techniques. Confidence thresholds involve evaluating the model's confidence in its predictions and using this information to make decisions about resource allocation and response handling. By focusing on predictions with high confidence and addressing those with low confidence differently, models can enhance their accuracy and efficiency. Research highlights the application of confidence thresholds in various contexts, such as uncertainty-aware in-context learning, which filters out responses with high uncertainty to improve reliability [32]. Generating confidence scores based on agreement between different prompts creates more accurate predictions, which is essential for decision-making processes [33]. Self-improvement techniques, where models use high-confidence answers for further learning, enhance reasoning abilities without needing labeled data [30]. Additionally, Pareto's optimal self-supervision aids in calibrating model responses by providing risk scores for each answer, boosting accuracy in critical fields such as biomedicine [34]. By integrating confidence thresholds into adaptive modeling techniques, LLMs deliver more accurate and reliable results, making them more effective for various applications [35].

In our study, a novel approach was introduced that uses confidence thresholds to filter LLM responses. This added an analytical layer that effectively halved the frequency of incorrect diagnoses from 29.4% to 14.1%, highlighting the potential of this approach to improve the clinical utility of LLMs. Implementing these thresholds led to a substantial decrease in insufficient responses, from 221 to 50, in a dataset of 751 cases. However, this method required greater human intervention in 53% of cases where the LLM did not meet the high-confidence criteria, revealing a significant trade-off between accuracy and practical usability. The model automatically recognizes uncertainty in scenarios where responses are not obtained and filters out high-uncertainty responses, enhancing reliability.

The success of diagnostic efforts depends on human expertise and the quality of data supplied to the LLM. High confidence thresholds significantly reduce the risk of incorrect diagnoses and restrict the number of cases the LLM can effectively address. Requiring medical professionals to evaluate multiple diagnostic proposals introduces additional cognitive load, affecting clinical workflows and decision-making processes. It is important to note that pursuing excessively high confidence thresholds does not yield beneficial results. Although setting the confidence threshold at 100% ensures perfect accuracy, it covers only 8 out of 751 cases, representing a mere 1% reduction in radiologists' workload. This outcome demonstrates that current AI technology cannot replace the capabilities of radiologists.

This study focused on precision in scenarios where sufficient information was provided for diagnosis, indicating the need for further research on LLM performance with real-world data, which may be incomplete or atypical, and in domains beyond neuroradiology. Future research should enhance LLM accuracy by expanding learning data, especially for tasks with low confidence levels, and implementing few-shot learning as part of prompt engineering to refine LLM reasoning processes by providing examples of human thought processes. Optimizing these methods to increase the proportion of high-confidence cases is crucial for future research.

To address the concerns raised about the composition of the AJNR Case of the Week Archive, we acknowledge that the cases included in our study are more specialized compared to those typically encountered in routine clinical practice. The AJNR Case of the Week Archive is curated by editors who select cases that are educational and designed to improve diagnostic skills by presenting unique and challenging scenarios. Consequently, the frequency and types of disease in the archive do not represent the actual distribution seen in everyday clinical settings. This selection bias is a limitation of our study, and we have taken it into account in our analysis. For example, when comparing the cases targeted in this study with those encountered in routine clinical practice, particularly in the context of trauma, there are several notable differences. The number of trauma cases in our dataset is relatively low. Additionally, the ability to detect abnormalities, which is crucial in trauma imaging, was not evaluated in this study. These factors should be considered limitations.

5. Conclusions

Prompt engineering strategies, including the appropriate setting of confidence thresholds, improve its diagnostic assistance capabilities. Currently, the simple diagnostic accuracy of GPT-4 Turbo in neuroradiology is not ideal, but AI-assisted image diagnosis and clinical decision-making with increased reliability are a promising path to improving medical outcomes. Our research results will encourage the continued development and refinement of these strategies to maximize the potential of AI in improving healthcare outcomes.

Author Contributions: Conceptualization, A.W. and T.A.; methodology, A.W.; software, G.S.; validation, M.N., Y.H., J.K. and K.S. (Katsuhiro Sano); formal analysis, A.W.; investigation, A.H., M.N. and Y.H.; resources, A.W.; data curation, K.S. (Keigo Shimoji); writing—original draft preparation, A.W.; writing—review and editing, T.A. and G.S.; visualization, K.S. (Keigo Shimoji); supervision, G.S., K.K., A.N. and S.A.; project administration, A.W.; funding acquisition, S.A. All authors have read and agreed to the published version of the manuscript.

Funding: This work was supported by the Japan Society for the Promotion of Science (JSPS) KAKENHI under Grant [22K07674]. The authors express their gratitude for the financial support provided, which has been instrumental in the advancement of this research.

Institutional Review Board Statement: This study was exempted from institutional review board oversight because it used publicly available data.

Informed Consent Statement: Not applicable.

Data Availability Statement: The logs of conversations with GPT-4 Turbo from this study will be made publicly available on GitHub at https://github.com/aki-wada/GPT4-Turbo, accessed on 17 July 2024.

Conflicts of Interest: The authors declare no conflicts of interest. The funders had no role in the design of the study, in the collection, analyses, or interpretation of data, in the writing of the manuscript, or in the decision to publish the results.

References

1. Hirosawa, T.; Harada, Y.; Yokose, M.; Sakamoto, T.; Kawamura, R.; Shimizu, T. Diagnostic Accuracy of Differential-Diagnosis Lists Generated by Generative Pretrained Transformer 3 Chatbot for Clinical Vignettes with Common Chief Complaints: A Pilot Study. *Int. J. Environ. Res. Public Health* **2023**, *20*, 3378. [CrossRef] [PubMed]
2. Chen, A.; Chen, D.O.; Tian, L. Benchmarking the Symptom-Checking Capabilities of ChatGPT for a Broad Range of Diseases. *J. Am. Med. Inform. Assoc.* **2023**, ocad245. [CrossRef] [PubMed]
3. Antaki, F.; Touma, S.; Milad, D.; El-Khoury, J.; Duval, R. Evaluating the Performance of ChatGPT in Ophthalmology: An Analysis of Its Successes and Shortcomings. *medRxiv* **2023**. [CrossRef]
4. Lallas, A.; Lallas, K.; Tschandl, P.; Kittler, H.; Apalla, Z.; Longo, C.; Argenziano, G. The Dermoscopic Inverse Approach Significantly Improves the Accuracy of Human Readers for Lentigo Maligna Diagnosis. *J. Am. Acad. Dermatol.* **2021**, *84*, 381–389. [CrossRef] [PubMed]
5. Yang, Z.; Yao, Z.; Tasmin, M.; Vashisht, P.; Jang, W.S.; Ouyang, F.; Wang, B.; Berlowitz, D.; Yu, H. Performance of Multimodal GPT-4V on USMLE with Image: Potential for Imaging Diagnostic Support with Explanations. *medRxiv* **2023**. [CrossRef]

6. Gertz, R.; Bunck, A.; Lennartz, S.; Dratsch, T.; Iuga, A.-I.; Maintz, D.; Kottlors, J. GPT-4 for Automated Determination of Radiological Study and Protocol Based on Radiology Request Forms: A Feasibility Study. *Radiology* **2023**, *307*, e230877. [CrossRef] [PubMed]
7. Biswas, S. ChatGPT and the Future of Medical Writing. *Radiology* **2023**, *30*, e223312. [CrossRef]
8. Bhayana, R.; Bleakney, R.R.; Krishna, S. GPT-4 in Radiology: Improvements in Advanced Reasoning. *Radiology* **2023**, *307*, e230987. [CrossRef] [PubMed]
9. Fink, M.A.; Bischoff, A.; Fink, C.A.; Moll, M.; Kroschke, J.; Dulz, L.; Heußel, C.P.; Kauczor, H.-U.; Weber, T.F. Potential of ChatGPT and GPT-4 for Data Mining of Free-Text CT Reports on Lung Cancer. *Radiology* **2023**, *308*, e231362. [CrossRef]
10. Jiang, S.-T.; Xu, Y.-Y.; Lu, X. ChatGPT in Radiology: Evaluating Proficiencies, Addressing Shortcomings, and Proposing Integrative Approaches for the Future. *Radiology* **2023**, *308*, e231335. [CrossRef]
11. Haver, H.L.; Ambinder, E.B.; Bahl, M.; Oluyemi, E.T.; Jeudy, J.; Yi, P.H. Appropriateness of Breast Cancer Prevention and Screening Recommendations Provided by ChatGPT. *Radiology* **2023**, *307*, e230424. [CrossRef] [PubMed]
12. Jeblick, K.; Schachtner, B.; Dexl, J.; Mittermeier, A.; Stüber, A.T.; Topalis, J.; Weber, T.; Wesp, P.; Sabel, B.O.; Ricke, J.; et al. ChatGPT Makes Medicine Easy to Swallow: An Exploratory Case Study on Simplified Radiology Reports. *Eur. Radiol.* **2023**, *34*, 2817–2825. [CrossRef] [PubMed]
13. Bhayana, R. Chatbots and Large Language Models in Radiology: A Practical Primer for Clinical and Research Applications. *Radiology* **2024**, *310*, e232756. [CrossRef] [PubMed]
14. Bhayana, R.; Krishna, S.; Bleakney, R.R. Performance of ChatGPT on a Radiology Board-Style Examination: Insights into Current Strengths and Limitations. *Radiology* **2023**, *307*, e230582. [CrossRef] [PubMed]
15. Ueda, D.; Mitsuyama, Y.; Takita, H.; Horiuchi, D.; Walston, S.L.; Tatekawa, H.; Miki, Y. Diagnostic Performance of ChatGPT from Patient History and Imaging Findings on the Diagnosis Please Quizzes. *Radiology* **2023**, *308*, e231040. [CrossRef]
16. Kottlors, J.; Bratke, G.; Rauen, P.; Kabbasch, C.; Persigehl, T.; Schlamann, M.; Lennartz, S. Feasibility of Differential Diagnosis Based on Imaging Patterns Using a Large Language Model. *Radiology* **2023**, *308*, e231167. [CrossRef]
17. Horiuchi, D.; Tatekawa, H.; Shimono, T.; Walston, S.L.; Takita, H.; Matsushita, S.; Oura, T.; Mitsuyama, Y.; Miki, Y.; Ueda, D. Accuracy of ChatGPT Generated Diagnosis from Patient's Medical History and Imaging Findings in Neuroradiology Cases. *Neuroradiology* **2024**, *66*, 73–79. [CrossRef]
18. Suthar, P.P.; Kounsal, A.; Chhetri, L.; Saini, D.; Dua, S.G. Artificial Intelligence (AI) in Radiology: A Deep Dive Into ChatGPT 4.0's Accuracy with the American Journal of Neuroradiology's (AJNR) "Case of the Month". *Cureus* **2023**, *15*, e43958. [CrossRef] [PubMed]
19. Shen, Y.; Heacock, L.; Elias, J.; Hentel, K.D.; Reig, B.; Shih, G.; Moy, L. ChatGPT and Other Large Language Models Are Double-Edged Swords. *Radiology* **2023**, *307*, e230163. [CrossRef]
20. Prompt Engineering—OpenAI API. Available online: https://platform.openai.com/docs/guides/prompt-engineering (accessed on 18 March 2024).
21. Case of the Week Diagnoses | American Journal of Neuroradiology. Available online: https://www.ajnr.org/cow/by/diagnosis (accessed on 18 March 2024).
22. GPT-4 Turbo in the OpenAI API. Available online: https://help.openai.com/en/articles/8555510-gpt-4-turbo (accessed on 26 May 2024).
23. Nori, H.; King, N.; McKinney, S.M.; Carignan, D.; Horvitz, E. Capabilities of GPT-4 on Medical Challenge Problems. *arXiv* **2023**, arXiv:2303.13375.
24. MD.Ai. Available online: https://www.md.ai/ (accessed on 26 May 2024).
25. Ickes, W.; Holloway, R.; Stinson, L.L.; Hoodenpyle, T.G. Self-Monitoring in Social Interaction: The Centrality of Self-Affect. *J. Pers.* **2006**, *74*, 659–684. [CrossRef] [PubMed]
26. Ye, Q.; Axmed, M.; Pryzant, R.; Khani, F. Prompt Engineering a Prompt Engineer. *arXiv* **2023**. [CrossRef]
27. Sylvester, J.; Reggia, J. Engineering Neural Systems for High-Level Problem Solving. *Neural Netw. Off. J. Int. Neural Netw. Soc.* **2015**, *79*, 37–52. [CrossRef] [PubMed]
28. Scandura, J.M. Algorithm Learning and Problem Solving. *J. Exp. Educ.* **1966**, *34*, 1–6. [CrossRef]
29. Zheng, C.; Liu, Z.; Xie, E.; Li, Z.; Li, Y. Progressive-Hint Prompting Improves Reasoning in Large Language Models. *arXiv* **2023**. [CrossRef]
30. Huang, J.; Gu, S.; Hou, L.; Wu, Y.; Wang, X.; Yu, H.; Han, J. Large Language Models Can Self-Improve. In Proceedings of the 2023 Conference on Empirical Methods in Natural Language Processing, Singapore, 6–10 December 2023; pp. 1051–1068. [CrossRef]
31. Savage, T.; Nayak, A.; Gallo, R.; Rangan, E.; Chen, J.H. Diagnostic Reasoning Prompts Reveal the Potential for Large Language Model Interpretability in Medicine. *NPJ Digit. Med.* **2024**, *7*, 20. [CrossRef] [PubMed]
32. Yang, Y.; Li, H.; Wang, Y.; Wang, Y. Improving the Reliability of Large Language Models by Leveraging Uncertainty-Aware In-Context Learning. *arXiv* **2023**. [CrossRef]
33. Wightman, G.P.; Delucia, A.; Dredze, M. Strength in Numbers: Estimating Confidence of Large Language Models by Prompt Agreement. In Proceedings of the 3rd Workshop on Trustworthy Natural Language Processing (TrustNLP 2023), Toronto, ON, Canada, 14 July 2023; pp. 326–362. [CrossRef]

34. Zhao, T.; Wei, M.; Preston, J.S.; Poon, H. Pareto Optimal Learning for Estimating Large Language Model Errors. *arXiv* **2023**. [CrossRef]
35. Schuster, T.; Fisch, A.; Gupta, J.; Dehghani, M.; Bahri, D.; Tran, V.Q.; Tay, Y.; Metzler, D. Confident Adaptive Language Modeling. *arXiv* **2022**. [CrossRef]

Journal of
Clinical Medicine

MDPI

Article

Deep Learning in Cardiothoracic Ratio Calculation and Cardiomegaly Detection

Jakub Kufel [1,*], Iga Paszkiewicz [2], Szymon Kocot [3], Anna Lis [4], Piotr Dudek [5], Łukasz Czogalik [5], Michał Janik [5], Katarzyna Bargieł-Łączek [6], Wiktoria Bartnikowska [6], Maciej Koźlik [7], Maciej Cebula [8], Katarzyna Gruszczyńska [1] and Zbigniew Nawrat [9,10]

1 Department of Radiology and Nuclear Medicine, Faculty of Medical Sciences in Katowice, Medical University of Silesia, Medyków 14, 40-752 Katowice, Poland
2 Tytus Chalubinski's Hospital in Zakopane, 34-500 Zakopane, Poland
3 Bright Coders' Factory, Technologiczna 2, 45-837 Opole, Poland
4 Faculty of Medicine in Katowice, Medical University of Silesia, Medyków 18, 40-752 Katowice, Poland
5 Students' Scientific Association of Computer Analysis and Artificial Intelligence, Department of Radiology and Nuclear Medicine, Medical University of Silesia, Medyków 14, 40-752 Katowice, Poland
6 Paediatric Radiology Students' Scientific Association, Division of Diagnostic Imaging, Department of Radiology and Nuclear Medicine, Faculty of Medical Science in Katowice, Medical University of Silesia, 40-752 Katowice, Poland
7 Division of Cardiology and Structural Heart Disease, Medical University of Silesia, 40-635 Katowice, Poland
8 Individual Specialist Medical Practice Maciej Cebula, 40-239 Katowice, Poland
9 Foundation of Cardiac Surgery Development, 41-800 Zabrze, Poland
10 Department of Biophysics, Faculty of Medical Sciences in Zabrze, Medical University of Silesia, 41-808 Zabrze, Poland
* Correspondence: jakubkufel92@gmail.com

Abstract: Objectives: The purpose of this study is to evaluate the performance of our deep learning algorithm in calculating cardiothoracic ratio (CTR) and thus in the assessment of cardiomegaly or pericardial effusion occurrences on chest radiography (CXR). **Methods**: From a database of 8000 CXRs, 13 folders with a comparable number of images were created. Then, 1020 images were chosen randomly, in proportion to the number of images in each folder. Afterward, CTR was calculated using RadiAnt Digital Imaging and Communications in Medicine (DICOM) Viewer software (2023.1). Next, heart and lung anatomical areas were marked in 3D Slicer. From these data, we trained an AI model which segmented heart and lung anatomy and determined the CTR value. **Results**: Our model achieved an Intersection over Union metric of 88.28% for the augmented training subset and 83.06% for the validation subset. F1-score for subsets were accordingly 90.22% and 90.67%. In the comparative analysis of artificial intelligence (AI) vs. humans, significantly lower transverse thoracic diameter (TTD) ($p < 0.001$), transverse cardiac diameter (TCD) ($p < 0.001$), and CTR ($p < 0.001$) values obtained using the neural network were observed. **Conclusions**: Results confirm that there is a significant correlation between the measurements made by human observers and the neural network. After validation in clinical conditions, our method may be used as a screening test or advisory tool when a specialist is not available, especially on Intensive Care Units (ICUs) or Emergency Departments (ERs) where time plays a key role.

Keywords: chest radiograph; cardiothoracic ratio; cardiomegaly; convolutional neural network; segmentation

1. Introduction

Chest radiography (CXR) is one of the most frequently performed imaging procedures in clinical diagnosis, representing 40% of the 3.6 billion imaging procedures performed worldwide every year [1]. The National Health Service (NHS) of the United Kingdom

(UK) reports that around 2.2 million CXRs are ordered by general practitioners performed each year [2]. According to the Federal Office for Radiation Protection in Germany, CXR accounted for about 13 million X-ray examinations in 2018 [3]. Its main advantage is high availability (regardless of the size and location of the medical facility), low cost, and wide diagnostic use in many diseases, including lung and heart diseases. One useful measurement determined on CXR is the cardiothoracic ratio (CTR), which is the ratio of the width of the heart silhouette (TCD—transverse cardiac diameter) to the widest dimension of the chest (TTD—transverse thoracic diameter). CTR helps in detecting enlargement of the heart silhouette, which usually indicates cardiomegaly, but can also be the result of pericardial effusion [4]. A value greater than 0.50 (normal: 0.42–0.50) in an adult who is considered pathological [5]. Although the diagnostic and predictive value of this parameter is losing importance in relation to modern methods such as echocardiography of determining the size of the heart, CXR and CTR are still valuable in the assessment of heart size in the hospital emergency room (ER) or intensive care unit (ICU) [6].

According to literature reports, the CTR should be determined in the posteroanterior (PA) projection [7,8], even though there are also studies containing appropriate values for CTR in the anteroposterior (AP) projection [5]. The cut-off value for CTR may vary, depending on the projection of the study and the group of patients in whom the study is performed. The PA projection is preferred because the silhouette of the heart is closest to its true dimensions. In the case of the AP projection, the heart is closer to the cassette, which makes its silhouette enlarged. Even so, AP is indispensable in the diagnosis of bedridden patients and small children.

Cardiomegaly is a broad term for various conditions that cause the heart's enlargement, often going undiagnosed until symptoms appear. It affects nearly 5.8 million people in the United States. There are many reasons for the development of cardiomegaly—from coronary artery disease and myocardial infarction, through valvular regurgitation, various cardiomyopathies, to physiological conditions such as the athlete's heart or pregnancy [9]. Many of these are pathological conditions, which may lead to heart failure, resulting in up to a 50% five-year survival rate [10]. Considering the potential risk underlying this pathology, CTR should be assessed in each chest X-ray examination. However, it is a time-consuming process. Artificial intelligence (AI) and its subset, deep learning (DL), have proven to be helpful in improving the effectiveness of diagnostic imaging in medicine. Thanks to the use of convolutional neural networks (CNNs), the diagnosis of pathology on CXR has reached a level comparable to the effectiveness of trained radiologists [11,12].

This article focuses on the possibility of more effective usage of deep learning in clinical diagnostics. To conduct the study, the standardized digital imaging and communications in medicine (DICOM) format was used, which enables efficient distribution of datasets. The aim was to evaluate the performance of our deep learning algorithm in calculating CTR, and thus predict the possibility of such diseases as cardiomegaly or pericardial effusion on chest X-rays. The algorithm was compared with physicians, whose assessment was used as a reference method. The correctness of anatomical segmentation of the heart and lungs performed by physicians and artificial intelligence (AI) was also analyzed.

2. Materials and Methods

2.1. Radiological Phase

To ensure the highest possible standard of this study, a preliminary analysis and selection of images was carried out from a database of about 8000 anonymized CXRs. The patients from whom the images were taken during their admission to the clinical hospital gave their consent to the collection and processing of their data. The exclusion criteria for CXR images were as follows: images were not of the chest; images with an abnormal range not covering all chest structures; rotated images; incorrectly exposed images; images with movement artifacts; and images of children.

The entire dataset was divided into 13 folders containing a comparable number of CXRs. In total, 4 investigators (3 doctor interns and 1 radiology resident doctor) pre-analyzed the contents of the folders to determine the projection in which the images were taken: standing (PA), or prone (AP). A total of 1020 CXRs were randomly selected from all analyzed images proportionally from each of the 13 folders. Because CXR images of both PA and AP were included in this study, different CTR threshold values were set depending on the position of the patient: >0.55 for the standing position, >0.58 for the supine position, based on previous studies [5,13–15].

Afterward, the same four investigators independently calculated the CTR by measuring the width of the heart and lungs separately. The CTR was calculated for all eligible studies using the freely available RadiAnt DICOM Viewer software (2023.1). The chest width was measured at the widest point, usually at the height of the diaphragm domes. Heart width measurements were made with respect to a vertical line drawn along the spinous processes of the vertebrae.

An orthogonal line segment was then drawn from the vertical line to the farthest border of the heart separately on the left and right sides. The sum of the left and right segments determined the measurement of the width of the heart silhouette (Figure 1). During CTR calculations, the time needed to estimate TCD and TTD was measured each time for all four researchers. A table containing the individual results of the measurements (TCD, TTD, CTR, measurement time) made by the researchers and AI can be found in the Supplementary Materials (Table S1).

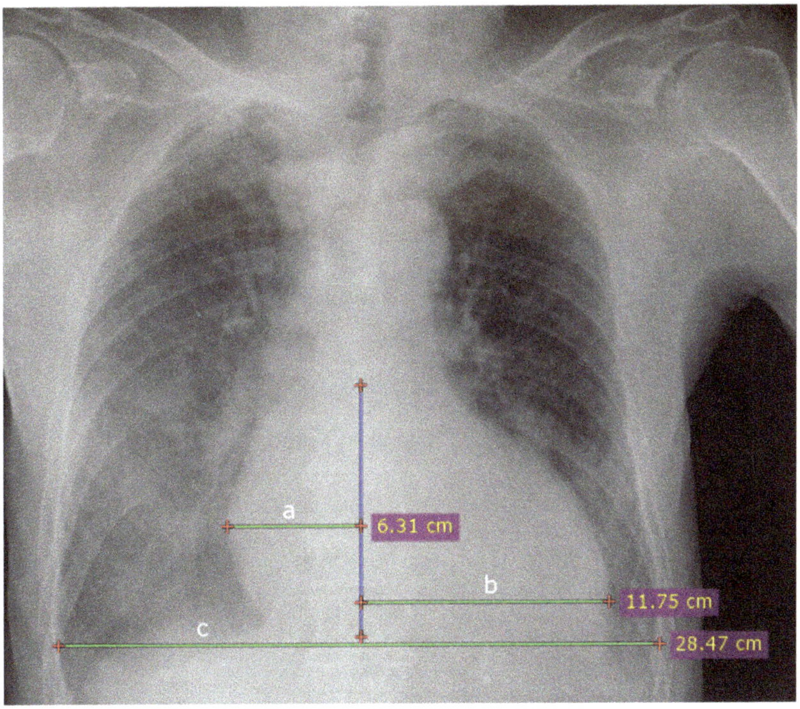

Figure 1. How measurements were manually determined using RadiAnt: blue vertical line—a line drawn through the spinous processes of the thoracic spine vertebrae; a—right side of the heart; b—left side of the heart; a + b = the widest dimension of the heart; c—the widest dimension of the chest.

Then, the four investigators independently marked a total of 1059 CXR anatomical areas of the heart and lungs in the 3D Slicer program, which is used to make annotations on radiological images. The masks were used in subsequent stages to train the artificial neural network model. The finished markings were re-checked by another two independent researchers with the most experience to eliminate potential errors. Both lungs were marked with the same color as mask #1. The lung mask covered the area from the inner surfaces of the ribs, including the shadow of the mediastinum, bilaterally to the paraspinal line. The heart has been marked with a separate color as mask #2 (Figure 2), excluding trunks of large venous and arterial vessels. It was decided to overlap the masks in the areas where the shadows of the heart overlap with the areas of the lungs to increase the accuracy of measurements and receive the most accurate mapping of anatomical structures.

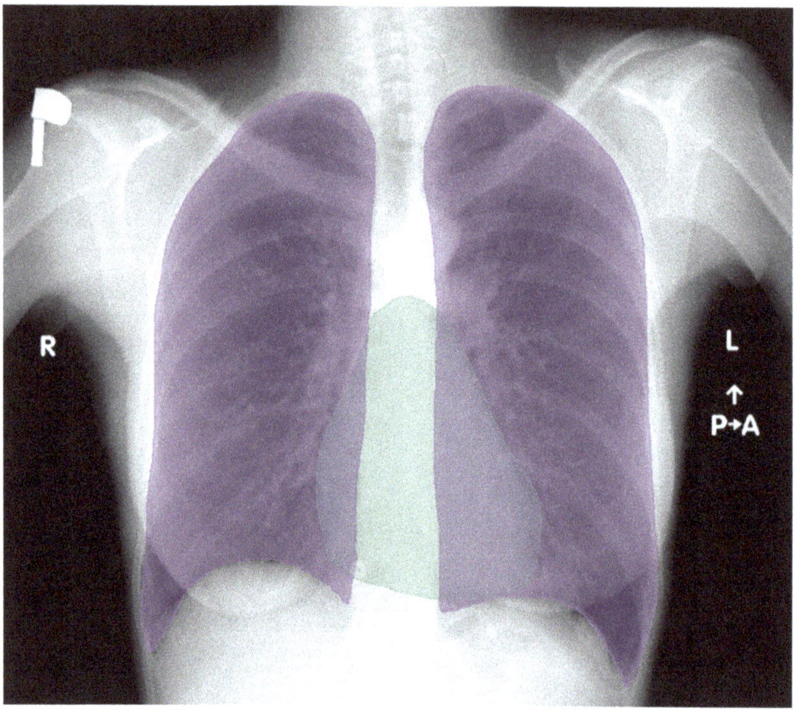

Figure 2. How annotations were applied to the anatomical areas of the heart (green) and lungs (purple).

2.2. Technical Materials

To conduct machine learning experiments in the radiological domain, usually non-standard software is required to combat such aspects as overlapping annotations, annotation management, annotation storage, versioning, and verification of resulting segmentations.

2.3. Slicer and Custom Workflow

We decided to use industry standard medical annotation software, 3D Slicer (5.1.0-2022-11-16) [16]. It supports DICOM files [17] as well as standard non-overlapping segmentations and plugins which can be developed in the Python 3.10 programming language [18].

The plugin was developed to improve and enable multi-class overlapping segmentation with minimal effort from the radiological team.

The label list can be updated from a remote server and users can select, visualize, annotate, load, and save segmentation classes. To standardize the format for saving segmentations in a replicable and robust way, the zarr library [19] was used. Annotations were uploaded to the Google Drive cloud, where each annotator had their own folder in which the annotations were saved. This allowed for rapid collaboration between team members of different specializations.

2.4. Data Preparation and Dataset

We sourced about 8000 images in total, out of which 1059 were segmented with the heart and lungs label and 4072 had their CTR measured, which we used for comparison. Segmented images were split into two subsets: training (80%—847 images), used for fitting the U-Net model; and validation (20%—212 images) used for monitoring and validation of the training process. Image preparation consisted of the following steps:

1. Inversion of values of Monochrome1 to Monochrome2 images.
2. Scaling to Hounsfield units (HU).
3. Downsampling to 256 × 256.
4. Standardization to zero mean and unit variance (computed with training dataset).

In order to increase robustness of the model, the training data were augmented by randomly flipping images vertically and horizontally, as well as rotating by −0.2:+0.2 radians and −20:+20% horizontal and vertical random shift.

2.5. Semantic Segmentation—U-Net

Semantic segmentation is a supervised task in which each pixel has a class label assigned to it according to a predicted object type. It usually forms clusters which can be grouped into objects. One of the models which has been successfully applied to segmentation tasks, especially medical segmentation, is U-Net [20]. U-Net combines down/up-sampling paths and skip connections, with activation maps from different stages of forward propagation. The resolution of activation maps decreases with the combination of convolutional and pooling layers until the middle of the network and then is gradually increased by transposed convolution layers.

2.6. Model—Training Details

U-net can be adjusted to one's hardware and time resources by adjusting the number of layers and filters. We have trained a 32-layer neural network with 1.94 M parameters. An Adam optimizer with learning rate 0.001 with lr reduction on plateau was used. The network was trained for 56 epochs. A combination of focal and dice loss was used as a loss function. Using Google Colab Pro (Tesla A100) training took 9.33 min total, with each step with a batch size of 64 taking 0.8 s.

2.7. Postprocessing and CTR Calculation

CTR was computed with a non-AI algorithm, utilizing standard computer vision operations. The goal was not only to compute the width of the object(s), but also eliminate any remaining artifacts that may be the result of AI-based segmentation.

3. Results

A total of 1059 hearts and 2118 lungs were segmented on 1059 chest radiographs.

Metrics were observed during and at the end of training for both augmented training and validation subsets. Results were saved after each completed epoch. The model achieved an Intersection over Union (IoU) metric of 88.28% for the augmented training subset and 83.06% for the validation subset. F1 scores for each subset were 90.22% and 90.67%. Higher validation metrics were recorded due to data augmentation technique, which regularizes the training-reducing factor model of previously seen data (Figure 3).

We also measured the average inference time (1.839 ms; P100 GPU) while total time, including segmentation post-processing and CTR calculation (4.706 ms).

A Lilliefors test ($p < 0.01$) and Kolmogorov–Smirnov test ($p < 0.05$) were used to assess the normality of the distribution of quantitative variables.

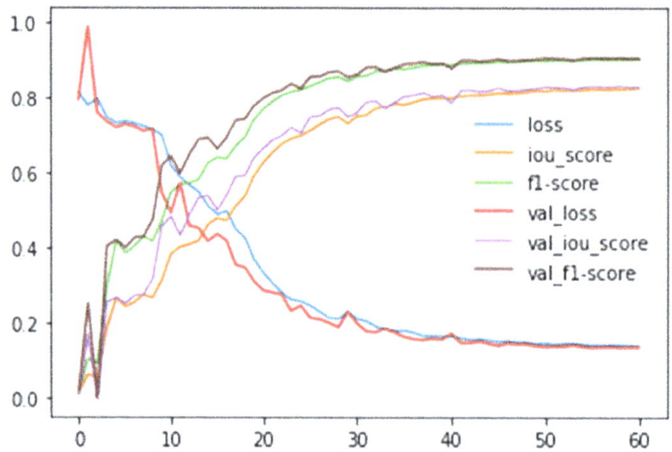

Figure 3. Metrics, loss, and learning rate during neural network training.

3.1. Comparative Analysis AI vs. Humans

The average combined measurement time for TCD, TTD, and CRT in the entire dataset was 17.00 s for the researchers and 0.004706 s for AI.

A U-Mann–Whitney test was used to assess the differences between the observers and the neural network. The results of all four observers were averaged. Extremes and outliers were discarded before comparison. Significantly lower TTD ($p < 0.001$), TCD ($p < 0.001$), and CTR ($p < 0.001$) values obtained using the neural network were observed (Figure 4).

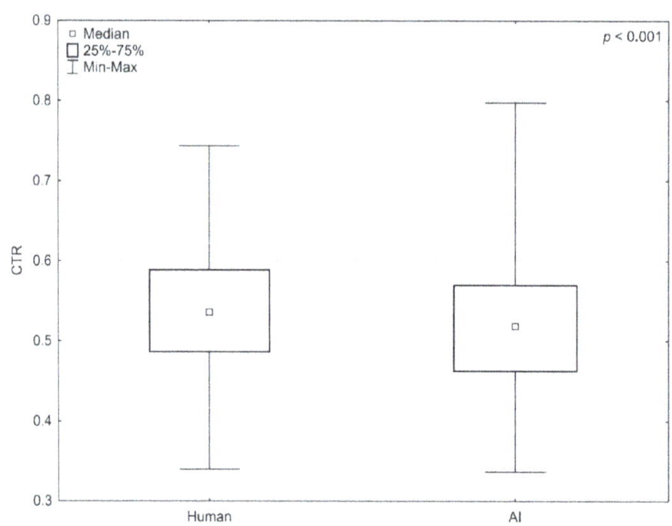

Figure 4. Difference in mean obtained by the humans observers and AI in the cardiothoracic ratio.

3.2. Comparative Analysis of the Observer vs. Observer

A Kruskal–Wallis test was used to assess differences between observers. There were no significant differences in TTD ($p = 0.823$), TCD ($p = 0.455$), and CTR ($p = 0.533$) measurements (Figure 5).

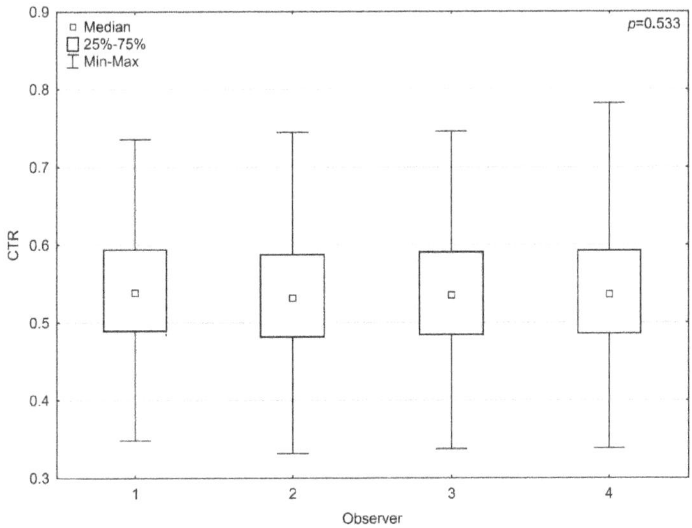

Figure 5. Difference between the human observers in the cardiothoracic ratio.

3.3. Correlation Strength Analysis (CTR_AI vs. CTR_Human)

To assess the strength of the correlation between the observers and the neural network, a Spearman rank correlation test was used, obtaining significant, positive, and strong correlations between TTD ($p < 0.01$, $r^2 = 0.875$), TCD ($p < 0.01$, $r^2 = 0.815$), and CTR ($p < 0.01$, $r^2 = 0.781$) (Figure 6).

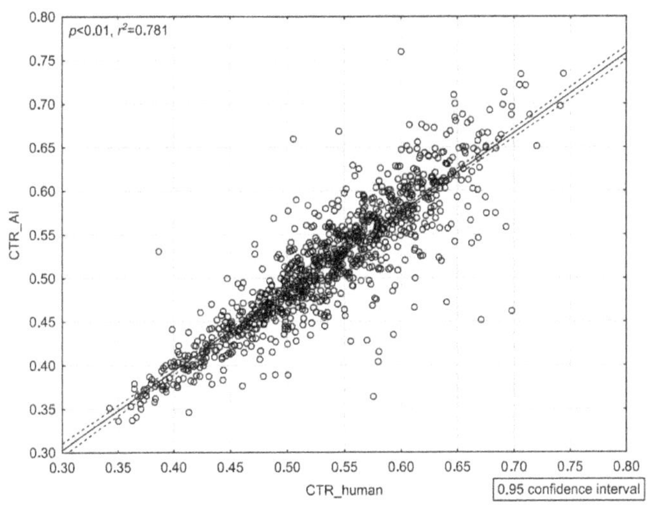

Figure 6. Correlation of the mean obtained by the human observers and AI for the cardiothoracic ratio.

4. Discussion

The CTR derived from CXR is an important tool for the assessment of heart diseases, such as cardiomegaly and pleural effusion [21,22]. However, because it requires manual measurement, is time consuming and is subject to error. The method of automatic determination of CTR has been technically validated in several studies [23,24]. However, there are few studies with clinical evaluation of this solution. Saiviroonporn et al., which validated manual CTR measurements and measurements performed with the use of artificial intelligence, rated AI assistance in diagnosing cardiomegaly at 40% as excellent, 56% as good and 4% as poor [25]. The authors of Arsalam et al. point out the time-consuming nature and the need to involve experienced medical experts in performing CTR measurements, who could be replaced by artificial intelligence and point out that cardiomegaly and related diseases have been successfully diagnosed with the use of artificial intelligence [26]. Ajmera et al. showed that the artificial intelligence model they used for CTR measurements not only achieved high specificity (>99%) and sensitivity (80%), but also contributed to increasing the efficiency of the radiologist assessing X-ray images. However, these studies concerned the comparison of CXR mainly unchanged and only in the standing position in the PA projection [27].

In our work, a broader dataset was used to train and validate a deep learning model. We are the first to include CXR in both PA and AP projections, which reflects the reality of working in a hospital with patients in various conditions. We are also the first to use a segmentation method in which anatomical areas overlap, which contributes to a better representation of these structures. All CXRs came from a hospital database, which contained many diseases and artifacts, such as drains, cables, and clothing. Our dataset thus represents conditions found in real clinical practice.

The trained model, based on the determinations carried out by our doctors, performed segmentation of the heart and lungs which were later used to calculate the CTR. The test set demonstrated high efficiency and accuracy of deep learning model segmentation, supported by qualitative (IoU, F1) and quantitative methods, comparing them with expert segmentations. The CTR values derived from the model correlated significantly with the average of the values obtained by four independent observers. The visible significant difference between the observers and AI in terms of the obtained CTR values, as well as TCD and TTD, suggests that the model underevaluates measurement values. In the retrospective analysis of some significantly underevaluated cases, it was noted that the discrepancies between the determined TCD and TTD resulted from significant scoliosis, asymmetry in the AP projection, or consolidation in the lung field projection. These factors did not significantly affect the values obtained by four independent observers, as the results of their measurements (CTR, TCD, TTD) did not significantly differ from each other. In our analysis, we decided to include studies that are difficult to assess due to our desire to reproduce the real work environment, realizing that this will affect the results. Therefore, CXR in the AP projection in bedridden patients, including ICU patients, was included in the study group.

The advantage of our tool is the fact that it allows you to shorten the interpretation time of CXR (17.00 s for researchers, 0.004706 s for AI). The radiologist usually must manually mark the segments on the image and calculate the index using the formula. Our tool takes only a few milliseconds to calculate CTR, freeing the radiologist to focus on interpreting other pathologies. Ajmera et al. obtained a CXR interpretation time of 2 s for the DL model they described [27]. Saiviroonporn et al. showed that the use of AI even as a supporting tool during manual determination of CTR values speeds up the performance of measurements almost five times (manual method—t 10.6 ± 1.5 s per case vs. manual + AI 2.2 ± 2.4 s) [25].

The application of AI in medical visualization, focusing on its role in medical imaging and image processing. AI, in particular machine learning and deep learning techniques, are being used to improve image quality, automate analysis, and support diagnosis. With AI, it is possible to detect subtle pathological changes, which contributes to early diagnosis and more precise treatment. In addition, AI plays a key role in the personalization of healthcare, providing doctors with advanced tools to interpret images and make clinical decisions [28].

5. Conclusions

To improve our model, it is necessary to train the neural network model on a larger amount of data. Moreover, CXRs should be used both in AP and PA positions with various pathologies so that they best reflect the working conditions in the hospital. In the future, after validation in clinical conditions, it will be able to provide an advisory tool for doctors to improve their work and act as a quick screening test when a specialist doctor is not available. Use can be made during chest screening, e.g., periodic examinations of employees or admission to a new job. The algorithm could have a significant impact on shortening the time of the diagnostic process (by three orders of magnitude), as well as extending CXR examination descriptions by automatically marked CTR each time. During this time, the physician describing the image could focus on the analysis of other pathologies visible in the examination. The results presented in this paper are very promising and confirm that there is a significant, positive, and strong correlation between the measurement results marked by the observers and the neural network model, which proves the great potential of using our tool to work in clinical conditions.

Supplementary Materials: The following supporting information can be downloaded at: https://www.mdpi.com/article/10.3390/jcm13144180/s1. Table S1: Measurements.

Author Contributions: Conceptualization, J.K.; Data curation, A.L., Ł.C., and W.B.; Formal analysis, I.P.; Funding acquisition, K.G.; Investigation, P.D., Ł.C., M.J., and W.B.; Methodology, J.K.; Software, S.K.; Supervision, M.C., K.G., and Z.N.; Validation, I.P.; Visualization, S.K. and Ł.C.; Writing—original draft, I.P., P.D., Ł.C., M.J., K.B.-Ł., W.B., M.K., and M.C.; Writing—review and editing, K.B.-Ł. and M.K. All authors have read and agreed to the published version of the manuscript.

Funding: This research received no external funding.

Institutional Review Board Statement: The study was conducted in accordance with the Declaration of Helsinki, and approved by the Institutional Review Board (or Ethics Committee) of Bioethical Committee of the Medical University of Silesia (PCN/0022/KB/195/20, 21 January 2021).

Informed Consent Statement: Not applicable.

Data Availability Statement: The original contributions presented in the study are included in the article/Supplementary Material; further inquiries can be directed to the corresponding author/s.

Acknowledgments: This research was supported in part by PLGrid Infrastructure. Medical University of Silesia, K. Gibiński Clinical University Center provided the data needed to perform this study.

Conflicts of Interest: Author Szymon Kocot was employed by the company Bright Coders' Factory. The remaining authors declare that the research was conducted in the absence of any commercial or financial relation-ships that could be constructed as a potential conflict of interest.

References

1. Murphy, K. How data will improve healthcare without adding staff or beds. In *The Global Innovation Index 2019*; World Intellectual Property Organization: Geneva, Switzerland, 2019; pp. 129–132.
2. NHS England. Diagnostic Imaging Dataset Annual Statistical Release 2017/18. Available online: https://www.england.nhs.uk/statistics/wp-content/uploads/sites/2/2018/11/Annual-Statistical-Release-2017-18-PDF-1.6MB-1.pdf (accessed on 31 October 2022).
3. X-ray Diagnostics: Frequency and Radiation Exposure of the German Population. Available online: https://www.bfs.de/EN/topics/ion/medicine/diagnostics/x-rays/frequency-exposure.html (accessed on 4 November 2022).
4. Gaillard, F.; Sharma, R.; Bell, D. Cardiothoracic ratio. Reference article, Radiopaedia.org. Available online: https://radiopaedia.org/articles/cardiothoracic-ratio?lang=us (accessed on 16 July 2024).
5. van der Jagt, E.J.; Smits, H.J. Cardiac size in the supine chestfilm. *Eur. J. Radiol.* **1992**, *14*, 173–177. [CrossRef] [PubMed]
6. Milne, E.N.C.; Burnett, K.; Aufrichtig, D.; McMillan, J.; Imray, T.J. Assessment of cardiac size on portable chest films. *J. Thorac. Imaging* **1988**, *3*, 64–72. [CrossRef] [PubMed]
7. Truszkiewicz, K.; Poręba, R.; Gać, P. Radiological Cardiothoracic Ratio in Evidence-Based Medicine. *J. Clin. Med.* **2021**, *10*, 2016. [CrossRef] [PubMed]
8. Simkus, P.; Gutierrez Gimeno, M.; Banisauskaite, A.; Noreikaite, J.; McCreavy, D.; Penha, D.; Arzanauskaite, M. Limitations of cardiothoracic ratio derived from chest radiographs to predict real heart size: Comparison with magnetic resonance imaging. *Insights Imaging* **2021**, *12*, 158. [CrossRef] [PubMed]
9. Amin, H.; Siddiqui, W.J. Cardiomegaly. In *StatPearls*; StatPearls Publishing: Treasure Island, FL, USA, 2022.
10. Bui, A.L.; Horwich, T.B.; Fonarow, G.C. Epidemiology and risk profile of heart failure. *Nat. Rev. Cardiol.* **2011**, *8*, 30–41. [CrossRef] [PubMed]

11. Rajpurkar, P.; Irvin, J.; Zhu, K.; Yang, B.; Mehta, H.; Duan, T.; Ding, D.; Bagul, A.; Langlotz, C.; Shpanskaya, K.; et al. CheXNet: Radiologist-Level Pneumonia Detection on Chest X-rays with Deep Learning. *arXiv* **2017**, arXiv:1711.05225.
12. Rajpurkar, P.; Irvin, J.; Ball, R.L.; Zhu, K.; Yang, B.; Mehta, H.; Duan, T.; Ding, D.; Bagul, A.; Langlotz, C.P.; et al. Deep learning for chest radiograph diagnosis: A retrospective comparison of the CheXNeXt algorithm to practicing radiologists. *PLoS Med.* **2018**, *15*, e1002686. [CrossRef] [PubMed]
13. Kabala, J.E.; Wilde, P. The measurement of heart size in the antero-posterior chest radiograph. *Br. J. Radiol.* **1987**, *60*, 981–986. [CrossRef]
14. Keats, T.E.; Anderson, M.W. *Atlas of Normal Roentgen Variants That May Simulate Disease*, 9th ed.; Saunders: Philadelphia, PA, USA, 2013.
15. Keats, T.E. *Atlas of Roentgenographic Measurement*, 6th ed.; Mosby Year Book: Saint Louis, MO, USA, 1990.
16. Fedorov, A.; Beichel, R.; Kalpathy-Cramer, J.; Finet, J.; Fillion-Robin, J.-C.; Pujol, S.; Bauer, C.; Jennings, D.; Fennessy, F.; Sonka, M.; et al. 3D Slicer as an image computing platform for the Quantitative Imaging Network. *Magn. Reson. Imaging* **2012**, *30*, 1323–1341. [CrossRef] [PubMed]
17. *NEMA PS3/ISO 12052*; Digital Imaging and Communications in Medicine (DICOM) Standard. National Electrical Manufacturers Association: Rosslyn, VA, USA. Available online: http://medical.nema.org/ (accessed on 31 October 2022).
18. van Rossum, G.; Drake, F.L. *The Python Language Reference. Release 3.0.1 [Repr.]*; Python Software Foundation: Hampton, NH, USA, 2010.
19. Zarr-Python. Available online: https://zarr.readthedocs.io/en/stable/ (accessed on 31 October 2022).
20. Ronneberger, O.; Fischer, P.; Brox, T. U-Net: Convolutional Networks for Biomedical Image Segmentation. In *Medical Image Computing and Computer-Assisted Intervention–MICCAI 2015: 18th International Conference, Munich, 5–9 Germany, October 2015, Proceedings, Part III 18*; Springer International Publishing: Berlin/Heidelberg, Germany, 2015.
21. Kearney, M.T.; Fox, K.A.A.; Lee, A.J.; Prescott, R.J.; Shah, A.M.; Batin, P.D.; Baig, W.; Lindsay, S.; Callahan, T.S.; Shell, W.E.; et al. Predicting death due to progressive heart failure in patients with mild-to-moderate chronic heart failure. *J. Am. Coll. Cardiol.* **2002**, *40*, 1801–1808. [CrossRef] [PubMed]
22. Dimopoulos, K.; Giannakoulas, G.; Bendayan, I.; Liodakis, E.; Petraco, R.; Diller, G.-P.; Piepoli, M.F.; Swan, L.; Mullen, M.; Best, N.; et al. Cardiothoracic ratio from postero-anterior chest radiographs: A simple, reproducible and independent marker of disease severity and outcome in adults with congenital heart disease. *Int. J. Cardiol.* **2013**, *166*, 453–457. [CrossRef] [PubMed]
23. Chamveha, I.; Promwiset, T.; Tongdee, T.; Saiviroonporn, P.; Chaisangmongkon, W. Automated Cardiothoracic Ratio Calculation and Cardiomegaly Detection using Deep Learning Approach. *arXiv* **2020**, arXiv:2002.07468.
24. Que, Q.; Tang, Z.; Wang, R.; Zeng, Z.; Wang, J.; Chua, M.; Gee, T.S.; Yang, X.; Veeravalli, B. CardioXNet: Automated Detection for Cardiomegaly Based on Deep Learning. In Proceedings of the 2018 40th Annual International Conference of the IEEE Engineering in Medicine and Biology Society (EMBC), Honolulu, HI, USA, 18–21 July 2018; pp. 612–615.
25. Saiviroonporn, P.; Rodbangyang, K.; Tongdee, T.; Chaisangmongkon, W.; Yodprom, P.; Siriapisith, T.; Wonglaksanapimon, S. Cardiothoracic ratio measurement using artificial intelligence: Observer and method validation studies. *BMC Med. Imaging* **2021**, *21*, 95. [CrossRef] [PubMed]
26. Arsalan, M.; Owais, M.; Mahmood, T.; Choi, J.; Park, K.R. Artificial Intelligence-Based Diagnosis of Cardiac and Related Diseases. *J. Clin. Med.* **2020**, *9*, 871. [CrossRef] [PubMed]
27. Ajmera, P.; Kharat, A.; Gupte, T.; Pant, R.; Kulkarni, V.; Duddalwar, V.; Lamghare, P. Observer performance evaluation of the feasibility of a deep learning model to detect cardiomegaly on chest radiographs. *Acta Radiol. Open* **2022**, *11*, 205846012211073. [CrossRef] [PubMed]
28. Obuchowicz, R.; Strzelecki, M.; Piórkowski, A. Clinical Applications of Artificial Intelligence in Medical Imaging and Image Processing—A Review. *Cancers* **2024**, *16*, 1870. [CrossRef] [PubMed]

diagnostics

MDPI

Article

Identifying Acute Aortic Syndrome and Thoracic Aortic Aneurysm from Chest Radiography in the Emergency Department Using Convolutional Neural Network Models

Yang-Tse Lin [1], Bing-Cheng Wang [2,*] and Jui-Yuan Chung [3,4,*]

1 Department of Emergency Medicine, Cathay General Hospital, Hsinchu Branch, Hsinchu 300003, Taiwan; qqyyog@gmail.com
2 Department of Emergency Medicine, Sijhih Cathay General Hospital, New Taipei City 221037, Taiwan
3 Department of Emergency Medicine, Cathay General Hospital, Taipei City 106438, Taiwan
4 School of Medicine, National Tsing Hua University, Hsinchu 300044, Taiwan
* Correspondence: kamejack@hotmail.com (B.-C.W.); bybarian@gmail.com (J.-Y.C.); Tel./Fax: +886-2-2708-2121 (J.-Y.C.)

Abstract: (1) Background: Identifying acute aortic syndrome (AAS) and thoracic aortic aneurysm (TAA) in busy emergency departments (EDs) is crucial due to their life-threatening nature, necessitating timely and accurate diagnosis. (2) Methods: This retrospective case-control study was conducted in the ED of three hospitals. Adult patients visiting the ED between 1 January 2010 and 1 January 2020 with a chief complaint of chest or back pain were enrolled in the study. The collected chest radiography (CXRs) data were divided into training (80%) and testing (20%) datasets. The training dataset was trained by four different convolutional neural network (CNN) models. (3) Results: A total of 1625 patients were enrolled in this study. The InceptionV3 model achieved the highest F1 score of 0.76. (4) Conclusions: Analysis of CXRs using a CNN-based model provides a novel tool for clinicians to interpret ED patients with chest pain and suspected AAS and TAA. The integration of such imaging tools into ED could be considered in the future to enhance the diagnostic workflow for clinically fatal diseases.

Keywords: acute aortic syndrome; thoracic aortic aneurysm; convolutional neural network; emergency department

1. Introduction

Acute aortic syndrome (AAS) encompasses patients with a similar clinical profile, including penetrating atherosclerotic aortic ulcer, intramural aortic hematoma (IMH), and classic aortic dissection (AD) [1]. AAS presents a life-threatening medical condition, challenging prompt diagnosis in the emergency department (ED) due to its atypical presentation. The long-term survival rate among AD patients ranges from 30% to 60% [2]. Thoracic aortic aneurysm (TAA) also represents a medical emergency, with an overall mortality rate of 97% to 100% upon rupture [3]. Immediate surgical repair is necessary for all symptomatic TAAs, underscoring the importance of early diagnosis for successful treatment.

Despite advancements in medical technology over the centuries since AD was first reported, the mortality rate remains high, ranging from 18% to 25% [4]. This high mortality rate may be due to the fact that, clinically, AAS can lead to rapid deterioration and requires immediate detection and management [5]. Current diagnostic tools, including electrocardiography, chest radiography (CXRs), and symptom assessment, exhibit poor sensitivity and specificity for TAA diagnosis. CXRs, however, offers a convenient diagnostic tool in the early stages due to its immediate availability and low radiation dose. Radiographic signs of AD in CXRs include widening of the mediastinum, double or irregular aortic knob, left pleural effusion due to a hemothorax, and displacement of intimal calcification [6–9].

Nevertheless, some studies have noted that 37.4% of Type A AD cases show no mediastinal widening, and 12.4% exhibit no radiographic abnormalities [4].

Currently, computed tomography angiography (CTA) serves as the gold standard diagnostic tool for AD due to its high sensitivity (100%) and specificity (98–100%) [10,11]. However, CTA may be more time consuming than single CXR, has a risk of contrast medium injection, and is more expensive, and thus it is not an easily accessible screen image tool clinically.

Traditionally, clinical physicians diagnose AAS primarily based on symptoms and signs and then proceed with basic diagnostics such as CXR, electrocardiogram, blood tests, and focused ultrasound to differentiate it from other diseases. If AAS is highly suspected, CTA will be arranged for confirmation. However, sometimes the symptoms and signs are not specific, making early diagnosis challenging. With the introduction of artificial intelligence (AI) in CXR imaging, we can detect AAS at an earlier stage, potentially accelerating the diagnostic process and consequently shortening the time to treatment or surgery.

In recent years, AI interpretation of medical images has gained traction, offering objective interpretation, examination of a large number of image features, automation, rapid diagnosis, and continuous improvement through rigorous database establishment [12–15]. For example, deep learning networks have been utilized in medical image processing to aid in the prognosis and diagnosis of diseases such as breast cancer, lung cancer, and brain tumors [16]. A particular study highlighted that the ResNet-18 model demonstrates exceptional performance in characterizing dense tissue patterns, which is a critical risk factor for the development of cancerous cells in women's breasts [17].

To date, AI applications in AD diagnosis have been limited to basic clinical data analysis (area under the curve, AUC: 0.857) [18] and computer tomography (CT) interpretation assistance [19]. Research on enhancing the efficiency of automated radiography interpretation remains scarce. Many medical imaging studies have employed existing public convolutional neural network (CNN) architectures for transfer learning, showing promising results in interpreting CXRs [20,21].

Reviewing the literature, most existing studies have focused on a single CNN model to predict AD via CXRs. However, research comparing different CNN models is lacking. Therefore, this study aims to utilize four different CNN-based models as objective imaging tools to expedite the diagnosis of aortic syndromes via CXRs. It also seeks to evaluate the performance of these models and discuss their potential application in the ED, with the expectation of improving the efficiency of CXR interpretation by emergency physicians and enhancing the accuracy of disease diagnosis.

Furthermore, this study also makes several contributions to the field of medical AI:

1. This study compares the performance of four various CNN architectures on medical imaging, demonstrating the varying effectiveness of different models in CXR diagnosis.
2. The ground truth for disease diagnosis in this study was established using CTA, which is the gold standard imaging tool for aortic disease.
3. By incorporating class activation mapping (CAM) in CXRs and comparing it with CTA, our study demonstrates that CNNs have the potential to accurately pinpoint aortic lesions.
4. This research highlights the specificity of CNNs in disease diagnosis, suggesting that they can be practically applied in emergency clinical settings.

2. Method

2.1. Study Design

This was a retrospective case-control study conducted in the ED of the Cathay Medical System (CMS), Taiwan, which comprises three hospitals: one medical center (located in Taipei), one regional hospital (located in New Taipei City), and one district hospital (located in Hisnchu City). The medical center has a capacity of 800 beds and an estimated annual ED visit volume of 60,000. The regional and district hospitals have capacities of 642 beds and 348 beds, respectively, with estimated annual ED visit volumes of 48,000 and 30,000. Patients who visited these three hospitals between 1 January 2010, and 1 January 2020, were enrolled in the study.

2.2. Data Collection and Assignment to Case and Control Groups

The experimental group included CXRs of patients who met the following criteria: (1) emergency patients who were older than 18 years old, with the chief complain of chest or back pain. (2) Patients underwent CXRs and computer tomography angiography in the ED. Patients in this group also fit the following image criteria: (1) diagnosed as AAS and IMH or (2) enlarged TAA (>5.5 cm) as confirmed by CTA. Exclusion criteria for the experimental group were: (1) trauma patients; (2) patients who had implants or a history of thoracic surgery; and (3) lesions on the CXRs, such as pneumonia, pulmonary edema, and tumors in the thorax cavity and mediastinum, as these lesions may interfere with the interpretation of the thoracic aorta. Other than chest images, patients' gender, age, and underlying medical conditions were also collected. The underlying medical conditions of each patient were identified via the ICD-9 and recorded during the ED visit, including hypertension, atherosclerosis, renal insufficiency, ischemic heart disease, diabetes, and cerebral vascular disease, which can be related to aortic disease [22]. The control group included the CXRs of patients who met the following criteria: (1) emergency patients who were older than 18 years; (2) with a complaint of chest and back pain and who underwent CXR and computer tomography in the ED; (3) and whose CTA diagnosis report showed no evidence of AAS or TAA. The CTA images were interpreted and confirmed by board-certified radiologists. Gender, age, and underlying medical conditions were collected to analyze the characteristics of the control group patients. The patients' demographic information was obtained from the electronic medical records of the CMS, while the images were sourced from the picture archiving and communication system (PACS) of the CMS. The flowchart of the study is illustrated in Figure 1.

2.3. Region of Interest

The ROI algorithm can extract specific signals from an image and maintain the anatomical structure we are interested in. It can maintain good image quality during the image decompression process of the CNN model. Therefore, such a method can prevent interference on the experimental results while accelerating the computational speed [23,24]. In order to train the ROI model, two hundred images were randomly selected from all image data, and the dataset was further divided into 80% for the training group (160 images) and 20% for the testing group (40 images). A board-certified emergency physician (the attending physician, who has 3 years of experience) manually annotated the training dataset to select the structures near the mediastinum, including the ascending aorta, aortic arch, descending aorta, and cardiac structure; After that, an aggregate channel features (ACF) object detector was used as the architecture for the ROI model training [25]. While detecting the CXRs automatically, the object detector model gave three sets of coordinates of ideal bounding boxes to show the rectangular area where the entire thoracic aorta may be located; the ROI was then defined as the intersection of the three ideal bounding boxes. The ROI selection step retained important structures in images while excluding other interfering factors such as text labels, abdominal images, neck bones, etc.

Finally, in the testing dataset, emergency physicians manually interpreted the model, and the ACF object detector trained a model that could automatically detect the ROI. In the testing dataset, the ROI area consisting of the thoracic aorta structure was marked with an accuracy rate of 100% (40/40). This ACF model was then used in the next experiment to detect the ROI of different CXRs before proceeding to the next step of image processing. In Figure 2A,B, the central black square area on the chest image demonstrates the regions of the aorta and mediastinum automatically labeled by our ROI model.

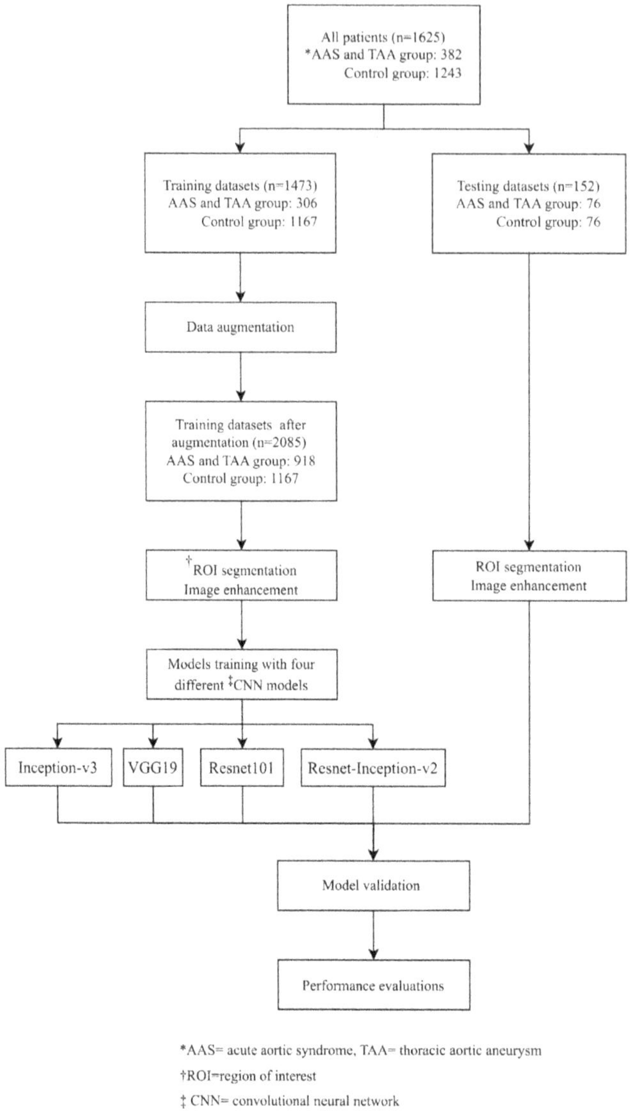

Figure 1. The flow chart of the study.

2.4. Image Enhancement

This study utilized contrast limited adaptive histogram equalization (CLAHE), a technique widely employed in medical imaging [26]. CLAHE has been found to offer enhanced visualization of the mediastinal cavity and thoracic aorta without over highlighting high-density structures, such as bones, compared to other algorithms like histogram equalization and adaptive histogram equalization. Consequently, CXR images processed with CLAHE exhibit improved performance in training both the ROI model and the CNN model (Figure 3).

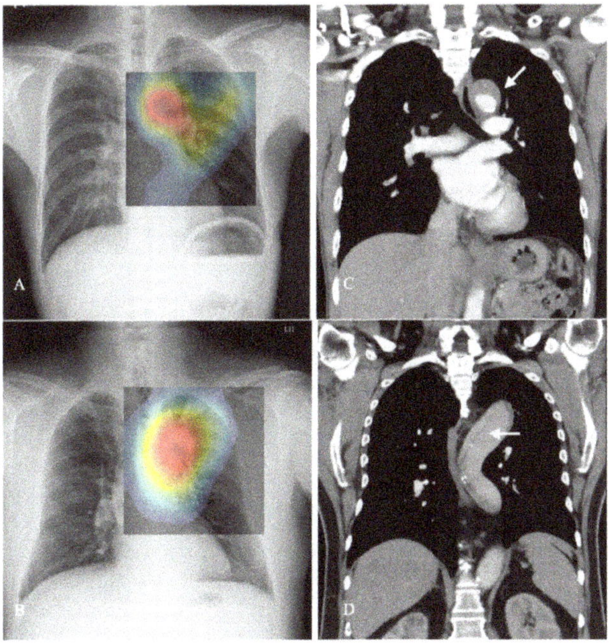

Figure 2. The images on the left (**A**,**B**) show the location of a possible aortic lesion on the CXR marked by the CNN model (VGG19), and these areas are colored by CAM to make it easy for users to interpret them. The pictures on the right (**C**,**D**) are the CTA images of the same patient showing the true location of the patient's aortic lesion. After comparing with the CAM image, it was found that the CNN model correctly interpreted the location of the lesion on the CXRs, arrow: false lumen of aortic dissection.

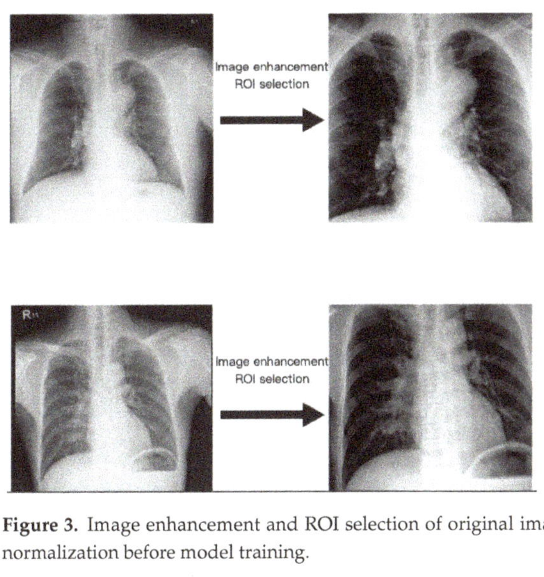

Figure 3. Image enhancement and ROI selection of original images for better image quality and normalization before model training.

2.5. Data Augmentation

Given the greater number of cases in the control group compared to the AAS and TAA groups (n = 1167 vs. 306), we augmented the images of patients with AAS and TAA in the training dataset to achieve data balance (n = 1167 vs. 918) (Figure 1). This augmentation involved rotating CXRs of the AAS and TAA groups in the training dataset. We decided to rotate these images (n = 306) by three degrees clockwise (n = 306) and counterclockwise (n = 306), and combined these images with the original CXRs (n = 306) to increase the data numbers (n = 918), as demonstrated in Figure 4.

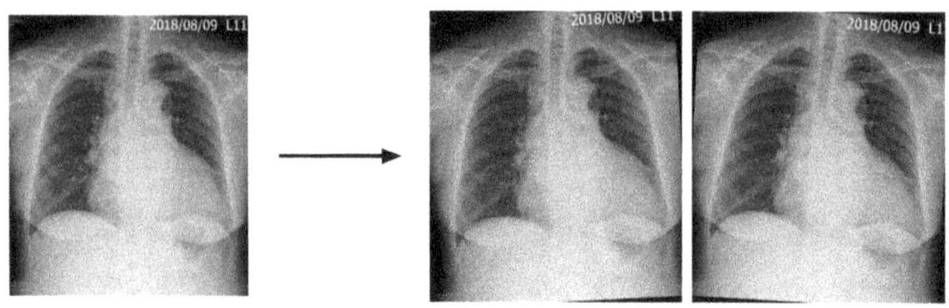

Figure 4. Image augmentation: original images were rotated by 3 degrees clockwise and counter-clockwise.

2.6. Pre-Trained CNN Model

CNNs have found extensive application in deep learning, encompassing tasks such as image classification, object detection, and feature extraction. A CNN typically comprises various types of neural network layers, including convolutional layers, MaxPooling layers, dropout layers, fully connected layers, and SoftMax. Over time, CNN architectures have evolved, with many medical imaging studies leveraging existing public architectures for transfer learning.

In this research, we utilized four pre-trained CNN models (InceptionV3 [27], Inception-ResNet-v2 [28], VGG19 [29], and ResNet101 [30]), all derived from the ImageNet Database, which was originally developed for interpreting natural images. After image augmentation and preprocessing, we resized the images and inputted them into these four different CNN architectures for transfer learning to establish models. Our data were divided into training datasets (80% of all images) and testing datasets (20% of all images). We then assessed the performance of these models on the testing dataset by evaluating their ability to interpret CXRs.

2.7. Statistical Analysis and Model Performance Evaluations

After testing the four different CNN-based models in the testing dataset, the final result of their confusion matrix was acquired. The contents of the confusion matrix for each model were analyzed for their sensitivity (precision), specificity, precision, F1 score, and accuracy of the testing dataset. The F1 score is a popular tool for evaluating the performance of AI models. The F1 score represents the classifier's performance in both precision and recall; thus, the F1 score was used in this study to decide which model was the most successful.

$$F1\ score = 2\frac{precision \times recall}{precision + recall}$$

The area under the receiver operating characteristic (AUROC) was used to evaluate the performance of the classifier models. Without threshold selection and calculation of precision and recall, the AUC represents the overall diagnostic performance of an AI model and is widely used in the machine learning field [31]. CAM is used to evaluate and weight each CNN-based model while interpreting the CXRs [32]. Although the CNN model can handle non-linear and high-degree-of-freedom data (such as images), it lacks interpretability, as the model itself could not identify the relationship between input data and output results [33]. Therefore, researchers often need to further verify the performance of the CNN model in order to increase users' confidence. CAM is currently an effective tool to visualize the featured maps extracted by CNN. In the research process, when it is necessary to adjust training parameters or select algorithm tools, CAM can help researchers to confirm whether the model's prediction results are accurate and whether adjustments are clinically reasonable when evaluating the model. CAM can provide a reference for researchers to adjust parameters and avoid model over fitting. In clinical applications, the visualized image features of CAM can allow clinical users to quickly enter the situation, thereby increasing the willingness of clinicians to use the CNN model tool (Figure 2C,D).

2.8. Training Parameters, Software, and Hardware

The software used in this study was Matlab 2020b; it was used for image pre-processing, model training, and statistical analysis of the results. The parameters used in the training CNNs were as follows: optimization algorithm; Adaptive Moment Estimation (ADAM); mini batch size: 20; max epochs: 6; and initial learn rate: 0.0001. We used an Intel® Core™ i7-10750H as the CPU (Central Processing Unit) and an AMD Radeon™ Pro 555X as the GPU (Graphics Processing Unit) for building and training our models.

3. Results

In total, 1625 patients' CXRs were included in this study, with 382 patients in the AAS and TAA group and 1243 patients in the control group. Analysis of patient demographics revealed a higher percentage of males in the AAS and TAA groups compared to the control group, accounting for 64.4% and 58.5%, respectively. Furthermore, the AAS and TAA groups exhibited a higher mean age ± standard deviation of 69.5 ± 15.5 years, compared to 65.1 ± 17.0 years in the control group. Hypertension was more prevalent in the AAS and TAA groups, with 69.1% of patients affected, compared to 55.3% in the control group. Similarly, the prevalence of all underlying medical conditions was higher in the AAS and TAA group, with 77% of patients affected, compared to 70% in the control group (Table 1).

Table 1. Patient characteristics.

Patient Characteristic	AAS and TAA Groups (*N* = 382)	Control Group (*N* = 1243)	*p* Value
Sex, *n* (%)			0.04
Male	246 (64.4)	727 (58.5)	
Female	136 (35.6)	516 (41.5)	
Age-yr (Mean ± SD)	69.5 ± 15.5	65.1 ± 17.0	<0.01
Underlying medical condition, *n* (%)	294 (77.0)	874 (70.3)	0.01
Hypertension	264 (69.1)	689 (55.4)	<0.01
Atherosclerosis	57 (14.9)	251 (20.2)	0.02
Renal insufficiency	63 (16.5)	205 (16.5)	0.10
Ischemic heart disease	77 (20.2)	378 (30.4)	<0.01
Diabetes mellitus	69 (18.1)	391 (31.5)	<0.01
Cerebral vascular disease	81 (21.2)	203 (16.3)	0.03

AAS, acute aortic syndrome; TAA, thoracic aortic aneurysm; *n*, number; SD, standard deviation.

In terms of demographic distribution, patients in the AAS and TAA groups were older and had a higher proportion of hypertension, which was significant ($p < 0.01$), consistent with the known risk factors for AAS. Although the difference was not statistically significant ($p = 0.04$), the AAS and TAA groups had a higher proportion of male patients. Previous literature has shown that patients with emergency chest pain or those in the AAS and TAA groups exhibit a similar gender distribution.

Regarding dataset organization, approximately 80% of the images from both groups were randomly allocated to the training datasets, resulting in 306 images in the AAS and TAA group and 1167 images in the control group, while the remaining 20% of images were assigned to the testing datasets, with 76 images in each group. To ensure data balance in the training datasets, data augmentation techniques were employed, resulting in a total of 2085 images (918 in the AAS and TAA group, and 1167 in the control group) (Figure 1).

For dataset arrangement, approximately 80% of images from both groups were randomly selected for training datasets (AAS and TAA group: 306, control group: 1167) and the remaining 20% for testing datasets (AAS and TAA group: 76, control group: 76). Data augmentation was used to increase the number of images to 2085 (AAS and TAA group: 918, control group: 1167) in order to achieve data balance in our training datasets.

During algorithm development, images processed without ROI selection via the ACF model sometimes caused the CNN model to lose focus, as shown in Figure 5(A1–A3). Conversely, images processed with ROI selection allowed the CNN to concentrate on the true anatomical structures, such as the aortic arch and thoracic aorta (Figure 5(B1–B3)), enhancing the clinical reliability of the CNN model.

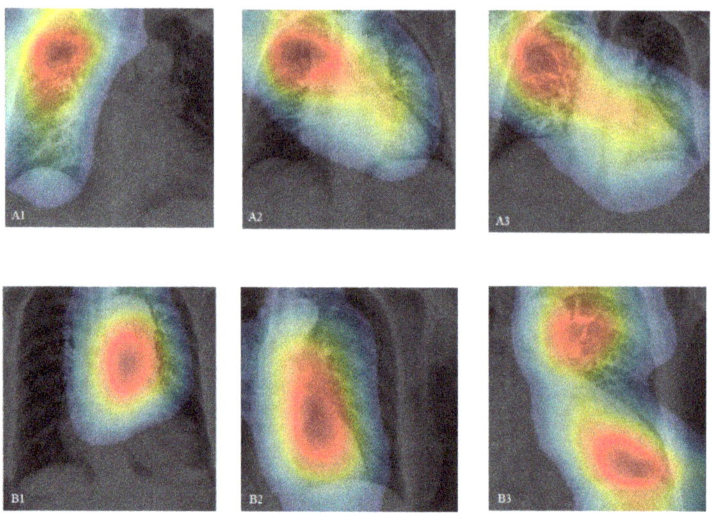

Figure 5. (**A1–A3**) The CAM images of the original CXRs interpreted by the CNN model show that some feature extraction areas are not logically related to the aortic structure. In contrast, (**B1–B3**) displays the results after the ACF-generated feature extraction model processed the images. Training the CNN model with ROI-focused images shows that the model focuses more on the anatomical structures of the mediastinum, without being distracted by surrounding organs.

We trained the processed images using four different CNN architectures for CXR interpretation and validated each model using the testing datasets (AAS and TAA group: 76, control group: 76). Analysis of model performance revealed that the Inception-v3 model attained the highest F1 score of 0.76, indicating strong overall performance. The VGG19-based model achieved the highest AUC of 0.84, highlighting its robust discrimination ability between classes. Both models demonstrated similar specificity, with the VGG19 model and the Inception-v3 model achieving specificities of 88%. Additionally, both the Inception-v3 and VGG19 models exhibited superior precision, at 85% and 82%, respectively, demonstrating their ability to correctly identify positive cases.

In contrast, the Resnet101 model showed lower sensitivity at 64%, suggesting it may miss more true positive cases compared to Inception-v3 and VGG19. It also had a lower AUC of 0.68, indicating less effective discrimination between classes compared to the other models. The Res-net-Inception-v2 model demonstrated consistent but modest performance across all models, with sensitivity, specificity, precision, and F1 scores all around 64%.

These findings highlight the varying effectiveness of different CNN architectures in the task of X-ray interpretation, with Inception-v3 and VGG19 outperforming Resnet101 and Res-net-Inception-v2 in key metrics (Table 2).

Table 2. Performance of AD detection in AAS and TAA predictions using different CNN models.

CNN Pre-Trained Models	Sensitivity (%, 95% CI)	Specificity (%, 95% CI)	Precision (%, 95% CI)	F1 Score (95% CI)	Accuracy (%, 95% CI)	* AUC
Inception-v3	68 [50, 86]	88 [75, 100]	85 [68, 100]	0.76 [0.58, 0.91]	78 [65, 92]	0.82
VGG19	56 [39, 73]	88 [73, 97]	82 [66, 92]	0.67 [0.53, 0.80]	72 [61, 83]	0.84
Resnet101	64 [45, 83]	68 [50, 87]	67 [48, 86]	0.65 [0.46, 0.84]	66 [58, 89]	0.68
Resnet-Inception-v2	64 [45, 83]	64 [45, 83]	64 [45, 83]	0.64 [0.45, 0,83]	64 [45, 83]	0.67

* Area under the curve (AUC) and area under the receiver operating curve (AUROC).

To enhance the model's reliability, we also collected digital CTA images of AAS and TAA patients and retrospectively compared them with CXRs. This was to determine whether the CNN model could not only correctly identify abnormal images but also pinpoint the lesion's location. CAM was applied to the original CXRs to visualize the feature maps extracted by the CNN models, enabling the localization of possible aortic lesions on CXRs and comparison with the same patients' aortic CTA images (Figure 4). This confirmed that the CNN has the potential to locate and visualize lesions, providing valuable diagnostic information to clinicians.

4. Discussion

The novelty of this study lies in the comparative analysis of four distinct CNN-based models to determine their diagnostic performance for AAS and TAA based on CXRs in the ED. Specifically, the study provides a comprehensive evaluation of four pre-trained CNN models (Inception-v3, VGG19, Resnet101, and Resnet-Inception-v2) across several key metrics, including sensitivity, specificity, precision, F1 score, accuracy, and AUC. The results showed that Inception-v3 had the highest F1 score, while VGG19 had the highest AUC. These findings align with a recent study using the ResNet18 CNN model to detect acute thoracic AD based on CXRs, which achieved a diagnostic accuracy of 90.20%, a precision of 75.00%, a recall of 94.44%, and an F1 score of 83.61% [34]. Another study explored the use of explainable AI methods like Grad-CAM to interpret the decisions of a CNN model for detecting aortic elongation, which can be an indicator of AD, from CXR images [35]. However, the algorithms, data sources, and study designs of these studies varied. Therefore, we have included a table that summarizes the comparison of three studies (current study and two recent studies [34,35]) on the use of CNNs for aortic disease detection in CXR images, detailing their case numbers, data sources, CNN types used, and targeted abnormalities in Table 3.

In current practice, the diagnosis of AAS and TAA is challenging and often overlooked by physicians in the ED due to several factors. Firstly, crowded EDs result in physicians having insufficient time to diagnose a patient [36]. Secondly, using CXRs to diagnose AAS and TAA lacks clear image feature definition, leading to subjective interpretation and inter-rater differences. Thirdly, AAS may present with atypical symptoms that can be easily overlooked. Fourthly, novice doctors, such as post-graduate-year doctors or junior residents, may be unfamiliar with the disease's characteristics. Finally, fatigue from long working hours or night shifts can contribute to diagnostic errors.

The CNN models used in the present study offer significant advantages by automatically screening all CXRs to identify patients who may potentially have AAS or TAA, especially in crowded EDs where physicians may have limited time to diagnose a patient. CNN models also provide more objective judgment, are not constrained by past research, and may identify new features of AAS on CXRs. CNN models are also helpful for novice doctors who are not familiar with the disease's characteristics. Unlike human physicians, CNN models are not affected by long working hours or fatigue. Moreover, the prompt diagnosis of AAS and TAA by CNN models allows ED physicians to initiate treatment before receiving the official radiology report from radiologists [37], thereby potentially enhancing the quality of medical care and prognosis. In Taiwan, several studies have reported using CNN models for interpreting X-rays [38], particularly for severe diseases that are easily missed in the ED, such as acute epiglottitis [39]. Furthermore, the combination of CAM technology demonstrated in this study (Figure 2) illustrates the CNN model's ability to accurately locate aortic lesions during diagnosis, further highlighting its utility as a valuable medical assistance tool.

Table 3. Comparison of this study with two recent studies on the use of CNN in aortic disease CXR research, including methods and results.

	This Study	Ribeiro et al. (2024) [35]	Lee et al. (2023) [34]
Case numbers	*N* = 1473 (normal= 1167, AAS and TAA= 306)	*N* = 8752 (Aortic elongation = 2350, non-aortic elongation = 6402)	*N* = 3331 (Positive images = 716, negative images = 2615)
Data source	Three hospitals: one medical center, one regional hospital, and one district hospital	VinDr-CXR dataset	Three tertiary academic hospitals
CNN type	Inception-v3 VGG19 Resnet101 Resnet-Inception-v2	DenseNet 121 EfficientNet B4	ResNet 18
Abnormalities targeted	AAS and TAA	Aortic elongation	Acute thoracic aortic dissection
Disease label	CTA report	Interpretation by radiologist	CTA report and surgery record
Image augmentation protocol	Rotation	Rotation, horizontal flipping, and vertical flipping	Rotation, horizontal flipping, and vertical flipping
ROI model architecture	Aggregate channel features object detector	* UNet	UNet
Image enhancement	CLAHE	Histogram equalization	Histogram equalization
CAM application	Yes, and comparison with patients' CTA image	Yes	Yes

* UNet is a convolutional network architecture for fast and precise segmentation of images.

While developing diagnostic AI models for medical images, the preprocessing of images is as crucial as selecting the appropriate CNN structure. Preprocessing images using suitable image enhancement algorithms and selecting an ROI segmentation model are vital in our study settings. Image preprocessing can expedite the CNN model training process and enhance diagnostic accuracy [23,24,26]. However, employing CNN models directly on medical images may not suffice, as real-world medical images often contain considerable noise. Noise reduction can be achieved by combining various algorithms at different stages of image preprocessing, enabling the CNN model to focus on relevant information in CXRs. In this study, the ACF detector was initially utilized as the ROI segmentation model to identify structures such as aortic vessels, heart borders, and the mediastinum. CLAHE was then applied for image enhancement, enhancing the density of these soft tissue structures. Subsequently, these images were fed into various CNN architectures for training. Throughout the training process, CNN model parameters were adjusted based on prediction results and the CAM analysis. The training outcomes were further deliberated by clinical physicians and programming engineers, and our group determined which algorithms to select and how to adjust the parameters accordingly.

Patients presenting with chest pain represent approximately 10% of total ED visits. While most of these patients may be discharged following evaluation, a subset may ultimately receive diagnoses of acute and potentially fatal conditions such as acute coronary syndrome and AAS [40]. Our study findings demonstrate that both Inception-v3 and VGG19 exhibited superior performance compared to other methods, with Inception-v3 achieving the highest scores for sensitivity, F1 score, and accuracy. VGG19, while slightly behind Inception-v3 in these areas, showed the highest AUC, indicating its strong discriminative ability. Resnet101 and Resnet-Inception-v2, although performing adequately, lagged in several key aspects, suggesting room for improvement in these models for detecting AAS and TAA from CXRs in EDs (Table 2). The high precision and accuracy of Inception-v3 offers a critical role in an ED setting where timely and accurate diagnosis can significantly impact patient outcomes. The high precision (85%, 95% CI: 68, 100) indicates that when the model predicts a positive case, it is likely to be correct, which is important for maintaining the credibility of the diagnostic tool among clinicians. The accuracy (78%, 95% CI: 65, 92) shows its overall effectiveness in correctly classifying both positive and negative cases. Therefore, Inception-v3 would be the recommended model for use in the ED for screening AAS and TAA from CXRs.

There are several limitations to this study. Firstly, despite fine model adjustment and image preprocessing, the sensitivity of the CNN model to identify AAS and TAA remains at 68%. Previous studies have also noted the limitations of CXRs in diagnosing aortic diseases [4]. This may be attributed to the inherent constraints of CXRs, which typically provides flat, binary-colored, and single-view images, making it challenging to diagnose vascular diseases such as AAS and TAA, which have complex 3D anatomical structures. In fact, delving into the detailed structure or blood flow changes in aortic dissection requires the aid of advanced imaging tools. For example, one study utilized computational fluid dynamics (CFD) to model blood flow in aortic dissection, enhancing the understanding of hemodynamics in these cases [41]. Another review article introduced the application of image-based CFD simulations and four-dimensional flow magnetic resonance imaging (4D-MRI) to predict risks in patients with aortic dissection [42]. These cutting-edge imaging tools provide valuable insights for identifying, managing, and treating aortic conditions.

In further exploration of this topic, we suggest considering the combination of CNN models with these advanced imaging tools (CFD, 4D-MRI, and 3D reconstruction techniques) and expanding the image database for CNN model training. Additionally, integrating CNN models for image analysis with other machine learning models that utilize clinical information and parameters such as age, risk factors, symptoms, and vital signs could form a multimodal solution to complement the limitations of a single CNN model.

Secondly, this study is retrospective in nature, which inevitably introduces some selection bias in patient selection and grouping, despite efforts to mitigate this bias in the study design. However, such selection bias is a common challenge encountered in similar AI medical research during the developmental stages. Therefore, based on our findings, we anticipate the emergence of more prospective studies in the future, focusing on the application of AI in real-world medical scenarios.

5. Conclusions

A CNN-based model (Inception-v3) can provide good diagnostic performance for AAS and TAA based on CXRs, as indicated by its F1 score of 0.76, demonstrating a good balance between sensitivity and precision. Furthermore, the use of this CNN-based model may help physicians speed up the diagnosis process and avoid possible misdiagnoses, resulting in a non-invasive, objective, accurate, and fast diagnostic tool for AAS and TAA patients before they undergo CTA examination.

Author Contributions: Conceptualization, J.-Y.C.; methodology, Y.-T.L. and J.-Y.C.; software, Y.-T.L.; validation, Y.-T.L.; formal analysis, J.-Y.C.; investigation, B.-C.W.; resources, B.-C.W.; data curation, B.-C.W.; writing—original draft preparation, Y.-T.L.; writing—review and editing, B.-C.W. and J.-Y.C.; visualization, B.-C.W.; supervision, B.-C.W. and J.-Y.C.; project administration, J.-Y.C.; funding acquisition, B.-C.W. and J.-Y.C. All authors have read and agreed to the published version of the manuscript.

Funding: This work was supported by Cathay General Hospital, Grant number CGH-MR-B11003.

Institutional Review Board Statement: The study was conducted in accordance with the Declaration of Helsinki and approved by the Institutional Review Board (or Ethics Committee) of Cathay General Hospital, CGH-P109083, 17 December 2020.

Informed Consent Statement: Patient consent was waived due to the retrospective nature of this study.

Data Availability Statement: All data generated or analyzed during this study are included in this manuscript.

Conflicts of Interest: The authors declare no conflicts of interest.

References

1. Vilacosta, I.; Román, J.A.S.; Aragoncillo, P.; Ferreirós, J.; Mendez, R.; Graupner, C.; Batlle, E.; Serrano, J.; Pinto, A.; Oyonarte, J.M. Penetrating atherosclerotic aortic ulcer: Documentation by transesophageal echocardiography. *J. Am. Coll. Cardiol.* **1998**, *32*, 83–89. [CrossRef]
2. Bossone, E.; LaBounty, T.M.; Eagle, K.A. Acute aortic syndromes: Diagnosis and management, an update. *Eur. Heart J.* **2018**, *39*, 739–749d. [CrossRef]
3. Johansson, G.; Markström, U.; Swedenborg, J. Ruptured thoracic aortic aneurysms: A study of incidence and mortality rates. *J. Vasc. Surg.* **1995**, *21*, 985–988. [CrossRef]
4. Hagan, P.G.; Nienaber, C.A.; Isselbacher, E.M.; Bruckman, D.; Karavite, D.J.; Russman, P.L.; Evangelista, A.; Fattori, R.; Suzuki, T.; Oh, J.K.; et al. The International Registry of Acute Aortic Dissection (IRAD). *J. Am. Med. Assoc.* **2000**, *283*, 897–903. [CrossRef]
5. Ahn, J.-M.; Kim, H.; Kwon, O.; Om, S.Y.; Heo, R.; Lee, S.; Kim, D.-H.; Kim, H.J.; Kim, J.B.; Jung, S.H.; et al. Differential clinical features and long-term prognosis of acute aortic syndrome according to disease entity. *Eur. Heart J.* **2019**, *40*, 2727–2736. [CrossRef]
6. Earnest, F.T.; Muhm, J.R.; Sheedy, P.F., 2nd. Roentgenographic findings in thoracic aortic dissection. *Mayo Clin. Proc.* **1979**, *54*, 43–50.
7. JaJagannath, A.; Sos, T.; Lockhart, S.; Saddekni, S.; Sniderman, K.; Jagannath, T.S.A.; LePage, M.A.; Quint, L.E.; Sonnad, S.S.; Deeb, G.M.; et al. Aortic dissection: A statistical analysis of the usefulness of plain chest radiographic findings. *Am. J. Roentgenol.* **1986**, *147*, 1123–1126. [CrossRef]
8. Klompas, M. Does this patient have an acute thoracic aortic dissection? *JAMA* **2002**, *287*, 2262–2272. [CrossRef]
9. vovon Kodolitsch, Y.; A Nienaber, C.; Dieckmann, C.; Schwartz, A.G.; Hofmann, T.; Brekenfeld, C.; Nicolas, V.; Berger, J.; Meinertz, T. Chest radiography for the diagnosis of acute aortic syndrome. *Am. J. Med.* **2004**, *116*, 73–77. [CrossRef]
10. Shiga, T.; Wajima, Z.I.; Apfel, C.C.; Inoue, T.; Ohe, Y. Diagnostic accuracy of transesophageal echocardiography, helical computed tomography, and magnetic resonance imaging for suspected thoracic aortic dissection: Systematic review and meta-analysis. *Arch. Intern. Med.* **2006**, *166*, 1350–1356. [CrossRef]
11. YoshidYoshida, S.; Akiba, H.; Tamakawa, M.; Yama, N.; Hareyama, M.; Morishita, K.; Abe, T. Thoracic involvement of type A aortic dissection and intramural hematoma: Diagnostic accuracy—Comparison of emergency helical CT and surgical findings. *Radiology* **2003**, *228*, 430–435. [CrossRef]
12. Sarle, W.S. Neural Networks and Statistical Models. 1994. Available online: https://people.orie.cornell.edu/davidr/or474/nn_sas.pdf (accessed on 24 August 2020).
13. Schmidhuber, J. Deep learning in neural networks: An overview. *Neural Netw. Off. J. Int. Neural Netw. Soc.* **2015**, *61*, 85–117. [CrossRef]
14. LeCun, Y.; Bengio, Y.; Hinton, G. Deep learning. *Nature* **2015**, *521*, 436–444. [CrossRef]
15. Topol, E.J. High-performance medicine: The convergence of human and artificial intelligence. *Nat. Med.* **2019**, *25*, 44–56. [CrossRef]
16. Bhatt, C.; Kumar, I.; Vijayakumar, V.; Singh, K.U.; Kumar, A. The state of the art of deep learning models in medical science and their challenges. *Multimed. Syst.* **2021**, *27*, 599–613. [CrossRef]
17. Kumar, I.; Kumar, A.; Kumar, V.D.A.; Kannan, R.; Vimal, V.; Singh, K.U.; Mahmud, M. Dense Tissue Pattern Characterization Using Deep Neural Network. *Cogn. Comput.* **2022**, *14*, 1728–1751. [CrossRef]
18. Huo, D.; Kou, B.; Zhou, Z.; Lv, M. A machine learning model to classify aortic dissection patients in the early diagnosis phase. *Sci. Rep.* **2019**, *9*, 2701. [CrossRef]
19. Hata, A.; Yanagawa, M.; Yamagata, K.; Suzuki, Y.; Kido, S.; Kawata, A.; Doi, S.; Yoshida, Y.; Miyata, T.; Tsubamoto, M.; et al. Deep learning algorithm for detection of aortic dissection on non-contrast-enhanced CT. *Eur. Radiol.* **2021**, *31*, 1151–1159. [CrossRef]
20. Rajpurkar, P.; Irvin, J.; Zhu, K.; Yang, B.; Mehta, H.; Duan, T.; Ding, D.; Bagul, A.; Langlotz, C.; Shpanskaya, K.; et al. Chexnet: Radiologist-level pneumonia detection on chest x-rays with deep learning. *arXiv* **2017**, arXiv:1711.05225v3.
21. Qin, C.; Yao, D.; Shi, Y.; Song, Z. Computer-aided detection in chest radiography based on artificial intelligence: A survey. *Biomedical engineering online* **2018**, *17*, 113. [CrossRef]
22. Ahmad, F.; Cheshire, N.; Hamady, M. Acute aortic syndrome: Pathology and therapeutic strategies. *Postgrad. Med. J.* **2006**, *82*, 305–312. [CrossRef]

23. Yee, D.; Soltaninejad, S.; Hazarika, D.; Mbuyi, G.; Barnwal, R.; Basu, A. Medical image compression based on region of interest using better portable graphics (BPG). In Proceedings of the 2017 IEEE International Conference on Systems, Man, and Cybernetics (SMC), Banff, AB, Canada, 5–8 October 2017; Volume 2017, pp. 216–221. [CrossRef]
24. Zhang, Q.; Xiao, H. Extracting regions of interest in biomedical images. In Proceedings of the 2008 International Seminar on Future BioMedical Information Engineering, Wuhan, China, 18 December 2008; pp. 3–6. [CrossRef]
25. Dollar, P.; Appel, R.; Belongie, S.; Perona, P. Fast Feature Pyramids for Object Detection. *IEEE Trans. Pattern Anal. Mach. Intell.* **2014**, *36*, 1532–1545. [CrossRef]
26. Reza, A.M. Realization of the contrast limited adaptive histogram equalization (CLAHE) for real-time image enhancement. *J. VLSI Signal Process. Syst. Signal Image Video Technol.* **2004**, *38*, 35–44. [CrossRef]
27. Szegedy, C.; Vanhoucke, V.; Ioffe, S.; Shlens, J.; Wojna, Z. Rethinking the inception architecture for computer vision. In Proceedings of the IEEE Conference on Computer Vision and Pattern Recognition (CVPR), Las Vegas, NV, USA, 26 June–1 July 2016; pp. 2818–2826.
28. Szegedy, C.; Ioffe, S.; Vanhoucke, V.; Alemi, A. Inception V4, inception-resnet and the impact of residual connections on learning. In Proceedings of the AAAI Conference on Artificial Intelligence, San Francisco, CA, USA, 4–9 February 2017; Volume 31.
29. Simonyan, K.; Zisserman, A. Very deep convolutional networks for large-scale image recognition. *arXiv* **2014**, arXiv:1409.1556.
30. He, K.; Zhang, X.; Ren, S.; Sun, J. Deep residual learning for image recognition. In Proceedings of the IEEE Conference on Computer Vision and Pattern Recognition (CVPR), Las Vegas, NV, USA, 26 June–1 July 2016; pp. 770–778.
31. Huang, J.; Ling, C. Using AUC and accuracy in evaluating learning algorithms. *IEEE Trans. Knowl. Data Eng.* **2005**, *17*, 299–310. [CrossRef]
32. Zhou, B.; Khosla, A.; Lapedriza, A.; Oliva, A.; Torralba, A. Learning deep features for discriminative localization. In Proceedings of the IEEE Conference on Computer Vision and Pattern Recognition (CVPR), Las Vegas, NV, USA, 26 June–1 July 2016; pp. 2921–2929.
33. Aneja, J.; Deshpande, A.; Schwing, A.G. Convolutional Image Captioning. In Proceedings of the 2018 IEEE/CVF Conference on Computer Vision and Pattern Recognition, Salt Lake City, UT, USA, 18–22 June 2018; pp. 5561–5570.
34. Lee, D.K.; Kim, J.H.; Oh, J.; Kim, T.H.; Yoon, M.S.; Im, D.J.; Chung, J.H.; Byun, H. Author Correction: Detection of acute thoracic aortic dissection based on plain chest radiography and a residual neural network (Resnet). *Sci. Rep.* **2023**, *13*, 2324. [CrossRef]
35. Ribeiro, E.; Cardenas, D.A.C.; Dias, F.M.; E Krieger, J.; A Gutierrez, M. Explainable AI in Deep Learning-Based Detection of Aortic Elongation on Chest X-ray Images. *Eur. Heart J. Digit. Health* **2024**, ztae045. [CrossRef]
36. Hautz, S.C.; Schuler, L.; Kammer, J.E.; Schauber, S.K.; Ricklin, M.E.; Sauter, T.C.; Maier, V.; Birrenbach, T.; Exadaktylos, A.; Hautz, W.E. Factors predicting a change in diagnosis in patients hospitalised through the emergency room: A prospective observational study. *BMJ Open* **2016**, *6*, e011585. [CrossRef]
37. Grant, K.; McParland, A. Applications of artificial intelligence in emergency medicine. *Univ. Tor. Med. J.* **2019**, *96*, 37–39.
38. Shih, B.-H.; Yeh, C.-C. Advancements in Artificial Intelligence in Emergency Medicine in Taiwan: A Narrative Review. *J. Acute Med.* **2024**, *14*, 9–19. [CrossRef]
39. Lin, Y.-T.; Shia, B.-C.; Chang, C.-J.; Wu, Y.; Yang, J.-D.; Kang, J.-H. Using Transfer Learning of Convolutional Neural Network on Neck Radiographs to Identify Acute Epiglottitis. *J. Digit. Imaging* **2023**, *36*, 893–901. [CrossRef] [PubMed]
40. Stepinska, J.; Lettino, M.; Ahrens, I.; Bueno, H.; Garcia-Castrillo, L.; Khoury, A.; Lancellotti, P.; Mueller, C.; Muenzel, T.; Oleksiak, A.; et al. Diagnosis and risk stratification of chest pain patients in the emergency department: Focus on acute coronary syndromes. A position paper of the Acute Cardiovascular Care Association. *Eur. Heart J. Acute Cardiovasc. Care* **2020**, *9*, 76–89. [CrossRef] [PubMed]
41. Polanczyk, A.; Piechota-Polanczyk, A.; Huk, I.; Neumayer, C.; Balcer, J.; Strzelecki, M. Computational Fluid Dynamic Technique for Assessment of How Changing Character of Blood Flow and Different Value of Hct Influence Blood Hemodynamic in Dissected Aorta. *Diagnostics* **2021**, *11*, 1866. [CrossRef] [PubMed]
42. Zhu, Y.; Xu, X.; Rosendahl, U.; Pepper, J.; Mirsadraee, S. Advanced risk prediction for aortic dissection patients using imaging-based computational flow analysis. *Clin. Radiol.* **2023**, *78*, e155–e165. [CrossRef] [PubMed]

diagnostics

MDPI

Article

Evaluation of Machine Learning Classification Models for False-Positive Reduction in Prostate Cancer Detection Using MRI Data

Malte Rippa [1,2,*], Ruben Schulze [2], Georgia Kenyon [3,4], Marian Himstedt [1], Maciej Kwiatkowski [5,6,7], Rainer Grobholz [8,9], Stephen Wyler [5,6], Alexander Cornelius [10], Sebastian Schindera [6,10] and Felice Burn [10,11]

1 Institute for Medical Informatics, University of Lübeck, 23562 Lübeck, Germany; marian.himstedt@uni-luebeck.de
2 Fuse-AI GmbH, 20457 Hamburg, Germany; ruben.schulze@fuse-ai.de
3 Australian Institute of Machine Learning, University of Adelaide, Adelaide, SA 5005, Australia; georgia.kenyon@adelaide.edu.au
4 Precision Imaging Beacon, University of Nottingham, Nottingham NG7 2RD, UK
5 Department of Urology, Cantonal Hospital Aarau, 5001 Aarau, Switzerland
6 Medical Faculty, University Hospital Basel, 4056 Basel, Switzerland
7 Department of Urology, Academic Hospital Braunschweig, 38126 Brunswick, Germany
8 Institute of Pathology, Cantonal Hospital Aarau, 5001 Aarau, Switzerland
9 Medical Faculty, University of Zurich, 8032 Zurich, Switzerland
10 Institute of Radiology, Cantonal Hospital Aarau, 5001 Aarau, Switzerland; felice.burn@ksa.ch (F.B.)
11 AI & Data Science CoE, Cantonal Hospital Aarau, 5001 Aarau, Switzerland
* Correspondence: malte.rippa@fuse-ai.de

Abstract: In this work, several machine learning (ML) algorithms, both classical ML and modern deep learning, were investigated for their ability to improve the performance of a pipeline for the segmentation and classification of prostate lesions using MRI data. The algorithms were used to perform a binary classification of benign and malignant tissue visible in MRI sequences. The model choices include support vector machines (SVMs), random decision forests (RDFs), and multi-layer perceptrons (MLPs), along with radiomic features that are reduced by applying PCA or mRMR feature selection. Modern CNN-based architectures, such as ConvNeXt, ConvNet, and ResNet, were also evaluated in various setups, including transfer learning. To optimize the performance, different approaches were compared and applied to whole images, as well as gland, peripheral zone (PZ), and lesion segmentations. The contribution of this study is an investigation of several ML approaches regarding their performance in prostate cancer (PCa) diagnosis algorithms. This work delivers insights into the applicability of different approaches for this context based on an exhaustive examination. The outcome is a recommendation or preference for which machine learning model or family of models is best suited to optimize an existing pipeline when the model is applied as an upstream filter.

Keywords: machine learning; deep learning; multiparametric MRI; medical imaging; prostate cancer

1. Introduction

According to the latest epidemiological data, prostate cancer (PCa) is the most frequently diagnosed cancer among men in 112 countries worldwide [1]. In 2022, 397,430 PCa-related deaths and 1,467,854 newly diagnosed PCa cases were reported worldwide [2], making PCa the eighth leading cause of cancer death in both sexes [2]. An increasing trend is expected as the population is aging, and age and risk of PCa are correlated [3]. In the case of early detection of PCa, curative treatment is possible, which causes a reduction in mortality. Multiparametric MRI (mpMRI) of the prostate plays an important role in the diagnostic pathway for the early detection of PCa. This is where computer-aided diagnosis can be utilized. Artificial intelligence (AI) has gained popularity in many fields, including medicine. Kufel et al. [4] provide a detailed introduction to AI and machine learning (ML) in medicine and highlight common challenges, such as the scarcity of labeled training data that would be needed to train a reliable classifier with distinctive generalization capabilities. Once trained successfully, AI can aid in the automation of intellectual tasks that are regularly performed by humans. However, the clinical adoption and validation of AI-based systems need to be carried out carefully since ML models may only predict true conditions within certain limits [4].

The current state-of-the-art medical AI solutions report AUC-ROC scores of 0.8328 ± 0.0878 for lesion detection and characterization [5]. These approaches often only cover the evaluation of the classifier as a standalone with known lesion locations but do not cover the big picture of lesion classification together with localization as a complete pipeline. In real-world applications, it can be necessary to construct holistic systems that locate and classify potentially malignant lesions. Such end-to-end pipelines exist in the literature [6,7] or as certified medical products developed by FUSE-AI GmbH in Hamburg, Germany. The architecture of such products is commonly based on a sequential pipeline utilizing one or more UNet models to predict the location of certain anatomies of the prostate. The FUSE-AI pipeline uses mpMRI sequences as input and predicts the segmentations of the prostate gland and its zones. It proceeds to generate voxel-wise lesion location predictions together with a label, i.e., background, benign, or malignant. These holistic solutions are often prone to delivering overly sensitive predictions, resulting in higher false-positive rates. This could possibly cause unnecessary surgery, e.g., prostate biopsy in the case of a false-positive finding. Therefore, there is a need for a reduction in the false-positive rate, i.e., an increase in the specificity with maintained or improved sensitivity.

In this work, several ML approaches are evaluated in terms of their ability to improve the lesion classification performance of the UNet-based pipeline, as shown in Figure 1. It is not desired to propose an entirely new method or apply broad changes to the pipeline but rather to analyze the impact of state-of-the-art methods on an existing pipeline with the overall aim of improving its performance for false-positive reduction in prostate cancer detection.

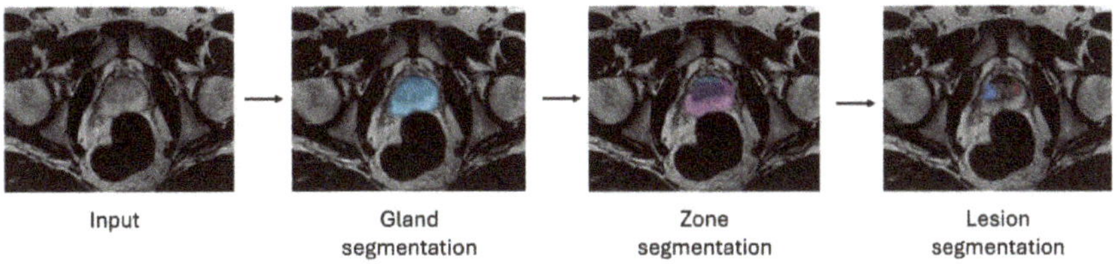

Figure 1. Simplified setup of a sequential lesion segmentation/classification pipeline.

However, during evaluation, it is best to use as little segmentation/localization as possible. A strong classifier that does not rely on voxel-wise annotations could have several advantages: (1) it benefits from a larger amount of data, as image-level labels are easier to obtain, resulting in a more robust and stable classifier; (2) it offers an immediate warning for extra attention if the case appears to contain malignant lesions, even before the image is reviewed by a radiologist; and (3) it can be used as an upstream filter without the need to run computationally expensive segmentation models. A robust and reliable whole-image classifier could save time and resources by minimizing unnecessary segmentation model inferences for MRI scans that do not contain PCa.

This study focuses on evaluating the tendency of different ML models best suited for this problem, considering how the performance is influenced by the inclusion of localization information and whether classical machine learning or deep learning is more beneficial. The emphasis of this study is on the process of model evaluation rather than model development.

Three main questions emerge that will be covered in this work:

- Is the classification performance affected by incorporating localization information using the ROI?
- Is classical machine learning or deep learning more beneficial in solving the issue?
- Can the pipeline performance be improved by adding a classification algorithm?

To assess these main questions, various well-established machine learning methods are evaluated using carefully chosen data, as detailed in Section 2. The results are presented in Section 3, with subsections comparing whole-image classification to region-based classification.

This paper then provides an extensive discussion of the results in Section 4, comparing the achieved results to the state of the art and highlighting the study's limitations. Finally, a brief conclusion is provided, answering the three main questions posed earlier.

2. Materials and Methods

2.1. Image Data and Labels

A total of 1166 cases from one public dataset (ProstateX [8], $n = 182$) and two private datasets were retrospectively collected. The private datasets were provided to FUSE-AI GmbH by Kantonsspital Aarau (Aarau, Switzerland) ($n = 895$), and Universitätsklinikum Jena (Jena, Germany) ($n = 89$). All data sources used SIEMENS Skyra 3.0T MRI devices for the image acquisition. Each image was normalized and then resampled to a voxel spacing of 0.75, 0.75, and 3 and cropped/padded to a size of $149 \times 149 \times 32$ voxels, using the transverse views of the T2-weighted (T2W), apparent diffusion constant (ADC), and diffusion-weighted images (DWI) sequence.

Cases containing a T2W image of insufficient quality due to artifacts that obscure the prostate in the image, such as those caused by endorectal coils, hip implants, or anatomical phenomena (e.g., bladder protruding into the prostate or similar), were excluded from the dataset. Patients were included if they were male and suspected of having prostate cancer.

Cases for patients meeting any of the following criteria were excluded from the dataset:

- Patients younger than 45 years;
- Patients who had undergone previous prostate surgeries (ICD-10-PCS 0VT0 Resection of Prostate, 0VB0 Excision of the Prostate);
- Patients (ICD 0VB-03ZX) who had a prostate biopsy less than six months ago.

Only the transverse view of all series was used; coronal and sagittal views, if present, were discarded.

Labels are based on the Gleason score, which provides reliable information about the condition of the tissue. According to the scoring system definition [9], a Gleason score of $>3 + 3 = 6$ is considered clinically significant. Therefore, the region of interest (ROI) that includes the lesion was labeled with a 1 for analysis purposes. To indicate clinically insignificant (benign) lesions or no lesions at all, a study label of 0 was assigned. This labeling was achieved by mapping histopathological report findings to the image.

Due to inconsistencies, errors, and incompleteness in human annotation, the ground truth was found to be of insufficient quality, and the entire study, including the image data, was excluded from the dataset.

In total, 718 benign and 448 malignant cases were included. The ROI can cover the entire image or certain anatomies within the image.

All cases included in the final dataset were fully anonymized and explicitly cleared for research (and/or commercial) use; therefore, no further ethics assessment was conducted.

2.2. Models

For classical ML, we used a support vector machine (SVM), multilayer perceptron (MLP), and random decision forest (RDF), specifically XGBoost (referred to as XGB). The hyperparameters for each of the classifiers were optimized as described in Section 2.3. In addition to classical ML methods, we investigated convolutional neural networks (ConvNet, ConvNeXt, and ResNet). A standard ConvNet was implemented, consisting of several blocks, each containing two convolutional layers followed by a MaxPooling layer with a pooling size of (2, 2, 2). The output feature map is pooled using global average pooling and classified using a linear layer and sigmoid output activation. The model has a total of 168,705 trainable parameters when using the smallest layout with two blocks. The second model utilized model was a residual network (ResNet) [10], implemented with eight convolutional blocks. Each block consists of a convolutional layer, a batch normalization, and a ReLU layer, resulting in a total of 4,527,906 trainable parameters. Recently, Liu et al. introduced a novel approach to further improve the ResNet by incorporating principles from vision transformers [11]. In the final 3D adaptation for this model, 31,321,561 parameters needed to be trained. All models were adapted to process anisotropic 3D data by replacing 2D convolution and pooling blocks with 3D convolution and pooling blocks, using respective anisotropic kernels. To evaluate a pure transfer learning approach, we utilized the architecture and CT pretrained weights from Models Genesis [12]. Models Genesis describes a self-supervised learning framework for deep models to learn common anatomical representations automatically. To enable the 3D models to learn a transferable image representation, the authors used sub-volumes of the original image (chest CT), deforming them so the model learns to restore the original sub-volume.

For this work, the weights and UNet architecture from lung cancer detection on CT data (Models Genesis) were applied and fitted to the prostate MRI data. Additionally, we evaluate the training of a UNet as autoencoder (AE) for input compression in combination with a Softmax classifier.

All models output either an integer label (0 or 1) or a probability vector that can be converted to a label of 0 or 1, indicating whether the analyzed region is likely to contain a malignant lesion (1) or not (0).

2.3. Methods

For classical ML, performance on the whole image was assessed using different combinations of feature sets and classifiers. The models required textural features, represented by Haralick features, 3D implementations of local binary pattern (LBP) [13], and histogram of oriented gradients (HOG) [14]. A total of 297 features per sequence were extracted, resulting in a total of 891 features when using T2W, ADC, and DWI. The maximum relevance—minimum redundancy (mRMR) feature-selection method [15], as well as the principal component analysis (PCA), were used. Additionally, SMAC3 hyperparameter tuning [16] was applied to optimize hyperparameters for the classical ML classifiers. CNN-based experiments on the whole image were carried out by incorporating techniques such as hyperparameter tuning, regularization, data augmentation, dropout, early stopping, and weighted losses. Convolutional autoencoders were used for the creation of an embedding to be classified by a softmax classifier. Anomaly detection was also investigated following [17]. Transfer learning approaches, such as transferring weights from segmentation models to classification models or using weights from Models Genesis to MRI tasks, were considered. Furthermore, a Jigsaw-puzzle-solving pretraining task was evaluated, where the model theoretically learns the image composition by ordering a sequence of permutations of systematically chosen image patches, consolidating methods proposed in [18,19].

To investigate the effect of incorporating localization information, various region-based classification approaches were implemented. Region-based approaches use the same models as whole image approaches but use bounding boxes around certain anatomical regions as input instead. The regions used included the prostate gland, the peripheral zone (PZ), and lesions, with each subsequent region gradually decreasing in size and increasing in localization information. During training, the anatomical regions were known from ground truth segmentations, and during inference, the pipeline models predicted the segmentation of the required anatomy. Reducing the input space to the gland size was expected to enhance the performance compared to the whole-image classification by minimizing background noise. Given that 70% of prostate lesions are found in the PZ [20], the reduction in the input space to the PZ was expected to be particularly beneficial. The tumors in the PZ are best seen on the ADC sequence [21], so only the ADC sequence was used as input for the analysis. Bounding boxes around known lesion locations were also tested, as suggested by [5].

A sliding window approach is useful when classifying small regions of an image without providing spatial information for ROI extraction during inference [22]. Therefore, a window of size 70, 65, and 3 voxels (x, y, and z directions, respectively) was moved across the image. The true label for the window content was determined by its overlap with a lesion. If the window/lesion over-lap ratio exceeded 0.5, the window was labeled with the lesion's label (benign or malignant); otherwise, it was labeled as background.

Due to the convolutional and pooling layers of the CNNs, the sliding window size was adjusted to 64x-64x-8 voxels for CNN-based approaches. The windows overlapped by 50% of their width. To obtain an image-based classification, the confidence scores of each window were used to generate a heatmap, highlighting areas likely to contain potentially malignant lesions. The heatmap was thresholded at a specific cut-off point determined from the ROC curve. If areas in the heatmap exceeded this confidence threshold, the image-level label was set to malignant; otherwise, it was assigned as benign.

2.4. Experiment Setup

All classifiers were first evaluated as standalone classifiers on the whole image as well as in region-based setups. To increase robustness, the performance metrics were averaged using 5-fold cross-validation. An 85/15 training/test split of the data was made, with 85% used for training (divided into the five folds) and 15% used as the test set.

After standalone training, the classifiers were combined with the lesion segmentation pipeline to evaluate their impact. Depending on the required input (whole image, gland, zone, or lesion), the classifier was positioned in the pipeline accordingly and triggered different mechanisms. The whole image, gland, and zone classifiers filtered out all images predicted to be lesion-free, omitting the inference of segmentation models for those images, as depicted in Figure 2. The lesion-based models used the segmentations proposed by the pipeline and assigned a label to each segmented lesion, as shown in Figure 3. To measure and compare the performance of the classifiers, both as standalone and in combination with the pipeline, the following metrics were used: Area under the Curve of the Receiver Operating Characteristic (AUC-ROC), sensitivity, and specificity. In these metrics, the positive class was the malignant class.

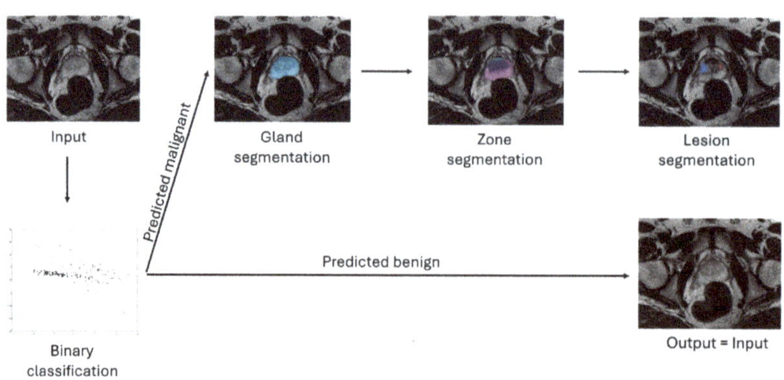

Figure 2. Pipeline evaluation mode 1: All classifiers that do not require lesion segmentations are placed at the beginning of the pipeline or after the model that predicts the required anatomy.

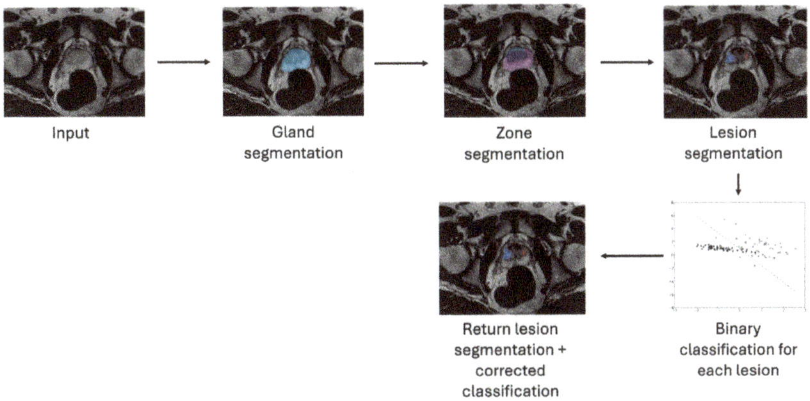

Figure 3. Pipeline evaluation mode 2: The lesion classifiers are placed at the end of the regular pipeline to produce a classification of the lesion candidates selected by the existing pipeline segmentation models.

3. Results

3.1. Whole-Image Results

The results of the classical ML image classifiers are presented in Table 1. The approaches were evaluated in different settings, achieving up to 0.6016 AUC-ROC on the test partition when using the whole image.

Table 1. Metric measurements for the whole-image classification using classical ML on the test partition with the best feature configuration, respectively. Values written in bold indicate the best performance in each class.

Model	AUC-ROC	Sensitivity	Specificity	Feature Set	Selection (# Features)
SVM	**0.6016**	**0.3611**	0.8421	LBP + HOG	PCA (95)
XGB	0.5782	0.2223	**0.9342**	LBP + HOG + Haralick	None (891)
MLP	0.5762	0.3056	0.8158	LBP + HOG + Haralick	None (891)

The different feature-extraction and feature-selection methods did not significantly impact the performance, nor did the SMAC3 hyperparameter optimization for any of the classifiers. SMAC3 evaluated the best parameter setting for each classifier, optimizing parameters such as the regularization parameter, kernel function, or class weight for the SVM. XGBoost was optimized by the learning rate, maximum depth of a tree, and the maximum number of leaf nodes. For the MLP, various numbers of layers and layer sizes were tested. During the experiments, XGB and SVM performed similarly both on the training partition and on the test partition compared to the MLP. The best overall performance was achieved by the SVM classifier, with the error tolerance parameter set to 60, using 95 principal components returned from PCA on LBP, HOG, and Haralick features. The standard ConvNet, ConvNeXt, and ResNet, in combination with standard optimization methods, returned AUC scores of about 0.5273 ± 0.0238. Table 2 shows that the best performance for the standard models was achieved by the ConvNeXt architecture, yielding a 0.5038 AUC-ROC. To improve the performance, pretraining and transfer learning were applied.

Table 2. Metric measurements for the whole-image classification using CNNs on the test partition with the best feature configuration. Values written in bold indicate "the best of class".

Architecture	AUC-ROC	Sensitivity	Specificity
ConvNet	0.4808	0.4172	0.5808
ConvNeXt	0.5038	0.3659	0.6353
ResNet	0.4958	**0.4832**	0.5159
Convolutional autoencoder (Softmax classifier)	**0.6553**	0.4722	0.7763
ConvNeXt (with Jigsaw Puzzle Pretraining)	0.5461	0.1500	**0.9105**
ConvNet (Encoding branch from Models Genesis)	0.5946	0.3611	0.6895

The Jigsaw-puzzle-solving approach did not deliver the anticipated performance improvement. However, applying an AE based on the ConvNeXt architecture (two mirrored ConvNeXt models comprising a UNet-like architecture) to create an embedding to be classified by a softmax classifier yielded the best results for the whole image with an AUC-ROC of 0.6553. The Genesis model, fine-tuned with MRI data using its CT pretrained weights, performed better than the plain CNN-based architectures but slightly worse than the AE. Using an autoencoder for anomaly detection by measuring the reconstruction Mean Squared Error (MSE) of images from different classes resulted in a random classifier, as no difference between the classes could be determined, as shown in Figure 4. The variational autoencoder yielded similar reconstruction probabilities from the latent space for benign and malignant images, preventing any distinction either.

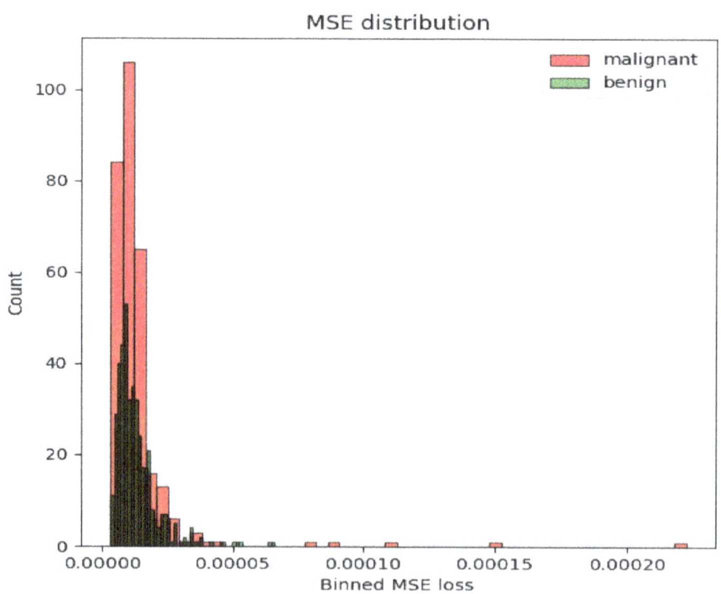

Figure 4. MSE loss distribution with respect to the two classes.

Averaging the five folds of the training and validation of the whole-image classification with the Genesis model indicated that the model was prone to overfitting, as shown in Figures 5 and 6. A diverging AUC-ROC score and binary cross-entropy (BCE) were observed after around 40 epochs (approximately 10,000 optimizer steps). Countermeasures such as dropout, regularization, and reduced model complexity did not show improvement.

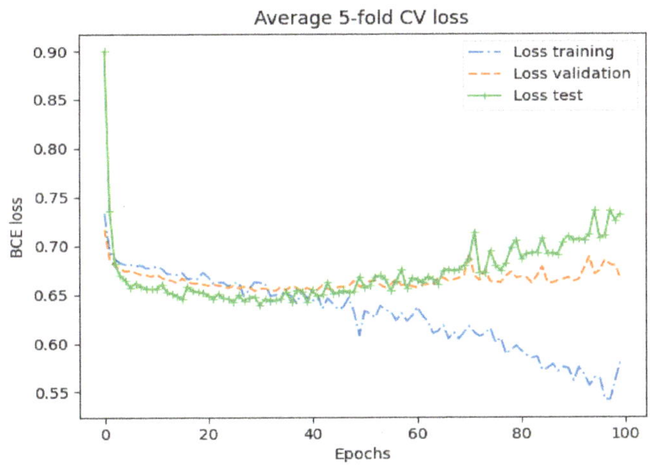

Figure 5. Average 5-fold cross validation loss (binary cross entropy loss) for the training, validation, and test partition on the whole image with the Genesis model over 100 epochs.

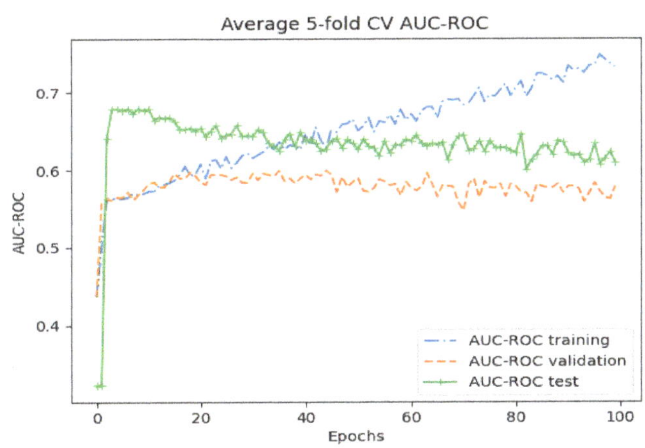

Figure 6. Average 5-fold cross-validation AUC-ROC for the training, validation, and test partition on the whole image with the Genesis model over 100 epochs.

3.2. Region-Based Results

Assessing the previously established methods on regions to introduce a stronger localization showed mixed results. Table 3 presents the best results for each region-based approach, along with the best-performing classifier for that region. While the SVM delivered the strongest results for whole-image classification in the area of the classical ML, the XGB classifier yielded the relatively best scores by a small margin across all regions. Using a segmentation of the prostate gland delivered no improvement compared to the classification of the whole image. The PZ setup led to significantly decreased scores compared to the whole-image classification approach. However, using lesion segmentations achieved the best performance, with an AUC-ROC of 0.6897. The sliding-window approach with classical ML classifiers delivered results close to random chance. For CNN-based methods, only the best-performing approaches (AE and Genesis) were compared. In Table 3, it can be observed that the Genesis model yielded the best scores for all regions. The Genesis model outperformed the AE by at least 10 percentage points in the AUC-ROC. Additionally, performance on the gland segmentation with CNN-based models did not improve by using a bounding box around the gland when compared to whole-image classification.

Table 3. Metric measurements for different regional inputs on the test partition. First four rows: classical ML methods, last four rows: CNN-based methods. Values written in bold indicate the best performance in each class.

Region	Model	AUC-ROC	Sensitivity	Specificity
Gland	XGB	0.5972	**0.6111**	0.5833
PZ (on ADC)	XGB	0.5467	0.4483	0.6452
Lesion	XGB	**0.6897**	0.5333	0.8462
Sliding Window	XGB	0.5291	0.1974	**0.8608**
Gland	Genesis	0.7192	0.6318	0.6578
PZ (on ADC)	Genesis	0.6393	0.5982	0.6502
Lesion	Genesis	**0.7343**	**0.7656**	0.7300
Sliding Window	Genesis	0.6598	0.5805	**0.8004**

Classifying the PZ decreased the performance on both the test partition and the training partition. Using lesion segmentation as input provided reasonable performance when transfer learning with the Genesis model. However, the sliding-window approach did not deliver the anticipated results as a standalone classifier.

3.3. *Performance Measurement in the Segmentation Pipeline*

The goal of this work is to reduce the false positives in a lesion segmentation pipeline. To measure the impact of the aforementioned classifiers, the best performing models were integrated into such a pipeline. Table 4 shows that none of the classifiers was able to achieve outstanding improvements compared to the baseline. Interestingly, the best results in the pipeline were not necessarily achieved by the best standalone classifiers. Overall, only the Genesis-based sliding window approach improved specificity by 0.0225 while maintaining the sensitivity.

Table 4. Performance measurements for each region approach as filter upstream to the lesion segmentation pipeline, listing only the best result for each region. Values written in bold indicate the best performance in each class.

Model	Region	Sensitivity	Specificity
Baseline UNet	Lesion	0.6170	0.4727
ConvNeXt	While Image	0.4231	0.4198
SVM	Gland	0.5106	0.4815
SVM	Zone	0.4894	0.4561
Genesis	Lesion	0.4808	0.3551
Genesis	Sliding window	**0.6170**	**0.4952**

Similar to the graphs presented in Figures 4 and 5, the Genesis model overfitted the training data, yielding perfect scores on the training partition. Applying countermeasures such as dropout, regularization, and reduced model complexity did not prevent the model from overfitting. However, the validation and test results were improved compared to the whole-image results.

4. Discussion

4.1. Discussion of Methods

The applied methods demonstrated the potential to improve the pipeline performance, but only one approach was beneficial. Most methods resulted in unbalanced metric values, indicating room for improvement. Exhaustive research of all parameter combinations was unfeasible due to the extensive range of investigated methods and models investigated. Minor changes might lead to better performance in the pipeline. Additionally, the methods based on the whole image, instead of lesion segmentations as originally proposed, likely compromised the performance. For example, Min et al. [15] selected 819 radiomics features from lesion segmentations and reduced the feature set to a total of 9 features by using mRMR and LASSO. The authors reported an AUC-ROC of 0.823, sensitivity of 0.841, and specificity of 0.727 (test dataset) when classifying csPCa vs. non-csPCa. In this work, applying the method to the whole image returned 0.5461 AUC-ROC, 0.5000 sensitivity, and 0.5921 specificity. Even when applied to lesion segmentations, Min et al.'s results could not be matched, achieving an AUC-ROC of 0.6768 with the SVM. The best result using a radiomic feature set and classical machine learning methods on lesion segmentations was an AUC-ROC of 0.6897 with a sensitivity of 0.8462 and 0.5333 specificity, obtained with an XGB model. This demonstrates that lesion-based methods using the whole image returned worse results compared to the results obtained with the intended use. Feature selection plays an important role, as Min et al. achieved higher scores with different feature compositions. The feature set used in this study could be improved by using different feature-extraction methods, such as stacked sparse autoencoders for dynamic feature selection, as proposed in [23], which perform better than PCA.

For zone-based classification, it could be beneficial to include only one specific subset of features, as proposed in [24]. The authors reported a high AUC-ROC of 0.92 in the PZ by using a total of 26 features, identified using a semi-exhaustive search to find the best feature composition to identify lesions within the PZ. In this study, the best score for zone-based classification was 0.5467 AUC-ROC using texture features. The number of features was regulated by applying PCA or mRMR, differing from the semi-exhaustive search. Better performance might be achieved by selecting a feature subset using a more effective sampling method.

The lesion-based classification has been reported with high scores with state-of-the-art methods. For instance, an AUC-ROC score of 0.95 for the binary classification of csPCa vs. non-csPCa was reported using 1281 radiomic features [25]. In this work, the highest AUC-ROC for lesion classification using classical machine learning was 0.6897. The lower scores may be due to the feature-extraction approach. The chosen extraction methods were originally designed and applied for 2D problems but were adapted to 3D for this study, potentially comprising their performance and leading to lower AUC-ROC scores compared to the state of the art. Common methods rely on 2.5D approaches to analyze 3D volumes with 2D feature extraction methods. However, 2.5D approaches were not utilized in this study and should be investigated in the future.

For localization-free classification, a sliding-window approach was chosen. A window was moved over the image to produce a heatmap of probabilities for malignant lesions following the method described in [18]. The applied sliding-window approach offered low localization performance, as the model favored lesion-like objects outside the prostate. Future approaches should incorporate further restrictions to limit findings only to the prostate gland.

Previous work reported 0.73 to 0.79 accuracy, sensitivity, and specificity using sliding windows by employing a tumor-candidate-detection model to propose regions for further classification [26]. By extracting various features (intensity features, first- and second-order statistics, region sizes, morphologic features, asymmetry features, and physiologic features), strong classification was realized. Despite this setup closely resembling the second pipeline evaluation mode presented in this work, the authors extracted different features that better represented the data. In contrast, the features extracted during the experiments could not represent the data well enough to grant strong classification performance.

A multiscale sliding window approach could also improve performance, achieving up to 0.96 sensitivity at 0.95 specificity [22]. For this purpose, voxel-wise classification was created by classifying textural features and incorporating clinical information such as the location and shape of the lesion. The absence of clinical features may account for the lower results achieved in this work. Furthermore, no voxel-wise classification was carried out due to the high computational effort. Both of the state-of-the-art sliding-window approaches [22,26] used relatively small window sizes and based their feature extraction on 2D windows instead of 3D cubical windows. Multiscale and 2.5D approaches were employed in state-of-the-art studies for both classical machine learning and deep learning [25,27]. In this work, the sliding-window approach to the whole image was utilized with a small z dimension, resembling a 2.5D approach. The obtained results led to an improvement in the pipeline performance. Considering that reformulating and solving tasks in 2D loses rich 3D anatomical information, which can comprise the model [12], a true 2.5D approach was not chosen to maintain the depth information contained in the 3D image. However, it is possible that the pipeline performance could be increased by adhering to a 2.5D approach using a modified ConvNet presented in [27]. The authors applied an XmasNet to classify modified 2D slices of ROIs around the lesion, yielding 0.95 AUC-ROC; however, due to time constraints, this method was not investigated in this work.

Different approaches were chosen for pretraining the CNN models. The Jigsaw puzzle-solver model, in particular, did not perform well in detecting permutations and thus did not benefit the PCa-classification task. It is possible that the task was overly complex for a 3D volume. Originally, the approach was used for the detection of large objects on natural two-dimensional images. There are adaptations to 3D [28] where the task was simplified. Instead of determining a permutation sequence, the model was trained to determine the spatial relation of one puzzle piece to another. This modification caused the model to be confronted with only two puzzle pieces, delivering better results.

In this section, the choice and performance of the applied methods were compared against state-of-the-art approaches. A broad selection of methods was carefully evaluated using sufficient training data with cross-validation. However, the results did not reach the levels achieved by state-of-the-art methods. The performance of the methods was improved by tuning the respective parameters to explore each method's full capacity. Although this work provides insights into the applicability of the chosen methods, it may have overlooked well-performing methods outside of the scope of this study. A broader search, with less parameter-tuning and a higher number of distinctive methods, could reveal better-performing approaches for this use case. Additionally, addressing the overfitting of models is crucial for improving their performance.

4.2. Discussion of Models

The results presented in this work did not fully reach state-of-the-art levels. In the previous section, method implementation was discussed, but the model choice should also be considered. The implemented models were inspired by the state of the art. However, certain choices were excluded.

This work focused exclusively on classification models and did not consider regression, as proposed in other studies [25]. For example, the authors reported an AUC-ROC of up to 0.88 using certain image features and L2-regularized SVM regression. Moreover, the classification performance could be improved by using model ensembles instead of single models [29]. Ensemble learning methods achieved an accuracy, precision, and recall of 0.8097, 0.7669, and 0.7732, respectively, by using ensembles of SVM or MLP classifiers. None of the classical machine learning approaches presented in this work returned comparable scores on the test partition. However, using deep learning models, scores comparable to those presented in [29] were achieved when running the models on lesion segmentations.

Three different architectures were used for CNN-based classification in this study: ConvNet, ResNet, and ConvNeXt. Multiscale approaches using the Xmas-Net architecture reportedly achieved high scores for the classification of csPCa vs. non-csPCa [27]. Xmas-Net is a modified ConvNet that extracts information from different ROI sizes of the same region.

The best performance in this work was achieved by using a pretrained model. Using self-supervised pretraining should be investigated further in future work. Further improvement could also be achieved by using larger pretrained models, such as the Segment Anything Model developed by Meta AI or the Inception V3 model from Google.

5. Conclusions

Altogether, the extensive evaluation of different methods and models provided an enhancement in overall performance. The pipeline performance increased by filtering out images that previously caused false-positive predictions. As the performance increase was slight, the outcome of this work indicates a direction for further research to improve medical pipeline products. It was shown that pretraining models in a self-supervised manner delivered reasonable results in the evaluated setup. The results revealed that providing models with the best available localization is beneficial, as even strong classifiers could not perform well in a pipeline with mediocre localization capabilities.

The incorporation of lesion segmentation data as localization positively impacted classification performance, addressing the first main question stated in the Introduction section. The pretraining approach based on the Genesis model improved the pipeline specificity by 0.0225, from 0.4727 to 0.4952, while maintaining the sensitivity at 0.6170, thus lowering the false positive rate. This indicated that the CNN-based approaches were more beneficial in this setup compared to the classical machine learning approaches, thereby addressing the second and third questions. It is recommended that future work focuses on the use of self-supervised or pretrained models. Investigating an end-to-end pipeline based on nn-UNet or similar models for simultaneous or staggered localization and classification could lead to further improvements.

The best-performing classifier could technically be integrated into existing pipeline products. However, given the slight performance increase on one specific dataset, it is uncertain whether products would perform similarly on new data. The small performance increase does not justify the additional time that is required to compute the image-level labels from the sliding windows. For changes to significantly impact existing medical products, higher pipeline performance would be necessary. The standalone lesion classification performance would need to translate directly into the pipeline performance. A robust and reliable image classifier could save time and resources by minimizing unnecessary inferences of segmentation models for benign prostate scans.

Author Contributions: Conceptualization, F.B. and M.R.; methodology, M.R. and F.B.; software, M.R. and R.S.; validation, M.R. and R.S.; formal analysis, M.R. and R.S.; investigation, M.R.; resources, M.R., M.H., A.C., S.S. and R.S.; data curation, A.C., S. S., F.B., M.K., R.G. and S.W.; writing—original draft preparation, M.R.; writing—review and editing, F.B. and G.K.; visualization, M.R.; supervision, M.H., R.S. and F.B.; project administration, F.B.; funding acquisition, F.B. and M.R. All authors have read and agreed to the published version of the manuscript.

Funding: We acknowledge financial support by Land Schleswig-Holstein within the funding program Open Access Publikationsfonds for this publication. Additionally, the fees for the ethical committee approval for this study were supported by a research grant from the Kantonsspital Aarau (FR1410.000.156).

Institutional Review Board Statement: This study was conducted in accordance with the Declaration of Helsinki and approved by the Ethics Committee EKNZ (protocol code 2021-01466 and date of approval 21 July 2021).

Informed Consent Statement: General research consent was obtained from all subjects involved in the study and herewith aligned with GCP and Helsinki Legislation.

Data Availability Statement: The data used in this study are not available due to ethical, legal, and privacy protection of the involved study subjects and to be compliant with national and international legislations of data privacy related to healthcare data for research purposes.

Acknowledgments: Thanks are given to Universitätsklinikum Jena and Kantonsspital Aarau, as well as to Quang Thong Nguyen for the implementation of ResNet3D, ConvNet3D, and ConvNeXt3D.

Conflicts of Interest: Authors Malte Rippa and Ruben Schulze were employed by the company FUSE-AI GmbH. The remaining authors declare that the research was conducted in the absence of any financial relationships that could be construed as a potential conflict of interest within the research collaboration.

References

1. Sung, H.; Ferlay, J.; Siegel, R.L.; Laversanne, M.; Soerjomataram, I.; Jemal, A.; Bray, F. Global cancer statistics 2020: GLOBOCAN estimates of incidence and mortality worldwide for 36 cancers in 185 countries. *CA Cancer J. Clin.* **2021**, *71*, 209–249. [CrossRef] [PubMed]
2. Ferlay, J.; Ervik, M.; Lam, F.; Laversanne, M.; Mery, L.; Piñeros, M.; Znaor, A.; Soerjomataram, I.; Bray, F. *Global Cancer Observatory: Cancer Today*; International Agency for Research on Cancer: Lyon, France, 2024. Available online: https://gco.iarc.who.int/today (accessed on 30 July 2024).
3. Siegel, R.L.; Miller, K.D.; Wagle, N.S.; Jemal, A. Cancer statistics. *CA Cancer J. Clin.* **2023**, *73*, 17–48. [CrossRef] [PubMed]
4. Kufel, J.; Bargieł-Łączek, K.; Kocot, S.; Koźlik, M.; Bartnikowska, W.; Janik, M.; Czogalik, Ł.; Dudek, P.; Magiera, M.; Lis, A.; et al. What Is Machine Learning, Artificial Neural Networks and Deep Learning?—Examples of Practical Applications in Medicine. *Diagnostics* **2023**, *13*, 2582. [CrossRef] [PubMed]
5. Li, H.; Lee, C.H.; Chia, D.; Lin, Z.; Huang, W.; Tan, C.H. Machine learning in prostate MRI for prostate cancer: Current status and future opportunities. *Diagnostics* **2022**, *12*, 289. [CrossRef] [PubMed]
6. Schelb, P.; Kohl, S.; Radtke, J.P.; Wiesenfarth, M.; Kickingereder, P.; Bickelhaupt, S.; Kuder, T.A.; Stenzinger, A.; Hohenfellner, M.; Schlemmer, H.P.; et al. Classification of cancer at prostate MRI: Deep learning versus clinical PI-RADS assessment. *Radiology* **2019**, *293*, 607–617. [CrossRef] [PubMed]
7. Arif, M.; Schoots, I.G.; Tovar, J.C.; Bangma, C.H.; Krestin, G.P.; Roobol, M.J.; Niessen, W.; Veenland, J.F. Clinically significant prostate cancer detection and segmentation in low-risk patients using a convolutional neural network on multi-parametric MRI. *Eur. Radiol.* **2020**, *30*, 6582–6592. [CrossRef] [PubMed]
8. Litjens, G.; Debats, O.; Barentsz, J.; Karssemeijer, N.; Huisman, H. SPIE-AAPM PROSTATEx Challenge Data (Version 2) [dataset]. The Cancer Imaging Archive. *Cancer Imaging Arch.* **2017**, *10*, K9TCIA. [CrossRef]
9. Gordetsky, J.; Epstein, J. Grading of prostatic adenocarcinoma: Current state and prognostic implications. *Diagn. Pathol.* **2016**, *11*, 25. [CrossRef] [PubMed]
10. He, K.; Zhang, X.; Ren, S.; Sun, J. Deep residual learning for image recognition. In Proceedings of the IEEE Computer Society Conference on Computer Vision and Pattern Recognition (CVPR), Las Vegas, NV, USA, 27–30 June 2016. [CrossRef]
11. Liu, Z.; Mao, H.; Wu, C.Y.; Feichtenhofer, C.; Darrell, T.; Xie, S. A convnet for the 2020s. In Proceedings of the 2022 IEEE/CVF Conference on Computer Vision and Pattern Recognition (CVPR), New Orleans, LA, USA, 18–24 June 2022. [CrossRef]
12. Zhou, Z.; Sodha, V.; Pang, J.; Gotway, M.B.; Liang, J. Models genesis. *Comput. Vis. Pattern Recognit.* **2020**, *67*, 101840. [CrossRef]
13. Zhao, G.; Pietikainen, M. Dynamic texture recognition using local binary patterns with an application to facial expressions. *IEEE Trans. Pattern Anal. Mach. Intell.* **2007**, *29*, 915–928. [CrossRef]
14. Dupre, R.; Argyriou, V.; Greenhill, D.; Tzimiropoulos, G. A 3d scene analysis framework and descriptors for risk evaluation. In Proceedings of the 2015 International Conference on 3D Vision, Lyon, France, 19–22 October 2015. [CrossRef]
15. Min, X.; Li, M.; Dong, D.; Feng, Z.; Zhang, P.; Ke, Z.; You, H.; Han, F.; Ma, H.; Tian, J.; et al. Multi-parametric MRI-based radiomics signature for discriminating between clinically significant and insignificant prostate cancer: Cross-validation of a machine learning method. *Eur. J. Radiol.* **2019**, *115*, 16–21. [CrossRef]
16. Lindauer, M.; Eggensperger, K.; Feurer, M.; Biedenkapp, A.; Deng, D.; Benjamins, C.; Ruhopf, T.; Sass, R.; Hutter, F. Smac3: A versatile bayesian optimization package for hyperparameter optimization. *Mach. Learn. (Stat.ML)* **2022**, *23*, 1–9. [CrossRef]
17. Guo, Y.; Liao, W.; Wang, Q.; Yu, L.; Ji, T.; Li, P. Multidimensional time series anomaly detection: A gru-based gaussian mixture variational autoencoder approach. *Proc. Mach. Learn. Res.* **2018**, *95*, 97–112. Available online: https://proceedings.mlr.press/v95/guo18a.html (accessed on 30 July 2024).
18. Blendowski, M.; Nickisch, H.; Heinrich, M.P. How to learn from unlabeled volume data: Self-supervised 3d context feature learning. In *International Conference on Medical Image Computing and Computer-Assisted Intervention*; Lecture Notes in Computer Science; Springer International Publishing: Berlin/Heidelberg, Germany, 2019; pp. 649–657. [CrossRef]
19. Noroozi, M.; Favaro, P. Unsupervised learning of visual representations by solving jigsaw puzzles. In *European Conference on Computer Vision*; Springer: Cham, Switzerland, 2016. [CrossRef]
20. McNeal, J.E.; Redwine, E.A.; Freiha, F.S.; Stamey, T.A. Zonal distribution of prostatic adenocarcinoma. *Am. J. Surg. Pathol.* **1988**, *12*, 897–906. [CrossRef]

21. Murphy, G.; Haider, M.; Ghai, S.; Sreeharsha, B. The expanding role of MRI in prostate cancer. *Am. J. Roentgenol.* **2013**, *201*, 1229–1238. [CrossRef] [PubMed]
22. Han, S.M.; Lee, H.J.; Choi, J.Y. Computer-aided prostate cancer detection using texture features and clinical features in ultrasound image. *J. Digit. Imaging* **2008**, *21*, 121–133. [CrossRef] [PubMed]
23. Abraham, B.; Nair, M.S. Computer-aided classification of prostate cancer grade groups from MRI images using texture features and stacked sparse autoen coder. *Comput. Med. Imaging Graph.* **2018**, *69*, 60–68. [CrossRef]
24. Jensen, C.; Carl, J.; Boesen, L.; Langkilde, N.C.; Østergaard, L.R. Assessment of prostate cancer prognostic gleason grade group using zonal-specific features extracted from biparametric MRI using a KNN classifier. *J. Appl. Clin. Med. Phys.* **2019**, *20*, 146–153. [CrossRef]
25. Toivonen, J.; Perez, I.M.; Movahedi, P.; Merisaari, H.; Pesola, M.; Taimen, P.; Bostrom, P.J.; Pohjankukka, J.; Kiviniemi, A.; Pahikkala, T.; et al. Radiomics and machine learning of multisequence multiparametric prostate MRI: Towards improved non-invasive prostate cancer characterization. *PLoS ONE* **2019**, *14*, e0217702. [CrossRef]
26. Cameron, A.; Khalvati, F.; Haider, M.A.; Wong, A. MAPS: A quantitative radiomics approach for prostate cancer detection. *IEEE Trans. Biomed. Eng.* **2015**, *63*, 1145–1156. [CrossRef]
27. Liu, S.; Zheng, H.; Feng, Y.; Li, W. Prostate cancer diagnosis using deep learning with 3d multiparametric MRI. *Comput. Vis. Pattern Recognit.* **2017**, *10134*, 581–584. [CrossRef]
28. Blendowski, M.; Bouteldja, N.; Heinrich, M.P. Multimodal 3d medical image registration guided by shape encoder–decoder networks. *Int. J. Comput. Assist. Radiol. Surg.* **2019**, *15*, 269–276. [CrossRef] [PubMed]
29. Zhang, L.; Li, L.; Tang, M.; Huan, Y.; Zhang, X.; Zhe, X. A new approach to diagnosing prostate cancer through magnetic resonance imaging. *Alex. Eng. J.* **2020**, *60*, 897–904. [CrossRef]

diagnostics

MDPI

Article

Brain Tumor Detection and Classification Using an Optimized Convolutional Neural Network

Muhammad Aamir [1,2], Abdallah Namoun [3,*], Sehrish Munir [1], Nasser Aljohani [3], Meshari Huwaytim Alanazi [4,*], Yaser Alsahafi [5] and Faris Alotibi [6]

1 Department of Computer Science, Sahiwal Campus, COMSATS University Islamabad, Sahiwal 57000, Pakistan; muhammadaamir@cuisahiwal.edu.pk (M.A.); sehrishjonaid@gmail.com (S.M.)
2 Department of Computer Science, Superior University Lahore, Lahore 54000, Pakistan
3 AI Centre, Faculty of Computer and Information Systems, Islamic University of Madinah, Madinah 42351, Saudi Arabia; naljohani@iu.edu.sa
4 Computer Science Department, College of Sciences, Northern Border University, Arar 73213, Saudi Arabia
5 School of Information Technology, University of Jeddah, Jeddah 23218, Saudi Arabia; yaalsahafi@uj.edu.sa
6 College of Computer Science and Engineering, Taibah University, Madinah 42353, Saudi Arabia; fotibi@taibahu.edu.sa
* Correspondence: a.namoun@iu.edu.sa (A.N.); meshari.alanazi@nbu.edu.sa (M.H.A.)

Abstract: Brain tumors are a leading cause of death globally, with numerous types varying in malignancy, and only 12% of adults diagnosed with brain cancer survive beyond five years. This research introduces a hyperparametric convolutional neural network (CNN) model to identify brain tumors, with significant practical implications. By fine-tuning the hyperparameters of the CNN model, we optimize feature extraction and systematically reduce model complexity, thereby enhancing the accuracy of brain tumor diagnosis. The critical hyperparameters include batch size, layer counts, learning rate, activation functions, pooling strategies, padding, and filter size. The hyperparameter-tuned CNN model was trained on three different brain MRI datasets available at Kaggle, producing outstanding performance scores, with an average value of 97% for accuracy, precision, recall, and F1-score. Our optimized model is effective, as demonstrated by our methodical comparisons with state-of-the-art approaches. Our hyperparameter modifications enhanced the model performance and strengthened its capacity for generalization, giving medical practitioners a more accurate and effective tool for making crucial judgments regarding brain tumor diagnosis. Our model is a significant step in the right direction toward trustworthy and accurate medical diagnosis, with practical implications for improving patient outcomes.

Keywords: brain tumor; classification; MRI; convolutional neural network; fine-tuning; hyperparameter; detection

1. Introduction

The human brain is the most sophisticated organ in the body, with several complex neuronal systems. These neurons are interlinked and work together with the help of instructions given by the other parts of the body. When these neurons start working abnormally, brain tumors occur. Brain tumors are the world's second leading cause of mortality, accounting for around 9.6 million deaths in 2018. Around one out of every ten deaths worldwide occurs due to brain tumors [1]. There are two categories of brain tumors: primary and secondary. Brain tumors are recognized as malignant (cancerous) and benign (non-cancerous). The benign tumors do not spread or harm the other parts of the body, while malignant tumors spread all over the human body and can lead to life-threatening situations. Glioma, meningioma, and pituitary tumors stand out as separate forms of brain tumors [2]. Gliomas are the most common primary brain tumors and are classified into four degrees of malignancy, with higher grades signifying increased aggressiveness. These cancers begin in the glial cells of the brain [3,4]. Meningiomas are benign tumors that arise from the meninges tissue layer and are characterized by sluggish growth and limited distribution. Pituitary tumors, on the other hand, form on the pituitary gland and are generally benign and less common [5,6].

The occurrence signs of brain tumors vary depending upon the size, shape, and location of tumors. Some of the common signs of brain tumors are headache, nausea, vomiting, seizures, and difficulty in thinking or speaking [7]. The most famous brain tumor diagnosis methods include a combination of imaging tests, such as MRI and CT scans, and biopsy, depending on the type and stage of the tumor [8]. Other treatment possibilities include surgery, radiation therapy, and chemotherapy [9]. The goal of treatment is to relieve signs, control the progression of the tumor, and prolong survival.

Brain tumors affect persons of diverse categories, like ages and genders, regardless of the identification of certain risk factors. Risk factors include genetic disposition, ionizing radiation revelation, and certain hereditary illnesses. Nonetheless, the particular causes of most brain tumors remain unidentified [10]. Moreover, progressions in medical imaging and diagnostic methods have made it promising to determine earlier brain tumors, increasing the probability that interference would be effective.

Brain tumor detection and classification accuracy are critical to selecting the best treatment method. Frequently, histological investigation of tumor tissue attained from operations is used in traditional classification methods. However, in the last numerous years, there have been significant developments in the classification and diagnosis of brain tumors without surgery. These approaches comprise magnetic resonance imaging [11], CT scans [12], positron emission tomography [13], progressive neuroimaging methods known as diffusion tensor imaging [14], and magnetic resonance spectroscopy [15]. These methods provide accurate information about the tumor biography, which aids in the exact diagnosis of a brain tumor. Recent studies have focused on developing several approaches for improving the classification and detection of brain tumors. One of the most state-of-the-art developments comprises the evaluation of imaging data using artificial intelligence and machine learning algorithms [16]. These methods can significantly increase the precision of brain tumor diagnosis, classification, and patient outcome prediction [17]. In oncology, the task of precisely classifying and identifying brain tumors is difficult due to the complex and diverse structure and functional location of brain tumor tissues. Even with the prominent development in medical imaging and diagnosis, brain tumor treatment requires significant care for patients to cure them [18].

Key Contributions of Our Work

Brain tumors constitute a major cause of cancer deaths, affecting individuals indiscriminately regardless of age or gender. Avoiding these causes requires thorough information on fundamental biological and behavioral factors due to their intricate structure and likelihood of severe neurological signs. Even though traditional diagnostic approaches are helpful, they frequently give an imprecise depiction of the extensive molecular and genetic distinctions initiated in these malignancies. The demand for sophisticated technologies that enable exact tumor characterization, leading to specific treatment plans and improved clinical findings, urges the improvement of brain tumor classification and detection approaches. This research contributes a fine-tuned CNN hyperparametric model with the following distinct characteristics:

- An optimized CNN hyperparameter model: The paper presents an advanced CNN hyperparameter model that has been carefully developed to optimize critical parameters in diagnosing brain tumors. The activation function, learning rate, batch, padding, filter size and numbers, and pooling layers are just a few of the carefully selected parameters that enhance the model performance and ability to generalize the model. The objective is to increase the model's overall diagnostic accuracy and dependability by fine-tuning these hyperparameters.

- Datasets used: In this study, three publicly available brain MRI datasets sourced from Kaggle were utilized to test and validate the proposed model.
- Outstanding predictions: The proposed approach demonstrates exceptional results in average precision, recall, and f1-score values of 97% and an accuracy of 97.18% for dataset 1. These outcomes indicate the effectiveness of the optimized CNN model in accurately diagnosing brain tumors.
- Comparative analysis: The study extensively compares our optimized model with established techniques, affirming the strength and reliability of the findings. The proposed method consistently surpasses these approaches, showcasing its superiority in accuracy and reliability when it comes to diagnosing brain tumors.
- Practical implications: This model offers medical professionals a more accurate and effective tool to aid their decision-making in diagnosing brain tumors. By enhancing diagnostic accuracy and reliability, the model has the potential to advance medical imaging and improve patient care.

Our research extends our work published in [19], where we introduced a CNN hyperparameteric model for brain tumor diagnosis. The main contribution was a CNN hyperparameter model tailored for brain tumor diagnosis, fine-tuning several crucial parameters like activation functions, learning rate, batch size, number of layers, stride padding, activation functions, and filter number and size. An improved tool for assisting decision-making processes in brain tumor diagnosis is realized by the paper's remarkable outcomes, which included high recall, accuracy, F1-score, and precision. Two datasets (containing 7023 and 253 images, respectively) [20] of various tumor types, including pituitary, glioma, meningioma, and no tumor, were used to validate the model. Additionally, the article compared the proposed model against current methods, showing superior performance results. However, our previous model suffered from several limitations. First, the model was tested on a small dataset to validate the optimized hyperparameters and assess its performance. Second, the model's accuracy and other performance values were not optimal. Third, the model needs to be generalized to explore the integration of different imaging modalities.

The remainder of this article is organized as a related work section providing an overview of relevant research in the field, followed by a methodology section describing the overall approach employed. Subsequently, the results section explains the outcomes resulting from the applied model. Lastly, the conclusion summarizes the findings and proposes existing gaps for future research.

2. Related Work

Recently, significant research has been conducted to detect and classify brain tumors and assist in saving human lives. Research in [21,22] presents a brain tumor classification model based on deep learning and optimization algorithms. The proposed approach improves the efficiency and accuracy of tumor diagnosis, addressing the limitations of manual methods and providing a potential solution for automated detection approaches. Another study [23] proposes a unique CNN-based MRI brain tumor classification technique. The study compares the performance of the optimized CNN model with five pre-trained models on the CE-MRIs dataset. The model achieves excellent validation accuracy, outperforming state-of-the-art approaches, and shows the possibility of automated hyperparameter optimization in MRI brain tumor classification. CNNs outperform traditional approaches in brain tumor diagnosis by automatically learning and extracting hierarchical characteristics, resulting in increased accuracy and performance. They provide scalability, versatility, and a comprehensive learning framework, making them more efficient and effective for medical imaging analysis. The research in [24] suggests a novel hybrid deep learning model combining SqueezeNet with SVM and fine-tuning for classifying brain tumors from MRIs. The model was tested on a dataset consisting of glioma, meningioma, pituitary, and no tumors, achieving an accuracy of 96.5%. This approach outperforms existing methods, offering a precise, efficient medical diagnosis tool, highlighting significance through innovative deep learning techniques.

The work in [25] presents a thorough overview of recent improvements in automatic segmentation of white matter hyperintensities (WMHs) from brain magnetic resonance imaging, emphasizing the role of deep learning and big data in enhancing segmentation accuracy and efficiency. It analyzes several deep learning models and datasets used in the field, providing information on their effectiveness and limits. Another research paper [26] compares many local thresholding techniques for segmenting white matter hyperintensities in brain magnetic resonance imaging. The study concludes that the adaptive thresholding algorithm surpasses others in terms of segmentation accuracy and robustness, making it the most effective method for WMH segmentation.

The study in [27] explores the performance of CNN in classifying MRI scans of brain tumors. Using two MRI datasets, the study analyzes various CNN architectures, including VGG, ResNet, EfficientNet, and ConvNeXt. The best model performed well in terms of accuracy, with average precision rates of 95.3% for images without tumors, 93.8% for meningioma, 97.9% for pituitary tumors, and 94% for gliomas. The authors in [28] use the Harris Hawks optimization algorithm to optimize CNN, achieving excellent tumor recognition accuracy on a Kaggle dataset. The proposed method enhances the identification of tumor regions and hidden edge details, offering potential benefits for early diagnosis and treatment of brain tumors. A fine-tuning method in [29] uses machine learning to categorize gliomas in brain magnetic resonance imaging (MRI), focusing on reducing picture inconsistencies across different medical facilities. The advantages of this approach include improved accuracy in glioma segmentation, as evidenced by the acquired accuracy rate of 87.5% in experimental data. However, there are some limitations to consider. The fine-tuning procedure can be computationally costly, and the method performance depends on data availability and quality. Despite these limitations, the work emphasizes the potential of the proposed approach to considerably increase glioma segmentation accuracy, making it an attractive route for future research and clinical applications. Another paper [30] blends handcrafted and deep learning characteristics for brain tumor diagnosis, attaining a high accuracy of 91.2%. The method produces reliable findings, although it may necessitate significant computational resources. However, the prediction performance is impacted by balancing varied features and data quality.

The study in [31] explores brain tumor detection by combining statistical and machine learning techniques, achieving 85.6% accuracy. However, problems arise as feature choice and the dataset size can improve the method performance. Despite its limitations, the study shows that merging these methods can lead to the effective detection of brain tumors. The research in [32] examines brain tumor identification using deep learning techniques for big data processing. One benefit is a notable accuracy of 94.3%, which signifies the efficiency of neural networks in tumor identification in medical imaging research. However, deep networks require significant data labeling and substantial computing power for training.

A technique for identifying and classifying brain tumors in MRIs is proposed in [33]. However, the method cannot be used for all tumor sizes and types. Another study [34] presents a novel, trustworthy BrainMRNet model for magnetic resonance imaging-based brain tumor detection. This model applies advanced neural networks to detect tumors with high accuracy. Training deep networks is computationally expensive and efficiency may fluctuate based on the range of tumor types and imaging conditions.

The research in [35] proposes a neural network-based technique for wireless infrared imaging sensor-based brain tumor detection, with an accuracy rate of 87.2%. Drawbacks include its dependency on high-quality data and the need for an optimal sensor site. A CNN method is used in [36] for detecting brain tumors, with a notable accuracy of 93.8%. Conversely, the prerequisite for a lot of labeled data and computing resources for training is a disadvantage. The CNNs are a valuable technique for precise brain tumor diagnosis, and this work highlights their importance in medical image processing.

The study in [37] shows that brain tumors are identified with an accuracy of 95.62% by applying a maximal fuzzy sure entropy improved CNN model. Disadvantages include the complexity of merging several methods and the need for a large amount of training data. This work shows the potential of the collective approach to improve brain tumor identification and depicts its role in enhancing medical image processing. In another work [38], brain tumors in MRIs are recognized and segmented using deep learning methods, achieving a 90% accuracy. However, extensive processing resources are required for the training and inference stages.

The study in [39] reviews how deep learning was used to identify brain tumors between 2015 and 2020, showing a notable rise in accuracy, reaching as high as 95.6%. A deep neural network correlation learning technique for classifying CT brain tumors is described in [40]. Drawbacks include the complexity of neural network architectures and their extensive computational demands.

3. Materials and Methods

This section explains the methodology workflow employed in this research, with detailed steps provided subsequently.

3.1. MRI Dataset

Our research utilized three publicly available brain tumor MRI datasets from Kaggle [20]. The details of the datasets and their divisions (i.e., training and testing) are listed in Table 1. The table presents three MRI datasets, their respective class distributions, and the number of images in the training and testing sets. Dataset 2 includes classes labeled as yes and no, with 239 images. The training set of Dataset 2 comprises 201 images, and the testing set contains 38 images, as shown in Figure 1. Dataset 3 focuses on the tumor classes, with 1500 images in total, as shown in Figure 2. The training set of Dataset 3 has 1200 images, and the testing set consists of 300 images. Dataset 3 also has an additional set of 3000 images, with 2400 in the training set and 600 in the testing set. Dataset 1 contains images of glioma, meningioma, pituitary, and no tumor classes, with a total of 7023 images, as shown in Figure 3a,b. The training set of Dataset 1 consists of 5712 images, while the testing set has 1311 images.

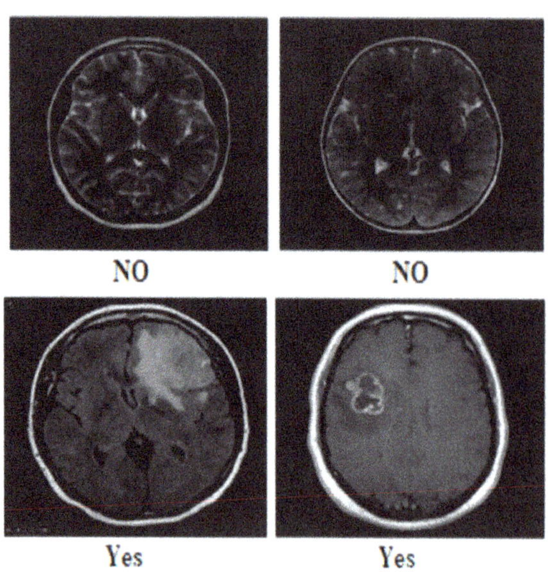

Figure 1. Sample images from Dataset 2.

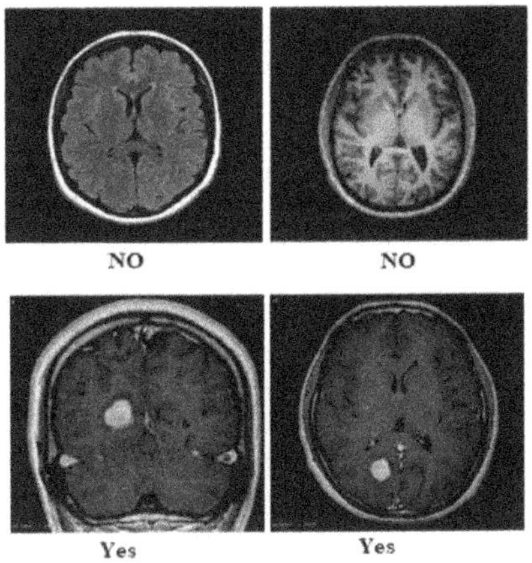

Figure 2. Sample images from Dataset 3.

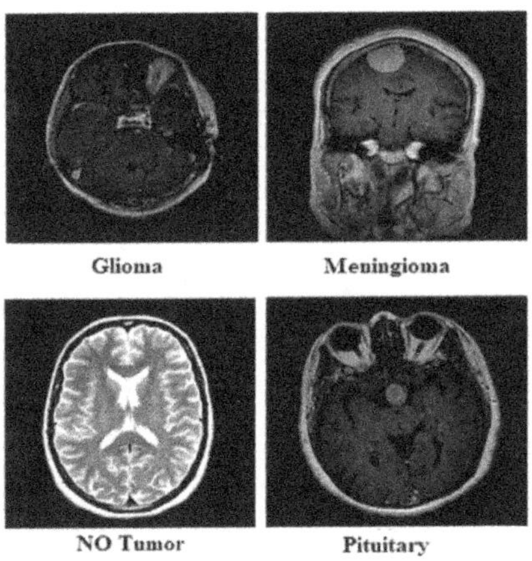

(a)

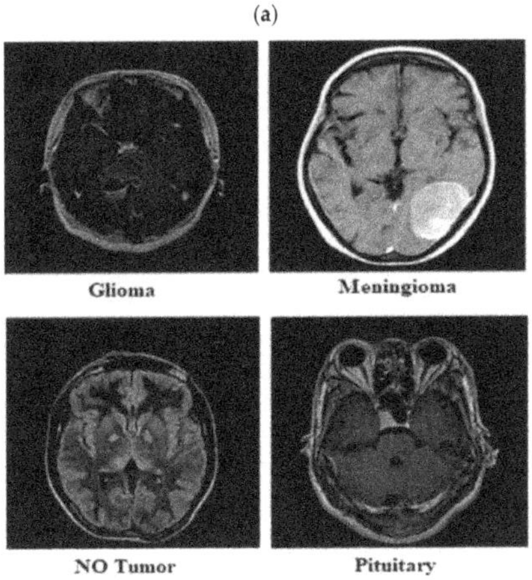

(b)

Figure 3. Samples from Dataset 1.

Table 1. Brain tumor MRI dataset.

Dataset 1				Dataset 2				Dataset 3			
Class	Images	Train	Test	Class	Images	Train	Test	Class	Images	Train	Test
Glioma	1621	1321	300	Yes	155	135	20	Yes	1500	1200	300
Meningioma	1645	1339	306	No	84	66	18	No	1500	1200	300
Pituitary	1757	1457	300								
No Tumor	2000	1595	405								
Total	**7023**	**5712**	**1311**	**Total**	**239**	**201**	**38**	**Total**	**3000**	**2400**	**600**

3.2. Pre-Processing

Several processes were completed to pre-process the MRI scans for precise brain tumor analysis and insightful conclusions. This involves resolving issues with MRI images of different resolutions and intensity ranges. Normalizing intensity values improves the performance of algorithms and models. Commonly used methods include z-score normalization [41] and rescaling pixel values to the specified range (0, 1) [42]. Due to changes in position and orientation, the MRI images must be aligned to a standard reference frame. Techniques for image registration [43] make it easier to match images spatially, which improves comparison and analysis. Furthermore, it is critical to address MRI image noise and abnormalities introduced by diverse variables, such as patient movements or equipment fluctuations. Techniques for denoising the images, such as non-local means filtering or Gaussian smoothing, efficiently reduce noise without sacrificing important information [44].

3.3. Hyperparameters of CCN for Training

In convolutional neural networks (CNNs), hyperparameters [45] are parameters the user configures before training the model and are not learned during the training process as shown in Figure 4 The input layer serves as the starting point for the CNN training process, while the classification layer marks its culmination in a feed-forward manner. Conversely, the reverse procedure initiates from the classification layer and progresses through the first convolutional layer. The neuron J forwards information computed based on Equation (1) to neuron N in layer L in a forward manner. The output is determined by the non-linear ReLU function [46], as described in Equation (2).

$$IP_N^L = \sum_{J=1}^{N} W_{NJ}^L x_j + b_N \quad (1)$$

$$OP_N^L = max\left(0, IP_N^L\right) \quad (2)$$

In the given equations, IP represents the input, OP denotes the output, W stands for weight, and b represents the neuron number. Equations (1) and (2) are utilized by all neurons to generate outputs and construct the non-linear activation function based on inputs. On the other hand, pooling adopts a k-by-k filter to aggregate and compute maximum average feature values. Equation (3) demonstrates the calculation process using the SoftMax function by minimizing the new weights with the help of Equation (4), given below.

$$OP_N^L = \frac{e^{IP_N^L}}{\sum_N e^{OP_k^L}} \quad (3)$$

$$C = -\frac{1}{S}\sum_N^S IP\left(X\left(\frac{a^i}{b^i}\right)\right) \quad (4)$$

During the training process, S represents a sample from the training set, b^i represents the ith example with its respective label a^i. The classification possibility $X\left(\frac{a^i}{b^i}\right)$ is a probabilistic measure related to the ratio of features or parameters $\left(\frac{a^i}{b^i}\right)$ for the i-th data point. This probability is used as part of a machine-learning model to improve its predictions. Using the stochastic gradient function, the model aims to iteratively update its parameters to minimize the overall cost or loss function C. In practice, this means that during each iteration of the training process, the stochastic gradient descent algorithm calculates the gradient of the cost function concerning the model parameters using only a randomly chosen subset of the data. This gradient is then used to adjust the parameters, ideally leading to a decrease in the cost function C. Over time, this process helps the model become more accurate in its classifications, as indicated by the improved classification possibility $X\left(\frac{a^i}{b^i}\right)$. Equation (5) illustrates the calculation of the weights for each convo layer known as L, with weight L having iteration t indicated as W_L^t.

$$W_L^{t+1} = W_L^t + V_L^{t+1} \tag{5}$$

In the given context, W_L^t represents the weight L, while V_L^{t+1} represents the updated weight value at iteration t. This plays a critical role in feature extraction within convolutional neural networks. It consists of multiple filters that extract features from input data. Equations (6) and (7) are employed to evaluate the resulting value and layer sizes. Here, n_L^i denotes the resulting feature map for images, σ represents the activation function, y_L signifies the input width, and $x_L^{i\epsilon f}, z^{i\epsilon f}$ are filter channels within the filter (f).

$$n_L^i = \sigma\left(x_L^i - y_L + z^i\right) \tag{6}$$

$$Convo\ layer\ ouput\ size = \left(\frac{input - size\ of\ filter}{stride}\right) + 1 \tag{7}$$

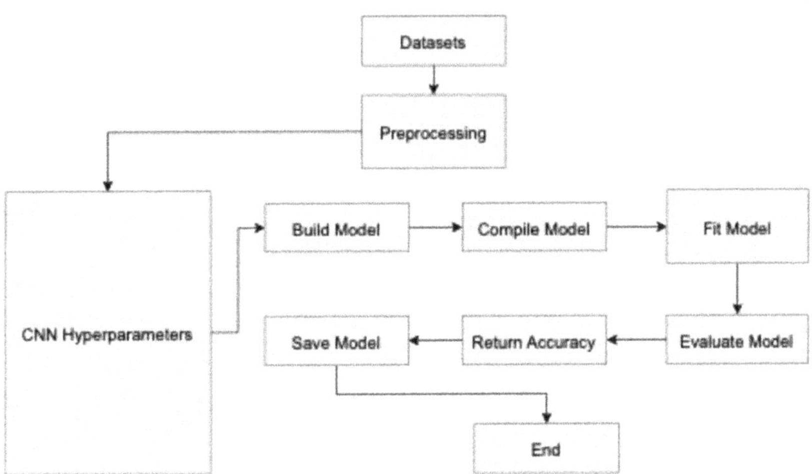

Figure 4. The workflow of the proposed model.

In convolutional neural networks, a pooling layer is expected to follow each convolutional layer. This layer plays a role in parameter management and helps prevent overfitting. Among the various types of pooling layers, such as min and average, max pooling [47] is the most commonly employed. The output and size for these layers are computed using Equations (8) and (9). The equation $Pool_{i,j} = max_{r,s\epsilon R}$ describes the max pooling operation where the value at the (*i,j*)-th position of the output feature map is determined by taking the maximum value from a specific region *R* of the input feature map. This region *R* consists of all positions (*r,s*) within the pooling window centered around the (*i,j*)-th position.

$$Pool_{i,j} = max_{r,s \epsilon R} \tag{8}$$

$$Pooling\ layer\ size = \left(\frac{convo\ output - Pooling\ Size}{stride}\right) + 1 \tag{9}$$

3.4. Hyperparametric Fine-Tuning of CNN

Table 2 illustrates the importance of improving many parts of network architecture to fine-tune the hyperparameters. The number and size of filters play a crucial role in determining the depth of the convolutional layers and the receptive field. It is beneficial to explore alternative filter numbers and different filter sizes while also adjusting the stride to control the dimensions of the output feature maps. A large stride leads to a decrease in spatial resolution, while a smaller stride increases it. Appropriate padding parameters are chosen to preserve the spatial size of the input volume during convolutional processes. Padding helps mitigate the impact of boundaries while retaining essential spatial information. The user manually sets several hyperparameters to control the structure and training process of the network. These hyperparameters include the learning rate, batch size, number of epochs, optimizer, learning rate schedule, shuffle, verbose, dropout rate, filters, filter size, and activation function.

Table 2. Steps for fine-tuning of CNN.

Fine-Tuning of CNN Hyperparameter
Step 1: Find the best hyperparameters to train the final model.
Step 2: Develop new model instances for the best hyperparameters.
Step 3: Train the model with the specified parameters.
Step 4: Test and evaluate the CNN model.
Step 5: Find the best performance metrics (e.g., accuracy).

On the other hand, the machine learning process automatically optimizes certain variables, primarily the weights and biases of the convolutional and fully connected layers. These parameters are adjusted during training to minimize the loss function and improve the network's performance on the given task. The optimization algorithm, such as stochastic gradient descent (SGD) or Adam, iteratively updates these weights and biases based on the gradients computed from the loss function.

Different pooling methods were utilized during the experiments, such as max, min, and average pooling. These methods assist in reducing spatial sizes. In a CNN, suitable activation functions known as ReLU, sigmoid, and tanh introduced non-linearity and assisted the system in developing complex relationships with inputs [48]. The choice of learning rate influences the convergence of the model. The lower learning rate may need further iterations and can lead to better convergence, and the higher one may result in more rapid convergence but with the risk of passing the optimal solution. In experiments, the batch sizes determine the number of training examples processed in each iteration. The number of fully connected and convolutional layers can be changed to change the depth of the network. Overfitting is reduced, and generalization is improved by using regularization techniques like L2 regularization or dropout. Weight updates during training are regulated by experimenting with optimization approaches such as Adam and stochastic gradient descent (SGD).

3.5. Working of Hyperparameteric CNN

The hyperparameterized CNN model uses hyperparameters to adjust its design and improve performance. The hyperparameter configuration for the proposed CNN model in the table appears to be a well-designed and consistent starting point for training on the three different datasets. The learning rate is set to a low value of 0.00001, the model is trained on a GPU environment, and the batch size is 8 with 50 training epochs for Datasets 2 and 3 and 8 epochs for Dataset 1. Both SGD and Adam optimizers are utilized, and the learning rate schedule follows a piece-wise approach, with the training data shuffled after each epoch. The model incorporates a 20% dropout rate and uses various filters (ranging from 2 to 128) with 3 × 3 and 5 × 5 filter sizes and the commonly used ReLU activation function. This hyperparameter configuration provides a solid foundation for the proposed CNN model and can be further refined through additional experimentation and tuning to achieve optimal performance on specific datasets. The particular configuration of the model hyperparameters is provided in Table 3.

Table 3. Hyperparameter configuration for proposed CNN.

Sr. No	Parameters	Dataset1	Dataset2	Dataset3
		Values	**Values**	**Values**
1	Batch size	8	8	8
2	Epochs	8	50	50
3	Optimizer	SGD, Adam	SGD, Adam	SGD, Adam
4	Learning rate	• Epochs 0–5, Learning Rate: 0.0001 • Epochs 6–8, Learning Rate: 0.00005 • Epochs 9–10, Learning Rate: 0.00001	• Epochs 0–20, Learning Rate: 0.0001 • Epochs 21–30, Learning Rate: 0.00005 • Epochs 31–50, Learning Rate: 0.00001	• Epochs 0–20, Learning Rate: 0.0001 • Epochs 21–30, Learning Rate: 0.00005 • Epochs 31–50, Learning Rate: 0.00001
5	Shuffle	Every epoch	Every epoch	Every epoch
6	Dropout rate	0.2	0.2	0.2
7	Number of filters	16, 32, 64, 128	2, 4, 16, 32, 64	4, 8, 16, 32, 64
8	Filter size	3 × 3, 5 × 5	3 × 3, 5 × 5	3 × 3, 5 × 5
9	Activation function	ReLU	ReLU	ReLU

4. Results

The CNN was implemented in Python on the system, which had an 8GB GTX 1060 GPU, a 12th generation i9 processor, and 32GB of RAM. This setup was utilized to predict brain tumors. The execution is available for other researchers at GitHub (https://github.com/muhammadaamir1234/Brain-tumor-hyperparameter-CNN (accessed on 11 June 2024)).

4.1. Evaluation Criteria

To evaluate the proposed model's performance in detecting and classifying brain tumors, several performance equations (i.e., (10)–(13)) were employed. True positive images, denoted as Tp, referred to correctly classified cases, while true negative images, denoted as Tn, represented correctly classified cases as negative. The quantity of incorrectly positive classified images was signified as Fp, and incorrectly negative classified images were denoted as Fn. Statistical metrics were calculated with the help of Equations (10)–(13) given below.

$$Precision\ (Pre) = \frac{Tp}{Tp + Fp} \tag{10}$$

$$Recall\ (R) = \frac{Tp}{Tp + Fn} \tag{11}$$

$$F1 - score\ (F1 - S) = \frac{2(R * Pre)}{R + Pre} \tag{12}$$

$$Accuracy\ (Acc) = \frac{Tp + Tn}{Tn + Tp + Fp + Fn} \tag{13}$$

4.2. Applied Model Results

The given classification confusion matrix represents model performance on the test dataset, displayed in Figures 5–7 for Datasets 1, 2, and 3, respectively. Four separate categories make up this dataset: glioma, pituitary, meningioma, and no tumor for Datasets 1 and 2 as a yes and no for Datasets 1 and 2. Regarding the number of images used for classification, the confusion matrix (CM) is the square matrix whose proportions are equivalent to the number of classes. It is a 4 × 4 matrix in this instance because there are four classes. Actual and anticipated class labels are combined to form each cell in the matrix. Every element within the matrix represents the number of photos associated with a particular class (rows) and anticipated to be a part of a particular forecasted class. The confusion matrix in Figure 5 shows a classification model with 97.18% accuracy, correctly predicting 1274 out of 1311 instances. The model performs best on no tumor cases (100% accuracy) but has minor misclassifications between glioma, meningioma, and pituitary cases. The CM in Figure 6 shows the classification results for two classes, "Yes" and "No", with the model achieving 93.33% overall accuracy. The model correctly predicted 18 "Yes" instances (60.00%) and 10 "No" instances (33.33%), with minor misclassifications resulting in 2 "Yes" instances and 2 "No" instances being incorrectly labeled. On the other hand, CM in Figure 7 shows the performance of a binary classification model with an overall accuracy of 96.49%. The model correctly predicted 302 "Yes" instances (50.50%) and 275 "No" instances (45.99%), with minor misclassifications resulting in 9 "Yes" instances and 12 "No" instances being incorrectly labeled. Additionally, Table 4 presents statistical data, including average precision, recall, and f1-score as 0.97 for each class.

TARGET / OUTPUT	Glioma	Meningioma	No Tumor	Pituitary	SUM
Glioma	284 21.66%	16 1.22%	0 0%	0 0%	300 94.67% 5.33%
Meningioma	10 0.76%	286 21.82%	0 0%	10 0.76%	306 93.46% 6.54%
No Tumor	0 0%	0 0%	405 30.89%	0 0%	405 100% 0%
Pituitary	0 0%	1 0.08%	0 0%	299 22.81%	300 99.67% 0.33%
SUM	294 96.60% 3.40%	303 94.39% 5.61%	405 100% 0%	309 96.76% 3.24%	1274 / 1311 97.18% 2.82%

Figure 5. The Confusion Matrix for Dataset 1.

Figures 8, 10 and 12 depict the training accuracy of Datasets 1, 2, and 3, respectively. It represents the proportion of correctly identified examples within the training dataset. It serves as a measure of how effectively the model absorbs and learns from the training data. During each training iteration, also known as an epoch, the model parameters are adjusted to better fit the training data, resulting in improved training accuracy.

The training loss illustrated in Figures 9, 11 and 13 for Datasets 1, 2, and 3 computes the variance between the models' predicted outputs and the actual targets. The objective is to decrease the training loss of the model and adapt the data. Loss functions such as categorical cross-entropy are typically used to compute the training loss. Validation and training accuracy (Figures 5, 7 and 9), which were ascertained to not be used during the training phase, are used to evaluate the model's capacity to generalize to new, unknown data. The x-axis displays the number of epochs, while the y-axis displays accuracy. The orange line represents the validation accuracy, the blue line represents the training accuracy. The graph is made up of these two lines. The validation loss (Figures 9, 11 and 13) means the deviation between the model predictions and the actual targets in the validation dataset. It serves as a gauge for the model performance on unseen data.

TARGET / OUTPUT	Yes	No	SUM
Yes	18 60%	2 6.67%	20 90% 10%
No	0 0%	10 33.33%	10 100% 0%
SUM	18 100% 0%	12 83.33% 16.67%	28 / 30 93.33% 6.67%

Figure 6. The Confusion Matrix for Dataset 2.

TARGET / OUTPUT	Yes	No	SUM
Yes	302 50.50%	9 1.51%	311 97.11% 2.89%
No	12 2.01%	275 45.99%	287 95.82% 4.18%
SUM	314 96.18% 3.82%	284 96.83% 3.17%	577 / 589 96.49% 3.51%

Figure 7. The Confusion Matrix for Dataset 3.

Table 4. Results of model performance.

Dataset 1					Dataset 2					Dataset 3				
Class	Pre	R	F1-S	Acc	Class	Pre	R	F1-S	Acc	Class	Pre	R	F1-S	Acc
Glioma	0.95	0.97	0.96		Yes	0.90	1.00	0.95		Yes	0.97	0.96	0.97	
Meningioma	0.93	0.94	0.94											
No Tumor	1.00	1.00	1.00	97.18	No	1.00	0.83	0.91	0.93	No	0.96	0.97	0.96	0.96
Pituitary	1.00	0.97	0.98											
Average	0.97	0.97	0.97			0.95	0.91	0.93			0.96	0.96	0.96	

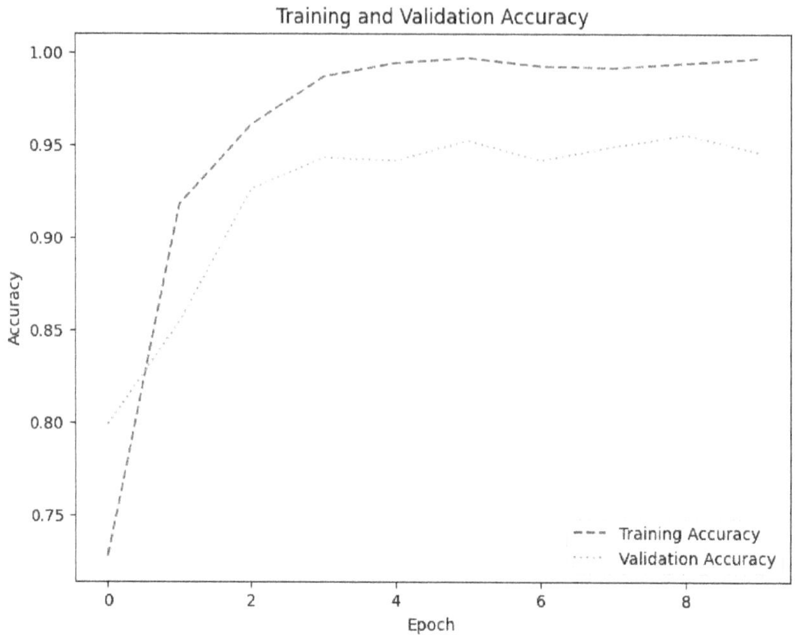

Figure 8. Accuracy of training and validation for Dataset 1.

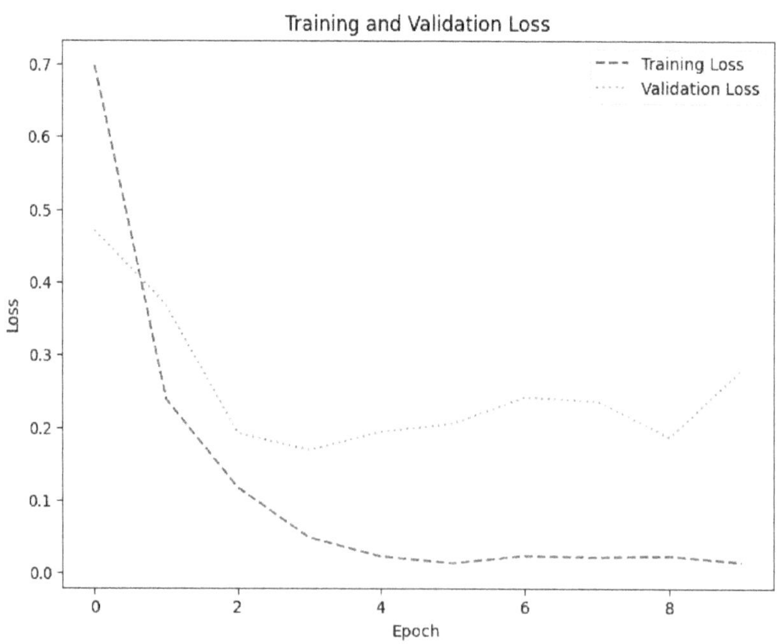

Figure 9. Training and validation loss in Dataset 1.

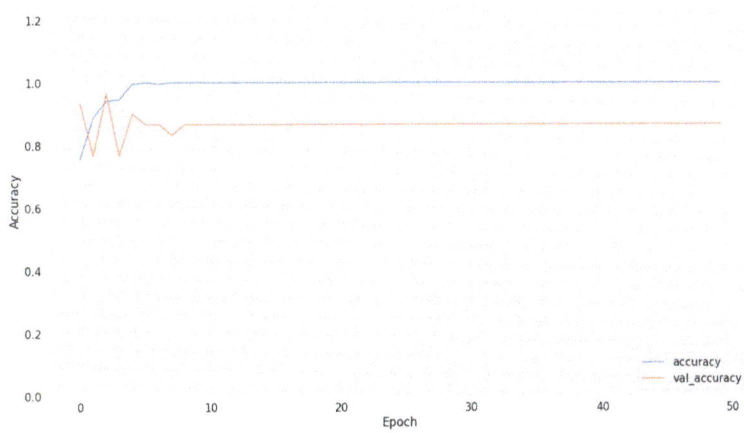

Figure 10. Accuracy of training and validation using Dataset 2.

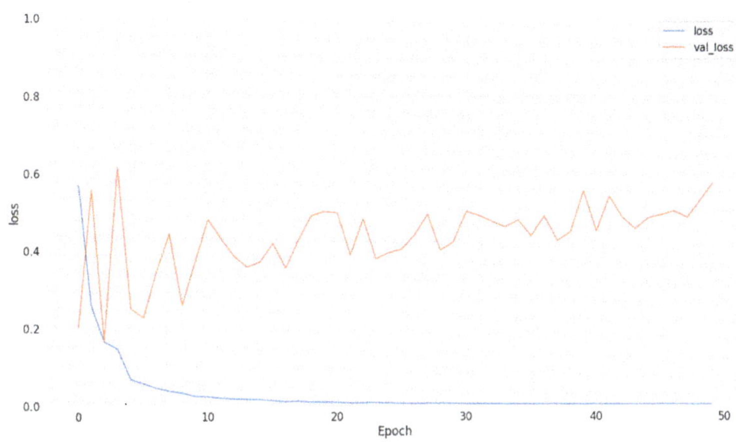

Figure 11. Training and validation loss in Dataset 2.

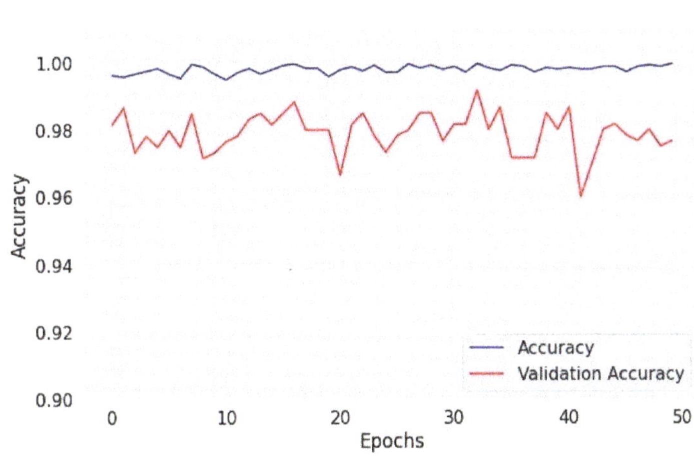

Figure 12. Accuracy of validation and training using Dataset 3.

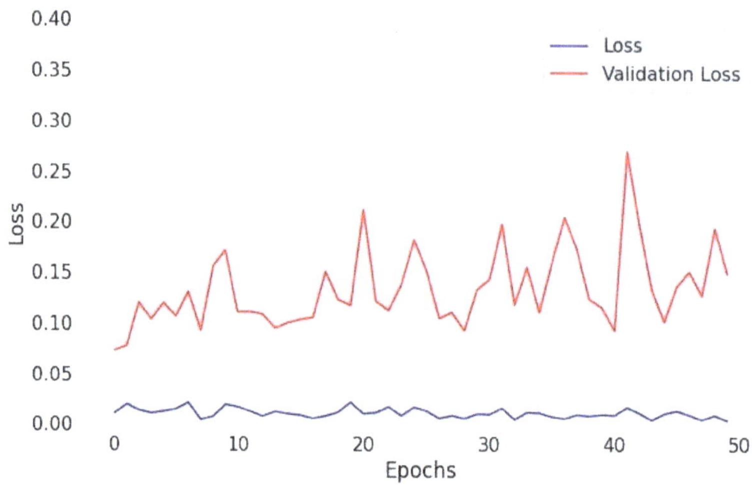

Figure 13. Losses in training and validation for Dataset 3.

5. Discussion

Table 4 provides a complete summary of the performance achieved in this work. The results presented in the table are highly impressive, showing an average statistical value of 0.97 for Dataset 1 for each term, and the overall accuracy of Dataset 1 is 97%. In Table 5, a comparison is made between the proposed techniques and state-of-the-art methods. By way of contrast, the effectiveness and consistency of the model in correctly detecting and categorizing brain tumors are illustrated. The model performs admirably and yields reliable results, as demonstrated by the statistics in these tables.

Table 5. Results comparison using the current techniques.

Method	Dataset	Acc	Pre	R	F1-S
Inception-V3 Fine-tuned model [49]	Brain MRI	0.94	0.93	0.95	0.94
MobileNetV2 [50]	Brain MRI	0.92	0.93	0.90	0.91
Deep-Net: Fine-Tuned model [51]	Brain MRI	0.95	0.93	0.94	0.95
CNN model [19]	Brain MRI Dataset1 Dataset 2	 0.96 0.88	 0.94 0.87	 0.94 0.87	 0.94 0.87
	Our model				
Dataset 1	Brain MRI	0.97	0.97	0.97	0.97
Dataset 2	Brain MRI	0.93	0.95	0.91	0.93
Dataset 3	Brain MRI	0.96	0.96	0.96	0.96

Table 5 compares different model performances in classifying brain MRI data. Our model demonstrated superior performance with an accuracy of 97%, with the same statistical values as 97% on Dataset 1. Our model produced results of 0.93 for accuracy, 0.95 for precision, 0.91 for recall, and 0.93 for f1-score on Dataset 2. Using the same statistical values as 96%, our model produced an accuracy of 0.96 on Dataset 3. These numerical values highlight the strong performance of our model compared to the other models, indicating its effectiveness in accurately classifying brain MRI data across multiple datasets. Our model provides the most reliable and balanced performance across accuracy and other statistical values for Dataset 1. This comparison demonstrates "our model" effectiveness and reliability in medical image analysis, demonstrating its potential to improve diagnostic accuracy and patient outcomes.

6. Limitations of the Model and Future Work

Although the CNN model employed for brain tumor detection demonstrates high accuracy and effectiveness, its limitations may involve potential overfitting due to its complexity and the need for specific tuning of hyperparameters to the dataset. This might reduce the model's generalizability to new, unseen data or medical imaging datasets. Additionally, the reliance on a large and diverse dataset for training may not account for all possible variations of brain tumors, which could impact the model's applicability to real-world diagnostic scenarios where data variability is high. Furthermore, the computational resources required for training and optimizing such a model could be substantial, limiting its accessibility for some medical facilities. This implies that while the model demonstrates impressive performance metrics, its effectiveness might diminish when applied to other datasets with different brain tumor characteristics, distributions, or types. This limitation emphasizes the need for further validation and testing across a broader range of datasets to ensure the model's robustness and applicability to diverse medical imaging contexts in the future.

7. Conclusions

A fine-tuned CNN hyperparametric model is proposed in this research. This model improves brain tumor diagnosis accuracy by optimizing the fine-tuning parameters of the CNN model. To this end, we employed a readily accessible dataset of brain tumor MRI scans. Our method proved highly effective, boasting an accuracy of 97%, indicating discrimination abilities, primarily attributed to the meticulous adjustment of CNN hyperparameters. Significant results, including an average precision, recall, and f1-score of 97%, demonstrate excellent accuracy in detecting brain tumors. Moreover, the statistical comparison with other recent models shows that our technique performs better using the same MRI dataset. The proposed method may serve as a guideline and assist in the future medical field for brain tumor detection and classification.

The implications of the hyperparametric CNN model used for brain tumor detection are significant and transformative for medical diagnostics. The model receives a high accuracy of 97% by methodically adjusting important hyperparameters, including the number of filters, filter sizes, and learning rate. Our optimization technique makes the diagnosis method more reliable and accurate for brain tumors, giving medical practitioners a more effective and accurate tool. The practical implications of such a model are profound, with the potential to improve patient care by offering more precise and reliable diagnostic information that supports critical decision-making processes in treating and managing brain tumors.

Author Contributions: M.A.: Conceptualization, data curation, formal analysis, writing-review and editing; A.N. and S.M.: conceptualization, methodology, writing-original draft, validation, supervision; N.A.: resources, investigation; M.H.A.: funding acquisition, validation, visualization; Y.A.: writing-original draft, formal analysis; F.A.: investigation, data curation. All authors have read and agreed to the published version of the manuscript.

Funding: The authors extend their appreciation to the Deanship of Scientific Research at Northern Border University, Arar, KSA for funding this research work through the project number "NBU-FFR-2024-1180-03".

Institutional Review Board Statement: Not applicable.

Informed Consent Statement: Not applicable.

Data Availability Statement: The data collected and analyzed during this study are available from the corresponding author upon reasonable request.

Conflicts of Interest: The authors declare no conflicts of interest.

References

1. Sadoon, T.A.; Ali, M.H. Deep learning model for glioma, meningioma and pituitary classification. *Int. J. Adv. Appl. Sci.* **2021**, *2252*, 8814. [CrossRef]
2. Cheng, J.; Huang, W.; Cao, S.; Yang, R.; Yang, W.; Yun, Z.; Wang, Z.; Feng, Q. Enhanced performance of brain tumor classification via tumor region augmentation and partition. *PLoS ONE* **2015**, *10*, e0140381. [CrossRef]
3. Wen, P.Y.; Kesari, S. Malignant gliomas in adults. *N. Engl. J. Med.* **2008**, *359*, 492–507. [CrossRef]
4. Goodenberger, M.L.; Jenkins, R.B. Genetics of adult glioma. *Cancer Genet.* **2012**, *205*, 613–621. [CrossRef]
5. Laws, E.R. *Pituitary Disorders*; Wiley Online Library: Hoboken, NJ, USA, 2013.
6. Devi, O.R.; Bindu, C.S.; Kumar, E.S. Identification and Classification of Brain Tumor from MRI Using Transfer Learning Approach. In Proceedings of the 2022 International Conference on Computing, Communication, and Intelligent Systems (ICCCIS), Greater Noida, India, 4–5 November 2022.
7. Nagaraj, P.; Muneeswaran, V.; Reddy, L.V.; Upendra, P.; Reddy, M.V. Programmed multi-classification of brain tumor images using deep neural network. In Proceedings of the 2020 4th international conference on intelligent computing and control systems (ICICCS), Madurai, India, 13–15 May 2020.
8. Jans, L.B.; Chen, M.; Elewaut, D.; Bosch, F.V.D.; Carron, P.; Jacques, P.; Wittoek, R.; Jaremko, J.L.; Herregods, N. MRI-based synthetic CT in the detection of structural lesions in patients with suspected sacroiliitis: Comparison with MRI. *Radiology* **2021**, *298*, 343–349. [CrossRef]
9. Ammirati, M.; Nahed, B.V.; Andrews, D.; Chen, C.C.; Olson, J.J. Congress of neurological surgeons systematic review and evidence-based guidelines on treatment options for adults with multiple metastatic brain tumors. *Neurosurgery* **2019**, *84*, E180–E182. [CrossRef]
10. Wahlang, I.; Maji, A.K.; Saha, G.; Chakrabarti, P.; Jasinski, M.; Leonowicz, Z.; Jasinska, E. Brain magnetic resonance imaging classification using deep learning architectures with gender and age. *Sensors* **2022**, *22*, 1766. [CrossRef]
11. Alanazi, M.F.; Ali, M.U.; Hussain, S.J.; Zafar, A.; Mohatram, M.; Irfan, M.; AlRuwaili, R.; Alruwaili, M.; Ali, N.H.; Albarrak, A.M. Brain tumor/mass classification framework using magnetic-resonance-imaging-based isolated and developed transfer deep-learning model. *Sensors* **2022**, *22*, 372. [CrossRef]
12. Wohlfahrt, P.; Möhler, C.; Troost, E.G.; Greilich, S.; Richter, C. Dual-energy computed tomography to assess intra-and inter-patient tissue variability for proton treatment planning of patients with brain tumor. *Int. J. Radiat. Oncol. Biol. Phys.* **2019**, *105*, 504–513. [CrossRef]
13. Lohmann, P.; Werner, J.-M.; Shah, N.J.; Fink, G.R.; Langen, K.-J.; Galldiks, N. Combined amino acid positron emission tomography and advanced magnetic resonance imaging in glioma patients. *Cancers* **2019**, *11*, 153. [CrossRef]
14. Hu, R.; Hoch, M.J. Application of diffusion weighted imaging and diffusion tensor imaging in the pretreatment and post-treatment of brain tumor. *Radiol. Clin.* **2021**, *59*, 335–347. [CrossRef]
15. Branzoli, F.; Pontoizeau, C.; Tchara, L.; Di Stefano, A.L.; Kamoun, A.; Deelchand, D.K.; Valabrègue, R.; Lehéricy, S.; Sanson, M.; Ottolenghi, C.; et al. Cystathionine as a marker for 1p/19q codeleted gliomas by in vivo magnetic resonance spectroscopy. *Neuro-Oncology* **2019**, *21*, 765–774. [CrossRef]
16. Islam, S.; Udhayakumar, R.; Kar, S.; Pavitha, N.; Aswal, U.S.; Saini, D.K. Enhancing Brain Tumor Detection Classification by Computational Intelligence. In Proceedings of the 2023 Second International Conference on Electronics and Renewable Systems (ICEARS), Tuticorin, India, 2–4 March 2023.
17. Chakraborty, P.; Das, S.S.; Dey, A.; Chakraborty, A.; Bhattacharyya, C.; Kandimalla, R.; Mukherjee, B.; Gopalakrishnan, A.V.; Singh, S.K.; Kant, S.; et al. Quantum dots: The cutting-edge nanotheranostics in brain cancer management. *J. Control. Release* **2022**, *350*, 698–715. [CrossRef]
18. Biratu, E.S.; Schwenker, F.; Ayano, Y.M.; Debelee, T.G. A survey of brain tumor segmentation and classification algorithms. *J. Imaging* **2021**, *7*, 179. [CrossRef]
19. Asiri, A.A.; Shaf, A.; Ali, T.; Aamir, M.; Irfan, M.; Alqahtani, S. Enhancing brain tumor diagnosis: An optimized CNN hyperparameter model for improved accuracy and reliability. *PeerJ Comput. Sci.* **2024**, *10*, e1878. [CrossRef]
20. Images, B.M. Available online: https://github.com/muhammadaamir1234/Dataset-Link (accessed on 7 May 2024).
21. ZainEldin, H.; Gamel, S.A.; El-Kenawy, E.-S.M.; Alharbi, A.H.; Khafaga, D.S.; Ibrahim, A.; Talaat, F.M. Brain tumor detection and classification using deep learning and sine-cosine fitness grey wolf optimization. *Bioengineering* **2022**, *10*, 18. [CrossRef]
22. Umirzakova, S.; Mardieva, S.; Muksimova, S.; Ahmad, S.; Whangbo, T. Enhancing the Super-Resolution of Medical Images: Introducing the Deep Residual Feature Distillation Channel Attention Network for Optimized Performance and Efficiency. *Bioengineering* **2023**, *10*, 1332. [CrossRef]
23. Ait Amou, M.; Xia, K.; Kamhi, S.; Mouhafid, M. A novel MRI diagnosis method for brain tumor classification based on CNN and Bayesian Optimization. *Healthcare* **2022**, *10*, 494. [CrossRef]
24. Rasool, M.; Ismail, N.A.; Al-Dhaqm, A.; Yafooz, W.M.S.; Alsaeedi, A. A novel approach for classifying brain tumours combining a squeezenet model with svm and fine-tuning. *Electronics* **2022**, *12*, 149. [CrossRef]

25. Balakrishnan, R.; Hernández, M.D.C.V.; Farrall, A.J. Automatic segmentation of white matter hyperintensities from brain magnetic resonance images in the era of deep learning and big data—A systematic review. *Comput. Med. Imaging Graph.* **2021**, *88*, 101867. [CrossRef]
26. Piórkowski, A.; Lasek, J. Evaluation of local thresholding algorithms for segmentation of white matter hyperintensities in magnetic resonance images of the brain. In Proceedings of the Applied Informatics: Fourth International Conference, ICAI 2021, Buenos Aires, Argentina, 28–30 October 2021; Proceedings 4; Springer International Publishing: Cham, Swizterland, 2021; pp. 331–345.
27. Reyes, D.; Sánchez, J. Performance of convolutional neural networks for the classification of brain tumors using magnetic resonance imaging. *Heliyon* **2024**, *10*, e25468. [CrossRef]
28. Kurdi, S.Z.; Ali, M.H.; Jaber, M.M.; Saba, T.; Rehman, A.; Damaševičius, R. Brain tumor classification using meta-heuristic optimized convolutional neural networks. *J. Pers. Med.* **2023**, *13*, 181. [CrossRef]
29. Takahashi, S.; Takahashi, M.; Kinoshita, M.; Miyake, M.; Kawaguchi, R.; Shinojima, N.; Mukasa, A.; Saito, K.; Nagane, M.; Otani, R.; et al. Fine-tuning approach for segmentation of gliomas in brain magnetic resonance images with a machine learning method to normalize image differences among facilities. *Cancers* **2021**, *13*, 1415. [CrossRef]
30. Saba, T.; Mohamed, A.S.; El-Affendi, M.; Amin, J.; Sharif, M. Brain tumor detection using fusion of hand crafted and deep learning features. *Cogn. Syst. Res.* **2020**, *59*, 221–230. [CrossRef]
31. Amin, J.; Sharif, M.; Raza, M.; Saba, T.; Anjum, M.A. Brain tumor detection using statistical and machine learning method. *Comput. Methods Programs Biomed.* **2019**, *177*, 69–79. [CrossRef]
32. Amin, J.; Sharif, M.; Yasmin, M.; Fernandes, S.L. Big data analysis for brain tumor detection: Deep convolutional neural networks. *Future Gener. Comput. Syst.* **2018**, *87*, 290–297. [CrossRef]
33. Amin, J.; Sharif, M.; Yasmin, M.; Fernandes, S.L. A distinctive approach in brain tumor detection and classification using MRI. *Pattern Recognit. Lett.* **2020**, *139*, 118–127. [CrossRef]
34. Toğaçar, M.; Ergen, B.; Cömert, Z. BrainMRNet: Brain tumor detection using magnetic resonance images with a novel convolutional neural network model. *Med. Hypotheses* **2020**, *134*, 109531. [CrossRef]
35. Shakeel, P.M.; Tobely, T.E.E.; Al-Feel, H.; Manogaran, G.; Baskar, S. Neural network based brain tumor detection using wireless infrared imaging sensor. *IEEE Access* **2019**, *7*, 5577–5588. [CrossRef]
36. Hossain, T.; Shishir, F.S.; Ashraf, M.; Al Nasim, M.A.; Shah, F.M. Brain tumor detection using convolutional neural network. In Proceedings of the 2019 1st international conference on advances in science, engineering and robotics technology (ICASERT), Dhaka, Bangladesh, 3–5 May 2019.
37. Özyurt, F.; Sert, E.; Avci, E.; Dogantekin, E. Brain tumor detection based on Convolutional Neural Network with neutrosophic expert maximum fuzzy sure entropy. *Measurement* **2019**, *147*, 106830. [CrossRef]
38. Sajid, S.; Hussain, S.; Sarwar, A. Brain tumor detection and segmentation in MR images using deep learning. *Arab. J. Sci. Eng.* **2019**, *44*, 9249–9261. [CrossRef]
39. Nazir, M.; Shakil, S.; Khurshid, K. Role of deep learning in brain tumor detection and classification (2015 to 2020): A review. *Comput. Med. Imaging Graph.* **2021**, *91*, 101940. [CrossRef]
40. Woźniak, M.; Siłka, J.; Wieczorek, M. Deep neural network correlation learning mechanism for CT brain tumor detection. *Neural Comput. Appl.* **2023**, *35*, 14611–14626. [CrossRef]
41. Majib, M.S.; Rahman, M.; Sazzad, T.M.S.; Khan, N.I.; Dey, S.K. Vgg-scnet: A vgg net-based deep learning framework for brain tumor detection on mri images. *IEEE Access* **2021**, *9*, 116942–116952. [CrossRef]
42. Alnowami, M.; Taha, E.; Alsebaeai, S.; Anwar, S.M.; Alhawsawi, A. MR image normalization dilemma and the accuracy of brain tumor classification model. *J. Radiat. Res. Appl. Sci.* **2022**, *15*, 33–39. [CrossRef]
43. Shehab, L.H.; Fahmy, O.M.; Gasser, S.M.; El-Mahallawy, M.S. An efficient brain tumor image segmentation based on deep residual networks (ResNets). *J. King Saud Univ.-Eng. Sci.* **2021**, *33*, 404–412. [CrossRef]
44. Sankareswaran, S.P.; Krishnan, M. Unsupervised end-to-end brain tumor magnetic resonance image registration using RBCNN: Rigid transformation, B-spline transformation and convolutional neural network. *Curr. Med. Imaging* **2022**, *18*, 387–397. [CrossRef] [PubMed]
45. Shukla, M.; Sharma, K.K. A comparative study to detect tumor in brain MRI images using clustering algorithms. In Proceedings of the 2020 2nd International Conference on Innovative Mechanisms for Industry Applications (ICIMIA), Bangalore, India, 5–7 March 2020.
46. Minarno, A.E.; Mandiri, M.H.C.; Munarko, Y.; Hariyady, H. Convolutional neural network with hyperparameter tuning for brain tumor classification. *Kinetik Game Technol. Inf. Syst. Comput. Netw. Comput. Electron. Control* **2021**, *6*. [CrossRef]
47. Latif, G.; Iskandar, D.A.; Alghazo, J.; Butt, M.M. Brain MR Image Classification for Glioma tumor detection using deep convolutional neural network features. *Curr. Med. Imaging* **2021**, *17*, 56–63.
48. Grampurohit, S.; Shalavadi, V.; Dhotargavi, V.R.; Kudari, M.; Jolad, S. Brain tumor detection using deep learning models. In Proceedings of the 2020 IEEE India Council International Subsections Conference (INDISCON), Visakhapatnam, India, 3–4 October 2020.
49. Noreen, N.; Palaniappan, S.; Qayyum, A.; Ahmad, I.; Alassafi, M.O. Brain Tumor Classification Based on Fine-Tuned Models and the Ensemble Method. *Comput. Mater. Contin.* **2021**, *67*, 3967–3982. [CrossRef]

50. Asiri, A.A.; Aamir, M.; Ali, T.; Shaf, A.; Irfan, M.; Mehdar, K.M.; Alqhtani, S.M.; Alghamdi, A.H.; Alshamrani, A.F.A.; Alshehri, O.M. Next-Gen brain tumor classification: Pioneering with deep learning and fine-tuned conditional generative adversarial networks. *PeerJ Comput. Sci.* **2023**, *9*, e1667. [CrossRef]
51. Khan, M.A.; Mostafa, R.R.; Zhang, Y.-D.; Baili, J.; Alhaisoni, M.; Tariq, U.; Khan, J.A.; Kim, Y.J.; Cha, J. Deep-Net: Fine-Tuned Deep Neural Network Multi-Features Fusion for Brain Tumor Recognition. *Comput. Mater. Contin.* **2023**, *76*, 3029–3047.

diagnostics MDPI

Article

Reproducibility and Repeatability in Focus: Evaluating LVEF Measurements with 3D Echocardiography by Medical Technologists

Marc Østergaard Nielsen *, Arlinda Ljoki, Bo Zerahn, Lars Thorbjørn Jensen and Bent Kristensen

Department of Nuclear Medicine, Herlev University Hospital, 2730 Herlev, Denmark;
arljinda.ljoki@regionh.dk (A.L.); bo.zerahn@regionh.dk (B.Z.); lars.thorbjoern.jensen@regionh.dk (L.T.J.);
bent.kristensen.01@regionh.dk (B.K.)
* Correspondence: marc.oestergaard.nielsen@regionh.dk

Abstract: Three-dimensional echocardiography (3DE) is currently the preferred method for monitoring left ventricular ejection fraction (LVEF) in cancer patients receiving potentially cardiotoxic anti-neoplastic therapy. In Denmark, however, the traditional standard for LVEF monitoring has been rooted in nuclear medicine departments utilizing equilibrium radionuclide angiography (ERNA). Although ERNA remains a principal modality, there is an emerging trend towards the adoption of echocardiography for this purpose. Given this context, assessing the reproducibility of 3DE among non-specialized medical personnel is crucial for its clinical adoption in such departments. To assess the feasibility of 3DE for LVEF measurements by technologists, we evaluated the repeatability and reproducibility of two moderately experienced technologists. They performed 3DE on 12 volunteers over two sessions, with a collaborative review of the results from the first session before the second session. Two-way intraclass correlation values increased from 0.03 to 0.77 across the sessions. This increase in agreement was mainly due to the recognition of false low measurements. Our findings underscore the importance of incorporating reproducibility exercises in the context of 3DE, especially when operated by technologists. Additionally, routine control of the acquisitions by physicians is deemed necessary. Ensuring these hurdles are adequately managed enables the adoption of 3DE for LVEF measurements by technologists.

Keywords: 3D echocardiography; left ventricular ejection fraction (LVEF); reproducibility; repeatability

1. Introduction

Left ventricular ejection fraction (LVEF) is the main variable of choice for monitoring heart function in cancer patients receiving potentially cardiotoxic treatments [1]. Precise evaluation of LVEF is therefore important since it guides therapeutic decision making and has prognostic implications [2]. While three-dimensional transthoracic echocardiography (3DE) is the recommended first-line modality for LVEF monitoring, its effectiveness hinges not only on the operator's skill but also on the agreement between observers. This highlights a critical aspect: the need to assess and ensure reproducibility of 3DE measurements, particularly when operated by technologists or other non-specialized medical personnel. Inconsistent results across different operators could significantly influence clinical decision making and subsequent outcomes. Therefore, our observational study primarily focused on evaluating the reproducibility and repeatability of real-time 3DE (RT-3DE) in the hands of technologists over a two-month period. The null hypothesis tested was whether the reproducibility of RT-3DE remains unchained, irrespective of the operator, within this timeframe.

2. Background

Two-dimensional echocardiography (2DE) dominates global practice for monitoring cancer-therapy-related cardiac dysfunction (CTRCD) [3]. Definitions and severity vary, but generally, non-symptomatic CTRCD can be defined as a significant decrease in LVEF ($\geq$10 percentage points) to below the lower limit of normal (50–53%) [1,4].

Recent European guidelines favor 3DE or cardiac MR (CMR) for serial LVEF estimation [5]. 3DE, whether real-time or not, offers superior accuracy and lower observer variability when compared to 2DE [6–8]; however, 3DE is more dependent on good acoustic windows and patient cooperation. Meanwhile CMR, the gold standard for volumetric assessment, is less suitable for serial monitoring for CTRCD given its limitations of cost and availability.

The shift towards 3DE and CMR has relegated the once staple equilibrium radionuclide angiocardiography (ERNA) to a secondary role in LVEF estimation, primarily due to concerns of radiation exposure from serial scans [9–11]. However, the guidelines base this recommendation on the tracer doses utilized for planar ERNA, an older technique that employs significantly higher radiotracer doses compared to what is possible utilizing cadmium–zinc–telluride (CZT)-based detectors [12]. The advantage of ERNA in general is its high accuracy and precision when compared with CMR [13], and its already impressive reproducibility can be further enhanced with CZT-based detectors [14]. It is also worth noting that other nuclear modalities such as myocardial perfusion imaging (MPI) including Rb-82 positron emission tomography (Rb-PET) and ^{99m}Tc-Sestamibi-SPECT also are fully capable of providing highly reproducible LVEF assessments [15,16].

These nuclear modalities all have in common that they are less user-dependent than 2DE [17]; however, it remains to be demonstrated if non-specialized health care professionals such as technologists can wield 3DE to reliably detect changes within $\pm$10 percentage points.

Studies investigating the reproducibility of 3DE among non-specialized medical staff are less common in real clinical settings. Nonetheless, previous research has provided valuable insights into this area. Notably Guppy-Coles et al. demonstrated the feasibility of training cardiac nurses in the analysis of pre-acquired 3D echocardiographic data [18]. Building upon this foundation, their subsequent research further revealed the potential for cardiac nurses to not only analyze but also acquire 3DE images for LVEF assessment. The results demonstrated a reasonable degree of agreement between the cardiac nurses and experienced echo-sonographers. However, in both studies, reproducibility was determined by analyzing the same image twice rather than through repeated acquisitions, and the Bland–Altman limits of agreement (LOA) for the nurses versus the echo-sonographers exceeded 10 percentage points without accompanying confidence intervals [19].

Our observational study was designed to evaluate the reproducibility of LVEF measurements made by technologists with intermediate experience. The objective was to evaluate its potential as a complete or partial substitute for the currently employed CZT-ERNA technology.

3. Materials and Methods

This longitudinal prospective observational study, conducted at the Department of Nuclear Medicine, Herlev University Hospital, Denmark, focused on evaluating the repeatability, reliability, and reproducibility of LVEF measurements from RT-3DE by two technologists. The participant cohort included twelve hospital staff volunteers and consisted of six age-matched men and women, all without known heart disease.

After receiving training from the system's vendor, the technologists applied RT-3DE for LVEF estimation in patients over an eight-month period, amounting to roughly 250 days of experience. During this period, the first technologist (OP1) successfully acquired usable 3D images in 75% (661/881) of the sessions, while the second technologist (OP2) had a success rate of 63% (349/558).

This study was conducted where each technologist performed three replicate LVEF measurements on each participant during two separate sessions, denoted as M1 and M2. To minimize a possible "carry-over" learning effect, the sessions were performed 1–2 months apart.

Between each replicate, the transducer was completely removed from the chest, while the participant remained in the left lateral decubitus position. After the scan, the technologists provided a combined grading of image quality and practical difficulty. The grading scale ranged from 0 to 3, where 0 indicated no difficulty, 1 a somewhat challenging acquisition, 2 a very difficult acquisition, and 3 an impossible task.

Operators were required to provide justification for scores of 1, 2, or 3, citing specific challenges such as poor endocardial definition or subjected-related issues like suboptimal positioning or problems with breath-hold maneuvers.

3.1. *Real-Time Three-Dimensional Transthoracic Echocardiogram*

Real-time full-volume three-dimensional transthoracic echocardiography was conducted using the Acuson SC2000 (Siemens Ultrasound, Mountain View, CA, USA) cardiovascular ultrasound system, equipped with a 4Z1c-phased array real-time volume transducer operating at a frequency range of 1.5–3.5 MHz.

Complete left-ventricular volumes were captured from the apical view during every cardiac cycle over a period of three consecutive cycles. Patients were positioned in the left lateral decubitus orientation and instructed to perform breath-hold maneuvers by the operator.

Subsequent analysis of the full-volume images was carried out off-line utilizing eSie LVA version 5.1. This software features a fully automated, knowledge-based algorithm for endocardial detection, removing the need for manual delineation of endocardial borders by the operators [20].

3.2. *Statistical Analysis*

The statistical analyses were conducted using the following:

'R' version 4.2.2 (R Core Team (2022): A language and environment for statistical computing, R Foundation for Statistical Computing, Vienna, Austria. URL https://www.R-project.org/ (accessed on 4 August 2024), including but not limited to the following packages: tidyverse (dplyr, ggplot2), LMMstar, irr, VCA, performance, and lme4.

Descriptive statistics included visualizations, medians, and ranges, and significance was determined using either Welch's t-test or the Mann–Whitney U test, depending on the data distribution. The whole dataset can be viewed from Figure A1 in the Appendix A, and the trend between measurement sessions is visualized through Figure A2.

Intraclass correlation coefficient (ICC) calculations were employed for evaluating operator agreement and consistency. We used a one-way model for intra-operator consistency and a two-way model for inter-operator agreement. For the Bland–Altman plot, the confidence intervals for the LOA were calculated using exact methods, providing a more precise estimation of the agreement levels [21].

It is worth noting ICC's limitations: Its values can vary based on the chosen model, type, and measures; it is sensitive to subject variability, potentially affecting reliability assessments; and its statistical nature can complicate clinical interpretation [22]. Appendix A contains Table A1, which serves as a guide for interpreting ICC values.

A linear mixed model (LMM) was constructed where operators were treated as a fixed effect to assess if they exerted a systematic, significant influence on the LVEF measurements. To further explore the operators' impact on the variability of the measurements, we developed a second model where the operators were considered a random effect. We made this adjustment to determine if the operators' influence varied across the subjects' measurements. In both models, variance component analysis included random effects for subjects, measurement sessions, and replicates, allowing us to quantify the variance attributed to each factor. These variances were used to calculate the repeatability and reproducibility coefficients detailed in Appendix A.

An important part of the statistical analysis is assessment of the assumptions and quality of the model. These analyses were carried out with the R package performance.

4. Results

Six males and six females were studied. Descriptive variables are presented in Table 1. Significant differences in all volumetric variables (LVEF, EDV, and ESV) were observed between men and women, as evidenced by the Mann–Whitney U test ($p < 0.01$).

Table 1. Descriptive variables presented as medians and (ranges).

Variable	Men	Women
Age	49 (28–66)	47 (26–62)
Body mass index (BMI)	23 (21–31)	22 (20–32)
Heart rate	58 (45–80)	55 (46–80)
LVEF	58 (35–69)	60 (24–73)
End-diastolic volume	124 (97–193)	117 (58–184)
End-systolic volume	53 (32–92)	43 (19–84)
LVEF (outliers excluded)	58 (50–69)	61 (49–73)

The boxplots show small differences in LVEF measurements between operators. Both operators observed an increase in LVEF values for women from M1 to M2 (Figure 1). No significant differences were found when comparing M1 to M2 for each gender for each operator using both the paired *t*-test and the Wilcoxon signed-rank test.

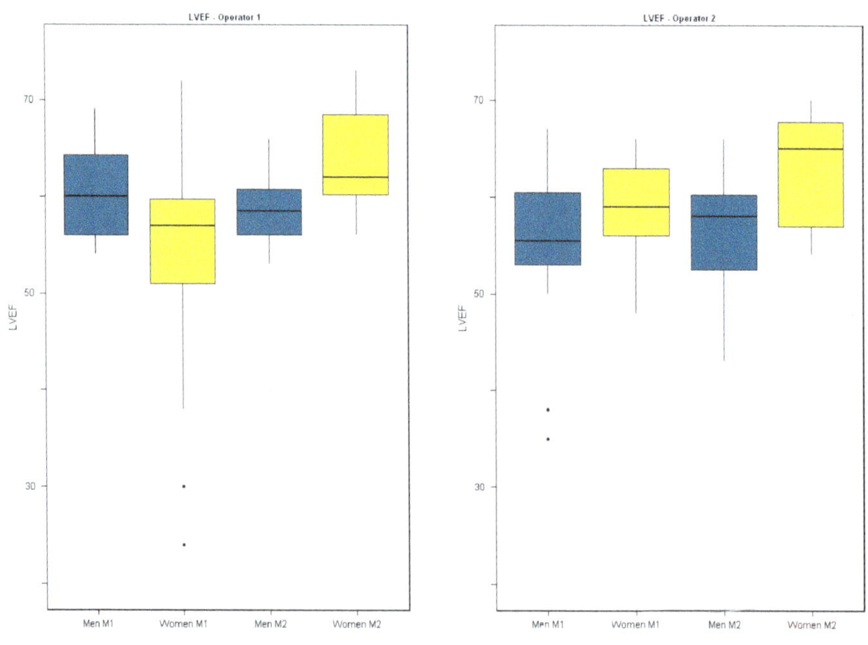

(**a**) (**b**)

Figure 1. Boxplots of LVEF measurements by OP1 (**a**) and OP2 (**b**), further split by sex and measurement session.

Inspection of the strip plots (Figure 2) identified seven deviant measurements under 50% LVEF, specifically (a) OP1's measurements for subject 12 in M1 (replicates 1, 2, and 3); (b) OP2's measurements for subject 8 (two outliers in M1 and one in M2) and one outlier from subject 11 in M1.

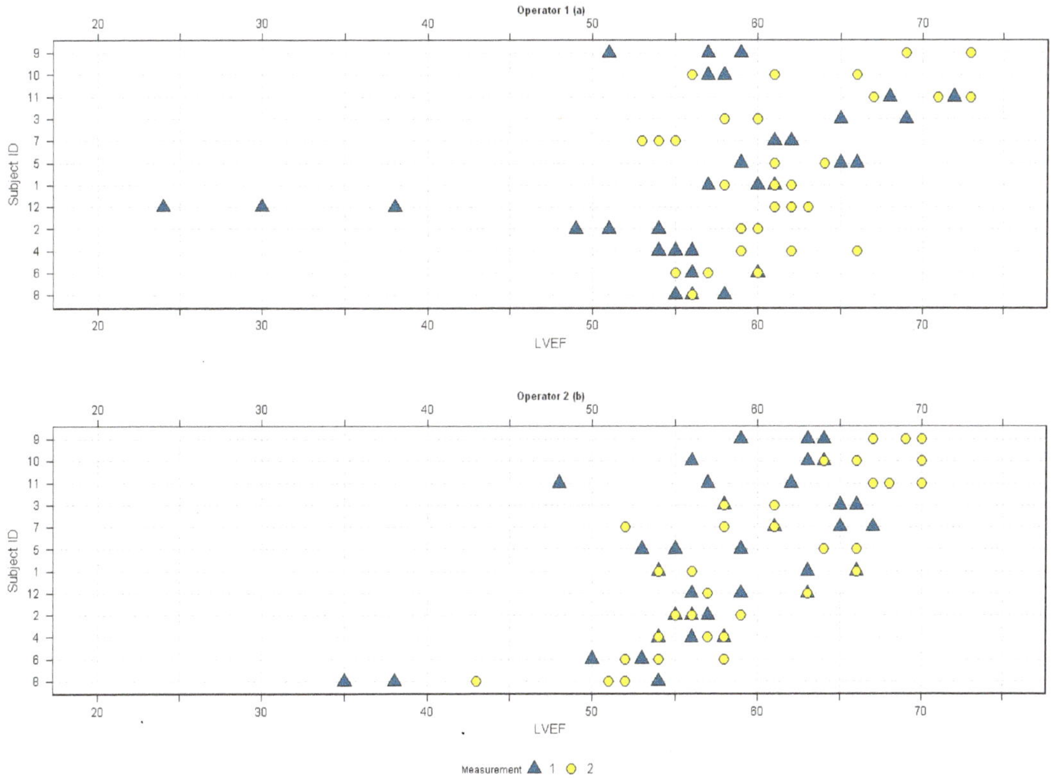

Figure 2. Strip-dot plots of LVEF percentages by OP1 (**a**) and OP2 (**b**). Triangles represent M1 and circles M2.

The Bland–Altman plot (Figure 3) illustrates the agreement of LVEF between OP1 and OP2 across the measurement sessions. The LOA for M1 spanned 45 percentage points (22.5 to −22.5), while LOA for M2 spanned 14.7 percentage points (6.1 to −8.6).

Removing the outlier (top left corner) narrowed the LOA of M1 to 29.3 percentage points (12.1 to −17.2).

Table 2 shows one-way ICC calculations, indicating the consistency of the operators in M1 and M2. The consistency of OP1 decreased from 0.91 in M1 to 0.80 in M2. In contrast, OP2's consistency increased from 0.55 in M1 to 0.75 in M2. All one-way ICC calculations were statistically significant ($p < 0.001$).

Table 3 details two-way ICC calculations for assessing observer agreement. The ICC for M1 was near 0, increasing to 0.35 after outlier removal, yet remained non-significant. The ICC for M2 was 0.77, improving slightly to 0.79 after excluding outliers; both these values were statistically significant.

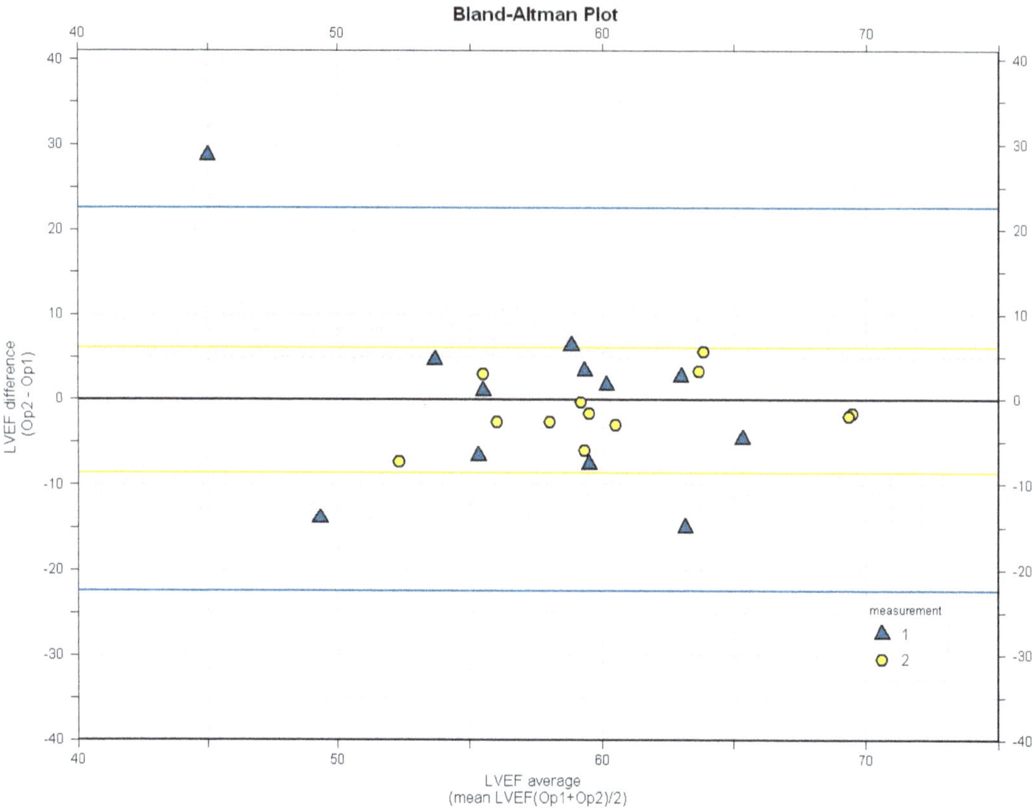

Figure 3. Bland–Altman plot with LOA (solid, colored lines) with confidence intervals (shaded grey areas). Triangles represent M1 and circles M2. The x-axis represents the average LVEF of OP1 and OP2, while the y-axis represents the difference.

Table 2. One-way ICC calculations of LVEF replicates grouped by operator and measurement session.

Operator, Measurement Session	ICC * (95% Confidence Intervals)
OP1, M1	0.91 (0.79–0.97) [1]
OP1, M2	0.80 (0.57–0.93) [1]
OP2, M1	0.55 (0.21–0.82) [1]
OP2, M2	0.75 (0.49–0.91) [1]

[1] $p < 0.001$; * intraclass correlation coefficient.

Table 3. Two-way ICC calculations of agreement between operators using LVEF means of the replicates grouped by measurement series.

Measurement Session	ICC (95% Confidence Intervals)
M1	0.03 (−0.61–0.60)
M2	0.77 (0.39–0.93) [1]
M1 *	0.35 (−0.31–0.77)
M2 *	0.79 (0.45–0.94) [1]

* After exclusion of outliers; [1] $p < 0.001$.

The two LMMs detailed in the statistical section where operators were considered either a fixed or random effect differed slightly. When considered as a fixed effect, operators were not statistically significant ($p = 0.277$). The estimated average decrease in LVEF was 1 percentage point for operator 2 compared to operator 1. Treating operators as a random effect accounted for only 2.5% of the overall variance. The estimated intercept for LVEF was 60.5. The second model's results, which considered operator as a random effect, are summarized below in Table 4.

Table 4. LMM variance component analysis with operators treated a random effect.

Variance Component	Standard Deviation (%,Total)
Within-subject (replicates)	2.6 (21%)
Between-subject	2.7 (24%)
Between-measurement	2.8 (26%)
Inter-observer	0.9 (2%)

Despite the relatively modest sample size, model checking did not reveal serious deviations from the model's assumptions.

Using these standard deviations, we calculated the repeatability coefficient for within-subject variation as 7.1. To evaluate the reproducibility of LVEF measurements, we applied the same formula but used different variance parameters. With variations between sessions and different operators, the reproducibility coefficient was determined to be 10.3. When we isolated the variability between sessions alone, the coefficient decreased to 7.9.

In the evaluation of scan performance, there were no patterns discernible when both operators were considered together. However, OP1 used the performance rating "somewhat difficult" (rating 2) 50% less, instead choosing "no problem" (rating 1) or "very difficult" (rating 3) from M1 to M2.

5. Discussion

We assessed the repeatability, reproducibility, agreement, and consistency of RT-3DE LVEF estimations by intermediately experienced technologists on 12 healthy subjects.

Our results show a marked increase in agreement between the two observers across measurement sessions. Additionally, our LMM analysis and coefficient calculations estimate the variability expected in LVEF values from replicate measures, between sessions, and between operators. With these insights, we are confidently positioned to identify clinically relevant changes in LVEF of ±10 percentage points, providing a level of precision that supports informed clinical decision making.

Following outlier exclusion, as detailed above Figure 2, LVEF values aligned with established normal ranges for a Scandinavian population [23]. End-diastolic and end-systolic values also aligned with publications utilizing the same echocardiographic system [24]. Gender-specific differences in volumetric measurements were anticipated, as this has been documented across various imaging modalities [25,26]. The study design ensured no significant age variance between groups.

Differences between operators were especially pronounced during M1, which translated to minimal agreement, evident by a low ICC (Table 3) and wide LOAs (Figure 3). Removing outliers improved this agreement, but it remained poor. The measurements in M2 demonstrated significantly improved agreement, which was marginally improved after excluding outliers. We attribute this increase in agreement primarily to the discussions and reflections that followed M1. These included a deeper focus on recognizing the necessary image quality for accurate endocardial tracing.

The Bland–Altman plot (Figure 3) illustrates the LOA between the two operators' LVEF measurements across M1 and M2. The LOA for M2 indicates that changes in LVEF exceeding 10 percentage points (−10–10) are discernible (in approximately 95% of cases) when different operators conduct the measurements. However, to enhance measurement precision, our future aim is to narrow the outer bounds of the LOAs CIs to within ±10 percent.

The outliers identified on the strip plots (Figure 2) were the main driver of the disparities observed between the boxplots (Figure 1). Reviewing the images confirmed suboptimal endocardial tracing by the automatic algorithm due to poor endocardial definition. After exclusion of these, the boxplots between the observers were nearly identical.

The small increase in LVEF for female participants from M1 to M2 was consistent for both operators even after outlier exclusion. Combined with a small increment in heart rate, this suggests that the increase in LVEF is most likely physiological in nature rather than the result of measurement error.

To ensure the inclusion of only physiologically accurate LVEF values in our linear mixed model, we excluded the outliers detailed in Figure 2. This was done to avoid bias and inaccuracies in representing variability. The repeatability coefficient of 7.1 indicates that replicate measurements on the same subject by the same operator are expected to fall within $\pm$7.1 percentage points in 95% of the time, providing an estimate of measurement error. This information is vital for physicians, as it offers a margin of error to consider when interpreting individual measurement results.

For reproducibility, we calculated the coefficient from the variation contributed by operators and between sessions. The resulting value of 10.3 suggests that an LVEF change greater than 10 percentage points is likely significant in practice. The variation between sessions without the effect of the operators was estimated at 7.9 percentage points. This lower value indicates the extent of LVEF variability over time within our healthy study population, highlighting another critical factor for physicians evaluating measurements longitudinally.

Our analysis revealed no significant systematic differences between operators. When modeled as a fixed effect, differences among operators were statistically insignificant; when treated as a random effect, operator-related variance contributed minimally to the total variance. This indicates that operator influence is predominantly random, aligning more with measurement error associated with the replicate measurement process. About 27% of the variance remains unexplained by our model, potentially encompassing factors such as environmental variations, subtle physiological changes not captured by other variables, or other unmeasured aspects of the LVEF measurement process.

To enhance the reliability of LVEF measurements in actual patient cohorts, we recommend conducting additional repeated measures, particularly for LVEF values around 50%. Furthermore, involving the reading physician in selecting the most representative measurement for reporting could improve accuracy and relevance.

Our evaluation of intra-operator consistency is summarized in Table 2. We observed a high consistency for OP1 overall, which decreased slightly in M2. However, despite high consistency, this operator performed false low measurements in subject 12 during M1, and this highlights that precision does not inherently imply accuracy. The discovery and subsequent discussion of these false low measurements could have affected the confidence of OP1, perhaps explaining the small decrease in ICC. Conversely, the ICC of OP2 improved from 0.55 to 0.75 across series, indicating potential learning-curve effects and increased confidence with the measurement protocol.

Interpreting our results in terms of completion rates might be viewed as somewhat forced. However, given the context of using RT-3DE for LVEF monitoring, we find that the measurements for subject 12 by OP1 are unreliable. The baseline measurements were consistently too low, making the subsequent M2 replicates clinically irrelevant, as they do not allow for accurate tracking of changes over time. Meanwhile, the outlier results from OP2, when grouped with measurements that displayed more realistic contouring, provide an opportunity for physicians to select the most clinically relevant replicate.

By excluding subject 12's results, OP1 achieved a completion rate of 92%. OP2, after discarding the four problematic replicates, reached a completion rate of 94%. These rates, though impressive, may not accurately reflect the broader patient demographic referred to the department. These patients are characterized by older age and higher body mass index—factors known to affect the quality of the acoustic window [27].

The issue of operator skill and its influence on reproducibility, particularly among non-specialized medical personnel in the context of RT-3DE, remains largely unexplored. This study highlights the variability in ICC values between operators, potentially influenced by several factors. OP1, who had more experience, demonstrated better consistency when compared to OP2.

Furthermore, the difference in experience, as detailed in the methods section, as well as the impact of the coronavirus pandemic, which necessitated a nearly two-month pause in scanning activities during a nationwide lockdown in Denmark in 2020, could have exacerbated these initial discrepancies. This interruption may have contributed to a drift in agreement between the operators, underlining the challenges faced in maintaining consistency in clinical measurements during unprecedented disruptions.

It remains unclear whether the operators were initially in closer agreement at the start of their patient scans before this study and subsequently diverged over time. However, this aspect is of lesser importance. The crucial observation is their eventual convergence towards greater agreement and enhanced ICC values as the study progressed. This trend suggests that discrepancies in operator skill can be markedly reduced with collaborative review of 3DE acquisitions.

The limitations of this pilot observational study include its small sample size and LVEF range above 50%. Secondarily, we are unable to verify the accuracy of the measurements obtained. This could have been remedied by including a third "expert" operator or by directly comparing the measurements to cardiac magnetic resonance; the latter, however, would significantly increase the cost and complexity of the study. Moreover, the rather modest sample size, all else being equal, entails a higher risk of false-positive results.

Additionally, OP1′s consistent measurement error across all replicates for subject 12 during the first measurement session underscores the necessity of alternative methods in cases of poor echocardiogram quality. Our current modality for LVEF determination, CZT-ERNA, boasts a high feasibility rate exceeding 98% in our patient cohort, with Rb-PET expected to achieve even higher success rates. These modalities could provide robust alternatives for LVEF quantification.

Furthermore, we did not evaluate the potential influence of chest wall conformation on the repeatability of our measurements. Previous research has shown that chest wall shape significantly affects the repeatability of 2D-derived LVEF measurements [28]. Future studies could consider these factors to better understand their impact on echocardiographic measurements.

6. Clinical Implications

RT-3DE proves effective for LVEF assessments by non-specialized medical personnel, provided that specific controls are in place to ensure reliability. Key practices include reproducibility exercises to manage inter-operator variability and improve agreement as well as physician oversight to address potential inaccuracies from suboptimal endocardial contouring due to poor image quality.

In individuals without cardiovascular diseases, natural LVEF variability over time was estimated at 8 percentage points. The within-session measurement error was estimated at 7 percentage points. No systematic variability due to operators was detected.

7. Conclusions

With our study, we demonstrated a significant improvement in observer agreement between two technologists using RT-3DE. This enhanced agreement is fundamental for identifying clinically relevant changes in LVEF of ±10 percentage points.

The improvement was the result of a collaborative review of measurements from the first measurement session. Such "reproducibility exercises" are deemed essential, particularly with major changes in personnel or technology and at regular intervals. Additionally, when measurements are made by non-specialized medical personnel, such as our moderately experienced technologists, physician oversight of image quality is crucial.

Although our sample size was small and consisted of healthy volunteers with normal LVEF values, our results support the use of RT-3DE by non-specialized medical personnel under the specified conditions.

Moving forward, we aim to study observer agreement and the precision of LVEF measurements in actual patient cohorts using RT-3DE. We plan to incorporate a secondary method like CZT-ERNA when echocardiogram quality is suboptimal. Exploring other methods, such as Rb-PET, will also be a key research focus.

Author Contributions: Conceptualization, L.T.J.; Methodology, A.L. and B.K.; Software, B.K.; Formal analysis, M.Ø.N. and B.K.; Investigation, A.L.; Data curation, M.Ø.N.; Writing—original draft, M.Ø.N.; Writing—review & editing, A.L., B.Z., L.T.J. and B.K.; Project administration, L.T.J.; Funding acquisition, L.T.J. All authors have read and agreed to the published version of the manuscript.

Funding: This research received no external funding.

Institutional Review Board Statement: Not applicable.

Informed Consent Statement: Not applicable.

Data Availability Statement: Dataset available upon request from authors.

Conflicts of Interest: The authors declare no conflicts of interest.

Appendix A

Regarding sample size for such a pilot study, "the recommendation of a sample size of 12 per group" was followed, viz. 6 women and 6 men covering the same age range. The justifications for this sample size are based on rationale about feasibility and precision about the mean and variance [29].

The analyses for repeatability, reproducibility, and reliability were carried out according to the recommendations described in detail in the following papers and books [30–35].

Appendix A.1. Unlinked Data

The repeated measurements on a subject are unlinked (or unpaired) if the measurements from the two methods/measurement sessions are obtained separately, and a measurement session's multiple measurements on a subject are independent replications of the same underlying measurement. A replication is a repeated a measurement under identical conditions, ensuring that the true value of the subject remains unchanged during the measurement period. The data for the present analysis are assumed to be unlinked.

Appendix A.2. Repeatability

Repeatability of measurements refers to the variation in repeat measurements made on the same subject under identical conditions. This means that measurements are made by the same instrument or method and by the same observer if human input is required, and the measurements are made over a short period of time, over which the underlying value can be considered to be constant. Variability in measurements made on the same subject in a repeatability study can then be ascribed only to errors due to the measurement process itself.

The repeatability is also called the smallest real difference, minimal detectable change, and minimum clinical difference because it is the smallest difference that can be interpreted as evidence for a real change in the subject's true value.

In a repeatability study, the possibility of bias between measurements is excluded so that agreement between measurements made on the same subject depends only on the within-subject standard deviation (*SD*), which measures the size of measurements errors. One way to describe the agreement is to report an estimate of the within-subject *SD*, which is the same as the *SD* of the measurement errors. An alternative is to report the *SD* of the differences between two measurements made on the same subject. This is equal to the following:

$$\sqrt{2} \cdot SD_{within-subject}$$

A further alternative is to report the estimated repeatability coefficient (*RC*) [36], which is defined by the following:

$$RC = 1.96 \cdot \sqrt{2} \cdot SD_{within-subject}$$

If the differences between two measurements made on a subject are approximately normally distributed, then in the long term, one can expect the absolute difference between two measurements on a subject to differ by no more than the repeatability coefficient on 95% of occasions—unless a pronounced (significant) change has occurred, e.g., due to a cardiotoxic treatment.

Appendix A.3. Reproducibility

Reproducibility refers to the variation in measurements made on a subject under changing conditions. The changing conditions may be due to different measurement methods or instruments being used, measurements being made by different observers, or measurements being made over time, within which the "error-free" level of the variable could undergo non-negligible change.

Appendix A.4. Reliability

The reliability of a measurement method is defined as the proportion of variation in observed measurements that is not explained by the error variation inherent in the method. Reliability relates the magnitude of the measurement error in observed measurements to the inherent variability in the "error-free", "true", or underlying level of the quantity between subjects.

These measures of variability is often expressed as *SD*s, and formally, reliability is defined as follows:

$$Reliability = \frac{\left(SD_{subjects' \ true \ value}\right)^2}{\left(SD_{subjects \ true \ values}\right)^2 + \left(SD_{measurement \ error}\right)^2}$$

If the reliability is high, measurement errors are small in comparison to the true differences between subjects so that subjects can be relatively well distinguished (in terms of the quantity being measured) based upon of the error-prone measurements.

Conversely, if measurement errors tend to be large compared with the true differences between subjects, reliability will be low because differences between the measurements of two subjects could be due purely to error rather than to a genuine difference in their true values.

The reliability parameter is also known as an intraclass correlation coefficient (ICC), as it equals the correlation between any two measurements made on the same subject. Reliability takes values between zero and one, with a value of one corresponding to zero measurement error and a value of zero meaning that all the variability in measurements is due to measurement error. As a dimensionless quantity, it may be difficult to interpret, and deciding what value constitutes sufficiently high reliability is often carried out in a subjective fashion. The following table may serve as a guide for interpreting the ICC:

The reliability of a method is a measure of its relative precision. A high value of reliability indicates that the error variation is small compared to the variation in the error free values.

Table A1. Interpreting ICC values.

Reliability Outcome	Koo et al. [37]	Cicchetti et al. [38]
Poor	<0.50	<0.40
Fair	0.50–0.75	0.40–0.60
Good	0.75–0.90	0.60–0.75
Excellent	0.90–1.00	0.75–1.00

The expression for reliability shows that it depends on the error variation of the method as well as the heterogeneity (or the between subject variation) in the population. In particular, the reliability increases as the population heterogeneity increases even if the precision of the method does not change. Thus, care must be taken in interpreting reliability, especially comparison with ICCs in other (similar) studies. Reporting the between individual and within individual variation together with the ICC is therefore important.

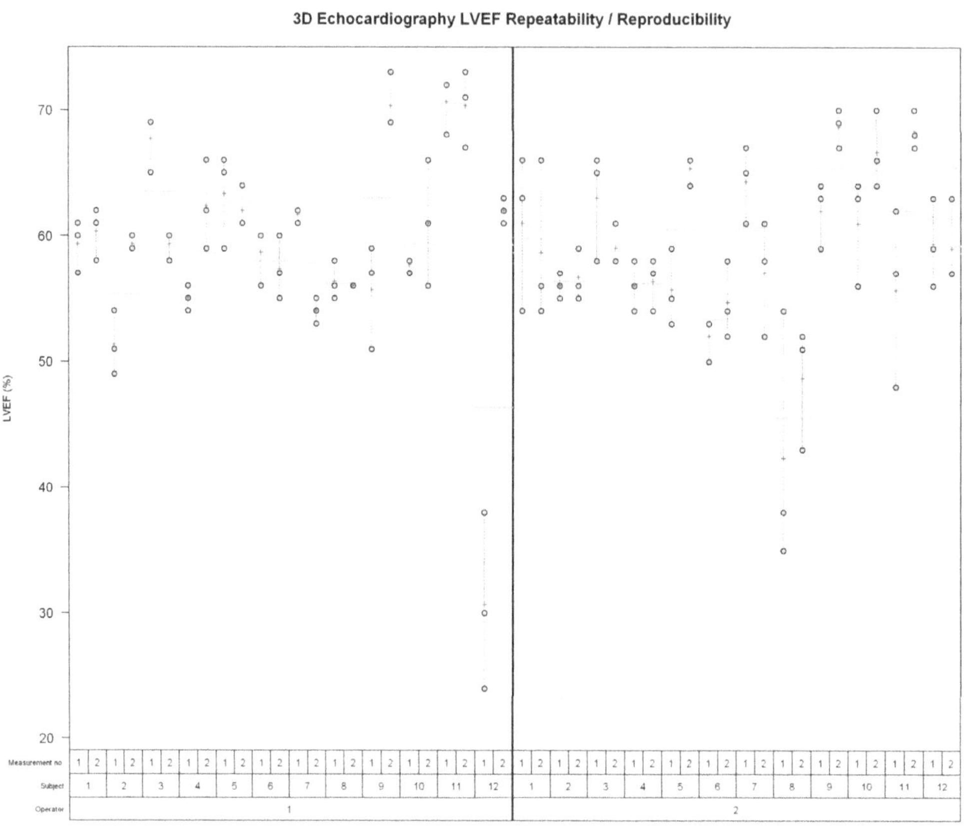

Figure A1. Variability chart of the total measurement dataset generated using the "VCR" R package. Individual measurements are depicted as points, with the red plus symbol representing the mean of each replicate set. Grey horizontal bars indicate the mean of all measurements for each subject, while light-blue bars represent the means of the entire measurement session.

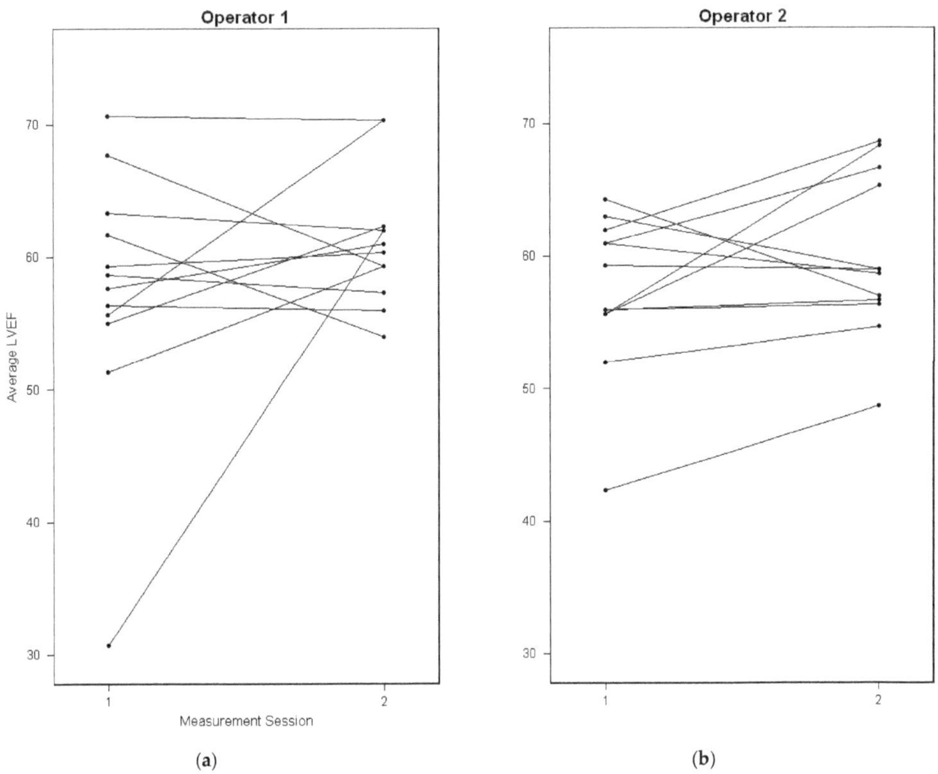

Figure A2. Paired-line plots or "spaghetti-plots", representing the change in mean-LVEF between measurement sessions for operator 1 in panel (**a**) and operator 2 in panel (**b**).

References

1. Herrmann, J.; Lenihan, D.; Armenian, S.; Barac, A.; Blaes, A.; Cardinale, D.; Carver, J.; Dent, S.; Ky, B.; Lyon, A.R.; et al. Defining Cardiovascular Toxicities of Cancer Therapies: An International Cardio-Oncology Society (IC-OS) Consensus Statement. *Eur. Heart J.* **2022**, *43*, 280–299. [CrossRef] [PubMed]
2. Armenian, S.H.; Lacchetti, C.; Barac, A.; Carver, J.; Constine, L.S.; Denduluri, N.; Dent, S.; Douglas, P.S.; Durand, J.B.; Ewer, M.; et al. Prevention and Monitoring of Cardiac Dysfunction in Survivors of Adult Cancers: American Society of Clinical Oncology Clinical Practice Guideline. *J. Clin. Oncol.* **2017**, *35*, 893–911. [CrossRef] [PubMed]
3. Plana, J.C.; Galderisi, M.; Barac, A.; Ewer, M.S.; Ky, B.; Scherrer-Crosbie, M.; Ganame, J.; Sebag, I.A.; Agler, D.A.; Badano, L.P.; et al. Expert Consensus for Multimodality Imaging Evaluation of Adult Patients during and after Cancer Therapy: A Report from the American Society of Echocardiography and the European Association of Cardiovascular Imaging. *J. Am. Soc. Echocardiogr.* **2014**, *27*, 911–939. [CrossRef] [PubMed]
4. Perez, I.E.; Taveras Alam, S.; Hernandez, G.A.; Sancassani, R. Cancer Therapy-Related Cardiac Dysfunction: An Overview for The. *Clin. Med. Insights. Cardiol.* **2019**, *13*, 13. [CrossRef] [PubMed]
5. Lyon, A.R.; López-Fernández, T.; Couch, L.S.; Asteggiano, R.; Aznar, M.C.; Bergler-Klein, J.; Boriani, G.; Cardinale, D.; Cordoba, R.; Cosyns, B.; et al. 2022 ESC Guidelines on Cardio-Oncology Developed in Collaboration with the European Hematology Association (EHA), the European Society for Therapeutic Radiology and Oncology (ESTRO) and the International Cardio-Oncology Society (IC-OS). *Eur. Heart J.* **2022**, *43*, 4229–4361. [CrossRef] [PubMed]
6. Thavendiranathan, P.; Grant, A.D.; Negishi, T.; Plana, J.C.; Popović, Z.B.; Marwick, T.H.; Carlos Plana, J.; Popovic, Z.B.; Marwick, T.H.; Cleveland, M.; et al. Reproducibility of Echocardiographic Techniques for Sequential Assessment of Left Ventricular Ejection Fraction and Volumes: Application to Patients Undergoing Cancer Chemotherapy. *J. Am. Coll. Cardiol.* **2013**, *61*, 77–84. [CrossRef] [PubMed]
7. Jenkins, C.; Bricknell, K.; Hanekom, L.; Marwick, T.H. Reproducibility and Accuracy of Echocardiographic Measurements of Left Ventricular Parameters Using Real-Time Three-Dimensional Echocardiography. *J. Am. Coll. Cardiol.* **2004**, *44*, 878–886. [CrossRef] [PubMed]

8. Mor-Avi, V.; Jenkins, C.; Kühl, H.P.; Nesser, H.J.; Marwick, T.; Franke, A.; Ebner, C.; Freed, B.H.; Steringer-Mascherbauer, R.; Pollard, H.; et al. Real-Time 3-Dimensional Echocardiographic Quantification of Left Ventricular Volumes: Multicenter Study for Validation With Magnetic Resonance Imaging and Investigation of Sources of Error. *JACC Cardiovasc. Imaging* **2008**, *1*, 413–423. [CrossRef]
9. Burke, L.M.B.; Bashir, M.R.; Neville, A.M.; Nelson, R.C.; Jaffe, T.A. Current Opinions on Medical Radiation: A Survey of Oncologists Regarding Radiation Exposure and Dose Reduction in Oncology Patients. *J. Am. Coll. Radiol.* **2014**, *11*, 490–495. [CrossRef]
10. Fazel, R.; Krumholz, H.M.; Wang, Y.; Ross, J.S.; Chen, J.; Ting, H.H.; Shah, N.D.; Nasir, K.; Einstein, A.J.; Nallamothu, B.K. Exposure to Low-Dose Ionizing Radiation from Medical Imaging Procedures. *N. Engl. J. Med.* **2009**, *361*, 849–857. [CrossRef]
11. Romero-Farina, G.; Aguadé-Bruix, S. Equilibrium Radionuclide Angiography: Present and Future. *J. Nucl. Cardiol.* **2021**, *28*, 1315–1322. [CrossRef]
12. Hansen, M.N.; Haarmark, C.; Kristensen, B.; Zerahn, B. An Algorithm for Individual Dosage in Cadmium–Zinc–Telluride Spect-Gated Radionuclide Angiography. *Diagnostics* **2021**, *11*, 2268. [CrossRef] [PubMed]
13. Walker, J.; Bhullar, N.; Fallah-Rad, N.; Lytwyn, M.; Golian, M.; Fang, T.; Summers, A.R.; Singal, P.K.; Barac, I.; Kirkpatrick, I.D.; et al. Role of Three-Dimensional Echocardiography in Breast Cancer: Comparison with Two-Dimensional Echocardiography, Multiple-Gated Acquisition Scans, and Cardiac Magnetic Resonance Imaging. *J. Clin. Oncol.* **2010**, *28*, 3429–3436. [CrossRef]
14. Jensen, M.M.; Schmidt, U.; Huang, C.; Zerahn, B. Gated Tomographic Radionuclide Angiography Using Cadmium-Zinc-Telluride Detector Gamma Camera; Comparison to Traditional Gamma Cameras. *J. Nucl. Cardiol.* **2014**, *21*, 384–396. [CrossRef] [PubMed]
15. Lertsburapa, K.; Ahlberg, A.W.; Bateman, T.M.; Katten, D.; Volker, L.; Cullom, S.J.; Heller, G.V. Independent and Incremental Prognostic Value of Left Ventricular Ejection Fraction Determined by Stress Gated Rubidium 82 PET Imaging in Patients with Known or Suspected Coronary Artery Disease. *J. Nucl. Cardiol.* **2008**, *15*, 745–753. [CrossRef] [PubMed]
16. Johnson, L.L.; Verdesca, S.A.; Aude, W.Y.; Xavier, R.C.; Nott, L.T.; Campanella, M.W.; Germano, G. Postischemic Stunning Can Affect Left Ventricular Ejection Fraction and Regional Wall Motion on Post-Stress Gated Sestamibi Tomograms. *J. Am. Coll. Cardiol.* **1997**, *30*, 1641–1648. [CrossRef] [PubMed]
17. Rydberg, J.; Andersen, J.; Haarmark, C.; Zerahn, B. The Influence of Anthropometric and Basic Circulatory Variables on Count Rate in Cadmium-Zinc-Telluride SPECT Gated Radionuclide Angiography. *J. Nucl. Cardiol.* **2019**, *26*, 1974–1980. [CrossRef]
18. Guppy-Coles, K.B.; Prasad, S.B.; Smith, K.C.; Hillier, S.; Lo, A.; Atherton, J.J. Evaluation of Training Nurses to Perform Semi-Automated Three-Dimensional Left Ventricular Ejection Fraction Using a Customised Workstation-Based Training Protocol. *J. Clin. Nurs.* **2015**, *24*, 1479–1488. [CrossRef]
19. Guppy-Coles, K.B.; Prasad, S.B.; Smith, K.C.; Lo, A.; Beard, P.; Ng, A.; Atherton, J.J. Accuracy of Cardiac Nurse Acquired and Measured Three-Dimensional Echocardiographic Left Ventricular Ejection Fraction: Comparison to Echosonographer. *Heart. Lung Circ.* **2020**, *29*, 703–709. [CrossRef] [PubMed]
20. Yang, L.; Georgescu, B.; Zheng, Y.; Meer, P.; Comaniciu, D. 3D Ultrasound Tracking of the Left Ventricle Using One-Step Forward Prediction and Data Fusion of Collaborative Trackers. In Proceedings of the 2008 IEEE Conference on Computer Vision and Pattern Recognition (CVPR), Anchorage, AK, USA, 23–28 June 2008.
21. Carkeet, A. A Review of the Use of Confidence Intervals for Bland-Altman Limits of Agreement in Optometry and Vision Science. *Optom. Vis. Sci.* **2020**, *97*, 3–8. [CrossRef]
22. Lee, K.M.; Lee, J.; Chung, C.Y.; Ahn, S.; Sung, K.H.; Kim, T.W.; Lee, H.J.; Park, M.S. Pitfalls and Important Issues in Testing Reliability Using Intraclass Correlation Coefficients in Orthopaedic Research. *Clin. Orthop. Surg.* **2012**, *4*, 149. [CrossRef] [PubMed]
23. Aune, E.; Bækkevar, M.; Rødevand, O.; Otterstad, J.E. Reference Values for Left Ventricular Volumes with Real-Time 3-Dimensional Echocardiography. *Scand. Cardiovasc. J.* **2010**, *44*, 24–30. [CrossRef] [PubMed]
24. Thavendiranathan, P.; Liu, S.; Verhaert, D.; Calleja, A.; Nitinunu, A.; Van Houten, T.; De Michelis, N.; Simonetti, O.; Rajagopalan, S.; Ryan, T.; et al. Feasibility, Accuracy, and Reproducibility of Real-Time Full-Volume 3D Transthoracic Echocardiography to Measure LV Volumes and Systolic Function: A Fully Automated Endocardial Contouring Algorithm in Sinus Rhythm and Atrial Fibrillation. *JACC. Cardiovasc. Imaging* **2012**, *5*, 239–251. [CrossRef] [PubMed]
25. Ababneh, A.A.; Sciacca, R.R.; Kim, B.; Bergmann, S.R. Normal Limits for Left Ventricular Ejection Fraction and Volumes Estimated with Gated Myocardial Perfusion Imaging in Patients with Normal Exercise Test Results: Influence of Tracer, Gender, and Acquisition Camera. *J. Nucl. Cardiol.* **2000**, *7*, 661–668. [CrossRef] [PubMed]
26. Lang, R.M.; Badano, L.P.; Mor-Avi, V.; Afilalo, J.; Armstrong, A.; Ernande, L.; Flachskampf, F.A.; Foster, E.; Goldstein, S.A.; Kuznetsova, T.; et al. Recommendations for Cardiac Chamber Quantification by Echocardiography in Adults: An Update from the American Society of Echocardiography and the European Association of Cardiovascular Imaging. *Eur. Heart J.-Cardiovasc. Imaging* **2015**, *16*, 233–271. [CrossRef]
27. de Geus-Oei, L.F.; Mavinkurve-Groothuis, A.M.C.; Bellersen, L.; Gotthardt, M.; Oyen, W.J.G.; Kapusta, L.; van Laarhoven, H.W.M. Scintigraphic Techniques for Early Detection of Cancer Treatment-Induced Cardiotoxicity. *J. Nucl. Med. Technol.* **2013**, *41*, 170–181. [CrossRef] [PubMed]
28. Sonaglioni, A.; Nicolosi, G.L.; Granato, A.; Bonanomi, A.; Rigamonti, E.; Lombardo, M. Influence of Chest Wall Conformation on Reproducibility of Main Echocardiographic Indices of Left Ventricular Systolic Function. *Minerva Cardiol. Angiol.* **2024**, *72*, 111–124. [CrossRef] [PubMed]

29. Julious, S.A. Sample Size of 12 per Group Rule of Thumb for a Pilot Study. *Pharm. Stat.* **2005**, *4*, 287–291. [CrossRef]
30. Bartlett, J.W.; Frost, C. Reliability, Repeatability and Reproducibility: Analysis of Measurement Errors in Continuous Variables. *Ultrasound Obstet. Gynecol.* **2008**, *31*, 466–475. [CrossRef]
31. Bland, J.M.; Altman, D.G. Agreement between Methods of Measurement with Multiple Observations per Individual. *J. Biopharm. Stat.* **2007**, *17*, 571–582. [CrossRef]
32. Jones, M.; Dobson, A.; O'brian, S. A Graphical Method for Assessing Agreement with the Mean between Multiple Observers Using Continuous Measures. *Int. J. Epidemiol.* **2011**, *40*, 1308–1313. [CrossRef] [PubMed]
33. Christensen, H.S.; Borgbjerg, J.; Børty, L.; Bøgsted, M. On Jones et Al.'s Method for Extending Bland-Altman Plots to Limits of Agreement with the Mean for Multiple Observers. *BMC Med. Res. Methodolody* **2020**, *20*, 304. [CrossRef] [PubMed]
34. Carstensen, B. *Comparing Clinical Measurement Methods*; Wiley: Hoboken, NJ, USA, 2010; ISBN 9780470694237.
35. Choudhary, P.K.; Nagaraja, H.N. *Measuring Agreement: Models, Methods and Applications*; Wiley Series in Probability and Statistics; Wiley: Hoboken, NJ, USA, 2017; ISBN 9781118078587.
36. *BS5497-1*; Precision of Test Methods—Guide for the Determination of Repeatability and Reproducibility for a Standard Test Method. British Standards Institution: London, UK, 1979.
37. Koo, T.K.; Li, M.Y. A Guideline of Selecting and Reporting Intraclass Correlation Coefficients for Reliability Research. *J. Chiropr. Med.* **2016**, *15*, 155. [CrossRef] [PubMed]
38. Cicchetti, D.V.; Sparrow, S.A. Developing Criteria for Establishing Interrater Reliability of Specific Items: Applications to Assessment of Adaptive Behavior. *Am. J. Ment. Defic.* **1981**, *86*, 127–137.

Journal of
Clinical Medicine

MDPI

Article

Preoperative OCT Characteristics Contributing to Prediction of Postoperative Visual Acuity in Eyes with Macular Hole

Yoko Mase [1,*], Yoshitsugu Matsui [1], Koki Imai [2], Kazuya Imamura [2], Akiko Irie-Ota [1], Shinichiro Chujo [1], Hisashi Matsubara [1], Hiroharu Kawanaka [2] and Mineo Kondo [1]

1 Department of Ophthalmology, Mie University Graduate School of Medicine, Tsu 514-8507, Mie, Japan
2 Department of Electrical and Electronic Engineering, Mie University, Tsu 514-8507, Mie, Japan
* Correspondence: yokosun9@gmail.com; Tel.: +81-59-232-1111

Abstract: Objectives: To develop a machine learning logistic regression algorithm that can classify patients with an idiopathic macular hole (IMH) into those with good or poor vison at 6 months after a vitrectomy. In addition, to determine its accuracy and the contribution of the preoperative OCT characteristics to the algorithm. **Methods:** This was a single-center, cohort study. The classifier was developed using preoperative clinical information and the optical coherence tomographic (OCT) findings of 43 eyes of 43 patients who had undergone a vitrectomy. The explanatory variables were selected using a filtering method based on statistical significance and variance inflation factor (VIF) values, and the objective variable was the best-corrected visual acuity (BCVA) at 6 months postoperation. The discrimination threshold of the BCVA was the 0.15 logarithm of the minimum angle of the resolution (logMAR) units. **Results:** The performance of the classifier was 0.92 for accuracy, 0.73 for recall, 0.60 for precision, 0.74 for F-score, and 0.84 for the area under the curve (AUC). In logistic regression, the standard regression coefficients were 0.28 for preoperative BCVA, 0.13 for outer nuclear layer defect length (ONL_DL), −0.21 for outer plexiform layer defect length (OPL_DL) − (ONL_DL), and −0.17 for (OPL_DL)/(ONL_DL). In the IMH form, a stenosis pattern with a narrowing from the OPL to the ONL of the MH had a significant effect on the postoperative BCVA at 6 months. **Conclusions:** Our results indicate that (OPL_DL) − (ONL_DL) had a similar contribution to preoperative visual acuity in predicting the postoperative visual acuity. This model had a strong performance, suggesting that the preoperative visual acuity and MH characteristics in the OCT images were crucial in forecasting the postoperative visual acuity in IMH patients. Thus, it can be used to classify MH patients into groups with good or poor postoperative visual acuity, and the classification was comparable to that of previous studies using deep learning.

Keywords: optical coherence tomography; macular hole; logistic regression; machine learning; clinical prediction models

1. Introduction

A macular hole (MH), typically idiopathic, is caused by an abnormal vitreomacular traction. It is a common ophthalmic abnormality that can rapidly progress to a reduction of the visual acuity. There have been significant advances in the diagnosis and treatment of MHs. The advanced surgical techniques include pars plana vitrectomy (PPV) and internal limiting membrane (ILM) peeling with or without an inverted ILM flap. The evolution of these diagnostic methods and treatments has been driven by advances in imaging technology, especially over the past 20 years. These advances have led to impressive advances in the interpretation of OCT images, and the ability to evaluate pathological conditions and disease progression using cross-sectional retinal images [1]. However, predicting the postoperative visual acuity remains difficult even with a surgical closure rate of 85%. The postoperative visual acuity is influenced by many factors associated with the MH, such as its preoperative minimum linear diameter, the MH index, the basal diameter, and the stage of the MH [2–6]. However, the causal relationships and the correlations are complicated.

Machine learning (ML) is a tool that can be trained to predict a subjective variable using explanatory variables that are statistically significant. It can analyze complex relationships between multiple variables. Relevant to this study, the application of ML in a Medical Decision Support System (MDSS) can enhance the quality of patient care by offering clinicians relevant information based on the patient's clinical characteristics. This provides a secondary and objective perspective to aid in the medical decision-making processes [7,8].

Our group has published the results of using a nonlinear ML algorithm to predict the BCVA in eyes with a macular edema (ME) due to a branch retinal vein occlusion (BRVO) during the first-year maintenance phase of anti-VEGF therapy [9]. The clinical information and OCT findings obtained at the first resolution of the ME after the initial treatment were used in that study. We have also shown that a linear algorithm can predict the BCVA in the same patients with good accuracy, and we have determined the accuracy of the linear classifiers and the degree of contribution by the explanatory variables [10].

Although there have been studies on the anatomic closure prognosis using the preoperative OCT features by ML for MHs [11,12], there are only two studies that examined the postoperative visual outcomes using artificial intelligence (AI) algorithms [13,14]. Both of these studies used deep learning (DL) for the preoperative OCT images, but these techniques had limited explanatory potential for prediction due to their 'black-box' nature.

Thus, the purpose of this study was to examine MH patients using ML, similar to the methods used in the BRVO study, to improve the predictive performance and to interpret the complex interplay of multiple factors of the OCT findings. More specifically, we aimed to determine the contribution of each explanatory variable on the classification and prediction of individual postoperative visual outcomes after a vitrectomy. This was accomplished by establishing single-label, two-class problems to categorize patients into Group A with good visual outcomes and Group B with poor visual outcomes. In addition, we determined the accuracy of the linear classifiers and the degree of contribution of the explanatory variables to the algorithm.

2. Materials and Methods

2.1. Patients and Treatment

This was a single-center, cohort study of the medical records of patients examined in the Department of Ophthalmology, Mie University Hospital, between January 2017 and October 2020 (ethical approval code: H2019-219). To create this prediction model, we followed the TRIPOD checklist [15].

Patients with a MH who had undergone surgery with at least 6 months of follow-up examinations were studied. The inclusion criteria were patients whose reduced visual acuity was solely due to the MH, an absence of concurrent retinal diseases, and no missing data of the explanatory variables. The exclusion criteria were cases of reoperation and cases where there was a failure to close the MH. All patients had undergone either a vitrectomy or phacovitrectomy, ILM peeling, and gas tamponade with gas as needed (2 with Air, 1 with C3F8, and the others with SF6) with several days of postoperative overhead bed rest at the same institution.

2.2. Dividing Patients into Two Groups Based on the Best-Corrected Visual Acuity

The best-corrected visual acuity (BCVA) was recorded at the baseline and at each examination following the treatment. The primary outcomes were the BCVA at 6 months post-operation. We defined Group A (good prognosis) as patients achieving a decimal BCVA of $\geq$0.7, and Group B (poor prognosis) consisted of patients with decimal BCVA of <0.7. A threshold of 0.15 logMAR units (approximate decimal BCVA of 0.7) was used, as this is the visual acuity required for the renewal of a Japanese driver's license and reflects the level of visual acuity desired by patients in a clinical setting.

2.3. Preprocessing of OCT Images and Features

Spectral domain (SD) optical coherence tomographic (OCT) images were recorded with the Spectralis OCT device (Spectralis HRA + OCT, Heidelberg Engineering, Heidelberg, Germany) at the baseline, and at the 1, 3, and 6 months postoperative examinations.

Instead of using the baseline OCT image as a feature, we annotated the OCT image and used the raster and vector data in that region as handcrafted features. The original OCT image size was 768 × 496 pixels (9 × 1.9 mm, 30°), and it was cropped to create a 256 × 256 pixels (0.98 × 0.98 mm, 3.26°) trimmed image. The trimming process was completed manually by an examiner (YM) with the outer retinal layer of the fovea as the center of the trimmed image (Figure 1A).

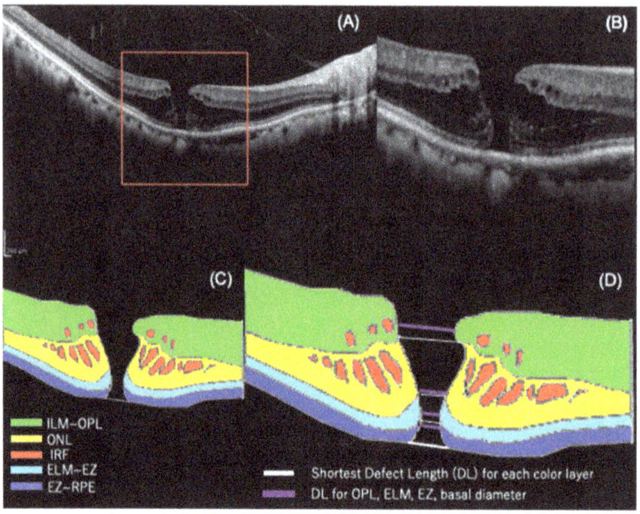

Figure 1. Preprocessing and annotation of OCT images to extract explanatory variables. (**A**) A preoperative optical coherence tomographic (OCT) image of an eye with a macular hole (MH). (**B**) Trimmed image of the OCT image in the red frame in (**A**). (**C**) Annotation for the outer plexiform (OPL) line, external limiting membrane (ELM) line, ellipsoid zone (EZ) line, and retinal pigment epithelial (RPE) line as demarcation lines in a trimmed image. The top layer of the image was painted green then in yellow, sky-blue, and blue in that order. The intraretinal fluid (IRF) was painted red. (**D**) The Shortest Defect Length (DL) for each color layer and DL for the OPL, ELM, EZ, and basal diameter.

In the cropped images, the vector and raster data were uniquely defined as handcrafted features in the structural regions related to the visual function of the macular hole, as in earlier studies [2–4,16,17]. The outer plexiform layer (OPL), external limiting membrane (ELM), ellipsoid zone (EZ), intraretinal fluid (IRF), and retinal pigment epithelium (RPE) were manually marked and highlighted on the trimmed images using the GNU Image Manipulation Program (GIMP) (v2.10.38), an image editing software (Figure 1C) [18].

This process yielded nine types of handcrafted features for objective evaluations. They included the following: (1) inter-edge distance for layers such as the OPL, ELM, and EZ, (2) minimum inter-layer distance (green, yellow, sky-blue, blue), and (3) minimum linear diameter and base diameter (Figure 1D). A total of 41 features were established from the patients' background information and features of the OCT images (Table 1). To ensure consistency and accuracy, the manual annotations of the OCT images were performed by a single retina specialist and subsequently reviewed by another retina specialist.

Table 1. Features established from the patients' background information and features of the OCT images.

Features	Definition	Variable Types 1 = Categorical 2 = Continuous
Sex	Man or woman	1
Age	N/A	2
Preoperative BCVA	N/A	2
Method	vitrectomy or phacovitrectomy	1
Affected eye	Right or left	1
Axial length	N/A	2
Stage	N/A	1
Disease duration	N/A	2
ILM	Peel or invert or not peel	1
VMT	Present or absent of VMT	1
PVD	PVD complete or not complete	1
BDM	basal diameter of MH	2
Hole-min	minimum linear diameter of MH	2
OPL-DL	DL for OPL	2
ELM-DL	DL for ELM	2
EZ-DL	DL for EZ	2
Green-sDL	shortest DL for green color area	2
Yellow-sDL (NL-DL)	shortest DL for yellow color area	2
Sky blue-sDL	shortest DL for sky blue color area	2
Blue-sDL	shortest DL for blue color area	2
Area IRF	Area of IRF	2
Area-green	Area from ILM to OPL not including boundary line	2
Area-yellow	Area from OPL to ELM not including boundary line, ONL	2
Area-sky_blue	Area from ELM to EZ not including boundary line	2
Area-blue	Area from EZ to RPE not including boundary line	2
(OPL-DL) − (ONL-DL)	(OPL-DL) minus (ONL-DL)	2
(ELM-DL) − (ONL-DL)	(ELM-DL) minus (ONL-DL)	2
(OPL-DL) − (Green-sDL)	(OPL-DL) minus (Green-sDL)	2
(ELM-DL) − (Sky blue-sDL)	(ELM-DL) minus (Sky blue-sDL)	2
(EZ-DL) − (Sky blue-sDL)	(EZ-DL) minus (Sky blue-sDL)	2
(EZ-DL) − (Blue-sDL)	(EZ-DL) minus (blue-sDL)	2
BDM − (Blue-sDL)	BDM minus (blue-sDL)	2
BDM − (hole-min)	BDM minus (hole-min)	2
(Green-sDL)/(OPL-DL)	(Green-sDL) divide by (OPL-DL)	2
(OPL-DL)/(ONL-DL)	(OPL-DL) divide by (ONL-DL)	2
(ELM-DL)/(ONL-DL)	(ELM-DL) divide by (ONL-DL)	2

Table 1. *Cont.*

Features	Definition	Variable Types 1 = Categorical 2 = Continuous
(ELM-DL)/(Sky blue-sDL)	(ELM-DL) divide by (Sky blue-sDL)	2
(EZ-DL)/(Sky blue-sDL)	(EZ-DL) divide by (Sky blue-sDL)	2
(EZ-DL)/(Blue-sDL)	(EZ-DL) divide by (Blue-sDL)	2
BDM/(Blue-sDL)	BDM divided by (Blue-sDL)	2
BDM/(Hole-min)	BDM divide by (Hole-min)	2

ILM = internal limiting membrane; VMT = vitreomacular traction; PVD = posterior vitreous detachment; MH = macular hole; OPL = outer plexiform layer; DL = defect length; ELM = external limiting membrane; EZ = ellipsoid zone; IRF = internal retinal fluid; sDL = shortest DL; ONL = outer nuclear layer; BCVA = best-corrected visual acuity.

2.4. Machine Learning Algorithms Considering AI Alignment

Logistic regression was used for the classifiers [19]. Features with statistically significant differences between the two groups served as the explanatory variables (Figure 2). A stratified cross-validation method for both test and parameter tuning was used so that the ratio of Group A to Group B was the same for each block when the data were divided. This resulted in dividing the dataset into five blocks [20]. One block was used for the test data and four blocks were used for the training data. For the test data, 100 pairs were randomly selected from all combinations of patients by performing 5 stratified cross-validation 100 times.

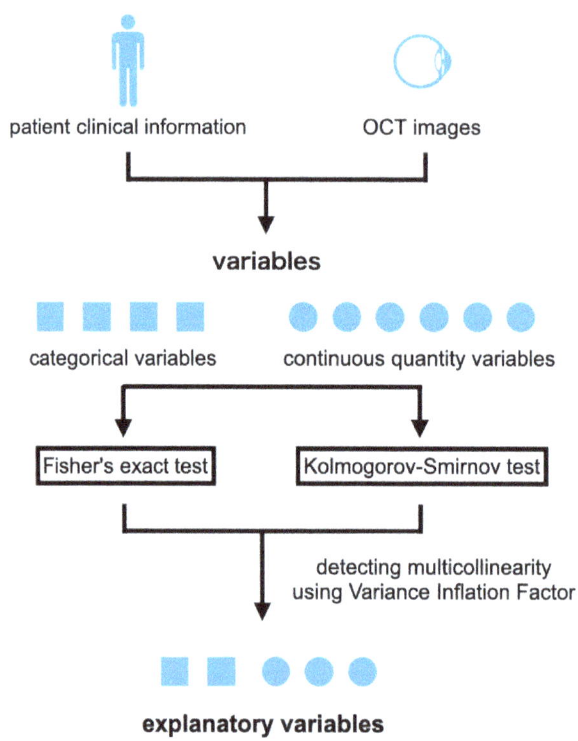

Figure 2. Fisher's probability of correct answer tests were performed for the categorical variables extracted from the clinical information and OCT images. Kolmogorov–Smirnov tests were performed

for continuous quantitative variables. Variables that had a statistically significant difference between Group A and Group B were used as candidates for the explanatory variables. Among these variables, those with a variance inflation factor values > 10, i.e., with R^2 scores > 0.9, were eliminated, and the tests were repeated until the R^2 score for all variables was <0.9. Finally, the remaining variables were used as the explanatory variables.

The AI alignment of the classifiers to predict the patient's visual function prior to treatment was carefully considered in terms of not compromising the patient's motivation for treatment [21]. For the adjusted classification thresholds, we adjusted the parameters of the algorithm so that the accuracy was higher than the recall. The tuning of the parameter was adjusted to maximize their accuracy (Figure 3).

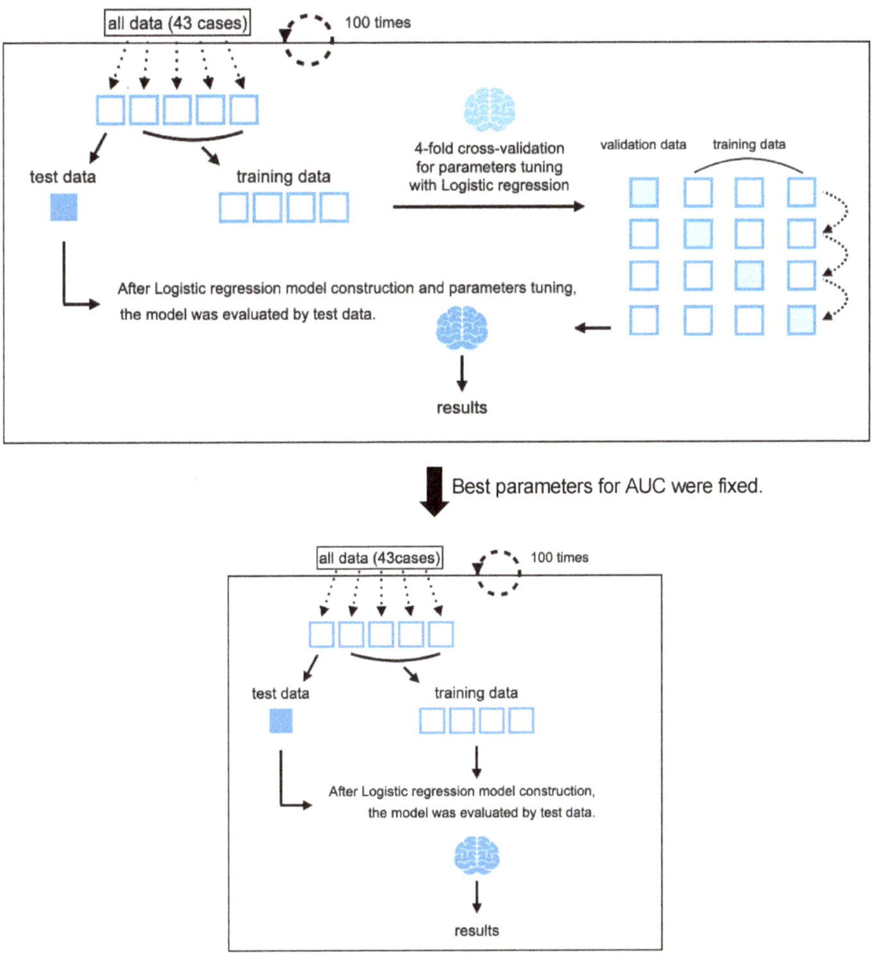

Figure 3. The algorithm shown in the upper box was used to adjust the parameters to maximize the area under the curve (AUC). Then, as shown in the algorithm in the lower box, a logistic regression model was created with the training data by fixing the parameters at the most frequent values among those explored in the upper box, and then the model was evaluated with the test data.

The accuracy, precision, recall, and F-measure were used to evaluate the cross-validation, and the interval estimation was also determined. The contribution of the explanatory variables to the predictions was assessed using standard regression coefficients. These tasks were implemented using the Python library "scikit-learn" [22].

2.5. Statistical Analyses

The explanatory variables were selected by comparing the features between the two groups and using the following tests. The Kolmogorov–Smirnov test was used for continuous quantitative variables. Fisher's exact test was used as a categorical variable. The Wilcoxon signed-rank test was also used to test the association between the preoperative BCVA and the 6-month BCVA. Each variable was considered statistically significant when $p < 0.05$. All statistical analyses were performed using the statistical programming language R (R version 3.1.3; e foundation for Statistical Computing, Vienna, Austria).

3. Results

3.1. Demographics of Group A and Group B

In total, 43 eyes of 43 patients met the eligibility criteria, and 32 eyes were placed in Group A and 11 eyes in Group B. The demographics of each group are presented in Table 2. Group A has a mean age of 65.6 years, whereas Group B has a mean age of 67.2 years. The male proportion is 30.3% in Group A and 36.4% in Group B. The majority of patients underwent phacovitrectomy procedures. Comparisons of the two groups showed that only the preoperative BCVA was statistically different between Groups A (BCVA = 0.46) and B (BCVA = 0.81).

Table 2. Baseline features of patients.

Variables	Group A	Group B	*p*-Value
Sex Men, n (%)	10 (30.3)	4 (36.4)	1.0
Age years	65.59 ± 6.51	67.18 ± 4.63	0.552
Preoperative BCVA	0.46 ± 0.24	0.81 ± 0.34	* 0.007
Methods PPV/phaco + PPV	1/31	0/11	1.0
Affected eye Right, n (%)	18 (54.5)	6 (36.0)	1.0
Axial length	23.98 ± 1.38	24.05 ± 1.56	0.987
Stage of MH (2, 3, 4)	3, 24, 5	3, 7, 1	0.524
Disease duration	1.72 ± 2.05	3.18 ± 3.46	0.481
ILM peeled, n (%)	22 (84.6)	4 (15.4)	0.147
VMT presence, n (%)	20 (76.9)	6 (23.1)	0.728
PVD exist, n (%)	27 (73.0)	10 (27.0)	1.0
BDM	724.66 ± 189.13	958.45 ± 399.37	0.162
Hole-min	295.50 ± 107.49	423.09 ± 175.49	0.053
OPL-DL	465.09 ± 140.14	492.36 ± 170.95	0.784
Yellow-sDL (ONL-DL)	313.28 ± 115.73	434.09 ± 186.22	0.015
ELM-DL	320.63 ± 120.25	480.82 ± 221.77	0.017
EZ-DL	359.00 ± 172.47	517.09 ± 263.87	0.217
Green-sDL	462.91 ± 134.37	533.73 ± 148.32	0.180
Sky blue-sDL	297.13 ± 120.35	458.27 ± 220.81	0.053
Blue-sDL	372.25 ± 168.61	530.82 ± 256.59	0.136

Table 2. *Cont.*

Variables	Group A	Group B	*p*-Value
Area IRF	1437.72 ± 910.70	2240.36 ± 1653.83	0.109
Area-green	7268.78 ± 1414.01	7122.45 ± 1195.36	0.721
Area-yellow	5263.59 ± 1220.27	5068.27 ± 1463.88	0.799
Area-sky_blue	1585.31 ± 327.78	1560.64 ± 215.41	0.721
Area-blue	1701.56 ± 417.81	1744.73 ± 472.78	0.552
(OPL-DL) − (ONL-DL)	151.81 ± 114.31	58.27 ± 46.37	0.020
(ELM-DL) − (ONL-DL)	7.34 ± 42.69	46.73 ± 76.45	0.336
(OPL-DL) − (Green-sDL)	2.19 ± 95.99	−41.36 ± 55.85	0.362
(ELM-DL) − (Sky blue-sDL)	23.50 ± 30.58	22.55 ± 22.67	0.843
(EZ-DL) − (Sky blue-sDL)	61.88 ± 82.83	58.82 ± 51.32	0.516
(EZ-DL) − (Blue-sDL)	−13.25 ± 25.11	−13.73 ± 22.21	0.984
BDM-(Blue-sDL)	352.41 ± 127.58	427.64 ± 231.34	0.616
BDM-(hole-min)	429.16 ± 134.12	535.36 ± 250.01	0.616
(Green-sDL)/(OPL-DL)	1.01 ± 0.17	1.12 ± 0.17	0.362
(OPL-DL)/(ONL-DL)	1.63 ± 0.60	1.19 ± 0.19	0.020
(ELM-DL)/(ONL-DL)	1.03 ± 0.14	1.11 ± 0.16	0.336
(ELM-DL)/(Sky blue-sDL)	1.10 ± 0.14	1.05 ± 0.06	0.843
(EZ-DL)/(Sky blue-sDL)	1.20 ± 0.23	1.11 ± 0.09	0.516
(EZ-DL)/(Blue-sDL)	0.95 ± 0.08	0.96 ± 0.05	0.984
BDM/(Blue-sL)	2.19 ± 0.81	1.92 ± 0.41	0.784
BDM/(Hole-min)	2.62 ± 0.75	2.33 ± 0.43	0.267

BCVA = best-corrected visual acuity; PPV = pars plana vitrectomy; phaco, phacoemulsification cataract surgery; MH = macular hole; ILM = internal limiting membrane; VMT = vitreomacular traction; PVD = posterior vitreous detachment; OPL = outer plexiform layer; DL = defect length; ELM = external limiting membrane; EZ = ellipsoid zone; IRF = internal retinal fluid; sDL = shortest DL; ONL = outer nuclear layer. Group A is postoperative BCVA < 0.7 and Group B is postoperative BCVA ≥ 0.7. p values were calculated by comparing each variable between Group A and Group B. * Significant at $p < 0.05$ (the Kolmogorov–Smirnov test was used for the continuous quantity variables. Fisher's exact test was used as the categorical variable).

3.2. Explanatory Variables

From 32 handcraft features extracted from the OCT images and 9 features obtained from the patients' clinical information, significant differences between Group A and Group B were observed in 5 features (Table 2). The R^2 values were calculated to exclude features with multicollinearity (Table 3). There were multicollinearities between the features that were statistically different between Groups A and B. These included the ELM defect length (DL), which was excluded, and the other features were selected as explanatory variables.

Table 3. Selection of explanatory variables.

Variables	1st R^2 Score	2nd R^2 Score
Preoperative BCVA	0.321	0.283
ELM DL	0.919	NA
ONL DL	0.918	0.521
(OPL DL) − (ONL DL)	0.722	0.660
(OPL DL)/(ONL DL)	0.767	0.755

3.3. Hyperparameters of Logistic Regression

The frequency of the occurrence of hyperparameters in 100 pre-tests for the adjustments of the hyperparameters with an F1 score is shown in Figure 4. Based on this, the hyperparameter used in the final test was fixed with a constant of 0.1.

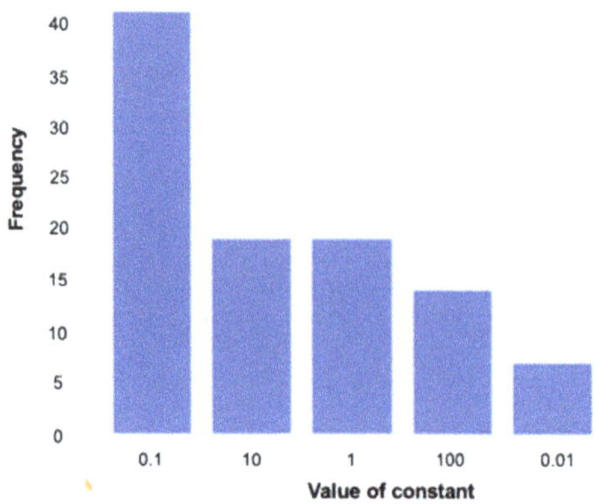

Figure 4. The frequency of each of the constant terms of the parameters is shown.

3.4. Classification Performance

The predictive performance of the classification between Groups A and B is shown in Table 4 and Figure 5. The precision was 0.92, recall was 0.73, accuracy was 0.74, F-score was 0.80, and AUC was 0.84.

Table 4. Results of classification accuracy.

Algorithm	Mean	Standard Deviation	95% Confidence Interval for Mean
Accuracy	0.738	0.130	0.712~0.764
Precision	0.921	0.088	0.903~0.938
Recall	0.734	0.162	0.702~0.766
F-measure	0.804	0.116	0.781~0.827
AUC	0.843	0.117	0.820~0.866

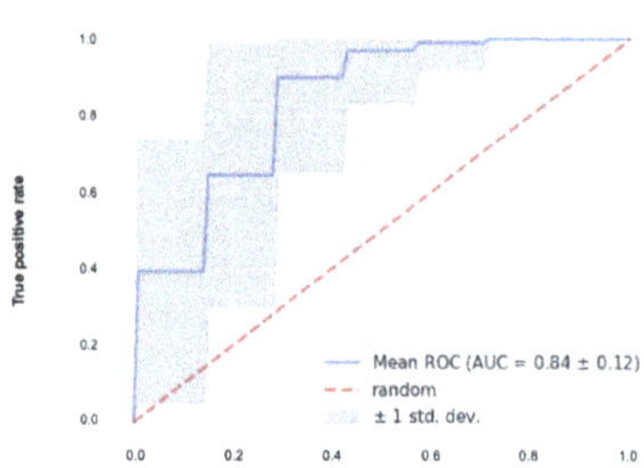

Figure 5. The mean receiver operating characteristic (ROC) curve of the classifiers for Group A and Group B at 6 months postoperation. The standard deviation (SD) is equivalent to the SD of the area under the ROC curve (AUC) obtained by evaluating the model 100 times with the test data.

3.5. Specific Contributions of Explanatory Variables

The regression coefficients determined are shown in Figure 6. The regression coefficients of the explanatory variables were as follows: preoperative BCVA was 0.281, ONL_DL was 0.130, (OPL_DL)/(ONL_DL) was −0.174, and (OPL_DL) − (ONL_DL) was −0.212 (Table 5).

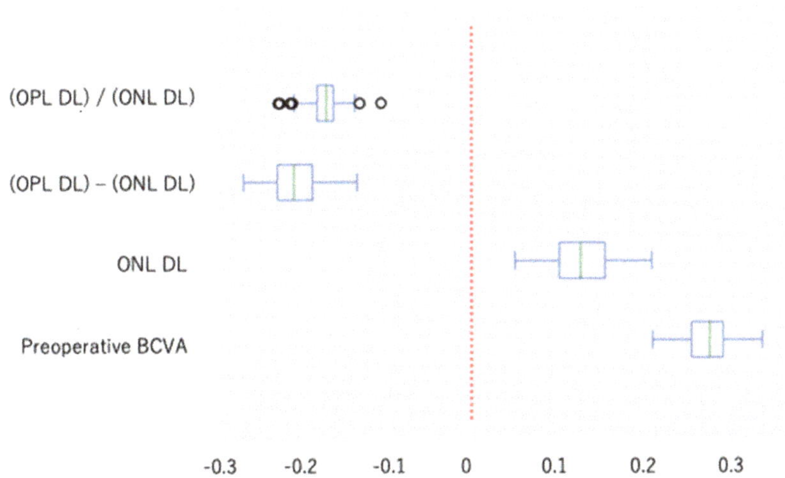

Figure 6. Box-and-whisker diagrams with outliers showing coefficients of the explanatory variables at 6 months postoperation. The maximum and minimum whisker lengths are set at the upper and lower limits of 1.5 times the interquartile range (IQR). The first quartile $-1.5 \times$ IQR is the lower limit of the whisker, and the third quartile $+1.5 \times$ IQR is the upper limit of the whisker. Values less than the lower end of the whisker or more than the upper end of the whisker are indicated by circles as outliers.

Table 5. Coefficients of explanatory variables.

Variables	Mean	Standard Deviation	95% Confidence Interval for Mean
Preoperative BCVA	0.281	0.028	0.275~0.286
ONL DL	0.130	0.038	0.123~0.138
(OPL DL)/(ONL DL)	−0.174	0.020	−0.178~−0.170
(OPL DL) − (ONL DL)	−0.212	0.029	−0.217~−0.206

3.6. Control Experiment

In a control experiment using only logistic regression on the nine features obtained from the patients' clinical information, significant differences were observed for the preoperative BCVA between Groups A and B. The hyperparameters used in the final test were fixed with a constant of 0.1. The precision was 0.863, recall was 0.764, accuracy was 0.715, F-score was 0.802, and AUC was 0.82 ± 0.12 (Figure 7).

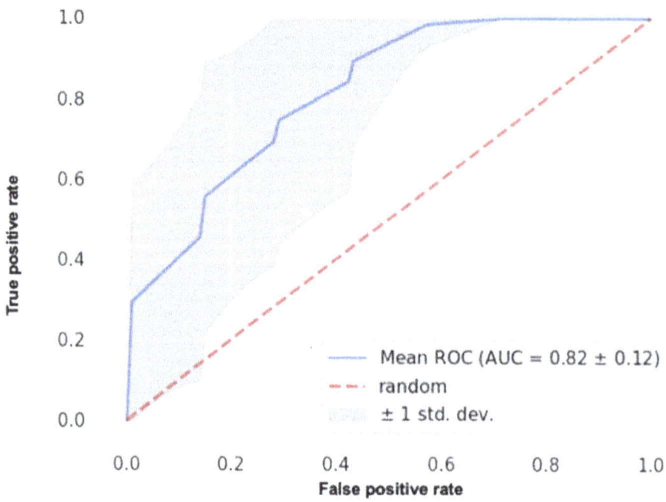

Figure 7. The mean receiver operating characteristic (ROC) curve of the classifiers for Group A and Group B at 6 months postoperation using only the patients' clinical information. The standard deviation (SD) is equivalent to the SD of the area under the ROC curve (AUC) obtained by evaluating the model 100 times with the test data.

4. Discussion

The methods used in our earlier study on BRVO were used in this study on MHs, which was intended to determine the individual contributions of each explanatory variable in classifying and predicting the postoperative BCVA [9,10]. A vitrectomy for MHs has improved the postoperative visual acuity, and the predicted AUC at 6 months postoperation during the recovery process was 0.84 ± 0.12.

We also created a high precision/low recall model aimed at encouraging patients to pursue treatment. At 6 months postoperation, the precision value was 0.92 and the recall value was 0.73. These values agree with our goals.

In a control experiment where the OCT features were removed from the explanatory variables, the AUC was 0.82 ± 0.12 (Figure 7), and the OCT features contributed only slightly to the improvement in the prediction of the postoperative BCVA in eyes with a MH.

ML was chosen over DL due to the small sample size and concerns about over-training leading to a poor generalizability performance and low explainability [23].

Previous reports on the predictions of the postoperative visual acuity have mainly used DL and not ML. For example, Lachance et al. employed a "hybrid regression model", which integrated clinical features with convolutional neural networks' (CNNs') predictions, and achieved an AUC of 0.81 ± 0.05. These findings indicated that, although the inclusion of OCT images slightly enhanced the preoperative data, its impact was minimal. Similarly, Obata et al. used the preoperative information and OCT images, and they reported a superior prediction outcome based on the OCT images alone, as compared to that including the preoperative patient information. However, the accuracy was similarly moderate at 46% vs. 40% [13,14]. The minimal impact of OCT images on preoperative data, as noted by these studies, may be attributed to the overlapping information obtained from both the clinical and OCT features. Our findings are consistent with the reports of Lachance et al. and Obata et al., which also highlight the importance of preoperative visual acuity. The predictive performance of our study is comparable to them. However, our study uniquely identified the significance of specific OCT-derived metrics that offered new insights into the predictors of the visual outcomes.

One strength of deep learning (DL) is its ability to process large datasets through direct image processing that improves the accuracy but reduces the interpretability. In contrast, ML can detect the relevant areas of the OCT images for evaluation that contribute to the postoperative predictions. This can then provide valuable information for understanding the pathological conditions in OCT research. The accuracy of the predictions was comparable to that reported by Lachance et al. [13]. In our study, the OCT images could not be used because this was not DL, and based on the prior literature, the features were designed by manually annotating the stratified structures and then calculating the length and area values as vector data. Obata et al. analyzed subsets of patients with inaccurate predictions and were unable to determine the causes due to the limited interpretability. In contrast, our ML approach allowed us to determine the contribution of each explanatory variable. The following section describes the characteristics of the explanatory variables that significantly contributed to our predictions.

Although the results are limited to the data used in this study, the originally defined explanatory variables for the combination of vector data focusing on the layer structure of OCT images were more effective in predicting than the reported explanatory variables contributing to the visual function.

There have been many reports on the preoperative OCT morphology and postoperative visual prognosis or anatomy of the MHs. Specifically, there is vector data information for distances such as the basal diameter, minimum linear diameter, ELM_DL, and EZ_DL [24–27]. There is also the diameter hole index (DHI) and the hole diameter ratio (HDR), which are combinations of the vector data information.

We used the filter method to select the explanatory variables from a stratified distance, minimum linear diameter, base diameter, ELM_DL, EZ_DL, stratified area, IRF area, and their combinations as features and examined the explanatory variables that contributed to the prediction.

We found that a poor preoperative BCVA was associated with a poor prognosis at 6 months postoperation, while a larger (OPL_DL) − (ONL_DL) and (OPL_DL)/(ONL_DL), and longer ONL_DL contributed to a good prognosis for the BCVA at 6 months postoperation.

In comparison with earlier reports, our study showed that poor preoperative visual acuity contributed to a poorer visual acuity at 6 months in our study, as well as in many other reports [28,29]. Furthermore, our study uniquely identified the significance of specific OCT-derived metrics, offering new insights into the predictors of visual outcomes. We found that the ELM_DL was likely to have a similar impact to the ONL_DL in terms of the contribution of the objective variable, which was eliminated because of multicollinearity (Table 3). It has been reported that the continuity of the outer retinal structure is correlated with the visual function, and that they were significantly correlated with the visual acuity prognosis [24–27]. We were able to confirm the similarity of the preoperative morphological information of the outer retina and the preoperative visual acuity.

On the other hand, (OPL_DL) − (ONL_DL) and (OPL_DL)/(ONL_DL) are combinations of distance information between layers and are novel features that have not been reported to contribute to the prognosis of the visual function. What these findings indicate is that the presence of a stenosis pattern with a narrowing from the OPL to the ONL is important for good postoperative visual function. In the previously reported DHI and HDR and stenotic MH, the morphology was reported to have a better anatomic prognosis [11,30]. However, the association with the visual function has not been reported in great detail.

The DHI was included in the features of the vector data combination, but it was not significantly related to the prediction of the visual function. Therefore, it is possible that we are the first to report that a stenosis of the MH is associated with the prognosis of the postoperative visual function.

The prognostic model created in this study is unique in that it was designed not only to improve the model's accuracy, but also to be fit for the purpose of its contribution to improve the patient's motivation. Assuming that the model is used in clinical practice, a vitrectomy for MH is the only method to improve vision, and it is necessary for patients who wish to improve their vision. Predicting the prognosis of the treatment is intended to motivate the patient, but it is a fact that not all patients have good postoperative vision. However, it is not a desirable prediction to reduce their motivation prior to treatment. Therefore, we believe that it is necessary to design an AI alignment that would contribute to improving the patient's motivation as much as possible.

Therefore, we created a model with high accuracy and low recall by adjusting the ROC curve of the accuracy–recall curve. We left open the possibility that even if the visual acuity prognosis was classified to less than 0.7 decimal visual acuity units, we could present the possibility that the prediction could be off because of the low recall. Such a prognosis could potentially allow us to choose to intervene earlier than usual for such cases, and it is known from other cases reported that earlier surgical intervention is associated with a better prognosis [31].

The use of AI in medical decision making raises ethical concerns, particularly on patient autonomy and the transparency of algorithmic predictions. When using such AI tools in real-world clinical settings, it is essential to ensure that the AI tools are used to support rather than replace clinical judgments.

The limitations of this study include the use of standard regression coefficients, which do not represent the interactions among the explanatory variables. The standard regression coefficients for the (OPL_DL) − (ONL_DL) and (OPL_DL)/(ONL_DL) categories are related to the stenosis of the MH form that was found. Each of the ONL_DL and OPL_DL coefficients is a common term in the explanatory variables, and there may be an interaction between ONL_DL and OPL_DL. Further investigations of our methods to assess the interaction of these explanatory variables would allow a better interpretation of the results of the contributions of the explanatory variables.

The next limitation was that we annotated the B-scan image clippings by stratum, and the distance information was measured automatically by the program. Our program was unable to measure the height information of the MH in the feature values because it was difficult to define the height of the MH in many cases because the bottom of MH was not horizontal in the images. For this reason, the MHI and THI [32], which have been associated with a postoperative visual function prognosis in the past, could not be examined. Future research should focus on developing a method for measuring MH height, even when the bottom is tilted.

In this study, annotation was performed manually, which proved to be costly and time-consuming. To address this, we are currently conducting joint research aimed at automating the annotation process using advanced clarification technology. This automation is expected to enhance consistency and reduce the labor involved in data preparation.

5. Conclusions

Our results indicate that the morphology of the MH, especially a stenosis pattern narrowing from the OPL to the ONL, may be an important factor in predicting the 6-month postoperative visual acuity. Thus, it can be used to classify MH patients into groups with good or poor postoperative visual acuity.

Although only a small number of data were available, we could obtain a good predictive performance for the postoperative visual acuity classification while ensuring explainability by using ML.

Author Contributions: Conceptualization, Y.M. (Yoko Mase), A.I.-O., Y.M. (Yoshitsugu Matsui) and S.C.; methodology, Y.M. (Yoshitsugu Matsui), K.I. (Koki Imai), K.I. (Kazuya Imamura) and H.K.; software, K.I. (Kazuya Imamura) and K.I. (Koki Imai); formal analysis, Y.M. (Yoko Mase), K.I. (Koki Imai) and K.I. (Kazuya Imamura); investigation, Y.M. (Yoko Mase); data curation, Y.M. (Yoko Mase), A.I.-O., Y.M. (Yoshitsugu Matsui), S.C. and H.M.; writing—original draft preparation, Y.M. (Yoko Mase); writing—review and editing, Y.M. (Yoko Mase), A.I.-O., Y.M. (Yoshitsugu Matsui) and H.M.; visualization K.I. (Koki Imai) and Y.M. (Yoshitsugu Matsui); supervision, H.K. and M.K.; project administration, M.K. All authors have read and agreed to the published version of the manuscript.

Funding: This research received no external funding.

Institutional Review Board Statement: This study was conducted in accordance with the Declaration of Helsinki, and approved by the Ethics Committee of Mie University Hospital (protocol code H2019-219 and the date of approval was 25 December 2019).

Informed Consent Statement: This study was retrospective and based on the information collected as a result of standard care. Identifiable information was de-identified in this study. The requirement for patients' individual written informed consent was approved to be waived.

Data Availability Statement: Data are unavailable due to privacy or ethical restrictions.

Acknowledgments: We thank Emeritus Duco Hamasaki of the Bascom Palmer Eye Institute of the University of Miami (Miami, FL, USA) for critical discussion and final manuscript editing.

Conflicts of Interest: All authors declare no competing interests.

References

1. Ong, J.; Zarnegar, A.; Corradetti, G.; Singh, S.R.; Chhablani, J. Advances in optical coherence tomography imaging technology and techniques for choroidal and retinal disorders. *J. Clin. Med.* **2022**, *11*, 5139. [CrossRef] [PubMed]
2. Kusuhara, S.; Teraoka Escaño, M.F.; Fujii, S.; Nakanishi, Y.; Tamura, Y.; Nagai, A.; Yamamoto, H.; Tsukahara, Y.; Negi, A. Prediction of postoperative visual outcome based on hole configuration by optical coherence tomography in eyes with idiopathic macular holes. *Am. J. Ophthalmol.* **2004**, *138*, 709–716. [CrossRef] [PubMed]
3. Chang, Y.C.; Lin, W.N.; Chen, K.J.; Wu, H.J.; Lee, C.L.; Chen, C.H.; Wu, K.-Y.; Wu, W.C. Correlation between the dynamic postoperative visual outcome and the restoration of foveal microstructures after macular hole surgery. *Am. J. Ophthalmol.* **2015**, *160*, 100–106. [CrossRef] [PubMed]
4. Oh, I.K.; Oh, J.; Yang, S.M.; Ahn, S.E.; Kim, S.W.; Huh, K. Hyperreflective external limiting membranes after successful macular hole surgery. *Retina* **2012**, *32*, 760–766. [CrossRef] [PubMed]
5. Gaudric, A. Macula hole surgery: Simple or complex? *Am. J. Ophthalmol.* **2009**, *147*, 381–383. [CrossRef] [PubMed]
6. Houly, J.R.; Veloso, C.E.; Passos, E.; Nehemy, M.B. Quantitative analysis of external limiting membrane, ellipsoid zone and interdigitation zone defects in patients with macular holes. *Graefe's Arch. Clin. Exp. Ophthalmol.* **2017**, *255*, 1297–1306. [CrossRef] [PubMed]
7. Aboudi, N.; Guetari, R.; Khlifa, N. Multi-objectives optimisation of features selection for the classification of thyroid nodules in ultrasound images. *IET Image Process.* **2020**, *14*, 1901–1908. [CrossRef]
8. Khachnaoui, H.; Guetari, R.; Khlifa, N. A review on deep learning in thyroid ultrasound computer-assisted diagnosis systems. In Proceedings of the 2018 IEEE International Conference on Image Processing, Applications and Systems (IPAS), Sophia Antipolis, France, 12–14 December 2018; pp. 291–297.
9. Matsui, Y.; Imamura, K.; Ooka, M.; Chujo, S.; Mase, Y.; Matsubara, H.; Kawanaka, H.; Kondo, M. Classification of good visual acuity over time in patients with branch retinal vein occlusion with macular edema using support vector machine. *Graefe's Arch. Clin. Exp. Ophthalmol.* **2022**, *260*, 1501–1508. [CrossRef] [PubMed]
10. Matsui, Y.; Imamura, K.; Chujo, S.; Mase, Y.; Matsubara, H.; Sugimoto, M.; Kawanaka, H.; Kondo, M. Which Explanatory Variables Contribute to the Classification of Good Visual Acuity over Time in Patients with Branch Retinal Vein Occlusion with Macular Edema Using Machine Learning? *J. Clin. Med.* **2022**, *11*, 3903. [CrossRef]
11. Zgolli, H.; k El Zarrug, H.H.; Meddeb, M.; Mabrouk, S.; Khlifa, N. Anatomical prognosis after idiopathic macular hole surgery: Machine learning based-predection. *Libyan J. Med.* **2022**, *17*, 2034334. [CrossRef]
12. Xiao, Y.; Hu, Y.; Quan, W.; Zhang, B.; Wu, Y.; Wu, Q.; Liu, B.; Zheng, X.; Lin, Z.; Li, T.; et al. Machine learning-based prediction of anatomical outcome after idiopathic macular hole surgery. *Ann. Transl. Med.* **2021**, *9*, 830. [CrossRef] [PubMed]
13. Lachance, A.; Godbout, M.; Antaki, F.; Hébert, M.; Bourgault, S.; Caissie, M.; Tourville, E.; Durand, A.; Dirani, A. Predicting visual improvement after macular hole surgery: A combined model using deep learning and clinical features. *Transl. Vis. Sci. Technol.* **2022**, *11*, 6. [CrossRef]
14. Obata, S.; Ichiyama, Y.; Kakinoki, M.; Sawada, O.; Saishin, Y.; Ito, T.; Tomioka, M.; Ohji, M. Prediction of postoperative visual acuity after vitrectomy for macular hole using deep learning–based artificial intelligence. *Graefe's Arch. Clin. Exp. Ophthalmol.* **2021**, *260*, 1113–1123. [CrossRef]
15. Collins, G.S.; Reitsma, J.B.; Altman, D.G.; Moons, K.G.M. Transparent reporting of a multivariable prediction model for individual prognosis or diagnosis (TRIPOD) the TRIPOD statement. *Ann. Intern. Med.* **2015**, *162*, 55–63. [CrossRef]
16. Miura, G.; Mizunoya, S.; Arai, M.; Hayashi, M.; Yamamoto, S. Early postoperative macular morphology and functional outcomes after successful macular hole surgery. *Retina* **2007**, *27*, 165–168. [CrossRef] [PubMed]
17. Unsal, E.; Cubuk, M.O.; Ciftci, F. Preoperative prognostic factors for macular hole surgery: Which is better? *Oman J. Ophthalmol.* **2019**, *12*, 20.
18. The Official Website of the GNU Image Manipulation Program. Available online: https://www.gimp.org (accessed on 1 April 2021).

19. Nick, T.G.; Campbell, K.M. Logistic regression. In *Topics in Biostatistics*; Springer: Berlin/Heidelberg, Germany, 2007; pp. 273–301.
20. Zeng, X.; Martinez, T.R. Distribution-balanced stratified cross-validation for accuracy estimation. *J. Exp. Theor. Artif. Intell.* **2000**, *12*, 1–12. [CrossRef]
21. Chen, J.H.; Asch, S.M. Machine learning and prediction in medicine—Beyond the peak of inflated expectations. *N. Engl. J. Med.* **2017**, *376*, 2507. [CrossRef] [PubMed]
22. The Official Website of Scikit-Learn. Available online: https://scikit-learn.org/stable/ (accessed on 1 April 2021).
23. Choosing the Right Estimator. Available online: https://scikit-learn.org/1.3/tutorial/machine_learning_map/index.html (accessed on 1 April 2021).
24. Daruich, A.; Matet, A.; Moulin, A.; Kowalczuk, L.; Nicolas, M.; Sellam, A.; Omri, S.; Jonet, L.; Zhao, M.; Behar-Cohen, F.; et al. Mechanisms of macular edema: Beyond the surface. *Prog. Retin. Eye Res.* **2018**, *63*, 20–68. [CrossRef]
25. Starr, M.R.; Salabati, M.; Mahmoudzadeh, R.; Patel, L.G.; Ammar, M.J.; Hsu, J.; Garg, S.; Ho, A.C.; Kuriyan, A.E. Fluctuations in central subfield thickness associated with worse visual outcomes in patients with diabetic macular edema in clinical trial setting. *Am. J. Ophthalmol.* **2021**, *232*, 90–97. [CrossRef]
26. Wakabayashi, T.; Oshima, Y.; Fujimoto, H.; Murakami, Y.; Sakaguchi, H.; Kusaka, S.; Tano, Y. Foveal microstructure and visual acuity after retinal detachment repair: Imaging analysis by Fourier-domain optical coherence tomography. *Ophthalmology* **2009**, *116*, 519–528. [CrossRef] [PubMed]
27. Otani, T.; Yamaguchi, Y.; Kishi, S. Correlation between visual acuity and foveal microstructural changes in diabetic macular edema. *Retina Phila. Pa* **2010**, *30*, 774–780. [CrossRef] [PubMed]
28. Fallico, M.; Jackson, T.L.; Chronopoulos, A.; Hattenbach, L.O.; Longo, A.; Bonfiglio, V.; Russo, A.; Avitabile, T.; Parisi, F.; Reibaldi, M.; et al. Factors predicting normal visual acuity following anatomically successful macular hole surgery. *Acta Ophthalmol.* **2021**, *99*, e324–e329. [CrossRef] [PubMed]
29. Gupta, B.; Laidlaw, D.A.H.; Williamson, T.H.; Shah, S.P.; Wong, R.; Wren, S. Predicting visual success in macular hole surgery. *Br. J. Ophthalmol.* **2009**, *93*, 1488–1491. [CrossRef] [PubMed]
30. Qi, Y.; Yu, Y.; You, Q.; Wang, Z.; Wang, J.; Liu, W. Hole diameter ratio for prediction of anatomical outcomes in stage III or IV idiopathic macular holes. *BMC Ophthalmol.* **2020**, *20*, 1–8. [CrossRef] [PubMed]
31. Murphy, D.C.; AI-Zubaidy, M.; Lois, N.; Scott, N.; Steel, D.H.; Qu, J.; Zhao, M.; Sadda, S.; Manasa, S.; Alvin, K.K.H.; et al. The effect of macular hole duration on surgical outcomes: An individual participant data study of randomized controlled trials. *Ophthalmology* **2023**, *130*, 152–163. [CrossRef] [PubMed]
32. Ruiz-Moreno, J.M.; Staicu, C.; Pinero, D.P.; Montero, J.; Lugo, F.; Amat, P. Optical coherence tomography predictive factors for macular hole surgery outcome. *Br. J. Ophthalmol.* **2008**, *92*, 640–644. [CrossRef] [PubMed]

cancers

MDPI

Article

MRI T2w Radiomics-Based Machine Learning Models in Imaging Simulated Biopsy Add Diagnostic Value to PI-RADS in Predicting Prostate Cancer: A Retrospective Diagnostic Study

Jia-Cheng Liu [1,†], Xiao-Hao Ruan [1,†], Tsun-Tsun Chun [2], Chi Yao [2], Da Huang [1], Hoi-Lung Wong [3], Chun-Ting Lai [3], Chiu-Fung Tsang [3], Sze-Ho Ho [3], Tsui-Lin Ng [3], Dan-Feng Xu [1,*] and Rong Na [2,3,*]

[1] Department of Urology, Ruijin Hospital, Shanghai Jiao Tong University School of Medicine, Shanghai 200025, China

[2] Department of Surgery, School of Clinical Medicine, LKS Faculty of Medicine, The University of Hong Kong, Hong Kong, China

[3] Department of Surgery, Queen Mary Hospital, Hong Kong, China; lct729@ha.org.hk (C.-T.L.)

[*] Correspondence: xdf12036@rjh.com.cn (D.-F.X.); narong.hs@gmail.com or yungna@hku.hk (R.N.); Tel.: +86-021-64370045 (D.-F.X.); +852-22554310 (R.N.)

[†] These authors contributed equally to this work.

Simple Summary: Prostate mpMRI is currently the most widely used image diagnosis approach to detect prostate cancer, while the PI-RADS system was developed to standardize and improve the accuracy of suspicious lesion identification on MRI. However, there still remain several limitations including inter-individual inconsistencies and naked-eye insufficiency. This study aims to apply AI technology to image interpretation to enhance diagnostic efficiency and explore the use of T2-weighted image-based stimulated biopsy in predicting prostate cancer (PCa). Using 820 lesions from The Cancer Imaging Archive database and 83 lesions from Hong Kong Queen Mary Hospital, we constructed 18 machine-learning models based on three algorithms and conducted both internal and external validation. We found that the logistic regression-based model provides additional diagnostic value to the PI-RADS in predicting PCa.

Abstract: Background: Currently, prostate cancer (PCa) prebiopsy medical image diagnosis mainly relies on mpMRI and PI-RADS scores. However, PI-RADS has its limitations, such as inter- and intra-radiologist variability and the potential for imperceptible features. The primary objective of this study is to evaluate the effectiveness of a machine learning model based on radiomics analysis of MRI T2-weighted (T2w) images for predicting PCa in prebiopsy cases. Method: A retrospective analysis was conducted using 820 lesions (363 cases, 457 controls) from The Cancer Imaging Archive (TCIA) Database for model development and validation. An additional 83 lesions (30 cases, 53 controls) from Hong Kong Queen Mary Hospital were used for independent external validation. The MRI T2w images were preprocessed, and radiomic features were extracted. Feature selection was performed using Cross Validation Least Angle Regression (CV-LARS). Using three different machine learning algorithms, a total of 18 prediction models and 3 shape control models were developed. The performance of the models, including the area under the curve (AUC) and diagnostic values such as sensitivity, specificity, positive predictive value (PPV), and negative predictive value (NPV), were compared to the PI-RADS scoring system for both internal and external validation. Results: All the models showed significant differences compared to the shape control model (all $p < 0.001$, except SVM model PI-RADS+2 Features $p = 0.004$, SVM model PI-RADS+3 Features $p = 0.002$). In internal validation, the best model, based on the LR algorithm, incorporated 3 radiomic features (AUC = 0.838, sensitivity = 76.85%, specificity = 77.36%). In external validation, the LR (3 features) model outperformed PI-RADS in predictive value with AUC 0.870 vs. 0.658, sensitivity 56.67% vs. 46.67%, specificity 92.45% vs. 84.91%, PPV 80.95% vs. 63.64%, and NPV 79.03% vs. 73.77%. Conclusions: The machine learning model based on radiomics analysis of MRI T2w images, along with simulated biopsy, provides additional diagnostic value to the PI-RADS scoring system in predicting PCa.

Keywords: prostate cancer; multi-parametric magnetic resonance imaging; prostate imaging reporting and data system; radiomics; machine learning; biopsy

1. Introduction

Prostate cancer (PCa) is one of the most prevalent cancers among males worldwide, with the highest incidence and leading to the second highest number of deaths [1,2]. In recent decades, the prevalence of prostate cancer has been on the rise in China. One notable difference is that the ratio of mortality-to-morbidity in prostate cancer is higher in China compared with Western countries [3,4].

Current diagnostic methods for detecting PCa typically involve various tests, such as prostate-specific antigen (PSA), prostate health index (*phi*), digital rectal examination (DRE), and multiparametric magnetic resonance imaging (mpMRI) [5–7]. These tests are used to identify potential cases of PCa. If the results indicate suspicion of PCa, a subsequent invasive biopsy, considered the gold standard in diagnostics, is performed for confirmation.

However, as an invasive procedure, prostate biopsy carries the risk of various side effects, such as bleeding, pain, infection, and, in severe cases, life-threatening sepsis [8]. Therefore, it is essential to assess the necessity of subjecting a patient to invasive biopsy. For individuals requiring biopsy, efforts should be made to enhance the accuracy of the procedure to mitigate the risk of false negatives and subsequent unnecessary interventions such as active surveillance or repeat biopsies.

The currently most widely used imaging method, mpMRI, provides a comprehensive depiction of different physiological and anatomical characteristics through the utilization of various imaging sequences. MRI-Targeted biopsy is one of the approaches to reduce the misclassification of clinically significant prostate cancer in men with MRI-visible lesions. This method involves superimposing T2w MRI images onto real-time ultrasound scans of the prostate, enabling clinicians to identify and biopsy suspicious. However, due to limitations inherent in mpMRI scans, current T2w targeted biopsy did not show a significantly improved PCa detection rate compared to systematic biopsy (51.5% vs. 52.5%, respectively) [9,10].

To standardize and improve the accuracy of suspicious lesion identification on MRI, the Prostate Imaging Reporting and Data System version 2.1 (PI-RADS v2.1) was developed. This system has demonstrated promising value in clinical practice [11]. Nevertheless, there still remain several limitations. Firstly, the PI-RADS assessment highly depends upon the individual interpreting the images, resulting in potential inconsistencies. Specifically, experienced radiologists tend to exhibit superior performance compared to their less experienced counterparts, and a group of radiologists collectively performs better than a single radiologist [12]. Secondly, there are certain features that are not visible to the naked eye and therefore cannot be directly observed or assessed [13]. These limitations can potentially compromise the accuracy and reliability of prostate cancer diagnoses.

Recently, the wide application of machine learning (ML) and artificial intelligence (AI) approaches has made it possible to overcome these disadvantages by establishing diagnostic tools based on radiomics data. Radiomics focuses on the extraction and analysis of a vast array of quantitative imaging features from medical images, enabling the analysis of characteristics that may be imperceptible to the naked eye and fostering a more objective approach. ML methods, which are increasingly being incorporated into radiomic studies, are used to analyze these high-dimensional features. Specifically, ML is a field of AI that focuses on the development of algorithms and models that enable computers to learn and make predictions or decisions without being explicitly programmed for each specific task. This combination of radiomics and ML has proved valuable for constructing medical prediction models [14–16].

Previous studies have already examined the diagnostic potential of radiomics in PCa diagnosis prior to biopsy by segmenting suspected areas [16–19]. In this study, our primary objective is to assess the efficacy of MRI T2w-based simulated biopsy. We aim to accomplish this by constructing a biopsy trajectory radiomics-based machine learning model for PCa prediction and comparing its incremental value to the current PI-RADS scoring system.

2. Method

This retrospective research involved lesion-to-lesion analysis. All the biopsy trajectories from two sources were delineated, and radiomic features were extracted from the MRI T2w images (T2W). After the feature selection process, ML algorithms were used to construct and validate prediction models. Figure 1 shows the workflow of this research.

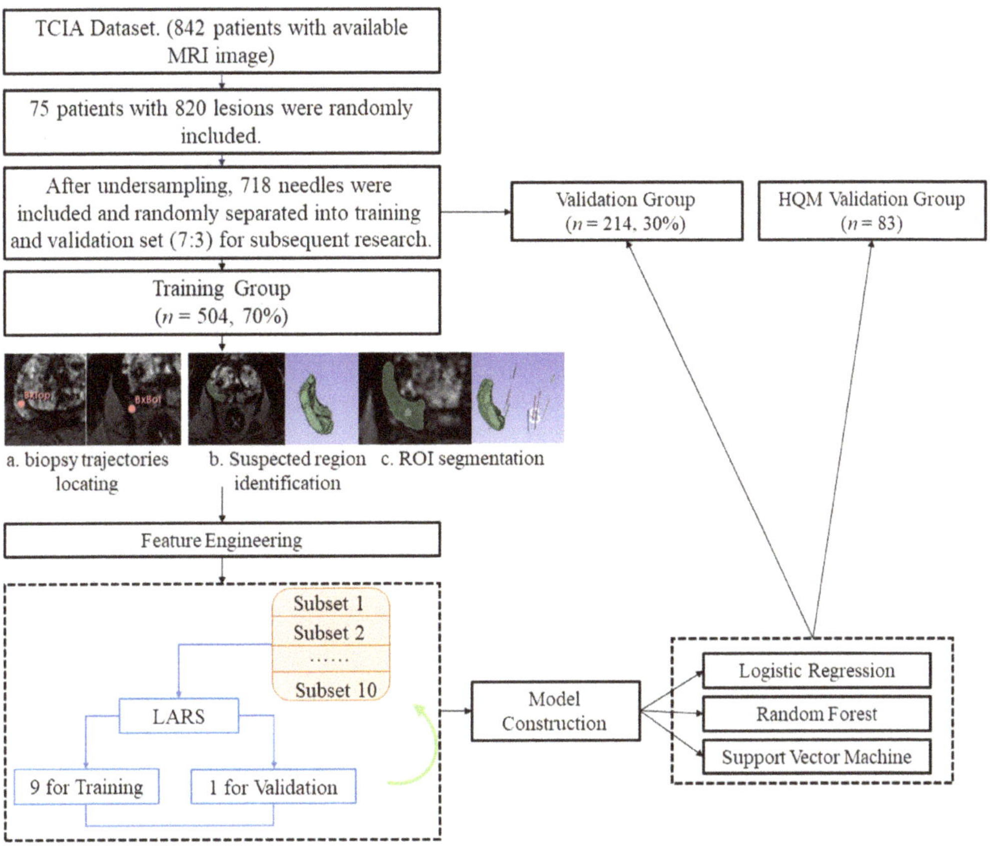

Figure 1. Workflow of models' construction and validation. Figure 1 describes the workflow of this study: (1) The MRI images were obtained from two sources: The Cancer Imaging Archive (TCIA) Database Collection (75 patients, 820 lesions) and Hong Kong Queen Mary Hospital (8 patients, 83 lesions); (2) The 820 lesions from TCIA were undersampled to 718 lesions and randomly separated to training group (n = 504, 70%) and validation group (n = 214, 30%); (3) Initial regions of interest (ROIs) were manually delineated on the MRI image, as indicated by the red markers (BxTop and BxBot); (4) ROIs were refined and segmented. The green overlay highlights the segmented prostate region; (5) A set of radiomic features was screened using the LARS (Least Angle Regression) algorithm. This step identified the most relevant features for prostate cancer prediction; (6) The extracted features were used to train logistic regression, random forest, and support vector machine models; (7) Performance of models was both validated internally and externally.

2.1. Patients and Data Collection

Data were retrospectively obtained from two sources: TCIA (The Cancer Imaging Archive) Database PROSTATE-US-MR Collection and Hong Kong Queen Mary Hospital. The PROSTATE-US-MR collection included a total of 1151 patients, of which 842 patients underwent MRI scans. Clinical characteristics including PSA, PI-RADS, and T2W MRI images were recorded for these 842 patients. Biopsy tracks were also labeled. MR imaging was performed on a 3 Tesla Trio, Verio, or Skyra scanner (Siemens, Erlangen, Germany). From the 842-patient collection, 75 patients with 820 available needle tracks were randomly selected for further model construction and internal validation. Additionally, 83 needles from 8 patients who experienced MRI-targeted biopsy at Queen Mary Hospital from June 2022 to October 2023, with available clinical variables and track recordings, were included for external validation. The study was approved by the Institutional Review Board of the University of Hong Kong/Hospital Authority Hong Kong West Cluster (UW20-462). All participants provided written informed consent to take part in the study.

2.2. PI-RADS

The PI-RADS score was evaluated at the needle level. When the biopsy trajectory intersected the suspected region, the score was determined based on the highest PI-RADS score assigned to any part of that region. The final PI-RADS score of suspected regions was a comprehensive evaluation considering the dataset results, as well as assessments by our own radiologists and urologists. A PI-RADS score ≥ 4 was considered a positive prediction, while ≤ 3 is regarded as negative.

2.3. Segmentation and Feature Extraction

2.3.1. ROI Segmentation

Biopsy trajectories were generated using the 3D Slicer software, employing the "draw tube" tool with a radius setting of 1.00. Along with each recorded trajectory, the suspected region (identified as suspicious in the dataset or by our researchers, consistent with the region of PI-RADS score region) was delineated.

2.3.2. Pyradiomics

The "PyRadiomics" package, developed by Harvard Medical School's Computational Imaging and Bioinformatics Lab, is widely adopted in contemporary radiomics research. It offers a wide range of radiomics features that are compliant with the Image Biomarker Standardization Initiative (IBSI), ensuring consistency and reproducibility. The features provided include First-order Statistics, Shape-based Features, Texture Features, and Wavelet Filtered Features. First-order Statistics describe the distribution of voxel intensities within the image region, without considering spatial relationships; Shape-based Features quantify the geometric properties of the segmented region; Texture Features include Gray Level Co-occurrence Matrix (GLCM), Gray Level Run Length Matrix (GLRLM), Gray Level Size Zone Matrix (GLSZM), Gray Level Dependence Matrix (GLDM) and Neighboring Gray Tone Difference Matrix (NGTDM). These texture features capture various aspects of the image's texture by analyzing the relationships and patterns of pixel intensities. Wavelet Filtered Features describe the characteristics of the region of interest by applying wavelet transformations, which can capture details at multiple scales. However, due to the uninterpretability of Wavelet Filtered Features, they were not included in the model construction.

There was also a previous study that constructed "MaZda" package for radiomic features extraction [20]. However, it is an older software package that predates the formalization of the IBSI standards. While MaZda includes a comprehensive set of texture features, it was not explicitly designed with IBSI standards in mind. Furthermore, MaZda is currently less widely used than PyRadiomics, with limited updates and community support, making it less suitable for ensuring reproducibility and consistency in modern research.

2.3.3. Feature Extraction

To enhance the robustness of the extracted features, several steps were performed, including the following image preprocessing and feature extraction were conducted using 3D Slicer (version 5.2.1): (1) The images were standardized by using "histogram matching" to eliminate the intensity variation; (2) we applied "N4ITK MRI Bias correction" to adjust the potentially corrupted MRI images caused by bias field signal; (3) the images were resampled to a voxel size of 1 × 1 × 1 mm to standardize voxel spacing and voxel intensity values were discretized using a fixed bin width of 25 HU; (4) based on the Image Biomarker Standardization Initiative (IBSI), 107 features were extracted by "Pyradiomics" package; (5) The images of 20 patients from TCIA dataset with 333 needles were re-evaluated by both two doctors twice, both intra- and inter-doctor intraclass correlation coefficient (ICC) for each feature were calculated and the variables with an ICC > 0.75 were included. Finally, 103 features were included for further model construction.

2.4. Model Construction

2.4.1. Data Undersampling

Commonly, only a portion of the biopsy needles from a single PCa patient will yield positive results. The imbalance in prostate cancer findings is more pronounced at the patient level compared to the needle level. Thus, in this research, we mainly focus on the needle level. The imbalance in the numbers of positive needles (n = 363) and negative needles (n = 457) could potentially impact the model's performance (Table 1). To address this issue, we employed the "ROSE" package in R for undersampling the data. This approach aims to create a more balanced dataset for data screening and model training, thereby preventing the predictive ability of the model from being influenced by dataset imbalance and potentially causing bias. We randomly selected a portion of the negative needles to make the number close to that of the positive group for further model construction.

Table 1. Patients' Characteristics.

	Patient Level Charcteristics	Needle Level before Resample	Needle Level after Resample	Needle Level Training	Needle Level Validation	Needle Level p Value *
Number	75	820	718	504	214	/
PSA	6.50 (4.50~9.50)	6.90 (5.40~11.00)	6.50 (5.40~12.00)	6.90 (5.30~11.00)	6.50 (5.40~12.00)	0.65
Prostate Cancer						0.98
Yes	64 (85.33%)	363 (44.27%)	363 (50.56%)	255 (50.60%)	108 (50.47%)	/
No	11 (14.67%)	457 (55.73%)	355 (49.44%)	249 (49.40%)	106 (49.53%)	/
Gleason Grade Group						0.88
Not PCa	11 (14.67%)	457 (55.73%)	355 (49.44%)	249 (49.40%)	106 (49.53%)	/
GG1	16 (21.33%)	184 (22.44%)	184 (25.63%)	129 (25.6%)	55 (25.70%)	/
GG2	22 (29.33%)	98 (11.95%)	98 (13.65%)	67 (13.29%)	31 (14.49%)	/
GG3	14 (18.67%)	35 (4.27%)	35 (4.87%)	24 (4.76%)	11 (5.14%)	/
GG4	3 (4.00%)	23 (2.80%)	23 (3.20%)	17 (3.37%)	6 (2.80%)	/
GG5	9 (12.00%)	23 (2.80%)	23 (3.20%)	18 (3.57%)	5 (2.34%)	/

PSA: prostate-specific antigen; PCa: prostate cancer; GG: grade group. * Wilcoxon signed-rank test comparing training dataset and validation dataset.

2.4.2. Feature Selection

Feature selection was performed using the step-forward 10-fold Cross Validation Least Angle Regression (CV-LARS) algorithm on the training set. Model performance was evaluated using the mean standard error (MSE). At the 8th step of the algorithm, the LARS achieved the lowest MSE, resulting in the extraction of 7 relevant features (Figure 2). Notably, the earlier a feature is included in the algorithm, the more significant it is in predicting the outcome.

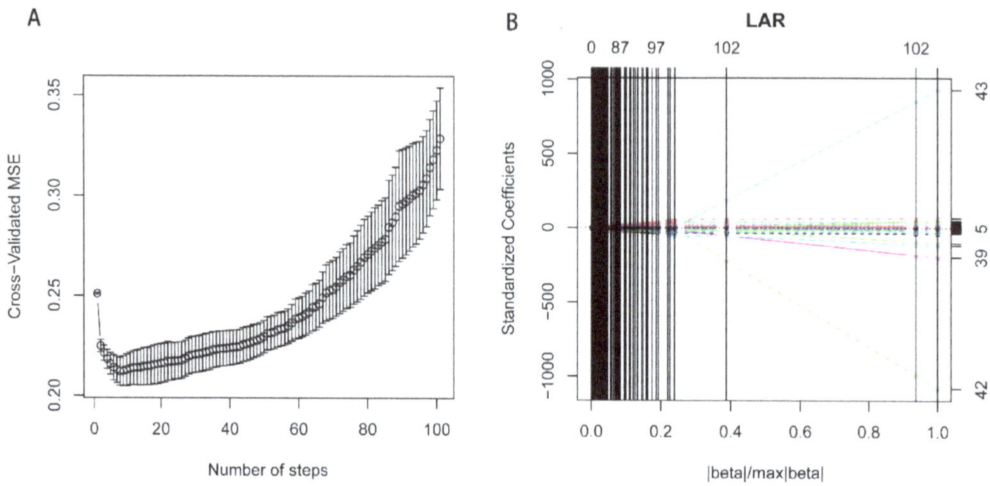

Figure 2. Ten-fold cross-validation least angle regression for feature selection. Figure 2 Plots describing the 10-fold cross-validation least angle regression (cv-LARS) based feature selection process and exhibits the results. (**A**). illustrating the changes in cross-validated Mean Squared Error (MSE) with the number of steps. At the 8th step, the LARS algorithm reaches the minimum MSE. (**B**). exhibiting the solution path plot of 10-fold cv-LARS.

2.4.3. Predictive Models and Control Models

To construct predictive models, we included the selected features along with a PI-RADS score. Three distinct machine learning classifiers, namely logistic regression (LR), random forest (RF), and support vector machine (SVM), were trained to predict the presence of PCa. Starting with the first feature among the seven, we gradually added more features to create multiple models. We compared the performance of these models to determine the optimal one.

In addition, we developed two control models for comparative analysis: a shape control model and a PI-RADS model. The "shape control model" was constructed by setting all non-shape-related features to zero, focusing solely on the impact of ROI shape in predicting PCa. This helped us eliminate the potential biases introduced by manual ROI drawing. The "PI-RADS model" was created using only the PI-RADS score as input variables. This model allowed us to assess the incremental value of radiomic features in predicting PCa beyond the information provided by current criteria, PI-RADS, alone.

2.5. Statistical Analysis

The variables in the training dataset and validation dataset were compared using the Wilcoxon signed-rank test. The performance of three machine learning models was evaluated by sensitivity, specificity, positive predictive value (PPV), and negative predictive value (NPV). The comparison between the different models (LR, RF, and SVM) was evaluated using Receiver Operating Characteristic (ROC) curves. The Area Under the Curve (AUC) was compared using DeLong's test. A two-tail p-value < 0.05 was considered significant. All the statistical analysis and model construction were performed using R version 4.2.2 [21].

3. Results

3.1. Patients

A total of 75 patients with 820 biopsy needles were finally included in this study, as indicated in Table 1. Among these, 363 needles (44.27%) were pathologically confirmed to be malignant, while 457 needles (55.73%) were pathologically proven to be benign. Following the undersampling process, the distribution of the target variable was balanced, with 363 needles (50.56%) classified as malignant and 355 needles (49.44%) classified as benign.

Subsequently, the resampled data were randomly divided into a training group and a validation group, with a ratio of 7:3, as shown in Table 1. The training group consisted of 504 needles, while the validation group consisted of 214 needles. There were no significant differences observed between these two groups in terms of PSA, biopsy outcome, GG, PI-RADS, or MRI results (p = 0.65, 0.98, 0.88, 0.2, and 0.42, respectively, Table 1 and Supplementary Table S1).

3.2. Feature Screening

For feature selection, we utilized the step-forward CV-LARS algorithm on the training set. Ultimately, at the 8th step, LARS achieved the lowest MSE (Supplementary Table S2). As a result, seven relevant features were extracted. The seven relevant features that were extracted are as follows, sorted in the order of inclusion according to LARS: (1) "originalglcmSumEntropy"; (2) "originalgldmDependenceNonUniformity"; (3) "originalfirstorderMaximum"; (4) "originalglrlmRunLengthNonUniformity"; (5) "originalglszmSizeZoneNonUniformity"; (6) "originalshapeSurfaceArea"; (7) "originalshapeMaximum2DDiameterColumn".

3.3. Model Performance

TCIA Dataset

Model construction was performed at each step of the LARS algorithm, and the performance was internally validated according to the TCIA Database as presented in Tables 2 and 3.

Table 2. Performance of different models.

	Variables	AUC	Sensitivity	Specificity	PPV	NPV	p Value (vs. PI-RADS Control) *	p Value (vs. Shape Control) *
LR	Shape Control	0.659 (0.596–0.723)	61.11%	70.75%	68.04%	64.10%	/	/
	PI-RADS Alone	0.701 (0.640–0.763)	67.59%	72.64%	71.57%	68.75%	/	/
	PI-RADS+2 Features	0.835 (0.779–0.89)	74.07%	77.36%	76.92%	74.55%	<0.001	<0.001
	PI-RADS+3 Features	0.838 (0.783–0.894)	76.85%	77.36%	77.57%	76.64%	<0.001	<0.001
	PI-RADS+4 Features	0.835 (0.780–0.891)	76.85%	76.42%	76.85%	76.42%	<0.001	<0.001
	PI-RADS+5 Features	0.833 (0.777–0.889)	79.63%	78.30%	78.90%	79.05%	<0.001	<0.001
	PI-RADS+6 Features	0.840 (0.784–0.896)	81.48%	78.30%	79.28%	80.58%	<0.001	<0.001
	PI-RADS+7 Features	0.841 (0.785–0.896)	81.48%	79.25%	80.00%	80.77%	<0.001	<0.001
RF	Shape Control	0.617 (0.552–0.682)	58.33%	65.09%	63.00%	60.53%	/	/
	PI-RADS Alone	0.701 (0.640–0.763)	67.59%	72.64%	71.57%	68.75%	/	/
	PI-RADS+2 Features	0.776 (0.720–0.831)	84.26%	70.75%	74.59%	81.52%	0.005	<0.001
	PI-RADS+3 Features	0.743 (0.684–0.801)	77.78%	70.75%	73.04%	75.76%	0.220	<0.001
	PI-RADS+4 Features	0.766 (0.709–0.822)	82.41%	70.75%	74.17%	79.79%	0.042	<0.001
	PI-RADS+5 Features	0.766 (0.709–0.823)	80.56%	72.64%	75.00%	78.57%	0.042	<0.001
	PI-RADS+6 Features	0.790 (0.735–0.844)	81.48%	76.42%	77.88%	80.20%	0.008	<0.001
	PI-RADS+7 Features	0.794 (0.740–0.849)	81.48%	77.36%	78.57%	80.39%	0.005	<0.001
SVM	Shape Control	0.655 (0.593–0.728)	55.56%	75.47%	69.77%	62.50%	/	/
	PI-RADS Alone	0.701 (0.640–0.763)	67.59%	72.64%	71.57%	68.75%	/	/
	PI-RADS+2 Features	0.771 (0.714–0.827)	81.48%	72.64%	75.21%	79.38%	<0.001	0.004
	PI-RADS+3 Features	0.780 (0.725–0.835)	84.26%	71.70%	75.21%	81.72%	<0.001	0.002
	PI-RADS+4 Features	0.799 (0.745–0.853)	83.33%	76.42%	78.26%	81.82%	<0.001	<0.001
	PI-RADS+5 Features	0.794 (0.74–0.848)	82.41%	76.42%	78.07%	81.00%	<0.001	<0.001
	PI-RADS+6 Features	0.827 (0.776–0.878)	85.19%	80.19%	81.42%	84.16%	<0.001	<0.001
	PI-RADS+7 Features	0.818 (0.766–0.870)	83.33%	80.19%	81.08%	82.52%	<0.001	<0.001

LR: logistic regression; RF: random forest; SVM: support vector machine; AUC; area under curve; PPV: positive prediction value; NPV: negative prediction value; * Compared by DeLong test.

When comparing with the shape control model, all the models demonstrated significant differences (all $p < 0.001$, except SVM model PI-RADS+2 Features $p = 0.004$, SVM model PI-RADS+3 Features $p = 0.002$). Furthermore, both the six LR prediction models and six SVM prediction models showed significant superiority when compared to PI-RADS alone ($p < 0.001$). Additionally, five out of the six RF prediction models performed better than PI-RADS alone ($p < 0.05$), except for the RF model PI-RADS+3 Features ($p = 0.220$).

Table 3. Comparisons between models' performances by Delong test.

	Models	Shape Control	PI-RADS Alone	+2 Features	+3 Features	+4 Features	+5 Features	+6 Features	+7 Features
LR	Shape Control								
	PI-RADS Alone								
	PI-RADS+2 Features	<0.001	<0.001						
	PI-RADS+3 Features	<0.001	<0.001	0.051					
	PI-RADS+4 Features	<0.001	<0.001	0.935	0.531				
	PI-RADS+5 Features	<0.001	<0.001	0.776	0.339	0.317			
	PI-RADS+6 Features	<0.001	<0.001	0.598	0.879	0.528	0.369		
	PI-RADS+7 Features	<0.001	<0.001	0.539	0.806	0.472	0.329	0.613	
RF	Models	Shape Control	PI-RADS Alone	+2 Features	+3 Features	+4 Features	+5 Features	+6 Features	+7 Features
	Shape Control								
	PI-RADS Alone								
	PI-RADS+2 Features	<0.001	0.005						
	PI-RADS+3 Features	<0.001	0.220	0.164					
	PI-RADS+4 Features	<0.001	0.042	0.688	0.280				
	PI-RADS+5 Features	<0.001	0.042	0.704	0.337	0.993			
	PI-RADS+6 Features	<0.001	0.008	0.553	0.076	0.364	0.317		
	PI-RADS+7 Features	<0.001	0.005	0.401	0.050	0.266	0.350	0.563	
SVM	Models	Shape Control	PI-RADS Alone	+2 Features	+3 Features	+4 Features	+5 Features	+6 Features	+7 Features
	Shape Control								
	PI-RADS Alone								
	PI-RADS+2 Features	0.004	<0.001						
	PI-RADS+3 Features	0.002	<0.001	0.422					
	PI-RADS+4 Features	<0.001	<0.001	0.055	0.148				
	PI-RADS+5 Features	<0.001	<0.001	0.055	0.302	0.317			
	PI-RADS+6 Features	<0.001	<0.001	0.004	0.016	0.106	0.051		
	PI-RADS+7 Features	<0.001	<0.001	0.016	0.066	0.312	0.193	0.155	

LR: logistic regression; RF: random forest; SVM: support vector machine; AUC; area under curve; PPV: positive prediction value; NPV: negative prediction value; PI-RADS: the Prostate Imaging Reporting and Data System. The performance differences between models are exhibited as the Delong test's p-value. The optimal models for each algorithm are highlighted with color coding.

When comparing the different models constructed by the same algorithm and different feature numbers, the model based on LR incorporated 3 radiomic features and yielded AUC = 0.838, sensitivity = 76.85%, and specificity = 77.36%. There are no significant differences in performance among LR models with 3, 4, 5, 6, or 7 features. Since models with fewer features are generally less prone to overfitting, which occurs when a model learns noise and details from the training data that do not generalize well to new data, we selected the LR model with 3 radiomic features as the best LR model for further research due to its simplicity and reduced risk of overfitting. Similarly, the best RF model exploited 2 radiomic features, yielding AUC = 0.775, and the best SVM model exploited 6 radiomic features with an AUC = 0.827 (Table 3).

In the further comparison, both the LR (3 features) model and the SVM (6 features) model showed significantly better predictive value than the RF (2 features) model (Figure 3, compared to the LR model $p = 0.003$, compared to the SVM model $p = 0.01$).

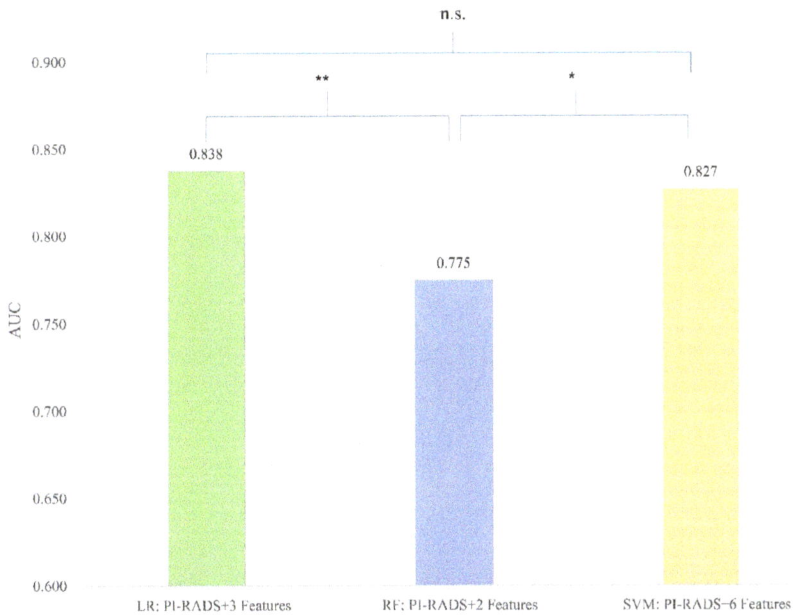

Figure 3. Comparison between best-performing models. Figure 3 column plots showing the area under the curve (AUC) of three best-performing models based on different algorithms. * $p < 0.05$; ** $p < 0.01$; n.s. indicates non-significance.

3.4. HQM Validation Dataset

External validation was performed in the HQM dataset based on eighty-three needles from 8 patients who experienced MRI-targeted prostate biopsy at Hongkong Queen Mary Hospital. The LR (3 features) model was compared to PI-RADS. The radiomics model outperforms PI-RADS in predictive value with AUC 0.870 vs. 0.658, sensitivity 56.67% vs. 46.67%, specificity 92.45% vs. 84.91%, PPV (positive predictive value) 80.95% vs. 63.64% and NPV (negative predictive value) 79.03% vs. 73.77%. Figure 4 is a visualization of the comparison between the LR (3 features) model and PI-RADS for the prediction of PCa.

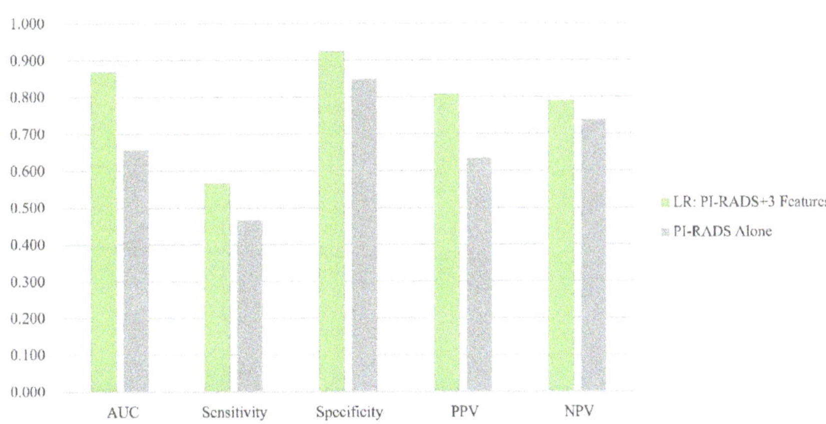

Figure 4. Comparison between the optimal model and PI-RADS in HQM set. Figure 4 column plot showing the area under the curve of the logistic regression model (3 features + PI-RADS).

4. Discussion

This study explored the prospective utility of simulated prostate biopsy using MRI T2-weighted (T2w) images to predict PCa before an actual invasive biopsy. We developed a diagnostic radiomics model based on selected MRI T2w features combined with PI-RADS, demonstrating superior performance compared to PI-RADS alone in predicting PCa.

PI-RADS stands out as the predominant system for standardizing the assessment of mpMRI in the evaluation of potential prostate disease. It classifies lesions into five levels based on their characteristics, offering a relatively standardized protocol for radiologists to interpret prostate MRI images. However, PI-RADS still has some limitations, such as variability in the interpretation of inter- or intra-radiologists with different levels of experience, and the potential features to be imperceptible to the naked eye, leading to unavoidable false-negative predictions. For instance, Moon Hyung Choi et al. reported variations in inter-reader agreements of PI-RADS scores among radiologists, with accuracy ranging from 54.5% to 82.6% and inter-reader agreements ranging from poor to good [12,13]. Moldovan, PC et al. conducted a meta-analysis based on 48 studies (involving 9613 patients) and found that the inter-observer reproducibility of existing scoring systems still requires improvement [22]. Samuel Borofsky et al. discovered that 16% of malignant lesions were missed on mpMRI, with 58% of these lesions either not visible or characterized as benign [23]. Additionally, in terms of MRI-targeted biopsy, Williams et al. noted that most misses are attributed to errors in lesion targeting, underscoring the importance of accurate co-registration and targeting techniques [24].

Radiomics, as a novel methodology, focuses on the quantitative and objective evaluation of medical images. It assists radiologists in achieving precise diagnoses of prostate cancer, thereby reducing the need for unnecessary follow-up procedures [25].

The radiomics research pipeline basically comprises several integral procedures, image preprocessing, feature extraction and selection, model construction, and validation. To enhance image homogeneity, we executed histogram calibration and N4ITK MRI bias correction. Subsequently, we extracted 107 features using the "Pyradiomics" package, adhering to the Image Biomarker Standardization Initiative (IBSI) to enhance robustness. During the feature selection process, we applied 10-fold cross-validation LARS rather than LASSO (least absolute shrinkage and selection operator), which is more commonly used in studies with high-dimensional features [26]. LARS is an iterative algorithm that adds features into the model one at a time based on their correlation with the residuals of the response variable. At each step, LARS adds the feature most correlated with the residuals of the model. The significance of a feature is indicated by how early it is included in the algorithm, as highly correlated features with the outcome are added first. This automated and objective process ensures that the most predictive features are prioritized, so as to mitigate the potential risk of overfitting by gradually incorporating fewer features step by step to meet optimal performance.

Previous studies have proved traditional machine learning algorithms' capability in constructing radiomics models focusing on prostatic areas. Hou et al. developed several radiomics models based on three algorithms, LR, RF as well as SVM to predict lymph node invasive. These models outperformed the MSKCC nomogram and helped to spare a large number of unnecessary extended pelvic lymph node dissections [27]. Zheng et al. trained an SVM model combining manually crafted radiomics features and clinical characteristics to predict biopsy results for patients with negative MRI findings. However, this research only included 330 lesions, with no external validation [28]. Although there have already been encouraging results proving the additional value of radiomics model in prostate cancer diagnosis, to our knowledge, only several studies validated their models in external cohorts [25].

In this study, we utilized the TCIA Database PROSTATE-US-MR Collection, which contains a large number of available recorded biopsy trajectories, corresponding PI-RADS scores, and pathological outcomes. This database enabled us to conduct the lesion-to-lesion study at the needle level, facilitating the training and validation of our models with a large sample size. Based on the 820 lesions from 75 patients randomly selected, we constructed 18 different prediction models by harnessing 3 machine learning algorithms. Remarkably, the LR radiomics model demonstrated optimal performance with the inclusion of only three features. When integrated with PI-RADS, it surpassed the performance of PI-RADS alone in PCa detection, validated both internally within the TCIA database and externally in the HQM cohort.

This outcome aligns with prior research, affirming the additional value of the radiomics model to clinical parameters, particularly PI-RADS. There was a previous study analyzing the correlation between PI-RADS and the radiomic features extracted from prostate MRI images using the qMaZda software (https://qmazda.p.lodz.pl/pms/SoftwareQmazda.html, accessed on 25 July 2024) [29]. Gibała et al. demonstrated that SVM models trained on texture features extracted from mpMRI images can achieve accurate diagnostic performance in detecting PCa. However, it is important to note that their study utilized qMaZda, an older software package that predates the formalization of the IBSI standards. Additionally, due to the limited sample size ($n = 92$), they relied on internal cross-validation without performing external validation. Building on this prior work, we refined our research methodology by splitting the patient-level images into needle-level datasets. This approach allowed us to significantly increase the sample size, thereby enhancing the robustness and generalizability of our results. Moreover, it underscores the capabilities of radiomics even in scenarios of incomplete lesion segmentation. Unlike many previous radiomics studies that manually delineate the complete suspicious region [8,18,25,30–33], our approach demonstrates the potential of radiomics within the biopsy trajectories, which are incomplete segmented lesions. Leveraging the "shape control model", we effectively mitigated potential shape bias introduced by manual crafting. This was evident in the significant difference observed between the LR model and the shape control model. The only three radiomic features incorporated into the LR model, namely "original glcm Sum Entropy", "original gldm Dependence NonUniformity", and "original first-order Maximum", illustrate the texture characteristics of the lesion. Our study indicates a promising future for simulated biopsy in prostate medical imaging, potentially enhancing the utility of the current PI-RADS system. Clinicians may consider conducting a simulated biopsy on MRI images for patients with suspicious PCa, aiding in identifying individuals who genuinely require invasive biopsy procedures. Furthermore, integrating the modeled suspected lesion into MRI-targeted biopsy procedures could enhance diagnostic accuracy. Further external validation in a much larger dataset is essential to evaluate the diagnostic performance and robustness of our model. Additionally, conducting large randomized controlled trials (RCTs) will be necessary to establish the efficacy and reliability of this approach in diverse clinical settings. If validated, this model could be developed into a software program accessible on both PC and mobile devices. Based on the widespread use of online medical imaging tools, such a program could be seamlessly integrated into current clinical workflows. In the future, clinicians, and potentially patients themselves, could simulate biopsy tracks on their devices, reducing the public health burden by minimizing unnecessary invasive procedures.

This study has several limitations. Firstly, only T2w images were incorporated due to the sole availability of this sequence in the PROSTATE-US-MR collection; DWI and ADC sequences were not accessible. Nonetheless, a prior radiomics study concentrating on predicting Gleason grade groups exclusively based on the T2w sequence yielded promising results [34]. Additionally, our model demonstrated robust performance in the external validation set. Nevertheless, for a more comprehensive understanding, further research encompassing multiple sequences is warranted. Secondly, to bolster the robustness and reliability of this model, it is advisable to conduct future multicenter validations with an expanded participant pool and a prospective design. In this study, the dataset was split into training and validation sets comprising 718 images, meaning that some validation lesions could have originated from the same patients present in the training set, potentially introducing bias. To mitigate this issue, we implemented several measures to ensure the independence of each needle track: (1) Biopsy trajectories on MRI images were generated by experienced urologists who were blinded to the pathology outcomes, ensuring unbiased assessments. (2) Rigorous standardization procedures, including histogram calibration and N4ITK MRI bias correction, were applied to all images to minimize variability and enhance data consistency. (3) During model construction, only PI-RADS scores of needle tracks and radiomic features were used, with deliberate exclusion of overall patient characteristics such as PSA or prostate volume. Additionally, we conducted an analysis with the training dataset split by subjects, as detailed in Supplementary Table S5. Following the application of the CV-LARS feature selection process, 10 features were chosen for further model development (Supplementary Table S6, Supplementary Figure S1). The resulting logistic regression (LR) model, which combined PI-RADS with 7 selected features, achieved an AUC of 0.864 (95% CI: 0.807–0.921), with a sensitivity of 81.25% and a specificity of 82.05% (Supplementary Table S7). These metrics surpassed those of the needle-level model. Furthermore, the optimal LR model demonstrated significantly superior performance compared to PI-RADS alone in external validation ($p < 0.001$, Supplementary Figure S2). While the features selected in the subject-based model differed from those in the needle-level model, the overall performance metrics remained consistent, thereby reinforcing the robustness of our original needle-level approach. This validation suggests that our approach is appropriate for the research objectives and does not suffer from significant data leakage or bias. However, for broader clinical applications, it will be crucial to further enhance the model's robustness and generalizability through larger, subject-based independent validation datasets. Lastly, this study exclusively considered PCa as the response variable, and clinical significance (csPCa) was not taken into account. However, previous research on the treatment patterns for PCa in China indicates that only a mere 2.33% of low-risk PCa patients opted for active surveillance or observation, despite AS (active surveillance) being widely recommended for such cases in guidelines [35]. This phenomenon may be attributed to cultural factors making it challenging to accept a malignancy without intervention and the relatively limited access to persistent healthcare and follow-up services.

5. Conclusions

Based on internal and external validation, we demonstrated that the logistic regression model incorporating three MRI T2w radiomic features and PI-RADS performs well in diagnosing prostate cancer. The machine learning and MRI T2w-based simulated biopsy radiomics model add diagnostic value to PI-RADS in predicting prostate cancer. In the prospective future, clinicians may contemplate performing a simulated biopsy on MRI images for patients with suspected prostate cancer, assisting in identifying those who truly necessitate invasive biopsy procedures.

Supplementary Materials: The following supporting information can be downloaded at: https://www.mdpi.com/article/10.3390/cancers16172944/s1, Figure S1: Dataset splitted into train and validation set based on subject level. Ten-fold cross-validation least angle regression for feature selection; Figure S2: Comparison between the optimal model trained based on subject level and PI-RADS in HQM set. Column plot showing the area under curve of the logistic regression model (7 features+PI-RADS). The LR model showed a significant superior performance than PI-RADS alone ($p < 0.001$); Table S1: Train dataset and Validation dataset; Table S2: LARS Steps; Table S3: Performance of different models in TCIA dataset; Table S4: Performance of different models in HQM dataset; Table S5: Train dataset and Validation dataset based on Subject Level; Table S6: LARS Steps based on Subject Level; Table S7: Performance of different models in TCIA dataset splitted based on subject level; Table S8: Comparisons between models' performances by Delong test based on subject level.

Author Contributions: All authors contributed to the study's conception. The methodology was designed by J.-C.L., X.-H.R., D.-F.X. and R.N. Software and Formal analysis were performed by J.-C.L., X.-H.R. and D.H. Resources was prepared by T.-T.C., H.-L.W., C.-T.L., C.-F.T., S.-H.H. and T.-L.N. Investigation was conducted by J.-C.L. and C.Y. Data Curation was performed by J.-C.L., T.-T.C. and C.Y. The first draft of the manuscript was written by J.-C.L. and all authors commented on previous versions of the manuscript. All authors have read and agreed to the published version of the manuscript.

Funding: This work was supported by (1) Shenzhen-Hong Kong-Macau Science and Technology Program (Category C; SGDX20220530111403024), Seed Fund for PI Research at HKU (No. 104006730) to Rong Na; (2) the National Natural Science Foundation of China (grants No. 81972405, No. 82372725, and No. 82173045 to Danfeng Xu); (3) The Science and Technology Commission of Shanghai Municipality (grants No. 20Y11904700, No. 22Y11905400 to Danfeng Xu); (4) Shanghai Sailing Program (No. 22YF1440500) to Dr. Da Huang.

Institutional Review Board Statement: The study was approved by the Institutional Review Board of the University of Hong Kong/Hospital Authority Hong Kong West Cluster (UW20-462, 4 August 2020).

Informed Consent Statement: All participants provided written informed consent to take part in the study.

Data Availability Statement: The HQM datasets generated and analyzed in this study are available from the corresponding authors upon reasonable request. The Cancer Imaging Archive (TCIA) Database PROSTATE-US-MR Collection can be accessed online (https://www.cancerimagingarchive.net/collection/prostate-mri-us-biopsy, accessed on 23 May 2023).

Conflicts of Interest: In the present study, we declare that the authors have no competing interests.

References

1. Siegel, R.L.; Miller, K.D.; Wagle, N.S.; Jemal, A. Cancer statistics, 2023. *CA Cancer J. Clin.* **2023**, *73*, 17–48. [CrossRef] [PubMed]
2. Sung, H.; Ferlay, J.; Siegel, R.L.; Laversanne, M.; Soerjomataram, I.; Jemal, A.; Bray, F.; Bsc, M.F.B.; Me, J.F.; Soerjomataram, M.I.; et al. Global Cancer Statistics 2020: GLOBOCAN Estimates of Incidence and Mortality Worldwide for 36 Cancers in 185 Countries. *CA Cancer J. Clin.* **2021**, *71*, 209–249. [CrossRef]
3. Chen, W.; Zheng, R.; Baade, P.D.; Zhang, S.; Zeng, H.; Bray, F.; Jemal, A.; Yu, X.Q.; He, J. Cancer statistics in China, 2015. *CA Cancer J. Clin.* **2016**, *66*, 115–132. [CrossRef] [PubMed]
4. Cao, W.; Chen, H.-D.; Yu, Y.-W.; Li, N.; Chen, W.-Q. Changing profiles of cancer burden worldwide and in China: A secondary anal-ysis of the global cancer statistics 2020. *Chin. Med. J.* **2021**, *134*, 783–791. [CrossRef] [PubMed]
5. Fanti, S.; Minozzi, S.; Antoch, G.; Banks, I.; Briganti, A.; Carrio, I.; Chiti, A.; Clarke, N.; Eiber, M.; De Bono, J.; et al. Consensus on molecular imaging and theranostics in prostate cancer. *Lancet Oncol.* **2018**, *19*, e696–e708. [CrossRef] [PubMed]
6. US Preventive Services Task Force; Grossman, D.C.; Curry, S.J.; Owens, D.K.; Bibbins-Domingo, K.; Caughey, A.B.; Davidson, K.W.; Doubeni, C.A.; Ebell, M.; Epling, J.W., Jr.; et al. Screening for Prostate Cancer: US Preventive Services Task Force Recommendation Statement. *JAMA* **2018**, *319*, 1901–1913.
7. Schaeffer, E.M.; Srinivas, S.; Adra, N.; An, Y.; Barocas, D.; Bitting, R.; Bryce, A.; Chapin, B.; Cheng, H.H.; D'Amico, A.V.; et al. NCCN Guidelines® Insights: Prostate Cancer, Version 1. 2023. *J. Natl. Compr. Canc. Netw.* **2022**, *20*, 1288–1298.
8. Zhao, L.-T.; Liu, Z.-Y.; Xie, W.-F.; Shao, L.-Z.; Lu, J.; Tian, J.; Liu, J.-G. What benefit can be obtained from magnetic resonance imaging diagnosis with artificial intelligence in prostate cancer compared with clinical assessments? *Mil. Med. Res.* **2023**, *10*, 29. [CrossRef]
9. Ahdoot, M.; Wilbur, A.R.; Reese, S.E.; Lebastchi, A.H.; Mehralivand, S.; Gomella, P.T.; Bloom, J.; Gurram, S.; Siddiqui, M.; Pinsky, P.; et al. MRI-Targeted, Systematic, and Combined Biopsy for Prostate Cancer Diagnosis. *N. Engl. J. Med.* **2020**, *382*, 917–928. [CrossRef] [PubMed]
10. Ahdoot, M.; Lebastchi, A.H.; Long, L.; Wilbur, A.R.; Gomella, P.T.; Mehralivand, S.; Daneshvar, M.A.; Yerram, N.K.; O'connor, L.P.; Wang, A.Z.; et al. Using Prostate Imaging-Reporting and Data System (PI-RADS) Scores to Select an Optimal Prostate Biopsy Method: A Secondary Analysis of the Trio Study. *Eur. Urol. Oncol.* **2022**, *5*, 176–186. [CrossRef] [PubMed]
11. Turkbey, B.; Rosenkrantz, A.B.; Haider, M.A.; Padhani, A.R.; Villeirs, G.; Macura, K.J.; Tempany, C.M.; Choyke, P.L.; Cornud, F.; Margolis, D.J.; et al. Prostate Imaging Reporting and Data System Version 2.1: 2019 Update of Prostate Imaging Reporting and Data System Version 2. *Eur. Urol.* **2019**, *76*, 340–351. [CrossRef] [PubMed]
12. Youn, S.Y.; Choi, M.H.; Kim, D.H.; Lee, Y.J.; Huisman, H.; Johnson, E.; Penzkofer, T.; Shabunin, I.; Winkel, D.J.; Xing, P.; et al. Detection and PI-RADS classification of focal lesions in prostate MRI: Performance comparison between a deep learning-based algorithm (DLA) and radiologists with various levels of experience. *Eur. J. Radiol.* **2021**, *142*, 109894. [CrossRef]
13. Turkbey, B.; Purysko, A.S. PI-RADS: Where Next? *Radiology* **2023**, *307*, 223128. [CrossRef] [PubMed]
14. Bektas, C.T.; Kocak, B.; Yardimci, A.H.; Turkcanoglu, M.H.; Yucetas, U.; Koca, S.B.; Erdim, C.; Kilickesmez, O. Clear Cell Renal Cell Carcinoma: Machine Learning-Based Quantitative Computed Tomography Texture Analysis for Prediction of Fuhrman Nuclear Grade. *Eur. Radiol.* **2019**, *29*, 1153–1163. [CrossRef] [PubMed]
15. Bhandari, M.; Nallabasannagari, A.R.; Reddiboina, M.; Porter, J.R.; Jeong, W.; Mottrie, A.; Dasgupta, P.; Challacombe, B.; Abaza, R.; Rha, K.H.; et al. Predicting intra-operative and postoperative consequential events using machine-learning techniques in patients undergoing robot-assisted partial nephrectomy: A Vattikuti Collective Quality Initiative database study. *BJU Int.* **2020**, *126*, 350–358. [CrossRef]

16. Bonekamp, D.; Kohl, S.; Wiesenfarth, M.; Schelb, P.; Radtke, J.P.; Götz, M.; Kickingereder, P.; Yaqubi, K.; Hitthaler, B.; Gählert, N.; et al. Radiomic Machine Learning for Characterization of Prostate Lesions with MRI: Comparison to ADC Values. *Radiology* **2018**, *289*, 128–137. [CrossRef] [PubMed]
17. Anari, P.Y.; Lay, N.; Gopal, N.; Chaurasia, A.; Samimi, S.; Harmon, S.; Firouzabadi, F.D.; Merino, M.J.; Wakim, P.; Turkbey, E.; et al. An MRI-based radiomics model to predict clear cell renal cell carcinoma growth rate classes in patients with von Hippel-Lindau syndrome. *Abdom. Imaging* **2022**, *47*, 3554–3562. [CrossRef]
18. Ogbonnaya, C.N.; Zhang, X.; Alsaedi, B.S.O.; Pratt, N.; Zhang, Y.; Johnston, L.; Nabi, G. Prediction of Clinically Significant Cancer Using Radiomics Features of Pre-Biopsy of Multiparametric MRI in Men Suspected of Prostate Cancer. *Cancers* **2021**, *13*, 6199. [CrossRef]
19. Bleker, J.; Kwee, T.C.; Rouw, D.; Roest, C.; Borstlap, J.; de Jong, I.J.; Dierckx, R.A.J.O.; Huisman, H.; Yakar, D. A deep learning masked segmentation alternative to manual segmentation in biparametric MRI prostate cancer radiomics. *Eur. Radiol.* **2022**, *32*, 6526–6535. [CrossRef]
20. Szczypiński, P.M.; Strzelecki, M.; Materka, A.; Klepaczko, A. MaZda – The Software Package for Textural Analysis of Biomedical Images. In *Computers in Medical Activity*; Kącki, E., Rudnicki, M., Stempczyńska, J., Eds.; Springer: Berlin/Heidelberg, Germany, 2009; pp. 73–84.
21. R: The R Project for Statistical Computing. Available online: https://www.r-project.org/ (accessed on 29 January 2024).
22. Moldovan, P.C.; Van den Broeck, T.; Sylvester, R.; Marconi, L.; Bellmunt, J.; van den Bergh, R.C.N.; Bolla, M.; Briers, E.; Cumberbatch, M.G.; Fossati, N.; et al. What Is the Negative Predictive Value of Multiparametric Magnetic Reso-nance Imaging in Excluding Prostate Cancer at Biopsy? A Systematic Review and Meta-analysis from the European Associa-tion of Urology Prostate Cancer Guidelines Panel. *Eur. Urol.* **2017**, *72*, 250–266. [CrossRef]
23. Borofsky, S.; George, A.K.; Gaur, S.; Bernardo, M.; Greer, M.D.; Mertan, F.V.; Taffel, M.; Moreno, V.; Merino, M.J.; Wood, B.J.; et al. What Are We Missing? False-Negative Cancers at Multiparametric MR Imaging of the Prostate. *Radiology* **2018**, *286*, 186–195. [CrossRef]
24. Williams, C.; Ahdoot, M.; Daneshvar, M.A.; Hague, C.; Wilbur, A.R.; Gomella, P.T.; Shih, J.; Khondakar, N.; Yerram, N.; Mehralivand, S.; et al. Why Does Magnetic Resonance Imaging-Targeted Biopsy Miss Clinically Signifi-cant Cancer? *J. Urol.* **2022**, *207*, 95–107. [CrossRef]
25. Ghezzo, S.; Bezzi, C.; Presotto, L.; Mapelli, P.; Bettinardi, V.; Savi, A.; Neri, I.; Preza, E.; Samanes Gajate, A.M.; De Cobelli, F.; et al. State of the art of radiomic analysis in the clinical management of prostate cancer: A sys-tematic review. *Crit. Rev. Oncol. Hematol.* **2022**, *169*, 103544. [CrossRef] [PubMed]
26. Wu, M.; Ma, S. Robust genetic interaction analysis. *Brief. Bioinform.* **2019**, *20*, 624–637. [CrossRef] [PubMed]
27. Hou, Y.; Bao, M.; Wu, C.; Zhang, J.; Zhang, Y.; Shi, H. A machine learning-assisted decision-support model to better identify patients with prostate cancer requiring an extended pelvic lymph node dissection. *BJU Int.* **2019**, *124*, 972–983. [CrossRef] [PubMed]
28. Zheng, H.; Miao, Q.; Liu, Y.; Raman, S.S.; Scalzo, F.; Sung, K. Integrative Machine Learning Prediction of Prostate Biopsy Results from Negative Multiparametric MRI. *J. Magn. Reson. Imaging* **2022**, *55*, 100–110. [CrossRef] [PubMed]
29. Gibała, S.; Obuchowicz, R.; Lasek, J.; Piórkowski, A.; Nurzynska, K. Textural Analysis Supports Prostate MR Diagnosis in PIRADS Protocol. *Appl. Sci.* **2023**, *13*, 9871. [CrossRef]
30. Wang, J.; Wu, C.-J.; Bao, M.-L.; Zhang, J.; Wang, X.-N.; Zhang, Y.-D. Machine learning-based analysis of MR radiomics can help to improve the diagnostic performance of PI-RADS v2 in clinically relevant prostate cancer. *Eur. Radiol.* **2017**, *27*, 4082–4090. [CrossRef]
31. Min, X.; Li, M.; Dong, D.; Feng, Z.; Zhang, P.; Ke, Z.; You, H.; Han, F.; Ma, H.; Tian, J.; et al. Multi-parametric MRI-based radiomics signature for discriminating between clinically significant and insignificant prostate cancer: Cross-validation of a machine learning method. *Eur. J. Radiol.* **2019**, *115*, 16–21. [CrossRef]
32. Bleker, J.; Kwee, T.C.; Dierckx, R.A.J.O.; de Jong, I.J.; Huisman, H.; Yakar, D. Multiparametric MRI and auto-fixed volume of inter-est-based radiomics signature for clinically significant peripheral zone prostate cancer. *Eur. Radiol.* **2020**, *30*, 1313–1324. [CrossRef]
33. Rabaan, A.A.; Bakhrebah, M.A.; AlSaihati, H.; Alhumaid, S.; Alsubki, R.A.; Turkistani, S.A.; Al-Abdulhadi, S.; Aldawood, Y.; Alsaleh, A.A.; Alhashem, Y.N.; et al. Artificial Intelligence for Clinical Diagnosis and Treatment of Prostate Cancer. *Cancers* **2022**, *14*, 5595. [CrossRef] [PubMed]
34. Shao, L.; Yan, Y.; Liu, Z.; Ye, X.; Xia, H.; Zhu, X.; Zhang, Y.; Zhang, Z.; Chen, H.; He, W.; et al. Radiologist-like artificial intelligence for grade group prediction of radical prostatectomy for reduc-ing upgrading and downgrading from biopsy. *Theranostics* **2020**, *10*, 10200–10212. [CrossRef] [PubMed]
35. Zhao, F.; Shen, J.; Yuan, Z.; Yu, X.; Jiang, P.; Zhong, B.; Xiang, J.; Ren, G.; Xie, L.; Yan, S. Trends in Treatment for Prostate Cancer in China: Preliminary Patterns of Care Study in a Single Institution. *J. Cancer* **2018**, *9*, 1797–1803. [CrossRef] [PubMed]

diagnostics

MDPI

Article

VerFormer: Vertebrae-Aware Transformer for Automatic Spine Segmentation from CT Images

Xinchen Li, Yuan Hong, Yang Xu and Mu Hu *

Department of Orthopedics, Ruijin Hospital, Shanghai Jiao Tong University School of Medicine, Shanghai 200025, China; leexingchen2011@163.com (X.L.); suppowerhong@163.com (Y.H.); dr_xuyang@163.com (Y.X.)
* Correspondence: 7200012731@shsmu.edu.cn

Abstract: The accurate and efficient segmentation of the spine is important in the diagnosis and treatment of spine malfunctions and fractures. However, it is still challenging because of large inter-vertebra variations in shape and cross-image localization of the spine. In previous methods, convolutional neural networks (CNNs) have been widely applied as a vision backbone to tackle this task. However, these methods are challenged in utilizing the global contextual information across the whole image for accurate spine segmentation because of the inherent locality of the convolution operation. Compared with CNNs, the Vision Transformer (ViT) has been proposed as another vision backbone with a high capacity to capture global contextual information. However, when the ViT is employed for spine segmentation, it treats all input tokens equally, including vertebrae-related tokens and non-vertebrae-related tokens. Additionally, it lacks the capability to locate regions of interest, thus lowering the accuracy of spine segmentation. To address this limitation, we propose a novel Vertebrae-aware Vision Transformer (VerFormer) for automatic spine segmentation from CT images. Our VerFormer is designed by incorporating a novel Vertebrae-aware Global (VG) block into the ViT backbone. In the VG block, the vertebrae-related global contextual information is extracted by a Vertebrae-aware Global Query (VGQ) module. Then, this information is incorporated into query tokens to highlight vertebrae-related tokens in the multi-head self-attention module. Thus, this VG block can leverage global contextual information to effectively and efficiently locate spines across the whole input, thus improving the segmentation accuracy of VerFormer. Driven by this design, the VerFormer demonstrates a solid capacity to capture more discriminative dependencies and vertebrae-related context in automatic spine segmentation. The experimental results on two spine CT segmentation tasks demonstrate the effectiveness of our VG block and the superiority of our VerFormer in spine segmentation. Compared with other popular CNN- or ViT-based segmentation models, our VerFormer shows superior segmentation accuracy and generalization.

Keywords: Vision Transformer; spine CT segmentation; attention mechanism

1. Introduction

Diagnosing and treating pathological diseases demands accurate spine segmentation and vertebrae identification. Vertebral segmentation and identification play a vital role in supporting spine-related clinical workflow, including diagnosing vertebral and spinal deformities and computer-assisted surgical planning [1]. However, manual segmentation by surgeons and radiologists is labor-intensive and time-consuming, motivating the development of automatic and semi-automatic tools [2]. The intricate nature of spine anatomy, characterized by its complex geometry and varying tissue intensities, poses significant challenges to traditional automatic segmentation techniques. However, the advent of deep learning (DL) algorithms has revolutionized the accuracy and efficiency of spine segmentation and vertebrae identification tasks [3,4]. Among various DL-based methods, convolutional neural networks (CNNs) have been widely used, and these CNN-based methods are performed for automatic spine segmentation and vertebrae identification in various medical image modalities, such as Computed Tomography (CT) [5], Magnetic Resonance Imaging (MRI) [6], and X-ray imaging [7]. However, spine segmentation by CNNs from CT images is still challenging. The spine has a complex anatomical structure and variability in the shape and size of the vertebrae. Additionally, the spine is always located across the whole CT image. However, due to the intrinsic characteristics of convolutional operations, CNNs are limited in utilizing image-level global contextual information to capture vertebrae-aware features. Thus, this lowers the capabilities of CNNs on accurate segmentation of the spine from CT images.

Unlike CNNs, the Vision Transformer (ViT) can capture and utilize image-level contextual information [8]. The significant factor in the success of ViT-based models is the application of the self-attention module, which enables them to utilize large receptive fields to capture global contextual information across the entire input image. Thus, this benefits ViTs in serving as a vision backbone for vertebrae segmentation from CT images, but few works are proposing ViT-based methods for vertebrae segmentation. To demonstrate the potential power of ViTs on vertebra and spine segmentation, we propose a ViT-based segmentation method. However, the standard ViT partitions the whole images into tokens and treats these tokens equally as the query in multi-head self-attention modules [8]. Thus, the ViT lacks the capabilities of highlighting vertebrae-related tokens and locating the region of interest in the spine from CT images, leading to the mis-segmentation or under-segmentation of the whole spine.

To tackle this limitation, we propose a novel and efficient ViT-based model for automatic spin segmentation from CT images, termed Vertebrae-aware Vision Transformer (VerFormer). Our method is designed based on employing a novel Vertebrae-aware Global (VG) block to efficiently and effectively capture vertebrae-related contextual information and facilitate the ViT to locate the spine from the whole input image, thus improving segmentation performance. This is achieved in the VG block by incorporating a novel Vertebrae-aware Global Query (VGQ) module. This VGQ module can capture vertebrae-aware contextual information with attention mechanisms and inject this information into query tokens to highlight vertebrae-related tokens based on their attention scores. When these tokens are encoded in the multi-head self-attention module, vertebrae-related tokens with higher attention scores are emphasized, and the spine is located. This mechanism can improve the capabilities of our VerFormer on spine segmentation from CT images. We evaluate our VerFormer for spine segmentation from CT images on two widely used public datasets. Our proposed model achieves superior segmentation performance in spine segmentation compared to other state-of-the-art methods on these two benchmarks. Our contributions can be summarized as follows.

- We propose a novel Vertebrae-aware Vision Transformer (VerFormer) for automatic spine segmentation from CT images. It employs the Vision Transformer as the backbone to utilize image-level global contextual information for accurate spine segmentation.
- We propose a novel Vertebrae-aware Global (VG) block to efficiently and effectively capture vertebrae-related contextual information and facilitate the ViT to locate the spine from the whole input image, thus improving segmentation performance.
- We incorporate a novel Vertebrae-aware Global Query (VGQ) module into the Vertebrae-aware Global (VG) block. This module can highlight vertebrae-related query tokens based on their attention scores when they are encoded in the multi-head self-attention module. Emphasizing vertebrae-related tokens empowers our VerFormer to locate the spine for accurate segmentation.
- We evaluate our VerFormer on two widely used spine segmentation datasets, VerSe 2019 and 2022. It achieves superior performance than other state-of-the-art methods.

2. Related Work

2.1. Vertebra Segmentation by Convolutional Neural Networks

Before deep learning was widely used in medical image analysis, vertebra segmentation was mainly solved by statistical shape models, including active shape models and shape-constrained deformable models [9–14]. In addition, some other traditional methods were proposed for vertebra segmentation, such as atlas-based models [15], level-sets with shape priors [16], and active contours [17,18].

Recently, deep learning-based models have been proposed for vertebra and spine segmentation. Korez et al. used a convolutional neural network (CNN) to generate probability maps for the vertebra regions and then used these maps to generate a deformable statistical model to segment the spine [3]. Sekuboyina et al. used a multi-class CNN to generate labels for the lumbar vertebrae in 2D spine CT slices [19]. Subsequently, these labels were used as prior information, and a multi-layer perception (MLP) was applied to generate a bounding box for the lumbar region and to identify the region of interest from the images. In subsequent work, Sekuboyina et al. designed a 3D patch-based CNN for vertebra segmentation by performing voxel classification from the whole image [4]. To further boost the performance by removing false positives outside the region of interest, a 2D network was used to predict a low-resolution mask for the vertebral region. Lessmann et al. applied a two-stage iterative approach for accurate vertebra segmentation [20]. Specifically, a CNN was used to segment vertebrae in downsampled images iteratively. Then, another CNN was used to analyze the full-resolution images to refine the low-resolution segmentation results. He et al. presented a dual densely connected U-shaped network (DDU-Net) to perform the extraction of multi-scale features and segmentation of different sizes of tissues automatically and precisely for automatic vertebral segmentation in CT images [21]. Liping et al. proposed a lightweight pyramid attention quick refinement network (LPAQR-Net) for efficient and accurate vertebra segmentation from biplanar whole spine radiographs [22].

2.2. Vision Transformer for Medical Image Segmentation

The recently proposed Vision Transformer (ViT) shows great success in computer vision tasks by utilizing a self-attention mechanism to capture long-range dependencies [8]. Because of its promising performance, ViT has been used as a backbone for medical image segmentation. TransUNet was the first ViT-based medical image segmentation model, which combines a ViT encoder with a CNN decoder [23]. Swin UNet was proposed as a pure Transformer-based model for medical image segmentation by incorporating the Swin Transformer block into a hierarchical architecture [24]. Subsequently, UNETR combined a Transformer backbone and a CNN architecture for 3D volumetric segmentation [25]. Similarly, Swin UNETR utilized the Swin Transformer in the encoder for brain tumor segmentation [26]. Following the idea of nnUNet [27], nnFormer was a self-configured ViT-based segmentation model for brain tumor segmentation [28]. CoTr incorporated a Deformable Transformer into a CNN architecture for accurate segmentation [29]. Hiformer was designed as a hierarchical multi-scale ViT-based model for medical image segmentation [30]. AgileFormer was proposed to capture spatially deformable features to improve the performance of medical image segmentation [31]. MS-Former employed a dual-branch Transformer network to encode global contextual dependencies while preserving local information by extracting two different scaled features [32].

2.3. Channel and Spatial Attention

Many methods and modules have been proposed to calculate channel attention to facilitate networks to utilize long-range dependencies. Squeeze-and-Excitation was proposed to model channel-wise inter-dependencies and use these channel attention values to recalibrate channel-wise features [33]. Then, another more efficient channel attention module was proposed to calculate channel attention in an efficient manner [34]. Channel attention is calculated in these independent modules. However, it is also calculated to improve convolution layers in CNNs and local-window-based self-attention in hierarchical ViTs.

The channel-wise inter-dependencies among features from two convolution layers were modeled in selective kernel networks [35] and channel attention networks [36]. Similarly, channel attention is calculated to model inter-dependencies among several convolutional layers [37]. Several methods have also been proposed to calculate spatial attention to enhance the capabilities of networks to model spatial-wise global contextual information. Specifically, spatial-wise attention was modeled in the CBAM [38] and dual attention networks [39]. The spatial-wise inter-dependencies among features from two convolution layers were modeled in spatial dynamic networks [40]. The attention gate was also designed to enable networks to suppress irrelevant regions and highlight salient spatial features by calculating spatial-wise attention values [41].

3. Methods

In this section, we first introduce the overall architecture of our Vertebrae-aware Vision Transformer (VerFormer) in Section 3.1. Then, we demonstrate the architecture of the Vertebrae-aware Global block, which is the basic block of the VerFormer in Section 3.2. This Vertebrae-aware Global block is built by incorporating the novel Vertebrae-aware Global Query module into the multi-head self-attention module. In Section 3.3, we introduce the loss function used for model training.

3.1. Overall Network

The overall architecture of the proposed Vertebrae-aware Vision Transformer (VerFormer) is demonstrated in Figure 1. The VerFormer is built as a U-shaped encoder-decoder architecture and consists of an encoder, a bottleneck, and a decoder. The overall architecture is designed based on a hierarchical Vision Transformer framework to obtain multi-scale feature representations. The basic block of our VerFormer is the Vertebrae-aware Global (VG) block, and two successive blocks are incorporated into each stage. The basic number of channels is $C = 96$, and the numbers of channels in the following stages are 192, 384, and 768. The number of channels in the bottleneck is 768. To extract more features in the deeper layers, the number of heads in the multi-head self-attention module at each stage is 2, 4, 8, and 16, respectively.

In the encoder, given an input image patch with the resolution $H \times W \times 1$, we obtain overlapping patches with the resolution $\frac{H}{2} \times \frac{W}{2} \times 1$ by applying a 3×3 convolutional layer with a stride of 2. Subsequently, these patches are projected onto a C-dimensional embedding space by another 3×3 convolutional layer with stride 2. In this convolutional layer, the dimension of these patches is $\frac{H}{4} \times \frac{W}{4} \times C$. The encoder consists of three stages. At each stage, two successive VG blocks are applied to extract spatial features. Subsequently, a downsampling layer is applied to decrease the spatial resolution by 2 while increasing the number of channels by 2 via a 3×3 convolutional layer with a stride of 2. The dimensions of patches in three stage are $\frac{H}{4} \times \frac{W}{4} \times C$, $\frac{H}{8} \times \frac{W}{8} \times 2C$, and $\frac{H}{16} \times \frac{W}{16} \times 4C$, respectively.

The bottleneck employs two successive VG blocks, which are used to learn the deep feature representations. In the bottleneck, the dimension and resolution of input and output features are kept unchanged as $\frac{H}{32} \times \frac{W}{32} \times 8C$.

We design a symmetric decoder as the encoder for dense prediction. The decoder also consists of three stages. At each stage in the decoder, we first apply an upsampling layer to increase the spatial resolution and decrease the channel number by 2 via a 2×2 transposed convolutional layer with a stride of 2. The dimension of patches is $\frac{H}{16} \times \frac{W}{16} \times 4C$. Then, the upsampled features are concatenated with features from the encoder via skip connections. Subsequently, a 1×1 convolutional layer is used to decrease the number of channels by 2 as $\frac{H}{16} \times \frac{W}{16} \times 4C$. In this stage, two successive VG blocks are applied to extract spatial features. The dimensions of patches in three stages are $\frac{H}{16} \times \frac{W}{16} \times 4C$, $\frac{H}{8} \times \frac{W}{8} \times 2C$, and $\frac{H}{4} \times \frac{W}{4} \times C$, respectively. To recover the feature to the original dimension of $H \times W \times C$, a final projection layer consisting of two transposed convolution layers with the kernel of 2×2 and a stride of 2 is used. Finally, a 1×1 convolutional layer is applied to produce the pixel-wise segmentation prediction.

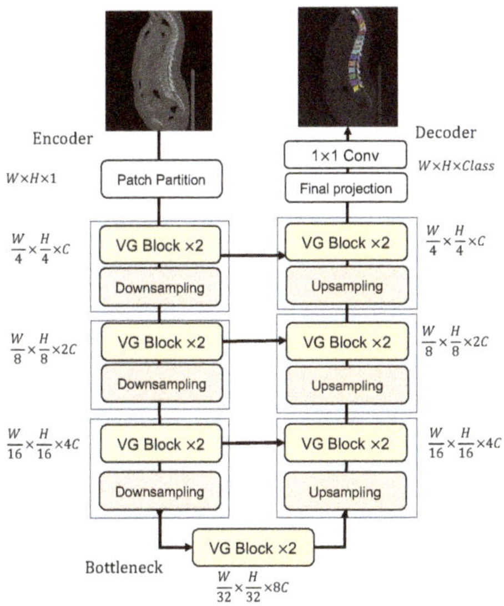

Figure 1. The overall architecture of the VerFormer. It consists of an encoder, a bottleneck, and a decoder. Both the encoder and the decoder consist of three stages, and in each stage, two successive VG blocks are used for learning feature representations. Two successive VG blocks are used in the bottleneck. A 3×3 convolutional layer with a stride of 2 is used for downsampling in each stage, and a 2×2 transposed convolutional layer with a stride of 2 is used for upsampling in each stage. Two 3×3 convolutional layers with a stride of 2 are used for the patch partition. Two 2×2 transposed convolution layers with a stride of 2 are used in the final projection.

3.2. *Vertebrae-Aware Global Block*

Figure 2 demonstrates the architecture of our Vertebrae-aware Global (VG) block. Our VG block is the basic block that is used in our VerFormer to capture vertebrae-aware global contextual features. The multi-head self-attention module is followed by a 2-layer MLP module with GELU non-linearity in between. A Layer Normalization (LN) layer is applied before each self-attention module and each MLP module, and a residual connection is applied after each module.

3.2.1. Vertebrae-Aware Global Query Module

Each VG block employs a Vertebrae-aware Global Query (VGQ) module to extract vertebrae-aware contextual information based on attention mechanisms. Then, this attention information can be utilized to highlight vertebrae-related tokens and suppress non-vertebrae-related tokens. Figure 2 demonstrates the architecture of our Vertebrae-aware Global Query (VGQ) module. Figure 3 demonstrates the mechanism of our Vertebrae-aware Global Query (VGQ) module. In our VGQ module, a channel attention-based module and a spatial attention-based module are both used to extract vertebra-related contextual information. This channel attention-based module cascades a 3×3 depth-wise convolutional layer (DWConv), a GELU activation function, a Squeeze-and-Excitation (SE) module [33], and a 1×1 convolutional layer (Conv). This SE module consists of an average pooling (AvgPool) layer and two fully connected (FC) layers with a ReLU activation function in between. This channel attention-based module can be formulated as Equation (1).

$$\begin{aligned} \hat{x} &= \mathrm{DWConv}(x), \\ \hat{x} &= \mathrm{SE}(\mathrm{GELU}(\hat{x})), \\ \hat{x} &= \mathrm{Conv}(\hat{x}) \end{aligned} \tag{1}$$

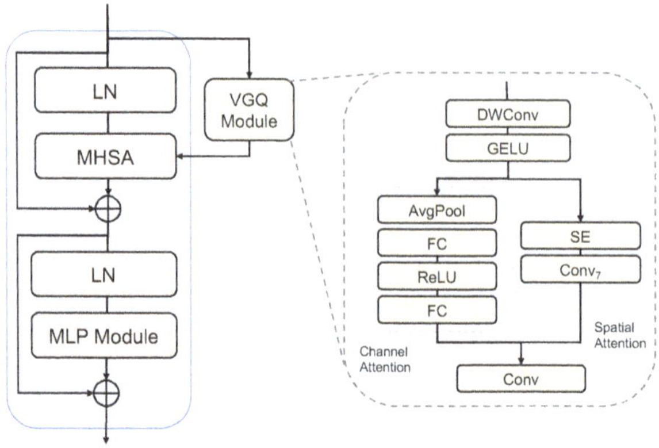

Figure 2. The overall architecture of the Vertebrae-aware Global (VG) block. In the VG block, a VGQ module is utilized to extract vertebrae-aware contextual information to highlight vertebrae-related query tokens. Then, these tokens are encoded in the multi-head self-attention (MHSA) module. In the VGQ module, two parallel paths are employed to extract global vertebrae-aware contextual information, including a channel attention path and a spatial attention path. In the channel attention path, an SE layer is used by cascading an average pooling (AvgPool) layer, a fully connected (FC) layer, a ReLu activation function, and a fully connected (FC) layer.

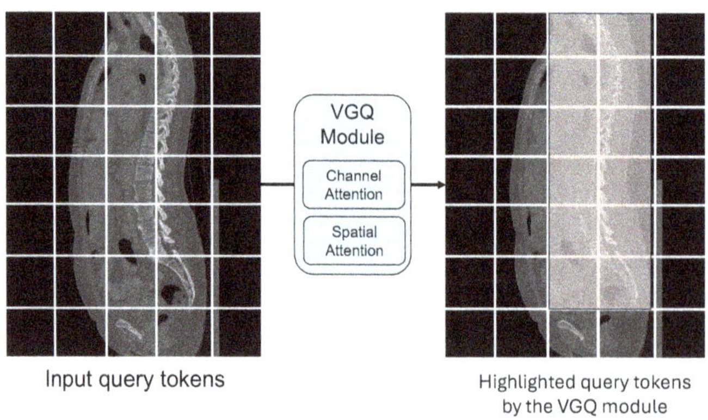

Figure 3. The mechanism of the Vertebrae-aware Global Query (VGQ) module. The input image is partitioned into patches, and these patches are converted into input query tokens. The VGQ module is utilized to extract vertebrae-aware contextual information by channel and spatial attention mechanisms. Then, vertebrae-related patches or tokens are highlighted by this contextual information. Thus, the VGQ module can leverage global information to locate the spine across the whole image, improving the segmentation capabilities of our VerFormer on the spine from CT images.

The spatial attention-based module cascades a 3×3 depth-wise convolutional layer (DWConv), a GELU activation function, an adaptive pooling (AvgPool) layer, a 7×7 convolutional layer (Conv_7), and a 1×1 convolutional layer (Conv). This channel attention-based module can be formulated as Equation (2).

$$
\begin{aligned}
\hat{x} &= \text{DWConv}(x), \\
\hat{x} &= \text{Conv}_7(\text{AvgPool}(\text{GELU}(\hat{x}))), \\
\hat{x} &= \text{Conv}(\hat{x})
\end{aligned} \tag{2}
$$

Features extracted from the channel attention-based module and spatial attention-based module are combined and then reshaped into tokenized features with the dimension $(h * w) \times C$. Subsequently, these are repeated and transformed to generate vertebrae-aware global queries q_v with the dimension of $B \times (h * w) \times C$. This output of our VGQ module is fed into the multi-head self-attention module.

3.2.2. Multi-Head Self-Attention Module

Unlike local self-attention in the Swin Transformer, which can only query patches within a local window [42], our multi-head self-attention (MHSA) module is designed to query vertebrae-related image regions. These vertebrae-related query tokens are generated by capturing global channel attention and spatial attention information in the VGQ module. Specifically, at each stage before the self-attention module, the VGQ module is used to pre-compute Vertebrae-aware Global Query tokens q_v based on global information. Then, vertebrae-related tokens are highlighted by their attention scores. The multi-head self-attention module utilizes the extracted vertebrae-aware global queries to interact with the key and value representations. With this design, our multi-head self-attention module can effectively utilize global information and capture spatial features. Theoretically, the Vertebrae-aware Global Query q_v has a size of $B \times C \times h \times w$, where B, C, h, and w denote batch size, embedding dimension, local window height, and width, respectively. q_v is further reshaped and fed into multi-heads in the self-attention modules, and the value v and key k are then computed using a linear layer. Since the partitioned windows only contain local information [42], utilizing rich global contextual information enlarges the receptive field of the network. Additionally, generating vertebrae-aware global queries provides an effective way of extracting localization information and related regions of vertebrae in the input feature maps. The multi-head self-attention module is computed in Equation (3).

$$Attention(q_v, k, v) = softmax(\frac{q_v k}{\sqrt{d}} + b)v \tag{3}$$

where d is a scaling factor and b is a learnable relative position bias term.

3.3. Loss Function

We employ a combo loss function (Equation (4)), which is a combination of dice loss and cross-entropy loss.

$$\mathcal{L} = \lambda_1 \mathcal{L}_{DICE} + \lambda_2 \mathcal{L}_{CE} \tag{4}$$

The optimal values for λ_1 and λ_2 are 0.6 and 0.4, respectively. Dice loss [43] is employed to measure the dissimilarity between the predicted segmentation and the group truth segmentation of the targeting object (Equation (5)).

$$\mathcal{L}_{DICE} = \frac{2 \times P \times Y + \epsilon}{P + Y + \epsilon} \tag{5}$$

Cross entropy loss [44] is employed to measure the error between two probability distributions of predicted segmentation of the targeting object (Equation (6)).

$$\mathcal{L}_{CE} = -\frac{1}{N}\left[\sum_{i=1}^{N} [p_i \log(p_i) + (1 - p_i) \log(1 - p_i)]\right] \tag{6}$$

4. Results

4.1. Datasets

To validate our segmentation methods, we used two publicly available datasets for automatic vertebra and spine segmentation from CT images, including VerSe 2019 and

VerSe 2020 [45–47]. These two datasets were prepared as vertebral labeling and segmentation challenges hosted at the 2019 MICCAI and 2020 MICCAI, respectively. Both datasets can be used by researchers to evaluate their segmentation models for the segmentation of the spine with multiple conditions, labeled vertebrae, and field of view from CT images. Specifically, the VerSe 2019 dataset includes 160 CT scans from 141 patients with metallic implants or spinal fractures, as well as a combination of isotropic and sagittal reformations. Centroids and segmented masks are provided for all scans, and these segmentation masks are used as ground truth in our experiment. The VerSe 2020 dataset consists of 300 CT scans with manually annotated voxel-wise labels. Scans from this dataset were collected across multiple centers from four different scanner manufacturers. This dataset was enriched with cases that exhibit anatomical variants, such as enumeration abnormalities and transitional vertebrae.

We implemented several pre-processing techniques for the data from two datasets. Three-dimensional scans were resampled to the target spacing of $1 \times 1 \times 1$ mm. Subsequently, voxel intensities were normalized by implementing the max–min normalization technique after being truncated by the percentage $[5\%, 95\%]$. Finally, normalized 3D volumes were prepared into 2D patches with the patch size of 224×224. Before training, several data augmentation techniques were applied. Specifically, patches were rotated with $[-30, 30]$ and scaled with $[0.8, 1.2]$ with both a probability of 0.3. Then, patches were mirrored along the X and Y axes with a probability of 0.5. Gaussian noise with a mean of zero and a variance of 0.1 was added to these patches with a probability of 0.2. Contrasts and brightness were added to pixel intensities in patches with a probability of 0.1.

4.2. Implementation Details

Our VerFormer was implemented based on PyTorch 3.9 and CUDA 11.3. During the training experiments, we used stochastic gradient descent (SGD) as the optimizer with a momentum of 0.99. Models were trained for 500 epochs by an initial learning rate of 0.005 with a poly weight decay factor of 3×10^{-5}. In all experiments, we adopted a batch size of 16. We trained all models on a single NVIDIA GeForce RTX 3090 GPU from the server of Shanghai Jiao Tong University (Shanghai, China) with 24 GB of memory. Similar to other ViT-based segmentation networks [24,26,31], we used the input patches with a resolution of 224×224. Five-fold cross-validation was implemented for evaluation to avoid overfitting and to provide a more accurate estimate of the model's generalization performance.

4.3. Evaluation Metrics

Five evaluation metrics were used to validate the segmentation performance of our proposed model. The dice similarity coefficient (DSC) is the most common and useful evaluation metric for segmentation tasks. It measures the similarity between the prediction mask and ground truth. The mathematical formula for calculating the DSC is shown as Equation (7), where P and Y are the predicted image and the ground truth, respectively.

$$\mathrm{DSC} = \frac{2 \times (P \times Y)}{P + Y} \tag{7}$$

Intersection over union (IoU) is also used to evaluate the performance of our automatic segmentation methods. It is used to compare a predicted mask with a known mask for semantic segmentation. The mathematical formula for the IoU is shown as Equation (8).

$$\mathrm{IoU} = \frac{TP}{TP + FN + FP} \tag{8}$$

Precision is calculated by quantifying the total number of correct positive outcomes made by the proposed model. The mathematical formula for calculating the precision is shown as Equation (9).

$$\mathrm{Precision} = \frac{TP}{TP + FP} \tag{9}$$

The recall is calculated as the total true positive divided by the sum of the true positive and false negative. The mathematical formula for the recall is shown as Equation (10).

$$\text{Recall} = \frac{TP}{TP + FN} \tag{10}$$

The 95% percentile Hausdroff Distance (95HD) is used to measure the maximum distance of the prediction set to the nearest point in the ground truth set. The mathematical formula for the 95HD is shown as Equation (11).

$$95\text{HD} = \max(\max_{x \in X} \min_{y \in Y} ||x - y||, \max_{y \in Y} \min_{x \in X} ||y - x||). \tag{11}$$

4.4. Experimental Results

We compared our VerFormer with 12 state-of-the-art (SOTA) methods. Four methods are CNN-based architecture, including U-Net [48], V-Net [49], Attention UNet (Att-UNet) [50], and nnU-Net [27]. Five methods are hybrid CNN and Transformer architecture, including TransUNet [23], UCTransNet [51], 3D UNETR [25], Swin UNETR [26], and 3D UX Net [52]. Among these methods, UNETR, Swin UNETR, and UX Net are 3D models. Three methods employ pure Vision Transformer as backbones, including Swin UNet [24], MissFormer [53], and AgileFormer-B [31]. We used the default configurations of these models provided in their papers.

Table 1 demonstrates the comparison results of the segmentation performance of our methods and other methods on the VerSe 2019 dataset. In comparison with other vertebra segmentation methods, our VerFormer outperformed previous methods on spine segmentation. Specifically, when compared with widely used 2D CNN baselines, U-Net and VNet, our VerFormer exceeded in performance by over 5% in DSC, IoU, and precision; 6% in recall; and six points in 95HD. Additionally, our VerFormer showed a better segmentation performance than 3D CNN-based models, including Att-UNet and nnU-Net, even though our VerFormer was evaluated as a 2D segmentation method. Moreover, our VerFormer showed a higher segmentation accuracy than other 2D or 3D CNN-Transformer methods with over 1–6% improvements in DSC, IoU, precision, recall, and 95HD points. Finally, our VerFormer had a much higher segmentation accuracy than other Vision Transformer-based segmentation methods, including Swin UNet, MissFormer, and AgileFormer.

Table 1. Comparison of spine segmentation between VerFormer and SOTA methods on the VerSe 2019. Segmentation performance was evaluated by mean DSC (%), standard deviation (SD) in DSC (%), IoU (%), precision (%), recall (%), and 95HD (mm). The best segmentation results are in **bold**. (*: $p < 0.01$ with Wilcoxon signed-rank test between our V-Former and each method).

Backbones	Methods	Mean DSC	SD DSC	IoU	Precision	Recall	95HD
CNN	UNet [48]	88.14	6.01	87.21	93.56	93.11	11.54
	VNet [49]	89.51	5.45	88.03	93.28	92.21	10.63
	Att-UNet [50]	89.97	5.36	90.25	93.68	92.74	10.21
	nnU-Net [54]	93.53	3.24	94.21	98.60	97.34	8.42
CNN+Transformer	TransUNet [23]	91.58	4.75	90.88	95.76	94.89	9.88
	UCTransNet [51]	90.12	4.89	90.42	94.12	93.92	10.02
	3D UNETR [25]	94.21	3.11	95.12	98.78	97.92	5.42
	Swin UNETR [26]	94.02	3.05	94.34	97.42	97.80	5.78
	3D UX Net [52]	94.37	3.02	95.19	98.89	97.96	5.24
Transformer	Swin UNet [24]	90.25	4.66	91.42	96.15	95.85	9.98
	MissFormer [53]	93.52	3.25	92.29	97.11	96.13	8.40
	AgileFormer [31]	94.15	3.17	93.98	98.88	97.41	5.62
	VerFormer (ours)	**95.28** *	2.89	**95.90** *	**99.57** *	**98.45** *	**4.24** *

Table 2 demonstrates the comparison results of the segmentation performance of our methods and other methods on the VerSe 2020 dataset. Similar to the results in the VerSe 2019 dataset, our VerFormer outperformed these baseline methods on spine segmentation from CT images. Specifically, when compared with widely used 2D CNN baselines, U-Net and V-Net, our VerFormer still exceeded in performance by over 4% in DSC, 5% in IoU, 4% in precision points, 5% in recall points, and five points in 95HD. Additionally, our VerFormer also showed a better segmentation performance than 3D CNN-based models, including Att-UNet and nnU-Net (+2.5 DSC, +2.5 IoU, +3.5 precision, +4 recall, and +4 95HD), even though our VerFormer was evaluated as a 2D segmentation method. Moreover, our VerFormerr showed a higher segmentation accuracy than all CNN-Transformers methods, including TransUNet, UCTransNet, 3D UNETR, Swin UNETR, and 3D UX Net. Finally, our VerFormer had a much higher segmentation accuracy than other Vision Transformer-based segmentation methods, including Swin UNet, MissFormer, and AgileFormer.

Table 2. Comparison of spine segmentation between VerFormer and SOTA methods on the VerSe 2020. Segmentation performance was evaluated by mean DSC (%), standard deviation (SD) in DSC (%), IoU (%), precision (%), recall (%), and 95HD (mm). The best segmentation results are in **bold**. (*: $p < 0.01$ with Wilcoxon signed-rank test between our V-Former and each method).

Backbones	Methods	Mean DSC	SD DSC	IoU	Precision	Recall	95HD
CNN	UNet [48]	87.98	6.27	88.45	92.62	92.41	12.56
	VNet [49]	88.11	6.32	87.24	93.45	93.04	11.62
	Att-UNet [50]	89.45	6.11	90.51	94.18	92.88	10.81
	nnUNet [54]	91.45	4.35	91.49	95.04	94.52	9.96
CNN+Transformer	TransUNet [23]	90.44	5.88	91.21	94.32	93.45	9.74
	UCTransNet [51]	90.02	5.21	90.12	93.76	93.16	10.36
	3D UNETR [25]	92.35	4.87	92.67	97.72	97.46	8.88
	Swin UNETR [26]	92.21	4.63	92.35	97.51	97.24	9.02
	3D UX Net [52]	92.73	4.52	92.75	97.81	97.66	8.62
Transformer	Swin UNet [24]	90.01	5.97	91.34	96.18	95.98	10.38
	MissFormer [53]	92.22	4.66	92.29	97.11	96.13	9.05
	AgileFormer [31]	92.64	4.14	92.80	98.02	97.22	8.74
	VerFormer (ours)	**93.98** *	3.21	**94.02** *	**99.10** *	**98.75** *	**5.88** *

5. Ablation Study

In the ablation study, we evaluated how the Vertebrea-aware Global (VG) block improves spine segmentation accuracy over the standard Vision Transformer block. It was implemented by comparing our VerFormerr with the standard ViT. Specifically, the standard ViT was built based on the standard Vision Transformer block by employing the multi-head self-attention (MHSA) module. Thus, we implemented the ablation study by deconstructing VerFormer by removing the VGQ module from the VG block.

The performance of our VerFormer and ViT was compared on two datasets, VerSe 2019 and VerSe 2020, and the results are shown in Table 3. In both datasets, our VerFormer demonstrated much better segmentation performance than the ViT. In these two datasets, our VerFormer outperformed the ViT by over four points in DSC, IoU, precision, and 95HD and five points in recall. Thus, our VerFormer improves the ViT on spine segmentation from CT images by incorporating VG block into it and utilizing the VGQ module to capture vertebrae-aware contextual information for spine localization. Figure 4 demonstrates the segmentation results from our VerFormer and global query tokens from the VGQ module.

Table 3. Comparison of spine segmentation between VerFormer and ViT on the VerSe 2019 and VerSe 2020 datasets. Segmentation performance was evaluated by DSC (%), IoU (%), precision (%), recall (%), and 95HD (mm). The best segmentation results are in **bold**. (*: $p < 0.01$ with Wilcoxon signed-rank test between our V-Former and ViT).

Datasets	Methods	DSC	IoU	Precision	Recall	95HD
VerSe 2019	ViT [8]	90.17	91.12	95.95	95.87	9.99
	VerFormer (ours)	**95.28** *	**95.90**	**99.57**	**98.45**	**4.24**

Table 3. *Cont.*

Datasets	Methods	DSC	IoU	Precision	Recall	95HD
VerSe 2020	ViT [8]	89.86	91.25	96.01	95.72	10.52
	VerFormer (ours)	**93.98**	**94.02**	**99.10**	**98.75**	**5.88**

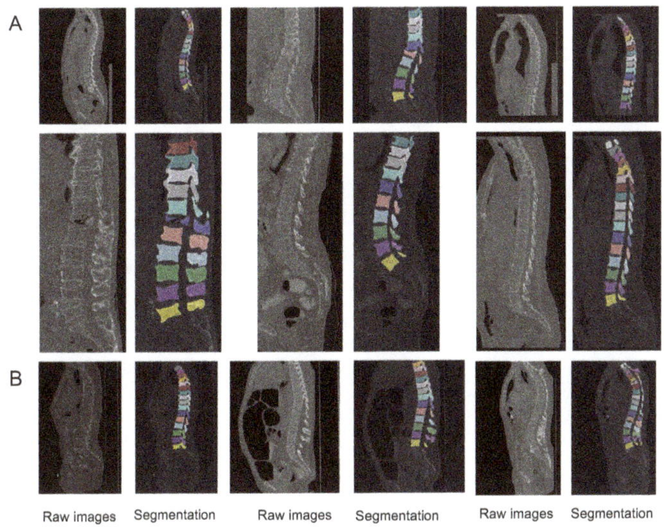

Figure 4. The visualization of segmentation results from our VerFormer. (**A**) The visualization of segmentation results from our VerFormer on the VerSe 2019 dataset. (**B**) The visualization of segmentation results from our VerFormer on the VerSe 2020 dataset.

6. Discussion

Our VerFormer was developed as a 2D ViT-based segmentation model for lower computational complexity. Our VerFormer cannot be developed as a 3D network because of the high computational complexity of multi-head self-attention. Our VerFormer generates tokens from the whole input image to capture image-level global contextual information. Then, features are extracted from these tokens in the multi-head self-attention (MHSA) module. If our VerFormer is designed as a 3D network, 3D tokens will be utilized in the MHSA module, thus leading to high computational complexity and high memory computation. Other 3D ViT-based networks, such as the Swin Transformer [26,42], utilize the local window and create 3D tokens within the window to avoid high computational complexity. However, employment of the local window limits these networks from capturing global information, thus lowering segmentation performance. Additionally, although our VerFormer is designed as a 2D model, it has achieved superior segmentation performance than other 3D methods, such as Att-UNet [41], 3D UNETR [25], Swin UNETR [26], and 3D UX Net [52].

Our VerFormer has high generalizability. It was evaluated on two datasets for spine segmentation from CT images. It can also be employed to spine CT images from other datasets since it is designed to extract data-driven features and can be trained end-to-end. Our VerFormer can also generalize across various medical image modalities. Our VerFormer can be applied to segment organs or lesions from 3D medical image modalities, such as CT and MRI. Additionally, it can also be used for other 2D medical images, such as X-rays and microscopy images. Thus, this 2D configuration improves the generalizability of our VerFormer over various medical image modalities.

The potential limitation of our VerFormer originates from the intrinsic characteristics of the ViT backbone. ViT extracts tokens of a fixed size from input images, and the VGQ module highlights vertebrae-related tokens. Thus, these fixed-sized tokens may limit our VerFormer from learning multi-scale features, and the size of the tokens may influence the segmentation performance. In future work, VerFormer can be improved by employing a dual path that extracts tokens of different sizes. Additionally, VerFormer can also be improved by utilizing an adaptive mechanism to find the optimal size of tokens based on input images.

7. Conclusions

In this paper, we proposed a Vertebrea-aware Vision Transformer, VerFormer, for automatic spine segmentation from CT images. Our VerFormer is designed by incorporating a novel Vertebrae-aware Global (VG) block into the ViT backbone. In the VG block, the vertebrae-related global contextual information is extracted by a Vertebrae-aware Global Query (VGQ) module. Then, this information is incorporated into query tokens to highlight vertebrae-related tokens in the multi-head self-attention module. Thus, this VG block can leverage global contextual information to effectively and efficiently locate spines across the whole input, thus improving the segmentation accuracy of VerFormer. We evaluate our VerFormer on two spine CT segmentation tasks, and experimental results demonstrate its superiority over other state-of-the-art methods.

Author Contributions: X.L.: investigation, formal analysis, validation, writing—original draft. Y.H.: investigation, formal analysis. Y.X.: investigation, formal analysis. M.H.: conceptualization, methodology, validation, writing—original draft. All authors have read and agreed to the published version of the manuscript.

Funding: This research received no external funding.

Institutional Review Board Statement: Not applicable.

Informed Consent Statement: Not applicable.

Data Availability Statement: All data included in this study are available upon request by contact with the corresponding author.

Conflicts of Interest: The authors declare no conflicts of interest.

References

1. Turnpenny, P.D.; Alman, B.; Cornier, A.S.; Giampietro, P.F.; Offiah, A.; Tassy, O.; Pourquié, O.; Kusumi, K.; Dunwoodie, S. Abnormal vertebral segmentation and the notch signaling pathway in man. *Dev. Dyn. Off. Publ. Am. Assoc. Anat.* **2007**, *236*, 1456–1474. [CrossRef] [PubMed]
2. Najjar, R. Redefining radiology: A review of artificial intelligence integration in medical imaging. *Diagnostics* **2023**, *13*, 2760. [CrossRef] [PubMed]
3. Korez, R.; Likar, B.; Pernuš, F.; Vrtovec, T. Model-based segmentation of vertebral bodies from MR images with 3D CNNs. In Proceedings of the International Conference on Medical Image Computing and Computer-Assisted Intervention, Athens, Greece, 17–21 October 2016; Springer: Berlin/Heidelberg, Germany, 2016; pp. 433–441.
4. Sekuboyina, A.; Rempfler, M.; Kukačka, J.; Tetteh, G.; Valentinitsch, A.; Kirschke, J.S.; Menze, B.H. Btrfly net: Vertebrae labelling with energy-based adversarial learning of local spine prior. In Proceedings of the Medical Image Computing and Computer Assisted Intervention–MICCAI 2018: 21st International Conference, Granada, Spain, 16–20 September 2018; Proceedings, Part IV 11; Springer: Berlin/Heidelberg, Germany, 2018; pp. 649–657.
5. Cheng, P.; Yang, Y.; Yu, H.; He, Y. Automatic vertebrae localization and segmentation in CT with a two-stage Dense-U-Net. *Sci. Rep.* **2021**, *11*, 22156. [CrossRef]
6. Peng, Z.; Zhong, J.; Wee, W.; Lee, J.H. Automated vertebra detection and segmentation from the whole spine MR images. In Proceedings of the 2005 IEEE Engineering in Medicine and Biology 27th Annual Conference, Shanghai, China, 17–18 January 2006; IEEE: Piscataway, NJ, USA, 2006; pp. 2527–2530.
7. Al Arif, S.M.R.; Knapp, K.; Slabaugh, G. Fully automatic cervical vertebrae segmentation framework for X-ray images. *Comput. Methods Programs Biomed.* **2018**, *157*, 95–111. [CrossRef] [PubMed]
8. Dosovitskiy, A.; Beyer, L.; Kolesnikov, A.; Weissenborn, D.; Zhai, X.; Unterthiner, T.; Dehghani, M.; Minderer, M.; Heigold, G.; Gelly, S.; et al. An image is worth 16 × 16 words: Transformers for image recognition at scale. *arXiv* **2020**, arXiv:2010.11929.
9. Castro-Mateos, I.; Pozo, J.M.; Pereanez, M.; Lekadir, K.; Lazary, A.; Frangi, A.F. Statistical interspace models (SIMs): Application to robust 3D spine segmentation. *IEEE Trans. Med. Imaging* **2015**, *34*, 1663–1675. [CrossRef] [PubMed]

10. Klinder, T.; Ostermann, J.; Ehm, M.; Franz, A.; Kneser, R.; Lorenz, C. Automated model-based vertebra detection, identification, and segmentation in CT images. *Med. Image Anal.* **2009**, *13*, 471–482. [CrossRef]
11. Korez, R.; Ibragimov, B.; Likar, B.; Pernuš, F.; Vrtovec, T. A framework for automated spine and vertebrae interpolation-based detection and model-based segmentation. *IEEE Trans. Med. Imaging* **2015**, *34*, 1649–1662. [CrossRef]
12. Mastmeyer, A.; Engelke, K.; Fuchs, C.; Kalender, W.A. A hierarchical 3D segmentation method and the definition of vertebral body coordinate systems for QCT of the lumbar spine. *Med. Image Anal.* **2006**, *10*, 560–577. [CrossRef] [PubMed]
13. Mirzaalian, H.; Wels, M.; Heimann, T.; Kelm, B.M.; Suehling, M. Fast and robust 3D vertebra segmentation using statistical shape models. In Proceedings of the 2013 35th Annual International Conference of the IEEE Engineering in Medicine and Biology Society (EMBC), Osaka, Japan, 3–7 July 2013; IEEE: Piscataway, NJ, USA, 2013; pp. 3379–3382.
14. Rasoulian, A.; Rohling, R.; Abolmaesumi, P. Lumbar spine segmentation using a statistical multi-vertebrae anatomical shape+ pose model. *IEEE Trans. Med. Imaging* **2013**, *32*, 1890–1900. [CrossRef]
15. Wang, Y.; Yao, J.; Roth, H.R.; Burns, J.E.; Summers, R.M. Multi-atlas segmentation with joint label fusion of osteoporotic vertebral compression fractures on CT. In Proceedings of the International Workshop and Challenge on Computational Methods and Clinical Applications for Spine Imaging, Munich, Germany, 5 October 2015; Springer: Berlin/Heidelberg, Germany, 2015; pp. 74–84.
16. Lim, P.H.; Bagci, U.; Bai, L. A robust segmentation framework for spine trauma diagnosis. In *Computational Methods and Clinical Applications for Spine Imaging Proceedings of the Workshop held at the 16th International Conference on Medical Image Computing and Computer Assisted Intervention, Nagoya, Japan, 22–26 September 2013*; Springer: Berlin/Heidelberg, Germany, 2014; pp. 25–33.
17. Athertya, J.S.; Kumar, G.S. Automatic segmentation of vertebral contours from CT images using fuzzy corners. *Comput. Biol. Med.* **2016**, *72*, 75–89. [CrossRef] [PubMed]
18. Hammernik, K.; Ebner, T.; Stern, D.; Urschler, M.; Pock, T. Vertebrae segmentation in 3D CT images based on a variational framework. In *Recent Advances in Computational Methods and Clinical Applications for Spine Imaging*; Springer: Berlin/Heidelberg, Germany, 2015; pp. 227–233.
19. Sekuboyina, A.; Valentinitsch, A.; Kirschke, J.S.; Menze, B.H. A localisation-segmentation approach for multi-label annotation of lumbar vertebrae using deep nets. *arXiv* **2017**, arXiv:1703.04347.
20. Lessmann, N.; Van Ginneken, B.; De Jong, P.A.; Išgum, I. Iterative fully convolutional neural networks for automatic vertebra segmentation and identification. *Med. Image Anal.* **2019**, *53*, 142–155. [CrossRef] [PubMed]
21. Tang, H.; Pei, X.; Huang, S.; Li, X.; Liu, C. Automatic lumbar spinal CT image segmentation with a dual densely connected U-Net. *IEEE Access* **2020**, *8*, 89228–89238. [CrossRef]
22. Zhang, L.; Shi, L.; Cheng, J.C.Y.; Chu, W.C.W.; Yu, S.C.H. LPAQR-Net: Efficient vertebra segmentation from biplanar whole-spine radiographs. *IEEE J. Biomed. Health Inform.* **2021**, *25*, 2710–2721. [CrossRef]
23. Chen, J.; Lu, Y.; Yu, Q.; Luo, X.; Adeli, E.; Wang, Y.; Lu, L.; Yuille, A.L.; Zhou, Y. Transunet: Transformers make strong encoders for medical image segmentation. *arXiv* **2021**, arXiv:2102.04306.
24. Cao, H.; Wang, Y.; Chen, J.; Jiang, D.; Zhang, X.; Tian, Q.; Wang, M. Swin-unet: Unet-like pure transformer for medical image segmentation. In Proceedings of the European Conference on Computer Vision, Tel Aviv, Israel, 23–27 October 2022; Springer: Berlin/Heidelberg, Germany, 2022; pp. 205–218.
25. Hatamizadeh, A.; Tang, Y.; Nath, V.; Yang, D.; Myronenko, A.; Landman, B.; Roth, H.R.; Xu, D. Unetr: Transformers for 3d medical image segmentation. In Proceedings of the IEEE/CVF Winter Conference on Applications of Computer Vision 2022, Waikoloa, HI, USA, 3–8 January 2022; pp. 574–584.
26. Hatamizadeh, A.; Nath, V.; Tang, Y.; Yang, D.; Roth, H.R.; Xu, D. Swin unetr: Swin transformers for semantic segmentation of brain tumors in mri images. In Proceedings of the International MICCAI Brainlesion Workshop, Virtual, 27 September 2021; Springer: Berlin/Heidelberg, Germany, 2021; pp. 272–284.
27. Isensee, F.; Jaeger, P.F.; Kohl, S.A.; Petersen, J.; Maier-Hein, K.H. nnU-Net: A self-configuring method for deep learning-based biomedical image segmentation. *Nat. Methods* **2021**, *18*, 203–211. [CrossRef]
28. Zhou, H.Y.; Guo, J.; Zhang, Y.; Yu, L.; Wang, L.; Yu, Y. nnformer: Interleaved transformer for volumetric segmentation. *arXiv* **2021**, arXiv:2109.03201.
29. Xie, Y.; Zhang, J.; Shen, C.; Xia, Y. Cotr: Efficiently bridging cnn and transformer for 3d medical image segmentation. In Proceedings of the Medical Image Computing and Computer Assisted Intervention–MICCAI 2021: 24th International Conference, Strasbourg, France, 27 September–1 October 2021; Proceedings, Part III 24; Springer: Berlin/Heidelberg, Germany, 2021; pp. 171–180.
30. Heidari, M.; Kazerouni, A.; Soltany, M.; Azad, R.; Aghdam, E.K.; Cohen-Adad, J.; Merhof, D. Hiformer: Hierarchical multi-scale representations using transformers for medical image segmentation. In Proceedings of the IEEE/CVF Winter Conference on Applications of Computer Vision 2023, Waikoloa, HI, USA, 3–7 January 2023; pp. 6202–6212.
31. Qiu, P.; Yang, J.; Kumar, S.; Ghosh, S.S.; Sotiras, A. AgileFormer: Spatially Agile Transformer UNet for Medical Image Segmentation. *arXiv* **2024**, arXiv:2404.00122.
32. Karimijafarbigloo, S.; Azad, R.; Kazerouni, A.; Merhof, D. Ms-former: Multi-scale self-guided transformer for medical image segmentation. In Proceedings of the Medical Imaging with Deep Learning. PMLR 2024, Paris, France, 3–5 July 2024; pp. 680–694.
33. Hu, J.; Shen, L.; Sun, G. Squeeze-and-excitation networks. In Proceedings of the IEEE Conference on Computer Vision and Pattern Recognition 2018, Salt Lake City, UT, USA, 18–23 June 2018; pp. 7132–7141.

34. Wang, Q.; Wu, B.; Zhu, P.; Li, P.; Zuo, W.; Hu, Q. ECA-Net: Efficient channel attention for deep convolutional neural networks. In Proceedings of the IEEE/CVF Conference on Computer Vision and Pattern Recognition 2020, Seattle, WA, USA, 13–19 June 2020; pp. 11534–11542.
35. Li, X.; Wang, W.; Hu, X.; Yang, J. Selective kernel networks. In Proceedings of the IEEE/CVF Conference on Computer Vision and Pattern Recognition 2019, Long Beach, CA, USA, 15–20 June 2019; pp. 510–519.
36. Bastidas, A.A.; Tang, H. Channel attention networks. In Proceedings of the IEEE/CVF Conference on Computer Vision and Pattern Recognition Workshops 2019, Long Beach, CA, USA, 15–20 June 2019.
37. Chen, Y.; Dai, X.; Liu, M.; Chen, D.; Yuan, L.; Liu, Z. Dynamic convolution: Attention over convolution kernels. In Proceedings of the IEEE/CVF Conference on Computer Vision and Pattern Recognition 2020, Seattle, WA, USA, 13–19 June 2020; pp. 11030–11039.
38. Woo, S.; Park, J.; Lee, J.Y.; Kweon, I.S. Cbam: Convolutional block attention module. In Proceedings of the European Conference on Computer Vision (ECCV) 2018, Munich, Germany, 8–14 September 2018; pp. 3–19.
39. Fu, J.; Liu, J.; Tian, H.; Li, Y.; Bao, Y.; Fang, Z.; Lu, H. Dual attention network for scene segmentation. In Proceedings of the IEEE/CVF Conference on Computer Vision and Pattern Recognition 2019, Long Beach, CA, USA, 15–20 June 2019; pp. 3146–3154.
40. Yang, J.; Qiu, P.; Zhang, Y.; Marcus, D.S.; Sotiras, A. D-Net: Dynamic Large Kernel with Dynamic Feature Fusion for Volumetric Medical Image Segmentation. *arXiv* **2024**, arXiv:2403.10674.
41. Oktay, O.; Schlemper, J.; Folgoc, L.L.; Lee, M.; Heinrich, M.; Misawa, K.; Mori, K.; McDonagh, S.; Hammerla, N.Y.; Kainz, B.; et al. Attention u-net: Learning where to look for the pancreas. *arXiv* **2018**, arXiv:1804.03999.
42. Liu, Z.; Lin, Y.; Cao, Y.; Hu, H.; Wei, Y.; Zhang, Z.; Lin, S.; Guo, B. Swin transformer: Hierarchical vision transformer using shifted windows. In Proceedings of the IEEE/CVF International Conference on Computer Vision 2021, Montreal, QC, Canada, 10–17 October 2021; pp. 10012–10022.
43. Sudre, C.H.; Li, W.; Vercauteren, T.; Ourselin, S.; Jorge Cardoso, M. Generalised dice overlap as a deep learning loss function for highly unbalanced segmentations. In Proceedings of the Deep Learning in Medical Image Analysis and Multimodal Learning for Clinical Decision Support: Third International Workshop, DLMIA 2017, and 7th International Workshop, ML-CDS 2017, Held in Conjunction with MICCAI 2017, Québec, QC, Canada, 14 September 2017; Proceedings 3; Springer: Berlin/Heidelberg, Germany, 2017; pp. 240–248.
44. Zhang, Z.; Sabuncu, M. Generalized cross entropy loss for training deep neural networks with noisy labels. *Adv. Neural Inf. Process. Syst.* **2018**, *31*, 8792–8802.
45. Sekuboyina, A.; Husseini, M.E.; Bayat, A.; Löffler, M.; Liebl, H.; Li, H.; Tetteh, G.; Kukačka, J.; Payer, C.; Štern, D.; et al. VerSe: A Vertebrae labelling and segmentation benchmark for multi-detector CT images. *Med. Image Anal.* **2021**, *73*, 102166. [CrossRef] [PubMed]
46. Löffler, M.T.; Sekuboyina, A.; Jacob, A.; Grau, A.L.; Scharr, A.; El Husseini, M.; Kallweit, M.; Zimmer, C.; Baum, T.; Kirschke, J.S. A vertebral segmentation dataset with fracture grading. *Radiol. Artif. Intell.* **2020**, *2*, e190138. [CrossRef] [PubMed]
47. Sekuboyina, A.; Rempfler, M.; Valentinitsch, A.; Menze, B.H.; Kirschke, J.S. Labeling vertebrae with two-dimensional reformations of multidetector CT images: An adversarial approach for incorporating prior knowledge of spine anatomy. *Radiol. Artif. Intell.* **2020**, *2*, e190074. [CrossRef]
48. Ronneberger, O.; Fischer, P.; Brox, T. U-net: Convolutional networks for biomedical image segmentation. In Proceedings of the Medical Image Computing and Computer-Assisted Intervention–MICCAI 2015: 18th International Conference, Munich, Germany, 5–9 October 2015; Proceedings, part III 18; Springer: Berlin/Heidelberg, Germany, 2015; pp. 234–241.
49. Milletari, F.; Navab, N.; Ahmadi, S.A. V-net: Fully convolutional neural networks for volumetric medical image segmentation. In Proceedings of the 2016 Fourth International Conference on 3D Vision (3DV), Stanford, CA, USA, 25–28 October 2016; IEEE: Piscataway, NJ, USA, 2016; pp. 565–571.
50. Schlemper, J.; Oktay, O.; Schaap, M.; Heinrich, M.; Kainz, B.; Glocker, B.; Rueckert, D. Attention gated networks: Learning to leverage salient regions in medical images. *Med. Image Anal.* **2019**, *53*, 197–207. [CrossRef]
51. Wang, H.; Cao, P.; Wang, J.; Zaiane, O.R. Uctransnet: Rethinking the skip connections in u-net from a channel-wise perspective with transformer. In Proceedings of the AAAI Conference on Artificial Intelligence 2022, Philadelphia, PA, USA, 27 February–2 March 2022; Volume 36, pp. 2441–2449.
52. Lee, H.H.; Bao, S.; Huo, Y.; Landman, B.A. 3d ux-net: A large kernel volumetric convnet modernizing hierarchical transformer for medical image segmentation. *arXiv* **2022**, arXiv:2209.15076.
53. Huang, X.; Deng, Z.; Li, D.; Yuan, X. Missformer: An effective medical image segmentation transformer. *arXiv* **2021**, arXiv:2109.07162.
54. Çiçek, Ö.; Abdulkadir, A.; Lienkamp, S.S.; Brox, T.; Ronneberger, O. 3D U-Net: Learning dense volumetric segmentation from sparse annotation. In Proceedings of the Medical Image Computing and Computer-Assisted Intervention–MICCAI 2016: 19th International Conference, Athens, Greece, 17–21 October 2016, Proceedings, Part II 19; Springer: Berlin/Heidelberg, Germany, 2016; pp. 424–432.

diagnostics

MDPI

Article

EpidermaQuant: Unsupervised Detection and Quantification of Epidermal Differentiation Markers on H-DAB-Stained Images of Reconstructed Human Epidermis

Dawid Zamojski [1,2], Agnieszka Gogler [3], Dorota Scieglinska [3] and Michal Marczyk [1,4,*]

1 Department of Data Science and Engineering, Silesian University of Technology, 44-100 Gliwice, Poland; dawid.zamojski@polsl.pl
2 Genetic Laboratory, Gyncentrum Sp. z o.o., 41-208 Sosnowiec, Poland
3 Center for Translational Research and Molecular Biology of Cancer, Maria Sklodowska-Curie National Research Institute of Oncology Gliwice Branch, 44-102 Gliwice, Poland; agnieszka.gogler@gliwice.nio.gov.pl (A.G.); dorota.scieglinska@gliwice.nio.gov.pl (D.S.)
4 Yale Cancer Center, Yale School of Medicine, New Haven, CT 06510, USA
* Correspondence: michal.marczyk@polsl.pl

Abstract: The integrity of the reconstructed human epidermis generated in vitro can be assessed using histological analyses combined with immunohistochemical staining of keratinocyte differentiation markers. Technical differences during the preparation and capture of stained images may influence the outcome of computational methods. Due to the specific nature of the analyzed material, no annotated datasets or dedicated methods are publicly available. Using a dataset with 598 unannotated images showing cross-sections of in vitro reconstructed human epidermis stained with DAB-based immunohistochemistry reaction to visualize four different keratinocyte differentiation marker proteins (filaggrin, keratin 10, Ki67, HSPA2) and counterstained with hematoxylin, we developed an unsupervised method for the detection and quantification of immunohistochemical staining. The pipeline consists of the following steps: (i) color normalization; (ii) color deconvolution; (iii) morphological operations; (iv) automatic image rotation; and (v) clustering. The most effective combination of methods includes (i) Reinhard's normalization; (ii) Ruifrok and Johnston color-deconvolution method; (iii) proposed image-rotation method based on boundary distribution of image intensity; and (iv) k-means clustering. The results of the work should enhance the performance of quantitative analyses of protein markers in reconstructed human epidermis samples and enable the comparison of their spatial distribution between different experimental conditions.

Keywords: immunohistochemistry; DAB-stained images; image pre-processing; segmentation; unsupervised methods

1. Introduction

Immunohistochemistry (IHC) allows the visualization of specific proteins in fixed tissue sections. It involves the application of antibodies specific to a target antigen, which ultimately allows microscopic observations of the antigen–antibody complex in situ [1]. The so-called secondary antibody that can be conjugated to an enzyme, such as horseradish peroxidase (HRP), is used to visualize antigen–antibody binding in DAB (3,3′-Diaminobenzidine)-mediated IHC staining. HRP oxidizes DAB and converts it into an insoluble brown precipitate [1]. The presence and localization of brown staining in tissue can be evaluated and imaged using a light microscope [2]. The use of quantitative digital analysis of images obtained by IHC staining is crucial for basic biomedical researchers and as a diagnostic tool in pathology [3]. The application of deep-learning and machine-learning algorithms for the analysis of IHC protein markers has been tested in precision medicine for the analysis of diagnostic biomarkers in pathological conditions such as malignant cancers (breast, prostate, lung), melanocytic proliferations, and hematologic conditions [4]. For example, routine molecular diagnostics of breast cancer [5] can be improved by deep-neural-network algorithms to help with the IHC analysis of biomarkers (estrogen receptor, progesterone receptor, epidermal growth factor receptor 2, and Ki67) [6–11]. Computational tools for the detection of IHC-stained epithelial-type biomarkers [12] to discriminate between benign, in situ, and malignant breast lesions are limited (if any), but for this purpose, several algorithms developed for slides stained with hematoxylin and eosin (H&E) can be adopted [13,14]. Quantitative IHC assessment is also important for basic research; e.g., it can provide a quantitative assessment of protein markers in tissue-like (organotypic) cultures generated using 3D-in vitro-cell-culture techniques. For example, the in vitro reconstructed human epidermis (RHE) is considered a representative and sufficient model of the human epidermis. RHEs can be obtained by culturing keratinocytes at the air–liquid interface on a collagen–fibroblast matrix. Such a 3D-in vitro cell culture is a valuable tool to study the impact of selected gene products on the integrity and function of the human epidermis [3].

The preparation of IHC slides, the method of image acquisition, technical differences during image capturing, and the presence of various artifacts are the main challenges in computational detection and segmentation of DAB-stained areas. The solution to this problem is to use an unsupervised algorithm for processing IHC images. Compared to the frequently used H&E-stained samples, the colors of DAB-stained samples are less consistent, which is considered a major problem in fully automated image processing systems. In addition, a multitude of obstacles and limitations make it difficult for both the specialist and the algorithm to produce consistent results [15]. The variability in shape, size, and color of interesting objects, the lack of clear criteria for cell type identification, and the presence of overlapping structures should be mentioned as the main difficulties. An effective image pre-processing concept should overcome all these limitations to ensure high quality and accuracy in the studies performed, especially clinical ones. With the help of computer-assisted evaluation of digital images of IHC-stained tissue (such as bioptates), a quick and more accurate prognosis or a new understanding of the mechanism of the disease is possible.

A variety of techniques have been proposed to segment and quantify tissue stained with H&E and stored as digital images [16]. Studies related to DAB staining are still limited. Patel et al. used the Otsu method for negative control slides to define the threshold that distinguishes tissue from the background, and all pixels considered tissue were evaluated for normalized red-minus-blue (NRMB) color intensity. Then, a user-defined error tolerance was applied to the negative control slides to set the NRMB threshold, distinguishing DAB-stained from unstained tissue. This threshold was used to calculate the pixel fraction of DAB-stained tissue on each test slide [17]. Bencze et al. compared semi-quantitative scoring and digital analysis of DAB-stained images using a Convolutional Neural Network. Semi-quantitative scoring was carried out using a four-point scale based on the IHC intensity of the cells. Users might submit images, which were then analyzed to determine whether the algorithm had correctly recognized the objects or if manual annotation of points of interest was required [18]. Eszter Sziva et al. proposed a mechanism for quantitative histomorphometric-mathematical image analysis of DAB-stained tissue as support in andrology and reproductive medicine. The quantitative analysis was based on the use of features such as area, circumference, and cross-sectional diameter of stained testes [19]. Roszkowiak et al. described a comprehensive system capable of quantifying digitized DAB&H-stained breast cancer tissue samples at different intensities. The researchers introduced segmentation based on regions of interest, as well as a step of dividing a cluster of nuclei, followed by boundary enhancement. The system used machine learning and local recursive processing to eliminate distorted and inaccurate regions of interest [15]. Deep-learning methods are gradually overtaking classical image-processing methods that deal with feature space partitioning. This is particularly evident in images where the features of objects are uncertain and variable, as is the case of IHC-stained tissue images [20,21]. Some

IHC image analysis methods have been developed and made available as freeware, for example, QuPath v0.5.1 or ImageJ version 1.54j software [22,23].

Here, we developed an unsupervised method for detecting protein markers of human epidermal keratinocyte differentiation on IHC images. The need to develop a new method was mainly due to (i) technological limitations of current IHC image-processing methods, which are not dedicated to epidermal images; (ii) problems with the structural complexity of the 3D tissue-like models resulting from their culture methodology; (iii) significant variability in the structure and shape of the areas of interest between the analyzed images, resulting from the specificity of the cell growth in the post-confluent cell density. We tested the effectiveness of various methods for pre-processing and segmentation of IHC-stained epidermal differentiation markers, proposed our solutions, and summarized the best methods into a freely available pipeline.

2. Materials and Methods

2.1. Data

The dataset consisted of 598 unannotated .jpg images (1936 × 1460 pixels) containing formalin-fixed and paraffin-embedded sections of in vitro reconstructed human epidermis, tissue-like structures generated by 3D culture in vitro of immortalized epidermal keratinocyte HaCaT line. Samples were processed by immunohistochemistry and subsequently stained using an antigen-specific primary antibody and an appropriate secondary antibody. After visualization of antigen–antibody binding by DAB-mediated reaction, cell nuclei were counterstained with hematoxylin (see examples in Figure 1). The details on tissue processing and IHC protocols are described in Gogler-Piglowska et al. [24]. Nine biological repeats in the form of positive control (specimens that contained the target molecule in its expected location and enabled the visualization of histomorphology) and negative control without primary antibodies (to confirm the specificity of the IHC staining) were prepared [25]. Four selected proteins (filaggrin (FLG), keratin 10 (K10), Ki67 protein (Ki67), and HSPA2 protein (HSPA2)) considered as markers of keratinocyte differentiation which are present in individual layers of the epidermis, indicative of epidermal development, were analyzed. The number of images per marker was as follows: FLG—189 images (163 positive and 26 negative controls); K10—131 images (113 positive and 18 negative controls); Ki67—96 images (96 positive and 0 negative controls); HSPA2—182 images (124 positive and 58 negative controls). Methods were tested using images of FLG, K10, and Ki67 markers, and the final pipeline was visually tested using HSPA2 marker data. Images were captured using a ZEISS AXIOCAM 503 color camera (Zeiss, Oberkochen, Germany) with a ZEN 2.6 photo archiving system at 40× magnification. Data preparation and scanning was done at the Center for Translational Research and Molecular Biology of Cancer, Maria Sklodowska-Curie National Research Institute of Oncology Gliwice Branch, Poland.

2.2. Color Normalization and Deconvolution

Reinhard's method, normalization by RGB histogram specification, and Macenko's method were tested as the implementation of the non-linear staining normalization algorithms [26]. Reinhard's method involved applying the mat2gray transformation to improve results. This operation converts a matrix to a grayscale image and stretches the histogram intensity values from 0 to 1. Then, to transform stained biological samples into images representing the concentrations of individual stains, color deconvolution was performed [27]. The method by Ruifrok and Johnston with different sets of parameters was used: (i) from the ImageJ Color Deconvolution 2 plug in; and (ii) from the Python scikit-image implementation (see details in the Supplementary Materials) [28].

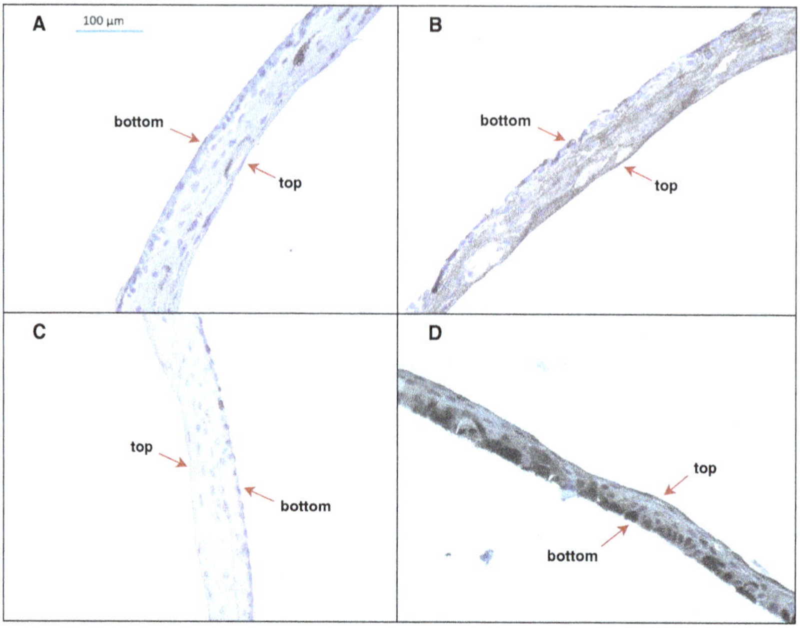

Figure 1. An example of IHC images of reconstructed human epidermis stained for: (**A**)—FLG marker; (**B**)—K10 marker; (**C**)—Ki67 marker; (**D**)—HSPA2 marker.

2.3. *Background Detection and Mask Creation*

The image on which Otsu's binarization method was performed was a greyscale hematoxylin channel. Morphological operations were implemented to remove noise and unnecessary regions in the specimen, including the image background. Morphological operations were applied in the following sequence: opening, closing, and hole filling. Opening removed unconnected light objects that were smaller than the structuring element (SE), while closing removed unconnected dark objects that were smaller than the SE. The SE was a disk with a radius of 15. The filling holes operation completed the background, that is, the empty spaces between pixels close to each other. Subsequently, artifacts were discarded by selecting the largest area of the tissue slide on a previously created black and white mask. In the end, the morphological operations were used once again to improve the quality of the results.

2.4. *Image Rotation and Crop*

Two methods of image rotation were tested: (i) the Hough transform and (ii) the proposed image rotation method based on the boundary distributions of pixel intensities.

The principle of the Hough transform is based on the spatially transformed points so that the lines in the image are represented by points in Hough space. Then, by analyzing the relationships between the points in Hough space, the algorithm can identify the lines in the image. The Hough space contains parameters that describe the shape being searched for. For example, to detect a straight line in an image, the Hough space is two-dimensional and consists of the angle of the line and the distance of that line from the origin of the coordinate system [29].

The proposed image rotation method automatically rotates the tissue to a horizontal position based on maximizing the boundary pixel intensities. The boundary intensity distribution is calculated as the sum of the intensities of the pixels in each row. When the orientation of the tissue is horizontal, the intensity distribution reaches maximum values, which allows the algorithm to accurately arrange the tissue to a horizontal position. The proposed algorithm is summarized in the following steps:

- The tissue mask (negation of background mask) is used as the input;
- The mask is rotated from 1 to 180 degrees with a step of 0.1 degrees;
- For each rotation position, the sum of pixels in each row of the mask is calculated to create boundary intensity distribution;
- For each rotation position, the maximum value of the boundary intensity distribution is found;
- The final rotation position is the one that maximizes the maximum value of the boundary intensity.

2.5. *Elimination of Images without DAB Stain*

To prevent the segmentation of images without DAB staining, an average proportion (AP) measure was introduced. The determination of minimum staining level was carried out for a set of images representing the FLG marker as the most difficult to analyze. The result for an individual DAB channel image was expressed as a percentage of the number of pixels passing the condition to the total number of pixels in the image:

$$\mathrm{AP} = \frac{\text{no. of pixels} < \text{threshold}}{\text{total number of pixels}} \times 100\ [\%] \quad (1)$$

To determine the appropriate threshold and the value of the average proportion, which is a determinant of the elimination of images without DAB stain, ROC curve analysis was performed, and the Youden index was calculated. The threshold for AP was searched in the range from 0.1 to 1% with a step of 0.01.

2.6. *DAB Region Segmentation*

Segmentation algorithms in the context of IHC imaging can be used to find areas stained with particular stains. From the existing segmentation methods, the k-means clustering algorithm was selected due to its efficiency and simplicity [30]. The process was divided into several steps: (i) reshape the DAB image into a new matrix retaining the original data; (ii) normalize DAB image channels independently using the mean and standard deviation; (iii) estimate the number of clusters using the Davies–Bouldin method, based on the ratio of distances within a cluster and between clusters in the range from 1 to 3; (iv) k-means clustering; (v) mask DAB image using obtained clusters; and (vi) arrange clusters from the darkest using the average DAB intensity per cluster.

2.7. *EpidermaQuant Framework*

The final pipeline for analysis was based on the custom algorithm written in the MATLAB® R2021b programming environment (see Supplementary Materials; Supplementary Figure S1). The algorithm is publicly available here: https://github.com/DawZam/EpidermaQuant (accessed on 28 August 2024).

3. Results

The analyzed pre-processing steps include image normalization, color deconvolution, background removal, and image rotation. Then, the image is segmented using the k-means clustering method. We tested selected methods, and the best algorithms chosen by visual investigation of resulting images by experts were implemented in the EpidermaQuant framework (Figure 2).

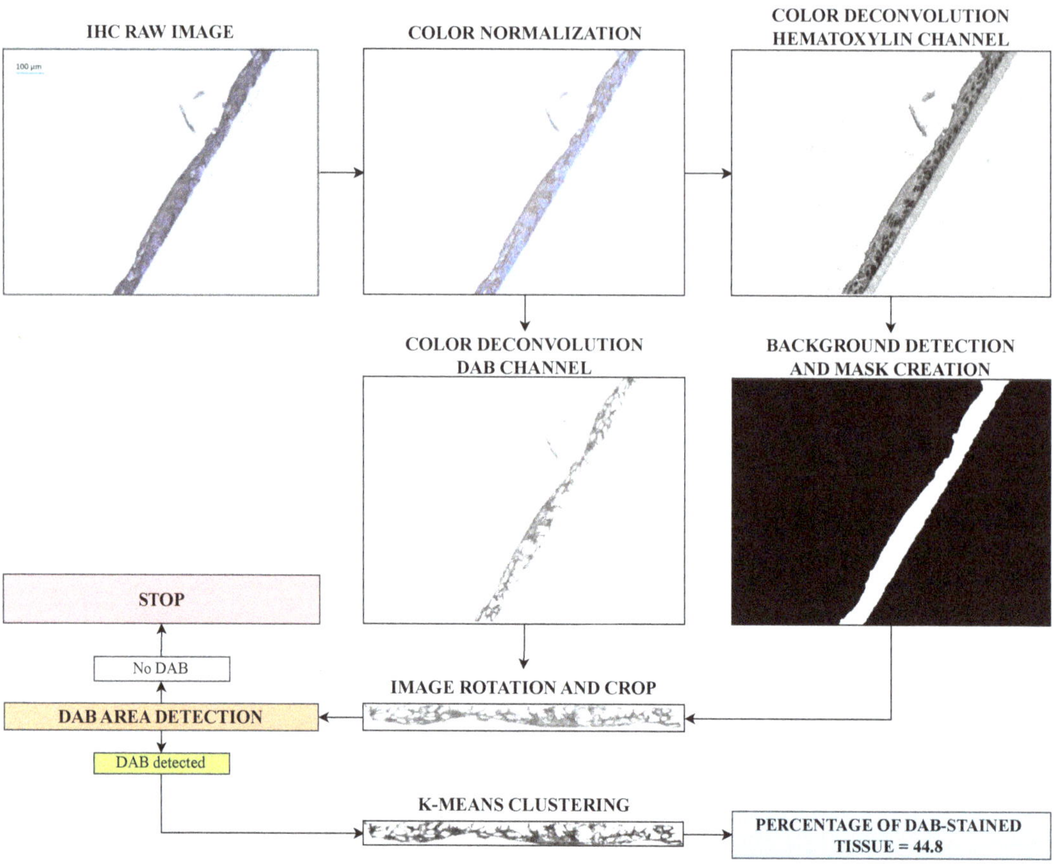

Figure 2. EpidermaQuant algorithm flowchart. The main steps of the pipeline include image color normalization, image color deconvolution, background detection, image rotation and crop, initial DAB-area detection step where the algorithm decides whether the image should be further analyzed, image segmentation, and calculation of the DAB percentage on tissue.

3.1. Color Normalization and Deconvolution Results

To better distinguish the interesting objects in the image and harmonize images from different scans, we tested several color-normalization and color-deconvolution methods (Supplementary Figure S2). The best normalization method was Reinhard's normalization. In most images, the brown staining was best exposed, and background noise was reduced in comparison to others (Figure 3A). Macenko's method gave the poorest visual results. The effectiveness of the color deconvolution method was tested using the results of the hematoxylin and DAB channels (Figure 3B). The best set of parameters was from ImageJ Color Deconvolution 2 plug-in. Only this method provided proper extraction of the DAB image, including only areas with brown staining representing the analyzed marker. Also, the residual image showed low intensities, which is preferential. In other methods, background noise was visible in the DAB image (Figure 3B).

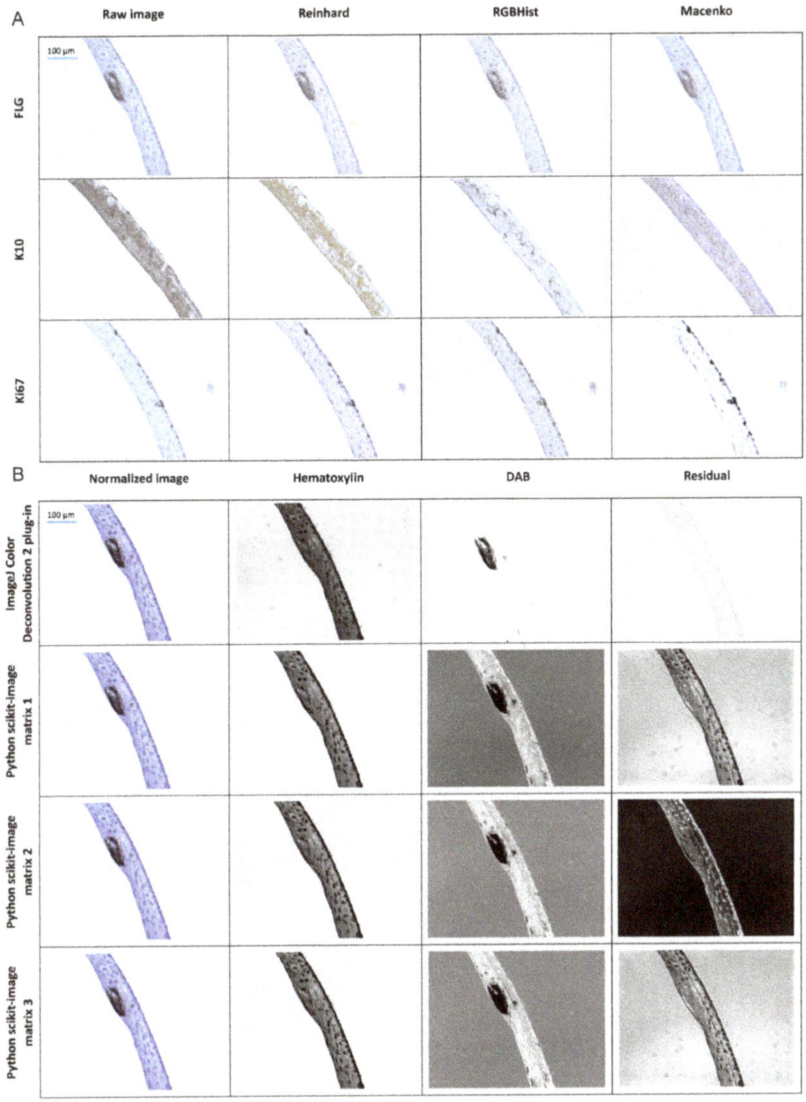

Figure 3. Comparison of normalization (**A**) and color-deconvolution (**B**) methods with the original image, depending on the selected marker using exemplary images.

3.2. Background Removal and Image Rotation

We detected a background region using the image of the hematoxylin channel since most tissue structures are visible here. The first step of the algorithm, image binarization, gives a rough estimate of tissue regions (Figure 4). By introducing a series of subsequent morphological operations and binarization, we found the background area of the image and created a mask without artifacts. Lastly, we discarded small artifacts by selecting the largest area of the mask. The mask allows the definition of a clear boundary between a tissue slice and an unnecessary image background.

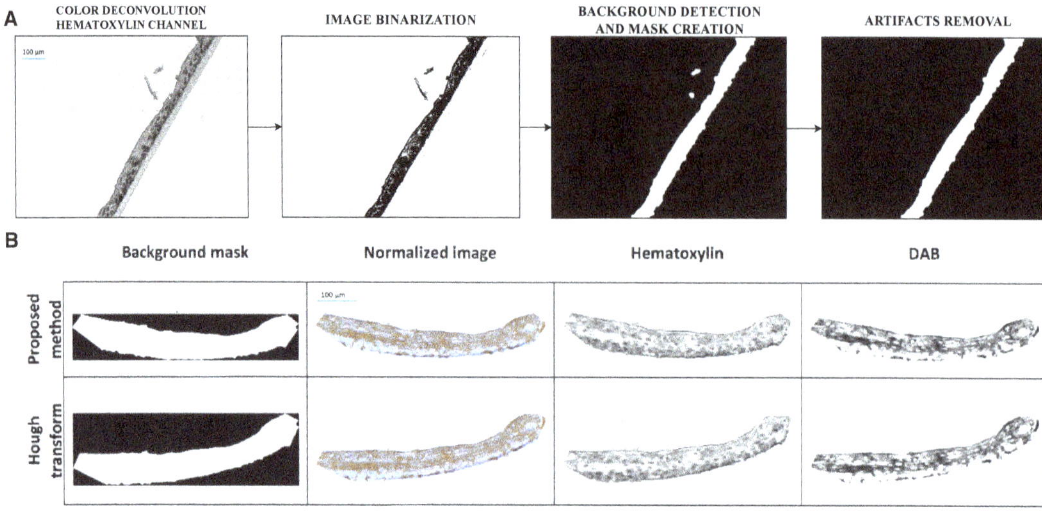

Figure 4. Subsequent steps of background removal (**A**) and comparison of two image rotation methods for an exemplary image of K10 marker (**B**).

The reconstructed epidermis forms a thin, single stripe on each stained slide. To reduce the scanned image size, we rotated the image and cropped as much background as possible (Supplementary Figure S3). At first, we tested functions implementing the Hough transform; however, its performance was not effective when tests were conducted on the entire set of images. Therefore, we developed the image-rotation method based on the boundary distribution of image intensity, which proved to work much more efficiently (Figure 4B). Based on the results of the mask rotation, we cropped the DAB channel image for further analysis.

3.3. Elimination of Images without DAB Stain Results

Some tissues may not contain the analyzed marker, so no DAB-stained regions should be observed on the image. Since we noticed brown-colored individual pixels in the negative samples, we developed a method to find and remove negative samples from further analysis. First, we calculated the AP for all images representing the FLG marker in both positive (with marker) and negative samples. By maximizing the AUC and Youden indices, we found the optimal threshold value as 0.6% (Supplementary Figure S4).

3.4. DAB Area Detection

Using the DAB channel of the image, we found areas of interest in the form of DAB staining in all images representing each marker. In most cases, two clusters were obtained using the k-means algorithm (Figure 5). The cluster containing the DAB image area with the largest number of darkest pixels forms the final segmentation of the analyzed marker region. These outcomes were used to quantitatively analyze the results, to determine the percentage of DAB-stained tissue, and to mark the outlines of the DAB areas on the original image.

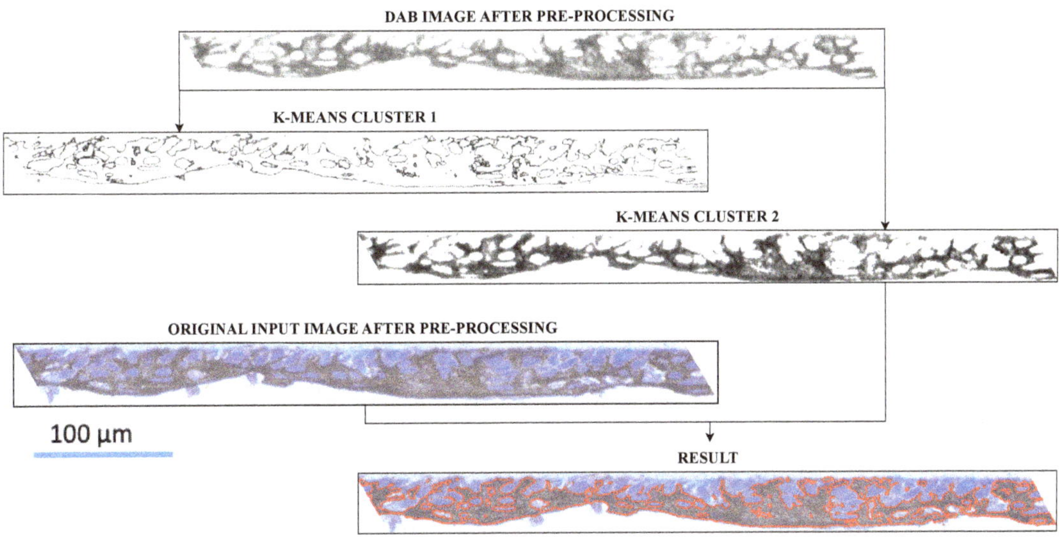

Figure 5. Example of DAB image segmentation result. Interesting regions of markers of human epidermal differentiation are segmented by the k-means method. The selected cluster outlines the DAB-stained areas (red line) on the original image with additional hematoxylin staining (blue).

3.5. Comparison of DAB-Staining Levels between Markers

The percentage of DAB-stained tissue area for the representatives of each study group is compared in Figure 6. Samples representing the K10 marker showed the biggest area with DAB staining in comparison to other markers (median equal to 39.5% vs. 4.1% in FLG, 2.5% in Ki67, and 25.3% in HSPA2). The spread of results obtained was also the largest. The smallest spread of results and, at the same time, the smallest area of the DAB staining were found for the Ki67 marker (see examples in Supplementary Figures S5–S8).

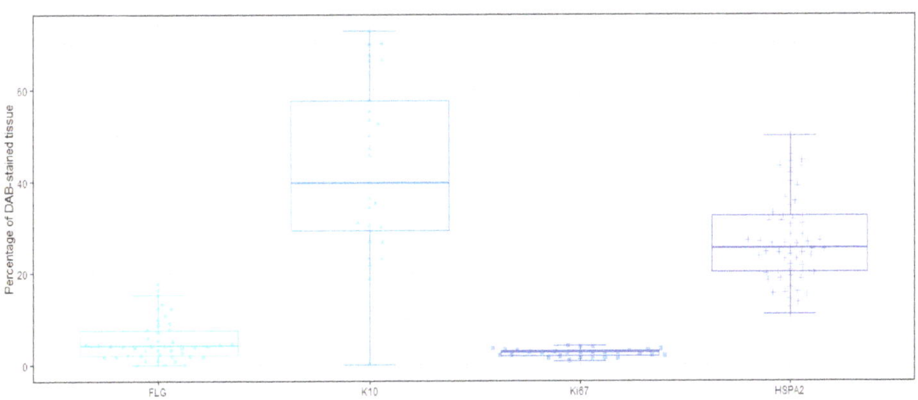

Figure 6. The percentage of DAB-stained tissue. The graph shows the percentage of DAB occupancy on the slide in each sample by study marker group.

3.6. Validation of Developed Pipeline on Human Protein Atlas Data

To verify if the proposed EpidermaQuant framework could determine the DAB-stained tissue correctly in an independent dataset, we use the images from The Human Protein Atlas (HPA). HPA contains images of histological sections from normal and tumor tissues obtained by tissue microarrays and immunohistochemistry procedures. Specimens comprising both normal and tumor tissue have been collected and sampled from anonymized paraffin-embedded surgical material. Antibodies are labeled with DAB and counterstained with hematoxylin to enable the visualization of microscopic features. The HPA dataset consisted of 66 unannotated .jpg images (3000 × 3000 pixels). Only tissues representing skin were selected. Thus, the number of images per marker was as follows: FLG—17 images; K10—12 images; Ki67—25 images; HSPA2—12 images. The percentage of DAB occupancy on the slide was for FLG: 0.501–8.3979; K10: 4.7549–16.7749; Ki67: 0.6336–21.9975; HSPA2: 6.3639–15.2822 (see Figure 7). Only one image was excluded and classified as negative.

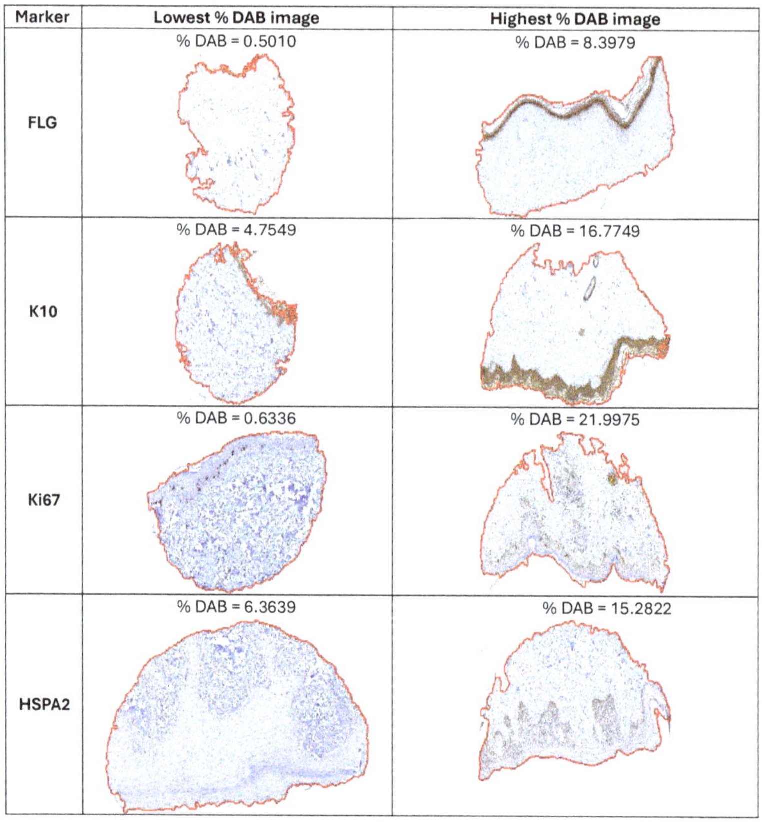

Figure 7. Exemplary results of EpidermaQuant on HPA dataset. For each analyzed marker (rows), images with the lowest and the highest estimated percentage of DAB occupancy were selected. The red line indicates the estimated area of the tissue.

3.7. Ablation Study

To demonstrate that the proposed steps of the pipeline are required for superior results, we selected parts of the algorithm that could be removed (normalization and image rotation) or that were optional (plastic removal) and tested these different configurations of the processing pipeline using the K10-marker images as an example. The four tested configurations are as follows: (i) full pipeline presented in the study (used as a baseline), (ii) pipeline without normalization step, (iii) pipeline without image rotation step and crop, and (iv) full pipeline with additional plastic removal step. Since no ground truth is given, for each scenario, we examined the difference in computational time (Figure 8A) and the difference in the percentage of DAB occupancy (Figure 8B). In the K10-marker dataset, turning off image normalization did not change computational time but increased the percentage of DAB occupancy by 17%, on average. Removing the image rotation step from the pipeline increased computational time by 15 s on average but did not change the percentage of DAB occupancy. When there is a visible plastic in the image, the method of its removal improves the estimate of DAB occupancy percentage (see example in Supplementary Figure S9) without a high increase in computational time.

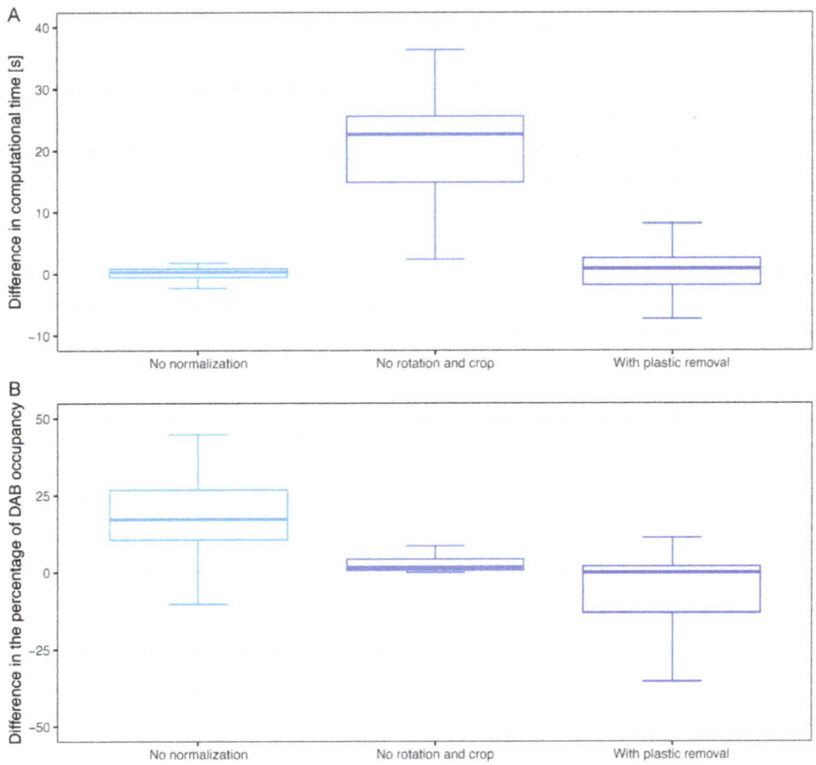

Figure 8. Summary of the ablation study using the K10-marker images. All results are compared to the full pipeline. Panel (**A**) shows the computational time comparison for selected configurations of pipeline, while panel (**B**) shows the difference in the percentage of DAB occupancy.

4. Discussion

We developed a new pipeline for automated detection, segmentation, and quantitative analysis of human epidermis differentiation markers in images containing slides of in vitro reconstructed human epidermis stained by DAB-mediated IHC and counterstained with hematoxylin. A performed analysis led to the choice of the best methods in subsequent processing steps.

Stain color inconstancy is a known problem that could be caused by several factors: The thickness of the tissue section, antibody concentration, stain timings, stain reactivity, characteristics of the scanner, and others. For the color normalization step, Reinhard's normalization was chosen because its results best reflected the colors of the staining used, especially for the brown areas of the DAB. The other two methods produced less satisfactory results. Both the RGB histogram specification and Macenko's normalization methods failed to sufficiently highlight areas of interest in the form of DAB staining. Our results were dissimilar from the study conducted by Khan et al. [26], where the authors selected Macenko's normalization method as the best. They mentioned that Reinhard's method was based on the false assumption of unimodal color distribution in each channel as the reason for rejecting it. This confirms that there are no gold standards and tests should be performed on each different tissue and staining type.

In the case of the image rotation method, it was decided to develop a new method that was more efficient compared to the Hough transform. In most cases, it excluded situations in which the image was not rotated maximally to a horizontal position or when it was incorrectly rotated to a vertical position. This step was important for the proper presentation of the segmentation results. Without it, it would have been difficult to compare images in different positions with each other, especially in the case of images representing the FLG marker, where the sizes of clusters of DAB staining areas are very small.

The analyzed images were mostly divided into two or three clusters, correctly reflecting the areas of interest. The k-means algorithm was also used in a publication by Vidhya et al., which presented an effective technique for segmenting and classifying IHC tissue images to detect colorectal tumors. This work also used the k-means method with morphological segmentation, such as erosion and dilation [31].

Quantification of staining intensity in histopathology is relevant only if the absorption of the stain into the preparation is stoichiometric [32]. IHC methods, like most histologic stains, are non-stoichiometric, making it impossible to accurately measure antigen expression based on DAB stain intensity. In addition, the IHC technique uses a series of amplification steps to visualize the results, making it difficult to control the actual signal intensity associated with the amount of antigen. It should be noted that the DAB chromogen does not follow Lambert–Beer's law, which describes a linear relationship between the concentration of a compound and its absorbance (optical density). The stain acts as a light scatterer with a broad, featureless spectrum, resulting in a darkly colored DAB, which has a different spectral shape than a lightly colored DAB [32]. Therefore, it was decided to quantitatively analyze the results by determining only the percentage of DAB stain occupancy on the slide relative to the entire surface of the tissue.

Considering the characteristics of the biological material in the form of a longitudinal tissue slide, its specific horizontal orientation, and the markers of keratinocyte differentiation used in the study, no publicly available annotated dataset was found to compare and validate the algorithm's results. Some studies concentrate on the examination of IHC tissue slides, which were generated through the utilization of techniques such as tissue microarrays or alternative methods of slide acquisition [5,6]. With the aforementioned facts, a decision was made to validate the EpidermaQuant algorithm using images provided by The Human Protein Atlas. The images were generated using the tissue microarray technique and did not resemble the shape of the reconstructed human epidermis images. However, from the visual analysis of the results, it can be concluded that the algorithm was able to successfully analyze the external dataset and may be used for other images that were prepared using the IHC procedure and stained with H-DAB.

The importance of selected steps of the algorithm reported here was established by the ablation study. The analysis without image rotation and crop required the greatest investment of time due to the size of the analyzed image. It proves that this step is crucial to maintain the time performance of the algorithm. Further analysis proved that a normalization step might decrease the false positive results resulting from color variation (too dark images; see Supplementary Figure S10). We assume that this step is especially important for some low-quality images or images acquired in different laboratories. However, since it does not increase computational time much, we suggest using it in all cases. In the case of tissue containing a plastic membrane, the optional plastic removal step allowed for a more precise definition of the region of interest (tissue) and did not require a significant investment of time, which is of particular importance in the context of this study.

Several different algorithms have been developed for the analysis of IHC images [7,10,11,13–15,18,20,21], but not strictly DAB-stained images of human epidermis. Many of these publications deal with artificial intelligence algorithms and neural networks or use commercially available but paid applications [8,9]. These supervised deep-learning models require complicated architecture systems, high computing power, and the availability of large and complex fully annotated datasets, which can be a challenge in the medical field [33]. Additionally, the heterogeneity of medical examples can present difficulties for deep learning and artificial intelligence models [33]. This excluded the possibility of using these types of algorithms to analyze images of reconstructed human epidermis. Our developed tool allows the quantitative analysis of protein markers in reconstructed human epidermis samples to facilitate a more accurate comparison of their spatial distribution between different experimental conditions.

As with every method, our solution also has drawbacks. The method may not work well when the plastic culture medium joins the slide and is additionally stained with DAB, or its color does not resemble the synthetic substrate. Moreover, the algorithm may also consider brown artifacts during segmentation. Another limitation is the MATLAB implementation. A likely gain could be achieved by implementing the proposed algorithm in a more commercial programming language. Lastly, the comparison of the methods was based only on visual evaluation by the expert. More precise methods would be needed to accurately evaluate the performance of the tested algorithms. To obtain automatic matching or mismatching of localized DAB-stained areas, it would have been necessary to compare them with ground truth results (segmentation based on manual labeling), which were not provided in our case.

5. Conclusions

The bioinformatics tool developed in the presented work enabled quantitative analysis of marker proteins and assisted the analysis of their spatial distribution by experts. These results might be useful for a better description of structural changes in the reconstructed epidermis and for staining analysis in bioptates, as biopsy material taken by pathologists for diagnostic purposes also has an elongated shape and undergoes IHC analysis. At the same time, it may inspire other researchers to fill the gap in the literature regarding the detection of markers of human epidermal differentiation on IHC images and may be further developed or adjusted to the other research problems in digital pathology.

Supplementary Materials: The following supporting information can be downloaded at https://www.mdpi.com/article/10.3390/diagnostics14171904/s1, Figure S1: epidermaquant application. The graphical interface allows the user to select the appropriate image by the marker used in the analysis and to preview the image entered, the final result, and the percentage of DAB-stained tissue; Figure S2: color normalization and deconvolution of IHC image. The first step of image processing is color normalization, which reduces the variability of pixel intensity values in different samples. In the color deconvolution step, the RGB image is split into three channels corresponding to the colors of the stains used (the residual-channel image is not further processed); Figure S3: automatic image rotation and crop. Based on the rotated and cropped mask, it is possible to scale the DAB-channel image accordingly. It allows us to remove the unnecessary in further analysis of the background. Rotation is performed by its method based on the boundary distribution of image intensity; Figure S4: summary of determining the optimal threshold value results. Comparison of potential threshold values based on ROC curves, including results of AUC and Youden index; Figure S5: final output of the algorithm, for example, images representing the FLG marker. Percentage of DAB occupancy on the tissue with the outlines of the DAB areas marked over the original image; Figure S6: final output of the algorithm, for example, images representing the K10 marker. Percentage of DAB occupancy on the tissue with the outlines of the DAB areas marked over the original image; Figure S7: final output of the algorithm, for example, images representing the Ki67 marker. Percentage of DAB occupancy on the tissue with the outlines of the DAB areas marked over the original image; Figure S8: final output of the algorithm, for example, images representing the HSPA2 marker. Percentage of DAB occupancy on the tissue with the outlines of the DAB areas marked over the original image; Figure S9: final output of the algorithm, for example, image with a plastic membrane (indicated by an arrow symbol) representing the K10 marker. Percentage of DAB occupancy on the tissue with the outlines of the DAB areas marked over the original image before (A) and after (B) removing the plastic culture medium; Figure S10: final output of the algorithm, for example, image with and without image normalization representing the K10 marker. Percentage of DAB occupancy on the tissue with the outlines of the DAB areas marked over the original image with (A) and without (B) normalization.

Author Contributions: Data, A.G. and D.S.; algorithm, computational framework, and data analysis, D.Z. and M.M.; writing—original draft preparation, D.Z.; writing—review and editing, M.M.; project administration, D.Z.; original idea, D.S.; supervision, M.M. All authors have discussed the results and reviewed the manuscript. All authors have read and agreed to the published version of the manuscript.

Funding: This research was funded by the Silesian University of Technology, grant number 02/070/BK_24/0052 for Support and Development of Research Potential (M.M.), by the Excellence Initiative—Research University program implemented at the Silesian University of Technology, grant number 02/070/SDU/10-21-02 (M.M.), by the Ministry of Science and Higher Education 'Implementation Doctorate', grant number DWD/7/0396/2023 (D.Z.), and by the National Science Centre, Poland, grant number 2017/25/B/NZ4/01550 (D.S.).

Institutional Review Board Statement: The study was conducted in accordance with the Declaration of Helsinki, and approved by the Ethics Committee of Maria Sklodowska-Curie National Research Institute of Oncology Gliwice Branch (protocol code KB/430-17/18 and date of approval 23 March 2018).

Informed Consent Statement: Informed consent was obtained from all subjects involved in the study.

Data Availability Statement: The datasets analyzed during the current study are available in the GitHub repository, https://github.com/DawZam/EpidermaQuant/tree/main/DATA (accessed on 28 August 2024).

Conflicts of Interest: Author Dawid Zamojski was employed by the Gyncentrum Sp. z o.o. The remaining authors declare that the research was conducted in the absence of any commercial or financial relationships that could be construed as a potential conflict of interest.

References

1. Magaki, S.; Hojat, S.A.; Wei, B.; So, A.; Yong, W.H. An Introduction to the Performance of Immunohistochemistry. *Methods Mol. Biol.* **2019**, *1897*, 289–298. [CrossRef] [PubMed]
2. Jahn, S.W.; Plass, M.; Moinfar, F. Digital Pathology: Advantages, Limitations and Emerging Perspectives. *J. Clin. Med.* **2020**, *9*, 3697. [CrossRef] [PubMed]
3. Gurcan, M.N.; Boucheron, L.E.; Can, A.; Madabhushi, A.; Rajpoot, N.M.; Yener, B. Histopathological Image Analysis: A Review. *IEEE Rev. Biomed. Eng.* **2009**, *2*, 147–171. [CrossRef] [PubMed]
4. Poalelungi, D.G.; Neagu, A.I.; Fulga, A.; Neagu, M.; Tutunaru, D.; Nechita, A.; Fulga, I. Revolutionizing Pathology with Artificial Intelligence: Innovations in Immunohistochemistry. *J. Pers. Med.* **2024**, *14*, 693. [CrossRef]
5. Sorlie, T.; Perou, C.M.; Tibshirani, R.; Aas, T.; Geisler, S.; Johnsen, H.; Hastie, T.; Eisen, M.B.; van de Rijn, M.; Jeffrey, S.S.; et al. Gene expression patterns of breast carcinomas distinguish tumor subclasses with clinical implications. *Proc. Natl. Acad. Sci. USA* **2001**, *98*, 10869–10874. [CrossRef]
6. Holten-Rossing, H.; Talman, M.-L.M.; Kristensson, M.; Vainer, B. Optimizing HER2 assessment in breast cancer: Application of automated image analysis. *Breast Cancer Res. Treat.* **2015**, *152*, 367–375. [CrossRef]
7. Saha, M.; Arun, I.; Ahmed, R.; Chatterjee, S.; Chakraborty, C. HscoreNet: A Deep network for estrogen and progesterone scoring using breast IHC images. *Pattern Recognit.* **2020**, *102*, 107200. [CrossRef]
8. Hartage, R.; Li, A.C.; Hammond, S.; Parwani, A.V. A Validation Study of Human Epidermal Growth Factor Receptor 2 Immunohistochemistry Digital Imaging Analysis and its Correlation with Human Epidermal Growth Factor Receptor 2 Fluorescence In situ Hybridization Results in Breast Carcinoma. *J. Pathol. Inform.* **2020**, *11*, 2. [CrossRef]
9. Shafi, S.; Kellough, D.A.; Lujan, G.; Satturwar, S.; Parwani, A.V.; Li, Z. Integrating and validating automated digital imaging analysis of estrogen receptor immunohistochemistry in a fully digital workflow for clinical use. *J. Pathol. Inform.* **2022**, *13*, 100122. [CrossRef]
10. Abele, N.; Tiemann, K.; Krech, T.; Wellmann, A.; Schaaf, C.; Länger, F.; Peters, A.; Donner, A.; Keil, F.; Daifalla, K.; et al. Noninferiority of Artificial Intelligence-Assisted Analysis of Ki-67 and Estrogen/Progesterone Receptor in Breast Cancer Routine Diagnostics. *Mod. Pathol.* **2023**, *36*, 100033. [CrossRef]
11. Erber, R.; Frey, P.; Keil, F.; Gronewold, M.; Abele, N.; Rezner, W.; Beister, T.; Daifalla, K.; Päpper, M.; Springenberg, S.; et al. 48P An AI System for accurate Ki-67 IHC assessment in breast cancer following the IKWG whole section global scoring protocol. *ESMO Open* **2023**, *8*, 101272. [CrossRef]
12. Kaufmann, O.; Fietze, E.; Mengs, J.; Dietel, M. Value of p63 and cytokeratin 5/6 as immunohistochemical markers for the differential diagnosis of poorly differentiated and undifferentiated carcinomas. *Am. J. Clin. Pathol.* **2001**, *116*, 823–830. [CrossRef]

13. Gandomkar, Z.; Brennan, P.C.; Mello-Thoms, C. MuDeRN: Multi-category classification of breast histopathological image using deep residual networks. *Artif. Intell. Med.* **2018**, *88*, 14–24. [CrossRef]
14. Sandbank, J.; Bataillon, G.; Nudelman, A.; Krasnitsky, I.; Mikulinsky, R.; Bien, L.; Thibault, L.; Shach, A.A.; Sebag, G.; Clark, D.P.; et al. Validation and real-world clinical application of an artificial intelligence algorithm for breast cancer detection in biopsies. *NPJ Breast Cancer* **2022**, *8*, 129. [CrossRef]
15. Roszkowiak, L.; Korzynska, A.; Siemion, K.; Zak, J.; Pijanowska, D.; Bosch, R.; Lejeune, M.; Lopez, C. System for quantitative evaluation of DAB&H-stained breast cancer biopsy digital images (CHISEL). *Sci. Rep.* **2021**, *11*, 9291. [CrossRef]
16. Belsare, A.D. Histopathological Image Analysis Using Image Processing Techniques: An Overview. *Signal Image Process. Int. J.* **2012**, *3*, 23–36. [CrossRef]
17. Patel, S.; Fridovich-Keil, S.; Rasmussen, S.A.; Fridovich-Keil, J.L. DAB-quant: An open-source digital system for quantifying immunohistochemical staining with 3,3′-diaminobenzidine (DAB). *PLoS ONE* **2022**, *17*, e0271593. [CrossRef]
18. Bencze, J.; Szarka, M.; Kóti, B.; Seo, W.; Hortobágyi, T.G.; Bencs, V.; Módis, L.V.; Hortobágyi, T. Comparison of Semi-Quantitative Scoring and Artificial Intelligence Aided Digital Image Analysis of Chromogenic Immunohistochemistry. *Biomolecules* **2022**, *12*, 19. [CrossRef]
19. Sziva, R.E.; Ács, J.; Tőkés, A.-M.; Korsós-Novák, Á.; Nádasy, G.L.; Ács, N.; Horváth, P.G.; Szabó, A.; Ke, H.; Horváth, E.M.; et al. Accurate Quantitative Histomorphometric-Mathematical Image Analysis Methodology of Rodent Testicular Tissue and Its Possible Future Research Perspectives in Andrology and Reproductive Medicine. *Life* **2022**, *12*, 189. [CrossRef]
20. Raza, S.E.A.; AbdulJabbar, K.; Jamal-Hanjani, M.; Veeriah, S.; Le Quesne, J.; Swanton, C.; Yuan, Y. Deconvolving Convolutional Neural Network for Cell Detection. In Proceedings of the 2019 IEEE 16th International Symposium on Biomedical Imaging (ISBI 2019), Venice, Italy, 8–11 April 2019; pp. 891–894. [CrossRef]
21. Swiderska-Chadaj, Z.; Pinckaers, H.; van Rijthoven, M.; Balkenhol, M.; Melnikova, M.; Geessink, O.; Manson, Q.; Sherman, M.; Polonia, A.; Parry, J.; et al. Learning to detect lymphocytes in immunohistochemistry with deep learning. *Med. Image Anal.* **2019**, *58*, 101547. [CrossRef]
22. Bankhead, P.; Loughrey, M.B.; Fernández, J.A.; Dombrowski, Y.; McArt, D.G.; Dunne, P.D.; McQuaid, S.; Gray, R.T.; Murray, L.J.; Coleman, H.G.; et al. QuPath: Open source software for digital pathology image analysis. *Sci. Rep.* **2017**, *7*, 16878. [CrossRef] [PubMed]
23. Schneider, C.A.; Rasband, W.S.; Eliceiri, K.W. NIH Image to ImageJ: 25 years of image analysis. *Nat. Methods* **2012**, *9*, 671–675. [CrossRef] [PubMed]
24. Gogler-Pigłowska, A.; Klarzyńska, K.; Sojka, D.R.; Habryka, A.; Głowala-Kosińska, M.; Herok, M.; Kryj, M.; Halczok, M.; Krawczyk, Z.; Scieglinska, D. Novel role for the testis-enriched HSPA2 protein in regulating epidermal keratinocyte differentiation. *J. Cell. Physiol.* **2018**, *233*, 2629–2644. [CrossRef] [PubMed]
25. Hewitt, S.M.; Baskin, D.G.; Frevert, C.W.; Stahl, W.L.; Rosa-Molinar, E. Controls for Immunohistochemistry. *J. Histochem. Cytochem.* **2014**, *62*, 693–697. [CrossRef] [PubMed]
26. Khan, A.M.; Rajpoot, N.; Treanor, D.; Magee, D. A Nonlinear Mapping Approach to Stain Normalization in Digital Histopathology Images Using Image-Specific Color Deconvolution. *IEEE Trans. Biomed. Eng.* **2014**, *61*, 1729–1738. [CrossRef]
27. Haub, P.; Meckel, T. A Model based Survey of Colour Deconvolution in Diagnostic Brightfield Microscopy: Error Estimation and Spectral Consideration. *Sci. Rep.* **2015**, *5*, 12096. [CrossRef]
28. Ruifrok, A.C.; Johnston, D.A. Quantification of histochemical staining by color deconvolution. *Anal. Quant. Cytol. Histol.* **2001**, *23*, 291–299.
29. Hassanein, A.S.; Mohammad, S.; Sameer, M.; Ragab, M.E. A Survey on Hough Transform, Theory, Techniques and Applications. *arXiv* **2015**, arXiv:1502.02160. [CrossRef]
30. Ashabi, A.; Sahibuddin, S.B.; Haghighi, M.S. The Systematic Review of K-Means Clustering Algorithm. In Proceedings of the 2020 The 9th International Conference on Networks, Communication and Computing, Tokyo Japan, 18–20 December 2020; ACM: New York, NY, USA; pp. 13–18. [CrossRef]
31. Vidhya, S.; Shijitha, M.R. Deep Learning based Approach for Efficient Segmentation and Classification using VGGNet 16 for Tissue Analysis to Predict Colorectal Cancer. *Ann. Romanian Soc. Cell Biol.* **2021**, *25*, 4002–4013.
32. van der Loos, C.M. Multiple Immunoenzyme Staining: Methods and Visualizations for the Observation with Spectral Imaging. *J. Histochem. Cytochem.* **2008**, *56*, 313–328. [CrossRef]
33. Raman, R.; Radha, R.H.; Inbamalar, T.M.; Subhahan, D.A.; Kumar, A.; Bathrinath, S.; Sarkar, S. Penetration of Deep Learning in Human Health Care and Pharmaceutical Industries; the Opportunities and Challenges. In Proceedings of the 2023 3rd International Conference on Innovative Practices in Technology and Management (ICIPTM), Nagar, India, 22–24 February 2023; pp. 1–6. [CrossRef]

tomography

MDPI

Article

Repurposing the Public BraTS Dataset for Postoperative Brain Tumour Treatment Response Monitoring

Peter Jagd Sørensen [1,2,3,*], Claes Nøhr Ladefoged [4,5], Vibeke Andrée Larsen [1], Flemming Littrup Andersen [2,4], Michael Bachmann Nielsen [1,2], Hans Skovgaard Poulsen [3], Jonathan Frederik Carlsen [1,2,†] and Adam Espe Hansen [1,2,3,†]

1 Department of Radiology, Centre of Diagnostic Investigation, Copenhagen University Hospital—Rigshospitalet, 2100 Copenhagen, Denmark; vibeke.andree.larsen@regionh.dk (V.A.L.); michael.bachmann.nielsen@regionh.dk (M.B.N.); jonathan.frederik.carlsen@regionh.dk (J.F.C.); adam.espe.hansen@regionh.dk (A.E.H.)
2 Department of Clinical Medicine, University of Copenhagen, 2100 Copenhagen, Denmark; flemming.andersen@regionh.dk
3 The DCCC Brain Tumor Center, 2100 Copenhagen, Denmark; hans.skovgaard.poulsen@regionh.dk
4 Department of Clinical Physiology and Nuclear Medicine, Centre of Diagnostic Investigation, Copenhagen University Hospital—Rigshospitalet, 2100 Copenhagen, Denmark; claes.noehr.ladefoged@regionh.dk
5 Department of Applied Mathematics and Computer Science, Technical University of Denmark, 2800 Lyngby, Denmark
* Correspondence: peter.jagd.soerensen@regionh.dk; Tel.: +45-31-1234-31
† These authors contributed equally to this work.

Abstract: The Brain Tumor Segmentation (BraTS) Challenge has been a main driver of the development of deep learning (DL) algorithms and provides by far the largest publicly available expert-annotated brain tumour dataset but contains solely preoperative examinations. The aim of our study was to facilitate the use of the BraTS dataset for training DL brain tumour segmentation algorithms for a postoperative setting. To this end, we introduced an automatic conversion of the three-label BraTS annotation protocol to a two-label annotation protocol suitable for postoperative brain tumour segmentation. To assess the viability of the label conversion, we trained a DL algorithm using both the three-label and the two-label annotation protocols. We assessed the models pre- and postoperatively and compared the performance with a state-of-the-art DL method. The DL algorithm trained using the BraTS three-label annotation misclassified parts of 10 out of 41 fluid-filled resection cavities in 72 postoperative glioblastoma MRIs, whereas the two-label model showed no such inaccuracies. The tumour segmentation performance of the two-label model both pre- and postoperatively was comparable to that of a state-of-the-art algorithm for tumour volumes larger than 1 cm^3. Our study enables using the BraTS dataset as a basis for the training of DL algorithms for postoperative tumour segmentation.

Keywords: brain tumour segmentation; treatment monitoring; postoperative; annotation protocol; automatic; deep learning algorithm; magnetic resonance imaging; MRI; Brain Tumor Segmentation Challenge; BraTS

1. Introduction

The measurement of the volume of brain tumours has the potential to be an important biomarker for both the routine response assessment of cancer patients as well as for clinical trials. In recent years, there have been substantial efforts towards automating the segmentation of brain tumours on magnetic resonance imaging (MRI), especially by deep learning (DL) algorithms [1,2]. Among these, the nnU-Net framework [3] has distinguished itself as a self-configuring method that adapts to varying segmentation tasks, demonstrating leading performance in multiple benchmark challenges, including the Brain Tumor Segmentation (BraTS) Challenge [4–6]. Today, DL brain tumour segmentation algorithms are achieving over 90% agreement with imaging experts [5,7]. The BraTS Challenge has been the main driver in the development of the field, providing by far the largest publicly available training dataset comprising 1251 MRI examinations of glioma patients with expert reference annotations [8]. However, the BraTS dataset derives exclusively from preoperative MRI examinations.

The majority of brain tumour patients undergo surgery as part of the initial treatment and are subsequently monitored by MRI [9–11]. Surgical procedures can result in cavities, tissue scarring and haematomas, all of which introduce image features typically absent preoperatively. The current BraTS annotation protocol is tailored for preoperative MRI and does not accommodate these postoperative features. Therefore, DL algorithms trained only by use of the BraTS dataset may be suboptimal for response assessment. The ideal source for training a DL algorithm for treatment response monitoring would be a comprehensive, expert-annotated dataset including postoperative MRIs. To the best of our knowledge, no suitable expert-annotated postoperative datasets are publicly available, hampering the development of DL algorithms for treatment response monitoring. HD-GLIO, an nnU-Net model trained on postoperative but non-public data, indicates the feasibility and potential of such endeavours [12–14], although its application in routine response-monitoring settings may be challenged when small contrast-enhancing tumours are prevalent [15].

The aim of this study is to aid the development of DL algorithms for postoperative brain tumour treatment response monitoring by facilitating the use of the preoperative BraTS dataset. We hypothesise that a state-of-the-art DL algorithm, when trained on the BraTS dataset with its current annotations, is unsuitable for postoperative segmentation due to the potential for misclassifying resection cavities as tumour regions. To remedy this shortcoming, we introduce a revised annotation protocol that aligns with postoperative tumour segmentation. Accordingly, we further hypothesise that when the DL algorithm is retrained using our proposed annotation protocol on the same MRI data, it will accurately exclude resection cavities from tumour volumes in postoperative cases, and thus significantly improve its usability in the postoperative setting. By validating these hypotheses, we seek to equip a broad community of researchers and clinicians with a large body of training data to develop algorithms tailored for postoperative brain tumour response assessment.

2. Materials and Methods

We trained a deep learning brain tumour segmentation algorithm using the BraTS dataset and annotation protocol as well as our proposed protocol. The datasets, annotation protocols and evaluations are described below.

2.1. Preoperative Public Dataset

We utilised the most recent BraTS adult glioma training dataset curated for the RSNA-ASNR-MICCAI BraTS 2021 Challenge [4,6,8,16] for training. The BraTS 2021 training dataset has been sourced from multiple institutions and comprises 1251 independent preoperative patient scans, each confirmed with a subsequent pathological diagnosis of glioma. Each scan encompasses four MRI sequences: T1-weighted before contrast infusion (T1), T1-weighted after contrast infusion (T1Gd), T2-weighted and fluid-attenuated inversion-recovery (FLAIR). These sequences have been preprocessed as described in [17–19], which includes co-registration, resampling to voxel size of 1 mm^3 and skull-stripping. For our study, we selected a subset consisting of the last 1000 out of the 1251 scans to train the DL algorithms. We used the remaining first 251 scans as a test set to evaluate preoperative tumour segmentation performance.

2.2. Postoperative Public Test Dataset

For testing the performance of the algorithms in a postoperative setting, we employed the publicly available Lumiere dataset [20]. The dataset encompasses scans of 91 patients with a confirmed diagnosis of glioblastoma. These patients underwent preoperative MRI between 2008 and 2013, received surgical resection treatment, underwent chemotherapy and had routine follow-up MRIs. The scans include T1, T1Gd, T2 and FLAIR sequences. In the Lumiere dataset, a version of these images has been preprocessed with HD-GLIO AUTO [12,21,22], complete with co-registration, resampling and skull-stripping. For our study, from the preprocessed dataset, we chose the earliest follow-up MRI after week 11 for each of the 72 patients where that particular scan was complete with all four sequences.

2.3. BraTS Three-Label Annotations

Historically, the BraTS Challenges have implemented an annotation protocol that subsegmented tumours into four distinct regions based on specific radiological observations. They include the active Gadolinium-enhancing tumour (AT), necrosis (NCR), non-enhancing tumour core (NET) and surrounding oedematous or infiltrated tissue (ED). In 2017, the protocol was simplified by merging NCR and NET into a single label (NCR+NET) [5]. Hence, NCR+NET encompasses both necrosis and non-enhancing tumour core. Recently, AT has been renamed to ET (enhancing tumour), and NCR+NET to just NCR [8]. For clarity, in this study, we will, however, refer to BraTS annotations by their original names, AT and NCR+NET as well as ED.

2.4. Proposed Two-Label Annotation Protocol

Our proposed annotation protocol adapts and expands the BraTS annotation protocol [5,8] to make it suitable for both pre- and postoperative settings. We employ two labels: the contrast-enhancing tumour (CE) and the non-enhancing hyperintense T2-FLAIR signal abnormalities (NEs) inspired by [12], with more detailed directions given below. The annotation protocol is in accordance with the relevant VASARI MR feature definitions [23] and with adaptations for postoperative compatibility. Specifically, necrotic and cystic regions are not incorporated in either label. They do not represent viable tumour tissue and may share image features with resection cavities.

The CE label is defined similarly to the BraTS AT label but with the morphological changes from surgery taken into consideration. If a region is hyperintense on T1, it should not be categorised under the CE label unless it distinctly enhances on T1Gd and exhibits a pattern different from that observed on T1. Enhancements on T1Gd with a simple, thin geometric configuration along the resection walls are interpreted as benign changes resulting from surgery and are thus excluded from the CE label. On the other hand, locally thickened or nodular enhancements seen along the resection walls should be included in the CE label. Dural thickening and leptomeningeal enhancement on T1Gd, much more often a result of surgery than glioma infiltration, should not fall under the CE label. We recognise that distinguishing between the two can occasionally pose challenges. Closely configured, sporadic enhancements in areas with high T2/FLAIR-signal are viewed as indicators of angiogenesis due to tumour growth and should thus be included in the CE label.

The NE label closely resembles a combination of the original BraTS NET and ED labels but comes with additional clarifications. T2/FLAIR hyperintensity, when adjacent to a resection cavity, indicating the presence of a previous tumour, should be equated with peritumoural oedema. As such, T2/FLAIR hyperintensity connected with a resection cavity should be allocated to the NE label. However, regions showing hyperintensity on T2/FLAIR, even if adjacent to an enhancing tumour, non-enhancing tumour core or a resection cavity, should be excluded from the NE label if they manifest a configuration mirrored contralaterally or if they evidently resemble typical periventricular oedema, a common treatment-induced feature, or white matter hyperintensities of probable vascular origin. We acknowledge the occasional difficulty in precisely determining the boundary between peritumoural oedema and unrelated periventricular oedema. Necrosis and cysts should not be allocated to the NE label.

2.5. HD-GLIO

HD-GLIO is a freely accessible DL brain tumour segmentation algorithm designed for postoperative treatment response assessment [12]. HD-GLIO differentiates between contrast-enhancing ($CE_{HD\text{-}GLIO}$) tumours and non-enhancing hyperintense T2/FLAIR signal abnormalities ($NE_{HD\text{-}GLIO}$), while excluding necrosis, obvious leucoaraiosis (white matter hyperintensities of probable vascular origin) and resection cavities. The algorithm employs the nnU-Net framework [21] and was trained on a non-public dataset comprising 455 independent pre- or postoperative adult glioma MRIs. It has been validated on two longitudinal datasets: a local set of 239 MRIs from 40 glioma patients and a large multi-centre set of 2034 MRIs from 532 glioblastoma patients in the EORTC-26101 cohort. In our study, HD-GLIO served two purposes: (1) it provided a reliable whole-tumour segmentation, excluding necrosis; and (2) it acted as a comparative benchmark for evaluating the performance of our algorithm. We used HD-GLIO version 1.5 [24].

2.6. Conversion of BraTS Annotations

To harmonise the BraTS training data annotations with our newly proposed annotation protocol, we devised an algorithm for the systematic conversion of the BraTS segmentation masks. This conversion process is outlined below:

1. With HD-GLIO, obtain a whole tumour segmentation that excludes necrosis, $WT_{HD\text{-}GLIO} = CE_{HD\text{-}GLIO} + NE_{HD\text{-}GLIO}$.
2. Assign the NCR+NET segmentations within $WT_{HD\text{-}GLIO}$ to the NE label. This is the only step where the HD-GLIO segmentation is used.
3. Add the ED segmentations to the NE label.
4. Remove voxels in the NE label that are entirely encapsulated by AT segmentations, as these typify necrosis.
5. Remove voxel clusters in the NE label that are less than 50 mm^3 to eliminate potentially isolated traces of what was previously NCR segmentations.
6. Add again the ED segmentations to the NE label to ensure complete incorporation of the ED segmentations.
7. Assign the AT segmentation to the CE label.

The result of the conversion is that the CE label is identical to the original AT label, and the NE label includes the full original ED label as well as the estimated NET regions of the original NCR+NET label. Thus, the conversion process exclusively removes voxels inside the NCR+NET regions of the BraTS segmentations. Assuming that the original masks adhere to the BraTS Challenge's annotation protocol, our process is designed to remove necrosis and cysts. Figure 1 illustrates the conversion process in one example, and Appendix A provides a schematic illustration of the process. The label conversion script is freely available on GitHub [25].

2.7. Training of Deep Learning Algorithm

We utilised the nnU-Net architecture with standard settings in the '3d_fullres' configuration to train our deep learning model on two distinct annotation sets. The first set was the expert-annotations from the BraTS 2021 dataset, adhering to the BraTS three-label annotation protocol. The second set, based on our newly proposed two-label protocol, was derived by conversion from the initial set as detailed in the previous section. Both training processes employed the same 1000 scans from the BraTS 2021 training dataset. See Appendix B for technical details.

2.8. Evaluation

To assess the conversion of the original three-label annotations in the BraTS dataset to our recommended two-label annotations, we conducted a subjective evaluation of every 10th case, 125 cases in total, and calculated the conversion success rate with 95% confidence interval (95% CI) using the conservative Clopper–Pearson (exact) method that does not assume a normal distribution.

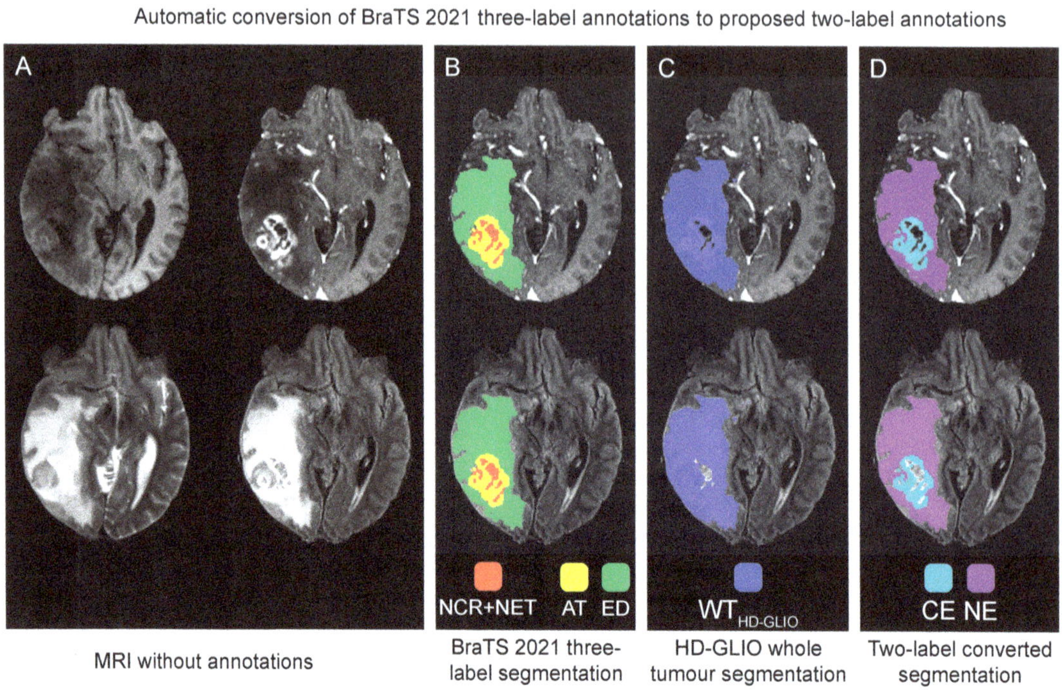

Figure 1. Conversion of the BraTS 2021 three-label segmentation masks for harmonisation with the proposed two-label annotation protocol. **Panel A**: Anatomical sequences without annotations. T1-weighted (T1) (top left), T1-weighted after contrast infusion (T1Gd) (top right), T2-weighted (bottom left) and fluid-attenuated-inversion-recovery (FLAIR) (bottom right). **Panels B–D**: annotations overlaid on T1Gd (top) and FLAIR (bottom). NCR+NET = necrosis, cysts and non-enhancing tumour core; AT = active contrast-enhancing tumour; ED = oedema and infiltrated tissue; $WT_{HD\text{-}GLIO}$ = automatic whole-tumour segmentation by HD-GLIO; CE = contrast-enhancing tumour; NE = non-enhancing hyperintense T2/FLAIR signal abnormalities. In essence, the conversion process labels the combination of the NCR+NET mask inside the $WT_{HD\text{-}GLIO}$ region and the ED mask as NE, thereby removing necrosis and cysts while retaining non-enhancing tumour core. AT is relabelled as CE without change. Only the regions inside the NCR+NET segmentations (red) are affected by the conversion.

We wished to examine how frequently the three-label and two-label deep learning models included parts of resection cavities in the postoperative test dataset. To this end, we employed a custom script that demarcated fluid-filled cavities in the brain, which on z-normalised (zero mean and unit variance) signal values were characterised by T1Gd < -1, FLAIR < 0 and T2 > 0 in a continuous volume of at least 2 cm^3, and subsequently validated these delineations by manual inspection before the analysis of all relevant volumes. We report how frequently the three-label and two-label models included parts of the identified cavities, and the volume included.

To verify that training of the deep learning model using converted labels did not compromise the tumour segmentation, we evaluated the segmentation both pre- and postoperatively. For evaluation of the preoperative tumour segmentation performance of the two-label model, we used as reference the converted annotations from the scans in the BraTS dataset that were kept out of the training dataset and determined Dice similarity scores (DSCs). As a benchmark, we also applied HD-GLIO and tested if its postoperative performance was significantly different from that of our model using the Wilcoxon rank sum exact test. Bootstrapping in R version 4.4.1 was used to calculate 95% CIs [26].

For evaluation of the postoperative tumour segmentation performance of the two-label model, we manually segmented the postoperative test dataset tumours using ITK-SNAP version 4.0.0 [27,28] in line with the two-label annotation protocol. Utilising these manual expert-provided segmentations as our reference, we determined DSCs for the segmentations generated by the two-label model. Likewise, for benchmarking, we evaluated the segmentations by HD-GLIO AUTO that was provided as part of the Lumiere dataset.

3. Results

We automatically converted all 1251 segmentations from the BraTS 2021 training dataset from the original three-label annotations to our proposed two-label annotations. A subjective evaluation of 125 cases (every 10th case) showed, with three exceptions, consistent success in the conversion process, yielding a conversion success rate of 122/125 = 97.6% (95% CI [93.2–99.5%]). Inspection showed that the removed internal areas from the original NCR+NET labels corresponded to probable necrotic and cystic regions, provided the original annotations adhered to the BraTS annotation protocol. The cases with discrepancies were two cases with substantial NET tumours in which the $WT_{HD\text{-}GLIO}$ left out parts of the less intense FLAIR hyperintensities, and one case where central necrosis was included in the $WT_{HD\text{-}GLIO}$ while not completely encapsulated in AT. Thus, in two cases, NET was erroneously excluded from the resulting NE label, and in one case, NCR was erroneously included in it. Typically, in cases with large NET volumes (lower grade gliomas), there were slight variations in the external boundary between the original three-label segmentation and the converted two-label segmentation. Generally, the dissimilarities between $WT_{HD\text{-}GLIO}$—used in step 2 of the conversion—and the original BraTS three-label segmentations were as desired within the internal probable necrotic and cystic regions and otherwise within the assessment of the lesion border.

We identified and segmented 41 fluid-filled resection cavities within the postoperative test set comprising MRI examinations from 72 patients. The deep learning model trained with expert annotations adhering to the BraTS three-label annotation protocol labelled a minimum of 1 cm^3 in 10 of the 41 cavities. On average, the labelled volume in a cavity was 10.7 cm^3. Conversely, the model trained with annotations adapted to our two-label protocol did not include a volume exceeding 0.1 cm^3 in any of the cavities (and neither did HD-GLIO AUTO). Figure 2 shows a case where the three-label model included parts of the resection cavity.

For the preoperative test set, the median DSC values between the two-label model and converted reference expert segmentations were 0.94 (95% CI [0.93; 0.95]) for CE tumours and 0.94 (95% CI [0.92; 0.94]) for NEs. HD-GLIO achieved median DSC values of 0.89 (95% CI [0.88; 0.90]) for CE tumours and 0.88 (95% CI [0.87; 0.90]) for NEs. The DSC distributions are illustrated by box plots in Figure 3.

For the postoperative test set, the median DSC values between the two-label model and reference expert segmentations were 0.48 (95% CI [0.30; 0.70]) for CE tumours and 0.68 (95% CI [0.63; 0.74]) for NEs. When focusing on CE tumours larger than 1 cm^3, the median DSC was 0.75 (95% CI [0.66; 0.83]). In contrast, the comparison of HD-GLIO's segmentations with reference expert segmentations produced median DSC values of 0.73 (95% CI [0.63; 0.79]) for CE tumours, 0.71 (95% CI [0.68; 0.74]) for NEs and 0.79 (95% CI [0.73; 0.83] for CE tumours larger than 1 cm^3. For CE tumours with volumes greater than 1 cm^3 and for NEs, the two models' performances were not significantly different (p = 0.40 and p = 0.29, respectively). The DSC distributions are illustrated by box plots in Figure 4. In 15 cases, the two-label model achieved CE DSC = 0 due to false positives. In all cases but one, the two-label model included either contrast enhancing dura above a superficial cavity or parts of an enhancing cavity wall. In one case, it included parts of plexus choroideus. In three cases, the two-label model achieved CE DSC = 0 due to false negatives. All three cases involved weakly contrast-enhancing lesions.

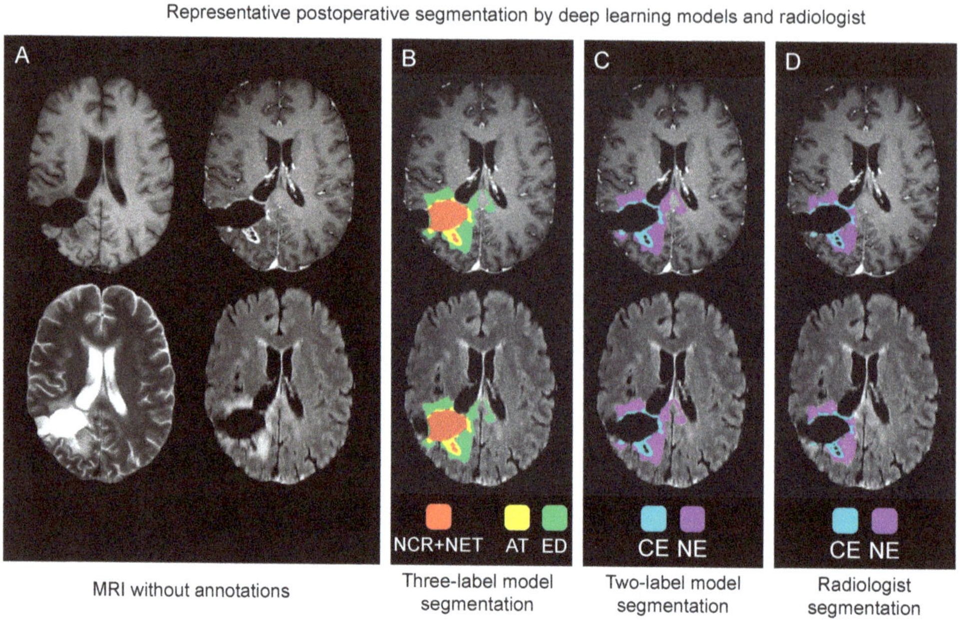

Figure 2. Representative case from the postoperative test set of segmentations performed by deep learning models trained utilising the BraTS three-label annotation protocol and our proposed two-label protocol and by radiologist as reference. **Panel A**: Anatomical sequences without annotations. T1 (top left), T1Gd (top right), T2 (bottom left) and FLAIR (bottom right). **Panels B–D**: Annotations overlaid on T1Gd (top) and FLAIR (bottom). NCR+NET = necrosis, cysts and non-enhancing tumour core; AT = active contrast-enhancing tumour; ED = oedema and infiltrated tissue; CE = contrast-enhancing tumour; NE = non-enhancing hyperintense T2/FLAIR signal abnormalities. The three-label model includes parts of the resection cavity (panel B) while the two-label model (**panel C**) and radiologist reference (**panel D**) do not.

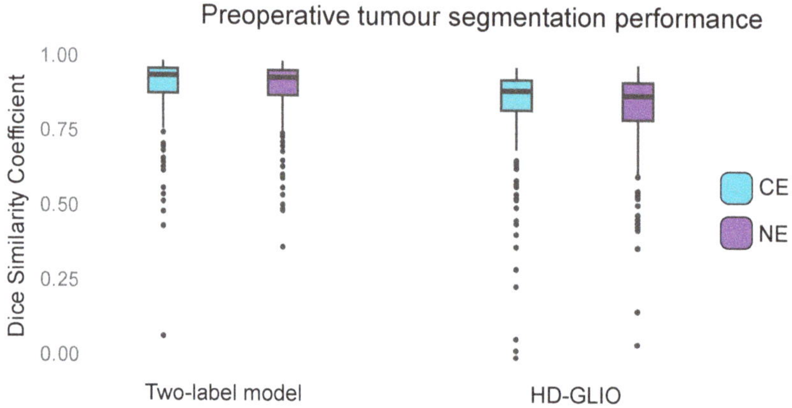

Figure 3. Agreement in preoperative brain tumour segmentations between deep learning models and two-label converted expert annotations across 251 cases from the BraTS 2021 training set, reserved for testing. The boxplots depict the distributions of Dice similarity coefficients (DSCs). CE = contrast-enhancing tumour; NE = non-enhancing hyperintense T2/FLAIR signal abnormalities.

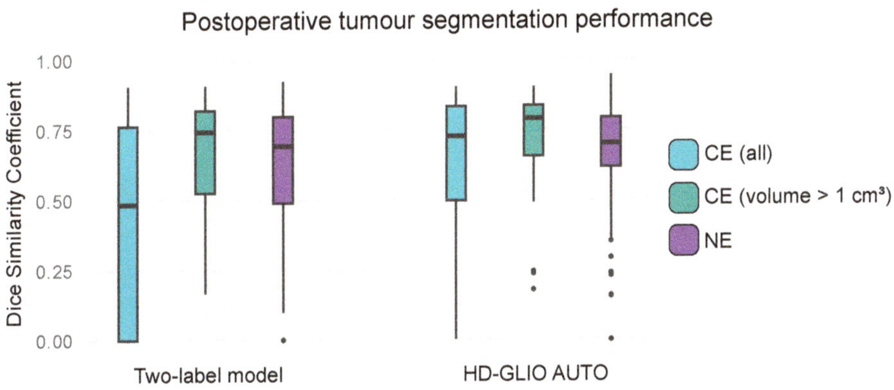

Figure 4. Agreement in postoperative brain tumour segmentations between deep learning models and our independent expert two-label annotations for 72 cases from the postoperative test set. The boxplots depict the distributions of Dice similarity coefficients (DSCs). CE = contrast-enhancing tumour; NE = non-enhancing hyperintense T2/FLAIR signal abnormalities; CE (volume > 1 cm^3) = CE segmentations with volumes exceeding 1 cm^3.

4. Discussion

In this study, we demonstrated that using the BraTS dataset, with its original three-label annotations, to train a DL algorithm for segmentation of brain tumours after surgery will result in substantial and frequent mislabelling of resection cavities. We automatically converted the three-label BraTS annotations to two-label annotations suitable for the postoperative setting and used them to train a model that excluded all cavities and showed a tumour segmentation performance comparable to that of a state-of-the-art algorithm for volumes exceeding 1 cm^3. Hence, our study enables the use of the largest publicly available expert annotated brain tumour (BraTS) dataset for training DL algorithms aimed at treatment response monitoring.

Prior research suggesting the harmonisation of pre- and postoperative brain tumour segmentation has typically incorporated the resection cavities into the NCR+NET label [29–31]. This approach is useful to radiotherapy-planning for glioblastoma, where, according to clinical guidelines [32], resection cavities are incorporated into the gross tumour volume (GTV). Conversely, Kickingereder et al. [12] and Chang et al. [33] opted to label the contrast-enhancing tumour and volumes of FLAIR hyperintense signal abnormalities but not the resection cavities, thereby emphasising the active tumour growth crucial for treatment response monitoring [10,11]. This perspective is underlined by Kickingereder et al., who illustrated that the time-to-progression based on these labels served as a superior surrogate endpoint for overall survival compared to RANO assessment with two-dimensional measurements.

The studies focusing on postoperative treatment response monitoring by Chang et al. [33] and Kickingereder et al. [12] relied on newly annotated pre- and postoperative data for training DL algorithms, which are not publicly available. Our study adds to the current literature by introducing a two-label annotation protocol that adapts and expands the BraTS annotation protocol with a focus on postoperative image features. Further, the study provides a fully automatic conversion of the existing, publicly available BraTS annotations to align with our proposed two-label annotation protocol. This latter contribution positions the large BraTS training dataset as a foundational resource in the public domain for the development of deep learning algorithms designed for brain tumour treatment response monitoring.

Central to this study is the novel conversion of the expert-validated BraTS three-label segmentations to our proposed two-label format. In one of its steps, the conversion process relies on an automatic whole-tumour segmentation by HD-GLIO ($WT_{HD\text{-}GLIO}$).

Typically, the dissimilarities between $WT_{HD\text{-}GLIO}$ and the original BraTS three-label segmentations occur as intended within the probable cystic and necrotic regions and otherwise within the assessment of the lesion border. Since only the NCR+NET label areas of the original annotations are altered in the conversion process, the cases most prone to potential conversion errors are tumours with large NET volumes (lower-grade gliomas) extending to the outer contour. In the majority of such cases, this results in only minor variations in the external NE contour. This is supported by the conversion success rate of 122/125 = 97.6% (95% CI [93.2–99.5%]). Based on our inspection, it is therefore unlikely that there are frequent issues in the conversion of the complete BraTS 2021 training dataset segmentations, and it demonstrates that the conversion remains robust against inconsistencies between $WT_{HD\text{-}GLIO}$ and the original BraTS segmentations.

A limitation of our study is that we employed a particular U-Net model and only a single postoperative dataset. Yet, evidence suggests the issue of misclassification of resection cavities is not isolated. DeepBratumIA [34] segmentations are provided along with the Lumiere dataset [20] using a different preprocessing method involving atlas registration. Our inspections of the segmentations revealed erroneously included cavity parts [20]. Additionally, Ramesh et al. shows an example segmentation of a Swin-UNETR model [35] trained on the same BraTS data, exhibiting cavity inclusion in their published figure [31]. Our own preliminary observations with nnU-Net on a local dataset reinforce this pattern. Thus, various U-Net architectures trained on the three-label BraTS 2021 training dataset demonstrate a consistent tendency to misclassify parts of resection cavities as tumour tissue across diverse postoperative datasets and preprocessing techniques, an error which is mitigated by our two-label annotation approach.

Our two-label model shows a high rate of false positives in the postoperative setting, particularly apparent by DSC = 0 achieved in some cases with CE tumour smaller than 1 cm^3. This is anticipated, given that the model was trained exclusively on preoperative MRI and thus was not exposed to the commonly occurring postoperative contrast enhancement patterns from non-tumorous tissue [36], like HD-GLIO was. Hence, some postoperative cases are necessary for training a model in this setting. However, our proposed conversion of the BraTS annotations enables the use of the large BraTS dataset for training, which may considerably reduce the need for expert-annotated postoperative data, which have limited availability [18]. The accuracy of our two-label model for larger CE tumours indicates the viability of this approach.

In assessing the automated conversion, we noted discrepancies in three out of 125 evaluated cases when compared to our expectations. Nevertheless, such discrepancies did not significantly impact the training efficacy of our two-label model, which sustained a high Dice coefficient of 0.94 for segmenting both CE tumour and NEs in the preoperative test set.

Although our two-label annotation protocol might differ slightly from the training approach used by HD-GLIO, the core criteria remain consistent: The CE label identifies contrast-enhancing tumours, while the NE label represents non-enhancing T2/FLAIR hyperintense signal abnormalities. Therefore, HD-GLIO's segmentations are a valid benchmark for direct comparisons with our model. The relevance of our protocol lies in its derivation from and full compatibility with the BraTS preoperative protocol, which allowed for the conversion to a two-label annotation but also ensures consistent segmentation of postoperative MRIs in future research and in the development and evaluation of DL segmentation models.

In perspective, our study underscores the capability of BraTS to serve as a foundational dataset for the training of DL algorithms for postoperative tumour segmentation, pivotal for treatment response monitoring. We demonstrate that by using the converted two-label annotations, DL algorithms can accurately exclude resection cavities postoperatively while maintaining robust tumour segmentation. However, we acknowledge that training solely on the preoperative BraTS dataset may not fully address all surgically induced lesions; incorporating some postoperative data remains necessary. The key contribution is enabling the research community to effectively utilise the extensive and high-quality BraTS dataset in training DL algorithms for postoperative applications, potentially reducing the reliance on scarce postoperative training data. This contribution is particularly significant given the notable scarcity of publicly available, high-quality postoperative datasets with expert annotations. Among the few available postoperative datasets, the UPenn-GBM dataset [37] includes 60 postoperative MRIs, and the Lumiere dataset [20], which we utilised for postoperative testing, encompasses longitudinally collected MRIs from 91 patients. Unfortunately, neither dataset offers expert annotations. To our knowledge, no other public datasets currently meet the requisite standards of quality and expert annotation.

With our work, the accessibility of adapted annotations for public use paves the way for significant advancements in research. Future studies could validate the potential of combining the BraTS dataset with a carefully selected or limited set of annotated postoperative MRI cases. This combination would ideally leverage datasets from the public domain, such as the Lumiere dataset [18], to efficiently train deep learning algorithms for postoperative treatment response monitoring.

5. Conclusions

In this study, we showed that a state-of-the-art DL algorithm, when trained on the BraTS 2021 training dataset with its current three-label brain tumour annotations, is unsuitable for postoperative segmentation due to the frequent misclassification of resection cavities as tumour regions. To remedy this shortcoming, we automatically converted the annotations of the BraTS 2021 training dataset to a revised two-label annotation protocol adapted for postoperative tumour segmentation. The DL algorithm trained using the two-label annotations accurately excluded resection cavities from tumour volumes while showing a good tumour segmentation performance for larger CE tumours. Our work enables the use of the BraTS 2021 training dataset for training DL algorithms aimed at a postoperative setting and thus equips a broad community of researchers and clinicians with a large body of essential training data to develop algorithms tailored for postoperative brain tumour response assessment, effectively reducing the need for the publicly scarce postoperative training data.

Author Contributions: Conceptualization, P.J.S., V.A.L., F.L.A., M.B.N., H.S.P., J.F.C., C.N.L. and A.E.H.; methodology, P.J.S., J.F.C., C.N.L. and A.E.H.; software, P.J.S.; validation, P.J.S.; formal analysis, P.J.S.; investigation, P.J.S., J.F.C. and C.N.L.; data curation, P.J.S.; writing—original draft preparation, P.J.S.; writing—review and editing, P.J.S., J.F.C., V.A.L., C.N.L., F.L.A., M.B.N., H.S.P. and A.E.H.; visualization, P.J.S.; supervision, J.F.C., C.N.L., M.B.N., H.S.P. and A.E.H.; project administration, P.J.S.; funding acquisition, A.E.H. All authors have read and agreed to the published version of the manuscript.

Funding: The project is part of the DCCC Brain Tumor Center funded by the Danish Cancer Society, Grant No. R295-A16770.

Institutional Review Board Statement: Not applicable. The studied data is in the public domain.

Informed Consent Statement: Not applicable. The studied data are in the public domain.

Data Availability Statement: The script for converting the BraTS three-label annotations to our proposed two-label annotation protocol and the original data generated in the study, i.e., the expert segmentations of the postoperative test dataset, are openly available at GitHub: https://github.com/DEPICT-RH/postoperative_brain_tumor_segmentation_with_brats (accessed on 7 August 2024). The preoperative image data and original three-label annotations used in this study are from the RSNA-ASNR-MICCAI Brain Tumor Segmentation (BraTS) Challenge 2021 and can be requested through: http://braintumorsegmentation.org/ (accessed on 7 August 2024). The postoperative image data and the HD-GLIO segmentation of these are from the public Lumiere dataset, and are available at FigShare: https://springernature.figshare.com/collections/The_LUMIERE_Dataset_Longitudinal_Glioblastoma_MRI_with_Expert_RANO_Evaluation/5904905 (accessed on 7 August 2024).

Acknowledgments: For the writing of this manuscript, we acknowledge the use of OpenAI's ChatGPT 4 for assistance with grammar and sentence structure.

Conflicts of Interest: The authors declare no conflicts of interest.

Appendix A

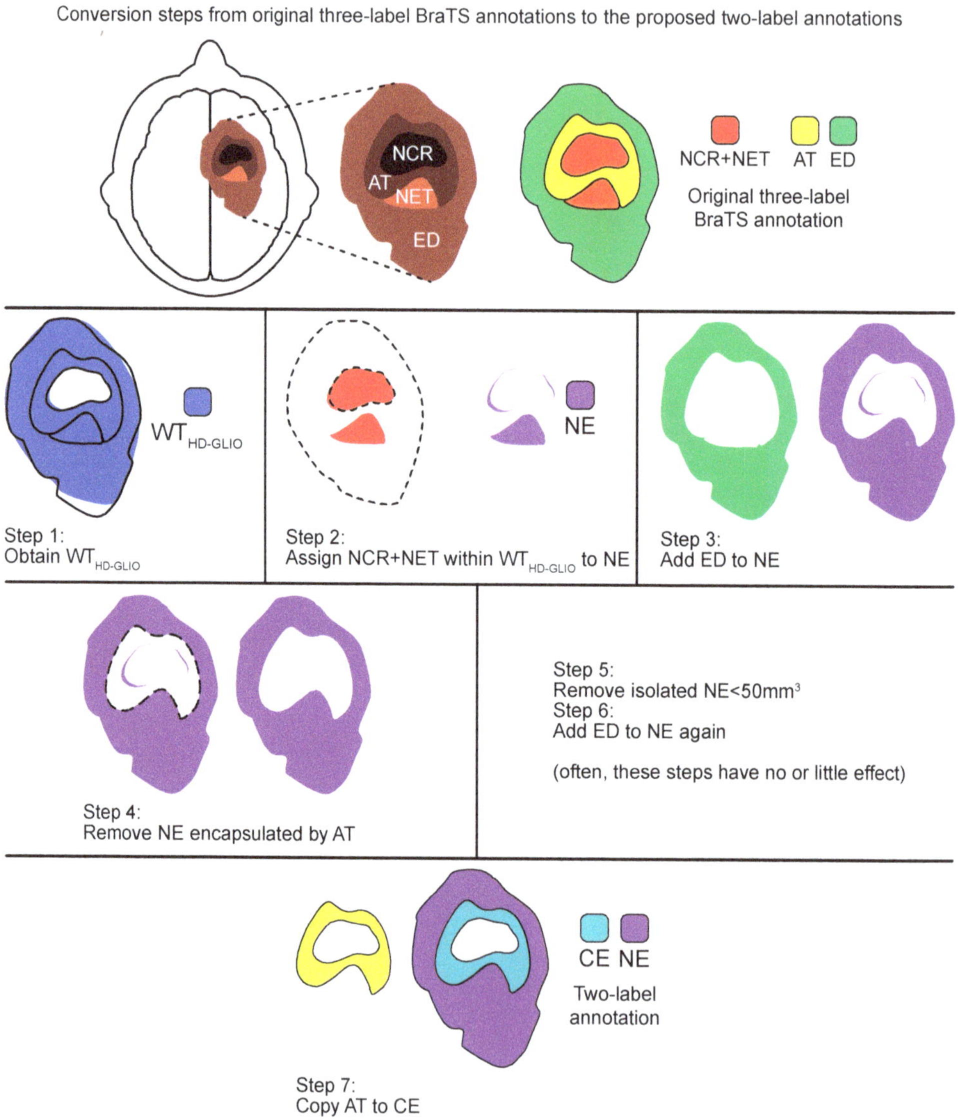

Figure A1. Schematic illustration of the steps of the conversion of the BraTS 2021 three-label segmentation masks for harmonisation with the proposed two-label annotation protocol. The top panel shows the original BraTS three-label annotations and the bottom panel the resulting two-label annotations. At each step, a left illustration shows what is currently treated and how, and a right illustration shows the current result of the process. AT = active contrast-enhancing tumour; ED = oedema and infiltrated tissue; $WT_{HD\text{-}GLIO}$ = automatic whole-tumour segmentation by HD-GLIO; CE = contrast-enhancing tumour; NE = non-enhancing hyperintense T2/FLAIR signal abnormalities.

Appendix B

The model was trained using nnU-Net [3]. nnU-Net is designed to require minimal optimisation for a new segmentation task, as it automatically extracts hyperparameters during network preprocessing. This is done by automatically defining a set of dataset fingerprints, including image sizes, voxel spacing and class ratios. From this fingerprint, hyperparameters such as the appropriate patch-size, batch-size, number of feature maps and the convolutional kernel size are set.

We utilised the default parameters set after extracting the dataset fingerprints. With the BraTS dataset, this resulted in 1 mm^3 spacing, a median matrix size of [140,171,136], a patch size of [128,160,112] and a batch size of 2. Image normalisation was performed with z-score normalisation. nnU-Net is publicly available at www.github.com/MIC-DKFZ/nnUNet, (accessed on 7 August 2024). A full description and further details about nnU-Net can be found in [3].

We used the default training setup, which involves training using five-fold cross validation for 1000 epochs, each lasting 250 batches. The training dataset (n = 1000) was randomly split into a training and a test set in each fold prior to training. In our study, we used the '3d_fullres' configuration of nnU-Net.

References

1. Liu, Z.; Tong, L.; Chen, L.; Jiang, Z.; Zhou, F.; Zhang, Q.; Zhang, X.; Jin, Y.; Zhou, H. Deep learning based brain tumor segmentation: A survey. *Complex Intell. Syst.* **2023**, *9*, 1001–1026. [CrossRef]
2. Magadza, T.; Viriri, S. Deep Learning for Brain Tumor Segmentation: A Survey of State-of-the-Art. *J. Imaging* **2021**, *7*, 19. [CrossRef]
3. Isensee, F.; Jaeger, P.F.; Kohl, S.A.A.; Petersen, J.; Maier-Hein, K.H. nnU-Net: A self-configuring method for deep learning-based biomedical image segmentation. *Nat. Methods* **2021**, *18*, 203–211. [CrossRef] [PubMed]
4. Brain Tumor Segmentation (BraTS) Challenge. Available online: https://www.med.upenn.edu/cbica/brats/ (accessed on 30 December 2023).
5. Bakas, S.; Reyes, M.; Jakab, A.; Bauer, S.; Rempfler, M.; Crimi, A.; Takeshi Shinohara, R.; Berger, C.; Ha, S.M.; Rozycki, M.; et al. Identifying the Best Machine Learning Algorithms for Brain Tumor Segmentation, Progression Assessment, and Overall Survival Prediction in the BRATS Challenge. *arXiv* **2018**, arXiv:1811.02629. [CrossRef]
6. Menze, B.H.; Jakab, A.; Bauer, S.; Kalpathy-Cramer, J.; Farahani, K.; Kirby, J.; Burren, Y.; Porz, N.; Slotboom, J.; Wiest, R.; et al. The Multimodal Brain Tumor Image Segmentation Benchmark (BRATS). *IEEE Trans. Med. Imaging* **2015**, *34*, 1993–2024. [CrossRef] [PubMed]
7. Mehta, R.; Filos, A.; Baid, U.; Sako, C.; McKinley, R.; Rebsamen, M.; Datwyler, K.; Meier, R.; Radojewski, P.; Murugesan, G.K.; et al. QU-BraTS: MICCAI BraTS 2020 Challenge on Quantifying Uncertainty in Brain Tumor Segmentation—Analysis of Ranking Scores and Benchmarking Results. *J. Mach. Learn. Biomed. Imaging* **2022**, *1*, 1–54. [CrossRef]
8. Baid, U.; Ghodasara, S.; Mohan, S.; Bilello, M.; Calabrese, E.; Colak, E.; Farahani, K.; Kalpathy-Cramer, J.; Kitamura, F.C.; Pati, S.; et al. The RSNA-ASNR-MICCAI BraTS 2021 Benchmark on Brain Tumor Segmentation and Radiogenomic Classification. *arXiv* **2021**, arXiv:2107.02314. [CrossRef]
9. Vogelbaum, M.A.; Jost, S.; Aghi, M.K.; Heimberger, A.B.; Sampson, J.H.; Wen, P.Y.; Macdonald, D.R.; Van den Bent, M.J.; Chang, S.M. Application of novel response/progression measures for surgically delivered therapies for gliomas: Response Assessment in Neuro-Oncology (RANO) Working Group. *Neurosurgery* **2012**, *70*, 234–243. [CrossRef]
10. Weller, M.; van den Bent, M.; Preusser, M.; Le Rhun, E.; Tonn, J.C.; Minniti, G.; Bendszus, M.; Balana, C.; Chinot, O.; Dirven, L.; et al. EANO guidelines on the diagnosis and treatment of diffuse gliomas of adulthood. *Nat. Rev. Clin. Oncol.* **2021**, *18*, 170–186. [CrossRef]
11. Wen, P.Y.; van den Bent, M.; Youssef, G.; Cloughesy, T.F.; Ellingson, B.M.; Weller, M.; Galanis, E.; Barboriak, D.P.; de Groot, J.; Gilbert, M.R.; et al. RANO 2.0: Update to the Response Assessment in Neuro-Oncology Criteria for High- and Low-Grade Gliomas in Adults. *J. Clin. Oncol.* **2023**, *41*, 5187–5199. [CrossRef]
12. Kickingereder, P.; Isensee, F.; Tursunova, I.; Petersen, J.; Neuberger, U.; Bonekamp, D.; Brugnara, G.; Schell, M.; Kessler, T.; Foltyn, M.; et al. Automated quantitative tumour response assessment of MRI in neuro-oncology with artificial neural networks: A multicentre, retrospective study. *Lancet Oncol.* **2019**, *20*, 728–740. [CrossRef] [PubMed]
13. Vollmuth, P.; Foltyn, M.; Huang, R.Y.; Galldiks, N.; Petersen, J.; Isensee, F.; van den Bent, M.J.; Barkhof, F.; Park, J.E.; Park, Y.W.; et al. AI-based decision support improves reproducibility of tumor response assessment in neuro-oncology: An international multi-reader study. *Neuro-Oncol.* **2022**, *25*, 533–543. [CrossRef]

14. Hannisdal, M.H.; Goplen, D.; Alam, S.; Haasz, J.; Oltedal, L.; Rahman, M.A.; Rygh, C.B.; Lie, S.A.; Lundervold, A.; Chekenya, M. Feasibility of deep learning-based tumor segmentation for target delineation and response assessment in grade-4 glioma using multi-parametric MRI. *Neurooncol. Adv.* **2023**, *5*, vdad037. [CrossRef] [PubMed]
15. Sorensen, P.J.; Carlsen, J.F.; Larsen, V.A.; Andersen, F.L.; Ladefoged, C.N.; Nielsen, M.B.; Poulsen, H.S.; Hansen, A.E. Evaluation of the HD-GLIO Deep Learning Algorithm for Brain Tumour Segmentation on Postoperative MRI. *Diagnostics* **2023**, *13*, 363. [CrossRef] [PubMed]
16. Bakas, S.; Akbari, H.; Sotiras, A.; Bilello, M.; Rozycki, M.; Kirby, J.S.; Freymann, J.B.; Farahani, K.; Davatzikos, C. Advancing The Cancer Genome Atlas glioma MRI collections with expert segmentation labels and radiomic features. *Sci. Data* **2017**, *4*, 170117. [CrossRef] [PubMed]
17. Davatzikos, C.; Rathore, S.; Bakas, S.; Pati, S.; Bergman, M.; Kalarot, R.; Sridharan, P.; Gastounioti, A.; Jahani, N.; Cohen, E.; et al. Cancer imaging phenomics toolkit: Quantitative imaging analytics for precision diagnostics and predictive modeling of clinical outcome. *J. Med. Imaging* **2018**, *5*, 011018. [CrossRef]
18. Pati, S.; Singh, A.; Rathore, S.; Gastounioti, A.; Bergman, M.; Ngo, P.; Ha, S.M.; Bounias, D.; Minock, J.; Murphy, G.; et al. The Cancer Imaging Phenomics Toolkit (CaPTk): Technical Overview. *Brainlesion* **2020**, *11993*, 380–394. [CrossRef]
19. Rathore, S.; Bakas, S.; Pati, S.; Akbari, H.; Kalarot, R.; Sridharan, P.; Rozycki, M.; Bergman, M.; Tunc, B.; Verma, R.; et al. Brain Cancer Imaging Phenomics Toolkit (brain-CaPTk): An Interactive Platform for Quantitative Analysis of Glioblastoma. *Brainlesion* **2018**, *10670*, 133–145. [CrossRef]
20. Suter, Y.; Knecht, U.; Valenzuela, W.; Notter, M.; Hewer, E.; Schucht, P.; Wiest, R.; Reyes, M. The LUMIERE dataset: Longitudinal Glioblastoma MRI with expert RANO evaluation. *Sci. Data* **2022**, *9*, 768. [CrossRef] [PubMed]
21. Isensee, F.; Jäger, P.F.; Kohl, S.A.A.; Petersen, J.; Maier-Hein, K.H. Automated Design of Deep Learning Methods for Biomedical Image Segmentation. *arXiv* **2019**, arXiv:1904.08128. [CrossRef]
22. Isensee, F.; Schell, M.; Pflueger, I.; Brugnara, G.; Bonekamp, D.; Neuberger, U.; Wick, A.; Schlemmer, H.P.; Heiland, S.; Wick, W.; et al. Automated brain extraction of multisequence MRI using artificial neural networks. *Hum. Brain Mapp.* **2019**, *40*, 4952–4964. [CrossRef] [PubMed]
23. VASARI Research Project. Available online: https://wiki.cancerimagingarchive.net/display/public/VASARI+Research+Project (accessed on 30 December 2023).
24. GitHub: HD-GLIO. Available online: https://github.com/NeuroAI-HD/HD-GLIO (accessed on 30 December 2023).
25. Postoperative Brain Tumour Segmentation with BraTS. Available online: https://github.com/DEPICT-RH/postoperative_brain_tumor_segmentation_with_brats (accessed on 7 August 2024).
26. R Core Team. *R: A Language and Environment for Statistical Computing*; R Foundation for Statistical Computing: Vienna, Austria, 2022. Available online: https://www.R-project.org/ (accessed on 22 August 2024).
27. Yushkevich, P.A.; Piven, J.; Hazlett, H.C.; Smith, R.G.; Ho, S.; Gee, J.C.; Gerig, G. User-guided 3D active contour segmentation of anatomical structures: Significantly improved efficiency and reliability. *Neuroimage* **2006**, *31*, 1116–1128. [CrossRef]
28. Yushkevich, P.A.; Pashchinskiy, A.; Oguz, I.; Mohan, S.; Schmitt, J.E.; Stein, J.M.; Zukic, D.; Vicory, J.; McCormick, M.; Yushkevich, N.; et al. User-Guided Segmentation of Multi-modality Medical Imaging Datasets with ITK-SNAP. *Neuroinformatics* **2019**, *17*, 83–102. [CrossRef] [PubMed]
29. Bianconi, A.; Rossi, L.F.; Bonada, M.; Zeppa, P.; Nico, E.; De Marco, R.; Lacroce, P.; Cofano, F.; Bruno, F.; Morana, G.; et al. Deep learning-based algorithm for postoperative glioblastoma MRI segmentation: A promising new tool for tumor burden assessment. *Brain Inform.* **2023**, *10*, 26. [CrossRef]
30. Lotan, E.; Zhang, B.; Dogra, S.; Wang, W.D.; Carbone, D.; Fatterpekar, G.; Oermann, E.K.; Lui, Y.W. Development and Practical Implementation of a Deep Learning-Based Pipeline for Automated Pre- and Postoperative Glioma Segmentation. *AJNR Am. J. Neuroradiol.* **2022**, *43*, 24–32. [CrossRef]
31. Ramesh, K.K.; Xu, K.M.; Trivedi, A.G.; Huang, V.; Sharghi, V.K.; Kleinberg, L.R.; Mellon, E.A.; Shu, H.G.; Shim, H.; Weinberg, B.D. A Fully Automated Post-Surgical Brain Tumor Segmentation Model for Radiation Treatment Planning and Longitudinal Tracking. *Cancers* **2023**, *15*, 3956. [CrossRef]
32. Niyazi, M.; Andratschke, N.; Bendszus, M.; Chalmers, A.J.; Erridge, S.C.; Galldiks, N.; Lagerwaard, F.J.; Navarria, P.; Munck Af Rosenschold, P.; Ricardi, U.; et al. ESTRO-EANO guideline on target delineation and radiotherapy details for glioblastoma. *Radiother. Oncol.* **2023**, *184*, 109663. [CrossRef]
33. Chang, K.; Beers, A.L.; Bai, H.X.; Brown, J.M.; Ly, K.I.; Li, X.; Senders, J.T.; Kavouridis, V.K.; Boaro, A.; Su, C.; et al. Automatic assessment of glioma burden: A deep learning algorithm for fully automated volumetric and bidimensional measurement. *Neuro Oncol.* **2019**, *21*, 1412–1422. [CrossRef] [PubMed]
34. ARTORG Center for Biomedical Engineering Research—University of Bern. *DeepBraTumIA*, 2021.
35. Hatamizadeh, A.; Nath, V.; Tang, Y.; Yang, D.; Roth, H.; Xu, D. Swin UNETR: Swin Transformers for Semantic Segmentation of Brain Tumors in MRI Images. *arXiv* **2022**, arXiv:2201.01266. [CrossRef]

36. Bette, S.; Gempt, J.; Huber, T.; Boeckh-Behrens, T.; Ringel, F.; Meyer, B.; Zimmer, C.; Kirschke, J.S. Patterns and Time Dependence of Unspecific Enhancement in Postoperative Magnetic Resonance Imaging After Glioblastoma Resection. *World Neurosurg.* **2016**, *90*, 440–447. [CrossRef]
37. Bakas, S.; Sako, C.; Akbari, H.; Bilello, M.; Sotiras, A.; Shukla, G.; Rudie, J.D.; Santamaria, N.F.; Kazerooni, A.F.; Pati, S.; et al. The University of Pennsylvania glioblastoma (UPenn-GBM) cohort: Advanced MRI, clinical, genomics, & radiomics. *Sci. Data* **2022**, *9*, 453. [CrossRef] [PubMed]

Journal of
Clinical Medicine

MDPI

Article

Interrater Variability of ML-Based CT-FFR in Patients without Obstructive CAD before TAVR: Influence of Image Quality, Coronary Artery Calcifications, and Location of Measurement

Robin F. Gohmann [1,2,*,†], Adrian Schug [1,2,†], Christian Krieghoff [2], Patrick Seitz [1], Nicolas Majunke [3], Maria Buske [3], Fyn Kaiser [1], Sebastian Schaudt [1], Katharina Renatus [1,2], Steffen Desch [3], Sergey Leontyev [4], Thilo Noack [4], Philipp Kiefer [4], Konrad Pawelka [1,2], Christian Lücke [2], Ahmed Abdelhafez [3], Sebastian Ebel [1,2], Michael A. Borger [4], Holger Thiele [3], Christoph Panknin [5], Mohamed Abdel-Wahab [3], Matthias Horn [6,‡] and Matthias Gutberlet [1,2,‡]

1 Department of Diagnostic and Interventional Radiology, Heart Center Leipzig, Strümpellstr. 39, 04289 Leipzig, Germany; adrian.schug@helios-gesundheit.de (A.S.); patrick.seitz@helios-gesundheit.de (P.S.); fyn.kaiser@helios-gesundheit.de (F.K.); sebastian.schaudt@helios-gesundheit.de (S.S.); katharina.renatus@helios-gesundheit.de (K.R.); paulkonrad.pawelka@helios-gesundheit.de (K.P.); sebastian.ebel@medizin.uni-leipzig.de (S.E.); matthias.gutberlet@helios-gesundheit.de (M.G.)
2 Medical Faculty, University of Leipzig, Liebigstr. 27, 04103 Leipzig, Germany; christian.krieghoff@helios-gesundheit.de (C.K.); christian.luecke@helios-gesundheit.de (C.L.)
3 Department of Cardiology, Heart Center Leipzig, University of Leipzig, Strümpellstr. 39, 04289 Leipzig, Germany; nicolas.majunke@medizin.uni-leipzig.de (N.M.); maria.buske@hmedizin.uni-leipzig.de (M.B.); steffen.desch@medizin.uni-leipzig.de (S.D.); ahmed.abdelhafez@medizin.uni-leipzig.de (A.A.); holger.thiele@medizin.uni-leipzig.de (H.T.); mohamed.abdelwahab@helios-gesundheit.de (M.A.-W.)
4 Department of Cardiac Surgery, Heart Center Leipzig, University of Leipzig, Strümpellstr. 39, 04289 Leipzig, Germany; sergey.leontyev@medizin.uni-leipzig.de (S.L.); thilo.noack@medizin.uni-leipzig.de (T.N.); philipp.kiefer@medizin.uni-leipzig.de (P.K.); michael.borger@medizin.uni-leipzig.de (M.A.B.)
5 Siemens Healthcare GmbH, Henkestr. 127, 91052 Erlangen, Germany; christoph.panknin@siemens-healthineers.com
6 Institute for Medical Informatics, Statistics and Epidemiology (IMISE), University of Leipzig, Härtelstr. 16-18, 04107 Leipzig, Germany; matthias.horn@imise.uni-leipzig.de
* Correspondence: robin.gohmann@gmx.de; Tel.: +49-341-865-1702
† These authors contributed equally to this work as first authors.
‡ These authors contributed equally to this work as senior authors.

Abstract: Objectives: CT-derived fractional flow reserve (CT-FFR) can improve the specificity of coronary CT-angiography (cCTA) for ruling out relevant coronary artery disease (CAD) prior to transcatheter aortic valve replacement (TAVR). However, little is known about the reproducibility of CT-FFR and the influence of diffuse coronary artery calcifications or segment location. The objective was to assess the reliability of machine-learning (ML)-based CT-FFR prior to TAVR in patients without obstructive CAD and to assess the influence of image quality, coronary artery calcium score (CAC), and the location of measurement within the coronary tree. **Methods**: Patients assessed for TAVR, without obstructive CAD on cCTA were evaluated with ML-based CT-FFR by two observers with differing experience. Differences in absolute values and categorization into hemodynamically relevant CAD (CT-FFR ≤ 0.80) were compared. Results in regard to CAD were also compared against invasive coronary angiography. The influence of segment location, image quality, and CAC was evaluated. **Results**: Of the screened patients, 109/388 patients did not have obstructive CAD on cCTA and were included. The median (interquartile range) difference of CT-FFR values was −0.005 (−0.09 to 0.04) ($p = 0.47$). Differences were smaller with high values. Recategorizations were more frequent in distal segments. Diagnostic accuracy of CT-FFR between both observers was comparable (proximal: Δ0.2%; distal: Δ0.5%) but was lower in distal segments (proximal: 98.9%/99.1%; distal: 81.1%/81.6%). Image quality and CAC had no clinically relevant influence on CT-FFR. **Conclusions**: ML-based CT-FFR evaluation of proximal segments was more reliable. Distal segments with CT-FFR values close to the given threshold were prone to recategorization, even if absolute differences between observers were minimal and independent of image quality or CAC.

Keywords: aortic stenosis; computed tomography coronary angiography; coronary angiography; coronary artery disease; transcatheter aortic valve implantation; diagnostic accuracy; machine learning

1. Introduction

Coronary computed tomography angiography (cCTA) is an excellent test for safely ruling out coronary artery disease [1] and is also employed in patients before transcatheter aortic valve replacement (TAVR) [2,3]. The diagnostic performance and specificity of cCTA can be improved by adding CT-derived fractional flow reserve (CT-FFR) to the diagnostic algorithm [4,5]. CT-FFR is a tool that in its original form is based on computational fluid dynamics (CFD) to simulate the blood flow in coronary vessels. CT-FFR combines this with the patient's vessel anatomy derived from cCTA. This way, the blood flow can be computed at every point of the coronary tree in a resting state and simulated hyperemia. The result is a 3D, color-coded model of the coronary tree from which the CT-FFR values can be read [6]. In contrast to commercially available CFD-based CT-FFR, machine-learning (ML)-based CT-FFR can be performed on-site without time delay and potentially at a significantly lower cost. ML-based CT-FFR is based on a less computationally demanding algorithm and immediately renders results [7] based on a semi-automatic segmentation of the coronary arteries performed by physicians or other staff on site. ML-based CT-FFR correlates well with CFD CT-FFR [4] and may also improve diagnostic performance compared to cCTA in patients before TAVR [5,8–12].

CT-FFR is particularly useful for ruling out hemodynamically relevant coronary artery disease (CAD) in patients with intermediate stenoses on cCTA [13], as the latter is limited by its low specificity. Validation studies of CT-FFR have focused on CAD-positive (CAD^+) patients and it is generally not recommended for patients without discrete stenoses (CAD^-). A recent study on CAD^- patients before TAVR reported a very high count of false-positive ratings with especially distal CT-FFR values frequently being pathologically decreased [14]. A similar gradual decrease has also been described in invasive FFR in patients with diffuse atherosclerosis [15]. It is still unclear whether these distal measurements in CT-FFR reflect true pathophysiology in severe aortic stenosis (AS; e.g., imbalance of left ventricular myocardium and vessel cross section), diffuse arteriosclerosis, or may stem from a cumulative segmentation error. An analysis of interobserver correlation in CAD^- patients could help differentiate between inaccurate, random measurements or true pathophysiology and remains to be assessed [16–18]. While CT-FFR is not recommended in this patient cohort, the results of this scientific approach will contribute to better interpretate pathologically decreased distal values in the clinical setting. The chosen cohort of patients with severe AS allows the evaluation of a gradual CT-FFR decrease without the influence of significant CAD.

In this study, we analyzed the interrater variability of ML-based CT-FFR in patients without obstructive CAD before TAVR. Secondarily, we examined the influence of image quality, coronary artery calcium score (CAC), and the location of measurement.

2. Materials and Methods

2.1. Study Design and Patient Population

The patient population and study design have been described previously [14]. Consecutive CT examinations within a 7-month period of patients with severe aortic valve stenosis undergoing TAVR planning were included. Patients also received invasive coronary angiography (ICA) within 3 months of the CT. Of 388 patients, 116 showed no relevant stenosis ($\geq$50%) on cCTA and were subsequently evaluated by two observers with CT-FFR.

The study was conducted in compliance with the Declaration of Helsinki (Medical Association 2013). The Ethics Committee of the University of Leipzig approved the study and written informed consent was waived (reference number: 435/18-ek).

2.2. CT Acquisition

The scan protocol has been described in a previous publication [3]. To reiterate, a non-enhanced scan for calcium scoring in standard technique was performed. This was followed by a single i.v. bolus of 70 mL iodinated contrast agent for a retrospectively ECG-gated helical CT scan of the heart and a non-gated high-pitch scan of the torso. No other medications were given. All examinations were performed on the same second-generation dual-source scanner (Somatom Definition Flash; Siemens, Erlangen, Germany).

2.3. Image Analysis

The cCTA scans and ICA were analyzed by segment, based on the 18-segment model (Figure 1) [16]. For both cCTA and ICA with quantitative coronary angiography (QCA), a diameter stenosis of ≥50% was deemed relevant. ICA was used as the standard of reference in this study. Results on vessel and patient levels were formed by considering the respective worst segment (highest-grade stenosis). The assessment of qualitative and quantitative image quality has previously been described in detail [3,5]. Quantitative image quality consisted of contrast opacification and contrast to noise ratio, qualitative image quality categorized the examination as one of the following: 0 = nondiagnostic (excluded from this analysis, as CAD could not be excluded); 1 = diagnostic; 2 = good; 3 = excellent.

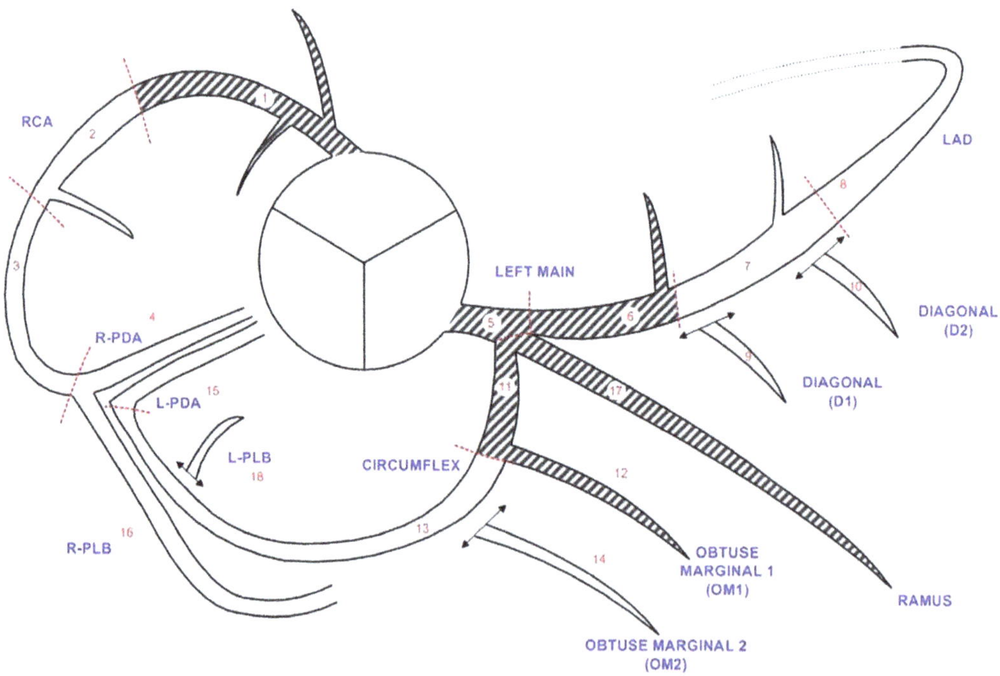

Figure 1. Diagram of the 18-segment model of the coronary tree. Diagram showing the coronary tree with its division into 18 segments according to the SCCT guidelines [16]. Shaded segments were defined as proximal in this study. L = left; LAD = left anterior descending artery; PDA = posterior descending artery; PLB = posterior-lateral branch; R = right; RCA = right coronary artery; SCCT = Society of Cardiovascular Computed Tomography.

ML-based CT-FFR (cFFR version 3.2.0, Siemens, Erlangen, Germany; not commercially available) was performed on all patients without morphological signs of obstruction twice on the same examination by two observers. Observers A and B received the same instructions, while observer A had additionally received clinical training beforehand [17]. The CT-FFR prototype for on-site evaluation used in this study has been described extensively elsewhere [4,5,7].

Readings were taken at the junction point of the middle and distal third of each segment for vessels with a luminal diameter of >1.5 mm [14]. CT-FFR values ≤ 0.80 were considered to be indicative of hemodynamically relevant CAD [18]. Per-vessel and per-patient gradings were generated by considering the respective minimal CT-FFR value of the comprising segments. Gradings were compared between both observers and mismatches were classified as recategorizations. Evaluation time was measured from the time the dataset was loaded till the CT-FFR was computed, with the largest proportion of time allocated to centerline definition and segmentation of the vessel lumen.

For subsequent analyses, segments 1, 5, 6, 17, and 11 were arbitrarily considered proximal; all other segments were considered distal (Figure 1). The methods in this study comply with the Guidelines for Reporting Reliability and Agreement Studies (GRRAS) [19].

2.4. Statistics

Body mass index and age were given as mean ± standard deviation. Asymmetric distributions for evaluation times and pairwise interobserver differences were given as median and interquartile range (IQR). In addition, 95% confidence intervals (CIs) of the median differences were specified. To assess differences in median CT-FFR values of the observers, a Wilcoxon signed-rank test was performed. Interrater agreement was calculated using the intra-class correlation coefficient (ICC) of type ICC (3,1) [20] with the corresponding 95% CI. For the interpretation of ICC values, Cicchetti's guidelines were employed [21] wherein values less than 0.4 and between 0.4 and 0.6 were considered indicative of poor and fair correlation, respectively. Values between 0.6 and 0.75 suggested good agreement; values exceeding 0.75 signified excellent correlation.

To determine the correlation between CT-FFR differences and covariates, Spearman's rank correlation (quantitative image quality measures and CAC) or Kendall's rank correlation (qualitative image quality) were calculated. The correlation of CAD categorization between both observers and covariates was assessed using point-biserial correlation (quantitative image quality and calcium burden) or rank-biserial correlation (qualitative image quality). p-values of all correlation analyses are with respect to the null hypothesis that the correlation coefficient equals zero. p-values < 0.05 were considered statistically significant.

Data curation and computation of inferential statistics were performed with spreadsheets (Microsoft Excel version 2010, Microsoft Corporation, Redmond, WA, USA). For further statistical analyses, R (v4.3.3, R Foundation for Statistical Computing, Vienna, Austria) was used.

3. Results

3.1. Study Population

In this study, 109 of 116 CT examinations of CAD^- patients were successfully evaluated by both observers. Initial exclusions occurred because of borderline image quality of cCTA rendering segmentation for CT-FFR not feasible (n = 3) and anatomical variants outside of the model boundaries of the CT-FFR prototype (n = 4) [14]. No additional exclusions occurred. The included patients had a mean body mass index of 28.4 ± 5.5 kg/m^2, a mean age of 78.4 ± 7.2 years, and 64.2% were female [3]. The median evaluation time of CT-FFR was 21 (16–28) min. and 24 (19–29) min. for observers A and B, respectively.

3.2. Absolute Differences

Absolute CT-FFR values were very similar between the observers (Figure 2) and showed no significant median difference on patient (n = 109; −0.005 [−0.09 to 0.04];

$p = 0.47$) or vessel level ($p \geq 0.12$; Table 1). On segment level, median differences were also very low, with few of these differences reaching statistical significance (Table 1). Between proximal and distal segments, there was no discernable trend toward higher or lower differences in CT-FFR values. All data is shown in Table 1.

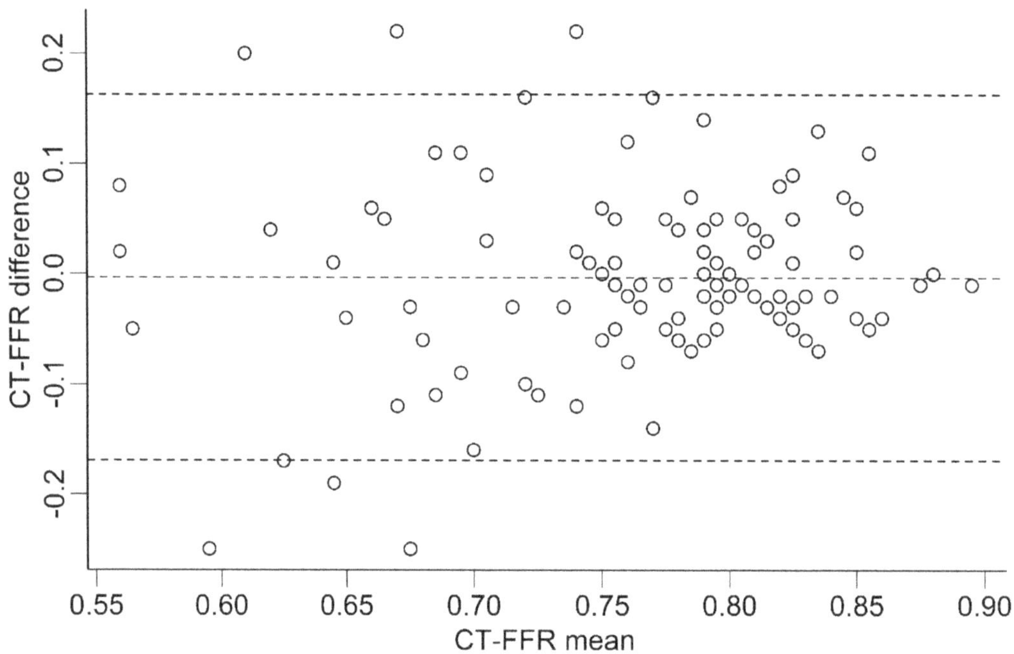

Figure 2. CT-FFR values at patient level. Bland-Altman plot showing the distribution of differences in CT-FFR values between both observers. Differences between both observers are overall very small. The plot shows no indication of a systematic bias. Lower mean CT-FFR values show one outlier (CT-FFR difference of −0.45 at a CT-FFR mean value of 0.58), which has been omitted from the plot for clarity. Lower mean CT-FFR values also show a larger heterogeneity of CT-FFR differences. CT-FFR = CT-derived fractional flow reserve. Dashed horizontal lines represent the mean difference (middle line) and the upper and lower limits of agreement (±1.96 SD, upper and lower lines).

Table 1. Interobserver variability of absolute CT-FFR values.

Level of Observation		n	Difference	95% CI	*p*	ICC	95% CI	*p*	RoR %	95% CI
Patient		109	−0.005 (−0.09 to 0.04)	−0.02, 0.01	0.47	0.421	0.25, 0.56	<0.001	29.4	21.6, 38.5
Vessel	**RCA**	109	0.0 (−0.03 to 0.05)	−0.01, 0.02	0.62	0.701	0.59, 0.79	<0.001	26.6	19.2, 35.6
	LM	109	0.0 (0.00 to 0.01)	0.00, 0.01	0.14	0.507	0.35, 0.63	<0.001	0.0	0.0, 3.4
	LAD	109	−0.015 (−0.08 to 0.04)	−0.03, 0.01	0.12	0.334	0.16, 0.49	<0.001	31.2	23.3, 40.4
	LCX	109	0.00 (−0.05 to 0.05)	−0.02, 0.01	0.76	0.588	0.45, 0.70	<0.001	20.2	13.7, 28.7
Segments	**S1**	109	0.01 (−0.01 to 0.01)	0.01, 0.02	<0.001	0.498	0.34, 0.63	<0.001	0.0	0.0, 3.4
	S2	108	0.015 (−0.01 to 0.03)	0.01, 0.02	<0.001	0.725	0.62, 0.80	<0.001	1.9	0.5, 6.5
	S3	101	0.015 (−0.02 to 0.04)	0.01, 0.03	0.003	0.724	0.62, 0.81	<0.001	13.9	8.4, 21.9
	S4	76	−0.005 (−0.04 to 0.03)	−0.02, 0.01	0.46	0.73	0.61, 0.82	<0.001	28.9	20.0, 40.0
	S16	80	0.00 (−0.04 to 0.04)	−0.01, 0.02	0.83	0.676	0.54, 0.78	<0.001	21.2	13.7, 31.4
	S5	109	0.00 (0.00 to 0.01)	0.00, 0.01	0.14	0.507	0.35, 0.63	<0.001	0.0	0.0, 3.4
	S6	109	0.015 (−0.01 to 0.02)	0.01, 0.02	<0.001	0.432	0.27, 0.57	<0.001	0.9	0.2, 5.0
	S7	109	0.00 (−0.05 to 0.03)	−0.02, 0.01	0.81	0.349	0.17, 0.50	<0.001	9.2	5.1, 16.1
	S8	108	−0.01 (−0.08 to 0.03)	−0.03, 0.01	0.17	0.362	0.19, 0.52	<0.001	29.6	21.8, 38.8

Table 1. *Cont.*

Level of Observation		n	Difference	95% CI	p	ICC	95% CI	p	RoR %	95% CI
	S9	88	0.00 (−0.05 to 0.04)	−0.02, 0.02	0.77	0.343	0.15, 0.52	<0.001	14.8	8.8, 23.7
	S10	56	−0.01 (−0.06 to 0.03)	−0.04, 0.01	0.42	0.475	0.24, 0.65	<0.001	17.9	10.0, 29.8
	S17	34	0.01 (−0.03 to 0.03)	−0.02, 0.04	0.35	0.304	−0.03, 0.58	0.04	14.7	6.4, 30.1
	S11	109	0.01 (−0.01 to 0.03)	0.01, 0.02	<0.001	0.485	0.33, 0.62	<0.001	2.8	0.9, 7.8
Segments	S12	88	0.005 (−0.03 to 0.04)	−0.01, 0.02	0.38	0.297	0.10, 0.48	0.002	10.2	5.5, 18.3
	S13	90	0.015 (−0.02 to 0.05)	0.01, 0.03	0.009	0.554	0.39, 0.68	<0.001	11.1	6.1, 19.3
	S14	58	0.00 (−0.06 to 0.04)	−0.02, 0.02	1.00	0.621	0.43, 0.76	<0.001	19.0	10.9, 30.9
	S15	11	0.005 (−0.03 to 0.06)	−0.06, 0.07	0.89	0.619	0.07, 0.88	0.02	9.1	1.6, 37.7
	S18	13	−0.024 (−0.06 to 0.06)	−0.09, 0.03	0.33	0.430	−0.13, 0.78	0.06	30.8	12.7, 57.6

Values are median difference (and IQR) of CT-FFR values, the intra-class correlation coefficient (ICC), and rate of recategorizations of the two observers. The first *p*-value column (and 95% CI) corresponds to the difference of median CT-FFR differences from zero while the second *p*-value column (and 95% CI) corresponds to the difference of the ICC from zero. *p*-values < 0.05 were statistically significant. CI = confidence interval; ICC = intra-class correlation coefficient; IQR = interquartile range; LAD = left anterior descending artery; LM = left main coronary artery; LCX = circumflex artery; RoR = rate of recategorization; RCA = right coronary artery.

3.3. Interobserver Variability

Analysis on patient level showed a fair correlation of absolute CT-FFR values between both observers (ICC = 0.421; $p < 0.001$). The LAD showed a poor correlation (ICC = 0.334; $p < 0.001$); the other vessels showed fair (LM: ICC = 0.507; $p < 0.001$; LCX: ICC = 0.588; $p < 0.001$) or good agreement (RCA: ICC = 0.701; $p < 0.001$) of CT-FFR values. The segments forming the LAD showed mostly a poor correlation. Segments forming the other vessels showed a better correlation (RCA > LM > LCX; Table 1). No trend towards higher or lower correlation in distal segments was found.

Between both observers, recategorizations into hemodynamically relevant CAD occurred in 29.4% of patients. On vessel level, the LAD showed the highest number of recategorizations, whereas the LM showed the lowest (LAD: 31.2% > RCA: 26.6% > LCX: 20.2% > LM: 0%) (Table 1). Recategorizations in proximal segments (median: 0.9%) were less frequent than in distal segments (median: 14.8%).

3.4. Diagnostic Performance

Diagnostic performance on patient level was identical between both observers (sensitivity: 100%; specificity: 29.0%; diagnostic accuracy: 30.3%; Table 2). On vessel level, observer B showed slightly better specificity and accuracy of Δ +1.8% and Δ +2.1%, respectively. The specificity and diagnostic accuracy of observer B were minimally higher for segmental measurements (Δ +0.4%). All values can be found in Table 2.

Table 2. Comparison of diagnostic performance of observer A and B.

Level of Observation	Observer	n	TP	TN	FP	FN	Sen. %	Spe. %	PPV %	NPV %	Acc. %
	Observer A		2	31	76	0	100.0%	29.0	2.6	100.0	30.3
Patient	Observer B	109	2	31	76	0	100.0%	29.0	2.6	100.0	30.3
	Difference Δ		0	0	0	0	0.0%	0.0	0.0	0.00	0.0
	Observer A		0	306	128	2	0.0%	70.5	0.0	99.4	70.2
Vessel	Observer B	436	1	314	120	1	50.0%	72.4	0.8	99.7	72.3
	Difference Δ		1	8	−8	−1	50.0%	+1.8	+0.8	+0.3	+2.1
	Observer A		0	1265	189	2	0.0%	87.0	0.0	99.8	86.9
Segment	Observer B	1456	0	1271	183	2	0.0%	87.4	0.0	99.8	87.3
	Difference Δ		0	6	−6	0	0.0%	+0.4	0.0	0.0	+0.4

ICA was used as the standard of reference. Thresholds for coronary artery disease were ICA ≥ 50% diameter and CT-FFR ≤ 0.80. Acc. = accuracy; CT-FFR = CT-derived fractional flow reserve; FN = false negative; FP = false positive; ICA = invasive coronary angiography; NPV = negative predictive value; PPV = positive predictive value; Sen. = sensitivity; Spe. = specificity; TN = true negative; TP= true positive.

3.5. Localization of Measurement

Proximal segments showed higher diagnostic accuracy and specificity than distal segments for both observers (accuracy: 98.9%/99.1% vs. 81.1%/81.6%; specificity: 98.9%/99.1% vs. 81.3%/81.8%; Table 3). Differences between both observers were very small with slightly smaller differences in proximal segments compared to distal ones (accuracy and specificity: Δ −0.2% vs. Δ −0.5%). Further detail is shown in Table 3.

Table 3. Comparison of diagnostic performance of observers A and B depending on segment location.

Segment Location	Observer	n	TP	TN	FP	FN	Sen. %	Spe. %	PPV %	NPV %	Acc. %
Proximal	Observer A	470	0	465	5	0	/	98.9%	0.0%	100.0%	98.9%
	Observer B		0	466	4	0	/	99.1%	0.0%	100.0%	99.1%
	Difference Δ		0	−1	1	0	/	−0.2%	0.0%	0.0%	−0.2%
Distal	Observer A	986	0	800	184	2	0.0%	81.3%	0.0%	99.8%	81.1%
	Observer B		0	805	179	2	0.0%	81.8%	0.0%	99.8%	81.6%
	Difference Δ		0	−5	5	0	0.0%	−0.5%	0.0%	0.0%	−0.5%

ICA was used as the standard of reference. Thresholds for coronary artery disease were ICA ≥ 50% diameter and CT-FFR ≤ 0.80. Acc. = accuracy; CT-FFR= CT-derived fractional flow reserve; FN = false negative; FP = false positive; ICA = invasive coronary angiography; NPV = negative predictive value; PPV = positive predictive value; Sen. = sensitivity; Spe. = specificity; TN = true negative; TP = true positive.

3.6. Influence of Image Quality and Coronary Artery Calcifications

On patient level, absolute and categorized CT-FFR values did not correlate with any image quality parameters. On vessel level, there were weak correlations between absolute CT-FFR values and contrast opacification in the LM (r = 0.204; $p = 0.03$) and between categorized values and contrast opacification in the RCA (r = 0.218; $p = 0.02$). Coronary artery calcium burden correlated weakly with absolute CT-FFR values on patient level (r = 0.394; $p < 0.001$) and in the LAD (r = 0.393; $p < 0.001$). Categorized CT-FFR values only showed a weak correlation with CAC in the LCX (r = 0.207; $p = 0.03$). Further detail is given in Table 4.

Table 4. Influence of image quality and coronary arterial calcifications on recategorization.

CT-FFR Values	Level of Observation		n	Image Quality									Calcium Burden		
				r CNR	95% CI	p	r HU	95% CI	p	r QIQ	95% CI	p	r CAC	95% CI	p
Absolute	Patient		109	−0.059	−0.241, 0.127	0.55	−0.073	−0.261, 0.120	0.45	−0.064	−0.208, 0.080	0.40	0.394	0.221, 0.542	<0.001
	Vessel	RCA	109	−0.032	−0.223, 0.157	0.74	−0.081	−0.276, 0.121	0.41	−0.127	−0.283, 0.033	0.10	0.078	−0.115, 0.264	0.42
		LM	109	0.173	−0.038, 0.363	0.07	0.204	−0.010, 0.396	0.03	0.004	−0.178, 0.184	0.97	0.001	−0.184, 0.192	1.00
		LAD	109	−0.122	−0.311, 0.075	0.21	−0.146	−0.340, 0.059	0.13	−0.094	−0.246, 0.066	0.22	0.393	0.200, 0.553	<0.001
		LCX	109	0.090	−0.102, 0.276	0.35	0.066	−0.135, 0.260	0.50	−0.026	−0.175, 0.128	0.73	0.129	−0.069, 0.311	0.18
Categorized	Patient		109	0.011	−0.177, 0.199	0.91	−0.040	−0.226, 0.149	0.68	0.009	−0.227, 0.243	0.94	0.133	−0.057, 0.313	0.17
	Vessel	RCA	109	0.114	−0.076, 0.296	0.24	0.218	0.031, 0.390	0.02	−0.226	−0.444, 0.016	0.05	0.013	−0.176, 0.200	0.90
		LAD	109	0.118	−0.071, 0.300	0.22	0.091	−0.098, 0.275	0.35	−0.019	−0.249, 0.213	0.86	0.099	−0.091, 0.282	0.31
		LCX	109	−0.020	−0.207, 0.169	0.84	-0.061	−0.246, 0.129	0.53	0.139	−0.131, 0.389	0.28	0.207	0.019, 0.380	0.03

Correlation of CNR, contrast opacification (measured in HU), qualitative image quality, or CAC with either absolute CT-FFR values or categorization into hemodynamically relevant CAD. The first p-value column (and 95% CI) corresponds to CNR, the second to HU, and the third to QIQ, while the fourth p-value column (and 95% CI) corresponds to CAC. All p-values are with respect to the null hypothesis that no correlation exists (correlation coefficient r = 0). p-values < 0.05 were considered statistically significant. Thresholds for significant CAD were ≥50% diameter for QCA and ≤0.80 for CT-FFR, respectively. The LM was excluded in categorized values because no recategorizations were observed in the cohort. CAC = coronary artery calcium score, CAD = coronary artery disease, CI = confidence interval; CNR = contrast-to-noise ratio; CT-FFR = CT-derived fractional flow reserve; HU = Hounsfield units; LAD = left anterior descending artery; LM = left main coronary artery; LCX = circumflex artery; QCA = quantitative coronary angiography; QIQ = qualitative image quality; RCA = right coronary artery.

4. Discussion

Overall, CT-FFR values of patients before TAVR without obstructive CAD on cCTA were highly consistent between the observers with only sporadic differences on segment level. Despite these small differences and identical diagnostic performance on patient level, numerous recategorizations into hemodynamically relevant CAD occurred, and correlation according to CT-FFR values ranged from good to even poor in several instances. Interestingly, differences in categorization were much smaller in proximal coronary artery segments and were generally independent of image quality and CAC.

Absolute CT-FFR values showed very small differences between both observers (Figure 2). In comparison to other studies on patients with obstructive CAD, our average differences on patient level were roughly one magnitude smaller (our results: −0.005 (−0.09 to 0.04), $p = 0.47$; CAD$^+$ patients before TAVR: −0.05 (−0.12 to 0.02); $p < 0.001$ [17]; Gaur et al.: 0.011 ± 0.034 [22]). The presence of CAD appears to be associated with an increase in variability, even more so in patients with multiple comorbidities. Gaur et al. were the first to publish data on the variation of values determined by the commercially available CFD CT-FFR algorithm [22]. Differences were higher than in this CAD$^-$ cohort, but similar to those of invasive FFR measurements. However, the details of the segmentation process or the observer experience remain undisclosed.

The sporadic statistically significant differences found in several segments should not be over-interpreted in light of the only weak associations found and the sheer number of tests performed. A possible explanation for the small differences may be that CT-FFR segmentation for computation of CT-FFR in CAD$^-$ patients could rely more heavily on the semi-automatic segmentation algorithm and is thus less susceptible to variation by manual intervention, e.g., correction of the luminal contours at calcified plaques. Interestingly, the interrater agreement of absolute CT-FFR values on patient level in comparison to our previous publication is lower than the much smaller absolute differences may lead to expect (our results: ICC = 0.421, $p < 0.001$; CAD$^+$ patients: ICC = 0.567, $p < 0.001$) [17]. One possible reason for this is the relatively homogenous data set compared to CAD$^+$ patients with reduced variability having the effect of potentially decreasing parameters like the ICC. Other studies thus showed higher ICC values, while examining different patient cohorts with also generally more experienced observers [8,23–25]. Less experienced observers typically achieve lower correlations in CT-FFR [26,27] as well as in the morphological assessment of cCTA and ICA [28–30]. However, in light of the low absolute differences, we do not believe this to be the primary explanation for the only moderate correlation of CT-FFR values, as supported by the reasons mentioned above [25,26]. Still, standardized training of observers is likely critical to secure robustness and reliability. Therefore, clinical application of ML-based CT-FFR should be carried out by experienced staff.

Evaluation on vessel level showed that the correlation of values in the LAD was the lowest. A possible explanation is that the LAD was the vessel with the most included segments in our cohort (mean: 4.6 segments/patient) thus entailing the highest potential for cumulative segmentation error. Additionally, segments 9, 10, and 17 (LAD side branches) with their respective bifurcation increase the difficulty of the segmentation process enabling potential errors in assignment.

Differences in categorization into hemodynamically relevant CAD between both observers occurred frequently, without affecting diagnostic accuracy on patient level at all. Considering these findings alongside the exceedingly small absolute median differences, it is evident that many reclassified segments likely possess CT-FFR values in close proximity to the threshold, thereby increasing the likelihood of 'threshold jumps' due to the minimal discrepancies observed during segmentation. A lower diagnostic power of CT-FFR values was described around the cut-off of ≤ 0.80 [31]. These values also correlated less well with invasive FFR in another study [32]. This study highlights that dichotomous decision-making should be discouraged with CT-FFR values around the cut-off (particularly values between 0.76 and 0.80), and additional risk stratification is needed before a treatment decision is made to account for the increased variability [13].

In our study, recategorizations were lower in proximal segments compared to distal ones (median: 0.9% vs. 14.8%). Thus, the assessment of proximal segments seems more reliable. The increasing number of recategorizations distally is most likely the result of a cumulative segmentation error. As this may alter CT-FFR values in either direction, threshold jumps for CT-FFR values close to the cut-off become more probable. Because this study was performed on CAD^{-} patients, the gradually decreasing values along any vessel occurred independently of discrete coronary artery stenoses. Generally, a decrease of 0.08 to 0.13 has been reported in the literature for CAD^{+} patients too [33]. The approach of this study enables the assessment of this phenomenon without the influence of stenoses. It can be assumed that these hemodynamic changes also occur in CAD^{+} patients. Similarly, Tsugu et al. recently reported that the lumen volume-to-vessel-length ratio was the strongest predictor after calcified plaque volume for CT-FFR $\leq$ 0.80 in the RCA in patients with non-obstructive CAD [34]. Additionally measuring the volume/length ratio might improve diagnostic performance distally for all patients undergoing CT-FFR in the future. Our study cohort before TAVR may present a special case because of severe AS with ultimately altered hemodynamics and frequent coinciding left ventricular myocardial hypertrophy and diffuse atherosclerosis. These may lead to an imbalance between vessel cross-section and muscle mass and thereby alter CT-FFR values [33].

To evaluate distal segments more reliably, changing the cut-off may be beneficial. The currently employed cut-off of $\leq$0.80 was proposed after evaluating lesions independent of their location [13,35]. A more lenient cut-off distally could factor in the gradual CT-FFR decrease and reduce the number of false positive ratings. Another way to mitigate this issue could be to apply ΔCT-FFR between two or more points of measurement along a vessel, rather than an absolute cut-off. An abrupt pressure drop along the coronary vessel has high diagnostic accuracy for relevant CAD [13,36,37]. Furthermore, in a recent study, Chen et al. found changes in CT-FFR values potentially useful for monitoring treatment efficacy in diffuse atherosclerosis [38].

The diagnostic performance of both observers was identical on patient level, with only minimal variances observed at vessel and segment levels. Looking at the high rate of recategorizations, especially on patient level, equal numbers of recategorizations from true to false and vice versa between both observers occurred (Tables 1 and 2; Δaccuracy: 0.0%; recategorizations: 29.4%). This reinforces the assumption that recategorizations are more likely caused by a random error affecting both, rather than, e.g., one observer's subpar/worse segmentation. As the prevalence of CAD is very low in our study cohort (n = 2), no meaningful findings could be generated concerning PPV, NPV, and absolute values of diagnostic accuracy. Hence, the values are listed to compare observers and should not be compared to other patient populations.

In proximal segments, higher diagnostic accuracy and specificity were observed (Table 3). This is analogous to the lower rate of recategorization in those segments discussed above and points towards a cumulative segmentation error with increasing importance distally. Conversely, the ICC showed no trend towards lower values distally. However, any trend could be masked by high ICC fluctuations due to the statistical impact of small differences within the otherwise homogenous data set. Similarly, Renker et al. reported in a CAD^{+} patient cohort lower lesion-specific diagnostic accuracy in distal segments with ML-based CT-FFR compared to invasive FFR serving as the standard of reference. Nonetheless, ML-based CT-FFR remained superior to cCTA alone [39] and is aimed at widespread clinical application. Current guidelines today already recommend (CFD) CT-FFR after cCTA evaluation for patients with intermediate pretest probability for CAD with intermediate stenosis [40]. Issues like relatively long evaluation time could be mitigated by further improving patient selection and image quality, e.g., with third-generation dual-source CTs.

Only sporadically, weak correlations between image quality or CAC burden and CT-FFR were found. The few sporadic significant correlations that were found in either absolute CT-FFR values or categorized values did not seem to be connected. Several other studies have published similar results [17,23,24,35]. On the other hand, for obvious reasons, a very high calcium burden may influence the readability of cCTA and ultimately CT-FFR [41]. Image quality parameters had no clinically meaningful influence on the consistency of CT-FFR values. A possible explanation for this may be that once image quality is sufficient to exclude relevant CAD reliably, neither image quality nor CAC burden significantly interferes with confident lumen segmentation.

Values obtained in proximally located segments appear more reliable. The gradual decrease of CT-FFR values distally leads to values falling closer to the cut-off of ≤ 0.80, making threshold jumps with the coinciding cumulative segmentation error more probable. Image quality and CAC seem not to have a major influence. A way to mitigate this would be the clinical application of a location-dependent threshold or ΔCT-FFR along a stenosis. Further studies of CT-FFR with correlation to invasive tests (e.g., invasive FFR) are needed. Lastly, an interesting subject for further studies is how reliable CT-FFR is on CAD^{-} patient cohorts without severe AS, as AS might facilitate low CT-FFR values.

Limitations

Several important limitations of this study must be mentioned. The cCTA data were acquired without the use of nitroglycerin or beta-blockers, likely adding to the challenges of interpretation, rather than artificially enhancing the results. Also, this study compared functional CT-FFR values with a morphological standard of reference (QCA $\geq$ 50%). A functional standard of reference would have been desirable to have more certainty of actual possible hemodynamic changes in patients before TAVR. These patients have severe AS and often have myocardial hypertrophy and comorbidities such as CAD. The aforementioned myocardial hypertrophy being relevant for the computation of CT-FFR is potentially contributing to the gradually decreasing CT-FFR values in our study cohort. As this was a single-center study employing a not commercially available prototype outside of its aimed for CAD^{+} patient cohort, the generalizability of our findings must be conducted cautiously.

Furthermore, both observers had a moderate amount of experience with the method beforehand, whereas other studies with better correlation were often carried out by experts with several years of clinical experience [24]. The comparability to the study on CFD CT-FFR variability is limited because a very small CAD^{+} patient cohort (n = 28) was assessed and their segmentation process remained undisclosed [22].

5. Conclusions

Differences in absolute CT-FFR values in CAD^{-} patients were very small, enabling a reliable evaluation of proximal segments. Nevertheless, a gradual decrease in CT-FFR value towards distal segments is known and in combination with a small coinciding cumulative segmentation error leads to a substantial amount of threshold jumps and consequently recategorizations, particularly in distal segments. Interobserver variability was independent of image quality and CAC, suggesting these abnormal measurements to be related to pathophysiological changes in severe AS. Though not useful for its original indication, these results are encouraging the use of CT-FFR also in challenging patient groups, potentially enabling novel uses, e.g., monitoring of diffuse CAD.

Author Contributions: Conceptualization, R.F.G., A.S. and M.G.; formal analysis, M.H. and A.S.; methodology, R.F.G., P.S., M.A.B. and M.G.; project administration, M.A.B. and M.G.; supervision, M.G.; data curation, R.F.G., A.S. and K.P.; investigation, all authors but A.S., K.P., C.P. and M.H.; visualization, R.F.G., P.S., K.P. and A.S.; Software, C.P.; Recourses, M.A.B. and M.G.; writing—original draft, R.F.G., A.S. and M.H.; writing—review and editing, all authors. All authors have contributed substantially to this work. All authors have read and agreed to the published version of the manuscript.

Funding: This research received no external funding.

Institutional Review Board Statement: The study was conducted in accordance with the Declaration of Helsinki, and approved by the Ethics Committee of the University of Leipzig (435/18-ek, 15 August 2019).

Informed Consent Statement: The ethics committee waived the requirement of written informed consent for participation from the participants or the participants' legal guardians/next of kin because of the retrospective design and no identifiable data was being used.

Data Availability Statement: The datasets generated and/or analyzed during the current study are not publicly available due to German Data Protection laws but are available from the corresponding author upon reasonable request after approval of the local ethics committee and data safety board.

Acknowledgments: The authors thank Siemens Healthcare for providing the prototype software. We acknowledge the position of Robin F. Gohmann to have been equally funded by Leipzig University and Leipzig Heart Center. We acknowledge support from Leipzig University for Open Access Publishing.

Conflicts of Interest: C. Panknin is an employee of Siemens Healthcare. None of the authors have relevant conflicts of interest to be stated. No grants or other forms of financial support were utilized for this work.

Abbreviations

AS	aortic stenosis
CAC	coronary artery calcium score
CAD	coronary artery disease
CAD^+	positive for coronary artery disease
CAD^-	negative for coronary artery disease
cCTA	coronary CT-angiography
CFD	computational fluid dynamics
CT-FFR	CT-derived fractional flow reserve
ICA	invasive coronary angiography
ICC	intra-class correlation coefficient
ML	machine learning
LM	left main coronary artery
LAD	left anterior descending coronary artery
LCX	circumflex coronary artery
QCA	quantitative coronary angiography
RCA	right coronary artery
TAVR	transcatheter aortic valve replacement

References

1. Maurovich-Horvat, P.; Bosserdt, M.; Kofoed, K.F.; Rieckmann, N.; Benedek, T.; Donnelly, P.; Rodriguez-Palomares, J.; Erglis, A.; Štěchovský, C.; Šakalyte, G.; et al. CT or Invasive Coronary Angiography in Stable Chest Pain. *N. Engl. J. Med.* **2022**, *386*, 1591–1602. [CrossRef] [PubMed]
2. van den Boogert, T.P.W.; Vendrik, J.; Claessen, B.E.P.M.; Baan, J.; Beijk, M.A.; Limpens, J.; Boekholdt, S.A.M.; Hoek, R.; Planken, R.N.; Henriques, J.P. CTCA for Detection of Significant Coronary Artery Disease in Routine TAVI Work-up: A Systematic Review and Meta-Analysis. *Neth. Heart J.* **2018**, *26*, 591–599. [CrossRef] [PubMed]
3. Gohmann, R.F.; Lauten, P.; Seitz, P.; Krieghoff, C.; Lücke, C.; Gottschling, S.; Mende, M.; Weiß, S.; Wilde, J.; Kiefer, P.; et al. Combined Coronary CT-Angiography and TAVI-Planning: A Contrast-Neutral Routine Approach for Ruling-Out Significant Coronary Artery Disease. *J. Clin. Med.* **2020**, *9*, 1623. [CrossRef] [PubMed]
4. Coenen, A.; Kim, Y.-H.; Kruk, M.; Tesche, C.; De Geer, J.; Kurata, A.; Lubbers, M.L.; Daemen, J.; Itu, L.; Rapaka, S.; et al. Diagnostic Accuracy of a Machine-Learning Approach to Coronary Computed Tomographic Angiography–Based Fractional Flow Reserve. *Circ. Cardiovasc. Imaging* **2018**, *11*, e007217. [CrossRef]
5. Gohmann, R.F.; Pawelka, K.; Seitz, P.; Majunke, N.; Heiser, L.; Renatus, K.; Desch, S.; Lauten, P.; Holzhey, D.; Noack, T.; et al. Combined CCTA and TAVR Planning for Ruling Out Significant CAD: Added Value of ML-Based CT-FFR. *JACC Cardiovasc. Imaging* **2022**, *15*, 476–486. [CrossRef]
6. Taylor, C.A.; Fonte, T.A.; Min, J.K. Computational Fluid Dynamics Applied to Cardiac Computed Tomography for Noninvasive Quantification of Fractional Flow Reserve: Scientific Basis. *J. Am. Coll. Cardiol.* **2013**, *61*, 2233–2241. [CrossRef]
7. Itu, L.; Rapaka, S.; Passerini, T.; Georgescu, B.; Schwemmer, C.; Schoebinger, M.; Flohr, T.; Sharma, P.; Comaniciu, D. A Machine-Learning Approach for Computation of Fractional Flow Reserve from Coronary Computed Tomography. *J. Appl. Physiol.* **2016**, *121*, 42–52. [CrossRef]
8. Langenbach, M.C.; Langenbach, I.L.; Foldyna, B.; Mauri, V.; Klein, K.; Macherey-Meyer, S.; Heyne, S.; Meertens, M.; Lee, S.; Baldus, S.; et al. Advanced CT Measures of Coronary Artery Disease with Intermediate Stenosis in Patients with Severe Aortic Valve Stenosis. *Eur. Radiol.* **2024**, *34*, 4897–4908. [CrossRef]

9. Brandt, V.; Schoepf, U.J.; Aquino, G.J.; Bekeredjian, R.; Varga-Szemes, A.; Emrich, T.; Bayer, R.R.; Schwarz, F.; Kroencke, T.J.; Tesche, C.; et al. Impact of Machine-Learning-Based Coronary Computed Tomography Angiography-Derived Fractional Flow Reserve on Decision-Making in Patients with Severe Aortic Stenosis Undergoing Transcatheter Aortic Valve Replacement. *Eur. Radiol.* **2022**, *32*, 6008–6016. [CrossRef]
10. Michail, M.; Ihdayhid, A.R.; Comella, A.; Thakur, U.; Cameron, J.D.; McCormick, L.M.; Gooley, R.P.; Nicholls, S.J.; Mathur, A.; Hughes, A.D.; et al. Feasibility and Validity of Computed Tomography-Derived Fractional Flow Reserve in Patients With Severe Aortic Stenosis: The CAST-FFR Study. *Circ. Cardiovasc. Interv.* **2021**, *14*, E009586. [CrossRef]
11. Peper, J.; Becker, L.M.; van den Berg, H.; Bor, W.L.; Brouwer, J.; Nijenhuis, V.J.; van Ginkel, D.J.; Rensing, B.J.M.W.; ten Berg, J.M.; Timmers, L.; et al. Diagnostic Performance of CCTA and CT-FFR for the Detection of CAD in TAVR Work-Up. *JACC Cardiovasc. Interv.* **2022**, *15*, 1140–1149. [CrossRef] [PubMed]
12. Wienemann, H.; Langenbach, M.C.; Mauri, V.; Banazadeh, M.; Klein, K.; Hohmann, C.; Lee, S.; Breidert, I.; Hof, A.; Eghbalzadeh, K.; et al. Feasibility and Comparison of Resting Full-Cycle Ratio and Computed Tomography Fractional Flow Reserve in Patients with Severe Aortic Valve Stenosis. *J. Cardiovasc. Dev. Dis.* **2022**, *9*, 116. [CrossRef] [PubMed]
13. Nørgaard, B.L.; Fairbairn, T.A.; Safian, R.D.; Rabbat, M.G.; Ko, B.; Jensen, J.M.; Nieman, K.; Chinnaiyan, K.M.; Sand, N.P.; Matsuo, H.; et al. Coronary CT Angiography-Derived Fractional Flow Reserve Testing in Patients with Stable Coronary Artery Disease: Recommendations on Interpretation and Reporting. *Radiol. Cardiothorac. Imaging* **2019**, *1*, e190050. [CrossRef] [PubMed]
14. Gohmann, R.F.; Seitz, P.; Pawelka, K.; Majunke, N.; Schug, A.; Heiser, L.; Renatus, K.; Desch, S.; Lauten, P.; Holzhey, D.; et al. Clinical Medicine Combined Coronary CT-Angiography and TAVI Planning: Utility of CT-FFR in Patients with Morphologically Ruled-Out Obstructive Coronary Artery Disease. *J. Clin. Med.* **2022**, *11*, 1331. [CrossRef]
15. De Bruyne, B.; Hersbach, F.; Pijls, N.H.J.; Bartunek, J.; Bech, J.W.; Heyndrickx, G.R.; Gould, K.L.; Wijns, W. Abnormal Epicardial Coronary Resistance in Patients With Diffuse Atherosclerosis but "Normal" Coronary Angiography. *Circulation* **2001**, *104*, 2401–2406. [CrossRef]
16. Leipsic, J.; Abbara, S.; Achenbach, S.; Cury, R.; Earls, J.P.; Mancini, G.J.; Nieman, K.; Pontone, G.; Raff, G.L. SCCT Guidelines for the Interpretation and Reporting of Coronary CT Angiography: A Report of the Society of Cardiovascular Computed Tomography Guidelines Committee. *J. Cardiovasc. Comput. Tomogr.* **2014**, *8*, 342–358. [CrossRef] [PubMed]
17. Gohmann, R.F.; Schug, A.; Pawelka, K.; Seitz, P.; Majunke, N.; El Hadi, H.; Heiser, L.; Renatus, K.; Desch, S.; Leontyev, S.; et al. Interrater Variability of ML-Based CT-FFR during TAVR-Planning: Influence of Image Quality and Coronary Artery Calcifications. *Front. Cardiovasc. Med.* **2023**, *10*, 1301619. [CrossRef]
18. Chinnaiyan, K.M.; Akasaka, T.; Amano, T.; Bax, J.J.; Blanke, P.; De Bruyne, B.; Kawasaki, T.; Leipsic, J.; Matsuo, H.; Morino, Y.; et al. Rationale, Design and Goals of the HeartFlow Assessing Diagnostic Value of Non-Invasive FFRCT in Coronary Care (ADVANCE) Registry. *J. Cardiovasc. Comput. Tomogr.* **2017**, *11*, 62–67. [CrossRef]
19. Kottner, J.; Audigé, L.; Brorson, S.; Donner, A.; Gajewski, B.J.; Hróbjartsson, A.; Roberts, C.; Shoukri, M.; Streiner, D.L. Guidelines for Reporting Reliability and Agreement Studies (GRRAS) Were Proposed. *J. Clin. Epidemiol.* **2011**, *64*, 96–106. [CrossRef]
20. Shrout, P.E.; Fleiss, J.L. Intraclass Correlations: Uses in Assessing Rater Reliability. *Psychol. Bull.* **1979**, *86*, 420–428. [CrossRef]
21. Cicchetti, D.V. Guidelines, Criteria, and Rules of Thumb for Evaluating Normed and Standardized Assessment Instruments in Psychology. *Psychol. Assess.* **1994**, *6*, 284–290. [CrossRef]
22. Gaur, S.; Bezerra, H.G.; Lassen, J.F.; Christiansen, E.H.; Tanaka, K.; Jensen, J.M.; Oldroyd, K.G.; Leipsic, J.; Achenbach, S.; Kaltoft, A.K.; et al. Fractional Flow Reserve Derived from Coronary CT Angiography: Variation of Repeated Analyses. *J. Cardiovasc. Comput. Tomogr.* **2014**, *8*, 307–314. [CrossRef]
23. Yang, D.H.; Kim, Y.H.; Roh, J.H.; Kang, J.W.; Ahn, J.M.; Kweon, J.; Lee, J.B.; Choi, S.H.; Shin, E.S.; Park, D.W.; et al. Diagnostic Performance of On-Site CT-Derived Fractional Flow Reserve versus CT Perfusion. *Eur. Heart J. Cardiovasc. Imaging* **2017**, *18*, 432–440. [CrossRef]
24. Donnelly, P.M.; Kolossváry, M.; Karády, J.; Ball, P.A.; Kelly, S.; Fitzsimons, D.; Spence, M.S.; Celeng, C.; Horváth, T.; Szilveszter, B.; et al. Experience With an On-Site Coronary Computed Tomography-Derived Fractional Flow Reserve Algorithm for the Assessment of Intermediate Coronary Stenoses. *Am. J. Cardiol.* **2018**, *121*, 9–13. [CrossRef]
25. Giannopoulos, A.A.; Keller, L.; Sepulcri, D.; Boehm, R.; Garefa, C.; Venugopal, P.; Mitra, J.; Ghose, S.; Deak, P.; Pack, J.D.; et al. High-Speed On-Site Deep Learning-Based FFR-CT Algorithm: Evaluation Using Invasive Angiography as the Reference Standard. *AJR Am. J. Roentgenol.* **2023**, *221*, 460–470. [CrossRef] [PubMed]
26. Ihdayhid, A.R.; Sakaguchi, T.; Kerrisk, B.; Hislop-Jambrich, J.; Fujisawa, Y.; Nerlekar, N.; Cameron, J.D.; Seneviratne, S.K.; Ko, B.S. Influence of Operator Expertise and Coronary Luminal Segmentation Technique on Diagnostic Performance, Precision and Reproducibility of Reduced-Order CT-Derived Fractional Flow Reserve Technique. *J. Cardiovasc. Comput. Tomogr.* **2020**, *14*, 356–362. [CrossRef] [PubMed]
27. Kumamaru, K.K.; Angel, E.; Sommer, K.N.; Iyer, V.; Wilson, M.F.; Agrawal, N.; Bhardwaj, A.; Kattel, S.B.; Kondziela, S.; Malhotra, S.; et al. Inter- and Intraoperator Variability in Measurement of On-Site CT-Derived Fractional Flow Reserve Based on Structural and Fluid Analysis: A Comprehensive Analysis. *Radiol. Cardiothorac. Imaging* **2019**, *1*, e180012. [CrossRef]
28. Nicol, E.D.; Stirrup, J.; Roughton, M.; Padley, S.P.G.; Rubens, M.B. 64-Channel Cardiac Computed Tomography: Intraobserver and Interobserver Variability (Part 1): Coronary Angiography. *J. Comput. Assist. Tomogr.* **2009**, *33*, 161–168. [CrossRef]

29. Kerl, J.M.; Schoepf, U.J.; Bauer, R.W.; Tekin, T.; Costello, P.; Vogl, T.J.; Herzog, C. 64-Slice Multidetector-Row Computed Tomography in the Diagnosis of Coronary Artery Disease: Interobserver Agreement among Radiologists with Varied Levels of Experience on a per-Patient and per-Segment Basis. *J. Thorac. Imaging* **2012**, *27*, 29–35. [CrossRef]
30. Murphy, M.L.; Galbraith, J.E.; de Soyza, N. The Reliability of Coronary Angiogram Interpretation: An Angiographic-Pathologic Correlation with a Comparison of Radiographic Views. *Am. Heart J.* **1979**, *97*, 578–584. [CrossRef]
31. Cook, C.M.; Petraco, R.; Shun-Shin, M.J.; Ahmad, Y.; Nijjer, S.; Al-Lamee, R.; Kikuta, Y.; Shiono, Y.; Mayet, J.; Francis, D.P.; et al. Diagnostic Accuracy of Computed Tomography-Derived Fractional Flow Reserve: A Systematic Review. *JAMA Cardiol.* **2017**, *2*, 803–810. [CrossRef] [PubMed]
32. Tanigaki, T.; Emori, H.; Kawase, Y.; Kubo, T.; Omori, H.; Shiono, Y.; Sobue, Y.; Shimamura, K.; Hirata, T.; Matsuo, Y.; et al. QFR Versus FFR Derived From Computed Tomography for Functional Assessment of Coronary Artery Stenosis. *JACC Cardiovasc. Interv.* **2019**, *12*, 2050–2059. [CrossRef]
33. Rajiah, P.; Cummings, K.W.; Williamson, E.; Young, P.M. CT Fractional Flow Reserve: A Practical Guide to Application, Interpretation, and Problem Solving. *Radiographics* **2022**, *42*, 340–358. [CrossRef] [PubMed]
34. Tsugu, T.; Tanaka, K.; Belsack, D.; Nagatomo, Y.; Tsugu, M.; Argacha, J.F.; Cosyns, B.; Buls, N.; De Maeseneer, M.; De Mey, J. Impact of Vessel Morphology on CT-Derived Fractional-Flow-Reserve in Non-Obstructive Coronary Artery Disease in Right Coronary Artery. *Eur. Radiol.* **2024**, *34*, 1836–1845. [CrossRef]
35. Van Hamersvelt, R.W.; Voskuil, M.; De Jong, P.A.; Willemink, M.J.; Išgum, I.; Leiner, T. Diagnostic Performance of On-Site Coronary CT Angiography–Derived Fractional Flow Reserve Based on Patient-Specific Lumped Parameter Models. *Radiol. Cardiothorac. Imaging* **2019**, *1*, e190036. [CrossRef] [PubMed]
36. Yan, H.; Gao, Y.; Zhao, N.; Geng, W.; Hou, Z.; An, Y.; Zhang, J.; Lu, B. Change in Computed Tomography-Derived Fractional Flow Reserve Across the Lesion Improve the Diagnostic Performance of Functional Coronary Stenosis. *Front. Cardiovasc. Med.* **2022**, *8*, 788703. [CrossRef]
37. Cami, E.; Tagami, T.; Raff, G.; Fonte, T.A.; Renard, B.; Gallagher, M.J.; Chinnaiyan, K.; Bilolikar, A.; Fan, A.; Hafeez, A.; et al. Assessment of Lesion-Specific Ischemia Using Fractional Flow Reserve (FFR) Profiles Derived from Coronary Computed Tomography Angiography (FFRCT) and Invasive Pressure Measurements (FFRINV): Importance of the Site of Measurement and Implications for Patient Referral for Invasive Coronary Angiography and Percutaneous Coronary Intervention. *J. Cardiovasc. Comput. Tomogr.* **2018**, *12*, 480–492. [CrossRef]
38. Chen, M.; Almeida, S.O.; Sayre, J.W.; Karlsberg, R.P.; Packard, R.R.S. Distal-Vessel Fractional Flow Reserve by Computed Tomography to Monitor Epicardial Coronary Artery Disease. *Eur. Heart J. Cardiovasc. Imaging* **2024**, *25*, 163–172. [CrossRef]
39. Renker, M.; Baumann, S.; Hamm, C.W.; Tesche, C.; Kim, W.K.; Savage, R.H.; Coenen, A.; Nieman, K.; De Geer, J.; Persson, A.; et al. Influence of Coronary Stenosis Location on Diagnostic Performance of Machine Learning-Based Fractional Flow Reserve from CT Angiography. *J. Cardiovasc. Comput. Tomogr.* **2021**, *15*, 492–498. [CrossRef]
40. Knuuti, J.; Wijns, W.; Saraste, A.; Capodanno, D.; Barbato, E.; Funck-Brentano, C.; Prescott, E.; Storey, R.F.; Deaton, C.; Cuisset, T.; et al. 2019 ESC Guidelines for the Diagnosis and Management of Chronic Coronary Syndromes: The Task Force for the Diagnosis and Management of Chronic Coronary Syndromes of the European Society of Cardiology (ESC). *Eur. Heart J.* **2020**, *41*, 407–477. [CrossRef]
41. Tesche, C.; Otani, K.; De Cecco, C.N.; Coenen, A.; De Geer, J.; Kruk, M.; Kim, Y.H.; Albrecht, M.H.; Baumann, S.; Renker, M.; et al. Influence of Coronary Calcium on Diagnostic Performance of Machine Learning CT-FFR: Results From MACHINE Registry. *JACC Cardiovasc. Imaging* **2020**, *13*, 760–770. [CrossRef] [PubMed]

MDPI AG
Grosspeteranlage 5
4052 Basel
Switzerland
Tel.: +41 61 683 77 34

MDPI Books Editorial Office
E-mail: books@mdpi.com
www.mdpi.com/books

www.ingramcontent.com/pod-product-compliance
Lightning Source LLC
Chambersburg PA
CBHW041933260926
51850CB00018B/131
* 9 7 8 3 7 2 5 8 4 5 1 3 2 *